SECOND EDITION

Essentials of HUMAN BEHAVIOR

To Hutch, Brad, Jennie, Abby, Darin, Auggie, Ruby, and Juliet. Family inspires, supports, and sustains. I am so lucky to have you along on my life journey.

Note From the Author

In 2008, the Council on Social Work Education adopted a competency-based framework for the accreditation of social work educational programs. The Educational Policy (EP), adopted in 2015, continues this approach to social work education, laying out 9 core social work competencies that should guide curriculum design in social work education programs. Competencies are practice behaviors that integrate knowledge, values, and skills. We have included material in this book to assist the reader in developing all 9 core competencies.

We present material to assist the reader to engage in personal reflection related to personal biases and social work values. Critical thinking questions appear in each chapter to assist the reader in ongoing critical examination of personal biases, conceptual frameworks, and empirical research. The content on diversity, oppression, human rights, and social and economic justice includes attention to issues of global social, economic, and environmental justice. Chapter 6, Culture and the Physical Environment, draws special attention to issues of environmental justice. All chapters draw on multidisciplinary sources and multiple ways of knowing about human behavior. A number of chapters include material on relevant social policies and historical, cultural, economic, and global influences on policy development. Theories of human behavior are a major focus of the book and are covered in every chapter. Each chapter includes practice principles for applying knowledge about human behavior for assessment and intervention. The multidisciplinary theoretical content includes theories of individual behavior, as well as theories of families, small groups, communities, formal organizations, social institutions, and social movements.

The 9 core competencies and the related practice behaviors are presented here, followed by a grid that indicates which of the core competencies are addressed in some fashion in each chapter. You might find it helpful to review these core competencies from time to time as you are learning more and more about what it means to be a social worker.

COMPETENCY 1: DEMONSTRATE ETHICAL AND PROFESSIONAL BEHAVIOR

Social workers

- make ethical decisions by applying the standards of the NASW Code of Ethics, relevant laws and regulations, models for ethical decision making, ethical conduct of research, and additional codes of ethics as appropriate to context;
- use reflection and self-regulation to manage personal values and maintain professionalism in practice situations;
- demonstrate professional demeanor in behavior; appearance; and oral, written, and electronic communication;
- use technology ethically and appropriately to facilitate practice outcomes; and
- use supervision and consultation to guide professional judgment and behavior.

COMPETENCY 2: ENGAGE DIVERSITY AND DIFFERENCE IN PRACTICE

Social workers

- apply and communicate understanding of the importance of diversity and difference in shaping life experiences in practice at the micro, mezzo, and macro levels;
- present themselves as learners and engage clients and constituencies as experts of their own experiences; and
- apply self-awareness and self-regulation to manage the influence of personal biases and values in working with diverse clients and constituencies.

COMPETENCY 3: ADVANCE HUMAN RIGHTS AND SOCIAL, ECONOMIC, AND ENVIRONMENTAL JUSTICE

Social workers

- apply their understanding of social, economic, and environmental justice to advocate for human rights at the individual and system levels; and
- engage in practices that advance social, economic, and environmental justice.

COMPETENCY 4: ENGAGE IN PRACTICE-INFORMED RESEARCH AND RESEARCH-INFORMED PRACTICE

Social workers

- use practice experience and theory to inform scientific inquiry and research;

- apply critical thinking to engage in analysis of quantitative and qualitative research methods and research findings; and
- use and translate research evidence to inform and improve practice, policy, and service delivery.

COMPETENCY 5: ENGAGE IN POLICY PRACTICE

Social workers

- identify social policy at the local, state, and federal level that impacts well-being, service delivery, and access to social services;
- assess how social welfare and economic policies impact the delivery of and access to social services; and
- apply critical thinking to analyze, formulate, and advocate for policies that advance human rights and social, economic, and environmental justice.

COMPETENCY 6: ENGAGE WITH INDIVIDUALS, FAMILIES, GROUPS, ORGANIZATIONS, AND COMMUNITIES

Social workers

- apply knowledge of human behavior and the social environment, person-in-environment, and other multidisciplinary theoretical frameworks to engage with clients and constituencies; and
- use empathy, reflection, and interpersonal skills to effectively engage diverse clients and constituencies.

COMPETENCY 7: ASSESS INDIVIDUALS, FAMILIES, GROUPS, ORGANIZATIONS, AND COMMUNITIES

Social workers

- collect and organize data and apply critical thinking to interpret information from clients and constituencies;
- apply knowledge of human behavior and the social environment, person-in-environment, and other multidisciplinary theoretical frameworks in the analysis of assessment data from clients and constituencies;
- develop mutually agreed-on intervention goals and objectives based on the critical assessment of strengths, needs, and challenges within clients and constituencies; and
- select appropriate intervention strategies based on the assessment, research knowledge, and values and preferences of clients and constituencies.

COMPETENCY 8: INTERVENE WITH INDIVIDUALS, FAMILIES, GROUPS, ORGANIZATIONS, AND COMMUNITIES

Social workers

- critically choose and implement interventions to achieve practice goals and enhance capacities of clients and constituencies;
- apply knowledge of human behavior and the social environment, person-in-environment, and other multidisciplinary theoretical frameworks in interventions with clients and constituencies;
- use interprofessional collaboration as appropriate to achieve beneficial practice outcomes;
- negotiate, mediate, and advocate with and on behalf of diverse clients and constituencies; and
- facilitate effective transitions and endings that advance mutually agreed-on goals.

COMPETENCY 9: EVALUATE PRACTICE WITH INDIVIDUALS, FAMILIES, GROUPS, ORGANIZATIONS, AND COMMUNITIES

Social workers

- select and use appropriate methods for evaluation of outcomes;
- apply knowledge of human behavior and the social environment, person-in-environment, and other multidisciplinary theoretical frameworks in the evaluation of outcomes;
- critically analyze, monitor, and evaluate intervention and program processes and outcomes; and
- apply evaluation findings to improve practice effectiveness at the micro, mezzo, and macro levels.

Essentials of Human Behavior and Social Work Core Competencies

CHAPTER	ETHICAL AND PROFESSIONAL BEHAVIOR	ENGAGE DIVERSITY & DIFFERENCE	HUMAN RIGHTS & JUSTICE	RESEARCH AND PRACTICE	POLICY PRACTICE	SOCIAL WORK ENGAGEMENT	ASSESSMENT	INTERVENTION	EVALUATION
1	√	√	√	√	√	√	√	√	√
2	√	√	√	√	√	√	√	√	√
3	√	√	√	√	√	√	√	√	√
4	√	√	√	√		√	√	√	√
5	√	√	√	√		√	√	√	√
6	√	√	√	√	√	√	√	√	√
7	√	√	√	√	√	√	√	√	√
8	√	√	√	√	√	√	√	√	√
9	√	√	√	√	√	√	√	√	√
10	√	√	√	√	√	√	√	√	√
11	√	√	√	√	√	√	√	√	√
12	√	√	√	√	√	√	√	√	√
13	√	√	√	√	√	√	√	√	√
14	√	√	√	√	√	√	√	√	√
15	√	√	√	√	√	√	√	√	√
16	√	√	√	√	√	√	√	√	√
Total Chapters	16	16	16	16	14	16	16	16	16

SECOND EDITION

Essentials of HUMAN BEHAVIOR

INTEGRATING PERSON, ENVIRONMENT, AND THE LIFE COURSE

Elizabeth D. Hutchison

Professor Emeritus
Virginia Commonwealth University

and Contributing Authors

Los Angeles | London | New Delhi
Singapore | Washington DC | Melbourne

FOR INFORMATION:

SAGE Publications, Inc.
2455 Teller Road
Thousand Oaks, California 91320
E-mail: order@sagepub.com

SAGE Publications Ltd.
1 Oliver's Yard
55 City Road
London, EC1Y 1SP
United Kingdom

SAGE Publications India Pvt. Ltd.
B 1/I 1 Mohan Cooperative Industrial Area
Mathura Road, New Delhi 110 044
India

SAGE Publications Asia-Pacific Pte. Ltd.
3 Church Street
#10-04 Samsung Hub
Singapore 049483

Acquisitions Editor: Nathan Davidson
eLearning Editor: Morgan Shannon
Editorial Assistant: Heidi Dreiling
Production Editor: Jane Haenel
Copy Editor: Mark Bast
Typesetter: C&M Digitals (P) Ltd.
Proofreaders: Christine Dahlin and Alison Syring
Indexer: Amy Murphy
Cover Designer: Scott Van Atta
Marketing Manager: Shari Countryman

Printed in Canada

Library of Congress Cataloging-in-Publication Data

Names: Hutchison, Elizabeth D., author.

Title: Essentials of human behavior : integrating person, environment, and the life course / Elizabeth D. Hutchison, Virginia Commonwealth University.

Description: Second edition. | Los Angeles : SAGE, [2017] | Includes bibliographical references and index.

Identifiers: LCCN 2016023305 | ISBN 9781483377728 (pbk. : alk. paper)

Subjects: LCSH: Human behavior. | Psychology. | Social psychology. | Social service.

Classification: LCC HM1033 .H87 2017 | DDC 302—dc23 LC record available at https://lccn.loc.gov/2016023305

This book is printed on acid-free paper.

16 17 18 19 20 10 9 8 7 6 5 4 3 2 1

Brief Contents

PART IV. The Changing Life Course

Detailed Contents

PART III. THE MULTIPLE DIMENSIONS OF THE ENVIRONMENT

6 CULTURE AND THE PHYSICAL ENVIRONMENT 157

Linwood Cousins and Elizabeth D. Hutchison

7 FAMILIES 191

Elizabeth D. Hutchison

PART IV. THE CHANGING LIFE COURSE

12 TODDLERHOOD AND EARLY CHILDHOOD 371

Debra J. Woody and David Woody III

13 MIDDLE CHILDHOOD 405

Leanne Wood Charlesworth

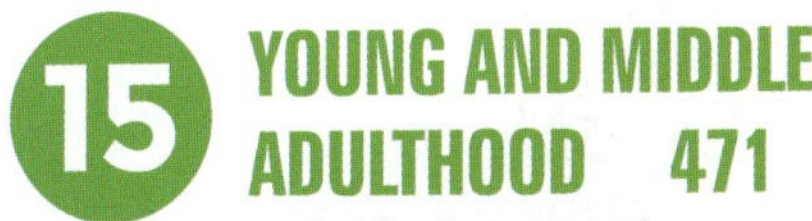

Case Studies

(Continued)

(Continued)

CHAPTER	CASE	CASE INFORMATION	PAGE
6. Culture and the Physical Environment	6.1 Stan and Tina at Community High School	Male and female African American students; navigating increasingly segregated high school in Newark, New Jersey	158
	6.2 Ben Watson's Changing Experience With the Physical Environment	20-something male, spinal cord injury	159
7. Families	The Sharpe Family's Postdeployment Adjustment	Four-generation African American family, small southwestern town, father deployed to both Iraq and Afghanistan in past decade, postdeployment adjustment issues	192
8. Small Groups, Formal Organizations, and Communities	8.1 The Sexuality and Gender Group at a Women's Residential Substance Abuse Treatment Facility	Support group for lesbian, bisexual, questioning, and transgender women in a residential substance abuse treatment facility	226
	8.2 Changing Leadership at Beacon Center	Different styles of leadership over time in a homeless advocacy and service organization in a midsize midwestern city	227
	8.3 Filipina Domestic Workers Creating Transnational Communities	Filipina domestic workers in Rome and Los Angeles, service workers of globalization	229
9. Social Structure, Social Institutions, and Social Movements	9.1 Leticia Renteria's Struggle to Make It in the United States	30-year-old married mother of three young children, living in Coachella Valley of California, undocumented immigrant from Mexicali, Mexico, impoverished seasonal laborer	264
	9.2 Fighting for a Living Wage	Start-up and development of the living wage movement, crossing national lines	265
10. The Human Life Journey: A Life Course Perspective	10.1 David Sanchez's Search for Connections	Native American male, early 60s, forced attendance at boarding school for Native American students in childhood and adolescence, veteran of Vietnam War, in substance abuse recovery, diabetes	304
	10.2 Phoung Le, Serving Family and Community	57-year-old Vietnamese refugee woman, intergenerational family acculturation issues	305
	10.3 The Suarez Family After September 11, 2001	Puerto Rican American family who lost a family member at the World Trade Center on September 11, 2001, trauma in a multigenerational family	307
11. The Journey Begins: Conception Pregnancy, Childbirth, and Infancy	11.1 Jennifer Bradshaw's Experience With Infertility	African American female, late 30s, infertility issues	332
	11.2 The Thompsons' Premature Birth	Military family with deployment in war zone, premature baby	333
	11.3 Sarah's Teen Dad	Teen father, primary caregiver to infant daughter	334
12. Toddlerhood and Early Childhood	12.1 Overprotecting Henry	Loss of toddler to community violence, traumatized mother caring for toddler son	372

Preface

In the preface to the first edition of this book, I noted that I have always been intrigued with human behavior. I didn't know any social workers when I was growing up—or even that there was a social work profession—but I felt an immediate connection to social work and social workers during my junior year in college when I enrolled in an elective titled Introduction to Social Work and Social Welfare. What attracted me most was the approach social workers take to understanding human behavior. I was a sociology major, minoring in psychology, and it seemed that each of these disciplines—as well as disciplines such as economics, political science, and ethics—added pieces to the puzzle of human behavior; that is, they each provided new ways to think about the complexities of human behavior. Unfortunately, it wasn't until several years later when I was a hospital social worker that I began to wish I had been a bit more attentive to my course work in biology, because that discipline increasingly holds other pieces of the puzzle of human behavior. But when I sat in that Introduction to Social Work and Social Welfare course, it seemed that the pieces of the puzzle were coming together. I was inspired by the optimism about creating a more humane world, and I was impressed with an approach to human behavior that clearly cut across disciplinary lines.

Just out of college, amid the tumultuous societal changes of the late 1960s, I became an MSW student. I began to recognize the challenge of developing the holistic understanding of human behavior that has been the enduring signature of social work. I also was introduced to the tensions in social work education, contrasting breadth of knowledge versus depth of knowledge. I found that I was unprepared for the intensity of the struggle to apply what I was learning about general patterns of human behavior to the complex, unique situations that I encountered in the field. I was surprised to find that being a social worker meant learning to understand my own behavior, as well as the behavior of others.

Since completing my MSW, I have provided services in a variety of social work settings, including a hospital, nursing homes, state mental health and mental retardation institutions, a community mental health center, a school-based program, public child welfare, and a city jail. Sometimes the target of change was an individual, and other times the focus was on bringing about changes in dyadic or family relationships, communities, organizations, or social institutions. I have also performed a variety of social work roles, including case manager, therapist, teacher, advocate, group facilitator, consultant, collaborator, program planner, administrator, and researcher. I love the diversity of social work settings and the multiple roles of practice. My varied experiences strengthened my commitment to the pursuit of social justice, enhanced my fascination with human behavior, and reinforced my belief in the need to understand human behavior holistically.

For 30 years, I have taught courses on human behavior to undergraduate students, MSW students, and doctoral students. The students and I have struggled with the same challenges that I encountered as a social work student in the late 1960s: the daunting task of developing a holistic understanding of human behavior, the issue of breadth versus depth of knowledge, and discovering how to use general knowledge about human behavior in unique practice situations. And, increasingly, over time, my students and I recognized a need to learn more about human and social diversity and to build a knowledge base that provides tools for promoting social justice. My experiences as student, practitioner, and teacher of human behavior led me, with the help of a dedicated and thoughtful group of contributing authors, to spend several years in the 1990s writing the first edition of the two-volume *Dimensions of Human Behavior* books, which are now in their fifth edition.

I have appreciated hearing from faculty and students who use the *Dimensions of Human Behavior* books, and their feedback has been enormously helpful as the contributing authors and I revised and updated the books for subsequent editions. Over the years, I was approached by faculty who would like to see a briefer one-volume version of those books. Sometimes the requests came from faculty who are teaching in universities organized by quarters rather than semesters, and they wanted text material better suited for this shorter term. Other requests came from faculty who wanted a somewhat less comprehensive, but still multidimensional, textbook. The contributing authors and I wrote the first edition of this book to respond to these requests, out of respect for the great variety of social work educational programs and the diversity of ways of organizing curriculum. We are pleased that it has been so well received and have worked diligently to reorganize and update the material to present what we think is a much improved book.

This book retains the multidimensional, multitheoretical approach of the two-volume *Dimensions of Human Behavior* and retains much of the content, as well, but it is organized into fewer chapters and is presented in a somewhat more simplified fashion. We have retained what we consider the essential themes of theory and research about human behavior.

MULTIDIMENSIONAL UNDERSTANDING OF HUMAN BEHAVIOR

Social work has historically used the idea of person-in-environment to develop a multidimensional understanding of human behavior. The idea that human behavior is multidimensional has become popular with most social and behavioral science disciplines. Recently, we have recognized the need to add the aspect of time to the person-environment construct, to capture the dynamic, changing nature of person-in-environment.

The purpose of this book is to help you to breathe life into the abstract idea of person-in-environment. As in the first edition of this book, I identify relevant dimensions of both person and environment, and my colleagues and I present up-to-date reports on theory and research about each of these dimensions in Parts II and III of the book. All the while, we encourage you to link the micro world of personal experience with the macro world of social trends—to recognize the unity of person and environment. We help you make this connection by showing how several of the same theories have been used to understand dimensions of both person and environment.

THE CHANGING LIFE COURSE

Part IV of the book builds on the multiple dimensions of person and environment analyzed in Chapters 3–9 and demonstrates how they work together with the dimension of time to produce patterns in unique life course journeys. The life course perspective puts equal value on individual agency and human connectedness; therefore, it serves as a good framework for social work's commitments to both the dignity and worth of the person as well as the importance of human relationships. The contributing authors and I draw on the best available evidence about the life course to assist the reader to develop and enhance expertise in serving people at all life stages.

BREADTH VERSUS DEPTH

The most difficult challenge I have faced as a student and teacher of human behavior is to develop a broad, multidimensional approach to human behavior without unacceptable sacrifice of depth. It is indeed a formidable task to build a knowledge base both wide and deep. After years of struggle, I have reluctantly concluded that although both breadth and depth are necessary, it is better for social work to err on the side of breadth. Let me tell you why.

Social workers are doers; we use what we know about human behavior to tell us what to do. If we have a narrow band of knowledge, no matter how impressive it is in its depth, we will "understand" the practice situations we encounter from this perspective. This will lead us to use the same solutions for all situations, rather than to tailor solutions to the unique situations we encounter. The emerging risk and resilience literature suggests that human behavior is influenced by the multiple risk factors and protective factors inherent in the multiple dimensions of contemporary social arrangements. What we need is a multidimensional knowledge base that allows us to scan widely for and think critically about risk factors and protective factors and to craft multipronged intervention programs to reduce risks and strengthen protective factors.

To reflect recent developments in the social and behavioral sciences, this book introduces dimensions of human behavior that are not covered in similar texts. Content on the biological and spiritual dimensions of person, the physical environment, social institutions, and social movements provides important insights into human behavior not usually covered in social work texts. In addition, we provide up-to-date information on the typically identified dimensions of human behavior.

GENERAL KNOWLEDGE AND UNIQUE SITUATIONS

The purpose of the social and behavioral sciences is to help us understand *general patterns* in person-environment transactions. The purpose of social work assessment is to understand *unique configurations* of person and environment dimensions. Those who practice social work must weave what they know about unique situations with general knowledge. To assist you in this process, as we did in the *Dimensions of Human Behavior* books, we begin each chapter with one or more case studies, which we then weave with contemporary theory and research. Many of the stories are composite cases and do not correspond to actual people known to the authors. Throughout the book, we call attention to the successes and failures of theory and research to accommodate human diversity related to gender, class, age, race and ethnicity, culture, sexual orientation, and disability. More important, we extend our attention to diversity, power, privilege, and oppression by being very intentional in our effort to provide a global context for understanding person-environment transactions. This global perspective becomes increasingly necessary in our highly interconnected world. It also calls us to examine the impact of new technologies on all dimensions of the person and environment and across the life course.

FEATURES OF THE BOOK

The task of developing a solid knowledge base for doing social work can seem overwhelming. For me, it is an exciting journey because I am learning about my own behavior as well as the behavior of others. What I learn enriches my personal life as well as my professional life. My colleagues and I wanted to write a book that gives you a state-of-the-art knowledge base, but we also wanted you to find pleasure in your learning. We have tried to write as we teach, with enthusiasm for the content and a desire to connect with your process of learning. We use some special features that we hope will aid your learning process.

- *Detailed chapter outlines*, presented at the beginning of each chapter, prepare the reader to understand what content will be covered before beginning to read the chapter.
- *Learning objectives* help readers anticipate what knowledge, values, and skills they should be able to exhibit following the reading of each chapter.
- *Case studies* put human faces on theory and research.
- *Critical thinking questions* are presented throughout all chapters to encourage critical analysis of theory and research and assist the reader in recognizing and managing personal values and biases.
- *Exhibits* are used throughout the chapters to summarize information in graphical or tabular form to help the reader understand and retain ideas.
- *Key terms* are presented in bold type in the chapters and defined in the Glossary.
- *Photographs* provide visual interest and human faces for abstract content.
- *Active learning exercises*, presented at the end of each chapter, suggest classroom activities that can be used to engage students in critical analysis of text materials.
- *Implications for social work practice* are included throughout the chapters and summarized as a set of practice principles at the end of each chapter to guide the reader's use of general knowledge in social work assessment and intervention.
- *Web resources* appear at the end of each chapter to assist readers with further exploration of issues.

NEW IN THIS EDITION

The bulk of this second edition will be familiar to instructors who used the first edition of *Essentials of Human Behavior: Integrating Person, Environment, and the Life Course*. Many of the changes came at the suggestion of instructors who have been using the first edition. The overall outline of the book has been reorganized in a number of places. To respond to the rapidity of changes in complex societies, all chapters have been comprehensively updated. As the contributing authors and I worked to revise the book, we were surprised to learn how much the knowledge base had changed since we worked on the first edition. We came to agree with the futurists who say that we are at a point where the rate of cultural change and knowledge development will continue to accelerate rapidly. You will want to use the many wonders of the World Wide Web to update information you suspect is already outdated.

The more substantial revisions for this addition include the following:

- The book now includes four parts instead of the three used in the first edition, with Part II, The Multiple Dimensions of Person and Environment, now divided into Part II, The Multiple Dimensions of the Person, and Part III, The Multiple Dimensions of the Environment.
- The chapters in Part III, The Multiple Dimensions of the Environment, have been reordered to move more smoothly from smaller systems to larger systems. The discussion of environmental dimensions continues to begin with Culture and the Physical Environment (Chapter 6) because those dimensions of the environment permeate all other dimensions. The Culture and the Physical Environment chapter is now followed by Families (Chapter 7), the most long-term and intimate social grouping. In the first edition, the discussion of families and small groups was joined in one chapter. In this second edition, one chapter is devoted to a fuller discussion of families, recognizing their important role as a social institution and their important impact on individual behavior. Following the chapter on families is Chapter 8, Small Groups, Formal Organizations, and Communities. This new organization reflects the important role that small groups play in both formal organizations and communities. Part III concludes with Chapter 9, Social Structure, Social Institutions, and Social Movements: Global and National, a discussion of large-scale societies and the social movements that attempt to create more just societies.
- Some reorganization of content is also presented in Part IV, The Changing Life Course. In the first

edition, Chapter 10, the first chapter in Part IV, included an overview of the life course perspective along with a discussion of conception, pregnancy, and childbirth. In this second edition, Chapter 10, The Human Life Journey: A Life Course Perspective, now presents a fuller discussion of the life course perspective that is used throughout the final six chapters of the book. We think this provides a clearer framework for the reading of those chapters. The discussion of infancy is now married to the discussion of conception, pregnancy, and childbirth in Chapter 11, a marriage that reflects increasing understanding of the close association of these two periods of life. Chapter 12 now covers the periods of toddlerhood and early childhood. The other chapters in Part IV are organized as they were in the first edition.

- Genetics content is moved from the discussion of conception, pregnancy, and childbirth to Chapter 3, The Biological Person.
- Significantly more content is added on the impact of the new information, communication, and medical technologies on person and environment.
- New content on neuroscience is added.
- Coverage of the global context of human behavior is expanded.
- New content on environmental and ecological justice has been added to Chapter 6, Culture and the Physical Environment.
- New content on gender identity has been added to several chapters.
- Eight new case studies have been added to reflect contemporary issues.
- The number of critical thinking questions is increased in every chapter.
- Visual metaphors are used in Chapter 2 to represent the major theoretical perspective used in the book.
- Several exhibits are added and others are updated.

INTERACTIVE eBOOK

A free interactive eBook is available with the text to expand the learning experience. Users of the eBook will have access to 45 original SAGE-produced videos. These videos are linked to learning objectives and assessments and serve to deepen readers' understanding of basic concepts. Also available in the eBook is a series of professionally narrated "Chalk Talks"—whiteboard-style animations that provide a visual overview of each part of the text.

SAGE edge INSTRUCTOR AND STUDENT RESOURCES

edge.sagepub.com/hutchisoness2e

For Instructors: SAGE edge is a robust online environment featuring an impressive array of free tools and resources. Instructors using this book can access customizable PowerPoint slides, along with an extensive test bank built on Bloom's taxonomy that features multiple-choice, true/false, essay, and short answer questions for each chapter. The instructor's manual is mapped to learning objectives and features lecture notes, sample syllabi for semester and quarter courses, discussion questions, class assignments, links to SAGE journal articles, and video and web resources.

For Students: The student study site provides access to eFlashcards, web quizzes, links to full-text SAGE journal articles with accompanying review questions, video and web resources, downloadable versions of in-text assessments, and a link to the author's blog on multicultural education.

ONE LAST WORD

I imagine that you, like me, are intrigued with human behavior. That is probably a part of what attracted you to social work. I hope that reading this book reinforces your fascination with human behavior. I also hope that when you finish this book, and in the years to come, you will have new ideas about the possibilities for social work action.

Learning about human behavior is a lifelong process. You can help me in my learning process by letting me know what you liked or didn't like about the book.

—Elizabeth D. Hutchison
Reno, Nevada
ehutch@vcu.edu

Acknowledgments

A project like this book is never completed without the support and assistance of many people. This second edition stands on the back of the first edition, as well as on five editions of *Dimensions of Human Behavior: Person and Environment* and *Dimensions of Human Behavior: The Changing Life Course*. Since I started work on the first edition of the *Dimensions* books in the mid-1990s a large number of people have helped me keep this project going. I am grateful to all of them, some of them known to me and others working behind the scenes in a way not visible to me.

Steve Rutter, former publisher and president of Pine Forge Press, shepherded every step of the many years of work to produce the first edition of the *Dimensions* books. Along with Paul O'Connell, Becky Smith, and Maria Zuniga, he helped to refine the outline for the second edition of those books, and that outline continued to be used in the third, fourth, and fifth editions. I am especially grateful to Becky Smith, who worked with me as a developmental editor for the first two editions of the *Dimensions* books. She taught me so much about writing, and I often find myself thinking *How would Becky present this?*

The contributing authors and I are grateful for the assistance Dr. Maria E. Zuniga offered during the drafting of the second edition of the *Dimensions* books. She provided many valuable suggestions on how to improve the coverage of cultural diversity in each chapter. Her suggestions have stayed with us as lasting lessons about human behavior in a multicultural society.

I am grateful once again to work with a fine group of contributing authors. They care about your learning and are committed to providing a state-of-the-art knowledge base for understanding the multiple dimensions of human behavior. I am also grateful for colleagues who have provided rich case studies for Chapters 1, 9, 10, 11, 15, and 16.

We are lucky to be working again with the folks at SAGE. Kassie Graves provided disciplined and creative editorial assistance from 2006 to 2016. She encouraged (gently nudged is more like it) me to bring the first edition of this book to fruition for several years. Nathan Davidson came on board at SAGE in time to help me turn months of research and writing into what you see in this book. He is just the editor I need at this time. Carrie Montoya and Heidi Dreiling have assisted me with tasks both large and small. I am so lucky to be working with Mark Bast as copy editor again; they don't get any better than Mark. He works with an eagle eye and a marvelous sense of humor. Likewise, I am lucky to once again have the disciplined, organized, and creative efforts of Jane Haenel to turn words and ideas into a beautiful book. I love these folks!

I am grateful to my former faculty colleagues at Virginia Commonwealth University (VCU), who set a high standard for scientific inquiry and teaching excellence. They also provided love and encouragement through both good and hard times. My conversations about the human behavior curriculum with colleagues Rosemary Farmer, Stephen Gilson, Marcia Harrigan, Holly Matto, Mary Secret, and Joe Walsh over many years have stimulated much thinking and resulted in many ideas found in this book.

My students over 30 years also deserve a special note of gratitude. They teach me all the time, and many things that I have learned in interaction with them show up in the pages of this book. They have also provided a great deal of joy to my life journey. Those moments when I learn of former students doing informed, creative, and humane social work are special moments indeed. I have also enjoyed receiving e-mail messages from students from other universities who are using the books and have found their insights to be very helpful.

I would also like to thank Goutham Menon, director of social work at the University of Nevada Reno, for inviting me back into the classroom. He is a thoughtful and supportive administrator.

My deepest gratitude goes to my husband, Hutch. Since work began on the first edition of the *Dimensions* books, we have weathered several challenging years and experienced many celebratory moments. He is constantly patient and supportive and often technically useful. But, more important, he makes sure that I don't forget that life can be great fun. He has now accompanied me through many changes for over three fourths of my life journey.

Finally, I am enormously grateful to a host of reviewers who provided very helpful feedback for the revisions found in this second edition. Their ideas were very helpful in framing our work on this book, and their ideas about the organization of the book were especially helpful:

Suzanne Rabon, *North Carolina State University*

Nicole Dubus, *Boston University*

Larry G. Morton, *Arkansas State University*

Joel L. Carr, *Texas A&M–Kingsville*

Carol S. Drolen, *University of Alabama*

Anne Sparks, *University of Rio Grande*

—*Elizabeth D. Hutchison*

About the Author

Elizabeth D. Hutchison received her MSW from the George Warren Brown School of Social Work at Washington University in St. Louis and her PhD from the University at Albany, State University of New York. She was on the faculty in the Social Work Department at Elms College from 1980 to 1987 and was chair of the department from 1982 to 1987. She was on the faculty in the School of Social Work at Virginia Commonwealth University from 1987 to 2009, where she taught courses in human behavior and the social environment, social work and social justice, and child and family policy; she also served as field practicum liaison. She has been a social worker in health, mental health, aging, and child and family welfare settings. She is committed to providing social workers with comprehensive, current, and useful frameworks for thinking about human behavior. Her other research interests focus on child and family welfare. She lives in Reno, Nevada, where she is a hands-on grandmother and teaches part-time in the School of Social Work at the University of Nevada, Reno.

PART I

A Multidimensional, Multitheoretical Approach for Multifaceted Social Work

- Caroline O'Malley is knocking at the door of a family reported to her agency for child abuse.
- Sylvia Gomez and other members of her team at the rehabilitation hospital are meeting with the family of an 18-year-old man who is recovering from head injuries sustained in a motorcycle accident.
- Mark Bernstein is on the way to the county jail to assess the suicide risk of an inmate.
- Helen Moore is preparing a report for a legislative committee.
- Juanita Alvarez is talking with a homeless man about taking his psychotropic medications.
- Stan Weslowski is meeting with a couple who would like to adopt a child.
- Andrea Thomas is analyzing the results of a needs assessment recently conducted at the service center for older adults where she works.
- Anthony Pacino is wrapping up a meeting of a cancer support group.
- Sam Belick is writing a social history for tomorrow's team meeting at the high school where he works.
- Sarah Sahair has just begun a meeting of a recreational group of 9- and 10-year-old girls.
- Jane Kerr is facilitating the monthly meeting of an interagency coalition of service providers for substance-abusing women and their children.
- Ann Noles is planning a fund-raising project for the local Boys Club and Girls Club.
- Meg Hart is wrapping up her fourth counseling session with a lesbian couple.
- Chien Liu is meeting with a community group concerned about youth gang behavior in their neighborhood.
- Mary Wells is talking with one of her clients at the rape crisis center.
- Nagwa Nadi is evaluating treatment for post-traumatic stress disorder at a Veterans Administration hospital.
- Devyani Hakakian is beginning her workday at an international advocacy organization devoted to women's rights.

What do these people have in common? You have probably guessed that they all are social workers. They work in a variety of settings, and they are involved in a variety of activities, but they all are doing social work. Social work is, indeed, a multifaceted profession. And because it is multifaceted, social workers need a multidimensional, multitheoretical understanding of human behavior. This book provides such an understanding. The purpose of the two chapters in Part I is to introduce you to a multidimensional way of thinking about human behavior and to set the stage for subsequent discussion. In Chapter 1, you will be introduced to the multiple dimensions of person, environment, and time that serve as the framework for the book, and you will learn about social work's emphasis on diversity, inequality, and social justice. You also will be given some tools to think critically about the multiple theories and varieties of research that make up our general knowledge about these dimensions of human behavior. In Chapter 2, you will encounter eight theoretical perspectives that contribute to multidimensional understanding. You will learn about their central ideas and their scientific merits. Most important, you will consider the usefulness of these eight theoretical perspectives for social work.

CHALK TALKS

Watch via the

SAGE Interactive eBook

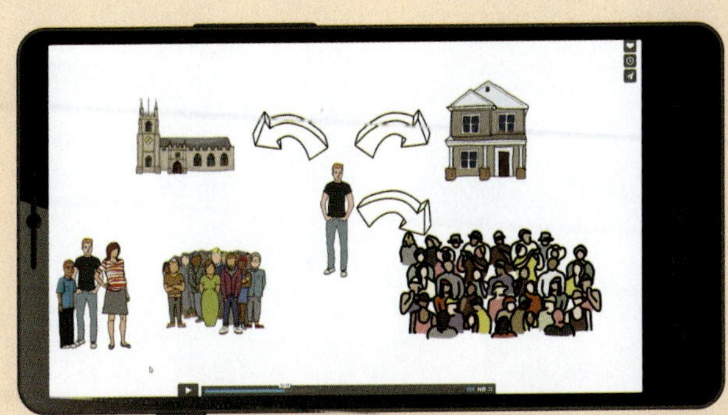

Created using Videoscribe, http://www.videoscribe.co

Human Behavior

A Multidimensional Approach

Elizabeth D. Hutchison

Learning Objectives

LO 1.1 Recognize one's emotional and cognitive reactions to a case study.

LO 1.2 Outline the elements of a multidimensional person-in-environment approach to human behavior.

LO 1.3 Advocate for an emphasis on diversity, inequality, social justice, and a global perspective in social work's approach to human behavior.

LO 1.4 Summarize four ingredients of knowing how to do social work.

LO 1.5 Analyze the roles of theory and research in guiding social work practice.

LO 1.6 Apply knowledge of the multidimensional person-in-environment framework, diversity, inequality, and the pursuit of social justice to recommend guidelines for social work assessment and intervention.

CASE STUDY

MANISHA AND HER CHANGING ENVIRONMENTS

Manisha is a 61-year-old Bhutanese woman who resettled in the United States in early 2009. She describes her childhood as wonderful. She was the youngest of seven children born to a farming family in a rural village of Bhutan. Although there was little support for education, especially for girls, Manisha's parents valued education, and she was one of five girls in her village school, where she was able to finish the second grade. As was tradition, she married young, at age 17, and became a homemaker for her husband, who was a contractor, and the four sons they later had. Manisha and her husband had a large plot of farmland, and Manisha enjoyed tending their large vegetable gardens. They were able to develop some wealth and were sending their children to school. They were managing well and living in peace.

In 1988, the political climate began to change and the good times ended. Manisha says she doesn't really understand how the problem started because in Bhutan, women were excluded from decision making and were given little information. As she talks, she begins to reflect that she has learned some things about what happened, but she still doesn't understand it. What she does recall is that the Bhutanese government began to discriminate against the Nepali ethnic group to which she belongs. News accounts indicate that the Druk Buddhist majority wanted to unite Bhutan under the Druk culture, religion, and language. The Nepalis had a separate culture and language and were mostly Hindu, whereas the Druks were Buddhist. Manisha says she does not know much about this, but she does recall that suddenly Nepalis were denied citizenship, were not allowed to speak their language, and could no longer get access to jobs.

Manisha recalls that the Nepali people began to raise their voices and question what was happening. When this occurred, the Bhutanese government sent soldiers to intimidate the villagers and undermine the Nepali resistance. Manisha tells about cases of rape of Nepali women at the hands of the Bhutanese soldiers and recalls that the soldiers expected Nepali girls and women to be made available to them for sexual activity. She reports that government forces targeted Nepali families who had property and wealth, arresting them in the middle of the night and torturing and killing some. Families were forcefully evicted from their property.

One day when Manisha was at the market, the soldiers arrested her husband and took him to jail; she didn't know where he was for 2 days. He was in jail for 18 months. She remembers that she and her sons would hide out, carefully watch for soldiers, and sneak back home to cook. She was afraid to be at home. Finally, one day she was forced to report to the government office and there was told to leave and go to Nepal. She told the government representative that she couldn't leave because her husband was in jail and she needed to care for her children. She tried to survive, living with other families, and she managed to live that way for a year.

Finally, Manisha heard that her husband would be released from jail on condition that he leave the country. By this time, neighbors had started to flee, and only four households were left in her village. She sent her youngest son with friends and neighbors who were fleeing. A few days later, her husband was released. He said he was too afraid to stay in their home, and they too had to flee. Manisha did not want to leave, and she still talks about the farm they had to leave behind. But the next morning, she and her husband and their other three sons fled the country. It was a 3-day walk to the Indian border, where Manisha and her family lived on the banks of a river with other Nepalis who had fled. Her sons ranged in age from 6 to 19 at this time. Manisha recalls that many people died by the river and that there was "fever all around."

After 3 months, Manisha and her family moved to a refugee camp in Nepal, the largest of seven Nepali refugee camps. They spent 17 years in this camp before coming to the United States. The 18 months of imprisonment affected her husband such that he was not able to tolerate the close quarters of refugee camp living; he lived and worked in the adjacent Nepali community and came to visit his family. The four boys were able to attend school in the camp.

The camp was managed by the United Nations High Commissioner for Refugees (UNHCR), whose representatives started to build a forum for women. Manisha says that many of the women were, like her, from rural areas where they had been self-reliant, eating what they grew and taking care of their families. Now they were dependent on other people. The facilities at the camps were closely built and crowded. There was always a need for cash; the refugees were given food, but money was needed for other things, like clothes and personal hygiene items. Oxfam, an international aid organization, started a knitting program, and the women were able to sell their knitted items, which provided much-needed cash. Manisha began to provide moral support to other women and to disabled children, and she worked as the camp's deputy secretary for 3 years.

Manisha's family wanted desperately to get back to Bhutan, but they began to realize that that would not happen. They also learned that Nepal would not give citizenship to the refugees even though they had a shared culture. So, Manisha and her family decided to resettle in the United States, where they had been assured by UNHCR workers that they would have a better life. The family resettled in three stages. First, Manisha and her husband came to the United States along with their youngest son and his wife. The older sons and their families resettled in two different waves of migration. They all live in proximity to one another. All of Manisha's sons and daughters-in-law are working, but some have only been able to find part-time work. They work in retail; hotel, hospital, and school housekeeping; and school food services. Her youngest son works at Walmart as a customer service manager and takes online college courses. Her grandchildren are all thriving and doing well in school. Manisha is pleased that they learned English so quickly.

In the camp in Nepal, Manisha had been working and was on the go. In her first year in the United States, she felt lonely, describing her life as "living behind closed doors." She and her husband took English as a second language (ESL) classes, but she felt strongly that she needed to be out at work so that she would have a chance to practice English. Five years after arriving in the United States, Manisha says that everything was so strange at first, and she found it difficult to adjust. For the past 4 years, she has worked part-time in a public school cafeteria, and she has been taking a citizenship preparation class. Her husband is not working, and he dropped out of the citizenship preparation class after a few weeks. English is still very hard for her, but her friends at work help her with the language. She has both American and Nepalese friends, and her friends are an important part of her life. She and her husband continue to practice their Hindu faith at home, but they are not able to attend the nearest Hindu Center, which is about 20 miles from their apartment, as often as they would like. The social worker at the refugee resettlement program is pleased that Manisha has found dignity and purpose in resettlement, but he continues to be concerned about other refugee men and women who are isolated and unhappy.

—Beverly B. Koerin and Elizabeth D. Hutchison

HUMAN BEHAVIOR: INDIVIDUAL AND COLLECTIVE

As eventful as it has been, Manisha's story is still unfolding. As a social worker, you will become a part of many unfolding life stories, and you will want to have useful ways to think about those stories and effective ways to be helpful to people like Manisha and her community of Bhutanese refugees. The purpose of this book is to provide ways for you to think about the nature and complexities of human behavior—the people and situations at the center of social work practice. To begin to do that, we must first clarify the purpose of social work and the approach it takes to individual and collective human behavior. This is laid out in the 2015 *Educational Policy* of the Council on Social Work Education (CSWE):

> The purpose of the social work profession is to promote human and community well-being. Guided by a person-in-environment framework, a global perspective, respect for human diversity, and knowledge based on scientific inquiry, the purpose of social work is actualized through its quest for social and economic justice, the prevention of conditions that limit human rights, the elimination of poverty, and the enhancement of the quality of life for all persons. (p. 1)

In discussion of social work competencies, the policy notes that "social workers apply knowledge of human behavior and the social environment, person-in-environment, and other multidisciplinary theoretical frameworks to engage with clients and constituencies" (p. 6).

As you think about Manisha's story, you may be thinking, as I was, not only about Manisha but also about the different environments in which she has lived and the ways in which both Manisha and her environments have changed over time. The person-in-environment framework noted in the CSWE Educational Policy is an old approach in social work, but it still is a very useful way to think about human behavior—a way that can accommodate such contemporary themes in human life as the emotional life of the brain, human–robot relationships, social media, human rights, economic globalization, and environmental justice. Social workers are concerned about both individual and collective behavior and well-being. When I talk about human behavior, I am referring to both the individual and collective behavior of humans. Sometimes we focus on individual behavior, and other times we are more concerned about the social systems created by human interaction.

This chapter overviews the person-in-environment framework that has guided social work intervention since the earliest days of the profession. The element of time is added to the person-in-environment framework to call attention to the dynamic, ever-changing nature of both people and environments. The chapter also presents a discussion of diversity, inequality, and the pursuit of social justice from a global perspective. After a brief description of the process by which professionals like social workers move from knowing to doing, the chapter ends with a discussion of how scientific knowledge from theory and research informs social work's multidimensional understanding of human behavior.

A MULTIDIMENSIONAL APPROACH

Social work's person-in-environment framework has historically recognized both person and environment as complex and **multidimensional**, that is, as having several identifiable dimensions. A **dimension** refers to a feature that can be focused on separately but that cannot be understood without also considering other features. This last piece is really important: Although we can focus on one dimension of a human story to help us think about it more clearly, no one dimension can be understood without considering other dimensions as well. With an explosion of research across a number of disciplines in the past few decades, the trend has been to expand the range of dimensions of both person and environment folded into the person-in-environment framework. Time too can be thought of as multidimensional. Let's look at some of the dimensions of person, environment, and time in Manisha's story.

If we focus on the *person* in Manisha's story, it appears that she was born with a healthy biological constitution, which allowed her to work in the family gardens and care for four sons. She describes no difficulty in managing the strenuous 3-day walk to the Indian border as she fled Bhutan. She survived while many people died by the river, and later, in the refugee camp, she survived and found new purpose when many others died of damaged bodies or broken spirits. Manisha appears to have emotional resilience, and she has maintained a belief in her ability to find dignity and purpose in life in the United States. She is able to learn a new language and culture and plan for the future. Her Hindu faith has been a source of comfort for her as she has adapted to different environments.

If we focus on the *environment*, we see many influences on Manisha's story. Consider first the physical environment. Manisha lived in relative comfort, first on her father's and then her husband's farm, for almost 40 years, where she was able to spend much of her day outside helping to turn gardens into food for her family. From there, she endured a long hike and a few months of survival in a poorly sheltered camp by the river. Her next stop was a crowded refugee camp. After 17 years, she and her family left the camp to establish a new life in the United States, where she lives with her husband in a small apartment that at first left her feeling isolated.

Culture is a dimension of environment that exerts a powerful influence in Manisha's story. Culture influenced the fact that she received limited, if any, education and that she be married at what may appear to us to be an early age. Her culture also held that women lack power and influence and are not involved in affairs outside the home, and yet Manisha assumed a powerful role in holding her family together after her husband was imprisoned. She also developed a very public role in the refugee camp and, on first coming to the United States, grieved the loss of that role. Although there were many challenges in the camp, she was living among people who shared her culture, language, and religion. She is adapting to a new, fast-moving culture where language is a constant barrier and her religious beliefs are in the minority. But culture is an important part of Manisha's story in another way. Culture clash and cultural imperialism led the Bhutanese government to discriminate against and then banish the Nepali ethnic group. Such cultural conflict is not new; historical analysis suggests that intercultural violence has actually declined in recent times (Pinker, 2011), but it continues to be a source of great international upheaval.

Another dimension of the environment, family, is paramount to Manisha. She is lucky to have her husband living with her again and all of her children nearby. None of her siblings was resettled in the same city, however, and they are spread across several countries at this time. She is not even sure what has happened to much of her large extended family. Manisha's children and grandchildren are central to her life, and they give her hope for the future. Manisha and her husband are devoted to each other but had to adjust to living together again after living in separate quarters for many years in Nepal. In some ways, Manisha led a much more independent life in the refugee camp than back in Bhutan, and she came to value that independence. She and her husband are still negotiating this change from traditional gender roles.

Small groups, organizations, and communities have been important forces in Manisha's life. In the refugee camp, she participated in some focus groups that the UNHCR conducted with the women in the camps. She is enjoying the relationships she is developing with her ESL class and her citizenship preparation class; she draws courage from the companionship and the collegial sense of "we are all in the same boat" that she gets from the weekly classes. She also has warm relationships with the other cafeteria workers at the school.

Several organizations have been helpful to Manisha and her family since they fled Bhutan. First, she is grateful for the UNHCR for all of the resources it put into running the Nepali refugee camps. Second, she has high praise for Oxfam International, which started the knitting program in the camps. In the United States, she is grateful for the assistance of the refugee resettlement program that sponsored her family and is especially appreciative of the ESL program they run and the moral support provided by the social worker. She is learning to work within the context of the public school bureaucracy. She would like to have more contact with the Hindu Center, but the distance does not make that easy.

Manisha has adapted her behavior to live within four different types of communities. In her Bhutanese farming village, she was surrounded by open land, extended family, and long-term friends. In the poorly sheltered camp by the river, fear and confusion were the driving force of relationships, and loss of loved ones was a much too common occurrence. In the crowded refugee camp, disease and despair were common, but she also found her voice and played an important role in helping other women and their children. She enjoyed her leadership position as deputy secretary of the camp and liked the active life she created in this role. Now, she has moved to a suburb of a U.S. city where she lives in a small apartment in a neighborhood with many other Bhutanese refugees. Suburban life is a new experience for her, and she has had many new behaviors to learn, such as how to use unfamiliar appliances, how to cook with unfamiliar foods, and how to navigate public transportation.

Manisha's story has been powerfully influenced by the geopolitical unrest that began just as she was entering middle adulthood. Her relationships with social institutions have changed over time, and she has had to learn new rules based on her changing place in the social structure. Prior to 1988, she enjoyed high status in her village and the respect that comes with it. She lived in peace. She still does not understand why the Bhutanese government suddenly began to discriminate against her ethnic group, and she grieves the loss of property, status, and homeland that came out of this unrest. She is grateful to the United Nations for its support of the Bhutanese refugees and to the United States for welcoming some to resettle here.

Manisha is aware that some members of her Nepali ethnic group developed a resistance social movement when the Bhutanese government began to discriminate against them. She is also aware that some refugees in the Nepali refugee camps resisted the idea of resettlement in the United States and other countries because they thought resettlement would dilute the pressure on Bhutan to repatriate the Nepalis. As much as Manisha would love to be repatriated, she and her family decided that resettlement in the United States was their best chance for a good future.

Time is also an important part of Manisha's story. Her story, like all human stories, is influenced by the human capacity to live not only in the present time but also in past and future times. Discrimination, imprisonment, escape, crowded camps, and resettlement are past events in her family's life and can be vividly recalled. There have been times in Manisha's life when she needed to focus on future possibilities with questions such as "Should we leave Bhutan or stay?" and "Should we resettle in the United States or continue to try to return to Bhutan?" This future thinking has had an enormous impact on the current circumstances of the family's lives. Manisha's husband spends a lot of time thinking about his past life in Bhutan and all that has been lost, but she likes to think about the pleasant aspects of her past life. Manisha sees that her children and grandchildren are living largely in the present while also imagining possibilities for their future life in the United States, and she is trying to do that as well.

Manisha's story is also influenced by the historical times in which she has lived and is living. If she had been born 50 years earlier, it is possible that she could have lived out life peacefully in her farm village. On the other hand, the UNHCR, which was so instrumental to her family's survival, was not established until December 1950, 2 years before her birth, and she is lucky to have lived in an era of international support for refugees. The family's adjustment to life in the United States was hampered in the early days by the global economic recession of the time. Her youngest son benefits from living in an era when college credits can be earned by online study. The times in which we live shape our behaviors in many ways.

Another way to think about the role of time in human behavior is to consider the way in which age, or life stage, influences behavior. Manisha notes that learning English and adapting to their new life in the United States is so much easier for her children and grandchildren than it is for her and her husband. She is enjoying the grandparent role that is a large part of her focus in this life stage. She is happy to have a job rather than spending all day in the small apartment, but she hopes that she and her husband will stay well enough for her to continue to work for many more years.

As suggested, social work has historically recognized human behavior as an interaction of person with environment, although the relative emphasis on different dimensions of person and environment has changed over time (see Kondrat, 2008). Today, a vast multidisciplinary literature is available to help us in our social work efforts. The good news is that the multifaceted nature of this literature provides a broad knowledge base for the varied settings and roles involved in social work practice. The bad news is that this literature is highly fragmented, scattered across a large number of fields. What we need is a structure for organizing our thinking about this multifaceted, multidisciplinary, fragmented literature.

The multidimensional approach provided in this book should help. This approach is built on the person–environment–time model described earlier. Although in this book we focus on each of these elements separately, keep in mind that no single element can be entirely understood without attention to other elements. The dimensions

Social work has historically recognized human behavior as an interaction of person with environment.

of person and environment identified in this book were traditionally studied as detached or semidetached realities, with one dimension characterized as causing or leading to another. In recent years, however, behavioral science scholars have begun to collaborate across disciplines, leading to exciting new ways of thinking about human behavior, which the contributing authors and I share with you. I want to be clear that I do not see the dimensions analyzed in this book as detached realities, and I am not presenting a causal model. I want instead to show how these dimensions work together, how they are interwoven with each other, and how many possibilities are opened for social work practice when we think about human behavior in a multidimensional way. I am suggesting that humans engage in **multidetermined behavior**, that is, behavior that develops as a result of many causes. I do think, however, that focusing on specific dimensions one at a time can help to clarify general, abstract statements about person-in-environment—that is, it can put some flesh on the bones of this abstract framework. Exhibit 1.1 is a graphic overview of the dimensions of person, environment, and time discussed in this book. Exhibit 1.2 defines and gives examples for each dimension.

CRITICAL THINKING Questions 1.1

What courses have you taken in the past that added to your understanding of human behavior? How does content from any of these courses help you to understand Manisha's story and how a social worker might be helpful to Manisha and her family? Do you agree that the person-in-environment framework is still useful for social work? Explain your answer.

PERSONAL DIMENSIONS

Any story could be told from the perspective of any person in the story. The story at the beginning of this chapter is told from Manisha's perspective, but it could have been told from the perspectives of a variety of other persons such as the Bhutanese king, Manisha's husband, one of Manisha's children, one of Manisha's grandchildren, a UNHCR staff member, one of the women supported by Manisha in the camp, the social worker at the refugee

EXHIBIT 1.1 • Person, Environment, and Time Dimensions

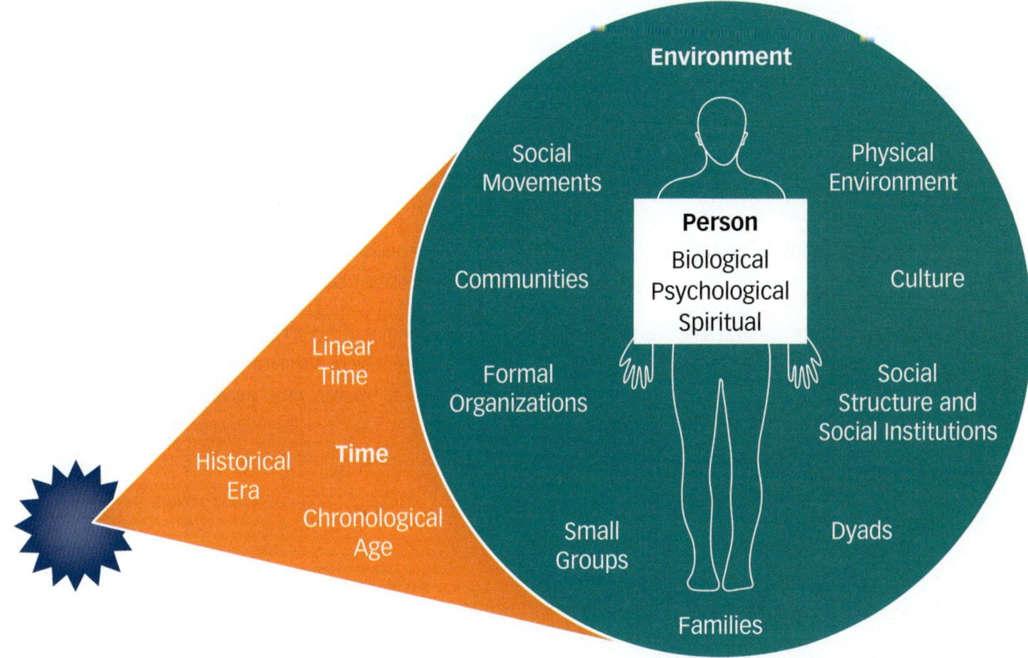

resettlement agency, or one of her coworkers. You will want to recognize the multiple perspectives held by different persons involved in the stories of which you become a part in your social work activities.

You also will want tools for thinking about the various dimensions of the persons involved in these stories. In recent years, social workers, like contemporary scholars in other disciplines, have taken a *biopsychosocial approach* that recognizes human behavior as the result of interactions of integrated biological, psychological, and social systems (see Melchert, 2013). In this approach, psychology is seen as inseparable from biology; emotions and cognitions affect the health of the body and are affected by it (Smith, Fortin, Dwamena, & Frankel, 2013). Neurobiologists are identifying the brain circuitry involved in thoughts and emotions (Davidson & Begley, 2012; Kurzweil, 2012). They are finding evidence that the human brain is wired for social life (Lieberman, 2013). They are also finding that the social environment has an impact on brain structure and functions and that environments actually turn genes on and off. Environments influence biology, but the same environment acts on diverse genetic material (Hutchison, 2014).

In recent years, social work scholars and those in the social and behavioral sciences and medicine have argued for greater attention to the spiritual dimension of persons as well (see Crisp, 2010). Developments in neuroscience have generated new explorations of the unity of the biological, psychological, and spiritual dimensions of the person. For example, recent research has focused on the ways that emotions and thoughts, as well as spiritual states, influence the immune system and some aspects of mental health (Davidson & Begley, 2012). One national longitudinal study examined the role of spirituality in physical and mental health after the collective trauma of the 9/11 attacks and found that high levels of spirituality were associated with fewer infectious ailments, more positive emotions, and more immediate processing of the traumatic event in the 3 years following the attacks (McIntosh, Poulin, Silver, & Holman, 2011). In this book, we give substantial coverage to all three of these personal dimensions: biological, psychological, and spiritual; they are covered in some detail in Chapters 3–5.

ENVIRONMENTAL DIMENSIONS

Social workers have always thought about the environment as multidimensional. As early as 1901, Mary Richmond presented a model of social work case coordination that took into account not only personal dimensions but also family, neighborhood, civic organizations, private charitable organizations, and public relief organizations. Several models for classifying dimensions of the environment have been proposed since Mary Richmond's time. Social workers (see, e.g., Ashford, LeCroy, & Lortie, 2010) have also been influenced by Uri Bronfenbrenner's (2005) ecological perspective, which identifies the five interdependent, nested categories or levels of systems presented in Exhibit 1.3. You might notice some similarities between Bronfenbrenner's model and the one presented in Exhibit 1.1. By adding

EXHIBIT 1.2 • Definitions and Examples of Dimensions of Person, Environment, and Time

DIMENSION	DEFINITION	EXAMPLES
PERSON		
Biological	The body's biochemical, cell, organ, and physiological systems	Nervous system, endocrine system, immune system, cardiovascular system, musculoskeletal system, reproductive system
Psychological	The mind and the mental processes	Cognitions (conscious thinking processes), emotions (feelings), self (identity)
Spiritual	The aspect of the person that searches for meaning and purpose in life	Themes of morality; ethics; justice; interconnectedness; creativity; mystical states; prayer, meditation, and contemplation; relationships with a higher power
ENVIRONMENT		
Culture	A set of common understandings, evident in both behavior and material artifacts	Beliefs, customs, traditions, values
Physical	The natural and human-built material aspects of the environment	Water, sun, trees, buildings, landscapes
Dyads	Two persons bound together in some way	Parent and child, romantic couple, social worker and client
Families	A social group of two or more persons, characterized by ongoing interdependence with long-term commitments that stem from blood, law, or affection	Nuclear family, extended family, chosen family
Small groups	Two or more people who interact with each other because of shared interests, goals, experiences, and needs	Friendship group, self-help group, therapy group, committee, task group, interdisciplinary team
Formal organizations	Collectivities of people, with a high degree of formality of structure, working together to meet a goal or goals	Civic and social service organizations, business organizations, professional associations
Communities	People bound either by geography or by network links (webs of communication), sharing common ties, and interacting with one another	Territorial communities such as neighborhoods; relational communities such as the social work community, the disability community, a faith community, a soccer league
Social structure and social institutions	Social structure: a set of interrelated social institutions developed by humans to impose constraints on human interaction for the purpose of the survival and well-being of the collectivity Social institutions: patterned ways of organizing social relations in a particular sector of social life	Social structure: social class Social institutions: government, economy, education, health care, social welfare, religion, mass media, and family
Social movements	Large-scale collective actions to make change, or resist change, in specific social institutions	Civil rights movement, poor people's movements, disability movement, gay rights movement
TIME		
Linear time	Time in terms of a straight line	Past, present, future
Historical era	A discrete block of time in human history	Progressive Era, the Great Depression, 1960s
Chronological age	Age of a person measured in years, months, and days from the date the person was born; may also be described in terms of a stage of the human life course	Six months old (infancy), 15 years old (adolescence), 80 years old (late adulthood)

EXHIBIT 1.3 • Five Categories or Levels of Systems as Presented by Uri Bronfenbrenner

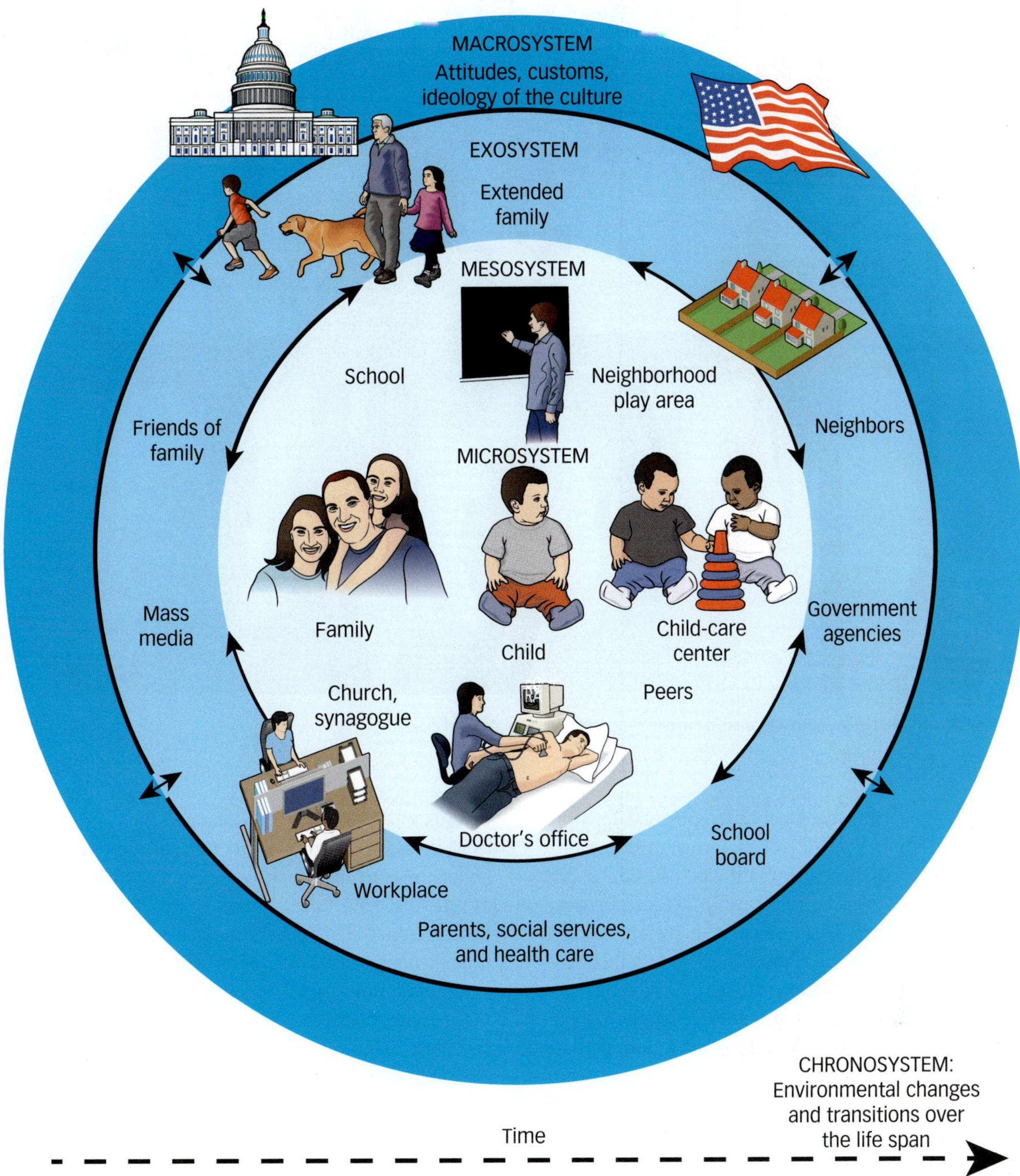

SOURCE: Adapted from Bronfenbrenner and Morris, 2006.

chronosystems in his later work, Bronfenbrenner was acknowledging the importance of time in person–environment transactions, but this book presents a more fluid, less hierarchical model of person-in-environment than presented by Bronfenbrenner. Some social work models have included the physical environment (natural and built environments) as a separate dimension (see Norton, 2009). There is growing evidence of the impact of the physical environment on human well-being and growing concern about environmental justice issues in the physical environment.

To have an up-to-date understanding of the multidimensional environment, I recommend that social workers have knowledge about the nine dimensions of environment described in Exhibit 1.2 and discussed in

Three elements of human behavior are captured in this photo—person, environment, and time.

Chapters 6–9 in this book: culture, physical environment, dyads, families, small groups, formal organizations, communities, social structure and social institutions, and social movements. Dyadic relationships—those between two people, the most basic social relationship—receive attention throughout the book and are emphasized in Chapter 4, in discussion of self in relationships. Simultaneous consideration of multiple environmental dimensions provides new possibilities for action, perhaps even new or revised approaches to social work practice.

These dimensions are neither mutually exclusive nor hierarchically ordered. For example, a family is sometimes referred to as a social institution, families can also be considered small groups or dyads, and family theorists write about family culture. Remember, dimensions are useful ways of thinking about person–environment configurations, but we should not think of them as detached realities.

The importance of time in human behavior is reflected in the finding that *time* is the most commonly used noun in print in the English language; *person* is the second most common (BBC News, 2006). There are many ways to think about time. Physics is generally seen as the lead discipline for studying time, and quantum physics has challenged much about the way we think about time. Various aspects of time are examined by other disciplines as well, and there are a number of different ways to think about time. In this book, we examine three dimensions of time that have been studied by behavioral scientists as important to the understanding of human behavior: linear time, historical era, and chronological age.

Linear time—time ordered like a straight line from the past through the present and into the future—is the most common way that humans think about time. Although it is known that people in some cultures and groups think of time as stationary rather than moving (Boroditsky, Fuhrman, & McCormick, 2011), contemporary behavioral science researchers are interested in what they call "mental time travel," the human ability to remember events from the past and to imagine and plan for the future (Eacott & Easton, 2012). The research on mental time travel has focused on the conscious processes of reminiscence and anticipation, but there is also considerable evidence that past events are stored as unconscious material in the brain and the body and show up in our thoughts and emotions (see Davidson & Begley, 2012; Kurzweil, 2012). Traces of past events also exist in the natural and built environments, for example, in centuries-old buildings or in piles of debris following a hurricane or tornado.

This approach to time has been called *clock time* (Zimbardo & Boyd, 2008). However, this approach to time is a relatively new invention, and many people in the contemporary world have a very different approach to time. In nonindustrialized countries, and in subcultures within industrialized countries, people operate on *event time*, allowing scheduling to be determined by events. For example, in agricultural societies, the most successful farmers are those who can be responsive to natural events—sunrise and sunset, rain, drought, temperature—rather than to scheduled events (Zimbardo & Boyd, 2008). Manisha's life was organized around cues from the natural world rather than the clock when she lived in Bhutan, just as my grandfather's was on his farm in rural Tennessee.

Clock time cultures often use the concept of **time orientation** to describe the extent to which individuals and collectivities are invested in the three temporal zones—past, present, and future. Research indicates that cultures differ in their time orientation. In most cultures, however, some situations call for us to be totally immersed in the present, others call for historical understanding of the past and its impact on the present, and still others call for attention to future consequences and possibilities. Psychologists Philip Zimbardo and John Boyd (2008) have been studying time orientation for more than 30 years and have identified the six most common time perspectives held in the Western world. They call these the *past-positive* (invested in the past, focused on its positive aspects), *past-negative* (invested in the past, focused on its negative aspects), *present-hedonistic* (invested in the present, focused on getting as much pleasure as possible from it), *present-fatalistic* (invested in the present, sees life as controlled by fate), *future* (invested in the future, organizes life around future goals), and *transcendental-future* (invested in the future, focuses on new time after death). Zimbardo and Boyd's research using the Zimbardo Time Perspective Inventory (ZTPI) in a number of Western societies indicates that human well-being is maximized when people in these societies live with a balance of past-positive, present-hedonistic, and future perspectives. People with biases toward past-negative and present-fatalistic perspectives are at greater risk of developing physical and mental health problems. Zimbardo and Boyd's (2008) book *The Time Paradox* suggests ways to become more past-positive, present, and future oriented to develop a more balanced time orientation. You might want to visit www.thetimeparadox.com and complete the ZTPI to investigate your own time orientation.

Zimbardo and Boyd have carried out their research in Western societies and acknowledge that the ZTPI may not accurately reflect time orientation in other societies. They make particular note that their description of present-hedonistic and present-fatalistic does not adequately capture the way Eastern religions think about the present. Recently, Western behavioral scientists have begun to incorporate Eastern mindfulness practices of being more fully present in the current moment (present orientation) to help people buffer the persistent stresses of clock time and goal monitoring (future orientation) (Davidson & Begley, 2012). Research also indicates age-related differences in time orientation, with older adults tending to be more past oriented than younger age groups (Yeung, Fung, & Kam, 2012). Women have been found to be more future oriented and men more present oriented (Zimbardo & Boyd, 2008). Researchers have found that trauma survivors who experienced the most severe loss are more likely than other trauma survivors to be highly oriented to the past (Martz, 2004). Zimbardo and Boyd (2008) suggest that trauma survivors may need assistance to think in different ways about past trauma and to enhance their capacity for present and future thinking. This is something to keep in mind when we interact with refugees, military men and women who have served in war zones, and other groups who have an increased likelihood of having a history of trauma. It is also important for social workers to be aware of the meaning of time for the individuals and communities they serve.

Two other dimensions of time have been identified as important to the understanding of human behavior. Both of these dimensions are aspects of linear time but have been separated out for special study by behavioral scientists. The first, *historical era*, refers to the specific block or period of time in which individual and collective lives are enacted. The historical era in which we live shapes our environments. The economies, physical environments, institutions, technologies, and geopolitical circumstances of a specific era provide both options for and constraints on human behavior. The second, *chronological age*, seems to be an important variable in every society. How people change at different ages and life stages as they pass from birth to death has been one of the most enduring ways of studying both individual and collective behavior. Historical era is examined throughout this book, and chronological age is the organizing framework for Part IV, "The Changing Life Course" (Chapters 10–16).

CRITICAL THINKING Questions 1.2

How would our understanding of Manisha's story change if we had no knowledge of her prior life experiences in Bhutan and the Nepali refugee camp—if we only assessed her situation based on her current functioning? What personal and environmental dimensions would we note in her current functioning?

DIVERSITY, INEQUALITY, AND THE PURSUIT OF SOCIAL JUSTICE: A GLOBAL PERSPECTIVE

The Council on Social Work Education (2015) proposes that social work practice is guided by a global perspective. What exactly does that mean, and why is it valued by social workers? We are increasingly aware that we are part of an interconnected world, and Manisha's story is one reminder of this. A global perspective involves much more than geography, however. Here are some aspects of what it means to take a global perspective:

- To be aware that my view of the world is not universally shared, and others may have a view of the world that is profoundly different from mine
- To have a growing awareness of the diversity of ideas and cultural practices found in human societies around the world
- To be curious about conditions in other parts of the world and how they relate to conditions in our own society
- To understand where I fit in the global social structure and social institutions
- To have a growing awareness of how people in other societies view my society
- To have a growing understanding of how the world works, with special attention to systems and mechanisms of inequality and oppression around the world

We have always been connected to other peoples of the world, but those connections are being intensified by **globalization**, a process by which the world's people are becoming more interconnected economically, politically, environmentally, and culturally. It is a process of increased connectedness and interdependence that began at least 5 centuries ago but has intensified in recent times and is affecting people around the world (C. Mann, 2011). This increasing connectedness is, of course, aided by rapid advancements in communication technology. There is much debate about whether globalization is a good thing or a bad thing, a conversation that is picked up in Chapter 9 as we consider the globalization of social institutions. What is important to note here is that globalization is increasing our experiences with social diversity and raising new questions about inequality, human rights, and social justice.

DIVERSITY

Diversity has always been a part of the social reality in the United States. Even before the Europeans came, the Indigenous people were divided into about 200 distinct societies with about 200 different languages (Parrillo, 2009). Since the inception of the United States of America, we have been a nation of immigrants. We value our nation's immigrant heritage and take pride in the ideals of equality of opportunity for all who come. However, there have always been tensions about how we as a nation handle diversity. Are we a *melting pot* where all are melted into one indistinguishable model of citizenship, or are we a *pluralist society* in which groups have separate identities, cultures, and ways of organizing but work together in mutual respect? Pioneer social worker Jane Addams (1910) was a prominent voice for pluralism during the early 20th century, and that stance is consistent with social work's concern for human rights.

Even though diversity has always been present in the United States, it is accurate to say that some of the diversity in our national social life is new. Clearly, there is increasing racial, ethnic, and religious diversity in the United States, and the mix in the population stream has become much more complex in recent years (Parrillo, 2009). The United States was 87% White in 1925, 80% White in 1950, and 72% White in 2000; by 2050, it is

FGP/Archive Photos/Getty Images

Diversity has always been a part of the social reality in the United States.

projected that we will be about 47% White (Taylor & Cohn, 2012). Why is this happening at this time? A major driving force is the demographic reality that native-born people are no longer reproducing at replacement level in the wealthy postindustrial nations, which, if it continues, ultimately will lead to a declining population skewed toward advanced age. One solution used by some countries, including the United States, is to change immigration policy to allow new streams of immigration. The current rate of foreign-born persons in the United States is lower than it has been throughout most of the past 150 years, but foreign-born persons are less likely to be White than when immigration policy, prior to 1965, strictly limited entry for persons of color. With the recent influx of immigrants from around the globe, the United States has become one of many ethnically and racially diverse nations in the world today. In many wealthy postindustrial countries, including the United States, there is much anti-immigrant sentiment, even though the economies of these countries are dependent on such migration. Waves of immigration have historically been accompanied by anti-immigrant sentiment. There appear to be many reasons for anti-immigrant sentiment, including fear that new immigrants will dilute the "purity" of the native culture, racial and religious bias, and fear of economic competition. Like other diverse societies, we must find ways to embrace the diversity and seize the opportunity to demonstrate the human capacity for intergroup harmony.

On the other hand, some of the diversity in our social life is not new but simply newly recognized. In the contemporary era, we have been developing a heightened consciousness of human differences—gender and gender identity differences, racial and ethnic differences, cultural differences, religious differences, differences in sexual orientation, differences in abilities and disabilities, differences in family forms, and so on. This book intends to capture the diversity of human experience in a manner that is respectful of all groups, conveys the positive value of human diversity, and recognizes differences *within* groups as well as *among* groups.

As we seek to honor differences, we make a distinction between heterogeneity and diversity. We use **heterogeneity** to refer to individual-level variations—differences among individuals. For example, as the social worker whom Manisha consults, you will want to recognize the ways in which she is different from you and from other clients you serve, including other clients of Bhutanese heritage. An understanding of heterogeneity allows us to recognize the uniqueness of each person and situation. **Diversity**, on the other hand, is used to refer to patterns of group differences. Diversity recognizes social groups, groups of people who share a range of physical, cultural, or social characteristics within a category of social identity. Knowledge of diversity helps us to provide culturally sensitive services.

I want to interject a word here about terminology and human diversity. As the contributing authors and I attempted to uncover what is known about human diversity, we struggled with terminology to define identity groups. We searched for consistent language to describe different groups, and we were dedicated to using language that identity groups would use to describe themselves. However, we ran into challenges endemic to our time related to the language of diversity. It is not the case, as you have probably observed, that all members of a given identity group at any given time embrace the same terminology for their group. As we reviewed literature from different historical moments, we recognized the shifting nature of terminology. In addition, even within a given historical era, we found that different researchers used different terms and had different decision rules about who composes the membership of identity groups. Add to this the changing way that the U.S. Census Bureau establishes official categories of people, and in the end, we did not settle on fixed terminology to consistently describe identity groups. Rather, we use the language of individual researchers when reporting their work, because we want to avoid distorting their work. We hope you will not find this too distracting. We also hope that you will recognize that the ever-changing language of diversity has both constructive potential to find creative ways to affirm diversity and destructive potential to dichotomize diversity into *the norm* and *the other*.

INEQUALITY

Attending to diversity involves recognition of the power relations and the patterns of opportunities and constraints for social groups. When we attend to diversity, we note not only the differences between groups but also how socially constructed hierarchies of power are superimposed on these differences.

Recent U.S. scholarship in the social sciences has emphasized the ways in which three types of categorizations—gender, race, and class—are used to develop hierarchical social structures that influence social identities and life chances (Rothenberg, 2010; Sernau, 2014). This literature suggests that these social categorizations create **privilege**, or unearned advantage, for some groups and disadvantage for other groups. In a much-cited article, Peggy McIntosh (2007, first printed in 1988) has pointed out the mundane, daily advantages of White privilege that are not available to members of groups of color, such as assurances "that my children will be given curricular materials that testify to the existence of their race," and "Whether I use checks, credit cards, or cash, I can count on my skin color not to work against the appearance of financial reliability." We could also generate lists of advantages of male privilege, adult privilege, upper-middle-class privilege, heterosexual privilege, ability privilege, Christian privilege, and so on. McIntosh argues that members of privileged groups benefit from their privilege but have not been taught to think of themselves as privileged. They take for granted that their advantages are normal and universal. For survival, members of nonprivileged groups must learn a lot about the lives of groups with privilege, but groups with privileged status are not similarly compelled to learn about the lives of members of nonprivileged groups.

Michael Schwalbe (2006) argues that those of us who live in the United States also carry "American privilege," which comes from our dominant position in the world. (I would prefer to call this U.S. privilege because people living in Canada, Ecuador, and Brazil also live in America.) According to Schwalbe, among other things, American privilege means that we don't have to bother to learn about other countries or about the impact of our foreign policy on people living in those countries. American privilege also means that we have access to cheap goods that are produced by poorly paid workers in impoverished countries. As Chapter 9 shows, the income and wealth gap between nations is mind-boggling. Sernau (2014) reports that the combined income of the 25 richest people in the United States is almost as great as the combined income of 2 billion of the world's poorest people. In 2011, the average per capita income in Bhutan was $2,346 in U.S. dollars, compared with $48,112 in the United States (World Bank, 2013a). It is becoming increasingly difficult to deny the costs of exercising American privilege by remaining ignorant about the rest of the world and the impact our actions have on other nations.

As the contributing authors and I strive to provide a global context, we encounter current controversies about appropriate language to describe different sectors of the world. Following World War II, a distinction was made between First World, Second World, and Third World nations, with *First World* referring to the Western capitalist nations, *Second World* referring to the countries belonging to the socialist bloc led by the Soviet Union, and *Third World* referring to a set of countries that were primarily former colonies of the First World. More recently, many scholars have used this same language to define global sectors in a slightly different way. *First World* has been used to describe the nations that were the first to industrialize, urbanize, and modernize. *Second World* has been used to describe nations that have industrialized but have not yet become central to the world economy. *Third World* has been used to refer to nonindustrialized nations that have few resources and are considered expendable in the global economy. However, this approach has begun to lose favor in the past few years (Leeder, 2004). Immanuel Wallerstein (1974, 1979) uses different language but makes a similar distinction; he refers to wealthy *core* countries, newly industrialized *semiperiphery* countries, and the poorest *periphery* countries. Other writers divide the world into *developed* and *developing* countries, referring to the level of industrialization, urbanization, and modernization. Still others divide the world into the *Global North* and the *Global South*, calling attention to a history in which the Global North colonized and exploited the resources of the Global South. Finally, some writers talk about the *West* versus the *East*, where the distinctions are largely cultural. We recognize that such categories carry great symbolic meaning and can mask systems of power and exploitation. As with diversity, we attempted to find a respectful language that could be used consistently throughout the book. Again, we found that different researchers have used different language and different characteristics to describe categories of nations, and when reporting on their findings, we have used their own language to avoid misrepresenting their findings.

It is important to note that privilege and disadvantage are multidimensional, not one-dimensional. One can be privileged in one dimension and disadvantaged in another; for example, I have White privilege but not gender privilege. As social workers, we need to be attuned to our own *social locations*—where we fit in a system of social identities, such as race, ethnicity, gender, social class, sexual orientation, religion, ability/disability, and age. We must recognize how our own particular social locations shape how we see the world, what we notice, and how we interpret what we "see."

It is important for social workers to acknowledge social inequalities because our interactions are constantly affected by inequalities of various types. In addition, there is clear evidence that social inequalities are on the rise in the United States. Although income inequality has been growing in all of the wealthy nations of the world over the past 2 decades, the United States gained the distinction as the most unequal wealthy nation in this period, and the gap has continued to widen since the deep economic crisis that began in 2008 (Organisation for Economic Co-operation and Development, 2011).

THE PURSUIT OF SOCIAL JUSTICE

There is another important reason why social workers must acknowledge social inequalities. The National Association of Social Workers (NASW) Code of Ethics identifies social justice as one of six core values of social work and mandates that "Social Workers challenge social injustice" (NASW, 2008). To challenge injustice, we must first recognize it and understand the ways it is embedded in a number of societal institutions. That is a major subject of Chapter 9 in this book.

The Council on Social Work Education (2015) notes that "social workers also understand the forms and mechanisms of oppression and discrimination and recognize the extent to which a culture's structures and values, including social, economic, political, and cultural exclusions, may oppress, marginalize, alienate, or create privilege and power" (p. 4). Suzanne Pharr (1988) has provided some useful conceptual tools that can help us with this. She identifies a set of mechanisms of oppression, whereby the everyday arrangements of social life systematically block opportunities for some groups and inhibit their power to exercise self-determination. Exhibit 1.4 provides an overview of these mechanisms of oppression. As you review the list, you may recognize some that are familiar to you, such as stereotyping and perhaps blaming the victim. There may be others that you have not previously given much thought to. You may also recognize, as I do each time I look at the list, that whereas some of these mechanisms of oppression are sometimes used quite intentionally, others are not so intentional but occur as we do business as usual. For example, when you walk into your classroom (or some place of business), do you give much thought to the person who cleans that room, what wage this person is paid, whether this is the only job this person holds, and what opportunities and barriers this person has experienced in life? Most likely, the classroom is cleaned in the evening after it has been vacated by teachers and students, and the person who cleans it, like many people who provide services that make our lives more pleasant, is invisible to you. Giving serious thought to common mechanisms of oppression can help us to recognize social injustice and think about ways to challenge it.

In recent years, social workers have expanded the conversation about social justice to include *global* social justice. As they have done so, they have more and more drawn on the concept of *human rights* to organize thinking about social justice (see Mapp, 2008; Reichert, 2006; Wronka, 2008). In the aftermath of World War II, the newly formed United Nations (1948) created a Universal Declaration of Human Rights (UDHR), which spelled out the rights to which all humans were entitled, regardless of

EXHIBIT 1.4 • Common Mechanisms of Oppression

MECHANISM	DEFINITION
Economic power and control	Limiting of resources, mobility, education, and employment options to all but a few
Myth of scarcity	Myth used to pit people against one another, suggests that resources are limited and blames people (e.g., poor people, immigrants) for using too many of them
Defined norm	A standard of what is good and right, against which all are judged
The other	Those who fall outside "the norm" but are defined in relation to it, seen as abnormal, inferior, marginalized
Invisibility	Keeping "the other's" existence, everyday life, and achievements unknown
Distortion	Selective presentation or rewriting of history so that only negative aspects of "the other" are included
Stereotyping	Generalizing the actions of a few to an entire group, denying individual characteristics and behaviors
Violence and the threat of violence	Laying claim to resources, then using might to ensure superior position
Lack of prior claim	Excluding anyone who was not originally included and labeling as disruptive those who fight for inclusion
Blaming the victim	Condemning "the others" for their situation, diverting attention from the roles that dominants play in the situation
Internalized oppression	Internalizing negative judgments of being "the other," leading to self-hatred, depression, despair, and self-abuse
Horizontal hostility	Extending internalized oppression to one's entire group as well as to other subordinate groups, expressing hostility to other oppressed persons and groups rather than to members of dominant groups
Isolation	Physically isolating people as individuals or as a "minority" group
Assimilation	Pressuring members of "minority" groups to drop their culture and differences and become a mirror of the dominant culture
Tokenism	Rewarding some of the most assimilated "others" with position and resources
Emphasis on individual solutions	Emphasizing individual responsibility for problems and individual solutions rather than collective responsibility and collective solutions

SOURCE: Adapted from Pharr, 1988.

their place in the world, and this document has become a point of reference for subsequent definitions of human rights. Cox and Pawar (2013) identify eight philosophical values suggested by the UDHR: life (human and nonhuman); freedom and liberty; equality and nondiscrimination; justice; solidarity; social responsibility; evolution, peace, and nonviolence; and relationships between humankind and nature.

A number of theories of social justice have been proposed. Probably the most frequently cited theory of social justice in the social work literature is John Rawls's (1971, 2001) theory of justice as fairness. In the past decade or so, some social work scholars (Banerjee & Canda, 2012; P. Morris, 2002) have recommended the capabilities approach to social justice, originally proposed by Amartya Sen (1992, 2009) and revised by Martha Nussbaum (2011). The capabilities approach draws on both Western and non-Western thinking. In this approach, capabilities are, in simplest terms, opportunities and freedoms to be or do what we view as worthwhile; justice is served when people have such opportunities and freedoms. Nussbaum carries the capabilities approach a step further and identifies 10 core capabilities that all people in all societies must have to lead a dignified life. She asserts that promotion of social justice involves supporting the capabilities of people who are denied opportunities and freedoms related to any of the core capabilities. See Exhibit 1.5 for an overview of the core capabilities identified by Nussbaum.

CRITICAL THINKING Questions 1.3

What impact is globalization having on your own life? Do you see it as having a positive or negative impact on your life? What about for Manisha? Do you think globalization is having a positive or negative impact on her life? Do you agree with Martha Nussbaum that it is important for all people to have opportunities and freedoms in relation to the 10 core capabilities she identifies? How do you see Manisha in relation to these core capabilities?

KNOWING AND DOING

Social workers, like other professional practitioners, must find a way to move from knowing to doing, from "knowing about" and "knowing that" into "knowing how to" (for fuller discussion of this issue, see Hutchison, Charlesworth, Matto, Harrigan, & Viggiani, 2007). We *know* for the purpose of *doing*. Like architects, engineers, physicians, and teachers, social workers are faced with complex problems and case situations that are unique and uncertain. You no doubt will find that social work education, social work practice, and even this book will stretch your capacity to tolerate ambiguity and uncertainty. That is important because, as Carol Meyer (1993) has suggested,

EXHIBIT 1.5 • Nussbaum's 10 Core Capabilities

CAPABILITY	DEFINITION
Life	To live to the end of a normal life course
Bodily health	To have good physical health and adequate nourishment and shelter
Bodily integrity	To exercise freedom of movement, freedom from assault, and reproductive choice
Senses, imagination, and thought	To have pleasant sensory experiences, pain avoidance, adequate education, imagination, free self-expression, and religious freedom
Emotion	To experience a full range of emotion and to love and be loved
Practical reason	To think critically and make wise decisions
Affiliation	To live with others with empathy and compassion, without discrimination
Concern for other species	To show concern for animals, plants, and other aspects of nature
Play	To laugh and play and enjoy recreational activities
Control over one's political and material environment	To participate freely in the political process and have equal access to employment and property

SOURCE: Adapted from Nussbaum, 2011.

"There are no easy or simple [social work] cases, only simplistic perceptions" (p. 63). There are four important ingredients of "knowing how" to do social work: knowledge about the case, knowledge about the self, values and ethics, and scientific knowledge. These four ingredients are intertwined in the process of doing social work. The focus of this book is on scientific knowledge, but all four ingredients are essential in social work practice. Before moving to a discussion of scientific knowledge, I want to say a word about the other three ingredients.

KNOWLEDGE ABOUT THE CASE

I am using *case* to mean the situation at hand, a situation that has become problematic for some person or collectivity, resulting in a social work intervention. Our first task as social workers is to develop as good an understanding of the situation as possible: Who is involved in the situation, and how are they involved? What is the nature of the relationships of the people involved? What are the physical, societal, cultural, and community contexts of the situation? What are the contextual constraints as well as the contextual resources for bringing change to the situation? What elements of the case are maintaining the problematic situation? How have people tried to cope with the situation? What preferences do the involved people have about the types of intervention to use? What is the culture, and what are the social resources of the social agency to whose attention the situation is brought? You might begin to think about how you would answer some of these questions in relation to Manisha's situation.

It is important to note that knowledge about the case is influenced by the quality of the relationship between the social worker and client(s). There is good evidence that people are likely to reveal more aspects of their situation if they are approached with commitment, an open mind, warmth, empathic attunement, authentic responsiveness, and mutuality (Hepworth, Rooney, Rooney, & Strom-Gottfried, 2013). For example, as Manisha became comfortable in the interview, feeling validated by both the interviewer and the interpreter, she began to engage in deeper reflection about what happened in Bhutan. At the end of the interview, she expressed much gratitude for the opportunity to tell her story, noting that it was the first chance she had to put the story together and that telling the story had led her to think about some events in new ways. This can be an important part of her grieving and adjustment process. The integrity of knowledge about the case is related to the quality of the relationship, and the capacity for relationship is related to knowledge about the self.

But knowledge about the case requires more than simply gathering information. We must select and order the information at hand and decide if further information is needed. This involves making a series of decisions about what is relevant and what is not. It also involves searching for recurring themes as well as contradictions in the information. For example, it was important for the refugee resettlement social worker to note Manisha's lingering confusion about why her peaceful world in Bhutan got turned upside down. This suggests that Manisha and other Bhutanese refugees might benefit from narrative exercises that help them to make sense of these experiences.

To assist you in moving between knowledge about the case and scientific knowledge, each chapter in this book begins, as this one does, with one or more case studies. Each of these unique stories suggests what scientific knowledge is needed. For example, to work effectively with Manisha, you will want to understand some things about Bhutan, the Nepali ethnic group, Hinduism, grief reactions, the acculturation process, challenges facing immigrant families, and cross-cultural communication. Throughout the chapters, the stories are woven together with relevant scientific knowledge. Keep in mind that scientific knowledge is necessary, but you will not be an effective practitioner unless you take the time to learn about the unique situation of each person or collectivity you serve. It is the unique situation that guides what scientific knowledge is needed.

KNOWLEDGE ABOUT THE SELF

In his book *The Spiritual Life of Children*, Robert Coles (1990) wrote about the struggles of a 10-year-old Hopi girl to have her Anglo teacher understand Hopi spirituality. Coles suggested to the girl that perhaps she could try to explain her tribal nation's spiritual beliefs to the teacher. The girl answered, "But they don't listen to hear *us*; they listen to hear themselves" (p. 25, emphasis in the original). This young girl has captured, in a profound way, a major challenge to our everyday personal and professional communications: the tendency to approach the world with preconceived notions that we seek to validate by attending to some information while ignoring other information (Kahneman, 2011). The capacity to understand oneself is needed in order to tame this very human tendency.

Three types of self-knowledge are essential for social workers: understanding of one's own thinking processes, understanding of one's own emotions, and understanding of one's own social locations. We must be able to think about our thinking, a process called *metacognition*. We all have biases that lead to thinking errors, and it is very difficult to get control of our biases. As Daniel Kahneman (2011) suggests in his book *Thinking Fast and Slow*, constant questioning of our own thinking can become tedious and immobilize us. The best we can do, therefore, is to understand the types of situations in which we are likely to make mistakes and slow down and use multiple sources of information to help correct for our biases. We also must be able to recognize what emotions get aroused in us when we hear stories like Manisha's and when we contemplate the challenges of the situation, and we must find a way to use those emotions in ways that are helpful and avoid using them in ways that are harmful. Although writing about physicians, Gunnar Biorck (1977) said it well when he commented that practitioners make "a tremendous number of judgments each day, based on inadequate, often ambiguous data, and under pressure of time, and carrying out this task with the outward appearance of calmness, dedication and interpersonal warmth" (p. 146).

In terms of social locations, as suggested earlier, social workers must identify and reflect on where they fit in a system of social identities, such as race, ethnicity, gender, social class, sexual orientation, religion, ability/disability, and age. The literature on culturally sensitive social work practice proposes that a strong personal identity in relation to important societal categories, and an understanding of the impact of those identities on other people, is essential for successful social work intervention across cultural lines (see Lum, 2011). This type of self-knowledge requires reflecting on where one fits in systems of privilege.

VALUES AND ETHICS

The process of developing knowledge about the case is a dialogue between the social worker and client system, and social workers have a well-defined value base to guide the dialogue. Six core values of the profession have been set out in a preamble to the Code of Ethics established by the National Association of Social Workers (NASW) in 1996 and revised in 2008. These values are service, social justice, dignity and worth of the person, importance of human relationships, integrity, and competence. The value of social justice was discussed earlier in the chapter. As demonstrated in Exhibit 1.6, the Code of Ethics articulates an ethical principle for each of the core values. Value 6, competence, requires that we recognize the science available to inform our work. It requires understanding the limitations of the available science for considering the situation at hand but also that we use the strongest available evidence to make practice decisions. This is where scientific knowledge comes into the picture.

CRITICAL THINKING Questions 1.4

If you were the social worker at Manisha's refugee resettlement program when she first arrived in the United States, what knowledge about the case would you like to have? What information would you find most important? What emotional reactions did you have to reading Manisha's story? What did you find yourself thinking about her story? Where do you see Manisha fitting in systems of privilege? Where do you see yourself fitting? How might any of this impact your ability to be helpful to Manisha?

SCIENTIFIC KNOWLEDGE: THEORY AND RESEARCH

The Council on Social Work Education (2015) proposes that social work practice is guided by knowledge based on scientific inquiry. Ethical social workers are always searching for or recalling what is known about the situations they encounter, turning to the social and behavioral sciences for this information. Scientific knowledge serves as a screen against which the knowledge about the case is considered. It suggests **hypotheses**, or tentative statements,

EXHIBIT 1.6 • Core Values and Ethical Principles in the NASW Code of Ethics

VALUE	ETHICAL PRINCIPLE
1. Service	Social workers' primary goal is to help people in need and to address social problems.
2. Social justice	Social workers challenge social injustice.
3. Dignity and worth of the person	Social workers respect the inherent dignity and worth of the person.
4. Importance of human relationships	Social workers recognize the central importance of human relationships.
5. Integrity	Social workers behave in a trustworthy manner.
6. Competence	Social workers practice within their areas of competence and develop and enhance their professional expertise.

SOURCE: Copyrighted material reprinted with permission from the National Association of Social Workers, Inc.

to be explored and tested, not facts to be applied, in transactions with a person or group. Because of the breadth and complexity of social work practice, usable knowledge must be culled from diverse sources and a number of scientific disciplines. **Science**, also known as scientific inquiry, is a set of logical, systematic, documented methods for answering questions about the world. Scientific knowledge is the knowledge produced by scientific inquiry. Two interrelated approaches to knowledge building, theory and empirical research, fit the scientific criteria of being logical, systematic, and documented for the public. Together, they create the base of knowledge that social workers need to understand commonalities among their clients and practice situations. In your coursework on social work research, you will be learning much more about these concepts, so I only provide a brief description here to help you understand how this book draws on theory and research.

THEORY

The Council on Social Work Education (2015) notes that "social workers understand theories of human behavior and the social environment, and critically evaluate and apply this knowledge" (p. 6). Social workers use theory to help organize and make sense of the situations they encounter. A **theory** is an interrelated set of concepts and propositions, organized into a deductive system that explains relationships among aspects of our world. As Elaine Leeder (2004) so aptly put it, "To have a theory is to have a way of explaining the world—an understanding that the world is not just a random series of events and experiences" (p. 9). Thus, theory gives us a framework for interpreting person and environment and for planning interventions. It seems to be human nature to develop theories to make sense of the world. As social workers we put our personal theories of the world to the test by studying theories proposed by serious scholars of human behavior. I want to emphasize that theories allow us to organize our thinking, but theories are not "fact" or "truth."

Other terms that you will often encounter in discussions of theories are *model*, *paradigm*, and *perspective*. *Model* usually is used to refer to a visual representation of the relationships between concepts, *paradigm* most often means a way of seeing the world, and *perspective* is an emphasis or a view. Paradigms and perspectives are broader and more general than theory. In this book, we will be focusing on theories and perspectives that attempt to explain human behavior, known as human behavior theories. You will also be studying another type of theory, known as practice theory, which provides guidelines for social work intervention. Many practice theories are drawn from human behavior theory; for example, psychoanalytic practice theory is derived from psychodynamic human behavior theory.

If you are to make good use of theory, you should know something about how it is constructed. **Concepts** are the building blocks of theory. They are symbols, or mental images, that summarize observations, feelings, or ideas. Concepts allow us to communicate about the phenomena of interest. Some relevant concepts in Manisha's story are culture, Hinduism, Buddhism, cultural conflict, refugee, resettlement, acculturation, loss, and grief.

Theoretical concepts are put together to form **propositions**, or assertions. For example, loss and grief theory proposes that the loss of a person, object, or ideal leads to a grief reaction. This proposition, which asserts a particular relationship between the concepts of loss and grief, may help the refugee resettlement social worker understand some of the sadness, and sometimes despair, that she sees in her work with Bhutanese refugee families. They have lived with an accumulation of losses—loss of land, loss of livelihood, loss of roles, loss of status, loss of extended family members, loss of familiar language and rituals, and many more.

Theories are a form of **deductive reasoning**, meaning they lay out general, abstract propositions that we can use to generate specific hypotheses to test in unique situations. In this example, loss and grief theory can lead us to hypothesize that Bhutanese refugees are grieving the many losses they have suffered, but we should understand that this may not be the case with all Bhutanese refugees. Theory is about likelihood, not certainty.

Social and behavioral science theories are based on **assumptions**, or beliefs held to be true without testing or proof, about the nature of human social life. These theoretical assumptions have raised a number of controversies, three of which are worth introducing at this point.

1. Do the dimensions of human behavior have an **objective reality** that exists outside a person's consciousness, or is all reality based on personal perception (**subjective reality**)?
2. Is human behavior determined by forces beyond the control of the person (**determinism**), or are people free and proactive agents in the creation of their behavior (**voluntarism**)?
3. Are the patterned interactions among people characterized by harmony, unity, and social cohesion or by conflict, domination, coercion, and exploitation?

The nature of these controversies will become more apparent to you in Chapter 2. The contributing authors and I take a middle ground on all of them: We assume that reality has both objective and subjective aspects, that human behavior is partially constrained and partially free, and that social life is marked by both cohesion and conflict.

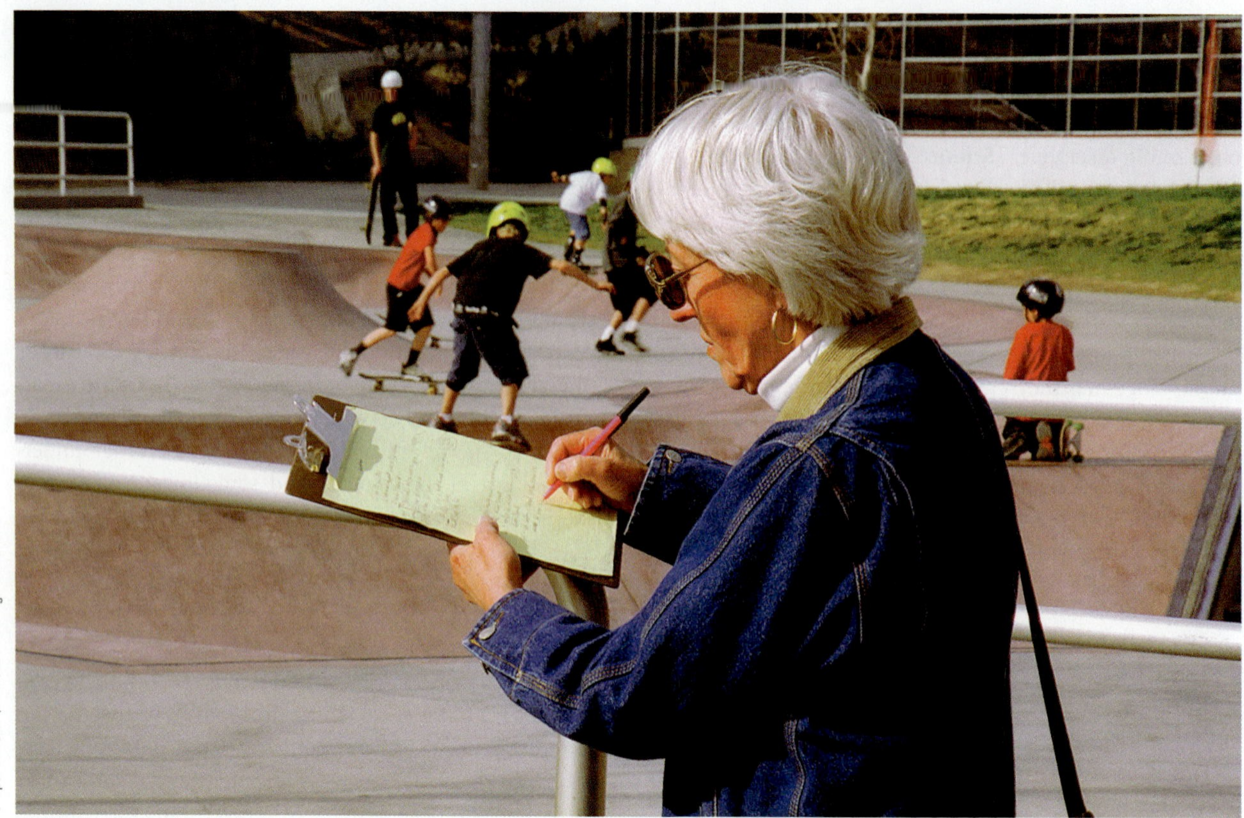

A research assistant records observations of children at a skate park.

EMPIRICAL RESEARCH

Traditionally, science is equated with empirical research, which is widely held as the most rigorous and systematic way to understand human behavior. Research is typically viewed, in simple terms, as a problem-solving process, or a method of seeking answers to questions. If something is empirical, we experience it through our senses, as opposed to something we experience purely in our minds. The process of **empirical research** includes a careful, purposeful, and systematic observation of events with the intent to note and record them in terms of their attributes, to look for patterns in those events, and to make our methods and observations public. Each empirical research project is likely to raise new questions, often producing more questions than answers. The new questions become grist for future research. Like theory, empirical research is a key tool for social workers. It is important to understand, however, that empirical research informs us about probabilities, not certainties (Firestein, 2012). For example, research can tell us what percentage of parents who were abused as children will become abusive toward their own children, but it cannot tell us whether a specific parent who was abused as a child will become abusive toward his or her children. Social workers, of course, must make decisions about specific parents, recognizing the probabilities found in research as well as considering the knowledge about the case.

Just as there are controversies about theoretical assumptions, there are also controversies about what constitutes appropriate research methods for understanding human behavior. Modern science is based on several assumptions, which are generally recognized as a **positivist perspective**: The world has an order that can be discovered, findings of one study should be applicable to other groups, complex phenomena can be studied by reducing them to some component part, findings are tentative and subject to question, and scientific methods are value-free. **Quantitative methods of research** are preferred from the positivist perspective. These methods use quantifiable measures of concepts, standardize the collection of data, attend only to preselected variables, and use statistical measures to look for patterns and associations (Engel & Schutt, 2013).

Over the years, the positivist perspective and its claim that positivism = science have been challenged. Critics argue that quantitative methods cannot possibly capture the subjective experience of individuals or the complex nature of social life. Although most of these critics do not reject positivism as *a way* of doing science, they recommend other ways of understanding the world and suggest that these alternative methods should also be considered part of science. Various names have been given to these alternative methods. I refer to them as the **interpretist perspective**, because they share the assumption that reality is based on people's definitions of it and research should focus on learning the meanings that people give to their situations. This is also referred to as a *constructivist perspective*.

Interpretists see a need to replace quantitative methods with **qualitative methods of research**, which are more flexible and experiential and are designed to capture how participants view social life rather than to ask participants to respond to categories preset by the researcher (Engel & Schutt, 2013). Participant observation, intensive interviewing, and focus groups are examples of qualitative methods of research. Interpretists assume that people's behavior cannot be observed objectively, that reality is created as the researcher and research participants interact. Researchers using qualitative methods are more likely to present their findings in words than in numbers and to attempt to capture the settings of behavior. They are likely to report the transactions of the researcher and participant as well as the values of the researcher, because they assume that value-free research is impossible.

In this controversy, it is our position that no single research method can adequately capture the whole, the complexity, of human behavior. Both quantitative and qualitative research methods have a place in a multidimensional approach, and used together they may help us to see more dimensions of situations. This position is consistent with the Council on Social Work Education (2015) Educational Policy that states that "social workers understand quantitative and qualitative research methods and their respective roles in advancing a science of social work and in evaluating their practice" (p. 5). Social workers must also understand the limitations of available science. Neuroscientist Stuart Firestein (2012) reminds us that we must learn to live with "unknowable unknowns" (p. 30) and become capable of working with uncertainties. Nevertheless, science remains the most rigorous and systematic way to understand human behavior.

CRITICAL USE OF THEORY AND RESEARCH

You may already know that social and behavioral science theory and research have been growing at a fast pace in modern times, and you will often feel, as McAvoy (1999) aptly put it, that you are "drowning in a swamp of information" (p. 19), both case information and scientific information. Ironically, as you are drowning in a swamp of information, you will also be discovering that the available scientific information is incomplete. You will also encounter contradictory theoretical propositions and research results that must be held simultaneously and, where possible, coordinated to develop an integrated picture of the situation at hand. That is, as you might guess, not a simple project. It involves weighing available evidence and analyzing its relevance to the situation at hand. That requires critical thinking. **Critical thinking** is a thoughtful and reflective judgment about alternative views and contradictory information. It involves thinking about your own thinking and the influences on that thinking, as well as a willingness to change your mind. It also involves careful analysis of assumptions and evidence. Critical thinkers also ask, "What is left out of this conceptualization or research?" "What new questions are raised by this research finding?" Throughout the book, we call out critical thinking questions to support your efforts to think critically.

As you read this book and other sources of scientific knowledge, begin to think critically about the theory and research they present. Give careful thought to the credibility of the claims made. Let's look first at theory. It is important to remember that although theorists may try to put checks on their biases, they write from their own cultural frame of reference, from particular locations in the social structure of their society, and from life experiences. So, when taking a critical look at a theory, it is important to remember that theories are generally created by people of privileged backgrounds who operate in seats of power. The bulk of theories still used today were authored by White, middle- to upper-class Western European men and men in the United States with academic appointments. Therefore, as we work in a highly diversified world, we need to be attentive to the possibilities of biases related to race, gender, culture, religion, sexual orientation, abilities/disabilities, and social class—as well as professional or occupational orientation. One particular concern is that such biases can lead us to think of disadvantaged members of society or of members of minority groups as pathological or deficient.

Social and behavioral science scholars disagree about the criteria for evaluating theory and research. However, I recommend the criteria presented in Exhibit 1.7 because they are consistent with the multidimensional approach of this book and with the value base of the social work profession. (The five criteria for evaluating theory presented in Exhibit 1.7 are also used in Chapter 2 to evaluate eight theoretical perspectives relevant to social work.) There is agreement in the social and behavioral sciences that theory should be evaluated for coherence and conceptual clarity as well as for testability and evidence of empirical support. The criterion of comprehensiveness is specifically related to the multidimensional approach of this book. We do not expect all theories to be multidimensional, but critical analysis of a theory should help us identify deterministic and unidimensional thinking where they exist. The criterion of consistency with emphasis on diversity and power arrangements examines the utility of the theory for a profession that places high value on social justice, and the criterion of usefulness for practice is essential for a profession.

EXHIBIT 1.7 • Criteria for Evaluating Theory and Research

CRITERIA FOR EVALUATING THEORY
Coherence and conceptual clarity. Are the concepts clearly defined and consistently used? Is the theory free of logical inconsistencies? Is it stated in the simplest possible way, without oversimplifying?
Testability and evidence of empirical support. Can the concepts and propositions be expressed in language that makes them observable and accessible to corroboration or refutation by persons other than the theoretician? Is there evidence of empirical support for the theory?
Comprehensiveness. Does the theory include multiple dimensions of persons, environments, and time? What is included and what is excluded? What dimension(s) is (are) emphasized? Does the theory account for things that other theories have overlooked or been unable to account for?
Consistency with social work's emphasis on diversity and power arrangements. Can the theory help us understand diversity? How inclusive is it? Does it avoid pathologizing members of minority groups? Does it assist in understanding power arrangements and systems of oppression?
Usefulness for social work practice. Does the theory assist in the understanding of person–environment transactions over time? Can principles of action be derived from the theory? At what levels of practice can the theory be used? Can the theory be used in practice in a way that is consistent with the NASW Code of Ethics?
CRITERIA FOR EVALUATING RESEARCH
Corroboration. Are the research findings corroborated by other researchers? Are a variety of research methods used in corroborating research? Do the findings fit logically with accepted theory and other research findings?
Multidimensionality. Does the research include multiple dimensions of persons, environments, and time? If not, do the researchers acknowledge the omissions, connect the research to larger programs of research that include omitted dimensions, or recommend further research to include omitted dimensions?
Definition of terms. Are major variables defined and measured in such a way as to avoid bias against members of minority groups?
Limitation of sample. Does the researcher make sufficient effort to include diversity in the sample? Are minority groups represented in sufficient numbers to show the variability within them? When demographic groups are compared, are they equivalent on important variables? Does the researcher specify the limitations of the sample for generalizing to specific groups?
Influence of setting. Does the researcher specify attributes of the setting of the research, acknowledge the possible contribution of the setting to research outcomes, and present the findings of similar research across a range of settings?
Influence of the researcher. Does the researcher specify his or her attributes and role in the observed situations? Does the researcher specify his or her possible contributions to research outcomes?
Social distance. Does the researcher attempt to minimize errors that could occur because of literacy, language, and cultural differences between the researcher and respondents?
Specification of inferences. Does the researcher specify how inferences are made, based on the data? What biases, if any, do you identify in the inferences?
Suitability of measures. Does the researcher use measures that seem suited to, and sensitive to, the situation being researched?

Just as theory may be biased toward the experiences of members of dominant groups, so too may research be biased. The results may be misleading, and the interpretation of results may lead to false conclusions about members of minority groups. Bias can occur at all stages of the research process.

- Funding sources and other vested interests have a strong influence on which problems are selected for research attention. In recent times, there has been controversy about how gun violence research was frozen in the United States in 1996 when Congress, under pressure from the National Rifle Association, passed legislation that banned funding by the Centers for Disease Control for research that could be used to advocate or promote gun control (American Psychological Association, 2013).

- Bias can occur in the definition of variables for study. For example, using "offenses cleared by arrests" as the definition of crime, rather than using a definition such as "self-reported crime involvement," may lead to an overestimation of crime among minority groups of color, because those are the people who are most often arrested for their crimes (Ritzer, 2013a).

- Bias can occur in choosing the sample to be studied. Because there are fewer of them, members of minority groups may not be included in sufficient numbers to demonstrate the variability within a particular minority group. Or a biased sample of minorities may be used (e.g., it is not uncommon to make Black/White comparisons on a sample that includes middle-class Whites and low-income Blacks). Recent analysis of articles in the major behavioral science journals indicates that most of the samples are drawn almost exclusively from Western, educated, industrialized, and democratic (WEIRD) societies (Henrich, Heine, & Norenzayan, 2010). This same analysis concludes that these research participants are different from most other people of the world in important ways. We need to keep this in mind as we review available empirical research.

- Bias can occur in data collection. The validity and reliability of most standardized measuring instruments have been evaluated by using them with White, non-Hispanic male respondents, and their cultural relevance with people of color, women, impoverished persons, or members of other groups is questionable. Language and literacy difficulties may arise with both written survey instruments and interviews. Some groups may be reluctant to participate in research because they don't trust the motives of the researchers.

- Bias can occur in interpretation of the data, because empirical research typically fails to produce uncontestable results (Firestein, 2012).

As with theory evaluation, there is no universally agreed-on set of criteria for evaluating research. I recommend the nine criteria presented in Exhibit 1.7 for considering the credibility of a research report. These criteria can be applied to either quantitative or qualitative research. Many research reports would be strengthened if their authors were to attend to these criteria.

CRITICAL THINKING Questions 1.5

If I drew a line on the floor with objective reality at one end and subjective reality at the other end, where would you place yourself on the line to demonstrate your own understanding of human behavior?

Objective Reality ________ Subjective Reality

And if I drew another line with determinism at one end and voluntarism at the other end, where would you place yourself on this line?

Determinism ________ Voluntarism

And if I drew a third line with harmony, unity, and social cohesion on one end and conflict, domination, coercion, and exploitation at the other end, where would you place yourself on this line to demonstrate your theory about what happens in human social interaction?

Harmony, Unity, Social Cohesion ________ Conflict, Domination, Coercion, Exploitation

A WORD OF CAUTION

In this book, Part I includes two stage-setting chapters that introduce the framework for the book and provide a foundation for thinking critically about the discussions of theory and research presented in Parts II, III, and IV. Part II comprises three chapters that analyze the multiple dimensions of persons—one chapter each on the biological person, the psychological person, and the spiritual person. The four chapters of Part III discuss environmental dimensions, including culture, the physical environment, families, small groups, formal organizations, communities, social structure and social institutions, and social movements. Part IV overviews the life course perspective and includes six chapters that examine theory and research about phases of the human life course.

Presenting personal and environmental dimensions separately, as we do in Parts II and III, is a risky approach. I do not wish to reinforce any tendency to think about human behavior in a way that camouflages the inseparability of person and environment. In our work as social workers, we engage in both *analysis* and *synthesis*. Sometimes, we need to think analytically, breaking down a complex situation by thinking more critically about specific aspects and dimensions of the situation, whether that is a biological system or a pattern of family relationships. But we also need to be able to put the puzzle pieces back together to see the whole story. That is synthesis. We are always working back and forth between analysis and synthesis.

IMPLICATIONS FOR SOCIAL WORK PRACTICE

The multidimensional approach outlined in this chapter suggests several principles for social work assessment and intervention, for both prevention and remediation services.

- In the assessment process, collect information about all the critical dimensions of the changing configuration of person and environment.
- In the assessment process, attempt to see the situation from a variety of perspectives. Use multiple data sources, including the person(s), significant others, and direct observations.
- Allow people to tell their own stories and pay attention to how they describe the pattern and flow of their person–environment configurations.
- Use the multidimensional database of information about critical dimensions of the situation to develop a dynamic picture of the person–environment configuration.
- Link intervention strategies to the dimensions of the assessment.
- In general, expect more effective outcomes from interventions that are multidimensional, because the situation itself is multidimensional.
- Pay particular attention to the impact of diversity and inequality on the unique stories and situations that you encounter.
- Allow the unique stories of people and situations to direct the choice of theory and research to be used.
- Use scientific knowledge to suggest tentative hypotheses to be explored in the unique situation.

KEY TERMS

assumptions, 21
concepts, 21
critical thinking, 23
deductive reasoning, 21
determinism, 21
dimension, 6
diversity, 15
empirical research, 22
globalization, 14
heterogeneity, 15
hypotheses, 20
interpretist perspective, 23
linear time, 12
multidetermined behavior, 8
multidimensional, 6
objective reality, 21
positivist perspective, 22
privilege, 15
propositions, 21
qualitative methods of research, 23
quantitative methods of research, 22
science, 21
subjective reality, 21
theory, 21
time orientation, 13
voluntarism, 21

ACTIVE LEARNING

1. We have used multiple dimensions of person, environment, and time to think about Manisha's story. If you were the social worker at the refugee resettlement agency that sponsored her family's resettlement, you would bring your own unfolding person–environment–time story to that encounter. With the graphic in Exhibit 1.1 as your guide, write your own multidimensional story. What personal dimensions are important? What environmental dimensions? What time dimensions? What might happen when these two stories encounter each other?
2. Working in small groups, select a social issue that interests you, such as child abuse or youth gangs. List five things you "know" about this issue. Talk about how you know what you know. How would you go about confirming or disproving your current state of knowledge on this topic?

WEB RESOURCES

No doubt, you use the Internet in many different ways and know your way around it. I hope that when you find something in this book that confuses you or intrigues you, you will use the incredibly rich resources of the Internet to do further exploration. To help you get started with this process, each chapter of this textbook contains a list of Internet resources and websites that may be useful to readers in their search for further information. Each site listing includes the address and a brief description of the contents of the site. Readers should be aware that the information contained on websites may not be truthful or reliable and should be confirmed before the site is used as a reference. Readers should also be aware that Internet addresses, or URLs, are constantly changing; therefore, the addresses listed may no longer be active or accurate. Many of the Internet sites listed in each chapter contain links to other sites containing more information on the topic. Readers may use these links for further investigation.

Information on topics not included in the Web Resources sections of each chapter can be found by using one of the many Internet search engines provided free of charge on the Internet. These search engines enable you to search using keywords or phrases, or you can use the search engines' topical listings. You should use several search engines when researching a topic because each will retrieve different Internet sites. We list the search engines first.

Aol Search: http://search.aol.com
Ask: www.ask.com
Bing: www.bing.com
Google: www.google.com
Yahoo! http://search.yahoo.com

There are several Internet sites maintained by and for social workers, some at university schools of social work and some by professional associations:

Council on Social Work Education (CSWE)
www.cswe.org
CSWE is the accrediting body for academic social work programs; site contains information about accreditation, projects, and publications.

Information for Practice
http://ifp.nyu.edu
Site developed and maintained by Professor Gary Holden of New York University's School of Social Work contains links to many federal and state Internet sites as well as journals, assessment and measurement tools, and sites maintained by professional associations.

International Federation of Social Workers
www.ifsw.org
Site contains information about international conferences, policy papers on selected issues, and links to human rights groups and other social work organizations.

National Association of Social Workers (NASW)
www.naswdc.org
Site contains professional development material, press room, advocacy information, and resources.

Society for Social Work and Research (SSWR)
www.sswr.org
SSWR is a nonprofit organization devoted to involving social workers in research and research applications. Site contains research news, job postings, and links to social work–related websites.

SAGE edge™ Sharpen your skills with SAGE edge at edge.sagepub.com/hutchisoness2e

SAGE edge for students provides a personalized approach to help you accomplish your coursework goals in an easy-to-use learning environment. watch listen read

LEARNING OBJECTIVES	FOR FURTHER EXPLORATION AND APPLICATION
LO 1.1: Recognize one's emotional and cognitive reactions to a case study.	(listen) The Stress of Social Work (read) How to Sustain Emotional Resilience
LO 1.2: Outline the elements of a multidimensional person-in-environment approach to human behavior.	(watch) Bhutanese Refugees in Nepal (watch) Bobby LeFebre—Social Worker (listen) Social Media Use and Social Work Practice: Boundary and Ethical Considerations
LO 1.3: Advocate for an emphasis on diversity, inequality, social justice, and a global perspective in social work's approach to human behavior.	(read) Human Rights Watch
LO 1.4: Summarize four ingredients of knowing how to do social work.	(read) Issues in International Social Work: Resolving Critical Debates in the Profession
LO 1.5: Analyze the roles of theory and research in guiding social work practice.	(read) The Science of Social Work and Its Relationship to Social Work Practice
LO 1.6: Apply knowledge of the multidimensional person-in-environment framework, diversity, inequality, and the pursuit of social justice to recommend guidelines for social work assessment and intervention.	(read) National Association of Social Workers

Theoretical Perspectives on Human Behavior

Elizabeth D. Hutchison, Leanne Wood Charlesworth, and Cory Cummings

Learning Objectives

LO 2.1 Recognize one's emotional and cognitive reactions to a case study.

LO 2.2 Recognize the major themes of eight different perspectives on human behavior: systems, conflict, exchange and choice, social constructionist, psychodynamic, developmental, social behavioral, and humanistic.

LO 2.3 Analyze the merits of a multitheoretical approach to human behavior.

LO 2.4 Apply knowledge of eight theoretical perspectives on human behavior to recommend guidelines for social work assessment and intervention.

CASE STUDY

INTERGENERATIONAL STRESSES IN THE MCKINLEY FAMILY

The hospice social worker meets three generations of McKinleys when she visits their home in an upper-midwestern city. She is there because the family has requested hospice services for Ruth McKinley, the 79-year-old mother of Stanley McKinley. Ruth has a recurrence of breast cancer that has metastasized to her lungs; she is no longer receiving aggressive treatment, and her condition is deteriorating. Upon entering the house, the social worker meets 50-year-old Stanley, his 51-year-old wife, Marcia, and their 25-year-old daughter, Bethany, who takes the social worker to a bedroom to meet her grandmother. She gives Ruth a gentle pat and introduces the social worker. Ruth smiles at Bethany and greets the social worker. Bethany leaves the room to give some privacy to the social worker and her grandmother. The social worker spends about 20 minutes with Ruth and finds her weak but interested in talking. Ruth says she knows that she is receiving hospice care because she is dying. She says she has lived a good life and is not afraid of dying. She goes on to say, however, that there are some things on her mind as she thinks about her life. She is thinking a lot about her estranged daughter who lives several states away, and she does not want to die with this "hardness between us." She also is thinking a lot about Stanley, who is unemployed, and hoping that he can find a spark in his life again. Bethany is very much on her mind, as well. She says she worries that Bethany is sacrificing too much of her young life to the needs of the family. As Ruth grows tired, the social worker ends the conversation, saying that she would like to visit with Ruth again next week so that they can talk some more about Ruth's life and the things that are on her mind.

Back in the living room, the social worker talks with Stanley, Marcia, and Bethany. She learns that Ruth moved into Stanley and Marcia's home 5 years ago after she had a stroke that left her with left-sided paralysis. At that time, Stanley and Marcia took out a second mortgage on their house to finance some remodeling to make the home more accessible for Ruth, providing her with a bedroom and bathroom downstairs. They also put in a much-needed new furnace at the same time. Bethany speaks up to say that her grandmother is the kindest person she knows and that they were all happy to rearrange their home life to make Ruth comfortable. Marcia notes that it seemed the natural thing to do, because Ruth had taken care of Bethany while Marcia worked during Bethany's early years. After Ruth came to live with them, Stanley continued to work at a print shop, and Marcia changed to the evening shift in her job as a police dispatcher. Bethany arranged her work and part-time community college studies so that she could be available to her grandmother between the time her mother left for work and her father returned from his workday. She took charge of preparing dinner for her dad and grandmother and giving Ruth a daily bath.

This arrangement worked well for 4 years. Bethany speaks fondly of the good times she and her grandmother had together as Bethany provided direct care to her grandmother, and her grandmother showered her with stories of the past and took a lively interest in her life, often giving her advice about her romantic life. Marcia breaks in to say that life has been tough for the past year, however, and her voice cracks as she says this. She recounts that they learned of the recurrence of Ruth's breast cancer 11 months ago and of the metastasis 5 months ago. For a few months, Stanley, Marcia, and Bethany juggled their schedules to get Ruth to doctor visits, chemotherapy treatments, and bone scans, until Ruth and the oncologist decided that it was time to discontinue aggressive treatment.

Then, 7 months ago, Stanley lost his job at the printing company where he had worked since getting out of the army, and he has been unsuccessful in finding new work. They were still managing financially with the help of unemployment checks until Marcia took a tumble down the stairs and injured her back and hip 4 months ago. She had surgery, which was followed by complications, and has been out of work on disability. She is expecting to go back to work next week. Bethany says she has wanted to work more to bring more money into the home, but she has also been needed at home more to fill in for Marcia. She lost one job because of too many absences and has pieced together two part-time jobs that give her a little more flexibility. She recently signed up for health insurance through the Affordable Care Act, but she is hearing scary stories about the likelihood that premiums will soon increase. Marcia says that Stanley has been a wonderful caregiver to her and his mom, but she knows that the caregiving has interfered with his job search and is wearing him down.

Stanley enters the conversation to report that they have been unable to make mortgage payments for the past 3 months, and the bank has notified him that they are at risk of facing foreclosure. He becomes despondent as he relates this. He says they have been in the house for 15 years and had always paid the mortgage on time. The second mortgage for the remodeling is adding to the current financial pinch. He says he is in a quandary about what to do. Marcia is going back to work soon, but she is still not strong enough to provide much physical care to Ruth. In addition, Stanley is not at all optimistic that he will find a job in the near future. His former boss has now closed the printing shop because she lost some of her large clients. Stanley wonders if he should retrain for another occupation but knows that this is not a good time for him to try to do that, with his mother's deteriorating condition.

Bethany suggests that she take some time off from school and find a job working nights so that she can give her dad time to look for jobs during the day. She has graduated from community college and been accepted into a bachelor's degree program in nursing. She says she is feeling too sad about her grandmother and too worried about the family's future to do well in school anyway. Besides that, she would like to be able to spend more time with her grandmother before she dies. At this point, Marcia breaks down and cries, sobbing that she just wants to give up: "We work so hard, but nothing goes our way. I don't know where we will go if we lose the house."

As the family talks about their problems and possible solutions, the social worker recalls that she has heard something about a community program that provides counseling to people who are in jeopardy of home foreclosure. She wonders if that could help the McKinley family.

MULTIPLE PERSPECTIVES FOR A MULTIDIMENSIONAL APPROACH

As you think about the details of the unfolding story of the multigenerational McKinley family, you may discover that you have some theory or theories of your own about what is happening with them and what can and should be done to help them. If we asked you what caught your attention as you read the story, we would begin to learn something about your theory or theories of human behavior, as you have developed it or them so far. There is much information in the case study as presented, but the case may have raised questions for you as well and left you wanting more information. What you see as gaps in the information might also tell us something about your theory or theories. Theories help us organize vast and multifaceted information. The purposes of this chapter are twofold: first, to help you identify and refine your own theory or theories of human behavior and, second, to help you think critically about commonly used formal theories of human behavior that have been developed by behavioral science scholars.

There is general agreement that contemporary social workers must use a range of theories that draw on a number of disciplines to help them understand the practice situations they encounter and to see the possibilities for change. As we have come more and more to recognize that human behavior is multidimensional, we have also recognized the need for multiple disciplines and a multitheoretical framework to understand it (K. Bell, 2012; Council on Social Work Education, 2015; Melchert, 2013). There are many theories from which to draw, general theories of human behavior as well as theories designed to understand the specific dimensions of person and environment covered in this book. There are also a number of ways of organizing existing theories into categories or perspectives. We have organized them into eight broad perspectives: the systems perspective, conflict perspective, exchange and choice perspective, social constructionist perspective, psychodynamic perspective, developmental perspective, social behavioral perspective, and humanistic perspective.

We have selected these eight perspectives for a number of reasons. Each has a wide range of applications across dimensions of human behavior and is used in empirical research. Each has been reconceptualized and extended over time to keep current with rapid knowledge development. Each paid little attention to diversity, and most paid little attention to inequality in early versions, but each has evolved over time to address both diversity and inequality. Each is European American in heritage, but in recent years, each has been influenced by thinking in other regions of the world. Some of the perspectives had interdisciplinary roots in their early versions, and each has benefited from collaboration across disciplines in more recent refinement and elaboration. Some blurring of the lines between perspectives has begun to occur. Theorists are being influenced by each other, as well as by societal changes, and have begun to borrow ideas from each other and to build new theory by combining aspects of existing theory. As you can see, theory, like other aspects of human behavior, is ever-changing.

Each of the perspectives presented in this chapter comprises a number of diverse theories. We present the "big ideas" of each perspective and not a detailed discussion of the various theories within the perspective. Although we trace the development of each perspective over time, we pay particular attention to some of the recent extensions of the perspectives that seem most useful in contemporary times.

We introduce the perspectives in this chapter, and you will see variations of them throughout subsequent chapters where theory and research about specific dimensions of person and environment are explored. We hope you will take time to analyze the connections between the perspectives discussed in this chapter and the specific theories you read about in subsequent chapters.

In this chapter, in addition to presenting an overview of the big ideas, we analyze the scientific merit of the perspectives and their usefulness for social work practice. The five criteria for critical understanding of theory identified in Chapter 1 provide the framework for our discussion of the perspectives: coherence and conceptual clarity, testability and empirical support, comprehensiveness, consistency with social work's emphasis on diversity and power arrangements, and usefulness for social work practice.

SYSTEMS PERSPECTIVE

When you read the case study at the beginning of this chapter, you probably thought of it as a story about a family system—a story about Ruth, Stanley, Marcia, and Bethany McKinley—rather than "Ruth McKinley's story," even though the hospice case file reads "Ruth McKinley." You may have noted how Ruth's, Stanley's, Marcia's, and Bethany's lives are interrelated, how they influence one another's behavior, and what impact each of them has on the overall well-being of the family. You may be thinking about the changing health statuses of Ruth and Marcia and about how the family members keep adjusting their caregiving roles to accommodate changing care needs. You also may note that this family, like other families, has a **boundary** indicating who is in and who is out, and you may be wondering if the boundary around this family allows sufficient input from friends, extended family, neighbors, religious organizations, and so on. You probably have noted the influence of larger systems on this family. For example, Medicare coverage for hospice care is an important resource for the family as they cope with the end-of-life care needs of Ruth, but Bethany's worries about continued access to health care reflect ongoing controversies about public policy. These are some of the ideas that the systems perspective suggests for understanding what is happening in the McKinley family.

The **systems perspective** sees human behavior as the outcome of interactions within and among systems of interrelated parts. Its roots are very interdisciplinary, and there are many theoretical variations. During the 1940s and 1950s, a variety of disciplines—including mathematics, physics, engineering, biology, psychology, cultural anthropology, economics, and sociology—began looking at phenomena as the outcome of interactions within and among systems. Mathematicians and engineers used the new ideas about system **feedback mechanisms**—the processes by which information about past behaviors in a system are fed back into the system in a circular manner—to develop military and communication technologies. The development of the computer and sophisticated computer models for analyzing information has influenced continuous revision of the systems perspective. Exhibit 2.1 provides a visual representation of the systems perspective.

Social workers were attracted to the systems perspective in the 1960s, and *general systems theory* was the dominant theoretical perspective in the social work literature during the 1960s and 1970s. This approach was based primarily on the work of biologist Ludwig

The pieces of this globe come together to form a unified whole—each part interacts with and influences the other parts—but the pieces are interdependent, as suggested by the systems perspective.

von Bertalanffy (1969), who defined systems as "sets of elements standing in interrelation" (p. 38). He proposed that any element is best understood by considering its interactions with its constituent parts as well as its interactions with larger systems of which it is a part. For example, the McKinley family is best understood by considering the interactions among the family members as well as the interactions the family has with other social systems, such as their neighborhood, the health care system, workplace systems, and educational systems. Von Bertalanffy identified two types of systems: closed systems and open systems. A *closed system* is isolated from other systems in its environment. An *open system* is in constant interaction with other systems.

EXHIBIT 2.1 • Systems Perspective

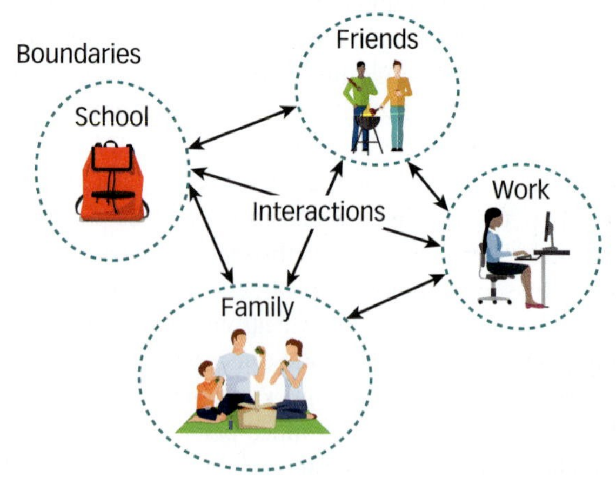

He emphasized that feedback mechanisms produce both stability (homeostasis) and change within and across systems. Socially and geographically isolated families and communities could be considered examples of closed systems. Internet-based social networks are examples of open systems.

In the 1980s, *ecological theory*, also known as ecosystems theory, became popular across several disciplines, including social work. This theory comes from the field of ecology, which focuses on the relationships and interactions between living organisms and their environments. Interdependence and mutual influence are emphasized. The environment exerts influence on an individual, family, or group, but individuals, families, and groups can also have an impact on external systems. Social workers who promoted the ecological perspective called for a holistic view of practice situations that considers the multiple environmental influences involved (Germain & Gitterman, 1996). The ecological perspective extended general systems theory by considering the important role of physical as well as social environments in human behavior.

Influenced by scientific inquiry in a number of disciplines, several new systems theories have emerged in the last 2 decades or so. Taken as a whole, these new theories are attempting to explain the complexity of contemporary life. One approach often used in social work is *risk and resilience theory*, which is an extension of the ecological perspective. It draws on concepts from epidemiology and public health to explain the complexity of influences on human behavior. This theory proposes risk factors and protective factors in both the person and the environment. Risk factors increase the likelihood of a harmful outcome of person and environment interactions, and protective factors support a positive outcome (see Jenson & Fraser, 2016). Proponents of the risk and resilience approach acknowledge the uncertainty of human behavior that derives from the complexity of influences on it.

Complex systems theory proposes that we are all part of numerous interacting systems that are linked through many dense interconnections (think of your social system, including your Facebook, Instagram, or Twitter networks). These complex interactions produce uncertainty and unpredictability (Fuchs, 2013). Systems, including systems of human behavior theory, are always evolving toward greater complexity (Green & McDermott, 2010).

Chaos theory suggests that although it appears that the complexity of numerous interacting systems produces disorder, there is actually an underlying order that can only be discovered by analysis using complex computer models (Gleick, 2008). Chaos theory recognizes *negative feedback loops* that work like a thermostat to feed back information that the system is deviating from a steady state and needs to take corrective action as important processes that promote system stability. In addition, it proposes that complex systems produce *positive feedback loops* that feed back information about deviation, or should we say innovation, into the steady state in such a way that the deviation reverberates throughout the system and potentially produces change, sometimes even rapid change. The change-producing feedback may come from within the system or from other systems in the environment. Small random changes in any area can lead to rapid large-scale change. Chaos theory has been recommended as a useful approach for clinical social workers and clinical psychologists as they assist clients in trying new solutions to long-standing problems (M. Lee, 2008) and to re-create themselves in times of transition (Bussolari & Goodell, 2009). Examples of such problems and transitions include addiction recovery and intimate partner violence.

Complex systems and chaos theories propose that it is the openness of systems that produces complexity. European social workers (see Ahmed-Mohamed, 2011; Kihlström, 2012) are drawing on another systems theory that conceptualizes the openness of systems in a very different way. German sociologist Niklas Luhmann (2011) has proposed a systems theory that suggests that in highly complex societies systems must find a way to reduce complexity to make life more manageable. They do this by developing cultures and structures that clearly differentiate the system from other systems. Systems are open to interaction with other systems, but they are operatively closed, meaning that system behavior is influenced only by the system's operations, its language, culture, and processes, not by the language, culture, and processes of other systems. The environment can affect the system only by causing it irritations or disruptions, but the system will have its own conditions for responding to these irritations. Luhmann argues that systems are *autopoietic*, meaning they are self-created and reproduced. We can think about the U.S. Supreme Court ruling (*United States v. Windsor*, 2013) regarding the Defense of Marriage Act, a ruling that found the act unconstitutional and determined that same-sex couples in recognized marriages could not be treated differently from other married couples in terms of federal benefits. Luhmann's approach would suggest that the gay rights movement and changing public opinion about same-sex marriage were irritations in the judicial system, but the system used its own language and processes to come to a decision.

Other newer systems theories take other positions on the issue of boundaries. Whereas Luhmann argues that boundaries between systems are clear and tight, some social work scholars (see DePoy & Gilson, 2012) suggest that social workers might benefit by considering *fuzzy set theory* developed in mathematics. Fuzzy set theory proposes that membership of a set is not binary (meaning you are either a member or you are not). You may be a member to a certain degree. In fuzzy sets, objects are assigned a number from 0 to 1 to indicate the degree to which the object belongs in the set. From this perspective, I am wondering what value we would give to Ruth McKinley's estranged daughter in relation to the family system described in this story. Would you give her a value of 0 or 1, or would you say her membership lies somewhere between "member" and "not member"? Reisch and Jani (2012) suggest that social workers should consider such theories that recognize the blurring of system boundaries in complex societies. As DePoy and Gilson (2012) suggest, fuzzy set theory could be a useful way to think about issues such as identity group membership, including race and ethnicity; for example, where should Barack Obama fit in racial categories? Fuzzy set theory is consistent with contemporary thinking about gender as a nonbinary identity.

Other theories emphasize the openness of systems. *Deep ecology* has emerged with an emphasis on the notion of the total interconnectedness of all elements of the natural and physical world (Besthorn, 2012). Sociologist John Clammer (2009) suggests that deep ecology, with its addition of connections to the natural and physical worlds, can help to bridge Western and Eastern social science. The emerging *globalization theories* also emphasize the openness of systems, calling our attention to, among other things, how Stanley McKinley's job opportunities are connected to the increasingly globalized economy (Giddens, 2000).

This is how the systems perspective rates on the five criteria for evaluating social work theory.

- *Coherence and conceptual clarity.* Although it has been popular over time, the systems perspective is often criticized as vague and somewhat ambiguous. Although consistency in use of terms has improved in recent theorizing, concepts in these theories remain highly abstract and often confusing in their generality.

- *Testability and empirical support.* Poorly defined and highly abstract concepts are difficult to translate into measurable variables for research. Nevertheless, a long tradition of research supporting a systems perspective can be found in anthropology and sociology (see White, Klein, & Martin, 2015a, for a discussion of the use of the systems perspective to study family systems). The systems perspective has been greatly strengthened in recent years with developments in neuroscience and epidemiology and a rapidly expanding empirical literature on ecological risk and resilience.

- *Comprehensiveness.* Clearly, the systems perspective is devoted to the ideal of comprehensiveness, or holism. It can incorporate, and has incorporated, the various dimensions of human systems as well as various dimensions of environmental systems, nonhuman as well as human. It does better than the other perspectives discussed here in accommodating rapid developments in neuroscience. Recent formulations have explicitly added a time dimension to accommodate both past and future influences on human behavior (see Bronfenbrenner, 2005).

- *Diversity and power.* Although diversity is not addressed in most systems theorizing, recent versions of the systems perspective, with their attention to complexity and continuous dynamic change, open many possibilities for diversity. Furthermore, whereas most systems theorists do not address the role of power in systems transactions, some can accommodate the idea of power differentials better than others. Traditional systems theories assumed that social systems are held together by social consensus and shared values. The emphasis on system stability can rightly be criticized as socially conservative and oppressive to those who lack power within the system. Contemporary systems theory has begun to recognize power and oppression; conflict is seen as necessary for change in chaos theory; and some versions of globalization theory call attention to how powerful nations exploit the cultures, economies, and political arrangements of less powerful nations (McMichael, 2012).

- *Usefulness for social work practice.* The systems perspective is perhaps more useful for understanding human behavior than for directing social work interventions, but several social work practice textbooks were based on the systems perspective in the 1970s and 1980s. The risk and resilience approach is informative for both program and policy development, suggesting ways to reduce risk and increase protection. The greatest value of the systems perspective is that it can be used at any level of practice. It also has merit because it surpasses other perspectives in suggesting that we should widen the scope of assessment and intervention and expect better outcomes from multidimensional interventions. Social workers who work from a family systems perspective have for some time used methods such as family genograms, and other forms of feedback about the family, as information that can produce change as it reverberates through the family system. Mo Yee Lee (2008) provides a number of examples of how clinical social workers can use chaos and turbulence to help clients open to new ways of looking at and resolving problems.

CONFLICT PERSPECTIVE

As she thinks about the McKinley family, the hospice social worker is struck by Stanley and Marcia's growing sense of powerlessness to manage the trajectories of their lives. A major theme in their story, like the stories of so many other families, is lack of power in both the labor market and the housing market. Worries about access to health care are another part of the story, and one is reminded of ongoing political debates about health care policy. Whereas the systems perspective helps us think about how interdependent the family members are, you may be thinking that they have some competing interests in relation to scarce resources of time and money. The hospice social worker knows that communications can become tense in families facing similar situations of scarce resources, and she wants to know more about how the McKinley family negotiates competing interests. These are some of the observations about the McKinley family suggested by the conflict perspective.

The **conflict perspective** has become popular over and over again throughout history, with roots that can be traced back to German philosopher Georg Hegel (1770–1831) and Italian philosopher Niccolò Machiavelli (1469–1527), and perhaps even further, drawing attention to conflict, dominance, and oppression in social life. The conflict perspective emphasizes conflicts that arise because of inequalities in the distribution of resources. It typically looks for sources of conflict in the economic and political arenas, and more recently in the cultural arena. Exhibit 2.2 provides a visual representation of the conflict perspective.

The roots of contemporary conflict theory are usually traced to the works of Karl Marx and his collaborator Friedrich Engels, as well as the works of Max Weber. Marx (1887/1967) and Engels (1884/1970) focused on economic structures, suggesting that the capitalist economic system is divided into capitalists and workers. Capitalists decide what is to be done and how to do it, and they own the products produced by the workers as well as the means of production. Capitalists pay workers as little as they can get away with, and they, not the workers, reap the benefits of exploiting natural resources. According to Marx, this system produces *false consciousness*: Neither capitalists nor workers are aware that the system is based on exploitation; workers think they are getting a fair day's pay, and capitalists think workers are fairly rewarded. Marx proposed, however, that workers are capable of recognizing the exploitation and achieving *class consciousness*, but capitalists are incapable of recognizing the exploitation in the system.

EXHIBIT 2.2 • Conflict Perspective

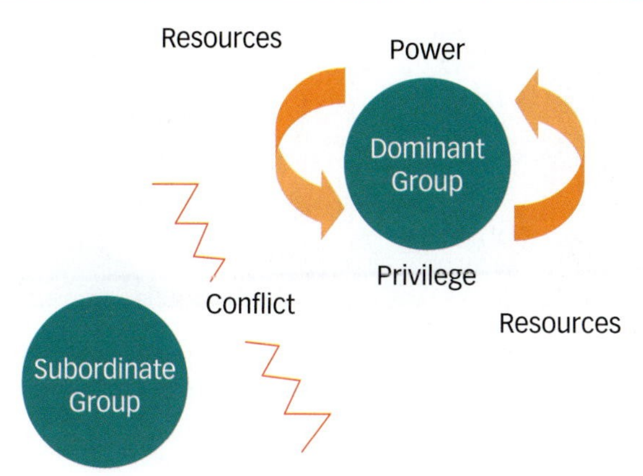

The roots of contemporary conflict theory are usually traced to the works of Karl Marx.

Weber (1904–1905/1958) rejected this singular emphasis on economics in favor of a multidimensional perspective on social class that included prestige and power derived from sources other than economics. Contemporary conflict theory tends to prefer Weber's multidimensional perspective, calling attention to a confluence of social, economic, and political structures in the creation of inequality. Jürgen Habermas (1984, 1981/1987) and other **critical theorists** argue that as capitalism underwent change, people were more likely to be controlled by culture than by their work position. Our lives became dominated by the culture industry, which is controlled by mass media. Critical theorists suggest that the culture industry plays a major role in turning workers into consumers, calling attention to the role of the advertising industry in exploiting consumers. They suggest that in the contemporary world, workers work very hard, sometimes at second and third jobs, in order to consume. They describe the exploitation of consumers as a pleasant kind of control: People spend more and more time working to be able to shop, and shopping becomes the major form of recreation. Working and shopping leave little time for reflective or revolutionary thinking. George Ritzer (2013a) suggested that the same might be said about the time we spend on Facebook, Twitter, and the like. But he also notes that besides informing us about what our friend ate for breakfast, social media is also used to spread the word about injustice and organize social protest.

Immanuel Wallerstein (2004) is a neo-Marxist who has focused on international inequality. He proposed that the capitalist world system is divided into three geographic areas with greatly different levels of power: A *core* of nations dominates the capitalist worldwide economy and exploits the natural resources and labor in other nations. The *periphery* includes nations that provide cheap raw materials and labor that are exploited to the advantage of the core. The *semiperiphery* includes nations that are newly industrializing; they benefit from the periphery but are exploited by the core.

Power relationships are a major focus of the conflict perspective. Some theorists in the conflict tradition limit their focus to the large-scale structure of power relationships, but many theorists, especially critical theorists, also look at the reactions and adaptations of individual members of nondominant groups. These theorists note that oppression of nondominant groups leads to their *alienation*, or a sense of indifference or hostility. **Critical race theory** was developed by legal scholars who wanted to draw attention to racial oppression in the law and society. They call attention to how *microaggressions*, brief, everyday exchanges that send denigrating messages and insults to people of color or members of any other minority identity group, create alienation for members of the group (Cappicci, Chadha, Bi Lin, & Snyder, 2012).

Lewis Coser (1956) proposed a *pluralistic theory of social conflict*, which recognizes that more than one social conflict is going on at all times and that individuals hold cross-cutting and overlapping memberships in status groups. Social conflict exists between economic groups, racial groups, ethnic groups, religious groups, age groups, gender groups, and so forth. Thus, it seeks to understand life experience by looking at simultaneous memberships—for example, a White, Italian American, Protestant, heterosexual, male semiskilled worker or a Black, African American, Catholic, lesbian, female professional worker. Feminist and critical race theorists have developed a pluralistic approach called **intersectionality theory**, which recognizes that all of us are jointly and simultaneously members of a number of socially constructed identity groups, such as gender, race, ethnicity, social class, sexual orientation, age, religion, geographical location, and disability/ability (see P. Collins, 2012). We live our lives at the intersection of these identities.

Although early social workers in the settlement house tradition recognized social conflict and structured inequality, and focused on eliminating oppression of immigrants, women, and children, most critics agree that social workers have not drawn consistently on the conflict perspective over time. In the past 2 decades, with renewed commitment to social justice in its professional code of ethics and in its curriculum guidelines, social work has drawn more heavily on the conflict perspective to understand dynamics of *privilege*, or unearned advantage, as well as discrimination and oppression. Social workers have used the conflict perspective as a base to develop practice-oriented **empowerment theories**, which focus on processes that individuals and collectivities can use to recognize patterns of inequality and injustice and take action to increase their own power (e.g., Gutiérrez, 1990, 1994; J. Lee, 2001; Rose, 1992, 1994; Solomon, 1976, 1987). Both in their renewed interest in domination and oppression and in their development of practice-oriented empowerment theories, social workers have been influenced by **feminist theories**, which focus on male domination of the major social institutions and present a vision of a just world based on gender equity. Feminist theories emphasize that people are socialized to see themselves through the eyes of powerful actors. Like Marx, most feminist theorists are not content to ask, "Why is it this way?" but also ask, "How can we change and improve the social world?"

George Rinhart/Contributor/Corbis Historical/Getty Images

Pioneer social worker Jane Addams was a prominent voice for pluralism during the early 20th century, and that stance is consistent with social work's concern for human rights.

This is how the conflict perspective rates on the five criteria for evaluating social work theory.

- *Coherence and conceptual clarity.* Most concepts of the conflict perspective are straightforward—conflict, power, domination, inequality—at least at the abstract level. Like all theoretical concepts, however, they become less straightforward when we begin to define them for the purpose of measurement. Across the various versions of the conflict perspective, concepts are not consistently used. One major source of variation is whether power and privilege are to be thought of as objective material circumstances, subjectively experienced situations, or both. In general, theories in the conflict tradition are expressed in language that is relatively accessible and clear. This is especially true of many of the practice-oriented empowerment theories developed by social workers.

- *Testability and empirical support.* Conflict theory has developed, in the main, through attempts to codify persistent themes in history. The preferred research method is empirical research that looks at large-scale patterns of history (see McMichael, 2012; Skocpol & Williamson, 2012; Wallerstein, 2004). As with other methods of research, critics have attacked some interpretations of historical data from the conflict perspective, but the historical analyses of Theda Skocpol and Immanuel Wallerstein are some of the most influential works in contemporary sociology. In addition to historical analysis, conflict theorists have used experimental methods to study reactions to coercive power (see Zimbardo, 2007) and naturalistic inquiry to study social ranking through interaction rituals (R. Collins, 2004). Contemporary conflict theorists are also drawing on network analysis, which plots the relationships among people within groups, and are finding support for their propositions about power and domination. Family researchers have used conflict theory, specifically the concept of power, to study family violence (White et al., 2015b).

- *Comprehensiveness.* Traditionally, the conflict perspective focused on large-scale social institutions and social structures, such as economic and political institutions. In the contemporary era, conflict theorists integrate conflict processes at the societal level with those at the community, small-group, and family levels. They suggest that we should recognize conflict as a central process in social life at all levels. Family theorists propose a conflict theory of families (White et al., 2015b). Traditional conflict theories propose that oppression of subordinate groups leads to a sense of alienation, and recent empowerment theories give considerable attention to individual perceptions of power. The conflict perspective does not explicitly address biology, but it has been used to examine racial and social class health disparities. Most conflict theories do consider dimensions of time. They are particularly noteworthy for recommending that the behavior of members of minority groups should be put in historical context, and indeed, as discussed, empirical historical research is the method many conflict theorists prefer.

- *Diversity and power.* The conflict perspective is about inequality, power arrangements, and systems of oppression. It, more than any other perspective presented in this chapter, helps us look at group-based patterns of inequality. In that way, it also assists us in understanding diversity. Intersectionality theory, which recognizes that individuals have overlapping memberships in a variety of status groups, is particularly useful for considering human diversity. A major strength of the conflict perspective is that it discourages pathologizing members of minority groups by encouraging recognition of the historical, cultural, economic, and political context of their behavior. Empowerment theories guide practice interventions that build on the strengths of members of minority groups.

- *Usefulness for social work practice.* The conflict perspective is essential for social workers to develop "Competency 3—Advance Human Rights and Social, Economic, and Environmental Justice" as required by the Council on Social Work Education (2015, p. 5). Concepts from the conflict perspective have great value for understanding power dimensions in societal, organizational, community, group, family, and dyadic relationships, as well as the power differential between social worker and client. Clearly, the conflict perspective is crucial to social work because it shines a spotlight on how domination and oppression might be affecting human behavior; it illuminates processes by which people become estranged and discouraged; and it encourages social workers to consider the meaning of their power relationships with clients, particularly nonvoluntary clients. In recent years, social workers have been in the forefront of developing practice-oriented empowerment theories, and the conflict perspective has become as useful for recommending particular practice strategies as for assisting in the assessment process. Empowerment theories provide guidelines for working at all system levels (e.g., individual, family, small group, community, and organization), but they put particular emphasis on group work because of the opportunities presented in small groups for solidarity and mutual support. Social movement theories (see Chapter 9), which are based in the conflict perspective, have implications for the mobilization of oppressed groups, but the conflict perspective in general provides little in the way of specific policy direction.

CRITICAL THINKING Questions 2.1

Both the systems and the conflict perspectives pay attention to the environment external to individuals. It could be argued that the hospice social worker should only be focusing on Ruth McKinley's personal needs and reactions. How would you argue in favor of that approach? How would you argue against it? To what extent do you see interactions within the family system to be important to meeting Ruth's personal needs? Explain. To what extent are conflicts external to the McKinley family influencing the well-being of the family? Explain. How might situating the McKinley family in the context of those conflicts help the social worker think about how to be helpful to the family? How would it not be helpful?

EXCHANGE AND CHOICE PERSPECTIVE

Another way to think about the McKinley family is to focus on the resources each member brings to the ongoing life of the family and each member's sense of fairness in the exchange of those resources. You might note that Ruth has diminishing resources to offer to the family, but the rest of the family seems to derive satisfaction, perhaps emotional energy, from caring for her. Marcia indicates that it is only fair that they care for her now because of the care Ruth provided to Bethany when she was a young child. Stanley's ability to provide economic resources to the family has diminished, but his contributions as caregiver have increased. Marcia has gotten satisfaction over the years from her caregiving role in the family, and her ability to bring this resource to the family has been compromised. On the other hand, the economic resources she brings into the family have become more important since Stanley became unemployed. Bethany provides economic resources as well as caregiving resources, and there is no evidence that she considers her contributions to the family to be unfair. She is weighing the long-term rewards of education against the short-term costs of adding a rigorous educational program to an already overtaxed life. This way of thinking about the McKinley family is suggested by the exchange and choice perspective.

The various streams of the **exchange and choice perspective**, which has roots in behavioral psychology, economics, anthropology, philosophy, and sociology, share the common focus on the processes whereby individual and collective actors seek and exchange resources and the choices made in pursuit of those resources. Resources may be material or nonmaterial: for example, time, money, material goods, sex, affection, loyalty, social contacts. These ideas are visually represented in Exhibit 2.3.

Social exchange theory, originally proposed by George Homans (1958), considered *social exchange*, defined as an interaction in which resources are exchanged, as the core process in social life. Homans started with the basic premise that social exchange is based on the desire to maximize benefits and minimize costs, a basic belief that social relationships occur in a social marketplace in which people give in order to get. Homans focused on individual motivation in exchanges in dyadic relationships. He saw individuals as always calculating the rewards and costs of relationships and making choices based on those calculations.

Peter Blau (1964) developed a social exchange theory that focused on how exchange works in organizations and complex institutions. He proposed that such exchanges are governed by a norm of **reciprocity**, that receiving resources requires giving resources of relatively equal value. He suggested that such exchanges build trust over time. Blau acknowledged, however, that imbalance of exchange occurs, and, when this happens, actors with the greatest resources hold power. He suggested that the most comfortable exchanges are those in which actors have equality of resources and that trust is fragile in unequal relationships. Karen Cook and colleagues (2005) share this concern about the fragility of trust and note the importance of "trust-nurturing bodies," like the U.S. Food and Drug Administration, whose purpose is to supervise and enforce trust.

The closely related *rational choice theory* (Coleman, 1990) shares with exchange theories the view that humans are rational (weighing rewards and costs), purposive, and motivated by self-interest. But rational choice theorists are particularly interested in the group dynamics that occur when rational actors make strategic decisions. They are

EXHIBIT 2.3 • Exchange and Choice Perspective

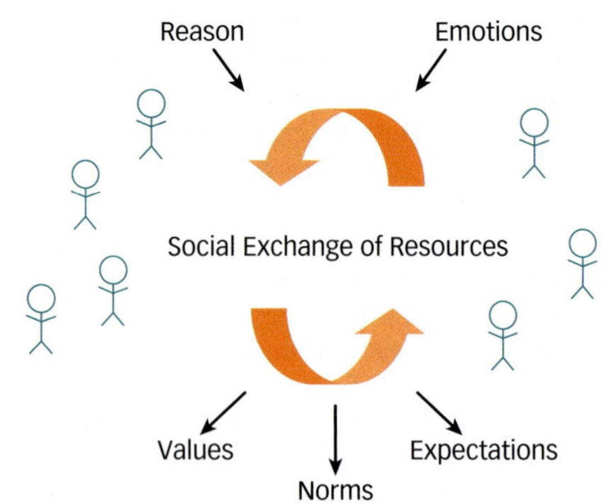

interested in the norms and networks formed by social exchanges and how, once created, norms and networks facilitate as well as constrain the behavior and choices of individuals. Coleman used rational choice theory to explore possible public policies that would offer incentives for actors to behave in ways that are more beneficial to others. Rational choice theory is currently popular in sociology, health promotion, and family studies.

Theorists in the rational choice tradition advanced **social network theory** (Cook, 1987). They introduced the concept of *exchange network*, which is a set of actors linked together, both directly and indirectly through exchange relationships. Social networks are typically presented visually, with members of the network—individuals, groups, or organizations—represented as points. Lines are drawn between pairs of points to demonstrate a relationship between them. Arrows are often used to show the flow of exchanges in a relationship. These graphic displays illuminate such issues as network size, density of relationships, strength of relationships, reciprocity of relationships, and access to power and influence. *Social capital theory* is a recent outgrowth of social network theory. Social networks provide social capital, both direct and indirect connections to others that are potential sources of a number of types of resources.

Traditional exchange and choice theories have been criticized on a number of grounds. Some critics have noted that exchange theory has a difficult time accounting for altruistic behavior. Others note that recent research indicates that humans are not really capable of considering all alternatives and their possible outcomes. Still other critics note that traditional exchange theory does not address why some rewards are valued more than others. We can imagine, for example, that some young adults in Bethany McKinley's position would consider it unfair to be involved in economic provider and caregiving roles in their family of origin, but she does not. What values are at play here? In response to these theoretical concerns, some behavioral scientists have proposed nonrational models of exchange and choice.

Sociologist Randall Collins (2004) introduced a form of exchange theory he calls *interaction ritual chains*. He proposes that social structures are developed by the aggregation of many exchanges over long periods of time. Rituals, or patterned sequences of behavior, develop out of these ongoing exchanges. Interaction rituals become linked or chained together by individuals who are members of multiple networks. Collins suggests that emotion, not reason, is the driving force of social exchange; emotional energy is the motive behind all exchanges. People are more likely to repeat interactions from which they take away emotional energy, and they engage in altruistic behavior because of the emotional energy they receive in the exchange. Collins proposes that physical copresence is necessary for rituals to develop; copresence produces common emotional mood, focused attention, and collective emotional energy. He supports this assertion by citing research indicating that the brain waves of participants in ritualized interactions become synchronized. Collins suggests that the self emerges from patterns of interaction; who we hang out with is the key to who we become.

An exchange network is a set of actors linked together through exchange relationships.

Political scientist Deborah Stone (2012) has criticized the dominance of rational choice models of policy analysis. She refers to rational choice models as *market* models and proposes, instead, a *polis model*, which starts from the point of view of the community rather than the individual. She suggests that a theory of the political process must recognize altruism and public interest as well as self-interest. She acknowledges that reasonable people can disagree about what the public interest is and proposes that the political process involves a negotiation of ideas about that. In the political process, participants are influenced in their choices by people in their networks and by their loyalties, operating by "laws of passion," rather than "laws of reason." They form alliances to gain power. Stone (2012) argues that whereas the market model proposes that participants in the political process have access to accurate and complete information for making political choices, in reality, information about policy issues is "ambiguous, incomplete, and sometimes deliberately withheld" (p. 30). She argues that we cannot be effective in influencing policy if we do not understand the nonrational aspects of the policy development process.

This is how the exchange and choice perspective rates on the five criteria for evaluating social work theory.

- *Coherence and conceptual clarity.* Early exchange theory contained a conceptual hole about the motivation for altruistic behavior, but recent formulations have addressed that hole. There is much consistency within each stream of the exchange and choice perspective. There is also much consistency across streams about the important role of exchange and choice in human behavior.

There is a great deal of inconsistency across theories, however, about issues of rationality and self-interestedness. Although concepts are sometimes presented at a high level of abstraction, most theories in the perspective define and measure terms in a clear and consistent manner.

- *Testability and empirical support.* The exchange and choice perspective has stimulated empirical research at several levels of analysis, with mixed results. Cognitive psychologists Daniel Kahneman and Amos Tversky (1982, 1984) dealt a blow to the rational choice perspective in the 1980s. They reported research findings that individual choices and decisions are often inconsistent with assumed rationality and that, indeed, situations are often too complicated for individuals to ascertain the most rational choice. On the other hand, more than modest support for the perspective has been found in research on dyads and families (see Sutphin, 2010). Researchers across a wide range of disciplines are using statistical methods to calculate the balance of costs and benefits of particular courses of action, such as conserving natural habitats (Naidoo & Adamowicz, 2006) or prescribing antidepressant medications instead of cognitive behavioral therapy (Hollinghurst, Kessler, Peters, & Gunnell, 2005).

- *Comprehensiveness.* Although all streams of the exchange and choice perspective are interested in human interactions, the different streams focus on different dimensions in which interactions occur. The perspective has been used to study dyads, families, small groups, networks, communities, organizations, and institutions (see White et al., 2015c). In general, the exchange and choice perspective is weak in exploration of personal dimensions, but Homans (1958) was interested in human motivation, and Randall Collins (2004) has been explicit in identifying the biological mechanisms involved in the emotional energy he sees as the engine of social exchange. The exchange and choice perspective attends to time in terms of the history of past exchanges.

- *Diversity and power.* Although they were designed to look at patterns, not diversity, early exchange and choice theories provided some tools for understanding diversity in behaviors that come out of particular social exchanges. All theories in this perspective recognize power as deriving from unequal resources in the exchange process. Some versions of rational choice theory emphasize the ways in which patterns of exchange lead to social inequalities and social injustices. Although the exchange and choice perspective does not explicitly pathologize members of minority groups, those versions that fail to put social exchanges in historical, political, and economic contexts may unintentionally contribute to the pathologizing of these groups.

- *Usefulness for social work practice.* Some versions of the exchange and choice perspective serve as little more than a defense of the rationality of the marketplace of social exchange, suggesting a noninterventionist approach. In other words, if all social exchanges are based on rational choices, then who are we to interfere with this process? This stance, of course, is inconsistent with the purposes of social work. However, the perspective has also been used to analyze the service participation decision making among clients and to guide decision making about recruitment of volunteers. Social network theory, with its recent emphasis on social capital, suggests tools for enhancing the resources of individuals and groups, including networks of social service providers. Randall Collins's (2004) theory of exchange rituals suggests ways to create and reinforce altruism and group solidarity. Deborah Stone's (2012) polis model provides tools for thinking about the complexities of the policymaking process and can help social workers be more realistic about how they might influence that process.

SOCIAL CONSTRUCTIONIST PERSPECTIVE

As the hospice social worker drives back to the office, the McKinley family is on her mind. She thinks about how they are coping with a great deal of change in the external world as well as within their family system. She is interested in learning more about how they are describing and explaining these changes. For example, how do they understand their struggles in the labor market and the housing market? How much do they attribute their struggles to personal failings, and how much do they see themselves as part of a bigger story? How do their attributions affect their sense of self-worth? She thinks of Marcia's words, "nothing goes our way," and wonders whether this understanding of the world is shared by Stanley and Bethany—and, if so, how she might help them construct a different ending to the story they are telling themselves. She thinks about Ruth and her end-of-life reflections about her life and social relationships. She hopes that she can be a good listener and a partner with Ruth as she makes meaning of her life. This way of thinking about the McKinley family is consistent with the social constructionist perspective.

To understand human behavior, the **social constructionist perspective** focuses on how people construct meaning, a sense of self, and a social world through their interactions with each other. They learn, through their interactions, to classify the world and their place in it. People interact with each other and the physical world based on *shared meanings*, or shared understandings about the world. In this view, people develop their understandings of the world and themselves from social interaction, and these understandings shape their subsequent social interactions. Reality is shaped through social interaction and is continuously reshaped by ongoing social interaction. A visual representation of this way of thinking about human behavior is presented in Exhibit 2.4.

The early roots of the social constructionist perspective come from *symbolic interaction theory* developed by sociologists in the United States in the mid-20th century. This theory proposes that as humans interact, they develop symbols to which they attach meaning. Words are symbols, but so are piercings, tattoos, national flags, and fashion styles. The symbolic interactionist would be interested in how the McKinley family came to attach particular meaning to the word *family*. For the symbolic interactionist, society is constructed by human beings engaging in symbolic interaction. Through interaction, humans consciously and deliberately create their personal and collective histories. You may recall that the social exchange theorists are also concerned with social interaction, but their focus is on social interaction as an exchange of resources rather than on how social interaction produces meaning, a sense of self, and social life (society), which is the focus of the interactionist (Blumer, 1998).

To the social constructionist, there is no singular objective reality, no true reality that exists "out there" in the world. There are, instead, the shared subjective realities created as people interact in different contexts. Constructionists emphasize the existence of multiple social and cultural realities. Both persons and environments are dynamic processes, not static structures. The sociopolitical environment and history of any situation play an important role in understanding human behavior because of the way they have shaped meaning over time.

EXHIBIT 2.4 • Social Constructionist Perspective

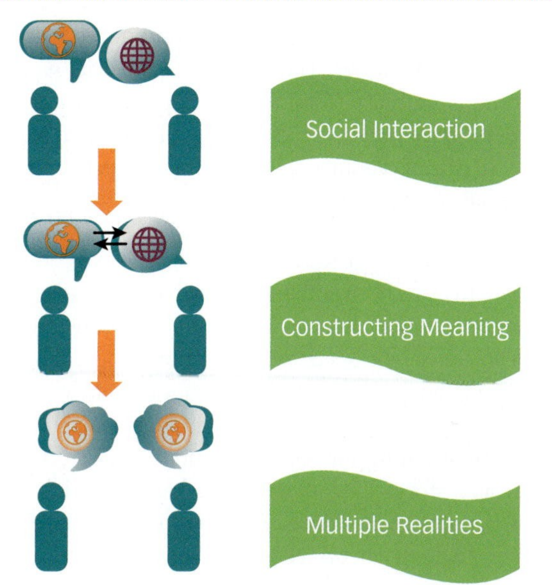

The social constructionist would, for example, call attention to how Stanley's understanding of himself as a worker is being influenced by current economic uncertainties.

The importance of subjective rather than objective reality has been summed up by the words of W. I. Thomas (Thomas & Thomas, 1928): "If men define situations as real, they are real in their consequences" (p. 128). Actually, social constructionists disagree about whether there is, in fact, some objective reality out there. Radical social constructionists believe there is not. They believe there is no reality beyond our personal experiences. Most *postmodern theorists* fall in this category, arguing that there are no universals, including no universal truth, reality, or morality (Dybicz, 2011; Lyotard, 1984). The postmodernists accept that the world is "messy" and see no need to impose order on it. More moderate social constructionists believe there are "real objects" in the world, but those objects are never known objectively; rather, they are only known through the subjective interpretations of individuals and collectivities (C. Williams, 2006).

Social constructionists also disagree about how constraining the environment is. Some see individual actors in social interactions as essentially free, active, and creative (Gergen, 1985). Others suggest that individual actors are always performing for their social audiences, based on their understanding of community standards for human behavior (Berger & Luckmann, 1966; Goffman, 1959). Although this idea has been around for a while, it is taking on new meaning in the current world of proliferating communication technology, which provides us with many modalities for performing for our audiences, for engaging in what Goffman (1959) refers to as *impression management*. The dominant social constructionist position is probably the one represented by Schutz's (1932/1967) *phenomenological sociology*. In arguing that people shape social reality, Schutz also suggests that individuals and groups are constrained by the preexisting social and cultural arrangements constructed by their predecessors.

The social constructionist perspective sees human understanding, or human consciousness, as both the product and the driving force of social interaction. Some social constructionists focus on individual consciousness, particularly on the human capacity to interpret social interactions and to have an inner conversation with oneself about them. They see the self as developing from the interpretation of social interaction. Cooley (1902/1964) introduces the concept of the *looking-glass self*, which can be explained as "I am what I think you think I am." The looking-glass self has three components: (1) I imagine how I appear to others, (2) I imagine their judgment of me, and (3) I develop some feeling about myself that is a result of imagining their judgments of me. George Herbert Mead (1959) suggests that one has a self only when one is in community and that the self develops based on our interpretation of the *generalized other*, which is the attitude of the entire community.

Other social constructionists put greater emphasis on the nature of social interactions, calling attention to gestures and language that are used as symbols in social interaction (Charon, 1998). These symbols take on particular meaning in particular situations. These social constructionists also see social problems as social constructions, created through claims making, labeling, and other social processes. Social workers have used the social constructionist approach to understand how society has constructed the meaning of phenomena such as parental incapability (Ben-David, 2011) and homelessness (Cronley, 2010) over time, as well as the processes by which these socially constructed definitions become internalized.

This is how the social constructionist perspective rates on the five criteria for evaluating social work theory.

- *Coherence and conceptual clarity.* Social constructionism, both the original phenomenological and symbolic interactional concepts as well as the contemporary postmodern conceptualizations, is often criticized as vague and unclear. Over the past few decades, a great diversity of theorizing has been done within this broad theoretical perspective, and there is much fragmentation of ideas. That situation is consistent, however, with postmodernist understanding of multiple realities. Sociologists in the conflict and exchange and choice traditions have begun to incorporate social constructionist ideas, particularly those related to meaning making, which has further blurred the boundaries of this perspective but also attests to the usefulness of that concept. One challenge to the consistency of the social constructionist perspective is that, in its most radical form, it denies the one-absolute-truth, objective approach to reality while arguing that it is absolutely true that reality is subjective. There is inconsistency among the various streams of the perspective about how constraining history is on human interaction and how free humans are to reconstruct their social interaction.

- *Testability and empirical support.* Because of the vagueness of its concepts, the social constructionist perspective has been criticized for being difficult to operationalize for empirical research. Like DePoy and Gilson (2012), we think the constructionist perspective has made a great contribution to scientific inquiry by calling attention to the limitations of positivist research methods to explain all of human behavior, for pointing out the possibilities for bias in those research methods. Social constructionists propose alternative research methodology that focuses more on narrative and storytelling. Social constructionism has stimulated a trend in the behavioral sciences to use a mix of quantitative and qualitative research methodologies to accommodate both objective and subjective reality. This is providing a richer picture of human behavior.

- *Comprehensiveness.* Social constructionism pays little attention to the role of biology in human behavior, with the exception of a few constructivist biologists (Stewart, 2001). In some versions of social constructionism, cognitive processes are central, and the social construction of emotions is considered in others. With the emphasis on meaning making, social constructionism is open to the role of religion and spirituality in human behavior. With its emphasis on social interaction, the social constructionist perspective is strong in attention to the social environment. It has been criticized, however, for failing to pay sufficient attention to the macro world of social institutions and social structure. It has been criticized for focusing on meaning making and interpretation processes at the micro level, but it is important to acknowledge that it has also been used to propose the culture-framing perspective on social movements. Time, and the role of history, is respected in the social constructionist perspective, with many authors drawing attention to the historical era in which behavior is constructed.

- *Diversity and power.* With its emphasis on multiple social realities, the social constructionist perspective is strong in its ability to accommodate diversity. It has been criticized, however, for failure to provide the theoretical tools necessary for the analysis of power relationships. Some critics have suggested that many contemporary postmodern versions of social constructionism, by ignoring power while focusing on multiple voices and multiple meanings in the construction of reality, reduce oppression to mere difference (C. Williams, 2006). These critics suggest that this reduction of oppression to difference masks the fact that some actors have greater power than others to privilege their own constructions of reality and to disadvantage the constructions of other actors. This criticism cannot be leveled at all versions of social constructionism, however. Social work scholars have been attracted to those versions of the social constructionist perspective that have incorporated pieces of the conflict tradition (see Freeman & Couchonnal, 2006). They propose that social workers can bring credibility to minority viewpoints by allowing oppressed individuals and groups to tell their own stories. Most theorizing about empowerment integrates conflict and social constructionist thinking.

- *Usefulness for social work practice.* Social constructionism gives new meaning to the old social work adage, "Begin where the client is." In the social constructionist perspective, the social work relationship begins with developing an understanding of how the client views the situation and what the client would like to have happen. The current strong interest in solution-focused and narrative and storytelling therapies is based on the social constructionist perspective. Solution-focused approaches attempt to help clients construct solutions rather than solve problems (Greene & Lee, 2011). They are based on the assumption that clients want to change and are capable of envisioning the change they would like to see. Narrative therapy starts with the assumption that we all tell ourselves stories about our lives, developing dominant story lines and forgetting material that does not fit into them. A goal of therapy is to help clients see more realities in their story lines, with other possible interpretations of events (J. Walsh, 2014). The social worker should engage the client in thinking about the social, cultural, and historical environments in which his or her version of reality was constructed, which, for members of oppressed groups, may lead to empowerment through *restorying*, or revision of the story line (Greene & Cohen, 2005). Joseph Walsh (2014) suggests that narrative therapy can be particularly helpful to hospice patients who are reflecting on their life stories. That is, indeed, the approach of the hospice social worker who is working with Ruth McKinley and her family. At the level of groups and organizations, the social constructionist perspective recommends getting discordant groups to engage in sincere discussion of their disparate constructions of reality and to negotiate lines of action acceptable to all (Riera, 2005).

CRITICAL THINKING Questions 2.2

Both the exchange and choice and the social constructionist perspectives focus on social interactions. What do you see as the main difference in these two perspectives? What resources, both material and nonmaterial, do you see being exchanged in the McKinley family? What resources must be secured by interactions with people and systems outside the family? How might the hospice social worker help the family to increase their social capital? What shared meanings do you think the McKinley family members hold? If you were their social worker, how would the meanings you hold about the social world be similar to and different from theirs? In what contexts have you developed your sense of self and your understandings of the social world?

PSYCHODYNAMIC PERSPECTIVE

Both Stanley and Marcia McKinley's despondence and loss of hope are apparent in their first meeting with the hospice social worker—and easy to understand. Think about the losses they have faced in the past year: loss of job (Stanley), loss of income (Stanley and Marcia), loss of valued roles (provider for Stanley and caregiver for Marcia), and loss of health (Marcia). They also face the impending loss of Ruth, the last surviving parent for them, and the possible loss of their home. This rapid accumulation of loss would challenge, even overwhelm, the adaptive capacities of most any human. Bethany is thinking of dropping out of school, a decision that will involve loss of a dream, at least temporarily. In the midst of all that loss, we also note the deep attachment that all four family members—Ruth, Stanley, Marcia, and Bethany—have for each other. This suggests that early nurturing environments supported the development of secure attachments. As we explore the McKinley family's situation from the psychodynamic perspective, these and other ideas emerge.

The **psychodynamic perspective** is concerned with how internal processes such as needs, drives, and emotions motivate human behavior. The perspective has evolved over the years, moving from the classical psychodynamic emphasis on innate drives and unconscious processes toward greater emphasis on the adaptive capacities of individuals and their interactions with the environment. The origins of all psychodynamic theories are in the work of Sigmund Freud. More recent formulations of the perspective include ego psychology, object relations, self psychology, and relational-cultural theories. We elaborate on these more recent developments later. Exhibit 2.5 presents a visual representation of the psychodynamic perspective.

To trace the evolution of the psychodynamic perspective, it is essential to begin with its Freudian roots. Sigmund Freud looked at the human personality from a number of interrelated points of view; the most notable are his drive or instinct theory, topographical theory, structural theory, and psychosexual stage theory, summarized shortly. Freud revised each of these approaches to human personality over time, and different followers of Freud have attended to different aspects of his theoretical works, further revising each of them over time.

- *Drive or instinct theory.* This theory proposes that human behavior is motivated by two basic instincts: *thanatos*, or the drive for aggression or destruction, and *eros*, or the drive for life (through sexual gratification). Revisions of drive theory have suggested that human behavior is also motivated by drives for mastery (see D. Goldstein, 1996) and for connectedness (Borden, 2009).

- *Topographical theory of the mind.* Topographical theory proposes three states of mind: conscious mental activities of which we are fully aware; preconscious thoughts and feelings that can be easily brought to mind; and unconscious thoughts, feelings, and desires of which we are not aware but that have a powerful influence on our behavior. Although all psychodynamic theorists believe in

EXHIBIT 2.5 • Psychodynamic Perspective

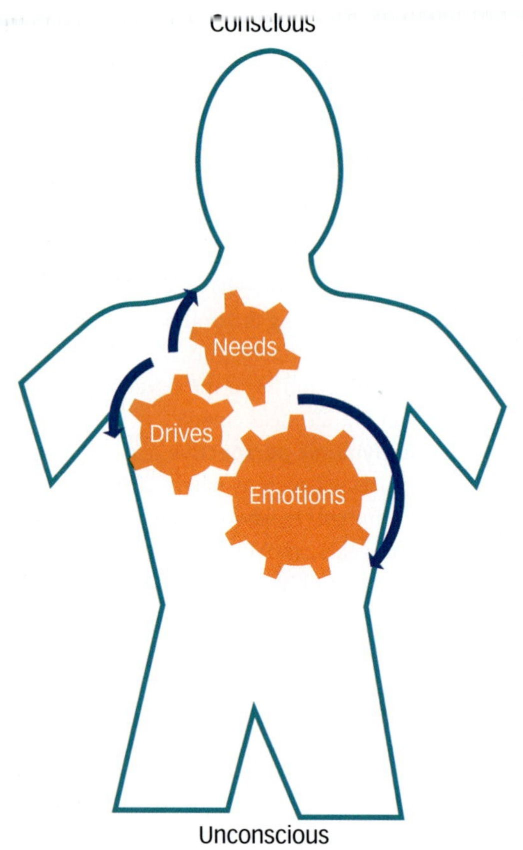

the unconscious, the different versions of the theory put different emphases on the importance of the unconscious in human behavior.

- *Structural model of the mind.* This model proposes that personality is structured around three parts: the *id*, which is unconscious and strives for satisfaction of basic instincts; the *superego*, which is made up of conscience and ideals and is the censor of the id; and the *ego*, which is the rational part of personality that mediates between the id and the superego. Freud and his early followers were most interested in the id and the pathologies that emanate from it, but later followers have focused primarily on ego strengths and the drive for adaptation. Both ego psychology and self psychology are part of this later tradition.

- *Psychosexual stage theory.* This theory proposes a five-stage model of child development, based on sexual instincts: the oral phase (birth to about 18 months), when the search for pleasure is centered in the mouth; the anal phase (from about 18 months to 3 years), when the search for pleasure is centered in the anus; the phallic phase (ages 3 to 6), when the search for pleasure is centered in the genitals; the latency phase (ages 6 to 8), when erotic urges are repressed; and the genital phase (adolescence onward), when the search for pleasure is centered in the genitals and sexual intimacy. Freud asserted that there was no further personality development in adulthood. Revisions of psychodynamic theory, starting with the work of Erik Erikson (1963), have challenged that idea. Although they still give primacy to the childhood years, they suggest that personality continues to develop over the life course. Recent theories also put less emphasis on sexual instincts in stage development.

Let's turn now to some revisions of Freudian theory. *Ego psychology* gives primary attention to the rational part of the mind and the human capacity for adaptation. It recognizes conscious as well as unconscious attempts to cope and the importance of both past and present experiences. Defense mechanisms, unconscious processes that keep intolerable threats from conscious awareness, play an important role in ego psychology (see E. Goldstein, 2001). *Object relations theory* studies how people develop attitudes toward others in the context of early nurturing relationships and how those attitudes affect the view of the self as well as social relationships. In this tradition, John Bowlby's attachment theory has become the basis for a psychobiological theory of attachment (Barnekow & Kraemer, 2005). *Self psychology* focuses on the individual need to organize the personality into a cohesive sense of self and to build relationships that support it (see E. Goldstein, 2001). *Relational-cultural theory*, also known as relational feminist theory, proposes that the basic human drive is for relationships with others. The self is understood to develop and mature through emotional connectedness in mutually empathic relationships, rather than through a process of separation and independence as proposed by traditional object relations theory. Human connectedness is emphasized, human diversity acknowledged, and human difference normalized rather than pathologized (Borden, 2009; Freedberg, 2007).

In recent years, social workers who practice from a psychodynamic perspective have drawn on both biological research and propositions from conflict theorists to extend the psychodynamic perspective. Joan Berzoff (2011) writes about why psychodynamically oriented social work practice with "vulnerable, oppressed, and at-risk clients" must be informed by biological research, particularly neuroscience research, concepts of power and privilege, and critical race theory with its emphasis on intersectionality (p. 132). She also analyzes the contribution that traditional psychodynamic theories can make to understanding discrimination, scapegoating, and oppression. You will read more about the psychodynamic perspective in Chapter 4.

This is how the psychodynamic perspective rates on the five criteria for evaluating social work theory.

- *Coherence and conceptual clarity.* Criticisms that the psychodynamic perspective lacks logical consistency are directed primarily at Freud's original concepts and propositions, which were not entirely consistent because they evolved over time. Ego psychology and object relations theorists strengthened the logical consistency of the psychodynamic perspective by expanding and clarifying definitions of major concepts. Theories in the psychodynamic perspective are also criticized for the vague and abstract nature of their concepts but perhaps no more than most other theoretical perspectives.

- *Testability and empirical support.* Much empirical work has been based on the psychodynamic perspective, and research in other disciplines provides some support for some of the propositions of the perspective. Recent long-term longitudinal studies support the importance of childhood experiences but also indicate that personality continues to develop throughout life. There is growing evidence of the supremely important role that attachment plays in shaping development over the life course. Research by cognitive psychologists indicates that much of human behavior is based on activity that is outside of consciousness; although they do not use this language, it appears that they are suggesting both preconscious and unconscious activity (Kahneman, 2011). Neuroscience research is indicating the important role of emotion in human behavior, demonstrating the brain mechanisms involved in emotion and suggesting that both genetics and life experiences shape the emotional brain (Davidson & Begley, 2012). Early life experiences are important in this process, but the brain is plastic and can be changed by ongoing life experiences and mental activity.

- *Comprehensiveness.* Early psychodynamic theories were primarily concerned with internal psychological processes. Strong attention is paid to emotions, and in recent formulations, cognitions are also acknowledged. Although Freud assumed that biology determines behavior, he developed his theory several decades before neurological science began to uncover the biological base of emotions. Recently, however, psychodynamic theorists have begun to incorporate new developments in neurological sciences about early brain development into their formulations (see, e.g., Berzoff, 2011). With the exception of Carl Jung, early psychodynamic theorists were not interested in the spiritual aspects of human behavior, typically viewing them as irrational defenses against anxiety. Some psychodynamically oriented social workers have attempted to integrate spirituality into their practice in recent times, often drawing on Eastern psychological theories (see Nagai, 2007). As for environments, most psychodynamic theory conceptualizes them as sources of conflicts with which the individual must struggle. Relational cultural theory, with its emphasis on supporting the growth of relationships and community, takes exception to that view. Overall, however, environments beyond the family or other close interpersonal relationships are ignored. This has led to criticisms of "mother blaming" and "family blaming" in traditional psychodynamic theories. Social, economic, political, and historical environments of human behavior are probably implied in ego psychology, but they are not explicated. As for time, the focus is on how people change across childhood. There has traditionally been little attempt to account for change after childhood or to recognize the contributions of historical time to human behavior, but this is changing.

- *Diversity and power.* Traditional psychodynamic theories search for universal laws of behavior and their applicability to unique individuals. Thus, diversity of experience at the group level has been quite neglected in this tradition until recently. Moreover, in the main, "universal" laws have been developed through analysis of European American, heterosexual, middle-class men. Feminists, as well as members of racial and ethnic minority groups, have criticized the psychodynamic bias toward thinking of people as autonomous individuals (Freedberg, 2007; Nagai, 2007). These critics suggest that viewing this standard as "normal" makes the connectedness found among many women and members of racial and ethnic minority groups seem pathological. Recently, proponents of the psychodynamic perspective have tried to correct for these biases and develop a better understanding of human diversity. Psychodynamic theories are strong in their recognition of power dynamics in parent-child relationships and in exploration of the lifeworlds of children. Until recently, they have been weaker in looking at power issues in other relationships, however, including gender relationships. In the contemporary era, psychoanalytic feminists have reworked Freud's ideas to focus on patriarchy, asking the question, "Why do men work so hard to maintain patriarchy, and why do women put so little energy into challenging patriarchy?" (Lengermann & Niebrugge-Brantley, 2007). They propose that the answer to this question is found in the gender-based early child-rearing environment. African American social workers have proposed that social workers can help to empower African American clients by integrating empowerment theory and an Afrocentric perspective with the ego-strengthening aspects of ego psychology (Manning, Cornelius, & Okundaye, 2004). Relational-cultural theory was developed out of concerns about the male bias in existing psychodynamic theories. These examples illustrate the psychodynamic perspective's growing attention to issues of diversity and power.

- *Usefulness for social work practice.* Most versions of the psychodynamic perspective have included practice theory as well as human behavior theory. Differences of opinion about principles of practice reflect the theoretical evolution that has occurred. Practice principles common to all versions of the psychodynamic perspective include the centrality of the professional–client relationship, the curative value of expressing emotional conflicts and understanding past events, and the goals of self-awareness and self-control. In contrast to the classical psychodynamic approach, recent formulations include directive as well as nondirective intervention, short-term as well as long-term intervention, and environmental manipulations—such as locating counseling regarding possible mortgage foreclosure for the McKinley family—as well as intrapsychic manipulations such as emotional catharsis. Ego psychology has also been used to develop principles for prevention activities in addition to principles of remediation (D. Goldstein, 1996). In general, however, the psychodynamic perspective does not suggest practice principles at the level of communities, organizations, and social institutions. Thus, from this perspective, it would not help you to think about how to influence public policy related to housing, income security, or access to health care.

DEVELOPMENTAL PERSPECTIVE

Another way to think about the McKinley family is to view their situation in terms of the developmental tasks they face. You might note that Ruth McKinley is in late adulthood and engaged in a review of her life journey, attempting to make peace with the life she has lived. You might also note that Stanley and Marcia assumed caregiving responsibilities for Ruth 5 years ago while also continuing to provide support to Bethany as she moved into young adulthood. At the current time, their struggles to stay employed and hold on to their house are situations that were once thought to be "off time," or atypical, for individuals in middle adulthood but have become more common for the current cohort of midlife adults. Bethany assumed a caregiving role with Ruth as she emerged into adulthood, and that also may seem off time. We can think about where she stands with the developmental markers typically associated with young adulthood: education/work, intimate relationship, leaving home, and starting career. These observations are consistent with the central ideas of the developmental perspective.

The focus of the **developmental perspective**, perhaps the most widely used of the perspectives presented in this chapter, is on how human behavior unfolds across the life course, how people change and stay the same over time. Human development is seen to occur in clearly defined stages based on a complex interaction of biological, psychological, and social processes. Each new stage involves new tasks and brings changes in social roles and statuses. A visual representation of these ideas is presented in Exhibit 2.6.

Although there are a great number of developmental theories, they can be categorized into two streams of theorizing: one based in psychology and one based in sociology. *Life span* or *life cycle theory*, based in psychology, focuses on the inner life during age-related stages. The study of life span development is rooted in Freud's (1905/1953) theory of psychosexual stages of childhood development, but Erikson (1963) has been the most influential developmental theorist to date because his model of development includes adult, as well as child, stages of development. Erikson (1963) proposed an *epigenetic model of human development*, in which the psychological unfolding of personality takes place in sequences influenced by biological, psychological, and social forces. Healthy development depends on the mastery of life tasks at the appropriate time in the sequence. Although life span theorists tend to agree with this epigenetic principle, there is also growing agreement that the stages are experienced in a more flexible way than

EXHIBIT 2.6 • Developmental Perspective

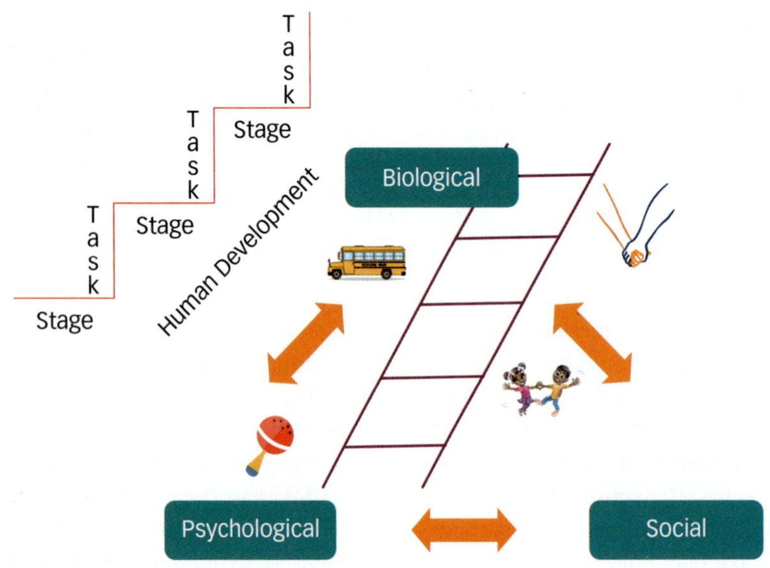

Erikson proposed, with cultural, economic, and personal circumstances leading to some differences in timing and sequencing (Sollod, Wilson, & Monte, 2009). For example, Bethany McKinley is thinking of postponing school and career development to be a support to her extended family in a stressful period in the life of the family. Stanley McKinley is faced with a need to rethink his occupational career at the age of 50. Erikson divided the life cycle into eight stages, each with a special psychosocial crisis (see Exhibit 4.11 in Chapter 4 for a summary of these stages).

Early life span theorists, including Erikson, saw their models of development as universal, applying equally well to all groups of people. This idea has been the target of much criticism, with suggestions that the traditional models are based on the experiences of European American, heterosexual, middle-class men and do not apply well to members of other groups. This criticism has led to a number of life cycle models for specific groups, such as women (Borysenko, 1996), gay and lesbian persons (e.g., Troiden, 1989), and African Americans (Cross, Parham, & Black, 1991). Life span theories have also been criticized for failing to deal with historical time and the cohort effects on human behavior that arise when groups of persons born in the same historical time share cultural influences and historical events at the same period in their lives.

These criticisms have helped to stimulate development of the *life course perspective* in sociology. This relatively new perspective conceptualizes the life course as a social, rather than psychological, phenomenon that is nonetheless unique for each individual, with some common life course markers, or transitions, related to shared social and historical contexts (George, 1993). Glen Elder Jr. (1998) and Tamara Hareven (2000) have been major forces in the development of the life course perspective. In its current state, there are six major themes in this perspective: interplay of human lives and historical time; biological, psychological, and social timing of human lives; linked or interdependent lives; human capacity for choice making; diversity in life course trajectories; and developmental risk and protection. As you may recall, the life course perspective is the conceptual framework for Part IV of this book and will be further analyzed in Chapter 10.

This is how the developmental perspective rates on the five criteria for evaluating social work theory.

- *Coherence and conceptual clarity.* Classical developmental theory's notion of life stages is internally consistent and conceptually clear. Theorists have been able to build on each other's work in a coherent manner. The life course perspective has developed some coherence and beginning clarity about the major concepts. When viewing these two developmental streams together, contradictions appear in terms of universality versus diversity in life span/life course development.

- *Testability and empirical support.* Many of Erikson's ideas have been employed and verified in empirical research, but until recently, much of developmental research has been based on European American, heterosexual, middle-class males. Another concern is that by defining normal as a statistical average, developmental research fails to capture the lifeworlds of groups who deviate even moderately from the average, or even to capture the broad range of behavior considered normal. Thus, empirical support for the developmental perspective is based to some extent on statistical masking of diversity. The life course perspective has offered a glimpse of diversity, however, because it has been developed, in general, from the results of longitudinal research, which follows the same people over an extended period of time. The benefit of longitudinal research is that it clarifies whether differences between age groups are really based on developmental differences or whether they reflect cohort effects from living in particular cultures at particular historical times. There is a growing body of longitudinal research in the life course tradition that suggests that age-graded differences in behavior reflect both developmental factors and historical trends (see Elder & Giele, 2009a).

- *Comprehensiveness.* The developmental perspective, when both theoretical streams are taken together, gets relatively high marks for comprehensiveness. Both the life span and the life course streams recognize human behavior as an outcome of complex interactions of biological, psychological, and social factors, although most theorists in both streams pay little attention to the spiritual dimension. The traditional life span approach pays too little attention to the political, economic, and cultural environments of human behavior; the life course perspective pays too little attention to psychological factors. Both approaches attend to the dimension of time, in terms of linear time, but the life course perspective attends to time in a more comprehensive manner, by emphasizing the role of historical era in human behavior. Indeed, the developmental perspective is the only one of the eight perspectives discussed here that makes time a primary focus.

- *Diversity and power.* The early life span models were looking for universal stages of human development and did not attend to issues of diversity. More recent life span models have paid more attention to diversity, and diversity of pathways through life is a major theme in the life course perspective. Likewise, the traditional life span approach did not take account of power relationships, with the possible exception of power dynamics in the parent–child relationship. Moreover, traditional life span models are based on the average European American, middle-class, heterosexual male and ignore the worlds of members of nondominant groups. Newer models of life span development have attempted to correct for that failure. Daniel Levinson's (1996) study of women's lives is noteworthy in that regard; it includes a sample of women diversified by race and social class and acknowledges the impact of gender power differentials on women's development. The life course perspective recognizes patterns of advantage and disadvantage in life course trajectories, and life course researchers have done considerable work on the accumulation of advantage and disadvantage over the life course (see Seabrook & Avison, 2012).

- *Usefulness for social work practice.* Erikson's theory has often been used for assessment purposes in social work practice, and in a positive sense, the theory can aid indirectly in the identification of potential personal and social developmental resources. Traditional life span theories should be applied, however, only with recognition of the ethnocentrism expressed in them. Although it is harder to extrapolate practice principles from the more complex, still-emerging life course perspective, it seems more promising for understanding diverse persons in diverse environments. It suggests that individuals must always be assessed within familial, cultural, and historical contexts. Overall, the developmental perspective can be viewed as optimistic. Most people face difficult transitions, life crises, and developmental or other challenges at some point, and many people have been reassured to hear that their struggle is "typical." Because the developmental perspective sees individuals as having the possibility to rework their inner experiences, as well as their family relationships, clients may be assisted in finding new strategies for getting their lives back on course. For example, Stanley McKinley could explore untapped talents and interests that might be used to get his occupational career moving again.

CRITICAL THINKING Questions 2.3

Both the psychodynamic and developmental perspectives provide stage theories of human behavior, but they put different emphases on the importance of childhood experiences. The psychodynamic perspective sees emotion as holding a central place in human behavior. What emotions do you experience as you read the story of the McKinley family? How do you think these emotions are related to your childhood experiences? To adult experiences? How do you think those emotions might be helpful for work with the McKinley family? How might they not be helpful? According to the developmental perspective, Bethany McKinley is in the phase of young adulthood. You are either in that phase or have already passed through it. How is Bethany's experience with young adulthood similar to yours? Different from yours? What biases do you have about the choices Bethany is making?

SOCIAL BEHAVIORAL PERSPECTIVE

The hospice social worker observed Bethany McKinley's warm and gentle interaction with her grandmother, Ruth. She wasn't surprised later to hear Bethany describe Ruth as kind. She imagined that Ruth modeled kind behavior as she cared for Bethany when she was a young child. She also observed that Stanley, Marcia, and Bethany seemed to reinforce kind behavior in each other. She noticed how Stanley and Bethany put their arms around Marcia when she began to cry. The social worker was also struck by statements by both Stanley and Marcia that seem to indicate that they have lost confidence in their ability to make things happen in their lives. She understands how recent events could have undermined their confidence, but she is curious whether she simply caught them on a down day or if, indeed, they no longer have expectations of being able to improve their situation. Viewing the McKinley family from a social behavioral perspective can lead to such assessment and questions.

Theories in the **social behavioral perspective**, sometimes called the social learning perspective, suggest that human behavior is learned as individuals interact with their environments. There are disagreements among the different streams of social behavioral theory, however, about the processes by which behavior is learned. Over time, three major versions of behavioral theory have been presented, proposing different mechanisms by which learning occurs. The general themes of the social behavioral perspective are represented visually in Exhibit 2.7.

Classical conditioning theory, also known as respondent conditioning, sees behavior as learned through association, when a naturally occurring stimulus (unconditioned stimulus) is paired with a neutral stimulus (conditioned stimulus). This approach is usually traced to a classic experiment by Russian physiologist Ivan Pavlov, who showed, first, that dogs naturally salivate (unconditioned response) to meat powder on the tongue (unconditioned stimulus). Then, a ringing bell (conditioned stimulus) was paired with the meat powder a number of times. Eventually, the dog salivated (conditioned response) to the ringing of the bell (conditioned stimulus) without the meat powder. In other words, an initially neutral stimulus comes to produce a particular behavioral response after it is repeatedly paired with another stimulus of significance. Classical conditioning plays a role in understanding many problems that social work clients experience. For example, a woman with an alcohol abuse problem may experience urges to drink when in a location where she often engaged in drinking alcohol before getting sober. Anxiety disorders are also often conditioned; for example, a humiliating experience with public speaking may lead to a deep-seated and long-lasting fear of it,

EXHIBIT 2.7 • Social Behavioral Perspective

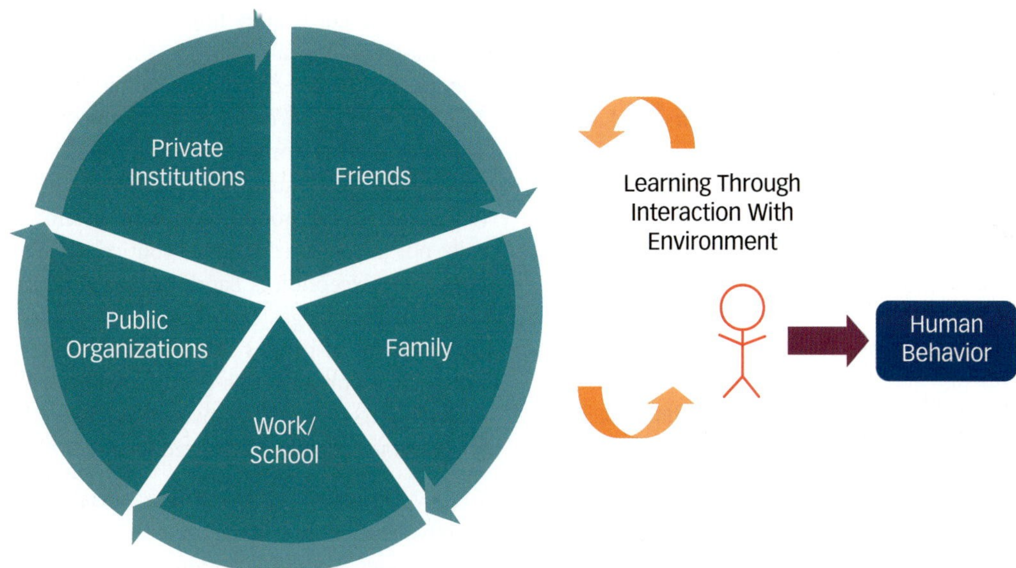

which can result in anxiety attacks in situations where the person has to speak publicly. This approach looks for antecedents of behavior—stimuli that precede behavior—as the mechanism for learning.

Operant conditioning theory, sometimes known as instrumental conditioning, sees behavior as the result of reinforcement. It is built on the work of two American psychologists, John B. Watson and B. F. Skinner. In operant conditioning, behavior is learned as it is strengthened or weakened by the reinforcement (rewards and punishments) it receives or, in other words, by the consequences of the behavior. Behaviors are strengthened when they are followed by positive consequences and weakened when they are followed by negative consequences. A classic experiment demonstrated that if a pigeon is given a food pellet each time it touches a lever, over time the pigeon learns to touch the lever to receive a food pellet. This approach looks for consequences—what comes after the behavior—as the mechanism for learning behavior. We all use operant conditioning as we go about our daily lives. We use positive reinforcers, such as smiles or praise, to reward behaviors we find pleasing, in hopes of strengthening those behaviors. Negative reinforcers are also used regularly in social life to stop or avoid unpleasant behavior. For example, an adolescent girl cleans her room to avoid parental complaints. Avoiding the complaints reinforces the room-cleaning behavior.

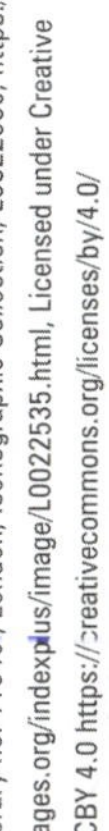

Classical conditioning is traced to an experiment Russian physiologist Ivan Pavlov performed with dogs.

Cognitive social learning theory, also known as cognitive behavioral theory or social cognitive theory, with Albert Bandura as its chief contemporary proponent, suggests that behavior is also learned by imitation, observation, beliefs, and expectations. In this view, the "learner" is not passively manipulated by elements of the environment but can use cognitive processes to learn behaviors. Cognitive-behavioral therapy (CBT), developed in the 1960s, focuses on helping people to better understand the thoughts and emotions that lead to problematic behavior and to develop new ways of thinking and behaving. Observing and imitating models is a pervasive method for learning human behavior. Bandura (1977a, 1986) proposes that human behavior is also driven by beliefs and expectations. He suggests that **self-efficacy** (a sense of personal competence) and **efficacy expectation** (an expectation that one can personally accomplish a goal) play an important role in motivation and human behavior. Bandura (2001, 2002) has extended his theory of self-efficacy to propose three models of **agency** (the capacity to intentionally make things happen): *personal agency* of the individual actor; *proxy* *agency*, in which people reach goals by influencing others to act on their behalf; and *collective agency*, in which people act cooperatively to reach a goal.

Although the different streams of social behavioral theorizing disagree about the mechanisms by which behavioral learning occurs, there is agreement that all human problems can be defined in terms of undesirable behaviors. Furthermore, all behaviors can be defined, measured, and changed.

This is how the social behavioral perspective rates on the five criteria for evaluating social work theory.

- *Coherence and conceptual clarity.* Although there are disagreements about the mechanisms of learning among the various streams of the social behavioral perspective, within each stream, ideas are logically developed in a consistent manner. The social behavioral perspective gets high marks for conceptual clarity; concepts are very clearly defined in each of the streams.

- *Testability and empirical support.* Social behavioral concepts are easily measured for empirical investigation because theorizing has been based, in very large part, on laboratory research. This characteristic is also a drawback of the social behavioral perspective, however, because laboratory experiments by design eliminate much of the complexity of person–environment configurations. In general, however, all streams of the social behavioral perspective have attained a relatively high degree of empirical support. Neuroscientists have found that CBT has a powerful effect on the brain activity involved in depression (Davidson & Begley, 2012). On the other hand, recent research in Sweden (Werbart, Levin, Andersson, & Sandell, 2013) found that CBT produced no better results than psychodynamic or integrative therapy in outpatient psychiatric care. Davidson and Begley (2012) suggest that the skill level of the CBT therapist for targeting specific neural circuits is an important variable, but understanding of this is in the early stages.

- *Comprehensiveness.* Overall, the social behavioral perspective sacrifices multidimensional understanding to gain logical consistency and testability. Little attention was paid to biology in early theorizing, but in his later work, Bandura (2001, 2002) recognized the role of biology in human behavior. Even so, biological research provides some of the best evidence for social behavioral theory. Besides the research on CBT already noted, research on neurophysiology and the immune system indicate that classical conditioning plays a role in physiological functioning (Farmer, 2009). Cognition and emotion are not included in theories of classical and operant conditioning, but they do receive attention in social cognitive theory. Spiritual factors are considered unmeasurable and irrelevant in classical and operant conditioning theories. For this reason, social behaviorism is sometimes seen as dehumanizing. Although environment plays a large role in the social behavioral perspective, the view of the environment is quite limited in classical and operant conditioning. Typically, the social behavioral perspective searches for the one environmental factor, or contingency, that has stimulated or reinforced one specific behavior. The identified contingency is usually in the micro system (such as the family) or sometimes in the meso system (e.g., a school classroom), but these systems are not typically put in social, economic, political, or historical contexts. One exception is Bandura's social cognitive theory, which acknowledges broad systemic influences on the development of gender roles. Time is important in this perspective only in terms of the juxtaposition of stimuli and reinforcement. The social behaviorist is careful to analyze antecedents and consequences of behavior.

- *Diversity and power.* The social behavioral perspective receives low marks in terms of both diversity and power issues. Very little attention has been paid to recognizing diversity in human behaviors, and it is assumed that the same mechanisms of learning work equally well for all groups. Likewise, the social behavioral perspective attends little to issues of power and oppression. Operant behavioral theory recommends rewards over punishment, but it does not account for the coercion and oppression inherent in power relationships at every system level. It is quite possible, therefore, for the professional behavior modifier to be in service to oppressive forces. On the other hand, behavioral methods can be used to serve social work values. Bandura (1986) writes specifically about power as related to gender roles. He and other theorists note that persons in nondominant positions are particularly vulnerable to **learned helplessness** in which a person's prior experience with environmental forces has led to low self-efficacy and expectations of efficacy, a point also made by some feminist theorists. You may find the concepts of self-efficacy and learned helplessness particularly useful in thinking about both Stanley and Marcia McKinley's situations. Both have experienced some setbacks that may be leading them to expect less of themselves.

- *Usefulness for social work practice.* A major strength of the social behavioral perspective is the ease with which principles of behavior modification can be extrapolated, and it is probably a rare person who has not used social behavioral principles in action at some point. Social workers and psychologists have used social behavioral methods primarily to modify undesirable behavior of individuals. For example, systematic desensitization techniques are used to diminish or eradicate anxiety symptoms. Parent training programs often teach parents how to make more effective use of reinforcements to strengthen positive behaviors and weaken negative behaviors in their children. Social workers often model how to enact new behaviors for their clients. Dialectical behavior therapy teaches adaptive coping related to emotion regulation, distress tolerance, cognitive distortions, and interpersonal communication (J. Walsh, 2014). However, although the potential exists, behavioral methods have not been used effectively to produce social reform. Bandura's (2002) conceptualization of proxy agency and collective agency has implications for social reform.

HUMANISTIC PERSPECTIVE

Consistent with the social work code of ethics, the hospice social worker who is making contact with the McKinley family believes in the dignity and worth of all humans. Her experiences as a hospice social worker have reinforced her belief that each person is unique, and even though she has worked with more than 100 hospice patients, she expects Ruth McKinley's story to be in some ways unlike any other story she has heard. She is eager to hear more about how Ruth sees her situation and whether there are any things she would like to change in the limited time she has left. The social worker takes note of strengths she sees in the McKinley family, their love and kindness toward each other and their courage in the face of an accumulation of stress. She wants to hear more about how Stanley, Marcia, and Bethany are thinking about their relationships with Ruth and whether there are any changes they would like to make in that relationship during Ruth's final days. Her thoughts and planned course of action reflect the humanistic perspective.

The humanistic perspective is often called the "third force" of psychology, because it was developed in reaction to the determinism found in early versions of both the psychodynamic (behavior as intrapsychically determined) and behavioral (behavior as externally determined) perspectives (Sollod et al., 2009). We are using the term **humanistic perspective** to include humanistic psychology and existential psychology, both of which emphasize the individual's freedom of action and search for meaning. We also extend the term to include the growing movement of positive psychology and the capabilities approach. The main ideas of the humanistic perspective are presented visually in Exhibit 2.8.

EXHIBIT 2.8 • Humanistic Perspective

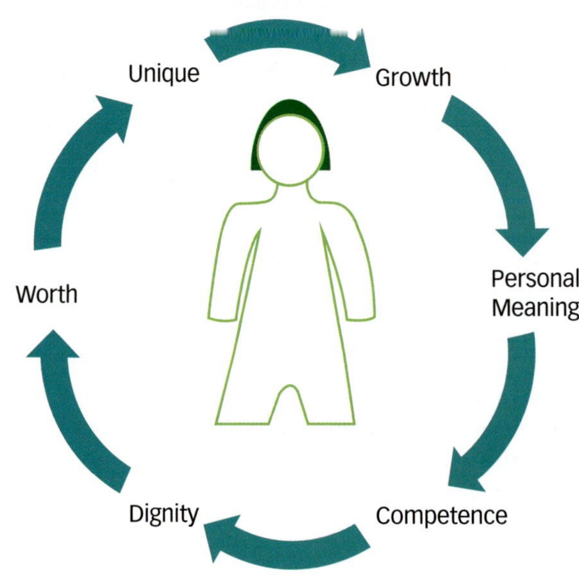

Perhaps the most influential contributions to humanistic psychology were made by Carl Rogers (1951) and Abraham Maslow (1962). Abraham Maslow was drawn to understand "peak experiences," or intense mystical moments of feeling connected to other people, nature, or a divine being. Maslow found peak experiences to occur often among self-actualizing people, or people who were expressing their innate potentials. Maslow developed a theory of a **hierarchy of needs**, which suggests that higher needs cannot emerge in full motivational force until lower needs have been at least partially satisfied. Physiological needs are at the bottom of the hierarchy, and the need for self-actualization is at the top:

1. *Physiological needs*: hunger, thirst, sex
2. *Safety needs*: avoidance of pain and anxiety; desire for security
3. *Belongingness and love needs:* affection, intimacy
4. *Esteem needs*: self-respect, adequacy, mastery
5. *Self-actualization*: to be fully what one can be; altruism, beauty, creativity, justice

Maslow is considered one of the founders of *transpersonal psychology*, which he labeled as the "fourth force" of psychology. We include transpersonal psychology under the umbrella of the humanistic perspective, but it is not discussed here because it receives considerable attention in Chapter 5, "The Spiritual Person."

Carl Rogers was interested in the capacity of humans to change in therapeutic relationships. He began his professional career at the Rochester Child Guidance Center, where he worked with social workers who had been trained at the Philadelphia School of Social Work. He has acknowledged the influence of Otto Rank, Jessie Taft, and the social workers at the Rochester agency on his thinking about the importance of responding to client feelings (Hart, 1970). He came to believe that humans have vast internal resources for self-understanding and self-directed behavior. He emphasized, therefore, the dignity and worth of each individual and presented the ideal interpersonal conditions under which people come to use their internal resources to become "more fully functioning." These have become known as the core conditions of the therapeutic process: empathy, warmth, and genuineness.

Existential psychology, which developed out of the chaos and despair in Europe during and after World War II, presented four primary themes (Krill, 1996):

1. Each person is unique and has value.
2. Suffering is a necessary part of human growth.
3. Personal growth results from staying in the immediate moment.
4. Personal growth takes a sense of commitment.

It is the emphasis on the necessity for suffering that sets existentialism apart from humanism.

Maslow is said to have coined the term *positive psychology* when he used it as a chapter title in his 1954 book, *Motivation and Personality.* As we know it today, **positive psychology** is a relatively recent branch of psychology that undertakes the scientific study of people's strengths and virtues and promotes optimal functioning of individuals and communities. Proponents of positive psychology argue that psychology has paid too much attention to human pathology and not enough to human strengths and virtues. Martin Seligman (1998, 2002), one of the authors of the concept of learned helplessness, has been at the forefront of positive psychology, contributing the important concept of learned optimism. Positive psychologists argue that prevention of mental illness is best accomplished by promoting human strength and competence. They have identified a set of human strengths that promote well-being and buffer against mental illness, including optimism, courage, hope, perseverance, honesty, a work ethic, and interpersonal skills (Snyder & Lopez, 2007). The positive psychology approach is drawing on both Western and Eastern worldviews. A large focus on hope is rooted in Western thinking (McKnight, Snyder, & Lopez, 2007); whereas emphasis on balance, compassion, and harmony comes more from Eastern thinking (Pedrotti, Snyder, & Lopez, 2007).

In Chapter 1, we described the capabilities approach to social justice, which can be classified with the humanistic perspective. The *capabilities approach* was proposed by welfare economist and political philosopher Amartya Sen (1999). Like other humanistic thinkers, Sen focuses on human agency or people's ability to pursue and realize goals that they value. He and collaborator Martha Nussbaum (2001) see humans as active, creative, and able to act on behalf of their aspirations. In contrast to earlier humanistic theorists, however, the capabilities approach puts individuals in a wider context and focuses on the idea that social arrangements should aim to support and expand people's capabilities. As suggested in Chapter 1, Nussbaum lists 10 core capabilities that all people in all societies must have to be able to pursue and realize valued goals. Sen argues, instead, that no such list can be arbitrarily delineated because of the great diversity of people and environments in the world. He recognizes the intersectionalities of diversity that exist in social life, that one person can belong to many different groups. He thinks that individuals should be left to decide which capabilities they choose to enhance or neglect.

This is how the humanistic perspective rates on the five criteria for evaluating social work theory.

- *Coherence and conceptual clarity.* Theories in the humanistic perspective are often criticized for being vague and highly abstract, with concepts such as "being" and "phenomenal self." The language of transpersonal theories is particularly abstract, with discussion of self-transcendence and higher states of consciousness. Indeed, theorists in the humanistic perspective, in general, have not been afraid to sacrifice coherence to gain what they see as a more complete understanding of human behavior. The positive psychology movement is working to bring greater consistency and coherence to humanistic concepts, and Nussbaum's core capabilities are quite explicit.

- *Testability and empirical support.* As might be expected, empirically minded scholars have not been attracted to the humanistic perspective, and consequently until recently there was little empirical literature to support the perspective. A notable exception is the clinical side of Rogers's theory. Rogers began a rigorous program of empirical investigation of the therapeutic process, and such research has provided strong empirical support for his conceptualization of the necessary conditions for the therapeutic relationship: warmth, empathy, and genuineness (Sollod et al., 2009). Recent research across several disciplines has demonstrated that a high level of practitioner empathy is associated with positive client outcomes (Gerdes & Segal, 2011). The positive psychology movement is focusing, with much success, on producing empirical support for the role of human strengths and virtues in human well-being. Some researchers have suggested that neuroscience research is calling the notion of free will (human agency) into question, arguing that it provides clear evidence that human behavior is determined by the gene–environment interactions that shape the brain (Kurzweil, 2012). Other neuroscientists provide evidence that humans have the power to "live our lives and train our brains" in ways that shift emotions, thoughts, and behaviors (Davidson & Begley, 2012, p. 225). That is a high endorsement for some of the tenets of the humanistic perspective.

- *Comprehensiveness.* The internal life of the individual is the focus of the humanistic perspective, and it is strong in consideration of both psychological and spiritual dimensions of the person. With its emphasis on a search for meaning, the humanistic perspective is the only perspective presented in this chapter to explicitly recognize the role of spirituality in human behavior. (Other theories of spirituality are discussed in Chapter 5.) In addition, Maslow recognizes the importance of satisfaction of basic biological needs. Most theorists in the humanistic tradition give limited attention to the environments of human behavior. The positive psychology movement has begun to examine positive environments that can promote human strengths and virtues, including school, work, and community environments (Snyder & Lopez, 2007). The capabilities perspective calls for social institutions to support and expand people's capabilities.

- *Diversity and power.* The humanistic perspective, with its almost singular consideration of an internal frame of reference, devotes more attention to individual differences than to differences between groups. The one exception is Sen's capabilities perspective, which emphasizes the great diversity of human capabilities and values. In general, far too little attention is given in the humanistic tradition to the processes by which institutional oppression influences the **phenomenal self**—the individual's subjectively felt and interpreted experience of "who I am." Like the social constructionist perspective, however, the humanistic perspective is sometimes quite strong in giving voice to experiences of members of nondominant groups. With the emphasis on the phenomenal self, members of nondominant groups are more likely to have preferential input into the telling of their own stories. The social worker's intention to hear and honor the stories of each member of the McKinley family may be a novel experience for each family member, and the social worker may, indeed, hear very different stories from what she expects to hear. Rogers developed his respect for the personal self, and consequently his client-centered approach to therapy, when he realized that his perceptions of the worlds of his low-income clients in the Child Guidance Clinic were very different from their own perceptions.

- *Usefulness for social work practice.* If the social constructionist perspective gives new meaning to the old social work adage "Begin where the client is," it is social work's historical involvement in the development of the humanistic perspective that gave original meaning to the adage. It is limited in terms of providing specific interventions, but it is consistent with social work's value of the dignity and worth of the individual. The humanistic perspective suggests that social workers begin by developing an understanding of how the client views the situation, and with its emphasis on the individual drive for growth and competence, it recommends a "strengths" rather than "pathology" approach to practice. George Vaillant (2002), a research psychiatrist, suggests that this attention to strengths is what distinguishes social workers from other helping professionals. From this perspective, then, we might note that the strong commitment to helping one another displayed by the McKinley family is one of several strengths that could be the basis for successful intervention. At the organizational level, the humanistic perspective has been used by organizational theorists, such as Douglas McGregor (1960), to prescribe administrative actions that focus on employee well being as the best route to organizational efficiency and effectiveness. Positive psychology is popular in clinical work and is beginning to propose guidelines for developing positive environments in schools, workplaces, and communities.

CRITICAL THINKING Questions 2.4

Both cognitive social learning theory and theories in the humanistic perspective emphasize the important role of human agency, the capacity to intentionally make things happen, in human behavior. Other theories in the social behavioral perspective and most of the other perspectives discussed here put less emphasis on human agency. Now that you have examined eight theoretical perspectives, how much agency do you think humans have over their behavior, in general? Explain. How much agency do you think members of the McKinley family have? Explain.

THE MERITS OF MULTIPLE PERSPECTIVES

You can see that each of these perspectives puts a different lens on the unfolding story of the McKinley family. Although they all are seeking to understand human behavior, different phenomena are emphasized. You can also see that each of the eight perspectives has been used to guide social work practice over time. It was suggested in Chapter 1 that each situation can be examined from several perspectives and that using a variety of perspectives brings more dimensions of the situation into view. Cognitive psychologists have provided convincing evidence that all of us, whether new or experienced social workers, have biases that predispose us to do too little thinking, rather than too much, about the practice situations we confront. We are particularly prone to ignore information that is contrary to our hypotheses about situations. Consequently, we tend to end our search for understanding prematurely. One step we can take to prevent this premature closure is to think about practice situations from multiple theoretical perspectives. Exhibit 2.9 overviews the big ideas of the eight perspectives presented in this chapter and cues you to where you can find these ideas reflected in theory and research in Chapters 3 through 9. As you read about research and specific theories in these chapters, occasionally look back at Exhibit 2.9 and think about which theoretical perspectives might be reflected in what you read.

EXHIBIT 2.9 • Big Ideas of Eight Theoretical Perspectives as Used in Chapters 3–9

PERSPECTIVE	BIG IDEAS	WHERE REFLECTED IN THEORY AND RESEARCH IN CHAPTERS 3–9
Systems	• Systems are made up of interrelated members that constitute a linked whole. • Each part of the system impacts all other parts and the system as a whole. • All systems are subsystems of other larger systems. • Systems maintain boundaries that give them their identities. • The dynamic interactions within, between, and among systems produce both stability and change, sometimes even rapid dramatic change.	Chapter 3 Chapter 4 Chapter 5 Chapter 6 Chapter 7 Chapter 8 Chapter 9
Conflict	• All social systems have inequalities in the distribution of valued resources. • Power is unequally divided, and powerful social groups impose their will on subordinate groups. • Conflict and the potential for conflict underlie unequal social relationships. • Members of subordinate groups often become alienated from society. • Social change may occur when subordinate groups recognize patterns of inequality and injustice and take action to increase their own power.	Chapter 3 Chapter 4 Chapter 5 Chapter 6 Chapter 7 Chapter 8 Chapter 9
Exchange and choice	• Individual and collective actors engage in social exchange of material and nonmaterial resources and make choices in pursuit of those resources. • Choices in social exchange are based on self-interest as well as community interest. • Choices in social exchange are based on both reason and emotion and on values, norms, and expectations. • Social exchange operates on a norm of reciprocity, but exchange relationships are often unbalanced. • Power comes from unequal resources in exchange.	Chapter 3 Chapter 7 Chapter 8 Chapter 9
Social constructionist	• People construct meaning, a sense of self, and a social world through their interactions with each other. • Social reality is created when people, in social interaction, develop shared meaning, a common understanding of their world. • There is no singular objective reality but rather the multiple realities that are created in different contexts. • Social interaction is grounded in language customs, as well as cultural and historical contexts. • People can modify meanings in the process of interaction.	Chapter 3 Chapter 4 Chapter 6 Chapter 7 Chapter 8 Chapter 9
Psychodynamic	• Emotions have a central place in human behavior. • Unconscious, as well as conscious, mental activity serves as the motivating force in human behavior. • Early childhood experiences are central in the patterning of an individual's emotions and, therefore, central to problems throughout life. • Individuals may become overwhelmed by internal or external demands. • Individuals frequently use ego defense mechanisms to avoid becoming overwhelmed by internal or external demands.	Chapter 4 Chapter 5 Chapter 6 Chapter 7 Chapter 8 Chapter 9

PERSPECTIVE	BIG IDEAS	WHERE REFLECTED IN THEORY AND RESEARCH IN CHAPTERS 3–9
Developmental	• Human development occurs in clearly defined, age-graded stages. • Each stage of life is qualitatively different from all other stages. • Each stage builds on earlier stages. • Human development is a complex interaction of biological, psychological, and social factors. • Moving from one stage to the next involves new tasks and changes in statuses and roles.	Chapter 3 Chapter 4 Chapter 5 Chapter 6 Chapter 8
Social behavioral	• Human behavior is learned when individuals interact with the environment. • Human behavior is learned through different mechanisms of learning, including association of environmental stimuli, reinforcement, imitation, and personal expectations and meaning. • All human problems can be formulated as undesirable behavior. • All behavior can be defined and changed.	Chapter 4 Chapter 5 Chapter 6 Chapter 8
Humanistic	• Each person is unique and has value. • Each person is responsible for the choices he or she makes within the limits of freedom. • People always have the capacity to change themselves, even to make radical change. • Human behavior can be understood only from the vantage point of the internal frame of reference of the person. • Human behavior is driven by a desire for growth, personal meaning, and competence and by a need to experience a bond with others.	Chapter 4 Chapter 5 Chapter 6 Chapter 7 Chapter 8

A number of behavioral science disciplines offer a variety of ways of thinking about changing person–environment configurations, ways that have been worked out over time to assist in understanding human behavior. They are tools that can help us make sense of the situations we encounter. We do not mean to suggest that all eight of the perspectives discussed in this chapter will be equally useful, or even useful at all, in all situations. But each of these perspectives will be useful in some situations that you encounter as a social worker. As a competent professional, you must view the quest for adequate breadth and depth in your knowledge base as an ongoing, lifelong challenge and responsibility. We hope that over time you will begin to use these multiple perspectives in an integrated fashion so that you can see the many dimensions—the contradictions as well as the consistencies—in stories like the McKinley family's. We encourage you to be flexible and reflective in your thinking and your "doing" throughout your career. We remind you, again, to use general knowledge such as that provided by theoretical perspectives only to generate hypotheses to be tested in specific situations, not as facts inherent in every situation.

CRITICAL THINKING Questions 2.5

At the beginning of the chapter, we wondered what got your attention when you read the story of the McKinley family. As you read about the eight theoretical perspectives, did you see any ideas that addressed the things that caught your attention about the story? If so, what were they? Were there things that caught your attention that did not seem to be addressed by any of the perspectives? If so, what were they? Which perspectives seemed more closely aligned with what caught your attention upon first reading the story? Which perspectives provided you with useful new ways to think about the story?

IMPLICATIONS FOR SOCIAL WORK PRACTICE

The eight perspectives on human behavior discussed in this chapter suggest a variety of principles for social work assessment and intervention.

- In assessment, consider any recent system changes that may be affecting the client system. Assist families and groups to renegotiate unsatisfactory system boundaries. Develop networks of support for persons experiencing challenging life transitions.
- In assessment, consider power arrangements and forces of oppression, and the alienation that emanates from them. Assist in the development of advocacy efforts to challenge patterns of dominance, when possible. Be aware of the power dynamics in your relationships with clients; when working with nonvoluntary clients, speak directly about the limits and uses of your power.
- In assessment, consider the patterns of exchange in the social support networks of individual clients, families, and organizations, using network maps where useful. Assist individuals, families, and organizations to renegotiate unsatisfactory patterns of exchange, when possible. Recognize the role of both reason and emotion in the policymaking process.
- Begin your work by understanding how clients view their situations. Engage clients in thinking about the environments in which these constructions of self and situations have developed. When working in situations characterized by differences in belief systems, assist members to engage in sincere discussions and to negotiate lines of action.
- Assist clients in expressing emotional conflicts and in understanding how these are related to past events, when appropriate. Help them develop self-awareness and self-control, where needed. Assist clients in locating and using needed environmental resources.
- In assessment, consider the familial, cultural, and historical contexts in the timing and experience of developmental transitions. Recognize human development as unique and lifelong.
- In assessment, consider the variety of processes by which behavior is learned. Be sensitive to the possibility of learned helplessness when clients lack motivation for change. Consider issues of social justice and fairness before engaging in behavior modification.
- Be aware of the potential for significant differences between your assessment of the situation and the client's own assessment; value self-determination. Focus on strengths rather than pathology; recognize the possibility of learned hopefulness as well as learned helplessness.

KEY TERMS

agency, 49
boundary, 32
chaos theory, 33
classical conditioning theory, 48
cognitive social learning theory, 49
conflict perspective, 35
critical race theory, 36
critical theorists, 35
developmental perspective, 46
efficacy expectation, 49
empowerment theories, 36
exchange and choice perspective, 38
feedback mechanism, 32
feminist theories, 36
hierarchy of needs, 51
humanistic perspective, 51
intersectionality theory, 36
learned helplessness, 50
operant conditioning theory, 49
phenomenal self, 53
positive psychology, 52
psychodynamic perspective, 43
reciprocity, 38
self-efficacy, 49
social behavioral perspective, 48
social constructionist perspective, 40
social exchange theory, 38
social network theory, 39
systems perspective, 32

ACTIVE LEARNING

1. Reread the case study of the intergenerational stresses in the McKinley family. Next, review the big ideas of the eight theoretical perspectives as presented in Exhibit 2.9. Choose three specific big ideas that you think are most helpful in thinking about the McKinley family. For example, you might choose this big idea from the systems perspective: Each part of the system affects all other parts and the system as a whole. You might also choose this big idea from the humanistic perspective: Human behavior is driven by a desire for growth, personal meaning, and competence and by a need to experience a bond with others. Likewise, you might choose another specific idea from any of the perspectives. The point is to choose the three big ideas that you find most useful. Now, in a small group, compare notes with three or four classmates about which big ideas were chosen. Discuss why these particular choices, and not others, were made by each of your classmates.

2. Break into eight small groups, with each group assigned one of the theoretical perspectives described in the chapter. Each group's task is to briefly summarize the assigned theoretical perspective and then explain the group's interpretation of the perspective's usefulness when applied to the McKinley family or another case study.

3. Choose a story that interests you in a current edition of a daily newspaper. Read the story carefully and then think about which of the eight theoretical perspectives discussed in this chapter is most reflected in the story.

WEB RESOURCES

Association for Behavioral and Cognitive Therapies

www.abct.org

ABCT is a multidisciplinary organization committed to the advancement of scientific approaches to the understanding and improvement of human functioning through the investigation and application of behavioral, cognitive, and other evidence-based principles to the assessment, prevention, and treatment of human problems and the enhancement of health and well-being.

Conflict Theory(ies) of Deviance

www.umsl.edu/~keelr/200/conflict.html

Site presented by Robert O. Keel at the University of Missouri at St. Louis contains information on the basic premises of conflict theory as well as specific information on radical conflict theory and pluralistic conflict theory.

International Humanistic Psychology Association

http://ihpaworld.org

Site maintained by the International Humanistic Psychology Association contains links to events, capacity-building training projects, professional collaboration and development, research, dialogues and networking, and publications and resources.

Personality Theories

webspace.ship.edu/cgboer/perscontents.html

Site maintained by C. George Boeree at the Psychology Department of Shippensburg University provides an electronic textbook on theories of personality, including the theories of Sigmund Freud, Erik Erikson, Carl Jung, B. F. Skinner, Albert Bandura, Abraham Maslow, Carl Rogers, Jean Piaget, and Buddhist psychology.

Sociological Theories and Perspectives

www.sociosite.net/topics/theory.php

Site maintained at the University of Amsterdam contains general information on sociological theory and specific information on a number of theories, including chaos theory, interaction theory, conflict theory, network theory, and rational choice theory.

William Alanson White Institute

www.wawhite.org

Site contains contemporary psychoanalysis journal articles, training programs, and a psychoanalysis-in-action blog.

SAGE edge™ **Sharpen your skills with SAGE edge at edge.sagepub.com/hutchisoness2e**

SAGE edge for students provides a personalized approach to help you accomplish your coursework goals in an easy-to-use learning environment. watch listen read

LEARNING OBJECTIVES	FOR FURTHER EXPLORATION AND APPLICATION
LO 2.1: Recognize one's emotional and cognitive reactions to a case study.	(watch) Overview of the Process of Conducting Focus Groups (read) Understanding Power and Powerlessness
LO 2.2: Recognize the major themes of eight different perspectives on human behavior: systems, conflict, exchange and choice, social constructionist, psychodynamic, developmental, social behavioral, and humanistic.	(read) American Sociological Association (read) American Psychological Association (read) National Organization for Human Services
LO 2.3: Analyze the merits of a multitheoretical approach to human behavior.	(read) Social Constructionist Family Systems Research: Conceptual Considerations
LO 2.4: Apply knowledge of eight theoretical perspectives on human behavior to recommend guidelines for social work assessment and intervention.	(watch) Theories of Social Work Practice (watch) The New Social Worker (listen) The New Social Worker (listen) The Social Work Podcast

The Multiple Dimensions of the Person

The multiple dimensions of person, environment, and time have unity; they are inseparable and embedded. That is the way I think about them and the way I am encouraging you to think about them. However, you will be better able to think about the unity of these three aspects of human behavior when you have developed a clearer understanding of the different dimensions encompassed by each one. A review of theory and research about the different dimensions will help you to sharpen your thinking about what is involved in the changing configurations of persons and environments.

The purpose of Chapters 3–5 is to provide you with an up-to-date understanding of theory and research about the dimensions of the person. Part II begins with a chapter on the biological dimension, is followed by a chapter on the complex psychological dimension, and ends with a chapter on the spiritual dimension.

With a state-of-the-art knowledge base about the multiple dimensions of persons, you will be prepared to consider the interactions between persons and environments, which is the subject of Part III. And then you will be able to think more comprehensively and more clearly about the ways configurations of persons and environments change across the life course. The discussion of the life course in Part IV attempts to put the dimensions of persons and environments back together and help you think about their embeddedness across time.

CHALK TALKS
Watch via the
SAGE Interactive eBook

Created using Videoscribe,
http://www.videoscribe.co

[566]

The Biological Person

Stephen French Gilson

Learning Objectives

LO 3.1 Compare and contrast one's emotional and cognitive reactions to six case studies.

LO 3.2 Use theory to summarize the intersection of the interior body and the exterior environment.

LO 3.3 Recognize the major functions of six biological systems: nervous, endocrine, immune, cardiovascular, musculoskeletal, and reproductive.

LO 3.4 Explain the association between health outcomes and socioeconomic circumstances.

LO 3.5 Apply knowledge of human biology to recommend guidelines for social work assessment and intervention.

Acknowledgments: The author wishes to thank Elizabeth DePoy and Elizabeth Hutchison for their helpful comments, insights, and suggestions for this chapter.

CASE STUDY 3.1

CHERYL'S BRAIN INJURY

Cheryl, who is in her early 20s, grew up in rural Idaho in a large extended family and enlisted as a private in the army just after she finished her 3rd year in high school. After basic training, she was first deployed to Iraq and subsequently to Afghanistan for active combat duty. Traveling en route to Ghorak Base in southern Afghanistan, Cheryl's Humvee contacted an explosive device, causing Cheryl to sustain a closed head injury and multiple fractures. She was in a coma for 3 weeks.

Over a 6-month period, all of Cheryl's external bodily injuries, including the fractures, healed, and she was able to walk and talk with no apparent residual impairments. Cognitively and socially, however, Cheryl experienced change. Although able to read, she could not retain what she had just read a minute ago. She did not easily recall her previous knowledge of math and was not able to compute basic calculations such as addition and subtraction without the use of a calculator. She was slow in penmanship, taking at least 5 minutes to write her own name. Unlike her social behavior prior to the accident, Cheryl was often blunt in her comments, even to the point of becoming confrontational with friends without provocation.

Because of her observable recovery, everyone expected Cheryl to return to active duty, but 2 years after the accident, her family knows that she is not going to return to military service. Cheryl's ex-boyfriend, Sean, is about to get engaged to another woman, but Cheryl thinks that she is still dating Sean and that he will soon marry her. People who knew Cheryl before the accident cannot understand why her personality has changed so markedly, and they even say, "She's a completely different person!"

CASE STUDY 3.2

A DIABETES DIAGNOSIS FOR BESS

Bess, a 52-year-old Franco American woman who lives in rural Maine, was enjoying her empty nest just before the social worker met her. The youngest of her three children had married 6 months earlier, and although Bess was proud of what she had accomplished as a single mother, she was now ready to get on with her life. Her first order of business was to get her body back into shape, so she started on a high-carbohydrate, low-fat diet that she had read about in a magazine. Drinking the recommended eight glasses of water or more each day was easy, because it seemed that she was always thirsty. But Bess was losing more weight than she thought possible on a diet, and she was always cheating! Bess had thought that she would have to get more exercise to lose weight, but even walking to and from her car at the grocery store tired her out.

One morning, Bess did not arrive at the country store where she worked. Because it was very unusual for her not to call and also not to answer her phone, a coworker went to her house. When there was no response to the knocking, the coworker and one of Bess's neighbors opened the door to Bess's house and walked in. They found Bess sitting on her couch, still in her nightclothes, which were drenched with perspiration. Bess was very confused, unable to answer simple questions with correct responses. Paramedics transported Bess to the local community hospital.

In the emergency room, after some bloodwork, a doctor diagnosed her with diabetes mellitus (diabetes). Because diabetes is common among middle-aged and older people in this poor rural town, a social worker had already established an educational support group for persons with diabetes that Bess now attends.

CASE STUDY 3.3

MELISSA'S HIV DIAGNOSIS

Melissa's "perfect life" has just fallen apart. As a young urban professional who grew up in a middle-class suburb in New York, Melissa had always dreamed of a big wedding at her parents' country club, and her dreams were about to come true. All the plans had been made, invitations sent out, bridesmaids' dresses bought and measured, and her wedding dress selected. All that remained was finalizing the menu and approving the flower arrangements. Because Melissa and her fiancé planned to have children soon after their marriage, she went to her physician for a physical exam 2 months before her wedding. As the doctor does with all of her patients, she asked if Melissa had ever been tested for HIV. Melissa said no and gave her permission for an HIV test to be run with all the other routine bloodwork.

One week after her physical, the doctor's office called and asked Melissa to return for more bloodwork because of what was thought to be an inaccuracy in the report. Melissa went back to the office for more blood tests. Another week passed, but Melissa did not think again about the tests because she was immersed in wedding plans. Her physician called her at home at 8:00 one morning and asked her to come to her office after work that day. Because she was distracted by the wedding plans and a busy schedule at work, Melissa did not think anything of the doctor's request.

When she arrived at the doctor's office, she was immediately taken to the doctor's private office. The doctor came in, sat down, and told Melissa that two separate blood tests had confirmed that she was HIV-positive. Melissa spent over 3 hours with her physician that evening, and soon thereafter she began to attend an HIV support group.

Melissa has never used illicit drugs, and she has only had two sexual partners. She and her fiancé had decided not to have unprotected intercourse until they were ready for children, and because they used condoms, he was not a prime suspect for passing along the infection. Melissa remembered that the man with whom she was involved prior to meeting her fiancé would not talk about his past. She has not seen this former lover for the past 3 years since she moved away from New York.

CASE STUDY 3.4

LIFESTYLE CHANGES FOR THOMAS

Thomas is a 30-year-old man who lives with his parents, both of whom are obese, as are his two older sisters. Thomas loves his mom's cooking, but some time ago he realized that its high-fat and high-sodium content was contributing to his parents' obesity and high blood pressure.

In contrast, Thomas takes pride in watching his diet (when he isn't eating at home) and is pretty smug about being the only one in the family who is not obese. Being called "the thin man" is, to Thomas, a compliment. He also boasts about being in great physical shape and exercises to the point of being dizzy.

After one of his dizziness episodes, a friend told him that he should get his blood pressure checked. Out of curiosity, the next time Thomas stopped at his local drug store, he decided to use a self-monitoring machine to check his blood pressure. To his astonishment, the reading came back 200/105, which is quite high. Thomas now seeks a social worker's help to adopt some major lifestyle changes.

CASE STUDY 3.5

MARY AND HER DIAGNOSIS OF MULTIPLE SCLEROSIS (MS)

Mary's follow-up appointment with her family practitioner was the week following her 43rd birthday. Mary's grandparents, both maternal and paternal, emigrated from Denmark. Mary's mother was raised in Brush, Colorado, and her father in Buffalo, Wyoming. Having grown up on a small ranch in rural Colorado, it seemed natural for her to eventually settle in the area near her family. In addition to working as a teacher at the local high school, she spent her time tending the garden; taking care of the chickens; and raising goats, a small herd of Belted Galloway cows, and her horses. She learned to ride before she ever attended grammar school. Although she enjoyed all types of equitation, her primary loves were barrel racing and team roping.

Over the past 5 years she began to experience several physical symptoms that made it difficult for her to always feel confident or even safe when she was riding, whether at her home barn practicing or competing in an event.

(Continued)

(Continued)

When she met with her physician, she described experiencing several seemingly unrelated symptoms. These included periods of intense ankle and knee discomfort, episodic vision difficulties, digestive and gastrointestinal distress, fevers, chest pains including shortness of breath and rapid heart rate, and periods of fatigue and exhaustion, among several other episodic conditions and symptoms. She regularly sought treatment for these illnesses, often being prescribed medications and a variety of treatment regimens.

Because Mary often talked about these symptoms and conditions, which seemed to vary in duration and intensity and were frequently nonspecific, she commonly referred to herself as a hypochondriac. Linked to this self-doubt was her feeling that her primary-care physician dismissed her experiences of pain and discomfort. Her physician did not refer her to outside consultation, and she set her own appointments with condition-specific health providers, such as her optometrist for her vision difficulties.

Finally, following 2 weeks of feeling constant exhaustion, regular heart palpitations when riding, and falling off her horse during a barrel racing competition, Mary's best friend convinced her to seek a medical evaluation from a neurologist. At this appointment, in addition to a general physical evaluation, Mary was referred for a comprehensive diagnostic workup. As a result of these tests, when combined with her medical history and symptom presentation, Mary was given a diagnosis of multiple sclerosis (MS).

CASE STUDY 3.6

JUAN AND BELINDA'S REPRODUCTIVE HEALTH

Juan and Belinda, now both 17 years old, grew up in the same neighborhood of a southwestern city in the United States and attend the same church, St. Joseph's Catholic Church. They do not attend the same school, however. Belinda has received all of her education at the schools at St. Joseph's; Juan has attended public schools. Since seventh grade, Juan has met Belinda after school and walked her home.

They both live in small, well-kept homes in a section of the community that is largely Spanish speaking with very strong influences from the wide variety of countries of origin represented by community residents: Mexico, Honduras, El Salvador, and Nicaragua, among others. The Catholic Church here is a dominant exterior environmental force in shaping community social, political, economic, and personal values and behaviors.

Both Juan's and Belinda's parents immigrated to the United States from Mexico, seeking to improve the opportunities for their families. Juan's mother found a job as a housekeeper at a local hotel, where she now manages the housekeeping staff. His father began as a day laborer and construction worker, eventually moving up to become foreman of the largest construction company in the area. He anticipates beginning his own construction company within the next year. Belinda's mother is a skilled seamstress and was able to start her own tailoring business shortly after immigrating. Belinda's father, with a background in diesel mechanics, was able to find work at a large trucking company where he continues to work today.

Like many teenagers, Juan and Belinda face the difficulties of sorting out the complexities and intricacies of their relationship. They feel very much in love, knowing in their hearts that they want to get married and raise a family. At 17, they are at the crossroads of intimacy, because they face conflicts about their sexuality with limited information and strong prohibitions against premarital sex. Following many of the teachings of their church and the urgings of their parents, Juan and Belinda have avoided much physical contact except for kissing and holding each other.

Like many communities in the United States, their community struggled with the question of just what information should be given to students about physical health and sexuality. Their community decided to limit the amount and type of information to the basics of female and male sexual anatomy and physiology. The result of this decision for Juan and Belinda was that they learned very little about sexual response and behavior, conception, pregnancy, childbirth, contraception, safe sex practices, and other areas that are critical in today's world. The decision by the school board was based on a belief that it was the family's responsibility to provide this information to their children. The school social worker at Cesar Chavez High School, where Juan attends school, is aware of the challenges that arise for youth in this community that in part result from limited sex education.

AN INTEGRATIVE APPROACH FOR UNDERSTANDING THE INTERSECTION OF INTERIOR BIOLOGICAL HEALTH AND ILLNESS AND EXTERIOR ENVIRONMENTAL FACTORS

As we think about the stories of Cheryl, Bess, Melissa, Thomas, Mary, and Juan and Belinda, we can see that biology is an important dimension of their behavior. Today, there is much agreement about the importance of biology in influencing human behavior and thus the need for social workers to be well informed in this arena. Although there are a variety of ways to think about our bodies, a central tenet of this chapter is the view that the body and its surroundings are a continuous environment that spans from *proximal* (most interior) to *distal* (or moving outward from the organic matter of the corpus). Thus environment is defined as the entire set of conditions under which one operates (DePoy & Gilson, 2012). For instructive purposes, however, the language of interior and exterior environment is used. Interior is concerned with the description and explanation of embodied organic conditions, such as internal organ systems, genetics, interior psychological structures, processes, and so forth. Exterior environments are characterized as nonorganic conditions that are not contained within the body (DePoy & Gilson, 2012).

Because social workers deal with people, social workers encounter human biology and its reciprocal influence with exterior environmental conditions such as poverty, violence, and child abuse each time they interact with individuals. We distinguish interior from exterior environments on the basis of corporeality, or material that relates to the body (DePoy & Gilson, 2012). However, the division between corporeal and noncorporeal is not clear. Consider for example a knee replacement. Whereas it is not organic in composition, it is located beneath the skin and functions as integral to body stability and movement. But is it interior or exterior? What about eyeglasses, prostheses, or even clothes that preserve body temperature? What about speech? Although articulated by an individual, sound is created by air vibrations and received by another.

Returning to the cases of Cheryl, Bess, Melissa, Thomas, Mary, and Juan and Belinda, their interior environments are the initial reason they are seeking social work assistance. To meet professional goals, social workers must have a working knowledge of the body's systems and the ways these systems interact with one another and with other interior and exterior environmental dimensions. Social workers also must be sufficiently informed to be able to discuss details of biological functioning with clients when indicated (H. Johnson, 2004; Tangenberg & Kemp, 2002). Professional decision making and activity require an understanding of the interactions of interior and exterior environments, as exemplified by each of the chapter-opening case studies. Two theoretical perspectives are particularly useful in this effort.

First, systems frameworks describe and explain human phenomena as sets of interrelated parts. There are many variations and applications of systems approaches ranging from those that look at embodied or interior systems, to those that examine human systems composed of both humans and their surroundings, and even extending to systems that do not contain embodied elements (DePoy & Gilson, 2007). At this point, there is a well-developed theory, supported by rigorously conducted empirical evidence, of the complex relationships among diverse embodied systems (DePoy & Gilson, 2007; Weitz, 2013). Several topics focusing on the interaction of exterior and interior environments are receiving intense research scrutiny—for example, the neurobiology of human emotions, early care and brain development, the biology of social interactions, socioeconomic status (SES) and health, neuroendocrinology of stress, and the role of sleep in health and cognition.

Although these attempts to understand mind–body connections have led to many important theories about health and illness, they may also be misinterpreted. Social workers therefore are advised to heed the warning of a number of medical researchers and social critics against explaining behavior and emotion through a purely medicalized lens (see Conrad, 2007; Lane, 2007; Watters, 2010). Such a reductionist perspective may undermine our ability to consider the full range of environmental

© iStockphoto.com/monkeybusinessimages

Medical researchers examine data to test a hypothesis.

influences on embodied phenomena. On the flip side of this caution, overattribution of physical experiences to psychological and social conditions fails to consider the interior environmental causes of illness (DePoy & Gilson, 2012; Saleebey, 2012). Comprehensive analysis requires knowledge of all biological systems, exterior environment conditions, and their reciprocal influence. Whereas the efficiency of a single explanatory framework is seductive, such thinking may limit our ability to identify the broad nature of problems and needs and constrain a range of appropriate interventions to resolve problems (DePoy & Gilson, 2004, 2011).

The second useful framework is the constructionist perspective, which suggests that human phenomena are pluralistic in meaning. For example, rather than being a singular, scientifically supported entity, through the lens of social construction, a disabling medical condition such as paralysis or low vision is defined in large part by its meaning from interior views as well as from political, social, cultural, technological, aesthetic, and economic exterior environments (DePoy & Gilson, 2004; Gilson & DePoy, 2000, 2002). Thus, using a social constructionist perspective, the experience of having atypical low vision can be understood in terms of shared cultural understandings of the "expected roles" for persons with atypical vision or in terms of actions or inactions of political institutions to promote or impede this subpopulation's access to physical, social, technological, and virtual environments. We may automatically assume that someone with atypical low vision is in need of professional intervention, but that person may in effect have his or her life well organized and function well in all chosen living and working environments. Thus, rather than being explained by the biological condition itself, limitation associated with an atypical biological condition may be a function of the exterior environment; the characteristics of the task; personal attitude; and available resources such as technology; assistance from family, friends, or employees; accessible transportation; and welcoming, fully accessible communities (DePoy & Gilson, 2011).

For example, although social workers do not make medical diagnoses for embodied conditions in the scope of their practice, the social work administrator who is developing or operating a shelter, a food kitchen, or an advocacy center may integrate medical and mental health services with employment, housing, financial, and companionship services (Colby, Dulmus, & Sowers, 2012; Strier, 2013). Miller, Pollack, and Williams (2011) have recommended a social model of practice that promotes healthy communities as well as working with individuals, families, and groups to help them identify and advocate for their own health needs if they so choose. DePoy and Gilson (2004, 2011) have built on this model by proposing *legitimate communities*, defined as those that practice acceptance of ideas and appreciate and respond to the full range of human diversity.

CRITICAL THINKING Questions 3.1

Which theoretical perspective (perspectives) from Chapter 2 is (are) the best fit with the way of thinking of human biology suggested in the previous section? How important is biology in your own life story? In what ways is it important or not important? How do you think of the relationship between your body and aspects of your exterior environment?

A LOOK AT SIX INTERIOR ENVIRONMENT SYSTEMS

Now we turn to six biological systems: the nervous system, endocrine system, immune system, cardiovascular system, musculoskeletal system, and reproductive system. All the other biological systems (such as the digestive system, respiratory system, and urinary system) also warrant our attention, but with the limitations of space, we have chosen these six because they are commonly involved in many of the biologically based issues social workers encounter and thus can serve as a model for thinking about other systems as well.

As you read the descriptions of these six interior environment systems, keep in mind their connectedness with each other as well as with all environmental conditions. As we emphasize throughout, just as human behavior is a complex transaction of person and environment, biological functioning is the result of complex interactions among all biological systems and the environments in which they function. No one system operates in isolation from other systems.

NERVOUS SYSTEM

In the first case study, Cheryl is considered to have a **brain injury (BI)**, or what is commonly termed a *traumatic brain injury* (TBI), defined as an insult to the brain caused by an external physical force that may result in a diminished or altered state of consciousness (Brain Injury Association of America, 2013). Included here are what might be classified as mild brain injuries or concussions. Traumatic brain injuries include head injuries that result from falls, automobile accidents, infections and viruses, insufficient oxygen, and poisoning. Explosions caused by land mines and improvised explosive devices have been identified as one of the primary causes of TBI in military personnel.

According to the Centers for Disease Control and Prevention (CDC; 2013a), approximately 1.7 million people sustain traumatic brain injury in the United States each year, accruing $76.5 billion yearly in hospital and injury-related costs (direct medical costs and indirect costs such as lost economic productivity) (CDC, 2013a). For children and young adults, TBI is the type of injury most often associated with deaths due to unintended injuries. It is estimated that one in four adults with TBI is unable to return to work within 1 year after the injury.

Although it has similar symptoms, *acquired brain injury* (ABI) is a different classification of brain injury. It does not result from traumatic injury to the head; is not hereditary, congenital, or degenerative; and it occurs after birth. Included in this category are oxygen deprivation (anoxia), aneurysms, infections to the brain, and stroke (Brain Injury Association of America, 2013).

Each type of BI may provoke specific issues and behaviors for the person. However, brain injury in general can affect cognitive, physical, and emotional functioning. Atypical cognitive functioning may present as atypical language and communication, information processing, memory, and perception. Cheryl's atypical writing is an example, as well as a reflection of atypical fine motor skill. Atypical physical functioning often occurs, such as walking differently or not at all (problems with ambulation) and changes in balance and coordination, strength, and endurance. Atypical emotional functioning may come from two different sources. It may be *primary*, or directly related to the BI, including such symptoms as irritability and judgment errors. Or it may be *reactive* to the adjustments required to live with the atypical functioning caused by BI and its consequences, typically resulting in a diagnosis of depression and changes in self-esteem. Cheryl's difficulty in recognizing that Sean is not going to marry her and her misjudgments in other social situations are symptoms of the psychological consequences of her BI.

The **nervous system** provides the structure and processes for communicating sensory, perceptual, and autonomically generated information throughout the body. Three major subsystems compose the nervous system:

1. *Central nervous system (CNS):* the brain and the spinal cord
2. *Peripheral nervous system (PNS):* spinal and cranial nerves
3. *Autonomic nervous system (ANS):* nerves controlling cardiovascular, gastrointestinal, genitourinary, and respiratory systems

The brain sends signals to the spinal cord, which in turn relays the message to specific parts of the body by way of the PNS. Messages from the PNS to the brain travel back by way of a similar pathway (Carter, 2009; Society for Neuroscience, 2012). Note that Cheryl's brain injury affects only a part of her nervous system—in fact, only part of the CNS. Damage to other parts of the nervous system can have significant atypical effects, but here we focus on her brain injury because it is so closely linked with behavioral changes.

The human brain, which constitutes only about 2% of one's total body weight, may contain as many as 10 million neurons. Its three major internal regions are referred to as the forebrain, midbrain, and hindbrain. Viewed from the side (see Exhibit 3.1), the largest structure visible is the *cerebral cortex*, part of the forebrain. The cerebral cortex is the seat of higher mental functions, including thinking, planning, and problem solving. This area of the brain is more highly developed in humans than in any other animal. It is divided into two hemispheres—left and right—that are interconnected by nerve fibers. The hemispheres are thought to be specialized, with a "conscious linguistic self" located in the left hemisphere and "a physical emotional self" located in the right hemisphere (Cozolino, 2014, p. 18). Each hemisphere controls the opposite side of the body, so that damage to one side of the brain may cause numbness or paralysis of the arm and leg on the opposite side.

The cerebral cortex has four lobes, depicted in Exhibit 3.1. As Exhibit 3.2 explains, functions such as vision, hearing, and speech are distributed in specific regions, with some lobes being associated with more than one function. The frontal lobe is the largest, making up nearly one third of the surface of the cerebral cortex. Lesions of any one of the lobes can have a dramatic impact on the functions of that lobe (Carter, 2009; Society

EXHIBIT 3.1 • Selected Areas of the Brain

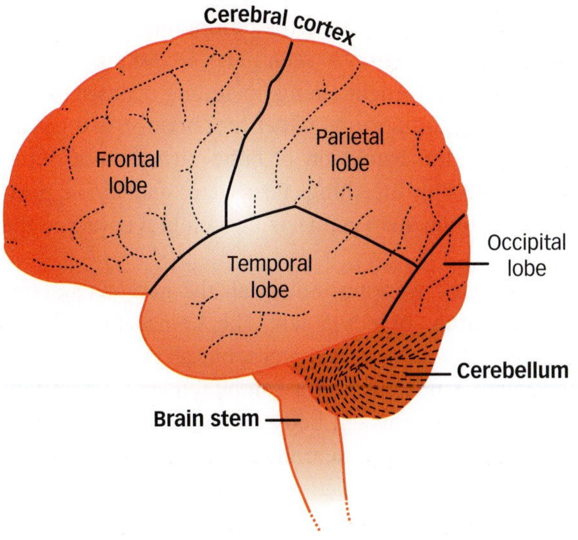

EXHIBIT 3.2 • Regions of the Cerebral Cortex

BRAIN REGION	FUNCTION
Frontal lobe	Motor behavior Expressive language Social functioning Concentration and ability to attend Reasoning and thinking Orientation to time, place, and person
Temporal lobe	Language Memory Emotions
Parietal lobe	Intellectual processing Integration of sensory information
Left parietal lobe	Verbal processing
Right parietal lobe	Visual/spatial processing
Occipital lobe	Vision

for Neuroscience, 2012). Other forebrain structures process information from the sensory and perceptual organs and structures and send it to the cortex, or receive orders from cortical centers and relay them on down through central nervous system structures to central and peripheral structures throughout the body. Also in the forebrain are centers for memory and emotion, as well as control of essential functions such as hunger, thirst, and biological sex drive.

The midbrain is a small area, but it contains important centers for sleep and pain as well as relay centers for sensory information and control of movement.

In Exhibit 3.1, part of the hindbrain, including the cerebellum, can also be seen. The *cerebellum* controls complex motor programming, including maintenance of muscle tone and posture. Other hindbrain structures are essential to the regulation of basic physiological functions, including breathing, heart rate, and blood pressure. The brain stem connects the cerebral cortex to the spinal cord.

The basic working unit of all the nervous systems is the **neuron**, or nerve cell. The human body has a great diversity of neuronal types, but all consist of a cell body with a nucleus and a conduction fiber, an **axon**. Extending from the cell body are *dendrites*, which conduct impulses to the neurons from the axons of other nerve cells. Exhibit 3.3 shows how neurons are linked by axons and dendrites.

The connection between each axon and dendrite is actually a gap called a **synapse**. Synapses use chemical and electrical **neurotransmitters** to communicate. As the inset box in Exhibit 3.3 shows, nerve impulses travel from the cell body to the ends of the axons, where they trigger the release of neurotransmitters. The adjacent dendrite of another neuron has receptors distinctly shaped to fit particular types of neurotransmitters. When the neurotransmitter fits into a slot, the message is passed along.

Although neurotransmitters are the focus of much current research, scientists have not yet articulated all that positivist research reveals about what neurotransmitters do. Essentially, they may either excite or inhibit nervous system responses. But medical research has revealed very little about many of the neurotransmitters and may not yet have identified them all. Here are a few.

- *Dopamine (DA)*. This neurotransmitter is an inhibitory substance that appears in many parts of the body and plays a role in regulation of motor behavior, the endocrine system, and the pleasure centers of the brain. Dopamine influences emotional behavior and

EXHIBIT 3.3 • Features of a Typical Neuron

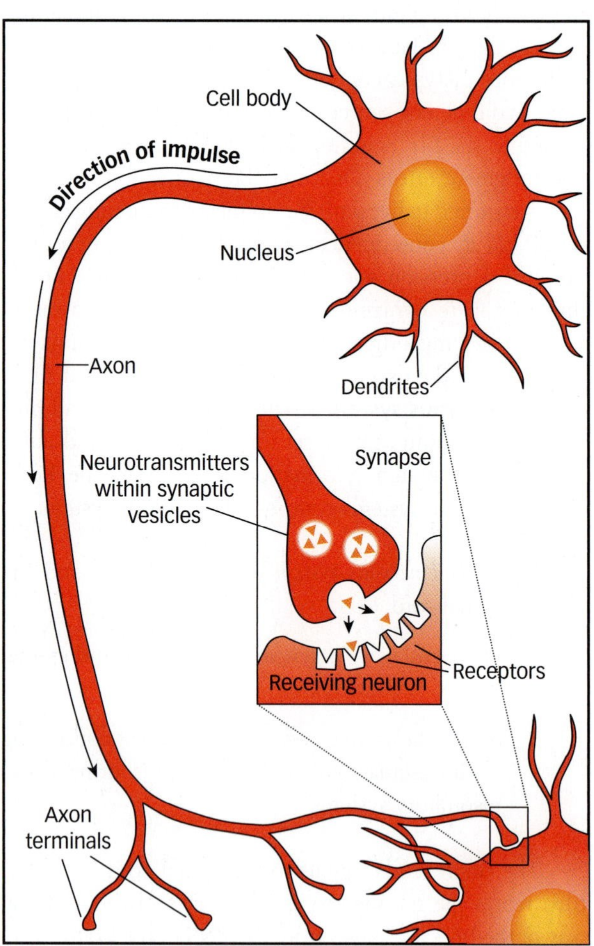

cognition. Dopamine abnormalities in the limbic system are thought to be involved in schizophrenia. Researchers are identifying a number of subtypes of dopamine (Bentley & Walsh, 2014).

- *Norepinephrine (NE)*. This neurotransmitter is an excitatory transmitter located in the sympathetic nerves of the peripheral and central nervous systems. It is also secreted by the adrenal glands in response to stress. It influences emotional behavior and alertness and plays a role in the regulation of anxiety and tensions (Bentley & Walsh, 2014).

- *Serotonin*. Present in blood cells, the lining of the digestive tract, and a tract from the midbrain to all brain regions, serotonin is an inhibitory transmitter. It is involved in sensory processes, muscular activity, thinking, regulation of states of consciousness, mood, depression, anxiety, appetite, sleep, and sexual behavior. Several subtypes have been identified in recent years (Bentley & Walsh, 2014).

- *Amino acids*. Some types of these molecules, found in proteins, are distributed throughout the brain and other body tissues. One amino acid, gamma aminobutyric acid (GABA), is believed to be instrumental in many functions of the CNS, such as locomotor activity, cardiovascular reactions, pituitary function, and anxiety diagnoses (Bentley & Walsh, 2014).

Biologically, behavior is affected not only by the levels of a neurotransmitter but also by the balance between two or more neurotransmitters. Psychotropic medications impact behaviors and symptoms associated with diagnoses of mental illness by affecting the levels of specific neurotransmitters and altering the balance among them. Social workers would be well advised to keep current on medical research about the effects of neurotransmitters on human behavior when working with people referred for medications evaluation and when following up with individuals who have been placed on medication treatment regimens (Bentley & Walsh, 2014).

Cheryl's injury has changed her brain, but brain injuries are not the only way the brain changes. For decades, neuroscientists thought that the adult brain was static, fixed, and unchanging. But now we know that is not true. Neuroscientists have learned a lot about **neuroplasticity,** the ability of the brain to change its structure and patterns of activity in significant ways throughout life. We have learned that the brain can be changed by experience with exterior environments as well as by activity in the interior environment (Davidson & Begley, 2012). Here is an example of change that results from experience with exterior environments: when a visually impaired person learns to read Braille, the "visual cortex" of the brain adapts to become a center for processing sensations from the fingers. Here is an example of how the brain is changed by activity in the interior environment: when an athlete engages in mental imagery practice, the motor cortex expands. Neuroscientists are also learning about the ways that the brain is shaped by activity in other biological systems. Here is a recent example of research on the complex relationships among exterior environments, the brain, and other biological systems. Chronic stress, often related to experiences with exterior environments, can cause high levels of cortisol secretion; cortisol is a glucocorticoid hormone produced in the adrenal gland (an endocrine gland). High levels of cortisol produce proinflammatory cytokines in the immune system. Recent research indicates that the secretion of proinflammatory cytokines to the brain influences the development and progression of major depressive disorder (Young, Bruno, & Pomara, 2014). This finding is important because we have tended to think, erroneously, of physical and mental illness as unrelated to each other.

For Cheryl, as for many people living with traumatic brain injury, her skills, abilities, and emotions may be affected by a variety of interior and exterior environment circumstances—including which parts of the brain were injured, her achievements prior to injury, her social and psychological supports, and the training and education she is offered following her accident. Tremendous advances are being made in rehabilitation following brain injuries (Gordon et al., 2006). The better social workers understand brain functions and brain plasticity, the more they can communicate with medical personnel in a well-informed manner. We may be able to help with adjustment or adaptation to changes as well as the recovery of functions. Cheryl could benefit from cognitive retraining, support in finding and maintaining employment, family counseling, and individual counseling to help her end her relationship with Sean. A key to recovery for many people who have experienced similar trauma is an opportunity to interact with peers and other individuals with similar experiences. Such peer networks may provide the individual with access to new skills and a key link to exterior environment social support. A social worker working with Cheryl may fill several roles: case manager, advocate, counselor, resource coordinator, and referral source.

ENDOCRINE SYSTEM

Remember Bess, the middle-aged woman diagnosed with diabetes? If you had first met her in a nonhospital setting, you might have interpreted her behaviors quite differently. Because of the recent rural health initiative in Bess's town, which has a number of residents who have relocated from French Canada, it was not unusual to hear women speaking in both French and English about their diets and exercise, and initially you may have been quite pleased for Bess's success. If Bess had told you she was tired, you might have suggested she slow down and get more rest or perhaps that she include vitamins in her diet. Sitting in the morning in her nightclothes on her couch and missing work might suggest alcohol or other drug use. Confusion, switching back and forth between speaking French and English in the same sentence, and inability to answer simple questions could signal stroke, dementia, or a mental illness such as schizophrenia. But only a thorough medical assessment of her interior environment revealed the primary and immediate cause of Bess's behaviors: a physical health condition traceable to a malfunction in the endocrine system.

The **endocrine system** plays a crucial role in our growth, metabolism, development, learning, and memory. It is made up of *glands* that secrete hormones into the blood system; those hormones bind to receptors in target organs, much as neurotransmitters do in the brain, and affect the metabolism or function of those organs (Rosenzweig, Breedlove, & Watson, 2010). Distinguishing differences between hormones and neurotransmitters are often the distance of travel from the point of release to the target, as well as the route of travel. Hormones travel long distances through the bloodstream; neurotransmitters travel shorter distances from cell to cell, across the synaptic cleft.

Endocrine glands include the pineal, pituitary, thyroid, parathyroid, pancreas, and adrenal. Endocrine cells

EXHIBIT 3.4 • Selected Endocrine Glands and Their Effects Within the Corpus

GLAND	HORMONE	EFFECT
Pituitary	Adrenocorticotropic (ACTH)	Stimulates adrenal cortex
	Growth (GH, somatotropic)	Stimulates cell division, protein synthesis, and bone growth
	Vasopressin	Stimulates water reabsorption by kidneys
	Prolactin	Stimulates milk production in mammary glands
Testes	Androgens (testosterone)	Stimulates development of sex organs, skin, muscles, bones, and sperm Stimulates development and maintenance of secondary male sex characteristics
Ovaries	Estrogen and progesterone	Stimulates development of sex organs, skin, muscles, bones, and uterine lining Stimulates development and maintenance of secondary female sex characteristics
Adrenal	Epinephrine	Stimulates fight-or-flight reactions in heart and other muscles Raises blood glucose levels
	Adrenal cortical steroids	Stimulates sex characteristics
Pancreas	Insulin	Targets liver, muscles, adipose tissues
	Glucagon	Regulates blood glucose levels Promotes formation of glycogen, proteins, and fats
Thymus	Thymosins	Triggers development of T lymphocytes, which orchestrate immune system response
Pineal	Melatonin	Maintains circadian rhythms (daily cycles of activity)
Thyroid	Thyroxin	Plays role in growth and development Stimulates metabolic rate of all organs

are also found in some organs that have primarily a non-endocrine function: the hypothalamus, liver, thymus, heart, kidney, stomach, duodenum, testes, and ovaries. Exhibit 3.4 lists some of the better-known glands and organs, the hormones they produce, and their effects on other body structures.

The most basic form of hormonal communication is from an endocrine cell through the blood system to a target cell. A more complex form of hormonal communication is directly from an endocrine gland to a target endocrine gland.

The endocrine system regulates the secretion of hormones through a **feedback control mechanism**. Output consists of hormones released from an endocrine gland; input consists of hormones taken into a target tissue or organ. The system is self-regulating. Similar to neurotransmitters, hormones have specific receptors, so that the hormone released from one gland has a specific target tissue or organ (Mader & Windelspecht, 2012).

A good example of a feedback loop is presented in Exhibit 3.5. The hypothalamus secretes the gonadotropin-releasing hormone (GnRH), which binds to receptors in the anterior pituitary and stimulates the secretion of the luteinizing hormone (LH). LH binds to receptors in the ovaries to stimulate the production of estrogen. Estrogen has a negative effect on the secretion of LH and GnRH at both the pituitary and hypothalamus, thus completing the loop. Loops like these allow the body to finely control the secretion of hormones.

Another good way to understand the feedback control mechanism is to observe the results when it malfunctions. Consider what has happened to Bess, who has been diagnosed with the most common illness caused by hormonal imbalance: **diabetes mellitus**. Insulin deficiency or resistance to insulin's effects is the basis of diabetes. Insulin and glucagon, which are released by the pancreas, regulate the metabolism of carbohydrates, the source of cell energy. These two substances are essential for the maintenance of blood glucose levels (blood sugar). High blood glucose levels stimulate the release of insulin, which in turn helps to decrease blood sugar by promoting the uptake of glucose by tissues. Low blood sugar stimulates the release of glucagon, which in turn stimulates the liver to release glucose, raising blood sugar. In people with insulin deficiency, muscle cells are deprived of glucose. As an alternative, those muscle cells tap fat and protein reserves in muscle tissue as an energy source. The results include wasting of muscles, weakness, weight loss, and *metabolic acidosis*, a chemical imbalance in the blood. The increase in blood acidity suppresses higher nervous system functions, leading to coma. Suppression of the respiratory centers in the brain leads to death (Kapit, Macey, & Meisami, 2000).

EXHIBIT 3.5 • An Example of a Feedback Loop

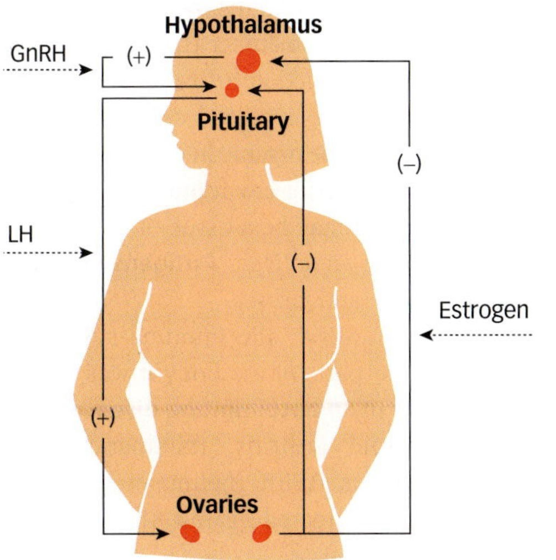

Epidemiologists report a dramatic increase in the incidence of diabetes worldwide in recent years. There are currently 25.8 million persons (8.3% of the population) in the United States who have diabetes, 18.8 million persons who have been diagnosed with diabetes, and an estimated 7 million who have undiagnosed diabetes (National Institute of Diabetes & Digestive & Kidney Diseases [NIDDK], 2011). Nearly 800,000 new cases of diabetes are diagnosed each year, or 2,200 per day. It is estimated that $1 out of every $5 spent on health care in the United States is spent on diabetes and its consequences (American Diabetes Association, 2013). Juvenile-onset diabetes (type 1) is found in children and young adults; risk factors may be autoimmune, genetic, or environmental. Non-Hispanic Whites are at greater risk of developing type 1 diabetes than other racial and ethnic groups. No known way to prevent type 1 diabetes exists. Maturity-onset diabetes (type 2), non-insulin-dependent diabetes mellitus, most commonly arises in people older than age 40 who are also obese. Type 2 diabetes is associated with older age, obesity, family history of diabetes, history of gestational diabetes, impaired glucose metabolism, physical inactivity, and particular races or ethnicities. Compared with non-Hispanic White adults, the risk of type 2 diabetes is 18% higher among Asian Americans, 66% higher among Hispanics/Latinos, and 77% higher among non-Hispanic Blacks (NIDDK, 2011).

For Bess, as for many people with symptoms indicating the presence of a medical condition, a crucial role for the social worker is to facilitate access to and comprehension of information about the symptoms and the diagnosed condition. Social workers can also aid in the translation of this information, so clients such as Bess, whose first language is French and who might not understand medical jargon, can grasp what is happening to them. The social worker may also help Bess begin to examine the lifestyle changes that may be suggested by this diagnosis. What might it mean in terms of diet, exercise, home and work responsibilities, and so forth? Bess may need assistance in working with her insurance company as she plans how her care will be financed. She may also need counseling as she works to adjust to life with this new medical diagnosis.

CRITICAL THINKING Questions 3.2

How important is it for Cheryl and Bess to be well informed about their medical conditions? Explain. How would you advise them about possible sources of information for their specific conditions? How should their social workers go about becoming better informed about their medical conditions?

IMMUNE SYSTEM

Melissa is far from alone in testing positive for HIV. The Centers for Disease Control and Prevention (CDC, 2013b) estimates that approximately 49,273 people in the United States were newly infected with HIV in 2011 (the most recent year that such diagnostic data were recorded). At the end of 2010, about 1.1 million Americans were living with the **human immunodeficiency virus (HIV)**, the virus that causes **acquired immunodeficiency syndrome (AIDS)**. According to the CDC, 16% of those individuals did not know they were infected. Males accounted for 79% of all new diagnoses among adults and adolescents in 2011 (CDC, 2013b).

It is estimated that, in 2012, 35.3 million people were living with HIV worldwide, 2.3 million people were newly infected, and somewhere between 1.7 and 2.4 million people died of AIDS-related illness (Joint United Nations Programme on HIV/AIDS [UNAIDS], 2013). The good news is that new infections of HIV were reduced 34% from 2000 to 2012, and the number of AIDS-related deaths declined 6% in the same period (UNAIDS, 2013).

Persons of all ages and racial and ethnic groups are affected. The cumulative estimates of the number of AIDS cases in the United States from the beginning of the epidemic through 2011 include 486,282 cases of AIDS among Blacks/African Americans; 435,613 cases among Whites (not Hispanic); 202,182 cases among Hispanics/Latinos; 9,054 cases among Asians; 3,787 cases among American Indians/Alaska Natives; and 901 cases among Native Hawaiians/Other Pacific Islanders. Among people identified as or who identify as multiple races, 17,804 cases were estimated (CDC, 2013c).

HIV/AIDS is a relatively new disease, and early in its history, it was assumed to be terminal. The introduction of highly active antiretroviral therapy (HAART), which became widespread in the United States in 1996, altered the perception of AIDS. It came to be seen as a chronic instead of terminal disease. The reality is that, although some are living longer with the disease, others are still dying young.

The Centers for Disease Control and Prevention (2013b) reports six common transmission categories for HIV: male-to-male sexual contact, injection drug use, male-to-male sexual contact *and* injection drug use, heterosexual contact, mother-to-child (perinatal) transmission, and other (includes blood transfusions and unknown causes). According to the CDC (2013c), 84% of women who acquire HIV do so through heterosexual contact, a group to which Melissa now belongs. Although HIV is more easily transmitted from men to women, it can be transmitted from women to men as well. Heterosexual transmission occurs mainly through vaginal intercourse.

Once a person is infected with HIV, the disease-fighting immune system gradually weakens. This weakened immune system lets other diseases begin to attack the body. Over the next few years, Melissa will learn a great deal about how her body does or does not protect itself against disease and infection. The **immune system** is made up of organs and cells that are commonly thought of as working together to defend the body against disease (Sarafino & Smith, 2010; Świątczak, 2012). When operating in an optimal manner, the immune system is able to distinguish our own cells and organs from foreign elements (Sarafino & Smith, 2010). When the body recognizes something as exterior or foreign, the immune system mobilizes body resources and attacks. Remember that we cautioned you about the arbitrary distinction between exterior and interior environments? Here is a good example: The foreign substance (which may be organic in composition and thus fit the definition of interior environment) that can trigger an immune response may be a tissue or organ transplant or, more commonly, an antigen. **Antigens** include bacteria, fungi, protozoa, and viruses.

Sometimes, however, the immune system is mistakenly directed at parts of the body it was designed to protect, resulting in an **autoimmune disease**. Examples include rheumatoid arthritis, rheumatic fever, and lupus erythematosus. With rheumatoid arthritis, the immune system is directed against tissues and bones

Wikimedia Commons, Public Domain

The AIDS Memorial Quilt is a powerful reminder of the people who have died from AIDS. HIV/AIDS is a relatively new disease, and early in its history it was assumed to be terminal.

at the joints. In rheumatic fever, the immune system targets the muscles of the heart. With lupus erythematosus, the immune system affects various parts of the interior environment, including the skin and kidneys (Sarafino & Smith, 2010).

Organs of the immune system are located throughout the body. They have primary involvement in the development of **lymphocytes**, or white blood cells (Sarafino & Smith, 2010). The main lymphatic organs include the following:

- *Bone marrow*. The largest organ in the body, it is the soft tissue in the core of bones. There are two types of bone marrow, red and yellow. Yellow bone marrow stores fat, which the body consumes only as a last resort in cases of extreme starvation. At birth, all bone marrow is red, but as the body ages, more and more red bone marrow is converted to yellow. In adults, red bone marrow is found in the sternum, ribs, vertebrae, skull, and long bones. The bone marrow produces both red (erythrocytes) and white (leukocytes and lymphocytes) blood cells.

- *Lymph nodes*. Small oval or round spongy masses distributed throughout the body (Sarafino & Smith, 2010). Lymph nodes are connected by a network of lymphatic vessels that contain a clear fluid called *lymph*, whose job is to bathe cells and remove bacteria and certain proteins. As the lymph passes through a lymph node, it is purified of infectious organisms. These vessels ultimately empty into the bloodstream.

- *Spleen*. An organ in the upper left quadrant of the abdomen. The spleen functions much like a very large lymph node, except that instead of lymph, blood passes through it. The spleen filters out antigens and removes ineffective or worn-out red blood cells from the body (Sarafino & Smith, 2010). An injured spleen can be removed, but the person becomes more susceptible to certain infections (Mader & Windelspecht, 2012).

• *Thymus*. Located along the trachea in the chest behind the sternum, the thymus secretes *thymosins*, hormones believed to trigger the development of T cells. *T cells*, white blood cells that mature in the thymus, have the task of slowing down, fighting, and attacking antigens (Mader & Windelspecht, 2012).

The immune system's response to antigens occurs in both specific and nonspecific ways. **Nonspecific immunity** is more general. "Scavenger" cells, or phagocytes, circulate in the blood and lymph, being attracted by biochemical signals to congregate at the site of a wound and ingest antigens (Parham, 2009; Sarafino & Smith, 2010; Sompayrac, 2012). This process, known as *phagocytosis*, is quite effective but has two limitations: (1) Certain bacteria and most viruses can survive after they have been engulfed, and (2) because our bodies are under constant attack and our phagocytes are constantly busy, a major assault on the immune system can easily overwhelm the nonspecific response. Thus, specific immunity is essential (Parham, 2009; Sarafino & Smith, 2010; Sompayrac, 2012).

Specific immunity, or acquired immunity, involves the lymphocytes. They not only respond to an infection but also develop a *memory* of that infection and allow the body to make rapid defense against it in subsequent exposure. Certain lymphocytes produce **antibodies**, protein molecules designed to attach to the surface of specific invaders. The antibodies recruit other protein substances that puncture the membrane of invading micro-organisms, causing the invaders to explode. The antibodies are assisted in this battle by T cells, which destroy foreign cells directly and orchestrate the immune response. Following the *primary response*, the antibodies remain in the circulatory system at significant levels until they are no longer needed. With reexposure to the same antigen, a *secondary immune response* occurs, characterized by a more rapid rise in antibody levels—over a period of hours rather than days. This rapid response is possible because, during initial exposure to the antigen, memory cells were created. *Memory T cells* store the information needed to produce specific antibodies. They also have very long lives (Parham, 2009; Sarafino & Smith, 2010; Sompayrac, 2012).

The immune system becomes increasingly effective throughout childhood and declines in effectiveness in older adulthood. Infants are born with relatively little immune defense, but their immune system gradually becomes more efficient and complex. Thus, as the child develops, the incidence of serious illness declines. During adolescence and most of adulthood, the immune system, for most people, functions at a high level of effectiveness. As we age, although the numbers of lymphocytes and antibodies circulating in the lymph and blood do not decrease, their potency diminishes.

The functioning of the immune system can be hampered by a diet low in vitamins A, E, and C and high in fats and cholesterol, and by excess weight (Parham, 2009; Sarafino & Smith, 2010; Sompayrac, 2012). There are also far more serious problems that can occur with the immune system, such as HIV, that are life threatening. HIV, like other viruses, infects "normal" cells and "hijacks" their genetic machinery. These infected cells in essence become factories that make copies of the HIV, which then go on to infect other cells. The hijacked cells are destroyed. A favorite target of HIV is the T cells that tell other cells when to start fighting off infections. HIV thus weakens the immune system and makes it increasingly difficult for the body to fight off other diseases and infections. Most of us host organisms such as fungi, viruses, and parasites that live inside us without causing disease. However, for people with HIV, because of the low T cell count, these same organisms can cause serious infection. When such a disease occurs or when the individual's number of T cells drops below a certain level, the person with HIV is considered to have AIDS (Cressey & Lallemant, 2007).

Melissa's life may undergo significant changes as symptoms of HIV infection begin to emerge. For example, Melissa may be at increased risk for repeated serious yeast infections of the vagina, and she may also be at increased risk for cancer of the cervix and pelvic inflammatory disease. Both men and women are vulnerable to opportunistic diseases and infections such as Kaposi's sarcoma, cytomegalovirus (CMV), AIDS retinopathy, pneumocystis carinii pneumonia (PCP), mycobacterium tuberculosis, and Candida albicans (thrush); atypical functioning such as AIDS dementia, loss of memory, loss of judgment, and depression; and other symptoms such as gastrointestinal dysfunction/distress, joint pain, anemia, and low platelet counts. (Details on these conditions can be found in medical sources.) The social worker may help to educate Melissa about these increased risks. In order to protect her health and the health of others, Melissa will most likely be advised to take special precautions. She can be supported in staying well by getting early treatment, adopting a healthy lifestyle, and remaining informed about new treatments (Voronin & Phogat, 2010).

The social worker also may have a role to play in working with Melissa as she tells her family and fiancé about her diagnosis. Melissa and her fiancé may need advice about how to practice safe sex. The social worker should also be available to work with Melissa, her fiancé, and her family as they adjust to her diagnosis and the grief they may feel, an experience frequently associated with a diagnosis of HIV. The social worker may explore reactions and responses of Melissa, her fiancé, and her parents to this health crisis.

Because of the tremendous costs for medications, particularly the new HAART, the social worker may link Melissa to sources of financial support. This aid will become increasingly critical if she gets sicker, her income declines, or her medical expenses increase. Given advances in medical diagnostics and therapeutics, recent estimates indicate that the lifetime costs of health care associated with HIV may be more than $567,000 per person diagnosed in adulthood (Nakagawa et al., 2015). Treatment with HAART is not a cure, but it allows the person with HIV to fight off other infections and increase life expectancy (Maggiolo & Leone, 2010; Pokorná, Machala, Rezáčová, & Konvalinka, 2009). However, side effects of some of the drugs are just as debilitating as the effects of AIDS.

In addition to providing Melissa with information about her immune system, HIV, AIDS, and other health issues, the social worker can advise Melissa about the protections guaranteed to her under the Americans with Disabilities Act of 1990 and the Amendments Act of 2008. Melissa has joined an HIV support group, but the social worker may also offer to provide her with or refer her to counseling. The social worker may also have a role to play on behalf of all people with HIV/AIDS, working to address prevention and public health in part by providing HIV/AIDS education to business groups, schools, civic and volunteer associations, and neighborhood groups and by influencing policy to support public health HIV prevention initiatives.

CARDIOVASCULAR SYSTEM

Thomas, from Case Study 3.4, is one of many people living with one or more types of *cardiovascular disease* (CVD), disease of the heart and blood vessels. The most common types of CVD are coronary disease, hypertension, and stroke. CVD is the most common cause of death in this country, responsible for one in three deaths, with one death every 40 seconds (American Heart Association, 2013a). Stroke is the fourth leading cause of death, having declined significantly since the 1970s, due in large part to improvement in both prevention and treatment. It is the leading cause of long-term disability (American Heart Association, 2013a).

In 2011, 6.6% of U.S. adults age 18 and older reported being told by a health professional that they had coronary disease, 25.5% had been told they had hypertension, and 2.7% reported a history of stroke (Schiller, Lucas, & Peregoy, 2012). Men were twice as likely as women to have coronary disease, but the prevalence of hypertension and stroke was about the same for men and women. American Indian or Alaska Natives were more likely than other racial and ethnic groups to have some type of CVD, and Hispanic or Latino adults were less likely than White and African American adults to have CVD. The highest prevalence occurred in adults reporting two or more races (Schiller et al., 2012). As educational and income level increased, the prevalence of CVD decreased (Schiller et al., 2012).

Thomas's cardiovascular diagnosis is **high blood pressure (hypertension)**, defined as a systolic blood pressure equal to or greater than (≥) 140 mm Hg and/or a diastolic blood pressure ≥ 90 mm Hg (his was 200/105). Blacks, Puerto Ricans, Cubans, and Mexican Americans are all more likely to suffer from high blood pressure than are Whites, and African Americans have the highest rates of high blood pressure in the world (American Heart Association, 2013b). An estimated 6.4 million Blacks have high blood pressure, with more frequent and severe effects than in other population subgroups. Blacks also develop high blood pressure earlier in life (American Heart Association, 2013b).

In 2013, it was estimated that one in three adults in the United States had high blood pressure, with 81.5% of those individuals aware of their condition and 52.5% having it under control (American Heart Association, 2013c). In 90% to 95% of the cases of individuals with high blood pressure, the cause is unknown. The death rate from high blood pressure steadily increased by 17.1% from 1999 to 2009, but with the rising population of older adults, the actual number of deaths rose by 43.6%. The death rate per 100,000 people from high blood pressure in 2009 was 17.0 for White males, 51.6 for Black males, 14.4 for White females, and 38.3 for Black females (American Heart Association, 2013c).

To better understand cardiovascular disease, it is first important to gain insight into the functioning of the **cardiovascular system**, which is composed of the heart and the blood circulatory system (Mader & Windelspecht, 2012). The heart's walls are made up of specialized muscle. As the muscle shortens and squeezes the hollow cavities of the heart, blood is forced in the directions permitted by the opening or closing of valves. Blood vessels continually carry blood from the heart to the rest of the body's tissues and then return the blood to the heart. Exhibit 3.6 shows the direction of the blood's flow through the heart.

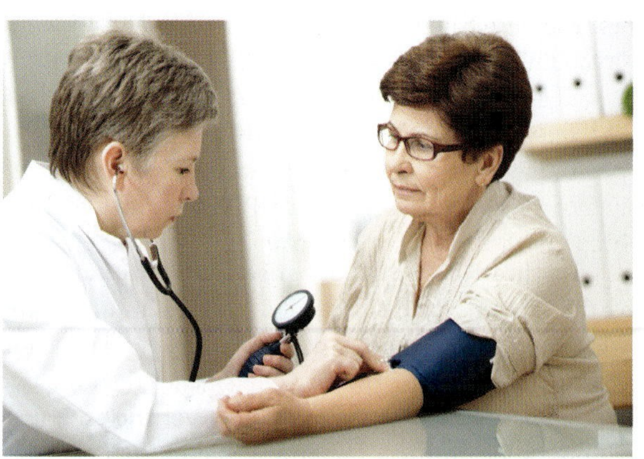

In 2013, it was estimated that one in three adults in the United States had high blood pressure.

EXHIBIT 3.6 • The Direction of Blood Flow Through the Heart

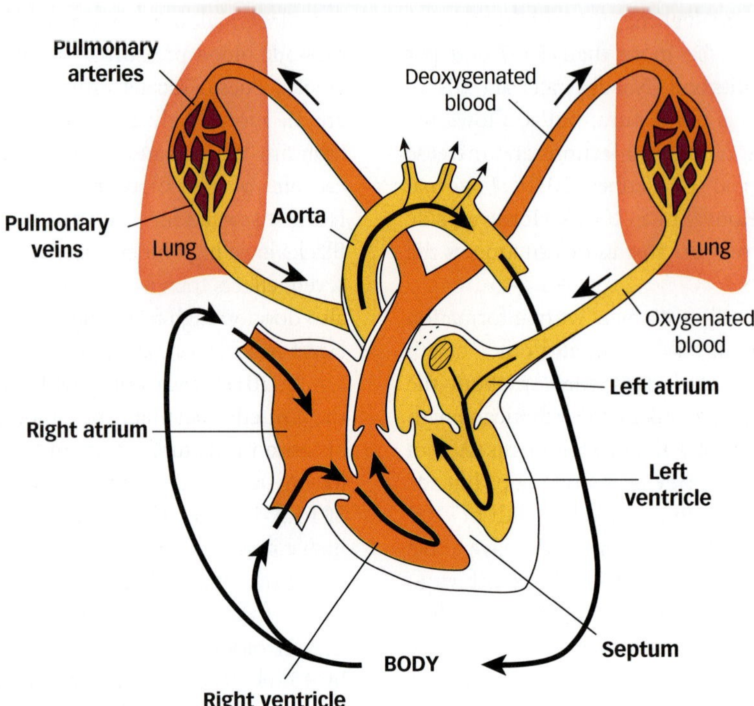

There are three types of blood vessels.

1. *Arteries*. These have thick walls containing elastic and muscular tissues. The elastic tissues allow the arteries to expand and accommodate the increase in blood volume that occurs after each heartbeat. Arterioles are small arteries that branch into smaller vessels called capillaries.
2. *Capillaries*. A critical part of this closed circulation system, they allow the exchange of nutrients and waste material with the body's cells. Oxygen and nutrients transfer out of a capillary into the tissue fluid in surrounding cells and absorb carbon dioxide and other wastes from the cells.
3. *Veins*. These take blood from the capillaries and return it to the heart. Some of the major veins in the arms and legs have valves allowing the blood to flow only toward the heart when they are open and block any backward flow when they are closed (Mader & Windelspecht, 2012).

The heart has two sides (right and left), separated by the septum. Each side is divided into an upper and a lower chamber. The two upper, thin-walled chambers are called **atria**. The atria are smaller than the two lower, thick-walled chambers, called **ventricles**. Valves within the heart direct the flow of blood from chamber to chamber and, when closed, prevent its backward flow (Mader & Windelspecht, 2012).

As Exhibit 3.6 shows, the right side of the heart pumps blood to the lungs, and the left side pumps blood to the tissues of the body. Blood from body tissues that is low in oxygen and high in carbon dioxide (deoxygenated blood) enters the right atrium. The right atrium then sends blood through a valve to the right ventricle. The right ventricle then sends the blood through another valve and the pulmonary arteries into the lungs. In the lungs, the blood gives up carbon dioxide and takes up oxygen. Pulmonary veins then carry blood that is high in oxygen (oxygenated) from the lungs to the left atrium. From the left atrium, blood is sent through a valve to the left ventricle. The blood is then sent through a valve into the aorta for distribution around the body (Mader & Windelspecht, 2012).

Contraction and relaxation of the heart moves the blood from the ventricles to the lungs and to the body. The right and left sides of the heart contract together—first the two atria, then the two ventricles. The heart contracts ("beats") about 70 times per minute when the body is at rest. The contraction and relaxation cycle is called the cardiac cycle. The sound of the heartbeat, as heard through a stethoscope, is caused by the opening and closing of the heart valves.

Although the heart will beat independently of any nervous system stimulation, regulation of the heart is primarily the responsibility of the ANS. *Parasympathetic activities* of the nervous system, which tend to be thought of as normal or routine activities, slow the heart rate. *Sympathetic activities*, associated with stress, increase the heart rate. As blood is pumped from the aorta into the arteries, their elastic walls swell, followed by an immediate recoiling. The alternating expansion and recoiling of the arterial wall is the pulse. The normal pulse rate at rest for children ages 6 to 15 is 70 to 100 beats per minute; for adults age 18 and older, the normal pulse rate at rest is 60 to 100 beats per minute (Cleveland Clinic, 2014).

Blood pressure is the measure of the pressure of the blood against the wall of a blood vessel. A *sphygmomanometer* is used to measure blood pressure. The cuff of the sphygmomanometer is placed around the upper arm over an artery. A pressure gauge is used to measure the *systolic blood pressure*, the highest arterial pressure, which results from ejection of blood from the aorta. *Diastolic blood pressure*, the lowest arterial pressure, occurs while the ventricles of the heart are relaxing. Medically desired and healthy blood pressure for a young adult is 120 mm of mercury systole over 80 mm of mercury diastole, or 120/80 (Mader & Windelspecht, 2012).

Blood pressure accounts for the movement of blood from the heart to the body by way of arteries and arterioles, but skeletal muscle contraction moves the blood through the venous system. As skeletal muscles contract, they push against the thin or weak walls of the veins, causing the blood to move past valves. Once past the valve, the blood cannot return, forcing it to move toward the heart.

High blood pressure has been called the silent killer, because many people like Thomas have it without noticeable symptoms. It is the leading cause of stroke and is a major risk factor for heart attack and kidney failure.

Suddenly faced with startling information, such as a dramatic change in what was believed to be good health, Thomas might experience a range of responses, including but not limited to denial, questioning, self-reflection, self-critique, and even anger. The social worker can play many critical roles with Thomas. Perceptions of exterior conditions such as daily hassles and stressful life events place him at increased risk for having a stroke or dying as a result of his high blood pressure (Paradies, 2006). Social workers are uniquely positioned to see the links between external environment issues—such as racism, sexism, and other forms of discrimination; lack of economic opportunity; and criminal victimization—and interior environment health issues.

On an individual level, being better informed about the cardiovascular system and its care can help Thomas maximize the benefits of medical examination and treatment. The social worker can participate in medical care by helping Thomas learn the essential elements of effective health practice, including what it means to have high blood pressure, what causes high blood pressure, and how to lower the risks of high blood pressure. If medication is prescribed, the social worker can support the medication regimen and Thomas's decision about how to follow it.

The social worker also can process with Thomas a strategy for identifying and deciding on his preferred lifestyle changes to help lower his blood pressure. These may include examination of sources of stress and patterns of coping, diet, how much exercise he gets on a regular basis, and his social and economic external environmental conditions.

Because high blood pressure has been shown to run in families, the social worker can also work with Thomas's family to discuss lifestyle factors that might contribute to high blood pressure, such as exposure to stress, cigarette/tobacco use, a diet high in cholesterol, physical inactivity, and excess weight.

The social worker may also work with community organizations, community centers, and religious organizations to advance policy and public health practices to support education and prevention programs as well as a physician and health care provider referral program. Given the ubiquity of smartphone use, the social worker might recommend that Thomas use contemporary technologies such as free smartphone apps for monitoring blood pressure and fitness activity.

CRITICAL THINKING Questions 3.3

Melissa and Thomas are both in the young adulthood period. What impact could their health conditions have on their young adult development? What are the implications for the later phases of their life journeys?

MUSCULOSKELETAL SYSTEM

After a number of years with a variety of physical symptoms, Mary from Case Study 3.5 was diagnosed with multiple sclerosis (MS). The symptoms and presentation of multiple sclerosis vary depending on the location of the affected nerve fibers. Symptoms can include weak or stiff muscles in one or more limbs, often with painful muscle spasms; tingling, pain, and/or numbness in the arms, legs, trunk of the body, or face; vision problems such as complete loss of central vision (usually in one eye), blurred or double vision, or pain in the eye; lack of coordination, clumsiness, unsteady gait, and difficulty staying balanced when walking; dizziness; slurred speech; and bladder control problems. Subsequent symptoms often include fatigue, mental or physical; changes in mood; difficulty concentrating or attending to multiple tasks; and difficulty making decisions, planning, or prioritizing (Mayo Foundation for Medical Education and Research, 2012; National Institute of Neurological Disorders and Stroke, 2013a).

It is quite common for people in the beginning stages of multiple sclerosis to experience periods of symptom expression followed by complete or partial remission of the symptoms. For some individuals this symptom presentation is followed by long periods of partial or apparent full recovery. Some individuals may have a mild course of the disease, with little functional impairment, whereas others may have a steadily worsening constellation of symptoms, with increasing severity of functional impairment. MS is often considered one of the most common functionally impairing neurological diseases of young adults. Although MS can affect children and adults age 60 and older, it most often occurs in individuals ages 20 to 40 years old (Mayo Foundation for Medical Education and Research, 2012; National Institute of Neurological Disorders and Stroke, 2013a).

Multiple sclerosis (MS) is a neuroinflammatory disease that affects myelin. Myelin is an insulating layer or membrane (called the myelin sheath) that wraps around nerve fibers (axons) of the brain and spinal cord. The role of the myelin sheath is to enable nerve impulses to transmit quickly and efficiently along a nerve fiber. The rapid transmission of nerve impulses allows individuals to function in a more typical fashion. MS is also considered an autoimmune disorder (a condition in which the immune system mistakenly attacks and destroys healthy body tissue), where the immune system attacks the myelin, resulting in lesions. These lesions then slow or halt the nerve impulse, leading to neurological signs and symptoms associated with MS.

The prevalence of people diagnosed with MS in the United States currently ranges from 250,000 to 350,000. It appears that the rate of the disease or at least the diagnosis of MS has steadily increased during the 20th century and the first part of the 21st century. It is suggested that approximately 200 individuals are diagnosed with MS each week (National Institute of Neurological Disorders and Stroke, 2013a).

About twice as many women are diagnosed with MS as men. MS seems to be more common in colder climates than more temperate climates. Caucasians (particularly those of northern European decent) seem to be more at risk for diagnosis than other ethnic groups, but people of African and Hispanic ancestry also develop the disease. Asian American populations and Native Americans of North and South America have relatively low rates of MS (National Institute of Neurological Disorders and Stroke, 2013a; National Multiple Sclerosis Society, n.d.).

Among the range of symptoms of MS is dysfunction in the **musculoskeletal system**, which supports and protects the body and provides motion. The contraction and relaxation of muscles attached to the skeleton is the basis for all voluntary movements. Over 600 skeletal muscles in the body account for about 40% of body weight (Mader & Windelspecht, 2012). When a muscle contracts, it shortens; it can only pull, not push. Therefore, for us to be able to extend and to flex at a joint, muscles work in "antagonistic" pairs. As an example, when the hamstring group in the back of the leg contracts, the quadriceps in the front relax; this allows the leg to bend at the knee. When the quadriceps contract, the hamstring relaxes, allowing the leg to extend.

The contraction of a muscle occurs as a result of an electrical impulse passed to the muscle by a controlling nerve that releases acetylcholine. When a single stimulus is given to a muscle, it responds with a twitch, a contraction lasting only a fraction of a second. But when there are repeated stimulations close together, the muscle cannot fully relax between impulses. As a result, each contraction benefits from the previous contraction, giving a combined contraction that is greater than an individual twitch. When stimulation is sufficiently rapid, the twitches cease to be jerky and fuse into a smooth contraction/movement called *tetanus*. However, tetanus that continues eventually produces muscle fatigue due to depletion of energy reserves.

Skeletal muscles exhibit tone when some muscles are always contracted. Tone is critical if we are to maintain body posture. If all the muscle fibers in the neck, trunk, and legs were to relax, our bodies would collapse. Nerve fibers embedded in the muscles emit impulses that communicate to the CNS the state of particular muscles. This communication allows the CNS to coordinate the contraction of muscles (Mader & Windelspecht, 2012). In its entirety, the musculoskeletal system both supports the body and allows it to move. The skeleton, particularly the large heavy bones of the legs, supports the body against the pull of gravity and protects soft body parts. Most essential, the skull protects the brain, the rib cage protects the heart and lungs, and the vertebrae protect and support the spinal cord.

Bones serve as sites for the attachment of muscles. It may not seem so, but bone is a very active tissue, supplied with nerves and blood vessels. Throughout life, bone cells repair, remold, and rejuvenate in response to stresses, strains, and fractures. A typical long bone, such as the arm or leg bone, has a cavity surrounded by a dense area. The dense area contains compact bone; the cavernous area contains blood vessels and nerves surrounded by spongy bone. Far from being weak, spongy bone is designed for strength. It is the site of red marrow, the specialized tissue that produces red and white blood cells. The cavity of a long bone also contains yellow marrow, which is a fat-storage tissue (Mader & Windelspecht, 2012).

Most bones begin as cartilage. In long bones, growth and calcification (hardening) begin in early childhood and continue through adolescence. Growth hormones and thyroid hormones stimulate bone growth during childhood. Androgens, which are responsible for the adolescent growth spurt, stimulate bone growth during puberty. In late adolescence, androgens terminate bone growth.

Bones are joined together at joints. Long bones and their corresponding joints are what permit flexible body movement (Mader & Windelspecht, 2012).

Joints are classified according to the amount of movement they permit. Bones of the cranium, which are sutured together, are examples of immovable joints. Joints between the vertebrae are slightly movable. Freely movable joints, which connect two bones separated by a cavity, are called *synovial joints*. Synovial joints may be hinge joints (knee and elbow) or ball-and-socket joints (attachment of the femur to the hipbone). Exhibit 3.7 shows the structure of the knee joint. Synovial joints are prone to arthritis because the bones gradually lose their protective covering and grate against each other as they move (Mader & Windelspecht, 2012).

The bones in a joint are held together by *ligaments*, whereas *tendons* connect muscle to bone. The ends of the bone are capped by cartilage, which gives added strength and support to the joint. Friction between tendons and ligaments and between tendons and bones is eased by fluid-filled sacs called *bursae*. Inflammation of the bursae is called bursitis.

Because of the commonly held perspective that individual independence is most desirable, it is not unusual for social workers and other health care professionals to discourage a person with a medical explanation for atypical function from using exterior environmental modifications and resources when they are not essential, even though they may be quite useful. These may include ramps, elevators, and electrically operated doors or assistive devices. **Assistive devices** are those products designated by the medical community to help an impaired person to communicate, see, hear, or maneuver. Examples used by individuals with atypical activity include manual wheelchairs, motorized wheelchairs, motorized scooters, and other aids that enhance mobility; hearing aids, telephone communication devices, listening devices, visual and audible signal systems, and other products that enhance the ability to hear; and voice-synthesized computer modules, optical scanners, talking software, and other communication devices. In suggesting technological devices, the social worker should be attentive to stigma that accompanies the term *assistive* and the medicalized appearance of many products named assistive technology.

EXHIBIT 3.7 • Structure of the Knee Joint

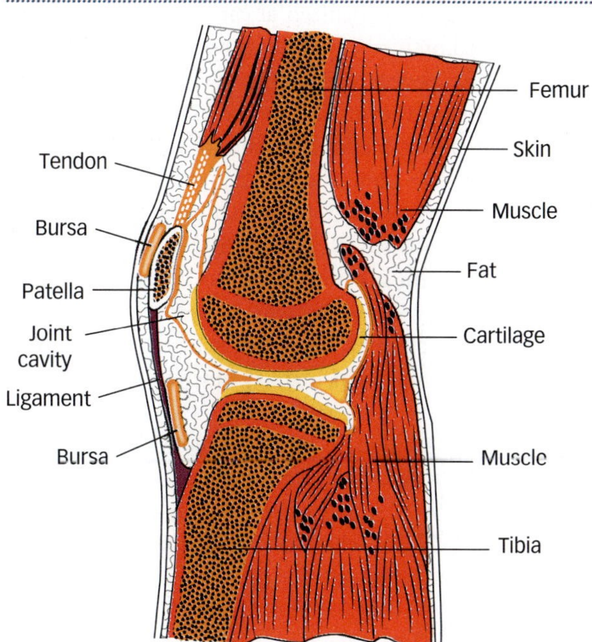

Those who believe that working to "overcome" challenges is a helpful approach in adjusting to or working with atypical function may be well meaning. But implicit within this belief system is the impression that being labeled as "disabled" ascribes deficiency that makes an individual less than whole, less than competent, and less than capable.

Although the most commonly held perspective of disability is one of medical deficiency, contemporary disability studies challenge this belief. DePoy and Gilson have theorized disability as disjuncture or an ill fit between body and context (DePoy & Gilson, 2011). Thus, using this perspective, the diagnosed body is not the sole locus for intervention. Social work addresses policy change, exclusion or lack of access, or other conditions that limit a person's progress toward meeting his or her desired goal.

Depending on the severity of symptom presentation, Mary may or may not benefit from social work assistance. If she does seek such assistance, it is important for the social worker to know that because there is no single test to diagnose MS, Mary may have been subjected to a wide range of tests to rule out or to confirm the diagnosis. In addition to providing a complete medical history and undergoing a physical examination and full neurological evaluation, Mary may have an MRI scan of the head and spine to look for the characteristic lesions of MS. An additional common medical procedure ordered when MS is suspected is a lumbar puncture (sometimes called a spinal tap) to obtain a sample of cerebrospinal fluid. It is also important for the social worker to know that during an acute phase or exacerbation, which may also be called a relapse, flare-up, or attack, there is a sudden worsening of symptoms that lasts for at least 24 hours (National Institute of Neurological Disorders and Stroke, 2013a). He or she may work with other rehabilitation professionals, such as physical therapists and occupational therapists, in identifying useful adaptions and modifications in Mary's work, recreation, and home environments. The social worker might provide counseling but also could refer Mary to a wide range of community groups ranging from yoga classes to MS peer support groups. Should Mary choose to acquire new technology to support any limitation connected with MS, the social worker may also intervene with insurance companies reluctant to purchase the needed technological equipment.

REPRODUCTIVE SYSTEM

Juan and Belinda are at an age when an understanding of reproduction and sexuality is critical. In the United States, as in many countries around the globe, the typical age for first experience of sexual intercourse is approximately 17. However, individuals tend not to marry until they reach their mid-20s (Guttmacher Institute, 2013a). According to the Centers for Disease Control and Prevention (2012a), 47.4% of high school students surveyed in 2011 reported having had sexual intercourse during their life. Nearly 34% reported having had sexual intercourse in the previous 3 months, with 39.8% reporting that they did not use a condom the last time they had sex and 76.7% reporting that they did not use birth control pills or Depo-Provera to prevent pregnancy the last time they had sexual intercourse. According to the Centers for Disease Control and Prevention (2012b), in 2011 44.3% of White high school students reported having sexual intercourse during their life; the percentage among Black students was 60% and 48.6% among Hispanic students. Less than 2% of adolescents have had sex by the time they are 12; the percentage rises to 16% by age 15, 33% by age 16, and 48% by age 17 (Guttmacher Institute, 2013a).

Contraception use has been increasing among sexually active teens in the United States. From 2006 to 2010, an estimated 78% of sexually active females and 85% of sexually active males used contraception during their first experience with sexual intercourse. For females, this is an increase from 48% in 1982 (Guttmacher Institute, 2013a). This is an encouraging trend, but sexually active U.S. teens still lag behind sexually active teens in other wealthy countries in contraceptive use. This contributes to a higher incidence of teen pregnancy and sexually transmitted infections (STIs) in the United States than in other wealthy countries. Annually, about 750,000 females aged 15 to 19 become pregnant in the United States, with 82% of teen pregnancies unintended, 59% ending in birth, and 26% ending in abortion (Guttmacher Institute, 2013a). Two thirds of all teen pregnancies occur in teens aged 18 to 19 years old. The highest teen pregnancy rates occur in Black and Hispanic women (117 and 107 per 1,000 women aged 15 to 19, respectively); White adolescent women have a rate of 43 per 1,000 (Guttmacher Institute, 2013a). The teen pregnancy rate in the United States has declined steadily from 117 pregnancies per 1,000 women aged 15 to 19 in 1990 to 68 per 1,000 in 2008 (Guttmacher Institute, 2013a). Among Black teenagers aged 15 to 19, the pregnancy rate fell by 48%, compared with the overall decline of 42% (Guttmacher Institute, 2013a). The teen abortion rate declined by 59% from 1988 to 2008 (Guttmacher Institute, 2012). The Guttmacher Institute (2013a) estimates nearly 19 million new STIs each year, with nearly half occurring among youth and young adults aged 15 to 24, even though this group is only about 25% of the sexually active population.

Adolescents consider parents, peers, and the media to be important sources of information about sexual health, but there is also strong evidence that comprehensive sex education programs help young people to delay sexual activity and to use responsible protection once beginning to engage in sexual activity (Guttmacher Institute, 2012). From 2006 to 2008, 93% of teens in the United States had received formal education about STIs, 89% had received formal education about HIV, and 84% had received formal education about abstinence. About one third of teens had not received formal education about contraception (Guttmacher Institute, 2012). A 2007 study found that federally funded abstinence-only education programs had no beneficial effect on teen sexual behavior (Boonstra, 2010), and in 2010, Congress eliminated the two federal programs that had funded abstinence-only education, the Adolescent Family Life (AFL) Prevention Program and the Community-Based Abstinence Education (CBAE) Program.

If adolescents are to make responsible decisions about their sexuality, they would be wise to develop an understanding of the structures and functions of the reproductive system. For some individuals, this information may come from the home; for others, from schools, community activity centers, websites, and social networking interactions; and for others, from family planning centers where social workers may work. The discussion that follows focuses on the interior environmental aspects of heterosexual sexuality and reproduction, but before beginning this discussion it is important to say some things about the intersections of sex, gender, and sexual orientation.

First, we want to provide working definitions of these three terms, but before we do so, we point out that the terms themselves are under dispute and receiving considerable reexamination. That said, *sex* is used to refer to a person's biological characteristics. In most cultures, two sex categories are recognized at birth: male and female, usually based on type of genitalia. However, in every culture, intersex people may present with both male and female genitalia (Levitt & Ippolito, 2014a, 2014b). In addition, it is possible for a person to be a chromosomal male with female genitals and vice versa. Chromosomal, genetic, anatomical, and hormonal aspects of sex are sometimes not aligned (Rudacille, 2005).

Gender, on the other hand, is a social construct based on socially accepted ideals of what it means to be male and female. In most cultures, two genders are designated: masculine and feminine, which are assumed to flow naturally from the two sex categories of male and female (Caron, 2011). In some cultures, however, more than two genders have been identified and accepted (S. Davies, 2006; McDermott, 1997). *Transgender* is an umbrella term that refers to individuals who have been assigned a gender (based on biological sex) that defies their understanding of who they are as a gendered person. These individuals may or may not alter their bodies through surgery or hormonal treatment. In recent years, *cisgender* has been used to describe situations in which people's gender identity matches their assigned gender based on biological sex.

Sexual orientation refers to erotic, romantic, and affectionate attraction to people of the same sex (gay or lesbian), the opposite sex (heterosexual), both sexes (bisexual), or the lack thereof. A person's sexual orientation is distinct from his or her gender identity or expression.

Let us now return to our discussion of the interior environment of heterosexual sexuality and gender. In humans, the reproductive system comprises internal and external structures. After conception, the sex-determining chromosome produced by the father unites with the mother's egg, and it is this configuration that determines the child's sex. At birth, boys and girls are distinguished by the presence of specific genitalia.

As Exhibit 3.8 shows, the external male organs are the penis and scrotum. Internal organs consist of the testes, the tubes and ducts that serve to transfer the sperm through the reproductive system, and the organs that help nourish and activate sperm and neutralize some of the acidity that sperm encounter in the vagina. The penis functions as a conduit for both urine and semen.

Externally, one can view the shaft and the glans (often referred to as the head or tip) of the penis. The shaft contains three cylinders. The two largest are called the corpa cavernosa (singular: *corpus cavernosum*). During sexual arousal, these become engorged with blood and stiffen. The corpus spongiosum, the third cylinder, contains the urethra. It enlarges at the tip of the penis to form a structure called the glans. The ridge that separates the glans from the shaft of the penis is called the corona. The frenulum is the sensitive strip of tissue connecting the underside of the glans to the shaft. At the base of the penis is the root, which extends into the pelvis.

Three glands are part of the feedback loop that maintains a constant level of male hormones in the bloodstream. The primary functions of the **testes**, or male gonads, are to produce sperm (mature germ cells that fertilize the female egg) and to secrete male hormones called *androgens*. *Testosterone* is one of the most important hormones in that it stimulates the development of the sex organs in the male fetus and the later development of secondary sex characteristics such as facial hair, male muscle mass, and a deep voice. The two other glands in the feedback loop are the hypothalamus and the pituitary gland. Both secrete hormones that serve a regulatory function, primarily maintaining a constant testosterone level in the blood.

Before we move forward, let's pause to briefly review heredity and genetics. For humans, chromosomes come in pairs, one member from the father and one from the mother, which are transferred at fertilization. Each individual has 22 pairs of uniquely shaped autosomal chromosomes (not sex chromosomes) plus 1 pair of sex chromosomes (XX or XY), for a total of 23 chromosome

EXHIBIT 3.8 • The Male Reproductive System

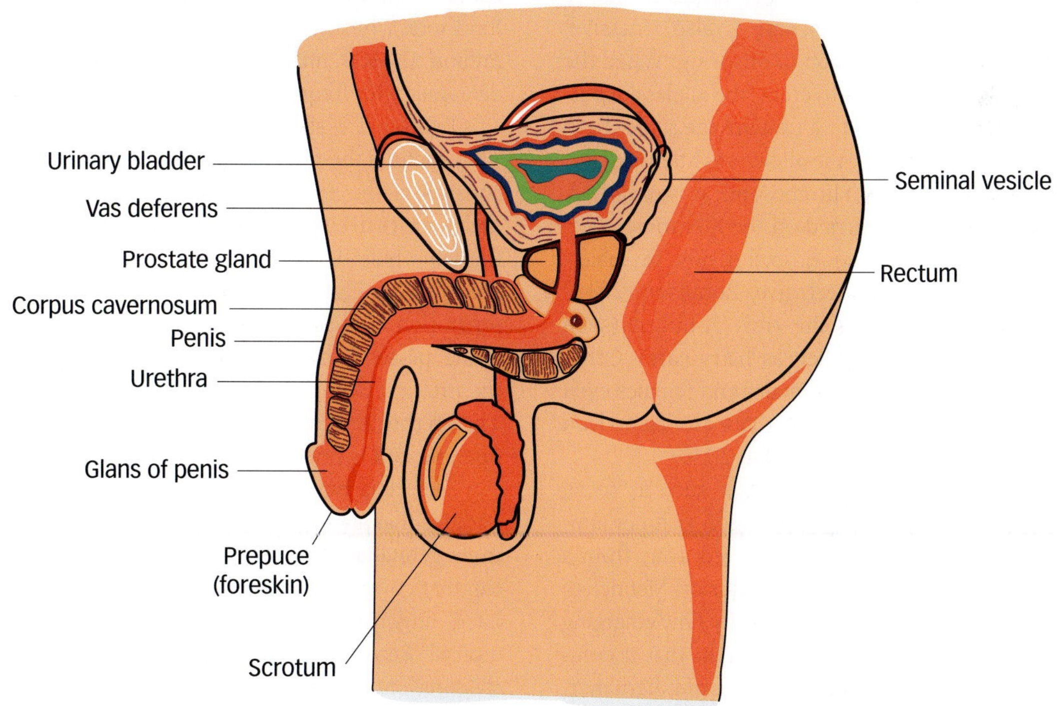

pairs. In the early stages of their development, sperm cells are called spermatocytes. Each contains 46 chromosomes, including both an X and a Y chromosome that determine sex. The X chromosome (female) is larger than the Y (male) chromosome. As the spermatocytes mature and divide, chromosomes are reduced by half, and only one (either the X or Y) sex-determining chromosome is retained. The mature sperm cell is called the spermatozoan. This cell fertilizes the female egg (ovum), which contains only X chromosomes. Thus, the spermatozoan is the determining factor for the child's sex. (Females have two X chromosomes, and males have one X and one Y chromosome.) Chromosomes are threadlike bodies found in the nucleus of a cell that contain the DNA molecule, with each DNA molecule being composed of many genes, or individual segments or subunits of DNA. Any gene that appears at a specific site on a chromosome is called an allele (one member of a pair). Genes carry the code or set of instructions for a specific trait (characteristic). These traits make up the physical, biochemical, and physiologic makeup of every cell in the body.

Robinson (2010) notes that "when genes are passed on, some are assertive and dominant while others are shy and recessive" (Kindle location 376). More commonly we refer to genes as either dominant or recessive. A *dominant gene* is one that expresses its effect in the cell regardless of whether its allele on the matching chromosome is the same or different from the dominant gene (a gene in one strand of DNA that is stronger than the corresponding gene in another strand of DNA), whereas a *recessive gene* is a gene in one strand of DNA that is weaker than the corresponding gene in another strand of DNA, the effect of which is not evident unless its paired allele on the matching chromosome is also recessive. Recessive genes can be passed on to offspring. When the matching genes for a trait are different, the alleles are heterozygous. When the genes for a trait are the same (both dominant or both recessive), the alleles are homozygous. Any trait carried on a sex chromosome is sex linked. Most sex-linked traits are carried on the X chromosome. Sex-linked traits appear almost exclusively in males, and most of these traits are recessive. Robinson (2010) reminds us that "some traits are truly X-linked (such as hemophilia) or Y-linked (such as hairy ears). Other traits are expressed differently in males and females even though the genes that control the traits are located on nonsex chromosomes" (Kindle location 2039).

Of particular interest for professions such as social work is Bonduriansky's (2012) observation that contemporary discussions of heredity have moved away from a "hard heredity" model associated with classical Mendelian genetics. In its place "the model of heredity now emerging is pluralistic, or 'inclusive' or 'extended,' in that it combines genetic and non-genetic mechanisms of inheritance. The pluralistic model therefore recognizes the reality of both hard and soft inheritance, and the potential for a range of intermediate phenomena" (Bonduriansky, 2012, p. 334). Mendelian genetics, or hard heredity, would assert a model of heredity whereby the characteristics of the offspring (child) are determined at the point of conception, "of a set of factors whose nature is unaffected by the environment or phenotype of the parents" (Bonduriansky, 2012, p. 330). Before discussing genetics and social work, we return to the reproductive system.

Before ejaculation, the sperm pass through a number of tubes and glands, beginning with a testis, proceeding through a maze of ducts, and then to an epididymis, which is the convergence of the ducts and serves as the storage facility for sperm in a testicle. Each epididymis empties into the vas deferens, which brings the mature sperm to the seminal vesicles, small glands that lie behind the bladder. In these glands, a nourishing and activating fluid combines with the sperm before the mixture is carried through the urethra to the outside of the penis. The *prostate gland*, through which the urethra passes, produces and introduces the milky fluid that preserves the sperm and neutralizes the alkalinity found in the female reproductive system. Cowper's glands also make their contribution to the seminal fluid before it leaves the male.

However, even if there is early ejaculation and the Cowper's glands do not have time to secrete fluid, viable sperm exist in the ejaculate and can fertilize the female egg. Early withdrawal of the penis from a woman's vagina therefore does not prevent the passage of some viable sperm cells. It is also important to know that sperm only compose about 1% of the ejaculate (3 to 5 milliliters of fluid total), but this small percentage contains from 200 million to 400 million sperm. The number of sperm decreases with frequent ejaculation and advancing age.

Exhibit 3.9 shows the external female sex organs. They include the pudendum, also called the vulva, which consists of the mons veneris, the fatty tissue below the abdomen that becomes covered with hair after puberty; the labia majora and minora; the clitoris; and the vaginal opening. Unlike the male, the female has a physical separation between excretion and reproductive organs. Urine passes from the bladder through the urethra to the urethral opening, where it is expelled from the body. The urethra is located immediately in front of the vaginal opening and is unconnected to it.

The labia majora, large folds of skin, contain nerve endings that are responsive to stimulation and protect the inner genitalia. Labia minora join the prepuce hood at the top that covers the clitoris. These structures, when stimulated, engorge with blood and darken, indicating sexual arousal. Resembling the male penis and developing from the same embryonic tissue, the clitoris is about 1 inch long

EXHIBIT 3.9 • The Female External Sex Organs

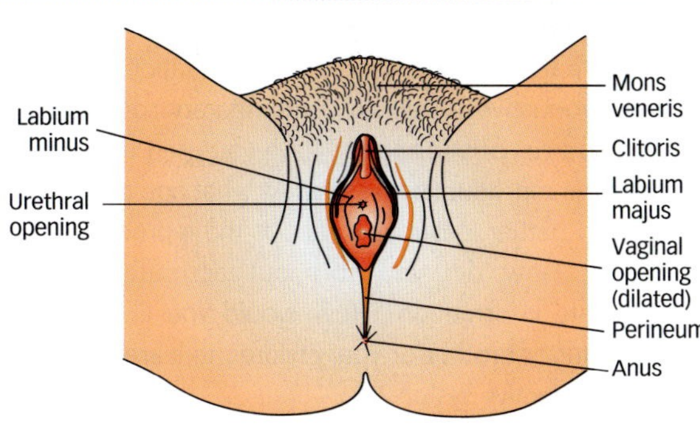

and ¼ inch wide. However, unlike the penis, the clitoris is not directly involved in reproduction but serves primarily to produce sexual pleasure. The vestibule located inside the labia minora contains openings to the urethra and the vagina. It is also a site for arousal because it is rich in nerve endings sensitive to stimulation.

Internal structures of the female reproductive system, shown in Exhibit 3.10, include the vagina, ovaries, fallopian tubes, cervical canal (cervix), and uterus. The vagina connects with the external sexual structures. Composed of three layers and shaped cylindrically, the vagina both receives the penis during intercourse and functions as the birth canal through which the child passes from the uterus to the world outside the mother. Because of its multiple functions, the vagina has the flexibility to expand and contract and to change its climate from dry to lubricated. The cervix is the lower end of the uterus and protrudes into the vagina. It maintains the chemical balance of the vagina through its secretions.

The **uterus**, also called the womb, serves as the pear-shaped home for the unborn child for the 9 months

EXHIBIT 3.10 • The Female Internal Sex Organs

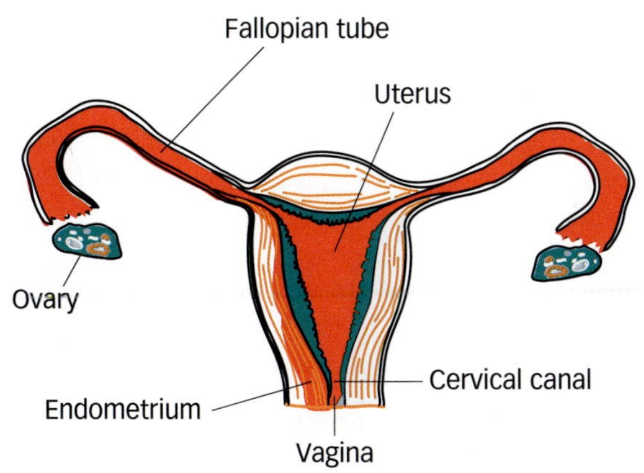

between implantation and birth. The innermost of its three layers, the endometrium, is the tissue that builds to protect and nourish the developing fetus. If pregnancy does not occur, the endometrium is shed monthly through the process of menstruation. If pregnancy does occur, the well-muscled middle layer of the uterus produces the strong contractions necessary at birth to move the fetus out of the uterus, into the vaginal canal, and then into the world. The external layer protects the uterus within the body.

The fallopian tubes connect the ovaries to the uterus and serve as a conduit for the ova (egg cells) from the ovaries to the uterus. Located on either side of the uterus, the ovaries have two major functions: the production of ova and the production of the female sex hormones, progesterone and estrogen.

Until recently it was believed that females were born with the total number of ova they would ever possess. However, several recent studies have strongly suggested that women may make new eggs throughout their reproductive years (Dell'Amore, 2012). This finding could prove to have profound implications not only in terms of overall fertility health but also in terms of our response to issues of women's health, aging, osteoporosis, muscle loss, menopause, and postmenopause (Dell'Amore, 2012).

Estrogen facilitates sexual maturation and regulates the menstrual cycle in premenopausal women. The benefits of estrogen in postmenopausal women, who can only obtain it from taking a supplement, are debatable. Some argue that estrogen maintains cognitive function and cardiac well-being in older women. However, estrogen supplements (also called hormone replacement therapy [HRT]) have been associated with increasing breast and uterine cancer risk, among other problems. Progesterone, though less discussed in the popular media, is critically important in preparing the uterus for pregnancy. It also is a regulator of the menstrual cycle.

Women's breasts are considered to be secondary sex characteristics because they do not have a direct function in reproduction. Mammary glands contained in the breast produce milk that is discharged through the nipples. The nipples are surrounded by the aureoles and become erect when stimulated. The size of the mammary glands is incidental to breast size and milk production. Rather, breast size is a function of the fatty tissue within the breast.

The social worker knowledgeable about interior environment mechanisms can clarify the specifics of male and female sexuality for Juan and Belinda. In the school setting or a local community agency or on virtual sites, youth may talk about their feelings for each other and ask questions regarding sexual and emotional intimacy. It is not unusual for youth to hold misconceptions about heterosexual and other types of sexuality and the biological aspects of sexual intimacy. Accurate information about sexuality could provide a basis for Juan and Belinda to make informed decisions about exercising their options related to sexuality.

Whereas it is beyond the scope of this chapter to discuss sexual activity among diverse genders and sexual orientations, we urge you to consider this important area and the implications for social work practice.

However, as promised, let's briefly return to the topic of genetics. In 1990, the National Institutes of Health and the Department of Energy joined forces with international partners to sequence the *human genome*, the complete set of DNA in the human body, in the Human Genome Project (HGP). Since its inception in 1990, this work has progressed exponentially. In April 2003, researchers announced that they had mapped the complete human genome (National Human Genome Research Institute, 2013). The initial primary goals of the HGP were "(i) to identify all genes of the human genome (initially estimated to be 100,000); (ii) to sequence the approximately 3 billion nucleotides (segments) of the human genome; (iii) to develop databases to store this information; (iv) to develop tools for data analysis; (v) to address ethical, legal, and social issues; and (vi) to sequence a number of 'model organisms'" (Gannett, 2008).

This knowledge has provided researchers and health care professionals with new strategies for diagnosis, treatment, and prevention of a variety of diseases and conditions. It is estimated that the HGP has enabled identification of more than 1,800 disease genes, with more than 2,000 genetic tests for human conditions (National Institutes of Health, 2010). Continued work on the HGP is intended to allow individualized analysis of each person's genome, leading to personalized strategies of intervention, prevention, and "preemptive medicine" (National Institutes of Health, 2010). For social workers, the National Institutes of Health (2010) has also identified that "the increasing ability to connect DNA variation with non-medical conditions, such as intelligence and personality traits, will challenge society, making the role of ethical, legal and social implications research more important than ever" (p. 2).

Given the mission of social work to celebrate diversity, it is incumbent on social workers to reexamine beliefs and practices that are and will be reshaped by the advancement of the HGP and genetic medicine intervention. For example, teasing apart the right to choose to have a child versus abortion as eugenics should be a major ethical debate engaged by social work. Questions such as which interior traits should be eliminated and how are critical bioethical concerns. Moreover, the intersection of economic disparity and unequal access to genetic medicine is a policy and praxis issue to be engaged within our profession.

CRITICAL THINKING Questions 3.4

What are the available sources of information about the reproductive system in contemporary societies? What sources of information have you used to learn about the reproductive system? At what age did you begin to gather information about the reproductive system? How did you sort out accurate from inaccurate information? How would you like your little sister or brother or your children to learn about the reproductive system?

EXTERIOR SOCIOECONOMIC ENVIRONMENT AND INTERIOR HEALTH ENVIRONMENT

Public health experts have long noted the association of poor health outcomes, in all body systems, with low income, low education, unsanitary housing, inadequate health care, unstable employment, and unsafe physical environments (Engels, 1892; Speybroeck et al., 2010). Until recently, however, researchers have made little attempt to understand the reasons behind this empirically supported connection of socioeconomic status (SES) and health. Beginning in 2000, there was a big jump in research on health inequalities related to SES, oppression, and discrimination in the United States (Adler & Stewart, 2010a).

In a review of research on socioeconomic status and health, Nancy Adler and Judith Stewart (2010b) noted that in the United States about twice as many Blacks and Hispanics report being in poor or fair health as Whites and that adults living in poverty are about five times as likely as adults with the highest incomes to report poor or fair health. Their review of the research indicates several mechanisms by which "socioeconomic status gets under the skin" (p. 11), including these:

- *Differential access to health care.* Health insurance alone does not guarantee access to health care. Other important access issues include "travel time, transportation availability and cost, scheduling flexibility, sense of self-efficacy and control" (p. 12). In addition, they note that health promotion is more important than disease treatment for overall health and longevity.

- *Environmental exposures.* People with lower SES have greater exposure to such environmental hazards as

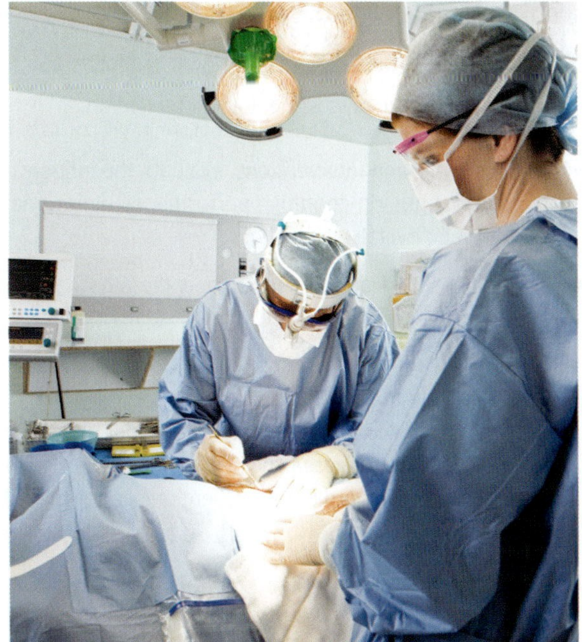

© Jupiterimages/Polka Dot/Thinkstock

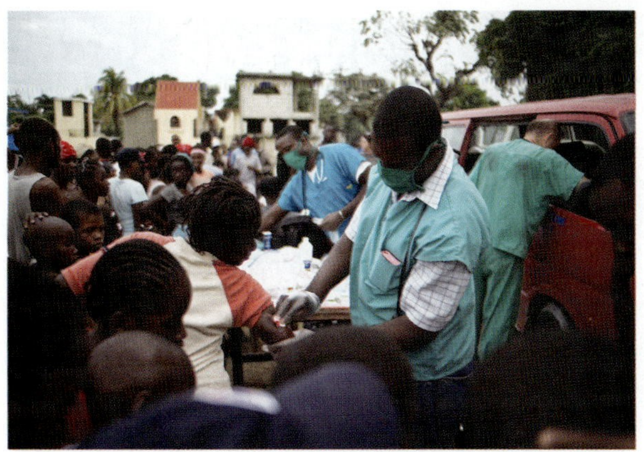

FRED DUFOUR/Staff/AFP/Getty Images

Biological health and illness greatly affect human behavior. Here, contrast how medical care is delivered in two very different situations: one in a high-tech operating room in the United States and the other in a temporary clinic in Haiti.

air, water, and noise pollution; hazardous waste; and toxins than people with higher SES. These environmental factors have received limited research to date.

- *Health behaviors.* People with lower incomes are more likely than people with higher incomes to be engaged in several types of risky health behaviors, including smoking, physical inactivity, and unhealthy diet. There is some evidence that these behaviors are used as coping strategies in the face of stress.
- *Exposures to stress.* Chronic stress has been linked to such adverse health outcomes as hypertension, susceptibility to infection, buildup of fat in blood vessels and the abdomen, and brain cell atrophy. It has also been linked to premature aging at the cellular level, indicated by reduced length of telomeres. A long line of research indicates that chronic stress increases as economic class decreases.
- *Neighborhood and community.* Individuals living in low-income neighborhoods have been found to have poorer health than individuals living in middle- or high-income neighborhoods, whether or not they themselves are poor.

The research so far supports the notion that the health care system alone cannot offset the effects of other external environment forces on health. Therefore, an important social work domain is public health research and practice. One study found that governmental policies aimed at reducing social inequalities result in lowered infant mortality rates and increased life expectancy at birth (Navarro et al., 2006).

An additional critical factor in health status (positive and negative) involves health literacy. The Institute of Medicine defines health literacy as "the degree to which individuals have the capacity to obtain, process, and understand the basic health information and services needed to make appropriate health decisions" (National Network of Libraries of Medicine, 2013, para. 1). Health literacy involves much more than simply translating health information into multiple languages. It also involves consideration of reading and listening skills; analytic and decision-making skills; and the freedom to be able to engage in dialogue, questioning, and critical evaluation of health information and health care options.

CRITICAL THINKING Questions 3.5

What could be some reasons why the incidence of heart attack, cancer, homicide, and infant mortality increases as the level of societal inequality increases? What are the implications of these statistics for public health policies?

IMPLICATIONS FOR SOCIAL WORK PRACTICE

This discussion of the interior biological person suggests several principles for social work assessment and intervention.

- Develop a working knowledge of the body's interior environmental systems, their interconnectedness, and the ways they interact with other dimensions of human behavior.
- In assessments and interventions, recognize that interior environmental conditions of health and illness are influenced by the exterior environmental social, political, cultural, and economic context.
- Recognize that the exterior environmental meanings attached to health and illness may influence not only the physical experience but also the values and socioemotional response assigned to health and illness.
- In assessment and intervention activities, look for the ways behavior affects biological functions and the ways biological functions affect behavior.
- In assessment and interventions, evaluate the influence of health status on cognitive performance, emotional comfort, and overall well-being.
- In assessment and intervention, consider the ways in which one person's interior environment health status is affecting other people in the person's exterior environment.
- Where appropriate, incorporate multiple social work roles into practice related to the health of the biological system, including the roles of researcher, clinician, educator, case manager, service coordinator, prevention specialist, and policy advocate.

KEY TERMS

acquired immunodeficiency syndrome (AIDS), 72
antibodies, 74
antigens, 72
assistive devices, 79
atria, 76
autoimmune disease, 72
axon, 68
blood pressure, 77
brain injury (BI), 66
cardiovascular system, 75
diabetes mellitus, 71
endocrine system, 70
feedback control mechanism, 71
high blood pressure (hypertension), 75
human immunodeficiency virus (HIV), 72
immune system, 72
lymphocytes, 73
musculoskeletal system, 78
nervous system, 67
neuron, 68
neuroplasticity, 69
neurotransmitters, 68
nonspecific immunity, 74
specific immunity, 74
synapse, 68
testes, 81
uterus, 83
ventricles, 76

ACTIVE LEARNING

1. You have been asked by the local public middle school to teach youth about the experience of living with one of the following conditions: brain injury, diabetes, HIV, high blood pressure, or multiple sclerosis. Working in small groups, locate literature and web resources on your chosen topic, select the material you wish to present, and prepare a presentation in lay terms that will be accessible to the youth audience.
2. Working in small groups, prepare two arguments, one supporting and one opposing sex education in public schools. Give some consideration to content that should or should not be included in sex education programs in public schools and the ages at which such education should occur. Provide evidence for your arguments.
3. *Theory analysis and application.* It might be said that much of the content in this chapter reflects the systems perspective as discussed in Chapter 2. Working in groups of three to four, review the big ideas of the systems perspective presented in Exhibit 2.9. Giving specific examples, discuss how these big ideas are reflected, or not, in the discussion of the biological person presented in this chapter. Do you see big ideas from other perspectives, as presented in Exhibit 2.9, that could be useful in thinking about the biological person? How could the systems perspective guide you in thinking about how to provide services to people with health challenges?

WEB RESOURCES

American Diabetes Association

www.diabetes.org

Site contains basic diabetes information as well as specific information on type 1 diabetes, type 2 diabetes, community resources, and healthy living.

American Heart Association

www.americanheart.org

Site contains information on diseases and conditions, healthy lifestyles, and health news and a heart and stroke encyclopedia.

Centers for Disease Control and Prevention (CDC) Division of HIV/AIDS Prevention

www.cdc.gov/hiv

Site contains basic science information on HIV/AIDS, basic statistics, fact sheets, and links to other resource sites.

Guttmacher Institute

www.guttmacher.org

Site presented by the Guttmacher Institute (formerly the Alan Guttmacher Institute)—a nonprofit organization that focuses on sexual and reproductive health research, policy analysis, and public education—contains information on abortion, law and public policy, pregnancy and birth, pregnancy and disease prevention and contraception, sexual behavior, sexually transmitted infections and HIV, and sexuality and youth.

MacArthur Research Network on SES & Health

www.macses.ucsf.edu

Site has overviews of questions of interest to four working groups: a social environment group, a psychosocial group, an allostatic load (physiological wear and tear on the body resulting from chronic stress) group, and a developmental group.

Multiple Sclerosis Association of America (MSAA)

www.mymsaa.org

Site contains news and helpful information for managing multiple sclerosis.

National Center for Health Statistics

www.cdc.gov/nchs

Site contains FastStats on a wide range of health topics as well as news releases and a publication listing.

Neuroscience for Kids

http://faculty.washington.edu/chudler/neurok.html

Site maintained by faculty at the University of Washington presents basic neuroscience information on the brain, spinal cord, peripheral nervous system, neurons, and sensory system, including the effects of drugs on the nervous system and neurological and mental disorders.

SAGE edge™ **Sharpen your skills with SAGE edge at edge.sagepub.com/hutchisoness2e**

SAGE edge for students provides a personalized approach to help you accomplish your coursework goals in an easy-to-use learning environment. watch listen read

LEARNING OBJECTIVES	FOR FURTHER EXPLORATION AND APPLICATION
LO 3.1: Compare and contrast one's emotional and cognitive reactions to six case studies.	(listen) Diabetes: 7 Lessons on the Basics (listen) Mutiple Sclerosis
LO 3.2: Use theory to summarize the intersection of the interior body and the exterior environment.	(watch) Expanded Maslow's Hierarchy of Needs
LO 3.3: Recognize the major functions of six biological systems: nervous, endocrine, immune, cardiovascular, musculoskeletal, and reproductive.	(read) Self-Reflective Meaning Making in Troubled Times: Change in Self-Identity After Traumatic Brain Injury (watch) Genetics and Pregnancy (read) Human Biology
LO 3.4: Explain the association between health outcomes and socioeconomic circumstances.	(read) "Macho Men" and Preventive Health Care: Implications for Older Men in Different Social Classes
LO 3.5: Apply knowledge of human biology to recommend guidelines for social work assessment and intervention.	(watch) The Affordable Care Act: Opportunities for Social Work Practice in Integrated Settings (read) NSWA Healthcare Standards

The Psychological Person

Joseph Walsh

Learning Objectives

LO 4.1 Analyze one's emotional and cognitive reactions to a case study.

LO 4.2 Define cognition and emotion.

LO 4.3 Compare and contrast five major theories of cognition (cognitive, information processing, social learning, multiple intelligences, and moral reasoning) and cognitive behavioral intervention theory.

LO 4.4 Compare and contrast four major categories of theories of emotion (physiological theories, psychological theories, social theories, and social work practice theories).

LO 4.5 Recognize how cognitive and emotional characteristics can be involved in cognitive and emotional "disorders."

LO 4.6 Describe four theories of self in relationships (relational, attachment, feminist, and social identity).

LO 4.7 Summarize the role of stress, crisis, and traumatic stress in human behavior.

LO 4.8 Analyze different styles of coping and adaptation in relation to stress.

LO 4.9 Critique four different approaches to normal and abnormal coping (medical, psychological, sociological, and social work).

LO 4.10 Apply knowledge of cognition, emotion, self, the self in relationship, stress, and coping to recommend guidelines for social work assessment and intervention.

GET MORE OUT OF YOUR STUDY TIME.

The **SAGE Interactive eBook** provides one-click access to integrated study tools that will enrich your understanding of course content.

- **Watch** video clips to learn actively
- **Think Critically** with SAGE Journals
- **Explore Further** with SAGE Reference
- **Connect** with relevant web resources
- **Listen** to podcasts for real-world context

CASE STUDY

THE PREMED STUDENT

Dan Lee was a 24-year-old single Chinese American male undergraduate student working toward admission into medical school when he came to the university counseling center to get help with his feelings of anxiety, tension, sadness, and anger and also for some ongoing interpersonal conflicts. Dan was having difficulty concentrating on his studies and was in danger of failing a course he needed to pass in order to stay on track for medical school. He was specifically preoccupied with perceived personal slights from several friends, his sister, and his mother. Dan told the social worker that he needed help learning how to get these significant others to behave more responsibly toward him so that he could focus more intensively on his own work. Dan reported that he also had been diagnosed several years ago with an auditory processing disorder, which meant he was slow to process other people's verbal communications at times and prepare his responses to them.

Dan is the older of two children (his sister was 22) born to a couple who had grown up in Taiwan and moved to the United States before the children were born. His father, a surgeon, and his mother, a homemaker, had divorced when Dan was 7. He and his sister had lived with their mother since then and only had occasional contact with their father. Dan had internalized the values of his family and culture; he understood that he needed to assume primary responsibility for the well-being of his mother and sister while also achieving high social status for himself. He also exhibited the cultural value of obedience to authority and saw himself as the family's primary authority figure, being the only male member. While a student at the diverse university, Dan maintained cultural ties through his membership in a church that served the Chinese American community.

Dan tried hard to be a good son and brother but held a firm position that others should always accede to his directives. He believed he was always "right" in decisions he made about his mother and sister (regarding where they lived, how his mother spent her time, and what kinds of friends and career choices his sister should make). Regarding his friends, who were mostly limited to casual contacts at school and at his volunteer job at a community health center, Dan felt that whenever there was a conflict or misunderstanding it was always "their fault." He felt disrespected at these times and became so preoccupied with these "unjust sleights" that he couldn't concentrate on much else for days afterward. Dan gave one example of a friend who had arrived more than 20 minutes late on two occasions for scheduled social outings. The second time he demanded that the friend apologize for being irresponsible and insensitive, and when the friend did not do so to Dan's satisfaction, the relationship ended. These kinds of relationship disruptions were common in his life. Dan's family and friends often did not accept his admonitions, and he wanted to learn from the social worker how to better help these other people see that he was always "rational" and "correct" in his thinking. Dan had warmer feelings toward his peers at church, all of whom were Asian Americans. He spent most of his Sunday afternoons there, participating in social events and singing in the choir. Dan was also in regular contact with an ex-girlfriend, mostly by e-mail but occasionally by phone. He had broken up with her 6 months ago, and whereas she hoped they would resume a romantic relationship, Dan did not think this would happen.

Spencer, the social worker, was a U.S.-born Caucasian male, several years older than Dan, who had some understanding of the Chinese value system in which the client was raised. He liked Dan, appreciating his intelligence, his motivation to get help, and his ability to articulate his concerns, but he also observed that Dan demonstrated a striking rigidity in his attitudes toward others. Still, he initially validated Dan's perspective on the presenting issues. Spencer easily engaged Dan in substantive conversations each time they met, reflecting back to Dan the difficulty of his competing demands and desire to help his family lead safe and productive lives. Before long, however, Dan began challenging Spencer's nondirective feedback. "I want to know what you think I should do here." "How can I approach my sister so she won't be so defensive about my input?" "I tell my mother she shouldn't speak to my dad so often, but she keeps doing so anyway. How can I get her to stop?"

Dan was having difficulty balancing his desires for personal development with his need to care for two adult family members in the manner he felt appropriate. He seemed to have internalized conditions of worth related to his family responsibility and, due to having begun doing so at such a young age, had become quite rigid in his approach to helping the family. Dan's defensive posture involved distorting the motives of others as oppositional rather than expressions of their own personal inclinations. Further, he never seemed to be able to relax and have fun, except when at church. In recognizing Dan's rigidity as a defense, Spencer helped him reflect on the possibility that the behaviors of others toward him might not be intentionally oppositional but reflective of differences of opinion and that perhaps Dan could feel good about his well-meaning efforts while recognizing that one's influence over others cannot be absolute.

Spencer was patient in his responses to Dan: "It's a difficult situation you are in, and you're trying your hardest to do the best for your family, and it's frustrating that you can't find ways to help them understand your concern." "It hurts you to see other people move in directions you believe are not good for them." "You feel strongly that certain people should do what you suggest even though they disagree." Still, despite these empathic responses that Spencer believed reflected positive regard, Dan became increasingly frustrated with the social worker. "I thought you were a professional. I thought you were trained to help people. Why can't you come up with some new ideas for me to try?"

Dan's emotions were not always evident beneath his rigid exterior. The primary feelings he expressed to the social worker were anxiety, anger, sadness, and frustration. Over time Dan continued to function with his rigid perspective. He tried to consider his situation from the points of view of others, but he always came back to the position that he was "rational" and others were "irrational." He occasionally accused the social worker of being incompetent for not answering his questions concretely enough. Spencer himself became frustrated with his inability to help Dan broaden his perspective on interpersonal differences and Dan's inability to distinguish disagreement from disrespect. During the course of their year of working together, Spencer employed the following interventions, which alternately focused on Dan's thinking and emotions: cognitive therapy (restructuring), behavioral change, and psychodynamic therapy (so that Dan might become more aware of the range of his feelings and how the sources of his anger might be based in his family history and early upbringing). Whereas Dan noted little progress for several months, Spencer was encouraged by the fact that he continued coming in faithfully, week after week.

Spencer's work with Dan experienced its most success with a series of behavioral interventions. Spencer helped Dan to use relaxation techniques and to consider the environments in which he was best able to focus on his studies. They determined, for example, that Dan was best able to concentrate during the middle of the day and when there were people around him. They set up a schedule of study in the medical library, where Dan could sit at a table with other students (whom he did not necessarily know). Spencer rehearsed deep-breathing activities with Dan, which helped calm his anxieties, and he further suggested that Dan study after a physical workout, when his body was calmer (Dan enjoyed swimming). Spencer also suggested that physical activity might help him release some of his anger after an interpersonal conflict.

Dan never articulated openly that his ideas about the appropriate behavior of others were anything but "correct," but over time he reported fewer conflicts with his sister, mother, and peers, and his study habits and grades improved to the point that he was admitted to medical school. After a year-long weekly intervention Dan finally decided to terminate because of his busy medical school schedule. During their final session together, he said to Spencer, "I don't know how much I've gotten out of this, but I know you tried to help, and I appreciate that."

Reviewing the intervention with his supervisor, Spencer regretted that he had felt such frustration with Dan, but he felt he had been able to contain those feelings. Further, despite Dan's ongoing misgivings about the quality of the intervention, he had continued meeting with Spencer for a full year and eventually demonstrated behaviors evident of improvement. It seemed that Dan had reached a higher level of adaptability even though it wasn't as apparent to him.

COGNITION AND EMOTION

Dan's problems at college reflect his personal **psychology**, which can be defined as his mind and his mental processes. His story illustrates the impact on social functioning of a person's particular patterns of cognition and emotion. **Cognition** can be defined as our conscious or preconscious thinking processes—the mental activities of which we are aware or can become aware with reflection. Cognition includes taking in relevant information from the environment, synthesizing that information, and formulating a plan of action based on that synthesis (Ronen & Freeman, 2007). *Beliefs*, key elements of our cognition, are ideas we hold to be true. Our assessment of any idea as true or false is based on the synthesis of information. Erroneous beliefs, which may result from misinterpretations of perceptions or from conclusions based on insufficient evidence, frequently contribute to social dysfunction.

Emotion is a difficult concept to define but can be understood as a feeling state characterized by our appraisal of a stimulus, changes in bodily sensations, and displays of expressive gestures (Mulligan & Scherer, 2012). The term *emotion* is often used interchangeably in the study of psychology with the term *affect*, but the latter refers only to the physiological manifestations of feelings. Affect may be the result of *drives* (innate compulsions to gratify basic needs), which generate both conscious and **unconscious** feelings (those of which we are not aware but that influence our behavior). In contrast, emotion is always consciously experienced. Likewise, emotion is not the same as *mood*, a feeling disposition that is more stable than emotion, usually less intense, and less tied to a specific situation.

The evolution of psychological thought since the late 1800s has consisted largely of a debate about cognition and emotion—their origins, the nature of their influence on behavior, and their influence on each other. The only point of agreement seems to be that cognition and emotion are complex and interactive.

THEORIES OF COGNITION

Theories of cognition, which emerged in the 1950s, assume that conscious thinking is the basis for almost all behavior and emotions. Emotions are defined within these theories as the physiological responses that follow our cognitive evaluations of input. In other words, thoughts produce emotions.

COGNITIVE THEORY

Jean Piaget's cognitive development theory is the most influential theory of cognition in social work and psychology (Lightfoot, Lalonde, & Chandler, 2004). In his system, our capacity for reasoning develops in stages, from infancy through adolescence and early adulthood. Piaget saw the four stages presented in Exhibit 4.1 as sequential and interdependent, evolving from activity without thought, to thought with less emphasis on activity—from doing, to doing knowingly, and finally to conceptualizing. He saw normal physical and neurological development as necessary for cognitive development.

A central concept in Piaget's theory is that of the **schema** (plural *schemata*), defined as an internalized representation of the world or an ingrained and systematic pattern of thought, action, and problem solving. Our schemata develop through *social learning* (watching and absorbing the experiences of others) or *direct learning* (our own experiences). Both of these processes may involve **assimilation** (responding to experiences based on existing schemata) or **accommodation** (changing schemata when new situations cannot be incorporated within an existing one). As children, we are motivated to develop schemata as a means of maintaining psychological *equilibrium*, or balance. Any experience that we cannot assimilate creates anxiety, but if our schemata are adjusted to accommodate the new experience, the desired state of equilibrium will be restored. From this perspective, you might interpret Dan's difficulties with his college peers as an inability to achieve equilibrium by assimilating new interactional experience within his existing schemata. Dan was accustomed to functioning within a relatively small group of family and friends from his own cultural background, where roles were clearly defined. He could not easily adjust to the challenge of managing relationships among a much larger and more diverse student population, where the members' motivations and worldviews were difficult to comprehend.

INFORMATION PROCESSING THEORY

Cognitive theory has been very influential, but, as you might guess, it leaves many aspects of cognitive functioning

EXHIBIT 4.1 • Piaget's Stages of Cognitive Operations

STAGE	DESCRIPTION
Sensorimotor stage (birth to 2 years)	The infant is egocentric; he or she gradually learns to coordinate sensory and motor activities and develops a beginning sense of objects existing apart from the self.
Preoperational stage (2 to 7 years)	The child remains primarily egocentric but discovers rules (regularities) that can be applied to new incoming information. The child tends to overgeneralize rules, however, and thus makes many cognitive errors.
Concrete operations stage (7 to 11 years)	The child can solve concrete problems through the application of logical problem-solving strategies.
Formal operations stage (11 to adulthood)	The person becomes able to solve real and hypothetical problems using abstract concepts.

© iStockphoto.com/BraunS

Information processing theory would suggest that the information these children are receiving from the computer flows through their senses to their minds, which operate much like computers.

unexplained. Whereas Piaget sought to explain how cognition develops, *information processing theory* offers details about how our cognitive processes are organized (Logan, 2000). This theory makes a clear distinction between the thinker and the external environment; each is an independent, objective entity in the processing of inputs and outputs. We receive stimulation from the outside and code it with sensory receptors in the nervous system. The information is first represented in some set of brain activities and is then integrated (by accommodation or assimilation) and stored for purposes of present and future adaptation to the environment. All of us develop increasingly sophisticated problem-solving processes through the evolution of our cognitive patterns, which enable us to draw attention to particular inputs as significant. Information processing is a *sensory theory* in that it depicts information as flowing passively from the external world inward through the senses to the mind. It views the mind as having distinct parts—including the sensory register, short-term memory, and long-term memory—that make unique contributions to thinking in a specific sequence. In contrast, a *motor theory* such as Piaget's sees the mind as playing an active role in processing—not merely recording but actually constructing the nature of the input it receives.

SOCIAL LEARNING THEORY

According to *social learning theory*, we are motivated by nature to experience pleasure and avoid pain. Social learning theorists acknowledge that thoughts and emotions exist but understand them as behaviors in need of explaining rather than as primary motivating factors. Social learning theory relies to a great extent on social behavioral principles of conditioning, which assert that behavior is shaped by its reinforcing or punishing consequences (operant conditioning) and antecedents (classical conditioning). Albert Bandura (1977b) added the principle of vicarious learning, or *modeling*, which puts forth that behavior is also acquired by witnessing how the actions of others are reinforced.

Social learning theorists, unlike other social behavioral theorists, assert that thinking takes place between the occurrence of a stimulus and our response. They call this thought process *cognitive mediation*. The unique patterns we learn for evaluating environmental stimuli explain why each of us may adopt very different behaviors in response to the same stimulus—for example, why Dan's reaction to the behavior of his peers is very different from how many of them might react to each other. Bandura takes this idea a step further and asserts that we engage in self-observations and make self-judgments about our competence and mastery.

EXHIBIT 4.2 • Gardner's Eight Intelligences

INTELLIGENCE	DESCRIPTION
Linguistic intelligence	The capacity to use language to express what is on your mind and to understand other people. Linguistic intelligence includes listening, speaking, reading, and writing skills.
Logical/ mathematical intelligence	The capacity for mathematical calculation, logical thinking, problem solving, deductive and inductive reasoning, and the discernment of patterns and relationships. Gardner suggests that this is the type of intelligence addressed by Piaget's model of cognitive development, but he does not think Piaget's model fits other types of intelligence.
Visual-spatial intelligence	The ability to represent the spatial world internally in your mind. Visual-spatial intelligence involves visual discrimination, recognition, projection, mental imagery, spatial reasoning, and image manipulation.
Bodily kinesthetic intelligence	The capacity to use your whole body or parts of your body to solve a problem, make something, or put on some kind of production. Gardner suggests that our tradition of separating body and mind is unfortunate because the mind can be trained to use the body properly and the body trained to respond to the expressive powers of the mind. He notes that some learners rely on tactile and kinesthetic processes, not just visual and auditory processes.
Musical intelligence	The capacity to think in musical images, to be able to hear patterns, recognize them, remember them, and perhaps manipulate them.
Intrapersonal intelligence	The capacity to understand yourself, to know who you are, what you can do, what you want to do, how you react to things, which things to avoid, which things to gravitate toward, and where to go if you need help. Gardner says we are drawn to people who have a good understanding of themselves because those people tend not to make mistakes. They are aware of their range of emotions and can find outlets for expressing feelings and thoughts. They are motivated to pursue goals and live by an ethical value system.
Interpersonal intelligence	The ability to understand and communicate with others, to note differences in moods, temperaments, motivations, and skills. Interpersonal intelligence includes the ability to form and maintain relationships and assume various roles within groups and the ability to adapt behavior to different environments. It also includes the ability to perceive diverse perspectives on social and political issues. Gardner suggests that individuals with this intelligence express an interest in interpersonally oriented careers, such as teaching, social work, and politics.
Naturalist intelligence	The ability to recognize and categorize objects and processes in nature. Naturalist intelligence leads to talent in caring for, taming, and interacting with the natural environment, including living creatures. Gardner suggests that naturalist intelligence can also be brought to bear to discriminate among artificial items such as sneakers, cars, and toys.

SOURCE: Based on Gardner, 1999, 2006.

We then act on the basis of these self-judgments. Bandura (2001) criticizes information processing theory for its passive view of human agency, arguing that it omits important features of what it means to be human, including subjective consciousness, deliberative action, and the capacity for self-reflection. For example, Dan may have made some negative self-judgments about his competence to complete his premed studies that are affecting his functioning.

THEORY OF MULTIPLE INTELLIGENCES

Howard Gardner's (1999, 2006) theory of **multiple intelligences** constitutes a major step forward in our understanding of how people come to possess different types of cognitive skills and how the same person is able to effectively use cognition and emotion in some areas of life but not others. In this theory, intelligence is defined as a "biopsychosocial potential to process information that can be activated in a cultural setting to solve problems or create products that are of value in a culture" (Gardner, 1999, p. 23).

The brain is understood not as a single cognitive system but as a central unit of neurological functioning that houses relatively separate cognitive faculties. During its evolution, the brain has developed separate organs, or modules, as information-processing devices. Thus, all of us have a unique blend of intelligences derived from these modules. Gardner has delineated eight intelligences, which are described in Exhibit 4.2, although in his ongoing research he is considering additional possibilities. Two intelligences, the *linguistic* (related to spoken and written language) and the *logical-mathematical* (analytic), are most consistent with traditional notions of intelligence. You may be interested to note that in one study, social work educators rated intrapersonal, interpersonal, and linguistic intelligences as the most important for social work practice, and the same educators rated bodily kinesthetic, musical, and spatial intelligences as important for culturally sensitive practice (Matto, Berry-Edwards, Hutchison, Bryant, & Waldbillig, 2006).

The theory of multiple intelligences is rather new and has not yet been empirically validated by research (Waterhouse, 2010). Still, it has proven useful in understanding a person's range of strengths and can even serve as a guide for social work practitioners in deciding on interventions that will maximize client motivation and participation (for example, art therapy for persons with strong visual-spatial intelligence) (Booth & O'Brien, 2008). One of the most positive implications of the theory of multiple intelligences is that it helps us see strengths in ourselves that lie outside the mainstream. Dan has a strong logico-mathematical intelligence that contributes to his ability to master difficult physiological concepts. He may benefit from help, however, in further development of his intrapersonal and interpersonal domains, especially outside his cultural group.

THEORIES OF MORAL REASONING

Morality is our sensitivity to, and perceptions of, what is right and wrong. It develops from our acquired principles of justice and ways of caring for others. Theories of moral reasoning are similar to those of cognitive development in that a sequential process is involved. Familiarity with these theories can help social workers understand how clients make decisions and develop preferences for action in various situations. Both of these issues are important in our efforts to develop goals with clients. The best-known theories of moral reasoning are those of Lawrence Kohlberg and Carol Gilligan. In reviewing these theories, it is important to keep in mind that they are based on studies of men and women in the United States.

Kohlberg (1969) formulated six stages of moral development, divided into three levels, which begin in childhood and unfold through adolescence and young adulthood (see Exhibit 4.3). The first two stages represent *preconventional morality* in which the child's primary motivation is to avoid immediate punishment and receive immediate rewards. *Conventional morality* emphasizes adherence to social rules. A person at this level of morality might be very troubled, as Dan is, by circumstances that make him or her different from other people. Many people never move beyond this level to *postconventional morality*, which is characterized by a concern with moral principles transcending those of their own society.

One limitation of Kohlberg's theory is that it does not take into account gender differences (his participants were all male). In fact, he claims that women do not advance through all six stages as often as men. Addressing this issue, Gilligan (1982, 1988) notes that boys tend to emphasize independence, autonomy, and the rights of others in their moral thinking, using a *justice-oriented* approach. Girls, on the other hand, develop an ethic of *care* and *interdependence* that grows out of a concern for the needs of others rather than the value of independence. To account for this difference, Gilligan proposed the three stages of moral development listed in Exhibit 4.4. Her stages place greater emphasis than Kohlberg does on the ethic of care and are meant to more accurately describe the moral development of females. The research findings on gender differences in moral reasoning are inconsistent, however (see, e.g., Donleavy, 2008; Hauser, Cushman, Young, Mikhail, & Jin, 2007; Malti, Gasser, & Buchmann, 2009).

With his great concern about individual achievement, along with a desire to care for his sister and mother, Dan seems to fall into Kohlberg's stage of conventional morality and Gilligan's stage of conventional care, but this may reflect both gender and culture. Researchers have found that culture may have a greater influence on moral reasoning than gender does, with Anglo Americans

EXHIBIT 4.3 • Kohlberg's Levels and Stages of Moral Development

STAGE	DESCRIPTION
PRECONVENTIONAL LEVEL	
Stage 1: Heteronomous morality	Accepting what the world says is right
Stage 2: Instrumental purpose	Defining the good as whatever is agreeable to the self and those in the immediate environment
CONVENTIONAL LEVEL	
Stage 3: Interpersonal experiences	Seeking conformity and consistency in moral action with significant others
Stage 4: The societal point of view	Seeking conformity and consistency with what one perceives to be the opinions of the larger community
POSTCONVENTIONAL LEVEL	
Stage 5: Ethics	Observing individual and group (societal) rights
Stage 6: Conscience and logic	Seeking to apply universal principles of right and wrong

EXHIBIT 4.4 • Gilligan's Three Stages of Moral Development

STAGE	DESCRIPTION
Survival orientation	Egocentric concerns of emotional and physical survival are primary.
Conventional care	The person defines as right those actions that please significant others.
Integrated care	A person's right actions take into account the needs of others as well as the self.

putting less emphasis on an ethic of care than members of other ethnic groups (Gardiner & Kosmitzki, 2011). Gardiner and Kosmitzki (2011) argue that moral development may not follow a universal script across cultures and suggest that the ecological system in which early social interactions occur shapes moral thought and behavior. For understanding moral reasoning across cultures, they recommend a social constructionist theory of moral development proposed by Haan (1991) and Neff and Helwig (2002), who suggest that moral reasoning comes from the understanding of the interdependence of self and others that develops through social interactions. They propose that the most mature moral reasoner is the one who makes moral decisions that balance the person's own needs and desires with those of others affected by the issue at hand. Haan found that people who are able to control their own emotions in order to think about possible solutions engage in higher levels of moral action than people who are not able to control their emotions. Research has tended to support the idea that moral development unfolds in stages across cultures (Gibbs, Basinger, Grime, & Snarey, 2007).

THEORIES OF COGNITION IN SOCIAL WORK PRACTICE

When theories of cognition first emerged, they represented a reaction against psychodynamic theories, which focused on the influence of unconscious thought. Many practitioners had come to believe that although some mental processes may be categorized as unconscious, they have only a minor influence on behavior. Rather, conscious thinking is the basis for almost all behavior and emotions (J. Walsh, 2014).

According to cognitive theory, we are "rational" to the extent that our schemata, the basis for our perceptions, accommodate available environmental evidence and our decisions do not rely solely on preconceived notions about the external world. So long as our cognitive style helps us to achieve our goals, it is considered healthy. However, thinking patterns can become distorted, featuring patterns of bias that dismiss relevant environmental information from judgment, which can lead in turn to the maladaptive emotional responses described in Exhibit 4.5. These *cognitive distortions* are habits of thought that lead us at times to distort input from the environment and experience psychological distress (A. T. Beck, 1976; J. S. Beck, 2005).

As a social worker, you could use cognitive theory to surmise that Dan is distressed because he subjectively assesses some of his life situations in a distorted manner. For example, *arbitrary inferences* may lead him to conclude that because other students do not share his perspectives on how they should behave, they do not respect his point of view. Because he concludes this, he may also conclude that he will continue to feel isolated from his peers, and this thought produces his emotional response of sadness.

To adjust his emotions and mood, Dan needs to learn to evaluate his external environment differently. He needs to consider changing some of the beliefs, expectations, and meanings he attaches to events, because they are not objectively true. He might conclude, for example, that people possess honest differences of opinion and that

EXHIBIT 4.5 • Common Cognitive Distortions

COGNITIVE ERROR	DESCRIPTION
Absolute thinking	Viewing experiences as all good or all bad and failing to understand that experiences can be a mixture of both
Overgeneralization	Assuming that deficiencies in one area of life necessarily imply deficiencies in other areas
Selective abstraction	Focusing only on the negative aspects of a situation and consequently overlooking its positive aspects
Arbitrary inference	Reaching a negative conclusion about a situation with insufficient evidence
Magnification	Creating large problems out of small ones
Minimization	Making large problems small and thus not dealing adequately with them
Personalization	Accepting blame for negative events without sufficient evidence

some of his peers appreciate him more than he assumes. He may even notice that their opinions are consistent with his more than he realizes. Cognitive theorists would make Dan's thinking the primary target of change activity, assuming that cognitive change will in turn produce changes in his emotional states.

Cognitive theory is a highly rational approach to human behavior. Even though the theory assumes that some of a person's beliefs are irrational and distorted, it also assumes that human beings have great potential to correct these beliefs in light of contradictory evidence. In clinical assessment, the social worker must assess the client's schemata and identify the source of his or her difficulties as being rooted in cognitive deficits, distortions, or accurate assessment of a situation. During intervention, the social worker helps the client adjust his or her cognitive processes to better facilitate the attainment of goals. As a result, the client will also experience more positive emotions. It is important to emphasize that clients are not encouraged to rationalize all of their problems as involving faulty assumptions, because many challenges people face are due to oppressive external circumstances. Still, Dan's belief that his family and peers do not value his feedback is an arbitrary inference. To help him overcome this distortion, the social worker could review the available evidence of that conclusion, helping Dan to understand that his significant others may often give consideration to his points of view even though they do not always accede to them.

Social learning theory takes the tendency in cognitive theory to deemphasize innate drives and unconscious thinking even further. Some practitioners in the social learning tradition make no attempt to understand internal processes at all and avoid making any inferences about them. Social workers who practice from the behavioral approach conceptualize thoughts and emotions as behaviors subject to *reinforcement contingencies* (Thyer, 2005). That is, we tend to behave in ways that produce rewards (material or emotional) for us. Thus, behaviors can be modified through the application of specific action-oriented methods, such as those listed in Exhibit 4.6. If Dan feels socially isolated due to his lack of skills at engaging in casual conversation, the social worker would first help him understand that improved social skills might help him feel more connected to his peers. Through behavioral rehearsal Dan could learn through step-by-step modeling and role-playing how to informally interact with his classmates more effectively. His positive reinforcers might include the sense of interpersonal connection, a new sense of efficacy, and reduced anxiety.

Assessing and intervening with a person's thought processes, and then helping the client to identify and develop reinforcers for new ways of thinking and behaving, is known as *cognitive-behavioral therapy* (CBT). Most cognitive practitioners use cognitive-behavioral methods because it is important to help the client experience rewards for any changes he or she risks.

The more we learn about cognition, however, the more complex it becomes. For example, psychologist and economist Daniel Kahneman (2011) suggests that people place too much confidence in the rationality of their judgment. In fact, his research concludes that we all have built-in cognitive biases. One of these is that we are more driven to avoid pain than to experience pleasure, but more problematic is our "optimistic bias," which generates a false sense of control of our lives. This bias may be adaptive in an evolutionary sense, but as a result we fail to comprehend and take complexity into account in assessing past and present events, and our understanding of the world consists of small, not necessarily representative sets of observations. One implication of this bias is that we tend to be overconfident in our judgments; our "rational" minds generally do not account for the role of chance in events and thus falsely assume that future events will mirror past ones. Kahneman's work provides a reminder that there is much to be learned about the nature of cognition and the potential for people to act "rationally."

CRITICAL THINKING Questions 4.1

How important do you think conscious thinking is in human behavior in general and for Dan Lee in particular? What do you think of Daniel Kahneman's thesis that we place too much confidence in the rationality of our judgments?

EXHIBIT 4.6 • Four Behavioral Change Strategies

STRATEGY	DESCRIPTION
Desensitization	Confronting a difficult challenge through a step-by-step process of approach and anxiety control
Shaping	Differentially reinforcing approximations of a desired but difficult behavior so as to help the person eventually master the behavior
Behavioral rehearsal	Role-playing a desired behavior after seeing it modeled appropriately and then applying the skill to real-life situations
Extinction	Eliminating a behavior by reinforcing alternative behaviors

THEORIES OF EMOTION

Emotion is physiologically programmed into the human brain (see Chapter 3). Its expression is primarily mediated by the hypothalamus, whereas the experience of emotion is a limbic function. But emotion also involves a cognitive labeling of these programmed feelings, which is at least partially a learned process. That is, some emotional experience is an interpretation and not merely given by our physiological state. For example, two students might feel anxious walking into the classroom on the first day of a semester. The anxiety would be a normal reaction to entering a new and unfamiliar situation. However, one student might interpret the anxiety as a heightened alertness that will serve her well in adjusting to the new students and professor, whereas the other student might interpret the same emotion as evidence that she is not prepared to manage the course material. The first student may become excited, but the second student becomes distressed.

Many theorists distinguish between primary and secondary emotions (Parkinson, Fischer, & Manstead, 2005). **Primary emotions** may have evolved as specific reactions with survival value for the human species. They mobilize us, focus our attention, and signal our state of mind to others. There is no consensus on what the primary emotions are, but they are usually limited to anger, fear, sadness, joy, and anticipation (Panksepp, 2008). **Secondary emotions** are more variable among people and are socially acquired. They evolved as humans developed more sophisticated means of learning, controlling, and managing emotions to promote flexible cohesion in social groups. Secondary emotions may result from combinations of primary emotions (Plutchik, 2005), and their greater numbers also imply that our processes of perception, though largely unconscious, are significant in labeling them. These emotions include (but are not limited to) envy, jealousy, anxiety, guilt, shame, relief, hope, depression, pride, love, gratitude, and compassion (Lazarus, 2007).

The autonomic nervous system is key to our processing of emotion (Bentley & Walsh, 2014). This system consists of nerve tracts running from the base of the brain, through the spinal cord, and into the internal organs of the body. It is concerned with maintaining the body's physical homeostasis. Tracts from one branch of this system, the sympathetic division, produce physiological changes that help make us more alert and active. These changes are sustained by the release of hormones from the endocrine glands into the bloodstream. Parasympathetic system nerve tracts produce opposite, or calming, effects in the body. The two systems work together to maintain an appropriate level of physical arousal.

Still, psychologists have debated for more than a century the sources of emotion. Theories range from those that emphasize physiology to those that emphasize the psychological or the purely social context, and they give variable weight to the role of cognition.

PHYSIOLOGICAL THEORIES OF EMOTION

Early physiological theories of emotion were proposed by William James (1890) and Walter Cannon (1924), but physiology-based theories of emotion lost favor in the mid-20th century. Recent brain research is once again suggesting a strong link between physiological processes and emotion. The *differential emotions theory* (Magai, 2001) asserts that emotions originate in our neurophysiology and that our personalities are organized around "affective biases." All of us possess the primary emotions of happiness, sadness, fear, anger, and interest/excitement. These emotions are instinctual, hardwired into our brains, and the source of our motivations. When our emotions are activated, they have a pervasive influence on our cognition and behavior. A key theme in this theory is that emotions influence cognition, a principle opposite to that stressed in cognitive theory.

For example, Dan has a persistent bias toward sadness, which may reflect some personal or material losses that occurred long before he started college. His episodes of sadness produce the temporary physical responses of a slowing down and decreased general effort. The sadness thus allows Dan time to reevaluate his needs and regain energy for more focused attempts to reach more achievable goals. It is also a signal for others to provide Dan with support. (You can certainly recall times when the sadness of another person prompted your own empathic response.) Of course, it is likely that "appearing sad" may have been more functional for Dan in his home community, where he was more consistently around people who knew and took an interest in him. In contrast, the emotion of anger tends to increase a person's energy and motivate behavior intended to overcome frustration. Furthermore, it signals others to respond with avoidance, compliance, or submission so that the person may resolve the problem. Dan becomes angry rather frequently, and his sullen demeanor clearly encourages his peers, but not necessarily his family, to give him space.

Researchers have speculated for decades about the precise locations of emotional processing in the brain. Much has been learned about structures that participate in this process, and it is clear that many areas of the brain have a role (Farmer, 2009). Furthermore, it is now widely accepted that cultural patterns shape the ways in which environmental input is coded in the brain (Kagan, 2007).

The physiology of emotion begins in the *thalamus*, a major integrating center of the brain. Located in the forebrain, the thalamus is the site that receives and relays sensory information from the body and from the environment to other parts of the brain. Any perceived environmental event travels first to the thalamus and then to the sensory cortex (for thought), the basal ganglia (for movement), and the hypothalamus (for feeling). The *amygdala*, part of the limbic system, is key in the production of emotional states. There are in fact two routes to the amygdala from the thalamus. Sensations that produce primary emotions described earlier may travel there directly from the thalamus, bypassing any cognitive apparatus, to produce an immediate reaction that is central to survival. Other inputs first travel through the cortex, where they are cognitively evaluated prior to moving on to the limbic system and amygdala to be processed as the secondary emotions.

Culture and the characteristics of the individual may influence the processing of stimulation because the cognitive structures (schemata) that interpret this stimulation may, through feedback loops to the thalamus, actually shape the neural pathways that will be followed by future stimuli. In other words, neural schemata tend to become rigid patterns of information processing, shaping subsequent patterns for making sense of the external world.

Richard Davidson's research has focused on the neurological processes underlying emotion, and he understands the interactions between the prefrontal cortex and amygdala to play an important role (Davidson & Begley, 2012). Through brain imaging research he has found that the greater the number of connections between the amygdala and prefrontal cortex, the better we tend to be at managing our emotions. As one example, activity in the left prefrontal cortex is higher in persons who are more resilient to negative emotions, and from this Davidson infers that the left prefrontal cortex sends inhibitory messages to the amygdala.

Davidson claims that we all have different *emotional styles*, composed of combinations of six components, that determine how we react to experiences in our lives and how likely we are to have particular moods (see Exhibit 4.7). The interrelation between the prefrontal cortex and amygdala plays a major role in determining these emotional styles. People with fewer connections tend to be less effective emotional regulators, making them more irritable, quick-tempered, and less able to manage their emotions in a healthy way. Davidson further cites research suggesting that genes associated with emotional styles can gradually change their expression based on our environments, behaviors, and life experiences.

PSYCHOLOGICAL THEORIES OF EMOTION

Perhaps the most contentious debates about the role of cognition in emotion have taken place among psychological theorists. Some psychologists have considered emotion as primary, and others have considered cognition as primary. Psychological theories in the social behavioral perspective, somewhat like physiology-based theories, assume an automatic, programmed response that is then interpreted as emotion, perhaps first consciously but eventually (through habit) unconsciously.

EXHIBIT 4.7 • Davidson's Six Components of Emotional Style

COMPONENTS	DESCRIPTION
Resilience	How quickly we recover from negative emotions.
Outlook	The duration of our positive emotions.
Context	The degree to which we modulate our emotional responses in a manner appropriate to the context (for example, not directly taking out our work-related anger on the boss).
Social intuition	Our sensitivity to social cues, including all verbal and nonverbal expressions, that reflect our ability to understand and empathize with other people's emotional worlds.
Self-awareness	The extent to which we are aware of emotional signals within our own bodies and minds. The more aware we are of our emotions, the better we will manage them.
Attention	The extent to which we can focus our attention on one thing at a time rather than becoming easily distracted.

Psychoanalytic Theory

Freud's landmark work, *The Interpretation of Dreams*, first published in 1899, signaled the arrival of **psychoanalytic theory**. Freud's theories became prominent in the United States by the early 1900s, immediately influencing the young profession of social work, and were a dominant force through the 1950s. Psychoanalytic thinking continues to be influential in social work today, through the theories of ego psychology, self psychology, object relations, and relational theory, among others.

The basis of psychoanalytic theory is the primacy of internal drives and unconscious mental activity in human behavior. Sexual and aggressive drives are not "feelings" in themselves, but they motivate behavior that will presumably gratify our impulses. We experience positive emotions when our drives are gratified and negative emotions when they are frustrated. Our conscious mental functioning takes place within the **ego**, that part of the personality responsible for negotiating between internal drives and the outside world. It is here that cognition occurs, but it is influenced by those unconscious impulses that are focused on drive satisfaction.

In psychoanalytic thought, then, conscious thinking is a product of the drives from which our emotions also spring. By nature, we are pleasure seekers and "feelers," not thinkers. Thoughts are our means of deciding how to gratify our drives. Defense mechanisms result from our need to indirectly manage drives when we become frustrated, as we frequently do in the social world, where

Emotion is physiologically programmed into the human brain.

we must negotiate acceptable behaviors with others. The need to manage drives also contributes to the development of our unconscious mental processes. According to psychoanalytic theory, personal growth cannot be achieved by attending only to conscious processes. We need to explore all of our thoughts and feelings to understand our essential drives. Change requires that we uncover unconscious material and the accompanying feelings that are repressed, or kept out of consciousness.

Let us grant, for example, that Dan has a normal, healthy drive for pleasure. He may also be angry with his father for breaking up the family, providing it with limited resources and leaving him in a responsible position at such a young age. This anger might be repressed into unconsciousness, however, because Dan is also emulating his father professionally and may believe, due to his cultural background, that it is not permissible for a child to be angry with a parent. Dan's unconscious anger, having been turned inward at himself, may be contributing to his frustrations and inability to experience joy. An analytical social worker might suspect from Dan's presentation that he experiences this anger but is not aware of it. The social worker might try to help Dan uncover the feeling by having him reflect on his family history in detail, in a safe clinical environment. With the insights that might result from this reflection, Dan's anger may become conscious, and he can then take direct measures to work through it.

Ego Psychology

Ego psychology, which emerged in the 1930s (E. Goldstein, 2009), shifted to a more balanced perspective on the influences of cognition and emotion in social functioning. As an adaptation of psychoanalytic theory, it signaled a reaction against Freud's heavy emphasis on drives and highlighted the ego's role in promoting healthy social functioning. Ego psychology represents an effort to build a holistic psychology of normal development. It was a major social work practice theory throughout much of the 20th century because of its attention to the environment as well as the person, and it continues to be taught in many schools of social work.

In ego psychology, the ego is conceived of as present from birth and not as derived from the need to reconcile drives within the constraints of social living, as psychoanalytic theory would say. The ego is the source of our attention, concentration, learning, memory, will, and perception. Both past and present experiences are relevant in influencing social functioning. The influence of the drives on emotions and thoughts is not dismissed, but the autonomy of the ego, and thus conscious thought processes, receives greater emphasis than in psychoanalytic theory. The ego moderates internal conflicts, which may relate to drive frustration, but it also mediates the interactions of a healthy person with stressful environmental conditions.

If we experience sadness, then, it is possible that we are having internal conflicts related to drive frustration. It is also possible that we are experiencing person–environment conflicts in which our coping efforts are not effective; the negative emotion may result from a frustration of our ability to manage an environmental stressor and thus may arise from cognitive activities. Dan may be experiencing both types of conflict. His anger at the lack of adequate nurturance in his early family history may have been turned inward and produced a moderate depression. At the same time, the mismatch between his personal needs for mastery and the demands of the academic environment may also be contributing to his negative feelings.

Attribution Theory: A Cognitive Perspective

Attribution theory was the first of the psychological theories of emotion to give primacy to cognition as a producer of emotions (Schacter & Singer, 1962). Attribution theory holds that our experience of emotion is based on conscious evaluations we make about physiological sensations in particular social settings. We respond to situations as we understand them cognitively, which leads directly to our experience of a particular emotion. For example, Dan has often experienced anxiety, but he interprets it differently in dealing with his family (frustration due to their lack of perceived loyalty) and his fellow students (being ridiculed). The nature of the social setting is key to the process of emotional experience.

Richard Lazarus (2001) has proposed a three-part psychological theory of emotion based on appraisals of situations. He suggests that emotion develops when we assess a situation as somehow relevant to a personal value or life concern. First, we make an unconscious appraisal of whether a situation constitutes a threat. This appraisal is followed by coping responses, which may be cognitive, physiological, or both and may be conscious or unconscious. Once these coping mechanisms are in place, we reappraise the situation and label our associated emotion. This process implies that our feelings originate with an automatic evaluative judgment. We decide whether there is a threat, take immediate coping action to deal with it, and then take a closer look to see exactly what was involved in the situation. At the end of this process, we experience a specific secondary emotion.

A major life concern for Dan is feeling secure in his interpersonal environments. He feels secure in familiar environments (such as his hometown, at his church, and with his family) but feels threatened in unfamiliar places. When he walks into a new classroom, he experiences anxiety. The feeling seems to Dan to be automatic, because his need for security is threatened in the situation. His means of coping is to ignore the other students, neither speaking to nor making eye contact with them, and to sit in a relatively isolated area of the room. Dan then makes at least a partly conscious appraisal that the room is occupied with strangers who are judging him in negative ways. Dan labels his emotion as resentment because he concludes that his classmates are incorrectly perceiving him as socially inferior.

Theory of Emotional Intelligence

Emotional intelligence is a person's ability to process information about emotions accurately and effectively and, consequently, to regulate emotions in an optimal manner (Goleman, 2005). It includes self-control, zest and persistence, and the ability to motivate oneself, understand and regulate one's own emotions, and read and deal effectively with other people's feelings. This is a relatively new concept in psychology.

Emotional intelligence involves recognizing and regulating emotions in ourselves and other people. It requires emotional sensitivity, or the ability to evaluate emotions within a variety of social circumstances. A person who is angry but knows that certain expressions of anger will be counterproductive in a particular situation, and as a result constrains his or her expressions of anger, is emotionally intelligent. On the other hand, a person with this same knowledge who behaves angrily in spite of this awareness is emotionally unintelligent.

People are not necessarily equally emotionally intelligent about themselves and other people. We may be more emotionally intelligent about other people than we are about ourselves, or vice versa. The first possibility helps to explain why some people, social workers included, seem to be better at giving advice to others than to themselves.

Emotional intelligence requires an integration of intellectual and emotional abilities. Recognizing and regulating emotions requires emotional self-awareness and empathy, but it also necessitates the intellectual ability to calculate the implications of behavioral alternatives. To understand how and why we feel as we do, and other people feel as they do, demands emotional awareness and intellectual reasoning. Emotional intelligence is more important to excellence in many aspects of life than pure intellect because it includes intellect plus other capacities. As we have already seen, Dan generally lacks emotional self-awareness.

SOCIAL THEORIES OF EMOTION

Social theories of emotion also take the view that perception, or the interpretation of a situation, precedes emotion. These interpretations are learned and become automatic (unconscious or preconscious) over time. Social theories emphasize the purpose of emotion, which is to sustain shared interpersonal norms and social cohesion. Two social theories are considered here.

James Averill's (2012) social constructionist theory states that emotions can be understood as socially constructed, transitory roles. They are socially constructed because they originate in our appraisals of situations, transitory in that they are time limited, and roles because they include a range of socially acceptable actions that may be performed in a certain context. We organize and interpret our physiological reactions to stimuli with regard to the social norms involved in the situations where these reactions occur. Emotions permit us, in response to these stimuli, to step out of the conventional social roles to which people not experiencing the emotion are held. For example, in our culture, we generally would not say that we wish to harm someone unless we were feeling anger. We would generally not lash out verbally at a friend or spouse unless we felt frustrated. We would generally not withdraw from certain personal responsibilities and ask others for comfort unless we felt sad. Because of the social functions of emotions, we often experience them as passions, or feelings not under our control. Experiencing passion permits unconventional behavior because we assume that we are somehow not "ourselves," not able to control what we do at that moment. Our society has adopted this mode of thinking about emotions because it allows us to distance ourselves from some of our actions. Emotions are thus legitimized social roles or permissible behaviors for persons in particular emotional states.

George Herbert Mead (1934), the originator of symbolic interaction theory, took a somewhat different view. He suggested that emotions develop as symbols for communication. He believed that humans are by nature more sensitive to visual than to verbal cues. Emotional expressions are thus particularly powerful in that they are apprehended visually rather than verbally. Our emotional expression is a signal about how we are inclined to act in a situation, and others can adjust their own behavior in response to our perceived inclinations. Dan's lack of eye contact and physical distancing from others are manifestations of his anxiety. Other persons, in response, may choose either to offer him support or, more likely in a classroom or lab setting, to avoid him if they interpret his expressions as a desire for distance. Dan was accustomed to people noticing his sadness at home, and responding to it by reaching out to him, but in the faster-paced, more impersonal context of the university culture, this was not happening. One reason he may be continuing contact with his ex-girlfriend is that, despite their differences, she perceives and affirms his sadness.

THEORIES OF EMOTION IN SOCIAL WORK PRACTICE

The preceding theories are useful in assessment and intervention with clients because they enhance the social worker's understanding of the origins of emotional experiences and describe how negative emotional states may emerge and influence behavior. The social worker can help the client develop more positive emotional responses by providing insight or corrective experiences. What follows, however, is a theory that is even more precise in identifying the processes of emotional experience.

L. S. Greenberg (2011) has offered an emotion-focused practice theory, similar to psychoanalytic theory, that may be helpful in social work interventions. Greenberg asserts that all primary emotions—those that originate as biologically based rapid responses—are adaptive. Every primary emotion we experience has the purpose of helping us adjust our relationship with an environmental situation to enhance coping. Secondary emotions emerge from these primary emotions as a result of cognitive mediation.

From this perspective, it is the unconscious or **preconscious** (mental activity that is out of awareness but can be brought into awareness with prompting) appraisal of situations in relation to our needs that creates emotions. Furthermore, as George Herbert Mead (1934) pointed out, we experience our emotions as images, not as verbal thoughts. Emotions are difficult to apprehend cognitively, and in our attempts to do so, we may mistake their essence. The bad feelings that trouble us come not from those primary emotional responses, which, if experienced directly, would tend to dissipate, but from defensive distortions of those responses. We tend to appraise situations accurately with our primary emotions, but our frustration in achieving affective goals can produce distortions. Thus, in contrast to the assumptions of cognitive theory, distortions of thought may be the *result* of emotional phenomena rather than their cause.

Consider Dan's distress as an example. Perhaps he accurately perceives wariness in others (due to his standoffish demeanor). His need to be in control is threatened by this appraisal, and the intensity of his reaction to this frustration becomes problematic, making it hard for him to concentrate on his studies. His emotional patterns evoke his tendencies at times to become confrontational almost to the point of verbal abuse.

Personal reality, then, may be as much a product of emotion as cognition. In any situation, the meanings we construct may automatically determine our conscious responses. It is when we directly experience primary emotions that we are functioning in an adaptive manner.

In emotion-focused practice, the social worker would attempt to activate the person's primary emotional reactions, making them more available to awareness within the safety of the social worker–client relationship and making secondary emotional reactions amenable to reflection and change when necessary. Emotional reactions, cognitive appraisals, and action tendencies may then be identified more clearly by the client. Affective needs can be identified, and a new sense of self may emerge along with an improved capacity for self-direction.

From this perspective, a social worker could help Dan understand that he carries much anger at his family because of their long-term lack of adequate support for his emotional development. Dan could be encouraged within the safety of the social worker–client relationship to experience and ventilate that anger and gain insight into his pattern. Once Dan can consciously identify and experience that negative emotion, he may be less incapacitated by the depression, which is a secondary emotion resulting from his suppression of anger. He might then have more energy to devote to his own social and academic goals and to develop new ways of interacting with others in the university setting.

CRITICAL THINKING Questions 4.2

We have just looked at three types of theories of emotion: physiological theories, psychological theories, and social theories. What did you find most interesting about these different ways of thinking about emotion? Which ideas did you find most appealing? Most convincing? Explain. Some research suggests that emotional intelligence is more important to career success than intelligence measured as IQ. Does that make sense to you? Why or why not?

COGNITIVE AND EMOTIONAL "DISORDERS"

As social workers, we are reluctant to label people as having cognitive or emotional "disorders." Instead, we conceptualize problems in social functioning as mismatches in the fit between person and environment. Still, in our study of the psychological person, we can consider how problems are manifested in the client's cognitive and emotional patterns.

Many social workers are employed in mental health agencies and use the *Diagnostic and Statistical Manual of Mental Disorders* (*DSM-5*; American Psychiatric Association [APA], 2013) to make diagnoses as part of a comprehensive client assessment. The *DSM* has been the standard resource for clinical diagnosis in the United States for more than half a century. The purpose of the manual is to provide clear descriptions of diagnostic categories so that practitioners of all disciplines can diagnose, communicate about, and treat people with mental and emotional disorders. The *DSM* includes 20 chapters of disorders that address, among others, neurodevelopmental (such as autism spectrum disorder), schizophrenia spectrum, bipolar, depressive, anxiety, obsessive-compulsive, trauma, dissociative, eating, elimination, sleep-wake, disruptive, substance-related, neurocognitive (such as Alzheimer's disease), personality, and paraphilic disorders, as well as sexual dysfunctions and gender dysphoria.

It is important to recognize that the *DSM* provides a medical perspective on human functioning. There is tension between the social work profession's person-in-environment perspective and the requirement in many settings that social workers use the *DSM* to "diagnose" mental, emotional, or behavioral disorders in clients (Corcoran & Walsh, 2010).

With this brief introduction, we can consider four examples of disorders selected from the *DSM* to illustrate how either cognitive or emotional characteristics may predominate in a client's symptom profile, even though both aspects of the psychological person are always present.

- Two disorders that feature cognitive symptoms are obsessive-compulsive disorder and anorexia nervosa. Obsessive-compulsive disorder is characterized by persistent thoughts that are experienced as intrusive, inappropriate, unwelcome, and distressful. The thoughts are more than excessive worries about real problems, and the person is unable to ignore or suppress them. In anorexia nervosa, an eating disorder, the person becomes obsessive about food, thinking about it almost constantly. The person refuses to maintain a reasonable body weight because of distorted beliefs about physical appearance and the effects of food on the body.

- Two disorders that feature emotional symptoms are persistent depressive disorder (PDD) and agoraphobia. PDD, a mood disorder, is characterized by a lengthy period of depression. It features the emotion of sadness, which tends to persist regardless of external events. Agoraphobia is an anxiety disorder characterized by fear. The person is afraid to be in situations (such as crowds) or places (such as large open areas) from which escape might be difficult or embarrassing. The person must restrict his or her range of social mobility out of fear of being overwhelmed by anxiety for reasons that are not consciously clear.

As a social worker, you might note that Dan displays symptoms of obsessive-compulsive disorder. He experiences persistent and unwanted ideas and thoughts that significantly intrude on his desire to do or think of other things. He does not, however, experience compulsions or illogical impulses to perform certain behaviors (such as repeatedly checking to see if his apartment door is locked). You might thus conclude that Dan's problems are primarily cognitive. However, Dan's cognitive patterns have contributed to, and been affected by, his development of negative emotions. His difficulties at school sustain his chronic anxiety, and his distorted beliefs about the attitudes of others contribute to his sadness at being isolated from them. It is rarely the case that only cognitive factors or only emotional factors are behind a client's problems.

THE SELF

It remains for us to integrate elements of cognition and emotion into a cohesive notion of the self. This is a difficult task—one that may, in fact, be impossible to achieve. All of us possess a sense of self, but it is difficult to articulate. How would you define *self*? Most of us tend to think of it as incorporating an essence that is more or less enduring. But beyond that, what would you say? Thinkers from the fields of philosophy, theology, sociology, psychology, and social work have struggled to identify the essence of the **self**, and they offer us a range of perspectives summarized here.

- *The self as soul.* A constant, unchanging self, existing apart from its material environment and material body, perhaps transcending the life of the physical body
- *The self as unfolding potential.* A conscious, fluid, unfolding self that strives to actualize inherent potentials
- *The self as organizing activity.* The initiator of activity, organizer of drives, and mediator of both internal and person–environment conflicts; an evolving entity in the synthesizing of experiences
- *The self as cognitive structure.* The thinker and definer of reality through conscious activities that support the primacy of thought
- *The self as shared symbolic experience.* A sense of meaning about who we are developed through interaction with our physical and social environments and through our perceptions of how others perceive us
- *The self as flow of experience.* The self in process, the changing self

© iStockPhoto.com/Christopher Futcher

Some see the self as shared symbolic experience. The shared play and exploration of these children contribute to their developing self-concepts.

THE SELF IN RELATIONSHIPS

Cultural psychologists suggest that all of these perspectives assume an independent self, but in many cultures of the world, the self is an interdependent one that cannot be detached from the context of human relationships (Markus & Kitayama, 2009). And, indeed, as Dan understood but had trouble managing, the ability to form, sustain, and use significant relationships with other people is a key to the process of successful coping and adaptation. With this theme in mind, we turn to examination of several theories that address the issue of how we exist in the context of relationships, including the relational, attachment, feminist, and social identity theories, and evidence demonstrating the importance of early nurturing in the ability to build relationships throughout life.

RELATIONAL THEORY

In recent years, an integration of the psychoanalytic and interpersonal theoretical perspectives (which focus on relationships as the driving force of personality development) has come to be called **relational theory** (Borden, 2009). In relational theory the basic human tendency (or drive) is for relationships with others, and our personalities are structured through ongoing interactions with others in the social environment. In this theory there is a strong value of recognizing and supporting diversity in human experience, avoiding the pathologizing of differences, and enlarging traditional conceptions of gender and identity. It assumes that all patterns of behavior are learned in the give-and-take of relational life and are adaptive ways of negotiating experience in the context of our need to elicit care from, and provide care for, others. Serious relationship problems are seen as self-perpetuating because we all have a tendency to preserve continuity in our interpersonal worlds. What is new is threatening because it lies beyond the bounds of our experience in which we recognize ourselves as cohesive beings.

For social work practice, the relational perspective enriches the concept of empathy by adding the notion of mutuality between the social worker and client. The ability to participate in a mutual relationship through empathic communication contributes to the client's growth. Contrary to traditional analytic notions, the relational social worker expresses a range of thoughts and feelings "in the moment" with the client to facilitate their mutual connection (Freedberg, 2007). Intervention focuses on here-and-now situations in the client's life, including those involving the social worker and client. Current social work literature reflects diverse views regarding the degree to which practitioners should self-disclose with their clients, but the general consensus calls for the worker to maintain a neutral, objective persona (J. Walsh, 2000). In relational theory, however, the more the worker expends energy on keeping parts of herself or himself out of the process, the more rigid and less genuine he or she will be with the client. Relational theorists encourage the social worker's natural, authentic manner of engagement; the strategic use of self-disclosure; and the encouragement of the client to regularly comment on the intervention process. The social worker also tries to avoid relegating the two parties into dominant and subordinate roles. This does not imply a neglect of appropriate boundaries, however, because the social worker must maintain a clear sense of self while engaged in the emotional and cognitive integration necessary for empathy to be effective.

Despite its limitations with regard to empirical validation, the assumptions of relational theory are consistent with the findings of the American Psychological Association (APA) on the significance of the worker–client relationship. The APA has systematically evaluated the significance of the practitioner–client relationship in determining intervention effectiveness and concluded that several relationship variables used in practice were *demonstrably* effective (the alliance in individual and family therapy; cohesion in group therapy; empathy; and collecting client feedback), and others were *probably* effective (attention to goal consensus, collaboration, and positive regard). Three other relationship elements (congruence or genuineness, repairing alliance ruptures, and managing countertransference) were deemed *promising* (Norcross & Wampold, 2011).

ATTACHMENT THEORY

To understand how we develop our initial relationship patterns, it may be useful to consider one model of parent–child attachment here (Shorey & Snyder, 2006). All children seek proximity to their parents, and they develop attachment styles suited to the types of parenting they encounter. Ainsworth and her colleagues (Ainsworth, Blehar, Waters, & Wall, 1978) identified three infant attachment styles—secure, anxious-ambivalent, and avoidant types. A fourth attachment style has been identified more recently—the disorganized type (Madigan, Moran, & Pederson, 2006).

All children seek proximity to their parents, and they develop attachment styles suited to the types of parenting they encounter.

Securely attached infants act somewhat distressed when their parent figures leave but greet them eagerly and warmly upon return. Parents of secure infants are sensitive and accepting. Securely attached children are unconcerned about security needs and are thus free to direct their energies toward nonattachment-related activities in the environment. Infants who are not securely attached must direct their attention to maintaining their attachments to inconsistent, unavailable, or rejecting parents, rather than engaging in exploratory behaviors. Because these children are only able to maintain proximity to the parents by behaving as if the parents are not needed, the children may learn not to express needs for closeness or attention.

Anxious-ambivalently attached infants, in contrast, are distraught when their parent figures leave. Upon their parent's return, these infants continue to be distressed even as they want to be comforted and held. These children employ "hyperactivation" strategies. Their parents, whereas not overtly rejecting, are often unpredictable and inconsistent in their responses. Fearing potential caregiver abandonment, the children maximize their efforts to maintain close parental attachments and become hypervigilant for threat cues and any signs of rejection.

Avoidantly attached infants seem to be relatively undisturbed both when their parent figures leave and when they return. These children want to maintain proximity to their parent figures, but this attachment style enables the children to maintain a sense of proximity to parents who otherwise may reject them. Avoidant children thus suppress expressions of overt distress and, rather than risk further rejection in the face of attachment figure unavailability, may give up on their proximity-seeking efforts.

The *disorganized attachment* style is characterized by chaotic and conflicted behaviors. These children exhibit simultaneous approach and avoidance behaviors. Disorganized infants seem incapable of applying any consistent strategy to bond with their parents. Their conflicted and disorganized behaviors reflect their best attempts at gaining some sense of security from parents who are perceived as frightening. When afraid and needing reassurance, these children have no options but to seek support from a caregiver who is frightening. The parents may be either hostile or fearful and unable to hide their apprehension from their children. In either case, the child's anxiety and distress are not lessened, and one source of stress is merely traded for another.

Although children with disorganized attachments typically do not attain senses of being cared for, the avoidant and anxious-ambivalent children do experience some success in fulfilling their needs for care.

IMPACT OF EARLY NURTURING ON DEVELOPMENT

We have been looking at theories that deem relationships to be important throughout our lives. Turning to both human and animal research, we can find physiological evidence that, as suggested by relational and attachment theory, the quality of our early relationships is crucial to our lifelong capacity to engage in healthy relationships and even to enjoy basic physical health.

A large body of research is devoted to studying the links between early life experiences and physical and mental health risks (e.g., Lally, 2011). This work demonstrates that negative early life experiences such as child abuse, family strife, poverty, and emotional neglect correlate with later health problems ranging from depression to drug abuse and heart disease. Relational elements of our early environments appear to permanently alter the development of central nervous system structures that govern our autonomic, cognitive, behavioral, and emotional responses to stress (Farmer, 2009). These findings tend to support the lifelong significance of specific relationship interactions.

Although much of this research is being conducted on rats, monkeys, and other animals, it has clear implications for human development. The concept of neuroplasticity (discussed in Chapter 3) is significant here (Bryck & Fisher, 2012). Humans may have a window of opportunity, or a critical period for altering neurological development, but this window varies, depending on the area of the nervous system. Even through the second decade of life, for example, neurotransmitter and synapse changes are influenced by internal biology, but perhaps by external signals as well. In other words, the brain is not a static organ.

Much research currently under way explores the relationship between the processes of attachment and specific neurological development in young persons (Diamond & Fagundes, 2010). Persistent stress in an infant or toddler results in an overdevelopment of areas of the brain that process anxiety and fear, and the underdevelopment of other areas of the brain, particularly the cortex. Of particular concern to one leading researcher (Schore, 2002) is the impact of the absence of nurturance on the orbitofrontal cortex (OFC) of the brain. Chronic levels of stress contribute to fewer neural connections between the prefrontal cortex and the amygdala, a process significant to psychosocial functioning. The OFC is particularly active in such processes as our concentration, judgment, and ability to observe and control internal subjective states. Further, the frontal cortex is central to our emotional regulation capacity and our experience of empathy. The amygdala, part of the limbic system, is attributed with interpreting incoming stimuli and information and storing this information in our implicit (automatic) memory. The amygdala assesses threat and triggers our immediate responses to it (the fight, flight, or freeze behaviors). A reduction in neural connections between these two areas suggests that the frontal cortex is not optimally able to regulate the processing of fear, resulting in exaggerated fear responses.

Stress can clearly affect brain development, but there is evidence that the first few years of life are not all-important (Korosi & Baram, 2010). A study of 2,600 undergraduate students found that even in late adolescence and early adulthood, satisfying social relationships were associated with greater autonomic activity and restorative behaviors when confronting acute stress (Cacioppo, Bernston, Sheridan, & McClintock, 2000).

In summary, research indicates that secure attachments play a critical role in shaping the systems that underlie our reactivity to stressful situations. When infants begin to form specific attachments to adults, the presence of warm and responsive caregivers begins to buffer or prevent elevations in stress hormones, even in situations that distress the infant. In contrast, insecure relationships are associated with higher CRH levels in potentially threatening situations. Secure emotional relationships with adults appear to be at least as critical as individual differences in temperament in determining stress reactivity and regulation (Eagle & Wolitzky, 2009).

Still, there is much to be learned in this area. Many people subjected to serious early life traumas become effective, high-functioning adolescents and adults. Infants and children are resilient and have many strengths that can help them overcome these early life stresses. Researchers are challenged to determine whether interventions such as foster care can remedy the physical, emotional, and social problems seen in children who have experienced poor nurturing and early problems with separation.

We now consider theories about social influences on one's sense of attachment to persons outside the family.

FEMINIST THEORIES OF RELATIONSHIPS

The term *feminism* does not refer to any single body of thought. It refers to a wide-ranging system of ideas about human experience developed from a woman-centered perspective. Feminist theories may be classified as liberal, radical, Marxist, socialist, existential, postmodern, multicultural, or ecofeminist (Lengermann & Niebrugge-Brantley, 2007). Among the psychological theories are psychoanalytic feminism (Angers, 2008) and gender feminism (Marecek, Kimmel, Crawford, & Hare-Mustin, 2003). We focus on these latter two as we consider how feminism has deepened our capacity for understanding human behavior and interaction. All of these theorists begin from the position that women and men approach relationships differently and that patriarchal societies consider male attributes to be superior.

Psychoanalytic feminists assert that women's ways of acting are rooted deeply in women's unique ways of thinking. These differences may be biological, but they are certainly influenced by cultural and psychosocial conditions. Feminine behavior features gentleness, modesty, humility, supportiveness, empathy, compassion, tenderness, nurturance, intuitiveness, sensitivity, and unselfishness. Masculine behavior is characterized by strength of will, ambition, courage, independence, assertiveness, hardiness, rationality, and emotional control. Psychoanalytic feminists assert that these differences are largely rooted in early childhood relationships. Because women are the primary caretakers in our society, young girls tend to develop and enjoy an ongoing relationship with their mothers that promotes their valuing of relatedness as well as other feminine behaviors. For young boys, on the other hand, the mother is eventually perceived as fundamentally different, particularly as they face social pressures to begin fulfilling male roles. The need to separate from the mother figure has long-range implications for boys: They tend to lose what could otherwise become a learned capacity for intimacy and relatedness.

Gender feminists tend to be concerned with values of separateness (for men) and connectedness (for women) and how these lead to a different morality for women. Carol Gilligan (1982, 1988) is a leading thinker in this area. As reported earlier, she elucidated a process by which women develop an ethic of care rather than an ethic of justice, based on the value they place on relationships. Gender feminists believe that these female ethics are equal to male ethics, although they have tended in patriarchal societies to be considered inferior. Gilligan asserts that all of humanity would be best served if both ethics could be valued equally. Other gender feminists go further, however, arguing for the superiority of women's ethics. For example, Noddings (2002, 2005) asserts that war will never be discarded in favor of the sustained pursuit of peace until the female ethic of caring, aimed at unification, replaces the male ethic of strenuous striving, aimed at dividing people.

All psychological feminist theories promote the value of relationships and the importance of reciprocal interpersonal supports. Dan was raised to be achievement- and task-oriented. These are admirable characteristics, but they represent male perspectives. Dan's inclinations for interpersonal experience may have been discouraged, which was harmful to his overall development.

SOCIAL IDENTITY THEORY

Social identity theory is a stage theory of socialization that articulates the process by which we come to identify with some social groups and develop a sense of difference from others (Hornsey, 2008; Nesdale, 2004). This is especially important to consider because the population in the United States and many other countries is becoming increasingly diverse. During the past decade, Hispanic and Asian populations have increased by 43% in the United States, compared with total population growth of 9.7% (U.S. Census Bureau, 2013a). It is estimated that by 2050 Latinos will make up 25%, and Asians 8%, of the nation's population.

Social identity development can be an affirming process that provides us with a lifelong sense of belonging and support. I might feel good to have membership with a Roman Catholic or Irish American community. Because social identity can be exclusionary, however, it can also give rise to prejudice and oppression. I may believe that my race is more intelligent than another or that persons of my cultural background are entitled to more social benefits than those of another.

Social identity development proceeds in five stages. These stages are not truly distinct or sequential, however; people often experience several stages simultaneously.

1. *Naïveté.* During early childhood, we have no social consciousness. We are not aware of particular codes of behavior for members of our group or any other social group. Our parents or other primary caregivers are our most significant influences, and we accept that socialization without question. As young children, we do, however, begin to distinguish between ourselves and other groups of people. We may not feel completely comfortable with the racial, ethnic, or religious differences we observe, but neither do we feel fearful, superior, or inferior. Children at this stage are mainly curious about differences.

2. *Acceptance.* Older children and young adolescents learn the distinct ideologies and belief systems of their own and other social groups. During this stage, we learn that the world's institutions and authority figures have rules that encourage certain behaviors and prohibit others, and we internalize these dominant cultural beliefs and make them a part of our everyday lives. Those questions that emerged during the stage of naïveté are submerged. We come to believe that the way our group does things is normal, makes more sense, and is better.

3. *Resistance.* In adolescence, or even later, we become aware of the harmful effects of acting on social differences. We have new experiences with members of

other social groups that challenge our prior assumptions. We begin to reevaluate those assumptions and investigate our own role in perpetuating harmful differences. We may feel anger at others within our own social group who foster these irrational differences. We begin to move toward a new definition of social identity that is broader than our previous definition. We may work to end our newly perceived patterns of collusion and oppression.

4. *Redefinition*. Redefinition is a process of creating a new social identity that preserves our pride in our origins while perceiving differences with others as positive representations of diversity. We may isolate from some members of our social group and shift toward interactions with others who share our level of awareness. We see all groups as being rich in strengths and values. We may reclaim our own group heritage but broaden our definition of that heritage as one of many varieties of constructive living.

5. *Internalization*. In the final stage of social identity development, we become comfortable with our revised identity and are able to incorporate it into all aspects of our life. We act unconsciously, without external controls. Life continues as an ongoing process of discovering vestiges of our old biases, but now we test our integrated new identities in wider contexts than our limited reference group. Our appreciation of the plight of all oppressed people, and our enhanced empathy for others, is a part of this process. For many people, the internalization stage is an ongoing challenge rather than an end state.

For all ethnic groups, higher levels of ethnic identity are associated with higher levels of self-esteem, purpose in life, and self-confidence (Rogers-Sirin & Gupta, 2012). Further, ethnic identity is associated with lower levels of depression among White, African American, and Asian youth. Social identity theory is sometimes used, however, to explain a process by which those who most strongly identify with their groups may come to hold less favorable attitudes about dissimilar groups (Negy, Shreve, Jensen, & Uddin, 2003). One study showed that the more Caucasian and Hispanic persons embraced their identity, the more negative views they held toward people who did not belong to their respective ethnic groups. Interestingly, this trend was not found among African American persons. Another theory, *multicultural theory*, proposes more positively that affirmations toward one's group, particularly with regard to ethnicity, should correspond with higher levels of acceptance toward dissimilar groups. Ethnic identity is defined as a sense of belonging to an ethnic group and the part of one's thinking, perceptions, feelings, and behavior that is due to group membership (Smith, Smith, Levine, Dumas, & Prinz, 2009).

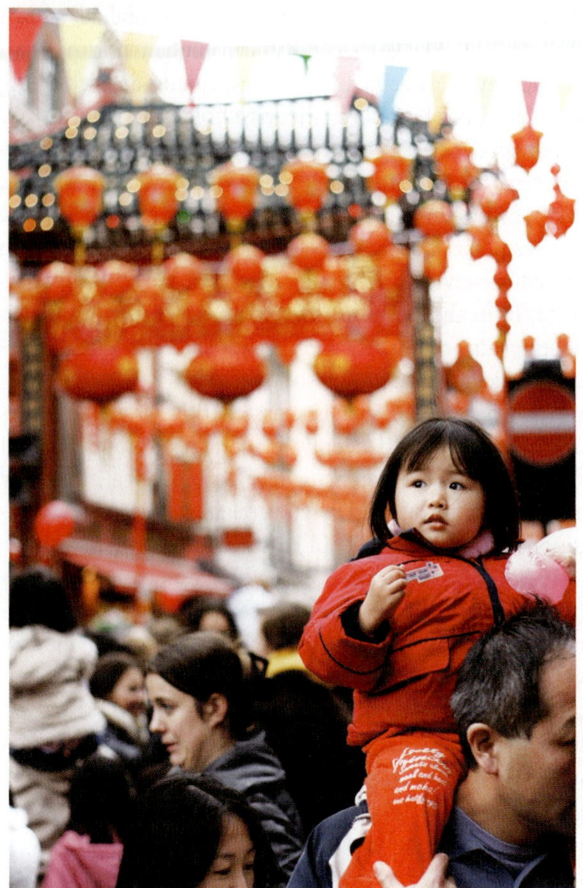

Ethnic identity is defined as a sense of belonging to an ethnic group and the part of one's thinking, perceptions, feelings, and behavior that is due to group membership.

CRITICAL THINKING Questions 4.3

How important is culture in influencing the nature of the self? How important do you think it is for your sense of self? For Dan Lee's sense of self? What are the policy implications of research on the impact of early nurturing on human development? Give some thought to social identity theory. With what social groups do you identify? How did you come to identify with these groups? How might your social identities affect your social work practice?

THE CONCEPT OF STRESS

One of the main benefits of good nurturing is, as you have seen, the way it strengthens our ability to cope with stress. **Stress** can be defined as any event in which environmental or internal demands tax our adaptive resources. Stress may be biological (a disturbance in bodily systems), psychological (cognitive and emotional factors involved in the evaluation of a threat), and even social (the disruption of a social unit). Dan experienced psychological stress, of course, as evidenced by his negative feelings resulting from marginalization and perceived rejection, but he also experienced other types of stress. He experienced biological stress because, in an effort to attend all his classes and study every day, he did not give his body adequate rest. As a result, he was susceptible to colds, which kept him in bed for several days each month and compounded his worries about managing coursework. Dan also experienced social stress, because he was functioning in a social system that he perceived to be threatening, and he had few positive relationships there.

Increasing emphasis is placed on the deleterious effects of stress on the immune system. This stressed father is comforted by his child.

THREE CATEGORIES OF PSYCHOLOGICAL STRESS

Psychological stress, about which we are primarily concerned in this chapter, can be broken down into three categories (Lazarus, 2007).

1. *Harm.* A damaging event that has already occurred. Dan minimized interactions with his classmates during much of the semester, which may have led them to decide that he is aloof and that they should not try to approach him socially. Dan has to accept that this rejection happened and that some harm has been done to him as a result, although he can learn from the experience and try to change in the future.

2. *Threat.* A perceived potential for harm that has not yet happened. This is probably the most common form of psychological stress. We feel stress because we are apprehensive about the possibility of the negative event. Dan felt threatened when he walked into a classroom because he anticipated rejection from his classmates. We can be proactive in managing threats to ensure that they do not in fact occur and result in harm to us.

3. *Challenge.* An event we appraise as an opportunity rather than an occasion for alarm. We are mobilized to struggle against the obstacle, as with a threat, but our attitude is quite different. Faced with a threat, we are likely to act defensively to protect ourselves. Our defensiveness sends a negative message to the environment: We don't want to change; we want to be left alone. In a state of challenge, however, we are excited, expansive, and confident about the task to be undertaken. The challenge may be an exciting and productive experience for us. Because Dan has overcome several setbacks in his drive to become a physician, he may feel more excited and motivated than before when resuming the program. He might be more aware of his resilience and feel more confident.

Stress has been measured in several ways (Aldwin & Yancura, 2004; Lazarus, 2007). One of the earliest attempts to measure stress consisted of a list of *life events*, uncommon events that bring about some change in our lives—experiencing the death of a loved one, getting married, becoming a parent, and so forth. The use of life events to measure stress is based on the assumption that major changes, even positive ones, disrupt our behavioral patterns.

More recently, stress has also been measured as *daily hassles*, common occurrences that are taxing—standing in line waiting, misplacing or losing things, dealing with troublesome coworkers, worrying about money, and many more. It is thought that an accumulation of daily hassles takes a greater toll on our coping capacities than do relatively rare life events.

Sociologists and community psychologists also study stress by measuring *role strain*—problems experienced in the performance of specific roles, such as romantic partner, caregiver, or worker. Research on caregiver burden is one example of measuring stress as role strain (Gordon, Pruchno, Wilson-Genderson, Murphy, & Rose, 2010).

Social workers should be aware that as increasing emphasis is placed on the deleterious effects of stress on the immune system, our attention and energies are diverted from the possibility of changing societal conditions that create stress and toward the management of ourselves as persons who respond to stress (D. Becker, 2005). For example, it is well documented that the experience of discrimination creates stress for many African Americans (K. Anderson, 2013). With the influence of the medical model, we should not be surprised when we are offered individual or biomedical solutions to such different social problems as discrimination, working motherhood, poverty, and road rage. It may be that the appeal of the stress concept is based on its diverting attention away from the environmental causes of stress. This is why social workers should always be alert to the social nature of stress.

STRESS AND CRISIS

A **crisis** is a major upset in our psychological equilibrium due to some harm, threat, or challenge with which we cannot cope (James & Gilliland, 2013). The crisis poses an obstacle to achieving a personal goal, but we cannot overcome the obstacle through our usual methods of problem solving. We temporarily lack either the necessary knowledge for coping or the ability to focus on the problem, because we feel overwhelmed. A crisis episode often results when we face a serious stressor with which we have had no prior experience. It may be biological (major illness), interpersonal (the sudden loss of a loved one), or environmental (unemployment or a natural disaster such as a flood or fire). We can regard anxiety, guilt, shame, sadness, envy, jealousy, and disgust as stress emotions (Zyskinsa & Heszen, 2009). They are the emotions most likely to emerge in a person who is experiencing crisis. Crisis episodes occur in three stages.

1. Our level of tension increases sharply.
2. We try and fail to cope with the stress, which further increases our tension and contributes to our sense of being overwhelmed. We are particularly receptive to receiving help from others at this time.
3. The crisis episode ends, either negatively (unhealthy coping) or positively (successful management of the crisis).

Crises can be classified into three types (Lantz & Walsh, 2007). *Developmental* crises occur when events in the normal flow of life create dramatic changes that produce extreme responses. Examples of such events include going off to college, college graduation, the birth of one's child, a midlife career change, and retirement from work. People may experience these types of crises if they have difficulty negotiating the typical developmental challenges outlined by Erikson (1968) and Gitterman (2009). *Situational* crises refer to uncommon and extraordinary events that a person has no way of forecasting or controlling. Examples include physical injuries, sexual assault, loss of a job, major illness, and the death of a loved one. *Existential* crises are characterized by escalating inner conflicts related to issues of purpose in life, responsibility, independence, freedom, and commitment. Examples include remorse over past life choices, a feeling that one's life has no meaning, and a questioning of one's basic values or spiritual beliefs.

Dan's poor midterm grades during his first semester of taking courses that would help him qualify for medical school illustrate some of these points. First, he was overwhelmed by the negative emotions of anger and sadness. Then, he occasionally retreated to church and his hometown, where he received much-needed support from his friends, mother, and sister. Finally, as the situation stabilized, Dan concluded that he could try to change some of his behaviors to relieve his academic-related stress.

TRAUMATIC STRESS

Although a single event may pose a crisis for one person but not another, some stressors are so severe that they are almost universally experienced as crises. The stress is so overwhelming that almost anyone would be affected. The term **traumatic stress** is used to refer to events that involve actual or threatened severe injury or death, of oneself or significant others (American Psychiatric Association, 2013). Three types of traumatic stress have been identified: natural (such as flood, tornado, earthquake) and technological (such as nuclear) disasters; war and related problems (such as concentration camps); and individual trauma (such as being raped, assaulted, or tortured) (Aldwin, 2007). People respond to traumatic stress with helplessness, terror, and horror.

Some occupations—particularly those of emergency workers such as police officers, firefighters, disaster relief workers, and military personnel in war settings—involve regular exposure to traumatic events that most people do not experience in a lifetime. Emergency workers, particularly police officers and firefighters, may experience threats to their own lives and the lives of their colleagues, as well as encounter mass casualties. Emergency workers may also experience *compassion stress*, a feeling of deep sympathy and sorrow for another who is stricken by misfortune, accompanied by a strong desire to alleviate the pain (Adams, Boscarino, & Figley, 2006). Any professionals who work regularly with trauma survivors are susceptible to compassion stress. Many social workers fall into this category.

VULNERABILITY TO STRESS

Many social work practitioners and researchers use a biopsychosocial *risk and resilience* framework for understanding how people experience and manage stress (Scholz, Blumer, & Brand, 2012). Although the biological and psychological levels relate to the individual, the social aspect of the framework captures the positive or adverse effects of the family, community, and wider social culture. The processes within each level interact, prompting risks for stress and impaired coping and the propensity toward *resilience*, or the ability to function adaptively despite stressful life circumstances. *Risks* can be understood as hazards occurring at the individual or environmental level that increase the likelihood of impairment. *Protective mechanisms* involve the personal, familial, community, and institutional resources that cultivate individuals' aptitudes and abilities while diminishing the possibility of problem behaviors. These protective influences may counterbalance or buffer against risk and are sometimes the converse of risk. For instance, at the individual level, poor physical health presents risks whereas good health is protective. The biopsychosocial framework provides a theoretical basis for social workers to conceptualize human behavior at several levels and can assist them in identifying and bolstering strengths as well as reducing risks. The framework offers a balanced view of systems in considering risks and strengths, as well as recognizing the complexity of individuals and the systems in which they are nested.

Individual factors encompass the biological and psychological realms. Within biology these include genes, temperament, physical health, developmental stage, and intelligence. At the psychological level it is useful to examine one's self-efficacy, self-esteem, and coping strategies. Social mechanisms include the family and household; the experience of traumatic events; the neighborhood; and societal conditions, including poverty, ethnicity, and access to health care.

Within the risk and resilience perspective, social workers can complete comprehensive assessments to determine the nature of their clients' problems. Knowledge of the risk and resilience influences helps social workers focus interventions onto the relevant areas of the client's life. Finally, the strengths perspective encourages social workers to build on the client's areas of real or potential resilience in recovering from, or adapting to, mental disorders and in so doing helps the client develop a greater sense of self-efficacy.

CRITICAL THINKING Questions 4.4

Why do you think we easily get diverted from thinking about societal conditions that create stress and come, instead, to focus on helping individuals cope with stress? How does such an approach fit with social work's commitment to social justice?

COPING AND ADAPTATION

Our efforts to master the demands of stress are referred to as **coping**. Coping includes the thoughts, feelings, and actions that constitute these efforts. One method of coping is **adaptation**, which may involve adjustments in our biological responses, perceptions, or lifestyle.

BIOLOGICAL COPING

The traditional biological view of stress and coping, developed in the 1950s, emphasizes the body's attempts to maintain physical equilibrium, or *homeostasis*, which is a steady state of functioning (Selye, 1991). Stress is considered the result of any demand on the body (specifically, the nervous and hormonal systems) during perceived emergencies to prepare for fight (confrontation) or flight (escape). A stressor may be any biological process, emotion, or thought.

In this view, the body's response to a stressor is called the *general adaptation syndrome* (explained in Exhibit 4.8). It occurs in three stages.

1. *Alarm*. The body first becomes aware of a threat.
2. *Resistance*. The body attempts to restore homeostasis.
3. *Exhaustion*. The body terminates coping efforts because of its inability to physically sustain the state of disequilibrium.

In this context, *resistance* means an active, positive response of the body in which endorphins and specialized cells of the immune system fight off stress and infection. Our immune systems are constructed for adaptation to stress, but the cumulative wear and tear of multiple stress episodes can gradually deplete our body's resources. Common outcomes of chronic stress include stomach and intestinal disorders, high blood pressure, heart problems, and emotional problems. If only to preserve healthy physical functioning, we must combat and prevent stress.

This traditional view of biological coping with stress came from research that focused on males, either male rodents or human males. Since 1995, the federal government has required federally funded researchers to include a broad representation of both men and women in their study samples. Consequently, recent research on stress has included female as well as male participants, and gender differences in responses to stress have been found. Recent research (Cardoso, Ellenbogen, Serravalle, & Linnen, 2013; Taylor & Stanton, 2007) suggests that females of many species, including humans, respond to stress with "tend-and-befriend" rather than the "fight-or-flight" behavior described in the general adaptation syndrome. Under stressful conditions, females have been found to protect and nurture their offspring and to seek social contact. Researchers suggest a possible biological basis for this gender difference in the coping response. More specifically, they note a large role for the hormone oxytocin, which plays a role in childbirth but also is secreted in both males and females in response to stress. High levels of oxytocin in animals are associated with calmness and increased sociability. Although males as well as females secrete oxytocin in response to stress, there is evidence that male hormones reduce the effects of oxytocin. This is thought to, in part, explain the gender differences in response to stress.

PSYCHOLOGICAL COPING

The psychological aspect of managing stress can be viewed in two ways. Some theorists consider coping ability to be a stable personality characteristic, or **trait**; others see it instead

EXHIBIT 4.8 • The General Adaptation Syndrome

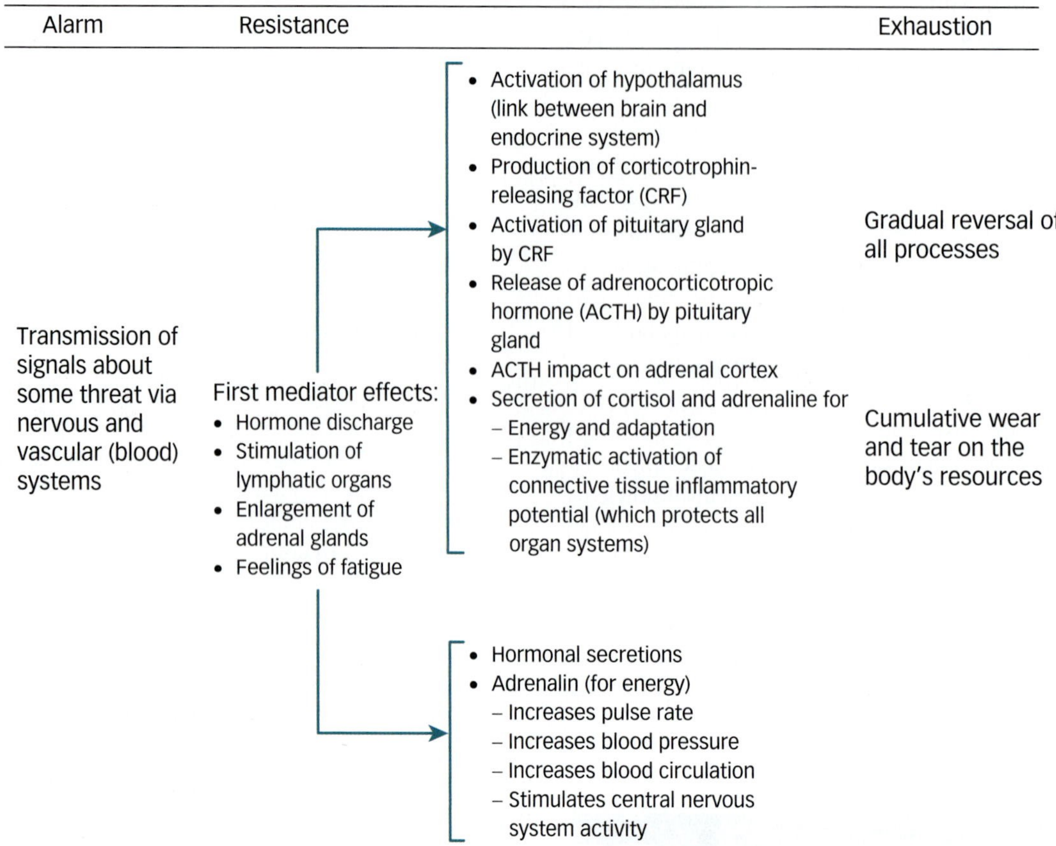

as a transient **state**—a process that changes over time, depending on the context (Lau, Eley, & Stevenson, 2006).

Those who consider coping to be a *trait* see it as an acquired defensive style. **Defense mechanisms** are unconscious, automatic responses that enable us to minimize perceived threats or keep them out of our awareness entirely. Exhibit 4.9 lists the common defense mechanisms identified by ego psychology. Some defense mechanisms are considered healthier, or more adaptive, than others. Dan's denial of his need for intimacy, for example, did not help him meet his goal of developing relationships with peers. But through the defense of sublimation (channeling the need for intimacy into alternative and socially acceptable outlets), he has been an effective and nurturing tutor for numerous high school science students.

Those who see coping as a *state*, or process, observe that our coping strategies change in different situations. After all, our perceptions of threats, and what we focus on in a situation, change. The context also has an impact on our perceived and actual abilities to apply effective coping mechanisms. From this perspective, Dan's use of denial of responsibility for relationship problems would be adaptive at some times and maladaptive at others. Perhaps his denial of needing support from classmates during the first academic semester helped him focus on his studies, which would help him achieve his goal of receiving an education. During the summer, however, when classes are out of session, he might become aware that his avoidance of relationships has prevented him from attaining interpersonal goals. His efforts to cope with loneliness might also change when he can afford more energy to confront the issue.

The trait and state approaches can usefully be combined. We can think of coping as a general pattern of managing stress that allows flexibility across diverse contexts.

COPING STYLES

Another way to look at coping is based on how the person responds to crisis. Coping efforts may be problem focused or emotion focused (Sideridis, 2006). The function of **problem-focused coping** is to change the situation by acting on the environment. This method tends to dominate whenever we view situations as controllable by action. For example, Dan was concerned about his professors' insensitivity to his learning disability (auditory processing disorder). When he took action to educate them about it and explain more clearly how he learns best in a classroom setting, he was using problem-focused

EXHIBIT 4.9 • Common Defense Mechanisms

DEFENSE MECHANISM	DEFINITION	EXAMPLE
DEVELOPMENTALLY EARLIER		
Acting out	Direct expression of impulses to avoid tension that would result from their postponement.	An adolescent steals money from her mother to buy alcohol and gets into constant arguments with her older sister who tries to monitor her behavior.
Denial	Negating an important aspect of reality that one may actually perceive.	A woman with anorexia acknowledges her actual weight and strict dieting practices but firmly believes she is maintaining good self-care by dieting.
Projection	Attributing unacceptable thoughts and feelings to others.	A man does not want to be angry with his girlfriend, so when he is upset with her, he avoids owning that emotion by assuming she is angry at him.
Regression	Resuming behaviors associated with an earlier developmental stage or level of functioning in order to avoid present anxiety. The behavior may or may not help to resolve the anxiety.	A young man throws a temper tantrum as a means of discharging his frustration when he cannot master a task on his computer. The startled computer technician, who had been reluctant to attend to the situation, now comes forth to provide assistance.
Splitting	The tendency to see the good and bad aspects of the self or others as separate; to see the self and others as alternately "all good" or "all bad."	A primary-school child "hates" his teacher when reprimanded and "loves" his teacher for praise and behaves accordingly.
DEVELOPMENTALLY LATER		
Displacement	Shifting feelings about one person or situation onto another.	A student's anger at her professor, who is threatening as an authority figure, is transposed into anger at her boyfriend, a safer target.
Intellectualization	Avoiding unacceptable emotions by thinking or talking about them rather than experiencing them directly.	A person talks to her counselor about the fact that she is sad but shows no emotional evidence of sadness, which makes it harder for her to understand its effects on her life.
Isolation of affect	Consciously experiencing an emotion in a "safe" context rather than the threatening context in which it was first unconsciously experienced.	A person does not experience sadness at the funeral of a family member but the following week weeps uncontrollably at the death of a pet hamster.
Rationalization	Using convincing reasons to justify ideas, feelings, or actions so as to avoid recognizing true motives.	A student copes with the guilt normally associated with cheating on an exam by reasoning that he was too ill the previous week to prepare as well as he wanted.
Reaction formation	Replacing an unwanted unconscious impulse with its opposite in conscious behavior.	A person cannot bear to be angry with his boss, so after a conflict he convinces himself that the boss is worthy of loyalty and demonstrates this by volunteering to work overtime.
Repression	Keeping unwanted thoughts and feelings entirely out of awareness.	A son may begin to generate an impulse of hatred for his father, but because the impulse would be consciously unacceptable, he represses the hatred and does not become aware of it.
Somatization	Converting intolerable impulses into somatic symptoms.	A person who is unable to express his negative emotions develops frequent stomachaches as a result.
Undoing	Nullifying an undesired impulse with an act of reparation.	A man who feels guilty about having lustful thoughts about a coworker tries to make amends to his wife by purchasing a special gift for her.
MOST "MATURE" DEFENSES		
Humor	The expression of painful or socially unacceptable feelings without discomforting the person who is being humorous or (often) the recipient.	An employee manages her discomfort at being in a supervisory meeting by making self-deprecating jokes.
Sublimation	Converting an impulse from a socially unacceptable aim to a socially acceptable one.	An angry, aggressive young man becomes a star on his school's debate team.

SOURCE: Adapted from E. Goldstein, 1995; Schamess & Shilkret, 2011.

coping. In contrast, the function of **emotion-focused coping** is to change either the way the stressful situation is attended to (by vigilance or avoidance) or the meaning to oneself of what is happening. The external situation does not change, but our behaviors or attitudes change with respect to it, and we may thus effectively manage the stressor. When we view stressful conditions as unchangeable, emotion-focused coping may dominate. If Dan learns that one of his professors has no empathy for students with learning disabilities, he might avoid taking that professor's courses in the future or decide that getting a good grade in that course is not as important as being exposed to the course material.

U.S. culture tends to venerate problem-focused coping and the independently functioning self and to distrust emotion-focused coping and what may be called relational coping. **Relational coping** takes into account actions that maximize the survival of others—such as our families, children, and friends—as well as ourselves (Zunkel, 2002). Feminist theorists propose that women are more likely than men to employ the relational coping strategies of negotiation and forbearance, and some research (Taylor & Stanton, 2007) gives credence to the idea that women are more likely than men to use relational coping. As social workers, we must be careful not to assume that one type of coping is superior to another. Power imbalances and social forces such as racism and sexism affect the coping strategies of individuals (Lippa, 2005). We need to give clients credit for the extraordinary coping efforts they may make in hostile environments.

We might note that Dan used many problem-focused coping strategies to manage stressors at the university, even though he was mostly ineffective because of the specific strategies he used. For example, he directly confronted his peers, teachers, family members, and social worker, and he also tried with limited success to control his moods through force of will.

COPING AND TRAUMATIC STRESS

People exhibit some similarities between the way they cope with traumatic stress (described earlier) and the way they cope with everyday stress. However, coping with traumatic stress differs from coping with everyday stress in several ways (Aldwin & Yancura, 2004).

- Because people tend to have much less control in traumatic situations, their primary emotion-focused coping strategy is emotional numbing, or the constriction of emotional expression. They also make greater use of the defense mechanism of denial.
- Confiding in others takes on greater importance.
- The process of coping tends to take a much longer time, months or even years.
- A search for meaning takes on greater importance, and transformation in personal identity is more common.

Although there is evidence of long-term negative consequences of traumatic stress, trauma survivors sometimes report positive outcomes as well. Studies have found that 34% of Holocaust survivors and 50% of rape survivors report positive personal changes following their experiences with traumatic stress (Koss & Figueredo, 2004). A majority of children who experience such atrocities as war, natural disasters, community violence, physical abuse, catastrophic illness, and traumatic injury also recover, demonstrating their resilience (Husain, 2012; Le Brocque, Hendrikz, & Kenardy, 2010).

However, many trauma survivors experience a set of symptoms known as *post-traumatic stress disorder (PTSD)* (American Psychiatric Association, 2013). These symptoms include the following:

- Persistent reliving of the traumatic event: intrusive, distressing recollections of the event; distressing dreams of the event; a sense of reliving the event; intense distress when exposed to cues of the event
- Persistent avoidance of stimuli associated with the traumatic event: avoidance of thoughts or feelings connected to the event; avoidance of places, activities, and people connected to the event; inability to recall aspects of the trauma; loss of interest in activities; feeling detached from others; emotional numbing; no sense of a future
- Negative alterations in cognition or mood after the event, such as memory problems, negative emotions, and distorted beliefs about the event (such as self-blame)
- Persistent high state of arousal: difficulty sleeping, irritability, difficulty concentrating, excessive attention to stimuli, exaggerated startle response

Symptoms of post-traumatic stress disorder have been noted as soon as 1 week following the traumatic event or as long as 20 years after (Middleton & Craig, 2012). It is important to understand that the initial symptoms of post-traumatic stress are normal and expectable and that PTSD should only be considered a disorder if those symptoms do not remit over time and result in serious, long-term limitations in social functioning. Complete recovery from symptoms occurs in 30% of cases, mild symptoms continue over time in 40%, moderate symptoms continue in 20%, and symptoms persist or get worse in about 10% (D. Becker, 2004). Children and older adults have the most trouble coping with traumatic events. A strong system of social support helps to prevent or to foster recovery from post-traumatic stress disorder. Besides providing support, social workers may be helpful by encouraging the person to discuss the traumatic event and by providing education about support groups.

SOCIAL SUPPORT

In coping with the demands of daily life, our social supports—the people we rely on to enrich our lives—can be invaluable. **Social support** can be defined as the interpersonal interactions and relationships that provide us with assistance or feelings of attachment to persons we perceive as caring (Hobfoll, 1996). Three types of social support resources are available (J. Walsh, 2000): *material support* (food, clothing, shelter, and other concrete items); *emotional support* (interpersonal support); and *instrumental support* (services provided by casual contacts such as grocers, hairstylists, and landlords). Some authors add "social integration" support to the mix, which refers to a person's sense of belonging (Wethington, Moen, Glasgow, & Pillemer, 2000).

This father provides emotional support to his son, increasing the son's sense of belonging.

Our **social network** includes not just our social support but all the people with whom we regularly interact and the patterns of interaction that result from exchanging resources with them (Moren-Cross & Lin, 2006). Network relationships often occur in *clusters* (distinct categories such as nuclear family, extended family, friends, neighbors, community relations, school, work, church, recreational groups, and professional associations). Network relationships are not synonymous with support; they may be negative or positive. But the scope of the network does tend to indicate our potential for obtaining social support. Having supportive others in a variety of clusters indicates that we are supported in many areas of our lives, rather than being limited to relatively few sources. Our *personal network* includes those from the social network who, in our view, provide us with our most essential supports (Bidart & Lavenu, 2005).

Virtual Support

I don't need to tell you, of course, that much social support is now provided through connective technologies that allow people to be "in contact" without being physically present with one another. Facebook, Skype, e-mail, blogging, tweets, and texts put people in touch with one another instantaneously, regardless of where they are or what they are doing. Whereas there is much to be admired about these developments, and they clearly allow us to be in touch with significant others we might never otherwise see, they also create the potential for us to reduce the frequency of, and even our desire for, face-to-face contacts and thus redefine the nature of relationships, support, and intimacy. The number of people with whom people physically interact has fallen in recent years. Dan, like many of his peers, spent several hours per day on the Internet communicating with others; in his case it was primarily through e-mail. Spencer believed this was a mixed blessing for his client, because whereas it did help Dan feel connected to his support system, it prevented any efforts he might otherwise expend for intimate interaction with people whose lives physically intersected with his own. Turkle (2011), among others, is concerned about the unpredictable ways social technology may alter the nature of our relationships.

How Social Support Aids Coping

The experience of stress creates a physiological state of emotional arousal, which reduces the efficiency of cognitive functions (Caplan & Caplan, 2000). When we experience stress, we become less effective at focusing our attention and scanning the environment for relevant information. We cannot access the memories that normally bring meaning to our perceptions, judgment, planning, and integration of feedback from others. These memory impairments reduce our ability to maintain a consistent sense of identity.

Social support helps in these situations by acting as an "auxiliary ego." Our social support—particularly our personal network—compensates for our perceptual deficits, reminds us of our sense of self, and monitors the adequacy of our functioning. Here are 10 characteristics of effective support (Caplan, 1990; Caplan & Caplan, 2000):

1. Nurtures and promotes an ordered worldview
2. Promotes hope
3. Promotes timely withdrawal and initiative
4. Provides guidance
5. Provides a communication channel with the social world
6. Affirms one's personal identity
7. Provides material help
8. Contains distress through reassurance and affirmation
9. Ensures adequate rest
10. Mobilizes other personal supports

Some of these support systems are formal (service organizations), and some are informal (such as friends and neighbors). Religion, which attends to the spiritual realm, also plays a distinctive support role (Caplan, 1990). This topic is explored in Chapter 5.

How Social Workers Evaluate Social Support

There is no consensus about how social workers can evaluate a client's level of social support. The simplest procedure is to ask for the client's subjective perceptions of support from family and friends (Procidano & Smith, 1997). One of the most complex procedures uses eight indicators of social support: available listening, task appreciation, task challenge, emotional support, emotional challenge, reality confirmation, tangible assistance, and personal assistance (Richman, Rosenfeld, & Hardy, 1993). One particularly useful model includes three social support indicators (Uchino, 2009):

1. *Listing of social network resources.* The client lists all the people with whom he or she regularly interacts.
2. *Accounts of supportive behavior.* The client identifies specific episodes of receiving support from others in the recent past.
3. *Perceptions of support.* The client subjectively assesses the adequacy of the support received from various sources.

In assessing a client's social supports from this perspective, the social worker first asks the client to list all persons with whom he or she has interacted in the past 1 or 2 weeks. Next, the social worker asks the client to draw from that list the persons he or she perceives to be supportive in significant ways (significance is intended to be open to the client's interpretation). The client is asked to describe specific recent acts of support provided by those significant others. Finally, the social worker asks the client to evaluate the adequacy of the support received from specific sources and in general. On the basis of this assessment, the social worker can identify both subjective and objective support indicators with the client and target underused clusters for the development of additional social support.

NORMAL AND ABNORMAL COPING

Most people readily assess the coping behaviors they observe in others as "normal" or "abnormal." But what does "normal" mean? We all apply different criteria. The standards we use to classify coping thoughts and feelings as normal or abnormal are important, however, because they have implications for how we view ourselves and how we behave toward those different from us (Francis, 2013). For example, Dan was concerned that other students at the university perceived him as abnormal because of his ethnicity and social isolation. Most likely, other students did not notice him much at all. It is interesting that, in Dan's view, his physical appearance and demeanor revealed him as abnormal. However, he was one of many Asian American students at the university, and his feelings were not as evident to others as he thought.

Social workers struggle just as much to define *normal* and *abnormal* as anybody else, but their definitions may have greater consequences. Misidentifying someone as normal may forestall needed interventions; misidentifying someone as abnormal may create a stigma or become a self-fulfilling prophecy. To avoid such problems, social workers may profitably consider how four disciplines define normal.

THE MEDICAL (PSYCHIATRIC) PERSPECTIVE

One definition from psychiatry, a branch of medicine, states that we are normal when we are in harmony with ourselves and our environment. Significant abnormality in perceived thinking, behavior, and mood may even classify as a mental disorder. In fact, the current definition of *mental disorder* used by the American Psychiatric Association (2013), which is intended to help psychiatrists and many other professionals distinguish between normality and abnormality, is a "syndrome characterized by clinically significant disturbance in an individual's cognition, emotion regulation, or behavior that reflects a dysfunction in the psychological, biological, or developmental processes underlying mental functioning" (p. 20). Such a disorder usually represents significant distress in social or occupational functioning. The medical definition focuses on underlying disturbances *within* the person and is sometimes referred to as the *disease model* of abnormality. This model implies that the abnormal person must experience changes within the self (rather than create environmental change) in order to be considered "normal" again.

In summary, the medical model of abnormality focuses on underlying disturbances within the person. An assessment of the disturbance results in a diagnosis based on a cluster of observable symptoms. Interventions, or treatments, focus on changing the individual. The abnormal person must experience internal, personal changes (rather than induce environmental change) in order to be considered normal again. Exhibit 4.10 summarizes the format for diagnosing mental disorders as developed by psychiatry in the United States and published in the *Diagnostic and Statistical Manual of Mental Disorders* (American Psychiatric Association, 2013). Many people in the helping professions are required to follow this format in mental health treatment facilities, including social workers.

EXHIBIT 4.10 • *DSM-5* Classification of Mental Disorders

- Record the mental disorder, beginning with the problem most responsible for the current evaluation. Many diagnoses also contain subtypes or specifiers (for example, "mild," "moderate," and "severe") for added diagnostic clarity.
- When uncertain if a diagnosis is correct, the social worker should use the "provisional" qualifier, which means he or she may need additional time or information to be confident about the choice.
- More than one diagnosis can be used for a client, and medical diagnoses should also be included if they are significant to the client's overall condition. Social workers cannot make medical diagnoses, of course, but they can be included if they are noted in a client's history or the client reports their existence.
- If a person no longer meets criteria for a disorder that may be relevant to his or her current condition, the qualifier "past history" can be used, although this would not be the primary diagnosis. For example, if a woman seeks help for depression while she is pregnant, it may be important to note if she had an eating disorder history.
- Social and environmental problems that are a focus of clinical attention may also be included as part of the diagnosis. A chapter in the *DSM* titled "Other Conditions That May Be a Focus of Clinical Attention" includes a list of conditions (popularly known as "V-codes") that are not considered formal diagnoses but can be used for that descriptive purpose.

PSYCHOLOGICAL PERSPECTIVES

One major difference between psychiatry and psychology is that psychiatry tends to emphasize biological and somatic interventions to return the person to a state of normalcy, whereas psychology emphasizes various cognitive, behavioral, or reflective interventions.

Psychological theory is quite broad in scope, but some theories are distinctive in that they postulate that people normally progress through a sequence of life stages. The time context thus becomes important. Each new stage of personality development builds on previous stages, and any unsuccessful transitions can result in abnormal behavior—that is, a deviant pattern of coping with threats and challenges. An unsuccessful struggle through one stage implies that the person will experience difficulties in mastering subsequent stages.

One life stage view of normality well known in social work is that of Erik Erikson (1968), who proposed eight stages of normal *psychosocial* development (see Exhibit 4.11 for a summary of these stages). Dan, at age 24, is struggling with the developmental stage of young adulthood, in which the major issue is intimacy versus isolation. Challenges in young adulthood include developing a capacity for interpersonal intimacy as opposed to feeling socially empty or isolated within the family unit. According to Erikson's theory, Dan's current difficulties would be related to his lack of success in negotiating one or more of the five preceding developmental phases or challenges, and reviewing this would be an important part of his intervention.

From this perspective, Dan's experience of stress would not be seen as abnormal, but his inability to make coping choices that promote positive personal adaptation would signal psychological abnormality. For example, at the university, he was having difficulty with relationship development and support seeking. He avoided social situations such as study groups, recreational activities, and university organizations in which he might learn more about what kinds of people he likes, what interests he might share with them, and what insecurities they might share as well. From a stage theory perspective, Dan's means of coping with the challenges of intimacy versus isolation might be seen as maladaptive, or abnormal.

THE SOCIOLOGICAL APPROACH: DEVIANCE

The field of sociology offers a variety of approaches to the study of abnormality, or deviance, one of which is

EXHIBIT 4.11 • Erikson's Stages of Psychosocial Development

LIFE STAGE	PSYCHOSOCIAL CHALLENGE	SIGNIFICANT OTHERS
Infancy	Trust versus mistrust	Maternal persons
Early childhood	Autonomy versus shame and doubt	Parental persons
Play age	Initiative versus guilt	Family
School age	Industry versus inferiority	Neighborhood
Adolescence	Identity versus identity diffusion	Peers
Young adulthood	Intimacy versus isolation	Partners
Adulthood	Generativity versus self-absorption	Household
Mature age	Integrity versus disgust and despair	Humanity

derived from symbolic interactionism. It states that those who cannot constrain their behaviors within role limitations that are acceptable to others become labeled as deviant. Thus, *deviance* is a negative label assigned when one is considered by a majority of significant others to be in violation of the prescribed social order (Curra, 2011). Put more simply, we are unable to grasp the perspective from which the deviant person thinks and acts; the person's behavior does not make sense to us. We conclude that our inability to understand the other person's perspective is due to that person's shortcomings rather than to our own rigidity, and we label the behavior as deviant. The deviance label may be mitigated if the individual accepts that he or she should think or behave otherwise and tries to conform to the social order. (It should be emphasized, however, that sociologists are increasingly using the term *positive deviance* to describe those persons whose outstanding skills and characteristics make them "outliers" in a constructive sense.)

From this viewpoint, Dan would be perceived as abnormal, or deviant, only by those who had sufficient knowledge of his thoughts and feelings to form an opinion about his allegiance to their ideas of appropriate social behavior. He might also be considered abnormal by peers who had little understanding of his Asian American cultural background. Those who knew Dan well might understand the basis for his negative thoughts and emotions and, in that context, continue to view him as normal in his coping efforts. However, it is significant that Dan was trying to avoid intimacy with his university classmates and work peers so that he would not become well known to them. Because he still views himself as somewhat deviant, he wants to avoid being seen as deviant (or abnormal) by others, which in his view would lead to their rejection of him. This circular reasoning poorly serves Dan's efforts to cope with stress in ways that promote his personal goals.

THE SOCIAL WORK PERSPECTIVE: SOCIAL FUNCTIONING

The profession of social work is characterized by the consideration of systems and the reciprocal impact of persons and their environments (the bio-psycho-social-spiritual perspective) on human behavior. Social workers tend not to classify individuals as abnormal. Instead, they consider the person-in-environment as an ongoing process that facilitates or blocks one's ability to experience satisfactory social functioning. In fact, in social work, the term *normalization* refers to helping clients realize that their thoughts and feelings are shared by many other individuals in similar circumstances (Hepworth, Rooney, Rooney, & Strom-Gottfried, 2013).

Three types of situations are most likely to produce problems in social functioning: stressful life transitions, relationship difficulties, and environmental unresponsiveness (Gitterman, 2009). Note that all three are related to transitory interactions of the person with other persons or the environment and do not rely on evaluating the client as normal or abnormal.

Social work's *person-in-environment (PIE) classification system* formally organizes the assessment of individuals' ability to cope with stress around the four factors shown in Exhibit 4.12: social functioning problems, environmental problems, mental health problems, and physical health problems. Such a broad classification scheme helps ensure that Dan's range of needs will be addressed. James Karls and Maura O'Keefe (2008), the authors of the PIE system, state that it "underlines the importance of conceptualizing a person in an interactive context" and that "pathological and psychological limitations are accounted for but are not accorded extraordinary attention" (p. x). Thus, the system avoids labeling a client as abnormal. At the same time, however, it offers no way to assess the client's strengths and resources.

With the exception of its neglect of strengths and resources, the PIE assessment system is appropriate for social work because it was specifically developed to promote a holistic biopsychosocial perspective on human behavior. For example, at a mental health center that subscribed to psychiatry's *DSM* classification system, Dan might be given an Axis I diagnosis of adjustment disorder or dysthymic disorder, and his auditory processing disorder might also be diagnosed. With the PIE system, the social worker would, in addition to addressing mental and physical health concerns, assess Dan's overall social and occupational functioning, as well as any specific environmental problems. For example, Dan's problems with the student role that might be highlighted

EXHIBIT 4.12 • The Person-in-Environment (PIE) Classification System

FACTOR I: SOCIAL FUNCTIONING PROBLEMS

A. Social role in which each problem is identified

1. Family (parent, spouse, child, sibling, other, significant other)
2. Other interpersonal (lover, friend, neighbor, member, other)
3. Occupational (worker/paid, worker/home, worker/volunteer, student, other)

B. Type of problem in social role

1. No problem	4. Dependency	7. Victimization
2. Ambivalence	5. Loss	8. Mixed
3. Responsibility	6. Isolation	9. Other

C. Severity of Problem

1. No Problem	3. Moderate severity	5. Very high severity
2. Low severity	4. High severity	6. Catastrophic

D. Duration of problem

1. More than five years	3. Six months to one year	5. Two weeks or less
2. One to five years	4. Two to four weeks	

E. Ability of client to cope with problem

1. Outstanding coping skills	3. Adequate	5. Inadequate
2. Above average	4. Somewhat inadequate	6. No coping skills

FACTOR II: ENVIRONMENTAL PROBLEMS

A. Social system where each problem is identified

1. Economic/basic need	3. Judicial/legal	5. Voluntary association
2. Education/training	4. Health, safety, social services	6. Affectional support

B. Specific type of problem within each social system

C. Severity of problem

D. Duration of problem

FACTOR III: MENTAL HEALTH PROBLEMS

A. Clinical syndromes (Axis I of *DSM*)

B. Personality and developmental disorders (Axis II of *DSM*)

FACTOR IV: PHYSICAL HEALTH PROBLEMS

A. Disease diagnosed by a physician

B. Other health problems reported by client and others

on PIE Factor I include his isolation, the high severity of his impairment and its 6-month to a year's duration, and the inadequacy of his coping skills. His environmental stressors on Factor II might include a deficiency in affectional support, of high severity, with a duration of 6 months to a year. Assessment with PIE provides Dan and the social worker with more avenues for intervention, which might include personal, interpersonal, and environmental systems.

CRITICAL THINKING Questions 4.5

What biases do you have about how people should cope with discrimination based on race, ethnicity, gender, sexual orientation, and so on? How might the coping strategy need to change in different situations, such as receiving service in a restaurant, being interviewed for a job, or dealing with an unthinking comment from a classmate? What do you see as the contributions of the medical, psychological, sociological, and social work perspectives on normal and abnormal coping? What do you see as the downsides of each of these perspectives?

IMPLICATIONS FOR SOCIAL WORK PRACTICE

The study of the psychological person as a thinking and feeling being and as a self in relationship has many implications for social work practice.

- Be alert to the possibility that practice interventions may need to focus on any of several systems, including family, small groups, organizations, and communities. The person's transactions with all of these systems affect psychological functioning.
- Where appropriate, help individual clients to develop a stronger sense of competence through both ego-supportive and ego-modifying interventions.
- Where appropriate, help individual clients to enhance problem-solving skills through techniques directed at both cognitive reorganization and behavioral change.
- Where appropriate, help individual clients strengthen their sense of self by bringing balance to emotional and cognitive experiences.
- Help clients consider their strengths in terms of the unique sets of intelligences they may have and show how these intelligences may help them address their challenges in unique ways.
- Always assess the nature, range, and intensity of a client's interpersonal relationships.
- Help clients identify their sources of stress and patterns of coping. Recognize the possibility of particular vulnerabilities to stress and to social and environmental conditions that give rise to stress.
- Help clients assess the effectiveness of particular coping strategies for specific situations.
- Where appropriate, use case management activities focused on developing a client's social supports through linkages with potentially supportive others in a variety of social network clusters.
- When working with persons in crisis, attempt to alleviate distress and facilitate a return to the previous level of functioning.

KEY TERMS

accommodation (cognitive), 93
adaptation, 111
assimilation (cognitive), 93
cognition, 91
coping, 111
crisis, 109
defense mechanisms, 112
ego, 99
ego psychology, 100
emotion, 92
emotional intelligence, 101
emotion-focused coping, 114
multiple intelligences, 94
preconscious, 102
primary emotions, 98
problem-focused coping, 112
psychoanalytic theory, 99
psychology, 91
relational coping, 114

relational theory, 104
schema (schemata), 92
secondary emotions, 98
self, 104
social network, 115
social support, 115
state, 112
stress, 108
trait, 111
traumatic stress, 110
unconscious, 92

ACTIVE LEARNING

1. *Theory analysis and application.* Working in small groups, reread the case study at the beginning of this chapter. As you read, discuss what you see as the driving force of Dan's behavior as he struggles with earning admission to medical school. Is it cognition? Is it emotion? What patterns of thinking and feeling might Dan have developed from his cultural background? What theories presented in the chapter are most helpful to you in thinking about this, and why? Now, review the big ideas of different theoretical perspectives presented in Exhibit 2.9 in Chapter 2. Find three big ideas that best reflect the way you understand Dan's situation. What are the implications of these big ideas for helping Dan to reach his goals?
2. What is your own perspective on the nature of the self? How does this affect your work with clients when you consider their potential for change?
3. Consider several recent situations in which you have used problem-focused or emotion-focused coping strategies. What was different about the situations in which you used one rather than the other? Were the coping strategies successful? Why or why not?

WEB RESOURCES

American Psychiatric Association DSM-5 Implementation and Support

www.dsm5.org/Pages/Default.aspx

Site includes information on implementation of the manual, answers frequently asked questions, lists DSM-5 *corrections, and provides a mechanism for submitting questions and feedback regarding implementation of the manual. Links are provided to educational webinars about the* DSM-5 *and trainings being conducted throughout the United States and abroad.*

Association for Moral Education (AME)

www.amenetwork.org

AME was founded in 1976 to provide an interdisciplinary forum for professionals interested in the moral dimensions of educational theory and practice. The association is dedicated to fostering communication, cooperation, training, curriculum development, and research that links moral theory with educational practice. It supports self-reflective educational practices that value the worth and dignity of each individual as a moral agent in a pluralistic society.

Howard Gardner

http://howardgardner.com

The website of Howard Gardner of Harvard Graduate School of Education includes information about his and others' research on multiple intelligences.

Jean Baker Miller Training Institute (JBMTI)

www.jbmti.org

The JBMTI at the Wellesley Centers for Women is the home of relational-cultural theory (RCT), which posits that people grow through and toward relationships throughout the life span and that culture powerfully impacts relationship. JBMTI is dedicated to understanding the complexities of human connections as well as exploring the personal and social factors that can lead to chronic disconnection.

MedlinePlus: Stress

www.nlm.nih.gov/medlineplus/stress.html

Site presented by the National Institute of Mental Health presents links to the latest news about stress research; coping; disease management; specific conditions; and stress in children, seniors, teenagers, and women.

Piaget's Developmental Theory

www.learningandteaching.info/learning/piaget.htm

Site maintained by James Atherton of the United Kingdom overviews Jean Piaget's key ideas and developmental stages.

University of Wisconsin–Madison Center for Healthy Minds

http://www.centerhealthyminds.org

The Center for Healthy Minds, directed by Dr. Richard Davidson, is engaged in a broad program of research on the brain mechanisms that underlie emotion and emotion regulation in normal individuals throughout the life course and in individuals with various psychiatric disorders.

SAGE edge™ Sharpen your skills with SAGE edge at edge.sagepub.com/hutchisoness2e

SAGE edge for students provides a personalized approach to help you accomplish your coursework goals in an easy-to-use learning environment. watch listen read

LEARNING OBJECTIVES	FOR FURTHER EXPLORATION AND APPLICATION
LO 4.1: Analyze one's emotional and cognitive reactions to a case study.	Drowning in Empathy: The Cost of Vicarious Trauma (watch)
LO 4.2: Define cognition and emotion.	The Cognitive-Emotional Brain (listen)
LO 4.3: Compare and contrast five major theories of cognition (cognitive, information processing, social learning, multiple intelligences, and moral reasoning) and cognitive behavioral intervention theory.	Howard Gardner's Theory of Multiple Intelligences (read) Kohlberg (read)
LO 4.4: Compare and contrast four major categories of theories of emotion (physiological theories, psychological theories, social theories, and social work practice theories).	Music Video Award: Social Work Theory (watch)
LO 4.5: Recognize how cognitive and emotional characteristics can be involved in cognitive and emotional "disorders."	Dysfunctional Cognitions and Their Emotional, Behavioral, and Functional Correlates in Adults With Attention Deficit Hyperactivity Disorder (ADHD): Is the Cognitive-Behavioral Model Valid? (read)
LO 4.6: Describe four theories of self in relationships (relational, attachment, feminist, and social identity).	Rethinking Compassion Fatigue Through the Lens of Professional Identity: The Case of Child-Protection Workers (read)
LO 4.7: Summarize the role of stress, crisis, and traumatic stress in human behavior.	How Social Media Shapes Identity (watch)
LO 4.8: Analyze different styles of coping and adaptation in relation to stress.	Coping With Stress (read)
LO 4.9: Critique four different approaches to normal and abnormal coping (medical, psychological, sociological, and social work).	Abnormal Ways to Cope With Stress (read)
LO 4.10: Apply knowledge of cognition, emotion, self, the self in relationship, stress, and coping to recommend guidelines for social work assessment and intervention.	Cognitive Behavioral Theory (listen)

iStockphoto.com/Bikeworldtravel

5

The Spiritual Person

Michael J. Sheridan

Learning Objectives

LO 5.1 Compare and contrast emotional and cognitive reactions to the seven case studies.

LO 5.2 Compare and contrast the definitions of spirituality and religion.

LO 5.3 Describe the major contributions of Fowler's and Wilber's transpersonal theories of human behavior.

LO 5.4 Give examples of the impact of spirituality and religion in the lives of oppressed groups and people coping with different problems of living.

LO 5.5 Demonstrate how to gather information about a client's religious or spiritual history.

LO 5.6 Apply knowledge of human spirituality to recommend guidelines for social work assessment and intervention.

CASE STUDY 5.1

CAROLINE'S CHALLENGING QUESTIONS

Caroline, who grew up in a large, close-knit family from North Carolina, is in her first year of college at a university in another state where she is encountering all kinds of new experiences. A devout Christian, Caroline is a member of a Baptist church back home, where her family has attended for generations. She was very involved in her home church, singing in the choir and actively engaged in several youth programs. Most of her high school friends attended her church, so she was more than a little uncomfortable when she learned that her roommate, Ruth, was Jewish. Caroline has met a number of other students who are from different faiths or who say that they don't belong to a church at all. This has been a new and challenging experience for her.

At first she tried to stay away from anyone who wasn't Christian but struggled with this because so many of her non-Christian classmates seemed like nice people and she really wanted to have friends. All sorts of questions began to emerge in her mind, like *How can they not believe in Jesus Christ?* and *What do they believe?* and *What will happen to them in the afterlife if they are not saved?* These questions only grew as she took a comparative religions class where she learned about faiths that she had never heard of before. In one class exercise, she was paired with a student from Turkey who said she was Muslim. At first, Caroline was anxious about talking with her, but as they moved through the exercise, she began to feel that they were more alike than different. They both were from very religious families, their faith was important to them personally, and they both were struggling with all the different perspectives they were encountering in college. Later that day, Caroline realized that if she had been born in Turkey, she would probably be a Muslim too. This thought both intrigued and unsettled her. More and more she is asking herself, *What do I really believe and why?*

CASE STUDY 5.2

NAOMI'S HEALTH CRISIS

Naomi is a 42-year-old mother of three children who are 10, 7, and 3 years old. Naomi discovered a lump in her breast a couple of weeks ago, and she and her husband, David, have been anxiously awaiting news regarding test results. When the diagnosis of cancer finally comes, they are both stunned and frightened but pull themselves together for the sake of the children. Naomi begins the long journey of doctors, surgery, chemotherapy, and radiation treatments while simultaneously trying to maintain family life and a part-time job as best she can. David takes on new duties as a more active parent and homemaker while still going to his full-time job. He struggles with his own fears and anger about what is happening, initially not sharing these with Naomi because he is determined to be her "rock."

Naomi and David are members of Temple Shalom, a local Reform Jewish congregation, which they joined after their first child was born. When they were growing up, Naomi's family were members of a Reform congregation, whereas David's family expressed their Jewish heritage in more secular and cultural terms, gathering annually for a Passover Seder but not attending services except occasionally on Yom Kippur. Naomi had not regularly attended services after her bat mitzvah, but both she and David decided that they wanted to be part of a spiritual community for their children. They had heard good things about the temple in their neighborhood and decided to explore it. They liked its open, welcoming atmosphere; its liberal viewpoints on social issues; and its active engagement in social action in the community. They both enjoy the weekly connection with other adults and are happy with the religious classes their children attend. Recently, Naomi and David have been engaged in weekly Shabbat Torah study sessions, to deepen their understanding of Jewish sacred texts.

Now that Naomi is facing this health crisis, both she and David are feeling a bit lost and are searching for answers. Although friends have been supportive, both of their families live far away, and their short visits and phone calls only provide minimal comfort. One night, when they both can't sleep, Naomi and David begin to share their doubts and fears with one another, even admitting that they feel angry with God and wondering if there is such a thing as God at all. Naomi finally suggests, "I think it would help to talk with Rabbi Shapiro and some of the people we've met at Temple Shalom." David agrees and adds that they should also explore the Jewish Healing Network that was described in the bulletin the previous week.

CASE STUDY 5.3

MATTHEW'S FAITH JOURNEY

Matthew will be 70 next month—a fact that is hard for him to believe. He's been a widower for 5 years now since his wife, Betty, died of a sudden heart attack. The first few years following her death were rough, but Matthew made it through with the help of his sons and their families and members of his Catholic parish, which he has been attending for 40 years. His faith has always been very important to him, even though he has struggled with periods of doubt and confusion—the latest following Betty's death. At one point when he was younger, he considered leaving the church, when disagreements about doctrine and rumblings about the new priest were causing uproar in the congregation. He even visited several other denominations to see if they were a better fit for him. But after much reflection and conversation with Betty, Matthew decided to stick with his commitment to the Catholic faith and his parish, saying, "No church is perfect, and this is where I truly belong."

For the past couple of years, he has been actively involved with the outreach activities of the church, working on the Food Bank and Affordable Housing committees. Recently, he has been a member of the Interfaith Dialogue Program, which promotes respect and mutual understanding across religious and cultural perspectives. Matthew finds the panel discussions, conferences, and interfaith community projects both challenging and invigorating. He's particularly looking forward to an upcoming conference on the role of interfaith dialogue in advancing world peace. He's also been involved with the National Religious Partnership for the Environment (NRPE), a Judeo-Christian association composed of many faiths that focuses on environmental stewardship. As a result of all of these activities, Matthew has also been reading a number of books on different religions and is struck by the similar themes reflected in the teachings of very diverse traditions. He is beginning to feel a new sense of purpose for his life, which both surprises and delights him as he heads into his 70s. Some of his friends have asked him if his involvement with the Interfaith Dialogue Program is making him question his own religion, but Matthew says, "No, quite the opposite. I feel more deeply connected to my faith as I understand more about other religions. It's not that I think mine is right and theirs is wrong, but I appreciate and respect other religions, while still knowing that mine is right for me."

CASE STUDY 5.4

TRUDY'S SEARCH FOR THE SACRED

Trudy is a 35-year-old single woman living in Berkeley, California—which is a long way from the little town in Arkansas where she lived until she left home at 18. She's moved several times since then, searching for a new home that feels right to her. She thinks she may have finally found it. A new job in a health food store, a small but comfortable and affordable apartment, a great yoga class, and a welcoming Buddhist Sangha (community) of like-minded people all make her feel like she's finally found what she's been looking for.

Trudy's early years were not easy. Her father was an alcoholic who flew into rages when drunk, which happened more often as the years went by. It was not an unusual event for someone in her family to be physically hurt during these episodes. Trudy, her mother, and her two sisters were afraid of her father and "walked around on eggshells" most of the time to avoid triggering his angry spells. Trudy found refuge in the woods in back of her house and in books, which she devoured because they took her to places beyond her current reality. She could stay curled up in a nook of her favorite tree for hours, transporting herself to somewhere else—anywhere else. She promised herself she would leave as soon as she finished high school.

Life since then has not been easy either. Trudy was briefly married in her 20s to a man who also had a hard time controlling his anger and began to drink more and more as problems in the marriage started to emerge. Trudy even found herself turning to alcohol as a way of numbing her pain, which really scared her. With the support of some friends, she finally left the marriage and was off again, searching for a new home. After a couple of other relationships that didn't work out, Trudy decided to avoid men and increasingly became isolated from all social ties. But in her new home in Berkeley, she finds that she likes the people who attend her Sangha and likes

(Continued)

(Continued)

even more the fact that they don't share a lot of personal information, focusing more on spiritual practices. She loves the group meditation and the dharma talks and has made a commitment to increased periods of solitary meditation when she is at home. Trudy is now rising at 4:00 a.m. to meditate for 3 hours before work, and she meditates an additional 2 hours most evenings. Her reading is now totally focused on books about spirituality, which support her quest to rise above personal concerns and ego to become an enlightened being. Although Trudy was not exposed to a particular religious tradition during childhood, her spiritual development is now her highest priority.

CASE STUDY 5.5

LEON'S TWO WORLDS

Leon is a 23-year-old man who is feeling torn in two. He is the oldest son in a family with five kids and the mainstay of his mother's life. Regina became a widow 8 years ago when her husband, Rodney, was killed in an accident at the mill yard where he worked. Since then, she's leaned heavily on Leon for help with his brothers and sisters and as a major contributor to the family's finances. He is also the one she confides in the most, sharing things with him that she once shared with her husband. The whole family also relies heavily on their African Methodist Episcopal (AME) church for both social support and spiritual nurturance.

Leon has grown up in the church and loves the fellowship and the joyous feeling that comes over him as he sings and worships on Sundays. But it is also a place that increasingly troubles him, because he has finally admitted to himself that he is gay. He has denied this for years, trying hard to follow church teachings about homosexuality being a sin and something that can be overcome with the help of God. He has prayed and prayed to God to change him, but this has not worked. Leon is now battling despair, and he fears that he will always be caught between his love for his faith and his church and a longing to be who he truly is. The idea of telling his mother about his sexual orientation seems unthinkable, but he's not sure how long he can go on living a lie. He knows he will have to leave the church if it ever becomes known that he is gay. That possibility also seems unthinkable. He has been feeling more and more depressed, to the point where his mother keeps asking him what's wrong. He's even had thoughts of suicide, which frightens him. In his nightly prayers to God he asks, "Why must I lose you to be who I am?"

CASE STUDY 5.6

JEAN-JOSEPH'S SERVING THE SPIRITS

Jean-Joseph is a 50-year-old man, originally from Haiti, who came with his family to the United States 10 years ago. He and his family were adherents of the Roman Catholic faith in Haiti and now attend a Catholic church near their new home. Jean-Joseph's family are also believers in Vodoun (known by most Westerners as Voodoo), which is widely practiced in Haiti and often integrated with belief in Catholicism. Most Roman Catholics who are active in this spiritual tradition refer to it as "serving the spirits." Although Vodoun holds that there is only one God, Bondye, who created the universe, he is considered to be too far away for a personal relationship with humans. Instead, believers in Vodoun center on *loa*, or spirits of ancestors and animals, natural forces, and good and evil spirits. Family loa are spirits who are seen to protect their "children"—the Haitian people—from misfortune. Jean-Joseph and his family regularly participate in rituals to feed the loa food and drink and offer them other gifts.

Recently, a loa visited Jean-Joseph in a dream, telling him that his youngest son was ill and needed healing. His son Emmanuel had indeed been listless for days, not wanting to eat or play, and his parents were very worried about him. Jean-Joseph decided that they needed to take him to a *mambo*, a Vodoun priestess, who could mediate between the human and spirit worlds to diagnose and treat Emmanuel's illness. The mambo agreed to perform a healing ceremony, which was held at a *hounfour,* or Vodoun temple, around a *poteau-mitan,* a center pole where the spirits can communicate with people. A *veve,* or pattern of cornmeal unique to the loa who was the focus of the ceremony, was created on the floor, and an altar was decorated with candles, pictures of Christian saints, and other symbolic items. A goat was also sacrificed for the ceremony. The mambo and her assistants began to chant and dance, accompanied by the shaking of rattles and beating of drums. Finally, the mambo was possessed by the loa and fell down. The loa then spoke through the mambo and told the family how to treat the distressed spirit that was causing Emmanuel's illness. After the ceremony, the mambo gave Jean-Joseph an herbal remedy to give to his son and instructions on how to continue feeding the spirit of the loa until Emmanuel was healed. The family also prayed to the Christian God and Catholic saints to bring healing to Emmanuel.

CASE STUDY 5.7

BETH'S FRAMEWORK FOR LIVING

Beth grew up as the only child of parents who were very clear about not wanting their child to be "brainwashed by religion." Beth's mother, Sarah, had been the daughter of a Presbyterian minister but had not spoken to her father for several years before he died over conflicts about her leaving the church. Beth's father, Sam, was raised by two union organizer parents who had not been involved with any particular religious faith throughout their lives. Both Sarah and Sam felt strongly that everyone needed a strong code of personal ethics, and they felt confident they could give Beth a solid "framework for living" that didn't involve religion. Instead they taught Beth to be honest and fair and to "always walk a mile in someone else's shoes" before she judged anyone. Beth didn't think much about religion during her growing-up years except when it came up in school or when she became aware that a few of her friends' families were very religious. She tended to feel more comfortable with kids from more secular families like hers, but she didn't let this stop her from making friends with kids from more religious families as well. As Beth grew older she relied more and more on her parents' "framework for living" to help her navigate challenges, like when some of her friends wanted her to go shoplifting with them or when other friends cheated on an exam. In both cases, she didn't go along with her friends, but she didn't tell on them either—telling herself that she didn't really know what it was like to "walk in their shoes" and she shouldn't judge them. She had many long talks with her father about the importance of having personal integrity and caring about social injustices that others faced. She also loved to hear him tell stories of his parents' union organizing days when they "fought the system" and sometimes won. So when it came time to choose her major in college she chose political science, and when she graduated she became a union organizer for the SEIU (Services Employees International Union). Her first job was as a field organizer in West Virginia, focused on organizing nursing home, home care, hospital, and other social service employees. The hours were long and the work was tough, but she felt she was living from a place of integrity and making the world a better place. She recently became close friends with Karen, another field organizer, who shared with Beth that her commitment to workers' rights was grounded in her deep Catholic faith—something Beth found surprising because she hadn't thought of religious people as being very concerned about the struggles ordinary people face. She began to wonder if she needed to rethink her views about "all those religious people." Was it time to walk a bit in *their* shoes?

THE SPIRITUAL DIMENSION

All of the stories presented in the seven case studies could be viewed through many different lenses. Knowledge of the biological components of health certainly would be useful in understanding the circumstances of Naomi's health crisis and Jean-Joseph's attempts at healing his son's illness. Psychological perspectives would shed light on Caroline's discomfort with encountering different beliefs, Matthew's deepening faith perspective, Trudy's search for a home and a different sense of self, Leon's despair at being torn between his faith and his sexual identity, and Beth's views about religious people. Social theories of family dynamics, ethnicity and culture, social movements, socioeconomic class, and social institutions would yield invaluable information about all of the people in these cases, providing a wider frame for understanding their individual lives. A spiritual lens can be added to help us understand Caroline's challenging questions, Naomi's health crisis, Matthew's faith journey, Trudy's search for the sacred, Leon's two worlds, Jean-Joseph's serving of the spirits, and Beth's framework for living.

Spirituality is understood and expressed differently by individuals but is generally associated with a person's search for meaning.

THE MEANING OF SPIRITUALITY

The concept of spirituality is often confused with religion, and Canda and Furman (2010) provide a detailed discussion of how the two terms are understood in social work and related fields, including medicine, nursing, and psychology. They also report findings from a series of national studies they have conducted in the United States, the United Kingdom, Norway, and New Zealand, which show relative consistency across countries. Specifically, the top six descriptors of *spirituality* across geographic locales were "meaning, personal, purpose, values, belief, and ethics." Similar congruence was found for the term *religion*, where the top six descriptors selected in all of the countries were "belief, ritual, community, values, prayer, and scripture" (Canda & Furman, 2010, p. 67). Drawing from these studies and additional research in the helping professions, Canda and Furman (2010) propose the following definitions for these two concepts.

Spirituality is "a process of human life and development

- focusing on the search for a sense of meaning, purpose, morality, and well-being;
- in relationship with oneself, other people, other beings, the universe, and ultimate reality however understood (e.g., in animistic, atheistic, nontheistic, polytheistic, theistic, or other ways);
- orienting around centrally significant priorities; and
- engaging a sense of transcendence (experienced as deeply profound, sacred, or transpersonal)" (p. 75).

Religion is "an institutionalized (i.e., systematic and organized) pattern of values, beliefs, symbols, behaviors, and experiences that involves

- spirituality;
- a community of adherents;
- transmission of traditions over time; and
- community support functions (e.g., organizational structure, material assistance, emotional support, or political advocacy) that are directly or indirectly related to spirituality" (p. 76).

Regardless of the scholarly definition of these terms, it is important as social workers to always inquire about and honor the client's definition of spirituality and religion and use the term that is most acceptable and relevant for that person, family, or community. *Spirituality*

EXHIBIT 5.1 • Symbolic Themes of Spirituality

1. Morality, ethics, justice, and right effort
2. The nature and meaning of self and the intention and purpose of human existence
3. Interconnection; wholeness; alignment; and integration of persons, place, time, and events
4. Creativity, inspiration, and intuition
5. Altruistic service for the benefit of others
6. The mystery and wonder woven into nature, the universe, and the unknown
7. Sociocultural-historical traditions, rituals, and myths
8. Virtues (such as compassion, universal love, peace, patience, forgiveness, hope, honesty, trust, faith)
9. Mystical, altered states of consciousness
10. Sexuality
11. Openness, willingness, surrender, and receptivity
12. The power of choice, freedom, and responsibility
13. Special wisdom or revealed knowledge
14. Prayer, meditation, and quiet contemplation
15. Answers to pain, suffering, and death
16. Identity and relation to the metaphysical grounds of existence, ultimate reality, and life force
17. The relationship of cause and effect regarding prosperity or poverty
18. Beliefs or experiences related to intangible reality or the unobstructed universe
19. The path to enlightenment or salvation
20. Sensitive awareness of the earth and the nonhuman world

SOURCE: Adapted from O'Brien, 1992.

is used in this chapter to include both religious and nonreligious expressions. Regardless of the precise words used to capture the meaning of spirituality, the term brings to mind many related themes. Exhibit 5.1 lists 20 symbolic themes of spirituality identified by Patrick O'Brien (1992). Which themes do you think are most applicable to the seven case studies presented at the beginning of this chapter?

SPIRITUALITY IN THE UNITED STATES AND GLOBALLY

The current spiritual landscape in the United States reveals both common threads and a colorful array of unique patterns. Recent Gallup (2014) polls report that 86% of people in the United States say they believe in God or a universal spirit, 78% report that religion is either "very important" or "fairly important" in their life, and 37% report attending religious services on a weekly basis. These statistics indicate a strong thread of spirituality in the United States. However, expressions of both religious and nonreligious spirituality have become increasingly diverse, making the United States likely the most religiously diverse country in the world today, with more than 1,500 different religious groups (Parrillo, 2009; Pew Forum on Religion & Public Life, 2008).

This diversity is due, in part, to ongoing schisms and divisions among many of the organized religions historically present within the United States. For example, the number of Christian denominations alone grew from 20 to more than 900 from 1800 to 1988 (Melton, 1993). In addition, there has been a significant rise in other spiritual traditions with each new influx of immigrants from other parts of the world. They have brought not only faiths recognized as major religions (e.g., Islam, Buddhism, Confucianism, Hinduism) but also various forms of spiritualism, folk healing, and shamanism (e.g., Santeria, espiritismo, Vodoun, curanderismo, santiguando, krou khmer, and mudang). This trend is further augmented by a growing interest in Eastern and Middle Eastern religions (e.g., Islam, Buddhism, and Hinduism) and earth-based spiritualities (e.g., neopaganism, goddess worship, and deep ecology). There has also been a revived or more visible involvement in traditional spiritual paths within Indigenous communities, as increasing numbers of Native Americans or First Nations peoples explore their tribal traditions or combine these traditions with faith in Christianity. Many of these "new" religions are among the fastest growing in the United States, although their overall numbers are still relatively small. Exhibit 5.2 shows the religious affiliation of the U.S. adult population in 2014, as well as changes in this profile since 2007 (Pew Research Center, 2015a).

It should be noted that estimates of members of any particular religious group vary widely depending on the source, data collection methods, and definition of "adherents" (e.g., self-identified, formal membership, or regular participant). For example, in the United States, figures for adherents of Islam range from 1 million to 8 million; adherents of Judaism from 1 million to 5 million; adherents of Buddhism from 1 million to 5 million; and adherents of Wicca and

EXHIBIT 5.2 • Change in Religious Affiliation of U.S. Adult Population, 2007–2014

RELIGIOUS AFFILIATION	2007 (%)	2014 (%)	CHANGE* (%)
Christianity	78.4	70.6	−7.8
Jewish	1.7	1.9	—
Muslim	0.4	0.9	+0.5
Buddhist	0.7	0.7	—
Hindu	0.4	0.7	+0.3
Other world religions**	<0.3	0.3	—
Other faiths**	1.2	1.5	+0.3
Unaffiliated	16.1	22.8	+6.7
Don't know/refused	0.8	0.6	−0.2

*The "change" column displays only statistically significant changes; blank cells indicate that the difference between 2007 and 2014 is within the margin of error.

**The "other world religions" category includes Sikhs, Baha'is, Taoists, Jains, and a variety of other world religions. The "other faiths" category includes Unitarians, New Age religions, Native American religions, and a number of other non-Christian faiths.

SOURCE: Pew Research Center, 2015a.

neopaganism from 10,000 to 770,000 (Canda & Furman, 2010; Kosmin & Keysar, 2009; Parrillo, 2009).

As tempting as it is to make overarching statements based on statistics concerning belief in God and religious identification—for example, that the U.S. population is highly religious—we must be cautious in drawing specific conclusions because the picture changes depending on the particular indicator. The percentage of U.S. adults who say they seldom or never attend religious services has increased from 25% in 2003 to 29% in 2013, while those who attend at least weekly has fallen from 39% to 37% (Lipka, 2013). Furthermore, recent data from the Pew Research Center (2015a) reveal that approximately 56 million (22.8%) adults report being unaffiliated, making them a substantial category second only to evangelical Protestants in the United States. The percentage of unaffiliated is even higher among younger adults, with over one third of younger people stating that they are not affiliated with any religion (34% for "older Millennials" born from 1981 to 1989 and 36% for "younger Millennials" born from 1990 to 1996). However, unaffiliated may not mean that spirituality is not important to this group of adults. Among unaffiliated Americans, 68% say they believe in God, 58% say they feel a deep connection with nature and the earth, 37% identify as "spiritual" but not "religious," and 21% report praying every day. Additionally, most of the religiously unaffiliated think "churches and other institutions benefit society by strengthening community bonds and aiding the poor" (Pew Research Center's Religion & Public Life Project, 2012, para. 4).

Moreover, there appears to be increasing fluidity in religious affiliation. Data on changes from one major religious tradition to another (e.g., from Protestantism to Catholicism or from Judaism to no religion) show that 34% of U.S. adults have changed their affiliation from that of their childhood (Pew Research Center, 2015a). A significant part of religious switching is due to the growth of the unaffiliated, in that "nearly one-in-five American adults (18%) were raised in a religion and are now unaffiliated, compared with just 4% who have moved in the other direction" (Pew Research Center, 2015a, p. 33), representing a leaving/joining ratio of 4.2 to 1. This contrasts with several groups of the religiously affiliated. For example, for every new convert to Christianity there has been a loss of four former Christians who no longer affiliate with the Christian religion. Catholicism has experienced the greatest net loss; there are currently more than six former Catholics for every one convert (ratio of 6.5 to 1). Both mainline Protestant denominations and historically Black Protestant denominations also show a net loss, with a 1.7 to 1 ratio for mainline Protestants and 1.6 to 1 ratio for historically Black Protestants. A major exception to this pattern is evangelical Protestantism, which has gained more adherents through religious switching than it has lost with a ratio of 1 to 1.2. Hindus, Muslims, and Jews have the highest percentages of retention of adherents at 80%, 77%, and 75%, respectively. Beyond religious switching, another key factor in religious fluidity is intermarriage, with 28% of American adults currently married or living with a partner who has a different religious affiliation than their own.

These figures concerning shifts in organized religious affiliation emerge at a time when people in the United States are expressing an unprecedented interest in spirituality in general. In 1994, an estimated 58% of the U.S. population said they felt the need to experience spiritual growth in their lives; by 2001, this percentage was 80% (Gallup, 2002; Gallup & Lindsay, 1999). Qualitative studies (Bender, 2010; Mercadante, 2014) have shown that although the diverse pathways to spiritual growth reported by many Americans may emphasize individual exploration and personal experience, they also involve communal sharing—albeit often outside of traditional religious institutions (e.g., yoga centers, spirituality groups, mind–body classes). Furthermore, these approaches may more closely reflect Ulrich Beck's (1992) understanding of spirituality as attending to the development of positive human qualities—such as generosity, gratitude, a capacity for awe and wonder, an appreciation of the interconnectedness among all beings, and deeper awareness and insight—as much as or even more than a search for any divine form of transcendence.

EXHIBIT 5.3 • World Religions, 2010

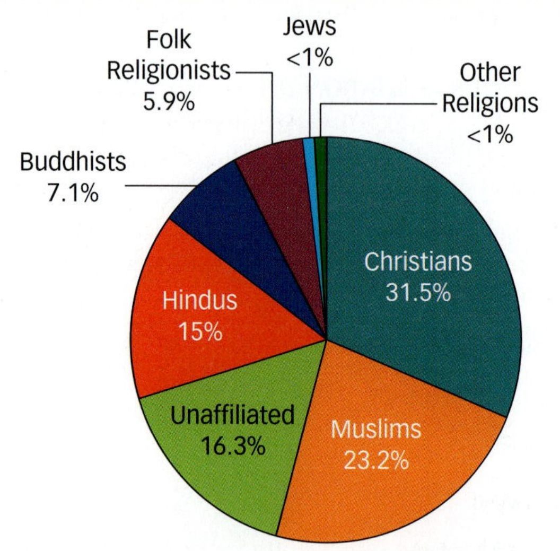

NOTE: Folk religionists include followers of African traditional religions, Chinese folk religions, Native American religions, and Australian aboriginal religions.

SOURCE: Pew-Templeton Global Religious Futures Project, 2014.

© iStockphoto.com/Robert Young

© iStockphoto.com/Bryan Busovicki

Religion involves the patterning of spiritual beliefs and practices into social institutions; different cultures focus their beliefs around different central figures.

It is important to consider all of these data within the context of global statistics (see Exhibit 5.3). Although adherents of Christianity remain the highest proportion of the population in the United States, they composed only 31.5% of the global population in 2010, with the remainder being composed of those who self-identified with other traditions: Muslims (23.2%), unaffiliated (16.3%), Hindus (15%), Buddhists (7.1%), folk religionists (5.9%), Jews (<1%), and other religions (<1%) (Pew Research Center's Religion & Public Life Project, 2010). However, projections of religious growth globally predict a different scenario, with Muslims increasing to 29.7% and percentages of other adherents remaining the same or dropping (Pew Research Center, 2015b). It is interesting to note that whereas the percentage of unaffiliated in the United States is projected to be 25.6% by 2050, globally that percentage is predicted to shrink to 13.2%.

Lester Kurtz (2012) posits three factors—modernism, multiculturalism, and modern technologies of warfare—significant to understanding religious conflict today. First, *modernism*, based on scientific, industrial, and technological revolutions, has had an ongoing contentious relationship with religious perspectives and institutions since the beginning of the 17th century, when church authorities charged Galileo with heresy for stating that the earth revolved around the sun. Present-day examples include debates regarding evolution versus creationism and intelligent design; the question of when life begins and ends; the ethics of stem cell research and genetic manipulation; the proper codes of behavior, especially sexual behavior; the rightful roles of women in society; the correct way to raise children; and the appropriate place of religion in the political sphere. Thus, this tension between science and religion continues during our current postmodern times as scientific and secular thought compete with religious traditions and doctrine as the authority for "truth" and moral guidelines for contemporary life.

Second, *multiculturalism* increasingly requires us to recognize myriad worldviews and ways of life, within the United States and globally. This pluralistic reality stands in contrast to unilateral belief systems, both religious and cultural, that have historically provided what Peter Berger (1969) calls a "sacred canopy," or the security and certainty of one view of the universe, one answer to profound and mundane questions, and one approach to organizing individual and collective life. Such a unified perspective is difficult to maintain as individuals and whole cultures are increasingly exposed to a religious and spiritual "marketplace" of diverse belief systems and practices, which often challenge the basic tenets previously held as absolute (Warner, 1993).

The potential for conflict is inherent in both modernism and multiculturalism, conflict that becomes especially deadly when combined with the third aspect of globalization—the dispersion of *modern technologies of warfare*. Violent conflict, often intertwined with religious issues, has been part of human history for thousands of years. But in the current period of globalization, the cost of such conflict has grown unimaginably high in that our arsenal now includes nuclear, biological, and chemical weapons of mass destruction as opposed to stones, clubs, and other primitive weapons. As Lester Kurtz (2012) succinctly states, "Given the destructive capabilities of modern weaponry and the consequent necessity for peaceful coexistence, the potential for religious traditions to promote either chaos or community becomes a crucial factor in the global village" (pp. 279–280).

In light of this complex and ever-changing picture, social workers gain very little real understanding of a person by simply knowing his or her primary religious affiliation. First, religious affiliation may or may not hold great significance for the person, and identification with a religion alone does not indicate depth of involvement. Second, belief, practice, and involvement can be quite varied, even among adherents of the same spiritual tradition or among members of the same family, kinship group, or faith community—even if they all self-identify as Methodist or Muslim or Wiccan. Third, some people feel connected to multiple spiritual perspectives simultaneously, such as a combination of Judaism and Buddhism or traditional Indigenous spiritual beliefs and Christianity. Fourth, the meaning of religious or spiritual affiliation may change across the life course; a person may feel more or less connected to a particular tradition at different points in his or her life. And finally, the meaning of a person's religious or spiritual affiliation must be understood within his or her broader historical, sociopolitical, and cultural context in order for its full significance to be realized. It is important to understand the range of spiritual influences (both religious and nonreligious) that may contribute to anyone's life story and the larger collective realities that impact that story at any particular point in time.

CRITICAL THINKING Questions 5.1

At the beginning of the chapter, you read about the spiritual and religious beliefs of seven people. With which of the stories were you most comfortable? For what reasons? With which of the stories were you least comfortable? For what reasons? How comfortable are you with the idea of including the spiritual person in social work's understanding of human behavior? What do you like about the idea? What don't you like about the idea?

TRANSPERSONAL THEORIES OF HUMAN DEVELOPMENT

The idea that spirituality is an important dimension of human behavior is not a new one in social work or in other helping professions. Although Sigmund Freud (1928) asserted that all religious and spiritual beliefs were either illusions or projections of unconscious wishes, many other early behavioral science theorists viewed the role of spirituality differently.

Notably, Carl Jung, a student of Freud's, differed with his former teacher and mentor in regard to the topic of spirituality. Jung's (1933a) theory of personality includes physical, mental, and spiritual selves, which all strive for unity and wholeness within each person. In Jung's (1959/1969) view, an important *archetype* (a universal unconscious idea) is "the Spirit" (p. 214). Jung further proposed that the evolution of consciousness and the struggle to find a spiritual outlook on life were the primary developmental tasks in midlife. If this task is successfully accomplished, the result is *individuation*, which Jung defined as "the moment when the finite mind realizes it is rooted in the infinite" (as quoted in Keutzer, 1982, p. 76).

Robert Assagioli (1965, 1973) also emphasized the spiritual dimension in his approach known as *psychosynthesis*. His understanding of the human psyche included the constructs of "higher unconscious" or "superconscious" as the source of creativity and spirituality. In Assagioli's view, some psychological disturbances are best understood as crises of spiritual awakening rather than symptoms of psychopathology. In such cases, the responsibility of the therapist is to facilitate the client's exploration of spiritual possibilities while dealing with the difficulties such awakenings can engender. As Assagioli (1989) defined it, "'spiritual' refers not only to experiences traditionally considered religious but to *all* the states of awareness, all the human functions and activities which have as their common denominator the possession of *values* higher than average" (p. 30, italics in original).

A third major contributor to early formulations on spirituality and human behavior was Abraham Maslow, founding father of humanistic psychology. Maslow (1971) described spirituality as an innate and key element in human nature. In his study of optimally functioning people, he characterized people at the top of his hierarchy as "transcendent self-actualizers" and described them as having (among other traits) a more holistic view of life; a natural tendency toward cooperative action; a tendency to be motivated by truth, goodness, and unity; a greater appreciation for peak experiences; an ability to go beyond their ego self to higher levels of identity; and more awareness of the sacredness of every person and every living thing. Maslow later came to believe that even this definition was not adequate to explain the highest levels of human potential. Near the end of his life, he predicted the emergence of a more expansive understanding of human behavior: "a still 'higher' Fourth Psychology; transpersonal, trans-human, centered in the cosmos, rather than in human needs and interests, going beyond humanness, identity, self-actualization, and the like" (as quoted in Wittine, 1987, p. 53).

Describing this evolution of forces within psychology, Au-Deane Cowley (1993, 1996) delineates four major therapeutic approaches that have emerged over the past century, each developed in response to our understanding of human behavior and human needs at the time.

1. **First force therapies** are based on dynamic theories of human behavior. The prime concern of these therapies is dealing with repression and resolving instinctual conflicts by developing insight.
2. **Second force therapies** evolved from behavioral theories. These therapies focus on learned habits and seek to remove symptoms through various processes of direct learning.
3. **Third force therapies** are rooted in existential/humanistic/experiential theories. They help the person deal with existential despair and seek the actualization of the person's potential through techniques grounded in immediate experiencing.
4. **Fourth force therapies**, based on transpersonal theories, specifically target the spiritual dimension. They focus on helping the person let go of ego attachments—identifications with the mind, body, and social roles—and transcend the self through various spiritually based practices. (Cowley, 1996)

The fourth force builds on the previous three forces and thus incorporates existing knowledge concerning human behavior within its framework. What differentiates the fourth force—the **transpersonal approach**—from other theoretical orientations is the premise that some states of human consciousness and potential go beyond our traditional views of health and normality. These states explicitly address the spiritual dimension of human existence (Cowley & Derezotes, 1994).

The term *transpersonal* literally means "beyond" or "through" the "persona" or "mask" (Wittine, 1987). When applied to theories of human behavior, transpersonal means going beyond identity tied to the individual body, ego, or social roles to include spiritual experience or higher levels of consciousness. The self is experienced as in unity with all others. A major focus of transpersonal theory is on "humanity's highest potential" (Lajoie & Shapiro, 1992, p. 91). Several branches of transpersonal thought are currently recognized, including Jungian psychology; depth or archetypal psychology; spiritual psychology; positive psychology; psychosynthesis, and approaches based on the writings of Abraham Maslow, Stanislav Grof, Ken Wilber, Michael Washburn, Frances Vaughan, Roger Walsh, Jorge Ferrer, and Charles Tart, among others. A major objective of all transpersonal theories is to integrate spirituality within a larger framework of human behavior. One key application of transpersonal theory is as a conceptual underpinning for theories that address spiritual development.

Two theorists who have developed comprehensive perspectives on spiritual development are James Fowler and Ken Wilber. Although these two theorists are not the only contributors to this area, they have produced two of the best-known approaches in the field today. The following sections give an overview of these two theories of spiritual development, providing key concepts and discussion of their respective models. Along the way, we consider the people you read about in the case studies at the beginning of this chapter and see how these two perspectives enhance our understanding of their current life situations and spiritual journeys.

FOWLER'S STAGES OF FAITH DEVELOPMENT

James Fowler's (1981, 1995) theory of faith development grew out of 359 in-depth interviews conducted from 1972 to 1981 in Boston, Chicago, and Toronto. The sample was overwhelmingly White (97.8%), largely Christian (over 85%), evenly divided by gender, and widely distributed in terms of age (3.5 years to 84 years). Each semistructured interview consisted of more than 30 questions about life-shaping experiences and relationships, present values and commitments, and religion. After the responses were analyzed, interviewees were placed in one of six **faith stages**. Fowler found a generally positive relationship between age and stage development; as age increased, so did the tendency for persons to be in higher stages. However, only a minority of persons revealed characteristics of Stages 5 or 6, regardless of age.

To Fowler (1996), **faith** is broader than religious faith, creed, or belief. It can, in fact, be expressed even by people who do not believe in God. Instead, faith is viewed as a universal aspect of human existence,

> an integral, centering process, underlying the formation of beliefs, values, and meanings that (1) gives coherence and direction to people's lives, (2) links them in shared trusts and loyalties with others, (3) grounds their personal stances and communal loyalties in a sense of relatedness to a larger frame of reference, and (4) enables them to face and deal with the limited conditions of life, relying upon that which has the quality of ultimacy in their lives. (p. 56)

Thus, Fowler's definition of faith is more aligned with the definition of spirituality given at the beginning of this chapter and is clearly distinguished from more specific notions of particular beliefs or religious traditions. Here is a brief description of Fowler's faith stages.

Prestage: primal faith (infancy). If consistent nurturance is experienced, the infant develops a sense of trust and safety about the universe and the divine. Negative experiences produce images of the universe and divine as untrustworthy, punitive, or arbitrary.

Stage 1: intuitive-projective faith (early childhood, beginning about age 2). The young child's new tools of speech and symbols give rise to fluid and magical thoughts, based on intuition and imagination. Faith is fantasy filled and imitative and can be powerfully influenced by examples, actions, stories of significant others, and familial and cultural taboos.

Stage 2: mythic-literal faith (middle childhood, beginning about age 6, and beyond). The child begins to take on stories, beliefs, and practices that symbolize belonging to his or her community. There is a high degree of conformity to community beliefs and practices. The ability to participate in concrete operational thinking allows distinction between fantasy and reality. There is increased capacity to take the perspective of others, and ideas about reciprocity and fairness become central.

Stage 3: synthetic-conventional faith (adolescence and beyond). For many adolescents, the capacity for abstract thinking and manipulation of concepts affects the process of developing faith as well as overall identity. Authority is perceived as external and is found in traditional authority figures, but there is an increased influence of peers, school and work associates, the media, and popular culture. Beliefs and values are often deeply felt but not critically examined or systematically reflected on. Symbols are not perceived as literally as in Stage 2.

Stage 4: individuative-reflective faith (young adulthood and beyond). Beginning in young adulthood, many people experience an increased responsibility for their own commitments, lifestyles, beliefs, and attitudes. Previously held creeds, symbols, and stories are demythologized through critical analysis. Beliefs become more explicit and personally meaningful, and symbols are reshaped into more powerful conceptualizations.

Stage 5: conjunctive faith (midlife and beyond). A minority of adults begin in midlife to rework the past and become open to voices of the "deeper self." They develop the capacity for "both/and" versus "either/or" thinking and come to tolerate ambiguity and paradox, taking into account and looking for balance in such polarities as independence and connection and determinism and free will. They recognize that there are many truths and engage in critical examination of their own beliefs, myths, and prejudices. They expand their definition of community and their sense of connection and responsibility to others.

Stage 6: universalizing faith (midlife and beyond). A very small minority of adults develop the capacity to truly embrace paradox. They develop an enlarged awareness of justice and injustice. The vision of truth is expanded to recognize partial truths. Symbols, myths, and rituals are appreciated and cherished at a deeper level. Divisions within the human family are felt with vivid pain because of the recognition of the possibility of the inclusive union of all beings. They lead selfless lives of service and action for justice aimed at the transformation of humankind.

Now let us consider the stories revealed in the seven case studies through the lens of Fowler's faith stages, based on both his early research and later theoretical refinements. In Fowler's model, our early experiences set the stage for later faith development. Given what we know about the seven people described in the case studies, it is probably safe to assume that most of them were able to develop at least a "good enough" fund of basic trust and mutuality during the *Prestage: primal faith* for later development of a relationship with the universe and the divine. A possible exception to this is Trudy, whose early years were marked by parental substance abuse and violence. It would be important to know when these problems first appeared within her family and how much they interfered with her initial bonding with her mother and father, because these factors would be influential in both her ability to trust and her internal sense of the ultimate as she moves through her life.

None of the seven case studies tells us much about the development of early images of the universe and the divine during *Stage 1: intuitive-projective faith*. However, we can speculate that these images were probably drawn from each person's particular faith affiliation. For Caroline, Matthew, and Leon, these initial conceptions of the divine would have been grounded within their particular Christian denominations, whereas Naomi would have developed her sense of the divine as it was reflected in her Jewish faith. Caroline's partner in the comparative religions class exercise would most likely have developed her sense of the divine based on examples, modes, actions, and stories that she experienced in her family's belief in Islam. Jean-Joseph's sense of the divine would have been influenced by a combination of Catholic symbols, narratives, and rituals and the spiritual beliefs and practices of Vodoun. Trudy and Beth were not raised in any particular religious tradition but found meaning and purpose in other ways. Trudy found solace in nature and Beth found significance through social justice activities. It would be important to talk with both of them about how their early experiences affected their sense of what they held to be most important in their lives and to not assume their lack of exposure to organized religion meant they had no early images or experiences with the ultimate, because spirituality is experienced and expressed through both religious and nonreligious means. In working with all seven people, we would want to understand how this process of image making was handled by their families and others in their lives and how much support they were given for their own intuition and imagination during this time.

If Fowler had interviewed any of the seven during middle childhood, he more than likely would have seen many of the aspects of *Stage 2: mythic-literal faith* reflected in this group. It would be important to understand the role of their childhood spiritual communities in shaping each person's sense of the world and his or her place in it. It would be particularly useful to explore the stories and narratives they remember from that time, especially as they transmitted values, attitudes, and norms for behavior. For example, discussing with Leon what he understood as his church's core principles relative to sin and redemption would be invaluable in comprehending his current struggle. It would also be important to understand the messages Caroline received regarding her own religion as the only true faith. For Naomi and Jean-Joseph, it would be key to talk about how their communities handled being believers of a nondominant (or "other") religion, in a culture where Christianity is the dominant faith and is generally seen as "the norm." For Beth, it might mean understanding the meaning of the stories she heard about her grandparents' experiences as union organizers. For all seven people, it would be vital to explore what helped create a sense of order and meaning at this stage of life and what provided a sense of guidance and belonging.

The events that occur during adolescence generally have a significant effect on faith development during *Stage 3: synthetic-conventional faith*, because this is the point where people are heavily engaged in the process of identity development, including spiritual identity. It is also a time when the person's world is greatly expanded, bringing diverse and complex ideas and experiences regarding all of life. Adolescents must make coherent meaning from all the different messages they receive from family, school, work, media, and the larger sociocultural realm. A person's faith understanding can help synthesize various values and viewpoints and provide a basis for forming a stable identity and worldview. There is a tendency to construct one's faith through conforming to a set of values and beliefs that are most familiar and to defer to whatever authority is most meaningful. As the two people most recently in this life stage, both Caroline and Leon illustrate the strong impetus to form a faith identity that provides a solid sense of self and a feeling of belonging to a particular group. For both of them, the faith of their families and their home churches were highly instrumental in this process. As another young person at this stage of life, Beth is also in the midst of developing an identity. For her this identity is composed of attributes of personal integrity and commitment to actions grounded in the socially conscious, ethical framework of her family. For all of them, entry into the next stage of life brought questions regarding the beliefs and values of these key social institutions and an urge to explore beyond what they had previously known.

If we look at Caroline's, Leon's, and Beth's lives as they move into *Stage 4: individuative-reflective faith*, we see young people grappling with key questions about themselves and their belief systems. Caroline's experiences at college have opened the door to considering different worldviews, which she handles with an approach-avoidance strategy. On the one hand, she is troubled by her experience with others who believe and practice differently from the way she does, but on the other hand, she is increasingly curious about these differences. For Leon, the struggle is more difficult, in that he is attempting to live with values, attitudes, and beliefs that tell him a core aspect of his identity is unacceptable. Beth is being challenged to reconsider whether she has misperceptions or even biases about people who are religious and the possible positive role religion might play in societal change. For all of these young adults, the task ahead is to construct a unique, individual self (identity) and outlook (**ideology**) from previously held conventional beliefs and develop an approach to faith that is both personal and workable. It is important to recognize that this task does not exclude Beth as a nonreligious person, in that "faith" in Fowler's (1996) terms involves developing "an integral, centering process, underlying the formation of beliefs, values, and meanings" for living one's life—whether or not this is found through a particular religious orientation (p. 56). Thus, the process at this point for all three young people requires a level of critical reflection and a capacity to struggle with conflicts and tensions that were not yet fully developed in the previous stage. As a social worker, you would want to facilitate this process while being mindful of the social work principles of self-determination and empowerment.

Naomi and David provide another example of *individuative-reflective faith*, even though they are considerably older than Caroline, Leon, and Beth. When they were in their late teens and early 20s, their identity formation led them to a more secular worldview, as Naomi lessened her involvement with her faith and David continued to base his identity and outlook on more humanistic understandings of self and the world. But the creation of a family caused them both to reconsider the role of Judaism in their lives as they realized their desire for a spiritual community. As their children grew, their involvement with their temple has provided the personal and workable framework characteristic of this phase. That framework is now being challenged by Naomi's illness and is leading both her and David to a deeper reflection of their faith. Social work with this couple would involve supporting this reflection, as well as exploring with them possible supports they could receive from their rabbi and larger faith community in dealing with Naomi's health crisis.

According to Lownsdale (1997), only 1 in 6 adults reflects characteristics of *Stage 5: conjunctive faith*. Of our seven life stories, only Matthew's provides glimpses of this faith stage. Although there is not much information about Matthew's internal reflection on the paradoxes of life (a key criterion of *conjunctive faith*), we do know that he was able to work through the loss of his wife, and other losses that inevitably come with aging, to embrace a new chapter in his life. As a social worker, you might find it useful to explore with Matthew his understanding of life's paradoxes (such as God being both personal and abstract and life being both rational and mysterious) and talk with him about any previously unrealized parts of himself that are now emerging. What is apparent in Matthew's story is his enthusiastic willingness to acknowledge and honor multiple faith perspectives, while being open to new depths within his own spirituality. We also see him engaging in service for others and concern for the natural world. All of these activities suggest a perspective that goes beyond egocentric and ethnocentric views to a more **worldcentric** (identification with the entire global human family) and **ecocentric** (identification with the whole ecosphere, of which humans are only one part) way of being in the world. As a result of these commitments, he is experiencing a renewed sense of purpose, meaning, and connection in his life. All of these are characteristic of persons of *conjunctive faith*, which brings a broader social consciousness, a passion for social justice, and a wider and deeper understanding of the sacred.

It is clear that none of the seven people reflects the self-sacrificial life of Fowler's *Stage 6: universalizing faith*. Persons at this stage are exceedingly rare, perhaps two to three individuals per thousand (Lownsdale, 1997). Given the exceptional nature of such persons, it is not surprising that the seven case studies do not reveal examples of this faith stage. Some might point to Trudy's total immersion in spiritual practices as evidence of this stage, but another perspective on her development is offered later in this chapter during discussion of the second theorist, Ken Wilber, and his integral theory of consciousness.

Finally, we must address Jean-Joseph's spiritual path, which includes a syncretism (combination) of Catholicism and Vodoun, or "serving the spirits." If a social worker embedded in dominant Western culture assessed his faith development solely from the standpoint of this context, he or she might determine that Jean-Joseph falls within an early stage, either *mythic-literal* or perhaps even *intuitive-projective*. This determination would no doubt lead to a conclusion that this 50-year-old man is an example of underdeveloped faith and may lead to interventions aimed at helping him give up his "primitive and immature" beliefs and practices for a worldview seen as more appropriate for mature adults. If this was the stance taken by a practitioner, he or she would be showing ethnocentric and religiocentric bias, as well as cultural insensitivity. Viewed within his sociocultural context, Jean-Joseph is exhibiting a faith stage that could be more accurately determined to be at least *synthetic-conventional*, given its congruence with the spiritual beliefs and practices of his Haitian culture. Upon further exploration with him—with an open mind, respect, and humility for the limits of one's knowledge about his religion—a social worker may discover that Jean-Joseph displays characteristics of higher stages of faith development. This highlights the need for social workers to constantly be aware of their own lack of knowledge and their internalized biases when working with religious and spiritual traditions unfamiliar to them, in order to engage in culturally sensitive service respectful of those traditions (Weaver, 2011).

WILBER'S INTEGRAL THEORY OF CONSCIOUSNESS

Ken Wilber first published his transpersonal theory of development in 1977 in *The Spectrum of Consciousness* but has continued to develop and refine his model in numerous writings. His work reflects a unique integration of biology, history, psychology, sociology, philosophy, and religion. It is rooted in both conventional Western knowledge and contemplative-mystical traditions of Eastern religions and other spiritual perspectives. Wilber (2006) explores human development across **four quadrants** or vantage points (interior-individual, exterior-individual, interior-collective, and exterior-collective) and through *three levels of consciousness* (prepersonal, personal, and transpersonal). He posits that human development must be understood through the lenses of subjective awareness of *personal meaning and sense of self* (the interior of individuals), objective knowledge of the *physical body and observable behaviors* (the external part of individuals), intersubjective understanding of *sociocultural values and shared meanings* (the interior of collectives), and interobjective knowledge of *institutional structures and systemic forces* (the external part of collectives). Within each quadrant, the three levels of consciousness unfold in a way that reflects the unique properties of that particular quadrant (see Exhibit 5.4). We look closer at Wilber's description of transpersonal levels within the

EXHIBIT 5.4 • Wilber's Integral Theory: Four Quadrants and Three Levels of Consciousness

	INTERIOR	EXTERIOR
Individual	Upper Left Quadrant (Individual Interior) "I" INTENTIONAL (Personal meaning and sense of self) subjective truthfulness	Upper Right Quadrant (Individual Exterior) "IT" BEHAVIORAL (Physical body and observable behaviors) objective truth
Collective	Lower Left Quadrant (Collective Interior) "WE" CULTURAL (Culture and shared values) intersubjective justness	Lower Right Quadrant (Collective Exterior) "ITS" SOCIAL (Institutions, systems, nature) intersubjective functional fit

SOURCE: Wilber, 1996, 2006.

interior of individuals, because this is a major contribution of his model to theories of spiritual development. But first we need to review some key concepts underpinning integral theory.

As already noted, Wilber (1995, 2000a, 2000b, 2006) agrees with other transpersonal theorists that consciousness spans from prepersonal to personal to transpersonal (matter to body to mind to soul to spirit). Wilber points out that this process is not strictly linear. There are five major components relative to the development of interior individual consciousness in Wilber's theory. The following gives an overview of each of these components, leading to a more detailed discussion of the higher or transpersonal levels of consciousness.

1. The term **levels** (or waves) **of consciousness** refers to various developmental milestones that unfold within the human psyche. A person does not have to master all the competencies of one level to move on to the next; in fact, most people at any given level will often respond about 50% from that level, 25% from the level above, and 25% from the level below. However, levels cannot be skipped over, because each level incorporates the capacities of earlier levels. Drawing from various cross-cultural sources, Wilber posits several major levels of consciousness, all of which are *potentials*—but not *givens*—at the onset of development. We consider these in more detail following introduction of the other major components.

2. Multiple **lines** (or streams) **of consciousness** flow through the basic levels of consciousness. Here are some examples of developmental lines identified by Wilber (2000a): morals, self-identity, ideas of the good, creativity, altruism, and empathy. He proposes that these lines or streams are relatively independent of one another in that they can develop at different rates within the same individual. Thus, a person can be at a relatively high level of development in some lines, medium in others, and low in still others. Thus, although most *individual* lines unfold sequentially, *overall development* does not and can be a relatively uneven process.

3. Wilber also includes in his model **states of consciousness**, which include both ordinary (e.g., waking, sleeping, dreaming) and nonordinary experiences (e.g., peak experiences, religious experiences, altered states, and meditative or contemplative states). In order for *temporary* experiences or states to become *permanent* aspects of a person's level of consciousness, they must become fully realized through continual development.

4. Wilber proposes that levels, lines, and states of consciousness are all navigated by the self or **self-system**. As a person negotiates each unfolding *level* and various *lines* of consciousness and integrates experiences from various *states* of consciousness, he or she moves from a narrower to a deeper and wider sense of self and self-identity.

5. At each point of development, the self goes through a **fulcrum**, or switch point. Specifically, each time the self moves to a different level on the developmental spiral, it goes through a three-step process. First, the self becomes comfortable and eventually identifies with the basic functioning of that level. Second, new experiences begin to challenge the way of being at this level, and the self begins to differentiate or "disidentify" with it. Third, the self begins to move toward and identify with the next

level while integrating the functioning of the previous basic structure into the sense of self. If the person is able to negotiate these fulcrum points successfully, development is largely nonproblematic. However, disturbances at different fulcrum points tend to produce various pathologies.

As noted earlier, Wilber's spectrum of consciousness can be further categorized into the three phases of development: the prepersonal (pre-egoic) phase, the personal (egoic) phase, and the transpersonal (transegoic) phase. The six levels of consciousness at the prepersonal and personal phases in Wilber's theory are very similar to the first five of Fowler's faith stages and are not presented in detail here. (See Wilber [1995, 1996, 1997a, 1997b] for a detailed discussion of these levels.) A review of the levels of prepersonal and personal phases of consciousness should sound familiar to students of conventional approaches to human development. In contrast, the levels of the transpersonal phase (and the language used to describe them) are most likely unfamiliar to those not well versed in contemplative Eastern ideas about human development. However, this synthesis of both conventional and contemplative approaches and the inclusion of higher-order levels of development is Wilber's primary contribution to our attempts to understand human behavior.

As one moves into the transpersonal or transegoic phase, the world and life in general are perceived in more holistic and interconnected terms. There is movement from an egocentric and ethnocentric perspective to a worldcentric and ecocentric grasp of the complete interdependence of all things in the cosmos. Here are brief descriptions of the three transpersonal levels.

1. *Level 7* (*psychic*) is characterized by a continuing evolution of consciousness as the self develops more and more depth. Wilber refers to this evolving inner sense as the *witness*, because it represents an awareness that moves beyond ordinary reality (sensorimotor, rational, existential) into the transpersonal (beyond ego) levels. A distinguishing spiritual experience at this level is a strong interconnectedness of self with nature. Because of this powerful experience of connection and identification, there is a natural deepening of compassion for all living things, including nature itself.

2. *Level 8* (*subtle*) is characterized by an awareness of subtler processes than are commonly experienced in gross, ordinary states of waking consciousness. Examples of such processes are interior light and sounds; awareness of transpersonal archetypes; and extreme states of bliss, love, and compassion. At this point, even nature is transcended. One's sense of connection and identification is extended to communion with a deity, or union with God, by whatever name. This level of consciousness can be experienced in many forms, often rooted in the person's personal or cultural history. For example, a Christian may feel union with Christ, whereas a Buddhist might experience connection with the Buddha.

3. *Level 9* (*causal*) transcends all distinctions between subject and object (even self and God). This level is said to be timeless, spaceless, and objectless. As Wilber (1996) describes it, "Space, time, objects—all of those merely parade by . . . never touching you, never tempting you, never hurting you, never consoling you" (p. 224). This level of consciousness is sometimes referred to as "full Enlightenment, ultimate release, pure nirvana" (Wilber, 1996, p. 226). But it is still not the final story.

Wilber also proposes a *Level 10* (*nondual*); there is no sense of two, there is only one (hence the name *nondual*). Essentially, the person's awareness has moved beyond nature, deity, and formless mysticism to *nondual mysticism*. Wilber does not depict the nondual as a separate level of consciousness because it represents the ground or origin of all other levels—the paper on which the figure is drawn.

With this model, Wilber is proposing that the personal phase of development, with its achievement of strong ego development and self-actualization, is not the highest potential of human existence, although a necessary point along the way. Rather, the ultimate goal of human development is the transpersonal or transegoic phase—beyond ego or self to self-transcendence and unity with the universe. The capacity for attaining the highest levels of consciousness is seen as innate within each human being, although Wilber acknowledges that very few people reach the higher transpersonal levels.

As for the characteristic pathologies, or problems in development at each level, all the disorders or conditions that Wilber identifies at the lower phases of development are well recognized within conventional diagnostic approaches (albeit with different labels). It is again at the transpersonal phase that Wilber (2000a) strikes new ground, by including what he calls psychic disorders and subtle or causal pathologies. Examples of such problems in living include unsought spiritual awakenings, psychic inflation, split life goals, integration-identification failure, pseudo nirvana, and failure to differentiate or integrate. Likewise, the treatment modalities that Wilber identifies at the prepersonal and personal phases are well known to most social workers. However, the approaches Wilber proposes for transpersonal phase disorders have been used in non-Western cultures for centuries. Furthermore, they are becoming more widely accepted in the United States as effective, complementary treatment approaches (e.g., prayer and meditation, yoga, visualization and spiritual imagery, focusing, dreamwork, disidentification techniques, bodywork, acupuncture, journaling, intuition techniques). Wilber (1996, 2000a) stresses that practitioners should be able to correctly identify the level of development in order to provide the most appropriate treatment. If not correctly identified, there is the probability of what Wilber (1995, 2000b) calls the "pre/trans fallacy," which occurs when a problem at a transpersonal level (such as a spiritual awakening) may be treated as if it were a prepersonal or personal disorder (a psychotic episode or existential crisis) or vice versa.

Let's revisit Trudy's story to better understand what Wilber is talking about here. Trudy is currently focusing most of her time and energy toward developing her spiritual self in order to achieve enlightenment. She is meditating 5 hours a day, is engaged with a daily yoga practice, and limits her reading and interpersonal contacts to those she identifies as spiritual. Given that most transpersonal theorists and spiritual leaders would agree that engagement in some type of spiritual practice is necessary for spiritual growth, one might characterize Trudy's behavior as that of a disciplined, spiritual seeker. But there is evidence in her story that Trudy is caught up in **spiritual bypassing**, a term first coined by John Welwood (2000), which he describes as "the tendency to use spiritual practice to bypass or avoid dealing with certain personal or emotional 'unfinished business'" (p. 11). He states that persons struggling with life's developmental challenges are particularly susceptible to spiritual bypassing, as they attempt to *find themselves by giving themselves up*—or prematurely trying to move beyond their ego to self-transcendence, ignoring their personal and emotional needs. This attempt to create a new "spiritual" identity in order to avoid the pain of working through unresolved psychosocial issues does not work and frequently causes additional problems. As Trudy's social worker, you would want to do a thorough assessment, taking into account the substantial unresolved trauma and losses in her life. To ignore these issues and focus only on supporting her quest for enlightenment would be to commit Wilber's pre/trans fallacy. As a responsible and ethical social worker, you would help her address these unresolved issues at the personal, and perhaps even prepersonal, level while maintaining respect for her spiritual perspective. You would also help her discern the appropriate role of her spiritual practices in support of her overall growth and development. Consulting with a spiritual teacher or a transpersonal practitioner, with Trudy's permission, also might be helpful in this case.

Likewise, if a practitioner identifies a client's spiritual practices as signs of a serious problem simply because they are unfamiliar or seem "strange," he or she would be moving to the other side of the pre/trans fallacy—treating potentially spiritual or transpersonal experiences as if they were psychological disorders. The potential for this type of error is evident in the case of Jean-Joseph and his family. If this family sought help from conventional health care services, while also following traditional spiritually based healing processes, as a social worker your task would be to help the family and the medical professionals find a way to work together. This is not always an easy task, as is poignantly illustrated in Anne Fadiman's (1998) book, *The Spirit Catches You and You Fall Down*, which tells the tragic story of a Hmong child with epilepsy who becomes brain-dead because of the failure of professionals to understand unfamiliar spiritual worldviews and negotiate cultural differences. This true account highlights the critical need for social workers to develop the knowledge, values, and skills of spiritually sensitive practice in order to serve clients from diverse spiritual traditions.

SUMMARY AND CRITIQUE OF FOWLER'S AND WILBER'S THEORIES

Both Fowler's and Wilber's models of individual spiritual development reflect fourth force theory in that they incorporate the first three forces (psychodynamic, behavioral, and existential/humanistic/experiential theories). In fact, Fowler and Wilber use many of the same theorists (e.g., Piaget, Kohlberg, Maslow) as foundations for their own work, and both are delineating higher and more transcendent levels of human development than have been previously proposed by Western theories. In later writings, both theorists also offer additional conceptual formulations at the larger sociocultural levels (Fowler, 1996; Wilber, 2000b).

The major difference between the two models in terms of individual development is that Wilber provides more substance and specification than Fowler does about what transpersonal levels of development look like and how they evolve. Wilber also provides more detailed descriptions of the potential pitfalls of spiritual development than Fowler, who provides only a general overview of the possible dangers or deficits of development at each of his faith stages. However, Fowler provides more specification about the content and process of spiritual development at the prepersonal and personal phases. In terms of their utility for social work practice, we could say that Fowler's model is more *descriptive* and Wilber's is more *prescriptive*. Both theories have been critiqued in a number of areas. An overview of these critiques is presented next.

First, as developmental models, Fowler's and Wilber's models are open to the criticisms of all developmental perspectives, including charges of dominant-group bias. Such perspectives do not pay enough attention to social, economic, political, and historical factors and the role of power dynamics and oppression in human development. Developmental perspectives are also said to convey the idea that there is only one right way to proceed down the developmental path and thus display an ethnocentrism often rooted in middle-class, heterosexual, Anglo-Saxon male life experience.

Both Fowler and Wilber might counter by pointing out that familial, cultural, and historical contexts are considered in their models. Wilber, in particular, would highlight the extensive use of cross-cultural knowledge in the development of his theory and point to the cessation of ethnocentrism as a major characteristic of his later stages of consciousness. He would also stress the nature of his more current theoretical developments, which pay equal attention to *exterior* impacts on spiritual development as to *interior* aspects (Wilber, 2000b, 2001, 2006). Both theorists would also support the notion of many paths in spiritual development, although they would say that these many paths have common features in their evolution.

A second critique of both theories is their relative lack of attention to the spiritual capacities and potentialities of children, focusing more on the emergence of spiritual issues in adulthood. This is due to the assertion that higher levels of cognitive functioning (capacity for formal operations and abstract thought) are necessary to fully experience and incorporate spiritual experience. A number of writers have contested this assertion, proposing that childhood is a unique time of enhanced, not diminished, spiritual awareness (R. Coles, 1990; Hay, Nye, & Murphy, 1996; Levine, 1999). They base this viewpoint on in-depth interviews with children ranging in age from 6 to 11 (Hay & Nye, 2006), which often revealed a richness and depth regarding spirituality that is generally not expected of people of this age, including a variety of spiritual experiences and epiphanies. Results from a national survey of seasoned social workers who work with children and adolescents reveal that practitioners generally see the relevance of religion and spirituality in the lives of children and that they encounter youth who present spiritual issues in practice (Kvarfordt & Sheridan, 2007).

Wilber (2000a) concedes that children can have a variety of spiritual experiences, including peak experiences that provide glimpses of the transpersonal realm, but he states that these incidents are experienced and incorporated within the child's prepersonal or personal stage of development. Regardless of the particular developmental level, there clearly is a need for further exploration of children's spirituality in order to understand their unique spiritual experiences, developmental processes, and needs. Similarly, there is also a need to revisit assumptions about the spiritual experiences and capacities of adults who have lower cognitive functioning, either congenitally or as a result of injury.

A third critique concerns empirical investigation of the theories. Although Fowler's model was developed through an inductive research process and Wilber's formulations are grounded in a synthesis of many lines of research and philosophical analysis, there is an ongoing need for empirical verification of both models. Empirical exploration of Fowler's faith stages has provided both support and critique for his framework (see Slee, 1996; Streib, 2005, for reviews of this work). Similarly, there have been more than 150 articles published on integral theory over the past decade (Esbjörn-Hargens, 2010), providing both support and challenge to some of the theory's key tenets. The fact that findings are not conclusive regarding Fowler's and Wilber's theories is understandable, given the difficulties of empirical investigation in such an abstract realm. Nonetheless, strategies from both positivist and constructivist research approaches are currently available to study interior states and subjective experiences of meaning as well as biophysical manifestations of different states of consciousness. (See Chapter 1 for a review of positivist and constructivist research approaches.) As is true for all theories of human behavior, transpersonal models such as Fowler's and Wilber's need to be specifically tested and refined through the research process. This research also must be replicated with different groups (defined by sex and gender, age, race, ethnicity, socioeconomic status, geopolitical membership, and the like).

In conclusion, both Fowler and Wilber provide perspectives beyond our traditional framework that allow us to better understand human development and functioning, and they suggest a direction for working with people from diverse spiritual perspectives. However, we also need viable practice theories and practice models that explicitly address the spiritual dimension. There have been promising developments in this area. Examples include Smith's (1995) transegoic model for dealing with death and other losses; Cowley's (1999) transpersonal approach for working with couples and families; Hickson and Phelps's (1998) model for facilitating women's spirituality; and Clark's (2007) model for working with spirituality, culture, and diverse worldviews. There are also practice models that directly integrate spirituality. Examples are Almaas's (1995, 1996) diamond approach, which incorporates object relations and body sensing within Sufism, and Grof's (2003; Grof & Bennett, 1992) holotropic breathwork model, which combines bodywork and altered states of consciousness to address unresolved psychological issues from earlier points in development. Finally, Cortright (1997) provides a good overview of how a transpersonal orientation can be generally incorporated within psychoanalytic and existential therapies, and Mikulas (2002) offers a practice approach that integrates a transpersonal perspective with behavioral approaches. All of these developments reflect a synthesis of transpersonal with earlier therapeutic modalities (first, second, and third force therapies). These practice theories and models also must be tested and continually refined to determine their utility and applicability for a wide range of client situations.

CRITICAL THINKING Questions 5.2

Fowler and Wilber both think of spirituality in terms of development to higher levels of faith or consciousness over time. Do you think this is a helpful way to think about spirituality? Explain. Is it a helpful way to think about your own spiritual life? Explain. Do you see any cultural biases in either of the theories? Explain.

THE ROLE OF SPIRITUALITY IN SOCIAL WORK

Canda and Furman (2010) outline five broad historical phases that trace the development of linkages between spirituality and social work in the United States. This history includes the early religious origins of social work, which was followed by a period of the profession distancing itself from its religious roots, and then to a period of resurgence of interest in spirituality. A number of publications address the relevance of spirituality for the profession, and the range of this literature has become extensive. Thus, the following sections provide examples of writings that examine the role of spirituality relative to human diversity or the human condition. Readers are encouraged to use these as a starting place for further exploration.

SPIRITUALITY AND HUMAN DIVERSITY

Commitment to issues of human diversity and to oppressed populations is a hallmark of the social work profession. At various times in history, some branches of organized religion have played a negative or impeding role in the attainment of social justice for various groups. Examples include the use of religious texts, policies, and practices to deny the full human rights of persons of color; women; and gay, lesbian, bisexual, and transgender persons. At the same time, organized religion has a rich heritage of involvement in myriad social justice causes and movements, including the civil rights movement, the peace movement, the women's movement, the gay rights movement, abolition of the death penalty, the antipoverty movement, and the deep ecology movement.

It is beyond the scope of this chapter to do an overall analysis of the role of religion in the struggle for social and economic justice. However, the following sections provide examples of the impact of both religious and nonreligious spirituality in the lives of oppressed groups as defined by race and ethnicity, sex and gender, sexual orientation, and other forms of human diversity.

Race and Ethnicity

Spirituality expressed in both religious and nonreligious forms has been pivotal in the lives of many persons of color and other marginalized ethnic groups. This brief discussion of spirituality and race/ethnicity emphasizes common experiences and themes in order to provide a general overview. However, remember that a great deal of diversity exists within these groups and that every person's story is unique.

1. *African Americans.* In a survey conducted by the Pew Research Center's Forum on Religion & Public Life (Sahgal & Smith, 2009), African Americans emerged as notably more religious than the general U.S. population based on a number of indicators. They have the highest percentage of religiously affiliated adults of all racial/ethnic groups (87%), and nearly 8 in 10 (79%) say that religion is very important in their lives, compared with 56% of all U.S. adults. Even the majority (72%) of African Americans who are not affiliated with any particular faith report that religion plays at least a somewhat important role in their lives, and almost half (45%) of this group say that it is very important. Furthermore, 53% report attending religious services at least once a week, 76% pray daily, and 88% declare that they are absolutely certain about the existence of God. Data from this survey show the majority of African Americans identifying as Protestant (78%), followed by Catholic (5%), and Jehovah's Witness (1%). Four percent reported some other type of affiliation, and 12% identify as "unaffiliated." African Americans account for about one fourth of adherents to Islam in the United States (Pew Forum, 2008), including membership in Sunni Islam or other mainstream Islamic denominations, the Nation of Islam, or smaller Black Muslim sects (Haddad, 1997). Black churches, in particular, have historically been a safe haven for African Americans facing racism and oppression, as well as an important source of social support, race consciousness and inspiration, leadership training, human services, and empowerment and social change (Franklin, 1994; Logan, 2001; Taylor, Chatters, & Levin, 2004). The legacy of slavery and the integrated heritage of African and African American spiritual values have emphasized collective unity and the connection of all beings (Nobles, 1980). Afrocentric spirituality stresses the interdependence among God, community, family, and the individual. Its central virtues include beneficence to the community, forbearance through tragedy, wisdom applied to action, creative improvisation, forgiveness of wrongs and oppression, and social justice (Paris, 1995). *Kwanzaa* is an important nonsectarian Afrocentric spiritual tradition developed by Maulana Karenga in the 1960s as a mechanism for celebrating and supporting African and African American strengths and empowerment. Seven principles represent the core values of Kwanzaa: *umoja* (unity), *kujichagulia* (self-determination), *ujima* (collective work and responsibility), *ujamaa* (collective economics), *nia* (purpose), *kuumba* (creativity), and *imani* (faith) (Karenga, 1995). Many writers stress the importance of paying attention to the role of spirituality in its various forms when working with African American clients, families, and communities (see, for example, Banerjee & Canda, 2009; Bennett, Sheridan, & Richardson, 2014; Freeman, 2006; Stewart, Koeske, & Pringle, 2007).

2. *Latino(a) Americans.* This category includes people with ties to 26 countries in North, South, and Central America; the Caribbean; and Europe (Spain). Thus, the categorizing of these peoples under a reductionist label such

as Latino(a) or Hispanic denies the considerable diversity within this population. (Although these two terms are often used interchangeably, *Hispanic* refers to coming from a Spanish-speaking family and *Latino[a]* refers to geographic origin in Latin America.) Keeping this in mind, the majority (58%) of Latino(a) Americans are Roman Catholic, but there is also a large and growing number (23%) of Protestants among this group. Almost 5% report other religious affiliations, including Muslim and Jewish, and 14% are unaffiliated (Pew Forum, 2008). In addition, many Latino(a) people follow beliefs and practices that represent a blending of Christian, African, and Indigenous spiritual traditions (Canda & Furman, 2010). Latino(a) American spirituality has been strongly affected by factors related to colonialism (Costas, 1991). This history includes military, political, economic, cultural, and religious conquest, forcing many Indigenous peoples to take on the Catholicism of their conquerors. Many traditional places of worship, spiritual texts, beliefs, and practices were destroyed, repressed, or blended with Catholic traditions (Canda & Furman, 2010). Today, Christian Latino(a) faith has several central features: a personal relationship with God that encompasses love and reverence as well as fear and dread; an emphasis on both faith and ritual behavior; belief in the holiness of Jesus Christ as savior, king, and infant God; special reverence shown to Mary as the mother of God; recognition of saints as models of behavior and as benefactors; significance of sacred objects as both symbols of faith and transmitters of luck or magic; and special events and celebrations, such as saints' feast days, Holy Week, Christmas Eve, feasts of the Virgin, and life passages (e.g., baptisms, first communions, confirmations, coming-of-age ceremonies, weddings, and funerals) (Aguilar, 2001; Ramirez, 1985). In addition to mainstream religions, a number of African and Indigenous spiritual healing traditions continue to be practiced by some Latino(a) groups today, including curanderismo, santiguando, espiritismo, Santeria, and Vodoun (Delgado, 1988; Paulino, 1995; Torrez, 1984). Social workers need to understand the importance of both religious institutions and folk healing traditions when working with Latino(a) populations. These various expressions of spirituality serve as important sources for social support, coping strategies, means of healing, socialization and maintenance of culture, and resources for human services and social justice efforts (Burke, Chauvin, & Miranti, 2005; Faver & Trachte, 2005).

3. *Asian Americans and Pacific Islanders.* This population represents many cultures, including Chinese, Filipino, Japanese, Korean, Asian Indian, Vietnamese, Hawaiian, Cambodian, Laotian, Thai, Hmong, Pakistani, Samoan, Guamanian, and Indonesian (Healey, 2012). These different peoples are affiliated with a wide range of spiritual traditions, including Hinduism, Buddhism, Islam, Confucianism, Sikhism, Zoroastrianism, Jainism, Shinto, Taoism, and Christianity (Tweed, 1997). In the United States, 27% of this group is Protestant, 17% Catholic, 14% Hindu, 9% Buddhist, and 4% Muslim. Approximately 6% report other religious affiliations, and 23% are unaffiliated (Pew Forum, 2008). There is much diversity within these various religious traditions as well, making it particularly difficult to discuss common elements of spiritual beliefs or practices. However, several themes can be discerned: the connection among and the divinity of all beings; the need to transcend suffering and the material world; the importance of displaying compassion, selflessness, and cooperation; the honoring of ancestors; a disciplined approach to life and spiritual development; and a holistic understanding of existence (Canda & Furman, 1999; Chung, 2001; Singh, 2001). Both religious institutions and traditional practices have been helpful to a variety of Asian and Pacific Islander immigrants and refugees and their descendants. For example, many southeast Asian refugee communities have established Buddhist temples and mutual assistance associations, which provide social, physical, mental, and spiritual resources (Canda & Phaobtong, 1992; Morreale, 1998), and the Korean church has been an essential provider of social services and community development efforts (Boddie, Hong, Im, & Chung, 2011). Some Asian Americans and Pacific Islanders also use Indigenous healers, such as the Cambodian krou khmer, the Korean mudang, the Hmong spirit medium, and the Hawaiian kahuna (Canda & Furman, 1999; Canda, Shin, & Canda, 1993; Hurdle, 2002). As with other groups, there is an emerging literature stressing the importance of attending to spirituality in practice with clients from this large and diverse cultural population (see, for example, Leung & Chan, 2010; Tan, 2006). In addition, several writers have proposed incorporating concepts and practices from Asian spiritual traditions into mainstream social work practice, including meditation (Keefe, 1996; Logan, 1997), Zen-oriented practice (Brandon, 1976), body–mind–spirit integration approaches (Leung, Chan, Ng, & Lee, 2009), and yoga (Fukuyama & Sevig, 1999).

4. *Native Americans.* Native Americans, or First Nations peoples, originally numbered in the millions and were members of hundreds of distinct tribes or nations, each with its own language, heritage, and spiritual traditions (Healey, 2012). As part of the effort to "humanize and civilize" Native Americans, Congress regularly appropriated funds for Christian missionary efforts beginning in 1819 (U.S. Commission on Human Rights, 1998). American Indian boarding schools were a major component of these efforts, where children were forbidden to wear their native attire, eat their native foods, speak their native language, or practice their traditional religion and were often severely punished for failure to adhere to these prohibitions (Haig-Brown, 1988; Snipp, 1998). See the case study of David Sanchez in Chapter 10 in this book for an example

Native American dance is a cultural and highly spiritual form of expression.

of the impact of these boarding school methods on Native American youth. Through a long history of resistance and renewal, however, Indigenous spiritual traditions have persisted and currently are being restored and revitalized (Swift, 1998). Various expressions of Native American spirituality have several common themes: the inseparability of spirituality from the rest of life; connection to and responsibility for the earth and all her creatures; the sacredness of all things, including animals, plants, minerals, and natural forces; the values of balance, harmony, and connectedness; the importance of extended family and community; and the use of myth, ritual, and storytelling as spiritual practices (Duran & Duran, 1995; Matheson, 1996; Yellow Bird, 1995). Many of these values are of increasing appeal to non-Indigenous people, producing great concern among Native American people regarding appropriation of their customs, ceremonies, rituals, and healing practices (Kasee, 1995; LaDue, 1994). This cross-tradition borrowing of spiritual practices requires sensitivity, respect, competence, and permission in such matters (Canda & Yellow Bird, 1996). Social workers also should become informed regarding ongoing efforts to protect Native American cultural and religious freedoms, including issues related to sacred lands, free exercise of religion in correctional and educational institutions, repatriation of human remains and sacred objects held in museums and scientific institutions, and protection of sacred and cultural knowledge from exploitation and appropriation (Harvard Pluralism Project, 2005). Many service providers also call for sensitivity and awareness of the effects of historical trauma on Native Americans and recommend the integration of traditional practices for more effective service delivery (see, for example, Chong, Fortier, & Morris, 2009; Limb & Hodge, 2008; Weaver, 2011). In addition, Indigenous worldviews and spiritual practices have application to social work in general (Canda, 1983; Voss, Douville, Little Soldier, & Twiss, 1999).

It is important to remember the experience of other groups that have been more extensively assimilated into the dominant culture of the United States (e.g., Irish, Italian, and Jewish Americans). Many of these groups also have histories of discrimination and religious intolerance, the effects of which are felt by succeeding generations. Since the terrorist attacks of September 11, 2001, we in the United States have witnessed increased discrimination and oppressive acts against Muslim Americans, especially those of Middle Eastern descent (Crabtree, Husain, & Spalek, 2008; Pew Research Center, 2009). Given this atmosphere and the growing Muslim population within the United States, it is imperative that social workers develop sensitivity and competence in working with Muslim clients (Carolan, Bagherinia, Juhari, Himelright, & Mouton-Sanders, 2000; Hodge, 2005a). Indeed, social workers must be sensitive to the particular history and spiritual traditions of all racial and ethnic groups.

Sex and Gender

Women are more likely than men to report that they are religious, church affiliated, and frequent users of prayer; are certain in their belief in God; feel close to God; hold a positive view of their church; and are more religiously engaged (Pew Forum, 2008). Women also are the majority of members in most religious bodies in the United States and play important roles in the life of many religious communities (Braude, 1997).

However, in several denominations, women's participation has been significantly restricted, prohibiting them from holding leadership positions or performing certain religious rites and ceremonies (Burke et al., 2005; Holm & Bowker, 1994; Reilly, 1995). In addition, women members of traditional Judeo-Christian and Islamic faiths generally experience conceptualizations and symbols of the divine as masculine, suggesting that men are closer to (and thus more like) God than women (Reuther, 1983). In response to this, some scholars are calling for increased ordination of women and more women in leadership positions in order to create a more woman-affirming environment within religious institutions (Roberts & Yamane, 2012).

Although most women who belong to mainstream denominations report being generally satisfied with their affiliations (Corbett, 1997), some struggle with the patriarchal aspects of their faith. One study conducted in-depth interviews of 61 women ages 18 to 71 who were affiliated with Catholic, United Methodist, Unitarian Universalist, or Jewish congregations (Ozorak, 1996). Most (93%) perceived gender inequality within their religions. Sixteen percent viewed these inequalities as appropriate, and thus accepted them; 8% left their faith in reaction to this issue and others. The remainder coped by using behavioral strategies (e.g., requesting equal treatment; requesting gender-inclusive language; substituting feminine words, images, or interpretations; participating in feminist activities), cognitive strategies (e.g., focusing on positive aspects of the religion, comparing their faith favorably to others, emphasizing signs of positive change), or a combination of both behavioral and cognitive mechanisms.

Christian and Jewish feminist theologians have made efforts to emphasize the feminine heritage of conventional faiths, and some Christian and Jewish denominations have increased opportunities for women in both lay leadership roles and clerical positions (Canda & Furman, 2010). There also has been a movement toward alternative women's spiritualities. Some women have become involved in spiritual support groups or explored other religious traditions, such as Buddhism (Carnes & Craig, 1998; Holm & Bowker, 1994). Others have pursued feminist-identified theology, such as Goddess worship (Manning, 2010), Wicca (Starhawk, 1979; Warwick, 1995), Jewish feminism (Breitman, 1995), or Christian womanist spirituality (Jackson, 2002). These spiritual traditions emphasize the feminine aspect of the divine; the sacredness of women's bodies, rhythms, and life cycles; the power and creativity of women's spirituality; a connection to earth-centered practices; and the care of all people and the planet (Ochshorn & Cole, 1995; Warwick, 1995). Some men are also turning to alternative spiritual traditions to overcome religious experiences and conceptions of God and masculinity they feel have been detrimental to them (Kivel, 1991; Warwick, 1995).

Sexual Orientation

Nonheterosexual persons are often linked together as the LGBT community (lesbian, gay, bisexual, and transgender persons). It should be noted, however, that transgender persons may identify themselves as heterosexual, bisexual, or homosexual; therefore, transgender status is a matter of sex and gender, not sexual orientation. However, as a group, transgender persons have much in common with gay men, lesbians, and bisexual persons when it comes to experiences with oppression and thus are included with these groups in this discussion of spirituality.

As an oppressed population, LGBT persons have suffered greatly at the hands of some groups affiliated with organized religion. Some egregious examples are the pronouncement by certain religious leaders that AIDS is a "punishment for the sins" of LGBT persons and the picketing of funerals of victims of antigay hate crimes by religiously identified individuals. More pervasively, many LGBT members of various faiths have had to struggle with religious teachings that tell them their feelings and behaviors are immoral or sinful. A growing body of literature reveals the serious impacts of religious rejection and abuse experienced by many LGBT persons, resulting in spiritual loss, depression, internalized shame, substance abuse, and thoughts of suicide (e.g., Barton, 2010; Hansen & Lambert, 2011; Super & Jacobson, 2011). Other studies show LGBT persons remaining connected to their faith despite negative experiences and relying on spirituality as an important source of coping and support (e.g., Bozard & Sanders, 2011; Yarhouse & Carr, 2012). In particular, involvement in gay-affirming congregations has been shown to provide significant benefits to LGBT persons facing conflict between their sexual and religious identities (Sherry, Adelman, Whilde, & Quick, 2010).

Every major religious and spiritual tradition has LGBT adherents. Furthermore, there are religious rationales within Christianity, Islam, Judaism, Buddhism, Confucianism, and Taoism for tolerance of nonheterosexual orientations, even though historically these religions have privileged heterosexuality (Ellison & Plaskow, 2007). There are also associations within every major religion that go beyond tolerance to work for full inclusion of LGBT persons. Examples include the following: Affirmation—United Methodists for Lesbian, Gay, Bisexual & Transgender Concerns; Association of Welcoming & Affirming Baptists; Integrity (Episcopal);

© iStockphoto.com/carterdayne

LGBT persons who grow up in less tolerant religious communities experience considerable tension between their faith and their sexuality.

Dignity USA (Catholic); Lutherans Concerned; More Light Presbyterians; United Church of Christ Coalition for Lesbian, Bisexual, Gay and Transgender Concerns; World Congress of Gay, Lesbian, Bisexual, and Transgender Jews; Keshet Ga'avah; Al-Fatiah (Muslim); Gay Buddhist Fellowship; the Gay and Lesbian Vaishnava Association (Hindu); and Seventh Day Adventist Kinship. There are also denominations that generally identify themselves as "open and gay affirming," including Metropolitan Community Church, Society of Friends (Quakers), United Church of Christ, Unitarian Universalism, and Reform and Reconstructionist branches of Judaism.

LGBT persons who grow up in less tolerant religious communities experience considerable tension between their faith and their sexuality. They, and others close to them, must decide how to respond to this tension. For social workers, it is important to respect the unique spiritual journeys that individual LGBT persons may take. If you were working with Leon as he struggles with the conflict between his church and his sexual orientation, it would be important to work collaboratively with him to discern what option was best for him, providing him information about alternatives while maintaining respect for his self-determination. As Barret and Barzan (1996) point out, regardless of the individual decisions LGBT persons make regarding religion, the process of self-acceptance is a spiritual journey unto itself.

Other Aspects of Diversity

The issues and implications relative to spirituality that pertain to race and ethnicity, sex and gender, and sexual orientation apply to other forms of human diversity as well. For example, some religious teachings have interpreted disability as a punishment for the sins of the person or family (Miles, 1995; Niemann, 2005) or as a means for nondisabled persons to acquire spiritual status through expressions of pity and charity (Fitzgerald, 1997). Conversely, spirituality has been noted as both a significant means of coping and a vehicle toward positive self-definition for persons with disabilities (Hurst, 2007; Niemann, 2005; Parish, Magana, & Cassiman, 2008; Swinton, 2012).

Spirituality and age is another area that has been widely addressed. Both religious and nonreligious forms of spirituality are important sources of social support for older persons and a pathway for coping, ongoing development, and successful aging (Burke et al., 2005; Hedberg, Brulin, & Alex, 2009; K. Lee, 2011). In addition, spirituality is viewed as an essential foundation for healthy development among young people (Hay & Nye, 2006; Myers, 1997; Roehlkepartain, King, Wagener, & Benson, 2006). Research has shown spirituality to be a significant protective factor against substance abuse, premature sexual activity, and delinquency for children and adolescents (Holder et al., 2000; Johnson, Jang, Larsen, & De Li, 2001; Miller, Davies, & Greenwald, 2000; Smith & Denton, 2005). Other research highlights the potential for the religious or spiritual abuse and neglect of youth (Bottoms, Nielsen, Murray, & Filipas, 2003; Kvarfordt, 2010). As our understanding of the interaction between religious and nonreligious spirituality and other forms of human diversity increases, social work will be in a better position to work sensitively, competently, and ethically with many diverse groups and communities.

CRITICAL THINKING Questions 5.3

With globalization, we have more regular contact with people of diverse religious and spiritual beliefs. How much religious and spiritual diversity do you come in contact with in your everyday life? How comfortable are you with honoring different religious and spiritual beliefs? How have you seen religious and spiritual beliefs used to discriminate against some groups of people? How have you seen religious and spiritual beliefs used to promote social justice?

SPIRITUALITY AND THE HUMAN EXPERIENCE

Social workers deal with every aspect of the human experience. They simultaneously focus on solving problems in living while supporting optimal human functioning and quality of life. The literature regarding spirituality in these two areas is immense, with significant development in social work, psychology, nursing, medicine, rehabilitation counseling, pastoral counseling, marital and family counseling, and other helping disciplines. The following discussion highlights examples of this continually evolving knowledge base. Similar to the previous discussion of spirituality and diversity, this brief overview will serve readers as an entry point to this expanding literature.

Problems in Living

It is difficult to find an area related to problems in living in which spirituality is not being explored. For example, much has been written about the link between spirituality and mental health. Various indicators of spirituality—such as religious commitment, involvement in spiritual or religious practices, and level of religiosity or spirituality—have been shown to have an inverse relationship with depression, anxiety, hopelessness, suicide, and other mental health problems while showing a positive relationship with self-esteem, self-efficacy, hope, optimism, life satisfaction, and general well-being (Koenig, 2005; Mueller, Plevak, & Rummans, 2001; Pargament, 1997).

Similar influences are found between spirituality and physical health, with spirituality linked to a variety of better health outcomes (Ellison & Levin, 1998; Koenig, King, & Carson, 2012; Matthews et al., 1998). Various propositions have been investigated to explain the exact mechanisms of this relationship. Findings suggest that religion and spirituality benefit physical health through their support of health-promoting behaviors and discouragement of risk behaviors, whereas others indicate possible biological processes that mediate the negative impacts of stress and support healthy immune functioning (Ray, 2004; Segerstrom & Miller, 2004). Specific spiritual practices, such as mindfulness-based stress-reduction techniques, have shown positive outcomes in several areas, including chronic pain, anxiety disorders, recurrent depression, psoriasis, and general psychological well-being (Grossman, Niemann, Schmidt, & Walach, 2004; Williams, Teasdale, Segal, & Kabat-Zinn, 2007), as well as benefits to the immune system (Davidson et al., 2003).

For both mental and physical health problems, religion and spirituality have been noted as major means of coping (Koenig, 2005; Koenig et al., 2012). In an extensive review of the social and behavioral science literature, Oakley Ray (2004) cites spirituality as one of four key factors significantly linked to positive coping, along with knowledge, inner resources, and social support. The specific benefits of spiritually based coping include relieving stress, retaining a sense of control, maintaining hope, and providing a sense of meaning and purpose in life (Koenig, 2005).

Higher levels of social support through religious and spiritual networks also play a significant role in positive coping with health issues (Reese & Kaplan, 2000). Both religious and nonreligious forms of spirituality have proven helpful to persons coping with caregiving demands related to health problems of family members (Bennett, Sheridan, & Richardson, 2014; Koenig, 2005; Vickrey et al., 2007). Similar effects are noted for coping with poverty (Greeff & Fillis, 2009; Parish et al., 2008) and homelessness (Ferguson, Wu, Dryrness, & Spruijt-Metz, 2007).

Still another body of scholarship explores spirituality and substance abuse. Both religiosity and spirituality have been noted as protective factors in this area for both adults and children (Smith & Denton, 2005; Wills, Yaeger, & Sandy, 2003). In addition, the spiritual dimension as a key factor in recovery from substance abuse has long been recognized in self-help groups such as Alcoholics Anonymous, Narcotics Anonymous, and other treatment approaches (Hsu, Grow, Marlatt, Galanter, & Kaskutas, 2008; Streifel & Servaty-Seib, 2009).

There is also a growing literature addressing the role of spirituality in understanding and dealing with the effects of various types of trauma—including physical and sexual abuse and assault (Bowland, Biswas, Kyriakakis, & Edmond, 2011; Robinson, 2000; Walker, Reid, O'Neill, & Brown, 2009); domestic and community violence (Benavides, 2012; Parappully, Rosenbaum, van den Daele, & Nzewi, 2002); serious injury and natural disasters (Ashkanani, 2009; Johnstone, Yoon, Rupright, & Reid-Arndt, 2009; Tausch et al., 2011); incarceration (O'Brien, 2001; Redman, 2008); and ethnic trauma, war, displacement, and terrorism (Drescher et al., 2009; Markovitzky & Mosek, 2005; Meisenhelder & Marcum, 2009). Certain spiritually oriented interventions, such as the use of ceremony and ritual, appear to have particular utility in helping persons recover from trauma and loss (Cairns, 2005; Lubin & Johnson, 1998).

Finally, nowhere has spirituality been viewed as more relevant than in the area of death and dying. Religious and spiritual issues often arise at the end of life, and thus practitioners need to be able to deal with these issues effectively (MacKinlay, 2006; J. Morgan, 2002; Nelson-Becker, 2006). Spiritual sensitivity is also needed in working with those grieving the loss of loved ones (Winston, 2006) or facing divorce or other kinds of loss (Coholic, 2011; Marsh, 2005).

Individual and Collective Well-Being

Spirituality also has a role to play in regard to the second major focus of social work: supporting and enhancing optimal human functioning and quality of life. This role is evident at all levels of human systems, including the individual, family, community, organizational, and societal spheres. The following discussion identifies key points of this influence on well-being at both the individual and collective levels.

At the individual level, interest in wellness, holistic health, and the mind–body connection has exploded in recent years, as evidenced by increasing numbers of workshops and retreats, weekly groups, self-help books, and media reports on the topic. Furthermore, there has been a marked increase in the use of complementary and alternative medicine (CAM), sometimes referred to as integrative medicine, which includes "an array of health care approaches with a history of use or origins outside of mainstream medicine" (National Center for Complementary and Alternative Medicine [NCCAM], n.d.). These approaches, which often are grounded in spiritual traditions and a holistic understanding of the human condition, include homeopathy and naturopathic medicine, acupuncture, massage therapy, mindfulness or transcendental meditation, movement therapies, relaxation techniques, spinal manipulation, Tai chi and Qi gong, yoga, healing touch, hypnotherapy, and Ayurvedic and traditional Chinese medicine (NCCAM, n.d.).

More than 1,200 research projects have been funded by NCCAM, which is the lead agency under the National Institutes of Health (NIH) charged with investigating the efficacy of these approaches for both physical and mental health. Many of these studies have found positive effects of various CAM modalities, while also identifying approaches that are ineffective. Regardless of the scientific results, Americans are increasingly using CAM processes and products. Findings from a 2007 national survey reveal that approximately 50% of Americans used some form of alternative or complementary medicine (Barnes, Bloom, & Nahin, 2008), compared with 34% in 1990 (Williamson & Wyandt, 2001). There is a rise in the use of CAM by physical health and mental health practitioners as well. In a study of social work practitioners, over 75% of the sample reported either direct use or referral to mind–body techniques or community health alternatives in work with their clients (L. Henderson, 2000).

In related research, investigations are uncovering the specific mechanisms of the mind–body connection. In a meta-analysis of 30 years of research, findings show clear linkages between psychological stress and lowered immune system functioning, the major biological system that defends the body against disease (Segerstrom & Miller, 2004). In another review of 100 years of research, Oakley Ray (2004) reports mounting evidence that stressors affecting the brain are harmful to the body at both a cellular and molecular level, and they diminish a person's health and quality of life. In addition, intriguing results are coming out of research on the neurobiology of consciousness. Several studies have shown demonstrable links between subjective experiences reported during meditation and noted alterations in brain function (e.g., EEG patterns, gamma activity, phase synchrony), as well as evidence of neuroplasticity (transformations of the brain) in long-term meditators (Lutz, Dunne, & Davidson, 2007). Taken together, these investigations suggest that many of our core mental and emotional processes not only are pivotal in maintaining optimal health but also affect our capacity for personal happiness and compassion for others. Results from the consciousness studies suggest that positive workings of the mind are trainable skills through practices such as meditation. This possibility has significant implications for both individual and communal well-being.

As a result of this research, a growing number of articles in the professional literature also promote the use of wellness or mind–body approaches for both clients and practitioners. Examples include the development of specialized wellness programs (Clark, 2002; Kissman & Maurer, 2002), the use of stress management and relaxation techniques (Finger & Arnold, 2002; McBee, Westreich, & Likourezos, 2004; Payne, 2000), and the use of mindfulness meditation and yoga (L. Bell, 2009; Brantley, Doucette, & Lindell, 2008; Lee, Ng, Leung, & Chan, 2009; Vohra-Gupta, Russell, & Lo, 2007; Wisniewski, 2008). Many of these approaches are rooted in spiritual traditions, especially Eastern traditions.

There also has been a great deal of recent development concerning spirituality and work. Much of this literature focuses on the search for "right livelihood," or the conscious choice of work consistent with one's spiritual values and supportive of ongoing spiritual growth (Neal, 2000; Sinetar, 2011). Other writers exploring the role of spirituality in the workplace discuss such issues as use of power, management style, workplace environment, and integrating spiritual values with overall work goals (Roberson, 2004; N. Smith, 2006). The social work enterprise itself has been the subject of such interest. Examples include Canda and Furman's (2010) identification of principles for spiritually sensitive administration of human service organizations and Chamiec-Chase's (2009) focus on measuring social workers' integration of spirituality in the workplace.

The connection between spirituality and creativity is another area being addressed by a variety of writers. Much of this writing emphasizes the potential that linking spirituality and creativity has for healing as well as nurturing self-expression and optimal development. Examples include use of the visual arts (Coholic, 2011; Farrelly-Hansen, 2009); journaling, poetry, and creative writing (Cameron, 1992; V. Wright, 2005); music and sound (D. Campbell, 1997; Goldman, 1996); and movement and dance, drama, and other performing arts (Pearson, 1996; Wuthnow, 2001). Engaging in the creative process seems to facilitate spiritual growth and well-being by encouraging the person to go beyond ego limitations, surrender to process, and tap into spiritual sources of strength and self-expression (Fukuyama & Sevig, 1999; K. Mayo, 2009).

Spirituality is also emerging as an important factor in the optimal functioning of various human collectives. In social work with couples and families, paying attention to the spiritual dimension of family life is viewed as important not only for the religiously affiliated but for the nonaffiliated as well (Duba & Watts, 2009; F. Walsh, 2009a). It has been identified as an important component in working with couples and families relative to a wide range of issues, including discord (Derezotes, 2001; Hunler & Gencoz, 2005), challenges of adoption and parenting (Belanger, Copeland, & Cheung, 2009; Evans, Boustead, & Owens, 2008), health issues (Cattich & Knudson-Martin, 2009), death and loss (F. Walsh, 2009b), and building on family strengths and resilience (H. Anderson, 2009; Bell-Toliver & Wilkerson, 2011; Gale, 2009; Hames & Godwin, 2008).

The literature also notes the role of spirituality in community-based and social change initiatives. Examples include community health promotion programs (C. Clark, 2002), collective action and social justice efforts (Hill & Donaldson, 2012; Hutchison, 2012; Perry & Rolland, 2009; Tripses & Scroggs, 2009), services to rural communities (Furman & Chandy, 1994; S. Johnson, 1997), and other types of community-focused practice (Garland, Myers, & Wolfer, 2008; Obst & Tham, 2009; Pargament, 2008; Tangenberg, 2008). Social workers are also becoming acquainted with the newly emerging spiritual activism movement, which goes beyond a focus on political and economic forces as primary mechanisms for social change to incorporate a spiritual framework for activism. Emerging principles of this new model include such themes as "recognition of interdependence," "acceptance of not knowing," "openness to suffering," and "outer change requiring inner work" (Sheridan, 2014). This more holistic approach is viewed as having greater potential for achieving liberation and social justice than previous efforts embedded in a conflict perspective.

Attention to religious and spiritual resources is also being identified in organizational practice. President Obama announced the reconfigured White House Office of Faith-Based and Neighborhood Partnerships on the 17th day of his first administration, while also stressing the importance of such partnerships remaining consistent with constitutional principles and American values:

> The goal of this office will not be to favor one religious group over another—or even religious groups over secular groups. It will simply be to work on behalf of those organizations that want to work on behalf of our communities, and to do so without blurring the line that our founders wisely drew between church and state. This work is important, because whether it's a secular group advising families facing foreclosure or faith-based groups providing job-training to those who need work, few are closer to what's happening on our streets and in our neighborhoods than these organizations. People trust them. Communities rely on them. And we will help them. (Office of Faith-Based and Neighborhood Partnerships, 2009, para. 1)

The proliferation of congregational and faith-based social services, which began with the George W. Bush administration in 2001, is being closely followed and evaluated by social work scholars. Some note positive opportunities and outcomes as a result of this trend, whereas others point to negative and unanticipated consequences (Belcher, Fandetti, & Cole, 2004; Boddie & Cnaan, 2006; Netting, O'Connor, & Singletary, 2007; M. Thomas, 2009). The National Association of Social Workers (NASW; 2002) response to the federal faith-based initiative remains cautious, stressing the need for services to be delivered in a way that makes them clearly voluntary and emphasizing the central role and responsibility of government in providing social services. Although acknowledging and supporting the role that religious social service providers play in providing essential services, NASW also has emphasized that social work "must not allow the vital series of faith-based groups to become co-opted by the government as mere government-funded religion" (NASW, 2006, para. 5). Although faith-based organizations clearly have an important role to play in the provision of social services, there is a need for ongoing research on the impact of these organizations for both clients and social workers employed in such agencies.

Finally, spirituality is being increasingly identified as a needed force in nurturing and sustaining life beyond the circle of the human family to include all living beings and our planet that is home to all. Growing numbers of religious congregations, both conservative and progressive, are identifying "stewardship of the planet" as part of their commitment to God's creation (National Religious Partnership for the Environment, 2014). Many writers are pointing to the critical link between our capacity to view all of nature as sacred and the mounting issues of environmental degradation, climate change, and ecojustice for vulnerable and marginalized populations (Berry, 2009; Coates, 2007; Dylan & Coates, 2012; Jenkins, 2008). This spiritually grounded perspective challenges us to redefine the meaning of community and re-envision our rightful place in the "sacred hoop" of life.

In sum, spirituality in both its religious and nonreligious forms holds much potential for promoting well-being and quality of life at all levels of the human experience, as well as for helping the profession address the problems and possibilities inherent in the human condition.

CRITICAL THINKING Questions 5.4

A study of social work practitioners in 2000 found that more than 75% of the sample reported either direct use of mind–body techniques or referral to community health practitioners who use complementary and alternative medicine (CAM). What CAM practices do you use in your own life? What CAM practices do you expect to incorporate into your own practice? To what types of CAM practitioners do you expect to make referrals?

SPIRITUAL ASSESSMENT

Given the important role of spirituality in understanding both human diversity and human experience, it has become evident that gathering information about a client's religious or spiritual history and assessing spiritual development and current interests are as important as learning about biopsychosocial factors. Assessment needs to go beyond the surface features of faith affiliation (such as Protestant, Catholic, Jewish, or Muslim) to include deeper facets of a person's spiritual life (Sheridan, 2002). For example, talking with Caroline about where she is in her unfolding spiritual development would be helpful in supporting her exploration of different faith perspectives. Asking Matthew what brings him meaning, purpose, and connection right now would be valuable in assisting him in the next chapter of his life. And in working with Leon, it would be useful to know what aspects of his current religious affiliation are the most important and meaningful to him as he struggles with the conflicts regarding his faith and his sexual identity. None of this knowledge would be gleaned by a simple response to "What is your current religious affiliation?"

Social workers also need to assess both the positive and negative aspects of clients' religious or spiritual beliefs and practices (Canda & Furman, 2010; Lewandowski & Canda, 1995). For example, Naomi and David's understanding of the meaning of illness may be either helpful or harmful in dealing with Naomi's health crisis; Trudy's current spiritual practices may be supportive or detrimental to her physical, emotional, and social well-being; and Jean-Joseph's synthesis of Catholic and Vodoun beliefs and practices may be very positive for his personal and family life but may be problematic in his interactions with the wider social environment. Assessing the role and impact of all of these factors would be important areas for exploration in developing a spiritually sensitive relationship with any of these individuals.

A growing number of assessment instruments and approaches are available to help social workers. These include brief screening tools, which can provide an initial assessment of the relevance of religion or spirituality in clients' lives. Examples include the HOPE (Anandarajah & Hight, 2001), the FICA (Puchalski & Romer, 2000), the MIMBRA (Canda & Furman, 2010), and the Brief RCOPE (Pargament, Koenig, & Perez, 2000). There are also several more comprehensive assessment tools that focus on religious/spiritual history and current life circumstances. For example, Bullis (1996) developed a spiritual history that includes questions about individuals, their parents or guardians, and their spouses or significant others. Canda and Furman (2010) provide a discussion guide for a detailed spiritual assessment, which covers spiritual group membership and participation; spiritual beliefs, activities, experiences, and feelings; moral and value issues; spiritual development; spiritual sources of support and transformation; spiritual well-being; and extrinsic/intrinsic styles of spiritual propensity.

EXHIBIT 5.5 • Examples of Questions for Implicit Spiritual Assessment

1. What nourishes you spiritually—for example, music, nature, intimacy, witnessing heroism, meditation, creative expression, sharing another's joy?
2. What is the difference between shame and guilt? What are healthy and unhealthy shame and guilt?
3. What do you mean when you say your spirits are low? Is that different from being sad or depressed?
4. What is an incident in your life that precipitated a change in your belief about the meaning of life?
5. What helps you maintain a sense of hope when there is no immediate apparent basis for it?
6. Do you need forgiveness from yourself or someone else?
7. What currently brings a sense of meaning and purpose to your life?
8. Where do you go to find a sense of deep inspiration or peace?
9. For what are you most grateful?
10. What are your most cherished ideals?
11. In what way is it important or meaningful for you to be in this world (or in this situation)?
12. What are the deepest questions your situation raises for you?

SOURCE: Canda & Furman, 2010; Titone, 1991.

There are also examples of more implicit assessment approaches, which do not directly include a reference to "religion" or "spirituality" but are composed of open-ended questions that tap into spiritual themes, such as those identified by Titone (1991) and Canda and Furman (2010). (See Exhibit 5.5 for examples of these kinds of questions.) A number of other creative, nonverbal strategies for gathering such information have also been developed, including the use of spiritual timelines (Bullis, 1996); spiritual lifemaps, genograms, ecomaps, and ecograms (Hodge, 2005b); and spiritual trees (Raines, 1997). Finally, Lewandowski and Canda (1995) and Canda and Furman (2010) provide questions for assessing the helpful or harmful impacts of participating in spiritual groups or organizations (e.g., satisfaction with leadership style, methods of recruitment, response to members leaving the group).

Assessment must also be able to distinguish between a religious/spiritual problem and a mental disorder. Peteet, Lu, and Narrow's 2011 book *Religious and Spiritual Issues in Psychiatric Diagnosis* provides guidance in this area. Spiritual problems may include distress due to mystical experiences, near-death experiences, spiritual emergence/emergency, or separation from a spiritual teacher (Turner, Lukoff, Barnhouse, & Lu, 1995). This framework would be helpful in understanding any extraordinary or mystical experiences that Trudy, Jean-Joseph, or any of the other people in the case studies might share with you. Accurate assessment of such an occurrence can help determine whether the experience needs to be integrated and used as a stimulus for personal growth or whether it should be recognized as a sign of mental instability.

Assessment is just one component of spiritually sensitive social work practice. The field is accumulating a number of publications that provide more comprehensive discussion of spiritually sensitive practice (see, for example, Bullis, 1996; Canda & Furman, 2010; Derezotes, 2006; Frame, 2003; Mijares & Khalsa, 2005; Pargament, 2007; Scales et al., 2002; Sheridan, 2002).

CRITICAL THINKING Questions 5.5

How comfortable are you in discussing religious and spiritual themes with others? Which of the questions in Exhibit 5.5 would you be comfortable asking a client? Which would you be comfortable answering?

IMPLICATIONS FOR SOCIAL WORK PRACTICE

Spiritually sensitive social work practice involves gaining knowledge and skills in the areas discussed in this chapter, always keeping in mind that this approach must be grounded within the values and ethics of the profession. The following practice principles are offered as guidelines for effective and ethical social work practice in this area.

- Maintain clarity about your role as a spiritually sensitive practitioner, making a distinction between being a social worker who includes a focus on the spiritual dimension as part of holistic practice and being a religious leader or spiritual director.
- Be respectful of different religious or spiritual paths and be willing to learn about the role and meaning of various beliefs, practices, and experiences for various client systems (individuals, families, groups, communities).
- Critically examine your own values, beliefs, and biases concerning religion and spirituality and be willing to work through any unresolved or negative feelings or experiences in this area that may adversely affect your work with clients.
- Inform yourself about both the positive and negative role of religion and spirituality in the fight for social justice by various groups and be sensitive to this history in working with members of oppressed and marginalized populations.
- Develop a working knowledge of the beliefs and practices frequently encountered in your work with clients, especially those of newly arriving immigrants/refugees or nondominant groups (for example, Buddhist beliefs of southeast Asian refugees, spiritual traditions of First Nations peoples).
- Conduct comprehensive spiritual assessments with clients at all levels and use this information in service planning and delivery.
- Acquire the knowledge and skills necessary to employ spiritually based intervention techniques appropriately, ethically, and effectively.
- Seek information about the various religious and spiritual organizations, services, and leaders pertinent to your practice and develop good working relationships with these resources for purposes of referral and collaboration.
- Engage in ongoing self-reflection about what brings purpose, meaning, and connection in your own life and make disciplined efforts toward your own spiritual development, however you define this process.

KEY TERMS

ACTIVE LEARNING

1. *Theory application.* Working in small groups, consider any of the case studies presented at the beginning of the chapter. Using either Fowler's stages of faith development or Wilber's integral theory of consciousness as the conceptual framework, construct a timeline of the person's spiritual development. Trace the overall growth patterns through the different stages, including any ups and downs, as well as plateau periods. Identify the significant points or transitions you consider pivotal to the person's spiritual development.
   - How would this information help you to better understand the person's story and overall development? How would this information help you work with him or her as a social worker at various points in his or her life?
   - What would your own spiritual timeline look like, including patterns throughout various stages and significant points or transitions that were particularly significant for your own growth and development?
2. Select a partner for this exercise. This chapter provides a brief overview of the spiritual diversity in the United States. Given both your knowledge and experiences with different spiritual traditions, both religious and nonreligious, address the following questions. Take a few moments to reflect on each question before answering it. Partners should take turns answering the questions.
   - To which spiritual perspectives do you have the most positive reactions (e.g., are in the most agreement with, feel an appreciation or attraction toward, are the most comfortable with, find it easiest to keep an open mind and heart about)? What is it about you that contributes to these reactions (e.g., previous knowledge, personal experiences, messages from family or larger culture)?
   - To which perspective do you have the most negative reactions (e.g., are in the most disagreement with, feel a repulsion or fear about, are the most uncomfortable with, find it most difficult to keep an open mind and heart about)? What is it about you that contributes to these reactions (e.g., previous knowledge, personal experiences, messages from family or larger culture)?
   - What impact(s) might your reactions (both positive and negative) have on work with clients (especially with those who may hold different spiritual perspectives from you)? What personal and professional "work" on yourself is suggested by your positive and/or negative reactions?
3. Select a partner for this exercise. Together select one of the open-ended questions listed in Exhibit 5.5 to consider as it applies to your own lives. After a few moments of quiet reflection, write your response to the question, allowing yourself to write freely without concern for the proper mechanics of writing (e.g., spelling, grammar). Then sit with what you've written, reading it over with fresh eyes. When you're ready, share this experience with your partner, sharing as much or as little of what you've written as you feel comfortable with. Then talk together about the following questions:
   - What was the experience like of answering this question and then reading the response to yourself (e.g., easy, difficult, exciting, anxiety producing, confirming)?
   - Are there previous times in your life when you considered this question? Did you share your thoughts about it with others? If so, what was that like? What is it like to do that now with your partner?
   - Can you see yourself asking this kind of a question with a client? What do you think that experience might be like for both the client and you?

WEB RESOURCES

Adherents.com

www.adherents.com

Site—not affiliated with any religious, political, educational, or commercial organization—contains a comprehensive collection of more than 41,000 statistics on religious adherents, geography citations, and links to other major sites on diverse religious and spiritual traditions.

Association of Religion Data Archives

www.thearda.com

Site sponsored by the Lilly Endowment, the John Templeton Foundation, and Pennsylvania State University provides more than 350 data files on U.S. and international religions using online features for generating national profiles, maps, overviews of church memberships, denominational heritage trees, tables, charts, and other summary reports.

Canadian Society for Spirituality and Social Work

http://stu.ca/~spirituality

Site includes information about the activities of this society, links to other websites, and other resources.

Pew Research Center Religion & Public Life Project

http://pewforum.org

Site sponsored by the larger Pew Research Center functions as both a clearinghouse for research and other publications related to issues at the intersection of religion and public affairs and also a virtual town hall for discussion of related topics.

Religious Tolerance

www.religioustolerance.org

Site presented by the Ontario Consultants on Religious Tolerance, an agency that promotes religious tolerance as a human right, contains comparative descriptions of world religions and diverse spiritual paths from Asatru to Zoroastrianism and links to other related sites.

Society for Spirituality and Social Work

http://societyforspiritualityandsocialwork.com

Site includes information about joining the U.S. Society for Spirituality and Social Work, a selected bibliography, and other resources.

Virtual Religion Index

www.virtualreligion.net/vri

Site presented by the Religion Department at Rutgers University contains analysis and highlights of religion-related websites and provides links to major sites for specific religious groups and topics.

LEARNING OBJECTIVES	FOR FURTHER EXPLORATION AND APPLICATION
LO 5.1: Compare and contrast emotional and cognitive reactions to the seven case studies.	(read) Spirituality and Social Work
LO 5.2: Compare and contrast the definitions of spirituality and religion.	(read) Spirituality and Social Work Practice
LO 5.3: Describe the major contributions of Fowler's and Wilber's transpersonal theories of human behavior.	(listen) Stages of Faith
LO 5.4: Give examples of the impact of spirituality and religion in the lives of oppressed groups and people coping with different problems of living.	(listen) Deepak Chopra—7 Spiritual Laws of Success (read) Racial/Ethnic Identity, Religious Commitment, and Well-Being in African Americans (watch) Ken Wilber: Introduction to Integral Spirituality
LO 5.5: Demonstrate how to gather information about a client's religious or spiritual history.	(read) The Islamic Perspective on Social Work: A Conceptual Framework; *International Social Work*
LO 5.6: Apply knowledge of human spirituality to recommend guidelines for social work assessment and intervention.	(read) Implicit Spiritual Assessment: An Alternative Approach for Assessing Client Spirituality (watch) Spiritual Diversity in Social Work: The Heart of Helping

The Multiple Dimensions of the Environment

Social workers have always recognized the important role the environment plays in human behavior and, equally important, have always understood the environment as multidimensional. The social work literature has not been consistent in identifying the significant dimensions of the environment, however. Although all dimensions of the environment are intertwined and inseparable, social scientists have developed specialized literature on several specific dimensions. Both the environment and the study of it become more complex with each new era of technological development, making our efforts to understand the environment ever more challenging.

The purpose of the four chapters in Part III is to provide you with an up-to-date understanding of the multidisciplinary theory and research about the dimensions of the environment. Chapter 6 examines two important dimensions that are present but not always recognized in every person–environment configuration: culture and the physical environment. Chapter 7 explores the all-important family dimension. Chapter 8 covers small groups, formal organizations, and communities. And, finally, Chapter 9 focuses on the macro world of social structure and social institutions and on the social movements that change them.

When you put together the person and environment dimensions covered in Parts II and III, you will be better prepared to understand the situations you encounter in social work practice. This knowledge base also prepares you well to think about the changing configurations of persons and environments across the life course—the subject of Part IV.

CHALK TALKS
Watch via the
SAGE Interactive eBook

Created using Videoscribe, http://www.videoscribe.co

HSBCPREMIERUSA.com
HSBC
SAMSUNG
JACK
TEXT JACK TO 58671
WELCOME
TIMES SQUARE
CROSSROADS OF THE WORLD
TIMESSQUARENYC.ORG
Coca-Cola
Corona
Light
W 46 ST
ONE WAY
tkts
tkts
PALACE
DARK SECRETS REVEALED
JULY 15
Tonight
NO

Culture and the Physical Environment

Linwood Cousins and Elizabeth D. Hutchison

Learning Objectives

LO 6.1 Compare and contrast one's emotional and cognitive reactions to two case studies.

LO 6.2 Describe ways that culture has been defined over time.

LO 6.3 Summarize mechanisms by which culture is maintained and changed over time.

LO 6.4 Summarize four categories of theories about the relationship between the physical environment and human behavior (stimulation, control, behavior settings, and ecocritical).

LO 6.5 Give examples of the benefits and costs of time spent in the natural environment.

LO 6.6 Give examples of the impact of the built environment on human behavior.

LO 6.7 Recognize the role of place attachment in human behavior.

LO 6.8 Suggest policy options for the social problem of homelessness.

LO 6.9 Demonstrate an ability to evaluate specific built environments for their accessibility for people with disabilities.

LO 6.10 Apply knowledge of culture and the relationship between the physical environment and human behavior to recommend guidelines for social work assessment and intervention.

GET MORE OUT OF YOUR STUDY TIME.

The **SAGE Interactive eBook** provides one-click access to integrated study tools that will enrich your understanding of course content.

- **Watch** video clips to learn actively
- **Think Critically** with SAGE Journals
- **Explore Further** with SAGE Reference
- **Connect** with relevant web resources
- **Listen** to podcasts for real-world context

CASE STUDY 6.1

STAN AND TINA AT COMMUNITY HIGH SCHOOL

Community High School in Newark, New Jersey, has approximately 1,300 students, the majority of whom are Black (African American, Afro-Caribbean, and West African). Most of the students live in the community of Village Park, which has a total population of approximately 58,000 people, also predominantly Black. Village Park has a distinct social history and identity as well as distinct physical boundaries that distinguish it from less prosperous communities and schools in Newark.

Village Park evolved from a middle- and working-class Jewish community that centered around its academic institutions, such as Community High. The school generated a national reputation for academic excellence as measured by the number of graduates who went on to become doctors, lawyers, scientists, professors, and the like. But after the Newark riots of the late 1960s, Jews and other Whites started moving out. By the early 1970s, upwardly mobile middle- and working-class Black families had become the majority in Village Park. The same process has occurred in other communities, but what's interesting about Village Park is that its Black residents, like the Jewish residents who preceded them, continued to believe in the ethic of upward mobility through schooling at Community High.

Since the mid-1980s, however, Village Park and Community High have undergone another transformation. Slumps in the economy and ongoing patterns of racial discrimination in employment have reduced the income base of the community's families. Many families who were able to maintain a middle-class income moved to the suburbs as crime and economic blight encroached on the community. Increasingly, Village Park was taken over by renters and absentee landlords, along with the social problems—drug abuse, crime, school dropouts—that accompany economically driven social despair.

By 1993, the population profile of Newark had become simultaneously Black and multiethnic. In the 1990s, the majority of Newark's residents were African American, but the city had a considerable population of other ethnic groups: Hispanics (Puerto Ricans, Colombians, Mexicans, Dominicans), Italians, Portuguese, Africans (from Nigeria, Sierra Leone, Liberia, Ghana, and other countries), Polish, and small groups of others. At the same time, the governing bodies of the city, the school system, and Community High in particular were predominantly composed of Black people. With an estimated population of 278,000 in 2008, Newark remains an ethnically diverse urban community.

The intermingling of such history and traditions has had an interesting impact on the students at Community High. Like many urban high schools all over the nation, Community High has suffered disproportionate levels of dropouts, low attendance, and violence. Yet a few parents, teachers, school staff, and community officials have tried hard to rekindle the spirit of academic excellence and social competence that are the school's tradition.

In this context, many of the students resist traditional definitions of academic success but value success nonetheless. Consider the behaviors of Stan and Tina, both students at Community High. Stan is the more troubled and more academically marginal of the two students. He is 17 years old, lives with his girlfriend who has recently had a baby, and has made a living selling drugs (which he is trying to discontinue). Stan was arrested (and released) for selling drugs some time ago. He was also under questioning for the drug-related murder of his cousin, because the police wanted him to identify the perpetrator. However, Stan has considerable social prestige at school and is academically successful when he attends school and is focused. Stan's mother—who has hammered into his head the importance of education—is a clerical supervisor, his stepfather works in a meat factory, and his biological father sells drugs.

Among his male and female peers, Stan is considered the epitome of urban maleness and style. He is an innovator. He mixes and matches the square-toe motorcycle boots normally associated with White bikers with the brand-name shirts and jeans commonly associated with urban, rap-oriented young people of color. At the same time, Stan is respected by teachers and administrators because he understands and observes the rules of conduct preferred in the classroom and because he can do his work at a level reflecting high intelligence. Before the end of his senior year, Stan visited Howard University in Washington, DC, and was smitten by the idea that young Black men and women were participating in university life. He says he will try very hard to go to that school after he graduates, but the odds are against him.

Tina is also 17 years old, but she is more academically successful than Stan. She ranks in the top 25 of her senior class and has been accepted into the premed program of a historically Black university. Tina talks about the lower academic performance of some of her Black peers. She sees it as a manifestation of the social distractions that seem to preoccupy Black youths—being popular and cool. On the other hand, Tina sees her successful academic performance, level of motivation, and assertive style of interacting in the classroom as part of being Black too—taking care of business and trying to make it in this world.

Tina is an only child. Her father is an engineer, and her stepmother is a restaurant manager. Tina has never known her biological mother, and she was raised primarily by her father until about 6 years ago. They moved to Village Park from Brooklyn, New York, around that time. Tina's is the kind of family that is likely to leave Village Park not for the suburbs, but for a more productive and less hostile urban community. Tina has been raised in a community that, despite its ills, centers around Black identity and culture.

Like Stan, Tina is an innovator. She adopted modes of language, demeanor, and clothing that are seen by some as decidedly mainstream in their origins. In fact, however, Tina mixes the aesthetics of Black and mainstream White culture as well as the contemporary urban flavor that textures the lives of many youths today. Perhaps the results are most apparent in the way Tina mixes and matches hip-hop-influenced clothing, attitudes, and hairstyles with mainstream clothing styles and the mannerisms associated with the norms and standards of professional, middle-class occupations.

However, anyone who would approach Tina as an ally of "the system"—defining the system as the White establishment—would meet with disappointment. He or she would discover that in Tina's view, and perhaps in Stan's, there is nothing generally wrong with Black people and their behavior. But there is something wrong with Black individuals who do things that are not in their own best interest and consequently not in the best interest of the Black community.

Furthermore, he or she would hear Tina, Stan, and other students at Community High describe academic success and failure not just in terms of students' actions. The person would hear these students indict uninterested and complacent teachers and staff, and schools that do not understand "how to educate Black people."

Source: Based on an ethnographic study of culture, race, and class during the 1992–1993 academic year in Cousins (1994). See Fordham (1996) and Ogbu (2003) for similar studies of Black high school students that confirm the persistence of the characteristics described here.

CASE STUDY 6.2

BEN WATSON'S CHANGING EXPERIENCE WITH THE PHYSICAL ENVIRONMENT

Author's Note: Ben narrates his own story.

I finished my final semester in the Bachelor of Architecture Program, and a couple of friends and I decided to spend a few days doing some rock climbing before graduation. I already had a job lined up with a small architecture firm down in North Carolina. Things were looking good, but it doesn't take but a minute for things to change forever. I fell 500 feet and knew, as soon as I came to, that something was very wrong. My legs were numb, I couldn't move them, and I had terrific pain in my back. My friends knew not to move me, and one stayed with me while the other went for help.

I don't remember much about the rescue, the trip to the nearest hospital, or the medivac to the closest trauma center. In my early days at the trauma hospital, I saw lots of medical people, but I vividly remember the doc who told me that I had an incomplete spinal cord injury, that I would have some sensation below my lesion but no movement. I didn't really believe it. Movement was what I was all about. I spent 5 months in the hospital and rehabilitation center, and I gradually began to understand that my legs were not going to move. I was depressed, I was angry (furious, really), and for 1 week I wanted to give up. My parents and my brothers pulled me

(Continued)

(Continued)

through. They showered me with love but were firm when I tried to refuse rehabilitation treatments. Oh yeah, some of my friends were terrific also. When things get rough, you learn who your real friends are. I also appreciated a chance to talk with the rehab social worker about my grief over this unbelievable turn in my life. It was good to talk with him because he wasn't dealing with his own grief about my situation the way my family and friends were.

I left rehab with my new partner, a sophisticated titanium wheelchair, and went home to live with my parents. They rearranged the house so that I could have the first-floor bedroom and bath. I appreciated the assistance from my parents and brothers, and my friends made heroic efforts to get me out of the house. As we did so, I began to learn the importance of the word *access*. The first time my friends took me out, we wanted to go to a bar; after all, that's what 20-something guys do. My friends called around to find a nearby bar that would be accessible to me and my wheelchair. That turned out to be tougher than they thought. Did you ever notice how many bars require dealing with stairs? Finally, they were assured that one bar was accessible—well, actually, nobody wanted to say their place wasn't accessible, given the law and all, plus most folks haven't given any thought to what that really means. So, my friends had to go through a set of questions about stairs, ramps, size of doors, etc., to make their own determination about accessibility. One question they didn't think to ask was whether there were stairs leading to the bathroom. So, we went out drinking, but I was afraid to drink or eat because I couldn't get to the bathroom.

After several months at home, I began to get restless and wanted to get on with my life. After my accident, the architecture firm down in North Carolina had told my parents that they would still be interested in having me work for them when I was strong enough. So, I began to talk with my parents about making the move to North Carolina. They understood that I needed to get on with my life, but they worried about me moving 350 miles away. I was still dependent on them for a lot of personal care, but I was gradually learning to do more for myself.

I knew from my interviews that the architecture firm was accessible by wheelchair—it was in a relatively new building with a ground-level entrance, spacious elevator, wide doors, and accessible bathrooms. With some trepidation, my dad drove me down to look for housing. There were plenty of new apartment complexes, but we found that everybody, not just people with disabilities, wanted ground-floor apartments with the open architectural features that make wheelchair mobility so much easier. After a lot of calls, we found a one-bedroom apartment that I could afford. I immediately loved the location, in a part of the city where there was a lot happening on the streets, with shops, restaurants, and a movie theater. The apartment was attractive, convenient, and accessible, but most important, it was mine. I was finally beginning to feel like an adult. I would have my privacy, but the open floor plan would allow me to have friends over without feeling cramped. And I loved the abundance of windows that would allow for good natural lighting from the sun. I couldn't afford to get my own car with hand controls yet, but the apartment luckily was only a short cab ride from my office.

My father and brothers helped me make the move, and my grandmother came for a visit to add some charming decorating touches. I hired a personal assistant to help me get ready in the mornings—well, actually, my parents paid him for the first few months, until I could get my finances worked out.

Given my profession, it is good that I still have excellent function of my upper body, particularly my hands. My colleagues at work turned out to be good friends as well as good colleagues. I never paid much attention to issues of accessibility in my design studios at school, but I have become the local expert on accessible design.

I learned a lot about accessible design from some of my own frustrating experiences. I have been lucky to develop a close set of friends, and we have an active life. My friends and I have learned where the streets are that don't have curb cuts, which bars and restaurants are truly accessible, places where the "accessible" entry is really some dark alley back entrance, and to watch out for retail doorways blocked by displays of goods.

My friends and I travel, and I find some airline personnel handle me and my wheelchair well and some are disastrous—imagine being rolled over on the ramp, and with an audience, no less. The natural environment was always an important part of my life—it provides beauty and serenity—and my friends and I could write a book about all the wonderful hiking trails that are wheelchair accessible. Hey, that's a good idea!

In the last three chapters, we focused on internal dimensions of the person—biological, psychological, and spiritual. These two case studies illustrate well the multiple dimensions of the external environment that influence our moment-to-moment behavior—and how our behavior influences those environments. We see evidence of the mutual influence of human behavior with culture, the physical environment, families, small groups, formal organizations, communities, social structure and social institutions, and social movements. In this chapter we focus on two aspects of the environment that are present, but not often recognized, in all other dimensions: culture and the physical environment.

THE CHALLENGE OF DEFINING CULTURE

The case of Tina and Stan has been selected because it makes a point we often miss in the United States in general and in social work and human services in particular: Culture is right under our noses and therefore often concealed from our awareness. Like Tina and Stan, you are actually immersed in many different cultures, including U.S. culture, family culture, school (university) culture, digital culture, consumer culture, peer culture, gender culture, entertainment culture, and more. For example, you may be involved in a work culture, a religious or spiritual culture, or some identity culture such as LGBT culture. You are continually learning the **norms**, the culturally defined standards or rules of conduct, of these different cultures.

When we think of culture, however, we are more likely to think of immigrants and non-Americans as the real examples of culture because they represent peoples who appear to be more different from us than perhaps they are. We may also think of Tina and Stan as more like you (or people you know) and me than perhaps they are. Their case study highlights not only race and ethnicity but also social class, power relations, gender, popular culture, and other significant features of interactions between people and their environments. In our everyday lives, we think we know what we see, but our life experiences lead us to see some things and not others. It is incredibly hard for us to take a detached viewpoint about our person–environment interactions.

The U.S. Census Bureau (2013b) tells us that there are now more than 7 billion people in the world. More than 313 million of them live in the United States. The United States is the third most populated country, behind China (just over 1.3 billion) and India (just over 1.2 billion), and the smallest population is found in Montserrat, a Caribbean island of 5,189 people. The U.S. population includes 199 million White (non-Hispanic) people of various ancestries, just over 46 million Hispanics/Latinos, just over 37 million African Americans/Blacks, more than 13 million Asians, and over 3 million American Indians and Alaska Natives, with Native Hawaiian, other Pacific Islanders, and other peoples constituting the rest (U.S. Census Bureau, 2013b). Finally, approximately 40 million of the U.S. population are foreign born (U.S. Census Bureau, 2013c).

Much diversity is concealed in this numerical portrait, but it is a good place to begin our discussion of the diverse society we live in. Given this scenario, how should we as social workers interpret the multifaceted contexts of Tina's and Stan's lives? Economics, race and ethnicity, traditions and customs, gender, political processes, immigration, popular culture, psychology, academic processes, technology, and a host of other factors are all involved. All this and more must be considered in our discussion of culture.

But let me caution you. Defining culture is a complex and arbitrary game. *Culture* is a word we use all the time but have trouble defining (Gardiner & Kosmitzki, 2011; Griswold, 2013). Long ago, Alfred Kroeber and Clyde Kluckhohn (1963, 1952/1978), two renowned anthropologists, catalogued more than 100 definitions of culture (see Exhibit 6.1). Definitions and discussions of culture tend to reflect the theoretical perspectives and purposes of the definers. Like other views of culture, the one presented here has its biases. In keeping with the emphases in this book, a view of culture is presented that exposes not only social differences or human variation but also the cultural bases of various forms of inequality. We look at the ways in which variations in human behavior have led to subjugation and have become the basis of, among other things, racial, ethnic, economic, and gender oppression and inequality.

According to Raymond Williams (1983), "Culture is one of the two or three most complicated words in the English language" (p. 87), partly because of its intricate historical development in several European languages but also because it is used as a concept that sometimes has quite different meanings in several incompatible systems of thought. For example, early German intellectual traditions merged with English traditions to define culture as general processes of intellectual, spiritual, and aesthetic development. A modified version of this usage is found in the contemporary field of arts and humanities, which describes culture in terms of music, literature, painting, sculpture, and the like. By contrast, U.S. tradition has produced the use of *culture* as we know it in contemporary social sciences to describe a particular way of life of a people, a period of time, or humanity in general. But even in this tradition, anthropologists have used the concept to refer to the material production of a people, whereas historians and cultural studies have used it to refer to symbolic systems such as language, stories, and rituals. Currently, and with the rise of postmodern theorizing, these uses of the concept overlap considerably.

One useful postmodern approach to human behavior sees culture as "a set of common understandings, manifest in act and artifact. It is in two places at once: inside somebody's head as understandings and in the external environment as act and artifact. If it isn't truly present in both spheres, it is only incomplete culture" (Bohannan, 1995, p. 47). **Culture**, in other words, includes both behavior (act or actions) and the material outcomes of that behavior (artifacts, or the things we construct from the material world around us—such as houses, clothing, cars, nuclear weapons, jets, the Internet, smartphones, texting, laptops, and the like). But at the same time, it is "inside our heads,"

EXHIBIT 6.1 • Categorical Definitions of Culture

ENUMERATION OF SOCIAL CONTENT

- That complex whole that includes knowledge, belief, art, morals, law, custom, and any other capabilities and habits acquired by humans as members of society; the sum total of human achievement

SOCIAL HERITAGE/TRADITION

- The learned repertory of thoughts and actions exhibited by members of a social group, independent of genetic heredity from one generation to the next
- The sum total and organization of social heritages that have acquired social meaning because of racial temperament and the historical life of the group

RULE OR WAY OF LIFE

- The sum total of ways of doing and thinking, past and present, of a social group
- The distinctive way of life of a group of people; their complete design for living

PSYCHOLOGICAL AND SOCIAL ADJUSTMENT AND LEARNING

- The total equipment of technique—mechanical, mental, and moral—by use of which the people of a given period try to attain their ends
- The sum total of the material and intellectual equipment whereby people satisfy their biological and social needs and adapt themselves to their environment
- Learned modes of behavior that are socially transmitted from one generation to another within a particular society and that may be diffused from one society to another

IDEAS AND VALUES

- An organized group of ideas, habits, and conditioned emotional responses shared by members of a society
- Acquired or cultivated behavior and thought of individuals; the material and social values of any group of people

PATTERNING AND SYMBOLS

- A system of interrelated and interdependent habit patterns of response
- Organization of conventional understandings, manifest in act and artifact, that, persisting through tradition, characterizes a human group
- Semiotics—those webs of public meaning that people have spun and by which they are suspended
- A distinct order or class of phenomena—namely, those things and events that are dependent upon the exercise of a mental ability peculiar to the human species—that we have termed symboling; or material objects (such as tools, utensils, ornaments, amulets), acts, beliefs, and attitudes that function in contexts characterized by symboling

SOURCE: Adapted from Kroeber and Kluckhohn (1952/1978), pp. 40–79.

or part of our thoughts, perceptions, and feelings. It is expressed through our emotions and thought processes, our motivations, intentions, and meanings as we live out our lives.

It is through culture that we construct meanings associated with the social and material world. Art, shelter, transportation, guns, cell phones, computers, the Internet, music, food, and clothing are material examples. The meanings we give these products influence how we use them. For example, some women's clothing is considered provocative, texting while in a meeting with others or while driving may be considered offensive or unsafe, and pork for some people is considered "polluted." In interaction with the social world and things around us, we construct religion, race and ethnicity, family and kinship, gender roles, and complex modern organizations and institutions.

Here's an example from U.S. history of how human beings construct meaning in a cultural context. Slaves of African descent tended to interpret their plight and quest for freedom in terms of Judeo-Christian religious beliefs, which were pressed on them by the slaveholders but were also adapted for better fit with their oppressive situations. They likened their suffering to that of the crucifixion and resurrection of Jesus Christ. Just like the biblical "children of Israel" (the Jews) who had to make it to the Promised Land, so it was that slaves had to find freedom in the promised land of Northern cities in the United States and Canada. The association of the plight of Christians and Jews in the Bible with racial oppression lives on today in the lives of many African Americans.

You may encounter clients who believe that their social, economic, and psychological difficulties are the

© iStockphoto.com/Pamela Moore

Family life is structured by meanings, values, and beliefs that fit our desires and imaginations about what is right and appropriate.

result of God's will, or issues of spirituality, rather than of the biopsychosocial causes we study and apply as social workers. Should a social work assessment include the various meanings that people construct about their circumstances? Applying a cultural perspective that considers this question will help you find more empowering interpretations and solutions to issues you face as a social worker, especially when working with members of oppressed communities.

Here is another example. Disability in our culture seems to be about its opposite: being seen as "normal." It is also about the desire for sameness or similarity (Ingstad & Whyte, 1995). But decisions about what is normal are embedded in culture. We may think that physical, mental, or cognitive disabilities are purely biological or psychological and therefore real in a scientific sense. But like race and gender, what they mean to the person possessing them and to those looking on and judging is a matter of the meanings derived from culture (Snyder & Mitchell, 2001; Thomson, 1996). These meanings play out in social, economic, and political relations that determine the distribution of resources and generate various types of inequality.

What are your emotional responses to thinking about Ben Watson in his wheelchair? How do you suppose he feels? Can you imagine his sexual attractiveness? Do you suppose he sees himself as a sexual being? What are the bodily images we hold for being "handsome" or "beautiful"? Do they correspond with the images that others, including Ben, hold? The point is that if the ethnically diverse people who reside in the United States see life in various ways, we must expect no less regarding those with different types and levels of ability.

The examples about African Americans and disability occur in a historical context. But history is about more than dates, names, inventions, and records of events. Rather, history is an ongoing story about the connections among ideas, communities, peoples, nations, and social transformations within the constraints of the natural world (Huynh-Nhu et al., 2008; McHale, Updegraff, Ji-Yeon, & Cansler, 2009). Think about how the historical experiences of Native Americans, Asian Americans, or Hispanic Americans in the United States influence how they perceive their lives today. Think about the historical development of the terms and ideas associated with disability: "crippled," "handicapped," "disabled," "differently abled," and so on.

Think about the history of social work. It is about more than mere dates and events. Think of the people involved in social work, such as Mary Richmond, a leader in the early charity movement, and Jane Addams, a leader in the early settlement house movement. Think about the philosophy and social practices they espoused in working with the disadvantaged people of their time. What do you know about their ethnic identity, socioeconomic status, gender, and living conditions? What about the dominant thinking and political, social, and economic trends of their time? What do you know about what may have influenced their very different conceptions of social work and how those influences connect to the ideas and practices of contemporary social work? Now, think about Ida B. Wells-Barnett, former slave, contemporary of Jane Addams, and founder of an African American settlement house. How much do you know about her achievements? This line of thought reveals a lot about U.S. culture and how it has interacted with the development of social work.

To sum up, culture includes multiple levels of traditions, values, and beliefs, as well as social, biological, and natural acts. These processes are driven by the meanings we give to and take from them. These meanings are fortified or changed in relations between people, as history unfolds. Culture affects all of us.

At Community High School, culture affects what curriculum is delivered, how, and by whom. A cultural interpretation would reveal competition and *strain*, or unequal power relations in this process. For example, many Village Park residents and Community High students have cultural frames of reference that give adversarial meanings to requirements that students act "studiously and behave a certain way" in class. These community members and students do not necessarily dismiss education and classroom rules, but they may see education and some of its rules as part of a system of mainstream institutions that have been oppressive and insensitive toward Blacks. They see schools as dismissing their norms and points of view, and the power to change things eludes them. When a teacher at Community High asks Black students like Stan and Tina to stop talking out of turn in class, these students hear more than an impartial and benign request. Of course, any adolescent student might resent being told to stop talking by an adult authority. However, the interpretation of that request by Black students is likely to reflect their understanding about what it means to be "put down" or "dissed" in front of one's peers by an "outsider" who represents the dominant White society and does not respect the Black community.

These are complex issues, but they are part of the everyday problems social workers encounter. Further examination of what culture is and how ideas about it have changed over time helps in our quest for multidimensional knowledge and skills.

CHANGING IDEAS ABOUT CULTURE AND HUMAN BEHAVIOR

Ideas about culture have changed over time, in step with intellectual, social, economic, and political trends. Exhibit 6.2 provides an overview of the evolution of culture as a concept since the 18th century. Some of the influential ideas that have remained with us from the past come from the Enlightenment and Romantic intellectual traditions, dating back to the 18th century.

Enlightenment thinking in the early 18th century ranked cultures and civilizations according to their developed logic, reason, and technology (or mastery and use of the physical environment). Africans and Native Americans, for example, were seen as less civilized and less valuable than Europeans because their technology was not on the same scale as some European countries. Can you think of situations that demonstrate Enlightenment biases today? Is this the same framework that justifies interpreting the actions of Tina and Stan as less developed, less mature, and less rational than the actions of more mainstream students?

Another set of ideas comes from a Romantic orientation dating from the late 18th century. This orientation suggests that all people and their cultures are relatively equal in value. Differences in culture reflect different frameworks of meaning and understanding and thus result in different lifestyles and ways of living (Benedict, 1946, 1934/1989; Shweder, 1984/1995). From this tradition comes the idea of **cultural relativism** that frames contemporary multiculturalism. For example, at some point you may have been asked which is superior, Islam or Christianity, Black culture or White culture, African culture or European culture. These religions and cultures differ in content and meaning, but is one better than the other? If so, what is the standard of measure, and in whose interest is it developed and enforced?

Some today dismiss cultural relativism as "politically correct" thinking, but it does have practical value. In social work at least, to start where individuals are, to understand their points of view and the context of their lives, has been an effective method of helping them gain control of their lives.

In the United States today, we still see conflicts between Enlightenment thinking and the cultural relativism of Romanticism. Romanticism is reflected by those who call for respect for diversity in our multicultural society. But Enlightenment thinking, with its emphasis on ranking of cultures, continues to have a great influence on our everyday understanding of culture. Consider recent public debates over crime, welfare, health insurance, Islam, and other issues that associate historical and contemporary social problems with people's race or ethnicity, religion, and socioeconomic status. Some social scientists and the popular media frequently express mainstream, Enlightenment-oriented values, attitudes, and morals in examining these issues, assigning more value to some things than to others (Lakoff, 2006; O'Reilly, 2007).

One outcome of such thinking is a belief in *biological determinism*—the attempt to differentiate social behavior on the basis of biological and genetic endowment.

EXHIBIT 6.2 • Ideas and Processes Influencing the Evolution of Culture as a Concept

TIME PERIOD	IDEAS AND HUMAN PROCESSES
18th and 19th centuries: Enlightenment and Romanticism	• Rankings of logic, reason, art, technology • Culture seizing nature • Psychic unity of humankind
19th and 20th centuries: Variation in human behavior and development	• Cultural relativism • Culture as patterns and structures • Culture and personality • Symbols as vehicles of culture
Contemporary understandings: Integration and synthesis of processes of human development and variation since 1950s	• Cultural psychology (cognitive psychology and anthropology) • Meaning, ecology, and culture • Political and economic systems and culture • Culture as private and public • Physical environment, biology, and culture • Ideology, history, common sense, tradition as cultural systems

One form of biological determinism is based on racial identity. For example, a person's intellectual performance is associated by some people with skin color and other physical differences believed to be related to race. **Race**, however, is a social construction based on biological differences in appearance. No racial differences in cognitive and intellectual capacities have been found to be biologically based. There is no verifiable evidence that the fundamental composition and functioning of the brain differs between Blacks and Whites, Asians and Hispanics, or whatever so-called racial groups you can identify and compare (Mukhopadhyay, Henze, & Moses, 2007; Mullings, 2005). Yet many still believe that race makes people inherently different. Such false associations are a vestige of Enlightenment thinking.

As a social work student, you can recognize the power and influence of such tendencies. Thinking in terms of natural, ordained, and inevitable differences based on race reinforces the social tendency to think in terms of "we-ness" and "they-ness," which often has unfortunate effects (Jandt, 2010). It leads to what has come to be called *othering*, or labeling people who fall outside of your own group as abnormal, inferior, or marginal. In your personal and professional lives, pay attention to the images and thoughts you use to make sense of the economic, social, and behavioral difficulties of Black people or other ethnic groups. Pay attention to the characterizations of English-speaking and non–English speaking immigrants, or of documented or undocumented immigrants.

The 20th- and 21st-century scholars of culture inherited both advances and limitations in thought from scholars of previous centuries. With these challenges in mind, anthropologist Franz Boas (1940/1948) encouraged us to understand cultural differences as environmental differences interacting with the accidents of history.

Before we go further, it is important to note that many contemporary culture scholars suggest that environmental differences interacting with accidents of history have produced three major types of culture in recent centuries (see Gotham, 2013; Griswold, 2013). They suggest the name *traditional culture*, or *premodern culture*, to describe preindustrial societies based on subsistence agriculture. They argue that this type of culture was markedly different from *modern culture*, which arose with the 18th-century Enlightenment and is characterized by rationality, industrialization, urbanization, and capitalism. **Postmodernism** is the term many people use to describe contemporary culture. They suggest that global electronic communication is the foundation of postmodern culture, exposing people in advanced capitalist societies to media images that span place and time and allow them to splice together cultural elements from these different times and places (Griswold, 2013). Exhibit 6.3 presents the primary characteristics usually attributed to these three types of culture. Whereas culture scholars who make these distinctions often present these three types as a historical timeline, running from traditional to modern to postmodern culture, we suggest that traits of all three types of culture can be found in advanced capitalist societies today and often become the source of contemporary culture wars within societies. Furthermore, many nonindustrial and newly industrializing societies can be characterized as either traditional or modern cultures, or some mixture of the two.

EXHIBIT 6.3 • Characteristics of Traditional, Modern, and Postmodern Culture

CHARACTERISTIC	TRADITIONAL CULTURE	MODERN CULTURE	POSTMODERN CULTURE
Role of rationality	Positive value for irrational aspects of life; religious traditions superior to reason	Supreme value of rationality; rational control of nature	Questions the limits of rationality
Status	Status based on blood line; hierarchy as natural order; patriarchy	Status based on achievement; egalitarianism	Emphasis on difference, not power
Source of authority	Religious authority	Nation-state; science	Globalization; national authority breaks down
Stability and change	Stability and order valued; order based on religion	Progress valued	Unpredictability and chaos
Unit of value	Communal values	Individualism	Diversity: multiplicity of perspectives and voices
Life structure	Agrarian, subsistence agriculture	Industrialization, urbanization, capitalism, commodity fetishism, specialization of function	Electronic communications, simulation, mass consumption

SOME IMPORTANT CULTURE CONCEPTS

The following concepts are central to contemporary thinking about culture.

- *Ideology.* Ideology is a set of shared ideas about the way things are and should work. Problems of inequality and discrimination arise when ideology supports social, economic, and political exploitation and subjugation of some people. Ideologies that justify exploitation and inequality get built into the everyday, taken-for-granted way the culture's members live their lives.

- *Ethnocentrism.* Through cross-cultural comparisons, anthropologists have demonstrated that Western culture is not universal. They have exposed our tendency to elevate our own ethnic group and its culture over others, a tendency known as **ethnocentrism**. For instance, theories of personality development are based on Western ideals of individuality and reliance on objective science rather than Eastern ideals of collective identity and reliance on subjective processes such as spirituality (Kottak, 2008).

- *Cultural symbols.* A **symbol** is something, verbal or nonverbal, that comes to stand for something else. The letters *d-o-g* have come to stand for the animal we call *dog*, golden arches forming a large *M* stand for McDonald's restaurants or hamburgers, and water in baptism rites stands for something sacred and holy and moves a person from one state of being to another (Kottak, 2008). Race, ethnicity, and gender are symbols that can be thought of in this way as well. For instance, beyond biological differences, what comes to mind when you think of a girl or woman? What about a boy or man? How do the images, thoughts, and feelings you possess about gender influence how you interact with boys and girls and men and women? With someone who is gender nonconforming or transgender? Gendered thinking undoubtedly influences your assessment of persons, even those you have not actually met. In short, symbols shape perception, or the way a person sees, feels, and thinks about the world, and they communicate a host of feelings, thoughts, beliefs, and values that people use to make sense of their daily lives and to guide their behavior (Wilkin, 2009). The idea that symbols express meaning within a culture is part of many recent models of practice in social work and psychology. For example, social constructionists focus on how narratives and stories can bring about emotional and behavioral changes in clinical social work practice.

- *Worldview and ethos. Worldview* is associated with the cognitive domain—what we think about things; *ethos* is associated more with the emotional or affective and stylistic dimensions of behavior—how we feel about things (Ortner, 1984). Like Stan and Tina, recent Hispanic/Latino and African immigrants are adept at using symbols such as clothing, language, and music to convey specific feelings and perceptions that express their worldview and ethos.

- *Cultural innovation.* Culture is not static; it is adapted, modified, and changed through interactions over time. This process is known as **cultural innovation**. For example, Stan and Tina were described earlier as innovators. Both restyle mainstream clothing to fit with their sense of meaning and with the values of their peers and their community. In addition, in the classroom and with peers, Stan and Tina can switch between Standard English and Black English. The mode of language they use depends on the social and political message or identity they want to convey to listeners. We see economic cultural innovation with immigrants, both recent and in the past.

- *Cultural conflict.* The symbols we use can mean one thing to you and something different to others. Therefore, *cultural conflict* over meanings can easily arise. For example, jeans that hang low on the hips of adolescents and young adults generally signify an ethos of hipness, toughness, and coolness. This is the style, mood, and perspective of a particular generation. However, the clothing, music, and language of politically and economically disadvantaged Black and Hispanic/Latino adolescents convey a different symbolic meaning to law enforcers, school officials, parents, and even social workers. In today's sociopolitical climate, these authority figures are likely to perceive low-slung jeans not only as signs of hip-hop culture but also as signs of drug and gang culture or as a form of social rebellion, decadence, or incivility.

In sum, culture is both private and public. It has emotional and cognitive components, but these play out in public in our social actions. Symbols are a way of communicating private meaning through public or social action. Furthermore, people's actions express their worldview (how they think about the world) and their ethos (how they feel about the world)—just as Tina and Stan do when they alternate between Black and mainstream styles.

These concepts have great relevance to social work. For example, arguments accompanying welfare reform legislation in the United States in the late 1990s represented shifting meanings regarding poverty, single parenting, and work. During the 1960s, it was considered society's moral duty to combat poverty by assisting the poor. Today, poverty does not just mean a lack of financial resources for the necessities of life; to many people, it symbolizes laziness, the demise of family values, and other characteristics that shade into immorality. Thus, to help people who are poor is now often purported to hurt them by consigning them to dependency and immoral behavior (Cousins, 2013).

As social workers, we depend on the NASW Code of Ethics for professional guidance in negotiating these shifts. But what is the source of the values and beliefs that guide our personal lives? And what happens when what we believe and value differs from our clients' beliefs and values? Exhibit 6.4 demonstrates several cultural conflicts that may arise as our personal social habits confront our principles, values, and ethics as professional social workers.

CRITICAL THINKING Questions 6.1

Which cultures are you a part of? What are three important norms of each of these cultures? Are there any conflicts in norms across the different cultures in which you participate? Explain. When you think of your day-to-day life, do you think you live in a traditional, modern, or postmodern culture? Explain. What do you see as the benefits and costs of each of these types of culture?

A POSTMODERN VIEW OF CULTURE

Forty or more years ago, the problems of Village Park and Community High School would have been explained largely in terms of a culture of poverty. The term **culture of poverty** was originally used to bring attention to the way of life developed by poor people to adapt to the difficult circumstances of their lives. Proponents of this theoretical orientation twisted it to suggest that Black schools and communities were impoverished because of Black people's own beliefs, values, traditions, morals, and frames of reference. Mainstream culture's racism and discrimination were not considered to be decisive factors. That Black people faced *redlining*, a practice that forced them to buy or rent homes only in Black communities, was not considered to be a factor. That Black people were working in low-income jobs despite qualifications for better ones was not considered to be a factor. That major colleges and universities were denying admission to qualified Black applicants was not considered to be a factor either. The list could go on. The culture of poverty orientation was used to argue both for and against publicly financed social programs. Even today, in public discourse, a culture of poverty line of reasoning is often used to explain people on welfare, poor single parents, and other problems of inner cities.

Contemporary and postmodern culture scholars (anthropologists, sociologists, psychologists, political scientists, economists, and social workers) have also adopted some of the tenets of past theorizing. However, they have taken the better parts of it to develop what has come to be called postmodern and **practice orientations** (Berger & Luckmann, 1966; Bourdieu, 1977; Giddens, 1979; Ortner, 1989, 1996, 2006; Sahlins, 1981). *Practice* as used here is different from its use in social work. This theoretical orientation seeks to explain what people do as thinking, intentionally acting persons who face the impact of history and the constraints of structures that are embedded in our society and culture. It asks how social systems shape, guide, and direct people's values, beliefs, and behavior. But it also asks how people, as human actors or agents, perpetuate or shape social systems.

History, social structure, and human agency are key elements in a practice orientation. *History* is made by people, but it is made within the constraints of the social, economic, political, physical, and biological systems in which people are living. To understand human diversity,

EXHIBIT 6.4 • Customary Social Habits Interacting With Social Work Principles, Values, and Ethics on a Continuum

What are your beliefs about the following interactions with clients and colleagues?

Continuum		
Most Professional (Formal)		**Least Professional (Informal)**
Greeting by handshake	hugging	kissing
Use of last name/title (e.g., Mr., Ms., Dr.)	first name	nickname
Authority by credentials (e.g., BSW, MSW)	age, experience, gender, marital status	religion/politics
Sharing no personal information	pertinent information	open-ended, mutual sharing
Confidentiality	sharing with professionals/ family	sharing with friends/ community members

especially as it relates to oppression, exploitation, and subjugation, we must listen to the memories of both official and unofficial observers. We must listen to clients as much as to social workers.

Structure refers to the ordered forms and systems of human behavior existing in public life (e.g., capitalism, family, public education). We carry forth meanings, values, and beliefs through social, economic, and political practices in our everyday personal lives and the institutions in which we participate. We reproduce structures when we assume the rightness of the values, beliefs, and meanings that undergird them and see no need to change them. When one set of values, beliefs, and meanings dominates, **cultural hegemony** results—the dominance of a particular way of seeing the world. Most observers of culture in the United States would agree that it is based on the hegemony of a Euro-American, or Anglo, worldview. People in many other parts of the world have observed a hegemony of the U.S. worldview. And there is much evidence that those whose cultures are overtaken by another culture often resent the hegemony.

Human agency asserts that people are not simply puppets, the pawns of history and structure; people are also active participants, capable of exercising their will to shape their lives. Thus, although racism is structured into society, it is not so completely dominant over Tina and Stan that they have no room for meaningful self-expression in their social and political lives. Human agency is a major source of hope and motivation for social workers who encounter people, organizations, and systems that seem unable to break away from the constraints of daily life. Human agency helps to counteract cultural hegemony as well. However, no individual or group is a fully free agent. All are constrained by external factors such as the climate, disease, natural resources, and population size and growth—although we may be able to modify these constraints through technology (Turkle, 2011). Examples of technologies that modify facts of biology and nature are medicines, agricultural breakthroughs, climate-controlled homes, telecommunications, transportation, and synthetic products that replace the use of wood in furniture and related items.

The issue of poverty offers one example of how the practice orientation can be applied. The practice orientation would not blame poverty's prevalence and influence in Tina and Stan's community solely on the failings of individuals. Rather, it would seek to identify the structural factors—such as low-income jobs, housing segregation, and racism—that impede upward mobility. It would also seek to understand how poor African Americans perceive and contribute to their conditions; how nonpoor, non-Black Americans perceive and contribute to the conditions of poor African Americans; and how all of these perceptions and actions shape the lives and influence the upward mobility of poor African Americans. Is there a "culture" of poverty, or do people in dire circumstances adapt their values and beliefs to the demands of survival?

We can use the practice orientation to ask how the values, beliefs, and practices of the social work profession help to maintain the profession and society as they are. When we label the people we have failed to help as resistant, unmotivated, and pathological, are we carelessly overlooking the ineffectiveness of our modes of understanding and intervention? Are we blaming the victim and reproducing his or her victimization? These and other questions are important for all of us to ponder.

CULTURAL MAINTENANCE, CHANGE, AND ADAPTATION

Tina's and Stan's experiences with mainstream schooling provide a good example of how cultural structures are maintained, how they change, and how they adapt. School systems are centered on the norms, values, and beliefs preferred by those who have had the power to decide what is or is not appropriate to learn and use in our lives. Some things we learn in school fit well with the needs of industry. Other things we learn fit well with the needs of our social and political institutions. From the outside looking in, schools look like benign or innocent institutions that are simply about academics and education. Yet which academic subjects are taught, how they are taught, who teaches them, and how they are to be learned involve an assertion of someone's values and beliefs, whether right or wrong, whether shared by many or few. Even in the face of evidence that schools do not work for many of us, they persist. Education is strongly correlated with economic and social success.

Culture provides stability to social life, but it does change over time. It does not change rapidly, however. First, we look at some ideas about how culture produces stability, and then we turn to how culture changes over time through immigration and processes of negotiating multicultural community life.

Common Sense, Customs, and Traditions

Over time, the ways in which families, schools, cities, and governments do things have come to seem natural to us. They seem to fit with the common sense, customs, and traditions of most people in our society.

Keep in mind, however, that **common sense** is a cultural system. It is what people have come to believe everyone in a community or society should know and understand as a matter of ordinary, taken-for-granted social competence. It is based on a set of assumptions that are so unself-conscious that they seem natural, transparent, and an undeniable part of the structure of the world (Geertz, 1983; Swidler, 1986).

Yet not everyone—especially not members of oppressed, subjugated, or immigrant groups within a society—is likely to share these common schemes of meaning and understanding. Thus, common sense becomes self-serving for those who are in a position of power to determine what it is and who has it. We believe common sense tells us what actions are appropriate in school or in any number of other contexts. But, as a part of culture, common sense is subject to historically defined standards of judgment related to maleness and femaleness, parenting, poverty, and so on. For better or worse, common sense helps to maintain cultures and societies as they are.

We need to approach customs and traditions with the same caution with which we approach common sense. **Customs**, or cultural practices, come into being and persist as solutions to problems of living (Goodenough, 1996). **Tradition** is a process of handing down from one generation to another particular cultural beliefs and practices. Traditions become so taken for granted that they seem "natural" parts of life, as if they have always been here and as if we cannot live without them (Hobsbawm, 1983; Swidler, 1986; Williams, 1977). They are not necessarily followed by everyone in the culture, but they seem necessary and ordained, and they stabilize the culture. They are, in a sense, collective memories of the group. They reflect meanings at a particular moment in time and serve as guides for the present and future (Chung, 2006; McHale et al., 2009).

Customs and traditions are selective, however. They leave out the experiences, memories, and voices of some group members while highlighting and including others. African American, Latino/Hispanic, and Native American students generally do not experience schooling as reflecting their traditions and customs. To reflect Village Park residents' traditions and customs, Community High would have to respect and understand the use of Nonstandard English as students are learning Standard English. Literature and history classes would make salient connections between European traditions and customs and those of West Africans, Afro-Caribbeans, and contemporary African Americans. In addition, processes for including a student's family in schooling processes would include kinship bonds that are not based on legalized blood ties or the rules of state foster care systems. What do you think a school social worker would have to learn to assist schools and to help immigrant families in your community to have a more successful experience in school?

Customs and traditions, moreover, play a role in the strain that characterizes shifts from old patterns and styles of living to new ones in schools and other institutions in society. To survive, groups of people have to bend their traditions and customs without letting them lose their essence. Nondominant ethnic, gender, religious, and other groups in the United States often have to assimilate or accommodate their host culture if they are to share in economic and political power. In fact, the general survival of the traditions and customs of nondominant groups requires adaptability.

Customs and traditions are parts of a cultural process that are changing ever so subtly and slowly but at times abruptly. Sometimes groups disagree about these changes, and some members deny that they are occurring because they believe they should still do things the old way. Social workers have to understand a group's need to hold onto old ways. They do this to protect their worldview about what life means and who they are as a people.

Immigration

It would be foolish to deny that the United States is a nation of immigrants (Parrillo, 2009). Immigration to this land began with the gradual migration of prehistoric peoples reported by anthropologists and picked up speed when Columbus and other Europeans arrived from across the Atlantic Ocean. It continued with the involuntary arrival of Africans and the voluntary and semivoluntary arrivals of various European ethnic groups. Later came Asian people and others. Forceful extension of the nation's borders and political influence incorporated Hispanics and Pacific Islanders. There have been many subsequent waves of immigration, with a great influx late in the 20th century that continues today. Now, more than ever, people are coming to the United States from all over the world. Today we define cultural diversity as a relatively new issue, but the nation's fabric has long included a rich diversity of cultures (Hing, 2004).

Although diversity has been a feature of life in the United States for centuries, immigration is an especially prominent feature of society today. According to U.S. Census estimates, 40 million foreign-born residents now reside in the United States (U.S. Census Bureau, 2013d). They represent 12.9% of the total U.S. population of just over 313 million. They are mostly from Latin America (53%; about 37% born in Central America). They constitute what the media have called the "browning" of the United States. As for the remaining immigrants, 28% of all foreign-born U.S. residents were born in Asia, 12% in Europe, and 7% in other regions of the world.

Population profiles of immigrants are complex and do not capture the dynamic complexity within and between groups based on, for example, region, language, and cultural traditions (Migration Policy Institute, 2013; Pew Research Hispanic Center, 2013). Whether they come from Mexico, South America, or Central America, Latinos and other immigrant groups bring with them their own cultural traditions and languages, which influence their worldview; ethos; and social, religious, economic, and political beliefs and values.

Although many immigrants realize their dream of economic opportunity, many, but not all, encounter resistance from the native-born. Consider the case of immigrants from Latin American countries (Central and South America and the Caribbean). This group recently surpassed African Americans as the largest minority in

© iStockphoto.com/maodesign

Mothers from different cultural backgrounds may have some different traditions and customs about child rearing, but they find their toddlers to have much in common.

the United States and is therefore the group that social workers are increasingly likely to encounter. New York City, Los Angeles, Chicago, San Antonio, Houston, and other southwestern cities are traditional sites for the settlement of Hispanic/Latino immigrants. However, they are also settling in increasing numbers in growing metropolitan areas.

Like other Americans, many Hispanic/Latino immigrants come to the United States to get a piece of the economic pie. However, they face a unique set of circumstances. One often hears complaints about "foreigners taking our jobs." African Americans and Latinos/Hispanics face social conflicts over lifestyles in the low-income neighborhoods they share. Social service and law enforcement agencies scramble for Spanish-language workers and interpreters. Banks decry the fact that many new Spanish-language residents don't trust banks and consequently don't open checking and savings accounts. As this book is going into production in the spring of 2016, immigration policy is once again a hot-button issue in the political campaigns of presidential candidates.

Processes of Cultural Change

In multicultural societies, cultural change can be understood in terms of four processes: assimilation, accommodation, acculturation, and bicultural socialization. They describe the minority individual's or group's response to the dominant culture and may have implications for clients' well-being.

- *Assimilation.* **Assimilation** is the process in which the cultural uniqueness of the minority is abandoned and its members try to blend invisibly into the dominant culture (Kottak, 2008). Some culture scholars have noted a prevailing assimilation ideology that asserts the ideal of Anglo conformity (M. Gordon, 1964). In keeping with this view, some people have argued that the root of the problems faced by African Americans and by economically marginal immigrants is that they have not assimilated successfully. This argument is oversimplified. First, to the extent that discrimination is based on obvious features such as skin color or lack of facility with Standard English, the ability to assimilate is limited. Second, capitalist economies and societies arbitrarily select different group characteristics as desirable at different times. Historically, we have done this in part through immigration policies that admit some groups but not others. For example, the Chinese Exclusion Act of 1882, which was not repealed until 1943, suspended the right of people from China to immigrate to the United States. Many minorities, especially first-generation immigrants, often resist giving up parts of their ethnic identity in order to protect their sense of meaning and purpose in life.

- *Accommodation.* This process is more common than assimilation in the multicultural, multiethnic society of the United States. **Accommodation** is the process of partial or selective cultural change. Nondominant groups follow the norms, rules, and standards of the dominant culture only in specific circumstances and contexts. When Punjabi Sikh children attended school in Stockton, California, in the 1980s, they generally followed the rules of the school (Gibson, 1988). They did not, however, remove their head coverings or socialize with peers of both sexes as is normal in mainstream U.S. society, nor did they live by U.S. cultural standards at home. Some of the Muslim students at Community High could be compared to the Punjabis. Black Muslim girls at Community High, for example, continue to wear head coverings and customary long gowns to attend school, even though the school asks them not to do so. Similar stories continue to turn up in local and national newspapers about students whose Islamic religious attire conflicts with school norms and rules, in Europe as well as the United States. Increasingly, Latino/Hispanic immigrants and native citizens are opting to retain their Spanish in many settings, even though they can and will speak English when necessary.

- *Acculturation.* **Acculturation** is a mutual sharing of culture (Kottak & Kozaitis, 2008). Although cultural groups remain distinct, certain elements of their culture change, and they exchange and blend preferences in foods, music, dance, clothing, and the like. As cities and towns grow in diversity, Mexican, Vietnamese, Asian Indian, and other cuisines are becoming more common. At the same time, these diverse cultural groups are incorporating parts of regional cultures into their lives.

- *Bicultural socialization.* The process of **bicultural socialization** involves a nonmajority group or its members mastering both the dominant culture and their own (Robbins, Chatterjee, & Canda, 2012). Bicultural socialization is necessary in societies that have relatively fixed notions about how a person should live and interact in school, work, court, financial institutions, and so on. A person who has achieved bicultural socialization has, in a sense, a dual identity. Mainstream economic, political, and social success (or "crossing over") requires nonmajority musicians, athletes, intellectuals and scholars, news anchors, bankers, and a host of others to master this process of cultural change and adaptation.

Social workers who conduct multidimensional cultural analyses should seek to uncover the processes by which culture is being maintained, changed, and adapted in the lives of the individuals and groups with whom they work. We must also be alert to the fact that the process of cultural change is not always voluntary, or a free and open exchange of culture. We must also pay attention to the political, social, and economic practices that undergird institutional norms and values. If these processes are harmful and oppressive for some people, we have a professional obligation, through our code of ethics, to facilitate change.

Women, people of color, immigrants, and poor people have historically not had a significant say in how cultural change proceeds. But having a limited voice does not eliminate one's voice altogether. As social workers, we must comprehend the process of cultural change affecting our clients and act in accord with such knowledge. We cannot accept only dominant notions about the meaning of the actions of exploited and subjugated groups. We cannot look only to mainstream culture and traditions of knowledge to determine the actions we take with nonmajority people. If we do, we are merely reproducing inequality and subjugation and limiting our effectiveness as human service providers.

Keep this discussion of culture in mind as we turn to a discussion of the physical environment and how it influences and is influenced by human behavior. As you do so, recall that culture is both inside our heads as understandings and in the external environment—as behavior and the things we construct from the material world around us. Anthropologists are particularly interested in the role of the material culture in shaping behavior and societies. That is the driving force of the multidisciplinary literature on the physical environment and human behavior.

CRITICAL THINKING Questions 6.2

Ann Swidler says that culture is a tool kit of symbols, stories, rituals, and worldviews people use to solve different kinds of problems. How does culture serve as a tool kit for Stan? What symbols, stories, rituals, and worldviews are in his tool kit? What problems is he trying to solve with this tool kit? How does culture serve as a tool kit for Tina? What symbols, stories, rituals, and worldviews are in her tool kit? What problems is she trying to solve with her tool kit? And how about you? How does culture serve as a tool kit for you? What symbols, stories, rituals, and worldviews are in your tool kit? What problems do you try to solve with your tool kit?

THE RELATIONSHIP BETWEEN THE PHYSICAL ENVIRONMENT AND HUMAN BEHAVIOR

As with most stories we hear as social workers, Ben Watson's story, as told at the beginning of the chapter, is a multidimensional story of person and environment interactions over time. The physical environment is a supremely important dimension of this unfolding story. Ben's story reminds us that all human behavior occurs not only in a cultural context but also in a physical one.

Although, historically, social work's person and environment construct considered the social environment but ignored the physical environment, in recent years, some social work scholars, like scholars in other behavioral science disciplines, have begun to pay attention to robust findings about the relationship between human well-being and the physical environment (see Gray, Coates, & Hetherington, 2013). The relationship between human behavior and the physical environment is a multidisciplinary study that includes contributions from the social, behavioral, and health sciences of psychology, sociology, geography, anthropology, neuroscience, and public health, as well as from the design disciplines of architecture, landscape architecture, interior design, and urban and regional planning. When thinking about human interactions with the physical environment, it is important to consider both the natural and the built environments.

Four broad categories of theory about human behavior and the physical environment are introduced in this chapter: stimulation theories, control theories, behavior settings theories, and ecocritical theories. Each of these categories of theory, and the research it has stimulated, provides useful possibilities for social workers to consider as they participate in person–environment assessments and consider possibilities for intervention at multiple levels of person and environment interactions. The ecocritical perspective is raising interesting and important new questions about the social work profession's responsibilities to the natural environment. Exhibit 6.5 presents the key ideas and important concepts of these four types of theory.

STIMULATION THEORIES

Have you thought about how you would react to the abundance of sunlight in Ben Watson's new apartment or the activity on his street? That question is consistent with **stimulation theories**, which focus on the physical environment as a source of sensory information that is essential for human well-being. The stimulation may be light, color, heat, texture, or scent, or it may be buildings, streets, and parks. Stimulation theorists propose that patterns of stimulation influence thinking, feelings, social interaction, and health.

Stimulation varies by amount—intensity, frequency, duration, number of sources—as well as by type. Stimulation theories based on theories of psychophysiological arousal assume that moderate levels of stimulation are optimal for

EXHIBIT 6.5 • Four Categories of Theories About the Relationship Between the Physical Environment and Human Behavior

THEORIES	KEY IDEAS	IMPORTANT CONCEPTS
Stimulation theories	The physical environment is a source of sensory information essential for human well-being. Patterns of stimulation influence thinking, emotions, social interaction, and health.	Stimulus overload Restricted environmental stimulation
Control theories	Humans desire control over their physical environments. Some person–environment configurations provide more control over the physical environment than others.	Privacy Personal space Territoriality Crowding
Behavior settings theories	Consistent, uniform patterns of behavior occur in particular settings. Behaviors of different persons in the same setting are more similar than the behaviors of the same person in different settings.	Behavior settings Programs
Ecocritical theories	All elements of nature and the physical world are interconnected. Humans have no more value than other forms of nature. Nondominant groups bear the burdens of environmental hazards.	Deep ecology Ecofeminism Environmental sustainability

human behavior (Gifford, 2007). Thus, both *stimulus overload* (too much stimulation) and *restricted environmental stimulation* (once called *stimulus deprivation*) have a negative effect on human behavior. Theorists interested in the behavioral and health effects of stimulus overload have built on Han Selye's work regarding stress (see Chapter 4).

Some stimulation theories focus on the direct, concrete effect of stimulation on behavior; others focus on the meanings people construct regarding particular stimuli (Gifford, 2007). In fact, people respond to both the concrete and the symbolic aspects of their physical environments. A doorway too narrow to accommodate a wheelchair has a concrete effect on the behavior of a person in a wheelchair; it will also have a symbolic effect, contributing to the person's feelings of exclusion and stigma. Stimulation theories alert social workers to consider the quality and intensity of sensory stimulation in the environments where their clients live and work.

Environmental design scholars have begun to incorporate recent advances in neuroscience research to understand how people's brains respond to different types of stimulation in physical environments (see Eberhard, 2008). Their goal is to use this knowledge to design environments that support brain development and functioning for the general population as well as for groups with special needs, such as premature newborns and persons with Alzheimer's disease (Zeisel, 2006, 2009). Neuroscientists are also working with architects and environmental psychologists to learn what aspects of the physical environment stimulate emotional and physical healing (Sternberg, 2009).

CONTROL THEORIES

The ability to gain control over his physical environment is a central theme of Ben Watson's story. In that way, the story is a good demonstration of the ideas found in **control theories**, which focus on the issue of how much control we have over our physical environments and the attempts we make to gain control (Gifford, 2007). Four concepts are central to the work of control theorists: privacy, personal space, territoriality, and crowding. Personal space and territoriality are *boundary regulating mechanisms* that we use to gain greater control over our physical environments.

Privacy

Altman (1975) defines *privacy* as "selective control of access to the self or to one's group" (p. 18). This definition contains two important elements: control over information about oneself and control over interactions with others. Virginia Kupritz (2003) has extended Altman's work by making a distinction between speech or conversational privacy (being able to hold conversations without being overheard) and visual privacy (being free of unwanted observation). Contemporary innovations in communication technologies have introduced new concerns about having control over information with respect to oneself and one's group and about how to balance national security with rights to privacy. Privacy is a frequent topic of articles in the journal *Computers in Human Behavior* (see, for example, Mohamed & Ahmad, 2012).

Some of us require more privacy than others, and some situations stimulate privacy needs more than other situations. Ben Watson was accustomed to sharing a house with his university pals and didn't mind the lack of privacy that came with that situation. He felt differently about the lack of privacy in his parents' home after rehab and was eager for a more private living situation, even though his privacy in some areas would be compromised by his need for a personal care assistant.

It appears that people in different cultures use space differently to create privacy. Susan Kent (1991) theorizes that the use of partitions, such as walls or screens, to create private spaces increases as societies become more complex. She particularly notes the strong emphasis that European American culture places on partitioned space, both at home and at work (see Duvall-Early & Benedict, 1992). More recent research supports this idea; for example, college students in the United States have been found to desire more privacy in their residence halls than Turkish students (Kaya & Weber, 2003). The situation appears to be different when it comes to privacy in online communications, however. For example, researchers have found college students in China and Japan to be more concerned about privacy in online communications than college students in the United States (Lowry, Cao, & Everard, 2011; Maynard & Taylor, 1996).

Researchers have examined the physical attributes of workplace offices that satisfy the privacy needs of the U.S. workforce. In recent decades employers have limited personal space of employees, using open-plan cubicles, based on the belief that such arrangements will facilitate communication among employees, as well as on a desire to cut costs. The consistent finding is that employees are not satisfied with the level of privacy in open-plan arrangements (see Lee, 2010). There is also evidence that employees tend to communicate less when they feel they cannot control the privacy of communications (Kupritz, 2003). Personal space and territoriality are two mechanisms for securing privacy.

Personal Space

Personal space, also known as *interpersonal distance*, is the physical distance we choose to maintain in interpersonal relationships. Robert Sommer (1969) has defined it as "an area with invisible boundaries surrounding a person's body into which intruders may not come" (p. 26). More recent formulations (Gifford, 2007) emphasize that personal space is not stable but contracts and expands with changing interpersonal circumstances and with variations in physical settings. The distance you desire when talking with your best friend is likely to be different from the distance you prefer when talking with a stranger or even with

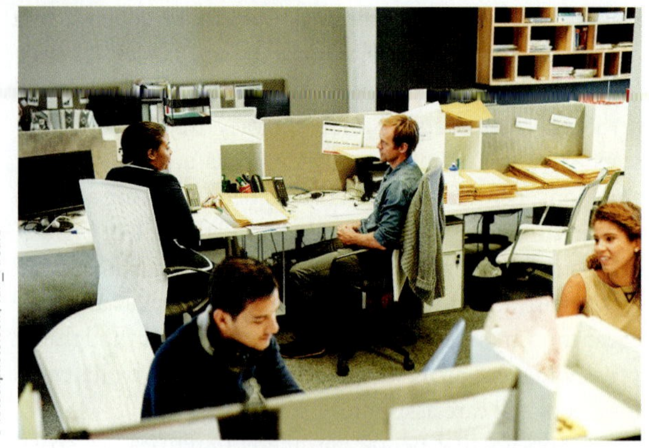

In recent decades employers have limited personal space of employees, using open-plan cubicles, but research finds that employees are not satisfied with the level of privacy in open-plan arrangements.

a known authority figure like your professor. The desired distance for any of these interpersonal situations is likely to expand in small spaces (Sinha & Mukherjee, 1996). We will want to recognize our own personal space requirements in different work situations and be sensitive to the personal space requirements of our coworkers and clients.

Variations in personal space are also thought to be related to age, gender, attachment style, previous victimization, mental health, and culture. Personal space requirements have been found to increase with age until early adulthood (Gifford, 2007). One recent research project found that, in shopping malls in the United States and Turkey, adolescents interacting with other adolescents kept the largest interpersonal distance of any age group (Ozdemir, 2008). Males have often been found to require greater personal space than females, and research indicates that the largest interpersonal distances are kept in male–male pairs, followed by female–female pairs, with the smallest interpersonal distances kept in male–female pairs (Ozdemir, 2008). There is evidence that adults with insecure attachment style require a larger personal space than children and adults with secure attachments (Kaitz, Bar-Haim, Lehrer, & Grossman, 2004). Physically abused children have also been found to keep significantly larger personal space than nonabused children, suggesting that personal space provides a protective function for these children (Vranic, 2003). A study of combat veterans in Croatia found that veterans diagnosed with PTSD preferred significantly larger interpersonal distance than veterans without PTSD (Bogovic, Mihanovic, Jokic-Begic, & Svagelj, 2013). Both groups of veterans maintained greater interpersonal distance when approached by a man than when approached by a woman. The veterans with PTSD required greater distance when they were approached from behind whereas the veterans without PTSD required greater distance when approached from the front. Individuals diagnosed with schizophrenia have also been found to require more personal space than people without such a diagnosis (Nechamkin, Salganik, Modai, & Ponizovsky, 2003).

In *The Hidden Dimensions*, Edward Hall (1966) reported field research indicating that members of contact-oriented, collectivist cultures (e.g., Latin, Asian, Arab) prefer closer interpersonal distances than members of non–contact oriented, individualist cultures (e.g., northern European, North American). More recent research has supported this suggestion; for example, pairs in Turkish malls have been observed to interact more closely than pairs in U.S. malls (Ozdemir, 2008), but within-culture differences in interpersonal distance preferences have also been noted (G. W. Evans, Lepore, & Allen, 2000). There is some evidence that people require less personal space when interacting with people they consider to be like themselves in some important way (Novelli, Drury, & Reicher, 2010).

Sommer (2002) has updated his discussion of personal space by raising questions about how personal space is affected by digital technology. For example, how much personal space do we need to have intimate conversations on our cell phones? Sommer also raises questions about the impact of the computer on personal space, noting that at work people sometimes communicate by e-mail with coworkers sitting beside them in the same office. Other researchers have examined how much personal space people need when using automated teller machines and other technology where private information is stored and found that people report larger desired space than the space actually provided (Shu & Li, 2007). Developers of artificial intelligence systems want to program service robots in such a way that they do not invade the personal space of humans (Banik, Gupta, Habib, & Mousumi, 2013).

Territoriality

Personal space is a concept having to do with individual behavior and about the use of space to control the interpersonal environment. **Territoriality** refers primarily to the behavior of individuals and small groups as they seek control over physical space (Taylor, 1988), but recently the concept has also been used to refer to attempts to control objects, roles, and relationships (Brown, Lawrence, & Robinson, 2005; Gifford, 2007). Territoriality leads us to mark, or personalize, our territory to signify our "ownership" and to engage in a variety of behaviors to protect it from invasion. The study of animal territoriality has a longer history than the study of human territorial behavior. For humans, there is much evidence that males are more territorial than females, but there is also some contradictory evidence (Kaya & Burgess, 2007; Kaya & Weber, 2003). For example, in crowded living conditions in Nigerian university residence halls, female students appeared to use more territorial strategies to cope, whereas male students used more withdrawal strategies (Amole, 2005). Other research shows that by their midteens, many youth in the United States want some territory of their own, as is sometimes demonstrated with graffiti, tagging, and gang behavior (Pickering, Kintrea, & Bannister, 2012).

Irwin Altman (1975) classifies our territories as primary, secondary, and public. A *primary territory* is one that evokes feelings of ownership that we control on a relatively permanent basis and that is vital to our daily lives. For most of us, our primary territories would include our home and place of work. *Secondary territories* are less important to us than primary territories, and control of them does not seem as essential to us; examples might be our favorite table at Starbucks or our favorite cardio machine at the gym. *Public territories* are open to anyone in the community, and we generally make no attempt to control access to them—places such as public parks, public beaches, sidewalks, and stores. For people who are homeless and lack access to typical primary territories, however, public territories may serve as primary territories.

Much of the literature on territoriality draws on the functionalist sociological tradition, emphasizing the positive value of territorial behavior to provide order to the social world and a sense of security to individuals (Taylor, 1988). We know, however, that territorial behavior can also be the source of conflict, domination, and oppression. Recently, it has been suggested that globalization is reducing territoriality among nation-states (Raustiala, 2005). And, indeed, globalization does blur national boundaries, but current national conversations about "securing our borders" are prime examples of territorial behavior.

Crowding

The term *crowding* has sometimes been used interchangeably with *density*, but environmental psychologists make important distinctions between these terms. **Density** is the ratio of persons per unit area of a space. **Crowding** is the subjective feeling of having too many people around. Crowding is not always correlated with density; the feeling of being crowded seems to be influenced by an interaction of personal, social, and cultural as well as physical factors. For example, in one study the perception of crowding was associated with density among older adults living with extended families in India, but perceived social support in high-density environments buffered the perception of crowding and decreased personal space requirements (Sinha & Nayyar, 2000). Researchers (Evans et al., 2000) have compared different ethnic groups that live in high-density housing in the United States and found that Latin American and Asian American residents tolerate more density before feeling crowded than Anglo Americans and African Americans. These researchers also found, however, that all four ethnic groups experienced

Crowding is the subjective feeling of having too many people around.

similar psychological distress from crowding. Another research team found that Middle Eastern respondents were less likely to perceive high-density retail situations as crowded than their North American counterparts (Pons, Laroche, & Mourali, 2006).

Research has also found gender differences in response to crowding. Women living in crowded homes are more likely to be depressed, whereas men living in crowded homes demonstrate higher levels of withdrawal and violence (Regoeczi, 2008). In crowded elementary school classrooms, girls' academic achievement and boys' classroom behavior are adversely affected (Maxwell, 2003).

Crowding has been found to have an adverse effect on child development (Evans & Saegert, 2000) and to be associated with elevated blood pressure and neuroendocrine hormone activity (Gifford, 2007), poor compliance with mental health care (Menezes, Scazufca, Rodrigues, & Mann, 2000), increased incidence of tuberculosis (Baker, Das, Venugopal, & Howden-Chapman, 2008; Wanyeki et al., 2006), and aggressive behavior in prison inmates (Lawrence & Andrews, 2004).

BEHAVIOR SETTINGS THEORIES

Would you expect to see the same behaviors if you were observing Ben Watson in different settings—for example, his parents' home, his apartment, running errands in his neighborhood, at work, at a party with friends, or on an outing in the natural environment? My guess is that you would not. A third major category of theories about the relationship between human behavior and the physical environment is **behavior settings theories**. According to these theories, consistent, uniform patterns of behavior occur in particular places, or *behavior settings*. Behavior is *always* tied to a specific place, and the setting may have a more powerful influence on behavior than characteristics of the individual (Scott, 2005).

Behavior settings theory was first developed by Roger Barker (1968), who unexpectedly found that observations of different persons in the same setting were more similar than observations of the same person in different settings. Barker suggested that *programs*—consistent, prescribed patterns of behavior—develop and are maintained in many specific settings. For example, when you enter a grocery store, you grab a cart, travel down aisles collecting items and putting them in the cart, and take the cart to a checkout counter where you wait while store employees tabulate the cost of the items and bag them (or you take your items to a self-serve checkout counter). Imagine how surprised you would be if you went into the grocery store to find everybody kicking soccer balls! Behavioral programs are created conjointly by individuals and their inanimate surroundings, and behavior settings are distinctive in their physical-spatial features as well as their social rules. The relationships of the social and physical environments to behavior can be summarized in these words: "It is the social situation that influences people's behavior, but it is the physical environment that provides the cues" (Rapoport, 1990, p. 57).

In recent years, behavior settings theory has been extended to explain behavior in nonplace settings, more specifically to explain behavior in *virtual behavior settings* such as online chat rooms and blogs (Stokols & Montero, 2002). This line of inquiry is interested in how interaction in such virtual behavior settings is integrated, or not, with the place-based settings in which it occurs, such as the home, workplace, or Internet café.

Behavior settings as conceptualized by Barker had a static quality, but Allan Wicker (2012) has more recently written about the changing nature—the life histories—of behavior settings. Some settings disappear (have you been to a barn raising lately?), and some become radically altered. These days, that trip to the grocery store often involves getting your own reusable grocery bags from the car before entering the store (or making a trip back to the car to get them when you are almost at the store door). Wicker (2012) also argues that behavioral scientists must pay attention to the larger contexts of settings, which often belong to networks that include a number of other settings.

Community psychologist Edward Seidman (2012) argues that focusing on the setting rather than the individual as the target for change opens the way for a wealth of interventions. Behavior settings theory has implications for social work assessment and intervention. It suggests that patterns of behavior are specific to a setting and, therefore, we must assess settings as well as individuals when problematic behavior occurs. Behavior settings theory also suggests that the place where we first learn a new skill helps re-create the state necessary to retrieve and enact the skill. When we are assisting clients in skill development, we should pay particular attention to the discontinuities between the settings where the skills are being "learned" and the settings where those skills must be used.

ECOCRITICAL THEORIES

In Chapter 2, we wrote about ecological theory in the systems perspective, a theory that focuses on the relationships and interactions between living organisms and their environments. This theory emphasizes the interdependence and mutual influence of organisms and their environments. In the past 2 decades, ecological theory has been extended in several disciplines to take a more critical view of human interactions with the natural environment. For the purpose of this discussion, we will call the theories in this tradition **ecocritical theories**, because they call attention to the ways that human behavior degrades and destroys the natural world, the unequal burden of environmental degradation on different groups, and ethical obligations that humans have to nonhuman elements of the natural environment. Given space limitations, this discussion touches on two such theories developed in the last quarter of the 20th century: deep ecology and ecofeminism.

Deep ecology is both a theory and a social movement. In simplest terms, deep ecology suggests that social work should focus on "person *with* environment," rather than "person *and* environment" (Besthorn, 2012). It emphasizes the total interconnectedness of all elements of the natural and physical world and the inseparability of human well-being and the well-being of planet Earth. It argues for the intrinsic value of all life forms, for the value of ecological diversity, and for the responsibility of humans to respect the rest of nature and live in ways that have minimal impact on the well-being of other life forms. It calls attention to the way that current human interactions with the natural environment are *unsustainable*, leading to global warming, atmospheric pollution, and other forms of environmental degradation that put the long-term survival of all elements of nature at risk. What distinguishes deep ecology from other theories discussed in this book is that it is *ecocentric* (earth centered) rather than *anthropocentric* (human centered). It insists on a nonhierarchical form of justice, in which humans do not control or have dominance over nature. Humans have no more value than other forms of nature. Deep ecologists note that some cultures have long held the view that ethical decision making must respect the interests of the natural world. Fred Besthorn (2012) has been a strong voice recommending that deep ecology is the theory that social workers should use to think about human–environment interactions.

Ecofeminism, also both a theory and a social movement, took shape about the same time as deep ecology, in the 1970s, but its roots go back much further. Although there are different strains of *ecofeminism*, the approach is best described as a feminist approach to environmental ethics. Ecofeminists see the oppression of women and the domination of nature as interconnected. They suggest that nature and women, as well as other groups such as children and people of color, have been conceptualized as separate and inferior in order to legitimate dominance over them by an elite male-dominant social order (Gaard, 2011). More than the deep ecologists, they call attention to the ways that women and other nondominant groups bear the burdens of environmental hazards such as toxic waste. Susan Mann (2011) argues that the intersection of feminism and environmentalism is not new, noting that throughout the Progressive Era in the United States, women played important roles in both wildlife conservation and activism to promote clean air, water, and food for people living in urban centers. Jane Addams, one of the founders of the social work profession, was such a woman.

CRITICAL THINKING Questions 6.3

What have you observed about the impact of the physical environment on your behavior and the behavior of others? How well do stimulation theories, control theories, or behavior settings theories account for the influence of the physical environment on your behavior and the behavior of other people you know? What do you think of the deep ecology argument that humans have no more value than other forms of nature?

THE NATURAL ENVIRONMENT

If I asked you to engage in a relaxation exercise by picturing yourself in your favorite place, where would that be? Research shows that places in the **natural environment**—the part of the environment made up of all living and nonliving things naturally occurring—are among people's favorite places (White, Pahl, Ashbullby, Herbert, & Depledge, 2013). This is, of course, not true for all people, but it appears to be true for the majority of people in all cultures (Wolsko & Hoyt, 2012). Most of the research on the relationship between human behavior and the natural environment has been in the stimulation theory tradition—looking for ways in which aspects of the natural environment affect our thinking, feeling, social interaction, and health. At a time of great international concern about the damage being done to the natural environment by human endeavors, ecocritical theorists are calling for humans to rethink their relationship with the natural environment.

The physical environment (both natural and human made) impacts our behavior. Researchers have found a strong preference for elements of the natural environment and positive outcomes of time spent in nature.

BENEFITS AND COSTS OF HUMAN INTERACTION WITH THE NATURAL ENVIRONMENT

Do you find that you feel refreshed from being in the natural environment—walking along the beach, hiking in the mountains, or even walking in your neighborhood? As it has for many people, the natural environment has always been a place of serenity for Ben Watson. There is a long tradition of research into the benefits of the natural environment for human behavior. In recent years, this research has been based on two theories developed by environmental psychologists. *Attention restoration theory* (ART) proposes that interacting with nature restores depleted cognitive resources (Kaplan & Berman, 2010). *Psychophysiological stress recovery theory* (PSRT) is interested in how interacting with nature helps people to recover emotionally and physiologically (Ulrich et al., 1991).

In general, this research finds many positive outcomes of time spent in the natural environment and suggests that you should consider the benefits of interacting with nature for both you and your clients. These benefits are summarized in Exhibit 6.6, but because of the extensive research in this area only a few of the recent findings are reported here.

There are consistent findings from research using a variety of methods that interaction with natural environments can restore depleted emotional and cognitive resources (see White et al., 2013, for a review of these findings). Our interaction with nature can help to recharge our attentional capacities (Felsten, 2009), reduce psychophysiological stress (Kjellgren & Buhrkall, 2010), and enhance emotional states (Bowler, Buyung-Ali, Knight, & Pullin, 2010). It is not clear which aspects of the natural environment provide benefit, but research indicates that environments with water have the greatest positive effect (Barton & Pretty, 2010; Karmanov & Hamel, 2008). Interactions with woodlands and mountains have also been found to have a positive effect (White et al., 2013), and there is considerable evidence that interactions with domestic and companion animals have emotional and physiological benefits for humans (Anderson, 2008).

A preponderance of the research has investigated the effects of interaction with nature in populations in good health, but recently researchers have been interested in whether nature has similar benefits for people with specific health concerns. Berman and colleagues (2012) studied the benefits of walking in nature, versus walking in an urban setting, for a group of people diagnosed with major depressive disorder (MDD). Participants were found to have improvements in memory span and positive emotion after both types of walks, but the improvements were significantly greater after the nature walks, and the effect sizes were larger than those found in populations without MDD. Kjellgren and Buhrkall (2010) studied a group of people identified as suffering from high stress and burnout and found improvements in stress level and energy after interaction with the natural environment. Walking in outdoor green spaces has been found to improve attention among children and adolescents with attention deficit disorder (ADD) (Taylor & Kuo, 2009).

Researchers have found synergistic effects between nature and physical activity, with moderate-intensity exercise in natural environments associated with the most positive effects (White et al., 2013). Thompson Coon et al. (2011) found that exercising in natural environments, compared with exercising indoors, was associated with greater revitalization and greater reduction in tension, confusion, anger, and depression. Research with individuals involved in both community gardening and backyard gardening indicates benefits that include a sense of tranquility, sense of control, and improved physical health (Shepard, 2013).

There is some evidence that you do not have to be active in the natural environment to derive benefits

EXHIBIT 6.6 • Benefits of Time Spent in the Natural Environment (Based on Stimulation Theory Research)

- Engaging children's interest
- Stimulating children's imagination
- Stimulating activity and physical fitness
- Increasing productivity
- Enhancing creativity
- Providing intellectual stimulation
- Aiding recovery from mental fatigue
- Improving concentration
- Increasing working memory
- Enhancing group cohesiveness and community cooperation
- Fostering tranquility and serenity
- Fostering a sense of oneness or wholeness
- Fostering a sense of control
- Fostering recovery from surgery
- Lowering heart rate, blood pressure, and muscle tension
- Improving emotional states, such as calmness, relaxation, and vitality
- Contributing to cognitive and emotional improvements in persons diagnosed with major depressive disorder (MDD)
- Reducing psychophysiological stress
- Decreasing vulnerability to illness

from it. Views of nature have been found to have positive benefits for cognitive and emotional functioning and to promote recovery from stress and surgery. Office workers have been found to experience less anger and stress when art posters depicting nature are present (Byoung-Suk, Ulrich, Walker, & Tassinary, 2008). Indoor plants have also been found to be associated with improved attention in office settings (Raanaas, Evensen, Rich, Sjostrom, & Patil, 2011). Researchers have begun to explore whether views of nature are as beneficial as time spent in nature. In a study of participants identified as suffering from stress and burnout, Kjellgren and Buhrkall (2010) investigated the similarities and differences in reactions to 30 minutes of relaxation in a natural environment versus 30 minutes of relaxation while viewing a slide show of photographs of the same natural environment. They found that pulse and diastolic blood pressure were lower after relaxation in both the natural environment and the simulated natural environment. They also found that the two types of relaxation situations were equally efficient in stress reduction. However, relaxation in the natural environment produced greater improvement in energy, sense of well-being, and tranquility than relaxation in the simulated natural environment.

Sociobiologists propose that humans have a genetically based need to affiliate with nature; they call it **biophilia** (Simaika & Samways, 2010; Wilson, 2007). They argue that humans have a 2-million-year history of evolving in natural environments and have only lived in cities for a small fraction of that time and that therefore we are much better adapted to natural environments than built environments. It is important to note that access to nature is not equally shared by all groups.

There is a growing call for **ecotherapy**, exposure to nature and the outdoors as a component of psychotherapy, as a major agenda for mental health promotion and treatment (see Buzzell & Chalquist, 2009; Wolsko & Hoyt, 2012). Proponents of ecotherapy propose such interventions as inquiring about clients' relationships with the natural environment, assigning a walk in the park as homework, use of plants and photos of natural settings in therapist offices, and developing forest experiences for adolescents (Hayward, Miller, & Shaw, 2013; Wolsko & Hoyt, 2012). The combination of green spaces with physical exercise has been found to be a particularly potent program for mood elevation in people experiencing symptoms of depression and anxiety (Mackay & Neill, 2010). This research indicates that the degree of perceived "greenness" of the environment has a greater influence than the intensity of the exercise on symptom relief, with the greater benefits coming from enhanced perception of greenness. Ecotherapy includes time spent with domestic and companion animals.

Ben Watson made special note of the ample sunlight in his apartment. Design innovations for older adults, particularly those with Alzheimer's disease, are emphasizing the benefit of natural over artificial light (Brawley, 2006, 2009). However, the relationship between sunlight and human behavior is curvilinear, with benefit coming from increasing amounts until a certain optimum point is reached, after which increasing amounts damage rather than benefit. Excessive sunlight can have negative impacts, such as glare and overheating, and inadequate sunlight has been identified as a contributor to depression, sometimes referred to as seasonal affective disorder (SAD), in some persons (Kurlanski & Ibay, 2012). Sunlight penetration in indoor spaces is related to feelings of relaxation, with patches of sunlight as the optimum situation, and both too little and too much penetration decreasing the feeling of relaxation (Brawley, 2009).

Although the natural environment can be a positive force, it also has the potential to damage cognitive, emotional, social, and physical well-being. The relationship between sunlight and human behavior provides a clue. Too little sun causes harm, but so does too much sun. Water is a favorite environmental feature for many people, but too little water causes drought and too much water causes flooding. The natural environment provides sensory stimulation in an uncontrolled strength, and the patterns of stimulation are quite unstable. Extremely stimulating natural events are known as natural disasters, including such events as hurricanes, tornadoes, floods, earthquakes, volcanic eruptions, landslides, avalanches, tsunamis, and forest fires. Natural disasters are cataclysmic events—a class of stressors with great force, sudden onset, excessive demands on human coping, and large scope. There is growing concern that climate change is leading to more frequent natural disasters (Datar, Liu, Linnemayr, & Stecher, 2013). Natural disasters have immediate effects on health and mortality, but they also have indirect long-term effects because they lead to disruptions in shelter, food supplies, income, and access to health care. Social workers play active roles in providing services to communities that have experienced natural disasters.

ENVIRONMENTAL JUSTICE AND ECOLOGICAL JUSTICE

Ben Watson says that he has become concerned about the damage he sees humans doing to the natural environment and about how some communities are suffering more than others from the health consequences of industrial and agricultural practices that put toxins into the soil, water, and air. Some social workers have also become concerned about these issues as indicated by recently published books, such as *Environmental Social Work* (Gray et al., 2013) and *Green Social Work: From Environmental Crises to Environmental*

Justice (Dominelli, 2012). The concerns raised by Ben Watson and the authors of these books are at the heart of two social movements—the environmental justice movement and the ecological justice movement. These movements share a concern about the ways in which human activities are exhausting natural resources and polluting air, water, and land. But they differ in one important way: The environmental justice movement is concerned about human rights in relation to degradation of the natural environment whereas the ecological justice movement is concerned about the rights of nature to be protected from human activity (Besthorn, 2013).

Environmental justice is thought to occur when all groups of people have equal share of the harmful environmental effects of policies and operations of business and governments. In the United States, there is considerable evidence that the toxic load of pollution from pesticides, fertilizers, and factories is generally heaviest in poor communities of color (Perkins, 2012), and considerable research establishes that such pollution is a risk factor for cancer and respiratory diseases. There is also clear evidence that hazardous waste facilities are more likely to be located in poor and minority communities. One research team found that brownfields—properties that are no longer operational because of the presence of hazardous substances—are much more likely to be located in poor and minority communities than in areas of higher socioeconomic status. They also found that brownfields are cleaned up much more slowly when they are located in communities with larger minority populations (Eckerd & Keeler, 2012). Internationally, wealthy nations are exploiting the natural resources of poor nations, exacerbating the poverty in those nations. The degradation of the world ecosystems is growing significantly worse, and the burdens of that degradation go increasingly to the most marginalized populations: poor people, people of color, older people, women, and children (Hetherington & Boddy, 2013). Social justice and environmental justice become more and more tightly entwined; in many communities it is not possible to promote social justice without working on issues of environmental justice.

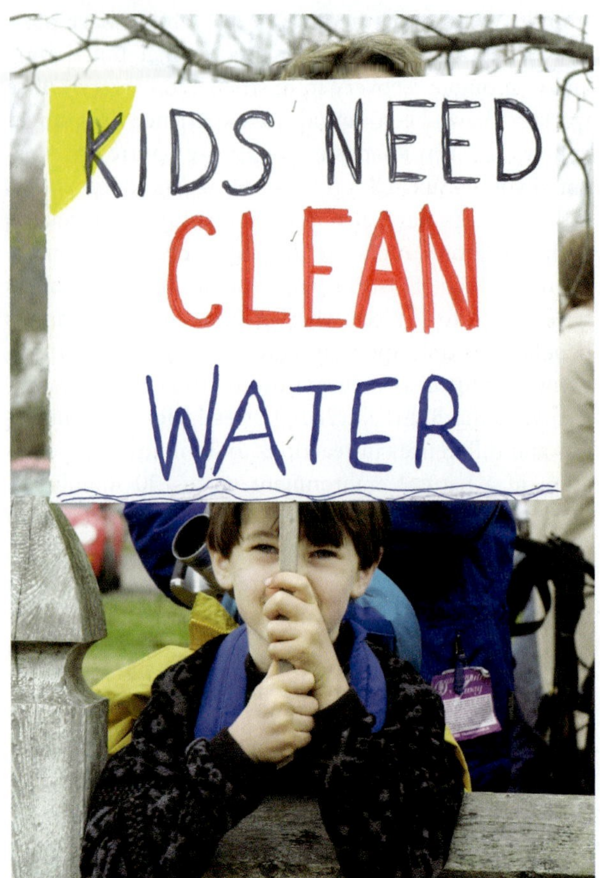

Both the environmental justice movement and the ecological justice movement are concerned about the ways in which human activities are exhausting natural resources and polluting air, water, and land.

THE BUILT ENVIRONMENT

It is the uncontrollable quality of the natural environment that humans try to overcome in constructing the **built environment**—the portion of the physical environment attributable solely to human effort. The built environment includes tools, structures, buildings, and technologies of various sorts designed and built by humans to create comfort and controllability and to extend their abilities to meet goals. The built environment is produced by human behavior, and what humans build has a great effect on human behavior.

For several decades, environmental psychologists have been studying the impact of the built environment on such factors as mood, problem solving, productivity, and violent behavior. They have examined physical designs that encourage social interaction, *sociopetal spaces*, and designs that discourage social interaction, *sociofugal spaces*. Researchers have studied design features of such institutional settings as psychiatric hospitals, state schools for persons with cognitive disabilities, college dormitories, and correctional facilities. Late 20th- and early 21st-century developments in biomedical science, particularly new understandings of the brain and the immune system, have allowed more sophisticated analysis of how the built environment affects physical and mental health and can be a source of healing. In the past 2 decades, researchers have also been interested in how information, communication, and other assistive technologies are affecting human behavior.

TECHNOLOGY

Ben Watson is in a partnership with his sophisticated titanium wheelchair. Since they first appeared on the earth, humans have used their cognitive capacities to build tools to manipulate and control the environment. Humans are not the only animals that have developed tools, but, to date, humans are the only animals to develop the types of complex tools resulting in rapid changes in our individual and collective behaviors. For the purposes of this discussion, **technology** is defined as the tools, machines, instruments, and devices developed and used by humans to enhance their lives. There are many types of technologies; examples include construction technology, industrial technology, information technology, communication technology, weapon technology, and medical technology. There is clear evidence that the pace of technological development is speeding up.

Across time, and certainly since the industrial revolution, there have been proponents and critics of technological development. Proponents have had confidence that technology will benefit society. The most optimistic have believed that technology will allow humans to master all problems and control the future. Critics have argued that technology can limit our freedoms and have negative effects on our psychological health. And recently, the ecological justice movement has emphasized the ways in which new technologies destroy the natural environment. As with earlier technological revolutions, the rapid developments in information and communication technologies we are currently experiencing have both proponents and critics. Recent work by Ray Kurzweil and Sherry Turkle highlights some of the arguments on both sides.

Ray Kurzweil is an author, inventor, futurist, and director of engineering at Google. Among other things, he has invented an image scanner, a reading machine that allows people with visual impairments to have computer text read out loud, and a music synthesizer. He is, as you might guess, a great proponent of technology. In his 2012 book *How to Create a Mind: The Secret of Human Thought Revealed*, Kurzweil notes, enthusiastically, that advancements in neurological science technologies are allowing us to understand our brains in more and more precise detail. This growing understanding will soon allow us to fix our brains when needed and vastly expand the powers of our own intelligence. He joyfully reminds us of the capacities of computers to route e-mails, produce an electrocardiogram, fly and land airplanes, and play games. He tells of efforts to build a computer that will read vast amounts of medical literature and become a master diagnostician. He reminds us that we have artificial intelligence all around us with the digital brain that stores old memories, e-mail, text messaging, and Siri on the iPhone. He predicts that Google self-driving cars will have fewer accidents than human-driven cars. Kurzweil argues that we build these tools to extend our own reach and are producing and will continue to produce very powerful abilities. He predicts that humans will sooner or later create an artificial neocortex that has the range and flexibility of the human neocortex. He says that the machines of the future will appear to be conscious and come to be accepted as "conscious persons" (Kurzweil, 2012, p. 209).

Sherry Turkle is professor of social studies and science and technology at the Massachusetts Institute of Technology. In her 2011 book *Alone Together: Why We Expect More From Technology and Less From Each Other*, Turkle reports on her research in two areas: human interaction with robots and human interaction with communication technologies. Whereas she finds some benefit of both types of human interactions, she is not optimistic about the way these technologies are reshaping human emotional life.

Turkle reports on the current state of development of robot companions being used to break the isolation of children and older adults. She notes that enthusiasm for robots is especially strong in Japan, where robot companions are used routinely in elder care facilities. Turkle acknowledges that robots can provide comfort and break isolation, but her own sensibilities coincide with those of a child in one of her studies who commented, "Don't we have people to do that?" She found that both children and older adults suggest that robots can be more dependable than people, and she worries that humans are not present enough to each other. She also worries that interactions with robots can become preferable to human–human interaction because robots are less complex than people.

Turkle (2011) is equally unenthusiastic about our thoroughly networked lives, which she describes as "always wirelessly connected" and "living full-time on the net" (pp. 151–152). She tells one story of attending a memorial service where attendees were using the memorial service program to hide their cell phones while they texted during the service. She suggests that our communication devices create new freedoms and pleasures but also create compulsions to use them. Turkle (2011) also writes about the part of human life lived in virtual space, creating virtual selves in Second Life, playing computer games, and interacting on social networking sites, suggesting that "we have moved from multi-tasking to multi-lifing" (p. 160), sometimes creating new selves to share in virtual environments. She is concerned about what is happening to human societies as people live in a "continual world of partial attention" (p. 160) and concludes that we have to find a way to live with the seductive technologies we have created and make them work to support our values and goals.

Ray Kurzweil emphasizes that we develop technologies to extend our capabilities. This is especially true in the rapidly expanding field of assistive technology. *Assistive technology* is technology developed and used to assist individuals with disabilities to perform functions that might otherwise be difficult or impossible. A tremendous variety of assistive technology is available today, including technology to assist with mobility, visual, hearing, and cognitive impairment; computer accessibility technology; and personal emergency response systems. Assistive technology can be as low-tech as colorful Post-it notes to serve as visual reminders for students who struggle with attention and organization or as high-tech as assistive robots for people with mobility impairments. Unfortunately, many of these technologies are quite expensive at this time and beyond the reach of most people.

HEALING ENVIRONMENTS

By many accounts, Roger Ulrich (1984) was the first researcher to measure the effects of the physical environment on physical health of hospital patients. He studied patients who had undergone gall bladder surgery and had different views out their hospital windows. One group had views of a brown brick wall, and the other group had views of a small stand of trees. The patients who had views of the trees left the hospital almost a day sooner than the patients with views of a brick wall. They also required less pain medication, received fewer negative comments from the nurses, and had slightly fewer postoperative complications.

The idea that nature is important to healing is not new; indeed, it has been around for thousands of years (Sternberg, 2009). There is a long tradition in architecture that proposes a connection of health with nature and building design (Joye, 2007). In the 19th century, hospitals were built with large windows, even skylights, and often in beautiful natural settings (Joye, 2007; Sternberg, 2009). Clinics and hospitals were particularly designed to take advantage of natural light because it was thought that sunlight could heal. Some public health scholars argue, however, that as medical technology became more sophisticated, hospital design began to focus more on care of the equipment than on care of the patient (Maller et al., 2005; Sternberg, 2009). These public health scholars are calling attention to biomedical research that links physical environments and human health.

Based on his early research, Roger Ulrich (2006), a behavioral scientist, has collaborated with architects, environmental psychologists, and public and private agencies and foundations to develop a field called *evidence-based design*, which uses physiological and health-outcome measures to evaluate the health benefits of hospital design features. Following on the earlier work of Ulrich, researchers use such measures as length of stay; amount of pain medication; rates of health complications; and patient satisfaction, stress, and mood to evaluate design innovations. By 2006, 700 rigorous studies had been identified (Ulrich, 2006), and the Center for Health Design had been established to engage in ongoing hospital design innovations and evaluations. Two foci of this research are discussed here: noise and sunlight.

A great deal of international research has focused on hospital noise as an impediment to healing. This research consistently finds that hospital noise has continued to increase over the past 50 years and exceeds the guidelines recommended by the World Health Organization (Eggerston, 2012). Hospital noise comes from a variety of sources, for example, overhead paging, moving of bedrails, medical equipment, and staff shift changes. The problem is exacerbated in hospitals that have hard, sound-reflecting floors and ceilings. It is also intensified in multibed rooms because of the activity of caring for multiple patients. Noise has been associated with high blood pressure and elevated heart rates, sleep loss, slower recovery from heart attack, and negative physiological responses such as apnea and fluctuations in blood pressure and oxygen saturation in infants in neonatal intensive care (Brown, 2009; Eggerston, 2012; Ulrich, 2006). Preterm infants exposed to prolonged high levels of noise are at risk for hearing loss, impaired brain development, and speech and language problems (Brown, 2009). Excessive noise also contributes to staff fatigue (Eggerston, 2012). A number of design innovations have been found to be effective in reducing hospital noise. These include single-bed rooms, replacing overhead paging with a noiseless system, covering neonatal incubators with blankets, and installing high-performance sound-absorbing ceiling tiles and floor carpets (Brown, 2009; Ulrich, 2006). These innovations have been found to be related to improved health outcomes and fewer rehospitalizations for patients as well as improved staff satisfaction and home sleep quality (Sternberg, 2009).

There is also growing evidence that 19th-century hospital designers were accurate in their belief that sunlight can heal. Beauchemin and Hays (1998) found that patients recovering from heart attacks in sunny hospital rooms had significantly shorter hospital stays than patients recovering in rooms without natural light. Another research team studied patients recovering from spinal surgery in one hospital and compared the experiences of patients in sunny rooms with the experiences of patients in rooms without sunlight. Patients in sunny rooms took 22% less pain medication and had 21% lower medication costs than similar patients recovering in rooms without sunlight (Walch, Day, & Kang, 2005). The patients in the sunny rooms also reported less stress than patients in the rooms without sunlight.

CRITICAL THINKING Questions 6.4

How might social workers incorporate ecotherapy into their practice in different settings? How do you think social workers should be involved with environmental or ecological justice, if at all? Do you consider yourself a proponent or critic of rapid advancements in information and communication technologies? Are you as optimistic as Ray Kurzweil? Why or why not? Are you as pessimistic as Sherry Turkle? Why or why not?

PLACE ATTACHMENT

Have you ever been strongly attached to a specific place—a beloved home, a particular beach or mountain spot, or a house of worship? **Place attachment**—the process in which people and groups form bonds with places—is the subject of a growing literature (Lewicka, 2011). Recent research on place attachment conceptualizes it as a multidimensional phenomenon involving person, place, and psychological process of attachment (Scannell & Gifford, 2010a). In terms of *person*, researchers explore how place attachment occurs at both the individual and group levels. At the individual level, place attachment develops out of personally important experiences. At the group level, attachment develops out of symbolic meanings shared by a group. In the context of place attachment, *place* is defined as a "space that has been given meaning through personal, group, or cultural processes" (Low & Altman, 1992, p. 5).

When a strong place attachment develops, it has been suggested that the place has become an important part of the self, that we can't think of who we are without some reference to the place (Rollero & Piccoli, 2010). When a particular place becomes an important part of our self-identity, this merger of place and self is known as **place identity**. Place attachment and place identity have been found to occur at several levels, including home, workplace, community, municipality, region, country, and continent (Lewicka, 2011). Place identity can develop where there is strong negative, as well as positive, place attachment, resulting in negative views of the self.

Much of the research on place attachment has focused on the social aspects of the attachment, suggesting that we become attached to places because of the satisfying social relationships we experience in those places. Some researchers have begun to examine attachment to physical places, particularly to places in the natural environment. They are particularly interested in how attachment to places in nature affects behavior toward the natural environment (Cheng & Monroe, 2012; Collado, Staats, & Corraliza, 2013). One research team (Scannell & Gifford, 2010b; 2013) found that attachment to the natural aspects of place contributes to proenvironmental behavior, but attachment to the social aspects of place, which they called civic place attachment, does not.

Researchers have been interested in the distress and grief people experience when a place of attachment and identity is lost, particularly in situations of forced relocation (Scannell & Gifford, 2010a). We should pay particular attention to issues of place attachment and place identity when we work with immigrant and refugee families and families displaced by disaster. We should also consider the long-term consequences of early experiences, such as homelessness or frequent movement between foster homes, in which no stable place of attachment forms or that result in a negative place attachment.

HOMELESSNESS

As suggested, place attachment can be quite problematic for people without homes. In January 2012, a new definition of *homeless* was implemented by the U.S. Department of Housing and Urban Development (HUD; 2011) to delineate who is eligible for HUD-funded homeless assistance. The new definition includes the four broad categories presented in Exhibit 6.7. In general, people are homeless because they cannot find housing they can afford; there is a real scarcity of affordable housing. HUD defines housing affordability as spending no more than 30% of monthly income on housing, but according to the National Alliance to End Homelessness (NAEH; 2013a) about 12 million households in the United States pay more than 50% of their annual incomes for housing.

It is a challenge to count the exact number of homeless people, and no recent estimates of the number of homeless persons worldwide are available. In the United States, HUD requires that each community do a point-in-time count on a single night in January every other year. According to the count in January 2012, 633,782 people experience homelessness on any given night in the United States. About 38% of these are people in families and 62% are individuals. For many people, homelessness is a short-lived experience, and only about 16% of those homeless on a given night are chronically homeless (NAEH, 2013b). More than half, 62.7%, of homeless persons are male, and 37.2% are female, but 79.3% of homeless persons in families are female. About equal proportions are White, Non-Hispanic (39.5%), and Black or African American (38.1%). The remainder are of other ethnicities. That means, of course, that Black or African American persons are greatly overrepresented in the homeless population, because they make up only about 13% of the total U.S. population. By age group, 22.1% of the homeless population is younger than age 18; 23.8% is 18 to 30; 35.8% is 31 to 50; 15.5% is 51 to 61; and 2.9% is 62 and older.

Place attachment can be quite problematic for people without homes.

NAEH has special concern about four groups of homeless persons: families, youth, veterans, and those who are chronically homeless (NAEH, 2013a). The reason for family homelessness is usually an unforeseen financial crisis such as a medical emergency or death in the family. Most homeless families are able to bounce back from homelessness with little public assistance, but they may need rent assistance, help finding permanent housing, or job assistance. Family conflict such as divorce, or neglect or abuse, is the most common reason youth become homeless. There is special concern about LGBTQ youth who become homeless because of family abuse or rejection. About 13% of homeless persons are veterans, who are often homeless because of war-related disabilities. Those counted among the chronic homeless either are homeless long-term or experience repeated bouts of homelessness. They often live in shelters and consume a large portion of the available homeless services. They are more likely than other homeless persons to have severe physical and mental health challenges.

The cost of homelessness can be quite high. When they become hospitalized, homeless people require, on average, 4 more days in the hospital than nonhomeless people. Homeless people are increasingly spending time

EXHIBIT 6.7 • Categories in the U.S. Department of Housing and Urban Development Definition of Homeless

1. People who are living in a place not meant for human habitation, in emergency shelter, in transitional housing, or are exiting an institution where they have temporarily resided for up to 90 days.
2. People who are losing their primary nighttime residence, which may include a motel or hotel or a doubled-up situation, within 14 days and lack resources or support networks to remain in housing.
3. Families with children or unaccompanied youth who are unstably housed and likely to continue in that state.
4. People who are fleeing or attempting to flee domestic violence, have no other residence, and lack the resources or support networks to obtain other permanent housing.

SOURCE: U.S. Department of Housing and Urban Development, 2011.

in jail or prison, often for violating regulations against loitering, sleeping in cars, or begging. Emergency shelter is a costly way to house people. Research indicates that providing chronically homeless persons with permanent supportive housing is less costly than current arrangements when medical, correctional, and shelter costs are considered (NAEH, 2013c).

ACCESSIBLE ENVIRONMENTS FOR PERSONS WITH DISABILITIES

In recent years, we have been reminded that environments, particularly built environments, can be disabling because of their inaccessibility to many persons, including most people with mobility and visual disabilities. Ben Watson provides us with several examples of how the physical environment curtailed his activity at times, and he is now in a professional position to try to minimize the barriers people with disabilities experience in the world. The *social model of disability* emphasizes the barriers people with impairments face as they interact with the physical and social world, arguing that disability is a result of the relationship between the individual and the environment (see Martin, 2013).

This way of thinking about disability was the impetus for development of the Disabled Peoples' International (2013) in 1981, a network of national organizations that promotes the rights of people with disabilities worldwide. In the United States, the social model of disability led to legislation at all levels of government during the 1970s and 1980s, most notably two pieces of federal legislation. The Rehabilitation Act of 1973 (Pub. L. No. 93-112) was the first federal act to recognize the need for civil rights protection for persons with disabilities. It required all organizations receiving federal assistance to have an affirmative action plan to ensure accessibility of employment to persons with disabilities. The Americans with Disabilities Act of 1990 (ADA) (Pub. L. No. 101-336) extended the civil rights of persons with disabilities to the private sector. It seeks to end discrimination against persons with disabilities and promote their full participation in society. The social model of disability was also the driving force behind the United Nations Convention on the Rights of Persons with Disabilities that entered into force in May 2008 (United Nations Enable, 2013).

The five titles of the ADA seek to eliminate environmental barriers to the full participation of persons with disabilities. You will want to be aware of the legal rights of your clients with disabilities. Ben Watson has discovered that, in spite of the law, he still encounters many physical barriers to his full participation in society.

- Title I addresses discrimination in the workplace. It requires reasonable accommodations, including architectural modification, for disabled workers.
- Title II requires that all public services, programs, and facilities, including public transportation, be accessible to persons with disabilities.
- Title III requires all public accommodations and services operated by private organizations to be accessible to persons with disabilities. It specifically lists 12 categories of accommodations: hotels and places of lodging; restaurants; movies and theaters; auditoriums and places of public gathering; stores and banks; health care service providers, hospitals, and pharmacies; terminals for public transportation; museums and libraries; parks and zoos; schools; senior centers and social service centers; and places of recreation.
- Title IV requires all intrastate and interstate phone companies to develop telecommunication relay services and devices for persons with speech or hearing impairments to allow them to communicate in a manner similar to that of persons without impairments.
- Title V covers technical guidelines for enforcing the ADA.

Under industrial capitalism, wages are the primary source of livelihood. People who cannot earn wages, therefore, tend to be poor. Around the world, people with disabilities are less likely than other people to be employed. In 2012, the unemployment rate in the United States for people with disabilities was 13.4%, compared with 7.9% for people without a disability (U.S. Bureau of Labor Statistics, 2013a). People with disabilities who lobbied for passage of the ADA argued that government was spending vast sums of money for what they called "dependency programs" but was failing to make the investments required to make environments accessible so that people with disabilities could become employed (Roulstone, 2004).

Social workers need to keep in mind the high prevalence of disabilities among older persons, the fastest growing group in the United States. More accessible environments may be an important way to buffer the expected deleterious effects of a large elderly population. As the baby boomers age, they will benefit from the earlier activism of the disability community. Exhibit 6.8 lists some of the elements of environmental design that

EXHIBIT 6.8 • Elements of Accessible Environments for Persons With Disabilities

- Create some close-in parking spaces widened to 8 feet to accommodate unloading of wheelchairs (1 accessible space for every 25 spaces).
- Create curb cuts or ramping for curbs, with 12 inches of slope for every inch of drop in the curb.
- Make ramps at least 3 feet wide to accommodate wheelchairs and provide a 5-by-5-foot square area at the top of ramps to entrances to allow space for door opening.
- Remove high-pile carpeting, low-density carpeting, and plush carpeting, at least in the path of travel. Put nonslip material on slippery floors.
- Avoid phone-in security systems in entrances (barriers for persons who are deaf).
- Make all doorways at least 32 inches wide (36 is better).
- Use automatic doors or doors that take no more than 5 pounds of force to open.
- Use door levers instead of doorknobs.
- Create aisles that are at least 3 feet wide (wider is better). Keep the path of travel clear.
- Connect different levels in buildings with ramps (for small level changes) or a wheelchair-accessible elevator.
- Place public phones no higher than 48 inches off the ground (35–42 is optimal).
- Place other things that need to be reached at this optimal height.
- Create brightly light foyers and areas with directories to assist persons with low vision. Use 3-inch-high lettering in directories.
- Install Braille signs about 5 feet off the ground.
- Make restroom stalls at least 3 feet deep by 4 feet wide (5 feet by 5 feet is optimal).
- Install toilets that are 17–19 inches in height. Provide grab bars at toilets.
- Hang restroom sinks with no vanity underneath, so that persons in wheelchairs can pull up to them.
- Avoid having low seats, and provide arm supports and backrests on chairs.
- Apply nonslip finish to tubs and showers. Install grab bars in tubs and showers.
- Use both visual and audible emergency warning systems.

SOURCES: Based on Brawley (2006); M. Johnson (1992).

improve accessibility for persons with disabilities. It is important to remember, however, that rapid developments in assistive technology are likely to alter current guidelines about what is optimal environmental design. For example, the minimum space requirements in the ADA's guidelines for wheelchairs are already too tight for the new styles of motorized wheelchairs like the one used by Ben Watson.

CRITICAL THINKING Questions 6.5

What do you think happens to place attachment among homeless persons? How easy would it be for Ben Watson to visit your home, your favorite restaurant, or your classroom? Explain.

IMPLICATIONS FOR SOCIAL WORK PRACTICE

This discussion of culture and the physical environment suggests several professional principles of action.

- Recognize the categories of knowledge—social science theories and orientations, folk or common everyday theories and orientations—that you rely on to understand human behavior in the social environment.
- Embrace the traditions, customs, values, and behaviors of disparate groups identified by race, ethnicity, sexual orientation, gender, physical differences, age, nationality, and religion. Avoid approaching these groups in a cookbook, stereotyped, or one-size-fits-all fashion.
- Examine culture through the lens of the practice orientation using a "strengths" and person-in-environment perspective that allows you to assess the simultaneous forces of history, social structure, human agency, and

the political context in which all of these forces work themselves out in the lives of your clients.

- Pay attention to processes of cultural change, including assimilation, accommodation, acculturation, and bicultural socialization, in the lives of individuals and groups with whom you work.
- Work to ensure that members of nondominant groups have a significant say in how cultural change proceeds.
- Assess the physical environment of your social service setting. Do clients find it accessible, legible, and comfortable? Do they find that it provides adequate privacy and control? Does it provide optimal quality and intensity of sensory stimulation? If it is a residential setting, does it promote social interaction?
- Routinely evaluate the physical environments of clients—particularly those environments where problem behaviors occur. Check your evaluation against clients' perceptions. If you have no opportunity to see these environments, have clients evaluate them for you. Provide space on the intake form for assessing the physical environments of clients.
- Know the physical environments of the organizations to which you refer clients. Assist referral agencies and clients in planning how to overcome any existing environmental barriers. Maximize opportunities for client input into design of their built environments.
- Keep the benefits of the natural environment in mind when planning both prevention and remediation programs. When possible, help clients gain access to elements of the natural environment, and where appropriate, help them plan activities in the natural environment.
- Become familiar with technology for adapting environments to make them more accessible.

KEY TERMS

accommodation (cultural), 171
acculturation, 171
assimilation (cultural), 170
behavior settings theories, 176
bicultural socialization, 171
biophilia, 179
built environment, 180
common sense, 168
control theories, 173
crowding, 175
cultural hegemony, 168
cultural innovation, 166
cultural relativism, 164
culture, 161
culture of poverty, 167
customs, 169
density, 175
ecocritical theories, 176
ecotherapy, 179
ethnocentrism, 166
natural environment, 177
norms, 161
personal space, 173
place attachment, 183
place identity, 183
postmodernism, 165
practice orientation, 167
race, 165
stimulation theories, 172
symbol, 166
technology, 181
territoriality, 174
tradition, 169

ACTIVE LEARNING

1. *The cultural construction of schooling.* Compare and contrast Stan's and Tina's experiences at Community High School with your own high school experience, considering the following themes:

    - Material and behavioral cultural symbols
    - Processes of cultural change (assimilation, accommodation, acculturation, bicultural socialization)
    - Ways in which race, ethnicity, social class, and gender play out in the school setting
    - Cultural conflict

    Next, imagine that you spend a day as a student at Community High, and Stan and Tina spend a day at your high school. How do you think you might react to the cultural symbols at Community High? How might Stan and Tina react to the cultural symbols at your high school? How do you account for these reactions?

2. Sitting with a small group of classmates, imagine that Ben Watson is visiting your community for the weekend. Your group would like to take him out to dinner. Working together, develop a list of questions that you will want to ask of restaurant managers about their accessibility for Ben to dine there. Now, each of you get out your cell phone and call one of your favorite restaurants and go through your list of questions. What did you learn?

3. *Theory analysis and application.* It might be said that the social constructionist perspective discussed in Chapter 2 is the most useful perspective for understanding culture. Working in small groups, review the big ideas of the social constructionist presented in Exhibit 2.9. Giving specific examples, discuss how these big ideas are reflected, or not, in the discussion of culture found in this chapter. Do you see big ideas from other perspectives as presented in Exhibit 2.9 as helpful for thinking about Stan and Tina at Community High School? Explain.

WEB RESOURCES

Academy of Neuroscience for Architecture

www.anfarch.org

Site contains information about the academy and its projects, upcoming workshops on neuroscience and specific design environments, and links to neuroscience and architecture organizations.

American Association of People With Disabilities

www.aapd.com

Site maintained by the American Association of People With Disabilities, a national nonprofit cross-disability organization, contains information on benefits, information on disability rights, news, and links to other disability-related sites.

The Center for Health Design

www.healthdesign.org

Site maintained by the Center for Health Design, a research and advocacy organization committed to using architectural design to transform health care settings into healing environments.

Critical Multicultural Pavilion

www.edchange.org/multicultural

Site maintained by Paul C. Gorski at Hamline University contains resources, research, awareness activities, and links to multicultural topics.

International Journal of Multicultural Education

http://ijme-journal.org/index.php/ijme

A peer-reviewed open-access e-journal published by Eastern University, St. Davids, Pennsylvania, site includes articles on multicultural education for an international audience.

Environmental Justice

https://www.epa.gov/environmentaljustice

Site maintained by the U.S. Environmental Protection Agency contains special topics on environmental justice, action agendas, resources, laws and regulations, and news and events.

Job Accommodation Network

www.jan.wvu.edu

Site maintained by the Job Accommodation Network of the Office of Disability Employment Policy of the U.S. Department of Labor contains ADA statutes, regulations, guidelines, technical sheets, and other assistance documents.

National Alliance to End Homelessness

www.endhomelessness.org

Site contains facts about and policy issues related to homeless families, chronic homelessness, rural homelessness, homeless youth, homeless veterans, domestic violence, and mental health and physical health; also contains case studies and best practices for ending homelessness.

SAGE edge™ Sharpen your skills with SAGE edge at edge.sagepub.com/hutchisoness2e

SAGE edge for students provides a personalized approach to help you accomplish your coursework goals in an easy-to-use learning environment. watch listen read

LEARNING OBJECTIVES	FOR FURTHER EXPLORATION AND APPLICATION
LO 6.1: Compare and contrast one's emotional and cognitive reactions to two case studies.	Culture and the Physical Environment
LO 6.2: Describe ways that culture has been defined over time.	Madness in Civilization: A Cultural History of Insanity
LO 6.3: Summarize mechanisms by which culture is maintained and changed over time.	How Culture Drives Behaviors
LO 6.4: Summarize four categories of theories about the relationship between the physical environment and human behavior (stimulation, control, behavior settings, and ecocritical).	The Place of Place in Social Work: Rethinking the Person-in-Environment Model
LO 6.5: Give examples of the benefits and costs of time spent in the natural environment.	The Role of the Built Environment in Healthy Aging: Community Design, Physical Activity, and Health Among Older Adults
LO 6.6: Give examples of the impact of the built environment on human behavior.	Repositioning Identity in Conceptualizations of Human–Place Bonding
LO 6.7: Recognize the role of place attachment in human behavior.	Place Attachment and Meaning
LO 6.8: Suggest policy options for the social problem of homelessness.	You're Homeless ... Now What?
LO 6.9: Demonstrate an ability to evaluate specific built environments for their accessibility for people with disabilities	Why Disability and Poverty Still Go Hand-in-Hand 25 Years After Landmark Law
LO 6.10: Apply knowledge of culture and the relationship between the physical environment and human behavior to recommend guidelines for social work assessment and intervention.	The Four Ways Sound Affects Us

Families

Elizabeth D. Hutchison

Learning Objectives

LO 7.1 Analyze one's emotional and cognitive reactions to a case study.

LO 7.2 Analyze the merits of different approaches to defining family.

LO 7.3 Compare and contrast five theoretical perspectives for understanding families (psychodynamic, family systems, feminist, family stress and coping, and family resilience).

LO 7.4 Identify a number of types of diversity in family life that might be encountered by social workers.

LO 7.5 Analyze three types of challenges to family life (family violence, divorce, and substance abuse).

LO 7.6 Apply knowledge of family theories, family diversity, and family challenges to recommend guidelines for social work assessment and intervention.

GET MORE OUT OF YOUR STUDY TIME.

The **SAGE Interactive eBook** provides one-click access to integrated study tools that will enrich your understanding of course content.

- **Watch** video clips to learn actively
- **Think Critically** with SAGE Journals
- **Explore Further** with SAGE Reference
- **Connect** with relevant web resources
- **Listen** to podcasts for real-world context

CASE STUDY

THE SHARPE FAMILY'S POSTDEPLOYMENT ADJUSTMENT

Bobby Sharpe's U.S. Army National Guard unit was deployed to Iraq in 2004 and to Afghanistan in 2010. Bobby suffered a relatively minor physical injury in Iraq and still has occasional nightmares about his tour in Afghanistan. He feels lucky, however, that he and his family have not suffered some of the traumatic postwar aftermath he has seen in the families of some members of his Guard unit.

Bobby Sharpe is a 40-year-old African American man who lives in a small southwestern town. He has been married to Vivian for 17 years, and they have a 16-year-old daughter, Marcie, and a 7-year-old son, Caleb, who has cerebral palsy. Back when Bobby finished high school, he served in the army for 4 years. He received some good training, enjoyed making friends with people from diverse backgrounds, and had two tours overseas but never served in a war zone. After 4 years, he was eager to return home to be near his close-knit family. Soon after returning home, he ran into Vivian, who had grown up in his neighborhood, and they were soon spending a lot of time together. A year later, they were married, and a year after that, Marcie was born.

Bobby wasn't sure what work he could do after he left the army, but a few months after he returned home, he got in touch with a high school friend who was working as a heating and air conditioning technician. After another technician was fired, Bobby got a job where his friend worked, and his friend helped him learn the technical aspects of the heating and air conditioning business. When Marcie was born, Vivian cared for her at home and also cared for her sister's small children while her sister, a single mother, worked. When Bobby's father had an automobile accident and had to miss work for 6 months, Bobby and Vivian provided some financial aid to Bobby's mother and younger siblings while his father was out of work. Finances were tight, and Bobby and Vivian were afraid they would not be able to keep up the mortgage on their house, which was a source of great pride to them. Bobby decided to join the army National Guard to bring in some extra money. He also looked forward to the type of camaraderie he had experienced in the army. He went to drills one weekend per month and took time off from work for a 2-week training each year. His unit was mobilized on two occasions to assist with floods in the state. The extra money helped to stabilize the family economics, and he enjoyed the friendships he developed, even though only one other person in his unit was from his small town. When Marcie entered public school, Vivian took a job in the cafeteria at her school, which allowed Bobby and Vivian to start a college fund for Marcie.

Bobby grew up in a close-knit family that included his mother and father and three younger sisters, as well as a maternal grandmother who lived with them. Several aunts, uncles, and cousins lived nearby. Both parents were hardworking people, and they created a happy home. Bobby's grandmother provided child care when the children were small and helped to keep the household running smoothly.

Vivian grew up a few blocks from Bobby. Her father died in Vietnam a few months before she was born, and her mother moved her two daughters back to the town where she had grown up. She struggled to raise her two daughters while working two jobs, with some help from her mother, who lived in town but also worked two jobs. Vivian was lucky that a neighborhood couple became her godparents and played an active role in her life. This couple was never able to have children of their own, and they were happy to include Vivian in their leisure activities. Vivian often turned to them for support and encouragement, and she continues to consider them family.

During Bobby's deployment to Iraq, Vivian and Marcie were able to get along fine, with the love and support of Bobby's family; Vivian's mother, sister, and godparents; and Bobby's boss. They missed Bobby and worried about him, but Marcie was very good about picking up more responsibilities to help Vivian with the chores usually performed by Bobby. When the furnace broke, Bobby's boss was generous about doing the repair. One of Bobby's sisters helped Vivian juggle taking Marcie to her afterschool activities and picking her up. Bobby was injured by shrapnel in his last week in Iraq and spent 2 weeks in the hospital in the nearest city when he returned home. The family and friends network took care of Marcie while Vivian juggled trips to the hospital with her work schedule.

But things were more complicated when Bobby was deployed to Afghanistan. Bobby's beloved grandmother had had a stroke 2 years before this deployment, and his mother and father were working opposite shifts at the local nursing home so that someone was always home to care for her. Bobby's aunts, uncles, and cousins were taking turns providing a few hours of care so that his mom and dad could get a break and run errands. One of Bobby's sisters had stayed in the city after she completed college and had a busy life there. Another sister, a single mother of a 2-year-old daughter, was serving in the army in Iraq when Bobby left for Afghanistan. Her daughter was living with Bobby and Vivian while she was deployed. Bobby and Vivian's son Caleb is the joy of the family, but he requires extra care. While Bobby was deployed, Vivian's mother moved in with Vivian and cared for Caleb and the 2-year-old niece during the day while Vivian worked and then turned their care over to Vivian so that she could do a 6-hour shift caring for an older woman with dementia. To help stabilize the family finances, Vivian accepted the offer to take a supervisory position in the school department's lunch program. She was excited about the new responsibilities, but the demands of the new job were often too much during a time of great family upheaval. Vivian was especially concerned about monitoring Marcie's afterschool activities now that she was approaching adolescence, but her godparents were a great help with that, just as they had been for Vivian during her adolescent years. Vivian had heard that the National Guard had family support groups, but there was nothing in the small town where she lives. Vivian did reach out to the women's group at her church, who provided emotional support as well as occasional meals and transportation for Marcie. Marcie and Caleb missed their dad, and Marcie worried a lot about his safety, especially during the weeks when they did not know his whereabouts.

Bobby returned from Afghanistan with no physical injuries, but his best friend from the Guard lost a leg to a roadside bomb. When Bobby came home, Vivian, Marcie, and Caleb were thrilled and were eager to pick up life where they left off. Bobby wanted to spend a lot of time by himself, however, and Vivian realized that he was having trouble sleeping, sometimes had nightmares, and was easily startled by loud noises. She did some research on the Internet and decided that she needed to give Bobby time to readjust. She did her best to help Marcie and Caleb understand this also. She was pleased, but also worried, when Bobby began to go for long walks and to spend time with a new puppy. After 4 months, Bobby was able to talk about the guilt he felt about surviving when other Guard members had died. He gradually began to be more like his old self and was happy to get back to work. He still makes time to spend with his friend who lost a leg in Afghanistan. He and Vivian are preparing for, but dreading, the day when Marcie will leave for college.

FAMILY DEFINED

We know that families are one of the key institutions in almost every society, past and present. Perhaps no other relationships contribute as much to our identity and have such pervasive influence on all dimensions of our lives as our family relationships (Floyd & Morman, 2006). Families address personal needs, but they also contribute to the public welfare by caring for each other and developing responsible members of society (Newman, 2012).

Families in every culture address similar societal needs, but there are many variations in family structure, family customs, and power arrangements. Around the globe, families are expected to provide economic security, emotional support, and a place in society for each family member; they also fulfill the critical social roles of bearing, providing for, and socializing children and youth. Families respond to these challenges in different ways, due in no small part to different cultures and different political and economic circumstances. Family situations and their access to resources differ as a function of their socioeconomic location. Social, cultural, and economic globalization is changing families in the United States and around the world (Gardiner & Kosmitzki, 2011; Leeder, 2004).

So what is a family? We were all born into some sort of family and may have created a similar or different sort of family. Take a break from reading and think about who is family to you. Who is in your family, and what functions does your family perform for you? We hear a lot of talk about family and family values, but family means different things to different people. Even family scholars struggle to define how family is different from other social groups. White, Klein, and Martin (2015d) suggest that family differs from other social groups in degree only. They suggest that nonfamily groups such as friend networks and coworkers often have some of the same properties as families but usually to a lesser degree. Family research is hampered by the lack of consensus about how to define family (Baxter & Braithwaite, 2006).

The family literature includes many definitions of family, but the many definitions center on three ways to form a family: biologically, legally, or socially (Floyd & Morman, 2006; Lepoire, 2006). *Biologically*, family refers to people related by blood and genetically bound to each other, however distantly. Examples of biological family relationships include parents, children, aunts, uncles, second cousins, grandparents, and great-grandparents. Families are created *legally* by marriage, adoption, or formalized fostering. There are many ways that families can be created *socially* when there is no biological or legal relationship. Sometimes neighbors, godparents, or longtime friends are considered family. These have been called fictive kin, but I prefer to refer to them as chosen family. Vivian Sharpe clearly thinks of her godparents as family, and they have come to be family for Marcie as well. Family is increasingly being created by cohabiting romantic partners of either opposite sexes or the same sex. Family may also be created by informal fostering.

Definitions of family include different configurations of biological, legal, and social relationships. Exhibit 7.1 provides a selection of definitions developed by family scholars in the United States, as well as the definition used by the U.S. Census Bureau. It is very difficult to develop one definition that includes all forms of families, but family scholars have attempted to develop inclusive definitions. As you can see, the Census Bureau definition includes families formed biologically and legally but not those formed socially without legal sanction. Think about what types of family would not be considered family by this definition. In contrast to the Census Bureau, the definitions of family scholars Baxter and Braithwaite (2006); Galvin, Bylund, and Brommel (2003); and Seccombe and Warner (2004) include families formed socially along with families formed biologically and legally. Leeder (2004) goes even further with a purely social definition of family. Which of these definitions is the best fit for who you call family?

How do the definitions fit for Bobby and Vivian Sharpe's family? The Census Bureau definition would certainly include Bobby, Vivian, Marcie, and Caleb. It also could embrace Vivian's mother when she lived in the household during Bobby's deployment to Afghanistan. Did it still include Bobby while he was deployed and not living in the household? It is clear that he and other family members still thought of him as family. But what about Bobby's 2-year-old niece? Was she family in the time she spent in the household? Could Vivian sign permission forms if she needed medical care? Who do you think Bobby, Vivian, Marcie, and Caleb consider to be family? How would they define family?

For the purposes of our discussion, I will use the Baxter and Braithwaite (2006) definition of family: **Family** is "a social group of two or more persons, characterized by ongoing interdependence with long-term commitments that stem from blood, law, or affection" (p. 2). Increasingly, we exercise the freedom to use the word *family* to describe the social group with whom we have emotional closeness (a social definition). However, our freedom to define our own families is limited (Newman, 2012). We must interact with organizations that have their own definitions of family and sometimes have the power to impose those definitions on us. Local, state, and federal governments have definitions of family and also have the power to enforce those definitions when providing goods, services, and legal sanctions. Examples include legal standards about who can marry, who inherits from whom, who can benefit from filing joint tax returns, who receives survivor benefits, and who can make medical decisions for another person.

In the United States and many other countries, the most contentious and public struggle over definitions of family involve families formed by same-sex couples. As social workers, we should be most interested in whom a person considers to be family, because that is where social resources can be tapped, but we must also be alert to situations where legal definitions do not recognize a given form of family.

In the United States, *monogamy*, or partnering with one spouse at a time, is the legal way to start a biological family. But anthropologists estimate that 75% of the world's societies prefer some type of *polygamy*, or having more than one spouse at a time (Newman, 2012). Polygamy can take the form of either polygyny (one man and multiple wives) or polyandry (one woman and multiple husbands). Polyandry is much less common than polygyny, however. Polygyny is found on every continent but is most common in Islamic countries, African countries, and parts of Asia (Gardiner & Kosmitzki, 2011). All societies allow monogamy, and, indeed, most people of the world cannot afford to support multiple spouses.

There are cultural variations in the process of mate selection. In most societies, mate selection is governed by both exogamy and endogamy rules. *Exogamy rules* require that mates must be chosen from *outside* the group. Most societies have either formal or informal rules prohibiting mating with specified family members, often referred to as the "incest taboo," but there are differences across cultures about which family members are prohibited. In the United States, 25 states prohibit marriage of first cousins, but 6 states allow it under some circumstances where the couple cannot reproduce, and North Carolina allows first-cousin marriage but prohibits double-cousin marriage (such as a sister and brother marrying cousins who are brother and sister; National Conference of State Legislatures, 2014). There are also some informal exogamy taboos against mating with people within other groups, such as in the same university dorm (dormcest) and with people in the workplace (workcest) (Newman, 2012). *Endogamy rules*,

EXHIBIT 7.1 • Selected Definitions of Family

SOURCE	DEFINITION
Baxter & Braithwaite (2006)	A social group of two or more persons, characterized by ongoing interdependence with long-term commitments that stem from blood, law, or affection
Galvin, Bylund, & Brommel (2003)	Networks of people who share their lives over long periods of time bound by ties of marriage, blood, or commitment, legal or otherwise, who consider themselves as family and who share a significant history and anticipated future of functioning in a family relationship
Leeder (2004)	A group of people who have intimate social relationships and have a history together
Seccombe & Warner (2004)	A relationship by blood, marriage, or affection, in which members may cooperate economically, may care for any children, and may consider identity to be intimately connected to the larger group
U.S. Census Bureau (2013e)	A group of two or more people who reside together and who are related by birth, marriage, or adoption

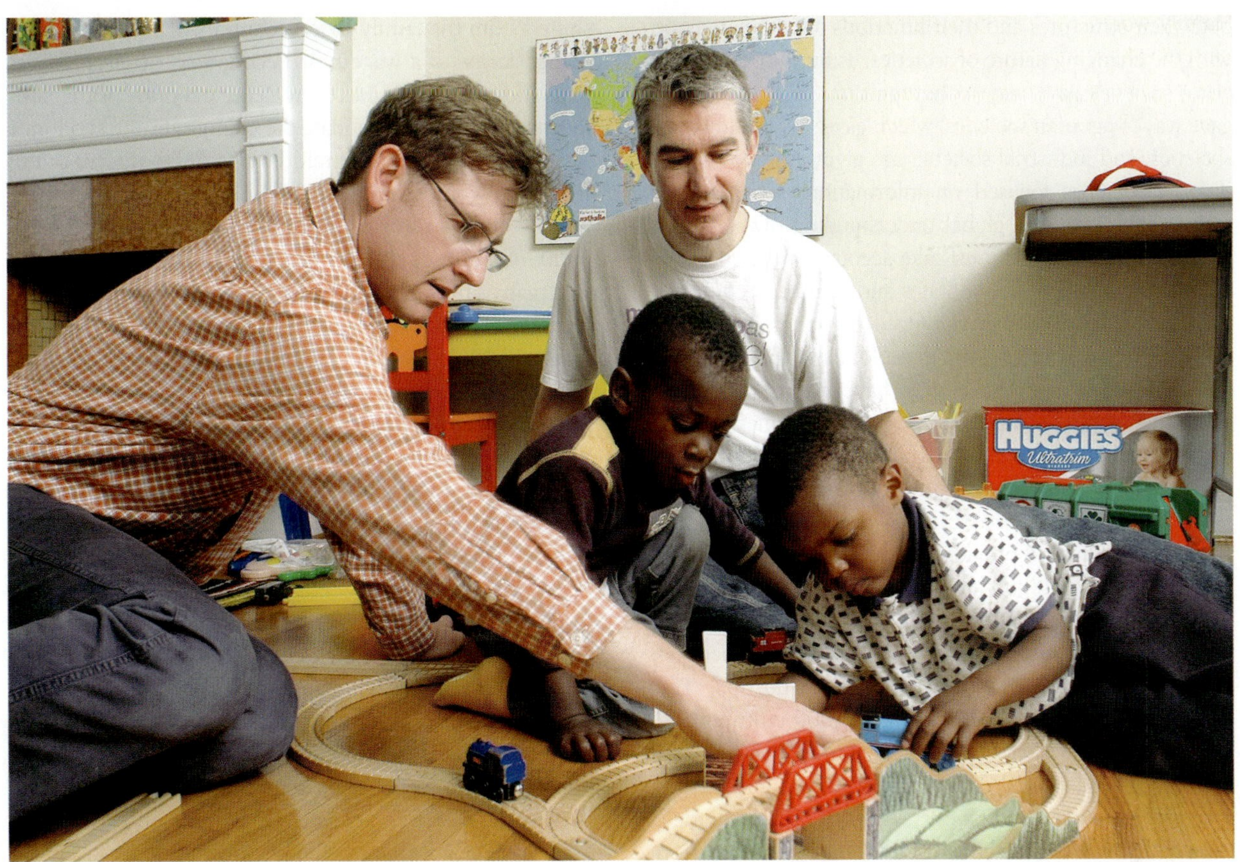

ShihWeber/SIPA/Newscom

Perhaps no other relationships contribute as much to our identity and have such pervasive influence on all dimensions of our lives as our family relationships.

on the other hand, require that mates should be selected from within the group on characteristics such as religion, race and ethnicity, and social class. Bobby and Vivian were honoring these rules when they chose each other, but endogamy rules are loosening in many places.

In the United States and other Western societies, mate selection is a culmination of romantic love, and it is often assumed that there is one true love in the world for each one of us. In many Eastern societies, marriages are arranged, and it is generally assumed that there are several possible mates with whom one can establish a successful long-term relationship. It is also assumed that parents will make wiser decisions than young people would make for themselves. In countries like Japan, however, love marriages are beginning to replace arranged marriages (Gardiner & Kosmitzki, 2011).

THE FAMILY IN HISTORICAL PERSPECTIVE

I often hear people lament the demise of the family. Maybe you hear this as well. To understand whether there is reality in this lament, it is necessary to place the contemporary family in a historical context. This is a daunting task, however. For one thing, the family has never been a monolithic institution. The structure and functions of families always varied according to race, ethnicity, religion, sexual orientation, social class, and so on. Most of what has been written about the family historically was written from the perspective of dominant members of society. It is only since the 1960s, when the discipline of social history began to describe the lives of women and other marginalized groups, that we have a more complete understanding of the variety of ways families have adapted to the challenges they've faced in their lives. When people in the United States talk about the "golden age of the traditional family," they are typically talking about one particular group of families: White, middle-class, heterosexual, two-parent families living in the 1950s. Social historians argue that the rosy picture usually painted about this group is really something that never existed. It is important to remember that a great diversity of family structures and functions has existed in the United States and around the world over time.

For another thing, in the United States, because we are a very young country, we tend to have a very short view of history. A longer-term tracing of the history of families worldwide would be the subject of multiple books. So, for the longer-term global view, I will simply note two important themes. First, it seems clear that families have adapted both their structures and their functions over time to cope with the changing nature of societies, as hunting and gathering societies gave way to horticultural societies, which gave way to agrarian societies, which gave way to industrial societies, and industrial societies are giving way to postindustrial societies focused on information, services, and technology. Second, a global understanding of the family in contemporary times must take account of the effects of colonialism. As the United States and European countries exploited local people in colonized countries, family life was directly impacted in both the colonizing and colonized countries. Most recently, families have been separated as some members relocate to find work, sometimes relocating from rural areas to cities within their own country and other times moving to wealthier countries where work is more plentiful. The case study of the Filipina domestic workers in Chapter 8 provides an example of the impact of these relocations on both families and communities.

Any discussion of the history of the family in the United States should begin with the Native peoples who predated the White settlers from Europe. The Native peoples included more than 2,000 cultures and societies, each with its own set of family customs and lifestyles (Leeder, 2004). There were some similarities across these societies, however. As with other societies, social life was organized around the family. Affection was lavished on children, who were never spanked or beaten. Children were instructed and disciplined by numerous caregivers in the extended family. There was a clear gender division of labor, with women growing crops and caring for the home and property and men hunting, fishing, and waging war. In many Native societies, however, women were afforded a great deal of respect and power (Ho, Rasheed, & Rasheed, 2004).

The White settlers established small, privately owned agricultural enterprises, and families performed many of the functions that have since been turned over to other institutions such as hospitals, schools, and social welfare agencies. David Fischer's (1989) historical analysis found regional differences in the organization of family life among the White settlers. From 1629 to 1775, four major waves of English-speaking immigrants settled in what became the United States of America. Each wave of immigrants came from a different part of what is now the United Kingdom and brought their own family customs with them. Family customs differed along several dimensions, including gender power arrangements, child-rearing practices, appropriate marriage partners, and nuclear versus extended family. Different attitudes about social inequality were also transmitted through the family. Fischer argues that in spite of later waves of immigration and much interregional mobility, these regional differences in family customs have endured to some degree over time.

During the industrial revolution, the economy of the United States and other newly industrializing nations shifted from the family-based economy of small, privately owned farms to a wage-based economic system of large-scale industrial manufacturing. The functions of the family changed to accommodate the changes in the economic system. In the upper and middle classes, men went out to work and women ran the household, but less advantaged women engaged in paid labor as well as family labor. By 1900, one fifth of U.S. women worked outside the home, and many children worked in mines, mills, and factories (Newman, 2012). The great majority of African American women engaged in paid labor, often serving as domestic servants in White households where they were forced to leave their own families and live in the employer's home. Women in other poor families took in piecework so they could earn a wage while also staying in the home. Poorer families also took in boarders to assist the family financially, something that also happened in the earlier agrarian period. Schools took over education, and family life began to be organized around segments of time: the workweek and weekends and summers off from school for children (Leeder, 2004). Rather than the center of work, the family home became a place to retreat from economic activities, and the primary role of the family was to provide emotional support to its members. A new ideal of marriage developed, based on sexual satisfaction, companionship, and emotional support. Family togetherness was never more emphasized than in the 1950s, a period of strong economic health in the United States.

Since the 1950s, personal fulfillment has become a major value in the United States and a number of other information/service/technology societies, but the great majority of people still view loving, committed relationships to be the most important source of happiness and well-being (Kamp Dush & Amato, 2005; Snyder & Lopez, 2007). Family members are often scattered across state and national lines, but the new technologies allow for continued connection. Recently, work and family time is once again comingled in many families, because the new technologies allow more work from home. Unfortunately, this often means that the workday is expanded.

As this discussion suggests, diversity of family structures is not new, but family forms have become increasingly varied in recent decades. Marriage and birthrates have declined, and more adults are living on their own. More children are born to unmarried parents. Divorce and remarriage are creating complex remarried families. Perhaps the biggest change in family structure in recent decades is the increase in dual-earner families, as women increased their involvement in paid labor (F. Walsh, 2012a).

There is general agreement that the most pronounced change in family life in the United States in the past 50 years is the change in gender roles. By 1960, one third of all workers were women (Gibbs, 2009), but employers typically paid women less than men performing the same job. In addition, women were often treated in a

Library of Congress, public domain

Families have adapted both their structures and their functions over time to cope with the changing nature of societies.

demeaning manner at work. Females were about half as likely as males to go to college, and less than 10% of students playing high school sports were girls (Gibbs, 2009). When women needed surgery or other medical treatment, they often had to secure the signed consent of husbands or fathers. In many settings, they were not allowed to wear pants in public. (For a comprehensive review of the changes in gender roles in the United States since 1960, see Collins, 2009.) By 2011, women made up 47% of the labor force, and the unemployment rate was slightly higher for men (9.4%) than for women (8.5%). In that same year, 58.1% of women were in the labor force, including 70.9% of mothers with children younger than age 18. Unmarried mothers have higher rates of labor force participation than married mothers, 74.9% compared with 69.1%. Women working full time earned 82% of what men earned in 2011, up from 62% in 1979 (U.S. Bureau of Labor Statistics, 2013b). In Bobby's family, as in many African American families, women have always been in the paid labor force, often working more than one job. In fact, research indicates that gender roles in African American families have typically been applied flexibly to manage work and family demands.

There is evidence that attitudes about women in the labor force are changing. In 1977, 74% of men and 52% of women agreed with the statement that "men should earn the money and women should take care of the children and family"; in 2008, only 40% of men and 37% of women agreed with the statement (Galinsky, Aumann, & Bond, 2011, p. 9). The attitudes of men in dual-earner couples have changed the most. In 2010, 29% of wives in dual-earning couples earned more than their spouses, compared with 18% in 1987 (U.S. Bureau of Labor Statistics, 2013b). In the 2005–2006 academic year, women earned 58% of all bachelor's degrees and 60% of master's degrees (Galinsky et al., 2011). The rate of girls participating in high school sports is also approaching that of males. In addition, women have a larger presence in the public arena, serving in leadership positions in both the private and public sectors. However, women are still underrepresented on university faculties and in boardrooms and legislatures. Although men are increasing their participation in child care and household labor, women still perform a larger share of this domestic work (Galinsky et al., 2011).

Unfortunately, business and government in the United States have been slow to respond to the changing needs of families who do not have a full-time mother at home. The Family and Medical Leave Act (FMLA) of 1993 requires employers with more than 50 employees to provide up to 12 weeks of *unpaid* leave per year for the birth or adoption of a child or to care for a sick child, parent, or spouse, excluding temporary and part-time workers. With the exemptions, about 40% of U.S. workers are not eligible for FMLA leave, but a good feature of the FMLA is that it covers both male and female workers (Ray, Gornick, & Schmitt, 2009). Compare this with the way that most other countries have responded to the increasing numbers of dual-earner families. One research project found that of 173 countries studied, 168 guarantee *paid* leave to women for childbirth and maternity, 98 countries guarantee at least 14 weeks of paid leave, and 66 guarantee paid paternity leave (Heymann, Earle, & Hayes, 2007). The combined leave employers must provide for both mothers and fathers in the five most generous countries ranges from 18 to 47 weeks. It is important to note, however, that the number of weeks of paid leave offered to fathers ranges from 2 to 7 in these same five countries (Ray et al., 2009).

Not all people in the United States agree that the changes in gender roles are a good trend. Certainly, around the world, there are many societies that have not embraced these changes, even though economic globalization has depended on the cheap labor of women in poor societies working long hours in low-wage jobs (McMichael, 2012).

CRITICAL THINKING Questions 7.1

Where have you gotten your ideas about what it means to be family? Have those ideas changed over time? If so, what influenced those changes? What beliefs do you have about appropriate gender relationships, child-rearing practices, appropriate marriage partners, and nuclear versus extended family? How might those beliefs affect your ability to work with different types of families and families facing different types of challenges?

THEORETICAL PERSPECTIVES FOR UNDERSTANDING FAMILIES

With an understanding of societal trends affecting families as background, you can use a number of theoretical lenses to understand family functioning and avenues for positive change. This section introduces five of these theoretical perspectives: the psychodynamic perspective, family systems perspective, feminist perspective, family stress and coping perspective, and family resilience perspective. The family life course perspective, also known as the family life cycle perspective, another important theoretical perspective, is discussed in Chapter 10, The Human Life Journey.

PSYCHODYNAMIC PERSPECTIVE AND FAMILIES

Psychodynamic approaches to thinking about families are a mix of ideas from psychodynamic and social systems perspectives. Social workers who approach family situations from this perspective assume that current personal and interpersonal problems are the result of unresolved problems in the **family of origin**, the family into which we were born and/or in which we were raised (Nichols & Schwartz, 2006; Walsh, 2014). They suggest that these unresolved problems continue to be acted out in our current intimate relationships. Patterns of family relationships are passed on from generation to generation, and intergenerational relationship problems must be resolved to improve current problems.

Some social workers who employ the psychodynamic perspective draw heavily on Murray Bowen's (1978) concept of differentiation of self. Bowen suggested two aspects of **differentiation of self** in the family system (see McGoldrick, Carter, & Garcia-Preto, 2011b; Walsh, 2014):

1. *Differentiation between thinking and feeling.* Family members must learn to own and recognize their feelings. But they must also learn to think about and plan their lives rather than reacting emotionally at times that call for clear thinking. It is assumed that many family problems are based on family members' emotional reactivity to each other. This aspect of differentiation is very similar to Daniel Goleman's concept of emotional intelligence, which was discussed in Chapter 4.

2. *Differentiation between the self and other members of the family.* While recognizing their interdependence with other family members, individuals should follow their own beliefs rather than make decisions based on reactivity to the cues of others or the need to win approval. They should do this, however, without attacking others or defending themselves. A clear sense of self allows them to achieve some independence while staying connected to other family members. This aspect of differentiation is similar to Howard Gardner's concept of interpersonal intelligence, also discussed in Chapter 4.

Another key concept in the psychodynamic perspective on families is triangulation. **Triangulation** occurs when two family members (a family subsystem) inappropriately involve another family member to reduce the anxiety in the dyadic relationship. For example, if a couple is having marital problems, they may focus their energy on a child's school problems to relieve the tension in the marital relationship. The child's school problems then become the stabilizing factor in the marriage, and this problem will not improve until the parents look at their relationship problem (and the origins of it in their own families of origin). In recent years, proponents of this approach have noted that it is not always another family member that gets "triangulated in." It may be an addiction, an overinvolvement in work, or an extramarital affair—all used to ease tension in a dyadic relationship.

The psychodynamic perspective has been criticized for its Anglo American emphasis on individualism versus collectivism. To some, it pathologizes the value of connectedness that prevails in some cultures. There is some merit to this criticism if the theory is misused to interpret a strong sense of familial responsibility as seen in the Sharpe family, and many ethnic minority families, to be a sign of lack of differentiation. A strong separate self is not a value in many cultures. The psychodynamic perspective can alert us, however, to any problematic triangles that emerge when the parental subsystem is expanded in times of stress, such as when a parent in the military is deployed.

If you use a psychodynamic perspective for thinking about the Sharpe family, you might want to do a multigenerational **genogram**, or a visual representation of a family's composition and structure (see Exhibit 7.2), to get a picture of the multigenerational family's patterns of relationships. (Females are indicated by circles, males by squares; lines indicate marriages and births.) The Sharpe genogram helps you to visualize the extended family relationships in Bobby Sharpe's family and Vivian's more limited extended family system in her family of origin. It may lead you to think about whether Bobby's deployments stirred unresolved grief about the loss of her father for Vivian and the loss of her husband for Vivian's mother.

FAMILY SYSTEMS PERSPECTIVE

A **family systems perspective** adds another lens—that of the family as a social system. As you might imagine, this approach requires a focus on relationships within the family rather than on individual family members. Persons are not thought of as individuals but as parts of overall patterns of roles and interactions (Galvin, Dickson, & Marrow, 2006). All parts of the family system are interconnected. Family members both affect and are affected by other family members; when change occurs for one, all are affected. Certainly, we can see that Bobby's and his sister's deployments and their grandmother's stroke affected the entire extended kinship system.

From the family systems perspective, families develop boundaries that delineate who is in the family at any given time. In the Sharpe family, the boundaries have shifted over time to cope with stressors of various kinds. Among members, families develop organizational structures and roles for accomplishing tasks, commonly shared beliefs and rules, and verbal and nonverbal communication patterns (White et al., 2015a). Like all systems, families have subsystems, such as a parental subsystem, sibling

EXHIBIT 7.2 • Sharpe Family Genogram

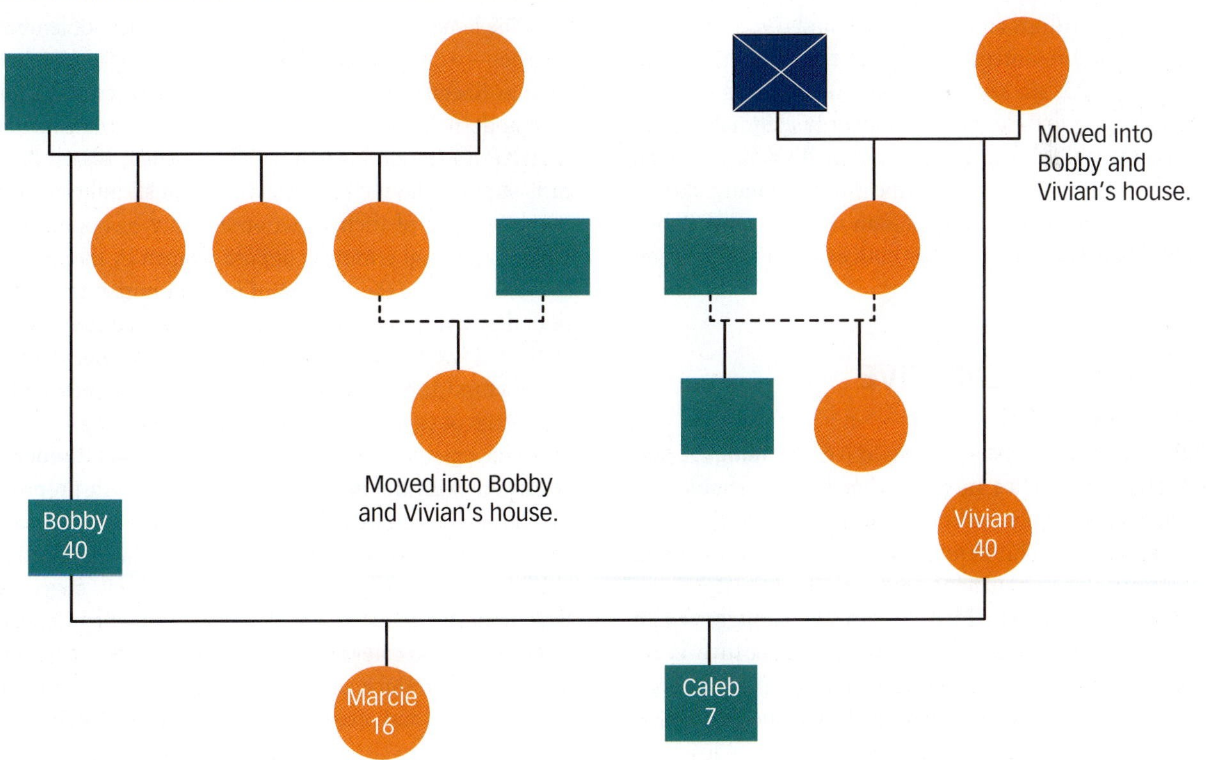

subsystem, or parent–child subsystem. When problems occur, the focus for change is the family system itself, with the assumption that changing the patterns of interaction between and among family members will address whatever problem first brought a family member to the attention of a social worker. Intervention may focus on helping to open communication across subsystems, helping the family explore the stated and unstated rules that govern interactions, or teaching members to communicate clearly with each other (Vetere, 2005; Walsh, 2014).

The **multilevel family practice model** (Vosler, 1996) widens the social worker's theoretical framework to include the larger systems in which the family system is embedded—including the neighborhood, local community, state, nation, and current global socioeconomic system. Thus, the multilevel model is broadly focused, acknowledging the economic, political, and cultural factors that affect resources available to the family and how family members view their current situation and future challenges. This model recognizes that the family institution is interrelated with other social institutions—religious, political, economic, educational, social welfare, health care, and mass media. Among other things, this perspective would call our attention to how the Sharpe family is affected by terrorism and war, global economic conditions, and health and social welfare policies related to elder care and children with disabilities. They are also influenced by mass media coverage of race issues and the U.S. involvement in war.

A *family ecomap* can be used to assess the way the Sharpe family is connected to larger social systems. The **family ecomap** uses circles, lines, and arrows to show family relationships and the strength and directional flow of energy and resources to and from the family (Hartman & Laird, 1983; see also Vosler, 1996). Ecomaps help the social worker and the family to identify external sources of stress, conflict, and social support. Exhibit 7.3 is an example of an ecomap for the Sharpe family during Bobby's deployment to Afghanistan. It shows that Bobby and Vivian's nuclear family has both external stressors and external resources.

FEMINIST PERSPECTIVE AND FAMILIES

Unlike the family systems perspective, the **feminist perspective on families** proposes that families should not be studied as whole systems, with the lens on the family level, because such attention results in failure to attend to patterns of dominance, subjugation, and oppression in families (Chibucos & Leite, 2005). As suggested in Chapter 2, the focus of the feminist perspective is on how patterns of dominance in major social institutions are tied to gender, with women devalued and oppressed. When applied to the family, the feminist perspective proposes that gender is the primary characteristic on which power is distributed and misused in the family (Allen, Lloyd, & Few, 2009). Although the Sharpe family, like many African American families, has relatively egalitarian approaches to enacting gender roles, they live in a world that gives men more power than women and are influenced by that bias. Men and women are both involved in nurturing care, but women are considered the primary caregivers. Bobby and Vivian have nieces and nephews whose fathers have taken no responsibility for their children, leaving the mothers to take full responsibility for their economic and emotional well-being.

The feminist perspective makes a distinction between sex and gender: Sex is biologically determined, but gender is socially constructed and learned from the culture. The feminist perspective questions how society came to assign male and female characteristics; seeks understanding of women's and children's perspectives on family life; analyzes how family practices create advantages for some family members and disadvantages for others; and raises questions about caregiving responsibilities in families (Wood, 2006). It argues that a diversity of family forms should be recognized and that the strengths and weaknesses of each form should be thoughtfully considered. It calls attention to the family as a site of both love and trauma (Allen et al., 2009). Although gender is the starting point of the feminist perspective, most feminist theories focus on disadvantage based on other characteristics as well, including race, ethnicity, social class, sexuality, age, religion, nationality, and ability status (Lloyd, Few, & Allen, 2009).

The feminist perspective includes a variety of feminist theories—we should speak of *feminisms*, not feminism—such as liberal, radical, interpretive, critical, cultural, and postmodern feminism. These varieties of feminism may disagree on important issues. For example, liberal feminists support the inclusion of women in all military positions, because of their focus on equality of opportunity, whereas cultural feminists oppose women in the military because they see the valuing of life and nurturing, rather than destroying, as a central part of female culture (White et al., 2015e). Bobby Sharpe's sister does not consider herself a feminist, but she is among the many women taking advantage of career opportunities in the military.

The emerging **intersectionality feminist theory** is consistent with the multidimensional approach proposed in this book. Feminists of color introduced the concept of *intersectionality* to challenge the idea that gender is a monolithic category (Collins, 2000). They suggested that no single category is sufficient to understand social oppression, and categories such as gender, race, and class intersect to produce different experiences for women of various races and classes. Bobby Sharpe's sister could

EXHIBIT 7.3 • Sharpe Family Ecomap

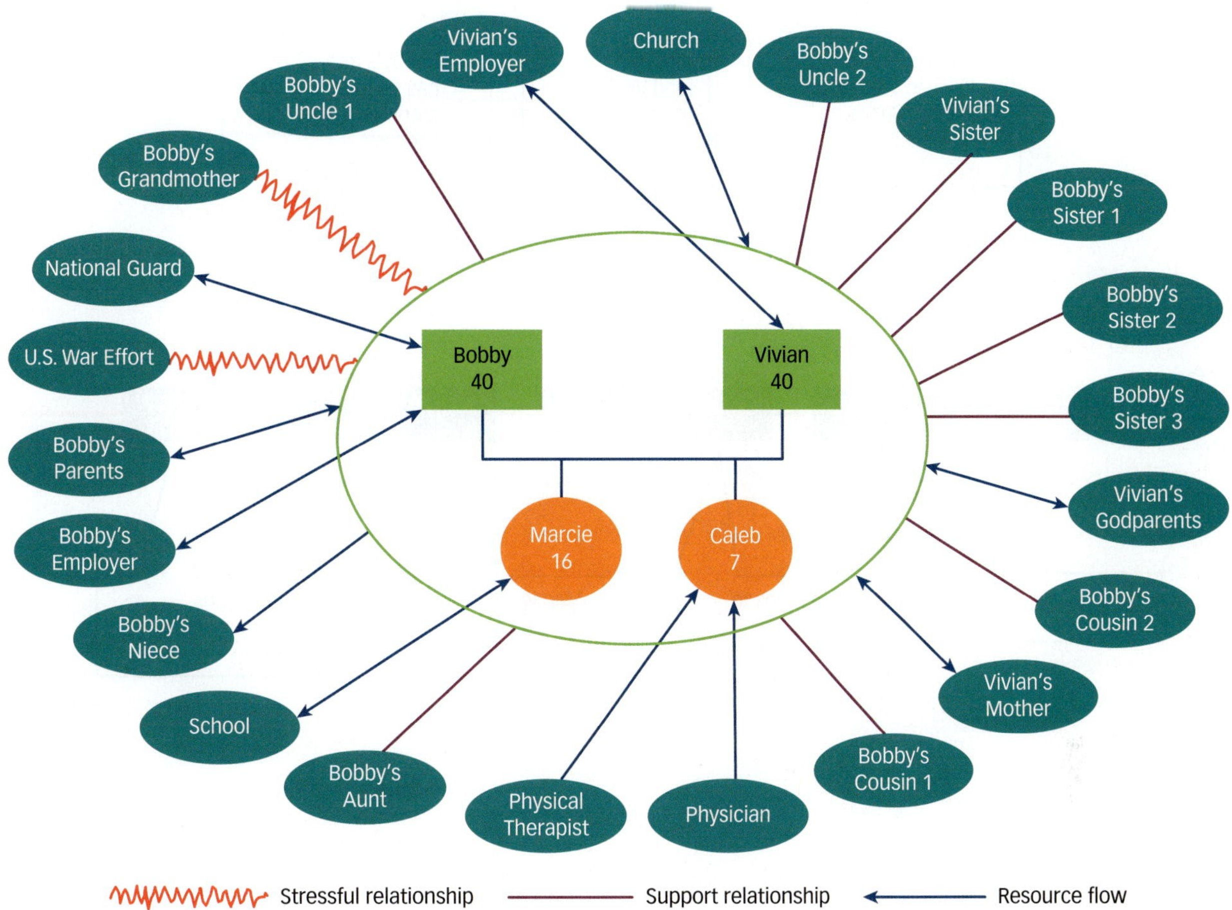

probably embrace this version of feminist theory, based on the observation that her e-mails from Iraq often included musings about what she was learning about how different her life experiences and life chances have been from other women in her unit, both White women and other African American women. She has also been shocked at the level of sexual harassment and sexual violence she has found in the military.

Intersectionality theory has also been used to look at other intersections in women's lives—for example, those related to sexuality, religion, disability, age, and nationality. From this perspective, a person may experience oppression based on gender or some other attribute but also experience privilege based on a different attribute. Some people may experience oppression related to several social categories. Intersectionality theory is being expanded to study transnational contexts, considering the consequences for women of colonialism and capitalism (Allen et al., 2009). Intersectionality theory would call attention to the ways that Bobby Sharpe and members of his family have experienced oppression related to race. But it would also suggest that Bobby has been able to build a middle-class life that has given him some class privilege compared with poor African American families. He also carries male privilege, heterosexual privilege, age privilege, and Christian privilege.

FAMILY STRESS AND COPING PERSPECTIVE

You read about theories of individual stress and coping in Chapter 4, and research in this area is incorporated into theorizing about stress and coping at the family level. The primary interest of the family stress and coping perspective is the entire family unit (Price, Price, & McKenry, 2010). The theoretical foundation of this perspective is the **ABC-X model of family stress and coping**, based on Rueben Hill's (1949, 1958) classic research on war-induced separation and reunion. It theorizes that to understand whether an event (A) in the family system becomes a crisis (X), we also need to understand both the family's resources (B) and the family's definitions (C) of the event. The main idea is that the impact of stressors on the family (the X factor) is

EXHIBIT 7.4 • Sharpe Family Timeline

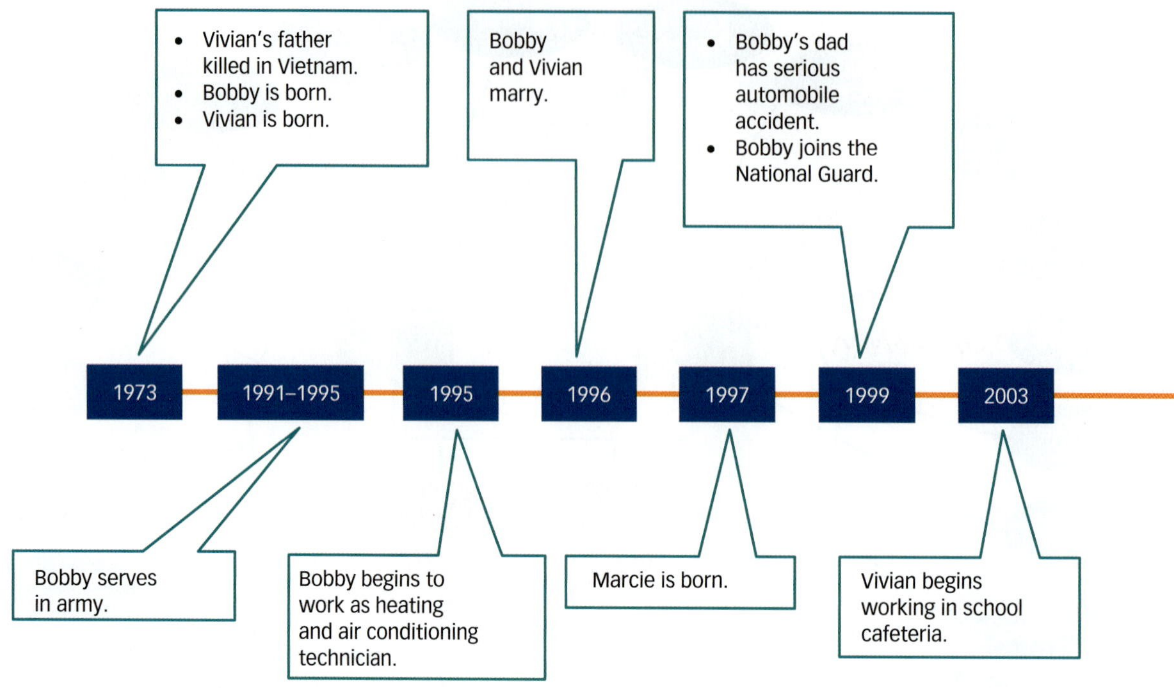

influenced by other factors, most notably the internal and external resources available and the meaning the family makes of the situation. With some updating, this theory continues to be the basis for examining family stress and coping (see Boss, 2006; Price et al., 2010).

The ABC-X model describes a family transition process following a stressful event. A period of disequilibrium is followed by three possible outcomes: (1) *recovery* to the family's previous level of functioning; (2) *maladaptation*, or permanent deterioration in the family's functioning; or (3) *bonadaptation*, or improvement in the family's functioning over and above the previous level. Thus, under certain circumstances, a stressor event can actually be beneficial, if the family's coping process strengthens the family in the long term. They might, for instance, come together to deal with the stressors. Vivian and Marcie Sharpe often talk about how their relationship was strengthened by the way they pulled together during Bobby's deployments.

A more complex, *double* ABC-X model incorporates the concept of **stress pileup** (McCubbin & Patterson, 1983). Over time, a series of crises may deplete the family's resources and expose the family to increasing risk of very negative outcomes (such as divorce, violence, or removal of children from the home). In this view, the balance of stressors and resources is an important consideration. Where there are significant numbers of stressors, positive outcomes depend on a significant level of resources being available to family members and the family as a whole. A **family timeline**, or chronology depicting key dates and events in the family's life (Satir, 1983; Vosler, 1996), can be particularly helpful in identifying times in the family's life when events have piled up. Family timelines can be used to identify the resources that have been tapped successfully in the past, as well as resource needs in the present. Exhibit 7.4 presents a family timeline for the Sharpe family. It suggests a pileup of stressors for the family in the period before, during, and after Bobby's deployment to Afghanistan; consequently, they needed a significant number of resources to allow for continued healthy individual and family functioning.

Two types of stressors are delineated in the ABC-X model (McCubbin & Figley, 1983). **Normative stressors** are the typical family life cycle transitions, such as the birth of a first child. **Nonnormative stressors** are potentially catastrophic events, such as natural disasters, medical trauma, drug abuse, unemployment, and family violence. These nonnormative events can quickly drain the family's resources and may leave family members feeling overwhelmed and exhausted. Lower-level but persistent stress—such as chronic illness or chronic poverty—can

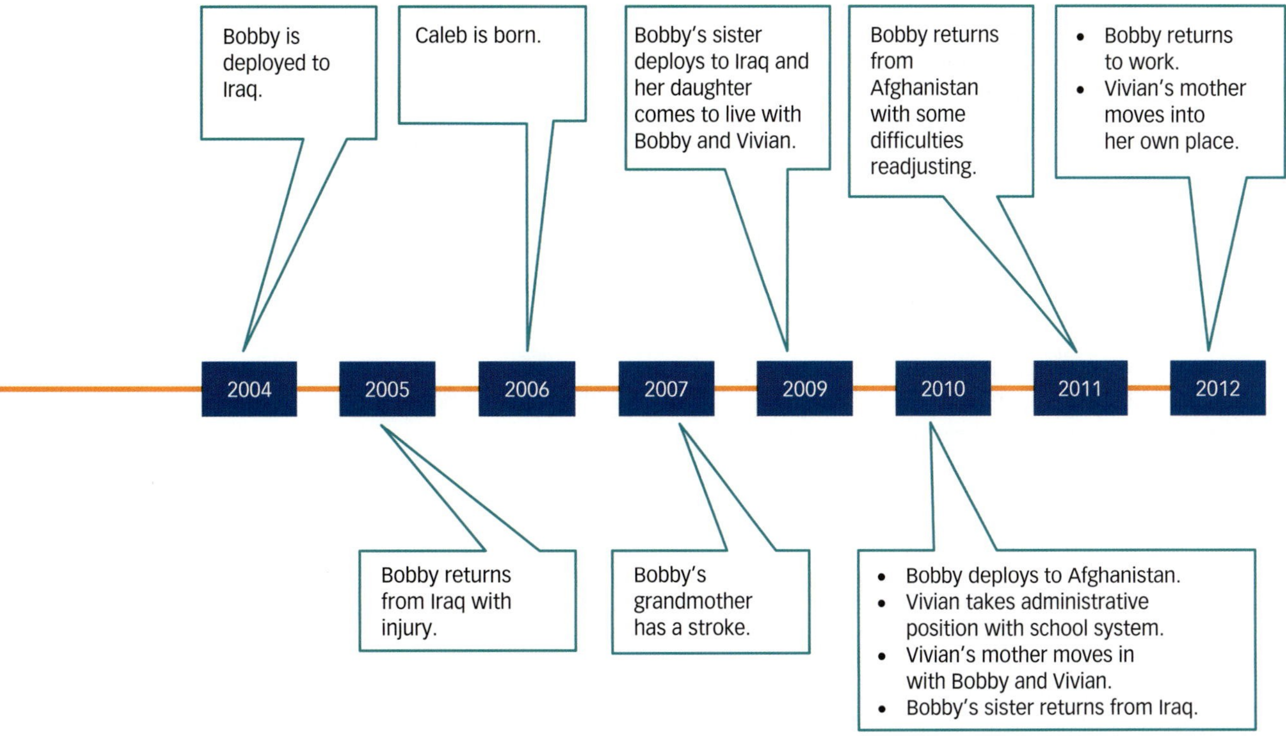

also create stress pileup, resulting in instability within the family system and a sense of being out of control on the part of family members.

FAMILY RESILIENCE PERSPECTIVE

The **family resilience perspective** extends the family stress and coping perspective by seeking to identify and strengthen processes that allow families to bear up under and rebound from distressing life experiences. From this perspective, distressed families are seen as challenged, not damaged, and they have the potential for repair and growth (Walsh, 2016). In her book *Strengthening Family Resilience*, Froma Walsh (2016) draws on existing research on risk and resilience to present a family resilience model for intervention and prevention, one that focuses on the family system as the target for intervention. She defines *resilience* as "the ability to withstand and rebound from serious life challenges . . . positive adaptation in the context of significant adversity" (p. 4). She describes this as "bouncing forward," rather than bouncing back. She assumes that all families face adversity, but resilient families "struggle well" and experience "both suffering and courage" (p. 5). She cautions social workers to avoid the tendency to pathologize the families they encounter in the midst of transitional distress, assessing families, instead, in the context of the situations they face and looking for family strengths.

Walsh (2012c, 2016) has taken the research on risk and resilience and organized the findings into a conceptual framework for targeting interventions to strengthen core processes of family resilience, whatever form the family takes. She organizes this framework into three dimensions: family belief systems, organizational patterns, and communication processes. Each dimension is summarized here.

- *Family belief systems.* How families view problems and possibilities is crucial to how they cope with challenges. Resilient families make meaning of adversity by viewing it as a shared challenge. They find a way to hold on to a shared confidence that they can overcome the challenge. They act on this shared hope by taking initiative and persevering. They draw on a spiritual value system to see their situation as meaningful and to imagine future possibilities.

- *Organizational patterns.* Resilient families have organizational patterns that serve as shock absorbers. They maintain flexibility in family structure and are able to make changes in roles and rules to respond to the demands of the moment, but in the midst of change, they hold on to some rituals and routines to provide stability and continuity. Strong family leaders provide nurturance and protection to children and other vulnerable family members, but they also leave some room to negotiate rules and roles, based on the situation at hand, and exercise leadership with warmth. Resilient families provide mutual support and commitment while honoring individual differences. They are able to mobilize extended kin and community resources.

- *Communication processes.* Good communication is vital to family resilience. Resilient families send clear, consistent, and genuine messages. They share a wide range of feelings and show mutual empathy and tolerance for differences. They can use humor to lighten threatening situations. They also engage in collaborative problem solving, identifying problems and possible solutions, sharing decision making, and taking concrete steps.

Froma Walsh (2012b) cautions that

> the concept of family resilience should not be misapplied to blame families that are unable to rise above harsh conditions, by simply labeling them as not resilient. Just as individuals need supportive relationships to thrive, families need supportive institutional polices, structures, and programs in workplace, health care, and other larger systems. (p. 412)

The Sharpe family has weathered a number of challenges along the way: health problems, war zone deployments for Bobby and his sister, the birth of a baby with special care needs, and intense elder care needs. According to Froma Walsh's model of family resilience, they are a resilient family. They view each adversity as a shared challenge for the extended kinship network, and they move forward with confidence that they can overcome each challenge. They take the initiative to devise plans for handling difficult situations, and they draw on a deeply held faith that makes meaning of their challenges. In terms of organizational patterns, they are flexible in the assignment of roles and resourceful in mobilizing extended care resources. They have made more use of family than community resources in the past, but Vivian was grateful for the support of their church during Bobby's deployment to Afghanistan. They communicate well, for the most part, often using humor to lighten stressful situations. Vivian, her sister, and her mother could benefit from more open communication about the struggles they had after Vivian's father was killed in Vietnam. They have never been able to talk about this, and it may well play a role in Vivian's sister's clinical depression and her mother's pervasive sadness.

CRITICAL THINKING Questions 7.2

Which one of the preceding theoretical perspectives on families do you find most useful for thinking about the multigenerational Sharpe family? Which perspective do you think offers the least insight into this family? Which of the perspectives do you find most useful for thinking about your own family? The least useful? Explain your answers.

DIVERSITY IN FAMILY LIFE

One question that must be asked about each of the theoretical perspectives on families is how well it applies to different types of families. As suggested earlier, diversity has always existed in the structures and functions of families, but that diversity is clearly increasing, and the reality today is that a great deal of diversity exists among families, both in the United States and globally. There is diversity in family structures, as well as economic and cultural diversity.

DIVERSITY IN FAMILY STRUCTURES

It is difficult, if not impossible, to catalog all of the types of family structures represented in the world's families. The following discussion is not meant to be exhaustive but rather to provide an overview of some relatively common structures that social workers might encounter.

Nuclear Families

There is a worldwide trend toward the nuclear family structure as societies become more industrialized and more people live in urban areas where smaller families are more practical (Ballantine & Roberts, 2014). The nuclear family is an adaptation to industrialization and urbanization. Some of the White settlers in the United States preferred the extended family structure, and others preferred the nuclear family, but the nuclear family has been the preferred family structure throughout most of U.S. history. Consequently, we would expect *nuclear family* to be easy to define. Actually, the family literature presents different definitions of this family structure. Some definitions specify that the nuclear family is composed of two parents and their biological or adopted offspring (LePoire, 2006). Others specify that a nuclear family is composed of at least one parent and one child (Leeder, 2004; Newman, 2012). This definition would include a broader brush of families, including lone-parent families and same-sex partners with children. But for the purpose of this discussion, we define the *nuclear family* as composed of two parents and their biological, adopted, or fostered offspring, because we think it is important to distinguish this idealized family structure from other family structures. Although, as mentioned, the nuclear family has been the preferred model throughout U.S. history, it has always been an ideal that was difficult to accomplish (Hareven, 2000). Families in colonial days and later were often marked by unplanned pregnancies and untimely death. Early parental death led to remarriage and stepfamilies and to children being placed with extended family or in foster care or orphanages. Nonkin boarders were brought in to provide income and companionship.

In 2012, according to the U.S. Census Bureau (Vespa, Lewis, & Kreider, 2013), 20% of households in the United States were married couples with children, down from 40% in 1970. We don't know a lot about the functioning of nuclear families because they are not often studied, except to compare other types of families with them. For example, children in lone-parent families are often compared with children in two-parent families, with the finding that children benefit from the resources—material and social—that come with two parents (see Shore & Shore, 2009). Recent U.S. Census data indicate that adults in married-couple families are older, more likely to be college educated, more likely to own their own homes, and more likely to have higher incomes than lone-parent families (Vespa et al., 2013). Both government (through marriage initiative programs) and religious groups are actively involved in trying to promote more two-parent families. Some social scientists see risk in nuclear families as compared with extended families, suggesting that the family can easily become too isolated with too much pressure put on the spousal relationship to fill each other's needs (F. Walsh, 2012b).

The often idealized nuclear family has a father in the labor force and a stay-at-home mother. That type of nuclear family peaked in the 1950s but was already beginning to decline by 1960. In 2010, 54% of married couples with children younger than age 18 had two parents in the labor force, down from 66% in 2007 (U.S. Bureau of Labor Statistics, 2013b). From 2005 to 2011, a period that included a steep recession, the number of two-parent families with children younger than 18 who had at least one unemployed parent rose by 33% (Vespa et al., 2013). Having two parents in the labor force puts married couples at an economic advantage over single parents but also raises concerns about who will provide child care and other domestic labor.

The idealized nuclear family, with a father in the labor force and a stay-at-home mother, peaked in the 1950s and was already beginning to decline by 1960.

Nuclear families may include adopted and foster children (as may lone-parent families, same-sex partner families, and stepfamilies). The 2000 U.S. Census found that 2.5% of children younger than 18 were adopted (cited in Galvin, 2006). More recent data indicate that 25% of adopted children in the United States are international adoptions, 40% are transracial, and 37% are foster care adoptions (Statistic Brain, 2013). Adoptive families face the same challenges as other families, but they also face some additional ones. Every adopted child has two families, and disclosure about and navigation of this complexity must be addressed. The adoptive family must also develop a coherent story about how they came to be family and cope with issues of loss, grief, and attachment (Rampage et al., 2012).

On September 30, 2014, an estimated 415,129 children were in foster care in the United States. Nearly half (46%) of these children were in nonrelative foster family homes, and about half (55%) of children in foster care had family reunification as the case goal. Almost half (46%) of children who left care in 2014 were in care for less than 1 year (Child Welfare Information Gateway, 2016). The challenge for foster families is to provide temporary care to children from troubled families, knowing that the family relationship is time limited.

Extended Families

An *extended family* is one in which the parent–child nuclear family lives along with other relatives, such as grandparents, adult siblings, aunts, uncles, or cousins. This is a common pattern in agricultural societies around the world. In the United States, this pattern exists in some rural families, as well as in some ethnic groups, particularly among Mexican Americans and some Asian American groups. This is financially practical, and it also

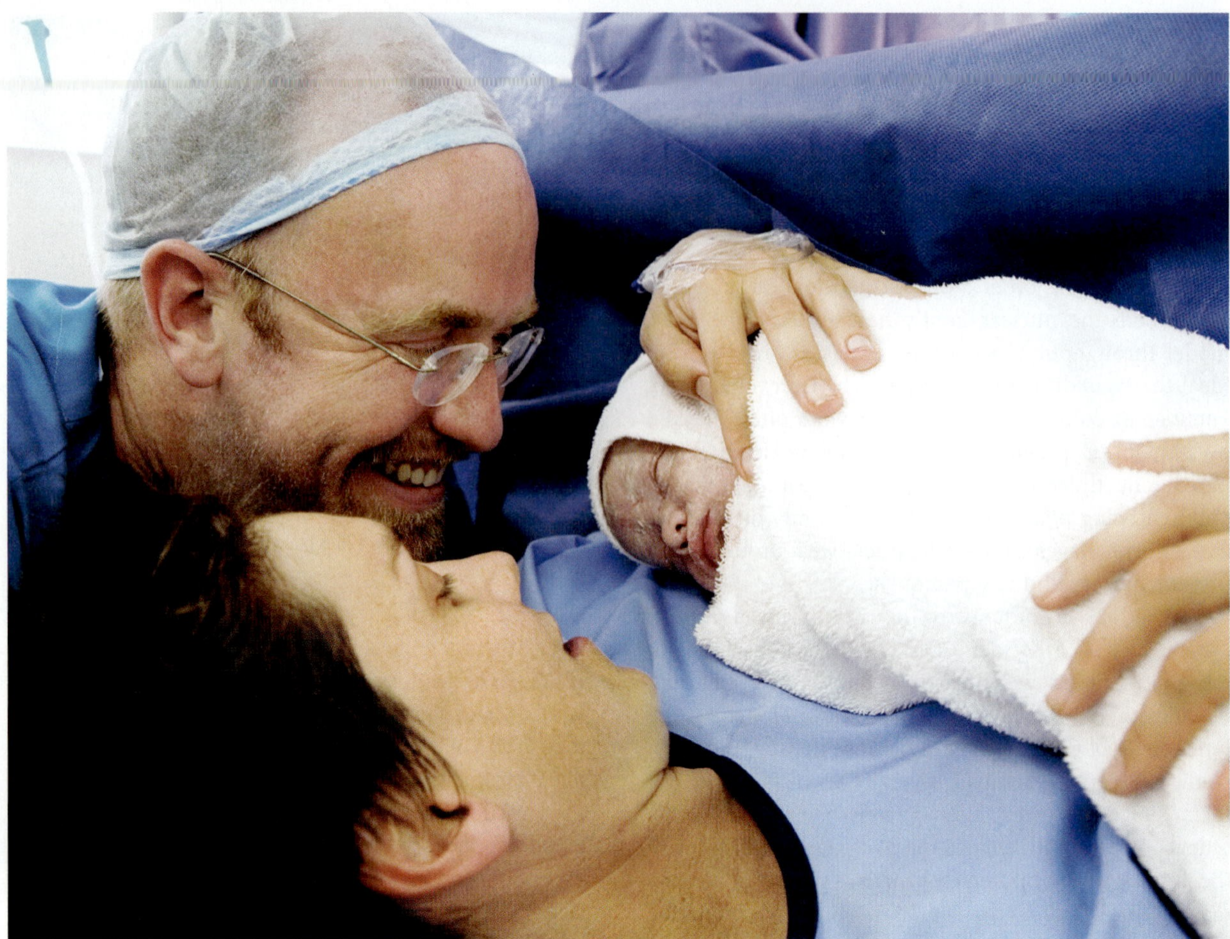
© iStockphoto.com/Don Bayley

The birth of a first child is a major transition for a family system, calling for new roles and the management of new tasks.

allows family groups to practice their ethnic traditions (Ballantine & Roberts, 2014). However, there are some downsides to the extended family. Sometimes family members exploit the labor of other family members. In other cases, the emotional and economic obligations to the extended family may come at the expense of individual development (Leeder, 2004).

Some family scholars suggest it is more appropriate to speak of the contemporary family in the United States and other industrialized nations as a *modified extended family* than a nuclear family (Knodel, Kespichayawattana, Saengtienchai, & Wiwatwanich, 2010). Members of the extended family network may not reside together, but they are involved with each other in ongoing emotional and economic action. They stay connected. This is clearly the pattern in the Sharpe family. It is also the pattern in the current migrations across national lines. Family members are often separated across thousands of miles, but money is shared and the new technologies allow ongoing communication. Often immigrant groups travel together in kin networks and live very close to each other when not living together. The extended kin network is a source of support in times of crisis. For example, children may be transferred from one nuclear family to another within the extended kin network as need arises, as happened when Bobby and Vivian cared for their niece while her mother was deployed to a war zone. The extended kin system also influences values and behaviors. For instance, Vivian Sharpe has expectations that her extended kinship system will have a positive influence on Marcie's values and behaviors as she grows through adolescence. Extended family ties are usually stronger in Asian and Pacific Islander Americans, Native American/First Nations peoples, African Americans, and Latino Americans than among middle-class White Americans (Ho et al., 2004). There is some evidence that the multigenerational family household has been making a comeback in Europe and the United States in recent years (Albuquerque, 2011).

Cohabiting Heterosexual Couples

Cohabiting is living together in a romantic relationship without marriage. This method of forming a romantic partnership has been on the increase in the United States and other Western societies since 1960. Cohabitation is now recognized as a family form by family scholars.

Sociologists Patrick Heuveline and Jeffrey Timberlake (2004) examined data from almost 70,000 women from 17 nations to learn how nonmarital cohabitation in the United States compares with that in 16 other industrialized nations. They examined the percentage of women in each of the nations estimated to experience at least one cohabiting relationship before the age of 45 and found a very large cross-nation range, from 4.4% in Poland to 83.6% in France. Spain and Italy were at the low end, with less than 15% of women in each country reporting cohabitation. The United States fell in the middle of the range, with about 50% of women estimated to ever cohabit before age 45, and more recent data indicate that the United States continues to rank in the middle globally in terms of cohabitation (Social Trends Institute, 2012). Heuveline and Timberlake (2004) suggest that the cross-national differences in rates of cohabitation are influenced by a number of sociocultural factors, including religion, the economy, partnership laws and benefits, and availability of affordable housing. Besides differences in rates of cohabitation, they also found different types of cohabiting relationships occurring in different nations. For example, cohabitation can be a prelude to marriage or an alternative to marriage. Heuveline and Timberlake (2004) found that cohabiting relationships are less stable in the United States than in other countries.

Cohabiting as a method of forming a romantic partnership has been on the increase in the United States and other Western societies since 1960.

Although the estimates vary, there is agreement that the rate of unmarried cohabiting partners in the United States has increased dramatically since the 1960s and that, currently, a majority of couples getting married are already living in a cohabiting relationship (Huang, Smock, Manning, & Bergstrom-Lynch, 2011). The increase in cohabitation is related to the increasing age at marriage. In the United States and other Western industrialized countries, cohabitation is most frequent among young adults ages 20 to 34 (OECD Family Database, 2013), but older adults are the fastest growing group of U.S. cohabiters as the baby boomers age (Vespa, 2012).

Qualitative research with a U.S. sample of cohabiting young adults identified three primary motives for cohabiting: wanting to spend more time together, wanting to share financial burdens, and wanting to test compatibility (Huang et al., 2011). There were gender differences in the perceived disadvantages of cohabitation. Women saw cohabitation as involving less commitment and less societal legitimacy than marriage, whereas men noted the loss of freedom involved in cohabitation. Both men and women reported that the benefits of cohabitation outweigh the disadvantages.

Another research team found that cohabitation is associated with greater economic well-being for adults with college degrees but not for adults without college degrees (Taylor et al., 2011). Adults without college degrees are more likely to cohabit than adults with college degrees, and college-educated cohabiters are more likely to marry within 3 years of moving in together than cohabiters without a college degree. Wealthier cohabiters are more likely than less wealthy cohabiters to report that cohabitation is a step toward marriage rather than a substitution for marriage.

As the age of marriage is pushed upward, researchers have begun to note the rise in *serial cohabitation*, defined as two or more cohabiting relationships over time, particularly among emerging adults (Cohen & Manning, 2010; Lichter, Turner, & Sassler, 2010). They have found that the majority of cohabiting unions dissolve, especially among economically disadvantaged cohabiting couples. Early sexual activity and teen childbearing are associated with serial cohabitation, and serial cohabiters are less likely than single-instance cohabiters to expect the cohabiting relationship to end in marriage. The researchers suggest that serial cohabitation is a new intensive form of dating among some emerging adults and an alternative to marriage among some older never-married women (Lichter et al., 2010). Another research team found that the unions of low-income mothers who were cohabiting at the time of giving birth were often dissolved; 46% dissolved within 3 years of giving birth and 64% dissolved within 5 years. Three quarters of these romantic relationships ended completely, but one quarter continued after cohabitation dissolution. Family stress and lack of human capital are associated with cohabitation dissolution, and mothers who have had more than one cohabitation partner are at special risk for cohabitation dissolution (Kamp Dush, 2011). Lichter and Qian (2008) speculate that serial cohabitation by women may "reflect demographic shortages of men who are good providers or companions (e.g., men with good jobs, who are faithful, or who are drug free)" (p. 874).

Couples With No Children

Over the past 3 decades, the United States and other wealthy nations have seen an increase in the proportion of married couples who are childless. Of note, relatively high rates of childlessness were experienced in these same societies from 1890 to 1920, followed by the lowest recorded prevalence of childlessness during the 1950s and early 1960s (Abma & Martinez, 2006; Kohli & Albertini, 2009). Thus, the current high rates of childlessness are a return to a trend started in the late 19th century. Couples may be temporarily or permanently childless. Permanently childless couples may be voluntarily or involuntarily childless. Although childlessness is a growing type of family structure, there is very little research on childless couples; the research that has been done focuses on childless women, with little or no attention to childless men (fertility of men is much harder to study) or to the childless couple system, except in cases of infertility. The research often does not distinguish between married and unmarried women.

The most comprehensive study of childless women in the United States was conducted by Joyce Abma and Gladys Martinez (2006) at the National Center for Health Statistics. Their study examined three types of childlessness: temporarily childless, voluntarily childless, and involuntarily childless. They studied both married and unmarried women and did not make distinctions between these two groups. They found that from 1976 to 2002, the percentage of women aged 35 to 39 who were childless increased from 11% to 20%, and the percentage of women aged 40 to 44 who were childless increased from 10% to 18%. The voluntarily childless was the largest group of childless women in 2002, making up 42% of all childless women; 30% were temporarily childless, and 28% were involuntarily childless. As might be expected, given declining fertility between the ages of 35 and 44, women who were temporarily childless were more likely to be in the younger cohort, ages 35 to 39, and women who were involuntarily childless were more likely to be in the older group, ages 40 to 44.

All three groups of childless women were found to have more egalitarian views on family relationships than the women who were parents. There were some differences in the profiles of these three groups of childless women, however. Consistent with earlier research, the voluntarily childless women, compared with parenting women and other childless women, were disproportionately White, tended to be employed full time, had the highest incomes, and were more likely to be nonreligious. However, from 1995 to 2002, the percentage of Black women among the voluntarily childless increased to where it was equivalent to their share of the total population of women ages 35 to 44. From 1976 to 2002, Hispanic women were consistently underrepresented among the voluntarily childless.

One finding from the Abma and Martinez (2006) study is that there was a slight downturn in the percentage of women who were voluntarily childless and a slight upturn in the percentage who were involuntarily childless from 1995 to 2002. They speculate that this change is probably related to the trend toward later marriage and childbearing, resulting in some couples discovering that they had fertility problems when they decided to become parents. Infertility can be caused by problems in the reproductive system of the man, the woman, or both. It is a global problem, but in countries with low resources it is most likely to be caused by sexually transmitted diseases, unsafe abortions, and home deliveries in unhygienic circumstances. Although there are many assistive technologies for dealing with fertility problems, these are inaccessible to most women in low-resource countries. In many countries of the world, childlessness is highly stigmatized, as well as an economic disadvantage where children are economic providers (Ombelet, 2014).

Research on the emotional impact of infertility indicates that it is a major source of stress. Infertility has been consistently associated with decreased scores in quality of life, affecting mental health, physical vitality, and social functioning (Drosdzol & Skrzypulec, 2008; El-Messidi, Al-Fozan, Lin Tan, Farag, & Tulandi, 2004; Lau et al., 2008). When couples experience similar levels of distress, they are more able to communicate about it and support each other (Peterson, Newton, & Rosen, 2003). However, it is not unusual for husbands and wives to have different reactions to infertility. The stressors related to infertility may go on over a long period of time. Treatments can be very costly and are often unsuccessful.

Although attitudes are changing, some social stigma is still attached to childlessness. Little is known about the lives of childless couples. In one attempt to understand the life trajectories of childless adults, an entire issue of the journal *Ageing & Society* was devoted to research on childless older adults. One researcher (Wenger, 2009) found that by the time they reached old age, childless people in rural Wales had made adaptations to their childless situation and developed closer relationships with kin and friends. This is the way Vivian Sharpe's godparents have adjusted to involuntary childlessness, and they draw great pleasure from being a part of the lively extended kin network in which Vivian and Bobby are embedded. On average, however, childless older adults in Wales entered residential care at younger ages than older adults who had children.

Lone-Parent Families

Lone-parent families are composed of one parent and at least one child residing in the same household. They are headed by either a divorced, widowed, or unmarried parent. Lone-parent families are on the increase in all wealthy industrialized nations but nowhere more than in the United States (U.S. Census Bureau, 2012a). In 2012, nearly one third (32%) of children in the United States lived with only one parent, 27% with the mother only and 5% with the father only (Vespa et al., 2013). This compares with less than 5% in Greece and Spain, 6% in Portugal, and 7% in Italy (U.S. Census Bureau, 2012a). Around the world, lone mothers are the great majority of parents in lone-parent families. In the United States, 55% of non-Hispanic Black children, 31% of Hispanic children, 21% of non-Hispanic White children, and 13% of Asian American children live with one parent. The share of children living with one parent in the United States has tripled since 1970, when the rate was 11% (Shore & Shore, 2009). It is important to exercise caution with these statistics, however. Sometimes people who get counted as lone-parent families reside with other family members and/or may have the support of a romantic partner.

Single mothers around the world have some common challenges: They are playing the dual roles of mother and worker with no partner assistance, receive lower earnings than men, and receive irregular paternal support (Anderson, 2012). If they became lone parents after divorce, they and their children must cope with loss and grief, may have to relocate, and face on average a 37% decline in their standard of living (Stirling & Aldrich, 2008). Lone-parent families headed by mothers are especially vulnerable to economic insecurity and poverty. Cross-national differences in government policies result in different circumstances for single mothers and their children, however. Some countries provide universal child allowances, paid maternity leave, and free child care. Children of single mothers have higher rates of poverty than children from two-parent families around the world, but the poverty rates among children of single parents are much lower in countries that provide such supports.

In 2005, the poverty rate (based on 55% of median income) for single-mother families in the United States was 51%, compared with 8% in Denmark (Casey & Maldonado, 2012). This is a very large range and primarily reflects differences in child and family policies in the two countries. Three other countries had poverty rates of over 40% for single-mother families: Canada, Germany, and Ireland. At the other end of the continuum, three other countries had poverty rates of less than 15% for single-mother families: Norway, Finland, and Sweden.

In the United States, social policy has focused on two priorities to improve the living situation of children in lone-parent families, as well as to decrease public expenditures on these families: improved child support payment by the nonresidential parent and marriage of the lone parent. The first of these priorities is to step up the enforcement of child support payment by the nonresidential parent. Research indicates that if nonresidential parents pay the child support required, the economic situation of residential children does indeed improve, although not to the level they would experience if both parents resided together. However, for impoverished families, the payment of child support is not sufficient to bring them out of poverty (see Stirling & Aldrich, 2008).

The second policy direction proposed in the United States in recent years is to encourage marriage of the lone parent. Some policy analysts conclude that this would, indeed, improve the economic situation of children currently being raised in lone-parent families (see Rector, Johnson, & Fagan, 2008). Others conclude that whereas this might be a good solution for some lone-parent families, male unemployment and marginal employment present serious barriers to marriage for many low-income couples (Edin & Reed, 2005; Gibson-Davis, Edin, & McLanahan, 2005). These latter researchers have found that men and women in impoverished neighborhoods often value marriage highly but do not see themselves as economically stable enough to have a viable marriage. Impoverished lone mothers have reported that they do not have a pool of attractive marriage partners who are economically stable, not addicted to drugs and alcohol, not involved with the criminal justice system, and able to be loving and kind parents to their children (Edin, Kefalas, & Reed, 2004).

It is important to note that in wealthy nations, the number of lone-parent families is growing across all socioeconomic groups, and in the United States, many affluent and well-educated women and men are choosing to become lone parents because they want to be a parent but do not have a partner with whom to share parenting (Anderson, 2012). These lone parents have the resources to afford full-time child care, private schools, and other domestic assistance.

One more point is important. Much of the research on lone-parent families has taken a deficit approach in looking at family interaction and functioning. Other researchers have attempted to look at lone parents from a strengths perspective and document how they function to adapt to the challenges they face. One example of this is a qualitative research project that asked low-income African American mothers and members of their families (who were sometimes not biologically related to them) to identify components of effective and ineffective family functioning (McCreary & Dancy, 2004). They found that all but 1 of the 40 respondents reported that they see or talk daily with at least one family member other than their children, a coping strategy that increases the effectiveness of family functioning by preventing isolation.

Stepfamilies

Stepfamilies have always been a relatively common family form in the United States, but they have changed over time. In colonial days, stepfamilies were typically the result of one parent dying and the other parent remarrying. Today, most stepfamilies are formed after biological parents divorce or dissolve their relationship and go on to form new romantic partnerships. We don't have good current data on the number of stepfamilies in the United States, but it is estimated that 10% to 20% of children younger than age 18 reside in stepfamilies (National Healthy Marriage Resource Center, 2009). The U.S. Census Bureau defines stepfamilies as those with two adults and children, where one adult is not the biological parent (cited in Pasley & Lee, 2010). Stepfamilies can be of several types. The most common is the stepfather family in which the mother has children from a previous relationship in the household. Another type is the stepmother family in which the father has children from a previous relationship in the household. Some stepfamilies have children from both partners' prior relationships living in the household. Any of these family forms can become more complex when children are born to the new partnership. Stepfamilies are also formed by same-sex partners where one or both partners have children from prior relationships living in the household. Although not counted by the U.S. Census Bureau as living in stepfamilies, many children reside with a single mother and make visits to the biological father and his new wife.

Stepfamilies are complex family structures. They involve complicated networks of relationships that include biological parents; stepparents; perhaps siblings and stepsiblings; and multiple sets of grandparents, aunts, uncles, and cousins. Children in stepfamilies may move back and forth between two homes and maintain connections with the nonresident parent. There are a number of subsystems in the stepfamily, including the new couple, the parent–child, the stepparent–stepchild, the child–nonresidential parent, the biological parents, the parent–stepparent–nonresidential parent, and sometimes the sibling or stepsibling subsystem. The parent–child subsystem is a more long-standing form than the new couple subsystem.

The new stepfamily must negotiate rules, roles, rituals, and customs. Things as simple as foods served in the household, bedtimes, chores, and methods of discipline may become points of tension. This works best when the issues and expectations are made explicit. It is quite common for loyalty conflicts to arise involving several subsystems, with family members feeling torn and caught between people they love (Pasley & Lee, 2010). The biological parent often feels torn between loyalty to the child(ren) and love for the new spouse or partner. Children may aggravate this situation by testing the biological parent's loyalty to them. Children may feel a conflict between their loyalty to the nonresidential parent and the need to form a relationship with the stepparent. Children can easily get triangulated into conflict between the parent and stepparent, between the residential parent and the nonresidential parent, or between the stepparent and the nonresidential parent. Events such as Parent Night at school can become a knotty situation.

The more children in the stepfamily situation, the more complicated the negotiations can become. First-marriage couples report that the biggest source of stress is finances, followed by child rearing. For stepfamilies, the biggest sources of stress are reversed, with child rearing coming first, followed by finances (Stanley, Markman, & Whitton, 2002). Stepparents are often treated as outsiders by children, and this is a difficult position from which to attempt to parent. Research indicates that stepfathers are less likely than stepmothers to try to engage in active parenting of stepchildren, no doubt because of expectations of gendered behavior; consequently, stepfathers tend to be perceived more positively than stepmothers (Pasley & Lee, 2010). Stepdaughters have been found to be more difficult to parent than stepsons (Hetherington & Kelly, 2002).

Same-Sex Partner Families

There is evidence that long-term relationships, even marriage, between same-sex partners were relatively common in premodern Europe (Boswell, 1994), but same-sex marriage is a new phenomenon in modern times (Chamie & Mirkin, 2011). In the 1990s, same-sex marriages were not legally recognized anywhere in the world. In 1989, Denmark was the first country to give legal rights to same-sex couples but did not allow them to marry. In 2001, the Netherlands became the first country to allow same-sex marriage, and by March 2014, 17 countries allowed same-sex marriage, up from 7 in December 2009 (Pew Research Center's Religion & Public Life Project, 2014). A number of other countries have some sort of federal civil union laws that grant partner registration and some rights and benefits of marriage. In the United States, in March 2014, same-sex marriage was legal or soon would be in 17 states and the District of Columbia, up from 5 states plus the District of Columbia in May 2010. In 2013, the U.S Supreme Court struck down part of the Defense of

Marriage Act, which was enacted in 1996, resulting in the requirement that the federal government recognize same-sex marriages from the states where they are legal (Pew Research Center's Religion & Public Life Project, 2014). On June 26, 2015, the U.S. Supreme Court ruled that state bans on same-sex marriage are unconstitutional, making same-sex marriage legal in all states (Human Rights Campaign, 2015). At the time of this writing same-sex marriage continues to be a hot-button issue in the United States and other countries, and it is likely that there will be further changes around the world by the time you read this.

It is important to remember that the preponderance of research about same-sex partner families was done in a time when such partnerships were not legally recognized. Most of the early research was based on convenience samples of White, middle-class families in lesbian partnerships, but in the past 10-plus years, researchers have begun to investigate the diversity in same-sex couple families and to consider the gay male family (Biblarz & Savci, 2010).

Same-sex partnerships share many characteristics with heterosexual partnerships, but they also are unique: the partners are of the same gender, they must often navigate a social world that continues to stigmatize same-sex relationships, and in many places the partners still lack legal protections, such as protection against being fired for sexual orientation. Some researchers have found that same-sex partners report about the same frequency of arguments as heterosexual couples (Peplau & Fingerhut, 2007), but others have found that same-sex couples report less conflict than heterosexual couples, more relationship satisfaction, and better conflict resolution (Balsam, Beauchaine, Rothblum, & Solomon, 2008). There is evidence that both same-sex and heterosexual partners tend to disagree about similar topics, such as sex, money, and household tasks (Kurdek, 2006). Some studies find that members of same-sex partnerships are more likely than married heterosexual couples to separate when they are unhappy, but the one longitudinal study that has followed the first same-sex partners to take advantage of Vermont's civil union laws found that same-sex couples in civil unions are less likely to separate than same-sex couples not in legally recognized unions (Balsam et al., 2008). Same-sex partners have been found to engage in less traditional division of labor than heterosexual married couples, even though heterosexual couples have become more egalitarian over time. Both same-sex and heterosexual couples reported greater commitment to monogamy in 2000 than in 1975 (Gotta et al., 2011).

Many lesbians and gay men became parents in earlier heterosexual relationships, before coming out as gay or lesbian. Increasingly, lesbians and gay men are also becoming parents in the context of their same-sex partner relationships, with the assistance of reproductive technology or by adoption (Green, 2012). Recent research indicates that, in the United States, more than 111,000 same-sex couples are raising an estimated 170,000 biological, step-, or adopted children. Same-sex couples are four times as likely to adopt as heterosexual couples and six times as likely to raise foster children. Half of children younger than 18 living with same-sex couples are non-White, and indeed, same-sex couples of color are more likely than White same-sex couples to be raising children. The median household income of same-sex couples with children is lower than the median for heterosexual couples with children, probably because the preponderance of these couples are lesbian (Gates, 2013). Lesbian couples may choose artificial insemination, and gay male couples may choose to use a surrogate mother; each method results in the child sharing a bloodline with one partner but not the other. There is very little research on gay men who become fathers via surrogacy, but one study found that these fathers reported greater closeness with their families of origin after becoming fathers and also reported heightened self-esteem (Bergman, Rubio, Green, & Padrón, 2010). Other research has found that when lesbian couples use artificial insemination, the biological mother is likely to be the primary child care provider and to have a somewhat closer relationship with the child (Bos, van Balen, & van den Boom, 2007).

Considerable research attention has been given to the question of how children fare in families of same-sex partners. This research, most of it conducted with children of lesbian couples, consistently finds that children who grow up with same-sex parents do not differ in any important way from children raised in families of heterosexual couples. They have similar emotional and behavioral adjustment; no differences are found in self-esteem, depression, or behavioral problems (Biblarz & Savci, 2010). This is remarkable, given the stigma such families often have to face. Children of same-sex parents have also been found to be no more likely than children of heterosexual couples to identify as homosexual. The school setting may present challenges, however; the children may face harassment, and their parents may find that they are not accepted on parent committees (Goldberg, 2010).

Military Families

Military families may have any of the family structures already discussed. They are included in this discussion of diversity of family structures, however, because of some special challenges they face in times of deployment to war zones. In the United States, military members may serve in either the active-duty or reserve components of the military. Active-duty members serve in the U.S. Army, Navy, Marine Corps, or Air Force. Reservists serve either in the Army National Guard or Air National Guard. Compared with other recent conflicts, deployments to Afghanistan and Iraq were more frequent and lengthier, usually lasting 12 to 15 months.

Wikimedia Commons, public domain

Cpl. Griselda Benjamin, an aviation supply clerk with Marine Aviation Logistics 16, hugs her daughter, Madison, after returning from a deployment to Iraq.

Approximately one third of both active-duty and reservist members have children; children of reserve members are a little older, on average, than children of active-duty members. The circumstances of reservist families are different in some ways from those of active-duty families. Active-duty military families typically live on or near military installations where the active-duty member receives daily military training. Reservist families live and work in a civilian community and receive military training one weekend per month (Faber, Willerton, Clymer, MacDermid, & Weiss, 2008).

Research indicates that active-duty families usually cope well with temporary separations during peacetime (Flake, Davis, Johnson, & Middleton, 2009). Active-duty military spouses are accustomed to managing as single parents for periods of time and then readjusting to operating in their predeployment family structure again when the deployment ends. Reservists and their families, on the other hand, are accustomed to occasional brief deployments to respond to state, local, and even national emergencies. They are not as prepared to deploy quickly for long periods of time and must deal with the break in civilian employment, as well as prepare the family for the coming separation. Consequently, active-duty families and reservist families face both similar and different challenges.

Spouses of both active-duty soldiers and reservists have reported loneliness, loss of emotional support, role overload, and worry about the safety and well-being of the deployed spouse (Padden & Agazio, 2013). Parents who are spouses or partners of soldiers deployed to war zones report higher levels of stress than the national average for parents. Communication with the military member in the war zone is spotty at best, because the deployed soldier is in and out of the range of adequate communications systems (Wadsworth & Southwell, 2011). During his deployment to Iraq, Bobby Sharpe was able to have only infrequent contact with his family, but he was able to have fairly regular contact by e-mail and Skype much of the time he was in Afghanistan. Both the family members at home and the deployed family member may try to avoid alarming each other about what is happening in their worlds, and together they must gauge how involved the deployed family member can be in making decisions about what is happening at home. Bobby Sharpe did not know his furnace was broken until he returned home from his first deployment, because Vivian did not want to bother him with that kind of family problem. She also avoided telling him that she was overwhelmed with the demands of work and family while he was in Afghanistan.

As the end of the deployment draws near, family members report that they begin to worry about what to expect when the soldier returns, in terms of possible war wounds or personality or behavior changes (Faber et al., 2008). Marcie Sharpe had heard scary stories of parents coming home with completely changed personalities. She worried a lot about this during Bobby's second deployment. Although it is often a joyous time, the military member's return home can be very stressful for families. Family members have to readjust to one another and realign family roles. Three out of four military families report that the first 3 months after coming home can be the most stressful period of the deployment process (Flake et al., 2009). Soldiers have to reacclimate to life away from the war zone and renegotiate roles, responsibilities, and boundaries with family members who had made adjustments in their absence (Faber et al., 2008). This readjustment is particularly difficult when there have been physical or mental injuries, such as traumatic brain injury or post-traumatic stress disorder (Martin & Sherman, 2010). Families tend to stabilize over time, but many families have needed to prepare for another deployment that can come in as quickly as 1 year.

Children of both active-duty and reservist families involved in the Iraq and Afghanistan wars have been found to be at increased risk for a range of problems in psychosocial functioning. In the time just before a parent's deployment, children may become withdrawn or engage in regressive behavior. Early in the deployment, they may be overwhelmed, sad, and anxious and have more somatic (physical) symptoms, but these symptoms usually diminish once children adjust to the deployment. They are usually excited and relieved when the soldier parent comes home but may experience conflict about the readjustments being made at home (Flake et al., 2009). One study of children of deployed National Guard members found that they reported missing their deployed parent as the biggest difficulty of the deployment. Their biggest worry was that their deployed parent would be injured or killed. The biggest change in their lives involved increased responsibility at home, more chores, and more responsibility for younger siblings. They reported concern about trying to avoid upsetting the parent at home. The children also described some positive aspects of deployment. Some reported being proud of what their deployed parents were doing for the country, although this pride was tempered when they heard talk from television, classmates, and other sources suggesting that the war is bad. Some children also reported pride in themselves for their ability to be more responsible while the deployed parent was away (Houston et al., 2009).

There is one important difference in the experiences of active-duty and reservist families. A large portion of active-duty military families continues to live in or near military installations during the family member's deployment. This allows them to have ongoing support from other military families as well as from military programs. Reservist families, on the other hand, are scattered across all 50 states and the U.S. territories, many of them living in rural communities. This is especially the case for National Guard members because the National Guard has a strong tradition in rural communities, where it serves as a point of pride as well as a supplement to the low wages often found in these communities (Martin & Sherman, 2010). Sometimes a National Guard family will be the only one in their area experiencing deployment at a given time. This is problematic because of the lack of access to other families facing similar experiences. Children of deployed reservists have reported that a chance to talk to other children with a deployed parent would be a big help (Houston et al., 2009). Likewise, the returning reservist soldier may be isolated from other returning soldiers, as well as from some of the medical and psychiatric resources available in and near military installations.

It is hard to say what the outcome of Operation Iraqi Freedom and Operation Enduring Freedom (the War in Afghanistan) is, but it is clear that the military families involved, both active-duty and reservist families, will continue to experience multiple challenges in the aftermath of the wars. According to a large-scale study sponsored by the RAND Corporation, many service members from the wars in Iraq and Afghanistan underwent prolonged periods of combat stress (Tanielian & Jaycox, 2008). In the aftermath of the trauma, many service members and veterans are experiencing horrific combat injuries; others are experiencing substance abuse, PTSD, relationship problems, and work problems (Wadsworth & Southwell, 2011). Social workers in all practice settings should be alert to possibilities for engaging these families in supportive services.

CRITICAL THINKING Questions 7.3

Which, if any, of the family structures discussed did you grow up in? What do you see as the major strength of this type of family structure? The major challenge? Which, if any, of these family structures are you living in now? If this is different from the type of family structure you grew up in, what do you consider to be its major strength and major challenge?

ECONOMIC AND CULTURAL DIVERSITY

Family structure is influenced by economic and cultural patterns, as well as immigration status. As you read the following sections on economic diversity, cultural diversity, and immigrant families, think about how your family structure is affected by the family's position in the economic structure; cultural heritage; and experience with immigration, where relevant.

Economic Diversity

Economic inequality exists in all societies, historical and contemporary, but the number of social classes and the amount of inequality vary from society to society. As indicated in Chapter 9, the United States has less inequality than some nations of the world, but it has more inequality than any other advanced industrialized nation. And, unfortunately, since 1970, the gap between the richest and poorest U.S. citizens has been growing. During the worst recession in the United States since the Great Depression of the 1930s, which began in December 2008, the national unemployment rate climbed to 10%. A number of wealthy families lost millions, even billions, of dollars in fraud schemes and investments gone bad. Middle-class families were devastated by job cutbacks, home foreclosures, and high debt, with middle-class men older than age 55 being particularly hard hit by job cutbacks. The poorest of families barely survived, not able to meet basic needs for food and shelter. Large numbers of U.S. families reported feeling a sense of financial insecurity (Bartholomae & Fox, 2010).

The question to be addressed here is, what impact do economic resources have on family life? How do family economic circumstances affect parental relationships, parent–child relationships, and child development? A large volume of research has found that individual physical and mental health, marital relationships, parent–child relationships, and child outcomes decline as economic stress increases. Two theoretical models have been proposed to explain the connection between economic resources and individual and family functioning: the family economic stress model and the family investment model.

The family economic stress model is based on Glen Elder's (1974) research on the impact of the Great Depression on parents and children. This research found that severe economic hardship disrupted family functioning in ways that negatively affected marital quality, parenting quality, and child outcomes. Similar results have been found in more recent studies of Iowa farm families facing a severe downturn in the agricultural economy in the 1980s (Conger & Elder, 1994) and of economic pressure in African American families (Conger et al., 2002). In the **family economic stress model** based on this research, economic hardship leads to economic pressure, which leads to parent distress, which leads to disrupted family relationships, which leads to child and adolescent adjustment problems (Conger & Conger, 2008).

There is a great deal of research to support the family economic stress model. Economic stress, such as unemployment, low income, and high debt, has been found to have negative effects on the physical and mental health of parents (Kahn & Pearlin, 2006; McKee-Ryan, Song, Wanberg, & Kinicki, 2005). Research has also found that psychological distress about economic pressures takes its toll on marital quality (Gudmunson, Beutler, Israelsen, McCoy, & Hill, 2007). Couple disagreements and fighting increase with financial strain. Parental psychological distress and marital conflict have been found to affect parenting practices, leading to less parental warmth and more inconsistent, punitive, and controlling discipline (Mistry, Lowe, Renner, & Chien, 2008; Waanders, Mendez, & Downer, 2007).

Family economic hardship has also been found to be associated with a number of child outcomes. Children in families experiencing economic hardship tend to have higher levels of depression and anxiety (Gutman, McLoyd, & Tokoyawa, 2005). They also have been found to demonstrate more aggressive and antisocial behaviors (Solantaus, Leinonen, & Punamaki, 2004). Economic disadvantage is associated with lower self-esteem and self-efficacy in children (Shek, 2003) and poorer school performance (Gutman et al., 2005). Adolescents who report worrying about the family's finances also report more somatic complaints, such as stomachaches, headaches, and loss of appetite (Wadsworth & Santiago, 2008).

Whereas the family economic stress model focuses on the impact of low income and economic hardship on family life, the **family investment model** focuses on the other end of the economic continuum, on how economic advantage affects family life and child outcomes. This theoretical model proposes that families with greater economic resources can afford to make large investments in the development of their children (Bornstein & Bradley, 2003; Bradley & Corwyn, 2002).

Families with abundant economic resources are able to make more learning materials available in the home; spend more time engaged in intellectually stimulating activities, such as visiting museums and traveling; secure education in enriched educational environments; secure outside assistance such as tutoring and specialized training; provide a higher standard of living in such areas as housing, clothing, nutrition, transportation, and medical care; and reside in a safe, clean, and roomy environment. They also are able to open doors to social networks that provide educational and career opportunities. This seems to go without saying, but there is empirical support for the proposal that family income affects the types of investments parents make in their children (Bradley & Corwyn, 2002), and this investment has been demonstrated to be positively associated with child cognitive development (Linver, Brooks-Gunn, & Kohen, 2002).

Cultural Diversity

The world over, we are living in a time when people are moving about from society to society and increasing the level of cultural diversity in small towns, suburbs, and cities. As suggested earlier, there has always

A combination photograph shows Los Angeles–area street signs that mark the boundaries of neighborhoods in Los Angeles, Long Beach, and San Pedro, California.

been cultural diversity in the United States, but with the new waves of immigration in recent years, the United States has become a microcosm of the whole world in terms of the complex mix of ethnic heritages and religions. Across cultural groups, families differ in how they define family; in how they organize family life; and in their customs, traditions, and communication patterns (McGoldrick & Ashton, 2012). Social workers face a daunting challenge in responding sensitively and appropriately to each and every family they encounter.

In the past, many of the clinical models for family practice were based on work with primarily middle-class and often two-biological-parent European American families. Working from these models often led to thinking of racial and ethnic minority families as deviant or deficient. One of the best examples of the damage this way of thinking can do is Anne Fadiman's (1998) story about the experience of a Hmong family with the health care and child protective systems in California. (If you haven't read *The Spirit Catches You and You Fall Down* yet, I suggest you put it on your to-do list during your next break between terms.) In recent years, however, there has been a concerted call for social workers and other professionals to practice in a culturally sensitive manner that moves from culturally aware to culturally competent practice (Lum, 2011). I prefer to talk in terms of culturally sensitive practice, because I doubt that we can ever be truly competent in a culture other than the one in which we were raised, and certainly not in the multiple cultures we are likely to encounter in our work over time. In light of the great diversity in contemporary life, the goal should be to remain curious and open-minded, taking a stance of "informed not knowing" (Dean, 2001).

Consequently, I do not present a cookbook approach to working with cultural differences but rather a process by which we can develop cultural awareness about the family groups with which we work. The first step, as suggested earlier, is to develop an intense understanding of the limitations of our own cultural perspective and a healthy respect for the integrity of all cultures. Starting from this position, we can set out to become as well informed as possible about the cultural groups represented by the families we serve. One thing social workers are particularly good at, when we are at our best, is putting people and situations into context. We will want to use that strength to learn as much as possible about the context of the culturally variant families we encounter. Juliet Rothman (2008, p. 38) suggests the types of knowledge needed to practice in a culturally sensitive manner; they are presented in modified form here:

- The group's history prior to arriving in the United States, if relevant
- The group's experience with immigration, if relevant
- The group's experience with settlement in the United States, if relevant
- The group's experience with oppression, discrimination, bias, and prejudice
- The group's relationship to the country of origin, if relevant
- The group's relationship to the country of residence
- The group's worldviews and beliefs about child rearing, family relationships, dating and marriage, employment, education, recreation, health and illness, aging, death and bereavement, and other life course issues
- Variations and differences within the group, particularly those related to social class
- Generational issues about acculturation within the group, if relevant

Some of this information may be more important for specific practice situations. There are a number of ways to learn this information: through Internet research, history books, biographies and autobiographies of group members, films and documentaries about the group, conversations with friends or colleagues who are members of the group, attendance at cultural festivals, and by asking your clients what you need to know to be helpful to them.

Even though we want to learn as much as we can about the cultural group, we must realize that there are many variations within all cultural groups. When I need to avoid stereotypical application of knowledge about a cultural group, it helps me to think about how many variations there are within my own cultural group and how well or poorly generalizations about my group apply to me. It is also helpful to hear different stories from members of the group, through books, videos, or personal conversations. It is particularly important to remember that there are social class differences among all cultural groups. You will want to consider whether the African American woman you are working with is middle class or working class and know something about her experiences with oppression. You will want to keep in mind that more than 500 distinct First Nations (or Native American) peoples exist within the United States, and they differ in language, religion, social structure, and many other aspects of culture (Weaver, 2011). You will want to know how a specific nation or tribe coped with attempts to eradicate their cultural practices. You will want to note whether the Latino immigrant family came from a rural or urban environment and what level of education they received in their home country; you will also want to note their country of origin and whether they are of documented or undocumented status. When working with an Asian or Pacific Island family, you will want to know not only the country of origin (out of 60 represented in the United States) but also the social class and education level of the family, religious beliefs, and when the family first immigrated to the United States. You will want to note how integrated the family from North Africa or the Middle East is into U.S. mainstream culture, as well as how traditional they are in religious and cultural beliefs. These are only a few examples of how you will need to individualize families while also putting them into cultural context.

Immigrant Families

The United States is built on successive waves of immigration and is currently the world's leader as a destination for immigrants. In 2011, approximately 40.4 million immigrants were living within the United States, making up 13% of the U.S. population (Pew Research Hispanic Trends Project, 2013). Immigrants are foreign-born people who plan to settle permanently in the United States. They may be economic migrants seeking better jobs and pay, family migrants who come to join family members already here, or refugees involuntarily fleeing political violence or extreme environmental distress. Current immigrants to the United States are more diverse than earlier immigrants in terms of country of origin, language, religion, and socioeconomic status. The places from which immigrants come have changed over time, influenced by immigration policies. For example, 1965 amendments to the Immigration and Nationality Act of 1952 created a "family reunification" category and gave preference to immigrants who had family members already in the United States. The 1986 Refugee Assistance Extension Act made it easier for families facing political persecution and extreme environments in their home countries to enter the United States. The Immigration Act of 1990 shifted policy away from family reunification to individuals with specific education and credentials and to wealthy individuals who could invest in the U.S. economy (Bush, Bohon, & Kim, 2010).

Immigrants may be *first generation* (moved from another country to the United States), *second generation* (children of first-generation immigrants), or *third generation* (grandchildren of first-generation immigrants). In general, first-generation immigrants experience more loss and grief than second- and third-generation immigrants, but the reaction to immigration differs by the degree of choice about migration, accessibility to the country of origin, gender and age, stage of family life cycle, number of family members immigrating and left behind, community social supports, and experiences with discrimination in the country of origin and the country of adoption (Falicov, 2011). Many losses are involved with migration, including loss of the family members and friends left behind, loss of familiar language, and loss of customs and traditions. Involuntary immigrants often have been traumatized in their country of origin and have no option to visit home. Other immigrants are able to make frequent visits home and maintain transnational families who are in frequent contact. Families may migrate together or in sequential stages, whereby one or two family members immigrate first, followed by others at later times.

In cases of sequential migration, family roles and relationships must be reorganized over time. The first immigrating family member must now perform some roles not carried out in the home country, whether those were domestic chores, paid labor, or managing finances. Likewise, the spouse left in the home country must now take on roles that had been filled by the immigrating family member. If the trailing spouse later immigrates, the spousal roles will have to be renegotiated, as happens when military families reunite. One difference in the reunifications of immigrant and military families is that sequential immigration may happen over a period of years and have unexpected delays, and the separations can be much longer than for military families. When children are left behind for a number of years, they may have trouble reattaching to the parents.

Immigrant families face a number of challenges. If they come from a non-English-speaking country, the language barrier will be a serious impediment to becoming comfortable in the new country. They will be unable to read street signs, job announcements and applications, food labels, and communications from the children's schools, unless they live where language translations are commonly used. Because children learn new languages more easily than adults, parent and child roles often are reversed as children become the language and cultural brokers. Children also learn the new cultural norms more quickly than parents, and this causes intergenerational tension about the appropriate level of acculturation, how much of the old to maintain and how much of the new to adopt. Parents may not understand the new culture's norms about child rearing and find themselves at odds with the school system and perhaps with the child protective system. Immigrant wives often come from cultures with traditional gender roles but need to engage in paid work in the United States to keep the family afloat. This often results in more independence and status for wives than they were accustomed to in their home countries and can cause marital conflict if men want to hold on to the traditional gender hierarchy. Research has found increased male-to-female violence in Asian families when wives earn as much or more than their husbands (Chung, Tucker, & Takeuchi, 2008). Many immigrant families come from collectivist cultures where harmony is valued over individual ambition and may feel a great deal of tension about how to respond to cultural pressures toward individualism. They may have had both the support and control of the extended family in the home country and find themselves struggling to maintain family stability with a much more limited support network.

CRITICAL THINKING Questions 7.4

Think of the economic and cultural locations of your family of origin and your current family. What experiences have you had with family economic and cultural diversity that will be helpful to you in your social work career? What are the limitations in your experience with family economic and cultural diversity? What can you do to build your understanding and skills in this area?

CHALLENGES TO FAMILY LIFE

Contemporary families of all types face many stressful situations that challenge their ability to provide nurturance and the necessary resources for healthy development of family members. Every historical era and every culture presents its own set of challenges to families. In the following sections, we discuss three challenges to contemporary families: family violence, divorce, and substance abuse.

FAMILY VIOLENCE

The family is the social group from whom we expect to receive our greatest love, support, nurturance, and acceptance. And yet family relationships are some of the most violent in many societies. It is estimated that wife beating occurs in about 85% of the world's societies, and husband beating occurs in about 27% (Newman, 2012). Children are even more vulnerable to violence within the family than adults. Children are abused by parents, but physical violence between siblings may be the most common form of family violence. Older adults are sometimes abused by their family caregivers, and teenage children sometimes abuse their parents, particularly their mothers (Gelles, 2010).

It is very difficult to produce accurate statistics about the amount of family violence in different categories because the family is the most intimate of social groupings; what happens in families is usually "behind closed doors," away from the watchful eyes of strangers, relatives, and neighbors. In addition, different definitions of violence are used by different researchers. The data presented here are the best available. According to the U.S. Department of Justice Statistics (Catalano, 2012), 775,650 women and 130,890 men in the United States were victims of intimate partner violence in 2009. This is a 64% decline since 1994. From 1994 to 2010, about 4 out of 5 victims of intimate partner violence were females. In 2012, an estimated 9.2 per 1,000 children were judged to be victims of child maltreatment by parents or other caregivers; of these situations where the type of maltreatment is known, 78% involved child neglect, 18.3% involved physical abuse, 9.3% involved sexual abuse, and 8.5% involved psychological maltreatment (U.S. Department of Health and Human Services, 2013). National surveys find much higher numbers of child maltreatment than these official numbers (see Finkelhor, Ormrod, Turner, & Hamby, 2005). One research team found that 35% of 2,030 children in a national survey reported being physically assaulted by a sibling in the past year (Finkelhor et al., 2005). There are no official statistics on elder abuse, but one national incidence study found that 1 in 10 adults older than age 60 reported emotional, physical, or sexual mistreatment or neglect during the past year (Acierno et al., 2010). It is estimated that 750,000 to 1 million violent acts are committed against parents by their adolescent children each year (Gelles, 2010).

How is it that the social group assigned the societal task of providing love and nurturance becomes a setting for so much violence? Research indicates that family violence is multidetermined and identifies a number of associated factors. Stress, social isolation, economic distress, substance abuse, mental health problems, and intergenerational modeling have all been found to increase the risk of family violence (Gelles, 2010; Newman, 2012). The United States is a relatively violent society, and violence is often seen as an appropriate way to resolve disputes (Hutchison, 2007). There are cultures of the world and subcultures in the United States that believe men have the right to beat women and parents have the right to beat children.

It can be argued that the very nature of family life makes it a breeding ground for conflict. Family members spend a great deal of time together and interact intimately in good times and bad. They tend to stir each other's most intense emotions, both positive and negative. If family members do not have good conflict resolution skills, they may not have a repertoire of behaviors other than violence to resolve conflicts.

Intervention in situations of family violence requires careful assessment, and even with the best assessment, it is difficult to predict future behavior. The decision that must be made is whether protective steps are necessary: Must children be removed? Are restraining orders necessary? Must the abused partner flee for safety? There are no ideal solutions. Removing children from abusive households may be necessary to protect them physically, but this solution carries its own risks. Children suffer emotional damage from the separation and loss and may blame themselves for the family disruption. They may be vulnerable to further abuse in the foster home if they have intense care needs. There are also risks to leaving children in homes where they have been abused, including the risk that the child will be killed. Unfortunately, the available resources are not often sufficient to meet a distressed family's needs. Clearly, no one solution fits every situation of child abuse.

The literature on domestic partner violence has proposed some useful typologies for thinking about intervention in such situations (Holtzworth-Munroe & Stuart, 1994; Johnson, 1995). Domestic partner violence can be one-way or mutual; mutual violence can be mutual fighting or involve self-defense or retaliation against a primary aggressor. It may be considered minor, involving shoving, pushing, grabbing, and slapping, or severe, involving choking, kicking, hitting with an object, beating up, or using a knife or gun. Mutual fighting tends to be less severe and more infrequent than other forms of intimate partner violence and does not usually escalate. It involves both partners who use physical means to resolve conflicts. On the other hand, one-sided use of severe forms of violence, sometimes called intimate terrorism, typically occurs more frequently and escalates over time. Many of the perpetrators of this type of violence are involved in other antisocial behaviors as well.

Just as with child abuse, different types of intervention are required for different types of domestic partner violence. Protective removal is imperative for intimate terrorism or any form of escalating violence. On the other hand, systemic couples work, in which couples are taught other methods of conflict resolution, may well be appropriate for couples who occasionally use mutual violence to resolve conflict. Support for this idea comes from a research project that looked at mutual and one-way spouse abuse in the army. The researchers found about even rates of these two types of intimate violence in 1998. After 4 years of prevention and education programs, mutual abuse had decreased by 58%, while one-way abuse had decreased by only 13% (McCarroll, Ursano, Fan, & Newby, 2004). This finding suggests that further attention to matching the intervention to the specific situation may be fruitful. The typologies discussed here do not cover every type of intimate partner violence situation, but they do make a good start at thinking about the multiple factors involved in family violence.

DIVORCE

Most people who get married do not anticipate that they will divorce, and yet divorce is very common. Almost all societies have mechanisms for dissolving marriages, whether it is divorce or civil or religious annulment. Worldwide, divorce rates tend to be higher in wealthier nations; for example, divorce rates are lower in the newly industrializing nations of Latin America and Asia than in the wealthy late-industrial nations of western Europe and North America (Newman, 2012). In the United States, however, the divorce rate is highest among low-income families.

There is much complexity in the analysis of divorce rates, but the divorce rate in the United States appears to have increased steadily from the mid-19th century through the 1970s, except for a sharp drop in the 1950s. It peaked in 1981 and has been dropping slightly since then but remains high compared with other wealthy industrialized countries (Greene, Anderson, Forgatch, Degarmo, & Hetherington, 2012). The lifetime probability of divorce in the United States still approaches 50% but appears to be lower for more recent marriages (Cherlin, 2010). Second and third marriages are more likely to end in divorce than first marriages. The average length of a marriage that ends in divorce is 8 years, and the average age of first divorce is 30 (Irvin, 2012). The likelihood of divorce is very small for couples that have been married for 35 or more years (divorcesource.com, n.d.).

It is thought that economic factors contribute to divorce. Wages have stagnated for non-Hispanic White men and have declined for African American men. Millions of lower-income wage earners are receiving poverty-level wages and are vulnerable to layoffs. Although women still earn less than men, they are becoming more economically independent, and about two thirds of divorces are initiated by women (Amato & Irving, 2006; Coleman, Ganong, & Warzinik, 2007). On the other hand, wives' earnings may reduce economic pressures and help to stabilize marriage (Fine, Ganong, & Demo, 2010).

There is a controversy in the empirical literature about the consequences of divorce for family members. Some researchers have found serious, long-term, postdivorce adjustment problems for both children and adults (Wallerstein & Blakeslee, 1990). Other researchers who use larger and more representative samples have found more modest and shorter-term effects for both adults and children (Barber & Demo, 2006; Braver, Shapiro, & Goodman, 2006).

Fine et al. (2010) suggest several reasons for the differences in findings. First, researchers tend to focus on one or two reactions to divorce and fail to measure other types of reactions. Second, few researchers have taken a longer-term longitudinal view of divorce adjustment, and consequently they are tapping reactions during the difficult acute adjustment phase. Third, researchers look for average reactions rather than for the variability of reactions to divorce. The feminist perspective, on the other hand, would emphasize that divorce is experienced and perceived differently by different family members and would be interested in these various perspectives. Fine et al. (2010) assert that the different conclusions about the effects of divorce on child and adult development may result partly from the fact that the effect sizes are often small and may vary with the nature and size of the sample, which would not happen if there was a stronger relationship between divorce and adjustment.

There is consistent evidence, however, that the economic well-being of women and children declines after divorce (Sayer, 2006). There are several reasons for this. Mothers devote more time to caring for children than fathers, and this restricts their time to devote to educational and occupational pursuits. Women do not earn as much as men. Moreover, many fathers do not comply fully with child support requirements (Pirog & Ziol-Guest, 2006), but even if they did, child support awards are typically too low to meet the costs of raising children (Stirling & Aldrich, 2008).

It seems clear that divorce is a crisis for most adults, lasting for approximately 2 years. Stress increases in the run-up to the divorce, during the divorce, and in the immediate aftermath. However, the stress level typically subsides within a year after divorce as families adjust relationships and routines (Demo & Fine, 2010). There is also evidence that African American women get more social support than White women following divorce (Orbuch & Brown, 2006).

After a careful review of the empirical evidence, Fine et al. (2010) agree with Emery (1999) on the following points about children's adjustment to divorce:

- Divorce is stressful for children.
- Divorce leads to adjustment and mental health problems for children.
- Most children are resilient and adjust well to divorce over time.
- Children whose parents divorce report pain, unhappy memories, and continued distress.
- Postdivorce family interaction has a great influence on adjustment to divorce.
- Children's adjustment is enhanced if they have a good relationship with at least one parent.

SUBSTANCE ABUSE

Substance abuse is often part of the fabric of family life and usually has an effect on the partner relationship and on child development. For the purposes of this discussion, substance abuse is defined as serious and persistent problems with alcohol and/or other substances and does not refer specifically to a clinical diagnosis. Substance abuse is often described as a family problem, not only because of its effect on the entire family system but also because of the growing evidence of a strong genetic component in the etiology of substance abuse (Bierut, 2011). The effect of substance abuse on the partner relationship and the impact of adolescent substance abuse on the family are discussed briefly here, followed by a larger discussion of the impact of parental substance abuse on children.

Kenneth Leonard and Rina Eiden (2007) reviewed the evidence about the impact of alcohol abuse on marital satisfaction and marital violence. They conclude that alcohol abuse has an adverse effect on marital satisfaction and stability, especially among couples where one partner is abusing alcohol and the other partner is not. They also conclude that there is evidence of a strong association between excessive alcohol consumption and intimate partner violence. Consistent with a family life cycle perspective, they found evidence that family transitions can affect patterns of alcohol use for both men and women, with excessive drinking declining in the transition to marriage and during pregnancy and increasing in the postnatal period. There is also strong evidence that excessive alcohol use increases after divorce but may decrease for women divorcing from spouses with alcohol problems.

Some evidence also exists that adolescent substance abuse problems change the nature of parent–child relationships, with parents changing their discipline methods in response to the substance abuse (Mezzich et al., 2007). There is also evidence that adolescent substance abuse increases parental stress and sometimes results in increased use of alcohol among parents (Leonard & Eiden, 2007). Parents may need family support and training in coping responses, as well as social policies that allow family leave from work when faced with an adolescent with substance abuse problems (Deater-Deckard, 2004).

By one estimate, one in four children in the United States is exposed to a family member's alcohol abuse, and one in six children live with parents who abuse illicit drugs (VanDeMark et al., 2005). Although research finds that parental substance abuse does not always lead to an unacceptable level of parenting (Coyle et al., 2009; Havnen, Breivik, Stormark, & Jakobsen, 2011; Street, Harrington, Chiang, Cairns, & Ellis, 2004), there is much empirical evidence that parental substance abuse often impairs parental functioning. Brynna Kroll (2004) reviewed the empirical literature on the experiences of children who grow up in families where adult use of alcohol and other substances is problematic. A number of negative effects on children were noted. In all the reviewed studies, secrecy and denial about the substance abuse were organizing features of family life, cutting the family off from extended family and community supports. Children often become afraid and mistrustful of outsiders who try to help, fearing being taken from their parent(s), among other fears.

Adult children of alcoholics report pervasive loss and grief, including loss of feeling loved, loss of a reliable parent, loss of a "normal" lifestyle, and loss of childhood itself. And whereas not all substance-abusing parents abuse their children, there is an increased risk of child maltreatment while using. Given that substance abuse is often characterized by cycles of relapse and recovery, parental substance abuse does not mean that everything falls apart, particularly during phases of abstinence or reduced use, but parental conflict and fighting do typically increase during periods of excessive substance use. Children's lives are often dominated by the needs, feelings, and behaviors of substance-abusing parents. The children sometimes become caregivers to their parents, putting them to bed when they are drunk or cleaning up after a parent who urinates on the floor. There is considerable evidence that substance-abusing parents engage in less monitoring of their children's behavior.

Research has also found parental substance abuse to be a risk factor for child behavior problems as well as depression and anxiety (Barnard & McKeganey, 2004). School performance often suffers in children of substance-abusing parents, as do peer relationships. Parental substance abuse during childhood is also associated with young-adult difficulties with romantic partnerships (Fischer, Lyness, & Engler, 2010).

Although parental substance abuse is a risk factor in child development, some substance-abusing parents are able to manage family life in a way that supports healthy child development. James Coyle and colleagues (2009) were interested in family functioning in families affected by parental alcohol abuse, particularly in the dimensions of family functioning that allowed these families to be resilient. Their statistical analysis identified families who were functioning at above-average, average, and below-average levels, according to standardized measures. Their research provides support for Froma Walsh's (2016) model of family resilience, in which aspects of belief systems, family organization, and communication processes allow families to be resilient in the face of adversity. They found that families who functioned well on one of these dimensions functioned well on all three. Levels of social functioning were not related to social class or parental education. They did find, however, that Black families with a substance-abusing parent were more likely to have above-average or average functioning than White and Native American families, even though the Black families were, overall, in the lower end of the range of economic resources and reported more stressful life events.

Other research that has looked at the strengths of substance-abusing parents has focused on those parents in treatment. This research finds that these parents are self-critical about their abilities to parent while abusing substances but also report making attempts to combine their substance abuse with efforts to ensure that the needs of their children were being met. The desire to look after their children properly or to get the children back from substitute care is a powerful motivator to stop using alcohol and/or other drugs (Fraser, McIntyre, & Manby, 2009; Tracy & Martin, 2007).

Some researchers report that substance-abusing mothers feel overwhelming guilt and shame about the impact their substance abuse has on their parenting (K. Cox, 2000). In a study of mothers in treatment, 68% of whom had "lost" children to substitute care, Tracy and Martin (2007) found that 90% of the mothers viewed their relationships with their children as close, and 84% reported that their children provide as much support for sobriety as the adults in their lives do. The emotional care provided by children of substance-abusing parents is often noted in the literature by such terms as "role reversal," "parental child," or "parentification," all of which suggest a negative impact on the child of providing such care. One research team (Godsall, Jurkovic, Emshoff, Anderson, & Stanwyck, 2004) examined the relationships between parental alcohol misuse and parentification and children's self-concept. They found that African American child participants scored higher on self-concept than European American children. They suggest that the concept of parentification, and similar concepts, may not be applicable to African American families and other collectivist-oriented families where close kinship networks are valued. They further suggest that considerable caregiving responsibilities in the context of close kinship ties may not have negative effects for children who are also receiving support and caring. Caregiving by children may be a part of a pattern of "filial responsibility" and not interpreted as unjust by the children.

In interpreting their finding that African American families with alcohol-abusing parents score better on family functioning than other such families, Coyle et al. (2009) note that Froma Walsh's (2016) model of family resilience indicates that flexibility in family structure in times of adversity serves as a shock absorber and fosters family resilience. Walsh (2006) also identifies family belief systems as sources for resilience, and Coyle et al. (2009) note that other researchers have found that cultural pride, kinship, spirituality, and high expectations for children are common in African American families. Coyle et al. (2009) suggest that struggling families may best be helped by identifying possible cultural beliefs, locating resources outside the nuclear family, becoming more flexible in family roles, and improving communication. You may recognize this as consistent with Walsh's model of family resilience that identifies belief systems, organizational patterns, and communication as the ingredients for family resilience.

CRITICAL THINKING Questions 7.5

Three challenges to family life are discussed in the previous section: family violence, divorce, and substance abuse. If you were to be my coauthor on this chapter for the third edition of the book, what advice would you give me about the most important challenges facing families today? Are family violence, divorce, and substance abuse new or enduring challenges for families in the United States? Do these challenges appear to occur across cultural lines—across traditional, modern, and postmodern cultures (review Chapter 6 for descriptions of these three types of culture)?

IMPLICATIONS FOR SOCIAL WORK PRACTICE

This discussion of families and family life, in the context of larger social systems, suggests several practice principles.

- Assess families from a variety of theoretical perspectives. Given recent economic shifts, be particularly aware of the impact of changes in larger systems on families' resources and functioning.
- Recognize the diversity of family structures represented by the families with whom you work and be sensitive to the relative strengths and weaknesses of each of these family structures.
- Develop awareness of economic diversity among families and the different economic and other resources available to the families you serve.
- Develop awareness of cultural diversity among families and a commitment to culturally sensitive practice that involves ongoing learning both about and from families that are different from your own.
- Use appropriate family assessment tools, including the genogram, ecomap, and timeline, to help you develop a more comprehensive understanding of the families with which you work.
- Give families credit for struggling well in adverse circumstances.
- Understand policies and changes at the state and national levels and the ways they affect both your own work and the lives of all families—particularly lower-income, stressed families.
- Where appropriate, encourage family members to become involved in neighborhood, local, state, and national efforts for positive change.
- As appropriate, work toward your agency's becoming involved in policy and advocacy work on behalf of families, including development of needed programs and services.

KEY TERMS

ABC-X model of family stress and coping, 201
cohabiting, 206
differentiation of self, 198
family, 194
family ecomap, 200
family economic stress model, 214
family investment model, 214
family of origin, 198
family resilience perspective, 203
family systems perspective, 199
family timeline, 202
feminist perspective on families, 200
genogram, 199
intersectionality feminist theory, 200
lone-parent families, 209
multilevel family practice model, 200
nonnormative stressors, 202
normative stressors, 202
stress pileup, 202
triangulation, 198

ACTIVE LEARNING

1. *Theory and your family.* We have used different theoretical lenses to look at the family of Bobby Sharpe. If you were a social worker working with a family similar to the Sharpes, you would want to be aware of how your own family experiences influence your practice with families. You can use theory to help you do that as well. To begin this process, working individually, reflect on the following questions related to your family of origin and your childhood:

   - What value was placed on connectedness, and what value was placed on the differentiated self?
   - What were the external boundaries—who was in and who was out of the family? What were the commonly shared beliefs? What roles did family members play? What were the patterns of communication?
   - How traditional were the gender roles in your family? How was power distributed?
   - Can you recall any periods of stress pileup? If so, how did your family cope during those periods?
   - How did your family use belief systems, organizational patterns, and communication to be resilient in the face of adversity?

   After you have reflected on these questions, pair up with one other student and discuss your reflections, sharing only what you are comfortable to share.

2. *Visualizing your family.* Sometimes we learn new things about families when we prepare visual representations of them. There are several tools available for doing this. You can use three of them here to visualize your own family.

   - Referring to Exhibit 7.2, prepare a multigenerational genogram of your family, going back to your maternal and paternal grandparents.
   - Referring to Exhibit 7.3, prepare a family ecomap of your current family situation.
   - Referring to Exhibit 7.4, prepare a family timeline, beginning at the point of your birth or earlier if you think there were significant earlier events that need to be noted.

   After you have prepared these materials, work in small groups in class to discuss how useful each tool was in helping you think about your family of origin. Were any new insights gained from using these visual tools? What is your overall reaction to using tools like these to understand your family?

3. *Theory analysis and application.* Working in small groups, review the big ideas of the eight theoretical perspectives presented in Exhibit 2.9 in Chapter 2. Discuss which of the theoretical perspectives is the best fit for how you think about families. Also discuss how your theory of families might affect your social work with families.

WEB RESOURCES

Administration for Children & Families (ACF)

www.acf.hhs.gov

Site of ACF, a government agency that is part of the U.S. Department of Health and Human Services, contains fact sheets about children and families and information about ACF programs such as child support enforcement, Head Start, and Temporary Assistance for Needy Families (TANF).

Council on Contemporary Families

www.contemporaryfamilies.org

Official site of the Council on Contemporary Families, a nonprofit organization that promotes an inclusive view of families, contains information and research on families, along with links to other Internet resources.

Families and Work Institute

www.familiesandwork.org

Site contains information on work–life research, community mobilization forums, information on the Fatherhood Project, and frequently asked questions.

Forum on Child and Family Statistics

www.childstats.gov

Official website of the Federal Interagency Forum on Child and Family Statistics offers easy access to federal and state statistics and reports on children and families, including international comparisons.

National Council on Family Relations (NCFR)

www.ncfr.org

Site contains publications, news, and professional resources.

SAGE edge™ **Sharpen your skills with SAGE edge at edge.sagepub.com/hutchisoness2e**

SAGE edge for students provides a personalized approach to help you accomplish your coursework goals in an easy-to-use learning environment. watch listen read

LEARNING OBJECTIVES	FOR FURTHER EXPLORATION AND APPLICATION
LO 7.1: Analyze one's emotional and cognitive reactions to a case study.	(listen) Putting the Post-Deployment Family Back Together
LO 7.2: Analyze the merits of different approaches to defining family.	(read) Family Diversity Projects
LO 7.3: Compare and contrast five theoretical perspectives for understanding families (psychodynamic, family systems, feminist, family stress and coping, and family resilience).	(listen) Strengthening Family Resilience (read) Families Parenting Adolescents With Substance Abuse—Recovering the Mother's Voice: A Narrative Literature Review
LO 7.4: Identify a number of types of diversity in family life that might be encountered by social workers.	(watch) How to Talk to Veterans About the War (watch) Blended Family (watch) Multigenerational Family (read) Work and Family Researcher's Network
LO 7.5: Analyze three types of challenges to family life (family violence, divorce, and substance abuse).	(watch) Why Domestic Violence Victims Don't Leave (read) Family Diversity Is the New Normal for America's Children
LO 7.6: Apply knowledge of family theories, family diversity, and family challenges to recommend guidelines for social work assessment and intervention.	(read) Doing Family Therapy as a New Social Worker: The Do's and Don'ts (read) What Is Family Diversity? Objective and Interpretive Approaches

Small Groups, Formal Organizations, and Communities

Elizabeth D. Hutchison and Elizabeth P. Cramer

Learning Objectives

LO 8.1 Compare and contrast one's emotional and cognitive reactions to three case studies.

LO 8.2 Define small groups and identify some of their uses in social work practice.

LO 8.3 Analyze the benefits and difficulties in using virtual groups in social work practice.

LO 8.4 Identify dimensions of small group structure, composition, and processes.

LO 8.5 Critique five theories of small group processes (psychodynamic, symbolic interaction, status characteristics and expectation states, exchange, and self-categorization).

LO 8.6 Define formal organizations.

LO 8.7 Critique four theoretical perspectives on formal organizations (rational, systems, interactional/interpretive, and critical).

LO 8.8 Recommend uses of information and communication technologies in social service organizations.

LO 8.9 Define community, territorial community, relational community, and sense of community.

LO 8.10 Critique five theoretical approaches to community (contrasting types, spatial arrangements, social systems, social capital, and conflict).

LO 8.11 Apply knowledge of small groups, formal organizations, and communities to recommend guidelines for social work assessment and intervention.

Jim West imageBROKER/Newscom

CASE STUDY 8.1

THE SEXUALITY AND GENDER GROUP AT A WOMEN'S RESIDENTIAL SUBSTANCE ABUSE TREATMENT FACILITY

The sexuality and gender group at the women's residential substance abuse treatment facility meets twice a month. This is a support group for lesbian, bisexual, and questioning women (those women who are unsure of their sexual orientation). Women who identify as transgender also attend the group. Women in the treatment facility are informed about the group by their counselors, and participation in the group is strictly voluntary. The facilitator is a licensed clinical social worker who is also a social work professor and a lesbian. The composition of the group can change each session because women are entering and exiting the facility regularly. Typically, 8 to 15 women attend the group. The duration of the treatment program is 90 days; however, some of the women choose to leave the program before treatment has been completed. Many of the women in the group are parents; some of them have brought their children into treatment with them because one of the treatment programs at this facility allows women and their children to come into residence. Most of the women in this group identify as African American or Hispanic and range in age from 19 to 50. The facilitator is Caucasian, Jewish, and in her early 40s. The following is an account of one of the group sessions. Pseudonyms for all the group members and facilitator are used in this case.

Deb has been facilitating the sexuality and gender group at the substance abuse treatment facility, the first of its kind at this facility, for about a year. It has been a good learning experience for her, and she has grown quite attached to the group. She particularly is impressed with the candidness of the group members and often refers to this population of women as superb "BS detectors," because they are not afraid to call each other out when denial or deceitfulness is surfacing.

The group members are already in the lounge where group meets when Deb arrives. She smiles and acknowledges each of the group members through eye contact. She notices that out of the dozen women in the room, about eight of them were there for the last group session. Deb introduces herself and makes a point to say that she is a lesbian but not in recovery, although she has worked with many women who are in recovery. She mentions where she works and how long she has been facilitating this group. She then asks the women to introduce themselves using first names. In their introductions, some of the women mention why they have come to group or how long they've attended group. Two of the women share that they were curious about the group but don't identify as lesbian or bisexual; however, they have considered same-sex relationships and have had feelings of same-sex attraction. One of the group members notes that she has recently exited the prison system and had relationships with other women while she was incarcerated but never while "on the streets."

Deb describes the purpose of the group as a place for members to talk about sexual orientation, whether they are lesbian, bisexual, or questioning. Deb stresses that what is said in the room stays in the room and that members should refrain from sharing someone's story with others outside of the group. Confidentiality is especially important to emphasize in residential programs. Deb also mentions that the group is open and that members can freely discuss what they want to.

Deb usually has a loosely planned agenda for each group session but also waits to see what issues may get raised in the introductions and check-in at the beginning of the group. Today, she brought the documentary film *All God's Children* to show the group (Mosbacher, Reid, & Rhue, 1996). The film highlights the experiences of African American lesbians, gays, and bisexuals, particularly related to family, church, and community. It's a powerful film and reminds the group members that their sexual orientations are not experienced in a bubble; rather, the intersections of faith, neighborhood, geography, and other identities and characteristics influence how they experience their sexual orientations.

One part of the film seems to arouse much energy and discussion: whether a person is born gay or makes a decision or choice to be gay. Tamika, one of the younger women in group, strongly asserts that a person chooses to be gay. She shuns the labels of "lesbian" and "bisexual"; instead, she prefers to allow herself to date or fall in love with whoever is attractive to her, whether that person is male, female, or transgender. Monica, a woman in her early 50s, disagrees that sexual orientation is a choice. She shares a story of how she "knew" she was a lesbian when she was 12 and she fell head over heels for a girl in her neighborhood. She tried to suppress those feelings and pretended she was into boys all through middle school and the beginning of high school. By her junior year, she just couldn't pretend anymore. She secretly would date girls, but no one in her family or her church knew. To this day, many years later, she has never openly said to any of her family members that she is a lesbian. They all seem to know that she is, but it isn't discussed. She experienced a deep hurt at her church when her pastor delivered a sermon that Monica thought was very antigay. Her parents insisted that she attend church. She really didn't want to go to church after that sermon, but she also didn't want to tell her parents the reason why. That wasn't the first and last time that antigay remarks were made in her church. Gail, usually quiet in group, shares that her experience at church has been the opposite of Monica's. Her family attended a progressive church and persons of all sexual orientations were welcomed. She still hesitated to come out to her family members when she first began dating women but then eventually began to disclose to the family members to whom she felt closest. Their positive responses encouraged her to continue to disclose to other family members and close friends.

The discussion of the film moves the group into deeper core themes related to their sexual orientation and their addiction. As the facilitator, Deb looks for opportunities to work the parallel process in group—to note the similarities between the negative consequences of an addiction and the experience of being a sexual minority who is often discriminated against and ostracized. A few of these common issues include shame, fear, emotional dependence, and despair and loneliness. Shame is a particularly powerful emotion; the women in the group connect shame to experiences they've had as sexual minorities and the guilt and embarrassment about behaviors in which they've engaged while they were using drugs. Negative judgments from others about their sexual orientations and/or their addictions exacerbated the shame. One of the group members shares with the group about how she would get high in order to allow herself to be intimate with women. She thought it was the only way she could mask her fear and shame about her attraction to other women. Many of the group members struggle with feelings of internalized homophobia. In the group, Deb emphasizes how acceptance of oneself is important to group members' emotional health.

The group is coming to a close. Most of the women have spoken in group today. The film seemed to strike a chord with many of them. On the way back to her workplace, Deb thinks about all the group members and what they shared that day. She feels fortunate to be let in to the inner lives of the women during a time when they are working hard to heal.

CASE STUDY 8.2

CHANGING LEADERSHIP AT BEACON CENTER

Beacon Center (BC) has a short but proud history of providing innovative services to persons who are homeless in River Run, the midsize midwestern city where it is located. It was established in 1980, thanks to one woman, Martha Green, and her relentless pursuit of a vision.

While serving as executive director of the YWCA, Martha became increasingly concerned about the growing homeless population in River Run. During the late 1960s and 1970s, she had worked in several positions in River Run's antipoverty agency, and she was well-known throughout the city for her uncompromising advocacy efforts for families living in poverty. Martha was also a skilled advocate and service planner, and she soon pulled together supporters for a new social service agency to address the special needs of homeless persons. A mix of private and public (both federal and local) funds were secured, and BC opened with Martha Green as director, working with the assistance of one staff social worker. The agency grew steadily, and within a decade it had a staff of 15, as well as several subcontracted programs.

Martha valued client input into program development and made sure that client voices were heard at all levels: at city council meetings, in community discussions of program needs, in BC discussions of program needs and issues, in staff interviews, and at board meetings. She remained uncompromising in advocacy efforts and often angered city officials because she was unyielding in her demands for fair treatment of homeless persons. She advocated for their

(Continued)

(Continued)

right to receive resources and services from other social service organizations as well as for their right to congregate in public places.

By the same token, Martha and the staff consistently reminded clients of their obligations as citizens and, gently but firmly, held them to those obligations. Clients were sometimes angered by this call for responsible behavior, but they appreciated the tireless advocacy of Martha and the staff. They also appreciated that they were kept fully informed about political issues that concerned them, as well as about actions taken by BC in relation to these issues.

Martha also had a vision regarding staff relationships. She was committed to working collaboratively, to trusting frontline workers to make their own decisions, and to securing the participation of all staff on important policy decisions. This commitment was aided by the fact that Martha and her staff came from similar backgrounds and had deep family roots in River Run. Rules were kept to a minimum, and staff relationships were very personal. Martha believed in hiring the best-trained and most experienced staff for frontline positions, and she had high expectations of her staff. She was also a nurturing administrator who was concerned about the personal well-being and professional development of each staff member. She established a climate of mutual respect where people could risk disagreeing.

Martha spent some time every week working in each program area to ensure that she understood the agency's programs as they were experienced by clients and frontline staff. She kept staff fully informed about economic and political pressures faced by BC and about her actions in regard to these issues. She regularly sought their input on these issues, and decisions were usually made by consensus. On occasion, however, around really sensitive issues—such as the choice between forgoing a salary increase and closing a program—she asked staff to vote by secret ballot to neutralize any potential power dynamics.

Martha had a vision, as well, about how a board of directors can facilitate a successful client-centered program. She saw the board as part of the BC system, just as staff and clients were part of the system. She worked hard to ensure that members chosen for the board shared the BC commitment to the rights of homeless persons, and she developed warm, personal relationships with them. She kept the board fully informed about issues facing BC and was successful in securing their support and active involvement in advocacy and resource development activities.

Over the years, BC became known as an innovative, client-centered service center, as well as a hardheaded advocacy organization. Staff and board members took pride in being part of what they considered to be a very special endeavor—one that outstripped other social service organizations in its expertise, commitment, and compassion. Clients were not always satisfied with the services but generally acknowledged among themselves that they were lucky to have the dedication of BC.

Reactions from the community were more mixed, however. The respect offered up was, in many circles, a grudging one. Many city officials as well as staff of other social service organizations complained about the self-righteous attitudes and uncompromising posture of Martha and the staff at BC. These detractors acknowledged that the tactics of BC staff were successful in countering discrimination against homeless persons but suggested that BC succeeded at much cost of goodwill. Although Martha believed in keeping staff, clients, and board members informed about the economic and political pressures faced by BC, she saw it as her job to carry the major responsibility for responding to, and absorbing, those pressures, to protect staff energy for serving clients.

Martha retired almost 20 years ago and relocated with her husband to be closer to their children. An acting director was appointed at BC while a search for a permanent director was under way. The acting director had worked several years at BC and shared much of Martha's administrative and service philosophy. She was not as good, however, at juggling the multiple demands of the position. Staff and clients felt a loss of support, board members lost some of their enthusiasm and confidence, and antagonists in the community saw an opportunity to mute some of BC's advocacy efforts. Staff maintained a strong commitment to the rights of homeless persons, but they lost some of their optimism about making a difference.

After 8 months, Helen Blue, a former community college administrator, was hired as the new executive director. Like Martha Green, she was of European American heritage, but she had only lived in River Run for a few years. She was excited about this new professional challenge but had a vision for BC that was somewhat different from Martha's. She was concerned about the alienation that had resulted, in some circles, from BC's hard-hitting advocacy stance, and she favored a more conciliatory approach. For example, after meeting with city officials, she assigned staff social workers the task of convincing clients to stop congregating in the city park near BC and to stay out of the business district during business hours. After meeting with directors of other social service organizations, she directed staff to be less demanding in their advocacy for clients. Helen was also concerned about the lack of rules and the looseness of attention to chain of command, and she began to institute new rules and procedures. Staff meetings and open community meetings with clients became presentations by Helen. Staff were no longer allowed to attend board meetings and were not informed about what happened at them. Frontline staff often found their decisions overturned by Helen. When the first staff resignation came, Helen hired the replacement with no input from staff, clients, or board members.

Helen stayed a few years at BC and then decided to return to community college administration. Since she left, BC has had three executive directors, two that stayed for only a short time. The current CEO, Roderick Wallace, has been with BC for 12 years and has guided it through a major funding and program expansion. When he came to BC, the organization was floundering. He spent time with different groups of stakeholders—staff, board members, clients, community leaders, and representatives of other social service organizations—to learn their vision for the organization. He invited the staff to begin to attend board meetings again. Working collaboratively with other organizations, he brought in some new federal and local funds to expand health care coverage for homeless persons. His meetings with stakeholding groups identified two issues for BC: (1) the need for a more ethnically diverse staff and board (Roderick is African American) and (2) the need to improve information technology to support administrative functions and program accountability. Roderick has had some success in both areas, but the introduction of greater ethnic diversity of the staff has introduced new tensions that continue to bubble up from time to time.

In the recession of 2009, as funding streams became more restricted at a time of growing homelessness caused by home foreclosures and a weakened economy, Roderick encouraged the board to begin a strategic planning process to ensure financial stability and continued service quality, with some success on both fronts. In the past 2 years, BC has forged new partnerships in the community and expanded the comprehensiveness of its health care services. Roderick depends on a dedicated professional staff to ensure the quality of the programs. As the organization has grown, he has maintained much of the structure developed by Helen Blue, but he emphasizes to all stakeholders the importance of staying flexible in a highly volatile environment.

CASE STUDY 8.3

FILIPINA DOMESTIC WORKERS CREATING TRANSNATIONAL COMMUNITIES

Filipina domestic workers scattered around the globe read the multinational magazine *Tinig Filipino*, now on Facebook and Twitter, and many contribute articles describing the realities of their lives as overseas domestic workers. Sometimes their children back in the Philippines write articles about the pain of separation from their mothers or about the heroic sacrifices their mothers make to provide much-needed economic resources to their families back home. Filipino women (Filipinas) work as domestic workers in more than 130 countries, working in elder care, child care, and housecleaning. They are among the ranks of service workers of globalization.

Globalization has created both a pull and a push for Filipinas to become global domestic workers. It has created a heightened demand (pull) for low-wage service workers in major global cities of affluent nations to maintain the lifestyles of professional and managerial workers. It has also produced large geographical economic inequalities, and many poor countries, like the Philippines, are depending on the export of labor to help with debt repayment (push). More than 6 million Filipinos work overseas as contract workers, and the money and goods these workers send home to families, known as remittances, are an important source of revenue at home. In 2013, the Philippines ranked third among countries receiving the largest remittances from overseas workers, with remittances amounting to $26 billion (World Bank, 2013b). The large outflow of labor also helps to decrease very high unemployment and underemployment rates.

Since the early 1990s, women have made up over half of Filipino contract workers. Filipino men work as seamen, carpenters, masons, and mechanics, many in the Middle East. Two thirds of migrant Filipinas are domestic workers, and they work in cities around the world. Many of them have a college education, but they earn more as domestic workers in affluent nations than they would as professional workers in the Philippines. They migrate for economic gain but also, in many instances, to escape domestic violence or other domestic struggles. Most migrate alone. The Philippine government has applauded the legion of female migrant workers as "modern-day heroes." The remittances they send home allow families to buy houses, computers, and college educations for siblings, children, and other relatives.

The two most popular destinations for Filipina domestic workers are Rome and Los Angeles. The community life of the Filipina domestic workers in these two cities is alike in a number of ways; most important, both groups see themselves as simultaneously members of more than one community.

(Continued)

(Continued)

They see themselves as part of a global community of Filipina domestic workers across geographic territories. They see themselves as part of their Philippine communities and only temporarily part of their receiving communities, referring to their sending communities as "home." While they are doing domestic work for class-privileged women in their receiving communities, they sometimes purchase the domestic services of even lower-paid women left behind in the Philippines to help care for their own families. They leave children, who are often very young, at home to be cared for by the extended family that benefits from the remittances they send. By 2008 they were keeping contact with their families in the Philippines by telephone, text messaging, e-mail, airmail letters and packages, and joint bank accounts. In both Rome and Los Angeles, they face anti-immigrant sentiment in their receiving communities, but the hostility is more severe in Rome.

There are great differences, however, in the local cultures of community life among Filipina domestic workers in Rome and Los Angeles. These differences seem to reflect the larger social and political contexts of the migration experience. Let's look first at the community of domestic workers in Rome. There, residence requirements restrict Filipina migrants to domestic work, and they live segregated lives in a society that is not welcoming. Consequently, they have built a community of much solidarity that congregates in multiple private and public gathering places. The domestic workers are residentially dispersed throughout the city, and gathering places are likewise geographically dispersed. Specific gathering places are associated with specific regions of the Philippines.

On their days off, the workers tend to congregate in private gathering places in church centers and apartments. Several churches, mostly Catholic, have opened day-off shelters or church centers where the workers can spend time watching television or listening to music, visiting, and purchasing Filipino food. These centers are often developed out of the joint efforts of local churches in the Philippines and in Rome. The Filipino Chaplaincy, a coalition of 28 Roman Catholic churches, is the strongest advocate for Filipino workers in Rome. It publishes a directory of religious, government, and civic organizations relevant to the Filipino workers. The Santa Prudenziana parish, besides offering regular spiritual activities, also provides a variety of social services, including job placement referrals, free medical care, legal assistance, and Italian language classes. The migrant workers can also participate in choirs, dance groups, and a theater group.

Apartments are another site of private gathering for the Filipinas in Rome. Domestic workers who can navigate the barriers to rent their own apartments sometimes rent out rooms or beds to other migrant workers. They also rent access to their apartments to live-in workers on their days off. Apartments are furnished with televisions and equipment for watching Filipino movies, and at night, renters congregate in the kitchen, eating and relaxing, playing card games and mahjong.

There are also particular train stations and bus stops that are known as public gathering places for Filipinos in Rome, but the city authorities have discouraged congregating in such public places. After much harassment at one bus stop, the Filipino migrants moved to a spot under an overpass, near the Tiber River. They subsequently turned the spot into a shopping bazaar that includes food shops, restaurants, hair salons, and tailoring shops.

These gathering spots allow for network building, sharing information, and providing a variety of assistance to new migrants. The domestic workers often discuss their problems at work and share information about housing. There is an ethic of mutual assistance and solidarity, although occasionally, some migrants take advantage of others in activities such as money lending.

The community of Filipina domestic workers in Los Angeles is not nearly as cohesive as the one in Rome. In contrast to Rome, the Los Angeles Filipino population is class stratified. There has been a long stream of migration from the Philippines to the United States, going back a century, and many earlier streams involved professional workers, particularly in the medical professions. Although many of the Filipina domestic workers have connections to more economically privileged Filipinos in Los Angeles, often securing work through these connections, they perceive the class distinctions as impeding cohesion and do not feel supported by the middle-class Filipino community. This is so even though they often spend their days off with relatives or friends in middle-class homes, or even live alongside middle-class neighbors. The domestic workers perceive the Filipino enclaves as middle-class spaces.

A subcommunity of Filipina domestic workers does seem to form from time to time, however. Live-in workers often congregate in the parks and playgrounds of the wealthy communities where they work. The minority who work as day workers rather than live-in workers often meet on the buses traveling to and from work. Like their counterparts in Rome, they talk about work situations, but these gatherings are neither as large nor as regular as they are in Rome. The domestic workers also often participate in parties in the homes of middle-class Filipinos, but these associations do not seem to lead to the type of solidarity that occurs among the workers in Rome (Parreñas, 2001, 2008).

EXHIBIT 8.1 • Definitions of Small Group, Formal Organization, and Community

CONCEPT	DEFINITION
Small group	Two or more people who interact with each other because of shared interests, goals, experiences, or needs
Formal organization	A collectivity of people, with a high degree of formality of structure, working together to meet a goal or goals
Community	People bound either by geography or by webs of communication, sharing common ties, and interacting with one another

These three case studies illustrate some of the many ways that contemporary social life is shaped by and also shapes human behavior. In this chapter, we look at how humans, in their attempt to work together for stability, survival, and a just world, create small groups, formal organizations, and communities, and how these social creations subsequently influence individual and collective behavior. The sexuality and gender group provides much needed support and information for women struggling with the combined consequences of addiction and being a sexual minority as well as an ethnic and racial minority. The Beacon Center case study illustrates a formal organization in leadership transition as it provides essential social services. The case study of Filipina domestic workers in two cities is an example of how globalization is shaping community life for many people. See Exhibit 8.1 for definitions of small groups, formal organizations, and communities.

SMALL GROUPS IN SOCIAL WORK

Much of human behavior takes place in small groups. The sexuality and gender group is a type of small group with special relevance to social work practice, but most people also become involved in other types of small groups: friendship groups, task groups at work, self-help groups, or sports teams, to name but a few. Donelson Forsyth (2011) reminds us that "people, no matter what they are doing—working, relaxing, studying, exercising, worshipping, or sleeping—are usually in a group rather than alone" (p. 19). We carry out our relationships with significant others in small groups, but it is important to remember that small groups also provide the structures on which communities, organizations, and the larger society are built.

In a mobile society, small groups serve a useful function. Exhibit 8.2 shows how group members may benefit from belonging to a small group. Small groups offer individuals an opportunity to meet others and work together to achieve mutual goals. They provide social support; they socialize us to the norms, values, behaviors, and skills for living in a given society; they provide a sense of belonging; they provide us with companionship and conversation; and they help us to connect to the wider world. Robert Putnam (2000) suggests that in our rapidly changing globalized society, small groups are an important source of *social capital*, or connections among individuals based on reciprocity and trustworthiness.

Small groups may be formally defined in a number of ways, but there is general agreement that small groups are more than a collection of individuals who may have similar traits or be in physical proximity. Persons who live on the same block may be in proximity but have little social interaction and not perceive themselves as a group. Thus, we may define a **small group** as "two or more people who interact with each other because of shared interests, goals, experiences and needs" (Ballantine & Roberts, 2014, p. 153).

A significant element of social work practice today is **group work**, which serves people's needs by bringing them together in small groups. Group work emerged in the United States in the late 1800s and early 1900s. Early group work took place within the settlement houses, YMCA/YWCA, Jewish community centers, and the Boy Scouts and Girl Scouts. These groups focused primarily on recreation, social integration, immigration issues, character building, and social reform. We are now seeing a resurgence in recreation and social skill–building groups, reminiscent of early group work (see Rosenwald et al., 2013). Social skills groups with elementary-age children (Lane et al., 2003); hoops groups (basketball) with adolescent males (Hansen, Larson, & Dworkin, 2003); and physical activity, reminiscence, and motivation groups for older adults (Hughes et al., 2005) are three examples.

Today, groups are viewed as a financially prudent method of service delivery (Coyne, 2014). In addition, empirical studies have shown the effectiveness of groups in addressing a number of social, health, and emotional problems, such as mental illness and substance abuse (Drake, Mueser, Brunette, & McHugo, 2004; Lau, Chan, Li, & Au, 2010) and cancer (Spiegel & Classen, 2000). One researcher (Garrett, 2004) found that a small sample of school social workers make extensive use of group work methods.

EXHIBIT 8.2 • Benefits of Small Groups

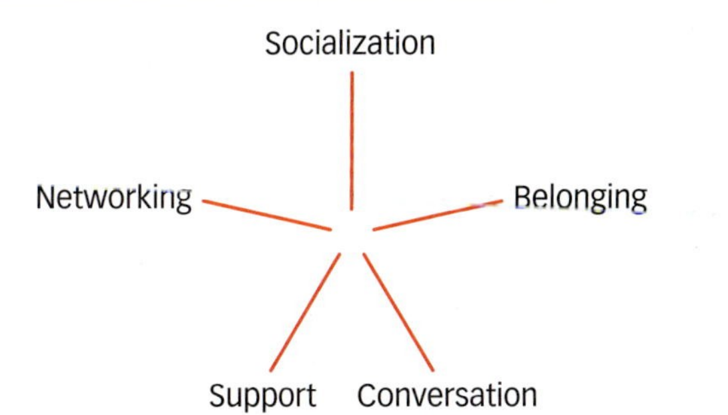

© Digital Vision/Thinkstock

Mothers' support group. Here, mothers join together to share stories, struggles, and insights about the adjustment of becoming a parent.

A number of scholars have established classifications for groups encountered in social work (see, e.g., Kottler & Englar-Carlson, 2010; Toseland & Rivas, 2012; Zastrow, 2009). Exhibit 8.3 compares five types of groups on several major features—purpose, leadership, size, duration—and gives examples of each. Groups may not fall exclusively into one category; rather, they may share elements of several group types. For example, a group for parents and friends of seriously mentally ill persons may include psychoeducational material about the nature of mental illness and its impact on family members, provide mutual aid to its members through discussion of taboo areas, and offer a therapeutic component in the examination of family patterns and dynamics. In recent years, all types of groups have been meeting in virtual format, and we take a look at this trend in the next section.

VIRTUAL GROUPS

Virtual groups are those where members do not meet face-to-face, meeting instead by telephone or through the Internet. Any of the group types covered in Exhibit 8.3 can and has used technology, either as the primary format for running the group or as a supplement to a group that meets face-to-face. Technological advances have made it possible to have telephone conversations among a number of people at very little cost. During the past 2 decades, some social workers and other helping professionals have been using the telephone to offer therapeutic and support groups (Toseland & Larkin, 2010; Toseland & Rivas, 2012). During this same time period, computer-mediated support groups have proliferated in the United States and around the world (Jones & Meier, 2011). We'll look first at telephone-mediated groups and then at computer-mediated groups.

Telephone-mediated groups have not been rigorously evaluated to date, but a number of good case studies have been reported. Toseland and Rivas (2012) reviewed 19 studies of telephone support groups. They found that these groups are most often used with persons with chronic and long-term illnesses or with caregivers of frail older adults. Their review found both advantages and disadvantages of telephone-mediated groups, but the findings were overwhelmingly positive for the types of groups noted earlier. Some researchers found that in some situations, telephone-mediated groups are more cohesive than face-to-face groups. They found that in telephone groups members

EXHIBIT 8.3 • Types of Groups

TYPE OF GROUP	PURPOSE	LEADERSHIP	SIZE	DURATION	EXAMPLES
Therapy	Uses group modality to assist individuals to resolve emotional and behavioral problems	Typically led by a trained clinician or psychotherapist	Typically small, sometimes six or fewer members	Brief therapy groups usually meet for 6 weeks or less. Long-term psychotherapy groups can last years.	Groups for college students run by university counseling centers; groups for male adolescents who engage in sexual harm
Mutual aid	Uses mutual aid processes to create a helping environment within the group milieu	Typically led by a facilitator who may be a professional or layperson trained to lead the group. The leader may or may not have experienced the issue on which the group is focused.	These groups may be small (fewer than 5 persons) or large (12 or more), especially if run in a drop-in format.	Drop-in mutual aid groups may be ongoing for a number of years with members coming in and out of the group. Time-limited mutual aid groups typically run for 4 to 12 weeks.	Groups for cancer survivors; groups in schools for children whose parents are going through a divorce
Psychoeducational	Focuses on the provision of information about an experience or problem	Typically led by a trained professional	Limiting the group size is usually not as critical with these types of groups because of their purpose.	One-time meetings of psychoeducational groups may be offered on a regular schedule; they might be offered in a series of sessions (e.g., a 4-week educational series), or they might be offered on an as-needed basis.	Groups for couples preparing to adopt a child; groups to teach parents how to use adaptive equipment for children with disabilities
Self-help	Uses the commonality of the problem or issue to build social support among members	Typically led by a layperson who has experience with the problem (e.g., a person in recovery from alcohol and drug addiction)	Typically, because self-help groups operate on a drop-in basis, the group size is not limited.	Most often, self-help groups are run on a drop-in basis; however, some may be offered in a time-limited format.	Twelve-step groups (e.g., AA, ACOA, NA)
Task	Created to accomplish a specific task or to advocate around a particular social issue or problem	These groups may be led by professionals or nonprofessionals; leaders may be appointed or elected.	Often limited in size to successfully accomplish the task. When advocating for change, membership may be larger.	Meet until the task has been accomplished or the desired social change has been accomplished	A committee to examine low-income housing needs that is instructed to submit a report of its findings to the city council

no longer focus on personal features such as skin color or other social status cues. Other advantages of telephone groups include convenience of meeting in one's own home, reduced time needed to participate because of no travel time, ability to reach people in rural areas and across greater distances, ability to reach people who are homebound or caring for someone who can't be left alone, and greater levels of self-disclosure. Disadvantages of telephone groups include difficulty for leaders to track individual participation and interpret subtle verbal cues, difficulty for group members to gauge each other's reactions because of the lack of visual cues, and distortions related to technological problems or background noise. Some researchers noted more hostility in telephone-mediated groups than in face-to-face groups, and others noted less hostility. Toseland and Larkin (2010) suggest that social group workers use the same skills in telephone-mediated groups as with face-to-face groups but need to be more active to ensure clear communication because of the lack of visual cues.

Computer technology offers several potential support group outlets, including e-mail-based groups, chat rooms, news groups, videoconferencing, and discussion forums. Computer-mediated support is particularly attractive to younger people for whom electronic communication is their primary means of communication. Computer-mediated groups may provide benefits to some of the same groups of people that benefit from telephone-mediated groups: people living in rural areas, people who are homebound, and caregivers who cannot leave their care recipients (Jones & Meier, 2011). As with telephone-mediated groups, some researchers have found that computer-mediated groups can speed up the process of group cohesiveness and heighten the sense of interdependence among members (Michinov, Michinov, & Toczek-Capell, 2004). Group identity and group cohesiveness do not appear to require member copresence. On the other hand, miscommunication has been found to be more frequent in computer-mediated team meetings (Levi, 2014).

Some people enjoy the anonymity of web-based groups. In some of these groups, the use of pseudonyms and withholding other identifying information is appealing for persons who desire support but don't want to feel too vulnerable. Social workers who refer clients to web-based groups may want to first discuss the potential negative consequences of using such groups. For example, because of the anonymity of the site, participants may engage in hostile or bullying behavior to an extent they would not do in person. A good group moderator will intervene in such behavior. Also, *cyberstalking* is another danger for those who desire to participate in web-based groups (Hitchcock, 2006).

It is a challenge for social workers to stay current with constant technological advances. Jones and Meier (2011) provide a case study of a computer-mediated support group that demonstrates the need to adapt to changing technology. They studied an online support group called Parents of Suicides (POS). The group started in 1998 as an e-mail-based mailing list of about 10 people. In the beginning, the group stayed small and developed quick bonding and a strong sense of identity. In the first year, however, the group grew substantially and lost some of its intimacy. In 2000, new technology allowed POS to add a web-based discussion forum to its e-mail-based list. A separate website was developed to create a memorial wall to honor members' deceased children. Along the way, an online newsletter was developed and then a chat room. As the group numbers grew into the hundreds, conflict and complaints grew. These new challenges were addressed through formalized rules and the formation of

Some people enjoy the anonymity of web-based groups.

subgroups. This case study reminds us that many online support groups are quite large and are better characterized as e-communities than as e-groups.

In deciding whether to use virtual groups, social workers must also give thought to groups that do not have access to telephone and computer technology or who do not have the skills to use the technologies (Mann, Belchior, Tomita, & Kemp, 2005). The digital divide is shrinking but still exists. Students facilitating groups using social network sites need to be particularly careful of potential ethical issues, especially personal privacy, boundaries, safety, and client confidentiality (Barsky, 2013; Judd & Johnston, 2012).

SMALL GROUP STRUCTURE, COMPOSITION, AND PROCESSES

The sexuality and gender group serves a variety of functions, but that one group cannot provide for all of the group members' needs. Group members are also involved in friendship circles, 12-step groups, and educational classes. Each group plays a unique part in group members' lives. For example, friendship circles are important to maintaining recovery when those friends reinforce the attitudes and behaviors that support staying clean and sober. But there is much variation among these groups in structure, composition, and processes (often referred to as group dynamics).

Group structures can be categorized along three dimensions:

1. *How they develop.* Some groups are formed (*formed groups*) specifically to meet a defined purpose. Other groups develop spontaneously based on friendship, physical location, or some naturally occurring event (*natural groups*) (Toseland & Rivas, 2012). The types of groups encountered in social work have typically been organized for a specific purpose.

2. *How long they last.* Some groups have a set time for termination (*time-limited groups*), whereas other groups have no defined endpoint (*ongoing groups*).

3. *How they determine membership.* Some groups permit the addition of new members throughout the group's life (*open groups*). Other groups limit the size of the group at the outset and do not add new members once the group is formed (*closed groups*).

Another important element of small groups is their composition—the types of people who are members. Some groups are welcoming of a wide range of member characteristics (heterogeneous), and other groups are more exclusive in member selection (homogeneous). Groups vary in the degree of heterogeneity/homogeneity among the membership, along dimensions such as age, race, sexual orientation, gender, level of education, coping style, religion, socioeconomic status, disabilities, and problem areas or strengths. The goal of promoting social justice may, at times, mean the development of groups that are homogeneous on an important identity dimension, where people can speak about common experiences, receive social support, and develop solidarity. Such groups can lead to empowerment, and social group workers can support self-advocacy while also advocating for the group when appropriate. At other times, inclusivity in the promotion of social justice will mean being intentional about having a group that is heterogeneous on important social identity issues, while being homogeneous on group purpose. In developing such heterogeneous groups, the group worker should avoid having a token member of a marginalized community group (the Noah's Ark principle). When working with heterogeneous groups, the group worker must work to ensure that all members have a voice and are treated with dignity and respect, paying particular attention to power dynamics that members bring into the group from the world beyond the group.

The overall development of the group is overlaid with patterns of interactions that can be characterized as group processes or dynamics—such issues as how leaders are appointed or emerge, which roles members take in groups, and how communication networks affect interactions in groups. One important variable related to group dynamics is **group cohesiveness**—the tendency of the group to stick together and be unified in pursuit of its objectives and the satisfaction of member emotional needs (May et al., 2008). Groups that are cohesive tend to have higher rates of attendance, participation, and mutual support. Cohesion in therapy groups has been found to contribute to group effectiveness (Norcross & Wampold, 2011), and cohesive task groups (teams) have been found to be more effective than task groups with low cohesion (Kogler Hill, 2013). But cohesiveness does not mean the absence of conflict or dislike among group members. Even a cohesive group may sometimes experience bickering, frustration, or alienation. It is important for group leaders to try to prevent heterogeneous groups from splitting into coalitions that are not committed to the interest of the whole group (Jones, 2005).

To be effective, group workers need tools for understanding the group processes in which they participate. *Group processes* are those unique interactions between group members that result from being in a group together. How people behave in groups is of interest to us because we spend much of our time in groups, and groups have a strong influence on our behaviors.

CRITICAL THINKING Questions 8.1

In what types of small groups have you participated? What benefits have you derived from participating in small groups? What frustrations have you faced from participating in small groups? What experiences have you had with small groups that were heterogeneous in race or ethnicity? What did you see as the benefits of heterogeneity? What challenges were presented by heterogeneous membership? Think of the most cohesive small group in which you have participated. What do you think contributed to that cohesion?

THEORIES OF GROUP PROCESSES

The fields of social psychology and sociology have been in the forefront of empirical research on group processes. Five of the major theories of group processes are discussed in this section: psychodynamic theory, symbolic interaction theory, status characteristics and expectation states theory, exchange theory, and self-categorization theory. Each one helps us understand, among other things, why and how certain members of a group develop and maintain more power than other members to influence the group's activities.

PSYCHODYNAMIC THEORY

You were introduced to the psychodynamic theoretical perspective in Chapter 2. When applied to small groups, **psychodynamic theory** "focuses on the relationship between the emotional unconscious processes and the rational processes of interpersonal interaction" (McLeod & Kettner-Polley, 2005, p. 63). It assumes that understanding the emotional processes in a group is essential for accomplishing the group's task. The psychodynamic theoretical perspective is especially important to therapy groups where understanding emotional processes is the central task of the group, but some group leaders argue that it is an important perspective for increasing the effectiveness of any type of group. Small groups can be challenging because they satisfy our need to belong, and yet they also arouse our fears about social acceptance and social competence (Geller, 2005).

McLeod and Kettner-Polley (2005) identify three broad assumptions of psychodynamic theory for understanding small groups:

1. Emotional, unconscious processes are always present in every group.
2. Emotional, unconscious processes affect the quality of interpersonal communication and task accomplishment.
3. Group effectiveness depends on bringing emotional, unconscious processes to group members' conscious awareness.

Group leaders in a psychodynamic therapy group would look for opportunities to assist group members to identify how their interactions within the group may mirror their patterns of interactions with others outside of the group; in other words, the group experience becomes a microcosm of members' lives outside the group. For example, a female group member who tends to defer to the opinions of male group members and who is afraid to confront them may be demonstrating a general theme in her life of being intimidated by males because of childhood experiences of physical or emotional abuse by her father.

SYMBOLIC INTERACTION THEORY

According to **symbolic interaction theory**, humans are symbol-using creatures. We make meaning of the world by interacting with others through symbols—words, gestures, and objects. Some small group theorists find it helpful to think about the small group as a place where symbols are created, exchanged, and interpreted and to think about individual and social change happening as meanings are made and changed through the use of symbols (Frey & Sunwolf, 2005). In fact, they think that a "group" is itself a symbol used to describe a relationship people understand themselves to have with each other. Group members create a sense of being a group through their symbolic actions with each other, through their language and their behaviors over time. Groups may use such symbols as metaphors, stories, and rituals to communicate and build cohesion. In this way, they also build a culture with its own symbols and meanings. The symbols provide group identity and stimulate commitment to struggle with the tensions of group life.

The symbols used in a group, and the meaning made of those symbols, are influenced by the environments in which the group is embedded (Frey & Sunwolf, 2005). Group members are also members of other groups and bring symbolic meanings with them from these groups. This may lead to tension and conflict in the group as members struggle to develop shared meaning about who they are as a group, what their goals are, and how they will operate as a group.

STATUS CHARACTERISTICS AND EXPECTATION STATES THEORY

Status characteristics and expectation states theory proposes that the influence and participation of group members during initial interactions are related to their status and to expectations others hold about their ability to help the group accomplish tasks (Fisek, Berger, & Moore, 2002; Oldmeadow, Platow, Foddy, & Anderson, 2003). **Status characteristics** are any characteristics evaluated in the broader society to be associated with competence. **Performance expectations**, or the expectations that group members have of other group members in terms of how they will act or behave in the group or how well they will perform a task, are influenced by status characteristics.

In the sexuality and gender group, Beverly carries some influence. She has attended group sessions for almost 3 months and is one of the core members who come to the group consistently. As an influential member, she is expected to articulate and enforce the group's rules and to assist new members in acclimating to the group. Group members expect Beverly to share her insights about the coming-out process and recovery from addiction, and they perceive her as a knowledgeable person, especially when discussing issues faced by African American lesbians. But in another setting, the color of Beverly's skin might negatively influence how she is perceived by other people. Stereotypes about African Americans may cause other people to question Beverly's interests, skills, or values. Such stereotypes are the basis of *diffuse status characteristics* whereby the power and prestige of group members are correlated with their status in the external world, regardless of their specific characteristics relative to the tasks at hand.

Gender is an influential diffuse status characteristic in our society, perhaps because it can often be easily discerned. In mixed-gender groups, males have greater participation and influence than females, and males or females with traditionally masculine personality traits are likely to exhibit more dominant behavior (Karpowitz et al., 2012; Toosi et al., 2012). In same-sex groups, gender is not an initial status differential; instead, members develop expectations of each other based on other status characteristics, such as education, race, or experience. Regardless of gender, a person's perceived ability also affects performance expectations. For example, a female may be perceived as incapable of handling a complex mechanical problem in a work group, but she may be able to develop influence if she shows she can accomplish the task successfully (Schneider & Cook, 1995).

One assumption of status characteristics and expectation states theory is that people rely on their stereotypes in the absence of proof that those characteristics are irrelevant. In the psychological literature, this phenomenon is often referred to as "self-fulfilling stereotypes" (Snyder, 2014).

EXCHANGE THEORY

Sometimes in coming-out groups, those who have been out for the longest time have implicit power over those newly out, the baby dykes. A "let me show you the ropes and tell you what this is about" attitude can be used to gain power and influence over another person and to create dependency: "You need me to help you understand what you are getting yourself into." But social power can also be used in a positive way in a coming-out group, as when those who have been in the lesbian community for a long time offer support and information to others with the intention of providing mutual aid. To understand power as a social commodity, we can look to **exchange theory** (Lovaglia, Mannix, Samuelson, Sell, & Wilson, 2005), which assumes that human interactions can be understood in terms of rewards and costs.

According to exchange theory, social power is what determines who gets valued resources in groups and whether those resources are perceived as being distributed in a just manner. Conflicts within the group often revolve around power issues among members—those who want the power in the group, those who have power and don't want to give it up, and those who don't want others to have power over them.

Small groups are particularly vulnerable to conflicts over power because social power arises within the context of the group itself rather than being an innate quality of an individual. Power not only determines the distribution of group resources but also influences people's expectations of others' abilities, even when the power results from structural conditions and not from innate personal ability (Lovaglia, 1995). Emotion also has an impact on perceived power and influence, regardless of status. If a person has negative emotions toward a high-status person, the power of the high-status person will lessen (Lovaglia, 1995).

The exercise of social power often brings with it a concern about justice, fairness, and equality. Most of us would agree that power should not be exercised to the special benefit or detriment of some group members. However, *justice* is a relative rather than absolute term. Any two persons may have quite different ideas about what constitutes justice. For some, justice would be an equal distribution of resources; for others, justice would be an equitable (but not necessarily equal) distribution.

How persons evaluate the equity of a situation depends on such factors as cultural values, self-interest, the situation, the relationships between those affected, and personal characteristics (Hegtvedt, 1994). People tend to operate more from self-interest in impersonal conditions than when they have personal bonds with others. The status of the person for whom justice claims are being considered also affects the definition of justice, the perception of injustice, and the resolution of injustices. In addition, what may be perceived as fair on an individual level may be perceived as unfair when viewed from a group perspective. For example, suppose a group member is in crisis and asks for extended time in the group. The other five group members agree to give the person an extra 10 minutes because of the crisis. This extension, however, requires each group member to give up 2 minutes of his or her floor time. Giving one individual an extra 10 minutes may not seem like much, but that one action has a cost for five other group members. And what if one group member decides that he or she has a pressing issue to discuss and does not want to give up the 2 minutes? How the group would resolve this dilemma relates to its spoken and unspoken guidelines for handling matters of justice within the group.

SELF-CATEGORIZATION THEORY

Self-categorization theory builds on social identity theory, which, as discussed in Chapter 4, is a stage theory of socialization that articulates the process by which we come to identify with some social groups and develop a sense of difference from other social groups. **Self-categorization theory** expands social identity theory by suggesting that in this process, we come to divide the world into *in-groups* (those to which we belong) and *out-groups* (those to which we do not belong). We begin to stereotype the attributes of in-groups and out-groups by comparing them with each other, with bias toward in-groups. When we encounter new group situations, we are more likely to be influenced by in-group members than by out-group members. We give more credence to those similar to us than to those different from us, particularly when situations are conflicted or unclear. Doing so is consistent with our categorization schemes, but it also helps us maintain distinctive and positive social identities (Abrams, Hogg, Hinkle, & Otten, 2005; Hogg, 2005). So, in this approach, we are influenced in group situations by members of our in-groups, whether or not they hold high status in society.

An example of this is Katie, a member of the sexuality and gender group, who was raised in an evangelical Protestant church. Katie struggled with her sexuality and what she was taught in church about homosexuality. Katie received approval from her counselor to go into the community on a day pass so that she could accompany her sponsor to a Metropolitan Community Church service. She immediately "felt at home" there. She felt she had found a place where both her sexual orientation and faith could be affirmed—a place where she could belong.

Researchers have studied the impact of both status characteristics and self-categorization on social influence in group settings, recording who agrees with whom and who defers to whom. They have found that group members are influenced by both status characteristics and social identity. More specifically, they found that group members are more highly influenced by high-status members who also belong to the in-group than by either a low-status in-group member or a high-status out-group member (Kalkhoff & Barnum, 2000).

CRITICAL THINKING Questions 8.2

The psychodynamic perspective on groups proposes that emotional processes in the small group affect the effectiveness of the group. Some proponents of this perspective argue that dealing with the emotional processes in the group is important in any type of group, not just therapy groups. What do you think about this argument? How important are emotional processes to mutual aid groups, psychoeducational groups, self-help groups, and task groups? Can you think of an example where unconscious emotional processes interfered with task accomplishment in a task group of which you were a member?

FORMAL ORGANIZATION DEFINED

Martha Green, in Case Study 8.2, saw a social condition that she thought needed a remedy, and she envisioned a formal organization as at least part of the remedy. For most of us who live in contemporary complex societies, formal organizations are pervasive in our lives, a most important but usually taken-for-granted part of life. **Formal organization** can be defined as a collectivity of people with a high degree of formal structure, working together to meet common goals. This definition, like most found in the organization literature, has three key components: a collectivity of people, a formal structure, and the common purpose of working together to meet common goals.

This definition leaves a lot of room for variation. Formal organizations differ in size, structure, culture, and goals. They also perform a variety of functions in contemporary society and influence human behavior in many ways. Formal organizations are intricately woven into the fabric of life in contemporary society, but they can be both functional and dysfunctional for society or for specific groups; some members of organizations benefit more than others from organizational goals and structure. Formal organizations meet our needs, help us fulfill goals, and nurture our development. They also make stressful demands, thwart our goals, inhibit our holistic development, and constrain our behavior.

PERSPECTIVES ON FORMAL ORGANIZATIONS

Three decades ago, the ways of thinking about organizational life in the United States had grown so numerous, and so fragmented, one observer noted that the state of organization theory can be described as "more of a weed patch than a well-tended garden" (Pfeffer, 1982, p. 1). That is still an apt description of current theorizing about organizations (Walsh, Meyer, & Schoonhoven, 2006). Likewise, the research on organizations and the related prescriptions for organizational administration reflect great variety, as you can see from the changing approaches at Beacon Center. Several people have attempted to organize the weed patch of U.S. organizational theory into a garden—to bring some order to the diversity of viewpoints without denying the complexity and multifaceted nature of contemporary formal organizations (e.g., Garrow & Hasenfeld, 2010; Greenwald, 2008; Morgan, 2006). Here we use a classification system that includes four perspectives: the rational perspective, systems perspective, interactional/interpretive perspective, and critical perspective. The rational perspective is presented first because of its dominance in the study of organizations (Godwyn & Gittell, 2012). None of these perspectives, taken individually, accounts for all functions of organizations, but taken together, they elaborate the multifaceted nature of organizations reflected in those functions. Each perspective encompasses both classical and contemporary theories, and each has relevance for social work practice.

As you read about these perspectives, you may want to keep in mind one author's suggestion that existing theories of organizations fail to consider the powerful impact that contemporary organizations have on human "social and material lives and on our planet's ecosystem" (Walsh et al., 2006, p. 661) and that new theorizing is needed that takes these issues into account (see Marti, Etzion, & Leca,

Formal organizations are defined as a collectivity of people with a high degree of formality, working together to meet common goals.

2008, for a similar argument). This argument is consistent with social work's interest in social justice, and in the following discussion, we have tried to incorporate contemporary theories that are beginning to address these issues.

Please keep the important role of culture in mind as you read the discussion of theoretical perspectives in this chapter, which focuses primarily on organization theory developed in the United States and Europe. National culture has a great influence on the theories that are developed, and this is nowhere more true than in theorizing about formal organizations (Hofstede, 1996, 2001, 2010). Recently, organization theorists have suggested the possibility of developing a more globally relevant theory of organizations (see Soulsby & Clark, 2007). They note that existing theories of organizations have been developed and studied in stable-market economic systems, usually in North America and Europe. However, at the moment, it appears that around the world, in Asia, Arab countries, eastern Europe, and Russia, business schools are using translations of North American books on organization theory (Czarniawska, 2007). It is possible that scholars in other countries will develop original theory as they try to adapt existing theory to fit their unique situations.

RATIONAL PERSPECTIVE

When Helen Blue became the executive director at Beacon Center, she was concerned about the lack of administrative formality, the lack of rules, and the ambiguous chain of command, among other things. She also wanted greater authority over planning and decision making. These concerns reflect the **rational perspective on organizations**, which views the formal organization as a "goal-directed, purposefully designed machine" (Garrow & Hasenfeld, 2010, p. 34). It assumes organizations can be designed with structures and processes that maximize efficiency and effectiveness, concepts that are highly valued in this perspective. *Efficiency* means obtaining a high ratio of output to input, achieving the best outcome from the least investment of resources. *Effectiveness* means goal accomplishment. Exhibit 8.4 summarizes the central theories in this perspective, as well as the other perspectives discussed next.

The Ideal-Type Bureaucracy

In modern culture, formal organization is often equated with bureaucracy. Indeed, Max Weber (1947), the German sociologist who formulated a theory of bureaucracy at the beginning of the 20th century, saw bureaucracy and capitalism as inseparable. Although he had concerns about the negative impact of bureaucracies, Weber proposed a **bureaucracy** as the most efficient form of organization for goal accomplishment. The characteristics of Weber's ideal-type bureaucracy include a clear hierarchy and chain of command, clear division of labor based on specialized skills, formal rules of operation, formal and task-oriented communications, merit-based recruitment and advancement, and files and records for administrative purposes. Although Weber was enthusiastic about the advantages of the ideal-type bureaucracy over other ways of organizing for goal accomplishment, he was concerned about the dehumanizing potential of bureaucracies—their potential to become an *iron cage of rationality*, trapping people and denying many aspects of their humanity. Researchers have noted that excessive use of rules and procedures often limits the efficiency and effectiveness of bureaucratic organizations, but bureaucracies continue to be the predominant form of organization in contemporary modern and postmodern societies.

There is evidence, however, that some newer organizations are using less bureaucratic structures. This is true for human service organizations as well as organizations formed for other purposes (Hasenfeld, 2010a). Indeed, as Mary Katherine O'Connor and Ellen Netting (2009) suggest, most organizations that employ social workers have been influenced by the rational perspective but do not typically operate purely from this perspective. And, as is the case with other types of organizations, their research has found that newer social service organizations are less likely than older ones to have traditional bureaucratic cultures.

Martha Green, Helen Blue, and Roderick Wallace might all be interested in one researcher's findings that client satisfaction decreased as the level of bureaucracy increased in transitional housing programs for homeless families (Crook, 2001). In addition, conflict among residents increased as the level of organizational bureaucracy increased. The indirect impact of organizational bureaucracy on clients is called *trickle-down bureaucracy*.

Scientific Management

Another early 20th-century approach to formal organizations has had lasting influence. Frederick W. Taylor's (1911) *scientific management*, sometimes referred to as Taylorism, was directed toward maximizing internal efficiency. The set of principles Taylor developed to guide the design of organizations was widely adopted by both industry and government, first in the United States and then worldwide. These principles are as follows: time and motion studies to find the "one best way" to perform each organizational task; scientific selection and training of workers; training focused on performing tasks in the standardized one best way; close managerial monitoring of workers to ensure accurate implementation of task prescriptions and to provide appropriate rewards for compliance; and managerial authority over planning and decision making, with no challenge from workers.

In his provocative book *The McDonaldization of Society*, George Ritzer (2013b) proposes that McDonald's Corporation is a prototype organization, whose organizational style is coming to dominate much of the world. This relatively new type of organization, which operates on the

EXHIBIT 8.4 • Summary of Perspectives on Formal Organizations

THEORY	CENTRAL IDEA
RATIONAL PERSPECTIVE: THE ORGANIZATION IS A GOAL-DIRECTED, PURPOSEFULLY DESIGNED MACHINE (CLOSED SYSTEM).	
The ideal-type bureaucracy (Weber, 1947)	Formal rationality—rules, regulations, and structures—is essential to goal accomplishment.
Scientific management (Taylor, 1911)	The most effective organizations maximize internal efficiency, the "one best way."
Human relations theory (Mayo, 1933)	Human relationships are central to organizational efficiency and effectiveness.
Management by objectives (Drucker, 1954)	Managers should focus on the desired outcomes (objectives) and create an organizational design to achieve those outcomes; strategic planning is key to organizational success.
Decision-making theory (March & Simon, 1958)	Organizational rationality is limited.
SYSTEMS PERSPECTIVE: THE ORGANIZATION IS IN CONSTANT INTERACTION WITH MULTIPLE ENVIRONMENTS.	
Political economy model (Wamsley & Zald, 1973)	The organization depends on the environment for political and economic resources.
Learning organization theory (Argyris & Schön, 1978)	The organization must be able to learn and change in a rapidly changing environment.
INTERACTIONAL/INTERPRETIVE PERSPECTIVE: THE ORGANIZATION IS A SOCIAL CONSTRUCTION OF REALITY.	
Social action model (Silverman, 1971)	The organization is defined by individual actors.
Organizational culture model (Schein, 1992)	Organizations are cultures with shared experiences and shared meanings.
Managing diversity model (Cox, 1993)	Organizational systems and practices should maximize the potential advantages of diversity in organizational membership.
CRITICAL PERSPECTIVE: ORGANIZATIONS ARE INSTRUMENTS OF DOMINATION.	
Organizations as multiple oppressions (Hearn & Parkin, 1993)	Organizations exclude and discriminate against multiple groups.
Nonhierarchical organizations (Follett, 1924)	Organizations run by consensus, with few rules and with informality, are least likely to oppress employees.

combined principles of bureaucratization and scientific management, has four key traits:

1. *Efficiency*, which is valued in a fast-paced society
2. *Calculability*, with an emphasis on quantity rather than quality of products and services
3. *Predictability*, with the assurance that a Big Mac will be the same in San Francisco as it is in Washington, DC, or Hong Kong
4. *Control*, with workers trained to do a limited number of things exactly as they are told to do them and with maximum use of nonhuman technology

Principles of scientific management are frequently followed in social service organizations. For example, some organizations undertake task and workload analyses to improve effectiveness and efficiency, and managers develop procedures, regulations, and decision trees to be implemented by direct service workers. The recent emphasis on *best practices*, *competencies*, and *evidence-based practice* is derivative of scientific management thinking, but these practices do not typically conceive of "one best way."

Human Relations Theory

Human relations theory introduced a new twist on maximizing organizational efficiency and effectiveness. The theory grew out of a series of studies conducted by Elton Mayo (1933) and associates and emphasized the heretofore unrecognized importance of human interaction in organizational efficiency and effectiveness. As the theory developed, it also proposed that democratic leadership is more effective than authoritarian management in securing worker cooperation. Seeking to improve the rationality of the organization, the researchers were studying the effects of working conditions, such as intensity of lighting, on productivity. As expected, the researchers found that productivity increased as the lighting intensity increased. To their surprise, however, productivity continued to increase even when they began to dim the lights in an attempt to confirm their findings. The researchers concluded that technical rationality—the development of rational structures, procedures, and processes—is not sufficient to ensure maximum productivity. Social factors, they concluded, are as important as, if not more important than, technical factors in accomplishing organizational goals. They based this conclusion, which became the central proposition of a new theory, on their observation that productivity appeared to be related to worker morale and sense of social responsibility to the work group. The researchers of the lighting study concluded that worker morale was enhanced by the attention from the researchers.

The human relations approach has been a favorite theory in social service organizations because it calls attention to how staff attitudes about the work situation can influence how they relate to clients (see Garrow & Hasenfeld, 2010). The social workers at Beacon Center did indeed respond more cooperatively to Martha Green's democratic leadership than to Helen Blue's more authoritarian leadership. Furthermore, it appears that staff cohesion did "trickle down" to improve consumer satisfaction as well.

It is important to note, however, that human relations theory is still in the rational tradition. Like scientific management, it focuses on maximizing efficiency and effectiveness, and it endorses the interests of owners and managers. Managers must become leaders capable of securing the cooperation of workers, but they are still in control of the organization. Although the consideration of human interaction opens the possibility of nonrational factors in organizational life, human relations theorists still assume that, with "leadership skills," human interactions can be as rationally managed as structures and procedures. After losing ground during the 1950s, human relations theory was reinvigorated in the 1960s by *organizational humanism* and a subfield called organizational development. These theories suggest that organizations can maximize efficiency and effectiveness while also promoting individual happiness and well-being (McGregor, 1960).

Management by Objectives (MBO)

In the 1950s, Peter Drucker (1954) suggested that organizational goals and objectives should be the primary concern of organizational managers. Managers should focus on the desired outcome (objectives) and create an organizational design to achieve that outcome. The planning process, known as *strategic planning*, is the key to organizational success. Both short-range and long-range planning are seen as important, although most organizations that follow the MBO approach have not gone beyond short-range planning. You may recall that Roderick Wallace saw strategic planning as the way to manage the challenge of the economic recession.

Decision-Making Theory

In the 1950s, another group of organizational theorists in the rational tradition began to write about the limits to organizational rationality. Herbert Simon (1957) presented a *decision-making theory* of organizations, focusing on how decisions of individuals in organizations affect the organization as a whole. James March and Simon (1958) argued that administrators cannot be perfectly rational in their decision making, because they face many constraints that limit their alternatives: incomplete information about alternatives for action, incomplete understanding of the consequences of those actions, and the incapacity to explore more than a limited number of alternatives at a time. March and Simon used the term *bounded rationality* to describe this limited rationality of organizational actors. They also suggested that bounded rationality leads administrators and other organizational actors to *satisfice* rather than maximize when making decisions—to seek satisfactory rather than perfect solutions and to discontinue the search for alternatives when a satisfactory solution is available. Cognitive psychologist Daniel Kahneman (2011) has presented research from several disciplines to support the argument that human rationality is much more limited than usually assumed.

Although the rational perspective on organizations has been dominant in the design of organizations, including social service organizations, and has had some positive impact on productivity, it has been criticized on a number of grounds. It fails to consider external pressures on organizational decision makers. As suggested by decision-making theory, it overstates the rational capacity of organizational actors. It fails to attend to the issue of power in organizational life. Garrow and Hasenfeld (2010) suggest that the rational perspective fails to take the moral basis of human service organizations into account.

SYSTEMS PERSPECTIVE

Martha Green and Helen Blue had different styles of managing what happened inside Beacon Center, but they also had different styles of managing external pressures and resources. Martha focused on giving homeless persons a voice in efforts to secure political and economic resources for Beacon Center; Helen focused on conciliation with community and political leaders. In her own way, however, each was attentive to Beacon Center's relationship with its environment, and Roderick Wallace has continued to pay attention to the multifaceted environment. He recognized the challenge that the recession presented to social service organizations, and he has been diligent in seeking community partners for expanding services for homeless persons in River Run. In this respect, they all have negated the rational perspective's view of the organization as a closed system that can be controlled by careful attention to internal structure and processes. During the 1950s and 1960s, the rationalist view of organizations was challenged by the systems perspective. All subsequent theorizing about organizations has been influenced by the systems perspective.

The **systems perspective on organizations** builds on the fundamental principle that the organization is in constant interaction with its multiple environments—social, political, economic, cultural, technological—and must be able to adapt to environmental change. Some systems theorists suggest mutual influence between organizations and their environments; other theorists see the influence as unidirectional, with organizational structure and processes being determined by the environment. A second important principle of the systems perspective is that organizations are composed of interrelated subsystems that must be integrated in order to achieve the organization's goals and meet environmental demands. Finally, in contrast to the rational approach, the systems perspective holds that there are many different ways, rather than one best way, to reach the same ends. The idea that a system can attain its goals in a variety of ways is known as *equifinality*.

Several systems theories of organizations have been developed over time, but we look at only two here: the political economy model and the learning organization theory. These two theories are summarized in Exhibit 8.4.

Political Economy Model

The *political economy model* focuses on the dependence of organizations on their environments for necessary resources and on the impact of organization–environment interactions on the internal structure and processes of the organization (Wamsley & Zald, 1973). More specifically, it focuses on two types of resources necessary to organizations: political resources (legitimacy and power) and economic resources. The greater the dependence of the organization on the environment for either of these types of resources, the greater the influence the environment will have on the organization. Likewise, the greater control one unit of the organization has over resources, the more power that unit has over the organizational processes.

The political economy model is particularly potent for clarifying how social service organizations resolve such important issues as which clients to serve, which services to provide, how to organize service provision, and how to define staff and client roles (Garrow & Hasenfeld, 2010). Both Martha Green and Helen Blue were trying to read their political and economic environments as they made these kinds of decisions, but their different ways of thinking led them to attend to different aspects of the environment. Roderick Wallace appears to be taking a broad look at the agency's political and economic environments. The political economy model recognizes clients as resources and as potential players in the political arena. Social workers have an important role to play in facilitating their inclusion in the political process, a role that was part of Martha Green's vision for Beacon Center.

Learning Organization Theory

The *learning organization theory* was developed on the premise that rational planning is not sufficient for an organization to survive in a rapidly changing environment such as the one in which we live. Formal organizations must become complex systems capable of constant learning (Argyris, 1999; Argyris & Schön, 1978, 1996; Senge, 1990). The learning organization is one that can

- scan the environment, anticipate change, and detect "early warning" signs of trends and patterns;
- question, challenge, and change customary ways of operating;
- allow the appropriate strategic direction to emerge; and
- evolve designs that support continuous learning.

Theories in the systems perspective have advanced organizational understanding by calling attention to the influence of the external environment on organizations. They provide useful concepts for considering how organizations survive in turbulent environments. But the systems perspective has little to say about the moral purposes of social service organizations or how organizations can be positive rather than negative forces in society. Recently, however, Stephen Gill (2010) has proposed learning organization theory as an appropriate model for nonprofit organizations. As we can see from the experience of Beacon Center, we live in a world that values the kind of order Helen Blue wanted to bring to Beacon Center, and there can be much environmental resistance to the development of learning organizations. As Beacon Center continues to grow, Roderick Wallace is attempting to balance the need for order with the need to be open to new environmental conditions. If nothing else, the idea of the learning organization serves as a bridge between the systems perspective and the interactional/interpretive perspective.

CRITICAL THINKING Questions 8.3

Think of a formal organization of which you have been a part, for which you have positive feelings. What words come to mind when you think of this organization? Can you use specific theoretical concepts from the rational or systems perspective to talk about that organization? Now, think of a formal organization of which you have been a part, for which you have negative feelings. What words come to mind when you think of this organization? Can you use specific theoretical concepts from the rational or systems perspective to talk about that organization?

INTERACTIONAL/ INTERPRETIVE PERSPECTIVE

As we have been suggesting, when Helen Blue became executive director at Beacon Center, she wanted to introduce more "rational order" and have fewer internal voices speaking about the kind of place the center should be. It might be said that she found Martha Green's vision for Beacon Center to be too interactional and interpretive. Theories of organizations within the **interactional/ interpretive perspective on organizations** are diverse, but they all share two basic premises: (1) Organizations provide members with a sense of connection and meaning, and (2) organizations reflect the worldviews of the creators; they are social constructions of reality created by ongoing interactions and emerging relationships (Godwyn & Gittell, 2012).

Although the rational perspective on organizations has received the most attention in the organizational literature, the interactional/interpretive approach is actually older. In the early 1900s, Mary Parker Follett (1918) suggested that organizational reality is created by relationships; she did not focus on either workers or managers but on the relationships that connected them. Her philosophy took account of both mutual influence and egalitarianism.

The interactional/interpretive perspective rejects both the rational and the systems perspectives. Contrary to the rational perspective, the interactional/interpretive perspective focuses on processes rather than goals, emphasizes flexibility rather than control and reason, and is interested in a diversity of approaches rather than one right way. From this perspective, organizations are seen as increasingly fragmented into multiple realities, and they should be studied through multiple voices rather than through the unitary voice of the manager. Contrary to the systems perspective, the interactional/interpretive perspective emphasizes human agency in creating organizations and challenges the constraining influence of external forces.

Different interactional/interpretive theorists focus on different themes in relation to the basic premises just stated. The three separate approaches summarized in Exhibit 8.4 provide some sense of these differences.

Social Action Model

One of the most influential contributions to the interactional/ interpretive study of organizations is that of British sociologist David Silverman, presented in his 1971 book *The Theory of Organizations: A Sociological Framework*. Criticizing both rational and systems perspectives, Silverman proposed an approach that emphasizes the active role of individual organizational actors in creating the organization—an approach known as *Silverman's social action model*.

In a more recent work, Silverman (1994) criticized the singular emphasis on organizational actors in his earlier model. He suggested that in reacting against deterministic theories of environmental constraints, he failed to acknowledge the influence of history and social structure. He further suggested that his portrayal of human behavior as free and undetermined failed to acknowledge the influence of cultural scripts and the tendency of humans to see their behavior as freer than it is. This self-critique is consistent with other criticisms of the limitations of the interactional/interpretive perspective, but Silverman's theory has had a large impact on European theorizing about organizations (Scott, 2014).

Organizational Culture Model

In contrast to Silverman's deemphasis on culture, Edgar Schein (1992) focuses on organizations as cultures whose members have shared experiences that produce shared meanings, or interpretations. Organizations, therefore, exist as much in the heads of their members as in policies, rules, and procedures. The *organizational culture model* views organizations as ongoing, interactive processes of reality construction, involving many organizational actors. Organizational culture is made up of language, slogans, symbols, rituals, stories, and ceremonies (Morgan, 2006) but also of mundane, routine, day-to-day activities. For example, under Martha Green's leadership, the slogan "client input" was an important feature of the Beacon Center culture, buttressed by the day-to-day practice of soliciting client opinions.

Organizational culture is always evolving, and it is not always unitary. In many organizations, competing beliefs and value systems produced subcultures. Given the evolution of organizational culture and rapid societal changes, it is not unusual to find a split between the old and new guard or to find cultural divisions based on organizational function. For example, fund-raisers in social service organizations may speak a different language from clinicians in the same agency. The result may be cultural fragmentation or cultural warfare.

Criticisms of the organizational culture approach are twofold (Morgan, 2006). One criticism is leveled at theorists who write about managing organizational culture. These theorists are sometimes criticized for being biased in favor of management and potentially exploitative of employees. They are also criticized for overstating managers' potential to control culture, negating the role of multiple actors in the creation of shared meaning. The second criticism of the organizational culture approach is that it fails to take account of the fact that some members have more power than others to influence the construction of culture.

Managing Diversity Model

In the 1990s, organizational theorists developed an approach to organizational management called the *managing diversity model*. Given the trend toward greater diversity in the labor force, several social scientists (e.g., Cox, 1993, 2001; Kossek, Lobel, & Brown, 2006; Mor Barak, 2014; Mor Barak & Travis, 2010) have suggested that contemporary organizations cannot be successful unless they learn to manage diverse populations. Diversity is a permanent, not transitory, feature of contemporary life.

The purpose in managing diversity is to maximize the advantages of diversity while minimizing its disadvantages. Taylor Cox (1993), a leading proponent of the model, says, "I view the goal of managing diversity as maximizing the ability of all employees to contribute to organizational goals and to achieve their full potential unhindered by group identities such as gender, race, nationality, age, and departmental affiliation" (p. 11). He argues that this goal requires that a new organizational culture must be institutionalized, a culture that welcomes diversity (Cox, 2001).

Mor Barak and Travis (2010) analyzed a decade of research about the linkages between organizational diversity and organizational performance. This research can be divided into the study of individual outcomes, work group outcomes, and organizational outcomes. The results were mixed in terms of individual outcomes, with some researchers finding that job satisfaction improves when workers find a higher proportion of people similar to themselves in values and ethnicity and other researchers finding no such association. Likewise, mixed results were found in regard to diversity and work group outcomes. Some researchers found that the quality of ideas produced by work groups increased as racial and ethnic diversity increased, other researchers found that racially diverse groups had more emotional conflict than racially homogeneous work groups, and still other researchers found no relationship between extent of diversity of work group cohesion and performance. The results were also mixed regarding the relationship between diversity and organizational performance, but the majority of studies report positive relationships in both the corporate sector and the human service sector, meaning that organizational performance improves as diversity in the workforce increases. Roderick Wallace recognizes some of the tension related to ethnic diversity in the Beacon Center staff, but he has also seen new ideas and new understandings come out of the tension. Mor Barak and Travis (2010) note that social service organizations have historically served a diverse client population but have not historically hired a diverse workforce.

CRITICAL PERSPECTIVE

Although it may appear that Martha Green administered Beacon Center from an interactional/interpretative perspective, it is probably more accurate to describe her worldview as a **critical perspective on organizations**. She tried to minimize the power differences in her organization, and when she asked her staff to vote on sensitive issues, she invoked the secret ballot to neutralize any possible power dynamics. Critical theorists share the interactional/interpretive perspective's bias about the role of human interaction and meaning making in human behavior, but critical theory undertakes, as its central concern, a critique of existing power arrangements and a vision for change suggested by this critique. More specifically, critical theories see organizations as instruments of exploitation and domination, where conflicting interests are decided in favor of the most powerful members. This focus distinguishes the critical perspective from the interactional/interpretive perspective, which generally ignores or negates issues of power and the possibility that people in power positions can privilege their own versions of reality and marginalize other versions, thus controlling the organizational culture. The critical perspective on organizations has been more popular in Europe than in the United States. Exhibit 8.4 summarizes the two contemporary critical approaches to formal organizations discussed here: organizations as multiple oppressions and nonhierarchical organizations.

Organizations as Multiple Oppressions

Have you ever felt oppressed—voiceless, powerless, abused, manipulated, unappreciated—in any of the organizations of which you have been a member? Do you think that whole groups of people have felt oppressed in any of those organizations? In the contemporary era, the critical perspective has taken a more focused look at who is oppressed in organizations and the ways in which they are oppressed. This approach was influenced by feminist critiques, during the 1970s and 1980s, of the failure of traditional organization theories to consider gender issues (Hearn & Parkin, 1993). Feminist critiques led to the recognition that other groups besides women had also been marginalized by formal organizations and by organization theory.

Jeff Hearn and Wendy Parkin (1993) recommend viewing *organizations as multiple oppressions*—social constructions that exclude and discriminate against some categories of people. They indicate that oppression happens through a variety of processes, including "marginalization, domination and subordination, degradation, ignoring, harassment, invisibilizing, silencing, punishment, discipline and violence" (p. 153). These processes may also be directed at a variety of organizational actors, including "staff, members, employees, residents, patients and clients" (p. 153). This idea that multiple oppressions are usually embedded in organizational life has also been addressed in a book by Sharon Kurtz (2002), who argues that addressing the situation of only one oppressed group will never get to the heart of the matrix of domination in organizations. You may recognize this as consistent with intersectionality theory as discussed in Chapter 2.

The critical perspective on organizations has special relevance to social workers. It helps us recognize the ways in which clients' struggles are related to oppressive structures and processes in the formal organizations with which they interact. It can help us to understand the ways in which social service organizations are gendered, with women constituting the majority of human service workers and men assuming key administrative roles. It also calls our attention to the power imbalance between clients and social workers and helps us think critically about how we use our power. We must be constantly vigilant about the multiple oppressions within the organizations where we work, as well as those with which we interact, as we try to promote social justice.

Nonhierarchical Organizations

Helen Blue preferred a more hierarchical organizational structure than the one developed at Beacon Center under Martha Green's leadership. A constant theme in critical theory is that hierarchical organizational structures lead to alienation and internal class conflict. Critical theorists directly challenge the rational perspective argument that hierarchy is needed to maximize efficiency; they point out that in fact hierarchy is often inefficient but is maintained because it works well to protect the positions of those in power. For example, the staff at Beacon Center wasted much time and energy trying to find ways to thwart Helen Blue's decisions.

The idea of the *nonhierarchical organization* is not new. Mary Parker Follett (1924) proposed that organizations, like other human collective efforts, should be based on nonhierarchical power, on energy that comes from the egalitarian interactions of people and ideas. Human relations theorists have recommended "participatory management," which involves lower-level employees in at least some decision making, for several decades. Historical evidence indicates that since the 1840s, experiments with nonhierarchical organizations have accompanied every wave of antimodernist social movements in the United States (Rothschild-Whitt & Whitt, 1986).

Beginning in the 1970s, feminist critiques of organizational theory helped to stimulate renewed interest in nonhierarchical organizations (Kravetz, 2004). Nevertheless, such organizations constitute only a small portion of the population of formal organizations, and research on nonhierarchical organizations constitutes a very small part of the massive body of research on organizations (Garrow & Hasenfeld, 2010; Iannello, 1992).

Studies of nonhierarchical organizations summarize some of the special challenges, both internal and external, faced by consensual organizations (Ferree & Martin, 1995; Kravetz, 2004; Rothschild-Whitt & Whitt, 1986). Internal challenges include increased time needed for decision making, increased emotional intensity due to the more personal style of relationships, and difficulty incorporating diversity. External challenges are the constraints of social, economic, and political environments that value and reward hierarchy (Garrow & Hasenfeld, 2010).

On the basis of her study of two successful feminist organizations, Iannello (1992) proposed that the internal challenges of the nonhierarchical organization could be addressed by what she calls a "modified consensual organization" model. Critical decisions continue to be made by the broad membership, but routine decisions are made by smaller groups; members are recognized by ability and expertise, not by rank and position; and there are clear goals, developed through a consensual process. Similarly, reporting on the life course of five feminist organizations initiated in the 1970s, Diane Kravetz (2004) found that these organizations developed "modified hierarchies" as they grew and faced new external challenges. They gradually delegated authority to individuals and committees but retained some elements of consensus decision making.

One trend to watch is toward worker-owned corporations, in both the United States and Europe. Sometimes these corporations are not truly democratic, with strong worker input into decisions, but evidence indicates they are moving toward greater democratization (Alperovitz, 2005). The fact that the number of worker-owned companies in the United States increased from 1,600 in 1975 to 11,000 in 2003 seems to be a sign that the idea of shared leadership is gaining in popularity (Alperovitz, 2005). In their book *The Citizen's Share*, Blasi, Freeman, and Kruse (2013) report on their 10-year study of profit-sharing and employee-owned businesses and argue that these arrangements offer a viable path for rebooting the U.S. economy and restoring the middle class.

Given the increasing diversity of the workforce in the United States, management of difference and conflict can be expected to become an increasing challenge in organizational life. This is as true for social work organizations as for others. The literature on consensual organizations has failed to address the difficult challenges of diverse ideological and cultural perspectives among organizational members—issues that are the focus of the managing diversity model. This is an area in which social work should take the lead.

In Canada, one notable exception has occurred. Feminist critiques of social service organizations have led to growing interest in *anti-oppressive* social work practice at both the direct practice and organizational practice levels. The anti-oppression model seeks to develop social service organizations free from all types of domination and privilege (Barnoff & Moffatt, 2007).

TECHNOLOGY AND SOCIAL SERVICE ORGANIZATIONS

The information and communication revolution has presented new challenges and opportunities to social service organizations. Information and communication technology (ICT) is an integral part of most social service organizations, but the literature on the topic is sparse. One researcher found that the costs of ICT are prohibitive for many small and economically poor social service organizations, whereas technically sophisticated organizations benefit from great access to government resources (Mano, 2009). Another researcher reviewed the applications of nonprofit organizations for technology innovation grants in the state of Georgia and found that social service organizations proposed a higher number of ICT innovations than other types of nonprofit organizations (Jaskyte, 2012). They were proposing to use innovations in ICT for both administrative and service activities. In the administrative area, they were proposing to upgrade their ability to use ICT for donor, member, client, and volunteer databases; internal communication and scheduling; online outcome databases; online donations; streamlining communication with community partners; and online surveys and assessments. In the service area, they were proposing to upgrade their ability to use ICT for online client education and to provide counseling and other services online. They expected ICT to help them increase the number of clients served, attract more donors and volunteers, and improve their communications with community partners.

There is a growing research literature on the use of Internet and wireless-supported mental health interventions, with most of the research addressing online counseling and psychotherapy, psychoeducational websites, and online support groups. The results of this research indicate positive outcomes of these technologically supported interventions but raise questions of confidentiality and access (Barak & Grohol, 2011). Here are two examples of recent innovations in the use of ICT to enhance service provision. Twenty veterans in outpatient treatment for alcohol abuse and dependence at a veterans hospital were given an iPod loaded with recovery-related audio podcasts. Most participants indicated that they used the device regularly, thought it was useful, and wished they had access to this type of support earlier (Shaw, Sivakumar, Balinas, Chipman, & Krahn, 2013). Another organization investigated the interest in an online coping skills training program for women living with a partner with a drinking problem and found that interest was high (Rychtarik, McGillicuddy, & Barrick, 2013). Both of these innovations were seen as an adjunct to ongoing face-to-face service provision.

CRITICAL THINKING Questions 8.4

Think back to your earlier ideas about the characteristics of an organization for which you have positive feelings. Can you use specific theoretical concepts from the interactional/interpretive or critical perspective to talk about that organization? Now, think of your ideas about the characteristics of an organization for which you have negative feelings. Can you use specific theoretical concepts from the interactional/interpretive and critical perspective to describe that organization? How have you seen information and communication technologies used in human service organizations? What is one idea you have about a way for social workers to make good use of these technologies?

COMMUNITY: TERRITORIAL AND RELATIONAL

As summarized in Case Study 8.3, Rhacel Salazar Parreñas (2001, 2008) first chronicled the lives of Filipina domestic workers from June 1995 to August 1996, a period before the wide use of the Internet and cell phones. By 2008, the workers were using these new technologies to keep connected to their multiple communities. We can imagine how even newer technologies, such as Facebook, YouTube, Twitter, and Instagram, are now supporting these connections. Although the circumstances of their lives are different in some important ways, the Filipinas in Rome and Los Angeles both appear to see themselves as members of multiple communities. But what, exactly, is community?

Historically, community had a geographic meaning in sociology. More recently, however, two different sociological meanings of community have developed: community as a geographic or territorial concept and community as an interactional or relational concept. Both meanings of community have relevance for human behavior in the contemporary era, and recently, researchers are finding more similarities than differences between these two types of community (Obst & White, 2004; Obst, Zinkiewicz, & Smith, 2002a, 2002b). The following definition can be used to cover both territorial and relational communities: **Community** is people bound either by geography or by webs of communication, sharing common ties, and interacting with one another. Communities can be distinguished from formal organizations in two ways: Communities have less formal structures, and they are not organized around specific goals.

The field of community psychology has been interested in how people develop a **sense of community**, which Seymour Sarason (1974) defined in this way:

> the perception of similarity with others, an acknowledged interdependence with others, a willingness to maintain this interdependence by giving to or doing for others what one expects from them, the feeling that one is part of a larger dependable and stable structure. (p. 157)

These characteristics of sense of community are very similar to the "common ties" element of the definition of community. Does it appear to you that the Filipina domestic workers in Rome have a sense of community with other domestic workers in the city? What about the Filipina domestic workers in Los Angeles?

Some would argue that community in the contemporary era is based on voluntary interaction (**relational community**), not on geography or territory (**territorial community**). For the Filipina domestic workers, community seems to be both relational and territorial. They are a part of a growing trend of transnational families who are also creating *transnational communities*. They maintain a sense of community connection to their sending communities in the Philippines as well as to other Filipina domestic workers in their territorial communities. In addition, they imagine themselves as a part of a global community of Filipina domestic workers, especially when they read magazines such as *Tinig Filipino*. Their sense of belonging to this global community is based on common ties but does not include much interaction. They do, however, draw support from feeling a part of this community. What about for you? Are your strongest supports based on territorial or relational community?

In premodern times, human groups depended, by necessity, on the territorial community to meet their human needs. But each development in communication and transportation technology has loosened that dependency somewhat. Electronic communications now connect people over distant spaces, with a high degree of both immediacy and intimacy. The development of the World Wide Web in the early 1990s allowed rapid growth in the use of e-mail; beginning in the mid-1990s, hundreds of millions of people around the world began to use e-mail to communicate with other individuals and to develop e-mail discussion groups. Toward the end of 2004, Web 2.0 technologies, a second generation of the World Wide Web that allows people to collaborate and share information online, came to prominence. Web 2.0 technologies include blogs, wikis, podcasting, multimedia sharing sites, and social networking sites (SNSs). By 2008, a major research study of the use of digital technologies by adults in 17 industrialized nations found an average use of these technologies for one third of leisure time (Harrison & Thomas, 2009). The SNS Facebook reportedly has more than 1.3 billion users worldwide communicating in 70 different languages, with more than 600 million users accessing the site by mobile devices (Statistic Brain, 2014). Other SNSs have sprung up in specific countries, for example, Cyworld (Korea), Hyves (Holland), LunarStorm (Sweden), Mixi (Japan), Orkut (Brazil), QQ (China), and Skyrock (France), but some have closed down or become gaming sites only because of competition from Facebook. SNSs have been defined as web-based services that allow individuals to "construct a public or semi-public profile within a bounded system, articulate a list of other users with whom they share a connection, and view and traverse their list of connections and those made by others within the system" (Boyd & Ellison, 2008, p. 5). This definition is consistent with the aspects of the earlier-stated definition of community: linked by webs of communication, common ties, and interaction. Recently, a boom in the growth of mobile social network applications, such as Foursquare, has been connecting virtual and territorial communities (Zhang, Wang, Vasilakos, & Ma, 2013).

For a number of years, researchers have been finding that local ties make up a decreasing portion of our social connections, interpreting that finding to mean that territorial community is no longer important in our lives (Hunter & Riger, 1986; Wellman, 1982; Wellman & Wortley, 1990). A more careful look at this research suggests, however, that even highly mobile people continue to have a lot of contacts in their territorial communities. One study in Toronto (Wellman, 1996) found that if we study *ties*, the number of people with whom we have connections, it is true that the majority of ties for most of us are nonterritorial. However, when we study *contacts*, our actual interactions, two thirds of all contacts are local, in the neighborhood or work setting. This may well be the case for the Filipina domestic workers who often complain about how isolating their domestic work is.

When technology opens the possibilities for relational communities, it does not necessarily spell the death of territorial community, but there have been conflicting findings about this. One research team found that Internet-wired suburbanites were more likely than their nonwired neighbors to engage in "active neighboring," actually using the Internet to support neighboring (Hampton & Wellman, 2003). A widely publicized 2006 study by McPherson et al. found the opposite. This study found that from 1985 to 2005, people in the United States became more socially isolated, the size of their discussion networks declined, and the diversity of their networks decreased. More specifically, the researchers found that people had fewer close ties in their neighborhoods and with voluntary associations (e.g., clubs). They suggested that use of the Internet and mobile phones pulls people away from neighborhood and other locally based social settings. Using the same

© iStockphoto.com/hanoded

ROBIN UTRECHT/AFP/Getty Images

Two contrasting communities: (*left*) a tribal community in Ethiopia and (*right*) a member of the Second Life (online) community.

database, with data collected 2 years later, DiPrete and colleagues (DiPrete, Gelman, McCormick, Teitler, & Zheng, 2011) found that people in the United States are not as isolated as suggested by the data used by McPherson, but their social networks are increasingly segregated along racial, social class, religious, and political lines.

To address the inconsistencies in prior research, the most comprehensive study of social isolation and new technology in the United States to date was reported by researchers with the Pew Internet & American Life Project (Hampton, Sessions, Her, & Rainie, 2009). These researchers undertook a study to compare the social networks of people who use particular technologies with those of demographically similar people who do not use these technologies. Here are their major findings about the trends in social networks since 1985:

- There has been a small-to-modest drop in the number of people reporting that they have no one to talk to about important matters; 6% of adults report they have no one with whom they can discuss such matters.
- The average size of people's core discussion networks has declined, with a drop of about one confidant.
- The diversity of people's core discussion network has markedly declined.

However, the research indicates that use of technology is not the driving force behind these changes. Here are the findings about the relationship between new technology and social networks:

- People who own a cell phone and use the Internet for sharing photos and messages have larger core discussion networks than those who do not use this technology.
- People who use these technologies have more nonkin in their networks than people who do not.
- People who use the Internet to share photos are more likely to have discussion partners that cross political lines.
- People who use Internet social networking sites have social networks that are about 20% more diverse.
- In-person contact remains the most frequent way to have contact in the geographical community.
- The mobile phone has replaced the landline as the most frequently used medium for communication.
- Text messaging tied with the landline as the third most popular way to communicate.
- Those who use SNSs are 25% less likely to use neighbors for companionship, but use of other technologies is associated with higher levels of neighborhood involvement.
- Internet users are less likely to depend on neighbors to provide concrete services.

More recent Gallup poll data (Newport, 2014) indicate that texting, using a cellphone, and sending and reading e-mail messages are the most common ways of communicating for U.S. adults. From 37% to 39% of poll respondents reported using each of these methods of communication a lot on the day prior to being interviewed. The poll data also indicate that texting is the dominant way of communicating in the United States for people younger than age 50.

Wendy Griswold (2013) proposes that people can have ties to both relational and territorial communities at the same time, and this does seem to be the case for the Filipina domestic workers in both Rome and Los Angeles. They maintain relationships with their sending communities while also building community in local gathering places in their receiving communities. Griswold recognizes the possibility that the new technologies will simply allow us to develop and maintain a larger network of increasingly

EXHIBIT 8.5 • Theoretical Approaches to Community

APPROACH	CENTRAL IDEA
Contrasting types approach	Communities can be dichotomized as either *gemeinschaft* (personal and traditional) or *gesellschaft* (impersonal and contractual).
Spatial arrangements approach	Territorial communities can be understood by considering their spatial arrangements.
Social systems approach	Communities can be understood by studying their patterns of social interaction, cultures, and social structures.
Social capital approach	Communities can be understood by examining their levels of social cohesion.
Conflict approach	Communities can be understood by examining their power structure and patterns of domination and coercion.

superficial relationships. But she also points out the possibility that the new capacity to be immediately and intimately connected across space could help us to develop more shared meanings and become more tolerant of our differences. Jeffrey Boase (2008) found that people who draw heavily on all types of available technology have larger and more diverse personal networks than people who make less use of available technology.

As social workers concerned about social justice, however, we must understand the multiple implications of inequality of access to the new technologies. These technologies open opportunities for relational community and the multitude of resources provided by such communities. Skill in using the new technologies is also increasingly rewarded in the labor market. Unless access to these technologies is equalized, however, territorial community will remain central to the lives of some groups—most notably, young children and their caregivers; older adults; poor families; and many persons with disabilities, who have their own special technological needs. On the other hand, the new technologies may make it easier for some people with disabilities to gain access to relational community, even while inaccessible physical environments continue to block their connections to territorial community.

Although both territorial and relational communities are relevant to social work, social work's commitment to social justice has led to continued concern for territorial communities. That same commitment also requires social workers to work toward equalization of access to both territorial and relational community.

THEORETICAL APPROACHES TO COMMUNITY

Five theoretical perspectives on community seem particularly relevant for social work: the contrasting types approach, spatial arrangements approach, social systems approach, social capital approach, and conflict approach (see Exhibit 8.5 for a summary of the main ideas of these approaches). The second of these, the spatial arrangements approach, applies only to territorial communities, but the other four can be applied equally well to both relational and territorial communities. In combination, these five approaches to community should enable you to scan more widely for factors contributing to the problems of living among vulnerable populations, to recognize community resources, and to think more creatively about possible interventions. Using approaches that are not only varied but even discordant should assist you in thinking critically about human behavior and prepare you for the often ambiguous practice situations you will encounter.

CONTRASTING TYPES APPROACH

The Filipina domestic workers in Rome and Los Angeles are concerned about commitment, identification, and relationships within their communities. The Los Angeles Filipinas seem especially concerned about the nature of their relationship to the wider Filipino community in their area. These concerns are at the heart of the oldest theory of community, Ferdinand Tonnies's (1887/1963) concepts of *gemeinschaft* and *gesellschaft* (translated from the German as *community* and *society*). Actually, Tonnies was trying to describe contrasting types of societies, rural preindustrial societies (gemeinschaft) versus urban industrial societies (gesellschaft), but his ideas continue to be used by community sociologists today to understand differences between communities, both spatial and relational (Ballantine & Roberts, 2014; Memmi, 2006; Ritzer, 2013a). In gemeinschaft communities, relationships are personal and traditional; in gesellschaft communities, relationships are impersonal and contractual.

Tonnies (1887/1963) saw gemeinschaft and gesellschaft as ideal types that will never exist in reality. However, they constitute a hypothetical dichotomy against which the real world can be compared. Although Tonnies's work

These photos of a small German village and the Seattle skyline represent the contrasting types of gemeinschaft and gesellschaft communities.

is more than a century old, the gemeinschaft/gesellschaft dichotomy has proven to be a powerful analytical construct, and it continues to be used and validated in community research.

Tonnies (1887/1963) shared the view of other early European sociologists, such as Max Weber and Émile Durkheim, that modernization was leading us away from gemeinschaft and toward gesellschaft. Capitalism, urbanization, and industrialization have all been proposed as causes of the movement toward gesellschaft. Many typology theorists lament the "loss of community" that occurs in the process. But some theorists suggest that electronic technology is moving us into a third type of community—sometimes referred to as a postgesellschaft, or postmodern, community—characterized by diversity and unpredictability (Griswold, 2013; Lyon, 1987; Smith, 1996). This view has become more prominent with increasing globalization, and it is well illustrated by the Filipina domestic workers and their families back in the Philippines. Back home in their rural, newly industrializing sending communities, children, relatives, and friends talk about the loss of emotional intimacy in their relationships with the migrant workers. Although the Filipina domestic workers feel the pain of separation from family and friends back home, they talk about relationships based on goal attainment—meeting the goal of improving the financial situation of their families.

Howard Becker (1957) sees the evolution of community in a different light. He suggests that modern society does not always move in one direction but instead moves back and forth a great deal on the gemeinschaft-gesellschaft continuum (which Becker called the *sacred-secular* continuum).

Tonnies and other theorists who have studied communities as contrasting types have focused their attention on territorial communities. Indeed, empirical research supports the idea that territorial communities vary along the gemeinschaft/gesellschaft continuum (Cuba & Hummon, 1993; Hunter & Riger, 1986; Keane, 1991; Woolever, 1992). More recently, however, Barry Wellman (1999) and research associates have attempted to understand contrasting types of relational communities that are based on networks of interaction rather than territory. In his early work, Wellman (1979) identified three contrasting types of communities:

1. *Community lost.* Communities that have lost a sense of connectedness, social support, and traditional customs for behavior
2. *Community saved.* Communities that have retained a strong sense of connectedness, social support, and customs for behavior
3. *Community liberated.* Communities that are loosely knit, with unclear boundaries and a great deal of heterogeneity

Wellman (1999) suggests that as societies change, community is not necessarily lost but becomes transformed, and new forms of community develop. Daniel Memmi (2006) argues that online communities are just another form of community and another example of the long-term evolution of looser social relationships. There are differences of opinion about whether community is lost or merely transformed in the exportation of labor around the world. As you ponder this question, think about this personal story told by Rhacel Salazar Parreñas (2008) in her book *The Force of Domesticity*. While she was doing fieldwork about the families of Filipina migrant domestic workers in a city in the Philippines, she ended up spending a night in jail with her cousin, Mimi, in a remote small town. She was surprised that word of their incarceration reached relatives in the United States before anyone in her Filipino household or neighborhood knew anything about it.

Wellman and associates have continued to study the idea of contrasting types of relational communities for more than 20 years, seeking to understand multiple dimensions of communities. Their work (e.g., Wellman & Potter,

1999) suggests that it is more important to think in terms of *elements* of communities rather than *types* of communities. Using factor analytic statistical methods, they have identified four important elements of community—contact (level of interaction), range (size and heterogeneity of community membership), level of intimacy, and proportion of community membership composed of immediate kin versus friends. These elements are configured in different ways in different communities and in the same community at different times.

Social workers might benefit by recognizing both the gemeinschaft and gesellschaft qualities of the communities they serve as well as the histories of those communities. Approaches like Wellman and Potter's multiple elements of communities could be helpful in this regard.

SPATIAL ARRANGEMENTS APPROACH

If we think about the Filipina community in Rome in terms of spatial arrangements, we note the dispersed gathering places where they congregate. We think about how their gathering places are segregated from the public space of the dominant society. We also think about the crowded apartments that sometimes hold as many as four residents in a small room. If we think about the Filipinas in Los Angeles, we think about domestic workers isolated in houses in wealthy neighborhoods and visiting middle-class Filipino neighborhoods where they feel like outsiders on their days off. We also think about their lack of transportation to get beyond their live-in and day-off neighborhoods.

Beginning with Robert Park's (1936) human ecology theory, a diverse group of sociological theorists have focused on community as spatial arrangements. Their interests have included city placement; population growth; land use patterns; the process of suburbanization; the development of "edge" cities (newly developed business districts of large scale located on the edge of major cities); and the relationships among central cities, suburbs, and edge cities. They are also interested in variations in human behavior related to the type of spatial community, such as rural area, small town, suburb, or central city, and more recently, in how human health and well-being are related to physical features of the community (Sternberg, 2009).

Symbolic interactionists have studied how symbolic images of communities—the way people think about their communities—are related to spatial arrangements (Wilson & Baldassare, 1996). A survey of a random sample of Denver employees found that a large majority thought of themselves as either a "city person" or a "suburbanite" (Feldman, 1990). Participants largely agreed about the spatial attributes that distinguish cities from suburbs. On the whole, both city people and suburbanites reported a preference for the type of spatial community in which they resided. Recently, however, there is evidence that, after 50 years of movement from U.S. cities to the suburbs, many suburbanites no longer want suburban life. Cities and high-density inner suburbs are now growing faster than the suburbs (Gallagher, 2013). Two of the reasons for this trend are a desire to spend less time in the car and a desire to live where human interactions are more convenient. The future of this suburban to urban migration is unclear. Stay tuned.

One research team set out to discover the meanings that residents of seven distressed neighborhoods in one midwestern city make of the physical aspects of their neighborhoods (Nowell, Berkowitz, Deacon, & Foster-Fishman, 2006). They used a *photovoice* methodology, putting cameras in the hands of participants and asking them to use the cameras to tell a story about their community. They found that physical aspects of the neighborhood carry many meanings for the residents. Positive physical landmarks, such as parks and monuments, communicate a message of pride and identity, but physical conditions such as dilapidated houses, graffiti, and overflowing garbage convey negative meaning that invites frustration and shame. The researchers concluded that community physical conditions are important because they carry symbolic meanings for the residents. We are reminded that the Los Angeles Filipina domestic workers interpret the middle-class neighborhoods where they visit on their days off as "middle-class spaces."

The multidisciplinary theory on human behavior and the physical environment, discussed in Chapter 6, has also been extended to the study of community as spatial arrangements. Social scientists have focused on elements of environmental design that encourage social interaction as well as those that encourage a sense of control and the motivation to look out for the neighborhood. They have identified such elements as large spaces broken into smaller spaces, personalized spaces, and spaces for both privacy and congregation. One research team that studied the spatial arrangements in a suburban region found that people who had a sense of adequate privacy from neighbors' houses also reported a greater sense of community (Wilson & Baldassare, 1996). Another researcher found that opportunities to visit nearby shared space and having views of nature from home are correlated with increased neighborhood satisfaction (Kearney, 2006). Still another researcher found that neighborhood physical environments that provide opportunity for physical activity are particularly valued by children and recommends that social work assessment with children include aspects of the child–neighborhood relationship (Nicotera, 2005). Recently, new urbanist designers have been interested in aspects of community design that encourage physical activity for people of all ages; they are thinking of the health benefits that physical activity provides.

Early settlement house social workers at Hull House in Chicago developed color-coded community maps for assessing the spatial arrangements of social and economic injustices in local neighborhoods (Schoech, 2013). Social work planners and administrators have recently returned to the idea of geographical mapping, making use of advancements in *geographic information system (GIS)* computer technology, which can map the spatial distribution of a variety of social data. In recent years, GIS has been used to map (1) the distribution of supermarkets in areas of high concentration of diet-related deaths (Giang, Karpyn, Laurison, Hillier, & Perry, 2008); (2) where foster care children are placed in relation to schools, community services, transportation, and other types of community resources (Potter, 2005); (3) the geographical distribution of rates of child physical abuse, neglect, and sexual abuse (Ernst, 2000); and (4) the clustering of outdoor advertisements for unhealthful products near child-serving institutions in low-income and minority communities (Hillier et al., 2009). GIS is also being used to map public health risk factors and to examine the match of physicians to community needs (see Cervigni, Suzuki, Ishii, & Hata, 2008); to study residents' views of neighborhood scale (Coulton, Jennings, & Chan, 2013); to target neighborhoods for community-building initiatives (Huber, Egeren, Pierce, & Foster-Fishman, 2009); and to study race disparities in the national distribution of hazardous waste treatment, storage, and disposal facilities (Mohai & Saha, 2007). Huber et al. (2009) emphasize that community resources and community risk factors can be identified through the use of GIS.

GIS holds much promise for future social work planning, administration, and research. Amy Hillier (2007), a leading proponent of the use of GIS by social workers, emphasizes the important role GIS can play in identifying where social work clients live in relation to both resources and hazards. She also argues that GIS has the potential to empower community groups, particularly disenfranchised groups, but that it is rarely used this way by social workers. One challenge for social service organizations is the lack of staff training in the use of GIS software and hardware (Hillier & Culhane, 2013). If you have access to GIS technology, you might want to do some mapping of your territorial community: its ethnic makeup, socioeconomic class, crime rate, libraries, parks, hospitals, social services, and so on. If you do not have access to GIS, you can accomplish the same task with a good map blowup and multicolored pushpins.

Thinking about territorial communities as spatial arrangements can help social workers decide which territorial communities to target, for which problems, and with which methods. An interdisciplinary literature has focused on the compounding and interrelated nature of problems in deteriorating, impoverished neighborhoods in central cities. Philanthropic funders have responded with comprehensive community initiatives (CCIs) to fund multifaceted community building programs that address the economic and physical conditions, as well as social and cultural issues, of these impoverished communities (Huber et al., 2009; Nowell et al., 2006). Typical elements of CCIs are economic and commercial development, education, health care, employment, housing, leadership development, physical revitalization, neighborhood security, recreation, social services, and support networks. Although CCIs have been thought of as a development strategy for impoverished urban neighborhoods, Lori Messinger (2004) argues that the model is also relevant for work in rural communities. She suggests, however, that in rural communities, it is particularly important to pay attention to both current and historical points of tension and conflict. Another development is that many communities are using neighborhood youth for neighborhood cleanup and revitalization (Delgado & Staples, 2013).

SOCIAL SYSTEMS APPROACH

A third way to think about communities is as social systems with cultures and patterns of interactions. We have looked at some of the ways the cultures and patterns of interactions of the Filipina community in Rome are similar to and different from those in Los Angeles. A closer look at these communities as social systems might help us understand both the differences and similarities. The social systems perspective focuses on social interaction rather than on the physical, spatial aspects of community. Social interaction in a community can be understood in two ways: as culture and as structure (Griswold, 2013). Community culture includes use of language; pattern of meaning; typical practices; common knowledge; and symbols that guide thinking, feelings, and behaviors. Community structure includes networks of relationships, institutions, and economic and political factors.

For thinking about community in terms of its culture, symbolic interaction theory is promising because of its emphasis on the development of meaning through interaction. *Ethnography* is particularly useful for studying community culture. The goal of ethnographic research is to understand the underlying rules and patterns of everyday life, in a particular location or among a particular group, from the native point of view rather than the researcher's point of view. One example of this is work by Italian community psychologists Donata Francescato and Manuela Tomai (2001). Their method of building a profile of a territorial community of interest combines demographic data with ethnographic methods that include "environmental walks, drawings, movie scripts, narratives, and telling jokes" (p. 376). For the movie script, they ask different groups in the community to develop a plot for a movie script about the future they imagine for the neighborhood; sometimes these different groups perform parts of their "movies" for each other. Francescato and Tomai have used the movie script method to build understanding between Blacks, Afrikaners, and Asian Indians in a college town in South Africa; old farmers and young students in an Austrian town; and immigrants and locals in several neighborhoods in Italy.

Community can also be studied in terms of its structure. Roland Warren (1963, 1978, 1987) made significant contributions to the understanding of patterns of interactions in communities. Warren pointed out that members of communities have two distinctive types of interactions. The first are those that create *horizontal linkage*, or interactions with other members of the community. The second are interactions that create *vertical linkage*, or interaction with individuals and systems outside the community. Warren suggested that healthy communities must have both types of interactions. Communities with strong horizontal linkage provide a sense of identity for community members, but without good vertical linkage they cannot provide all the necessary resources for the well-being of community members. Communities with strong vertical linkage but weak horizontal linkage may leave community members searching and yearning for a sense of community.

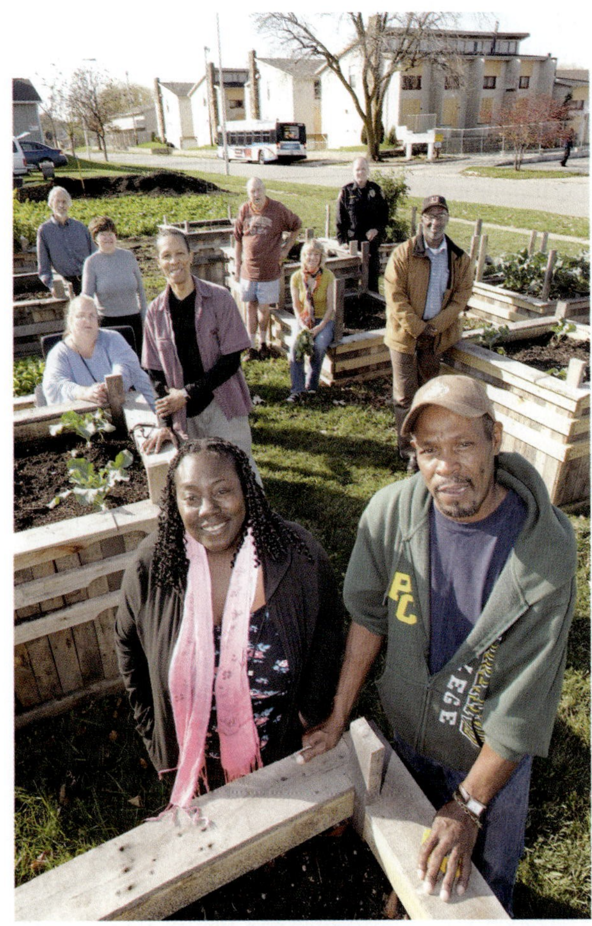
AP Photo/The News-Gazette, Robin Scholz

One way to think about communities is as social systems with cultures and patterns of interactions.

More recently, a similar distinction has been made by scholars who write about community as social capital (to be discussed later; see Putnam, 2000). They differentiate between bonding social capital and bridging social capital. **Bonding social capital** is inward looking and tends to mobilize solidarity and in-group loyalty, and it leads to exclusive identities and homogeneous communities. It may also lead to strong out-group hostilities. This type of social capital is often found in minority ethnic enclaves that provide psychological, social, and economic support to members. **Bridging social capital** is outward looking and diverse, and it links community members to assets and information across community boundaries. Robert Putnam (2000) describes the difference between the two types of social capital this way: "Bonding social capital constitutes a kind of sociological superglue, whereas bridging social capital provides a sociological WD-40" (p. 23). One research team (Ellison, Steinfield, & Lampe, 2007) found that the SNS Facebook is particularly useful for bridging social capital but much less useful for bonding social capital. Tomai et al. (2010) found that both bridging and bonding social capital were increased for youth who joined an online community of high school students outside Rome; however, increased intensity of use was associated with increased bridging social capital but not with increased bonding social capital.

Researchers have found support for the advantages and disadvantages of horizontal and vertical linkage. But consider also the experiences of the Filipina domestic workers in Rome and Los Angeles. We see much evidence that the workers in Rome have built strong horizontal linkages, but their opportunities to build vertical linkages are hampered by anti-immigrant sentiment. Unfortunately, the Filipina domestic workers in Los Angeles seem to be limited in both horizontal and vertical linkages, although middle-class Filipinos appear to be a source of bridging social capital for them.

For almost 3 decades, network theorists and researchers have been using network analysis to study community structure (Borgatti & Halgin, 2011). They suggest that communities, like small groups and organizations, should be thought of as networks of social interaction (Wellman, 1999, 2005). They have tended to define community as *personal community*, which is composed of ties with friends, relatives, neighbors, workmates, and so on. Community is personal because the makeup of community membership varies from person to person. Another name for personal community is *network*, which has been defined as "a set of actors with a set of ties of a specified type" (Borgatti & Halgin, 2011, p. 1169). Network theorists suggest that new communication technologies, particularly the Internet, have played a large role in transforming community from *solidarity community*, which seeks the participation of all members in an integrated fashion, to what Barry Wellman has called community as *networked individualism*, where individuals operate in large, personalized, complex networks (Boase, Horrigan, Wellman, & Rainie, 2006). Some network theorists value this transformation (see, e.g., Boase et al., 2006). Others argue that communication technologies, and particularly the Internet, can and should be used to develop solidarity community, which is friendlier, richer, and more socially binding than networked individualism, which they argue is a North American idea (see, e.g., Day & Schuler, 2004). It seems that both sides are correct. Certainly, we know that the Internet has been used to develop support groups as one form of solidarity community. It is interesting to note that the Los Angeles Filipina domestic workers seem to be closer to a network individualism model, whereas the Rome Filipinas seem to have built solidarity community.

In the mid-1990s, when Parreñas (2001) first did her study of Filipina domestic workers, the Internet was a tool accessible only to the technically elite, but a decade later, it was a part of everyday life for a large majority of people. That represents an unusually rapid diffusion of innovation, which has been accompanied by debates about whether it is helping to build or destroy community. In 2004–2005, the PEW Internet & American Life Project undertook a research project to study this question (Boase et al., 2006). Using a random-digit sample of telephone numbers in the United States, the researchers studied two types of connection people have in their social networks: *core ties*, or our closest relationships, and *significant ties*, or relationships that are only somewhat closely connected. They found surprisingly large networks among the respondents, a median of 15 core ties and 16 significant ties. There was no difference in the number of core ties between Internet users and nonusers, but Internet users were found to have larger numbers of significant ties.

Network analysis has been used to study social ties in both territorial and relational communities. In doing so, researchers have found that for many people, community is based more on relationships than territory. One research team (Lee & Campbell, 1999) did find, however, that barriers of segregation and discrimination make neighborhood relationships more important for Blacks than for Whites. They found that Blacks have more intimate and long-standing ties with neighbors than Whites do in similar neighborhoods, and they engage in more frequent contact with neighbors. Similarly, it would seem that the network of relationships built in Filipina gathering places in Rome is highly important to the Filipinas, who face much segregation and anti-immigrant discrimination.

SOCIAL CAPITAL APPROACH

When the Filipinas in Rome talk about solidarity in their migrant community, they are talking about the quality of the connections community members make with each other and the commitment they feel to one another. They are thinking about community as a social bond that unifies people. Similarly, when the Filipinas in Los Angeles talk about the lack of camaraderie in the Los Angeles Filipino community, they are talking about a lack of a social bond in the community.

In the midst of globalization, it is not unusual to hear both the general public and social scientists lamenting the weakening of community bonds and talking longingly about searching for community, strengthening community, or building a sense of community. These concerns have been consistently voiced in public opinion polls for some time in the United States, and they were the subject of Robert Putnam's (2000) best-selling book *Bowling Alone: The Collapse and Revival of American Community*. To be sure, concerns about the waxing and waning of community are not new, but the nature of those concerns has shifted over time. In the past decade or so, community psychologists and community sociologists have turned to the concept of social capital to conceptualize this social bond aspect of community.

In simplest terms, **social capital** is community cohesion, which is thought to be based in dense social networks, high levels of civic engagement, a sense of solidarity and equality among members, and norms of reciprocity and trustworthiness (see Kay, 2006; Putnam, 1993). In *Bowling Alone*, Putnam (2000) argues that for the first two thirds of the 20th century, social capital was expanding in the United States, but that tide reversed in the final decades of the century. He calls for reconnection and revitalization of networks, civic engagement, solidarity and equality, and reciprocity and trustworthiness. Putnam (2000) presents much empirical evidence to build a powerful argument for the loss of community in the United States.

Though respecting his empirical analysis, network researchers are critical of Putnam's conceptual analysis. They argue that community has been changing rather than declining and that, whereas people in the United States may not be participating in group-based community activities to the same extent as in the past, their networks remain large and strong (Boase et al., 2006). They see no inherent disadvantage to the more fragmented nature of contemporary social networks, whereas Putnam (2000) suggests that it takes dense integrated networks that exist over time to build cohesion and trust. The work of Robert Sampson and colleagues (see Sampson, 2003; Sampson, Morenoff, & Earls, 1999) seems to support and expand this concern of Putnam's. They have proposed a theory of **collective efficacy**, which is "the capacity of community residents to achieve social control over the environment and to engage in collective action for the common good" (Sampson, 2003, p. S56). Collective efficacy involves a working trust, a shared belief in the neighborhood's ability for action, and a shared willingness to intervene to gain social control. Research indicates that as collective efficacy in a neighborhood decreases, a host of individual and social ills increase (Odgers et al., 2009; Sampson, 2003).

It is important to note, however, that Sampson and colleagues (1999) have found that the spatial dynamics and quality of the physical environment of the neighborhood have an impact on collective efficacy. The Filipinos in Rome showed a great deal of collective efficacy when they developed their shopping bazaar by the Tiber River after the city authorities challenged their right to congregate in public spaces.

This idea of a social bond among community members is what Seymour Sarason (1974) had in mind when he declared the enhancement of a *psychological sense of community* (PSOC) as the mission of community psychology. Community psychologists David McMillan and David Chavis (McMillan, 1996; McMillan & Chavis, 1986) turned to the literature on group cohesiveness to understand how to enhance the social bonds of community. They presented a theory of PSOC that identified four essential elements.

1. *Membership* is a sense of belonging, of being part of a collective, something bigger than oneself.
2. *Influence* is bidirectional.
3. *Integration and fulfillment of needs* refers to individual reinforcement or reward for membership.
4. *Shared emotional connection* is based on a shared history and identification with the community.

On the basis of this definition of PSOC, McMillan and Chavis (1986) developed a 12-item Sense of Community Index (SCI) that has been used extensively for research. PSOC is one of the most widely studied concepts in community psychology (Townley, Kloos, Green, & Franco, 2011). Sense of community has been found to be related to positive health behaviors, positive mental health, and citizen participation. More recently, researchers have suggested some need to make minor revisions to the SCI (Obst & White, 2004). Some research teams caution that the SCI was developed and validated in Western societies and may not be a good fit for the meaning of community for non-Western people, particularly those from collectivist societies (Mak, Cheung, & Law, 2009; Xu, Perkins, & Chow, 2010). Measures of sense of community have been developed for specific cultural groups, including gay men (Proescholdbell, Roosa, & Nemeroff, 2006), Italians (Prezza & Costantini, 1998), and individuals with serious mental illness (Townley & Kloos, 2011).

An Australian research team (Obst et al., 2002a, 2002b) has used McMillan and Chavis's theory of PSOC to compare PSOC in territorial and relational communities. More specifically, the researchers asked 359 science fiction aficionados attending a World Science Fiction Convention to complete questionnaires rating PSOC both for their fandom community and for their territorial community. Research participants reported significantly higher levels of PSOC in their fandom communities than in their territorial communities. They also found that although the ratings on all dimensions of McMillan and Chavis's four theorized dimensions of PSOC were higher in the fandom communities than in the geographical communities, the dimensions received essentially the same rank ordering in both communities. The researchers also suggest that a fifth dimension, *conscious identification* with the community, should be added to McMillan and Chavis's theory of PSOC. They found this cognitive identification to be an important component of PSOC. Other researchers have found that social bonding and intimacy take time to mature in computer-mediated communication (Harrison & Thomas, 2009).

In a theoretical turn particularly useful for considering the situations of the Filipina migrants in Rome and Los Angeles, some community psychologists have introduced the concept of **multiple psychological senses of community (MPSOC)**. They note that people live in multiple territorial and relational communities, such as neighborhood, city, workplace, university, religious group, sports league, SNS, and so on, and have multiple senses of community representing each of these communities (Brodsky, 2009). This conceptualization helps us to think about the different senses of community experienced by the Filipina migrant workers with their sending communities, their receiving communities, and their global communities. Beard and Sarmiento (2010) chronicle how immigrants from Oaxaca, Mexico, to Southern California establish hometown associations to maintain a positive sense of community in both their sending community and their receiving community. The associations in Southern California hold social and cultural events, such as fiestas and danzas, to fund-raise for community-planning projects back in their hometowns in Oaxaca.

In recent years, the social work literature has paid attention to the issue of community building. This literature often focuses broadly on community revitalization, in terms of the economic and physical, as well as the social relationship dimensions of communities. The literature on youth leadership development is particularly noteworthy for its attention to building a sense of community among youth in neighborhoods. Recent social work literature on community youth development has returned to its settlement house roots, recommending the use of arts, humanities, and sports to build a sense of community, as well as to empower youth and help them build skills (Delgado & Staples, 2013; Tilton, 2009).

Social capital theorists acknowledge that social capital can be used for antisocial as well as prosocial purposes. Think of the elements of social capital and sense of community and you will have to agree that they apply equally well to the Ku Klux Klan (KKK) and a neighborhood committee formed to welcome the influx of new immigrants.

The literature on networks often suggests that birds of a feather flock together. It is possible, as the KKK example demonstrates, that groups can be socially cohesive and yet exclusionary, distrustful, and hostile (even violently so) to outsiders. That has led Putnam (2000) and others (Townley et al., 2011) to accede the dark side of social capital. Townley et al. (2011) note that both sense of community and the positive value of diversity are core values in community psychology, and these two values can conflict in community life. Fisher and Karger (1997) have made a similar observation about social work. Putnam (2000) notes that in the same time period that social capital was declining in the United States, social tolerance was growing. On another dark note, Australian public health educator Fran Baum (1999) states a fear that has also been presented by European community psychologists (see Riera, 2005):

> Social capital may come to be seen as a shorthand way of putting responsibility on communities that do not have the economic, educational or other resources to generate social capital. Networks, trust and cooperation are not substitutes for housing, jobs, incomes and education even though they might play a role in helping people gain access to them. (p. 176)

We would suggest that the dark side of social capital calls for a conflict approach to understanding community.

CONFLICT APPROACH

The Filipina domestic workers in Rome and Los Angeles have confronted anti-immigrant sentiment. They often feel exploited by their privileged employers. They feel shut out of all sectors of the labor market except for low-status domestic work. In Los Angeles, they have felt marginalized by and alienated from middle-class Filipinos. Back in the Philippines, some were abused or abandoned by their husbands. They blame the Philippine government for providing so little security to its residents, but they seldom blame the inequities of economic globalization for their limited options. Conflict theory's emphasis on dissension, power, and exploitation adds another dimension to our understanding of their story.

Writing about how European approaches to community psychology differ from U.S. community psychology, Francescato and Tomai (2001) suggest that European theorizing is much more in the conflict tradition than U.S. theorizing. They propose that, particularly in continental Europe (Germany, Italy, Spain, and Portugal), the work of community psychologists shows that they "do not believe in the myth of the self-made man" (p. 372) that undergirds much of the work in the United States. They further suggest that the longer historical view in Europe leads to more critical emphases in European theory on social and economic inequalities, the historical interpretations that have been presented by power elites to legitimize existing social hierarchies, and the historical collective struggles by which groups of people have become empowered. Indeed, they report that European textbooks on community psychology typically devote chapters to historical social struggles that have led to greater empowerment for specific groups. Francescato and Tomai (2001) argue that Putnam's findings of declining social capital in the United States can be explained by U.S. fascination with neoliberal economics and individual success, which has led to increasing inequality. They insist that social capital cannot exist at the community level without state policy that supports it. In their view, community practice should involve strategies that focus on unequal power distribution and stimulate community participants to challenge community narratives that legitimize the status quo.

Writing from the United Kingdom, Isabelle Fremeaux (2005) criticizes the social capital approach on several fronts. She argues that it typically romanticizes community and fails to recognize the internal coercion and divisions often at play in communities. Failure to recognize the power politics operating in communities does damage to the least powerful members. And, much like Francescato and Tomai, she criticizes Putnam and other social capital theorists for neglecting to analyze the impact of the macro political and economic contexts on local networks. The story of the Filipinas in Rome and Los Angeles is an excellent example of the influence of macro political and economic contexts on social networks among migrant domestic workers.

Other European social scientists argue that community is "as much about struggle as it is about unity" (Brent, 1997, p. 83). Community workers are often faced with heterogeneous settings with diverse opinions, attitudes, and emotional attachments (Dixon, Dogan, & Sanderson, 2005). Carles Riera (2005), community development specialist from Spain, argues that managing the conflicts in such diversity should be the focus of community theorists and practitioners. Riera notes that European society, like U.S. society, is becoming more and more multicultural, caused by migrations from non-European countries as well as by the loosening of the borders of the European Union. Migrating groups often have strong internal cohesion, but the receiving communities are often fragmented. The task for community workers is to work for both inclusion and equality of opportunities in a framework of coexistence.

Riera (2005) describes a model of practice developed in Barcelona, Spain, called the Intercultural Mediation Programme. The program is three-pronged: It strives (1) to facilitate the resolution of intercultural community conflicts that occur in public spaces, (2) to facilitate the resolution of intercultural conflict situations among neighbors living in the same buildings, and (3) to provide information and advice to service professionals struggling with intercultural conflicts. The program is carried out by community mediator teams who use both linguistic and sociocultural interpreters. Perhaps such mediation could have helped when the Filipinos in Rome were being harassed to stop congregating in public spaces, and it might also be helpful to bridge divisions in the Los Angeles Filipino community.

Conflict theory is not new to U.S. social workers and social scientists, but its popularity has waxed and waned over time. Like European theorists, Robert Fisher and Eric Shragge (2000) argue that the worldwide spread of neoliberal faith in the free market (see discussion in Chapter 9) has "dulled the political edge" of community social workers (p. 1). They argue for renewed commitment to a form of community social work willing to build opposition and use a range of confrontational tactics to challenge privilege and oppression. Given economic globalization, Fisher and Shragge (2000) recommend that effective community organizing in the current era will need to be tied to a global social movement. To work effectively with community conflict, social workers must be able to analyze the structure of community power and influence (Martinez-Brawley, 2000). They must understand who controls which types of resources and how power brokers are related to one another. That means understanding the power held internally in the community as well as the power that resides external to the community. This type of analysis allows social workers to understand both the possibilities and limits of community empowerment. Emilia Martinez-Brawley (2000) suggests that social workers working in small communities should keep in mind that memories are usually long in such places, and conflictual relationships established on one issue may have an impact on future issues. Historical understanding is important.

Contemporary life also calls for the type of mediation programs recommended by Riera (2005). In many areas of life, from race relations to family relations, the mediator role is becoming more prominent for social workers. We will have to become more comfortable with conflict if we are to take leadership roles in healing these social fractures. In recent years, some rural communities have faced sudden influxes of refugees from a particular trouble spot in the world. Some of these communities have responded in exclusionary and punitive ways, whereas others have responded in inclusive and collaborative ways. It is more than likely that communities in the United States and other affluent countries will continue to face such influxes, and social workers should be able to assist communities in managing such change. One suggestion is that restorative justice programs similar to the ones used in criminal justice could be used to heal friction and conflict within neighborhoods (Verity & King, 2007). Restorative justice gatherings would allow storytelling and dialogue about social fractures and allow communities to move toward a more just future. This suggestion is consistent with Riera's Intercultural Mediation Programme.

CRITICAL THINKING Questions 8.5

Of which communities are you a part? Is territorial or relational community more important to you? Explain. Think of the community that is most meaningful to you. Which approach to community (contrasting types, spatial arrangements, social systems, social capital, or conflict) is most useful for thinking about that community?

IMPLICATIONS FOR SOCIAL WORK PRACTICE

Several principles for social work action are recommended by this discussion of small groups, formal organizations, and communities.

- In the assessment process, identify any small groups to which the person or family belongs.
- In the assessment process, determine whether the group modality or another intervention modality would be most appropriate for the client.
- Be aware of various groups in your community for referral and networking purposes.
- Develop and implement small groups when it is clear that a group would benefit the population you serve. Determine what type(s) of groups would be most appropriate for that population. Consider groups for prevention when appropriate.
- In the groups you facilitate, understand the stated and unstated purposes and functions of the group and pay careful attention to issues of group structure, development, composition, and dynamics.
- Be alert to the influence of formal organizations on the client's behavior. Be particularly alert to the ways in which the social service organization where you work, as well as other social service organizations to which you frequently refer clients, influence the client's behavior.

- Develop an understanding of the organization goals of the social service organization where you work and how the tasks that you perform are related to these goals. Develop an understanding of the shared meanings of the organization where you work and of the processes by which those meanings are developed and maintained.
- Develop an understanding of the social, political, economic, cultural, and technological environments of the social service organization where you work.
- Be informed about the communities you serve; learn about their readiness to change, their spatial arrangements (for territorial communities), their cultures, their patterns of internal and external relationships, their social capital, and their conflicts.
- Where appropriate, strengthen interaction within the community (horizontal linkages) to build a sense of community and maximize the use of internal resources. Strengthen intercommunity interactions (vertical linkages) to ensure there are adequate resources to meet the community's needs.
- Where appropriate, collaborate with others to challenge exploitation and oppression in communities. Use consciousness-raising tactics to help oppressed groups understand their situations.
- Where appropriate, assist communities to negotiate differences and resolve conflicts.

KEY TERMS

bonding social capital, 253
bridging social capital, 253
bureaucracy, 239
collective efficacy, 254
community, 246
critical perspective on organizations, 244
exchange theory (small groups), 237
formal organization, 238
group cohesiveness, 235
group work, 231
interactional/interpretive perspective on organizations, 243
multiple psychological senses of community (MPSOC), 255
performance expectations, 236
psychodynamic theory (small groups), 235
rational perspective on organizations, 239
relational community, 247
self-categorization theory (small groups), 237
sense of community, 247
small group, 231
social capital, 254
status characteristics, 236
status characteristics and expectation states theory (small groups), 236
symbolic interaction theory (small groups), 236
systems perspective on organizations, 242
territorial community, 247

ACTIVE LEARNING

1. In personal reflection, think about your behavior and roles in important groups throughout your life, groups such as your family of origin, friendship groups, social groups, sports teams, work groups, therapy groups, and so on. What roles have you played in these different groups? Are there any patterns to the roles you have played across various types of groups? Do you notice any changes in your roles over time or in different types of groups? How do you understand both the patterns and the changes?
2. In Case Study 8.2, you read about the transition in leadership at Beacon Center. You have also read about four theoretical perspectives on formal organizations. Imagine that you, and not Roderick Wallace, are the current CEO at Beacon Center. In small groups, talk about the following points: What vision would you have for Beacon Center? What would you want to keep the same as it had been, and what would you want to change? Use theory to back up your position.
3. You have read about two communities with geographical properties, one based in Rome and one based in Los Angeles. Now think about your own geographic community. Compare and contrast it with the communities of Filipina domestic workers in Rome and in Los Angeles according to the following characteristics:
    - Sense of community
    - Physical environment
    - Horizontal and vertical linkages
4. *Theory analysis.* Working in small groups, review the big ideas of the eight theoretical perspectives presented in Exhibit 2.9 in Chapter 2. Discuss which of the eight perspectives seems to do the best job of helping you to understand all three of the social groupings discussed in this chapter: small groups, formal organizations, and communities. Are there specific big ideas that are particularly helpful for thinking about these three types of social groupings?

WEB RESOURCES

The Annie E. Casey Foundation

www.aecf.org

Site maintained by the Annie E. Casey Foundation, a grant-making organization that works to build better futures for disadvantaged children and their families, contains a description of initiatives, projects, and publications.

ARNOVA

www.arnova.org

Site presented by the Association for Research on Nonprofit Organizations and Voluntary Action contains a member directory, conference information, publications, and a job center.

Google Groups

Groups.google.com

Site for creating or finding groups on the Internet, including support-related groups.

International Association for Social Work with Groups (IASWG)

http://iaswg.org

Formerly the Association for the Advancement of Social Work with Groups, this professional organization promotes group work practice, research, and education. Information about state chapters, conferences, and group work projects is available on the site as well as a resources page, which includes information on group-related journals, IASWG practice standards, sample group work course syllabi, and member publications.

National People's Action (NPA)

www.npa-us.org

Site maintained by NPA, an advocacy organization that helps neighborhood people take on corporate America and political institutions, contains news and information about campaigns.

Social Psychology Network: Community Psychology

www.socialpsychology.org

This online guide to community psychology maintained by Scott Plous at Wesleyan University contains links to sites covering a wide range of community psychology issues.

United Neighborhood Houses

www.unhny.org

Site maintained by United Neighborhood Houses, a federation of 38 settlement houses in New York City, includes information about the settlement house movement, current activities of settlement houses in the United States, and job vacancies.

SAGE edge™ **Sharpen your skills with SAGE edge at edge sagepub.com/hutchisonc332e**

SAGE edge for students provides a personalized approach to help you accomplish your coursework goals in an easy-to-use learning environment. watch listen read

LEARNING OBJECTIVES	FOR FURTHER EXPLORATION AND APPLICATION
LO 8.1: Compare and contrast one's emotional and cognitive reactions to three case studies.	There's a Place for "Us"—How Community Fits Into Social Work.
LO 8.2: Define small groups and identify some of their uses in social work practice.	Types of Groups Commonly Used in Substance Abuse Treatments
LO 8.3: Analyze the benefits and difficulties in using virtual groups in social work practice.	Developing Online Community Accessibility Guidelines for Persons With Disabilities and Older Adults
LO 8.4: Identify dimensions of small group structure, composition, and processes.	What Is Group Work?
LO 8.5: Critique five theories of small group processes (psychodynamic, symbolic interaction, status characteristics and expectation states, exchange, and self-categorization).	Self-Categorization
LO 8.6: Define formal organizations.	Difference Between Formal and Informal Groups
LO 8.7: Critique four theoretical perspectives on formal organizations (rational, systems, interactional/interpretive, and critical).	Formal Organizations
LO 8.8: Recommend uses of information and communication technologies in social service organizations.	Around the Next Curve: Using Technology in Addiction Social Work Practice Utilizing Mutual Aid in Reducing Adolescent Substance Use and Developing Group Engagement
LO 8.9: Define community, territorial community, relational community, and sense of community.	The Secret to Lasting Community Change Transnational Lives
LO 8.10: Critique five theoretical approaches to community (contrasting types, spatial arrangements, social systems, social capital, and conflict).	Social Capital: The Key to Community
LO 8.11: Apply knowledge of small groups, formal organizations, and communities to recommend guidelines for social work assessment and intervention.	Working With Small Groups

Jim West imageBROKER/Newscom

We March For
PEACE

Social Structure, Social Institutions, and Social Movements

Global and National

Elizabeth D. Hutchison

Learning Objectives

LO 9.1 Compare and contrast one's emotional and cognitive reactions to two case studies.

LO 9.2 Recognize national and global trends in seven major social institutions (government and political, economic, education, health care, social welfare, religious, and mass media).

LO 9.3 Analyze different theories of social inequality.

LO 9.4 Define social movements.

LO 9.5 Compare and contrast three theoretical perspectives on social movements (political opportunities, mobilizing structures, and cultural framing).

LO 9.6 Apply knowledge of social institutions, social structure, and social movements to recommend guidelines for social work assessment and intervention.

GET MORE OUT OF YOUR STUDY TIME.

The **SAGE Interactive eBook** provides one-click access to integrated study tools that will enrich your understanding of course content.

- **Watch** video clips to learn actively
- **Think Critically** with SAGE Journals
- **Explore Further** with SAGE Reference
- **Connect** with relevant web resources
- **Listen** to podcasts for real-world context

CASE STUDY 9.1

LETICIA RENTERIA'S STRUGGLE TO MAKE IT IN THE UNITED STATES

Leticia Renteria is a 30-year-old woman who, along with her husband Marcos Vargas, is a parent to three young children, ages 4, 5, and 7. She lives in the Coachella Valley of California, which is a dichotomous region hosting both extreme wealth and extreme poverty. Leticia, unfortunately, fits into the latter category. Born in the border town of Mexicali, Baja California, Mexico, Leticia grew up poor, in proximity to the United States and surrounded by American culture. As a youth, she enjoyed a renewable visitor visa, which allowed her to travel back and forth across the border to visit an aunt and several cousins (some of whom were born in the United States) who lived not far away in the Imperial and Coachella Valleys of California. Leticia's experiences in the United States gave her even more understanding of the differences in opportunities between the United States and Mexico and made her yearn for those available in the United States, especially as she grew to working age. Work in Mexicali mostly consisted of very long hours at the maquiladoras (U.S. factories producing products for export in a free trade zone) or in various other low-paying informal occupations, such as selling *raspados* on street corners. Mexico's minimum wage remained at less than US$5.00 per day, and actual average wages for industries in which she was qualified to work with her high school–equivalent degree only rose slightly to US$8.00 to US$10.00 per day. With prices in the border region growing steadily to match U.S. prices in some areas, these wage rates simply became unfeasible for Leticia, and she soon made one of the most difficult decisions of her life: At age 19, she entered the United States legally on her visitor visa and decided to stay past her permissible time of visit—she thusly became an *undocumented immigrant*.

Leticia moved outside of the heavier border patrol enforcement zone, a zone within 60 miles of the border, to the nearby Coachella Valley, where she was able to stay with a relative for a low amount of rent. At age 20, she met Marcos. The two married within a year. Marcos is a *lawful permanent resident* of the United States, having gained *adjusted status* many years ago after immigrating without papers from Mexico. Marcos works year-round in a landscaping company that provides services to the lush golf courses and country clubs of the affluent part of the Coachella Valley; Leticia toils in seasonal positions in produce packing houses and landscaping crews, those positions beginning and ending based on seasonal need. In between her periods of employment, Leticia is without income altogether due to her inability to qualify for unemployment benefits because of her immigration status.

Despite their employment challenges, Leticia and Marcos were able to get together enough money to buy a used mobile home in a nearby settlement, where they pay rent for the space upon which their home sits. Leticia has mixed feelings about their home ownership—whereas she is excited to accomplish this version of the "American dream," she is frustrated and disappointed by the conditions of their mobile home park. The park is located in a rural area, several miles outside of the nearest city, and is not connected to water and wastewater services offered by the local municipal water district. The park's owner pipes water to the spaces from a well independently dug on the site, and the water coming from the well has recently been tested and reveals impermissibly high levels of arsenic contamination. The lack of wastewater services means that all of the homes are relying on septic systems, which unfortunately frequently fill or clog up, resulting in overflow, stench, and other problems. Moreover, not far down the street sits an illegal dump, which was created by the landowner "under the radar" without the knowledge of enforcement authorities and which now causes unbearable stench and sometimes smoke in Leticia's settlement. To make matters worse, when Leticia is not working and Marcos has the family's only car at his work, she is stuck at home, given that the nearest public transportation stop is more than 5 miles away and the nearest grocery stores, services, and recreation are more than 10 miles away.

Leticia does her best to find child care for the children with neighbors and acquaintances during the times she is able to work and continues working at night at home to complete the cooking, cleaning, and other tasks that Marcos and others expect her to do as a woman. All three of the children suffer from varying degrees of asthma, which Leticia believes is related to the dusty nature of their desert mobile home park, as well as the fumes and smoke that frequently come from the nearby dump. However, the community clinic where Leticia takes the children to be treated does not keep any data related to these kinds of causes and does not connect patients' health indicators to any environmental factors, so Leticia is left to rely on her own suspicions. The children receive medical care in the clinic, thanks to the state insurance program, because they are citizens of the United States. Leticia cannot qualify for any such assistance, given that she remains undocumented. Leticia and Marcos hope that their children will succeed in school, but they are not really sure how the system works, and they are really intimidated by the English-speaking teachers and big buildings and campuses, so they have mostly thus far refrained from getting involved with their children's school. Leticia tries her best to access some of the few other resources in the area for her children to help them supplement their education and get their minds off other stressors. The children particularly enjoy spending time at the new Boys and Girls Club in the nearby town of Mecca when the family has the time and transportation to get there.

Despite her marriage to a lawful permanent resident, Leticia has not yet applied for legal immigration status because she and Marcos cannot afford the immigration and attorney fees, which would cost more than $4,000. Even with their hard work, Leticia and Marcos remain at the minimum wage rate of $8.00 per hour and are only bringing home a little more than $20,000 per year. This is far from enough to support their family of five and to cover the $50 to $100 per month they try to send to family back in Mexico. Leticia does not apply for food stamps or other cash assistance for her children (though they do qualify because they are U.S. citizens) because she has heard that children who receive government benefits are the first ones sent to war when they turn 18 and that the children have to pay back all the benefits they received when they become adults. She just wishes that someday there will be an increase in the minimum wage, so that she and Marcos could make ends meet on their own. From everything Leticia hears on television, though, a lot of companies and politicians really don't want to see that happen. She figures that nothing ever happens unless powerful people want it to happen, so she thinks her minimum wage will never change.

Leticia finds her low wage rate doubly unjust because of all the things she has to tolerate in her workplace. As is common in landscaping and agricultural jobs, Leticia frequently encounters supervisors and coworkers who make unwelcome sexual comments to her and who sometimes even touch her in uncomfortable ways. Though these interactions would constitute illegal sexual harassment, Leticia, like most other women, never complains, for fear of losing her job, fear of immigration enforcement, and even fear of stigma among acquaintances as well as consequences in her own relationship with Marcos if he were to find out.

Early one morning, Leticia was detained by immigration authorities on her way to work, after having been originally stopped by a sheriff's deputy for a supposed violation related to a frame around her license plate. In immigration detention, she is offered the right to stay in detention and present her deportation defenses to a judge—which could take months—or the option to leave the country immediately through *voluntary departure*. Leticia has heard horror stories about deported mothers whose children get placed into the state foster care system and lose connection with their families. She tries to reach a local nun who helps in the community, to see if she can get any advice. However, even the nun isn't sure what to do or where to turn. So, even though Leticia knew that she could apply for status through her husband, she was scared to wait out the multimonth process and decided to leave voluntarily. She returned to the United States with her cousins by car with no papers only a few days later, simply telling the immigration officers at the border that she was a U.S. citizen just like her cousins. What Leticia wouldn't realize until much later, when she and Marcos finally went to apply for her status, is that her voluntary departure followed by her quick illegal return effectively disqualified her for any legal immigration status until she spends 10 years outside of the United States as a penalty.

—*Megan Beaman*

CASE STUDY 9.2

FIGHTING FOR A LIVING WAGE

Greg Halpern was in his senior year at Harvard University in 1998 when Aaron Bartley, his labor activist roommate and childhood friend, "dragged" him to a meeting of the Harvard Living Wage Campaign (Terkel, 2003). Greg remembers that he was in the lunch line a few days later when a friend made a joke about how bad the food was. Greg laughed, and then

(Continued)

(Continued)

he looked up and exchanged glances with one of the young women working behind the lunch counter. He saw her anger and hurt. He was deeply embarrassed and realized that most Harvard students had never been taught about the people who clean the bathrooms, serve the food, or clean the classrooms. Greg became active in the living wage campaign at Harvard, attending weekly rallies and sending letters to the university president, calling for the custodians, security guards, and food service workers at Harvard to be paid a living wage. In March 1999, the campaign presented the university president with the "Worst Employer in Boston" award while he was addressing a group of high school students. At graduation, some students chartered an airplane to pull a sign behind it that read "Harvard needs a living wage" (Tanner, 2002).

That same spring, in his final year at Harvard, Greg Halpern did an independent study in which he interviewed and photographed university workers. He decided to blow the interviews up on 10-foot pages and stick them up in the public space provided for students, so that other students could know the stories of the low-wage workers. Greg had never been an activist, but he was dismayed at what he was hearing from workers, and he remained active in the Harvard Living Wage Campaign after he graduated. The campaign had been holding rallies at Harvard for 3 years, but nothing was happening. During the spring of 2001, 2 years after Greg graduated from Harvard, there was growing interest among the members of the Harvard Living Wage Campaign to engage in a sit-in. As they discussed this option, Greg remembered the custodian he had interviewed 2 years earlier. Bill Brook, who cleaned the room in which they were meeting, was 65 years old, worked two full-time jobs, and slept 4 hours per night (Terkel, 2003).

Greg became one of the leaders of the Harvard Living Wage Campaign sit-in strike that occupied Massachusetts Hall, the president's building, for 21 days, demanding that the university raise the wages for 1,400 employees who were making less than a living wage. Throughout the strike, the students, who had never participated in such an event before, kept in touch with the media by cell phones and e-mail (sent and received on their laptops).

There were 50 students inside Massachusetts Hall and a growing group of students on the outside. Three hundred professors or more took out a full-page ad in the *Boston Globe* in support of the students. The dining hall workers and food workers began to deliver pizzas to the students on the inside, and many workers took the risk to wear buttons on the job that said "We Support the Living Wage Campaign." Every local labor union in Cambridge, Massachusetts, endorsed the students, and national labor leaders came to speak. The AFL-CIO union sent one of its top lawyers to negotiate with the university administration. Several high-profile religious leaders made appearances to support the students. On the 15th day of the sit-in, the Cambridge mayor and city council, along with other sympathizers, marched from City Hall to Harvard Yard in support of the students. During the second week of the sit-in, 30 to 40 Harvard Divinity School students held a vigil, chanting, "Where's your horror? Where's your rage? Div School wants a living wage." On the last night of the sit-in, there was a rally of about 3,000 people outside Massachusetts Hall (Tanner, 2002; Terkel, 2003).

In the end, the Harvard administration agreed to negotiate higher wages with the unions. Higher wages were paid, but the students were not fully satisfied with the results of their campaign. Two of the student activists later coproduced an advocacy film based on the sit-in, *Occupation: The Harvard University Living Wage Sit-in*, narrated by Ben Affleck (Raza & Velez, 2002). The sit-in at Harvard was neither the beginning nor the end of the gathering living wage movement in the United States. The sit-in built on the momentum that had started in Baltimore, Maryland, in 1994, and it fueled new actions on other university campuses. It was one piece of a story of a rapidly growing social movement.

In 1993, religious groups in Baltimore were seeing an increase in use of soup kitchens and food pantries by the working poor (Quigley, 2001; Tanner, 2002). They were angry that private companies involved in the city's urban renewal projects were paying low wages in order to bid low to win contracts with the city. They took their concerns to Baltimoreans United in Leadership Development (BUILD), a coalition of 50 Baltimore churches that had been advocating for services and subsidies for Baltimore's poor residents since the 1980s (Snarr, 2007). BUILD decided to join forces with the American Federation of State, County, and Municipal Employees (AFSCME) and low-wage service workers to create a local campaign to develop a law that would require businesses that had contracts with the city to pay their workers a "living wage," a pay rate that would lift a family of four over the federal poverty level. At the time, the federal minimum wage was $4.25 an hour, a wage that could not lift a family out of poverty. The living wage law was enacted in July 1996, requiring city contractors with municipal contracts over $5,000 to pay a minimum wage of $6.16 an hour in 1996, with increments to reach $7.70 an hour in 1999. The law is estimated to have affected 1,500 to 2,000 workers (Quigley, 2001; Tanner, 2002).

The BUILD coalition had no intention of sparking a national social movement, but its success helped to trigger a nationwide alliance of religious and labor groups that has come to be known as the living wage movement. Local grassroots coalitions of activists have used a variety of tactics, including lobbying, postcard campaigns, rallies, door knocking, leafleting, workshops, and sit-ins to achieve their goals in more than 120 localities. Each local coalition is different. The policy solutions have varied from locality to locality, with some bolder than others, but all have established a wage above the federal minimum wage for some group of workers. Some of the local living wage ordinances, like the one in Baltimore, cover only municipal workers. Others have been more expansive in their approach, like the ones in San Francisco and San Jose that cover all workers, public and private (Roosevelt, 2013). The living wage movement has also helped to enact legislation at the state rather than local level. As of January 1, 2015, a total of 29 states plus the District of Columbia have enacted minimum wage laws that set the minimum wage higher than the federal requirement (U.S. Department of Labor, Wage and Hour Division, 2015).

Along the way, the living wage movement has benefited from the support of a number of organizations. The Economic Policy Institute developed a guide to living wage initiatives and their economic impacts on its website. The National Low Income Housing Coalition compiled a report that calculated the amount of money a household needs to afford a rental unit in specific localities. The Brennan Center for Justice, located at the New York University School of Law, provided assistance to design and implement living wage campaigns, including economic impact analysis, legislative drafting, and legal analysis and defense. Responsible Wealth, a national network of businesspeople, investors, and affluent citizens, developed a living wage covenant for businesses interested in economic fairness. The Political Economy Research Institute (PERI), at the University of Massachusetts at Amherst, collected a number of research reports on the effects of living wage laws.

One of the more promising developments in the living wage social movement was the entry of university and high school students into the movement. The Living Wage Action Coalition (LWAC), made up of university students and recent graduates who had participated in living wage campaigns around the country, was created in the summer of 2005. LWAC toured around colleges and universities in the United States, running workshops about strategies for successful living wage campaigns for low-wage workers on campus (Living Wage Action Coalition, n.d.).

The living wage movement started in the United States, but by 2001, it had crossed national lines to London, England, where it has spread to hospitals, finance companies, universities, art galleries, and hotels (Living Wage Foundation, 2014). In October 2009, Asia Floor Wage, a loose coalition of labor and other groups, was formed to propose a floor wage for garment workers in Asia. Activists in 11 European countries participated in events to demand that retailers pay a living wage to all garment workers in their supply chains; the events included leafleting, public debates, visiting corporate headquarters, and hosting film screenings. These events were organized by a coalition of activists involved in a "clean clothes campaign" (fighting for the rights of workers in the global garment industry) (Clean Clothes Campaign, 2009). In 2013, a coalition of community activists, faith-based organizations, and unions concerned about the growing gap between the rich and the poor in New Zealand began a campaign called Living Wage Aotearoa New Zealand (2014).

Back in the United States, 2014 and 2015 were marked by an energetic debate about growing income inequality and the plight of low-wage workers. Fast-food workers around the country demanded wages of $15 an hour. One small town in Washington State voted to set the wage floor at $15 an hour, instead of the $9 state minimum wage. President Obama recommended that the federal minimum wage be raised from $7.25 to $10.10 (Kelly, 2014). Minimum wage laws apply to all employers, whereas living wage laws have typically applied only to employers in government-subsidized jobs. In December 2013, Liz Halloran, a reporter for National Public Radio, noted that in the midst of rising agitation for increasing the minimum wage, the living wage movement hadn't been getting much attention lately. Paul Sonn of the National Employment Law Project (NELP) responded that living wage and minimum wage are part of the same policy movement to promote wage fairness (Halloran, 2013).

PATTERNS OF SOCIAL LIFE

As you read Leticia Renteria's story, you were probably aware of both the people and the environments involved. A number of people are involved in the story, and you may be observing how they are interacting with each other and what each contributes to the current situation. Although you do not want to lose sight of the personal dimensions of Leticia Renteria's story, in this chapter consider the broad patterns of social life that she and her family have encountered and continue to encounter. I want you to see the connections between the personal troubles of this family and broader social conditions. One way to think about Leticia Renteria's story is to think of it as a globalization story. In Chapter 1, we defined globalization as a process by which the world's people are becoming more interconnected economically, politically, environmentally, and culturally.

Sociologists and anthropologists have given much thought to how social conditions are created as people work together to try to ensure the survival of a society. They have identified two concepts—social structure and social institutions—as central to understanding those endeavors. Social structure and social institutions are among the more abstract concepts used by sociologists. In the broadest sense, social structure is another term for *society*, or simply an acknowledgment that social life is patterned, not random. It provides the framework within which individual behavior is played out in daily life. **Social structure** is a set of interrelated social institutions developed by human beings to support and constrain human interaction for the purpose of the survival and well-being of the collectivity. Certainly, we can see some supports as well as some constraints that various social institutions provide and impose on Leticia Renteria's family.

Our understanding of social institutions is complicated by the casual, everyday use of the term *institution* to cover a variety of meanings. In this book, however, we use the definition of **social institutions** as "patterned ways of solving the problems and meeting the requirements of a particular society" (D. Newman, 2012, p. 30). To provide stability, social institutions organize rights and duties into statuses and roles and the expected behaviors that accompany them. **Statuses** are specific social positions; **roles** are the usual behaviors of persons occupying particular statuses. Sociologists have identified a set of interrelated social institutions—such as family, religion, government, economy, and education—with each institution organizing social relations in a particular sector of social life. We see evidence of each of these institutions in the lives of Leticia Renteria and her family.

Sociological treatment of social structure and social institutions emphasizes the ways in which they persist and contribute to social stability. But often they persist despite unintended consequences and evidence that they are ineffective. In addition, although social institutions are relatively stable, they also change—whether by accident, by evolution, or by design (McMichael, 2012; W. Scott, 2014). Social institutions persist only when they are carried forward by actors and only when they are actively monitored.

W. Richard Scott (2014) suggests three types of processes that contribute to the stability of social institutions: regulatory processes, normative processes, and cultural-cognitive processes. Different types of processes are at work in different social institutions. *Regulatory processes* involve rules, monitoring, and enforcement through rewards and punishment. *Normative processes* involve values and norms about how things should be done. *Cultural-cognitive processes* involve beliefs about the world and how to behave in it.

Seven interrelated social institutions are discussed in this chapter: the government and political institution, economic institution, educational institution, health care institution, social welfare institution, religious institution, and mass media institution. The family and kinship institution, the most basic institution in every society, received special attention in Chapter 7 in this book. We can see how important each of these institutions is in the current lives of Leticia Renteria and her family. Exhibit 9.1 presents these social institutions and the major functions they perform for society.

EXHIBIT 9.1 • Key Social Institutions and the Functions They Perform

SOCIAL INSTITUTION	FUNCTIONS PERFORMED
Government and political institution	• Making and enforcing societal rules • Resolving internal and external conflicts • Mobilizing collective resources to meet societal goals
Economic institution	• Regulating production, distribution, and consumption of goods and services
Educational institution	• Passing along formal knowledge from one generation to the next • Socializing individuals
Health care institution	• Promoting the general health
Social welfare institution	• Allocating goods, services, and opportunities • Enhancing social functioning of individuals • Contributing to the social health of the society
Religious institution	• Answering questions about the meaning and purpose of life • Socializing individuals • Maintaining social control • Providing mutual support
Mass media institution	• Managing the flow of information, images, and ideas

CONTEMPORARY TRENDS IN GLOBAL AND U.S. SOCIAL INSTITUTIONS

As suggested, social institutions are relatively stable, but they also change. They have undergone great changes over time, yet they often seem so resistant to change. Contemporary futurists suggest that we have entered a time when the pace of technological change will continue to accelerate rapidly, and we might expect that continued rapid technological change will produce change, sometimes rapid change, in most if not all major social institutions (Kurzweil, 2012). Writing about global social structure and social institutions at the beginning of the 21st century, Anthony Giddens (2000), a British social scientist, suggested that the recent pace and scope of change has produced a "runaway world." Some social scientists suggest that the pace and scope of change in the past few decades has produced several crises for global as well as U.S. social institutions, for example, a food crisis, energy crisis, climate crisis, and social inequality crisis. They propose that these combined crises are leading to a quest for new ways of organizing the global social structure and that we may now be at a turning point transitioning to yet unclear new ways of organizing social life (see McMichael, 2012). It is important for social workers to think about their work in the context of contemporary trends and to imagine the possibilities for how they might help to shape future trends in such a way that they bend toward social justice.

It is increasingly difficult to understand the changes in our own society without recognizing the global context of those changes. Globalization is affecting all aspects of social life around the world. Indeed, the process of globalization has been stimulating changes in the major social institutions for several decades, but in a pronounced way for the past few decades. The discussion that follows positions trends in U.S. social institutions within a global context. Doing so illuminates how U.S. society is both different from and the same as other societies, and it aids critical thinking about the question of why we do things the way we do.

Perhaps the most important and troubling trend in contemporary life is the continued extremely high level of social inequality, both between nations and within nation-states. Although globalization has brought some improvements in literacy, health, and living standards for many, we pay particular attention to trends in social inequality because the profession of social work has historically made a commitment to persons and groups that are disadvantaged in the distribution of resources by social institutions. To carry out this commitment, we must have a way of understanding social inequality and its influence on human behavior. In this chapter, I demonstrate how social inequality is created and maintained in seven major interrelated social institutions. But first we take a closer look at inequality globally and in the United States.

There are many debates about whether globalization is leading to increased or decreased global inequality, and the answer depends on how the question is asked. McMichael (2012) argues that although a global middle class has emerged in some previously low-income countries such as Brazil, Russia, India, China, and South Africa, global inequality is deepening if China, which has both the largest population in the world and growing wealth, is removed from the calculations. He reports that 80% of the world's population lives in countries where income differentials are widening. On the other hand, the United Nations Development Programme (UNDP; 2013) reports that, in recent years, a large number of developing countries have been transformed into dynamic major economies. It notes, however, that economic growth does not automatically translate into reduced inequality. Its most recent report (UNDP, 2013) indicates that in the recent great economic growth for some developing countries, most regions of the world had declining inequality in health and education but rising income inequality. Although different data sources report different numbers, there is agreement that we are talking about comparatively huge disparities in the contemporary world. For example, the richest 1% of the world's people receives more income than the poorest half of the world's people (Sernau, 2014).

It is clear that not all regions of the world have shared equally in the benefits of globalization and that high levels of inequality exist in regions of the world experiencing recent economic growth. During a time of massive income growth worldwide, average incomes fell in most of Sub-Saharan Africa, and much of that region is now further behind the rest of the world than in 1990 (Sernau, 2014). Twenty years ago, 93% of poor people lived in low-income countries; now 75% of the world's poorest people live in middle-income countries (McMichael, 2012). So, whereas available data show a slight average decline in global inequality, they also indicate that income inequality is growing between the poorest 10% and the richest 10% of the world's people.

Although most of the global inequality is due to inequality *between* countries, as you see from this discussion, the gap within nations is also staggering. Let's look at income inequality in the United States. In the period from 1947 to 1973, income inequality in the United States declined slightly. Since 1974, however, income inequality has grown substantially. The most commonly used measure of income inequality is the **Gini index**, which measures the extent to which the distribution of income within a country deviates from a perfectly equal distribution. Gini index scores range from 0 (perfect equality) to 100 (perfect inequality). As Exhibit 9.2 shows, the Gini index in the United States grew from 39.4 in 1970 to 47.7 in 2012. Emmanuel Saez (2012) reports that the incomes of the top 1% of earners in the United States captured more than half of the overall economic growth in the country in the period from 1993 to 2010. Looking at wealth instead of income, Ritzer (2013a) reports that 80% of the wealth gained in the United States from 1983 to 2009 went to the wealthiest 5% of the population, while the poorest 60% saw a 7.5% decline in wealth.

The United States has the highest level of inequality of all the wealthy industrialized nations (Sernau, 2014). Exhibit 9.3 shows the income inequality ranking of 19 advanced industrialized countries from 2000 to 2010, based on the Gini index, moving from the country with the least inequality at the bottom (Sweden, Gini index of 23.0) to the country with the greatest inequality at the top (United States, Gini index of 45.0). The 19 countries presented in Exhibit 9.3 are used throughout this chapter to make comparisons between the United States and other wealthy

EXHIBIT 9.2 • Gini Index of Inequality in the United States, 1970–2012

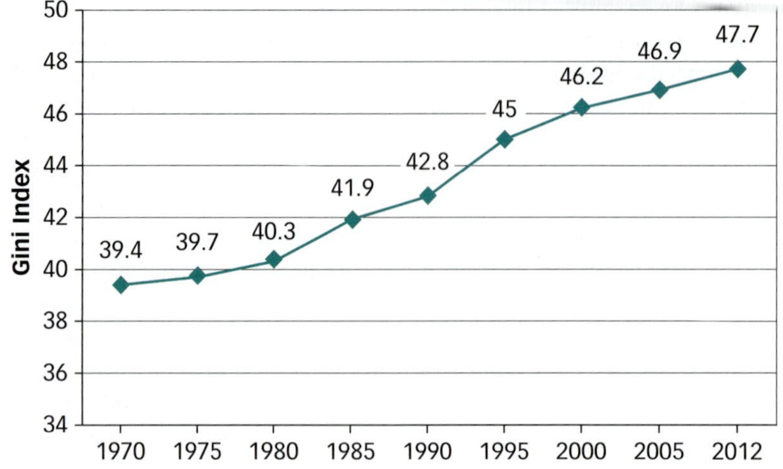

SOURCES: DeNavas-Walt, Proctor, & Hill Lee, 2006; DeNevas-Walt, Proctor, & Smith, 2013.

countries. I call these countries the comparison countries. Of course, the United States does not have more inequality than all countries in the world. In a general sense, highly industrialized, high-income countries have much lower levels of inequality than nonindustrial or newly industrializing countries. The rate of inequality is much lower in the United States than in many low- to middle-income countries. Overall, the highest rates of inequality can be found in some African and Latin American countries, but the rate of inequality is not consistent within these regions.

Leticia Renteria came to the United States to escape brutal poverty in Mexico. In recent years, Mexico has developed trade agreements with a number of other countries and has moved from being the world's 26th largest economy to being the 8th largest. Most of Mexico's recent industrial growth has been in the maquiladoras, and real wages in Mexico have declined by about 20% in this period of growth. A large percentage of workers, about 40% of Mexico's workforce, are poorly paid and have few employment options (Sernau, 2014). Half of Mexican families live in poverty, a rate that has not changed since the early 1980s. Half of the country's rural population earns less than US$1.40 per day (McMichael, 2012). Although Leticia Renteria and Marcos Vargas are struggling for economic survival in the United States, they do not wish to return to Mexico.

Some social analysts argue that social inequality is the price of economic growth and suggest that the poorest families in the United States enjoy a much higher standard of living than poor families in other countries (Hederman & Rector, 1999). But a comparison of the United States with other advanced industrialized countries suggests that societal health is best maintained when economic growth is balanced with attention to social equality. A growing international research literature suggests that high levels of inequality are bad for the social health of a nation. Let's look at

EXHIBIT 9.3 • Ranking of Social Inequality in 19 Advanced Industrial Countries from 2000 to 2010

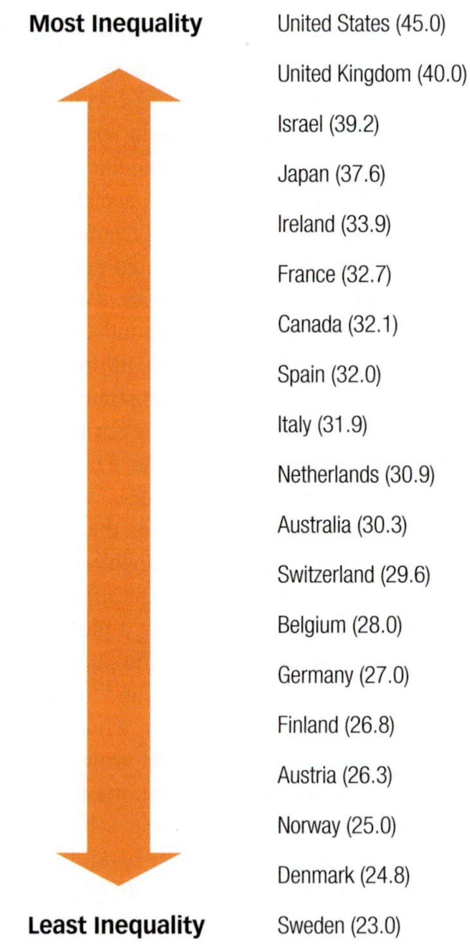

SOURCE: Based on Central Intelligence Agency, 2013a.

three social indicators for the 19 industrialized countries in Exhibit 9.3: childhood mortality (probability of dying before age 5), life expectancy, and secondary school enrollment. In 1960, the United States had a lower childhood mortality rate than 10 of the comparison countries listed in Exhibit 9.3. In 2012, the United States had the highest childhood mortality rate of the 19 countries (World Bank, 2013c). Likewise, all of the comparison countries have longer life expectancies than the United States (Central Intelligence Agency, 2013b). The United States does better in terms of educational equality; looking at the 25- to 34-year-old age group, the United States has higher secondary education completion rates than 12 of the comparison countries (Organisation for Economic Co-operation and Development [OECD], 2013a). These data suggest that education does not reduce economic inequality as much as sometimes suggested.

There is growing support for the idea that economic inequality is associated with a number of social ills, including low social cohesion, distrust, violence, poor health, and economic stagnation (see Fairbrother & Martin, 2013; Karlsson, Nilsson, Lyttkens, & Leeson, 2010; Stiglitz, 2012; van de Werfhorst & Salverda, 2012). The evidence of a correlation between economic inequality and a variety of social ills is strong, but because most of the research is cross-sectional we must be cautious about concluding that economic inequality is the cause of the other social ills. Researchers are currently taking a hard look at that issue (see van de Werfhorst & Salverda, 2012).

Poverty is one measure of social inequality, but there are different approaches to measuring poverty across the world. It is estimated that in 2013 1.4 billion, or about 20%, of the world's population lived in extreme poverty on less than US$1.25 a day (Global Poverty Project, 2013). Women and children are overrepresented in the world's poor. People living in extreme poverty go to bed hungry every night, and children living in these circumstances are vulnerable to death caused by malnutrition. It is estimated that one third of all deaths in the world each year are due to poverty-related causes (Ballantine & Roberts, 2014).

Poverty rates in the United States demonstrate that social inequality is related to race and ethnicity, age, gender, family structure, and disability (DeNavas-Walt et al., 2013). The overall poverty rate in 2012 was 15.0%, up from 12.5% in 2007. Although the majority of people living below the poverty level are White, and people of color can be found in all income groups, Blacks and Hispanics are more than 2.5 times as likely as Whites to be poor. The poverty rate in 2012 was 27.2% for Blacks, 25.6% for Hispanics, 11.7% for Asians, and 9.7% for non-Hispanic Whites. The good news is that the differential between Whites and groups of color has decreased in recent years. The bad news is that the differential remains quite large. For example, in the 1940s, the median income of Black families was about 50% of that of White families; by 2005, the median income of Black families was 61% of that of non-Hispanic White families (Bradshaw, Healey, & Smith, 2001; DeNavas-Walt et al., 2006). Unfortunately, Black families did not recover as well as White families from the 2007 recession, and in 2012, the median income of Black families was 58% of non-Hispanic White families (DeNavas-Walt et al., 2013). Foreign-born *noncitizens* have a higher poverty rate (24.9%) than foreign-born *naturalized citizens* (12.4%) (DeNavas-Walt et al., 2013). You can see from Leticia Renteria's story how lack of citizenship makes people particularly vulnerable in the labor market.

Over the past 50 years, vulnerability to poverty has shifted from older adults to children. From 1959 to 2012, the percentage of the U.S. population 65 years and older living in poverty decreased from about 35% to about 9.1% (DeNavas-Walt et al., 2006, 2013). The proportion of the population younger than age 18 living in poverty showed a smaller decrease in this same period, from about 27.0% to 21.8%. Since 1974, the poverty rate for persons younger than 18 has been higher than for those 65 and older.

Women are more likely than men to be poor in the United States as well as globally. In the United States, women's poverty rate (16.3%) is higher than men's (13.6%), and this difference continues to grow across the life course, rising to 11.0% of women 65 and older compared with 6.6% of men of the same age (DeNavas-Walt et al., 2013). Single-parent, mother-only families are more likely to live in poverty (30.9%) than two-parent families (6.3%) or single-parent father-only families (16.4%) (DeNavas-Walt et al., 2013).

The poverty rate for adults with a disability is more than twice the poverty rate for adults without a disability. In 2012, the poverty rate for people aged 18 to 64 with a disability was 28.4%, compared with 12.5% for adults of the same age without a disability (DeNavas-Walt et al., 2013).

We turn now to analysis of trends in seven major social institutions, both globally and in the United States. We look for the good news in these trends, but we also pay close attention to how social inequality and social conflict are created or maintained in each institution.

TRENDS IN THE GOVERNMENT AND POLITICAL INSTITUTION

Leticia Renteria lives in fear of agents of the government, particularly immigration agents. For the most part, she sees the government as a coercive force rather than a supportive one in her life. She believes that only powerful people can influence government actions. The **government and political institution** is responsible for how decisions get made and enforced for the society as a whole. It is expected to resolve both internal and external conflicts and mobilize collective resources to meet societal goals.

Political systems around the world vary widely, from authoritarian to democratic. Authoritarian systems may have a hereditary monarchy or a dictator who seized power; sometimes democratically elected leaders become dictators.

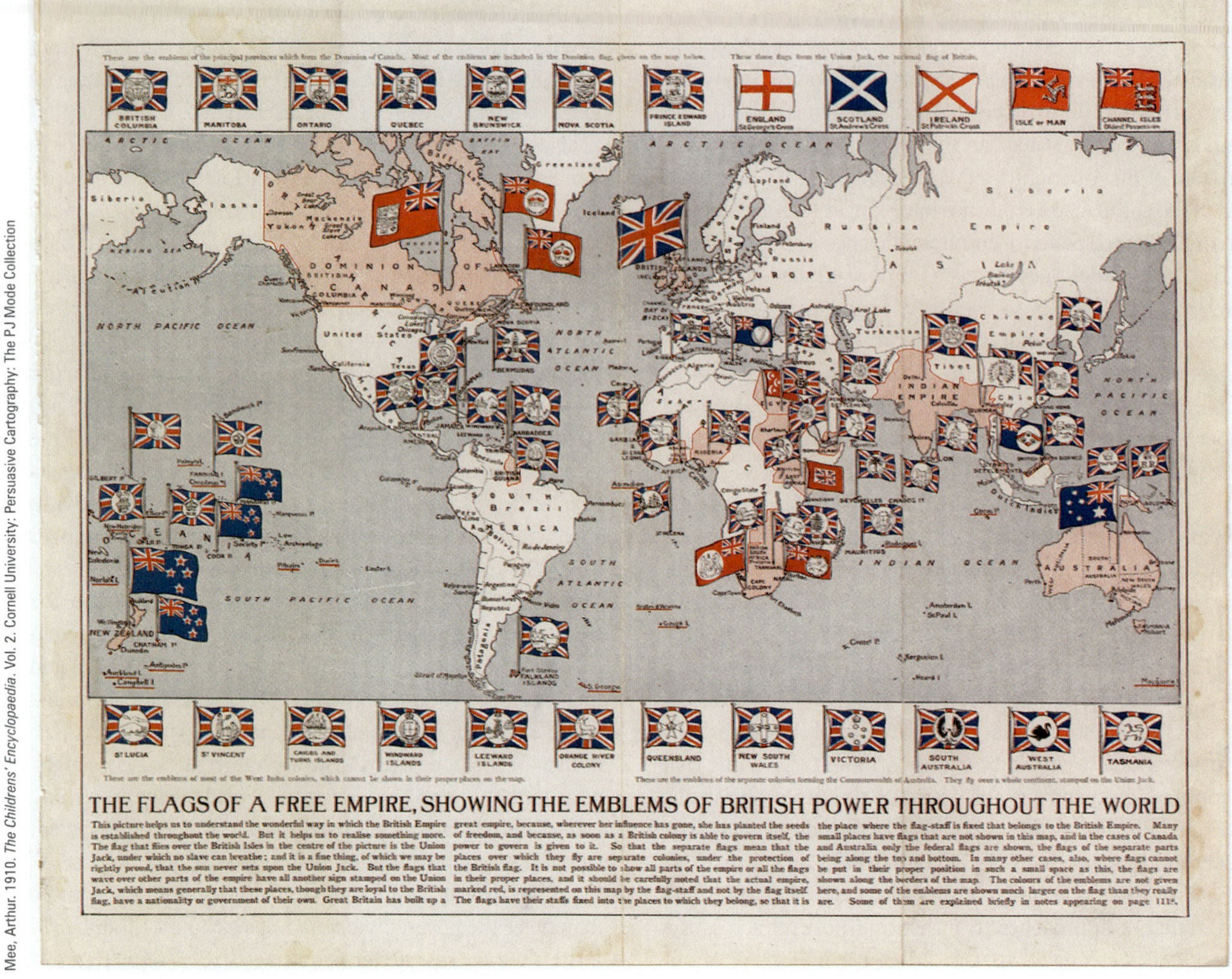

Mee, Arthur. 1910. *The Childrens' Encyclopaedia*. Vol. 2. Cornell University: Persuasive Cartography: The PJ Mode Collection

The contemporary global political landscape must be understood in the historical context of colonialism. This photo shows the emblems of the British Empire throughout the world in 1910.

Leaders in democratic systems are elected by their citizens and are accountable to them; they must govern in the context of written documents (Ballantine & Roberts, 2014). Evidence suggests that the government institution is in transition globally, including in the United States. There is much complexity in global trends in government and politics, but the following historical factors are supremely important for beginning to understand current complexities.

1. *Colonialism.* The contemporary global political landscape must be understood in the historical context of **colonialism** (Kurtz, 2012; McMichael, 2012). Eight European countries (Belgium, Britain, France, Germany, Italy, the Netherlands, Portugal, and Spain) and Japan were involved over several centuries in setting up colonial empires, which allowed them to strengthen their own economies by exploiting the raw materials and labors of the colonized countries. Colonial governments took power away from local governance and prevented the localities from establishing stable political systems. Most of these empires came to a rather abrupt end after World War II, but they left a disorganized political legacy in their wake in much of Africa, Central and South America, and parts of Asia and the Middle East. After the colonized countries established their independence, the United States and other Western powers advanced a new institutional framework that called for free trade and transformation of the formerly colonized countries into democracies. This new institutional framework, sometimes referred to as **neocolonialism**, is promoted by such international organizations as the World Bank, the International Monetary Fund (IMF), and the World Trade Organization (WTO). These organizations, which are led by the United States and western Europe, regulate relations between countries, and this role carries much power over political and economic institutions (Loomis, 2013). The United States and western Europe also played a major role in coercing former colonies to organize into nation-states and imposed national boundaries that were inconsistent with age-old ethnic divisions. This has resulted in ongoing ethnic clashes throughout the former colonies (McMichael, 2012).

2. *International power struggles.* Across time, groups have tried to assert their will over other groups, and the struggle for power over people, ideas, and natural resources is very much a part of the contemporary geopolitical scene. Sometimes nations or transnational organizations use the hard power of military force. Other times, they use the soft power of persuasion and inducement. After World War II, during the Cold War between the United States and the Soviet Union, the United States made extensive use of the soft power of foreign aid to encourage loyalty to its political (democracy) and economic (free market capitalism) visions. In the contemporary era, powerful countries are using foreign aid to ensure access to scarce natural resources (Brautigam, 2009). For some time now, the United States has outpaced all other nations in military spending. In 2013, U.S. military spending was 37% of total global military spending and was roughly the size of the next nine largest military budgets (National Priorities Project, 2015).

3. *Economic globalization.* Changes in the government institution are intertwined with changes in the economic institution, and these changes taken together are playing a large role in global inequality. Beginning in the 1970s, economic globalization started to present serious challenges to nationally based democracies (D. Newman, 2012). For a number of centuries, political and economic life had been organized into nation-states with bureaucracies for maintaining order and mobilizing resources to meet societal needs. Starting in the 1970s, however, new information and transportation technologies made possible the development of *transnational corporations (TNCs)*, which carry on production and distribution activities in many nations. These corporations cross national lines to take advantage of cheap labor pools, lax environmental regulations, beneficial tax laws, and new consumer markets. It is hard for any nation-state to monitor or get control over TNCs, and no international government exists (Sernau, 2014). Under these circumstances, around 1970, governments began to retrench in their efforts to monitor and control the economic institution. A **neoliberal philosophy** that governments should keep their hands off the economic institution took hold, perhaps nowhere more than in the United States.

4. *Transnational centers of power.* Although no international government exists, the United States played a leadership role in the development of several transnational political and economic organizations and policies at the end of World War II. The United Nations (UN) was developed to ensure international peace and security. The World Bank was developed to promote reconstruction in war-torn nations but has, in recent years, taken on a concern for poverty. The World Bank president is appointed by the U.S. president. The International Monetary Fund (IMF) was developed to promote international monetary cooperation and a fair balance of trade. The managing director of the IMF is appointed by the United Kingdom, France, and Germany. The General Agreement on Tariffs and Trade (GATT) was designed to provide an international forum for developing freer trade across national boundaries; the WTO was developed under GATT in 1995 to regulate the global economy according to principles of free trade. The United States, Canada, and Mexico signed the North American Free Trade Agreement (NAFTA) in 1994. European nations joined together as the EU, adopting a common currency, a set of common legal and economic structures, and other joint endeavors. Similar organizations are in various stages of development in Latin America, Asia, and Africa. The World Bank, IMF, and WTO, all governed by unelected officials, have become very powerful in dictating how nation-states should govern. For example, when making loans, the World Bank requires that borrowing nations follow the principles of neoliberalism, including reducing their social welfare programs, privatizing their public services, and becoming more open to imports. The IMF has enforced these principles, sometimes overriding decisions made at the national level. The deliberations of the WTO are secret; members can lodge complaints, but the decision of the WTO's dispute settlement program is binding unless every member of the WTO votes to reverse it. There is much evidence that the decisions of the World Bank, IMF, and WTO have been more favorable to some nations than others (McMichael, 2012).

Growing faith across the world in the wisdom and efficiency of the economic institution led many nation-states to withdraw from direct control of activities they had hitherto controlled. They do this in several ways. The government sells enterprises that produce goods or deliver services to the private sector. Another approach is for the government to retain ultimate control over a program but contract with private organizations for some activities. The United States makes heavy use of contracting in many governmental sectors. And, finally, governments sometimes give up their claims to the right to regulate particular activities they have previously regulated but not controlled. It is widely noted that deregulation of financial institutions over several decades in the United States and Europe was a primary factor in the 2008 financial crisis (Jeffers, 2013).

Economic globalization combined with war and political strife has produced mass cross-national migration. Most of this migration has occurred within regions; for example, most refugees fleeing Syria originally flee to neighboring countries Turkey, Lebanon, Jordan, and Iraq (Migration Policy Centre, 2013). But there is also a trend of migration from low-wage to high-wage countries (D. Newman, 2012). This has led to considerable political attention to immigration issues around the globe. In the United States and Europe, immigration issues are the

Syrians, including children, are at a refugee camp near the Turkish border in Atmeh, Syria.

source of intense political debate. As we think about the trials of Leticia Renteria and her family, we are reminded of this increased attention to immigration issues.

In the United States, three issues are creating concern in the government and political institution: a sharply divided electorate, the role of money in the political process, and voter turnout. Concerning a sharply divided electorate, recent elections and attempts at legislation have been more acrimonious than at any time in recent history. There are sharp divisions about what kind of country the United States should be. Concerning money in the political process, a Supreme Court decision and subsequent federal court of appeal ruling in 2010 resulted in wealthy individuals, corporations, and unions having the right to make unlimited political expenditures as long as the contributions are independent of specific candidates or political parties. The United States is next to the bottom of comparison countries in terms of voter participation, with an average voter turnout of 47.5% compared to 85.3% in Belgium, a country with one of the highest turnout rates (International Institute for Democracy and Electoral Assistance, 2011).

What happens in the government and political institution has enormous impact on the life chances of every group in society. For example, two important political issues play a large role in the level of inequality in a society: tax policy and minimum wage policy. European governments tax their wealthier citizens at a much higher rate than the United States does and set higher minimum wages. These actions of the government impact what social workers can and cannot do to promote individual and collective well-being. Social workers cannot afford to ignore processes and trends in the political arena, and they must be aware of the possibilities of what can be accomplished by collective action.

TRENDS IN THE ECONOMIC INSTITUTION

As you read the story of Leticia Renteria and her family, their economic struggles seem paramount, and yet, both Leticia and Marcus are employed and working hard to provide for their family. The **economic institution** has primary responsibility for regulating the production, distribution, and consumption of goods and services. The nature of the economy has been ever changing since premodern times, but the rate of change has accelerated wildly since the beginning of the industrial revolution, particularly in recent decades under neoliberalism and economic globalization.

Economic life can be organized in many ways, and a great variety of ways have been used over time. In recent times, different approaches to organizing the economic institution around the world fall on a continuum with market capitalism at one end and a centralized or planned economy at the other end. In market capitalism, the economy operates by voluntary exchange in a free market and is not planned or controlled by a central authority. The goods and services produced by human labor are exchanged in the market and not produced for consumption by the laborer. The means of production are privately owned by one group, and another group, the workers hired through a labor market, own little besides their capacity to work. No governmental interference is thought to be needed because "the invisible hand of the market" will ensure fair production and distribution, including fair profit for some and not for others. Investment is privately controlled. In a centralized or planned economy, the government plans and controls production and distribution of goods and services. The means of production are collectively rather than privately owned, and the terms of labor are regulated by the government rather than by the market. In such economies, there is deep distrust of the exploitation of labor thought to occur in a market run by a financial elite in pursuit of their own self-interests (Ballantine & Roberts, 2014; Ritzer, 2013a).

In reality, no country in the world today practices either pure market capitalism or a pure planned (centralized) economy. The U.S. economy is thought to be a special case of capitalism in the world today, coming the closest to pure market capitalism. And, yet, there are a number of ways in which national and state governments in the United States interfere with market-based production and distribution of goods and services, including labor regulations, public education, public libraries, social security legislation, Medicare, and Medicaid. A number of countries have mixed economies where the good of the whole society is considered paramount and private profit is less important than in pure capitalism. In these countries, collective planning is engaged in an attempt to balance societal needs with individual economic freedom. The Scandinavian and most European countries are the best examples of mixed economies. The former Soviet Union was once considered to be the best example of a planned economy, but since its fall in 1991, the region no longer holds that distinction. China is often thought to be the current best example of a pure planned economy today but, in fact, is becoming a dominant capitalist force while holding on to its highly centralized government (McMichael, 2012). There is much agreement that economic globalization is pushing all countries toward some embrace of market capitalism.

Before further discussion, some clarity is needed about what we mean by *economic globalization*. The primary ingredients are a global production system, a global labor force, and global consumers organized through a global market. Much of what we wear, eat, and use has global origins. If you look around your room, you will see many examples of economic globalization, but much of the global process will be invisible to you.

The global economy is driven by corporate desire for the bigger profits that come from cheap raw materials and cheap labor and by consumer desire for cheap and novel products. Corporations are constantly seeking cheaper labor sites to stay competitive. Much of the global economy is controlled by TNCs. TNCs have become very powerful over the past several decades; in fact, UN data indicate that TNCs account for two thirds of world trade and hold most product patents (cited in McMichael, 2012). Most TNCs are headquartered in France, Germany, Japan, the United Kingdom, or the United States.

Proponents of economic globalization argue that in time it will bring modernity and prosperity to all regions of the world. Critics argue that it is just an unsustainable pyramid scheme that must end because prosperity of victors is always paid for by the losses of latecomers or because the physical environment can no longer sustain the economic activities (Sernau, 2014). This is a good place to point out that not all peoples of the world put a high value on consumerism and chasing economic growth, values that are central to globalization. Unfortunately, however, policies of the World Bank, IMF, and WTO have made it impossible to make a living on subsistence farms and small-craft enterprises. Some globalization scholars argue

Walmart is a growing symbol of economic globalization.

that economic globalization as we have known it is not sustainable because of the social disruption and environmental degradation it has wrought and that we may be seeing the beginning of a transition to a different form of capitalism that puts greater emphasis on sustainability (see McMichael, 2012). The future of globalization is not certain, but several trends can be identified at its current stage of development.

1. *Regional disparities.* Rich nations have been getting richer, a few nations have made impressive gains, most poor nations have made few gains, and the poorest nations have lost ground.

2. *Labor force bifurcation.* As globalization progressed, wage labor began to *bifurcate*, or divide into two branches. One branch is the *core* of relatively stable, skilled, well-paid labor. The other branch is the *periphery* of periodic or seasonal (often referred to as casual) low-wage labor. In the new global division of labor, the upper tier of jobs is found disproportionately in the wealthy advanced industrialized countries, and the lower tier of jobs is found disproportionately in the previously colonized countries. Recently, bifurcation of labor has occurred all over the world, in advanced industrial societies as well as in poor, newly industrializing societies (McMichael, 2012). In the United States, the period of labor force bifurcation has been accompanied by a precipitous increase in CEO salaries and stagnation in wages of other workers. From 1978 to 2011, CEO compensation grew by more than 876% while the annual compensation of a typical private-sector worker grew by 5.4% (Mishel, 2013). This is an important contributor to growing inequality in the United States.

3. *Outsourcing.* Outsourcing relocates the production of goods and services from one place to another as a strategy to reduce costs. Information and communication technologies allow corporations to coordinate these outsourcing projects. Under neoliberalism, governments as well as corporations have been outsourcing service contracts. In an interesting twist to the outsourcing trend, as wages have risen in India, India began to outsource some of the work outsourced there to other countries such as the Philippines, Thailand, Poland, China, and Mexico (McMichael, 2012).

4. *Displacement.* Automation and outsourcing of work shed stable jobs. At the beginning of the 21st century, it is estimated that 1 billion workers, or one third of the world's labor force, mostly in the Global South, were either unemployed or underemployed (M. Davis, 2006).

5. *Labor exportation.* Migration for the purpose of finding work is not a new phenomenon, but it has become an important part of economic globalization. As many formerly colonized countries struggled to repay debt incurred during the 1980s, exporting workers became a way for countries to gain access to foreign currency, as we saw with the case study of the Filipina domestic workers in Chapter 8. In 2013, the World Bank (2013d) estimated that nearly 1 billion people, one in every seven in the world, had migrated either internally or across international borders to seek better opportunities. It further reports that remittance flows to developing countries more than quadrupled from 2000 to 2012, providing a vital lifeline for many countries. Although they are struggling financially, Leticia Renteria and Marcos Vargas are committed to sending remittances back home to Mexico because they are well aware of the extreme poverty in which many of their relatives live. A majority of labor migrants are women and children, and both women and children are vulnerable to human trafficking, a form of modern-day slavery (World Health Organization, 2012a). Although it is difficult to find reliable data on the extent of trafficking, UNICEF (2013a) reports human trafficking in all 50 U.S. states.

AP Photo/GURINDER OSAN

An employee at a call center in Bangalore, India, provides service support to international customers.

6. *Limited protection by organized labor.* Since the beginning of industrial capitalism, labor unions have been the force behind governmental protection of workers' rights, fighting successfully for such protection as workplace safety, a minimum wage, a reduced workweek, and pensions. Economic globalization has seriously weakened the bargaining power of nationally based labor unions, because companies can always threaten to take their business somewhere else. In the United States, the rate of union membership, or the percentage of all workers who are union members, decreased from 20.1% in 1983 to 11.3% in 2012 (U.S. Bureau of Labor Statistics, 2013c). However, labor unions are still strong in some countries, and the data indicate that the countries with the highest rates of union membership have the lowest rates of inequality. In the United States, the union membership rate of public-sector workers (35.9%) is more than five times that of private-sector workers (6.6%) (OECD, 2013b). In 2012, among full-time workers, the median usual weekly earnings of union members was $943, compared with $742 for nonunion workers.

Social workers who participate in policy development must be informed about the serious challenges to job security in the contemporary era. They are also called on to deal with many of the social problems arising out of these changes in the economic institution—problems such as inadequate resources for family caregiving, domestic violence, substance abuse, depression, and anxiety.

CRITICAL THINKING Questions 9.1

What have you heard about the benefits of economic globalization? What have you heard about harms from economic globalization? What do you make of the controversy about whether economic globalization is a good or bad thing? How is economic globalization affecting the government institution? How is economic globalization affecting Leticia Renteria and her family? Do you agree with social scientists who suggest that recent developments in social institutions have produced a food crisis, energy crisis, climate crisis, and social inequality? Explain.

TRENDS IN THE EDUCATIONAL INSTITUTION

Leticia Renteria and Marcos Vargas know that education is important for their children, but they are not sure how to help their children succeed at school. Traditionally, the primary purpose of the **educational institution** has been to pass along formal knowledge from one generation to the next—a function that was largely performed by the family, with some help from the religious institution, until the 19th century. Formal education, schooling that includes a predetermined curriculum, has expanded dramatically around the world in the past several decades.

However, in an era of a knowledge-based global economy, there continue to be large global gaps in opportunities for education. There is much evidence of long-term benefits of quality early childhood education, but in both low-income and wealthy nations, children from low-income families have less access to early childhood education than other children (UNESCO, 2012). Although educational participation is almost universal from the ages of 5 to 14 in affluent countries, 61 million of the world's children of primary school age, most residing in Sub-Saharan Africa or South and West Asia, are out of school. Lack of access to primary school education in low-income countries was worsened by conditions the World Bank set on debt refinancing in the late 1980s, which mandated reductions in education expenditure. The result was reduced educational levels in Asia, Latin America, and Africa and a widening gap in average years of education between rich and poor countries (McMichael, 2012). An international drive for universal primary education made good progress from 1999 to 2004 but stagnated from 2008 to 2010 during the international financial crisis that started with the banking collapse in high-income countries. Both nations and families found it necessary to cut back on education spending. This happened in wealthy nations such as the United States, but the impact was greatest in low-income nations (UNESCO, 2012).

Nations around the world structure their educational systems in different ways, and we have heard a lot recently about how educational outcomes in the United States stack up against those in other high-income countries. U.S. educational historian Diane Ravitch (2013) sums up much of what I have heard from the mass media:

> In the early years of the twenty-first century, a bipartisan consensus arose about education policy in the United States. Right and left, Democrats and Republicans, the leading members of our political class and our media elite seemed

AP Photo/Michael Sohn

© Sam Panthaky/AFP/Getty Images

The contrast between these two classrooms—one in a well-resourced suburban school in the United States and the other on a footpath in Ahmedabad, India—demonstrates global inequality in resources for education.

> to agree: Public education is broken. Our students are not learning enough. Public schools are bad and getting worse. We are being beaten by other nations with higher test scores. Our abysmal public schools threaten not only the performance of our economy but our national security, our very survival as a nation. This crisis is so profound that half measures and tweaks will not suffice. Schools must be closed and large numbers of teachers fired. Anyone who doubts this is unaware of the dimensions of the crisis or has a vested interest in defending the status quo. (p. 3)

Ravitch (2010) provides some context for this contemporary concern about the U.S. educational institution. Her historical research indicates that in almost every decade of the 20th century, critics loudly proclaimed that the public education system was in crisis. The nature of the proposed crisis shifted over time: Sometimes the schools were considered too academic and not sufficiently tied to the needs of the industrial economy, and other times the schools were attacked for their lack of academic rigor. Most recently, the proposed crisis in the educational institution has focused on the achievement gap between children of different racial and ethnic groups, but contemporary criticisms also emphasize the poor performance of U.S. students on international tests. Just as the nature of the proposed crisis has shifted over time, so has the nature of the proposed solutions, with each generation of policymakers assuming they have found the "silver bullet" to "fix" the educational institution.

The story told by the mass media is often one of decline in the educational institution, suggesting that there was a time when U.S. students performed better than all other students in the world but are now falling behind. Let's take a closer look at that story of decline. The 2012 performance of 15-year-old students on testing by the Program for International Student Assessment (PISA) found that 18 education systems had higher average scores than the United States in the three literacy areas: math, science, and reading. So, it is, indeed, true that U.S. students are not the top-ranked students in international testing. Long-term data suggest that this is not a sign of decline of the U.S. educational institution, however. In fact, there has not been a time when U.S. students were first on international tests. When the first international tests were administered in the mid-1960s, U.S. students ranked at or near the bottom of all students tested. In the 1970s, 1980s, and 1990s, U.S. students typically scored in the bottom quartile or near the international average (Ravitch, 2010). U.S. students do not stand out on international tests but are not faring worse over time, nor are they faring much better after years of ongoing national policy experiments. National test scores tell a different story, a story of constant improvement over time. U.S. fourth- and eighth-grade students have made significant, even remarkable, gains in national reading and mathematics test scores since 1978 (Ravitch, 2013; Rothstein, 2011).

But what of the recent concern about the achievement gap between White and minority students of color, more specifically Black and Hispanic students? This is a more complicated question. There is, no doubt, a substantial gap between the educational achievement of the White and Black populations in the United States, a gap that is as old as the nation, and there is strong evidence of a White–Hispanic gap as well. Paul Barton and Richard Coley (2010) of the Educational Testing Service examined the White–Black gap in educational achievement from the beginning of the 20th century to 2010. They found a large reduction in the gap in the 1970s and 1980s, when Black students made greater gains than White students. They also found that improvement in reducing the gap stagnated in the 1990s, and progress has continued to slow since that time. The gap remains large. Ravitch (2013) provides evidence that Black and Hispanic students have continued to make impressive gains since 1990, but White students have been making gains as well, slowing the pace of reduction in the gap. For example, in 1990, 83% of Black fourth graders and 67% of Hispanic fourth graders scored "below basic" in mathematics; in 2011 the percentages dropped to 34% for Black fourth graders and 28% for Hispanic fourth graders. The improvements in reading scores were not as dramatic but impressive nonetheless. The Black–White achievement gap is now smaller than the achievement gap between the poorest and most affluent students in the United States (Reardon, 2011). The income achievement gap has been growing for the past 50 years and continues to increase. Given the high rate of inequality in the United States, the income gap is probably a chief factor in the less than stellar average performance of U.S. students on international comparisons (Carnoy & Rothstein, 2013).

This analysis suggests that the U.S. educational institution needs some improvement, but it does not suggest an institution in a crisis of steep decline as the architects of recent policy experiments have often suggested. Since the beginning of the 21st century, two national policy experiments have created instability in the U.S. educational institution: the 2001 No Child Left Behind (NCLB) legislation passed during the George W. Bush administration and the Race to the Top policy direction of the Obama administration. The stated goals of both policies are to raise academic achievement for all students, out of concern that U.S. students are falling behind those in other wealthy nations, and to close the achievement gaps that divide low-income students and students of color from their peers.

NCLB was based on the belief that testing and school accountability would lead to significant improvement in student performance and narrow the achievement gap. The law required all states to engage in annual testing of every child in Grades 3 through 8 in reading and mathematics and to report the test scores by race, ethnicity, low-income status, disability status, and limited English proficiency. All students in every group were expected to achieve proficiency on state tests by 2014. Any school that failed to meet its annual target would be labeled "in need of improvement," and punishments were to increase over time, with the eventual punishments including staff firings, school closings, state control or private management, or some other form of "restructuring." The schools most likely to be labeled as failing were schools with high proportions of students with disabilities and poor and minority students. As 2014 approached, most schools in the country were considered failing by NCLB standards, including 80% of the public schools in Massachusetts, the state with the highest test performance. Ravitch (2013) points out that 100% proficiency is an impossible goal that no country has ever achieved.

Barack Obama became president in the midst of an economic crisis in January 2009. The economic stimulus bill passed by Congress included $5 billion to be used in a competition among the states known as Race to the Top. Secretary of Education Arne Duncan established the conditions for receipt of the moneys: Recipient states had to agree to adopt new Common Core standards and tests, expand charter schools, evaluate teacher effectiveness using student test scores as a major component of evaluation, and turn around their lowest-performing schools by such methods as firing staff and closing schools (and subsequently opening new privately managed charter schools). The most important piece added by Race to the Top was the wedding of teacher evaluation to value-added student test scores (Ravitch, 2010, 2013). In other words, teachers were considered effective if they could "cause" their students' test scores to go up every year. This aspect of recent educational policy is interesting, given that in this same time period, corporate CEO pay has become disconnected from the economic success of the corporation; teachers are responsible for student performance, but CEOs are not responsible for the bottom line of the corporation.

Both NCLB and Race to the Top greatly expanded the role of the federal government in the educational institution, but they also favored the neoliberal principles of privatization and market competition. Even though both policies have had wide support across the political spectrum, the data do not support the success of these two policy initiatives. There is increasing international evidence that the achievement gap is highly correlated with economic inequality, and school policy has limited impact. Students begin their journey through the public school system with an already existing achievement gap. Changes in the governmental and economic institutions would be the most effective way to close that gap. There is clear evidence that the most effective educational changes for reducing the achievement gap are quality early childhood education and smaller class size (Ravitch, 2010). Testing alone has not proven to raise student scores (Ravitch, 2013), and reliance on test-based teacher and school accountability has led to score inflation and cheating in some school systems (see Severson, 2011). When schools have been closed and replaced by new charter schools, the charter schools have not performed better than the closed schools (Gleason, Clark, Clark Tuttle, Dwoyer, & Silverberg, 2010). Wedding teacher evaluation to student test scores ignores the many variables that can go into test scores, including the specific makeup of a teacher's class in a given year (Baker et al., 2010).

Diane Ravitch (2010) reminds us that the U.S. educational institution has contended with three major policy changes in the government and political institution since 1960. First, legally sanctioned racial segregation of schools came to an end. Unfortunately, the legal rulings that ended it were followed by the flight of Whites and middle-class Blacks from some urban schools, leaving behind school districts struggling with racial isolation and concentrated poverty. Second, court rulings and legislation required public schools to serve students with disabilities. This change in policy direction was long overdue but also expensive and challenging for the schools. Third, changes in federal immigration policy brought millions of non-English-speaking students into the public schools. In addition, the educational institution has needed to adjust to changes in the family institution, growing societal inequality, and ever-changing information and communication technology. In recent years, teachers and school administrators have had to live with persistent attacks from politicians and the mass media.

Around the world, citizens and leaders are concerned about whether their educational institution is responding well to globalization and the rapid pace of change in other institutions (Ballantine & Roberts, 2014). Certainly, there is a need for improvements in the U.S. educational institution, and it makes sense to look for ideas from the countries that have successful educational institutions based on two criteria: first, their students score well on international testing, and second, their students' socioeconomic status does not have a large impact on learning outcomes. Evidence suggests that the best educational outcomes occur in countries where there are universal early childhood education programs; where the teachers are well trained, experienced, well paid, highly respected, and given professional autonomy; where the curriculum is broad-based and rigorous; and where there are resources to address the needs of students in every school (Ravitch, 2013; Ripley, 2013; Tucker, 2011).

Leticia and Marcos value education for their children but are intimidated by the schools their children attend. The children are often aware of their parents' lack of comfort in interacting with the school. Social workers can help schools and parents become more comfortable with each other. Social workers should also become active partners in efforts at educational reform, particularly those that equalize educational opportunities, but to be effective in these efforts, we need to be informed about trends in the educational institution. By the time you read this, the public conversation about the educational institution and ways to improve it may have shifted again. We must carefully evaluate whether what we see and hear in the mass media about circumstances in the educational institution is supported by available evidence.

TRENDS IN THE HEALTH CARE INSTITUTION

Health is an important issue for Leticia Renteria and her family. Leticia is concerned that environmental hazards are the cause of her children's asthma. She is happy that the children are able to receive health care at the community clinic and hopes to stay healthy herself because she does not qualify for health insurance. Health is important to this family, but health is also important to a society. Child development, adult well-being, and family stability are all affected by health. The **health care institution** is the primary one for promoting the general health of a society. At one time, health care was addressed primarily in the home, by families. Today, in wealthy countries, health care is a major social institution, and health care organizations are major employers (Ballantine & Roberts, 2014).

Unfortunately, there is much disparity in the global health care institution, both between and within countries (OECD, 2013c; World Health Organization, 2013a). Global inequalities in child and adult mortality are large and growing. In 2012, globally, more than 29 million children younger than age 5 suffered from acute malnutrition or wasting. Although more children of the world survive their 5th birthday than ever before, in 2012 6.6 million children younger than age 5 died, about 18,000 per day (UNICEF, 2013b). Almost all of the children who die each year live in poor countries.

In poor countries, basic health prevention and treatment services have been slowly improving, but serious gaps remain. In 2011, 67% of the population in low-income countries had access to safe drinking water, compared with 99% of the population in high-income countries. Likewise, 37% of the population in low-income countries was using adequate sanitation methods, compared with 100% of the population in high-income countries (World Health Organization, 2013a). The lowest rates of safe drinking water and adequate sanitation occurred in the African region. More than 1 billion people in the world lack sanitation facilities and must continue practices that pose serious health and environmental risks (UNICEF, 2013c). You may be as shocked as I am that Leticia Renteria and her family, living in the United States, have neither safe drinking water nor adequate sanitation. Unfortunately, they are not alone in this circumstance.

Within-country health disparities are prominent in the United States, where deep inequalities are related to socioeconomic status, race, and ethnicity, and poverty is seen as the driving force behind the growing health disparities (Centers for Disease Control and Prevention, 2013d). Research consistently finds that life expectancy increases as personal income increases (Burtless, 2012). The infant mortality rate for non-Hispanic Blacks is more than double the rate for non-Hispanic Whites, and the rates are higher in the South and Midwest than in other parts of the country. Non-Hispanic Black adults are 50% more likely than other adults to die of heart disease or stroke before age 75. Compared with Asian and non-Hispanic White adults, the prevalence of diabetes is higher among Hispanic and non-Hispanic Black adults, as well as among adults of mixed races. The prevalence is also higher among adults with lower incomes (Centers for Disease Control and Prevention, 2013d). It is clear that race and social class critically impact health disparities in the United States. Even at the higher ends of education, there are large health gaps between African Americans and Whites (Williams, Mohammed, Leavell, & Collins, 2010). Although morbidity and mortality rates rose among middle-aged White non-Hispanic adults between 1999 and 2013, a period in which there was decline in morbidity and mortality rates among other age groups and other races and ethnicities, middle-aged White non-Hispanic adults still have lower morbidity and mortality rates than middle-aged adults from other racial and ethnic groups (Case & Deaton, 2015). The increased death rates for middle-aged non-Hispanic Whites have been attributed to drug and alcohol poisoning, suicide, and chronic liver disease. Whites with the least education had the most marked increases. This pattern of increased morbidity and mortality among Whites was not found in other rich countries.

Although much of the health disparities in the United States are related to factors in other social institutions, aspects of the health care institution play a large role. The United States and Mexico are the only two countries of the 34 in the OECD without universal health coverage, and the United States is the only one of the wealthy comparison countries used in this chapter without such coverage (OECD, 2013c). The proportion of the population covered has grown rapidly in Mexico since health care reform in 2004, reaching nearly 90% by 2011. The percentage of the U.S. population without health insurance decreased sharply between 2012 and 2014, from 15.4% to 10.4%, with the bulk of that decrease occurring between 2013 and 2014 during a period of expanded coverage through the Affordable Care Act. The uninsured rate varied by race and ethnicity in 2014: 7.6% of non-Hispanic Whites, 9.3% of Asians, 11.8% of Blacks, and 19.9% of Hispanics (any race) were uninsured (Smith & Medalia, 2015).

Jeanne Ballantine and Keith Roberts (2014) suggest that the United States has both the best and the worst health care system in the industrialized world. It is one of the best in the world in terms of quality of care, trained practitioners, facilities, and medical technology. But it is the worst in terms of costs, inefficiency, equality of access, and fragmentation. The United States spends a much greater percentage of its GDP on health care than any of the other wealthy countries covered in this chapter. Israel is the comparison country that spends the smallest amount of its GDP on health (7.7%); the Netherlands is the second highest country with 12.1% of GDP spent on health, compared to 17.6% for the United States. This expenditure does not pay off in terms of the most often used measure of the health of a nation, life expectancy, which is 82 for Israel, 81 for the Netherlands, and 79 for the United States (World Health Organization, 2013a).

The reasons why the health care institution is so costly in the United States are complex, but two contributing factors are discussed here. First, compared with the health care systems in other countries, the U.S. approach to financing health care is extremely complex, and the administrative cost of this complex system is greater than in the more streamlined universal systems in other industrialized countries (Reinhardt, Hussey, & Anderson, 2004). Second, the health care institution is influenced by culture. Health care in the United States reflects the aggressive, can-do spirit of the mainstream culture (Gardiner & Kosmitzki, 2011). For example, compared with European physicians, U.S. physicians recommend more routine examinations and perform many more bypass surgeries and angioplasties than European doctors. These are both examples of a more aggressive approach to treatment that could be attributed to a reimbursement system that rewards such aggressiveness as much as to a cultural bias toward aggressive treatment (Reinhardt, Hussey, & Anderson, 2002).

Societies around the world struggle with health care costs and quality, access to care, and medical technology (OECD, 2013c; Rapoport, Jacobs, & Jonsson, 2009). Most governments in Europe made a decision in the late 1800s and early 1900s to support health care as a human right and put some form of national health care system into place. It appears that they were operating out of a belief that maintaining a healthy population is necessary to maintain a strong society (Ballantine & Roberts, 2014). In the United States, health care has not been viewed as a human right, historically, and the health care system developed with less direction and made piecemeal policies over time. Medical research has been a major strength in the U.S. health care system, but the two biggest challenges in the past 3 decades have been lack of universal access to care and continuously escalating costs. Access to health care was improved with the passage of Medicare and Medicaid in the 1960s, but large numbers continue to have no health care insurance. Several attempts were made to develop federal legislation to address these problems for a number of decades, but these efforts failed because politicians had conflicting philosophical positions on the role of government in health care delivery and because of considerable opposition from private insurance companies, physicians, and pharmaceutical companies.

After a year-long contentious debate, the U.S. Congress passed the Patient Protection and Affordable Care Act and the Health Care and Education Reconciliation Act of 2010, and both bills were signed into law in March 2010. The health insurance reforms were to roll out over several years. Here are some of the key pieces of the legislation (Cockerham, 2012; U.S. Department of Health and Human Services, 2013):

- Young adults can stay on their parents' health insurance policies until age 26.
- People with Medicare can get key preventive services for free and receive a 50% discount on drugs in the "donut hole."
- An additional 32 million people are to be covered by health insurance by 2014, and it is projected that 95% of people in the United States will be covered by the end of 2018.
- Medicaid coverage will be expanded for the poor, extending coverage to people with incomes of up to 133% of the federal poverty line.
- Almost all people will be required to have health insurance (individual mandate) or be fined.
- Employers with more than 50 employees will be required to provide health insurance for their employees or be fined.
- Health insurance companies will be unable to reject applicants because they have preexisting conditions, charge excessive rates, or cancel policies after policyholders become sick.

The future of this health care reform remains uncertain. Several states challenged the legality of the law, and the challenges went to the U.S. Supreme Court in 2012. The Supreme Court upheld the individual mandate provision but ruled that states could refuse to participate in the Medicaid expansion piece of the legislation. As of July 2015, 30 states plus the District of Columbia had decided to provide Medicaid expansion (Families USA, 2015). Republican senators and representatives continue to challenge the health care reforms, and the House of Representatives has voted to repeal the law so many times I have lost count. Individual states were encouraged to create their own health care exchanges to assist the uninsured in getting enrolled in insurance plans, but the great majority of states decided to rely on a federal exchange rather than run their own. The rollout of the federal government exchange in October 2013 had massive technical problems that were mostly worked out by early December 2013. Another legal challenge to the law was heard by the U.S. Supreme Court in 2015, this one challenging the right of persons who obtained health coverage through the federal exchange (instead of through a state exchange) to receive federal subsidies. The Court ruled in favor of subsidies to this group on June 25, 2015 (Leonard, 2015), another ruling that helped to protect the law. Proponents of the legislation argue that it will make health insurance more affordable, but the reform is off to a rough start. Early in the formulation of the policy, a public insurance option, whose intent was to keep prices down by competing with private insurance, was dropped from the plan. It was hoped that Medicaid expansion would lower the costs for many people, but the Supreme Court made that piece optional. The hopes for cost containment rest to a great extent on the willingness of uninsured healthy young adults to become insured and join the risk pools of insurance companies. This is key to lowering the overall costs of insurance, and some progress was made with this group in 2014 (Smith & Medalia, 2015). We continue to be a deeply divided country about the appropriate role for government in the health care institution. Stay tuned.

Like many other families, the family of Leticia Renteria may need social work assistance to navigate the complex, fragmented health care system if the children's health problems worsen. Social workers need to be particularly sensitive to the situation of some immigrant families who try to integrate traditional healing traditions with Global North, technology-oriented medical practices.

CRITICAL THINKING Questions 9.2

As this chapter was being written, there were many conflicting stories in the mass media about the performance of both the educational institution and the health care institution in the United States. How is what you have seen in the mass media about these social institutions in the past week similar to and different from what is reported in this chapter? How do you understand the strengths and limitations of these two social institutions in the United States, as compared with their counterparts in other wealthy countries? Why are these social institutions so controversial in the United States?

TRENDS IN THE SOCIAL WELFARE INSTITUTION

People in the community where Leticia Renteria and her family live are very excited about the new Boys and Girls Club in the nearby town. However, Leticia has heard many stories that make her fear the U.S. social welfare institution. Although food stamps and cash assistance programs might help bring some economic stability to the family, Leticia fears that receiving such assistance would make her children vulnerable to oppressive governmental intervention later in life. Her decision to voluntarily depart when she was faced with immigration detention was driven by fears about her children being placed in the state foster care system. Social workers working in such situations must have a good understanding of the special stressors of undocumented immigrants. We can play an important role in such communities to counter misinformation about social welfare services, such as what Leticia has heard. As social workers, we are well aware of the network of social welfare agencies and programs that could help such families; we are also aware of the gaps in the contemporary social welfare institution.

The **social welfare institution** is concerned with the fair allocation of goods, services, and opportunities to enhance social functioning of individuals and contribute to the social health of the society. The social welfare institution also engages in social control, in programs such as child protective services. The social welfare institution developed in all industrialized countries in the 19th and 20th centuries as these nations tried to cope with the alienation and disruption caused by social inequalities from industrial market capitalism (Teeple, 2000). It was an expression of altruism toward the people who did not fare well in this economic arrangement, but it also was an expression of concern that the inequalities inherent in the system could destabilize a society and undermine its social health.

The social welfare institution, like any other social institution, reflects the culture of the society. Social welfare scholars often call attention to the cultural attitudes toward social welfare in the United States compared with European countries (Karger & Stoesz, 2014). The U.S. social welfare institution has, historically, put primary emphasis on promoting independence and preventing dependence. In contrast, the European social welfare states have put more emphasis on promoting social inclusion and using the social welfare institution as an investment to protect the health of the society, which they refer to as social protection (European Commission: Employment, Social Affairs & Inclusion, 2013; Sernau, 2014). Public expenditure on social welfare (including old age, survivors, disability, health, family, unemployment, housing, and other policies), as a percentage of GDP, varies among affluent societies, ranging from 15.8%

in Israel to 33.0% in France in 2013. The United States spent 20.0% of GDP on social welfare in 2013, with 14 of the 18 wealthy comparison countries spending a larger percentage (OECD, 2013d).

Four things are important to remember when interpreting this trend. First, countries suffered a decline in GDP during and in the aftermath of the 2008 financial crisis, as always occurs at such times (Papell & Prodan, 2011). Second, in the midst of economic decline, many countries stepped up their social welfare expenditures in some areas to cushion the blow of the crisis and stimulate the economy. Third, in the aftermath of the financial crisis, governments around the world are being encouraged to engage in austerity measures, including trimming back the social welfare institution. Fourth, even though public expenditures for social welfare have been growing as a portion of GDP, it is important to note that as wealthy societies gray, expenditures on old-age benefits are increasing at a much faster rate than those in other social welfare sectors. In many affluent countries, government expenditures for children and families have been falling, and child poverty rates have been growing while poverty rates for older adults have not (UNICEF, 2012a). Given what we are learning about the long-term negative health consequences of early deprivation, cost cutting in programs serving children and their families in order to fund programs for older adults could pose serious challenges for the social welfare institution in the future. For all wealthy nations, the social welfare needs of an aging society pose a serious challenge for the social welfare institution going forward.

Social welfare policy is driven by political and economic philosophies. The United States is a diverse society, and there is much competition of ideas about what constitutes the public good and what type of social welfare institution is needed, if at all. Although the philosophical differences are more complex than this, we can divide them into conservative and liberal views of social welfare. Conservatives believe that the public good is best served when the federal government has a minimal role in social welfare. They believe that to the extent that social welfare programs are needed, they should be run by a combination of state and local governments and the private sector. They believe that income inequality and some level of unemployment are good for society, and any attempt by the government to stabilize the economy is harmful. Liberals believe that the government institution, particularly the federal government, should be the primary force in the social welfare institution because it is the institution most capable of promoting social justice, thereby promoting the public good. In their view, social justice is incompatible with high levels of inequality and unemployment, and the government has a role to play in minimizing the harms of market capitalism (for a fuller discussion, see Karger & Stoesz, 2014).

Social welfare policy in the United States, as in any society, varies with who holds political power at any given time and has shifted over time. From the 1930s to the 1970s, beginning with the presidency of Franklin Delano Roosevelt, the general policy direction was for the federal government to play a strong role in the social welfare institution. The Social Security Act of 1935 began a process of government protections that was expanded during the 1960s and 1970s, with the passage of Medicare, Medicaid, the Food Stamp Program, and Head Start, among other programs (J. Marx, 2012). In the late 1970s, the traditional liberal belief in a federally based social welfare system began to lose favor. The new liberals (neoliberals) began to assume some of the conservative philosophy, which led to a diminishing sense of public responsibility and an increasing emphasis on individual responsibility for the social well-being of the nation. Neoliberal philosophy, under the democratic administration of Bill Clinton in the 1990s, led to welfare reform that greatly curtailed supports to poor children and their families. Since the 1980s, the conservative philosophy has been in ascendancy with ongoing attempts to privatize social security (unsuccessful to date) and to otherwise limit the role of the federal government in the social welfare system. (At the same time, however, cultural conservatives have called for an increased role for the federal government in issues such as contraception, abortion, and school prayer.) With a huge federal debt caused by tax cuts, two wars, and a financial crisis, it does not appear that a liberal philosophy of social welfare will regain prominence in the near future. There is some evidence, however, that the millennial generation is more open than older generations to rethinking the role of federal government in securing the welfare of all people.

Given ambivalence about government and a strong belief in the market, the United States has developed a mixed social welfare system made up of federal, state, and local governmental programs; private nonprofit social welfare organizations; and a growing number of private for-profit organizations. It is hard to compare this system with the European model in terms of expenditures, but it is safe to say that the welfare institution in the United States is more fragmented than the European model, and its family support policies, such as family leave, family allowances, and early childhood education and care, are much less comprehensive. Indeed, the European countries are not alone in providing more generous public support to families than is offered in the United States. Parental leave policies are a good example. In the United States, parents are offered 12 weeks of *unpaid* leave under the Family and Medical Leave Act, which exempts companies with fewer than 50 paid employees. All other wealthy countries used as comparison in this chapter as well as many low- and middle-income countries provide *paid* parental leave. For example, Venezuela offers 18 weeks of paid leave, and Pakistan, South Africa, and Mexico each offer 12 weeks of paid leave (Yost, 2012). The average number of paid weeks of parental leave for the 34 countries in the OECD is 19 (OECD, 2012).

Some welfare scholars suggest a social welfare institution in transition (Karger & Stoesz, 2014). Across the Global North, countries pursued liberal social policies after World War II. As a result of the competition inherent in economic globalization, Western industrial nations have been cutting or slowing the growth of their social welfare programs since the 1970s. At the same time, demand for social services has increased as workers have tried to cope with the insecurities in the global labor market. Retrenchment of the social welfare institution in combination with increased concentration of income and wealth has produced political unrest across Europe and the United States and spurred rage across the political spectrum. In the United States, this rage produced both the very conservative Tea Party and the liberal Occupy movement at the beginning of the 2nd decade of the 21st century. The future of the social welfare institution is uncertain.

Leticia seems to think of the social welfare institution only as a coercive institution, one that tries to control behavior rather than provide compassionate support. Indeed, the social welfare institution in the United States has always played a social control function as well as a social reform function (Hutchison, 1987). In recent times, it has moved toward greater attention to social control than to social reform (Hutchison & Charlesworth, 2000; Teeple, 2000). Social workers cannot be active participants in moving that balance back to social reform unless they clearly understand trends in the interrelated social institutions discussed in this chapter.

TRENDS IN THE RELIGIOUS INSTITUTION

Although the Catholic Church was a very important part of the life of Leticia Renteria back in Mexico, she and Marcos do not regularly attend church. However, when Leticia was frantic at being detained by immigration officials, one person she thought might be able to help her was a nun in her community. The **religious institution** is the primary one for addressing spiritual and ethical issues. It also serves important socialization, social control, and mutual support functions. Sociologists study three components of the institution: a belief system, religious rituals, and an organizational structure that provides networks of support as well as roles and statuses (Roberts & Yamane, 2012).

Although there is a long history of conflict and adaptation as the major world religions confronted each other in the same political and geographic areas, globalization has urgently increased the need for religious communities to find ways to coexist globally as well as locally. A religious belief system helps people to feel secure, and exposure to different belief systems can be unsettling and sometimes perceived as a threat to the integrity of one's own beliefs and identity. Today, however, it is almost impossible for believers in one religious tradition to be isolated from other religious traditions. We are increasingly exposed to the beliefs, rituals, and organizations of diverse religious groups, and this is not a trend that is likely to be reversed. There are few choices about how to cope with this trend. We can attempt to impose one belief system on the world and commit genocide if that doesn't work. Or we can attempt to find a unified ethical code that is consistent with all religious traditions and respectfully agree to disagree if that doesn't work, giving legal protections to all groups. In the past, both of these choices have been put into practice at one time or another.

We have been living in a time of much religious strife. Serbian Orthodox Christians recently engaged in ethnic cleansing of Muslims in the former Yugoslavia. Catholics and Protestants have waged a long and often violent battle in Northern Ireland. The Ku Klux Klan in the United States has used religious arguments to vilify and sometimes persecute Jews, African Americans, and other groups. Terrorists have killed and injured thousands in the name of Islam. The United States has called on the name of God, and the language of good and evil, to justify the war on terror and the invasion of Afghanistan and Iraq. Hindus and Muslims kill each other in India. When religious differences are woven with other forms of struggle, such as social class, ethnic, or political struggle, the conflict is likely to be particularly intense (Kurtz, 2012).

On the other hand, there are also historical and current stories of peaceful coexistence of religious groups. In 1893, representatives of a wide range of religions were brought together to create the Parliament of the World's Religions. The second meeting of the parliament did not convene until a century later, in 1993 (Kurtz, 2012). It met again in 1999, 2004, 2009, and 2015. The mission of the parliament is "to cultivate harmony among the world's religious and spiritual communities and foster their engagement with the world and its other guiding institutions in order to achieve a just, peaceful and sustainable world" (Council for a Parliament of the World's Religions, 2015). Among the issues discussed and debated at the 2015 parliament were women, dignity, and human rights; income inequality; confronting war, violence, and hate speech; climate change; and solidarity with Indigenous communities.

It is not surprising that both violence and nonviolence have been used in the name of religion. The texts of all the major world religions include what Lester Kurtz (2012) calls both a "warrior motif" and a "pacifist motif" (pp. 283–284). All major religions justify violence on occasion, but no religion justifies terrorism. All religions also include norms of mercy, compassion, and respect. In the contemporary era, Islam is sometimes characterized as a violent religion, but Christianity was seen as the most violent world religion during the Crusades and the

Wikimedia Commons, public domain

Religious leaders attended the first Parliament of the World's Religions in 1893.

Inquisition. All of the major world religions have proven capable of perpetrating violence in the name of religion, and all have demonstrated compassion and tolerance.

It is good to get a sense of the global religious landscape. Consider a group of 10 people that represent the distribution of world religions. Three will be Christian, two will be Muslim, two will be unaffiliated or atheists, one will be Hindu, one will be Buddhist or from another East Asian religion, and the remaining one will represent every other religion of the world (Kurtz, 2012). This landscape includes two Eastern religions (Hinduism and Buddhism) and three Western religions (Judaism, Christianity, and Islam). The Western religions are *monotheistic*, believing that there is only one God, whereas the Eastern religions are either *polytheistic*, believing in multiple Gods (most forms of Hinduism and some forms of Buddhism) or not believing in a deity (e.g., some forms of Hinduism and Buddhism). Eastern religions are less insistent on the primacy of their "truth" than the Western religions and are more likely to embrace nonviolence. Eastern religions have also tended to be less centrally organized than the Western religions.

Each of the major world religions has changed over time and place and become more diverse. Lester Kurtz suggests that we should speak of all the major world religions in the plural: Hinduisms, Buddhisms, Judaisms, Christianities, and Islams. He also argues that some of the most violent contests occur *within* these religious traditions and not *between* them, as experienced by the Christian Catholics and Protestants in Northern Ireland and the Muslim Sunnis and Shias in some Muslim countries.

Each of the major world religions, but especially the Western religions, has an internal struggle, sometimes called a culture war (J. Hunter, 1994), between a branch of traditionalists and a branch of modernists (Kurtz, 2012). *Traditionalists* believe that moral obligations are rigid, given, and absolute. *Modernists* believe that moral commitment is voluntary, conditional, and fluid. These two branches often engage in a struggle for the heart and soul of the religious tradition, sometimes using violence to press their case.

Although many religious peoples around the world fear that modernism and postmodernism are destroying religion, there is clear evidence that the religious institution is quite resilient. Public opinion polls consistently report that religion is important in the lives of a great majority of people in the United States, yet a great majority of people also believe that religion is losing its influence

(Gallup, 2013). International data indicate that people in the United States have much higher weekly attendance at religious services than Europeans; they spend more time in private devotions and more money on religious activities than residents of other advanced industrialized countries. In 2012, about 60% of the U.S. population were church members, compared with about 10% in 1776 (Gallup, 2013; Kurtz, 2012). As suggested in Chapter 5, diversity is the hallmark of the religious institution in the United States today.

Christianity remains dominant within the United States, but there are intense culture wars between traditionalists and modernists, with the conflict centering on such issues as the definition of family, the role of women, the beginning and end of life, same-sex relationships, prayer in school, and theories of the creation of the world. Both traditionalists and modernists base their arguments on their understanding of biblical texts, but each tends to see the other as immoral. Some examples will help to clarify the competing moral precepts regarding some of these questions. Traditionalists see the push for women's rights as destructive to the traditional family and motherhood. Modernists see women's rights as necessary in a just society. Likewise, traditionalists see the gay rights movement as a particularly vicious attack on the traditional family, and modernists see it as a struggle for dignity. Traditionalists argue that school prayer is essential to help students develop a moral code, and modernists argue that it is an intrusion on religious freedom and tolerance. The culture wars are intense because both groups wish for dominance in the political institution.

Given the clear evidence of the central importance of religion in the lives of billions of people in the world, social workers must become comfortable in assessing the role of religion and spirituality in the lives of their client systems at the individual, family, and community levels. We should not assume that all persons of a religious group hold the same beliefs regarding social issues. But we must be aware of religious beliefs—both our own and those of clients—when working with controversial social issues.

TRENDS IN THE MASS MEDIA INSTITUTION

As she does her household chores, Leticia Renteria often watches television, but she has considered taking a break from TV. More often than not, she feels devalued, frightened, and dismayed by what she sees and hears about such political issues as the minimum wage and immigration policy. On the other hand, watching Telemundo (a U.S. network that broadcasts in Spanish with closed captions in both English and Spanish) helps her stay in touch with her Latino heritage and make connections between the English and Spanish languages.

The **mass media institution** is the primary institution for managing the flow of information, images, and ideas among all members of society. Mass media serves an entertainment role for society, but it also influences how we understand ourselves and the world. Mass media technology is the engine of globalization, giving people worldwide immediate access to other cultures and other markets. Rapid advances in electronic communication technology since the 1950s have resulted in widespread access to multiple forms of mass communication—"old media" such as newspapers, magazines, books, radio, television, and film and "new media" such as the Internet, digital television and radio, ever more elaborate multifunctional smartphones, and video games. Electronic media now allow two-way as well as one-way communication, and they can store and manipulate vast amounts of information. The mass media is thoroughly embedded in our daily lives and a larger focus of our leisure time than any other social institution (Devereux, 2013).

There are several important trends in the mass media landscape.

1. Growth in media outlets and media products
2. More time and money spent on media products
3. Integration of media functions
4. Audiences as communicators and creators
5. Globalization of media markets
6. Concentration of ownership

In totalitarian societies, such as North Korea, the flow of information, images, and ideas is controlled by the government. In the United States, we have a long tradition of freedom of the press—a belief that the media must be free to serve as a public watchdog. Traditionally, the emphasis has been on the watchdog role in relation to the government and political institution—in other words, a press that is not controlled by the government. In the current era of media mergers and acquisitions, concerns have centered on media censorship by the economic institution. Critics suggest that powerful multinational media corporations censor the coverage of news to protect their economic or political interests. Organizations that analyze freedom of the press report that after 2 decades of improvement around the world, there was a decline in press freedom in recent years, and in 2013 only 14.0% of the world's citizens lived in countries with a free press (Freedom House, 2015a). These organizations rated the United States as 49th in freedom of the press in 2015, down from 21st in 2009. The highest marks went to the northern European countries (Freedom House, 2015a; Reporters Without Borders, 2015). Around the world, freedom on the Internet declined for the 5th consecutive

Mass media technology is the engine of globalization, and people around the world are saturated with images from multiple media forms.

year in 2015. Authorities in 42 of the 65 countries studied prohibited Internet users, including private companies, from including web content that deals with political, religious, or social issues (Freedom House, 2015b).

In recent years, there is considerable concern about how the media abuses citizen privacy. There is concern about how social networking sites like Facebook violate users' privacy. There is concern about how commercial sites engage in information gathering, profiling, and data mining on "free" online platforms in order to market their products (Croteau, Hoynes, & Milan, 2012). There is concern about how media companies hack phones to gather information for news stories. As this chapter is being written in early 2016, there is considerable concern in the United States about how the government uses a variety of technologies to mine data on its citizens. Another growing concern is website hacking in which hackers are able to gain unauthorized access to sensitive data, from personal information to international secrets.

Mass media critics suggest that control of the media by political and economic elites results in control of cultural meanings to benefit elites and silence dissident views. The mass media in the United States has historically been controlled by White, middle- and upper-class men, who have presented their worldviews. Mass media owners are interested in attracting affluent consumers and choose content with this aim in mind (Croteau et al., 2012). Women, people of color, low-income people, sexual minorities, and people with disabilities are underrepresented in media presentations, and when they are represented, the images are often unflattering. There has been some improvement in this situation in the past 2 decades, but there is still a long way to go. Historically, nondominant groups have developed alternative media to compensate for their absence or poor treatment in the dominant media. That is still the case today and is becoming a much easier task with the new Internet-based media (Wilson, Gutiérrez, & Chao, 2013). Leticia Renteria is well aware of the negative images of immigrants that are often seen in the mass media in the United States. Social workers should be aware of how national and local media represent nondominant groups in their communities and collaborate with others to develop fairer representations.

CRITICAL THINKING Questions 9.3

What would life be like without the mass media? How would you find out about national and global events? Where would you get your ideas about social welfare, religion, and family? How would your daily life be different? What are some recent media images you have observed about the social welfare institution? About immigration?

THEORIES OF SOCIAL INEQUALITY

Throughout this chapter, we have presented information on how social inequality is created and maintained in seven interrelated major social institutions. **Social class** is the term generally used by sociologists to describe contemporary structures of inequality. Perhaps no question regarding the human condition has generated more intense and complex controversies and conflicts than the related issues of inequality and distributive justice. Unequal distribution of resources is probably as old as the human species and certainly has existed in all complex societies. Long before the discipline of sociology arose, thoughtful people constructed explanations and justifications for these inequalities (Lenski, 1966; Sernau, 2014). Although social class has been an important topic for sociology, by no means do sociologists agree about the role it plays in human behavior.

The contributing authors and I have presented inequality as a problem, but as you have probably noted, not everyone agrees with this view. Gerhard Lenski (1966) did a careful study of how societies over time have answered the question of whether inequality is a good or bad thing. He divided the way societies have responded to this question into a conservative thesis and a radical antithesis. In the **conservative thesis**, inequality is the natural, divine order, and no efforts should be made to alter it. In the **radical antithesis**, equality is the natural, divine order; inequality is based on abuse of privilege and should be minimized.

When social inequality is considered to be the natural order and divinely ordained, there is no need to search further for explanations of inequality. But as this traditional assumption gave way to a belief that human beings are born equal, persistent social inequalities required explanation and justification. Explanation of inequality and its relationship to human behavior became central to the emerging social and political sciences. As discussed in Chapter 2, two classical theorists, Karl Marx (1818–1883) and Max Weber (1864–1920), have had lasting impact on the sociological analysis of social inequality. These two theorists differed in perspective about the inevitability of class consciousness or class action. Marx saw class consciousness and communal action related to class as inevitable. Weber saw social class as a possible, but not inevitable, source of identity and communal action.

THE CONTEMPORARY DEBATE

Attempts to determine the cause of persistent social inequalities have led to debate among sociologists who embrace functional theories and sociologists who embrace conflict theories. *Functional theories* of social stratification present structural inequality (social classes) as necessary for society. According to this view, unequal rewards for different types of work guarantee that the most talented persons will work hard and produce technological innovation to benefit the whole society. *Conflict theorists* (see Chapter 2 for more discussion of conflict theories), on the other hand, emphasize the role of power, domination, and coercion in the creation and maintenance of inequality. According to this view, persons with superior wealth and income also hold superior social and political power and use that power to protect their privileged positions.

Sociological functionalism was dominant in U.S. sociology during the 1940s and 1950s, but it faded in importance after that. However, functionalism was the root for *modernization theory*, which attempted, in the 1960s, to explain on the global level why some countries are poor and others are rich (Rostow, 1990). These theorists suggested that poverty is caused by traditional attitudes and technology—by the failure to modernize. The conflict perspective counterargument to modernization theory was *dependency theory*, which argued that poor societies are created by worldwide industrial capitalism, which exploits natural resources and labor (Frank, 1967). These theorists emphasized the tremendous power of foreign multinational corporations to coerce national governments in poor nations. They called attention to colonial imperialism as the historical context of contemporary global inequalities (Sernau, 2014).

The recent debate has been between neoliberalism and the world systems perspective. *Neoliberalism* is based in classic economics and argues that free trade and free markets, with limited government interference, will result in a fair distribution of resources. As suggested earlier, this philosophy has been dominant across the world for the past few decades but is currently being challenged on several fronts. Economists at the World Bank and IMF have been strong voices in favor of neoliberalism, which informed the ideals of their structural adjustment program for dealing with the debts of impoverished nations. *Structural adjustment* called for poor countries to "clean house" by reducing government spending and bureaucracy and increasing exportation and entrepreneurship. To counter this view, the *world systems perspective* suggests that inequality is created and maintained by economic globalization (Wallerstein, 1974, 1980, 1989). According to the world systems perspective, the hegemony of the core sector of the United States and western Europe is reinforced by neocolonial practices of such transnational institutions as the World Bank, the IMF, and the WTO.

STRUCTURAL DETERMINISM VERSUS HUMAN AGENCY

Will knowledge of my social class position help you to predict my attitudes and behaviors? That question has become a controversial one for contemporary social science. Social scientists who see human behavior as highly determined by one's position in the social class structure (*structural determinism*) are challenged by social scientists who emphasize the capacity of humans to create their own realities and who give central roles to human actors, not social structures (*human agency*).

Macro-oriented sociologists have taken Émile Durkheim's lead in arguing that human action is a by-product of social institutions external to human consciousness. Micro-oriented sociologists have taken Max Weber's lead in the counterargument that humans are proactive agents who construct meaning in interaction with others. In a position more consistent with the multidimensional framework of this book, Anthony Giddens (1979) has proposed *structuration theory*, a theory of the relationship between human agency and social structure. Giddens notes that social practices repeat themselves in patterned ways over time and in space, structured by the rules and resources embedded in social institutions. While acknowledging the constraints that rules and resources place on human action, he also notes that human agents have the ability to make a difference in the social world. Human actions produce social structure, and at all times human action is serving either to perpetuate or to transform social structure. You may recognize that this is very similar to the practice approach to culture presented in Chapter 6. Some critics have suggested that Giddens is too optimistic about how much agency humans have, but Giddens acknowledges that those with the most power have a disproportionate opportunity to reinforce institutional arrangements that perpetuate their positions of power.

Structuration theory is a good framework for social workers. It calls our attention to power arrangements that constrain the behaviors of some actors more than others in a way that perpetuates social injustice. But it also calls our attention to the possibilities for human action to transform social institutions. Mary Ellen Kondrat (1999) suggests that structuration theory poses two questions that, when raised, provide critical consciousness, a necessary ingredient for progressive change agents. **Critical consciousness** can be defined as an ongoing process of reflection and knowledge seeking about mechanisms and outcomes of social, political, and economic oppression that requires taking personal and collective action toward fairness and social justice. The first question raised by Kondrat is, "How aware are we of the ways in which social institutions and social structure condition our behaviors?" The second question is, "How aware are we of the ways in which our day-to-day activities over time perpetuate or transform social structure?" Just as individual agency is essential for individual change, collective agency is essential for changing social institutions. That is the central point of social movements.

SOCIAL MOVEMENTS: A DEFINITION

What happens when a group of people, like the many people involved in living wage campaigns (see Case Study 9.2), think that certain arrangements are unjust and need to be changed? Sometimes they work together to try to bring about the desired changes—not just for themselves but for a large group of people. These joint efforts are **social movements**—ongoing, large-scale, collective efforts to bring about (or resist) social change.

We can think of social movements as either proactive or reactive (Ballantine & Roberts, 2014). *Proactive social movements* seek to reform existing social arrangements and try out new ways of living together. The living wage, Occupy Wall Street, and marriage equality movements are examples of proactive social movements. *Reactive social movements*, on the other hand, seek to defend traditional values and social arrangements. Christian and Islamic fundamentalist and property rights movements are examples of reactive social movements. Both types of social movements are common today in the United States and across the world.

Mario Diani (della Porta & Diani, 2006) identifies the following properties that distinguish social movements from other social collectivities. They

- are involved in conflictual relations with clearly identified opponents,
- are linked by dense informal networks, and
- share a distinct collective identity. (p. 20)

It is protest that distinguishes social movements from other types of social networks, but a single episode of protest is not a social movement unless it is connected to a longer-lasting network of public action (Tilly & Wood, 2013).

PERSPECTIVES ON SOCIAL MOVEMENTS

Theory and research about social movements have flourished in the past 4-plus decades, and in 2012 Roberta Garner and Mayer Zald suggested that the study of social movements is "hotter" than ever. I would agree that it is hotter than at any period since I started work on the first edition of this book in the mid-1990s. In the past 25 years, U.S. and European social movement scholars have worked together and engaged in comparative analysis of social movements across place and time (della Porta, Kriesi, & Rucht, 2009). Originally, these collaborative efforts focused only on social movements in the United States and western Europe, but in recent years international events have captured the attention of social movement scholars.

Three major perspectives on social movements have emerged out of this lively interest. I refer to these as the political opportunities perspective, the mobilizing structures perspective, and the cultural framing perspective (see Exhibit 9.4 for a summary of the main ideas of these perspectives). There is growing agreement among social movement scholars that none of these perspectives taken alone provide adequate tools for understanding social movements (Buechler, 2011; Edwards, 2014). Each perspective adds important dimensions to our understanding, however, and taken together they provide a relatively comprehensive theory of social movements. Social movement scholars recommend research that synthesizes concepts across the three perspectives. The recent social movement literature offers one of the best examples of contemporary attempts to integrate and synthesize multiple theoretical perspectives to give a more complete picture of social phenomena.

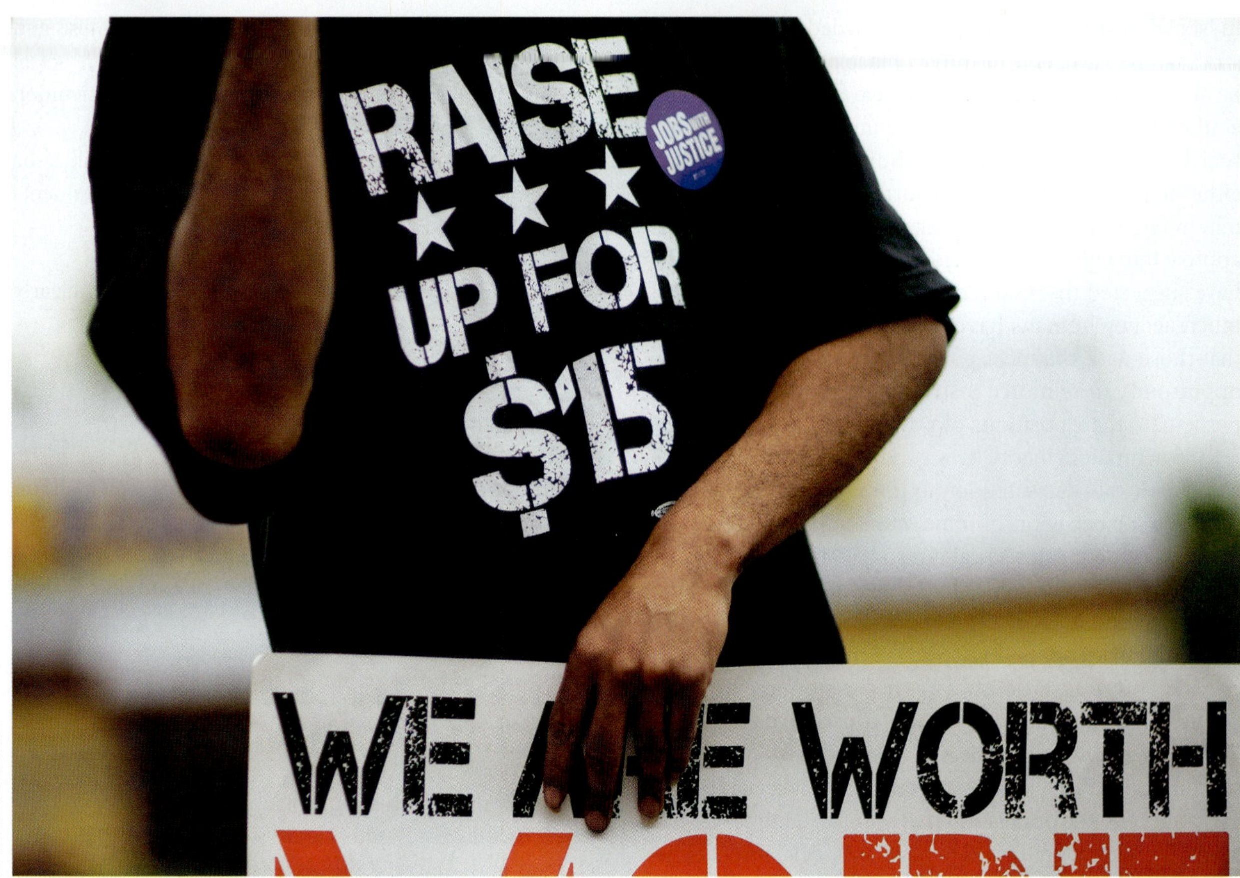

AP Photo/David Goldman

Living wage and minimum wage are part of the same policy movement to promote wage fairness.

POLITICAL OPPORTUNITIES PERSPECTIVE

Many advocates have been concerned about the deteriorating economic situation of low-wage workers in the United States for some time. After Republicans regained control of Congress in 1994, advocates saw little hope for major increases in the federal minimum wage. The federal minimum wage was increased slightly, from $4.25 an hour to $5.15 an hour in 1996, with a Democratic president and a Republican Congress. However, under the circumstances, advocates of a living wage decided it was more feasible to engage in campaigns at the local rather than federal level to ensure a living wage for all workers. A shift occurred at the federal level when the Democrats regained control of Congress in November 2006. After being stalled at $5.15 for 10 years, the minimum wage received a three-step increase from Congress in May 2007, and Republican president George W. Bush signed the new wage bill into law. The law called for an increase of the federal minimum wage to $5.85 in the summer of 2007, to $6.55 in the summer of 2008, and to $7.25 in the summer of 2009 (U.S. Department of Labor, 2014). In early 2014, Democratic president Barack Obama recommended an increase in the federal minimum wage to $10.10, but this proposal had little chance in a highly polarized Congress. In the meantime, state and local governments continue to consider the issue of fair wages.

These observations are in line with the *political opportunities perspective*, which begins with the assumption that social institutions—particularly political and economic institutions—benefit the more powerful members of society, often called *elites*, and disadvantage many. The elites typically have routine access to institutionalized political channels, whereas disadvantaged groups are denied access. Power disparities make it very difficult for some groups to successfully challenge existing institutions, but the **political opportunities (PO) perspective** suggests that institutions are not consistently invulnerable to challenge by groups with little power, and social movements develop when windows of opportunity open. Social movements can at times take advantage of institutional arrangements vulnerable to challenge. The BUILD coalition (see Case Study 9.2) was convinced that it was morally unjust for workers to receive wages that kept them below the federal poverty line, but they astounded even themselves by setting in motion a process that would spark a national social movement. Theories of social movements often underestimate the ability of challengers to mount and sustain social movements (Morris, 2004).

The political system itself may influence whether a social movement will emerge at a given time, as well as the form the movement will take. Social movement scholars have identified several influential dimensions of political

EXHIBIT 9.4 • Perspectives on Social Movements

PERSPECTIVE	MAIN IDEAS
Political opportunities perspective	Social movements emerge when political opportunities are open. Political systems differ from each other, and change over time, in their openness to social movements. A given political system is not equally open or closed to all challengers. Success of one social movement can open the political system to challenges from other social movements. A given political system's openness to social movements is influenced by international events. Opportunities for social movements open at times of instability in political alignments. Social movements often rely on elite allies.
Mobilizing structures perspective	Social movements must be able to mobilize various kinds of formal and informal networks. Resource mobilization theory focuses on the coordination of movement activists through social movement organizations (SMOs). The network model focuses on mobilization of the movement through informal networks. Mobilizing structures have a strong influence on the life course of social movements. To survive, social movements must be able to attract new members and sustain the involvement of current members.
Cultural framing perspective	Social movements must be able to develop shared understandings that legitimate and motivate collective action. Social movements actively participate in the naming of grievances and injustices. Social movement leaders must construct a perception that change is possible. Social movements must articulate goals. Social movements must identify and create tactical choices for accomplishing goals. Contests over cultural frames are common in social movements. Social movements must be able to create cultural frames to appeal to diverse audiences.

systems and analyzed the ways in which changes in one or more of these dimensions make the political system either receptive or vulnerable to challenges (della Porta & Diani, 2006; Tarrow, 2006). Here, we examine four of those dimensions: openness of the political system, stability of political alignments, availability of elite allies, and international relations.

Openness of the Political System

It might seem reasonable to think that activists will undertake collective action when political systems are open and avoid such action when political systems are closed. The relationship of system openness or closure to social movement activity is not that simple, however. They have instead a curvilinear relationship: Neither full access nor its total absence encourages the greatest degree of collective action. Some resistance stimulates movement solidarity, but too much resistance makes collective action too costly for social movement participants (D. Meyer, 2004). The nature of the political structure will also affect the types of social movement activities that emerge in a given society (Koopmans, 2004).

More generally, but in a similar vein, democratic states facilitate social movements and authoritarian states repress them (Tilly & Wood, 2013). Indeed, social movements as a form of collective action arose with the development of the modern democratic state (Marks & McAdam, 2009). However, because democratic states invite participation, even criticism, many challenging issues that might spark social movements are "processed" out of existence through electoral processes. It is hard to mount a social movement if it seems that the political system is easily influenced without serious collective action. On the other hand, the repression found in authoritarian states may serve to radicalize social movement leaders, as was evident during the Arab Spring uprisings of 2011 (Castells, 2012). Furthermore, as was evident in eastern Europe in the late 1980s, authoritarian states are not always effective in repressing challenges. The political leadership's efforts to appease the population by offering small liberties had a snowball effect. Relaxation of social control in a previously repressive political system often has the unintended consequence of fueling the fire of long-held grievances.

Social movement researchers are interested in how police handle protest events. They have identified two contrasting styles of policing: the escalated-force model and the negotiated control model. The *escalated-force model* puts little value on the right to protest, has low tolerance for many forms of protest, favors little communication between the police and demonstrators, and makes use of coercive and even illegal methods to control protests. The *negotiated control model* honors the right to demonstrate peacefully, tolerates even disruptive forms of protest, puts high priority on communication between police and demonstrators, and avoids coercive control as much as possible (della Porta & Diani, 2006).

A given political system is not equally open or closed to all challengers at a given time; some social movements are favored over others. Even in a democracy, universal franchise does not mean equal access to the political system; wealth buys access not easily available to poor people's movements (Bornstein, 2009). Indeed, the rapid success and growth of the living wage movement has been a surprise to many who support it ideologically, because it has been hard to sustain poor people's movements in the past.

The success of one social movement can open the political system to challenges by other social movements. For example, successful legislative action by the Black civil rights movement during the 1960s opened the way for other civil rights movements, particularly the women's movement, which benefited from Title VII of the Civil Rights Act of 1964, which included prohibiting employment discrimination on the basis of sex (McAdam, 1996a). But the successful movement may also open the way for opponent movements, called **countermovements**, as well as for allied movements. The living wage movement has engendered opposition coalitions that have launched intensive lobbying campaigns to convince state legislators in several states to bar cities from establishing their own minimum wages (Murray, 2001; Quigley, 2001).

Stability of Political Alignments

PO theorists agree that the routine transfer of political power from one group of incumbents to another, as when a different political party takes control of the U.S. presidency or Congress, opens opportunities for the development or reactivation of social movements (Tarrow, 2006). At such times, some social movements lose favor and others gain opportunity. In the United States, in both the 1930s and the 1960s, changes in political party strength appear to have been related to increased social movement activity among poor people. Some observers note that social movements on the Left mobilized during the Kennedy and Johnson administrations, and social movements on the Right mobilized during the Reagan and George H. W. Bush administrations and again when Republicans took over Congress in 1994 (McAdam, McCarthy, & Zald, 1996). Some researchers (see Amenta, Caren, & Stobaugh, 2012) have found, however, that Left regimes can incite Right-oriented social movements, and even more so, Right regimes can incite Left-oriented social movements.

Disruption of political alliances occurs at times other than political elections, for both partisan and nonpartisan reasons, and such disruptions produce conflicts and divisions among elites. When elites are divided, social movements can sometimes encourage some factions to take a stand for disenfranchised groups and support the goals of the movement. The Harvard Living Wage Campaign garnered the support of the mayor and city council in Cambridge, Massachusetts. Disruptions in political alliances also occur when different branches of the government—such as the executive branch and the legislative branch—are at odds with each other. New coalitions may be formed, and the uncertainty that ensues may encourage groups to make new or renewed attempts to challenge institutional arrangements, hoping to find new elite allies.

The events in eastern Europe in the late 1980s and the Arab Spring of 2011 represent another type of political opportunity—one that has received little attention by social movement scholars—the opportunity that opens when a political regime loses legitimacy with those it governs. Some social movement scholars suggest that this sort of instability is contributing to the global spread of social movement activity (Castells, 2012).

Availability of Elite Allies

Participants in social movements often lack both power and resources for influencing the political process. But they may be assisted by influential allies who play a variety of supportive roles. These elite allies may provide financial support, or they may provide name and face recognition that attracts media attention to the goals and activities of the movement. Research indicates a strong correlation between the presence of elite allies and social movement success (della Porta & Diani, 2006). The Harvard students, who mostly came from elite families themselves, were able to attract a number of elite allies, including Congressman Edward M. Kennedy, former Labor secretary Robert Reich, chairman of the NAACP Julian Bond, high-profile religious leaders, and actors Ben Affleck and Matt Damon. Michael Moore and Cornel West showed up to address the assembly of Occupy Wall Street in 2011. Social movement participants often have ambivalent relationships with their elite allies, however. On the one hand, powerful allies provide needed resources; on the other hand, they may limit or distort the goals of the movement (della Porta & Diani, 2006).

International Relations

Since the 18th century, social movements have diffused rapidly across national boundaries, and the fate of national social movements has been influenced by international events. In the 19th century, the antislavery movement spread from England to France, the Netherlands, and the Americas (Tarrow, 2006). The mid-20th-century Black civil rights movement in the United States was influenced by international attention to the gap between our national image as champion of human rights and the racial discrimination that permeated our social institutions (McAdam, 1996a). The fight for the right of women to vote was first won in New Zealand in the 1880s; the United States followed almost 40 years later, in 1920. It took some time, but gradually the movement for women's suffrage spread around the world (Sernau, 2014).

The recent revolution in communication technology is quickening the diffusion of collective action, as evidenced by recent democracy and justice movements. Democracy movements surged across the Arab world in 2011 after the successful democracy movements in Tunisia and Egypt. In the midst of the deep financial crisis that began in late 2007, unemployment reached 22% in Spain by 2011. After ignoring the severity of the situation for some time, the Spanish government, under pressure from Germany and the International Monetary Fund, instituted austerity policies that resulted in deep cuts in health, education, and social services. In protest, activists put out the call to occupy Barcelona's Catalunya Square on May 16, 2011, an action so successful it was followed up on in 100 other Spanish cities as well as 800 cities around the world. The Occupy Wall Street action that began in the United States in September 2011 was modeled on this social movement (Castells, 2012).

CRITICAL THINKING Questions 9.4

Have you participated in any social movement activities? If so, what were your reasons? If not, what have been the reasons? Are there particular historical social movements that you think have had a good impact on U.S. or global societies? Are there particular historical social movements that you think have had a detrimental impact on U.S. or global societies? Are there recent social movements you would like to know more about? If so, how might you go about learning about them?

MOBILIZING STRUCTURES PERSPECTIVE

Most analysts would agree that much of the success of the living wage movement can be attributed to strong existing networks of local progressive advocates. The movement also benefited from strong advocacy organizations that developed and provided resources to grassroots organizers. These views are consistent with the **mobilizing structures (MS) perspective**, which starts from this basic premise: Given their disadvantaged position in the political system, social movement leaders must seek out and mobilize the resources they need—people, money, information, ideas, and skills—in order to reduce the costs and increase the benefits of movement activities. In the MS perspective, social movements have no influence without effective organization of various kinds of *mobilizing structures*—existing informal networks and formal organizations through which people mobilize and engage in collective action. Mobilizing structures are the collective building blocks of social movements.

Informal and Formal Structures

MS scholars agree that social movements typically do not start from scratch but build on existing structures. They disagree, however, on the relative importance of informal versus formal structures. The MS perspective has two theoretical building blocks, one that emphasizes formal mobilizing structures and another that emphasizes informal mobilizing structures.

Resource mobilization theory focuses on the organization and coordination of movement activities through formal organizations called *social movement organizations (SMOs)* (Davis, McAdam, Scott, & Zald, 2005). Theorists in this tradition are particularly interested in *professional social movement organizations* staffed by leaders and activists who make a professional career out of reform causes (della Porta & Diani, 2006; A. Morris, 2004). The professional staff engages in fund-raising and attempts to speak for the constituency represented by the movement. There are advantages to professional SMOs, because social movements are more likely to meet their goals when they have a well-structured organization to engage in continuous fund-raising and lobbying. There are also problems, however. Professional SMOs must respond to the wishes of the benefactors who may be comfortable with low-level claims only. Theda Skocpol (2003) argues that professionalization can lead to movement defeat by taming protest. This may explain why the Occupy Wall Street movement (also known as the Occupy movement) was vehemently opposed to a leadership role for SMOs in their movement (Castells, 2012).

Global social movements are being supported by growing numbers of *transnational social movement organizations (TSMOs)*, or social movement organizations that operate in more than one nation-state. The number of TSMOs grew each decade of the 20th century, with particularly rapid growth in the last 3 decades of the century. There were 183 in 1973 and 1,011 in 2003 (Tilly & Wood, 2013). Some examples of TSMOs are Green Peace and Amnesty International.

In contrast to the resource mobilization theory, the *network model* focuses on everyday ties between people, in grassroots settings, as the basic structures for the communication and social solidarity necessary for mobilization (della Porta & Diani, 2006; Tindall, 2004). The focus is thus on naturally existing networks based in family, work, religious, educational, and neighborhood relationships or such networks as those that can be found at alternative cafés and bookshops and social and cultural centers. Naturally existing social networks facilitate recruitment to movement activities and support continued participation. These natural networks are hard to repress and control because, in a democratic society, people have the right to congregate in their private homes and other informal settings.

Although resource mobilization theory and the network model disagree about the relative merits of formal and informal structures, they do agree that the costs of mobilizing social movements are minimized by drawing on preexisting structures and networks (Davis et al., 2005; Tindall, 2004). The living wage campaign in Baltimore got its start in an existing coalition of religious leaders, and the growing living wage movement was able to generate support from existing social movement organizations and university students. This is very common in the life of social movements. Black churches and Black colleges played an important role in the U.S. civil rights movement of the 1950s and 1960s (Hutchison, 2012). The global justice movement depends on a broad coalition of organizations with a strong background in activism, including trade unions and other worker organizations, ethnic organizations, farmers, religious organizations, consumer groups, environmental groups, women's groups, and youth groups (della Porta & Diani, 2006; Tarrow, 2006). Research indicates that the vast majority of active participants in the Occupy movement in the United States had participated in other social movements and been involved in activist networks on the Internet (Castells, 2012).

Information and Communication Technology (ICT)

Social movement leaders have always made use of new communication technologies to mobilize, using the telephone, radio, television, and computer as they became available. However, as new communication technologies became available, they did not replace previously existing technologies but were, instead, used alongside them. In recent years, the Internet and wireless communication networks have been used extensively in the mobilization of social movements, and the dynamic force of their use is the primary reason the study of social movements is so hot now. Here are two fascinating examples of recent use of these technologies to mount social movements around the world.

In May 2007, activists in the southern China city of Xiamen were fighting the construction of a chemical plant in their city. They sent out text messages from their cell phones encouraging recipients to participate in a protest at a particular location on June 1 at 8:00 a.m. Discussion of the hazards of the chemical plant was taken up by bloggers. On June 1, tens of thousands of protesters marched against the project, uploading photographs, videos, and text messages to blogging sites as they marched. When one blogging site was blocked, another blogger would pick up the material and distribute it. In December 2007, the Chinese government announced that the plant would be moved to another city, Guangzhou. In March 2008, residents of Guangzhou and nearby towns engaged in 3 days of protest against the decision to move the plant to their city. In one nearby town, the protesters staged a sit-in to block traffic on a main road. The local government sent loudspeakers to the street to deny that the plant would be moved to Guangzhou. In 2011, thousands of people used text messaging to organize protests against a similar plant in another part of China, and that plant was closed by local authorities (Tilly & Wood, 2013).

On December 17, 2010, street vendor Mohamed Bouazizi set fire to himself in front of a government building in a small town in Tunisia to protest the constant confiscation of his fruit and vegetables by the local police after he refused to pay them a bribe. A few hours later, hundreds of youth, sharing similar experiences, led a protest in front of the same building. Mohamed's cousin, Ali, recorded the protest and distributed the video over the Internet. A few days later, spontaneous demonstrations were held around the country and continued in spite of brutal repression by the police. When the French government removed its support from the dictator Ben Ali, he and his family fled Tunisia. The protesters were not satisfied, however, and the demonstrations continued. The protesters posted videos (of the protests and police brutality), messages, and songs on Facebook, YouTube, and Twitter. They used the Twitter hashtag #sidibouzid to debate and communicate. Bloggers played an active role, and Al Jazeera television broadcast images that had been posted on YouTube. The mobilization was not all digital, however. The protesters also occupied the Place du Gouvernement, the site of most government offices, and covered the walls of the government square with slogans. Hundreds of cars converged on the capital. The Tunisian protesters continued their actions throughout 2011 and were rewarded with open elections on October 23, 2011 (Castells, 2012; Tilly & Wood, 2013).

Communication scholars suggest that the Internet and wireless communication technologies are a rich resource for social movements because they can be used to bypass mainstream media, which often ignores or distorts movement activity. Recent research indicates that YouTube is probably the most powerful mobilizing tool in the early stages of a movement because the visual images arouse strong emotions in the viewer (Castells, 2012). Research is also suggesting that the greatest power comes from connecting virtual relationships with occupation of a shared physical space (Bennett, 2004; Castells, 2012). In recent large-scale social movements, new technologies have been used to call people to gather in specific physical spaces and to occupy those spaces over time.

The Life Course of Social Movements

Social movements are by definition fluid. The MS perspective asserts that mobilizing structures have a strong influence on the life course of a social movement. Although most social movements fade relatively soon, some last for decades. Movements typically have brief periods of intense activity and long latent periods when not much is happening. One pattern for the movements that persist is as follows: At the outset, the movement is ill defined, and the various mobilizing structures are weakly organized (Kriesi, 1996; Marx & McAdam, 1994). Once the movement has been in existence for a while, it is likely to become larger, less spontaneous, and better organized. The mature social movement is typically led by the SMOs developed in the course of mobilization. The living wage movement seems to be in this position currently, with several organizations, including some transnational ones, playing a major role, but it was not always so.

Social movement scholars disagree about whether the increasing role of formal organizations as time passes is good or bad. Many suggest that movements cannot survive without becoming more organized and taking on many of the characteristics of the institutions they challenge (Tarrow, 2006). On the other hand, this tendency of social movements to become more organized and less spontaneous has often doomed them—particularly poor people's movements—to failure (Skocpol, 2003). Organizations that become more formal commonly abandon the oppositional tactics that brought early success and fail to seize the window of opportunity created by the unrest those tactics generated. But that is not always the case. Sometimes SMOs become more radical over time, and most current large-scale social movements are strengthened by the support of many types of organizations (della Porta & Diani, 2006). One of the most important problems facing social movement organizers is to create mobilizing structures that are sufficiently strong to stand up to opponents but also flexible enough to respond to changing circumstances (Tarrow, 2006). The living wage movement appears to have managed that tension in its first 2 decades, but it is still a work in progress. It is too early to tell what the long-term trajectory of the living wage movement will be. One possibility is that it will merge with other movements focused on economic justice.

CULTURAL FRAMING PERSPECTIVE

The **cultural framing (CF) perspective** asserts that a social movement can succeed only when participants develop shared understandings and definitions of the situation. These shared meanings develop through a transactional process of consciousness raising, which social movement scholars call cultural framing. *Cultural framing* involves "conscious strategic efforts by groups of people to fashion shared understandings of the world and of themselves that legitimate and motivate collective action" (McAdam et al., 1996, p. 6).

Social movement leaders and participants engage in a delicate balancing act as they construct cultural frames. To legitimate collective action, cultural frames must impel people to feel aggrieved or outraged about some situation they consider unjust. But to motivate people to engage in collective action, cultural frames must be optimistic about the possibilities for improving the situation. Consider the chant developed by the divinity students at Harvard: "Where's your horror? Where's your rage? Div School wants a living wage." The chant dramatized the severity of the situation and the fairness of their cause, but it also expressed hope for a solution. Simultaneously, social movements want to draw heavily on existing cultural symbols so that the movement frame will resonate with people's cultural understandings while they add new frames to the cultural stock, thus sponsoring new ways of thinking about social conditions. The challenge of this balancing act is "how to put forward a set of unsettling demands for unconventional people in ways that will not make enemies out of potential allies" (Tarrow, 1994, p. 10). The BUILD coalition was wise in choosing to call their cause a "living wage" rather than a "minimum wage." The notion that workers should draw a wage that allows them to "live" is morally persuasive, and even those who oppose the living wage movement have suggested that it is hard to take a public stance that you are opposed to such an idea (Malanga, 2003).

Cultural frames are "metaphors, symbols, and cognitive cues that cast issues in a particular light and suggest possible ways to respond to these issues" (Davis et al., 2005, pp. 48–49). A complication in the process of constructing frames is that frames attractive to one audience are likely to be rejected by other audiences, as we have recently seen with the slogan "Black lives matter." Movement activists are particularly concerned about the impact of the mass media on their *conscience constituency*—people attracted to the movement because it appears just and worthy, not because they will benefit personally. The students at Harvard gave serious thought to whether a sit-in demonstration would cause them to lose some support for their cause. They also were aware that they could face repercussions, such as being expelled from the university.

Activists desire media attention because that is the most effective way to reach wide audiences, but they also know they cannot control the way the movement will be framed by the mass media. That is why some social movement scholars see so much promise in the use of the Internet and wireless communication technology that allow participants to control their own messages. The mass media are attracted to dramatic, even violent, aspects of a movement, but these aspects are likely to be rejected by other audiences (Stein, 2009). They are often more interested in scandal than in providing substantive information on movement issues (della Porta & Diani, 2006). Successful social movements must always contend with the likelihood that successful advocacy will lead to a conservative backlash and countermovement.

Social movement framing is never a matter of easy consensus building, and intense *framing contests* may arise among a variety of actors, particularly in the later stages. Representatives of the political system and participants in countermovements influence framing through their own actions and public statements, and internal conflicts may become more pronounced. Leaders and followers often have different frames for the movement (Marx & McAdam, 1994), and there are often splits between moderate and radical participants. It is not at all unusual for movements to put forth multiple frames, with different groups sponsoring different frames. When a movement captures mass media attention, there is often an intense struggle over who speaks for the movement and which cultural frame is put forward.

Frames for Understanding That a Problem Exists

Social movements are actively involved in the "naming" of grievances and injustices. They do so in part by drawing on existing cultural symbols, but they also underscore, accentuate, and enlarge current understanding of the seriousness of a situation. In essence, they call attention to contradictions between cultural ideals and cultural realities. For example, the living wage movement calls attention to the discrepancy between working and receiving a wage that does not allow a person to rise out of poverty. Calling attention to this discrepancy is important in the United States, where the public tends to believe that people are poor because they don't work.

In the United States, movement frames are often articulated in terms of rights—civil rights, disability rights, GLBT rights, animal rights, children's rights. In Europe, where there is less emphasis on individual liberty, rights frames are far less common in social movements (Hastings, 1998; Tarrow, 1998). Recently, equality has been a powerful frame in the United States: "We are the 99%" and "Marriage equality." In the past 2 decades, fundamentalist religious movements have sprung up in many countries, including the United States. These movements have used morality frames, focusing on good and evil rather than justice versus injustice. Compared with Europe, the United States has historically produced a high number of such movements (Marx & McAdam, 1994). Prohibition, abolition, anticommunism, and antiabortionism have all had religious roots.

Frames for Recognizing a Window of Opportunity

The perception of opportunity to change a troublesome situation is also culturally framed, to some extent (Castells, 2012; della Porta & Diani, 2006). On occasion, it is easy to develop a shared frame that opportunity exists or does not exist, but most situations are more ambiguous. Social movement leaders must successfully construct a perception that change is possible, because an opportunity does not exist unless it is recognized. They typically attempt to overcome concerns about the dangers and futility of activism by focusing on the risks of inaction, communicating a sense of urgency, and emphasizing the openness of the moment. They are intent on keeping hope alive.

Calibrating this type of frame is a difficult task. On the one hand, overstating an opportunity can be hazardous. Without "fortifying myths," which allow participants to see defeats as mere setbacks, unrealistically high expectations can degenerate into pessimism about possibilities for change (Voss, 1996). On the other hand, "movement activists systematically overestimate the degree of political opportunity, and if they did not, they would not be doing their job wisely" (Gamson & Meyer, 1996, p. 285). Unrealistic perceptions about what is possible can actually make change *more* possible. The Harvard students were not happy with the size of the worker raise that came out of their sit-in, but their expectations led them to bold action, which brought some improvements in the lives of workers and has been an inspiration for students at other universities around the country.

Frames for Establishing Goals

Once it has been established that both problem and opportunity exist, the question of social movement goals arises. Is change to be narrow or sweeping, reformist or revolutionary? Will the emphasis be on providing opportunities for individual self-expression or on changing the social order? U.S. social movements have generally set goals that are more reformist than revolutionary (Marx & McAdam, 1994).

Typically, goals are poorly articulated in the early stages of a movement but are clarified through ongoing negotiations about the desired changes. Both the Occupy movement and the Black Lives Matter movement have been criticized for having no clear goal or goals, but George Lakoff (2011) aptly described the Occupy movement as a moral movement whose aim was to have an impact on the public discourse about democracy and economic justice. One could also suggest that the Black Lives Matter movement is serving an important role by reopening a recurring conversation about racial relations in the United States.

Manuals for social activism suggest that modest and winnable objectives in the early stages of a movement help to reinforce the possibility of change (Gamson & Meyer, 1996). Indeed, the early goals for the living wage movement were modest. The wage increase secured by

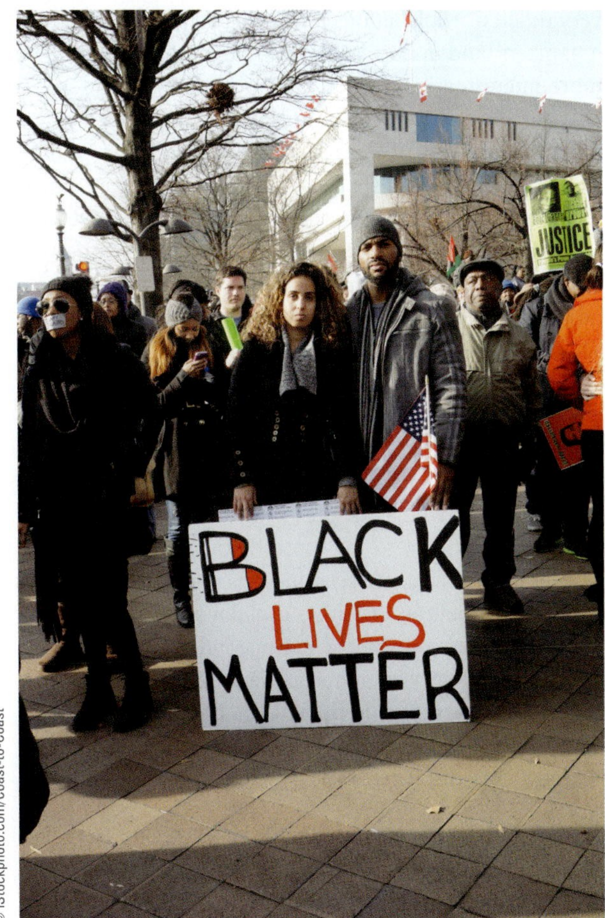

Although the Black Lives Matter movement has been criticized for having no clear goals, it is serving an important role by reopening a recurring conversation about racial relations in the United States.

BUILD only covered 1,500 to 2,000 workers. By 2001, it was estimated that the combined efforts of all local living wage campaigns had brought the number to only about 100,000 workers. Some progressives were critical of a movement that was yielding so little, but other analysts argued that it was the modest and winnable nature of the early campaigns that neutralized opposition and built a momentum of success (Murray, 2001). Certainly, it is true that the movement has become more ambitious in its goals over time, moving from improving the wages of a small number of municipal contract workers to large-scale, city-wide ordinances, as well as to statewide minimum wage laws. Likewise, the European activists' demands that all garment workers in retail supply chains be paid a living wage would have far-reaching results across national lines (Clean Clothes Campaign, 2009).

Frames for Identifying Pathways for Action

Some of the most important framing efforts of a social movement involve tactical choices for accomplishing goals. Social movement scholars generally agree that each society has a repertoire of forms of collective action that are familiar to social movement participants as well as the elites they challenge (Tarrow, 2006). New forms are introduced from time to time, and they spread quickly if they are successful. The sit-down strike is no longer as common as it once was, but occupying a physical space over time has been a hallmark of recent social movements. Contemporary social movements draw power from the large selection of forms of collective action currently in the cultural stock, and many movements have wisely used multiple forms of action (della Porta & Diani, 2006; Tarrow, 2006). As noted in Case Study 9.2, the living wage movement has made use of lobbying, postcard campaigns, door-knocking campaigns, leafleting, rallies, sit-ins, workshops, newspaper ads, and advocacy videos.

Just as social movement goals fall on a continuum from reform to revolution, forms of collective action can be arranged along a continuum from conventional to violent. Nonviolent forms of collective action are the core of contemporary U.S. movements, and nonviolence as a way of life was a cornerstone of the camp sites of the Occupy movement. Nonviolent disruption of routine activities is today considered the most powerful form of activism in the United States and in other Western democracies with relatively stable governments (della Porta & Diani, 2006). The power of nonviolent disruption is that it creates uncertainty and some fear of violence yet provides authorities in democratic societies with no valid argument for repression. Violent collective action, on the other hand, usually destroys public support for the movement. Martin Luther King was ingenious in recognizing that the best path for the U.S. civil rights movement was "successfully courting violence while restraining violence in his followers" (McAdam, 1996b, p. 349). Consequently, it was the police who lost public favor for their brutality, not the demonstrators.

Some action forms, such as marches, petitions, and Net strikes, are used to demonstrate numerical strength. Other action forms, such as conferences, concerts, documentaries, and "buycotts" of fair products, are used to bear witness to the substantive issues. Still other action forms are designed to do damage to the parties reputed to be to blame for an unfair situation, but violent action forms run the risk of escalating repression and alienating sympathizers.

EMERGING PERSPECTIVES

Some social movement scholars have suggested that the three dominant perspectives discussed—political opportunities, mobilizing structures, and cultural framing—fail to attend to some important dimensions of social movements. Two emerging perspectives are discussed here.

First, a few social movements scholars are arguing that social movement researchers should take another look at the role of emotions in motivating people to participate in social movement activities. They contend that the social movement literature has fallen short by attending to rationality but not emotions of movement participants. Drawing on recent neuroscience research about the role of emotion in human behavior, Manuel Castells (2012) theorizes that the energy of a social movement "starts with the transformation of emotion into action" (p. 13). He suggests that anger is the triggering emotion in social activism, and extreme anger or outrage helps to override fear of the consequences of action. Enthusiasm and hope, which are generated in social interaction, also play an important role in overriding the fear of activism. Visual images are powerful stimulants of both anger and hope. Deborah Gould (2004) applauds the rejection of earlier attempts to understand social movement actors in terms of psychopathologies but suggests that social movements are passionate political processes and emotions must be considered. She proposes that social movement researchers should study the role that emotions such as anger, indignation, hope, and pride play in motivating social movement involvement.

When reconsidering the living wage campaign, it seems that these scholars have a point. Certainly, it appears that Greg Halpern was touched emotionally as well as intellectually by the stories he heard from workers at Harvard. The divinity students who participated in the vigil chanted, "Where's your horror? Where's your rage?" Perhaps they were thinking that such strong emotions move people to action. We know that the religious leaders who started the action in Baltimore were angry at the plight of the working poor. This raises an important question for social movement leaders: Should they appeal to both emotional and intellectual understandings of injustice? If so, what are the best methods to do this?

Second, Richard Flacks (2004) suggests that the literature on resource mobilization has failed to consider the fundamental differences in the way different members participate in social movements. He asserts that there may be very different explanations for the participation of leaders, organizers, and mass participants. He thinks we should be more interested in why some people come to see societal change as a major priority in their lives whereas others don't and suggests that social movement scholars should study the biographies of activists to learn more about that. Studs Terkel was an activist, not a social movement scholar, but he was interested in exactly the same question that Flacks raises. For Terkel's (2003) book *Hope Dies Last*, he interviewed 55 activists about what motivated them to activism. As the title of the book indicates, he found hope to be a major motivator.

From another perspective, Robert Putnam (2000) notes that many people are participating at a very superficial level in contemporary social movements, responding to direct mail campaigns with a one-time contribution but making no greater commitment to the cause. Putnam argues that this type of involvement in social movements fails to build the social capital built in grassroots coalitions like those driving the living wage movement. There are, indeed, different ways to participate in social movements, and social movement leaders need to understand the different motivations involved.

CRITICAL THINKING Questions 9.5

Think of a social justice issue about which you have some passion. What existing networks might be available to organize change efforts regarding the issue? What are two or three cultural frames that would motivate people to engage in collective action on the issue? How important do you think emotions are in motivating people to participate in social movement activity? How important are social movements in the search for social justice?

IMPLICATIONS FOR SOCIAL WORK PRACTICE

The trends in social institutions and social structure, as well as the literature on social movements discussed in this chapter, suggest several principles for social work practice. These practice principles have the greatest relevance for social work planning and administration, but some are relevant for direct social work practice as well.

- Develop adequate information retrieval skills to keep abreast of trends in the interrelated social institutions and the impact of these trends on human interdependence and dependence.
- Monitor the impact of public policies on poverty and inequality.
- Be particularly aware of the impact of trends in the economic institution on client resources and functioning.

- Collaborate with other social workers and human service providers to advocate for greater equality of opportunity in the educational institution.
- Work to ensure that the voices of poor and other oppressed people are included in ongoing public dialogue about health care reform.
- Consider the extent to which contemporary social welfare programs, especially those with which you are personally involved, are responsive to recent changes in the other major social institutions.
- Be aware of the role religious organizations play in social service delivery and the role religion plays in the lives of clients.
- Collaborate with other social workers and human service providers to influence media coverage of vulnerable populations and patterns of social inequality.
- Become skillful in assessing political opportunities for social reform efforts.
- Become skillful in recognizing and mobilizing formal and informal networks for social reform activities.
- Become skillful in developing cultural frames that legitimate and motivate collective action.

KEY TERMS

colonialism, 272
conservative thesis, 288
countermovement, 292
critical consciousness, 289
cultural framing (CF) perspective, 295
economic institution, 274
educational institution, 277
Gini index, 269
government and political institution, 271
health care institution, 280
mass media institution, 286
mobilizing structures (MS) perspective, 293
neocolonialism, 272
neoliberal philosophy, 273
political opportunities (PO) perspective, 290
radical antithesis, 288
religious institution, 284
role, 268
social class, 287
social institution, 268
social movements, 289
social structure, 268
social welfare institution, 282
status, 268

ACTIVE LEARNING

1. We have looked at the conservative thesis and the radical antithesis in an ongoing debate about the role of inequality in social life. Talk to one classmate about this issue, asking each other the following questions:
   - Is inequality a good thing for a society? If not, why not? If so, in what way, and good for whom?
   - If we accept inequality as inevitable, how much is necessary? Should society try to maximize or minimize the amount of inequality?
   - On what criteria should we measure inequality?
   - If we seek equality, is it equality of opportunity or of outcomes?
   - How do you think members of your family would answer these questions? Your friends? Do you think you would find more support for the conservative thesis or the radical antithesis among your family and friends? How do these people support their arguments for the positions they take?
2. In this chapter, I suggested that successful social movements often open the way for countermovements. I also suggested that social movements may be either proactive or reactive. In considering these ideas, it is helpful to look at two social movements that hold competing views on issues related to women. Go to the websites of the National Organization for Women (NOW) at www.now.org and the National Right to Life Committee (NRLC) at www.nrlc.org. Study carefully the positions that each of these social movement organizations takes on the issue of abortion. What language and symbols does each organization use for framing the issue?
3. *Theory analysis and application.* It might be said that the content on social structure, social institutions, and social movements found in this chapter best reflects the conflict perspective discussed in Chapter 2. Working in small groups, review the big ideas of the conflict perspective presented in Exhibit 2.9. Giving specific examples, discuss how these big ideas are reflected, or not, in this discussion of social institutions, social structure, or social movements. Do you see big ideas from other perspectives, as presented in Exhibit 2.9, that are helpful for thinking about these social collectives? Explain.

WEB RESOURCES

Center for Responsive Politics

www.opensecrets.org

Site maintained by the nonpartisan Center for Responsive Politics contains information on major organizational and individual contributors, the money collected and spent by major political candidates, and political news and issues.

National Organizers Alliance (NOA)

www.noacentral.org

Site maintained by NOA, a nonprofit organization with the mission to advance progressive organizing for social, economic, environmental, and racial justice, contains information about national gatherings, a job bank, a newsletter, a calendar of events, and links to other activist organizations.

United Nations Children's Fund

www.unicef.org

Site contains cross-national information on the well-being of children.

U.S. Census Bureau

www.census.gov

Official site of the U.S. Census Bureau contains statistics on a wide variety of topics, including race and ethnicity, gender, education, birthrates, disabilities, and many other topics.

Wellstone

www.wellstone.org

Site maintained by the nonprofit Wellstone, devoted to progressive change and the training of young political organizers for progressive campaigns, contains information about training programs, internships, and jobs, as well as news and a blog.

World Health Organization (WHO)

www.who.int

Site contains information on the health and the health care institutions of countries around the world.

SAGE edge™ **Sharpen your skills with SAGE edge at edge.sagepub.com/hutchisoness2e**

SAGE edge for students provides a personalized approach to help you accomplish your coursework goals in an easy-to-use learning environment. watch listen read

LEARNING OBJECTIVES	FOR FURTHER EXPLORATION AND APPLICATION
LO 9.1: Compare and contrast one's emotional and cognitive reactions to two case studies.	(listen) Basic Income: An Antipoverty Strategy for Social Work
LO 9.2: Recognize national and global trends in seven major social institutions (government and political, economic, education, health care, social welfare, religious, and mass media).	(read) Five Global Health Trends You Just Can't Ignore (watch) Poor Kids (read) Neoliberal Education Reform and the Perpetuation of Inequality
LO 9.3: Analyze different theories of social inequality.	(read) Global Inequality and Wealth (read) What Explains Inequality?
LO 9.4: Define social movements.	(watch) Social Movements
LO 9.5: Compare and contrast three theoretical perspectives on social movements (political opportunities, mobilizing structures, and cultural framing).	(read) Social Movements (read) We've Been Framed! A Focus on Identity and Interaction for a Better Vision of Racialized Social Movements
LO 9.6: Apply knowledge of social institutions, social structure, and social movements to recommend guidelines for social work assessment and intervention.	(watch) Change the World, Join a Movement (listen) Modern Slavery: Social Work's Role in Addressing Human Trafficking

The Changing Life Course

"How old are you?" You have probably been asked that question many times, and no doubt you find yourself curious about the age of new acquaintances. Every society appears to use age as an important variable, and many social institutions in advanced industrial societies are organized, in part, around age—the age for starting school, the age of majority, retirement age, and so on. In the United States, our speech abounds with expressions related to age: "terrible 2s," "sweet 16," "20-something," "life begins at 40," "senior discounts," and lately "60 is the new 40." This interest in how humans change and stay the same across time is one important way that behavioral scientists introduce the idea of time into the understanding of person and environment.

We have chosen a life course perspective to capture the dynamic, changing nature of person–environment transactions. In the life course perspective, human behavior is not a linear march through time, nor is it simply played out in recurring cycles. Rather, the life course journey is a moving spiral, with both continuity and change, marked by both predictable and unpredictable twists and turns. It is influenced by changes in the physical and social environment as well as by changes in the personal biological, psychological, and spiritual dimensions.

The life course perspective recognizes *patterns* in human behavior related to biological age, psychological age, and social age norms. The life course perspective also recognizes *diversity* in the life course related to historical time, gender, race, ethnicity, social class, and so forth, and we emphasize group-based diversity in our discussion of age-graded periods. Finally, the life course perspective recognizes the *unique life stories* of individuals—the unique configuration of specific life events and person–environment transactions over time.

Chapter 10 provides an overview of current theory and research about the life course perspective. The remaining chapters of the book examine theory and research in relation to specific phases of the human life course. These chapters consider how the human life course is shaped by the constant interaction of persons and their environments. Chapter 11 examines the beginning of the life course journey, covering conception, pregnancy, childbirth, and infancy. Chapter 12 looks at toddlerhood and early childhood, Chapter 13 at middle childhood, Chapter 14 at adolescence, Chapter 15 at young and middle adulthood, and Chapter 16 at late adulthood.

CHALK TALKS
Watch via the
SAGE Interactive eBook

Created using Videoscribe,
http://www.videoscribe.co

The Human Life Journey

A Life Course Perspective

Elizabeth D. Hutchison

Learning Objectives

LO 10.1 Compare and contrast one's emotional and cognitive reactions to three case studies.

LO 10.2 List important words in the definition of the life course perspective.

LO 10.3 Identify some of the theoretical roots of the life course perspective.

LO 10.4 Summarize five basic concepts of the life course perspective (cohorts, transitions, trajectories, life events, and turning points).

LO 10.5 Critique six major themes of the life course perspective (interplay of human lives and historical time, timing of lives, linked or interdependent lives, human agency in making choices, diversity in life course trajectories, and developmental risk and protection).

LO 10.6 Demonstrate use of the family life course perspective to understand three case studies.

LO 10.7 Evaluate the strengths and limitations of the life course perspective.

LO 10.8 Recognize where themes of the life course perspective are consistent with eight major theoretical perspectives on human behavior discussed in earlier chapters.

LO 10.9 Apply basic concepts and major themes of the life course perspective to recommend guidelines for social work assessment and intervention.

GET MORE OUT OF YOUR STUDY TIME.

The **SAGE Interactive eBook** provides one-click access to integrated study tools that will enrich your understanding of course content.

- **Watch** video clips to learn actively
- **Think Critically** with SAGE Journals
- **Explore Further** with SAGE Reference
- **Connect** with relevant web resources
- **Listen** to podcasts for real-world context

CASE STUDY 10.1

DAVID SANCHEZ'S SEARCH FOR CONNECTIONS

David Sanchez has a Hispanic name, but he is a member of the Navajo tribe. He was raised by his maternal grandmother after his father was killed in a car accident when David was 7. His mother had been very ill since his birth and was too overwhelmed by her husband's death to take care of David. Just as David became attached to his grandmother, the Bureau of Indian Affairs (BIA) moved him to a boarding school. His hair was cut short with a tuft left at his forehead, which gave the teachers something to pull when he was being reprimanded.

Like most American Indian children, David suffered this harshness in silence. But, for some time, he has felt that it is important to break this silence. He has told his grandchildren about having his mouth washed out with soap for speaking Navajo. He jokes that he has been baptized in four different religions—Mormon, Catholic, Lutheran, and Episcopalian—because these were the religious groups running the boarding schools he attended. He also remembers the harsh beatings for not studying, or for committing other small infractions, before the BIA changed its policies for boarding homes and the harsh beatings diminished. David often spent holidays at the school, because his grandmother had no money for transportation. He remembers feeling so alone. When he did visit his grandmother, he realized he was forgetting his Navajo and saw that she was aging quickly.

David joined the Marines when he was 18, like many high school graduates of that era, and his grandmother could not understand why he wanted to join the "White man's war." David now recognizes why his grandmother questioned his decision to go to war. During his alcohol treatments, especially during the use of the Native sweat lodge, he often relived the horrible memories of the bombings and killings in Vietnam; these were the memories he spent his young adult life trying to silence with his alcohol abuse. Like many veterans, he ended up on the streets, homeless, seeking only the numbness his alcoholism provided. But the memories were always there. Sometimes his memories of the children in the Vietnam villages reminded him of the children from the boarding schools who had been so scared; some of the Vietnamese children even looked like his Native American friends. David receives a disability check for a partial disability from the war.

David has spent most of his life in New Mexico, but about a decade ago, he began to make trips to Los Angeles to visit his son, Marco, and his family. During these visits, David started to recognize how much his years of alcohol abuse hurt his son. After Mrs. Sanchez divorced David, he could never be relied on to visit Marco or to provide child support. Now that Marco has his own family, David hopes that by teaching his grandchildren the ways of the Navajo, he will pay Marco back a little for neglecting him. During visits, David began to talk about his own childhood, and Marco realized how much his father suffered as a child. After several visits, Marco asked David to teach him and his son how to speak Navajo. This gesture broke down some of the bad feelings between them.

During one of his trips to Los Angeles, David was taken to the emergency room and then hospitalized for what turned out to be a diabetic coma. He had been aware of losing weight during the past year, and felt ill at times, but thought these symptoms were just signs of getting older or perhaps the vestiges of his alcoholism from the ages of 20 to 43. Now in his early 60s and sober for the last 7 years, he was never surprised when his body reminded him how he had abused it. The social worker at the Los Angeles hospital helped David make plans to return to New Mexico and receive services at the local Veterans Administration (VA) hospital outpatient clinic. He had not been back to the VA since his rehabilitation from alcohol abuse, and he was happy to find that the social worker he had known during his rehabilitation was now working in the outpatient clinic.

It was through the Native American medicine retreats during David's rehabilitation that he began to touch a softer reality.

He began to believe in a higher order again. Although his father's funeral had been confusing, David experienced his grandmother's funeral in a more spiritual way. It was as if she was there guiding him to enter his new role. David now realizes this was a turning point in his life. At his grandmother's funeral, David's great-uncle, a medicine man, asked him to come and live with him because he was getting too old to cut or carry wood. He also wanted to teach David age-old cures that would enable him to help others struggling with alcohol dependency, from Navajo as well as other tribes. Although David is still learning, his work with other alcoholics has been inspirational, and he finds he can make special connections to Vietnam veterans.

David recently attended a conference where one of the American Indian speakers talked about the transgenerational trauma that families experienced because of the horrible beatings children encountered at the boarding schools. David is thankful that his son has broken the cycle of alcoholism and did not face the physical abuse to which he was subjected. But he is sad that his son was depressed for many years as a teen and young man. Now, both he and Marco are working to heal their relationship. They draw on the meaning and strength of their cultural and spiritual rituals. David's new role as spiritual and cultural teacher in his family has provided him with respect he never anticipated. Finally he is able to use his grandmother's wise teachings and his healing apprenticeship with his great-uncle to help his immediate family and his tribe.

A social worker like the one who helped Mr. Sanchez with his discharge plans from the L.A. hospital must be aware that discharge planning involves one life transition that is a part of a larger life trajectory.

—Maria E. Zuniga

CASE STUDY 10.2

PHOUNG LE, SERVING FAMILY AND COMMUNITY

Le Thi Phoung, or Phoung Le as she is officially known in the United States, grew up in Saigon, South Vietnam, in the midst of war and upheaval. She has some fond memories of her first few years when Saigon was beautiful and peaceful. She loves to remember riding on her father's shoulders down the streets of Saigon on a warm day and shopping with her grandmother in the herb shops. But she also has chilling memories of the military presence on the streets, the devastation caused by war, and the persistent fear that pervaded her home.

Phoung, 57, got married at age 17 to a man chosen by her father. She smiles when she recounts the story of her future groom and his family coming to visit with the lacquered boxes full of betrothal gifts of nuts, teas, cake, and fruit. She admits that, at the time, she was not eager to marry and wondered why her father was doing this to her. But she is quick to add that her father made a wise choice, and her husband Hien is her best friend and is, as his name suggests, "nice, kind, and gentle." Their first child, a son, was born just before Phoung's 20th birthday, and Phoung reveled in being a mother.

Unfortunately, on Phoung's 20th birthday, April 30, 1975, life in Saigon turned horrific; that is the day that the North Vietnamese army overran Saigon. For Phoung and Hien, as well as for most people living in South Vietnam, just surviving became a daily struggle. Both Phoung's father and her father-in-law were in the South Vietnamese military and both were imprisoned by the Viet Cong for a few years. Both managed to escape and moved their families around until they were able to plan an escape from Vietnam by boat. Family members got separated during the escape, and some were lost when pirates attacked their boats. Phoung's father and one brother have never been heard from since the pirate attack.

Phoung and Hien and their son spent more than 2 years in a refugee camp in Thailand before being resettled in Southern California. Their second child, a daughter, was born in the camp, and a second daughter was born 1 year after they resettled in California. Over time, other family members were able to join them in the large Vietnamese community where they live. Phoung's and Hien's opportunities for education were limited during the war years, but both came from families who valued education, and both managed to receive several years of schooling. Luckily, because they were living in a large Vietnamese community, language did not serve as a major barrier to employment in the United States. Phoung found a job working evenings as a waitress at a restaurant in Little Saigon, and Hien worked two jobs, by day as a dishwasher in a restaurant and by night cleaning office buildings in Little Saigon. Phoung's mother lived with Phoung and Hien and watched after the children while Phoung and Hien worked. Hien's parents lived a few blocks away, and several siblings and cousins of both Phoung and Hien were in the neighborhood. The Vietnamese community provided much social support and cultural connection. Phoung loved taking

(Continued)

(Continued)

the children to visit the shops in Little Saigon and found special pleasure in visiting the herb shops where the old men sat around and spoke animatedly in Vietnamese.

Phoung grieved the loss of her beloved father and brother, but she wanted to create a positive life for her children. She was happy that she was able to stay connected to her cultural roots and happy that her children lived in a neighborhood where they did not feel like outsiders. But she also wanted her children to be able to be successful outside the Vietnamese community as well as a resource for the community. She was determined that her children would have the education that she and Hien had been denied. Although she could have gotten by well in her neighborhood without English, she studied English along with her children because she wanted to model for the children how to live a bilingual, bicultural life. She was pleased that the children did well in school and was not surprised at how quickly the older two adapted to life in their adopted country. Sometimes there was tension in the multigenerational family about how the children were acculturating, and Phoung often served as the mediator in these tensions. She understood the desire of the older generation to keep cultural traditions, and she herself loved traditions such as the celebration of the Chinese New Year, with the colorful dresses and the little red lai-see envelopes of good luck money that were given to the children. She wanted her children to have these traditional experiences. But she also was tuned in to the children's desire to be connected with some aspects of the dominant culture, such as the music and other popular media. She was also aware of how hard it was for the family elders to enforce the traditional family hierarchy when they were dependent on younger family members to help them navigate life in the English-speaking world outside their cultural enclave.

When her children reached adolescence, Phoung herself was uncomfortable with the Western cultural ideal for adolescent independence from the family, but she found ways to give her children some space while also holding them close and keeping them connected to their cultural roots. Other mothers in the neighborhood began to seek her advice about how to handle the challenging adolescent years. When her own adolescent children began to be impatient with the pervasive sadness they saw in their grandparents, Phoung suggested that they do some oral history with their grandparents. This turned out to be a therapeutic experience for all involved. The grandparents were able to sift through their lives in Vietnam and the years since, and give voice to all that had been lost, but also begin to recognize the strength it took to survive and their good fortune to be able to live among family and a community where much was familiar. The grandchildren were able to hear a part of their family narrative that they did not know because the family had preferred not to talk about it. Phoung was so pleased with this outcome that she asked to start a program of intergenerational dialogue at the Vietnamese Community Service Center. She thought that this might be one way to begin to heal the trauma in her community while also giving the younger generation a strong cultural identity as they struggled to live in a multicultural world. She continues to be an active force in that program, even though her own children are grown.

Their 40s and early 50s brought both great sorrow and great joy to Phoung and Hien. Within a 2-year period, Phoung's mother and Hien's mother and father died. Phoung and Hien became the family elders. They provided both economic and emotional support during times of family crisis, such as a sibling's cancer, a niece's untimely pregnancy, and a nephew's involvement with a neighborhood gang. But there was also great joy. Phoung was very good at her job and became the supervisor of the wait staff at the best restaurant in Little Saigon. Hien was able to buy his own herb shop. After attending the local community college, the children were all able to go on to university and do well. Their son became an engineer, the older daughter became a physician, and the younger daughter recently finished law school. Their son is now father to two young children, and Phoung finds great joy in being a grandmother. She is playing an important role in keeping the grandchildren connected to some Vietnamese traditions. Phoung finds this phase of life to be a time of balance in all areas of her life, and she is surprised and pleased to find renewed interest in spiritual growth through her Buddhist practices.

Phoung has come to talk to the social worker at the Vietnamese Community Services Center. Her younger daughter has recently informed Phoung that she is lesbian. Phoung says that she has struggled with this news and has not yet told Hien. She knows that the Vietnamese community does not engage in "gay bashing" the way some communities do, but she also knows that homosexuality carries some stigma in her Vietnamese community. She has done much soul searching as she tries to integrate what her daughter has told her. But she knows one thing: She loves her daughter very much and wants her daughter to feel loved and supported by her family and her community. Her daughter plans to march with a Vietnamese gay rights group in the upcoming Tet Celebration march and has asked Phoung to march with her. Phoung is trying to decide what to do. She has come to ask the social worker if the Community Services Center runs any groups for parents of gays and lesbians. If not, she wants to start one.

Social workers working with refugee families must be aware of the conditions that led these families to flee their home countries as well as the adjustments they have made upon resettlement.

CASE STUDY 10.3

THE SUAREZ FAMILY AFTER SEPTEMBER 11, 2001

Maria is a busy, active 16-year-old whose life was changed by the events of September 11, 2001. Her mother, Emma Suarez, worked at the World Trade Center and did not survive the attack.

Emma was born in Puerto Rico and came to the mainland to live in the South Bronx when she was 5, along with her parents, a younger brother, two sisters, and an older brother. Emma's father, Carlos, worked hard to make a living for his family, sometimes working as many as three jobs at once. After the children were all in school, Emma's mother, Rosa, began to work as a domestic worker in the homes of a few wealthy families in Manhattan.

Emma was a strong student from her first days in public school and was often at the top of her class. Her younger brother, Juan, and the sister closest to her in age, Carmen, also were good students, but they were never the star pupils that Emma was. The elder brother, Jesus, and sister, Aida, struggled in school from the time they came to the South Bronx, and both dropped out before they finished high school. Jesus has returned to Puerto Rico to live on the farm with his grandparents.

During her summer vacations from high school, Emma often cared for the children of some of the families for whom her mother worked. One employer was particularly impressed with Emma's quickness and pleasant temperament and took a special interest in her. She encouraged Emma to apply to colleges during her senior year in high school. Emma was accepted at City College and was planning to begin as a full-time student after high school graduation.

A month before Emma was to start school, however, her father had a stroke and was unable to return to work. Rosa and Aida rearranged their work schedules so that they could share the care of Carlos. Carmen had a husband and two young children of her own. Emma realized that she was now needed as an income earner. She took a position doing data entry in an office in the World Trade Center and took evening courses on a part-time basis. She was studying to be a teacher, because she loved learning and wanted to pass on that love to other students.

And then Emma found herself pregnant. She knew that Alejandro Padilla, a young man in one of her classes at school, was the father. Alejandro said that he was not ready to marry, however. Emma returned to work a month after Maria was born, but she did not return to school. At first, Rosa and Aida were not happy that Emma was pregnant with no plans to marry, but once Maria was born, they fell hopelessly in love with her. They were happy to share the care of Maria, along with Carlos, while Emma worked. Emma cared for Maria and Carlos in the evenings so that Rosa and Aida could work.

Maria was, indeed, an engaging baby, and she was thriving with the adoration of Rosa, Carlos, Aida, Juan, and Emma. Emma missed school, but she held on to her dreams to be a teacher someday.

On the morning of September 11, 2001, Emma left early for work at her job on the 84th floor of the south tower of the World Trade Center, because she was nearing a deadline on a big project. Aida was bathing Carlos when Carmen called about a plane hitting the World Trade Center. Aida called Emma's number, but did not get through to her.

The next few days, even weeks, are a blur to the Suarez family. Juan, Carmen, and Aida took turns going to the Family Assistance Center, but there was no news about Emma. At one point, because Juan was worried about Rosa, he brought her to the Red Cross Disaster Counseling Center where they met with a social worker who was specially trained for working in disaster situations. Rosa seemed to be near collapse.

Juan, Rosa, and Aida all missed a lot of work for a number of weeks, and the cash flow sometimes became problematic. They were blessed with the generosity of their Catholic parish, employers, neighbors, and a large extended family, however, and financial worries were not their greatest concerns at that time. They struggled to understand the horrific thing that happened to Emma, and although she didn't understand what had happened, Maria was aware of a great sadness in the household for several years. Emma's remains were never identified, but the Catholic parish helped the family plan a memorial service.

Maria is lucky to have such a close, loving family, and they have tried to give her a good life. She continues to live with Aida and Rosa. Juan has married and has two young children now, living around the corner from Aida and Rosa. Carlos died in 2011, 10 days before the 10-year anniversary of the 9/11 attacks. Carmen and her family also live nearby, and Maria has become close friends with Carmen's two daughters. She also has a special relationship with Carmen, who reminds her of the pictures she has seen of her mother.

Maria is a good student and hopes to attend college and study to be a teacher. She loves to hear stories about the mother she can't remember, and one of Rosa's favorite stories

(Continued)

(Continued)

is about how smart Emma was and what a great teacher she would have been. On Maria's 13th birthday, Rosa gave her the necklace that had been Emma's 13th birthday gift, and Maria wears it every day. Growing up in the Bronx, Maria has seen many television images of those airplane attacks at the World Trade Center. She was disturbed, however, by all of the media coverage at the time of the 10th anniversary of the attack. She began to think a lot about what her mother might have suffered before her death, and she had nightmares for several nights. She built a small memorial to her mother in the backyard and goes there to talk with her mother when she is feeling particularly sad or when good things happen.

A social worker doing disaster relief must be aware of the large impact that disasters have on the multigenerational family, both in the present and for years to come.

A DEFINITION OF THE LIFE COURSE PERSPECTIVE

One of the things that the stories of David Sanchez, Phoung Le, and the Suarez family have in common is that they unfolded over time, across multiple generations. We all have stories that unfold as we progress through life. A useful way to understand this relationship between time and human behavior is the **life course perspective**, which looks at how biological, psychological, and social factors act independently, cumulatively, and interactively to shape people's lives from conception to death, and across generations. Of course, time is only one dimension of human behavior; characteristics of the person and the environment in which the person lives also play a large part (see Exhibit 1.1 in Chapter 1 for a visual representation of person, environment, and time dimensions). But it is common and sensible to try to understand a person by looking at the way that person has developed throughout different periods of life.

The life course perspective puts equal value on individual agency and human connectedness; therefore, it serves as a good framework for social work's commitments to both the dignity and worth of the person as well as the importance of human relationships. The contributing authors and I draw on the best available evidence about the life course to assist you to develop and enhance expertise in serving people of all life stages. You could think of the life course as a path. But note that it is not a straight path; it is a path with both continuities and twists and turns. Certainly, we see twists and turns in the life stories of David Sanchez, Phoung Le, and Emma Suarez.

If you want to understand a person's life, you might begin with an **event history**, or the sequence of significant events, experiences, and transitions in a person's life from birth to death. An event history for David Sanchez might include suffering his father's death as a child, moving to live with his grandmother, being removed to a boarding school, fighting in the Vietnam War, getting married, becoming a father, divorcing, being treated for substance abuse, participating in medicine retreats, attending his grandmother's funeral, moving to live with his great-uncle, and reconnecting with Marco. Phoung Le's event history would most likely include observing a new military presence in the streets, getting married, becoming a mother, escaping from Saigon, time spent in a refugee camp, resettlement in California, family loss, and promotion at work. For young Maria Suarez, the events of September 11, 2001, will become a permanent part of her life story, even though she has no memory of that day. She looks forward to the time when she will realize her mother's dream of starting college.

You might also try to understand a person in terms of how that person's life has been synchronized with family members' lives across time. David Sanchez has begun to have a clearer understanding of his linkages to his great-uncle, father, son, and grandchildren. Phoung Le's and Maria Suarez's stories are thoroughly entwined with those of their multigenerational families.

Finally, you might view the life course in terms of how culture and social institutions shape the pattern of individual lives. David Sanchez's life course was shaped by cultural and institutional preferences for placing Native American children in boarding schools during middle childhood and adolescence and for recommending the military for youth and young adults. Phoung Le lives biculturally and has taught her children to do that as well. Maria Suarez's life course was changed forever by culture-related geopolitical conflict.

THEORETICAL ROOTS OF THE LIFE COURSE PERSPECTIVE

The life course perspective (LCP) is a theoretical model that has been emerging over the last 50 years, across several disciplines. Sociologists, anthropologists, social historians, demographers, epidemiologists, and psychologists—working independently and, more recently, collaboratively—have all helped to give it shape.

Glen Elder Jr., a sociologist, was one of the early authors to write about a life course perspective, and his

Chris Rank/Corbis Historical/Getty Images

The life course perspective emphasizes ways in which humans are interdependent and gives special emphasis to the family as the primary arena from which to experience the world.

work is still foundational to the ongoing development of the perspective. In the early 1960s, he began to analyze data from three pioneering longitudinal studies of children that had been undertaken by the University of California, Berkeley. As he examined several decades of data, he was struck with the enormous impact of the Great Depression of the 1930s on individual and family pathways (Elder, 1974). He began to call for developmental theory and research that looked at the influence of historical forces on family, education, and work roles.

At about the same time, social history emerged as a serious field. Social historians were particularly interested in retrieving the experiences of ordinary people, from their own vantage point, rather than telling the historical story from the vantage point of wealthy and powerful persons. Tamara Hareven (1978, 1982a, 1996, 2000) played a key role in developing the subdiscipline of the history of the family.

As will become clearer later in the chapter, the life course perspective also draws on traditional theories of developmental psychology, which look at the events that typically occur in people's lives during different stages. The life course perspective differs from these psychological theories in one very important way, however. Developmental psychology looks for universal, predictable events and pathways, but the life course perspective calls attention to how historical time, social location, and culture affect the individual experience of each life stage.

The life course perspective is still relatively young, but its popularity has grown across a broad range of disciplines (Alwin, 2012). In recent years, it has begun to be used to understand the pathways of families (Min, Silverstein, & Lendon, 2012), organizations (King, 2009), and social movements (della Porta & Diani, 2006). I suggest that it has potential for understanding patterns of stability and change in all types of social systems. Gerontologists increasingly use the perspective to understand how old age is shaped by events experienced earlier in life (Seabrook & Avison, 2012), but it has also become an increasingly popular perspective for considering adolescent and young-adult transitions, such as the transition to high school (Benner, 2011) and the transition to motherhood (Black, Holditch-Davis, & Miles, 2009). LCP has become a major theoretical framework in criminology

(Chen, 2009; Schroeder, Giordano, & Cernkovich, 2010) and the leading perspective driving longitudinal study of health behaviors and outcomes (Bauldry, Shanahan, Boardman, Miech, & Macmillan, 2012; Evans, Crogan, Belyea, & Coon, 2009). It has been proposed as a useful perspective for understanding patterns of lifetime drug use (Hser, Longshore, & Anglin, 2007) and is a commonly used perspective for understanding the effects of childhood trauma on subsequent physical and mental health (Hovens et al., 2012; Lee, Tsenkova, & Carr, 2014).

CRITICAL THINKING Questions 10.1

Think of your own life path. How straight has your path been to date? What continuities can you identify? What, if any, twists and turns have been a part of your life journey to date?

BASIC CONCEPTS OF THE LIFE COURSE PERSPECTIVE

Scholars who write from a life course perspective and social workers who apply the life course perspective in their work rely on a handful of staple concepts: cohorts, transitions, trajectories, life events, and turning points (see Exhibit 10.1 for concise definitions). As you read about each concept, imagine how it applies to the lives of David Sanchez, Phoung Le, and Maria Suarez as well as to your own life.

EXHIBIT 10.1 • Basic Concepts of the Life Course Perspective

CONCEPT	DEFINITION
Cohort	Group of persons who were born during the same time period and who experience particular social changes within a given culture in the same sequence and at the same age
Transition	Change in roles and statuses that represents a distinct departure from prior roles and statuses
Trajectory	Long-term pattern of stability and change, which usually involves multiple transitions
Life event	Significant occurrence involving a relatively abrupt change that may produce serious and long-lasting effects
Turning point	Life event or transition that produces a lasting shift in the life course trajectory

COHORTS

As noted, Glen Elder Jr.'s observation that historical, sociocultural forces have an impact on individual and family pathways was a major inspiration for development of the life course perspective. With their attention to the historical context of developmental pathways, life course scholars have found the concept of a cohort to be very useful. In the life course perspective, a **cohort** is a group of persons who were born during the same time period and who experience particular social changes within a given culture in the same sequence and at approximately the same age (Bjorklund, 2011; D. Newman, 2012). *Generation* is another term used to convey a similar meaning. Generation is usually used to refer to a period of about 20 years, but a cohort may be shorter than that, and life course scholars often distinguish between the two terms, suggesting that a birth cohort becomes a generation only when it develops some shared sense of its social history and a shared identity (see Alwin, McCammon, & Hofer, 2006).

Cohorts differ in size, and these differences affect opportunities for education, work, and family life. For example, the baby boom that followed World War II (1946 to 1964) in the United States produced a large cohort. When this large cohort entered the labor force, surplus labor drove wages down and unemployment up (Pearlin & Skaff, 1996; Uhlenberg, 1996).

Some observers suggest that cohorts develop strategies for the special circumstances they face (K. Newman, 2008). They suggest that "boomers"—the large cohort born from 1946 to 1964—responded to the economic challenges of their demographic bubble by delaying or avoiding marriage, postponing childbearing, having fewer children, and increasing the presence of mothers in the labor force. However, one study found that large cohorts in affluent countries have higher rates of suicide than smaller cohorts, suggesting that not all members of large cohorts can find positive strategies for coping with competition for limited resources (Stockard & O'Brien, 2002). Other researchers have been interested in the adaptations of the millennial generation, born from 1980 to the late 1990s. The millennial generation is more ethnically diverse than previous cohorts and grew up in a time of great technological innovation. They have been found to be more tolerant of diversity and more media connected than earlier cohorts (Pew Research Center, 2010).

One way to visualize the configuration of cohorts in a given society is through the use of a **population pyramid**, a chart that depicts the proportion of the population in each age group. As Exhibit 10.2 demonstrates, different regions of the world have significantly different population pyramids. The first pyramid shows that affluent countries in the Global North have both low birth rates and low death rates. The populations are getting older in these societies, with a declining youthful population. These countries are becoming increasingly dependent on immigration (typically more attractive to young adults) for a workforce and taxpayers to support the aging population. It is predicted that 82% of the projected U.S. population increase from 2005 to 2050 will be the result of immigration (Passel & Cohn, 2008). Despite the economic necessity of immigrants in societies with aging populations, in the United States, as in many other affluent countries, there are strong anti-immigrant sentiments and angry calls to close the borders.

The second pyramid in Exhibit 10.2 shows that less affluent countries in the Global South have high birth rates and shorter life expectancy, leading to a situation in which the majority of people are young. In these countries, young people tend to overwhelm labor markets and education systems, and national standards of living decline. Some of these countries, such as the Philippines, have developed policies that encourage out-migration, whereas other countries, such as China, have developed policies to limit fertility.

Exhibit 10.2 also shows the ratio of males to females in each population. A cohort's **sex ratio** is the number of males per 100 females. Sex ratios affect a cohort's marriage rates, childbearing practices, crime rates, and family stability. Although there are many challenges to getting reliable sex ratio data, it is estimated that there are 105 males born for every 100 females in the world (Central Intelligence Agency, 2013c). However, several countries have a sex ratio at birth of more than 110 males per 100 females. It is thought that high sex ratios at birth represent a kind of sex discrimination in some countries, where it might be attributed to sex-selected abortion and infanticide. As you can see in Exhibit 10.2, sex ratios decline across adulthood because males die at higher rates at every age. Sex ratios can be further unbalanced by war (which leads to greater male mortality) or death at childbirth (which leads to greater female mortality) or to high rates of either male or female out-migration or in-migration.

TRANSITIONS

A life course perspective is stagelike because it proposes that each person experiences a number of **transitions**, or changes in roles and statuses that represent a distinct departure from prior roles and statuses (Andrew & Ruel, 2010; Black et al., 2009). Life is full of such transitions: starting school, entering puberty, leaving school, getting a first job, leaving home, migrating, retiring, and so on. Leaving his grandmother's home for boarding school and enrolling in the military were important transitions for David Sanchez. Phoung Le has experienced a number of transitions, including the beginning of war, becoming a mother, escaping, moving to a refugee camp, and resettling in California. A transition is a process of gradual change that usually involves acquiring or relinquishing roles, but it can be any change in status, such as a change in health status (Andrew & Ruel, 2010). A transition can produce both stress and opportunity (Benner, 2011).

EXHIBIT 10.2 • Population Pyramids by Level of Affluence, 2010

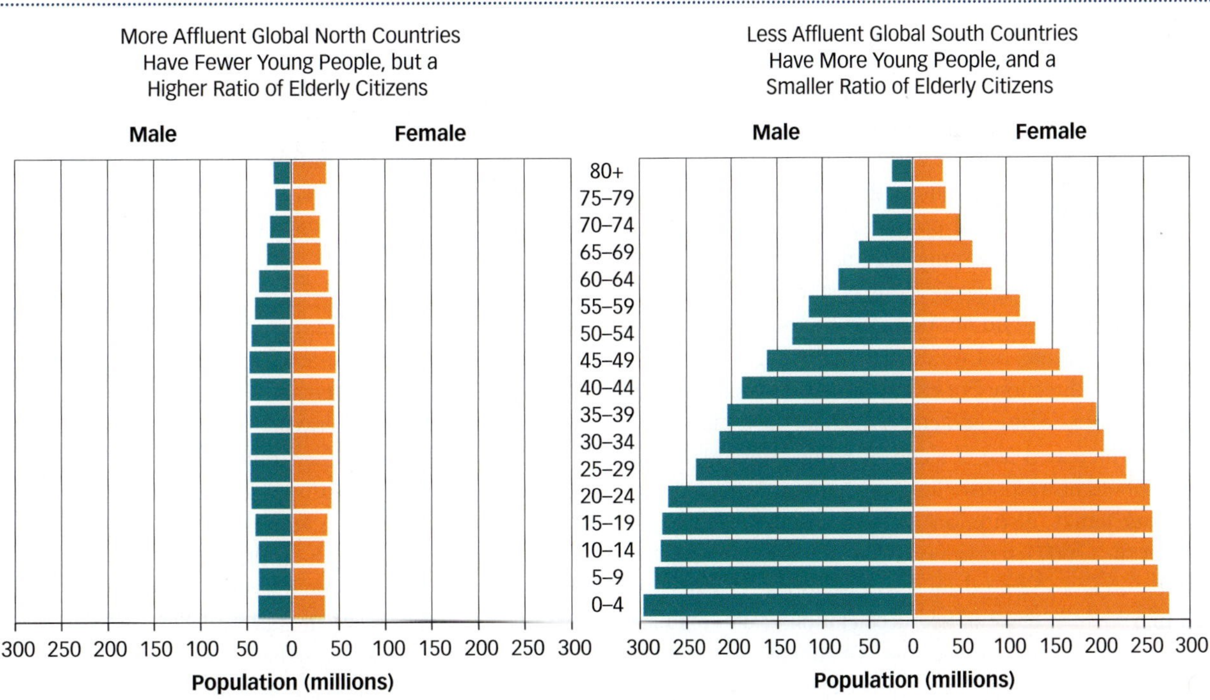

SOURCE: PRB Staff, "World Population Highlights: Key Findings From PRB's 2009 World Population Data Sheet," *Population Bulletin 64*, no. 3 (2009).

© iStockphoto.com/PeopleImages

The life course is full of transitions in roles and statuses; graduation from college or university is an important life transition that opens opportunities for future statuses and roles.

Transitions in the family as well as in collectivities other than the family, such as small groups, communities, and formal organizations, involve exits and entrances of members as well as changes in statuses and roles. In college, for example, students pass through in a steady stream. Some of them make the transition from undergraduate to graduate student, and in that new status they may take on the new role of teaching or research assistant.

TRAJECTORIES

Each life course transition is embedded in a trajectory that gives form to the life course (Alwin, 2012). They are entry points to a new life phase. In contrast with transitions, **trajectories** involve a longer view of long-term patterns of stability and change in a person's life, involving multiple transitions. For example, you may look forward to graduating from your program of social work study. Graduation is a transition, but it is a transition that will be embedded in a career trajectory that will probably involve a number of other transitions along the way, such as a licensing exam, job changes, promotions, and perhaps periods of discontent or burnout. At some point, you may look back on your career path and see some patterns that at the moment you can't anticipate. Trajectories are best understood in the rearview mirror. We do not necessarily expect trajectories to be a straight line, but we do expect them to have some continuity of direction. For example, we assume that once David Sanchez became addicted to alcohol, he set forth on a path of increased use of alcohol and deteriorating ability to uphold his responsibilities, with multiple transitions involving family disruption and job instability. Indeed, Hser et al. (2007) recommend the life course perspective for understanding drug use trajectories (or careers) that may include onset of use, acceleration of use, regular use, cessation of use, and relapse. Treatment may or may not be included in this trajectory. Because individuals and families live in multiple spheres, their lives are made up of multiple, intertwined trajectories—such as educational trajectories, family life trajectories, health trajectories, and work trajectories (Benner, 2011). These strands are woven together to form a life story.

LIFE EVENTS

Specific events predominate in the stories of David Sanchez, Phoung Le, and Maria Suarez: death of a parent, escape from the homeland, terrorist attack. A **life event** is a significant occurrence involving a relatively abrupt change that may produce serious and long-lasting effects (Settersten, 2003). The term refers to the happening itself and not to the transitions that will occur because of the happening. For example, loss of a spouse is a relatively common life event in all societies. The death of the spouse is the life event, but it precipitates a transition that involves changes in roles and statuses. When we reflect on our own lives, most of us can quickly recall one or more major life events that had long-lasting impact.

One common method for evaluating the effect of life events is the use of a life events rating scale such as Thomas Holmes and Richard Rahe's Schedule of Recent Events, also called the Social Readjustment Rating Scale (Holmes, 1978; Holmes & Rahe, 1967). The Schedule of Recent Events, along with the rating of the stress associated with each event, appears in Exhibit 10.3. Holmes and Rahe constructed their schedule of events by asking respondents to rate the relative degree of adjustment required for different life events.

Inventories like the Schedule of Recent Events can remind us of some of the life events that affect human behavior and life course trajectories, but they also have limitations:

> Life events inventories are not finely tuned. One suggestion is to classify life events along several dimensions: major versus minor, anticipated versus unanticipated, controllable versus uncontrollable, typical versus atypical, desirable versus undesirable, acute versus chronic. (Settersten & Mayer, 1997, p. 246)

Most existing inventories are biased toward undesirable, rather than desirable, events. Not all life events prompt harmful life changes. Indeed, researchers have begun to distinguish between positive and negative life events and to measure their different impacts on human behavior (Brennan & Spencer, 2009; Garcia & Siddiqui, 2009; Ogden, Stavrinaki, & Stubbs, 2009). However, the preponderance of research on the impact of life events on human behavior focuses on the negative impact of negative life events, and researchers still find life events scales to be useful tools. Some researchers are trying to understand the mechanisms that link stressful life events with immune system pathology (Herberth et al., 2008). Other often researched topics include the role of negative life events

EXHIBIT 10.3 • Life Change Events From the Holmes and Rahe Schedule of Recent Events

LIFE EVENT	STRESS RATING
Death of a spouse	100
Divorce	73
Marital separation from mate	65
Detention in jail or other institutions	63
Death of a close family member	63
Major personal injury or illness	53
Marriage	50
Being fired at work	47
Marital reconciliation with mate	45
Retirement from work	45
Major change in the health or behavior of a family member	44
Pregnancy	40
Sexual difficulties	39
Gaining a new family member (e.g., through birth, adoption, elder moving in)	39
Major business readjustment (e.g., merger, reorganization, bankruptcy)	39
Major change in financial state (a lot worse off or a lot better off than usual)	38
Death of a close friend	37
Changing to a different line of work	36
Major change in the number of arguments with spouse (more or fewer)	35
Taking out a mortgage or loan for a major purchase	31
Foreclosure on a mortgage or loan	30
Major change in responsibilities at work (e.g., promotion, demotion, lateral transfer)	29
Son or daughter leaving home	29
Trouble with in-laws	29
Outstanding personal achievement	28
Wife beginning or ceasing work outside the home	26
Taking out a mortgage or loan for a lesser purchase (e.g., a car, TV, freezer)	26
Major change in sleeping habits (a lot more or a lot less sleep, or change in part of day when asleep)	25
Major change in number of family get-togethers (e.g., a lot more or a lot less than usual)	24
Major change in eating habits (a lot less food intake or very different meal hours or surroundings)	23
Vacation	20
Christmas	20
Minor violations of the law (e.g., traffic tickets, jaywalking, disturbing the peace)	20
Beginning or ceasing formal schooling	19
Major change in living conditions (e.g., building a new home, remodeling, deterioration of home or neighborhood)	19
Revision of personal habits (e.g., dress, manners, associations)	18
Trouble with the boss	17
Major change in working hours or conditions	16
Change in residence	15
Major change in usual type and/or amount of recreation	13
Major change in church activities (e.g., a lot more or a lot less than usual)	12
Major change in social activities (e.g., clubs, dancing, movies, visiting)	11
Change to a new school	5

SOURCE: Holmes, T. H., & Rahe, R. H. (1967). The social readjustment rating scale. *Journal of Psychosomatic Research, 11*(2), 213–218.

in depressive symptoms (Miklowitz & Johnson, 2009) and the impact of traumatic life events on mental health (Mongillo, Briggs-Gowan, Ford, & Carter, 2009). One research team found the Holmes-Rahe scale to be helpful in predicting suicide risk in a Madrid, Spain, sample (Blasco-Fontecilla et al., 2012). A Chinese research team used Zhang's life events scale and found death of a spouse and financial crisis to be associated with higher risk of cognitive impairment in older adults (Deng et al., 2012).

Specific life events have different meanings to various individuals and to various collectivities. Those distinctive meanings have not been measured in most research on life events (Hareven, 2000). In an effort to capture the meanings that people make of life events, researchers have used the approach of asking respondents to recall life events rather than using existing life events inventories (Garcia & Siddiqui, 2009). For life events inventories to be useful, they must include events commonly experienced by the respondents.

TURNING POINTS

David Sanchez describes becoming an apprentice medicine man as a turning point in his life. It would be interesting to ask Phoung Le whether she identifies any turning points in her life. Even though Maria Suarez was too young to think of September 11, 2001, as a turning point in her life, there is no doubt that the events of that day changed the course of her life. A **turning point** is a time when major change occurs in the life course trajectory. We sometimes call these "defining moments." The turning point may involve a transformation in how the person views the self in relation to the world and/or a transformation in how the person responds to risk and opportunity (Cappeliez, Beaupré, & Robitaille, 2008; Ferraro & Shippee, 2009). It serves as a lasting change and not just a temporary detour. As significant as they are to individuals' lives, turning points usually become obvious only as time passes (George, 2009).

The addition of the concept of turning point is an important way that the life course perspective departs from traditional developmental theory. According to traditional developmental theory, the developmental trajectory is more or less continuous, proceeding steadily from one phase to another. But life course trajectories are seldom so smooth and predictable. They involve many discontinuities, or sudden breaks, and some special life events become turning points that produce a lasting shift in the life course trajectory. Inertia tends to keep us on a particular trajectory, but turning points add twists and turns or even reversals to the life course. For example, we expect someone who is addicted to alcohol to continue to organize his or her life around that substance unless some event becomes a turning point for recovery (Hser et al., 2007).

One research team interviewed older adults aged 60 to 87 about perceived turning points in their lives and found that the most frequently reported turning points involved health and family. The perceived turning points occurred across the entire life course, but there was some clustering at midlife (ages 45–64), a period in which 32.2% of the reported turning points occurred (Cappeliez et al., 2008). Gender differences have been found in reported turning points in samples of young adults as well as samples of older adults, with women reporting more turning points in the family domain and men reporting more turning points in the work domain (Cappeliez et al., 2008; Rönkä et al., 2003). It is not clear whether this gender difference will be manifested in future cohorts if women's work trajectories continue to become more similar to men's. Researchers have studied the turning points that lead women to leave abusive relationships (Khaw & Hardesty, 2007) and the turning points in the caregiving careers of Mexican American women who care for older family members (Evans et al., 2009). This latter research identifies a "point of reckoning" turning point when the caregiver recognizes the need for extensive caregiving and reorganizes her life to accept responsibility for providing care.

Loss of a parent is not always a turning point, but when such a loss occurs early in life as it did with David Sanchez and Maria Suarez, it is often a turning point. Emma Suarez may not have thought of her decision to take a job in the World Trade Center as a turning point, because she could not foresee the events of September 11, 2001.

Most life course pathways include multiple turning points, some that send life trajectories off track and others that bring life trajectories back on track. David Sanchez's Vietnam experience seems to have gotten him off track, and his grandmother's death seems to have gotten him back on track. In fact, we could say that the intent of many social work interventions is to get life course trajectories back on track. We do this when we plan interventions to precipitate a turning point toward recovery for a client with an addiction. Or we may plan an intervention to help a deteriorating community reclaim its lost sense of community and spirit of pride. It is interesting to note that many social service organizations have taken "Turning Point" for their name.

CRITICAL THINKING Questions 10.2

Consider the life course story of either David Sanchez or Phoung Le. Based on the information you have, what do you think would be the chapter titles if David Sanchez wrote a book about his life? What would be the chapter titles if Phoung Le wrote about her life? How about a book about your own life to date? What would be the chapter titles of that book? Which show up more in the chapter titles: life transitions (changes in roles and statuses) or life events (significant happenings)?

EXHIBIT 10.4 • Major Themes of the Life Course Perspective

THEME	DESCRIPTION
Interplay of human lives and historical time	Individual and family development must be understood in historical context.
Timing of lives	Particular roles and behaviors are associated with particular age groups, based on biological age, psychological age, social age, and spiritual age.
Linked or interdependent lives	Human lives are interdependent, and the family is the primary arena for experiencing and interpreting wider historical, cultural, and social phenomena.
Human agency in making choices	The individual life course is constructed by the choices and actions individuals take within the opportunities and constraints of history and social circumstances.
Diversity in life course trajectories	There is much diversity in life course pathways as a result of, e.g., cohort variations, social class, culture, gender, and individual agency.
Developmental risk and protection	Experiences with one life transition or life event have an impact on subsequent transitions and events and may either protect the life course trajectory or put it at risk.

MAJOR THEMES OF THE LIFE COURSE PERSPECTIVE

Two decades ago, Glen Elder Jr. (1994) identified four dominant, and interrelated, themes in the life course approach: interplay of human lives and historical time, timing of lives, linked or interdependent lives, and human agency in making choices. The meaning of these themes is discussed shortly, along with the meaning of two other related themes that Elder (1998) and Michael Shanahan (2000) have more recently identified as important: diversity in life course trajectories and developmental risk and protection. These six themes continue to be the framework for life course researchers across a number of disciplines, although different researchers emphasize different themes. The meaning of these themes is summarized in Exhibit 10.4.

INTERPLAY OF HUMAN LIVES AND HISTORICAL TIME

As sociologists and social historians began to study individual and family life trajectories, they noted that persons born in different years face different historical worlds, with different options and constraints—especially in rapidly changing societies, such as the United States at the beginning of the 21st century. They suggested that historical time may produce **cohort effects** when distinctive formative experiences are shared at the same point in the life course and have a lasting impact on a birth cohort (Alwin & McCammon, 2003). The same historical events may affect different cohorts in different ways. For example, Elder's (1974) research on children and the Great Depression found that the life course trajectories of the cohort who were young children at the time of the economic downturn were more seriously affected by family hardship than the cohort who were in middle childhood and late adolescence at the time. He also notes, however, that these young children were adolescents when fathers were fighting in World War II and mothers were often in the workplace. More recently, Australian researchers (Page, Milner, Morrell, & Taylor, 2013) found that the cohort born after 1970–1974 was more prone to suicide across the young-adult period than earlier cohorts. The researchers also found that this cohort faced higher rates of unemployment and underemployment as they entered young adulthood than earlier cohorts and propose a relationship between these two factors.

Analysis of large data sets by a number of researchers provides forceful evidence that changes in other social institutions impinge on family and individual life course trajectories (Vikat, Speder, Beets, Billari, & Buhler, 2007). Researchers have examined the impact of globalization, declining labor market opportunities, and rising housing costs on young-adult transitions (see K. Newman, 2008; Scherger, 2009). These researchers are finding that transitions associated with young adulthood (leaving the parental home, marriage, first parenthood) are occurring later for the current cohort of young adults than for their parents in many countries, particularly in countries with weak welfare states. The popular media in the United States has described the relationship between some parents and their millennial young adults as helicopter parents and landing pad kids, suggesting that the intense support offered by many parents to their adult offspring violates earlier norms of the young-adult transition. One research team found, however, that young adults who received such intense support reported better psychological adjustment and life satisfaction than young adults who did not receive such support. The parents were less satisfied with provision of intense support, however (Fingerman et al., 2013).

No doubt researchers will be studying the impact of the global economic recession that began in late 2007 on life course trajectories of different cohorts. Other aspects of the current historical era that will most likely generate life course research are the wars in Afghanistan and Iraq and the election of the first African American president of the United States.

Tamara Hareven's (2000) historical analysis of family life documents the lag between social change and the development of public policy to respond to the new circumstances and the needs that arise with social change. One such lag today in the United States is between trends in employment among mothers and public policy regarding child care during infancy and early childhood. Social work planners and administrators confront the results of such a lag in their work. Thus, they have some responsibility to keep the public informed about the impact of changing social conditions on individuals, families, communities, and formal organizations.

TIMING OF LIVES

Age is a prominent attribute in efforts by social scientists to bring order and predictability to our understanding of human behavior. Life course scholars are interested in the age at which specific life events and transitions occur, which they refer to as the timing of lives. They may classify entrances and exits from particular statuses and roles as "off-time" or "on-time," based on social norms or shared expectations about the timing of such transitions (McFarland, Pudrovska, Schieman, Ellison, & Bierman, 2013). For example, child labor and childbearing in adolescence are considered off-time in late industrial and postindustrial countries, but in much of the world such timing of roles is seen as a part of the natural order (Dannefer, 2003a, 2003b). One research team found that people who were diagnosed with cancer at earlier ages had a greater increase in religiosity than people diagnosed at later ages, suggesting that off-time transitions are more stressful or life changing than on-time transitions (McFarland et al., 2013). Survivors' grief is probably deeper in cases of "premature loss" (Pearlin & Skaff, 1996), which is perhaps why Emma Suarez's family continues to say, "She was so young; she had so much life left." Certainly, David Sanchez reacted differently to his father's and his grandmother's deaths.

Dimensions of Age

Chronological age itself is not the only factor involved in timing of lives. Age-graded differences in roles and behaviors are the result of biological, psychological, social, and spiritual processes. Thus, age is often considered from each of the perspectives that make up the biopsychosocial framework (Solomon, Helvitz, & Zerach, 2009). Although life course scholars have not directly addressed the issue of spiritual age, it is an important perspective as well.

Biological age indicates a person's level of biological development and physical health, as measured by the functioning of the various organ systems. It is the present position of the biological person in relation to the potential life cycle. There is no simple, straightforward way to measure biological age. One method is to compare an individual's physical condition with the conditions of others; for example, bone density scans are compared with the scans of a healthy 20-year-old.

Psychological age has both behavioral and perceptual components. Behaviorally, psychological age refers to the capacities that people have and the skills they use to adapt to changing biological and environmental demands. Skills in memory, learning, intelligence, motivation, emotions, and so forth are all involved (Bjorklund, 2011). Perceptually, psychological age is based on how old people perceive themselves to be. Life course researchers have explored the perceptual aspect of psychological age since the 1960s; recent research has referred to this perceptual aspect of age as "subjective age" or "age identity." The preponderance of research on subjective age has focused on older adults and found that older adults in Western societies feel younger than their chronological age (Stephan, Chalabaev, Kotter-Grühn, & Jaconelli, 2013). This has not been found to be the case among Chinese oldest old, but recent research finds that the percentage of China's oldest old reporting not feeling old has increased in the past decade (Liang, 2014). It is important to remember that, traditionally, Chinese culture has accorded high status to old age, but the traditions are weakening. A French research team found that a sample of older adults performed significantly better on a physical test when they were told that their earlier performance on the same test was better than 80% of the people their age; the improvement did not happen in the control group who did not receive this feedback (Stephan et al., 2013). Researchers in Switzerland found that older adults identify more strongly with their generation than with their specific age group and feel more positive about their generation identity than their age-group identity (Weiss & Lang, 2012). Young adults have been found to feel their same age or slightly older. Middle-aged and older adults' subjective age is related to their self-reported health, but that is not the case for younger adults (Stephan, Demulier, & Terracciano, 2012).

Social age refers to the age-graded roles and behaviors expected by society—in other words, the socially constructed meaning of various ages. The concept of **age norm** is used to indicate the behaviors expected of people of a specific age in a given society at a particular point in time. Age norms may be informal expectations, or they may be encoded as formal rules and laws. For example, cultures have an informal age norm about the appropriate age to leave the parental home. Conversely, many countries have developed formal rules about the appropriate age for driving, drinking alcohol, and voting. Life course scholars suggest that age norms vary not only across historical time and across societies but also by gender, race, ethnicity, and social class within a given time and society. They have paid particular attention to recent changes in age norms for the transitions of young adulthood (K. Newman, 2008; Scherger, 2009).

Although biological age and psychological age are recognized in the life course perspective, social age receives special emphasis. For instance, life course scholars use life phases such as middle childhood and middle adulthood, which are based in large part on social age, to conceptualize human lives from birth to death. Keep in mind, however, that the number and nature of these life phases are socially constructed and have changed over time, with modernization and mass longevity leading to finer gradations in life phases and consequently a greater number of them. Such fine gradations do not exist in most nonindustrial and newly industrializing countries (Dannefer, 2003a, 2003b).

Spiritual age indicates the current position of a person in the ongoing search for meaning, purpose, and moral relationships. David Sanchez is certainly at a different position in his search for life's meaning than he was when he came home from Vietnam. Although life course scholars have not paid much attention to spiritual age, it has been the subject of study by some developmental psychologists and other social scientists. In an exploration of the meaning of adulthood edited by Erik Erikson in 1978, several authors explored the markers of adulthood from the viewpoint of a number of spiritual and religious traditions, including Christianity, Hinduism, Islam, Buddhism, and Confucianism. Several themes emerged across the various traditions: contemplation, moral action, reason, self-discipline, character improvement, loving actions, and close community with others. All the authors noted that spirituality is typically seen as a process of growth, a process with no end.

James Fowler (1981) has presented a theory of faith development, based on 359 in-depth interviews, that strongly links it with chronological age. Ken Wilber's (2000a, 2001) integral theory of consciousness also proposes an association between age and spiritual development, but Wilber does not suggest that spiritual development is strictly linear. He notes, as do the contributors to the Erikson book, that there can be regressions, temporary leaps, and turning points in a person's spiritual development.

Standardization in the Timing of Lives

Life course scholars debate whether the trend is toward greater standardization in age-graded social roles and statuses or toward greater diversification (Brückner & Mayer, 2005; Scherger, 2009). Simone Scherger (2009) examined the timing of young-adult transitions (moving out of the parental home, marriage, becoming a parent) among 12 cohorts in West Germany. Cohorts of a 5-year range (e.g., born 1920–1924) were used for the analysis, beginning with the cohort born in 1920–1924 and ending with the cohort born in 1975–1979. This research indicated a trend toward destandardization. There was greater variability in the timing of transitions (moving out of the parental home, marriage, and becoming a parent) among the younger cohorts than among the older cohorts. Scherger also found the transitions were influenced by gender (men made the transitions later than women) and education level (higher education was associated with delay in the transitions). It is important to note, however, that another research team found that young-adult transitions have remained stable in the Nordic countries where strong welfare institutions provide generous supports for the young-adult transitions (K. Newman, 2008). The implication for social workers is that we must pay attention to the uniqueness of each person's life course trajectory, but we can use research about regularities in the timing of lives to inform social policy.

Many societies engage in **age structuring**, or standardizing of the ages at which social role transitions occur, by developing policies and laws that regulate the timing of these transitions. For example, in the United States there are laws and regulations about the ages for compulsory education, working (child labor), driving, drinking alcohol, being tried as an adult, marrying, holding public office, and receiving pensions and social insurance. However, countries vary considerably in the degree to which age norms are formalized (K. Newman, 2008). It is often noted that formal age structuring becomes more prevalent as nations modernize. European life course scholars suggest that U.S.-based life course scholars have underplayed the role of government in age structuring, suggesting that, in Europe, strong centralized governments play a larger role than in the United States in structuring the life course (Leisering, 2003; Marshall & Mueller, 2003). Indeed, there is evidence that life course pathways in Germany and Switzerland are more standardized than in the United States and Britain (Perrig-Chiello & Perren, 2005). There is also evidence that events and transitions in childhood and adolescence are much more age-normed and structured than in adulthood (Perrig-Chiello & Perren, 2005).

In spite of formal age structuring, as suggested earlier, there is much diversity in the sequencing and timing of adult life course markers, such as completing an education, beginning work, leaving home, marrying, and becoming a parent (K. Newman, 2008). An increasing number of students are delaying the entry into higher education (Roksa & Velez, 2012). The landscape of work is also changing, with less opportunity for continuous and stable employment, and this is creating greater diversity in work trajectories (Sweet & Meiksins, 2013). Life course trajectories also vary in significant ways by gender, race, ethnicity, and social class (Scherger, 2009). For example, although educational trajectories remain standardized for the most well-off, who move smoothly from secondary to higher education, they are less structured for other members of society (Roksa & Velez, 2012). Sources of diversity in life course perspectives are discussed later.

LINKED OR INTERDEPENDENT LIVES

The life course perspective emphasizes the interdependence of human lives and the ways in which people are reciprocally connected on several levels. It calls attention to how relationships both support and control an individual's behavior. *Social support*, which is defined as help rendered by others that benefits an individual or collectivity, is an obvious element of interdependent lives. Relationships also control behavior through expectations, rewards, and punishments. Social and behavioral scientists have paid particular attention to the family as a source of support and control. In addition, the lives of family members are linked across generations, with both opportunity and misfortune having an intergenerational impact. The cases of David Sanchez, Phoung Le, and Maria Suarez are rich examples of lives linked across generations. But they are also rich examples of how people's lives are linked with those of people outside the family.

Links Between Family Members

Certainly, parents' and children's lives are linked. Elder's (1974) longitudinal research of children raised during the Great Depression found that as parents experienced greater economic pressures, they faced a greater risk of depressed feelings and marital discord. Consequently, their ability to nurture their children was compromised, and their children were more likely to exhibit emotional distress, academic trouble, and problem behavior. The connection between family hardship, family nurturance, and child behaviors and well-being is now well established (e.g., Barajas, Philipsen, & Brooks-Gunn, 2008; Conger & Conger, 2008). In addition to the economic connection between parents and children, parents provide social capital for their children, in terms of role models and networks of social support (Szydlik, 2012).

It should also be noted that parents' lives are influenced by the trajectories of their children's lives. For example, parents may need to alter their work trajectories to respond to the needs of a terminally ill child. Or parents may forgo early retirement to assist their young-adult children with education expenses. Parents may be negatively affected by stressful situations that their children face. Emma Suarez's tragedy was a source of great stress for her mother and her siblings. One research team found a relationship between the problems of adult children and the emotional and relational well-being of their parents. Research participants who reported having adult children with a greater accumulation of personal and social problems (e.g., chronic disease, mental health problems, substance abuse problems, work-related problems, relationship problems) also reported poorer levels of well-being than reported by participants whose children were reported to have fewer problems (Greenfield & Marks, 2006). Without longitudinal research, it is impossible to know which came first, reduced parental well-being or adult child problems, but this research does lend strong support for the idea that lives are linked across generations.

The pattern of mutual support between older adults and their adult children is formed by life events and transitions across the life course. It is also fundamentally changed when families go through historical disruptions such as wars or major economic downturns. For example, the traditional pattern of intergenerational support—parents supporting children—is often disrupted when one generation migrates and another generation stays behind. It is also disrupted in immigrant families when the children pick up the new language and cultural norms faster than the adults in the family and take on the role of interpreter for their parents and grandparents (Clark, Glick, & Bures, 2009).

What complicates matters is that family roles must often be synchronized across three or more generations at once. Sometimes this synchronization does not go smoothly. Divorce, remarriage, and discontinuities in parents' work and educational trajectories may conflict with the needs of children. Similarly, the timing of adult children's educational, family, and work transitions often conflicts with the needs of aging parents (Huinink & Feldhaus, 2009). The "generation in the middle" may have to make uncomfortable choices when allocating scarce economic and emotional resources. When a significant life event in one generation (such as death of a grandparent) is juxtaposed with a significant life event in another generation (such as birth of a child), families and individual family members are especially vulnerable (McGoldrick et al., 2011b).

Links With the Wider World

Although the life course perspective has its origins in Elder's (1974) research on the ways that families and individuals are linked to situations in the economic institution, it seems that we know a lot more at this point about the ways that individuals and their multigenerational families are interdependent than about the interdependence between individuals and families and other groups and collectivities. However, in recent years life course researchers have been documenting the ways that individual and family life course trajectories are linked to situations in the labor market, the housing market, the education system, and the welfare system (K. Newman, 2008; Scherger, 2009; Szydlik, 2012). This line of research is well illustrated by one research project that examined young-adult transitions in western Europe and Japan (K. Newman, 2008). Katherine Newman (2008) reports two divergent trends in the timing of young-adult transitions in postindustrial societies. On the one hand, young adults are staying in the parental home for a prolonged period in Japan and the southern European countries. For example, in Japan, the age of marriage has been rising, and more than 60% of unmarried men and 70% of unmarried women aged 30 to 34 live with their parents. On the other hand, youth typically leave home at the age of 18 in the Nordic countries of northern Europe (Denmark, Finland, Norway, and Sweden). This raises a question about the structural arrangements in these countries that are producing such divergent trends in life course trajectories.

First, changes in the labor market are driving the delayed departure of young adults from the parental home

© iStockphoto.com/Rawpixel Ltd

Parents' and children's lives are linked—when parents experience stress or joy, so do children, and when children experience stress or joy, so do parents.

in southern Europe and Japan (K. Newman, 2008). In the 1980s, when globalization began to produce higher unemployment, governments in southern Europe and Japan began to loosen their commitment to lifetime employment. As a result, companies began to hire part-time and temporary workers; such tenuous connection to the labor market is associated with continued coresidence of young adults with their parents. Unemployment has always been higher in southern Europe than in northern Europe, but the divergence in young-adult transitions in these two European regions is not fully explained by conditions in the labor market.

Second, timing of departure from the parental home is linked to situations in the housing market. In the United States, there are a number of housing options for marginally employed young adults, including pooling resources with a roommate or romantic partner or finding rental housing in a less desirable neighborhood. Such options are dependent on a strong rental housing market, however. In southern European countries, great emphasis is put on owner-occupied housing and relatively little rental housing is available. For example, more than 85% of the population in Spain lives in homes they own. In addition, European banks typically are willing to lend only 50% of the cost of a house. In contrast, in the Nordic countries, there is a large rental sector in the housing market, with only 60% to 65% of the population living in homes that they own. Katherine Newman (2008) builds the case that these conditions in the housing market influence the timing of departure from the parental home.

Third, it is often suggested that there is a linkage between the education system and timing of departure from the parental home. More specifically, it is argued that young adults who participate in higher education leave the parental home later than those who do not participate in higher education and that the trend toward greater participation in higher education is an important factor in the trend toward later departure from the parental home (see Scherger, 2009). This is not the whole story, however, because the Nordic countries have a higher proportion of emerging adults in higher education than countries in southern Europe, and yet young adults in the Nordic countries depart the parental home earlier than those in southern Europe (K. Newman, 2008).

And, finally, there is strong evidence of a linkage between the welfare system and the timing of departure from the parental home (K. Newman, 2008). More specifically, the early departure from the parental home in Nordic countries is subsidized by a welfare system that provides generous housing and educational benefits. The Nordic governments provide much of what families are expected to provide in the weaker welfare systems in southern Europe and Japan.

Katherine Newman (2008) argues convincingly that it is a confluence of situations in different societal institutions that impact individual and family life trajectories. In terms of linked lives, she found some evidence that young adults feel more closely linked to their families in Japan and southern Europe than in Nordic countries—a situation that carried both positive and negative consequences. Nordic young adults, conversely, feel more closely linked to the government and the welfare institutions than young adults in Japan and southern Europe.

Using data from 11 European countries, Marc Szydlik (2012) has taken a similar look at the influence of the social welfare system on family solidarity between older adults and their adult children. He found strong family solidarity across the 11 countries but some differences in how the state and family are linked across national lines. He found that adult children in countries with strong social welfare systems provided more practical household help (home repairs, gardening, transportation, shopping, household chores, and paperwork) to their aging parents than adult children in countries with weaker social welfare systems. On the other hand, adult children in countries with weak social welfare systems provided more personal care (dressing, bathing, eating, getting in and out of bed, using the toilet) to their aging parents than adult children in countries with stronger social welfare systems. Szydlik suggests that societies with an aging population need family-friendly policies to protect family members from excessive demands, noting that middle-aged adults may get overburdened from the need to care for aging adults while also supporting their young-adult offspring who are struggling in a labor market that is becoming increasingly less secure.

It is important for social workers to remember that lives are also linked in systems of institutionalized privilege and oppression. The life trajectories of members of minority groups in the United States are marked by discrimination and lack of opportunity, which are experienced pervasively as daily insults and pressures. However, various cultural groups have devised unique systems of social support to cope with the oppressive environments in which they live. Examples include the extensive and intensive natural support systems of Hispanic families like the Suarez family (Falicov, 2005) and the special role of the church for African Americans (Billingsley, 1999). Others construct lives of desperation or resistance in response to limited opportunities.

Philip McMichael (2012) reminds us that, in the global economy, lives are linked around the world. The lifestyles of people in affluent countries depend on cheap

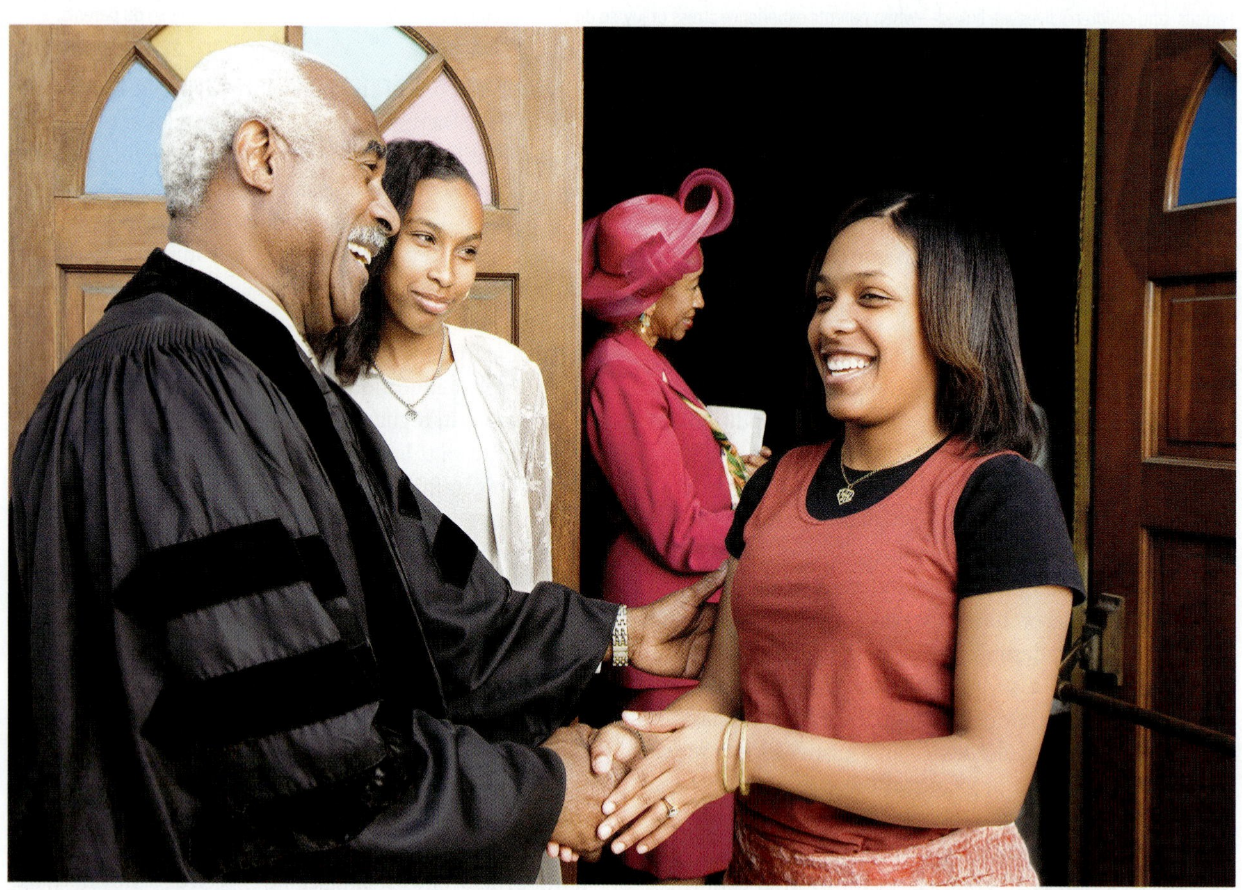

Hill Street Studios/Walter Jimenez Blend Images/Newscom

Various cultural groups have devised unique systems of social support to cope with the oppressive environments in which they live.

labor and cheap raw products in Africa, South America, the Caribbean, parts of Asia, and other places. Children and women in impoverished countries labor long hours to make an increasing share of low-cost products consumed in affluent countries. As we saw in the case study of the Filipina domestic workers in Chapter 8, women migrate from impoverished countries to become the domestic laborers in affluent countries, allowing women in affluent countries to leave the home to take advantage of career opportunities and allowing the domestic workers to send the money they make back home to support their own families.

CRITICAL THINKING Questions 10.3

What, if any, historical event or events have had a large impact on your cohort? In your family of origin, what were the norms about when young adults should leave the parental home, complete formal education, establish a committed romantic relationship, or become a parent? How consistent are your own ideas about these young-adult transitions with the ideas of your family of origin? Cross-national research indicates that the social welfare system has an influence on intergenerational family relationships. Do you think that research supports a strong welfare system or a weak welfare system? Explain.

HUMAN AGENCY IN MAKING CHOICES

Phoung Le and her husband made a decision that they wanted to live a bilingual, bicultural life, and this decision had a momentous impact on their own life course as well as the life course trajectories of their children. In other words, they participated in constructing their life courses through the exercise of **human agency**, or the use of personal power to achieve one's goals. The emphasis on human agency may be one of the most positive contributions of the life course perspective. Steven Hitlin and Glen Elder Jr. (2007) note that the concept of human agency is used by different theorists in different ways, but when used by life course theorists it refers to "attempts to exert influence to shape one's life trajectory" (p. 182). It involves acting with an orientation toward the future, with an eye for "possible selves" (Markus & Nurius, cited in Hitlin & Elder, 2007, p. 183).

A look at the discipline of social history might help to explain why considering human agency is so important to social workers. Social historians have attempted to correct the traditional focus on lives of elites by studying the lives of common people (Hareven, 2000). By doing so, they discovered that many groups once considered passive victims—for example, working-class people and slaves—actually took independent action to cope with the difficulties imposed by the rich and powerful. Historical research now shows that couples tried to limit the size of their families even in preindustrial societies (Wrigley, 1966), that slaves were often ingenious in their struggles to hold their families together (Gutman, 1976), and that factory workers used informal networks and kinship ties to manage, and sometimes resist, pressures for efficiency (Hareven, 1982b). These findings are consistent with social work approaches that focus on individual, family, and community strengths (Saleebey, 2012).

Emphasis on human agency in the life course perspective has been greatly aided by the work of psychologist Albert Bandura. Bandura proposes that humans are agentic, meaning they are capable of intentionally influencing their own functioning and life circumstances (Bandura, 2002, 2006). In his early work, he introduced the two concepts of *self-efficacy*, or sense of personal competence, and *efficacy expectation*, or expectation that one can personally accomplish a goal. More recently (Bandura, 2006), he has presented a psychological theory of human agency. This theory proposes three modes of human agency:

1. *Personal agency* is exercised individually, using personal influence to shape environmental events or one's own behavior.
2. *Proxy agency* is exercised to influence others who have greater resources to act on one's behalf to meet needs and accomplish goals.
3. *Collective agency* is exercised on the group level when people act together to meet needs and accomplish goals.

Bandura argues that everyday life requires use of all three modes of agency. There are many circumstances, such as those just discussed, where individuals can exercise personal agency to shape situations. However, there are many situations over which individuals do not have direct control, and they must seek out others who have greater influence to act on their behalf. Other circumstances exist in which goals are only achievable or more easily and comprehensively achievable by working collectively with others.

Cultural psychology critics of the concept of human agency have argued that it is a culture-bound concept that does not apply as well in collectivist societies as in individualistic societies (see Markus & Kitayama, 2003). They argue that individualistic societies operate on a model of *disjoint agency*, where agency resides in the independent self. In contrast, collectivist societies operate on a model of *conjoint agency*, where agency resides in relationships between interdependent selves. Markus and Kitayama (2003) provide empirical support for their proposal that agency is experienced differently by members of individualistic and collectivist societies. They cite several studies providing evidence that European American children perform better and are more confident if they are allowed to make choices (of tasks, objects, and so on), but Asian American children perform no better if allowed to make such choices. Markus and Kitayama do not deny that individuals from collectivist cultures sometimes think in terms of personal agency and individuals from individualistic cultures sometimes think in terms of collective agency. They argue, however, that there is a difference in the emphasis placed on these approaches to agency in different cultures. Gretchen Sisson (2012) suggests that in the United States, working-class individuals are more likely than middle-class individuals to follow a conjoint model of agency concerned with obligations to others. She notes that pregnancy prevention programs typically are based on a disjoint model, which may be inappropriate for the intended audience.

Bandura (2002, 2006) argues that although people in all cultures must use all three modes of agency (personal, proxy, and collective), there are cultural variations in the relative emphasis put on the different modes. He also argues that there are individual variations of preferences within cultures and that globalization is producing some cultural sharing.

Clearly, however, human agency has limits. Individuals' choices are constrained by the structural and cultural arrangements of a given historical era. For example, Phoung Le and her family did not have the choice to continue to live peacefully in Saigon. David Sanchez may have assumed that his choices were to voluntarily enlist or be drafted. Unequal opportunities also give some members of society more options than others have (Stephens, Hamedani, Markus, Bergsieker, & Eloul, 2009). Hitlin and Elder (2007) suggest both biological and social structural limits to agency. They note research indicating that greater perceptions of personal control contribute to better health among older adults but also propose that agency declines across the life course because of declining physical functioning.

The concepts of proxy agency and collective agency bring us back to linked and interdependent lives. These concepts add important dimensions to the discussion of human agency and can serve to counterbalance the extreme individualism of U.S. society. The modes of agency also raise important issues for social workers. When do we encourage clients to use personal individual agency, when do we use our own influence as proxy agents for clients, and when is collective agency called for?

DIVERSITY IN LIFE COURSE TRAJECTORIES

Life course researchers have long had strong evidence of diversity in individuals' life patterns. Early research emphasized differences between cohorts, but increasing attention is being paid to variability within cohort groups. However, the life course research has been based on samples from affluent societies and fails to account for global diversity, particularly for the life course trajectories of the great majority of the world's people who live in nonindustrial or early industrializing countries (Dannefer, 2003a, 2003b). Consequently, the life course perspective has the potential to accommodate global diversity but has not adequately done so yet.

Life course researchers have recently begun to incorporate intersectionality theory to understand diversity in life course trajectories (see Warner & Brown, 2011). As noted in Chapter 2, *intersectionality theory* recognizes that all of us are jointly and simultaneously members of a number of socially constructed identity groups, such as gender, race, ethnicity, social class, sexual orientation, age, religion, geographical location, and disability/ability. The theory is rooted in the writings of U.S. Black feminists who challenged the idea of a universal gendered experience (see P. Collins, 2012). For any one of us, our *social location*, or place in society, is at the intersection of our multiple identity groups. Either advantage or disadvantage is associated with each identity group, and when considering the life journey of any one individual, it is important to consider the multiple identity groups of which he or she is a part (see Hankivsky, 2012; Seng, Lopez, Sperlich, Hamam, & Meldrum, 2012).

An important source of diversity in a country with considerable immigration is the individual experience leading to the decision to immigrate, the journey itself, and the resettlement period (Clark et al., 2009). The decision to immigrate may involve social, religious, or political persecution, and it increasingly involves a search for economic gain. Or, as in Phoung Le's case, it may involve war and a dangerous political environment. The transit experience is sometimes traumatic, as was the case for Phoung Le and her relatives, who were attacked by pirates and separated, never to see some family members again. The resettlement experience requires establishment of new social networks, may involve changes in socioeconomic status, and presents serious demands for acculturating to a new physical and social environment. Phoung Le and her family were lucky to be able to settle into a large community of Vietnamese immigrants, a situation that eased the process of acculturation. Gender, race, social class, and age all add layers of complexity to the migration experience. Family roles often have to be renegotiated as children outstrip older family members in learning the new language. Tensions can also develop over conflicting approaches to the acculturation process (Falicov, 2011). Just as they should investigate their clients' educational trajectories, work trajectories, and family trajectories, social workers should be interested in the migration trajectories of their immigrant clients.

DEVELOPMENTAL RISK AND PROTECTION

As the life course perspective has continued to evolve, it has more clearly emphasized the links between the life events and transitions of childhood, adolescence, and adulthood (Gilman, 2012; O'Rand, 2009). Studies indicate that childhood events sometimes shape people's lives 40 or more years later (Ferraro & Shippee, 2009). Indeed, recent biomedical research has suggested we should look at factors that occur earlier than childhood, focusing on fetal undernutrition as a contributing factor in late-life cognition and late-life health conditions such as coronary heart disease, type 2 diabetes, and hypertension (see Joss-Moore & Lane, 2009; Rooij, Wouters, Yonker, Painter, & Roseboom, 2010).

It is an old idea that what happens at one point in the life journey influences what happens at later points. No doubt, you have heard some version of this idea for most of your life. However, the idea of earlier life experience affecting later development has taken on new energy since the explosion of longitudinal research a few decades ago (Elder & Giele, 2009b). In longitudinal research, researchers follow a group of people over a period of time, rather than comparing different groups at one point in time. This allows them to study individual lives over time, noting the factors that influence individual life trajectories.

Two different research traditions have examined how early life experiences affect later outcomes, one based in sociology and the other based in ecological developmental psychology. The sociological tradition is interested in cumulative advantage/cumulative disadvantage (see Dannefer, 2003c). The ecological developmental tradition is interested in risk, protection, and resilience. As you can see, we are borrowing language from the ecological developmental tradition. For a long time, there was little cross-flow of ideas between these two disciplinary traditions, but recently there has been some attempt to integrate them.

Let's look first at research that focuses on **cumulative advantage** and **cumulative disadvantage**. Life course scholars have borrowed these concepts from sociologist Robert Merton to explain inequality within cohorts across the life course (Ferraro & Shippee, 2009). Merton (1968) found that in scientific careers, large inequalities in productivity and recognition had accumulated. Scholarly productivity brings recognition, and recognition brings resources for further productivity, which of course brings further recognition and so on. Merton proposed that, in this way, scientists who are productive early in their careers accumulate advantage over time, whereas other scientists accumulate disadvantage. Sociologists propose that cumulative advantage and cumulative disadvantage are socially constructed; social institutions and societal structures develop mechanisms that ensure increasing advantage for those

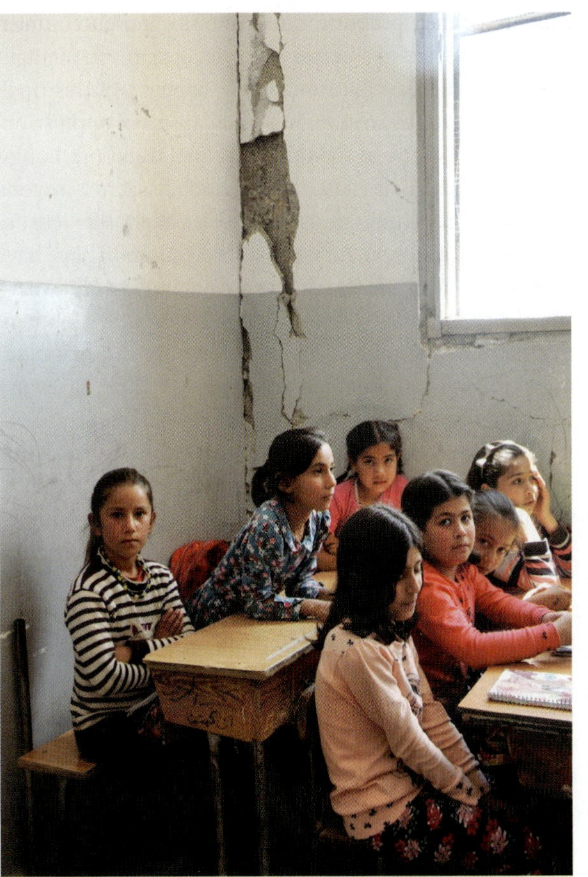

Anadolu Agency/Contributor/Anadolu Agency/Getty Images

These students receive their education at a damaged school in Kobani, Syria.

who succeed early in life and increasing disadvantage for those who struggle (Ferraro & Shippee, 2009). Researchers have applied the concepts of cumulative advantage and cumulative disadvantage to study racial health disparities across the life trajectory (see Shuey & Willson, 2008).

Consider the effect of advantages in schooling. Young children with affluent parents attend enriched early childhood programs and well-resourced primary and secondary schools, which position them for successful college careers, which position them for occupations that pay well, which provide opportunities for good health maintenance, which position them for healthy, secure old age. As reported in Chapter 1, this trajectory of unearned advantage is sometimes referred to as *privilege* (P. McIntosh, 1988). Children who do not come from affluent families are more likely to attend underequipped schools, experience school failure or dropout, begin work in low-paying sectors of the labor market, experience unemployment, and arrive at old age with compromised health and limited economic resources. **Oppression** is the intentional or unintentional act or process of placing restrictions on an individual, group, or institution; it may include observable actions but more typically refers to complex, covert, interconnected processes and practices (such as discriminating, devaluing, and exploiting a group of individuals) reflected in a perpetuating exclusion and inequalities over time. See Exhibit 1.4 in Chapter 1 of this book for descriptions of 16 common mechanisms of oppression.

Now let's look at the other research tradition. Longitudinal research has also led researchers across several disciplines to study human lives through the lens of ecological developmental risk protection. They have attempted, with much success, to identify multidimensional **risk factors**, or factors at one stage of development that increase the probability of developing and maintaining problem conditions at later stages. They have also been interested in individuals who have adapted successfully in the face of risk and have identified **protective factors**, or factors (resources) that decrease the probability of developing and maintaining problem conditions (Hutchison, Matto, Harrigan, Charlesworth, & Viggiani, 2007; Jenson & Fraser, 2016).

Recently, gerontologists in the life course tradition have tried to integrate the cumulative advantage/disadvantage and the ecological developmental risk and protection streams of inquiry. Kenneth Ferraro and Tetyana Shippee (2009) present a cumulative inequality (CI) theory. They propose that advantage and disadvantage are created across multiple levels of systems, an idea similar to the multidimensional aspect of the ecological risk and protection approach. They also propose that "disadvantage increases exposure to risk but advantage increases exposure to opportunity" (p. 335). They further submit that "life course trajectories are shaped by the accumulation of risk, available resources, and human agency" (p. 335).

It is important to note that neither cumulative advantage/disadvantage theory nor the ecological developmental risk and protection approach argue that early deprivations and traumas inevitably lead to a trajectory of failure. Research on cumulative advantage and disadvantage is finding that cumulative processes are reversible under some conditions, particularly when human agency is exercised, resources are mobilized, and environmental conditions open opportunities (Ferraro & Shippee, 2009; O'Rand, 2009). For example, it has been found that when resources are mobilized to create governmental safety nets for vulnerable families at key life transitions, the effects of deprivation and trauma on health are reduced (Gilman, 2012).

In the ecological developmental risk and protection stream of inquiry, protective factors provide the antidote to risk factors and minimize the inevitability of a trajectory of failure. Researchers in this tradition have begun to recognize the power of humans to use protective factors to assist in a self-righting process over the life course to fare well in the face of adversity, a process known as **resilience** (Jenson & Fraser, 2016). For example, researchers have found that disadvantaged children who participated in an enriched preschool program had higher levels of education, employment, and earnings and lower levels of crime in adulthood than a control group of similar children who did not participate in the program (Heckman, Moon, Pinto, Savelyev, & Yavitz, 2010). Werner and Smith (2001) found that a relationship with one supportive adult can be a strong protective factor across the life course for children with an accumulation of risk factors.

The life course perspective and the concept of cumulative disadvantage are beginning to influence community epidemiology, which studies the prevalence of disease across communities (e.g., Dupre, 2008; Mishra, Cooper, & Kuh, 2010). Researchers in this tradition are interested in social and geographical inequalities in the distribution of chronic disease. They suggest that risk for chronic disease gradually accumulates over a life course through episodes of illness, exposure to unfavorable environments, and unsafe behaviors, which they refer to as a *chain-of-risk model*. They are also interested in how some experiences in the life course can break the chain of risk.

CRITICAL THINKING Questions 10.4

Do you think David Sanchez would endorse a disjoint or conjoint form of agency? What about Phoung Le? Maria Suarez? Explain. Of what identity groups are you a member? Which identities provide you with privilege? Which provide you with disadvantage? How might your social location affect your ability to provide social work services to someone like David, Phoung, or Maria? What risk factors do you see in the lives of David, Phoung, and Maria? What protective factors do you see?

THE FAMILY LIFE COURSE

The family life course perspective (also known as the **family life cycle perspective**) looks at family systems over time (McGoldrick et al., 2011a). Families are seen as multigenerational systems moving through time, composed of people who have a shared history and a shared future. Relationships in families go through transitions as they move along the life cycle; boundaries shift, rules change, and roles are constantly redefined. Each transition changes family statuses and roles and generally is accompanied by family members' exits and entrances. We can see the dramatic effects of birth and death on the Suarez family as Maria entered and Emma exited the family circle. Health professionals have recently used the life course perspective, the concept of transitions in particular, to understand role changes that occur in family caregiving of older adults (Carpentier, Bernard, Grenier, & Guberman, 2010; Evans et al., 2009). The concept of transitions is also increasingly used to study the migration/immigration process (Gong, Xu, Fujishiro, & Takeuchi, 2011).

The family life course perspective proposes that **transition points**, when the family faces a transition in family life stage or in family composition, are particularly stressful for families. Many individual transitions relate to family life: marriages, births, divorces, remarriages, deaths (McGoldrick, Carter, & Garcia-Preto, 2011a). Many families also face unpredictable challenges, even crises, which also serve as transition points and complicate their normative life course development. Such nonnormative transition points are especially stressful to those with a family or cultural history of trauma or disruption. The family moving through time is influenced by cultural factors and by the historical era in which they live. McGoldrick et al. (2011a) recognize that contemporary families are undergoing changes and have many forms, but they delineate seven stages that many U.S. families seem to pass through: leaving home: emerging young adults; joining of families through marriage/union; families with young children; families with adolescents; launching children and moving on at midlife; families in late middle age; and families nearing the end of life. Each of these stages involves normative changes and challenging tasks, both for individual family members and for the family system as a whole. In this view, change is inevitable in families, and transitions offer opportunities for positive adaptation and growth. The identified life stages may not fit many of the families in today's society, however, including divorced and remarried families and families without children.

From the family life course perspective, we can see that David Sanchez has faced many transition points across the phases of his life and happily reconnected to his son and grandsons after many years of alienation. As he enters late adulthood, he is finding meaning in his role as a spiritual and cultural teacher in his family. Phoung Le is part of a family in late middle age, a time of launching children and moving on (Garcia-Preto & Blacker, 2011). Phoung's family is a part of the increasing diversity in the current cohort of midlife families, and Phoung is playing an important role in keeping her grandchildren connected to some Vietnamese traditions. She and Hien have grieved the loss of their parents, arrived at the peak of their work lives, and derived pleasure from the expansion of family through marriage and grandchildren. The Suarez family has had to negotiate nontraditional family roles through migration, sickness, and loss. They struggled with the unpredictable transition point that came out of the September 11 tragedy, but they seem to be responding resiliently to the challenges of being a family with adolescents.

STRENGTHS AND LIMITATIONS OF THE LIFE COURSE PERSPECTIVE

As a framework for thinking about the aspect of time in human behavior, the life course perspective has several advantages over traditional theories of human development. It encourages greater attention to the impact of historical and sociocultural change on human behavior, which seems particularly important in rapidly changing global societies. Its emphasis on linked lives shines a spotlight on intergenerational relationships and the interdependence of lives. At the same time, with its attention to human agency, the life course perspective is not as deterministic as some earlier theories and acknowledges people's strengths and capacity for change. Life course researchers are also finding strong evidence for the malleability of risk factors and the possibilities for preventive interventions. With attention to the diversity in life course trajectories, the life course perspective provides a good conceptual framework for culturally sensitive practice. And finally, the life course perspective lends itself well to research that looks at cumulative advantage and cumulative disadvantage, adding to our knowledge about the impact of power and privilege and subsequently suggesting strategies for social justice.

To answer questions about how people change and how they stay the same across a life course is no simple task, however. Take, for example, the question of whether there is an increased sense of generativity, or concern for others, in middle adulthood. Should the researcher study different groups of people at different ages (perhaps a group of 20-year-olds, a group of 30-year-olds, a group of 40-year-olds, a group of 50-year-olds, and a group of 60-year-olds) and compare their responses, in what is known as a cross-sectional design? Or should the researcher study the same people over time (perhaps at 10-year intervals from age 20 to age 60) and observe whether their responses stay the same or change over time, in what is known as a longitudinal design? I hope you are already raising this question: What happens to the cohort effect in a cross-sectional study? This question is, indeed, always a problem with studying change over time with a cross-sectional design. Suppose we find that 50-year-olds report a greater sense of generativity than those in younger age groups. Can we then say that generativity does, indeed, increase in middle adulthood? Or do we have to wonder if there was something in the social and historical contexts of this particular cohort of 50-year-olds that encouraged a greater sense of generativity? Because of the possibility of cohort effects, it is important to know whether research was based on a cross-sectional or longitudinal design.

EXHIBIT 10.5 • Overlap of the Life Course Perspective and Eight Theoretical Perspectives on Human Behavior

THEORETICAL PERSPECTIVE	LIFE COURSE THEMES AND CONCEPTS
Systems perspective: Human behavior is the outcome of reciprocal interactions of persons operating within linked social systems.	*Themes:* Timing of lives; linked or interdependent lives *Concepts:* Biological age, psychological age, social age, spiritual age
Conflict perspective: Human behavior is driven by conflict, dominance, and oppression in social life.	*Theme:* Developmental risk and protection *Concepts:* Cumulative advantage; cumulative disadvantage
Exchange and choice perspective: Human behavior is based on individual and collective actors seeking and exchanging resources and the choices made in pursuit of those resources.	*Theme:* Human agency in making choices *Concepts:* Choices; opportunities; constraints
Social constructionist perspective: Social reality is created when actors, in social interaction, develop a common understanding of their world.	*Themes:* Timing of lives; diversity in life course trajectories; developmental risk and protection *Concepts:* Making meaning of life events; social age; age norms; age structuring; acculturation; cumulative advantage and disadvantage
Psychodynamic perspective: Internal processes such as needs, drives, and emotions motivate human behavior; early childhood experiences are central to problems of living throughout life.	*Themes:* Timing of lives; developmental risk and protection *Concepts:* Psychological age; capacities; skills
Developmental perspective: Human behavior both changes and stays the same across the life span.	*Themes:* Interplay of human lives and historical time; timing of lives; developmental risk and protection *Concepts:* Life transitions; biological age, psychological age, social age, spiritual age; sequencing
Social behavioral perspective: Human behavior is learned when individuals interact with the environment; human behavior is influenced by personal expectations and meanings.	*Themes:* Interplay of human lives and historical time; human agency in making choices; diversity in life course trajectories; developmental risk and protection *Concepts:* Life events; human agency
Humanistic perspective: Human behavior can be understood only from the internal frame of reference of the individual; human behavior is driven by a desire for growth and competence.	*Themes:* Timing of lives; human agency in making choices *Concepts:* Spiritual age; meaning of life events and turning points; individual, family, and community strengths

Although attention to diversity may be the greatest strength of the life course perspective, heterogeneity may be its biggest challenge. I am using diversity to refer to group-based differences and heterogeneity to refer to individual differences. The life course perspective, like other behavioral science perspectives, searches for patterns of human behavior. But the current level of heterogeneity in countries such as the United States limits our capacity to discern patterns. Along with trying to understand patterns, social workers must try to understand the unique circumstances of every case situation. Another challenge related to diversity—perhaps a larger challenge—is that most of the research of the life course perspective has been done with samples from wealthy advanced industrial societies. This is true of all existing social and behavioral science research. I would suggest, however, that there is nothing inherent in either the basic conceptions or the major themes of the life course perspective that make it inappropriate for use to understand human behavior at a global level. This is particularly true if human agency is understood to include proxy agency and collective agency, conjoint as well as disjoint agency.

Another possible limitation of the life course perspective is a failure to adequately link the micro world of individual and family lives to the macro world of social institutions and formal organizations. Social and behavioral sciences have, historically, divided the social world up into micro and macro and studied them in isolation. The life course perspective was developed by scholars like Glen Elder Jr. and Tamara Hareven, who were trying to bring those worlds together. Sometimes, however, this effort is more successful than at other times, and this remains a challenge for the future.

INTEGRATION WITH A MULTIDIMENSIONAL, MULTITHEORETICAL APPROACH

In Chapters 1 and 2, we recommended a multidimensional, multitheoretical approach for understanding human behavior. This recommendation is completely compatible with the life course perspective presented here in Part IV. The life course perspective clearly recognizes the biological and psychological dimensions of the person and can accommodate the spiritual dimension. The life course emphasis on linked or interdependent lives is consistent with the idea of the unity of person and environment presented in Chapter 1. It can also easily accommodate the multidimensional environment discussed in the chapters in Part III of this book.

Likewise, the life course perspective is consistent with the multitheoretical approach presented in Chapter 2. The life course perspective has been developed by scholars across several disciplines, and they have increasingly engaged in cross-fertilization of ideas from a variety of theoretical perspectives. Because the life course can be approached from the perspective of the individual or from the perspective of the family or other collectivities, or seen as a property of cultures and social institutions that shape the pattern of individual lives, it builds on both psychological and sociological theories. Exhibit 10.5 demonstrates the overlap between the life course perspective and the eight theoretical perspectives presented in Chapter 2.

CRITICAL THINKING Questions 10.5

Which concepts and themes of the life course perspective seem most useful to you? Explain. Which, if any, concepts and themes would you want to argue with? Explain.

IMPLICATIONS FOR SOCIAL WORK PRACTICE

The life course perspective has many implications for social work practice, including the following.

- Help clients make sense of their unique life's journeys so they can use that understanding to improve their current situations.
- Try to understand the historical contexts of clients' lives and the ways that important historical events have influenced their behavior.
- Where appropriate, use life event inventories to get a sense of the level of stress in a client's life.
- Be aware of the potential to develop social work interventions that can serve as turning points that help individuals, families, small groups, communities, and organizations get back on track.
- Work with the media to keep the public informed about the impact of changing social conditions on individuals, families, communities, and formal organizations.
- Recognize the ways that the lives of family members are linked across generations and the impact of circumstances in one generation on other generations.
- Recognize the ways lives are linked in the global economy.
- Use existing research on risk, protection, and resilience to develop prevention programs.
- When working with recent immigrant and refugee families, be aware of the age norms in their countries of origin.
- Be aware of the unique systems of support developed by members of various cultural groups and encourage the use of those supports in times of crisis.
- Support and help to develop clients' sense of personal competence for making life choices.

KEY TERMS

age norm, 316
age structuring, 317
biological age, 316
cohort, 310
cohort effects, 315
cumulative advantage, 323
cumulative disadvantage, 323
event history, 308
family life cycle perspective, 324
human agency, 321
life course perspective, 308
life event, 312
oppression, 323
population pyramid, 310
protective factors, 324
psychological age, 316
resilience, 324
risk factors, 324
sex ratio, 311
social age, 316
spiritual age, 317
trajectories, 312
transition points, 325
transitions, 311
turning point, 314

ACTIVE LEARNING

1. One research team found that 99% of young-adult respondents to a survey on turning points reported that there had been turning points in their lives. Divide into small groups of 3–5 people. Each student can share whether or not they think they have had any turning points in their lives to date. If the answer is no, talk about whether the student sees her or his life as a straight path or a path with twists and turns. If the answer is yes, talk about the nature of the turning point(s). Compare the events of your lives with the events in the lives of David Sanchez, Phoung Le, and Emma Suarez.
2. Divide into small groups of 3–5 people. Each student should think of someone whom he or she thinks of as resilient, someone who has been successful against the odds. This may be the student, a friend, a coworker, a family member, or a character from a book or movie. Each student will tell some of the story of the resilient person he or she has identified. In discussion, the group will speculate about the reasons for the success. What risk and protective factors seem to have been at play in this person's life?

WEB RESOURCES

Bronfenbrenner Center for Translational Research (BCTR)

www.bctr.cornell.edu

Site presented by the Bronfenbrenner Center for Translational Research at Cornell University contains information on the center, publications, and news and resources.

Institute for Lifecourse and Society

www.nuigalway.ie/lifecourse

Site presented by the Lifecourse Institute at the National University of Ireland, Galway, home of three research centers, including the Centre for Disability Law & Policy, UNESCO Child and Family Research Centre, and the Irish Centre for Social Gerontology, contains information about the life course and critical and working papers.

Maternal and Child Health Life Course Resource Guide

http://mchb.hrsa.gov/lifecourse

Site maintained by the Health Resources and Services Administration contains information on the life course approach to conceptualizing health care needs and services and a bibliography.

Michigan Study of Adolescent and Adult Life Transitions (MSALT)

www.rcgd.isr.umich.edu/msalt/home.htm

Site presented by the Michigan Study of Adolescent and Adult Life Transitions project contains information about the longitudinal study begun in 1983, publications on the project, and family-oriented web resources.

Project Resilience

www.projectresilience.com

Site presented by Project Resilience, a private organization based in Washington, DC, contains information on teaching materials; products; and training for professionals working in education, treatment, and prevention.

Twin Study at University of Helsinki

https://wiki.helsinki.fi/display/twineng/Twinstudy

Site presented by the Department of Public Health at the University of Helsinki contains information on an ongoing project begun in 1974 to study environmental and genetic factors in selected chronic diseases with links to other related resources.

U.S. Census Bureau

www.census.gov

Site presented by the U.S. Census Bureau provides current and historical population data related to diversity and the life course.

SAGE edge™ Sharpen your skills with SAGE edge at edge.sagepub.com/hutchisoness2e

SAGE edge for students provides a personalized approach to help you accomplish your coursework goals in an easy-to-use learning environment. watch listen read

LEARNING OBJECTIVES	FOR FURTHER EXPLORATION AND APPLICATION
LO 10.1: Compare and contrast one's emotional and cognitive reactions to three case studies.	(read) Gender and the Work–Family Interface: Exploring Differences Across the Family Life Course
LO 10.2: List important words in the definition of the life course perspective.	(watch) Life Course Approach
LO 10.3: Identify some of the theoretical roots of the life course perspective.	(read) Life Course Theory: Key Principles and Concepts
LO 10.4: Summarize five basic concepts of the life course perspective (cohorts, transitions, trajectories, life events, and turning points).	(watch) How the Worst Moments in Our Lives Make Us Who We Are (watch) Subjective Age
LO 10.5: Critique six major themes of the life course perspective (interplay of human lives and historical time, timing of lives, linked or interdependent lives, human agency in making choices, diversity in life course trajectories, and developmental risk and protection).	(read) Integrating Varieties of Life Course Concepts
LO 10.6: Demonstrate use of the family life course perspective to understand three case studies.	(listen) Cultural and Historical Trauma: Affecting Lives for Generations
LO 10.7: Evaluate the strengths and limitations of the life course perspective.	(read) Theories: Life Course and Disengagement
LO 10.8: Recognize where themes of the life course perspective are consistent with eight major theoretical perspectives on human behavior discussed in earlier chapters.	(read) Toward a Psychology of Human Agency
LO 10.9: Apply basic concepts and major themes of the life course perspective to recommend guidelines for social work assessment and intervention.	(listen) 72 Is the New 65

The Journey Begins

Conception, Pregnancy, Childbirth, and Infancy

Marcia Harrigan, Debra J. Woody, Suzanne Baldwin, and Cara Wallace

Learning Objectives

LO 11.1 Compare and contrast one's emotional and cognitive reactions to three case studies.

LO 11.2 Recognize the sociocultural context of childbearing and child-rearing.

LO 11.3 Give examples of how humans attempt to exercise human agency to get control over conception and pregnancy.

LO 11.4 Summarize three trimesters of fetal development.

LO 11.5 Describe the special challenges faced by premature and low-birth-weight newborns and newborns with congenital anomalies.

LO 11.6 Summarize the typical physical, cognitive, and socioemotional development of infants.

LO 11.7 Analyze the role of play in infant development.

LO 11.8 Analyze cross-national differences in infant care policies.

LO 11.9 Identify issues that face multigenerational families with infants.

LO 11.10 Give examples of risk factors and protective factors during infancy.

LO 11.11 Apply knowledge of conception, pregnancy, childbirth, and infancy to recommend guidelines for social work assessment and intervention.

CASE STUDY 11.1

JENNIFER BRADSHAW'S EXPERIENCE WITH INFERTILITY

Jennifer Bradshaw always knew that she would be a mom. Now, at 36, the dream of having her own baby is still just a dream as she struggles with infertility. Like many women in her age group, Jennifer spent her late teens and 20s trying not to get pregnant. She focused on education, finding the right relationship, finances, and a career. As an African American woman, and the first person in her family to earn an MSW, she wanted to prove that she could be a successful clinical social worker. She thought that when she wanted to get pregnant, it would just happen, that it would be as easy as scheduling anything else on her calendar. When the time finally was right and she and her husband, Allan, decided to get pregnant, they couldn't.

With every passing month and every negative pregnancy test, Jennifer's frustration grew. First, she was frustrated with herself and had thoughts like, *What is wrong with me? Why is this happening to us?* and *We don't deserve this*. She would look around and see pregnant teens and think, *Why them and not me?* She also was frustrated with her husband for not understanding how devastating this was to her and wondered to herself, *Could it be him with the problem?* In addition, she was frustrated with her family and friends and started avoiding them to escape their comments and the next baby shower. Now, she is babyless and lonely. It has also been hard for Allan. For many men, masculinity is connected to virility; Allan would not even consider that he might be the one with the fertility problem, even though it is a male-factor issue in about 50% of infertility cases.

After months of struggling to get pregnant, multiple visits to the obstetrician and gynecologist, a laparoscopic surgery, a semen analysis, and timed intercourse (which began to feel like a chore), and after taking Clomid, a fertility drug that made her feel horrible, she and Allan finally accepted that they might need to see a specialist. She will never forget the first visit with the reproductive endocrinologist (RE). She was expecting a "quick fix," thinking that the RE would give her some special pills and then she would get pregnant. But, instead, he casually said to her, "I think your only option is in vitro fertilization [IVF], which runs about $16,000 per cycle, including medications." The RE also told her that for someone in her age range the success rate would be about 35% to 40%.

From her clinical practice and her friendship circle, Jennifer knows that many women think of in vitro as being a backup plan when they delay pregnancy. But she is learning that in vitro is a big deal. First, it is expensive. The $16,000 per cycle does not include the preliminary diagnostic testing, and in Jennifer's age group, the majority of women pursuing IVF will need at least two IVF cycles, $32,000 for two tries; three tries brings the bill up to $48,000. Jennifer has heard of couples spending close to $100,000 for infertility treatments.

Although about 15 states mandate insurance companies to cover fertility treatments, in the state where Jennifer lives, there is no fertility coverage mandate; consequently, her insurance company does not cover any infertility treatments. So at the very least, Jennifer and Allan would need to come up with $16,000 to give one IVF cycle a try. It's heartbreaking for them because they don't have $16,000, and their parents can't help them out. So to give IVF even one try, they need to borrow the money. They are considering taking out a home equity loan to pay for the needed IVF cycles and know that they are lucky to be in a position to do that. They have heard of people packing up and moving to states with mandated fertility coverage and/or quitting their jobs and finding jobs that carry specific insurance that will cover fertility treatments. Some couples are even traveling abroad for fertility treatments that can be had for much less than in the United States.

Jennifer has heard that IVF is physically and emotionally exhausting. First the in vitro patient is forced into menopause, and then the ovaries are hyperstimulated to release numerous eggs (up to 15 to 17 instead of 1), which can be painful. The eggs are surgically extracted, and finally the fertilized embryos are introduced to the IVF patient's body. Throughout this process, various hormone treatments are given via daily injections, multiple blood tests are taken, and at any point during the procedure something could go wrong and the IVF cycle could be called off. If all goes well, the IVF patient is left to keep her fingers crossed for the next 2 weeks waiting for a positive pregnancy test. If the test is negative, the treatment starts over again. Jennifer has heard that most women are an emotional wreck during the entire process because of the high stakes and the artificial hormones.

Jennifer and Allan decided to go the IVF route 7 months after visiting the RE. Before they made this decision, however, Jennifer carefully tracked her BBT (basal body temperature), purchased a high-tech electronic fertility monitor, used an ovulation microscope, took multiple fertility supplements, and used sperm-friendly lubricant during intercourse. Still nothing helped. When she heard that acupuncture has been found to increase the success rate of IVF, she started seeing a fertility acupuncturist on a weekly basis for both herbal formulas and acupuncture treatments. The acupuncture treatments and herbs are averaging about $100 per week, also not covered by insurance in her state.

Jennifer and Allan have decided to give IVF three tries, and after that they will move on to the next plan, adoption. They adore each other and want more than anything to have their own little one, but if they cannot have that, they will adopt, and Jennifer will realize her dream of being a mom.

—Nicole Footen Bromfield

CASE STUDY 11.2

THE THOMPSONS' PREMATURE BIRTH

Within days of discovering she was pregnant, Felicia Thompson's husband, Will, suddenly deployed to a combat zone. Through e-mails, occasional cellular phone calls, and Skype, Felicia told Will details about the changes she experienced with the pregnancy, but his world was filled with smoke, dirt, bombs, and danger, punctuated with periods of boredom. Six months into the pregnancy, Felicia's changing figure was eliciting comments from her coworkers in the office where she worked part-time as an office administrator. With weeks of nausea and fatigue behind her, she was experiencing a general sense of well-being. She avoided all news media as well as "war talk" at the office to protect herself from worry and anxiety. Yet even the sound of an unexpected car pulling up to the front of her home produced chills of panic. Was this the time when the officers would come to tell her that Will had been killed or wounded in combat? Her best friend only recently had experienced what every military wife fears may happen.

Then, with dawn hours away, Felicia woke to cramping and blood. With 14 more weeks before her delivery date, Felicia was seized with fear. Wishing that Will were there, Felicia fervently prayed for herself and her fetus. The ambulance ride to the hospital became a blur of pain mixed with feelings of unreality. When she arrived in the labor and delivery suite, masked individuals in scrubs took control of her body while demanding answers to a seemingly endless number of questions. Suddenly the doctors were telling her to push her son into the world.

In the newborn intensive care unit (NICU), a flurry of activity revolved around baby boy Thompson. Born weighing only 1 pound 3 ounces, this tiny red baby's immature systems were unprepared for the demands of the extrauterine world. He was immediately connected to a ventilator, intravenous lines were placed in his umbilicus and arm, and monitor leads were placed on all available surfaces. Nameless to his caregivers, the baby, whom his parents had already named Paul, was now the recipient of some of the most advanced technological interventions available in modern medicine. About an hour after giving birth, Felicia saw Paul for the first time. Lying on a stretcher, she tried to find resemblance to Will, who is of Anglo heritage, or herself, a light-skinned Latina, in this tiny form.

Later, alone in her room, she was flooded with fear, grief, and guilt. What had she done wrong? Could Paul's premature birth have been caused by paint fumes from decorating his room? From her anxiety and worry about Will?

The Red Cross sent the standard message to Will. Was he in the field? Was he at headquarters? It mattered because Paul may not even be alive by the time Will found out he was born. Who would be nearby to comfort him? Would the command allow him to come home on emergency leave? If he were granted permission for emergency leave, it could be days of arduous travel, waiting for space on any military plane, before he landed somewhere in the United States. Felicia knew that Will would be given priority on any plane available; even admirals and generals step aside for men and women returning

(Continued)

(Continued)

home to meet a family crisis. But, then again, the command may consider his mission so essential that only official notification of Paul's death would allow him to return home.

Thirteen days after his arrival, Paul took his first breath by himself. His hoarse, faint cry provoked both ecstasy and terror in his mother. A few days earlier Felicia had been notified by the Red Cross that her husband was on his way home, but information was not available regarding his arrival date. Now that her baby was off the ventilator, she watched Paul periodically miss a breath, which would lead to a decreased heart rate followed by monitors flashing and beeping. She longed for Will's physical presence and support.

Will arrived home 2 days later. He walked into the NICU having spent the last 72 hours flying. He started the trip being delivered to the airport in an armed convoy and landed stateside. Although Paul would spend the next 10 weeks in the hospital, Will had 14 days before starting the journey back to his job.

Paul's struggle to survive was the most exhilarating yet terrifying roller-coaster ride of his parents' lives. Shattered hopes were mended, only to be reshattered with the next telephone call from the NICU. Now Felicia dreaded the phone as well as the sound of an unfamiliar car. For Felicia, each visit to Paul was followed by the long trip home to the empty nursery. For Will, stationed thousands of miles away, there was uncertainty, guilt, helplessness, and sometimes an overwhelming sense of inadequacy. Felicia feared the arrival of a car with officers in it, and Will dreaded a Red Cross message that his son had died.

Great joy and equally intense anxiety pervaded Paul's homecoming day. After spending 53 days in the NICU and still weighing only 4 pounds, 13 ounces, Paul was handed to his mother. She made sure that a video was made so that Will could share in this moment. With more questions than answers about her son's future and her ability to take care of him, Felicia took their baby to his new home.

For the NICU social worker at the military hospital, the major goal is to support the family as they face this challenging transition to parenthood. In the past 53 days, the social worker has helped Felicia answer her questions, understand the unfamiliar medical language of the health care providers, and understand and cope with the strong emotions she is experiencing. The social worker also helped during the transition of Will's arrival from war and his departure back to war. Understanding the dynamics of the NICU, families in crisis, and the needs of the military family separated by an international conflict is critical to providing this family the level of support they need to manage their multifaceted role transitions.

CASE STUDY 11.3

SARAH'S TEEN DAD

Chris Johnson is the only dad in the teen fathers group, facilitated by the social worker at a local high school, who has sole custody of his infant daughter. Initially Sarah, Chris's infant daughter, lived with her mom and maternal grandparents. Chris was contacted by the social worker from Child Protective Services (CPS), who informed him that Sarah was removed from the mom's care because of physical neglect. The referral to CPS was made when Sarah was seen in a pediatric clinic and the medical staff noticed that she had not gained weight since the last visit and was generally unresponsive in the examination. Further investigation by the CPS worker revealed that Sarah was left in her crib for most of the day, and few of Sarah's basic daily care needs were being fulfilled. Although Chris's contact with Sarah had been sporadic since her birth, he did not hesitate to pursue custody, especially given that the only other alternative was Sarah's placement in foster care. Chris's parents were also supportive of Chris's desire to have Sarah live with all of them. However, although they were willing to help, they were adamant that the responsibility for Sarah's care belonged to Chris, not them. They were unwilling to raise Sarah themselves and in fact required Chris to sign a written statement indicating that he, not they, would assume primary responsibility for Sarah's care. Chris's parents also insisted that he remain in school and earn his high school diploma.

Thus far the situation seems to be working well. At the last medical appointment, Sarah's weight had increased significantly and she responded to the nurse's attempts to play and communicate with her. Chris is continuing his education at the alternative high school, which also has a day care for Sarah. Chris admits that it is much more difficult than he anticipated. He attends school for half the day, works a part-time job the other half, and then has to care for Sarah in the evenings. Chris has shared several times in the group that it is a lot for him to juggle. He still mourns the loss of his freedom and "carefree" lifestyle. Like most of the other teens in the group, whether they physically live with the child or not, Chris is concerned about doing the best he can for Sarah; he states that he just wants to be a good dad.

SOCIOCULTURAL ORGANIZATION OF CHILDBEARING AND CHILD-REARING

All aspects of childbearing and early child-rearing have deep meaning for a society and, as seen in these three stories, are experienced in different ways by different people. Procreation allows a culture to persist, as children are raised to follow the ways of their predecessors. But, consistent with the life course perspective, pregnancy, childbearing, and child-rearing practices change with historical time. We can draw on the social constructionist perspective to think about this. This perspective proposes that social reality is created when people, in social interaction, develop shared meaning, a common understanding of their world (you can read more about this perspective in Chapter 2 in this book).

In the United States, the social meaning of childbearing and child-rearing has changed rather dramatically in several ways over the past several decades. Here are a few examples of this change (McGoldrick, Carter, & Garcia-Preto, 2011b):

- Various options for controlling reproduction are more available and accessible but oftentimes only to the economically advantaged.
- Medical advances are raising new ethical issues.
- Childbirth is more commonly delayed, and more people are seeking fertility treatment and remaining involuntarily childless.
- The marriage rate has declined, and more children are born to unmarried mothers.
- The birth rate has declined, resulting in smaller families.
- Teen pregnancy declined over the last decade.
- There are greater variations in family values and sexual mores than in previous generations.
- Parents are less subject to traditional gender-role stereotyping.
- It is becoming much more common for gay and lesbian individuals and couples to become parents.
- More mothers are in the paid labor force.

This chapter presents a multidimensional overview of current knowledge about conception, pregnancy, childbirth, and infancy gleaned from the literatures of anthropology, genetics, medicine, nursing, psychology, social work, and sociology.

CONCEPTION AND PREGNANCY IN CONTEXT

The emotional reaction to conception may vary widely. Jennifer Bradshaw is frustrated about her failure to conceive; the Thompsons' conception brought joy, but we do know that for many people conception is seen as a major crisis, as it may have been for Sarah Johnson's mother. The conception experience is influenced by many factors, including the parents' ages, health, marital status, social status, cultural expectations, peer expectations, school or employment circumstances, the social-political-economic context, and prior experiences with conception and childbearing, as well as the interplay of these factors with those of other people significant to the mother and father. The conception experience may also be influenced by organized religion. The policies of religious groups reflect different views about the purpose of human sexual expression, whether for pleasure, procreation, or perhaps both (Kurtz, 2012).

Just as the experience of conception has varied over time and across cultures, so has the experience of pregnancy. For example, societal expectations of pregnant women in the United States have changed, from simply waiting for birth to actively seeking to maintain the mother's—and hence the baby's—health, preparing for the birth process, and sometimes even trying to influence the baby's cognitive and emotional development while the baby is in the uterus.

CHILDBIRTH IN CONTEXT

Throughout history, families—and particularly women—have passed on to young girls the traditions of childbirth practices. These traditions are increasingly shaped by cultural, institutional, and technological changes. The multiple influences on and changing nature of childbirth practices are exemplified in three related issues: childbirth education, place of childbirth, and who assists childbirth.

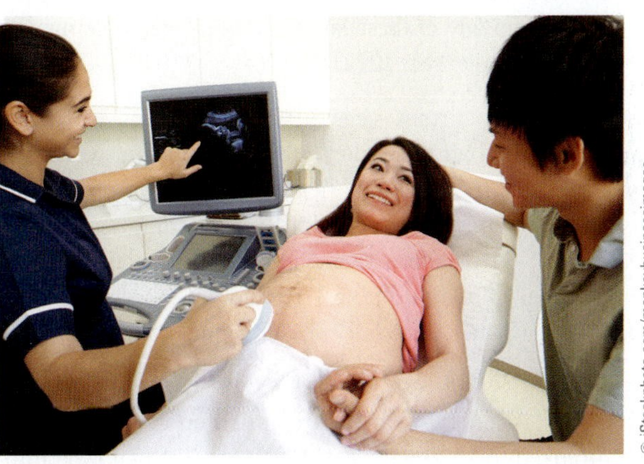

Societal views of pregnancy in the United States have changed from simply waiting to being actively involved in nurturing the mother's and baby's health.

Childbirth Education

Childbirth education, as a formal structure, took hold in the United States and other wealthy countries in the 1960s, fueled by the women's and grassroots consumer movements. Pioneers in the childbirth education movement were reacting against the increasing medicalization of childbirth, and they encouraged women to regain control over the childbirth process. Early childbirth education classes were based on books by Grantly Dick-Read (1944), *Childbirth Without Fear*, and French obstetrician Dr. Fernand Lamaze (1958), *Painless Childbirth*. Lamaze proposed that women could use their intellect to control pain while giving birth if they were informed about their bodies and used relaxation and breathing techniques. Early classes involved small groups meeting outside the hospital during late pregnancy and emphasized unmedicated vaginal birth. The movement had an impact on the development of family-centered maternity practices such as the presence of fathers in labor and delivery and babies rooming in with mothers after birth. Over time, childbirth education became institutionalized and was taught in large classes based in hospitals (Lothian, 2008).

There have been many societal changes in the 50 years since childbirth education was formalized. Here are some examples of how the experience of pregnancy and childbirth has changed since the early days of the childbirth education movement.

- Pregnant women had few sources of information about pregnancy and birth in the 1960s, but women today are overloaded with information from a number of sources. Research indicates that besides maternity care providers and childbirth education classes, women get information from family and friends, books, reality television, educational e-mails and text messages, and increasingly from Internet sites, including social media sites (Declercq, Sakala, Corry, Applebaum, & Herrlich, 2013; Lagan, Sinclair, & Kernohan, 2010; Morris & McInerney, 2010). Unfortunately, women may need help in sorting out inaccurate and out-of-date information from any of these sources (Lima-Pereira, Bermudez-Tamayo, & Jasienska, 2012).

- The current generation of pregnant women is more likely than the earlier cohort of pregnant women to be involved in a variety of health promotion activities that will help them manage childbirth. For example, they may be involved in alternative modalities for relaxation and fitness, such as mindfulness meditation, yoga, Pilates, or massage (Fisher, Hauck, Bayes, & Byrne, 2012; Morton & Hsu, 2007).

- Pregnant women are much more likely to be employed today than in the 1960s and 70s, and the multisession formats of most models of childbirth education often seem like an extra burden for contemporary pregnant women. One new trend in maternity care is to provide group appointments for prenatal care, incorporating education and group support along with maternity checkups (Walker & Worrell, 2008).

The current generation of pregnant women is more likely than earlier cohorts to be involved in a variety of health promotion activities that will help them manage childbirth.

© iStockphoto.com/laflor

- With the current cohort of pregnant women more likely to be unmarried than was true 50 years ago, the emphasis on husband involvement in traditional models of childbirth education may not resonate with many of these women.

- The current population of pregnant women is much more culturally diverse than the White, middle-class women for whom childbirth education was designed, and childbirth education classes are still made up largely of White, middle-class women (Lothian, 2008).

- Many new technological and pharmaceutical childbirth interventions have been introduced in the past 15 years, and many contemporary pregnant women prefer high-tech, pain-free, and scheduled (if possible) birth. This is not a good fit with models of childbirth education from the earlier era that discourage medical intervention, and women today are often strongly encouraged to use medical interventions (Declercq et al., 2013).

There have been a number of government initiatives that promote access to childbirth resources, initiated by the Maternity Care Access Act of 1989, which provided support for low-income women (Rabkin, Balassone, & Bell, 1995). Healthy People 2000, 2010, and 2020, programs by the federal government to enhance the nation's health, support prenatal education (Healthy People, 2014).

The research is inconclusive about whether childbirth education classes in the traditional model produce better pregnancy and childbirth outcomes (Koehn, 2008; Lothian, 2008), and there are mixed results as to whether the father's role is enhanced through childbirth education (Premberg, 2006; Premberg, Hellström, & Berg, 2008). As childbirth education branches from the traditional classroom model to home-based services and interactive media presentations, it is important for social workers to help women negotiate the changing landscape to make the choice that fits them the best (Lothian, 2008) while ensuring that the educational needs of women of all racial and ethnic groups, disabilities, and localities are met.

Place of Childbirth

Large changes in the place of childbirth have occurred in many parts of the world in the past century. In 1900, almost all births in the United States as well as other countries occurred outside of hospitals, usually at home (MacDorman, Mathews, & Declercq, 2012). Today, in high- and moderate-income countries, labor wards in hospitals are the usual settings for childbirth (Hodnett, Downe, & Walsh, 2012). In the United States, the percentage of births occurring outside of the hospital dropped to 44% in 1940 and to 1% in 1969 (MacDorman et al., 2012). As formalized medical training developed, so did the medicalization of childbirth, and the current childbirth experience commonly includes such medical interventions as intravenous lines, electronic fetal monitors, and epidural anesthesiology (Lothian, 2008). Induced labor and cesarean delivery are becoming increasingly common.

In the early part of the 20th century, the feminist movement advocated for hospital childbirth because it was considered to be safer than home birth, but beginning in the 1960s, feminists began to advocate for less invasive deliveries in more friendly environments that give women more choices over their care (DeVries & DeVries, 2007). In the past few decades, in the United States and other wealthy countries, a variety of institutional care settings have been developed, ranging from freestanding birth centers located near a hospital to more homelike birthing rooms within hospital labor departments (Hodnett et al., 2012). The Patient Protection and Affordable Care Act (PPACA) passed by the U.S. Congress in 2010 mandates payments for birthing centers. In 2012, the Centers for Medicare and Medicaid Services (2012) included birthing center care as one of three options for enhanced prenatal care under the Strong Start Initiative. A very small minority of pregnant women, less than 1% in the United States, give birth at home (MacDorman et al., 2012; Wyckoff, 2013). The same is true for most European countries. It is important to remember that in many low-income countries, high maternal mortality rates are due, in great part, to poor women in remote rural areas having no option but to give birth at home without access to emergency health care (Kristof & WuDunn, 2009). In some of these countries, birthing shelters are providing dormitory rooms near hospitals so that women can receive emergency care during childbirth if the need arises (First Ladies Community Initiative, 2013).

Although alternatives to conventional hospital settings, such as birthing centers and homelike birthing rooms, have been somewhat slow to develop in the United States, they are not considered controversial, and available research indicates some benefits and no drawbacks to them. Women giving birth in such settings have reduced likelihood of medical interventions, increased likelihood of spontaneous vaginal birth, and increased satisfaction (Hodnett et al., 2012; Stapleton, Osborne, & Illuzzi, 2013). Home birth has been very controversial, however (World Bank, 2013e; Wyckoff, 2013). The cross-national data on maternal and infant mortality suggest that place of birth is not the only, and probably not the most important, factor affecting birth outcomes (World Bank, 2013e).

Who Assists Childbirth

Before childbirth became medicalized, midwives, trained birthing specialists, assisted most births. Midwifery went into decline in the United States for a few decades, but today 1 in 8 vaginal deliveries are attended by a nurse midwife (Declercq, 2012). Most midwives work in a hospital setting (95.7%), 2% attend home deliveries, and 2.2% work in birthing centers (Martin et al., 2012). Most birthing centers have midwives as the primary care provider (Stapleton et al., 2013).

In most times and places, fathers have been excluded from participation in childbirth. This began to change in the United States and other countries in the 1970s, and worldwide there is an increasing trend for fathers to be present at the birth of their babies (Steen, Downe, Bamford, & Edozien, 2012). In some cultures, however, there is still a taboo about fathers witnessing childbirth (Sengane, 2009). In the past 40 years of having fathers involved in the birthing process, research has indicated a number of benefits of this involvement, including improved maternal well-being, improved father–infant attachment, and paternal satisfaction (Alio, Lewis, Scarborough, Harris, & Fiscella, 2013; Premberg, Carlsson, Hellström, & Berg, 2011). In recent years, however, several pieces of qualitative research have reported that fathers are struggling with their role in the birthing process. One research team (Steen et al., 2012) examined the qualitative research on fathers' involvement with childbirth published from 1999 to 2009. They found that most fathers saw themselves as a partner, had a strong desire to support their partner, and wanted to be fully engaged. They also found that fathers often felt uncertain, excluded, and fearful. They felt frustrated about their helplessness to relieve their partner's pain, they felt good when they could support their partner but bad when they did not feel supported by the childbirth team, and they found the transition to fatherhood to be profoundly life changing. Another research team (Bäckström & Hertfelt Wahn, 2011) found that fathers want to be recognized as part of the laboring couple.

In the past 3 decades, birth doulas have become a part of the childbirth experience for increasing numbers of women. *Doulas* are laywomen who are employed to stay with the woman through the entire labor, assisting with the nonmedical aspects of labor and delivery, encouraging her, and providing comfort measures. A systematic review of the research on the effects of continuous labor support found that women receiving such support had higher rates of spontaneous vaginal birth, lower rates of cesarean delivery, lower rates of epidural anesthesia, lower rates of instrument-assisted delivery, shorter labors, and higher levels of maternal satisfaction (Hodnett, Gates, Hofmeyr, Sakala, & Weston, 2012). It is important that the doula support the role of the father when he is present. Some policy analysts have pointed out that neither private nor public health insurance covers the cost of doulas but should consider doing so given the cost savings from reduced cesarean delivery, epidurals, and instrument-assisted delivery (Kozhimannil, Law, & Virniq, 2013). The PPACA allocated $1.5 million for community-based doula programs, following the success of a model program for disadvantaged and teen mothers (Sonfield, 2010). Think about the Thompsons' situation with Will in Afghanistan, unaware of the pending birth of his first child, and Felicia in premature labor without any family present. Perhaps a doula would have been a great benefit in that situation, as well as situations of other military wives.

DEVELOPMENTAL NICHE OF CHILD-REARING

Each **neonate** (newborn) enters a **developmental niche**, in which culture guides every aspect of the developmental process (Harkness & Super, 2003, 2006). Parents get their ideas about parenting and about the nature of children from the cultural milieu, and parents' ideas are the dominant force in how the infant and toddler develop. Harry Gardiner and Corinne Kosmitzki (2011) identify three interrelated components of the developmental niche: physical and social settings of everyday life, child-rearing customs, and caretaker psychology. Exhibit 11.1 provides an overview of these three important components of the developmental niche encountered by every newborn. As you review this exhibit, think about the developmental niches encountered by Paul Thompson and Sarah Johnson as they begin their life journeys.

EXHIBIT 11.1 • Components of Developmental Niche

PHYSICAL AND SOCIAL SETTINGS OF DAILY LIFE
Size, shape, and location of living space
Objects, toys, reading materials
Ecological setting and climate
Nutritional status of children
Family structure (e.g., nuclear, extended, single parent, blended)
Presence of multiple generations (e.g., parents, grandparents, other relatives)
Presence or absence of mother or father
Presence of multiple caretakers
Role of siblings as caretakers
Presence and influence of peer group members
CUSTOMS OF CHILD CARE AND CHILD-REARING
Sleeping patterns (e.g., co-sleeping vs. sleeping alone)
Dependence versus independence training
Feeding and eating schedules
Handling and carrying practices
Play and work patterns
Initiation rites
Formal versus informal learning
PSYCHOLOGY OF THE CARETAKERS
Parenting styles (e.g., authoritarian, authoritative, laissez-faire)
Value systems (e.g., dependence, independence, interdependence)
Parental cultural belief systems or ethnotheories
Developmental expectations

SOURCE: Gardiner, H., & Kosmitzki, C. (2011). *Lives across cultures: Cross-cultural human development* (5th ed.), p. 31. Printed and electronically reproduced by permission of Pearson Education, Inc., Upper Saddle River, NJ.

In the United States and other wealthy postindustrial societies, many newborns enter a developmental niche in which families have become smaller than in earlier eras. This results in a great deal of attention being paid to each child. Parents take courses and read books about how to provide the best possible care for their infants. Infant safety is stressed, with laws about car seats, guidelines about the position in which the baby should sleep, and a "baby industry" that provides a broad range of safety equipment (baby monitors, baby gates, and so on) and toys, books, and electronics to provide sensory stimulation. Of course this developmental niche requires considerable resources, and many families in wealthy nations cannot afford the regulation car seat or the baby monitor. Chris Johnson is attending school, working, and caring for Sarah; he probably would be hard-pressed to find time to read parenting books, but he does find time to attend a group for teen fathers. And, of course, the developmental niches in nonindustrial and newly industrializing countries are very different from the niche described earlier. Unfortunately, many infants of the world live in developmental niches characterized by infection and malnutrition. Please keep these variations in mind as you read about infant development.

CRITICAL THINKING Questions 11.1

What were your reactions to the situations of the people in the three case studies at the beginning of this chapter? How would your reactions be helpful if you were to encounter each person in your social work practice? How would your reactions complicate your ability to be helpful to each one of them?

CONTROL OVER CONCEPTION AND PREGNANCY

One way that humans exercise human agency is to attempt to get control over conception and pregnancy. The desire to plan the timing of childbearing is an ancient one, as is the desire to stimulate pregnancy in the event of infertility. Contraception and induced abortion have probably always existed in every culture but continue to generate much controversy. Effective solutions for infertility are more recent. It is important to remember that not all methods of controlling conception and pregnancy are equally acceptable to all people. Cultural and religious beliefs, as well as personal circumstances, make some people more accepting of certain methods than others. Social workers must be aware of this diversity of attitudes and preferences related to the control of conception and pregnancy. Cultural and religious beliefs also drive social policy in this area.

Although there is evidence that many women of the world want to control conception and pregnancy, unintended pregnancy is a global problem (Blumenthal, Voedisch, & Gemzell-Danielsson, 2011). About 49% of all pregnancies in the United States are unintended, and the unintended pregnancy rate is significantly higher in the United States than in many other wealthy nations (Guttmacher Institute, 2013b). A greater percentage of unintended pregnancies are reported by teenagers, women aged 18 to 24, cohabiting women, low-income and less educated women, and minority women (Guttmacher Institute, 2013b; Mosher, Jones, & Abma, 2012). For those pregnancies resulting in birth, unintended births (vs. intended births) are associated with delayed or no prenatal care (19% of unintended vs. 8.2% intended births), smoking during pregnancy (16% vs. 10%), low birth weight (12% vs. 7.2%), and no breastfeeding (39% vs. 25%) (Mosher et al., 2012). Unintended pregnancy and birth are also associated with increased likelihood of pathological anger and rejection of the infant after birth (Brockington, Aucamp, & Fraser, 2006); increased stress; higher incidence of intimate partner violence both during the pregnancy and after delivery (Charles & Perreira, 2007); and more prenatal illicit drug use (Orr, James, & Reiter, 2008).

CONTRACEPTION

The range of birth control options available today provides women and men in many parts of the world with the ability to plan pregnancy and childbirth more than ever before. Currently 62% of U.S. women of reproductive age use some form of contraception, and 99.1% of sexually active women use a contraceptive during their lifetime (Jones, Mosher, & Daniels, 2012). However, it is estimated that 222 million women in low-income countries who don't want to get pregnant have no access to contraceptives (World Health Organization [WHO], 2013b). Forms of birth control are varied, in both effectiveness and costs. Complete sexual abstinence is the only form of contraception that has no financial cost and is completely effective. It is important for social workers to be familiar with the choices women have. Each birth control option needs to be considered in light of its cost, failure rate, potential health risks, and probability of use, given the user's sociocultural circumstances. Exhibit 11.2 summarizes the types of currently available female and male contraception, including mode of delivery, failure rate, advantages, and complications and side effects.

INDUCED ABORTION

Induced abortion may be the most politicized, hotly debated social issue related to pregnancy today in the United States and in other parts of the world. Researchers have found that highly restrictive abortion laws do not lead to fewer abortions. Global data indicate that the abortion rate is lowest in regions of the world that have liberal abortion laws (Sedgh et al., 2012). Abortion laws do make a difference, however, in whether abortion is safe or unsafe.

In 1973, in *Roe v. Wade*, the U.S. Supreme Court legalized abortion in the first trimester and left it to the discretion of the woman and her physician. Three years later, in 1976, the Hyde Amendment limited federal funding for abortion, and the Supreme Court ruled in 1989, in *Webster v. Reproductive Health Services*, that Medicaid could no longer fund abortions, except in cases of rape, incest, or life endangerment (Guttmacher Institute, 2013b). Renewed annually, this ban on the use of federal funds for abortion has now extended to all federal employees and women in the military and the Indian Health Service. With much of the decision making related to abortion left to the states, there is wide variation in who has access to abortion, when, how, and at what cost. In some states, new rules are effectively decreasing access, particularly for poor and minority populations and others who are educationally disadvantaged. Seventeen states and the District of Columbia use

EXHIBIT 11.2 • Types of Male and Female Contraception

TYPE	MODE OF DELIVERY	FAILURE RATE	ADVANTAGES	COMPLICATIONS/SIDE EFFECTS	REFERENCE
Breastfeeding (lactational amenorrhea method)		2% with perfect use	Free; 98% effective with perfect use	17.2%–26% of U.S. women have perfect use (still experiencing amenorrhea, breastfeeding exclusively, nursing at least 6 times every 24-hour period); no protection from sexually transmitted infection (STI)	CDC, 2014a; Garad, McNamee, Bateson, & Harvey, 2012; Warboys, 2015
Coitus interruptus		18%	Free; can be used during breastfeeding	No protection for STI; hard to predict when to withdraw penis; some sperm may enter vagina; may be harder for woman to have an orgasm	CDC, 2015a; Mayo Clinic 2015; Reproductive Health Access Project, 2014
Fertility awareness based methods (FABMs) (periodic abstinence; rhythm method). Six subcategories: (1) basal body temperature, (2) cervical mucus or ovulation, (3) symptothermal method, (4) calendar method, (5) standard days method, (6) two-day method		24%	Minimal costs; no health risks	Requires careful recordkeeping; no protection from STI; abstinence required several days every month	CDC, 2015b; Cooper & RelayHealth, 2013; Garad et al., 2012
Barrier methods: male condom	Personal application	18%	Easily obtained; low cost; most effective protection from STI	Can break or slip off; decreases sensation	CDC, 2015b; Garad et al., 2012
Barrier methods: female condom	Can be inserted in vagina up to 8 hours before intercourse	21%; failure rate decreases with use over time	Inexpensive; can help prevent STI	Can decrease sensation; can be noisy; can be hard to insert; may slip out of place during sex	Beksinska, Smit, Greener, Piaggio, & Joanis, 2015; Reproductive Health Access Project, 2014
Implant (only Nexplanon approved in the United States)	Insertion by MD under skin of upper arm; effective for up to 3 years	0.05% (highest effectiveness of any contraceptive)	Simple office procedure; dysmenorrhea will improve	Obese women have increased chance of bleeding; acne flares; amenorrhea; no STI protection	CDC, 2015b; Jacobstein & Polis, 2014; Kolman, Hadley, & Jordahllafrato, 2015
Contraceptive patch	Applied to skin (lower abdomen, buttocks, upper body) and changed once weekly for 3 weeks; removed for 1 week	9%; increased failure for women who weigh more than 198 pounds	Periods can be less painful and more regular	Possible increase in blood clots compared to combined oral contraceptive pill; can irritate skin; no STI protection	Garad et al., 2012; M. Perry, 2015

TYPE	MODE OF DELIVERY	FAILURE RATE	ADVANTAGES	COMPLICATIONS/SIDE EFFECTS	REFERENCE
Injectables	Injection by health professional, usually every 12 weeks (note: A new form has been developed that is subcutaneous and could be self-administered)	0.40%	Can be used up to age 50; immediate effectiveness; no drug interactions	Decreased bone density; irregular bleeding	CDC, 2015b; Garad et al., 2012; Garner, 2014; Kolman et al., 2015
Intrauterine device (IUD): 4 devices approved by U.S. FDA (3 hormonal and 1 copper)	Insertion by health professional; 86% required two or more visits for insertion	<0.01%	May be left in place 3–12 years (depending on type); can be used when breastfeeding	Possible uterine perforation at insertion or removal; increased bleeding and pain (primarily with copper IUD); expulsion of device; increased or decreased bleeding at menses; no STI protection	Branum & Jones, 2015; Luchowski et al., 2014; Reproductive Health Access Project, 2014
Oral contraceptives: progesterone-only pill	Oral	0.01%–0.08%	May reduce arterial disease; good option for women who cannot have estrogen; safe for breastfeeding women	Poor efficacy in younger women; can cause depression, hair or skin changes, changed sex drive, changes in bleeding patterns; no STI protection	Hall, Trussell, & Schwartz, 2012; Jacobstein & Polis, 2014; Reproductive Health Access Project, 2014
Oral contraceptives: estrogen and progesterone	Oral	0.01%–0.08%	Periods more regular, less painful; improves acne; prevents ovarian cancer	Nausea; weight gain; higher risks if woman has migraines; arterial cardiovascular disease, hypertension; no STD protection	Daniels, Daugherty, & Jones, 2014; Reproductive Health Access Project, 2014; Yu & Hu, 2013
Male oral contraceptive (in development, may take 10 years)	Oral		Only current contraceptives for men are condoms or vasectomy	Concern by women that men may not take it; possible change in blood pressure and heart rate; possible change in ejaculation volume	Anguita, 2014
Emergency contraception (EC)	Oral or vaginal insertion	0.1%–50%; most effective is insertion of copper IUD	Some over the counter	No STI protection; time limitations to use; costs; need for medical care for some forms of EC	Cleland, Raymond, Westley, & Trussell, 2014; Roy & Chakraborty, 2012
Vaginal ring	Insertion; remains in place for 3 weeks and is removed for 1 week	9%	Less menstrual discomfort; ability to manipulate hormonal cycles; long-term dosing; ease of administration; reversibility	Contraindicated for obese women and those with migraines with auras; increased vaginal discharge; heavy bleeding; acne; no STI protection	Nappi, 2013; Reproductive Health Access Project, 2014
Surgical sterilization: female	Surgical	0.002%–0.01%, depending on procedure	Possible reversal; can prevent cancer	Surgical complications	CDC, 2015a; Daniels et al., 2014; Gariepy, Creinin, Smith, & Xiao, 2014
Surgical sterilization: male (vasectomy)	Surgical	0.10%	55% can be reversed in first 10 years, 25% after 10 years	Surgical complications	American College of Obstetricians and Gynecologists, 2013; Guttmacher Institute, 2015a

state-only funds to cover abortions for women on Medicaid whereas four other states ban abortion coverage by private insurers. Eighty-seven percent of U.S. counties have no abortion provider, and 35% of women aged 15 to 44 live in these counties (Guttmacher Institute, 2013b), resulting in rural disparities in access to abortion.

During the first trimester and until **fetal viability** (the point at which the baby could survive outside the womb) in the second trimester, U.S. federal law allows for a pregnant woman to legally choose an abortion, although states can narrow this option. Almost 88% of abortions in the United States are performed during the first 12 weeks of pregnancy, 10.4% from 13 to 20 weeks, and 1.5% after 21 weeks (Guttmacher Institute, 2013b). Recent controversy regarding procedures for terminating a pregnancy after fetal viability has called attention to ethical and legal dilemmas that are being addressed in the legal system, by most religions, and in other parts of U.S. culture. Opinion polls reveal, however, that the majority of Americans favor abortion as an option under specified conditions (Gallup, 2013). These attitudes have been relatively consistent since 1975. Two types of abortion are available to women:

1. *Medical abortion*. *Medical abortion* is the term used to refer to an abortion brought about by medication taken to end pregnancy. Most commonly, the drugs mifepristone (also known as RU-486) and misoprostol are used in combination in the first 9 weeks after the woman's last period. In the United States, a few states limit their use to 49 days after the last period. In 2011, medical abortions made up 23% of all nonhospital abortions and 36% of abortions before 9 weeks' gestation (Guttmacher Institute, 2015b). The number of medical abortions increased from 2001 to 2011 (growing from 6% to 23% of all abortions) while the overall number of abortions declined. Medical abortion works about 97% of the time.

2. *Surgical abortion*. Surgical abortions must be done in a health provider's office or clinic. There are several surgical options, depending on how far along a woman is in her pregnancy. The standard first-trimester vacuum aspiration, also called D&A (dilation and aspiration), is the type most frequently performed in the first 16 weeks after the woman's last period. A suction device is threaded through the cervix to remove the contents of the uterus. The use of this procedure decreased by 14% from 2001 to 2009. Sometimes, a spoon-shaped instrument called a curette is used to scrape the uterine lining, a procedure called a D&C. In the second trimester (between the 13th and 24th week), dilation and evacuation (D&E) is typically performed. This involves instruments, such as a forceps, to empty the uterus (CDC, 2012c).

Regardless of the timing or type of abortion, most women should be carefully counseled before and after the procedure. One research team (Fergusson, Horwood, & Boden, 2009) found that more than 85% of women reported feeling at least one negative reaction, such as grief, guilt, sadness, or sorrow, after having an abortion. These negative reactions were offset by positive reactions, and over 85% of the women also reported feeling relief, happiness, and satisfaction. The researchers also found that looking back at the abortion decision at a later date, nearly 90% reported that the decision to have an abortion was the correct decision, and only 2% reported that it was the wrong decision. Women who reported more negative reactions were more likely to have later mental health problems. Another research team (Steinberg & Finer, 2011) found that women who had risk factors such as physical or sexual abuse prior to abortion were more likely to have mental health issues after abortion. They also found that women with prior mood and anxiety disorders were more likely to have multiple abortions. It is important for social workers working with clients with unintended pregnancy to assess for prior traumatic experiences as well as know the current federal and state legalities and resources, especially when clients have limited income. They also need to be mindful of their personal views about abortion in order to help clients make informed decisions that reflect their own values, religious beliefs, and available options as well as agency or organization policy related to abortion.

INFERTILITY TREATMENT

Infertility, the inability to create a viable embryo after 1 year of intercourse without contraception (CDC, 2013e), is a major life stressor. It is estimated that 40% of infertility problems reside with the female, 45% with the male, and 25% of the time both contribute to the problem (Center for Human Reproduction, 2013a). Jennifer and Allan Bradshaw are struggling to find a way to afford infertility treatment as they encounter staggering costs. Jennifer Bradshaw poignantly conveys her emotional distress about infertility, but we don't know much about what her husband was experiencing. Whereas it is thought that infertility causes emotional distress to both women and men (Mascarenhas et al., 2012), little is known about the impact on men. Available research indicates that infertility places women at risk for depression, anxiety, substance abuse, social stress, isolation, and marital dissatisfaction (see, e.g., Baldur-Felskov et al., 2013; Karjane, Stovall, Berger, & Svikis, 2008). Both the experience of infertility and the treatment of infertility can cause emotional distress (Greil, McQuillan, Lowry, & Shreffler, 2011). The causes of infertility are many and complex. Infertility, like other aspects of human behavior, is multidetermined, and medical causes, environmental causes, and health and lifestyle causes have been identified.

In the past, infertile couples could keep trying and hope for the best, but medical technology has given today's

EXHIBIT 11.3 • Treatments for Infertility

MALE INFERTILITY		FEMALE INFERTILITY	
PROBLEM	**TREATMENT**	**PROBLEM**	**TREATMENT**
Low sperm count	Change of environment; antibiotics; surgery; hormonal therapy; artificial insemination	Vaginal structural problem Abnormal cervical mucus	Surgery Hormonal therapy
Physical defect affecting transport of sperm	Microsurgery	Abnormal absence of ovulation	Antibiotics for infection; hormonal therapy
Genetic disorder	Artificial insemination	Blocked or scarred fallopian tubes	Surgery; IVF
Exposure to work environment substances	Early detection and changes in work environment	Uterine lining unfavorable to implantation	Hormone therapy; antibiotics; surgery
Alcohol and caffeine use and cigarette smoking	Reduction or abstinence preconception	Obesity	Weight reduction
Advancing age	Sperm banking at younger age; artificial insemination	Alcohol and caffeine use and cigarette smoking	Abstinence preconception (and postconception to maximize pregnancy outcome)

couples a variety of options, summarized in Exhibit 11.3. Today, approximately 1% of infants born in the United States are the result of **assisted reproductive technologies** (ART) (CDC, 2013f). ART is any fertility treatment in which the egg and sperm are handled. As demonstrated by the Jennifer Bradshaw case, by the time a couple considers the use of ART, they have often struggled with infertility for some time, emotionally and physically, and may be desperate. But the high cost and limited success rates deter some prospective candidates. The most common types of ART include the following:

- *IVF.* In vitro fertilization (IVF) is the most common and most effective ART used today. The woman is treated with a drug that causes the ovaries to produce multiple eggs. Mature eggs are surgically removed from the woman and combined with sperm in a dish in the lab. Healthy embryos are then implanted in the woman's uterus (American Society for Reproductive Medicine, 2013). Success rates vary, but most clinics suggest that with a single cycle of IVF, there is a 30% to 40% success rate for women younger than age 34, to less than 5% for women older than 40 (Center for Human Reproduction, 2013b; Gordon et al., 2013). Previously frozen eggs may also be used, but the rate of success decreases.

- *Intracytoplasmic sperm injection (ICSI).* ICSI is typically used for couples when there are serious problems with the sperm. In ICSI, rather than mixing egg and sperm in a dish, a single sperm is injected into a single mature egg (American Society for Reproductive Medicine, 2013).

- *Egg donors and gestational carriers.* A couple may use donor eggs to be fertilized with the sperm of the male partner and then have the fertilized egg placed in the uterus of the female partner. The resulting child will be genetically related to the egg donor and the male partner. Another option is to implant a gestational carrier with the couple's embryo produced through IVF. This option may be used when the woman can produce healthy eggs but is unable to carry a pregnancy to term. Donor eggs or sperm may also be used in IVF to produce the embryo, which is then placed in the gestational carrier. The resulting child has no genetic relationship to the gestational carrier (American Society for Reproductive Medicine, 2013).

- *Intrauterine insemination (IUI).* Healthy sperm are collected, washed, and concentrated, then placed directly into the uterus through a fine tube inserted through the cervix around the time the ovary releases one or more eggs (American Society for Reproductive Medicine, 2013). It is the primary treatment for male infertility. It is also the treatment of choice for lesbian couples and single parents, using sperm of a male donor (De Brucker et al., 2009). The sperm of the male partner of a couple may also be placed in the uterus of a surrogate who gestates and carries the pregnancy for the couple. The resulting child will be biologically related to the male partner and the surrogate, but not to the female partner in the couple.

Each ART procedure carries risks. These include multiple gestations, which carry higher risks of maternal and neonate complications. In 2009, almost half of ART births resulted in more than one neonate (CDC, 2013f).

AP Photo/Argus Leader, Elisha Page

Some infertile individuals and couples prefer adoption to the demands and uncertainties of infertility treatment and are committed to giving a home to children in need of care.

Sometimes IVF-conceived children have rare genetic malformations (Ceelen, van Weissenbruch, Vermeiden, van Leeuwen, & Delemarre-van de Waal, 2008), and genetic counseling is strongly encouraged for this population (Geary & Moon, 2006).

Adoption is another alternative for the infertile couple. From 2007 to 2008, 136,000 children were adopted in the United States, a 6% increase since 2000 and a 15% increase since 1990. Over half of these adoptions were private or tribal, about 40% were accomplished through public agency, and the remainder were intercountry (Child Welfare Information Gateway, 2011). Adoption is almost as emotionally daunting as infertility treatment. A time-consuming multiphase evaluation, which includes a home study, is required before finalization of custody. The idea of parenting an infant with an unknown genetic heritage may be a challenge for some people, particularly because an increasing number of problems previously thought to be environmentally induced are being linked—at least in part—to genetics. On the positive side, however, some individuals and couples prefer adoption to the demands and uncertainties of ART, and some adoptive parents are also committed to giving a home to children in need of care.

CRITICAL THINKING Questions 11.2

In recent years, there has been much controversy about sex education in public schools. Some people argue that there should be no sex education in public schools. What is your opinion on this topic? If you think there should be sex education in public schools, at what age do you think it should start? If you think there should be sex education in public schools, which topics covered in this chapter should be included? Explain.

FETAL DEVELOPMENT

The 40 weeks of **gestation**, during which the fertilized ovum becomes a fully developed infant, are a remarkable time. *Gestational age* is calculated from the date of the beginning of the woman's last menstrual period, a fairly easy time for the woman to identify. In contrast, *fertilization age* is measured from the time of fertilization, approximately 14 days after the beginning of the last menstrual period. The average pregnancy lasts 280 days when calculated from gestational age and 266 days from the time of fertilization. Conventionally, the gestation period is organized by trimesters of about 3 months each. This is a convenient system, but note that these divisions are not supported by clearly demarcated events.

FIRST TRIMESTER

In some ways, the first 12 weeks of pregnancy are the most remarkable. In an amazingly short time, sperm and ovum unite and are transformed into a being with identifiable body parts. The mother's body also undergoes dramatic changes.

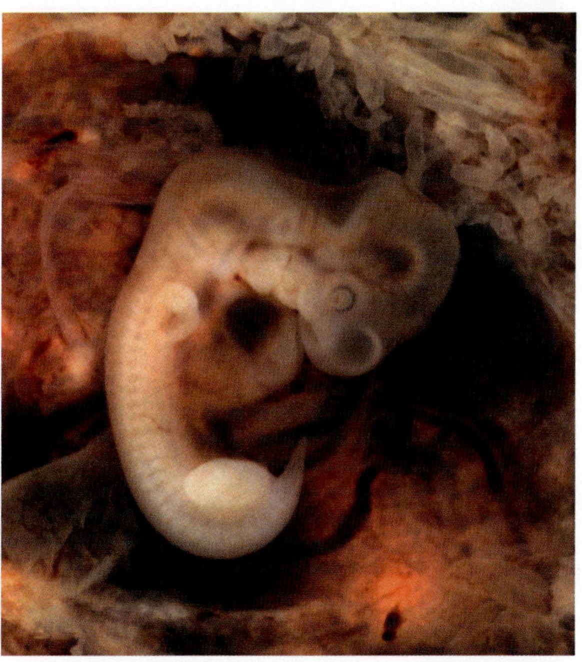

Wikimedia Commons, public domain

Following implantation in the uterine wall, the zygote matures into an embryo.

Fertilization and the Embryonic Period

Sexual intercourse results in the release of an average of 200 million to 300 million sperm. Their life span is relatively short, and their journey through the female reproductive tract is fraught with hazards. Thus, only about one or two in 1,000 of the original sperm reach the fallopian tubes, which lead from the ovaries to the uterus. Typically, only one sperm penetrates the ripened ovum, triggering a biochemical reaction that prevents entry of any other sperm. The **zygote** (fertilized egg) continues to divide and begins an approximately 7-day journey to the uterus.

Following implantation in the uterine wall, the zygote matures into an **embryo**. The placenta, which acts like a filter between the mother and the growing embryo, also forms. The umbilical cord connects the fetus to the placenta. Oxygen, water, and glucose, as well as many drugs, viruses, bacteria, vitamins, and hormones, pass through the placenta to the embryo. Amniotic fluid in the uterus protects the embryo throughout the pregnancy.

By the 3rd week, tissue begins differentiating into organs. During this period, the embryo is vulnerable to **teratogens**—substances that may harm the developing organism—but most women do not know they are pregnant. Exhibit 11.4 shows how some relatively common drugs may have a teratogenic effect in the earliest stage of fetal development. The importance of a healthy diet for the pregnant woman cannot be overestimated because her choices can have a lifelong impact on her baby (C. Anderson, 2010). Studies have found that nutritional deficiency in the first trimester results in an increase in brain abnormalities. High-fat diets negatively affect the development of the hippocampus, which helps control long-term memory and spatial navigation. Ongoing research seems to support the interaction of environment and the nutritional status of the pregnant woman as a risk factor for the child developing cancer in later years. Isothiocyanate and cruciferous vegetables (such as broccoli, brussels sprouts, radishes, turnips), beta-carotenes (found in yellow, red, and orange fruits, vegetables, and whole grains), and carotenoid lycopenes (found in tomatoes, guava, apricots, watermelons, papaya) have been found to promote healthy cellular growth in the fetus (Kaur, Shorey, Ho, Dashwood, & Williams, 2013). The development of a healthy cellular structure promotes health throughout the life span, and the positive effects appear to extend into future generations because the change occurs at the cellular level (Kaur et al., 2013). Moreover, a protein supplement used throughout the pregnancy has been shown to reduce the incidence of small-for-gestational-age babies, especially among undernourished women (Imdad & Bhutta, 2012).

The Fetal Period

By about the 8th week after fertilization, the embryo implanted in the uterine wall is mature enough to be called a **fetus**, or unborn baby, and the mother is experiencing signs of her pregnancy. A *multigravida*, or woman who has had a previous pregnancy, often recognizes the signs of excessive fatigue and soreness in her breasts as a sign of pregnancy. Approximately 80% of women experience nausea and vomiting (morning sickness) during the first trimester, as was the case for Felicia Thompson.

EXHIBIT 11.4 • Potential Teratogens During the First Trimester

SUBSTANCE	EFFECTS ON FETAL DEVELOPMENT
Antacids	Increase in anomalies
Antianxiety medications	Cranial facial defects
Anticonvulsant medications	Facial defects, neural tube defects
Barbiturates	Increase in anomalies
Bisphenol A (BPA)	Negative effects on mammary glands, immune system, brain, reproductive tract
Glucocorticoids (steroids)	Cleft palate, cardiac defects
Haloperidol	Limb malformations
Insulin	Skeletal malformations
Lithium	Goiter, eye anomalies, cleft palate
LSD	Chromosomal abnormalities
Podophyllin (in laxatives)	Multiple anomalies
Selective serotonin reuptake inhibitors (SSRIs)	May lead to neurobehavioral disturbances
Tetracycline (antibiotic)	Inhibition of bone growth, discoloration of teeth
Tricyclic antidepressants	Central nervous system and limb malformations

From the 7th to 12th week, the fetal heart rate can be heard using a Doppler fetal monitor (Merce, Barco, Alcazar, Sabatel, & Trojano, 2009). Early ultrasounds are being used to predict prenatal complications (Parra-Cordeno et al., 2013). At 12 weeks, the sex of the fetus usually can be detected, and the face is fully formed. The fetus is moving within the mother, but it is still too early for her to feel the movement.

Newly pregnant women often feel ambivalence. Because of hormonal changes, they may experience mood swings and become less outgoing. Anxiety and depression have been found to be higher during the first trimester and in the postpartum period than the second and third trimesters (Fan et al., 2009; Figueiredo & Conde, 2011). Concerns about the changes in their bodies, finances, the impact on their life goals, lifestyle adjustments, and interpersonal interactions may cause anxiety. Often the father experiences similar ambivalence, and he may be distressed by his partner's mood swings.

Miscarriage, or *spontaneous abortion*, is a pregnancy loss prior to 20 weeks of gestation and is most prevalent in the first trimester. Approximately 10% to 15% of all clinically recognized pregnancies end in spontaneous abortion, often unrecognized by the mother and without a discernible cause (American College of Nurse-Midwives, 2013). Recurrent miscarriage, three or more consecutive miscarriages, occurs in 1% of women (Horn & Alexander, 2005). It is estimated that about half of all miscarriages are caused by abnormalities in the genetic makeup of the embryo or fetus. Chronic conditions such as uncontrolled diabetes, thyroid disease, and other underlying maternal health conditions increase the risk of miscarriage, as do smoking and alcohol use (American College of Nurse-Midwives, 2013; Medical News Today, 2013). Other potential causes are problems in placental development, womb structure abnormalities, polycystic ovary syndrome, obesity and underweight, environmental toxins, and some medications (Medical News Today, 2013).

The signs and symptoms of miscarriage include vaginal spotting or bleeding, cramping or pain in the abdomen, lower backache, fluid or tissue discharge from the vagina, and feeling faint or light-headed (Medical News Today, 2013). These symptoms do not always mean a woman is having a miscarriage, and sometimes miscarriage happens with no symptoms (American College of Nurse-Midwives, 2013). Miscarriage is most commonly diagnosed these days by ultrasound; blood tests may also be done. Some women choose to allow the miscarriage to pass naturally; this may take 2 weeks. Sometimes it is not possible to pass all of the pregnancy without further assistance. Women may take medication to help the body pass the miscarriage, and sometimes surgery is needed to complete the miscarriage (American College of Nurse-Midwives, 2013). Social workers need to understand the possibility of both short-term and long-term grief following a pregnancy loss and be prepared to talk with women about whether a subsequent pregnancy is planned, the importance the mother attributes to motherhood, and fertility issues (Price, 2008a, 2008b; Shreffler, Greil, & McQuillan, 2011; P. Wright, 2011).

SECOND TRIMESTER

By the 16th week, the fetus is approximately 19 centimeters (7.5 inches) long and weighs 100 grams (3.3 ounces). The most rapid period of brain development is during the second trimester (van de Beek, Thijssen, Cohen-Kettenis, van Goozen, & Buitelaar, 2004). Recent evidence cautions pregnant women to monitor the eating of fish with higher levels of mercury to avoid negative impact on the infant's cognitive skills (Jain, 2013; Zeilmaker et al., 2013). Insufficient weight gain by the pregnant woman during this trimester has been shown to be associated with a small-for-gestational-age (SGA) neonate (Drehmer, Duncan, Kac, & Schmidt, 2013). The second trimester is generally a period of contentment, with the fatigue, nausea and vomiting, and mood swings that often accompany the first few weeks gone for most women. For problem pregnancies, or in troubled environments, quite the opposite may occur.

Hearing the heartbeat and seeing the fetus via ultrasound often bring the reality of the pregnancy home. As seen in the story of the Thompsons, *quickening*—the experience of feeling fetal movement—usually occurs around this time, further validating the personhood of the fetus.

THIRD TRIMESTER

The third trimester is critical for continued fetal development and preparation for birth. The mother must be able to effectively meet both her nutritional needs and those of the growing fetus. Women who have an excessive weight gain are at risk for preterm delivery and higher rates of cesarean section (Drehmer et al., 2013). Maternal smoking decreases fetal circulation and has been correlated with lower birth weight (Lindell, Marsal, & Kallen, 2012). Spouses who smoke increase the nicotine level in the nonsmoking pregnant woman, even if the spouse smokes outside (Sang-Ho, 2010).

More than 30% of women are iron-deficient by the third trimester, placing the neonate at risk for anemia. Low iron levels can result in permanently altered developmental and metabolic processes and negatively impact brain development (Cao & O'Brien, 2013). In addition, maternal stress can reduce fetoplacental blood flow and fetal weight gain (Helbig, Kaasen, Mait, & Haugen, 2013). Today, a transvaginal neurosonography can visualize the fetal brain anatomy and identify specific neurological problems (Ginath et al., 2013; Loureiro, Ferreira, Ushokov, Montenegro, & Nicolaides, 2012). By 24 weeks, the fetus is considered viable in many hospitals. In spite of fetal viability, parents are not usually prepared for childbirth early in the third trimester. Felicia Thompson, for instance, was not prepared for the birth of her son, Paul, who at 26 weeks' gestation struggled to survive.

The tasks of the fetus during the third trimester are to gain weight and mature in preparation for delivery. As delivery nears, the increased weight of the fetus can cause discomfort for the mother, and often she looks forward to delivery with increasing anticipation. Completing preparations for the new baby consumes much of her attention.

LABOR AND DELIVERY OF THE NEONATE

Predicting when labor will begin is impossible. However, one indication of imminent labor is *lightening* (the descent of the fetus into the mother's pelvis). For a *primipara*—a first-time mother—lightening occurs approximately 2 weeks before delivery. For a *multipara*—a mother who has previously given birth—lightening typically occurs at the beginning of labor. Often the mother experiences Braxton Hicks contractions, brief contractions that prepare the mother and fetus for labor—what is often referred to as "false labor." Usually, true labor begins with a show or release of the mucous plug that covered the cervical opening.

Labor is divided into three stages:

1. In the first stage, the cervix thins and dilates. The amniotic fluid is usually released during this stage ("water breaking"), and the mother feels regular contractions that intensify in frequency and strength as labor progresses. Near the end of this phase, "transition" occurs, marked by a significant increase in the intensity and frequency of the contractions and by heightened maternal emotionalism. The head crowns (is visible at the vulva) at the end of this stage.

2. The second stage is delivery, when the neonate is expelled from the mother. If the newborn is born breech (feet or buttocks first) or is transverse (positioned horizontally in the birth canal) and cannot be turned prior to birth, the mother may require a cesarean section.

3. Typically, within 1 hour after delivery, the placenta, the remaining amniotic fluid, and the membrane that separated the fetus from the uterine wall are delivered with a few contractions. If the newborn breastfeeds immediately, the hormone oxytocin is released to stimulate these contractions.

Following birth, the neonate undergoes rapid physiological changes, particularly in its respiratory and cardiac systems. Prior to birth, oxygen is delivered to the fetus through the umbilical vein, and carbon dioxide is eliminated by the two umbilical arteries. Although the fetus begins to breathe prior to birth, breathing serves no purpose until after delivery. The neonate's first breath, typically in the form of a cry, creates tremendous pressure within the lungs, which clears amniotic fluid and triggers the opening and closing of several shunts and vessels in the heart (Petty, n.d.). The blood flow is rerouted to the lungs.

Many factors, such as maternal exposure to narcotics during pregnancy or labor, can adversely affect the neonate's attempts to breathe—as can prematurity, congenital anomalies, and neonatal infections. To measure the neonate's adjustment to extrauterine life, Apgar scores—simple measures of breathing, heart rate, muscle tone, reflexes, and skin color—are assessed at 1, 5, and 10 minutes after birth. Apgar scores determine the need for resuscitation and indicate whether there are heart problems. The other immediate challenge to the newborn is to establish a stable temperature. Inadequately maintained body temperature creates neonatal stress and thus increased respiratory and cardiac effort, which can result in respiratory failure. Close monitoring of the neonate during the first 4 hours after birth is critical to detect any such problems in adapting to extrauterine life.

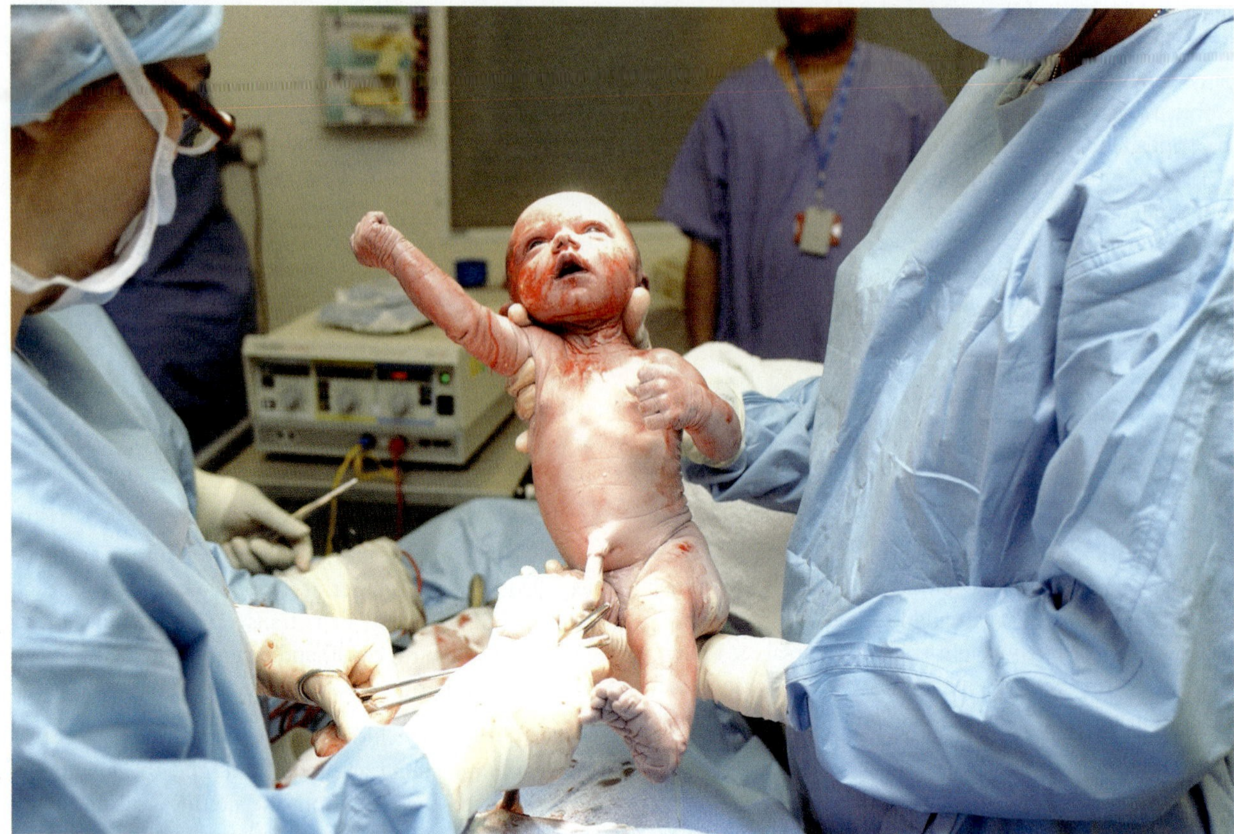

A typical delivery—here a newborn baby is delivered by medical professionals in a hospital delivery room.

Sometimes the baby is born showing no signs of life; this is known as *stillbirth*. The World Health Organization (WHO, 2013c) defines stillbirth as "a baby born with no signs of life at or after 28 weeks' gestation." The WHO reports that in 2009, there were more than 2.6 million stillbirths around the world, the majority occurring in impoverished countries (World Health Organization, 2013c). In the United States 1 in 160 pregnancies ends in stillbirth, a statistic that has stabilized over the past 10 years yet remains higher compared with other developed countries (Stillbirth Collaborative Research Network Writing Group, 2011). In up to 50% of stillbirths, the causes are not determined. For those where a possible or probable cause is found, approximately 15% to 20% are caused by chromosomal and genetic abnormalities; placental abruption accounts for 25%; infection 10% to 20%; maternal illness 8% to 10%; and birth trauma 2% to 4% (March of Dimes, 2010; Stillbirth Collaborative Research Network Writing Group, 2011). There is a greater chance of subsequent pregnancies ending in stillbirth once this has occurred (Barclay, 2009). In cases of fetal death, labor generally proceeds immediately and is allowed to occur naturally. But the pregnancy may continue for several days following cessation of movement. Although this wait can be distressing for the mother, cesarean sections are usually avoided because of the potentially high number of complications for the mother (Barclay, 2009). Stillbirths are often unexpected, resulting in great stress and anguish for parents, who blame themselves and struggle with unresolved guilt. Social workers can help parents understand and cope with the strong emotions they are experiencing due to such a significant loss (Price, 2008a, 2008b).

CRITICAL THINKING Questions 11.3

How is ultrasound technology changing the process of fetal development for the mother? What are the benefits to these technologies? What ethical issues are raised by the use of these technologies?

AT-RISK NEWBORNS

Not all pregnancies proceed smoothly and end in routine deliveries. There are 15 million preterm births per year worldwide, and the rate is increasing (World Health Organization, 2013d). One in nine births in the United States is premature, defined as before 37 weeks' gestation, with prematurity the leading cause of neonatal illness and responsible for 35% of infant deaths (March of

Dimes, 2012a). More than 90% of babies born at less than 28 weeks' gestation (the smallest and most vulnerable of preemies) die in the first days of life in low-income countries, whereas in high-income countries (like the United States), the survival rate for these fragile neonates is more than 90% (March of Dimes, 2012a). Seventy-five percent of the deaths of premature infants are preventable with low-cost interventions such as providing warmth, basic care, and breastfeeding (Hamilton, Martin, and Ventura, 2013; March of Dimes, 2012a; World Health Organization, 2013d). There is a global initiative to lower premature births by expanding birth control options and addressing adolescent pregnancy, preventing and treating STIs, increasing prenatal education, and enhancing prenatal nutrition (World Health Organization, 2013a, 2013d). Compared with 34 developed countries, the United States ranks 31st in infant mortality, despite having state-of-the-art medical services (Heisler, 2012).

PREMATURITY AND LOW BIRTH WEIGHT

The World Health Organization estimated that 9.6% of all global births were preterm in 2005. Approximately 85% of the preterm births occurred in Africa and Asia, but the highest rates of prematurity were in Africa and North America (Beck et al., 2010). Prematurity has a profound long-term effect on the family, including parental mental health problems related to parental stress (Mathews & MacDorman, 2013; Treyvaud et al., 2011). Prematurity costs more than $26 billion per year in the United States, with the average cost of a premature neonate 10 times greater than a full-term neonate (CDC, 2013g; National Business Group on Health, 2009). It is estimated that the care of one preemie costs $51,600, with 65% covering medical costs; 22% representing lost wages; and the remaining costs covering maternal care, special education services, and early intervention programs (CDC, 2013g).

In the United States, approximately 70% of premature births (8% of all births) occur from 34 to 36 weeks (40 weeks is full gestation), and the rate of these late-term preterm births has increased by 25% since 1990 (Loftin, Habli, & DeFranco, 2010). Most of these *late preterm births* are precipitated by induced labor, an elective cesarean, or maternal medical complications (including incorrect gestational estimation) (Loftin et al., 2010; March of Dimes, 2012b). These babies may weigh more than 2,500 grams (5.5 pounds) but are still premature. They are at risk for respiratory distress during the neonatal period as well as increased respiratory problems during the first year of life, feeding problems, hypoglycemia (low blood sugar), hypothermia (low body temperature), and hyperbilirubinemia (jaundice) (Colin, McEvoy, & Castile, 2010; Loftin et al., 2010). These babies have a threefold greater chance of dying than a full-term infant (McFarlin, 2009).

Low-birth-weight (LBW) neonates (weighing from 1,500 to 2,500 grams, 3.3 to 5.5 pounds) may be *small for gestational age (SGA)*, generally weighing below the 10th percentile for sex and gestational age (Mandy, 2013; MedlinePlus, 2011). In other situations, the LBW infant is premature. These neonates have an increased risk for death in the neonatal period when they need support in feeding, temperature maintenance, and respiration (Colin et al., 2010). Later, they have an increased risk for developing asthma, showing delayed growth patterns, developing eye problems, and experiencing cardiovascular and renal disorders (McCormick, Litt, Smith, & Zupancic, 2011; Simeoni, Ligi, Buffat, & Boubred, 2011). Additionally, they are at higher risk for later depression, anxiety, and inattention or hyperactivity than are full-term newborns (Hall, Jaekel, & Wolke, 2012; Sullivan, Msall, & Miller, 2012). The risks continue into the next generation; it has been shown that women who themselves were premature or SGA had a higher risk for pregnancy complications (Boivin et al., 2012).

Very-low-birth-weight (VLBW) infants—infants weighing less than 1,500 grams (3 pounds, 3 ounces)—have a 100 times greater risk of death than a full-term neonate (U.S. Department of Health and Human Services, Maternal and Child Health Bureau, 2011) and are at greater risk for poor physical growth, lower IQ, learning problems, and dropping out of high school (Child Trends Data Bank, 2013; Tamaru et al., 2011). Some will develop cerebral palsy (2 to 3 per 1,000 live births) (Lie, Groholt, & Eskild, 2010) and experience a lower quality of life (McCormick et al., 2011). There is a higher incidence of anxiety disorder and attention deficit/hyperactivity disorder in VLBW and SGA children compared with their full-term counterparts (Lund et al., 2011).

Extremely low-birth-weight (ELBW) infants—infants weighing less than 1,000 grams (2.2 pounds)—add dramatically to the neonatal and infant mortality rates (Lau, Ambalavanan, Chakraborty, Wingate, & Carlo, 2013). The smallest survivors have a very high risk of lifelong neurological, psychological, and physical problems, including cerebral palsy, blindness, deafness, cognitive delays, feeding intolerance, chronic lung disease, failure to thrive, anxiety, and attention deficit/hyperactivity disorder (Boat, Sadhasivam, Loepke, & Kurth, 2011; M. Boyle et al., 2011; Dewey et al., 2011). Paul Thompson is considered an ELBW newborn, and at approximately 540 grams, he has a 50% chance of survival.

Several policy initiatives in the United States address the issue of prematurity. Passage of the Prematurity Research Expansion and Education for Mothers Who Deliver Infants Early (PREEMIE) Act in 2006 (Pub. L. No. 109-450) mandated interagency coordination, improved data collection, and education for health care professionals. In 2013, the PREEMIE Reauthorization Act (S-252, 113th Congress) was passed to promote further federal

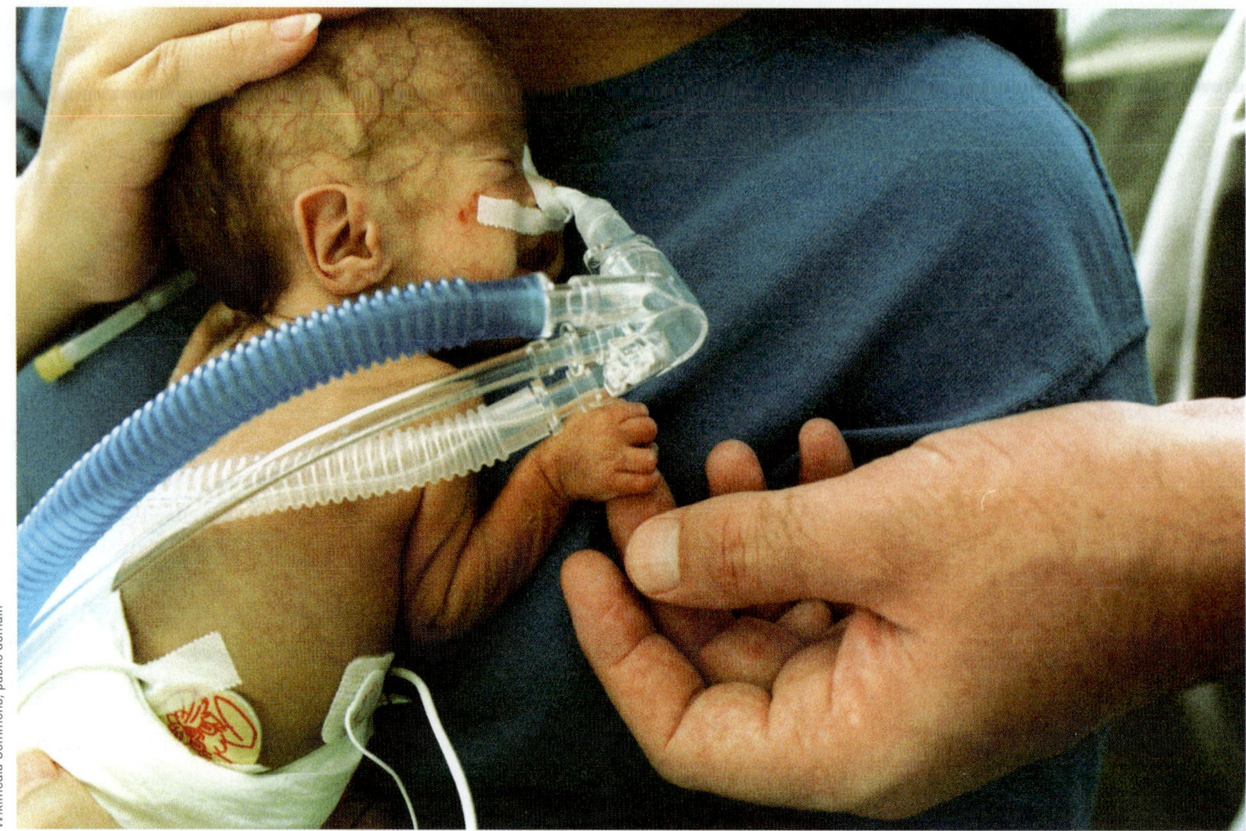
Wikimedia Commons, public domain

Prematurity costs more than $26 billion per year in the United States, with the average cost of a premature neonate 10 times greater than a full-term neonate.

funding and awareness campaigns (Congress.gov, 2013). The March of Dimes has promoted a National Prematurity Campaign since 2003 and has been at the forefront in bringing attention to this serious health problem (March of Dimes, 2012c). The Affordable Care Act of 2010 has a provision for in-home services for pregnant women and mothers, but the states have the option to opt out of the block grants that fund this initiative (Health Resources and Services Administration, 2010).

The survival rates of premature infants in high-income countries have improved largely because of explosive growth in the field of neonatal medicine and the establishment of regional Neonatal Intensive Care Units (NICUs). Studying the long-term effects of prematurity is difficult because today's 5-year-old who was born at LBW received significantly less sophisticated care than will the current patients in the NICU.

As the Thompsons know all too well, parents' expectations for a healthy newborn are shattered when their child is admitted to an NICU. Their fear and anxiety often make it hard for them to form a strong emotional bond with their newborn. About 90% of mothers and 80% of fathers report that they develop an attachment to the infant during the third trimester of pregnancy (Latva, Lehtonen, Salmelin, & Tamminen, 2007). But when an infant is premature, the parents have not had the same opportunity. In addition, the fear that a sickly newborn may die inhibits some parents from risking attachment. Mothers of VLBW infants visit the newborn significantly less than do mothers of infants who weigh more; for fathers, visitation is influenced by geographical distance and the number of other children in the home (Latva et al., 2007). Some parents are consumed with guilt about their baby's condition and believe that they will only harm the newborn by their presence. The NICU experience places the mother at risk for depression, but it also has been found that short-term psychotherapy can reduce stress and promote visitation (Friedman, Kessler, & Martin, 2009). Felicia and Will Thompson had to work hard to contain their anxiety about Paul's frailties.

Early disruption in bonding may have a larger long-term impact on the child than the infant's actual medical condition (Wigert, Johannson, Berg, & Hellstrom, 2006). The response has been a movement toward family-centered NICU environments, which are structured to promote interaction between the infant and the parents, siblings, and others in the family's support system. Mothers seem to more readily engage in caring for their infants in this environment than fathers (A. N. Johnson, 2008). Ample opportunity to interact with Paul facilitated Felicia and Will Thompson's attempts to bond with him.

CONGENITAL ANOMALIES

Overall, only 2% to 4% of all surviving newborns have a congenital disorder, some type of medical condition that occurs at or before birth, often referred to as a birth defect. However, the number of neonates born with anomalies caused by genetics, exposure to teratogens, or nonhereditary factors that affect development of the fetus does not reflect the number of abnormal embryos. Fewer than half of all fertilized ova result in a live birth; the rest are spontaneously aborted, oftentimes before a woman knows she is pregnant. Based on data from a 10-year study of placental tissue following pregnancy loss, 80.5% of these spontaneous abortions were caused by a genetic anomaly (Osterweil, 2013). Another study of subsequent pregnancy outcomes after a pregnancy loss attributed to a genetic anomaly revealed that two thirds of these women had a live birth (Osterweil, 2013).

In 2006 the American College of Medical Genetics with the March of Dimes established a recommended list of 28 core metabolic, endocrine, and hemoglobin disorders for which newborns should be screened because early intervention for these hereditary yet rare diseases is essential (Watson, Mann, Lloyd-Puryear, Rinaldo, & Howell, 2006). Twenty-one of these tests are required in all states whereas some states screen for more than 30 disorders. The National Newborn Screening and Global Resource Center (NNSGRC) provides genetic and newborn screening information, including resources for parents and providers to respond to positive testing results (NNSGRC, 2013). A *screening* test may not be definitive, however, and, if positive, is usually followed by a *diagnostic* test to confirm a genetic mishap. Some screening may be done before birth (CDC, 2011).

Congenital anomalies fall into four categories (B. Pierce, 2012):

1. *Inheritance of a single abnormal gene.* An inherited anomaly in a single gene may lead to a serious disorder.
2. *Multifactorial inheritance.* The expression of some genetic traits varies because of multifactorial inheritance, meaning they are controlled by multiple genes.
3. *Chromosomal aberration.* Some genetic abnormalities are not hereditary but rather caused by a genetic mishap during development of the ovum or sperm cells.
4. *Exposure to teratogens.* Teratogens can be divided into four categories: radiation, infections, maternal metabolic imbalance, and drugs and environmental chemicals.

Today most pregnant women in the United States undergo a maternal blood screen and ultrasound between Week 11 and Week 13. Most recently recommended is the noninvasive prenatal screening, or NIPS (American College of Medical Genetics, 2013). Second-trimester screening, Weeks 15 to 20, includes a maternal serum screen and an anomaly ultrasound (18 to 20 weeks), which produces a visual image of the developing fetus. Based on these results, the doctor may offer diagnostic tests such as high-resolution ultrasound and chorionic villi testing (CVT). CVT involves the insertion of a catheter through the cervix into the uterus to obtain a sample of the developing placenta and can be done as early as 10 to 12 weeks. *Amniocentesis* is the extraction of amniotic fluid for chromosomal analysis; it involves inserting a hollow needle through the abdominal wall during the second trimester. At greater risk of a genetic anomaly are women older than age 35, carriers of sex-linked genetic disorders and single gene defects, parents with chromosomal disorders, and women who have had previous and recurring pregnancy loss. When any of these risks is present, screening or diagnostic tests may be offered earlier in pregnancy (American Pregnancy Association, 2012; CDC, 2011).

TYPICAL INFANT DEVELOPMENT

What happens during the prenatal period and the earliest months and years of a child's life (young children are typically referred to as **infants** in the first year) has a lasting impact on the life course journey. In the earliest moments, months, and years, interactions with parents, family members, and other adults and children influence the way the brain and the rest of the body develop, as do such factors as nutrition and environmental safety.

In all three of the case studies at the beginning of this chapter, factors can be identified that may adversely affect development. However, we must begin by understanding what is traditionally referred to as "normal" development. But because *normal* is a relative term with some judgmental overtones, we use the term *typical* instead, meaning typical in a statistical sense.

To make the presentation of ideas about infancy manageable, we follow a traditional method of organizing the discussion by type of development: physical development, cognitive development, emotional development, and social development. In this chapter, emotional development and social development are combined under the heading "Socioemotional Development." Of course, all these types of development and behavior are interdependent, and often the distinctions blur.

PHYSICAL DEVELOPMENT

Newborns depend on others for basic physical needs. They must be fed, cleaned, and kept safe and comfortable until they develop the ability to do these things for themselves. At the same time, however, newborns have an amazing set of physical abilities and potentials right from the beginning.

In Case Study 11.3, the pediatrician and CPS social worker were concerned that Sarah Johnson was not gaining weight. With adequate nourishment and care, the physical growth of the infant is quite predictable and rapid. The WHO undertook a project, called the Multicentre Growth Reference Study (MGRS), to construct standards for evaluating children from birth through 5 years of age. One part of that project was to construct growth standards to propose how children *should* grow in *all* countries, of interest because of WHO's commitment to eliminate global health disparities. MGRS collected growth data from 8,440 affluent children from diverse geographical and cultural settings, including Brazil, Ghana, India, Norway, Oman, and the United States. To be eligible for the study, mothers needed to be breastfeeding and not smoking, and the environment needed to be adequate to support unconstrained growth.

The researchers found that there were no differences in growth patterns across sites, even though there were some differences in parental stature. Given the striking similarity in growth patterns across sites, they concluded that the data could be used to develop an international standard. Across sites, the average length at birth was 19.5 inches (49.5 cm), 26.3 inches (66.7 cm) at 6 months, and 29.5 inches (75.0 cm) at 12 months (WHO Multicentre Growth Reference Study Group, 2006a). By 1 year of age, infant height was about 1.5 times birth height.

Most newborns weigh from 5 to 10 pounds at birth, and infants triple their weight in the first year. Evidently, the size of individual infants can vary quite a bit. Some of the difference is the result of nutrition, exposure to disease, and other environmental factors; much of it is the result of genetics. The importance of nutrition in infancy cannot be overstated. Nutrition affects physical stature, motor skill development, brain development, and most every other aspect of development. Some ethnic differences in physical development have also been observed. For example, Asian American children tend to be smaller than average, and African American children tend to be larger than average (Tate, Dezateux, Cole, and the Millennium Cohort Study Child Health Group, 2006). The WHO child growth standards, calculated by different methods, can be found at www.who.int/childgrowth/standards/en.

Self-Regulation

Before birth, the bodily functions of the fetus are regulated by the mother's body. After birth, the infant must develop the capacity to engage in self-regulation (Davies, 2011). At first, the challenge is to regulate bodily functions, such as temperature control, sleeping, eating, and eliminating. That challenge is heightened for the premature or medically fragile infant, as Paul Thompson's parents are learning. Growing evidence indicates that some self-regulatory functions that allow self-calming and organize the wake-sleep cycles get integrated and coordinated during the third trimester, from 30 to 34 weeks' gestation (Institute of Medicine, 2006). Born at 26 weeks' gestation, Paul did not have the benefit of the uterine environment to support the development of these self-regulatory functions.

As any new parent will attest, however, infants are not born with regular patterns of sleeping, eating, and eliminating. With maturation of the central nervous system in the first 3 months, and with lots of help from parents or other caregivers, the infant's rhythms of sleeping, eating, and eliminating become much more regular (Davies, 2011). A newborn usually sleeps about 16 hours a day, dividing that time evenly between day and night. Of course, this is not a good fit with the way adults organize their sleep lives. At the end of 3 months, most infants are sleeping 14 to 15 hours per day, primarily at night, with some well-defined nap times during the day. Parents also gradually shape infants' eating schedules so that they are eating mainly during the day.

There are cultural variations in, and controversies about, the way caregivers shape the sleeping and eating behaviors of infants. The management of sleep is one of the earliest culturally influenced parenting behaviors. In some cultures, infants sleep with parents, and in other cultures, infants are put to sleep in their own beds and often in their own rooms. In some cultures, putting an infant to sleep alone in a room is considered to be neglectful (Gardiner & Kosmitzki, 2011). Co-sleeping, the child sleeping with the parents, is routine in most of the world's cultures (McKenna, 2002). There are also cultural variations and controversies about breastfeeding versus bottle feeding. It is interesting to note that both breastfeeding and sleeping with parents induce shorter bouts of sleep and less sound sleep than the alternatives (Blunden, Thompson, & Dawson, 2011). Some researchers have speculated that the infant's lighter and shorter sleep pattern may protect against sudden infant death syndrome (SIDS). The connection between co-sleeping and SIDS has been a controversial research issue. One research team conducted a meta-analysis of research of the issue published from 1970 to 2010; they found that co-sleeping increased the risk for SIDS, and the risk is highest for infants younger than 12 weeks and when parents smoke (Vennemann et al., 2012).

Parents become less anxious as the infant's rhythms become more regular and predictable. At the same time, if the caregiver is responsive and dependable, the infant becomes less anxious and begins to develop the ability to wait to have needs met.

Cultural variations exist in beliefs about how to respond when infants cry and fuss, whether to soothe them or leave them to learn to soothe themselves. When parents do attempt to soothe infants, interestingly, they seem to use the same methods across cultures: "They say something, touch, pick up, search for sources of discomfort, and then feed" (Shonkoff & Phillips, 2000, p. 100). Infants who have been consistently soothed usually begin to develop the ability to soothe themselves after 3 or 4 months.

Sensory Abilities

Full-term infants are born with a functioning **sensory system**—the senses of hearing, sight, taste, smell, touch, and sensitivity to pain—and these abilities continue to develop rapidly in the first few months. Indeed, in the early months the sensory system seems to function at a higher level than the motor system, which allows movement. The sensory system allows infants, from the time of birth, to participate in and adapt to their environments. A lot of their learning happens through listening and watching (Newman & Newman, 2012). The sensory system is interconnected, with various sensory abilities working together to give the infant multiple sources of information about the world.

Hearing is the earliest link to the environment; the fetus is sensitive to auditory stimulation in the uterus (Moraru et al., 2011). The fetus hears the mother's heartbeat, and this sound is soothing to the infant in the early days and weeks after birth. Newborns show a preference for their mother's voice over unfamiliar voices, but one research team found that this is not the case for newborns whose mothers were anxious or depressed during the third trimester (Figueiredo, Pacheco, Costa, Conde, & Teixeira, 2010). Early infants can also distinguish changes in loudness, pitch, and location of sounds, and they can use auditory information to differentiate one object from another and to track the location of an object (Bahrick, Lickliter, & Flom, 2006). These capacities grow increasingly sensitive across the first 6 months after birth. Infants appear to be particularly sensitive to language sounds, and the earliest infant smiles are evoked by the sound of the human voice (Benasich & Leevers, 2003). Unfortunately, research indicates that malnutrition during the infant's first 3 months increases the likelihood of early onset hearing loss (Olusanya, 2010).

The newborn's vision improves rapidly during the first few months of life. By about the age of 4 months, the infant sees objects the same way an adult does. Of course, infants do not have cognitive associations with objects as adults do. Infants respond to a number of visual dimensions, including depth, brightness, movement, color, and distance. Human faces have particular appeal for newborns. Although conflicting evidence exists, research suggests that several days after birth infants are able to discriminate between facial expressions (Farroni, Menon, Rigato, & Johnson, 2007). By 3 months, most infants are able to distinguish a parent's face from the face of a stranger (Nelson, 2001). From 4 to 7 months, infants are able to recognize emotional expressions, particularly happiness, fear, and anger (McClure, 2000). Some researchers have found that infants are distressed by a lack of facial movement in the people they look at, showing that they prefer caregivers to have expressive faces (Muir & Lee, 2003).

Touch plays a very important role in infant development.

Taste and smell begin to function in the uterus, and newborns can differentiate sweet, bitter, sour, and salty tastes. A preference for sweet tastes is innately present for both preterm and full-term newborns (Pepino & Mennella, 2006). Research suggests that the first few minutes after birth is a particularly sensitive period for learning to distinguish smells (Delaunay-El Allam, Marlier, & Schaal, 2006). Breastfed babies are particularly sensitive to their mother's body odors. One research team found that newborns undergoing a heel prick were soothed by the smell of breast milk, but only if the milk came from the mother's breast (Nishitani et al., 2009).

Both animal and human research tells us that touch plays a very important role in infant development. In many cultures, swaddling, or wrapping a baby snugly in a blanket, is used to soothe a fussy newborn. We also know that gentle handling, rocking, stroking, and cuddling are all soothing to an infant. Regular gentle rocking and stroking are very effective in soothing low-birth-weight (LBW) babies, who may have underdeveloped central nervous systems. Skin-to-skin contact between parents and their newborns has been found to have benefits for both infants and their parents. Preterm babies who have lots of skin contact with their parents, including gentle touching and massage, gain weight faster, have better temperature regulation, have better capacity for self-soothing, and are more alert compared with preterm babies who do not receive extensive skin contact (Feldman, 2004; Jean & Stack, 2012). Infants also use touch to learn about their world and their own bodies. Early infants use their mouths for exploring their worlds, but by 5 or 6 months of age, infants can make controlled use of their hands to explore objects in their environment.

They learn about the world and keep themselves entertained by exploring small details, transferring objects from one hand to the other, and examining the differences in surfaces and other features of the object (Streri, 2005).

Clear evidence exists that from the first days of life, babies feel pain. Researchers have been studying newborn reactions to medical procedures such as heel sticks, the sticks used to draw blood for lab analysis. One researcher found that newborns who undergo repeated heel sticks learn to anticipate pain and develop a stronger reaction to pain than other infants (Taddio, Shah, Gilbert-Macleod, & Katz, 2002). These findings are leading pediatricians to develop guidelines for managing pain in newborns (Spence et al., 2010).

Reflexes

Although dependent on others, newborns are equipped from the start with tools for survival that are involuntary muscle responses to certain stimuli, called **reflexes**. Reflexes aid the infant in adapting to the environment outside the womb. The presence and strength of a reflex is an important sign of neurological development, and the absence of reflexes can indicate a serious developmental disorder (Goldenring, 2011). Given Paul Thompson's early arrival, his reflex responses were thoroughly evaluated.

Newborns have two critical reflexes:

1. *Rooting reflex.* When infants' cheeks or the corners of their mouths are gently stroked with a finger, they will turn their head in the direction of the touch and open their mouths in an attempt to suck the finger. This reflex aids in feeding, because it guides the infants to the nipple.
2. *Sucking reflex.* When a nipple or some other suckable object is presented to the infant, the infant sucks it. This reflex is another important tool for feeding.

Many infants would probably perish without the rooting and sucking reflexes. Imagine the time and effort it would require for one feeding if they did not have them. Instead, infants are born with the ability to take in nutriment.

A number of reflexes disappear at identified times during infancy but in some cases change into voluntary behavior; others persist throughout adulthood (see Exhibit 11.5 for an overview of infant reflexes) (Goldenring, 2011; healthychildren.org, 2013). Both the rooting reflex and sucking reflex disappear at 2 to 4 months. By this time, the infant has mastered the voluntary act of sucking and is therefore no longer in need of the reflexive response. Several other infant reflexes appear to have little use now but probably had some specific survival purposes in earlier times. The presence of an infant reflex after the age at which it typically disappears can be a sign of damage to the brain or nervous system (Goldenring, 2011).

Motor Skills

The infant gradually advances from reflex functioning to motor functioning. The development of **motor skills**—the ability to move and manipulate—occurs in a more or less orderly, logical sequence. It begins with simple actions such as lifting the chin and progresses to more complex acts such as walking, running, and throwing. Infants usually crawl before they walk.

Motor development is somewhat predictable, in that children tend to reach milestones at about the same age and in the same sequence. As a part of the Multicentre Growth Reference Study (MGRS), the WHO undertook a project to construct standards for evaluating the motor development of children from birth through 5 years of age. MGRS collected longitudinal data on six gross motor milestones of children ages 4 to 24 months in Ghana, India, Norway, Oman, and the United States. The milestones studied were sitting without support, standing with assistance, hands-and-knees crawling, walking with assistance, standing alone, and walking alone. Because WHO was trying to establish standards for evaluating child development, healthy children were studied in all five study sites. The researchers found that 90% of the children achieved five of the six milestones in the same sequence, but 4.3% of the sample never engaged in hands-and-knees crawling (WHO Multicentre Growth Reference Study Group, 2006b).

Based on the data collected, MGRS developed "windows of milestone achievement" for each of the six motor skills, with achievement at the 1st and 99th percentiles as the window boundaries. All motor achievement within the windows is considered normal variation in ages of achievement for healthy children. The windows of achievement for the six motor skills studied are reported in Exhibit 11.6. The results reveal that the range of the windows varies from 5.4 months for sitting without support (from 3.8 months at the 1st percentile to 9.2 months at the 99th percentile) to 10.0 months for standing alone (from 6.9 at the 1st percentile to 16.9 at the 99th percentile). This is quite a wide range for normal development and should be reassuring to parents who become anxious if their child is not at the low end of the window. Many parents, for example, become concerned if their child has not attempted to walk unassisted by age 1. However, some children walk alone at age 9 months; others do not even attempt to walk until almost 18 months.

Culture and ethnicity appear to have some influence on motor development in infants and toddlers. MGRS found that girls were slightly ahead of boys in gross motor development, but the differences were not statistically significant. They did find small, but statistically significant, differences between sites of the study, however. The researchers speculate that these differences probably reflect culture-based child care behaviors, but the cause cannot be determined from the data, and a genetic component is

EXHIBIT 11.5 • Infant Reflexes

REFLEX	DESCRIPTION	VISIBLE
Sucking	The infant instinctively sucks any object of appropriate size that is presented to the infant.	First 2 to 4 months
Rooting	The head turns in the direction of a stimulus when the cheek is touched. The infant's mouth opens in an attempt to suck.	First 4 months
Moro/startle	The arms thrust outward when the infant is released in midair, as if attempting to regain support.	First 2 months
Swimming	When placed facedown in water, the infant makes paddling, swimlike motions.	First 3 months
Walking/ stepping	When the infant is held in an upright position with the feet placed on a firm surface, the infant moves the feet in a walking motion.	First 2 months
Grasping	The infant grasps objects placed in his or her hand.	First 4 months
Babinski	The toes spread when the soles of the feet are stroked.	First year
Blinking	The eyes blink when they are touched or when sudden bright light appears.	Lifetime
Cough	Cough occurs when airway is stimulated.	Lifetime
Gag	Gagging occurs when the throat or back of mouth is stimulated.	Lifetime
Sneeze	Sneezing occurs when the nasal passages are irritated.	Lifetime
Yawn	Yawning occurs when the body needs additional oxygen.	Lifetime

possible. The earliest mean age of achievement for four of the six milestones occurred in the Ghanaian sample, and the latest mean age of achievement for all six milestones occurred in the Norwegian sample (WHO Multicentre Growth Reference Study Group, 2006c). The U.S. sample mean was in the middle range on all milestones except for hands-and-knees crawling, where it had the lowest mean achievement age.

A longitudinal study of almost 16,000 infants in the United Kingdom took up this issue of cultural differences in developmental motor milestones. In this study, Black Caribbean infants, Black African infants, and Indian infants were, on average, more advanced in motor development than White infants. Pakistani and Bangladeshi infants were more likely than White infants to show motor delays. Although the delays among Pakistani and Bangladeshi infants appear to be explained by factors associated with poverty, the earlier development of Black Caribbean, Black African, and Indian infants could not be explained by economic advantage. The researchers suggest that parental expectations and parenting practices play a role in cultural differences in motor development (Kelly, Sacker, Schoon, & Nazroo, 2006). The development of motor skills (and most other types of skills, for that matter) is a continuous process. Children progress from broad capacities to more specific refined abilities.

EXHIBIT 11.6 • Windows of Milestone Achievement in Months

MOTOR MILESTONE	WINDOW OF MILESTONE ACHIEVEMENT
Sitting without support	3.8–9.2 months
Standing with assistance	4.8–11.4 months
Hands-and-knees crawling	5.2–13.5 months
Walking with assistance	5.9–13.7 months
Standing alone	6.9–16.9 months
Walking alone	8.2–17.6 months

SOURCE: WHO Multicentre Growth Reference Study Group, 2006b.

The Growing Brain

We are living in the midst of a neuroscientific revolution clarifying the important role of the brain in helping to shape human behavior (Matto, Strolin-Goltzman, & Ballan, 2014). Like the brains of other primates, human brains contain *neurons*, or specialized nerve cells that store and transmit information; they carry sensory information to the brain, and they carry out the processes involved in thought, emotion, and action. Between the neurons are *synapses*, or gaps that function as the site of information exchange from one neuron to another (see Exhibit 3.3 in Chapter 3 in this book for an illustration of a neuron and synapse). **Synaptogenesis**, the creation of synapses, begins to accelerate during the last trimester of pregnancy.

The available evidence suggests that both genetic processes and early experiences with the environment influence the timing of brain development. Brain plasticity, also known as neuroplasticity, has been a major finding of neuroscientific research of the past few decades. There are two elements of *brain plasticity* (see Chapter 3 in this book for a discussion of neuroplasticity): first, research indicates that the brain changes throughout life, and second, the brain changes in response to what it experiences—it is shaped by experience (Farmer, 2009). The human brain is genetically designed to accommodate an incredibly wide range of human experiences, and the environmental context helps to shape the brain for life in a particular developmental niche. What is used gets strengthened, and what is not used gets pruned. Infants contribute to their own brain development by repeating certain actions, attending to certain stimuli, and responding in particular ways to caregivers.

Exposure to speech in the first year expedites the discrimination of speech sounds; exposure to patterned visual information in the first few years of life is necessary for normal development of some aspects of vision. Some suggest that the entire infancy period is a crucial and sensitive time for brain development, given the quantity and speed at which the neurons develop and connect (K. Pierce, 2011). Positive physical experiences (feeding, safety, and so on) and positive psychological experiences (touching, cooing, and playing) activate and stimulate brain activity (D. Davies, 2011). Good nutrition and infant stimulation are essential for brain development, and exposure to environmental toxins, abuse, emotional trauma, and deprivation is hazardous. Persistent stress for the infant has been found to result in overdevelopment of areas of the brain that process anxiety and fear and underdevelopment of other brain areas, particularly the frontal cortex (Schore, 2002).

Certain risks to brain development are associated with prematurity. Premature infants like Paul Thompson have high rates of serious intracranial hemorrhage, which can lead to problems in cognitive and motor development, including cerebral palsy and mental retardation. Less serious intracranial hemorrhage can lead to later behavioral, attentional, and memory problems (Tam et al., 2011). It is not yet clear whether Paul Thompson suffered any type of brain hemorrhage and what impact it will have on his future development if he did.

COGNITIVE DEVELOPMENT

As the brain develops, so does its ability to process and store information and to solve problems. These abilities are known as *cognition*. When we talk about how fast an infant is learning, we are talking about cognitive development. Researchers now describe the infant as "wired to learn" and agree that infants have an intrinsic drive to learn and to be in interaction with their environments. A central element of cognition is language, which facilitates both thinking and communicating.

Piaget's Stages of Cognitive Development

To assess children's cognitive progress, many people use the concepts developed by the best-known cognitive development theorist, Jean Piaget (1936/1952). As discussed in Chapter 4 in this book, Piaget believed that cognitive development occurs in successive stages, determined by the age of the child (see Exhibit 4.1 in Chapter 4 in this book for an overview of Piaget's four stages of cognitive development). His overall contention was that as a child grows and develops, cognition changes not only in quantity but also in quality.

The first of Piaget's stages, *sensorimotor*, applies to infants and toddlers. During the **sensorimotor stage**, they respond to immediate stimuli—what they see, hear, taste, touch, and smell—and learning takes place through the senses and motor activities. Piaget suggests that infant and toddler cognitive development occurs in six substages during the sensorimotor stage, the first four of which typify infancy.

Substage 1: Reflex activity (birth to 1 month). Because reflexes are what the infant can "do," they become the foundation to future learning. Reflexes are what infants build on.

Substage 2: Primary circular reactions (1 to 4 months). During this stage, infants repeat (thus the term *circular*) behaviors that bring them a positive response and pleasure. The infant's body is the focus of the response, thus the term *primary*. If, for example, infants by chance hold their head erect or lift their chest, they will continue to repeat these acts because they are pleasurable. Infants also have limited anticipation abilities.

Substage 3: Secondary circular reactions (4 to 8 months). As in the second substage, the focus is on performing acts and behaviors that bring about a response. In this stage, however, the infant reacts to responses from the environment. If, for example, 5-month-old infants cause the rattle to sound inadvertently as their arms move, they will continue attempts to repeat this occurrence.

Substage 4: Coordination of secondary circular reactions (8 to 12 months). During this substage, the infant begins to engage in intentional actions, and the mastery of **object permanence** is a significant task during this stage. Piaget contended that around 9 months of age, infants develop the ability to understand that an object or a person exists even when they don't see it. Piaget demonstrated this ability by hiding a favored toy under a blanket. Infants are able to move the blanket and retrieve the toy. Object permanence is related to the rapid development of memory abilities during this period and is necessary for mental representation to develop

(Bruce & Vargas, 2013). Two other phenomena are related to this advance in memory. **Stranger anxiety**, in which the infant reacts with fear and withdrawal to unfamiliar persons, has been found to occur at about 9 months across cultures. Babies vary in how intensely they react to the strange situation and in how they express their anxiety (Rieser-Danner, 2003). **Separation anxiety** also becomes prominent in this period. The infant is able to remember previous separations and becomes anxious at the signs of an impending separation from parents. With time, the infant also learns that the parent always returns.

As much as Piaget's work has been praised, it has also been questioned and criticized. Piaget constructed his theory based on his observations of his own three children. Thus, one question has been how objective he was and whether the concepts can really be generalized to all children. Also, Piaget has been criticized for not addressing the influence of environmental factors—such as culture, family, and significant relationships and friendships—on cognitive development. However, for the past 30 years, researchers around the world have put Piaget's theory to the test. This research literature is immense but has been summarized by several reviewers (see, for example, Bronfenbrenner, 1993; Rogoff & Chavajay, 1995; Segall, Dasen, Berry, & Poortinga, 1999). Piaget's sensorimotor stage has been studied less than his other cognitive stages, but the existing research tends to support Piaget's theory, even though some minor cultural differences are noted (Gardiner & Kosmitzki, 2011). For example, some research has found that African infants receive more social stimulation and emotional support than European and American infants, whereas European and American infants get more experience with handling objects. This leads to African infants and toddlers developing more social intelligence and European and American children developing more technological intelligence (cited in Gardiner & Kosmitzki, 2011). This supports the idea of the importance of the developmental niche but, overall, suggests much more similarity than difference in cognitive development across developmental niches during infancy and toddlerhood.

Research findings have called into question some aspects of Piaget's theory. For example, Piaget described infants as being incapable of object permanence until at least 9 months of age. However, infants as young as 3½ and 4½ months of age have been observed who are already proficient at object permanence (Ruffman, Slade, & Redman, 2005). Other researchers (Munakata, McClelland, Johnson, & Siegler, 1997) have found that although infants seem aware of hidden objects at 3½ months, they fail to retrieve those objects until about 8 months of age. These researchers suggest that cognitive skills such as object permanence may be multifaceted and gradually developed (Baillargeon, 2004). Cognitive researchers have been interested in the development of object permanence in children with very low birth weight and in children with a range of intellectual and physical disabilities. One research team found that toddlers born full-term were more than six times more likely to have developed object permanence than children born prematurely with very low birth weight (Lowe, Erickson, MacLean, & Duvall, 2009). Susan Bruce and Zayyad Muhammad (2009) reviewed the research on the development of object permanence in children with intellectual disability, physical disability, autism, and blindness. They concluded that this research indicates that children with these disabilities develop object permanence in a similar sequence as children without disabilities, but at a slower rate. They also found evidence that children with severe disability benefit from systematic instruction in object permanence. Bruce and Vargas (2013) provide a case example of a successful team effort to teach object permanence to a 4-year-old girl with severe multiple developmental delays and visual impairment. It is interesting to note that much of the recent research on object permanence studies nonhuman animals. For example, one research team who studied Piagetian object permanence in carrion crows found support for Piagetian stages of cognitive development in this avian species (Hoffman, Rüttler, & Nieder, 2011).

Categorization is a cognitive skill that begins to develop in the first year of life. *Categorization*, or recognizing similarities in groups of objects, is a fundamental element of information processing. There is evidence that by 6 months, infants begin to see patterns in and make distinctions about human faces (Ramsey, Langlois, Hoss, Rubenstein, & Griffin, 2004). There is also evidence that by 3 months of age, infants can make a distinction between people and inanimate objects. They have been observed to smile and vocalize more and become more active when they are interacting with people than when interacting with inanimate objects (Rakison & Poulin-Dubois, 2001). Research has also found that 4½-month-old babies indicate recognition when two objects are different from each other (Needham, 2001).

Prelanguage Skills

Although babies seem to be born ready to begin processing language and infants communicate with their caretakers from the beginning (primarily by crying), language development truly begins around 2 months of age. The first sounds, cooing, are pleasing to most parents. By age 4 months, infants babble. Initially, these babbles are unrecognizable. Eventually, at about 8 to 12 months, infants make gestures to indicate their desires. The babble sounds and gestures together, along with caretakers' growing familiarity with the infant's "vocabulary," make it easier for infants to communicate their desires. For example, 12-month-old infants may point to their bottle located on the kitchen cabinet and babble "baba." The caretaker soon learns that "baba" means "bottle." Across cultures, there is an overall bias in infancy to use nouns

(Gardiner & Kosmitzki, 2011). The most important thing that adults can do to assist with language development is to provide opportunity for interactions and to read to infants. The opportunity for interaction is important for deaf children as well as hearing children, but deaf children need interaction that involves hand and eye, as with sign language (Shonkoff & Phillips, 2000).

Research indicates that early infants are capable of recognizing and making sounds from a wide range of languages. However, as they have repeated interactions with caregivers and family members, they strengthen the neural connections for the sounds of the language(s) spoken in the home environment, and the neural connections for sounds from other languages are lost (Hoff, 2009). Miraculously, infants and toddlers who are bilingual from birth learn two languages as fast as monolingual infants learn one (Kovács & Mehler, 2009). Of course, ability in any language is not retained unless the environment provides an opportunity for using the language.

CRITICAL THINKING Questions 11.4

What have you observed about variations in infant physical development? What variations have you observed in parental attitudes about the management of infant sleep and responding to infant crying? What are your own attitudes about management of infant sleep and responding to infant crying? What have you seen the adults in your family, or other families you know, do to support language development in infants?

SOCIOEMOTIONAL DEVELOPMENT

Infants begin to face vital developmental tasks in the emotional arena as well as in the social arena. The emotional life of the newborn is centered on physical states, but by 3 months of age, emotional life may begin to be centered on relationships. By the end of the first year, emotional life becomes sensitive to emotion cues from other people. Development during infancy and toddlerhood may set the stage for socioemotional development during all other developmental ages.

Erikson's Stages of Psychosocial Development

As discussed in Chapter 4 in this book, Erik Erikson's (1950) theory explains socioemotional development in terms of eight consecutive, age-defined stages (see Exhibit 4.11 in Chapter 4 in this book for an overview of these stages). Each stage requires the mastery of a developmental task. Mastery at each stage depends on mastery in the previous stages.

Infants are in Erikson's stage of *trust versus mistrust* where the overall task is to develop a sense that their needs will be met by the outside world and that the outside world is an okay place to be. In addition, the infant develops an emotional bond with an adult, which Erikson believes becomes the foundation for being able to form intimate, loving relationships in the future. The most important factor facilitating growth in this stage is consistency in having physical and emotional needs met: being fed when hungry, being kept warm and dry, and being allowed undisturbed sleep. In addition, the infant has to be protected from injury, disease, and so on and receive adequate stimulation. Infants who develop mistrust at this stage become suspicious of the world and withdraw, react with rage, and have deep-seated feelings of dependency. These infants lack drive, hope, and motivation for continued growth. They cannot trust their environment and are unable to form intimate relationships with others.

Erikson does not address whether tasks that should be mastered in one stage can be mastered later if the facilitating factors—such as a dependable, nurturing caregiver—are introduced. For example, we know that Sarah suffered neglect until Chris Johnson and his parents provided a dependable, nurturing environment for her.

Emotional Control

Researchers have paid a lot of attention to the strategies infants develop to cope with intense emotions, both positive and negative, finding that they use a range of techniques, including turning the head away, sucking on hands or lips, and closing their eyes (Shonkoff & Phillips, 2000). However, researchers who do experimental infant research note that a number of infants must be discontinued from the research process because they cannot be calmed enough to participate (Newman & Newman, 2012).

You may not be surprised to learn that researchers have found that one of the most important elements in how an infant learns to manage strong emotions is the assistance provided by the caregiver for emotion management (see, for example, Lowe et al., 2012). Caregivers may offer food or a pacifier, or they may swaddle, cuddle, hug, or rock the infant. By the time the infant is 6 months old, caregivers often provide distraction and use vocalization to soothe. One research team found that for all levels of infant distress, the most effective methods of soothing were holding, rocking, and vocalizing. Feeding and offering a pacifier were effective when the infant was moderately distressed but not at times of extreme distress (Jahromi, Putnam, & Stifter, 2004). Infants who demonstrate greater emotion regulation are much more likely to have parents who use higher levels of positive parenting behaviors, such as sensitivity, positive regard, stimulation, and animation (Ursache, Blair, Stifter, & Voegtline, 2013). Another important element that impacts an infant's ability to manage emotions is whether the infant is receiving an

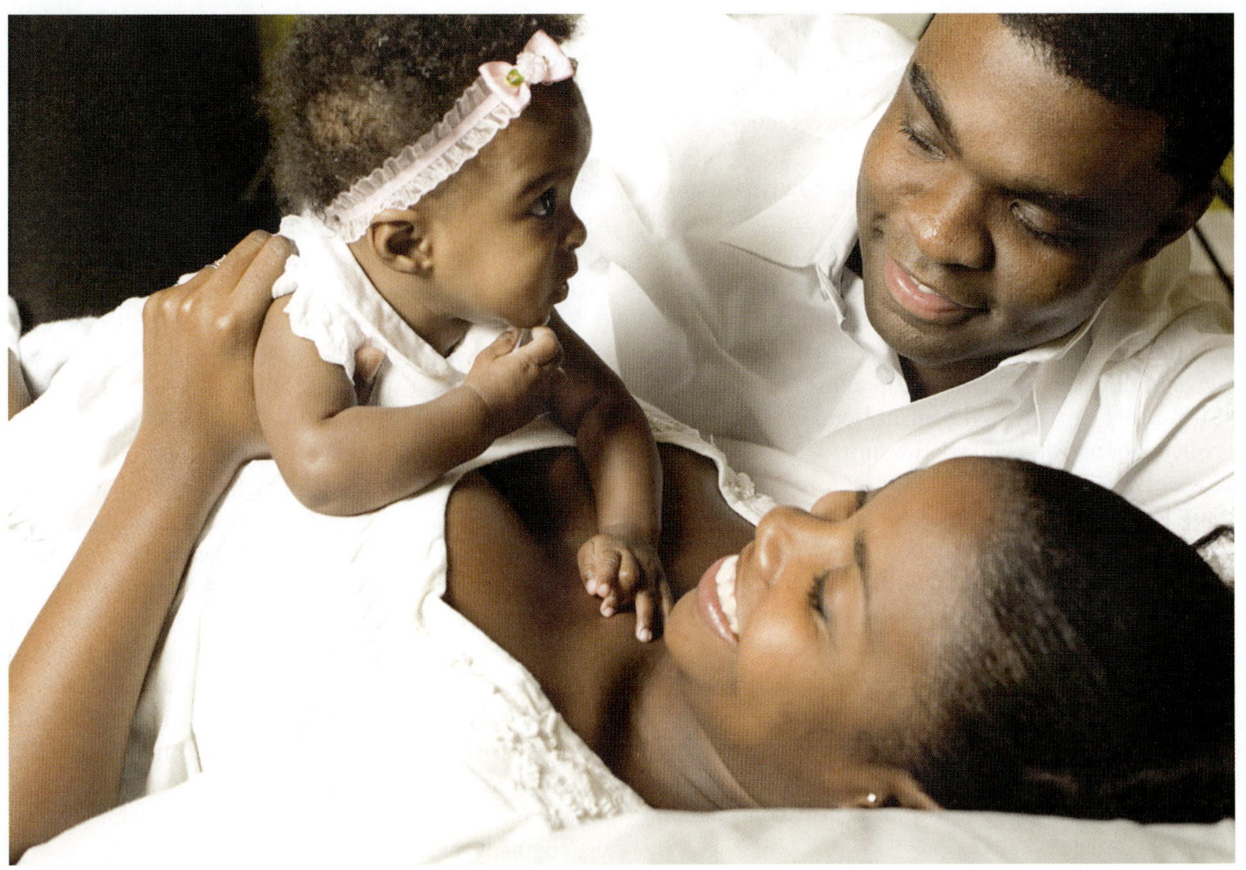

Infants depend on others for basic physical and emotional needs. Family support and affection are important factors in healthy development.

adequate amount of sleep (Kurcinka, 2006). The child's temperament also makes a difference, as you will see in the next section.

Finally, there are cultural differences in expectations for management of emotions in infants. For example, Japanese parents try to shield their infants from the frustrations that would invite anger. In other words, some emotions are regulated by protecting the infant from situations that would arouse them (Kitayama, Karasawa, & Mesquita, 2004). Cultural differences also exist in how much independence infants and toddlers are expected to exercise in managing emotions. In one study comparing Anglo and Puerto Rican mothers, Harwood (1992) found that Anglo mothers expected their infants to manage their stranger anxiety and separation anxiety without clinging to the mother. The Puerto Rican mothers, conversely, expected their infants to rely on the mother for solace.

Temperament

Another way to look at emotional development is by evaluating **temperament**—the individual's innate disposition. The best-known study of temperament in infants and young children was conducted by Alexander Thomas, Stella Chess, and Herbert Birch (1968, 1970). They studied nine components of temperament: activity level, regularity of biological functions, initial reaction to any new stimulus, adaptability, intensity of reaction, level of stimulation needed to evoke a discernible response, quality of mood, distractibility, and attention span or persistence. From their observations, the researchers identified three types of temperament: easy, slow to warm up, and difficult. The *easy* baby is characterized by good mood, regular patterns of eating and sleeping, and general calmness. The *slow to warm up* baby has few intense reactions, either positive or negative, and tends to be low in activity level. The *difficult* baby is characterized by negative mood, irregular sleeping and eating patterns, and difficulty adapting to new experiences and people. There is a tendency for recent researchers to focus on two clusters of temperamental traits, negative emotions (irritability, fear, sadness, shyness, frustration, and discomfort) and regulatory capacity (ability to self-regulate behavior and engage in self-soothing), as important to parent–infant relationships as well as to future personality and behavior development (see Bridgett et al., 2009).

Thomas and his colleagues believed that a child's temperament appears shortly after birth and is set, or remains unchanged, throughout life. Whether temperament is permanent is still unresolved. Neurobiologists are suggesting that infants come into the world with preexisting temperaments or emotional styles (Davidson & Begley, 2012). They report strong evidence for a genetic basis of emotional styles, with the genetic contribution varying from 20% to 60% for different emotional style traits. But even traits with a strong genetic base can be modified by how parents, teachers, and other caregivers interact with the child.

Families who have an infant with negative emotion and poor regulatory capacity may be in special need of social work interventions to prevent a troubling developmental trajectory for the infant and the relationship between the parents. Researchers are finding that negative emotion in the first 3 months is related to decreases in regulatory capacity from 4 to 12 months. And decreases in regulatory capacity in the infant from 4 to 12 months predict poor parent–child relationships when the child is 18 months old (Bridgett et al., 2009). Another research team found a relationship between infant regulatory capacity and marital satisfaction. Following a group of infants and their families from the time the infants were 7 months old until they were 14 months, these researchers found that marital satisfaction increased as infants developed greater regulatory capacity and decreased when infants failed to gain in regulatory capacity (Mehall, Spinrad, Eisenberg, & Gaertner, 2009). The good news is that neuroscience research suggests that how easily a baby can be soothed has little or no genetic contribution (Davidson & Begley, 2012).

Researchers have also been interested in whether there are cultural and socioeconomic differences in infant temperament. Several studies have found small to moderate cross-cultural differences in infant temperament and have attributed these differences mainly to genetics (see Gartstein, Knyazev, & Slobodskaya, 2005; Gartstein et al., 2006). To begin to examine the contributions of the role of genetics and environment to temperament, one research team compared three groups of Russian infants aged 3 to 12 months: infants living in Russia, infants of parents who immigrated to Israel, and infants of parents who immigrated to the United States. They found some differences in temperament across these three situations and concluded that the differences in temperament between the Russian Israeli infants and the Russian American infants probably reflect the different acculturation strategies used to adapt to different host societies (Gartstein, Peleg, Young, & Slobodskaya, 2009). Findings about the relationship between socioeconomic status and temperament are contradictory. Some researchers find no socioeconomic differences (Bridgett et al., 2009) whereas other researchers find that infants in more economically disadvantaged families have more difficult temperaments and conclude that this difference is largely explained by family stress (Janssen et al., 2009). The difference in findings about socioeconomic status and temperament could be caused by different samples, with socioeconomic variations in temperament more likely to show up when the sample includes greater income variability.

Attachment

Another key component of emotional development is **attachment**—the ability to form emotional bonds with other people. Many child development scholars have suggested that attachment is one of the most important issues in infant development, mainly because attachment is the foundation for emotional development and a predictor of later functioning. Note that this view of attachment is similar to Erikson's first stage of psychosocial development.

The two most popular theories of attachment were developed by John Bowlby (1969) and Mary Ainsworth and colleagues (Ainsworth, Blehar, Waters, & Wall, 1978). Bowlby's theory is discussed here, and you can read about Ainsworth's theory in Chapter 4 in this book. Bowlby, who initially studied attachment in animals, concluded that attachment is natural, a result of the infant's instinct for survival and consequent need to be protected. Attachment between infant and mother ensures that the infant will be adequately nurtured and protected from attack or, in the case of human infants, from a harsh environment. The infant is innately programmed to emit stimuli (smiling, clinging, and so on) to which the mother responds. This exchange between infant and mother creates a bond of attachment. The infant initiates the attachment process, but later the mother's behavior is what strengthens the bond.

Bowlby hypothesized that attachment advances through four stages: preattachment, attachment in the making, clear-cut attachment, and goal-corrected attachment. This process begins in the first month of life, with the infant's ability to discriminate the mother's voice. Bowlby contends that infants can demonstrate attachment behavior to others; however, attachment to the mother occurs earlier than attachment to others and is stronger and more consistent. It is thought that the earliest attachment becomes the child's **working model** for subsequent relationships (Bowlby, 1982). Attachment explains the child's anxiety when the parents leave. However, children eventually learn to cope with separation.

In both Bowlby's and Ainsworth's attachment theories, only mother–infant attachment is relevant to healthy infant development. This assumption probably seemed unquestionable when these theories were constructed. Today, however, many fathers have prominent, equal, and/or primary responsibilities in child-rearing and child care, sometimes by choice and other times because of necessity. Sarah Johnson's dad, for example, became the primary caregiver for Sarah out of necessity. The gender of the parent is irrelevant in the development of secure infant attachment. Rather, it is the behavior of the primary caregiver, regardless of whether it is a mother or father, that has the most influence on infant attachment (Geiger, 1996). When fathers who are the primary caregivers are able to provide infants with the warmth and affection they need, infants develop secure attachments to their fathers.

In fact, under stress, fathers become a greater source of comfort to their infants than the mothers who are the secondary caregivers (Geiger, 1996). Perhaps the best scenario is when infants develop secure attachments to both parents. In one study, infants with secure attachments to both parents demonstrated fewer behavioral difficulties as toddlers, even fewer problems than toddlers with only secure mother–infant attachment (Volling, Blandon, & Kolak, 2006). And, of course, these days some infants have two mothers or two fathers.

In addition to a more prominent role by fathers over the past 20 to 30 years, more women have entered the workforce, and many more children experience alternative forms of child care, including day care. The effect day care has on the development of attachment in young children continues to be a hotly debated topic. Friedman and Boyle (2008) reviewed 23 studies based on the National Institute of Child Health and Human Development (NICHD) data that tracked 1,000 children from birth through age 15. These studies found that the number of hours infants spend in nonmaternal care is not associated with the infants' security of attachment at age 15; they also found that working mothers interact with their infants almost as much as mothers who are not employed. The most robust finding was that mothers' sensitivity to their infants during interaction is a consistent predictor of secure attachment and positive child development. However, hours in alternative child care was a risk factor for mother–infant attachment if combined with other risk factors such as maternal insensitivity and poor quality of child care.

Let's look at one other issue concerning attachment. The manner in which infant attachment is measured raises some concerns. Most studies of attachment have used the Ainsworth group's strange situation method. However, this measure may not yield valid results with some groups or under certain conditions. For example, the avoidant pattern of attachment some investigators have noted among children in day care may not indicate lack of attachment, as some have concluded. These children may be securely attached but seem indifferent to the exit and return of the mother (or other primary caregiver) simply because they have become accustomed to routine separations and reunions with this caregiver.

The appropriateness of using the strange situation method with certain ethnic groups has also been questioned. An early study found Japanese infants to demonstrate more anxious attachment style than infants in other parts of the world and attributed this finding to the fact that Japanese mothers left their infants in the care of others much less often than mothers in a number of other cultures (Takahashi, 1990). A more recent study found that the distribution of attachment styles of Japanese infants was consistent with worldwide norms when the researchers controlled for the unfamiliarity of separation from the mother (Behrens, Hesse, & Main, 2007).

Conversely, in many cultures infants are cared for by a collective of mothers, older siblings, cousins, fathers, aunts, uncles, and grandparents. The level of sense of security in these infants depends on coordinated care of a number of caregivers. The strange situation does not capture the fluid nature of caregiving and the degree to which it supports infants' feelings of security and safety (Lewis, 2005). One study found that in Israeli kibbutz-reared children, one negative caregiving relationship could negatively affect other attachment relationships (Sagi, Koren-Karie, Gini, Ziv, & Joels, 2002).

In spite of these concerns, findings from a large number of studies using the strange situation in Europe, Africa, Asia, and the Middle East as well as North America indicate that the attachment patterns identified by Ainsworth occur in many cultures (Gardiner & Kosmitzki, 2011). It is important to remember that attachment theory was developed by European American theorists who conceptualized attachment as the basis for developing subsequent independence. However, in more collectivist cultures, attachment is seen as the basis for developing obedience and harmony (Weisner, 2005).

Attachment has been found to have a direct effect on brain development (Gerhardt, 2004; B. Perry, 2002). Gerhardt concludes that without emotional bonding with an adult, the orbitofrontal cortex in the brain of infants (the part of the brain that allows social relationships to develop) cannot develop well. During the first year of life, the infant must develop the capacity to tolerate higher and higher levels of emotional arousal. The caregiver helps the infant with this by managing the amount of stimulation the infant receives. As the right orbitofrontal cortex develops, the infant is able to tolerate higher levels of arousal and stimulation. However, when the caregiver is not attuned to the needs of the infant in regard to managing stimulation during the first year of life, negative emotions result and growth of the right orbitofrontal cortex is inhibited (Farmer, 2009). This process has been called the social brain. Supporters of this perspective cite several studies to support these conclusions, including an investigation of infants reared in orphanages in Romania conducted by Chugani et al. (2001). The infants had little contact with an adult, were left in their cots for most of the day, were fed with propped-up bottles, and were never smiled at or hugged. Research with these infants found that their brain development was severely impaired.

One question of concern is whether these deficiencies in brain development are permanent. Some suggest that the brain impairments can be reversed if changes in care and attachment occur early enough (Zigler, Finn-Stevenson, & Hall, 2002). They highlight the strides in brain development made by the Romanian orphans who were adopted into caring homes before they were 6 months of age. Perhaps Sarah Johnson's improvement was the result of early intervention and moving her quickly to live with her dad. Others suggest that the brain impairments caused by lack of attachment with a primary caregiver are permanent (B. Perry, 2002). Gerhardt concludes that the best advice we can offer parents of newborns is to forget about holding flashcards in front of their babies but instead, hold and cuddle the infants and simply enjoy them.

THE ROLE OF PLAY

Play is crucial to child development. Play enhances motor, cognitive, language, emotional, social, and moral development. Infants engage in vocal play, interactive play, exploratory play with objects, and parent-initiated ritualized games, such as peek-a-boo. The objective is to provide stimulation and opportunities for play. Fergus Hughes (2010, p. 68) makes the following suggestions about the appropriate toys for infants:

- *Birth to 3 months:* toys for sensory stimulation, such as rattles, bells, colorful pictures and wallpaper, crib ornaments, mobiles, music boxes, and other musical toys
- *3–6 months:* toys for grasping, squeezing, feeling, and mouthing, such as cloth balls, soft blocks, and teething toys
- *6–12 months:* colorful picture books, stacking toys, nesting toys, sponges for water play, mirrors, toy telephones, toys that react to the child's activity

Recently, researchers have become interested in the impact of new technologies and the effect they have on type of play, types of toys, and the amount of time spent in play (Bergen & Davis, 2011). It is not uncommon for children as young as several months old to be seen playing with technology-augmented toys or with apps on their parents' cell phones or tablets. The American Academy of Pediatrics and the government of Australia recommend that children under the age of 2 should not watch any television or video material (cited in Courage & Howe, 2010). Courage and Howe (2010) reviewed the empirical literature on the effects of screen time on infant and toddler development and found the evidence was not all bad. They found evidence for the following statements about infants and technology:

- Infants do not learn as readily from screen materials as do older children and adults.
- Infants learn more readily from people than from television and videos.
- Infants spend more time looking at a video if a parent views it with them and talks with them about it.
- Television can provide a route to early language development in impoverished environments.

Another important aspect of play is parent–child interaction. Parent–infant play may increase the likelihood of secure attachment between the parent and child (D. Davies, 2011; F. Hughes, 2010). The act of play at least provides the opportunity for infants and parents to feel good about themselves by enjoying each other and by being enjoyed. Even before infants can speak or understand language spoken to them, play provides a mechanism of communication between the parent and infant. Infants receive messages about themselves through play, which promotes their sense of self (Scarlett, Naudeau, Salonius-Pasternak, & Ponte, 2005).

Many similarities exist in the way that mothers and fathers play with infants but also some differences. Both mothers and fathers are teachers and sensitive communicators, and both enjoy rough-and-tumble play with their babies (Roggman, Boyce, Cook, Christiansen, & Jones, 2004). But research has also noted some differences in the ways that mothers and fathers play with infants and toddlers. Fathers engage in more rough-and-tumble play; they are more likely to lift their babies, bounce them, and move their legs and arms. Mothers are more likely to offer toys, play conventional games of peek-a-boo and pat-a-cake, and engage in constructive play. However, mothers have been found to play differently with infant sons than with infant daughters, engaging in more conversation with daughters and making more statements about the baby's feelings when talking with daughters; conversely, they engage in more direction with sons and make more comments to call the baby's attention to his surroundings (Clearfield & Nelson, 2006). Mothers have also been found to be more likely to follow the child's lead, whereas fathers are more likely to steer play activity according to their preferences. It is important to note, however, that these mother/father differences have not been found in Sweden and Israel, both societies with more egalitarian gender roles than found in the United States (F. Hughes, 2010).

It is not uncommon for children as young as several months old to be seen playing with technology-augmented toys or with apps on the parents' cell phones or tablets.

Play also is a vehicle for developing peer relations. A few decades ago, it was thought that babies really weren't interested in each other and could not form relationships with each other. Recent research challenges this view (F. Hughes, 2010). The peer group becomes more important at earlier ages as family size decreases and siblings are no longer available for daily social interaction. Researchers have found that very young infants, as young as 2 months, get excited by the sight of other infants; by 6 to 9 months, infants appear to try to get the attention of other infants; and by 9 to 12 months infants imitate each other (F. Hughes, 2010).

CHILD CARE ARRANGEMENTS IN INFANCY

Human infants start life in a remarkably dependent state, in need of constant care and protection. On their own, they would die. Societal health is dependent on finding good solutions to the question of who will care for infants and toddlers. With large numbers of mothers of infants in the paid workforce and not at home, this question becomes a challenging one. The United States seems to be responding to this challenge more reluctantly than other highly industrialized countries are. This difference becomes clear in comparative analysis of two solutions for early child care: family leave and paid child care.

FAMILY LEAVE

Because of changes in the economic institution in the United States from 1975 to 1999, the proportion of infants with mothers in paid employment increased from 24% to 54% and leveled off at 57% by 2012 (Shonkoff & Phillips, 2000; U.S. Bureau of Labor Statistics, 2013d). A similar trend is occurring around the world. In response, most industrialized countries have instituted social policies that provide for job-protected leaves for parents to allow them to take off from work to care for their infants. Sweden was the first country to develop such a policy in 1974. The Swedish policy guaranteed paid leave.

By the early 1990s, the United States was the only industrialized country without a family leave policy (Kamerman, 1996). But in 1993, the U.S. Congress passed the Family and Medical Leave Act (FMLA) of 1993 (Pub. L. No. 103-3). FMLA requires businesses with 50 or more employees to provide up to 12 weeks of unpaid, job-protected leave during a 12-month period for workers to manage childbirth, adoption, or personal or family illness. Eligible workers are entitled to continued health insurance coverage during the leave period, if such coverage is a part of their compensation package.

EXHIBIT 11.7 • Maternal Leave Policies in Selected Wealthy Countries (in weeks of leave)

COUNTRY	PAID	UNPAID
France	20	142
Austria	16	96
Sweden	40	45
United Kingdom	12	53
Australia	0	52
Canada	29	23
Denmark	19	31
Greece	34	13
Netherlands	16	13
Switzerland	11	3
United States	0	12

SOURCE: Ray, Gornick, & Schmitt, 2008. http://cepr.net/documents/publications/parental_2008_09.pdf. Licensed under CC BY 4.0, https://creativecommons.org/licenses/by/4.0/

Exhibit 11.7 highlights the maternal leave policies in selected wealthy countries. Most of the countries listed, including the United States, require that fathers are entitled to the same leave as mothers. That means, for example, that mother and father could each take a 12-week leave in the United States, or 24 weeks total. In 2015, the United States was the only affluent country of the world that did not offer some paid parental leave at the time of birth and adoption. European countries also provide birth or maternity grants and family allowances. This is an area for social work advocacy in the United States.

PAID CHILD CARE

Historically in the United States, mothers were expected to provide full-time care for infants and toddlers at home. If mothers were not available, it was expected that children would be cared for by domestic help or a close relative but still in their home setting. Even in the 1960s, with the development of Head Start programs, the focus was on preschool-age children; infants and toddlers were still expected to be cared for at home. Thus, historically there was very little provision of alternative child care for most children younger than school age.

Many advocates for infant day care refer to the European model as an ideal for the United States. Countries in Europe provide "universal" child care for all children, regardless of the parents' income, employment status, race, age, and so forth. These programs are supported through national policy and funded through public funds. If they pay at all, parents pay no more than a quarter of the monies needed. Parents in Europe thus pay far less than parents in the United States typically pay. For parents in the United States, only 1 in 6 eligible low-income families is receiving federal child care assistance (Lombardi, 2012), and the average annual cost of child care for an infant in a child care center is higher than a year's tuition at the average four-year public college in most states (Glynn, 2012).

As suggested earlier, there are controversies about whether child day care centers are harmful to infants, but there is growing consensus that nonparental child care is not inherently harmful. The type of nonparental child care must be put in ecological context and considered along with other variables such as the quality of the child care, the amount of time spent in nonparental care, the sensitivity of both parental and nonparental care providers, and characteristics of the child.

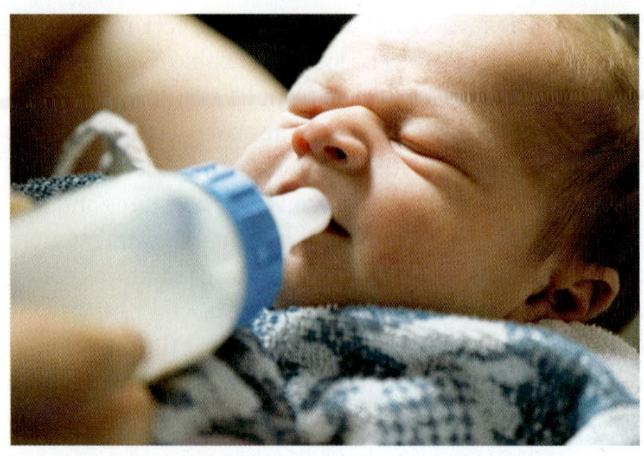

The American Academy of Pediatrics recommends that infants be breastfed, or fed with human milk, exclusively for the first 6 months.

INFANTS IN THE MULTIGENERATIONAL FAMILY

The birth of a child, especially of a first child, brings about a major transition not only for parents but also for the entire kin network. Partners become parents; sons and daughters become fathers and mothers; fathers and mothers become grandfathers and grandmothers; and brothers and sisters become aunts and uncles. Cultures of the world have different norms about who is involved, and in what ways, in the care of infants (see Carter, McGoldrick, & Petkov, 2011). Two issues, among many, that may involve the multigenerational family are the breastfeeding versus bottle feeding decision and postpartum depression.

BREASTFEEDING VERSUS BOTTLE FEEDING DECISION

Throughout history, most infants have been breastfed. However, alternatives to breastfeeding by the mother have always existed, and following World War II, breastfeeding ceased to be the primary nutritional source for infants because of the promotion of manufactured formula in industrialized and nonindustrialized countries. Since the 1980s, cultural attitudes have shifted again in favor of breastfeeding. The American Academy of Pediatrics (AAP) argues that infant nutrition should be considered a public health issue, not a lifestyle choice (Eidelman & Schanler, 2012). The AAP recommends that infants be breastfed, or fed with human milk, exclusively for the first 6 months, followed by continued breastfeeding with some supplementary use of foods until the infant is at least 1 year old.

In 2010, 76% of new mothers in the United States initiated breastfeeding, but only 13% breastfed exclusively for 6 months. The extended family could play a role in supporting mothers to persist with breastfeeding. There are racial, ethnic, and social class differences in the rate of breastfeeding, suggesting that family and culture play a role in the breastfeeding decision. The rate of breastfeeding initiation is 80.6% for Latina mothers and 58.1% for African American mothers. It is 67.5% for low-income mothers. Some employed mothers of infants are provided a space and flexible schedule for milk expression while at work, but workplace policies can be a barrier to breastfeeding for other mothers. Societal customs can support or discourage breastfeeding.

POSTPARTUM DEPRESSION

Family dynamics are often altered when mothers are depressed following childbirth. There is evidence that, around the world, 10% to 15% of mothers will have postpartum depression in the first year of the infant's life (Pearlstein, Howard, Salisbury, & Zlotnick, 2009; Wisner, Chambers, & Sit, 2006). Although social factors no doubt contribute to postpartum depression, it is generally accepted that the precipitous hormonal changes at birth, to which some women seem especially sensitive, play a large role. Postpartum depression often goes undiagnosed and untreated across cultural groups (Dennis & Chung-Lee, 2006), but it is more likely to receive attention in societies that have regular postpartum visits from midwives or nurses. For example, in the United Kingdom, new parents receive seven visits from midwives in the first 2 weeks postpartum (Posmontier & Horowitz, 2004). Postpartum depression can be very disruptive to the early mother–infant relationship and increases risk of impaired cognitive, emotional, and motor development (Wisner et al., 2006). Both social support and pharmacological interventions have been found to be helpful (Sword, Watt, & Krueger, 2006). Different cultures have different expectations for maternal adaptation, and it is important for health providers to recognize these cultural influences (Posmontier & Horowitz, 2004).

Very little research exists on psychosocial and mental health issues for new fathers, but the Australian First Time Fathers Study attempted to address this gap in knowledge (Condon, 2006). This study found no evidence of male postnatal depression but did find that male partners of women with postpartum depression are at risk for depression, anxiety, and abusing alcohol. At first, most men are confused by their wives' depression but supportive. If the depression lasts for months, which it often does, support is usually gradually withdrawn. Men report that they find their wives' irritability and lack of physical affection more troubling than the sadness and tearfulness. This study also found that male partners and other family members of depressed mothers often take on more and more of the care of the infant over time, which reinforces the mother's sense of incompetence. Communication breakdowns are very common in these situations.

RISK AND PROTECTIVE FACTORS IN CONCEPTION, PREGNANCY, CHILDBIRTH, AND INFANCY

As the life course journey begins, human behavior is being shaped by risk factors and protective factors. Throughout this chapter, you have read about factors that either increase risk or offer protection for healthy processes of conception, pregnancy, childbirth, and infancy. A confluence of biological, psychological, and social factors determines whether a couple can conceive. Once the woman is pregnant, an interplay of biological, psychological, and social factors influences the growth and development of the fetus, the childbirth experience, and the health of the new baby. This same interplay of factors continues to influence infant development, and indeed, the health of the new baby has long-term implications across the life course.

There is growing evidence from life course epidemiological research that experiences in these earliest days of a human life course have health impacts at every stage of the life course. This has led to a new "developmental" model for the origins of disease (for an overview of this model, see Barker & Thornburg, 2013). This model proposes that nutrition during fetal life is a key factor in later chronic disease. The fetal response to malnutrition is to slow growth and alter the metabolism in order to survive. It is not just the mother's diet during pregnancy that matters but also her nutrient stores at the time of conception. There is much research evidence that a range of chronic diseases have their origin in malnutrition during fetal life and infancy, including cardiovascular disease, type 2 diabetes, some cancers, and chronic infections. Research also indicates that a baby's birth weight is affected not only by maternal nutrition before and during pregnancy but also by the shape and size of the placenta at birth. And certain patterns of shape and size of the placenta have been found to be a risk factor for heart disease, hypertension, and some forms of cancer. How and why the placenta develops a particular shape and size is not well understood, but animal research has found that the placenta enlarges in response to malnutrition in midpregnancy. Barker and Thornburg (2013) conclude that this research on fetal nutrition indicates that "protecting the nutrition and health of girls and young women should be the corner stone of public health" (p. 518).

Unfortunately, not all infants get the start they need in life. Millions of infants around the world are impoverished, abandoned, neglected, and endangered. Most disturbing is the link between poverty and **infant mortality**—the death of a child before his or her first birthday. In general, infant mortality rates are the highest in the poorest countries (UNICEF, 2013b). Infant mortality rates in the United States are high compared with other economically advanced nations (World Bank, 2013e), but Bosnia and Herzegovina, a country with less than one fifth the average income of the United States, has achieved the same infant mortality rate as the United States (Central Intelligence Agency, 2012). Within the United States, mortality rates for infants are higher among poor infants, and the rate among African American infants is over twice that of Hispanic and non-Hispanic White infants (CDC, 2013h).

Poverty, inadequate caregiving, and child maltreatment in infancy are three factors that have negative consequences for the infant's immediate development but also have negative consequences on physical and mental health across the life course (read more about these risk factors in Chapter 12 in this book). Seldom is one environmental, social, or biological risk factor solely responsible for an outcome. Most outcomes are influenced by several factors, and ongoing research is showing an ever-increasing complexity of interacting factors.

Several factors have been found to mediate risk factors during the prenatal period and infancy. Key protective factors are family life education, social and economic support, and maternal education. Social workers can play an important role by advocating for better state and national policies that enhance good prenatal and infant health.

CRITICAL THINKING Questions 11.5

In your multigenerational family, what have you observed about the expectations parents have for how infants should manage emotions? Why do you think that the United States was slower than other advanced industrial countries to develop family leave policies? Why do you think the United States' policy does not include paid family leave as is the case in other advanced industrial societies? Do you think the United States should have "universal" child care for all children, regardless of parents' income, as they do in Europe? Why or why not?

IMPLICATIONS FOR SOCIAL WORK PRACTICE

Social workers practicing with persons at the stage of life concerned with conception, pregnancy, childbirth, and infancy should follow these principles.

- When working with clients, both females and males, of childbearing age, always consider the possibility of conception, pregnancy, and childbirth; their potential outcomes; and their impact on the changing person–environment configuration.
- Identify the needs of vulnerable or at-risk groups and work to provide services for them. For example, structure birth education classes to include not only family but family-like persons and provide interpreters for the hearing impaired or use appropriate technology to deliver content.
- Assume a proactive stance when working with at-risk populations to limit undesirable reproductive outcomes and to help meet their reproductive needs. At-risk groups include adolescents; low-income women; women involved with substance abuse; women with eating disorders; and women with disabilities who lack access to financial, physical, psychological, and social services.
- Establish collaborative relationships with other professionals to enhance and guide assessment and intervention.
- Become well acquainted with theories and empirical research about growth and development among infants.
- Assess infants in the context of their environment, culture included.
- Promote continued use of formal and informal social support networks for parents with infants.
- Advocate for more affordable, quality child care.
- Help parents understand the potential effects of inadequate caregiving on their infants, including the effects on brain development.
- Help parents and others understand the association between infant development and consequential outcomes across the life course.
- Provide support and appropriate intervention to parents to facilitate effective caregiving for infants.

KEY TERMS

assisted reproductive technologies (ART), 343
attachment, 360
developmental niche, 338
embryo, 345
fetal viability, 342
fetus, 345
gestation, 345
infant, 351
infant mortality, 365
infertility, 342
motor skills, 354
neonate, 338
object permanence, 356
reflex, 354
sensorimotor stage, 356
sensory system, 353
separation anxiety, 357
stranger anxiety, 357
synaptogenesis, 355
temperament, 359
teratogens, 345
working model, 360
zygote, 345

ACTIVE LEARNING

1. Locate the National Association of Social Workers Code of Ethics on the organization's website at www.socialworkers.org. Choose an ethical issue from the following list. Using the Code of Ethics as a guide, what values and principles can you identify to guide decision making related to the issue you have chosen?
   - Should employers have the right to prevent their female employees from having insurance coverage for contraception?
   - Should all women and men, regardless of marital status or income, be provided with the most current technologies to conceive when they are unable to do so?
   - What are the potential issues of gestational surrogacy in terms of social justice and diversity?
   - Should pregnant women who abuse substances be incarcerated to protect the developing fetus?
   - Do adoptive parents have the right to know the genetic background of an adoptee?

2. Divide into groups of three or four. The instructor will assign each group the task of discussing what variations of conception, pregnancy, and childbirth they would anticipate for one specific population of pregnant and parenting mothers. The specific populations might include teen mothers, lesbian mothers, undocumented immigrant mothers, mothers with a substance abuse problem, mothers with an eating disorder, HIV-infected mothers, homeless mothers, incarcerated mothers, or mothers with any type of disability—intellectual, emotional, or physical. Each group will write themes of their discussion about their assigned group of mothers on newsprint and post them on the wall. The whole class will take about 10 minutes to walk around and review each of the posted themes, adding any that they think should be included.

3. Divide into groups of three or four. Each group will select one of the three life journeys that introduced this chapter: Jennifer Bradshaw's, the Thompsons', or Sarah Johnson and her dad. Identify the risk and protective factors related to their conception, pregnancy, childbirth, and early parenting experience. Then change one factor in the story; for example, assume that Jennifer Bradshaw had only a 10th-grade education. How does that change the trajectory of her story? Or assume that Felicia Thompson was being treated for depression when she became pregnant. Again, how does that factor alter her life course and that of her child? Or you might assume that Chris Johnson's parents are wealthy and want to adopt Sarah. How might that change the life course of this multigenerational family?

4. Divide into groups of three or four. You have been told that you will be touring an infant day care program or a family-based infant day care home next week. What will you be looking for to assess the quality of care the infants in the program or home are receiving? What will you want to see to feel assured that the care providers are meeting the infants' physical, cognitive, and socioemotional developmental needs?

WEB RESOURCES

The American Pregnancy Association

americanpregnancy.org

Site presented by the American Pregnancy Association contains information on a number of pregnancy-related topics, including infertility, adopting, pregnancy options, multiples pregnancy, and the developing baby.

Childbirth.org

www.childbirth.org

Award-winning site maintained by Robin Elise Weiss contains information on conception, pregnancy, and birth, including recommended pregnancy books and access to a free online childbirth class.

National Center for Children in Poverty (NCCP)

www.nccp.org

Site presented by the NCCP of the Mailman School of Public Health of Columbia University contains media resources and child poverty facts as well as information about child care and early education, family support, and public welfare.

National Healthy Mothers, Healthy Babies Coalition (HMHB)

www.hmhb.org

Site maintained by HMHB, an informal coalition dedicated to improving the quality and reach of public education about prenatal and infant care, contains a blog, newsroom, and virtual library.

Zero to Three

www.zerotothree.org

Site presented by Zero to Three, a national nonprofit charitable organization with the aim to strengthen and support families, contains information about infant and toddler behavior and development, child maltreatment, child care and education, and public policy.

SAGE edge™ **Sharpen your skills with SAGE edge at edge.sagepub.com/hutchisoness2e**

SAGE edge for students provides a personalized approach to help you accomplish your coursework goals in an easy-to-use learning environment. watch listen read

LEARNING OBJECTIVES	FOR FURTHER EXPLORATION AND APPLICATION
LO 11.1: Compare and contrast one's emotional and cognitive reactions to three case studies.	(watch) A Journey Through Infertility: Over Terror's Edge
LO 11.2: Recognize the sociocultural context of childbearing and child-rearing.	(watch) The Partner's Role During Pregnancy and Birth
LO 11.3: Give examples of how humans attempt to exercise human agency to get control over conception and pregnancy.	(read) How Social Workers Help Couples Recover From Pregnancy Loss
LO 11.4: Summarize three trimesters of fetal development.	(read) Fetal Development (watch) Labor: Preparation and Process
LO 11.5: Describe the special challenges faced by premature and low-birth-weight newborns and newborns with congenital anomalies.	(listen) Weak Brain Connections May Link Premature Birth and Later Disorders
LO 11.6: Summarize the typical physical, cognitive, and socioemotional development of infants.	(watch) Object Permanence (watch) Motor Development in Infancy (read) How Important Is Physical Contact With Your Infant?
LO 11.7: Analyze the role of play in infant development.	(watch) Play Is More Than Just Fun
LO 11.8: Analyze cross-national differences in infant care policies.	(watch) Quality Child Care
LO 11.9: Identify issues that face multigenerational families with infants.	(watch) Developmental Milestones: Parent Views (watch) Transition to Parenthood
LO 11.10: Give examples of risk factors and protective factors during infancy.	(listen) Does Swaddling Babies Really Boost the Risk of SIDS? (read) A Problem-Solving Therapy Intervention for Low-Income, Pregnant Women at Risk for Postpartum Depression
LO 11.11: Apply knowledge of conception, pregnancy, childbirth, and infancy to recommend guidelines for social work assessment and intervention.	(read) What Is a Perinatal Social Worker? (read) Inequalities in Reproductive Health: What Is the Challenge for Social Work and How Can It Respond?

Owen Franken/Corbis Documentary/Getty Images

Toddlerhood and Early Childhood

Debra J. Woody and David Woody III

Learning Objectives

LO 12.1 Compare and contrast one's emotional and cognitive reactions to three case studies.

LO 12.2 Summarize typical physical, cognitive and language, moral, personality and emotional, and social development during toddlerhood and early childhood.

LO 12.3 Analyze the role of play in toddler and early childhood development.

LO 12.4 Identify major social policies regarding developmental disruptions during toddlerhood and early childhood.

LO 12.5 Evaluate the possible benefits of early childhood education.

LO 12.6 Identify some special issues that face the multigenerational family with toddlers and young children.

LO 12.7 Give examples of risk factors and protective factors during toddlerhood and early childhood.

LO 12.8 Apply knowledge of toddlerhood and early childhood to recommend guidelines for social work assessment and intervention.

CASE STUDY 12.1

OVERPROTECTING HENRY

Irma Velasquez is still mourning the death of her little girl Angel, who was 2 years old when she was killed by a stray bullet that came into their home through the living room window. Although it has been about a year since the incident, no one has been arrested. The police do know, however, that neither Ms. Velasquez's daughter nor her family was the intended victim. The stray bullet was the result of a shoot-out between two rival drug dealers in the family's neighborhood.

Ms. Velasquez is just glad that now 14-month-old Henry was in his crib in the back of the house instead of in the living room on that horrible evening. He had fallen asleep in her lap a few minutes before, but she had just returned from laying him in his crib when the shooting occurred. Irma Velasquez confides in her social worker at Victim Services that her family has not been the same since the incident. For one thing, she and her husband barely speak. His method of dealing with the tragedy is to stay away from home. She admits that she is angry with her husband because he does not make enough money for them to live in a safer neighborhood. She thinks that he blames her because she did not protect Angel in some way.

Ms. Velasquez admits that she is afraid that something bad will also happen to Henry. She has limited their area in the home to the back bedroom, and they seldom leave the house. She does not allow anyone, even her sister, to take care of him and confesses that she has not left his side since the shooting. Even with these restrictions, Ms. Velasquez worries. She is concerned that Henry will choke on a toy or food or become ill. She still does not allow him to feed himself, even dry cereal. He has just begun walking, and she severely limits his space for movement. Ms. Velasquez looks worn and exhausted. Although she knows these behaviors are somewhat irrational, she states that she is determined to protect Henry. She further states that she just could not live through losing another child.

CASE STUDY 12.2

TERRI'S TERRIBLE TEMPER

Terri's mother and father, Mr. and Mrs. Smith, really seem at a loss about what to do. They adopted Terri, age 3, when she was an infant. They describe to their social worker how happy they were to finally have a child. They had tried for many years, spent a lot of money on fertility procedures, and had almost given up on the adoption process when Terri seemed to be "sent from heaven." Their lives were going well until a year ago, when Terri turned 2. Mrs. Smith describes an overnight change in Terri's behavior. Terri has become a total terror at home and at preschool. In fact, the preschool has threatened to dismiss Terri if her behavior does not improve soon. Terri hits and takes toys from other children, she refuses to cooperate with the teacher, and she does "what she wants to do."

Mr. and Mrs. Smith admit that Terri runs their household. They spend most evenings after work coaxing Terri into eating her dinner, taking a bath, and going to bed. Any attempt at a routine is nonexistent. When the Smiths try to discipline Terri, she screams, hits them, and throws things. They have not been able to use time-outs to discipline her because Terri refuses to stay in the bathroom, the designated time-out place. She runs out of the bathroom and hides. When they attempt to hold her in the bathroom, she screams until Mr. Smith gets too tired to continue to hold her or until she falls asleep. Mr. and Mrs. Smith admit that they frequently let Terri have her way because it is easier than saying no or trying to discipline her.

The "straw that broke the camel's back" came during a family vacation. Mrs. Smith's sister and family joined the Smiths at the beach. Mr. Smith describes the vacation as a total disaster. Terri refused to cooperate the entire vacation. They were unable to eat at restaurants because of her tantrums, and they were unable to participate in family activities because Terri would not let them get her ready to go. They tried allowing her to choose the activities for the day, which worked until other family members tired of doing only the things that Terri wanted to do. Terri would scream and throw objects if the family refused to eat when and where she wanted or go to the park or the beach when she wanted. Mrs. Smith's sister became so frustrated with the situation that she vowed never to vacation with them again. In fact, it was the sister who insisted that they get professional help for Terri.

CASE STUDY 12.3

A NEW ROLE FOR RON AND ROSILAND'S GRANDMOTHER

Ron, age 3, and Rosiland, age 5, have lived with Ms. Johnson, their grandmother, for the last year. Their mother, Shirley, was sent to prison a year ago after conviction of drug trafficking. Shirley's boyfriend is a known drug dealer and had asked Shirley to make a "delivery" for him. Shirley was arrested as she stepped off the bus in another state where she had taken the drugs for delivery. Ron and Rosiland were with her when she was arrested, because she had taken them with her. Her boyfriend thought that a woman traveling with two young children would never be suspected of delivering drugs.

Ron and Rosiland were put into foster care by Child Protective Services until Ms. Johnson arrived to pick them up. It had taken her 2 weeks to save enough money to get to the children and fly them all home. Ms. Johnson shares with the social worker how angry she was that Shirley's boyfriend refused to help her get the children home. Shirley calls the children when she can, but because her crime was a federal offense, she has been sent to a prison far away from home. The children ask about her often and miss her terribly. Ms. Johnson has told the children that their mom is away but has not told them that she will be away for some time. She is also unsure how much they understand about what happened, even though they were present when their mom was arrested.

Ms. Johnson shares that she has no choice but to care for the children, although this is definitely not the life she had planned. She was looking forward to living alone; her husband died several years ago. With her small savings, she was planning to visit her sister in another state for an extended visit. But that money is gone now, because these funds were used to help get the children home. She seems to love both of the children but confides that the children "drive her crazy." She is not accustomed to all the noise, and they seem to need so much attention from her. Getting into the habit of having a scheduled day is also difficult for Ms. Johnson. Both children attend preschool, an arrangement Shirley made before her incarceration. Ms. Johnson describes the fact that the children attend preschool as a blessing, because it gives her some relief. Her social worker suspects that preschool is a blessing for the children as well.

TYPICAL DEVELOPMENT IN TODDLERHOOD AND EARLY CHILDHOOD

At 14 months, Henry Velasquez is considered a **toddler**, the designation usually given to young children between the ages of 12 to 36 months of age. Terri Smith and Ron and Rosiland Johnson are in the stage referred to as early childhood (ages 3–6), also referred to as preschool age and early school age by child development scholars. Toddlers are extremely busy, continuing the struggle for self-control and emotion regulation begun in infancy, making great strides in language development, and continuing to expand motor skills. Not all toddlers leave infancy with the foundation of trust and optimism needed for the new developmental tasks, and many parents struggle with the energy level and drive for mastery that distinguishes toddlerhood from infancy.

In the early childhood stage, young children turn their attention more and more to the external environment, working to discover some stability and regularity in the external world. That is not always an easy task, given their limitations in cognitive and language development. Some children emerge from toddlerhood with a sense of confidence in the availability of support and a beginning sense of confidence in themselves. Other children, unfortunately, leave toddlerhood more challenged than when they entered that stage (Sroufe, Egeland, Carlson, & Collins, 2005). Much happens in all interrelated dimensions of development from age 2 to 6, however, and most children emerge from early childhood with a much more sophisticated ability to understand the world and their relationship to it. They work out this understanding in an increasingly wider world, with major influences coming from family, school, peer groups, the neighborhood, and the media (Mokrova, O'Brien, Calkins, Leerkes, & Marcovitch, 2012). Remember as you read that the various types of development discussed in this chapter under separate headings actually are interdependent, and sometimes the distinctions between the dimensions blur.

International literature criticizes the notion of a universal early childhood. It suggests, instead, multiple and diverse early childhoods, based on class, race, gender, geography, and time (see Dahlberg, Moss, & Pence, 2007; Waller, 2009). The same can be said about the experience of toddlers. There are growing criticisms that all children of the world are evaluated against Western developmental psychology science, which is a mix of statistical averages and historically and culturally specific value judgments (Dahlberg et al., 2007; Nybell, Shook, & Finn, 2009). In this chapter, we have tried to broaden the view of toddlerhood and early childhood, where the literature allows, but please keep this criticism in mind as you read. Also keep in mind the great inequity in the environments children are born into. Many children of the world are still reared in households without access to even basic necessities such as safe drinking water and sanitation; this is also true of some children in the United States (UNICEF, 2012b).

PHYSICAL DEVELOPMENT

As Chapter 11 explained, infants grow rapidly, and rapid growth continues in toddlerhood. The toddler nearly doubles the birth height, and by age 2 most toddlers are quadruple their original weight. Thus, the average 2-year-old weighs 20 to 40 pounds. From ages 3 to 6, physical growth slows. On average, height during this stage increases about 2 to 3 inches per year, and the young child adds about 5 pounds of weight per year. As a result, young children look leaner. However, globally, one quarter of children younger than 5 years of age are stunted in growth due to malnutrition, with the highest prevalence in Sub-Saharan Africa and South Asia, where about 38% of children younger than 5 have stunted growth. At the same time, increasing rates of children have been found to be overweight in most regions of the world. Globally, 7% of children younger than 5 years of age were overweight in 2012, a 43% increase since 1990 (UNICEF, 2013d). There are two forms of malnutrition: undernutrition caused by inadequate intake of nutrients and obesity caused by excessive intake of foods high in calories (Ritzer, 2013a). As suggested in the previous chapter, the importance of adequate nutrition cannot be overemphasized; poor nutrition is involved in at least half of the child deaths in the world each year. It magnifies the effect of every disease.

Nutrition affects physical stature, motor skill development, brain development, and most every other aspect of development. A 2013 report by the *Lancet* ("Maternal and Child Nutrition," 2013) indicates that, globally, malnutrition contributes to 3.1 million deaths of children age 5 and younger each year. Nutritional deficiencies during the first 1,000 days of the child's life can result in damage to the immune system and impair social and cognitive capacities.

Great variation exists in the height and weight of toddlers and young children, and racial and ethnic differences in height and weight are evident in the toddler and early childhood years, as they were in infancy. For example, in the United States, African American children in early childhood on average are taller than White and Hispanic children of the same age, and there is some evidence that Hispanic American children weigh more on average than other young children (Dennison, Edmunds, & Stratton, 2006). Children of low economic status are more likely than other children to be overweight during early childhood, but severe food insecurity may lead to growth inhibition (Wang & Zhang, 2006).

The brain continues to be shaped by experience throughout toddlerhood, early childhood, and beyond. Brain growth continues at a rapid pace but is slower than in infancy. The creation of new synapses peaks in toddlerhood, at 2 to 3 years of age, when the brain has about twice the synapses it will have in adulthood (K. Pierce, 2011; Urban Child Institute, 2013). This rapid synaptogenesis results in an overabundance of synapses and a tripling in brain weight during the first 3 years. The period of overproduction of synapses, or **blooming**, is followed by a period of **pruning**, or reduction, of the synapses to improve the efficiency of brain functioning. It is through this process of creating elaborate communication systems between the connecting neurons that more and more complex skills and abilities become possible. Thus, during these early years of life, children are capable of rapid new learning. The blooming and pruning of synapses process continues well into childhood and adolescence at different timetables in different regions of the brain. By age 5, the brain is 90% of its adult size (Christen & Narvaez, 2012).

Synaptic pruning and myelination continue, and motor and cognitive abilities increase by leaps and bounds during early childhood because of increased interconnections between brain cells, which allow for more complex cognitive and motor capability (Davies, 2011). These abilities are perhaps even more accelerated with the availability of technology and media appropriate for young children that further stimulate brain development (Courage & Setliff, 2009). There is little research to date to clarify the benefits of and drawbacks to use of information and communication technology with young children, but what little research there is suggests that brain development may be enhanced with the use of interactive technologies that help children develop curiosity, problem solving, and independent thinking skills but hampered by passive engagement with technology (Mercer, 2013). Because of the great plasticity of the brain, each new wave of technological advancement, like earlier development of written language, results in new brain-mediated capabilities that had previously been unexpressed (Kneas & Perry, 2011).

Through a process called **lateralization**, the two hemispheres of the brain begin to operate slightly differently, allowing for a wider range of activity. Simply stated, brain functioning becomes more specialized. The left hemisphere is activated during tasks that require analytical skills, including speaking and reading. Tasks that involve emotional expression and spatial skills, such as visual imagery, require a response from the right hemisphere. With the development of the right hemisphere and the social-emotional components there, young children develop the ability to reflect on the feelings and thoughts of others (James & Bose, 2011). Brain lateralization was identified early in neuroscientific research, but current thinking is that we should avoid applying the right hemisphere/left hemisphere paradigm too rigidly. The hemispheres are in constant communication, and the tasks performed by each hemisphere are much more complex than once thought (Fogarty, 2009; Peng & Wang, 2011).

Because of other developments in the brain, children also obtain and refine some advanced motor skills during this time, such as running, jumping, and hopping, but less is known about motor development in early childhood compared with infancy and toddlerhood (Keenan & Evans, 2016). Early intervention specialists suggest the gross motor milestones presented in Exhibit 12.1. In addition to these **gross motor skills**—skills that require use of the large muscle groups—young children develop **fine motor skills**, including the ability to scribble and draw and cut with scissors. Suggested fine motor milestones are also presented in Exhibit 12.1. As you review these suggested milestones, remember that there is much variability in motor development in toddlerhood and early childhood. For example, one child may be advanced in gross motor skills and lag in fine motor skills, or the opposite. In addition, different motor skills are valued in different developmental niches, and the expression of motor skills will depend on the tools available to the child. With these cautions, parents and other adults who spend time with young children will find the milestones presented in Exhibit 12.1 to be helpful to keep in mind as they interact with young children.

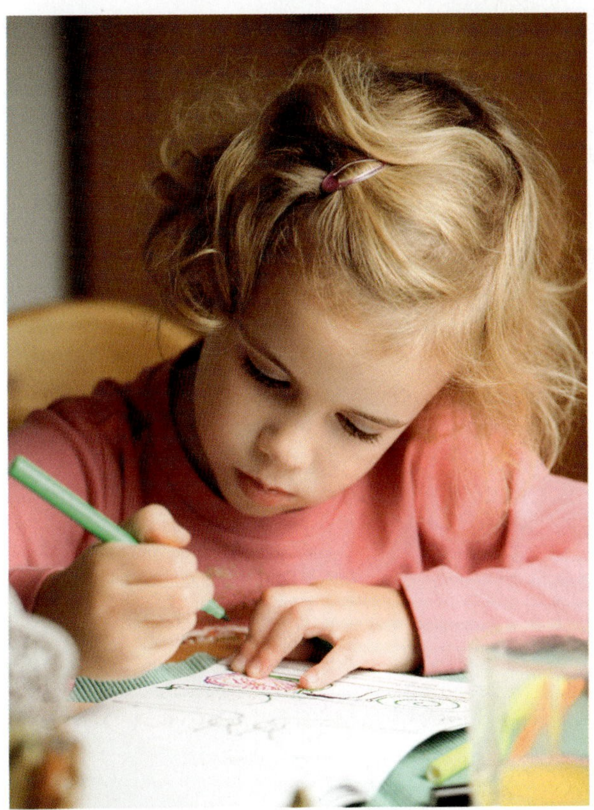

© iStockphoto.com

During toddlerhood and early childhood, young children make advancements in the development of fine motor skills, including the ability to draw.

Increases in fine motor skills allow young children to become more self-sufficient. However, allowing the extra time needed for young children to perform self-care tasks can be frustrating to adults. Ms. Johnson, for example, has lived alone for some time now and may need to readjust to allowing extra time for the children to "do it themselves." Spills and messes, which are a part of this developmental process, are also often difficult for adults to tolerate.

Parents are usually quite patient with their child's motor development. However, toilet training (potty training) is often a source of stress and uncertainty for new parents. Every human culture has mechanisms for disposing of human waste and socializes infants and toddlers to that method. One of the basic issues in this socialization is whether it should be in the hands of the child or the caregiver (Valsiner, 2000). In places in the world where there are no disposable diapers and no access to a washing machine, parents, even in

EXHIBIT 12.1 • Gross Motor and Fine Motor Skills in Toddlerhood and Early Childhood

AGE	GROSS MOTOR SKILLS	FINE MOTOR SKILLS
Most toddlers, age 12–18 months, can	Walk independently Attempt to run Squat to pick something up Crawl up stairs and creep back down Seat self on small chair Pull a toy behind themselves while walking Throw underhand when sitting	Point to pictures in books Build a tower using 2 blocks Scribble with a crayon Point with the pointer finger Hold own cup and drink, with some spilling Feed self using a spoon, with some spilling Remove own socks Put hat on own head
Most toddlers, age 18–24 months, can	Walk up and down the stairs while holding a hand Run fairly well Jump down and forward Squat to play Stand on tiptoe with support Start to use ride-on toys Throw a ball into a box Kick a ball forward	Build a tower with 4–6 blocks Put 4 rings on a stick Put large pegs in a pegboard Turn pages of a book, 2–3 at a time Scribble Turn knobs Throw a small ball Paint on paper using whole arm to move the paintbrush Imitate the drawing of a vertical line and a circle Begin to string large beads Feed self, using a fork and spoon Pull up a large zipper Start to hold a crayon with fingers Put large shapes into a shape sorter
Most toddlers, age 2–3, can	Stand on tiptoes if shown first Jump from bottom step Begin to ride a tricycle, moving forward with feet on floor Stand on balance beam with 2 feet and attempt to move forward Catch a large ball with arms straight out Stand on 1 foot momentarily (by age 2½) Walk up the stairs with alternating feet (by age 2½) Walk down stairs with 2 feet on same step (by age 2½) Walk on tiptoe (by age 2½) Start riding a tricycle using the pedals (by age 2½) Catch a ball with arms bent (by age 2½) Kick a ball forward (by age 2½)	Hold a crayon with thumb and fingers Draw a circle Begin to cut paper with scissors Draw simple shapes such as a triangle and a circle Make simple objects from Play-Doh Begin to draw detailed pictures Unfasten a button Build a tower of more than 6 blocks Get dressed with help
Most 3-year-olds can	Run forward Jump in place Stand on one foot with support Walk on tiptoe Avoid obstacles in path Catch an 8-inch ball Climb and walk up stairs with alternating feet Kick a ball forward Ride a tricycle Climb a ladder	Turn single pages Snip with scissors Hold crayons with thumb and finger Use one hand consistently Imitate circular, vertical, and horizontal strokes Paint with some wrist action Make dots, lines, and circular strokes Roll, pound, squeeze, and pull clay Build a tower of up to 9 cubes String ½-inch beads Cut along a line Use a fork Manage large buttons Dress self with supervision

AGE	GROSS MOTOR SKILLS	FINE MOTOR SKILLS
Most 4-year-olds can	Run around obstacles Walk on a line Balance on one foot for 5–10 seconds Hop on one foot Push, pull, and steer wheeled toys Use a slide independently Jump over a 6-inch-high object and land on both feet Throw a ball overhead Catch a bouncing ball	Copy crosses and squares Print some letters Use table utensils Cut on a line Build a tower of 9 small blocks
Most 5-year-olds can	Walk backward toe to heel Jump forward 10 times without falling Walk up and down stairs independently with alternating feet Turn a somersault Walk on tiptoes Walk on a balance beam Jump rope	Lace shoes but not tie Grasp pencil like an adult Color within lines Cut and paste simple shapes

SOURCES: Based on Aussie Childcare Network, 2015; Children's Therapy & Family Resource Centre, 2015a, 2015b; Destefanis & Firchow, 2013; Early Intervention Support, 2013.

the early months, become sensitive to signs that the infant is about to defecate or urinate and hold him or her over whatever type of toilet is available. This method, referred to as "assisted infant toilet training," is expected to work by about age 6 months. Although this method is not typically followed in the middle- to high-income countries, there is a current movement in the United States to raise diaper-free babies by using "elimination communication," based on timing, cues, and intuition (see the website www.diaperfreebaby.org). There is no clear consensus in the United States about the best method for toilet training (Howell, Wysocki, & Steiner, 2010). The U.S. American Academy of Pediatrics recommends a child-oriented approach that emphasizes the child's interest in toilet training and tries to minimize the demands made by parents. Toddlers are introduced to a potty-chair and gradually encouraged to sit on it and over time actually use it, followed by positive rewards. Reprimands or punishments are to be avoided. This can take weeks or months. In contrast, some parents use the train-in-a-day method developed by Azrin and Foxx (1989), which is recommended to start about the age of 20 months. Researchers have found that both the child-centered and the train-in-a-day method can lead to successful toilet training (Howell et al., 2010).

In the United States, the average age to complete toilet training has increased steadily over the past few decades, from 18 months in the 1940s to 27 months in 1980 and 37 months in 2003. There are subcultural variations, however. On average, girls achieve toilet training 2 to 3 months ahead of boys. Family stressors such as divorce, death, or birth of a new baby may lead to a delay in toilet training (Howell et al., 2010).

COGNITIVE AND LANGUAGE DEVELOPMENT

As memory improves, and the store of information expands, toddlers and young children begin to think much more in terms of categories (Davies, 2011; Newman & Newman, 2012). Young children are full of big questions such as where do babies come from, what happens to people when they die, where does the night come from, and so on. They can think about themselves and about other people. They engage in creative and imaginative thought and begin to develop humor, empathy, and altruism. They make great strides in language development and the ability to communicate. And they make gradual progress in the ability to judge right and wrong and to regulate behavior in relation to that reasoning.

Piaget's Stages of Cognitive Development

According to Piaget, the toddler, age 1–2 years, is still in the first stage of cognitive development, the sensorimotor stage, with cognitive development occurring in the last two substages of this period, Substages 5 and 6 (refer back to Chapter 11 in this book for a discussion of the sensorimotor stage):

Substage 5: Tertiary circular reactions (12 to 18 months). During this substage, toddlers become more creative in eliciting responses and are better problem solvers. For example, if the first button on the talking telephone does not make it talk, they will continue to press other buttons on the phone until they find the correct one.

Substage 6: Mental representation (18 months to 2 years). Piaget described toddlers in this stage as actually able to use thinking skills and retain mental images of what is not immediately in front of them. For example, the toddler will look in a toy box for a desired toy and move other toys aside that prohibit recovery of the desired toy. Toddlers can also remember and imitate observed behavior, for example, rolling a toy lawn mower over the lawn, imitating their parents' lawn mowing.

In late toddlerhood and throughout early childhood, children fit into the second stage of cognitive development described by Piaget, the **preoperational stage**, a stage when young children learn to use symbols to represent their earlier sensorimotor experiences. This stage is in turn divided into two substages:

Substage 1: Preconceptual stage (ages 2 to 3). The most important aspect of the preoperational stage is the development of symbolic representation, which occurs in the preconceptual stage. Through play, children learn to use symbols and actively engage in what Piaget labeled deferred imitation. Deferred imitation refers to the child's ability to view an image and then, significantly later, recall and imitate the image. For example, 3-year-old Ella, who watches the *Dora the Explorer* cartoon on TV, fills her backpack with a pretend map and other items she might need, such as a blanket and a flashlight; puts it on; creates a pretend monkey companion named Boots; and sets off on an adventure, using the kitchen as a barn, pretending the space under the dining table is the woods, and keeping her eyes open all the while for the "mean" Swiper the Fox.

Substage 2: Intuitive stage (ages 4 to 7). During the second part of the preoperational stage, children use language to represent objects. During the preconceptual stage, any object with long ears may be called "bunny." However, during the intuitive stage, children begin to understand that the term *bunny* represents the entire animal, not just a property of it. However, although young children are able to classify objects, their classifications are based on only one attribute at a time. For example, given a set of stuffed animals with various sizes and colors, the young child will group the animals either by color or by size. In contrast, an older child who has reached the intuitive stage may sort them by both size and color.

In early childhood, children also engage in what Piaget termed *transductive reasoning*, or a way of thinking about the relationship between two or more concrete experiences without using abstract logic. This can be explained best with an illustration. Imagine that 5-year-old Sam immediately smells chicken when he enters his grandmother's home. He comments that she must be having a party and asks who is coming over for dinner. When the grandmother replies that no one is coming over and that a party is not planned, Sam shakes his head in disbelief and states that he will just wait to see when the guests arrive. Sam recalls that the last time his grandmother cooked chicken was for a party. Because his grandmother is cooking chicken again, Sam thinks another party is going to occur.

One last related preoperational concept described by Piaget is *egocentrism*. According to Piaget, in early childhood, children perceive reality only from their own experience and believe themselves to be at the center of existence. They are unable to recognize the possibility of other perspectives on a situation. For example, a 3-year-old girl who stands between her sister and the television to watch a program believes that her sister can see the television because she can. This aspect of cognitive reasoning could be problematic for Ron and Rosiland who may attribute their mother's absence to their behavior, especially given that they were present when she was arrested. More recent experimental research has found that the ability to see another's point of view begins to develop by age 2 and continues to develop throughout early childhood (Davies, 2011). Researchers are finding that young children have the capacity for nonegocentric thinking but do not consistently demonstrate that capacity (Engel, 2005).

Language Skills

By the age of 18 to 24 months, the toddler learns about one new word each week (CTParenting.com, 2014). Most of the words spoken at this age relate to people and significant objects in the toddler's environment. These include words such as *mama*, *dada*, *cat*, and *sissy* (sister), for example. Toddlers' first words also include situational words such as *hot*, *no*, and *bye*. Around the age of 2, toddlers have a vocabulary of about 50 to 100 words, can follow directions, and are able to put two to three words together (CTParenting.com, 2014). For example, children can say "all gone" as they develop an understanding of object permanence (Berk, 2005). Even with these skills, toddlers may be difficult to understand on occasion. At age 2 toddlers can be understood by adults about half of the time (CTParenting.com, 2014).

At the end of toddlerhood, on average, young children have a vocabulary of about 1,000 words, and they are increasing that store by about 50 words each month (Davies, 2011). They can speak in two-word sentences, and they have learned the question form of language. They are asking "why" questions, persistently and often assertively, to learn about the world. Three-year-old speech is generally clear and easy to understand. At every point in development, however, children differ in the size of the vocabularies they command, the complexity of the language structure used, and the skill with which they communicate (Hoff, 2009).

By the fourth year of life, language development is remarkably sophisticated. The vocabulary is becoming more and more adequate for communicating ideas, and 4-year-olds are usually speaking in sentences of 8 to 10 words. They have mastered language well enough to tell a story mostly in words, rather than relying heavily on gestures, as toddlers must do. But perhaps the most remarkable aspect of language development in early childhood is the understanding of grammar rules. By age 4, young children in all cultures understand the basic grammar rules of their language (Gardiner & Kosmitzki, 2011). They accomplish this mostly by a figuring-out process. As they figure out new grammar rules, as with other aspects of their learning, they are overly regular in using those rules, because they have not yet learned the exceptions. So we often hear young children make statements such as "she goed to the store," or perhaps "she wented to the store."

There are two different approaches to studying language development. One approach focuses on the mental processes by which language is acquired and conceptualizes language ability as primarily a function of genetics. Although somewhat influenced by the environment, children are thought to develop language skills as long as the appropriate genetic material is in place (Chomsky, 1968; Hoff, 2005). The other approach focuses on the way that the social contexts in which children live shape language acquisition (Bronfenbrenner & Morris, 1998). Erika Hoff (2006) proposes a model that synthesizes these two approaches, a model that considers both "how the mind acquires language" and "how the social context shapes language development" (p. 56). She argues that children need both a language model and opportunities for communicative interaction to support language development. Language is not learned simply by overhearing it, as many of us have learned from our efforts to learn a new language in adolescence or adulthood. Language development is a social process; children learn language by listening to others speak and by asking questions. Past toddlerhood, children increasingly take charge of their own language acquisition by asking questions and initiating dialogues (Hoff, 2006). Parents can assist children by asking questions, eliciting details, and encouraging children to reflect on their experiences. As children grow older, they are often corrected by caregivers and preschool teachers in the misuse of words or phrases (Chapin & Altenhofen, 2010).

It appears that the developmental niche has an impact on the development of language skills. Children are talked to a great deal in some cultures and very little in other cultures (Hoff, 2006). North American parents tend to talk a lot about objects when speaking to their infants and toddlers, whereas Asian parents tend to use more verbs and fewer nouns. Considerable research indicates that infants and toddlers who are talked to a great deal acquire language skills earlier than infants and toddlers who are talked to less (Hoff, 2006). Across cultures, there is consistent evidence that parents with higher socioeconomic status, on average, speak more to their children, elicit more conversations with their children, use larger vocabularies in conversations with their children, and engage in fewer verbal behavioral prohibitions than parents with lower socioeconomic status (Hoff, 2006; Zhang, Jin, Shen, Zhang, & Hoff, 2008). This means that many low-income children enter elementary school with smaller vocabularies than their more privileged peers unless they are provided with support for language development. Some research indicates that both low-income and high-income mothers use more complex speech when reading books to their children, and book reading can attenuate the language disadvantage of low-income children (Hoff, 2003).

Two special types of language learners deserve greater attention: multilingual language learners and deaf and hard-of-hearing language learners. Hoff (2006) reports that half of the children in the world live in multilingual situations. And yet research on language acquisition among multilingual children is very young. There is some evidence that children learning two languages tend to have smaller vocabularies in each language than monolingual children, but vocabulary size depends on the amount of exposure to each language and the opportunities to speak each language (Hoff, 2006). Recent research indicates, however, that learning two languages simultaneously in the first 3 years of life lays down the brain structures for later language learning (Klein, Mok, Chen, & Watkins, 2013).

Language development is a particularly important area of development for deaf and hard-of-hearing (DHH) children. Unless they have deaf parents, who will teach them sign language, these children require intervention to acquire language. Three common methods provide DHH children with access to language: sign language, simultaneous communication, and spoken language. Various sign languages, using manual signs, have developed in deaf communities around the world. Simultaneous communication uses signs from traditional sign languages plus newly created signs to correspond to spoken language. These new sign systems can theoretically be used simultaneously with speech, but

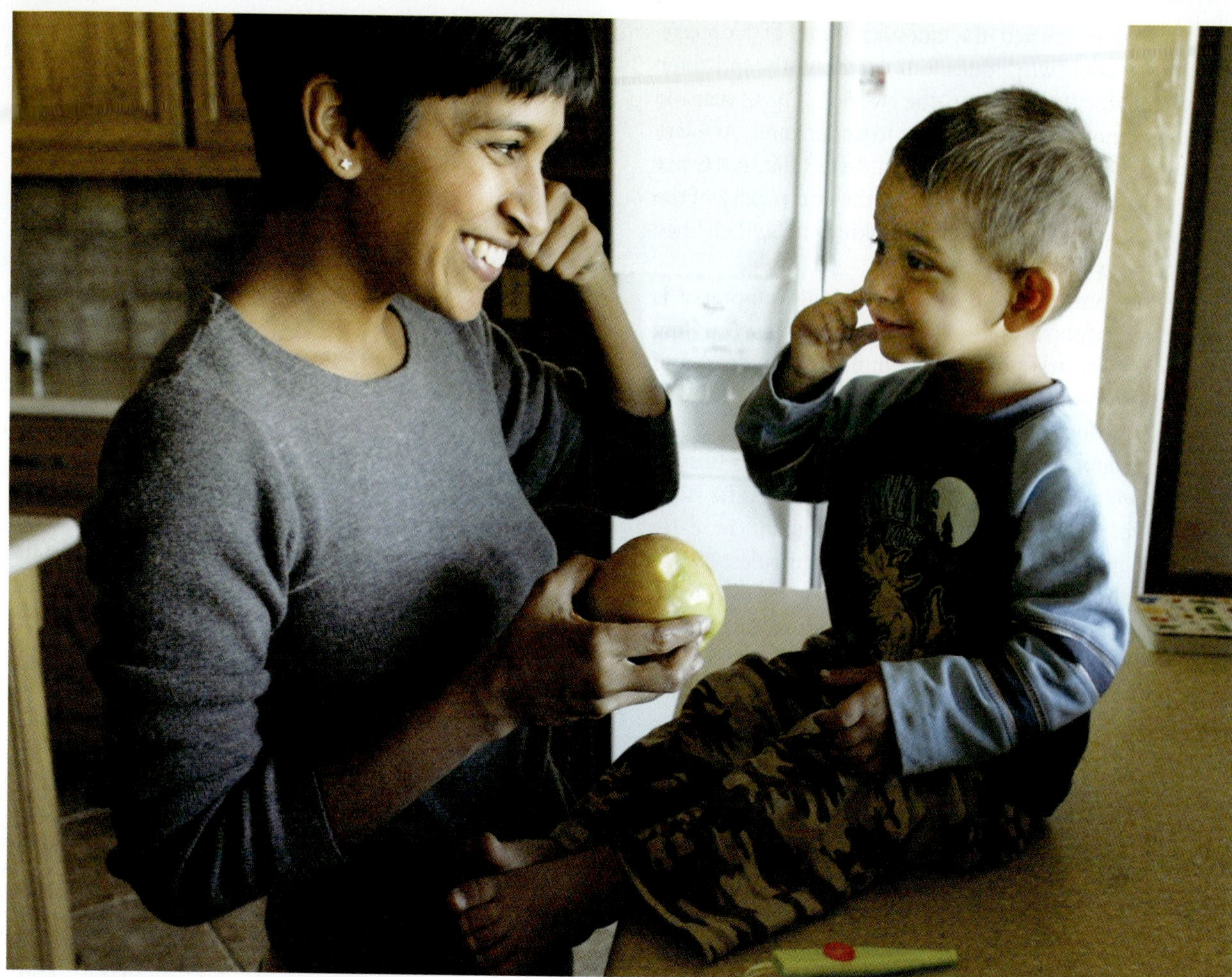
M.L. GRAY/KRT/Newscom

Language development is a particularly important area of development for deaf and hard-of-hearing children.

in reality, this is very challenging because signs are longer in duration than words. Some children are exposed to spoken language only, and technological innovations, such as hearing aids and cochlear implants, are making that a more realistic choice for children with less severe hearing loss. The choice of method is influenced by attitudes about how important it is for children to fit into a mainstream hearing world. Of paramount importance is that hearing loss be detected at birth or shortly after, which is now possible, and that access to language begin in the early days and weeks. There is strong evidence that not having access to language in the early months has long-term negative consequences for language development. The method of language exposure should fit the specific nature of the hearing loss (Lederberg, Schick, & Spencer, 2013).

MORAL DEVELOPMENT

During early childhood, children move from a moral sense based on outside approval to a more internalized moral sense, with a rudimentary moral code. They engage in a process of taking society's values and standards as their own. They begin to integrate these values and standards into both their worldview and their self-concept. There are three components of moral development during early childhood (Newman & Newman, 2012):

1. *Knowledge* of the moral code of the community and how to use that knowledge to make moral judgments
2. *Emotions* that produce both the capacity to care about others and the capacity to feel guilt and remorse
3. *Actions* to inhibit negative impulses as well as to behave in a **prosocial** or helpful and empathic manner

Understanding Moral Development

Moral development has been explored from several theoretical perspectives found to have merit. Three of these approaches to moral development are explored here.

1. *Psychodynamic approach.* Sigmund Freud's psychoanalytic theory proposed three distinct structures of the personality: id, ego, and superego. According to Freud, the superego is the personality structure that guides moral development. There are two aspects to the superego: the *conscience*, which is the basis of a moral code, and the *ego ideal*, which is a set of ideals expected in a moral person. Freud (1927) thought the superego is formed from the ages of 4 to 7, but more recent psychodynamic formulations suggest that infancy is the critical time for the beginning of moral development (Kohut, 1971). Freud thought children would have more highly developed superegos when their parents used strict methods to inhibit the children's impulses. Contemporary research indicates the opposite, however, finding that moral behavior is associated with parental warmth, democratic decision making, and modeling of temptation resistance (Kochanska, Forman, Aksan, & Dunbar, 2005). New psychodynamic models emphasize a close, affectionate bond with the caregiver as the cornerstone of moral development. This is supported by recent neuroscience research that finds the following caregiving practices to foster the type of brain development that underlies moral behavior in adults: breastfeeding, prompt response to needs, touch, play, and support (see Christen & Narvaez, 2012). Freud also believed that males would develop stronger superegos than females, but research has not supported this idea.

2. *Social learning approach.* From the perspective of social learning theory, moral behavior is shaped by environmental reinforcements and punishments. Children are likely to repeat behaviors that are rewarded, and they are also likely to feel tension when they think about doing something that they have been punished for in the past. From this perspective, parental consistency in response to their children's behavior is important. Social learning theory also suggests that children learn moral conduct by observing models. Albert Bandura (1977b) found that children are likely to engage in behaviors for which they see a model rewarded and to avoid behaviors that they see punished. This can be problematic for children who watch a lot of television, because they may come to view violence as an acceptable way to solve interactional conflict if they see violence go unpunished.

3. *Cognitive developmental approach.* Piaget's theory of cognitive development has been the basis for stage models of moral reasoning, which assume that children's moral judgments change as their cognitive development allows them to examine the logical and abstract aspects of moral dilemmas. Moral development is assisted by opportunities to encounter new situations and different perspectives. The most frequently researched stage model is that presented by Lawrence Kohlberg (1969, 1976) and summarized in Exhibit 4.3 in Chapter 4 in this book. Kohlberg described three levels of moral reasoning, with two stages in each level. According to Kohlberg, in early childhood, children operate at the **preconventional level of moral reasoning**, with their reasoning about moral issues based, in Stage 1, on what gets them rewarded or punished. This type of moral reasoning is thought to be common among toddlers. In the second stage of the preconventional level, moral reasoning is based on what benefits either the child or someone the child cares about. This is consistent with the child's growing capacity for attachments. There is some empirical evidence that children ages 3 to 6 do, indeed, begin to use the type of moral reasoning described in Stage 2 (Walker, 1989). The idea of a hierarchical sequence of stages of moral development has been challenged as being based on a Western cultural orientation, but longitudinal studies in a variety of countries have produced support for the idea of evolution of moral reasoning (Gielen & Markoulis, 2001).

All of these approaches to moral development in early childhood have been criticized for leaving out two key ingredients for moral development: **empathy**, or the ability to understand another person's emotional condition, and **perspective taking**, or the ability to see a situation from another person's point of view (Eisenberg, 2000). Neuroscientific research is currently suggesting that a special type of brain cell, called a *mirror neuron*, is key to the development of empathy. Have you ever noticed how you instinctively smile when you see someone else smiling? Mirror neurons allow us to sense the move another person is about to make and the emotions he or she is experiencing. Emotion is contagious, because mirror neurons allow us to feel what the other person feels through a brain-to-brain connection. Daniel Goleman (2006) has coined the term *social intelligence* to refer to this ability to be attuned to another person. It appears that humans have multiple systems of mirror neurons, and scientists are in the early stages of learning about them. Studies have found that people with autism have a dysfunctional mirror neuron system (Goleman, 2006).

There is growing agreement that empathy begins in infancy and grows throughout early childhood (Meltzoff, 2002). By age 3 or 4, children across cultures have been found to be able to recognize the type of emotional reaction that other children might have to different situations. Perspective taking, which is a thinking rather than feeling activity, grows in early childhood and is another important ingredient in moral development. One research team studied children at ages 3½ years and 5½ years and found that a sophisticated understanding of both emotional and mental states was associated with increased consideration of the emotional and mental states of others

(Lane, Wellman, Olson, LaBounty, & Kerr, 2010). Longitudinal research has found that children who show empathy and perspective taking at 4 and 5 years of age are more likely to exhibit prosocial behavior and sympathy during adolescence and early adulthood (Eisenberg et al., 1999).

In addition, there has been considerable examination of the degree to which Kohlberg's model is responsive to gender and cultural experience, in view of the study population on which his theory is based—Harvard male undergraduates (Donleavy, 2008; Sherblom, 2008). Carol Gilligan (1982) notes that gender plays a significant role in how one experiences and acts on themes of ethical thinking, justice, and notions of individuality and connectedness. She suggests strong gender bias in Kohlberg's theory, and her research indicated that women's moral thought is guided by caring and maintaining the welfare of others, whereas men use more abstract principles of justice. As you can see from Exhibit 4.3, caring for others and maintaining harmony in relationships would put women in Stage 3, at the highest. A similar criticism has been lodged about the poor fit of Kohlberg's theory with many non-European cultures that are more collectivist oriented than European and North American societies. Indeed, studies of Buddhist monks find that older monks barely reach Kohlberg's Stage 4, indicating that their moral reasoning is not as well developed as Western male adolescents, according to Kohlberg's model (Huebner & Garrod, 1993). Researchers suggest that the moral ideal in Western cultures is an autonomous individual with strong convictions who sticks up for those convictions. In contrast, the Buddhist moral ideal is guided by compassion and detachment from one's own individuality. How such themes are transmitted to young children can be indelible guideposts for managing and participating in interpersonal relationships.

One aspect of moral reasoning is *distributive justice*, or the belief about what constitutes a fair distribution of goods and resources in a society. Cross-cultural studies suggest that cultures hold different views on what constitutes a "fair" distribution of resources. Some societies see fairness in terms of need, whereas other societies see fairness in terms of merit. Reasoning about distributive justice starts in early childhood but is not well articulated until middle childhood (Gardiner & Kosmitzki, 2011).

Helping Young Children Develop Morally

Growing evidence indicates that some methods work better than others for helping children develop moral reasoning and conduct. Particularly helpful activities are those that help children control their own behavior, help them understand how their behavior affects others, show them models of positive behavior, and get them to discuss moral issues (Arsenio & Gold, 2006). It is important, however, to consider a child's temperament when undertaking disciplinary actions. Some children are more sensitive to messages of disapproval than others; sensitive children require a small dose of criticism, and less sensitive children usually require more focused and directive discipline (Kochanska, 1997). Brian Edmiston (2010) suggests that one important way for adults to assist young children to develop morally is to engage in dramatic play that helps children develop ethical identities.

Although religious beliefs play a central role in most societies in clarifying moral behavior, little research has been done to explore the role of religion in moral development in young children. Research (Roof, 1999) has indicated that adults often become affiliated with a religious organization when their children are in early childhood, even if the parents become "religious dropouts" after the children are out of the home. Religious rituals link young children to specific actions and images of the world as well as to a community that can support and facilitate their moral development. The major world religions also teach parents about how to be parents. Young children, with their comfortable embrace of magic, easily absorb religious stories on topics that may be difficult for adults to explain. Religion that emphasizes love, concern, and social justice can enrich the young child's moral development. Conversely, religion that is harsh and judgmental may produce guilt and a sense of worthlessness, which do not facilitate higher levels of moral reasoning.

CRITICAL THINKING Questions 12.1

What have you observed about the differences in gross and fine motor development among toddlers and young children, as outlined in Exhibit 12.1? How do you think culture and social class affect gross and fine motor development during this period? What types of social policies might help to narrow the social class disparities in language development? What do you see as the benefits and drawbacks to being multilingual during early childhood? What special challenges might caregivers face in their attempts to assist Terri Smith and Ron and Rosiland Johnson with moral development?

PERSONALITY AND EMOTIONAL DEVELOPMENT

A key concern for Henry Velasquez, Terri Smith, and Ms. Johnson's grandchildren—Ron and Rosiland—is their emotional development. Specifically, will they grow into happy, loving, well-adjusted people despite the disruptions in their lives? Writing about the early childhood years, Sroufe and colleagues (2005) suggest this as the period of life when a coherent personality emerges: "It is no exaggeration to say that the person emerges at this time" (p. 121). Based on a longitudinal study of 180 children born into poverty, they conclude that behavior and adaptation during early childhood predict later behavior and adaptation, something they did not find to be the case with the predictive power of behavior and adaptation in infancy and toddlerhood. They suggest that the important themes of development during this period are self-direction, agency, self-management, and self-regulation. Young children do face important developmental tasks in the emotional arena. This section addresses these tasks, drawing on Erikson's theory of psychosocial development.

Erikson's Stages of Psychosocial Development

Erikson proposed that toddlers, ages 1½ to 3, are in the stage of emotional development known as *autonomy versus shame and doubt* (refer back to Exhibit 4.11 in Chapter 4 in this book for a complete list of Erikson's stages). A child with autonomy has a growing sense of self-awareness and begins to strive for independence and self-control. These children feel proud that they can perform tasks and exercise control over bodily functions. They relate well with close people in the environment and begin to exercise self-control in response to parental limits. At the other end of the spectrum are children who doubt themselves. They fear a loss of love and are overly concerned about their parents' approval. These children are ashamed of their abilities and develop an unhealthy kind of self-consciousness. To develop autonomy, children need firm limits for controlling impulses and managing anxieties but at the same time still need the freedom to explore their environment. Exhibit 12.2 summarizes possible sources of anxiety for toddlers (Davies, 2011). Toddlers also need an environment rich with stimulating and interesting objects and with opportunities for freedom of choice. Adults must accept the child's bodily functions as normal and good and offer praise and encouragement to enhance the child's mastery of self-control.

Erikson labeled the stage of emotional development that takes place during the early childhood years as *initiative versus guilt* (ages 3 to 6). Children who pass

© iStockphoto.com/monkeybusinessimages

During early childhood, children engage in cooperative play and enjoy both sharing and competing with peers.

successfully through this stage learn to get satisfaction from completing tasks. They develop imagination and fantasies and learn to handle guilt about their fantasies. At the beginning of this stage, children's focus is on family relationships. They learn what roles are appropriate for various family members, and they learn to accept parental limits. Age and sex boundaries must be appropriately defined at this stage, and parents must be secure enough to set limits and resist the child's possessiveness. By the end of this stage, the child's focus turns to friendships outside the family. Children engage in cooperative play and enjoy both sharing and competing with peers. Children must also have the opportunity to establish peer relationships outside the family. This is one of the functions the preschool program serves for Ms. Johnson's grandchildren. Some children are not successful with the

EXHIBIT 12.2 • Possible Sources of Anxiety for Toddlers

Difficulty understanding what is happening
Difficulty communicating
Frustration over not being able to do what others can do or what they imagine others can do
Conflicts between wanting to be independent and wanting their parents' help
Separation or threat of separation from caregivers
Fears of losing parental approval and love
Reactions to losing self-control
Anxieties about the body

SOURCE: Adapted from Davies, 2011.

developmental tasks of this stage and are plagued with guilt about their goals and fantasies. These children are overly anxious and self-centered.

Emotions

Emotional life becomes centered on regulation of emotional states in toddlerhood, and struggles for self-control and mastery over powerful emotions are a major task in this stage. Growing cognitive and language skills give young children the ability to understand and express their feelings and emotions. Children ages 3 to 5 can recognize and label simple emotions, and they learn about themselves when they talk about their anxieties and fears (Hansen & Zambo, 2007). Children in early childhood can also identify feelings expressed by others—as the earlier discussion of empathy illustrated—and use creative ways to comfort others when they are upset.

The ability to understand emotion continues to develop as young children have more opportunity to practice these skills. Children reared in homes in which emotions and feelings are openly discussed are better able to understand and express feelings (Bradley, 2000). Early childhood educators Cory Cooper Hansen and Debby Zambo (2007) recommend the use of children's literature to help children understand and manage emotions. Here are some of their recommendations for how to do that (p. 277):

- Respect all responses to talks about emotions.
- Ask children to describe the emotions of story characters.
- Talk about your own emotions about story characters.
- Encourage children to draw, write, or paint about the emotions of story characters as well as their own emotional reactions.
- Sing or chant about emotions and how to handle them.
- Brainstorm ways that story characters can handle their emotions.
- Practice reading emotions from pictures in books.
- Use stuffed animals to "listen" to children's stories.

Most child development scholars agree that all emotions, including those that have been labeled "negative" (anger, sadness, guilt, disgust), are adaptive, but more needs to be learned about how the "negative" emotions can become problematic for children (Cole, Luby, & Sullivan, 2008). We know that by the first grade, most children can regulate their emotions well enough to learn, obey classroom rules, and develop friendships (Calkins & Hill, 2007). But we also know that emotional receptivity makes young children vulnerable to environmental stress, and early exposure to adverse situations can have a negative effect on the brain, cardiovascular, and endocrine processes that support emotional development (Gunnar & Quevedo, 2007). It is important to recognize when emotional development is getting off course, and researchers are at work to develop understanding of that issue. For example, we know that most young children have tantrums. For most children, anger and distress are expressed in quick peaks in anger intensity that decline into whining and comfort-seeking behavior. Researchers are finding, however, that the tantrums of depressed young children are more violent, destructive, verbally aggressive, and self-injurious; they also have a longer recovery time (Belden, Thompson, & Luby, 2008). It is important to avoid both overreacting and underreacting to children's difficulties in regulating their emotions (Hane, Cheah, Rubin, & Fox, 2008).

Aggression

One behavior that increases during the early childhood years is aggression. Two types of aggression are observed in young children: **instrumental aggression**, which occurs while fighting over toys and space, and **hostile aggression**, which is an attack meant to hurt another individual. Recently, researchers have studied another typology of aggression: physical aggression and relational aggression. **Physical aggression**, as the name suggests, involves using physical force against another person. **Relational aggression** involves behaviors that damage relationships without physical force, behaviors such as threatening to leave a relationship unless a friend complies with demands or using social exclusion or the silent treatment to get one's way. Researchers are finding that boys make greater use of physical aggression than girls, and girls make greater use of relational aggression (Ostrov, Crick, & Stauffacher, 2006).

Although some children continue high levels of aggression into middle childhood, usually physical aggression peaks early in the early childhood years (Alink, Mesmon, & van Zeijl, 2006). By the end of the early childhood years, children learn better negotiation skills and become better at asking for what they want and using words to express feelings. Terri Smith, in the second case study in this chapter, obviously has not developed these moderating skills.

Attachment

In toddlerhood and early childhood, children still depend on their attachment relationships for feelings of security. Toddlers often make use of a **transitional object**, or comfort object, to help them cope with separations from parents and to handle other stressful situations. During such times, they may cuddle with a blanket, teddy bear, or other stuffed animal. The transitional object is seen as a symbol of the relationship with the caregiver, but toddlers also see it as having magical powers to soothe and protect them (Davies, 2011). In particularly stressful times, the attachment behavior of the child ages 3 to 5 may look very much like the clinging behavior of the 2-year-old. For the most part, however, securely attached children will handle their anxieties by verbalizing their needs. For example, at bedtime, the 4-year-old child may say, "I would like you to read one more story before you go." This increased ability to verbalize wants is a source of security. In addition, many young children continue to use transitional objects, such as blankets or a favorite teddy bear, to soothe themselves when they are anxious (Davies, 2011).

In their longitudinal study of 180 children born into poor families, Sroufe et al. (2005) examined, among other things, how attachment style in infancy and toddlerhood affected the developmental trajectory into early childhood. Here are some of the findings:

- Anxiously attached infants and toddlers were more dependent on their mothers and performed more poorly on teaching tasks at age 3½ than either securely or avoidant attached toddlers.
- Securely attached infants and toddlers rated higher on curiosity, agency, activity, self-esteem, and positive emotions at age 4½ than either anxiously or avoidant attached toddlers.
- Securely attached infants and toddlers had better emotion regulation in early childhood than anxiously attached toddlers.

You might want to review the discussion of these attachment styles in Chapter 4.

Sroufe and colleagues also found that temperament was not a powerful predictor of early childhood behavior.

SOCIAL DEVELOPMENT

In early childhood, children become more socially adept than they were as toddlers, but they are still learning how to be social and how to understand the perspectives of other people. The many toddlers and young children who enter group care face increasing demands for social competence. In 2011, 48% of 3- and 4-year-olds in the United States were enrolled in nursery school, at least part time, compared with 10% in 1965 (Davis & Bauman, 2013).

Peer Relations

Although toddlers are capable of establishing relationships, their social play is a struggle, and a toddler play session is quite a fragile experience. Toddlers need help in structuring their play with each other. And yet researchers have found that groups of toddlers in preschool settings develop play routines that they return to again and again over periods of months (Corsaro, 2011). These toddler play routines are primarily nonverbal, with a set of ritualized actions. For example, Corsaro (2011) notes a play routine in one Italian preschool in which a group of toddlers would rearrange the chairs in the room and work together to move them around in patterns. They returned to this routine fairly regularly over the course of a year, modifying it slightly over time. Peer relations are being built by "doing things together."

In early childhood, children form friendships with other children of the same age and sex; boys gravitate toward male playmates and girls choose girls. Across cultures, young children's friendship groups are likely to be segregated by sex (Barbu, Le Maner-Idrissi, & Jouanjean, 2000; Maccoby, 2002a). When asked about the definition of a friend, most children in this age group think of someone with whom they play (Corsaro, 2011). As peer relationships become more important, around age 3, children are motivated to be accepted by peers. This motivation is the incentive for development of such skills as sharing, cooperating, negotiating, and perspective taking. Nevertheless, peer relations in early childhood are often marked by conflict and falling-outs (Davies, 2011).

Research indicates that young children are at a higher risk of being rejected by their peers if they are aggressive and comparatively more active, demonstrate a difficult temperament, are easily distracted, and demonstrate lower perseverance (S. Campbell, 2002). One would wonder, then, how young peers respond to Terri Smith. The rejection of some children is long lasting. It is important, therefore, to intervene early to help children like Terri Smith learn more prosocial behavior.

Peer relationships in early childhood are associated with early attachments. A child who has had secure relationships with parents in the first 3 years is likely to have good social skills and to expect peer relations to be positive. In contrast, peer interactions are often difficult for young children with insecure working models.

Self-Concept

In early childhood, the child seems to vacillate between grandiose and realistic views of the self (Davies, 2011). Children are aware of their growing competence, but at the same time, they have normal doubts about the self, based on realistic comparisons of their competence with the competence of adults. In early childhood, children begin to develop a self-concept, which includes a perception of oneself as a person who has desires, attributes, preferences, and abilities.

Some investigators have suggested that during early childhood, the child's ever-increasing understanding of the self in relation to the world begins to become organized into a **self-theory** (Epstein, 1973, 1991, 1998). As children develop the cognitive ability to categorize, they use categorization to think about the self. By age 2 or 3, children can identify their gender and race (discussed in greater detail shortly) as factors in understanding who they are. From ages 4 to 6, young children become more aware that different people have different perspectives on situations (Ziv & Frye, 2003). This helps them to begin to understand cultural expectations and sensitizes them to the expectations that others have for them.

This growing capacity to understand the self in relation to others leads to self-evaluation, or **self-esteem**. Very early interpersonal experiences provide information that becomes incorporated into self-esteem. Messages of love, admiration, and approval lead to a positive view of the self (Brown, Dutton, & Cook, 2001). Messages of rejection or scorn lead to a negative view of the self (Heimpel, Wood, Marshall, & Brown, 2002). In addition to these interpersonal messages, young children observe their own competencies and attributes and compare them with the competencies of other children as well as adults. And they are very aware of being evaluated by others, their peers as well as important adults (Newman & Newman, 2012).

Of course, a young child may develop a positive view of the self in one dimension, such as cognitive abilities, and a negative view of the self in another dimension, such as physical abilities. Children also learn that some abilities are more valued than others in the various environments in which they operate. For example, in individualistic-oriented societies, self-reliance, independence, autonomy, and distinctiveness are valued whereas interdependence and harmony are valued in most collectivistic-oriented societies. Self-esteem is based on different values in these different types of cultures (J. Brown, 2003). It is probably the case that every culture includes both individualistic and collectivistic beliefs (Turiel, 2004), but the balance of these two belief systems varies greatly from culture to culture. An example of the way these beliefs play out and influence self-development from an early age was described by Markus and Kitayama (2003), who noted that in U.S. coverage of the Olympics, athletes are typically asked about how they personally feel about their efforts and their success. In contrast, in Japanese coverage, athletes are typically asked who helped them achieve. This idea of an interdependent self is consistent with relational and feminist perspectives on relationships (see Chapter 4 in this book for discussion of these theoretical perspectives).

Recently, cognitive neuroscientists have been exploring the ways the brain gives rise to development of a sense of self. They have found that a right fronto-parietal network, which overlaps with mirror neurons, is activated during tasks involving self-recognition and discrimination between the self and the other (Kaplan, Aziz-Zadeh, Uddin, & Iacoboni, 2008). Viewing one's own face leads to greater signal changes in the inferior frontal gyrus (IFG), the inferior occipital gyrus, and the inferior parietal lobe. In addition, there is greater signal change in the right IFG when hearing one's own voice compared with hearing a friend's voice (Kaplan et al., 2008). Beginning evidence also indicates that the cortical midline structures (CMS) of the brain are involved in self-evaluation and in understanding of others' emotional states. In addition, there is beginning evidence of at least one pathway that connects the mirror neurons and the CMS, allowing for integration of self and other understanding (Uddin, Iacoboni, Lange, & Keenan, 2007).

Gender Identity and Sexual Interests

During early childhood, gender becomes an important dimension of how children understand themselves and others. Researchers have suggested four components to gender identity during early childhood (Newman & Newman, 2012):

1. *Making correct use of the gender label.* By age 2, children can usually accurately identify others as either male or female, based on appearance.
2. *Understanding gender as stable.* Later, children understand that gender is stable, that boys grow up to be men and girls to be women.
3. *Understanding gender constancy.* It is not until some time from ages 4 to 7 that children understand *gender constancy*, the understanding that one's gender does not change, that the girl dressed as a boy is still a girl.
4. *Understanding the genital basis of gender.* Gender constancy has been found to be associated with an understanding of the relationship between gender and genitals (Bem, 1998).

Gender includes the cognitive, emotional, and social schemes associated with being female or male; *gender identity* refers to one's sense of being male or female (review the discussion of these terms in Chapter 3 in this book and read more about gender identity in Chapter 14). It appears that gender identity development begins with a recognition of sex differences in early childhood but continues throughout life. Increasingly we are learning that the assigned gender at birth, based on genitalia, is not consistent with how some children, even some young children, understand their gender and that gender identity is much more fluid than researchers of gender identity once thought. The American Psychological Association (2015) has recommended a move away from considering gender as binary, suggesting that "psychologists understand that gender is a nonbinary construct that allows for a range of gender identities and that a person's gender may not align with sex assigned at birth" (p. 834).

That being said, researchers have found evidence of gender differences in multiple dimensions of human behavior, but there is also much debate about just how pervasive these differences are and, if they exist, how to explain them. In terms of the pervasiveness of gender differences, the findings are not at all consistent. In 1974, Eleanor Maccoby and Carol Jacklin reviewed more than 2,000 studies that included sex differences and found evidence of four sex differences: (1) girls have greater verbal abilities than boys, (2) boys excel in visual-spatial ability, (3) boys excel in mathematical ability, and (4) boys are more aggressive. Thirty years later, Janet Hyde (2005) reviewed a large number of studies and found that in 78% of them, gender differences were close to zero or quite small and that there was evidence of much within-group difference. In other words, the differences among girls were as great or greater than the differences between boys and girls. There were substantial gender differences in a few areas, however: some aspects of motor performance, some sexual attitudes and behaviors, and physical aggression. Indeed, research subsequent to the Maccoby and Jacklin review has found that the cognitive differences they reported are very limited. Females do seem to have an advantage in verbal fluency and writing, but not in reading comprehension. Males' visual-spatial advantage seems to occur only in tasks requiring mental rotation of a three-dimensional object. Although males perform better on tests of broad mathematical ability, females score better on computation (B. Garrett, 2009).

There are two competing perspectives on the causes of gender differences: the biological determination perspective and the socially constructed perspective. There is some evidence to support each of these perspectives, suggesting, not surprisingly, that behavior is multiply determined. In terms of verbal ability, there is some evidence that females use both hemispheres of the brain for solving verbal problems whereas males use mostly the left hemisphere, but the findings in this regard are not consistent. Relatively strong evidence indicates that estrogen probably does contribute to women's verbal advantage. Men who take estrogen in their transsexual treatments to become female score higher on verbal learning than men who do not take estrogen as part of their transsexual transformation. Testosterone appears to play a role in spatial ability. Males who produce low levels of testosterone during the developmental years have less well-developed spatial ability; in addition, testosterone replacement therapy in older men improves their spatial functioning. Interestingly, there is only a small sex difference in aggression when behavior is studied in the laboratory but a very large difference outside the laboratory. That is not convincing evidence for a biological basis for the gender differences in aggression (B. Garrett, 2009).

In terms of the socially constructed perspective, we know that human societies use gender as an important category for organizing social life. There are some rather large cultural and subcultural variations in gender role definitions, however. Existing cultural standards about gender are pervasively built into adult interactions with young children and into the reward systems developed for shaping child behavior. Much research indicates that parents begin to use gender stereotypes to respond to their children from the time of birth (Gardiner & Kosmitzki, 2011). They cuddle more with infant girls and play more actively with infant boys. Later, they talk more with young girls and expect young boys to be more independent. Recent studies have found that the nature of parental influence on children's gender role development is more complex than this. Parents may hold to stereotypical gender expectations in some domains but not in others. For example, parents may have similar expectations for boys and girls in terms of sharing or being polite (McHale, Crouter, & Whiteman, 2003). (Note: Unless otherwise specified by researchers, we have used the language of "gender difference" rather than "sex difference" because research indicates that these differences are both biologically and socially constructed.)

Once toddlers understand their gender, they begin to imitate and identify with the same-sex parent, if he or she is available. Once young children begin to understand gender role standards, they become quite rigid in their playing out of gender roles—only girls cook, only men drive trucks, only girls wear pink flowers, only boys wear shirts with footballs. This gender understanding also accounts for the preference of same-sex playmates and sex-typed toys (Davies, 2011). Remember, though, that the exaggeration of gender stereotypes in early childhood is in keeping with the struggle during this period to discover stability and regularity in the environment.

Evidence that gender differences in verbal, visual, and mathematical skills are at least partially socially constructed can be found in data that indicate that differences in all three areas have decreased over the same time period that gender roles have changed toward greater similarity. The dramatic difference in murder rates across societies suggests a strong cultural influence on aggression (B. Garrett, 2009).

During early childhood, children become increasingly interested in their genitals. They are interested, in general, in how their bodies work, but the genitals seem to hold a special interest as the young child learns through experimentation that the genitals can be a source of pleasure. From 3 to 5, children may have some worries and questions about genital difference; little girls may think they once had a penis and wonder what happened to it. Little boys may fear that their penises will disappear, like their sister's did. During early childhood, masturbation is used both as a method of self-soothing and for pleasure. Young children also "play doctor" with each other and often want to see and touch their parents' genitals. Many parents and other caregivers are confused about how to handle this behavior, particularly in our era of heightened awareness of childhood sexual abuse. In general, parents should not worry about genital curiosity or about children experimenting with touching their own genitals. They should remember, however, that at this age children may be overstimulated by seeing their parents' genitals. And we should always be concerned when children want to engage in more explicit adultlike sexual play that involves stimulation of each other's genitals (Davies, 2011; Newman & Newman, 2012).

Racial and Ethnic Identity

Findings from research suggest that children first learn their own racial identity before they are able to identify the race of others (Kowalski, 2003). Elements of racial and ethnic identity awareness have been found to occur as early as age 3. Most children begin to self-identify as a member of a racial group by age 3 to 4, but identification with an ethnic group does not usually occur until later in childhood, from 5 to 8 years of age (Blackmon & Vera, 2008). Early identification of others by race is limited to skin color, which is more easily recognized than ethnic origin. Young children may label a Latino/Latina individual, for example, as either Black or White, depending on the individual's skin color. Young children also show a preference for members of their own race over another, but they do not reject others on the basis of race (Brewer, 1999). Perhaps this choice is similar to the preference for same-sex playmates, a result of young children attempting to learn their own identity.

Social scientists concerned about the development of self-esteem in children of color have investigated racial bias and preference using children in early childhood as research participants. The most famous of these studies was conducted by Kenneth Clark and Mamie Clark in 1939. They presented African American children with Black dolls and White dolls and concluded that African American children responded more favorably to the White dolls and had more negative reactions to the Black dolls. A similar study 40 years later, observing young Black children in Trinidad and in New York, reported similar results (Gopaul-McNicol, 1988). The young children from both New York and Trinidad preferred and identified with the White dolls. Interestingly, the same results have been reported more recently in studies of Taiwanese young children (Chang, 2001). Most of the Taiwanese children in the study indicated a preference for the White dolls and demonstrated a "pro-white attitude." Another study found that African American children growing up in a mainly European American community tend to choose White images or dolls, but those growing up in a predominantly African American community tend to choose Black images or dolls (Cameron, Alvarez, Ruble, & Fuligni, 2001). Furthermore, when young children were not asked to make a preference between images, they showed interest in Asian, White, and Black images or dolls and did not make judgments based on race or ethnicity (Kowalski, 2003).

It is questionable, however, whether preferences and biases found in research are equated with self-concept and low self-esteem for children of color. Many argue that they are not. For example, racial bias and self-concept were not related among the young Taiwanese children (Chang, 2001). Likewise, findings from studies about young African American children indicate high levels of self-esteem despite the children's bias in favor of the White culture and values (Crain, 1996; Spencer, 1984). Spencer concludes that young Black children compartmentalize personal identity (self-concept) from knowledge about racial stereotypes in the dominant culture.

> **CRITICAL THINKING Questions 12.2**
>
> What types of children's literature might be particularly useful to help Henry Velasquez, Terri Smith, and Ron and Rosiland Johnson in their emotional development? What types of stories would you look for if you were to work with these children? How concerned should we be about Terri Smith's tantrums? Do you think her emotional development is getting off course? What challenges might each of these children face in developing self-esteem? How might a social worker help each of these children to develop a positive self-evaluation?

THE ROLE OF PLAY

The toddler and young child love to play, and play is essential to all aspects of early child development. We think of the play of young children as fun-filled and lively. And yet it serves a serious purpose. Through play, children develop the motor skills essential for physical development, learn the problem-solving skills and communication skills fundamental to cognitive development, express the feelings and gain the self-confidence needed for emotional growth, and learn to cooperate and resolve social conflicts. Essentially, play is what young children are all about; it is their work.

As children develop in all areas during early childhood, their play activities and preferences for play materials change over time. Hughes (2010) makes the following recommendations about the preferred play materials at different ages during toddlerhood and early childhood:

© iStockphoto.com

Play is one of the few elements in the development of children that is universal—regardless of culture.

- *12–18 months:* push toys; pull toys; balls; plain and interlocking blocks; simple puzzles with large, easy-to-handle pieces; stacking toys; riding toys with wheels close to the ground
- *18–24 months:* toys for the sandbox and water play; spoons, shovels, and pails; storybooks; blocks; dolls, stuffed animals, and puppets
- *3-year-olds:* props for imaginative play, such as dress-up clothes, doctor kits, and makeup; miniature toys that represent adult models, such as toy trucks, gas stations, dolls, doll houses, and airplanes; art materials, such as paint brushes, easels, marker pens, and crayons
- *4-year-olds:* vehicles, such as tricycles and wagons; play materials to develop fine motor skills, such as materials for sewing, stringing beads, coloring, painting, and drawing; books that involve adventure
- *5-year-olds:* play materials to develop precision in fine motor skills, such as coloring books, paints and brushes, crayons, marker pens, glue, scissors, stencils, sequins and glitter, clay, and Play-Doh; play materials that develop cognitive skills, such as workbenches, play cards, table games, and board games

In recent years, there has been a dramatic increase in the availability of computers and other instructional technology. These technologies have made their way into early childhood education programs, but there is controversy among early childhood educators about the positive and negative aspects of these technologies for early childhood development. There is evidence of benefits of instructional technologies in the preschool classroom. For example, 4- and 5-year-old children can use technology to develop language, art, mathematics, and science skills. Conversely, some early childhood educators are concerned that computers and other instructional technologies contribute to social isolation and limit children's creative play (Hughes, 2010). Adults must give serious consideration to how to balance the positive and negative aspects of these technologies.

Toddlers engage in simple repetitive motor movements, construct objects, act out everyday functions, and play with imaginary friends. The predominant type of play in early childhood, beginning around the age of 2, is **symbolic play**, otherwise known as fantasy play, pretend play, or imaginary play (Hughes, 2010). Young children continue to use vivid imaginations in their play, as they did as toddlers, but they also begin to put more structure into their play. Thus, their play is intermediate between the fantasy play of toddlers and the structured, rules-oriented play of middle childhood. Although toddler play is primarily nonverbal, the play of young children often involves highly sophisticated verbal productions. There is some indication that this preference for symbolic play during early childhood exists across cultures, but the themes of the play reflect the culture in which it is enacted (Roopnarine, Shin, Donovan, & Suppal, 2000).

Symbolic play during early childhood has five primary functions: providing an opportunity to explore reality, contributing to cognitive development, practicing for morality, allowing young children to gain control over their lives, and serving as a shared experience and opportunity for development of peer culture. Play that is focused on language and thinking skills has been described as **learning play** (Meek, 2000). Many researchers who study the play of young children suggest that **sociodramatic play**, or group fantasy play in which children coordinate their fantasy, is the most important form of play during this time. Young children are able to develop more elaborate fantasy play and sustain it by forming friendship groups, which in turn gives them experience with group conflict and group problem solving that carries over into the adult world (Corsaro, 2011). Group play also helps young children learn to understand and follow rules.

Children in preschool settings have been observed trying to get control over their lives by subverting some of the control of adults. Corsaro (2011) describes a preschool where the children had been told they could not bring any play items from home. The preschool teachers were trying to avoid the kinds of conflicts that can occur over toys brought from home. The children in this preschool found a way to subvert this rule, however; they began to bring in very small toys, such as Matchbox cars, that would fit in their pockets out of sight when teachers were nearby. Corsaro provides a number of other examples from his cross-cultural research of ways that young children use play to take some control of their lives away from adults.

© iStockphoto.com/Erna Vader

Young children use play to think and learn about the world.

DEVELOPMENTAL DISRUPTIONS

Children develop at different rates. Most developmental problems in infants, toddlers, and young children are most accurately described as **developmental delays**, offering the hope that early intervention, or even natural processes, will mitigate the long-term effects (Rosenberg, Ellison, Fast, Robinson, & Lazar, 2013). The delay may be temporary or may be a symptom of a lifelong condition. Developmental delays may exist in cognitive skills, communication skills, social skills, emotion regulation, behavior, and fine and gross motor skills. Developmental problems in school-age children are typically labeled *developmental disabilities* and classified into groups, such as cognitive disability, learning disabilities, and motor impairment (Parish, Saville, Swaine, & Igdalsky, 2016).

Part C of the Individuals with Disabilities Act (IDEA) is a nationwide program that provides services to infants and toddlers with developmental delays in cognitive, motor, communication, and social and emotional development, but there is no standard definition of what constitutes a developmental delay (Rosenberg et al., 2013). Premature infants, such as Paul Thompson in Case Study 11.2, often need time to catch up in terms of physical, cognitive, and emotional development. At what point do his parents and professional caregivers decide that he is not developing fast enough and label him developmentally delayed? At what point would it be appropriate to decide that he has a lifelong developmental disability?

Because early interventions for infants and toddlers produce better outcomes in comparison with interventions for school-aged children (Matson, Fodstad, & Dempsey, 2009; McMahon, 2013), early detection and diagnosis is key. The Centers for Disease Control and Prevention (2012d), along with the American Academy of Pediatrics, recommends screening for all types of developmental delays and disabilities at 9, 18, and 24 or 30 months of age.

In recent years, researchers have been studying the early impairments of developmental disabilities such as cerebral palsy, Down syndrome, and seizure disorder (Hattier, Matson, Sipes, & Turygin, 2011). A more aggressive research agenda has focused on early identification of autism spectrum disorders (ASD), because early intervention is seen as so critical for this developmental disability. Typical behaviors with these disorders include impairments in social and communication development and restricted and repetitive behaviors. Barbaro and Dissanayake (2012) investigated the early markers of ASD at the ages of 12, 18, and 24 months in an attempt to understand how infants and toddlers with ASD could be distinguished from infants and toddlers with developmental delays that would disappear with time and early intervention. They found that infants with the most severe symptoms at 24 months had pervasive impairment on all social and communication items at 12 and 18 months. There was more variability in the impairments of 12- and 18-month-old infants and toddlers who would later demonstrate less severe impairments at 24 months but were still on the autism spectrum. The infants and toddlers with developmental delays at 12 and 18 months had typical development in every area but language at 24 months. At 12 months the markers of later ASD were deficits in pointing, waving, imitation, eye contact, and response to name. At 18 months, the key markers were deficits in pointing, eye contact, and showing items to a communication partner. The same markers were present at 24 months, plus an added marker of deficits in pretend play. The children with developmental delay showed earlier deficits in pretend play but were performing at the typical level by age 24 months.

After interviewing professionals who work with children age 6 and younger, one research team compiled a list of traits observed in young children that indicate emotional and behavioral problems: extreme aggressive behavior, difficulty with change, invasion of others' personal space, compulsive or impulsive behavior, low ability to trust others, lack of empathy or remorse, and cruelty to animals (Schmitz & Hilton, 1996). Parents and teachers often handle these behaviors with firmer limits and more discipline. However, environmental risk factors, such as emotional abuse or neglect and domestic violence, may be the actual cause.

Given the difficulty of accurate assessment, assessment in young children should include many disciplines to gain as broad an understanding as possible (Parish, Saville, & Swaine, 2011). Assessment and service delivery should also be culturally relevant. In other words, culture and other related issues—such as family interaction patterns and stress, the surrounding community, ethnicity, acculturation, and developmental expectations—should all be considered when evaluating a child's developmental abilities.

For those children who have been labeled developmentally delayed, the main remedy has been social skill development (T. Lewis, 1994; Roberts, Burchinal, & Bailey, 1994).

It is also important to recognize the parental stress that often accompanies care of children with developmental delays. Researchers have found that an educational intervention with parents that teaches behavioral management and how to plan activities that minimize disruptive behavior results in improved child behavior, improved parent–child relationship, and less parental stress (Clare, Mazzucchelli, Studman, & Sanders, 2006).

In the 1980s, concern about the quality of education in the United States led to upgrades in the elementary school curriculum. Many skills previously introduced in the first grade became part of the kindergarten curriculum. This has led to increased concern about kindergarten readiness, the skills that the young child should have acquired before entering kindergarten, as well as how to provide for the needs of developmentally delayed children in the kindergarten classroom. It has also led to controversies about when to begin to think of developmental delays as disabilities. A growing concern is that children with developmental problems should not be placed in kindergarten classrooms that do not provide support for their particular developmental needs (Litty & Hatch, 2006). States vary in how much support they provide to children with developmental delays to allow them to participate in fully inclusive classrooms (classrooms where they are mainstreamed with children without developmental delays), but a growing number of children with developmental delays in the United States are participating as full citizens in inclusive classrooms during preschool and kindergarten (Guralnick, Neville, Hammond, & Connor, 2008).

Before leaving this discussion, we would like to emphasize one important point. When working with young children, we want to recognize and respect the variability of developmental trajectories. At the same time, however, we want to be attentive to any aspects of a child's development that may be lagging behind expected milestones so that we can provide extra support to young children in specific areas of development (Spinrad et al., 2007).

CRITICAL THINKING Questions 12.3

How could play be used to help Henry Velasquez, Terri Smith, and Ron and Rosiland Johnson in their multidimensional development? What do you see as particular needs each of them have that could be at least partially addressed with play?

EARLY CHILDHOOD EDUCATION

It is a relatively new idea to provide formalized education for young children, but three strands of research are indicating the importance of formal education to support social awareness, group interaction skills, and cognitive development during early childhood to prepare children to live in contemporary knowledge-driven economies. First, neuroscientific research indicates the critical importance of brain development in the early years. Second, social science research indicates that high-quality early childhood education programs improve readiness for primary school. And third, econometric research indicates that high-quality early childhood education programs save societies significant amounts of money over time (Economist Intelligence Unit, 2012). Early childhood education has been found to be especially important for children from low-income households in highly unequal societies who are likely to enter primary school far behind their peers and experience an achievement gap throughout their schooling years (Heckman, 2006, 2008). In spite of mounting evidence that greater investment in early childhood education reduces costs at later stages of education, most societies continue to prioritize tertiary, secondary, and primary education over early childhood education (Economist Intelligence Unit, 2012).

Rates of enrollment in early childhood education vary across the world, and program quality varies as well. In 2011, 47% of 3- and 4-year-olds in the United States were involved in formal education, compared with 100% in France, Germany, and Italy; 95% in the United Kingdom; and 86% in Japan (Miller, Warren, & Owen, 2011). With increasing concern about the need for early childhood learning, the Lien Foundation of Singapore commissioned the Economist Intelligence Unit (EIU) to study "preschool education" (which we are calling early childhood education) on a global scale. The EIU developed an index, which they call the Starting Well Index, to rank early childhood education in 45 countries on four indicators: social context, availability, affordability, and quality (Economist Intelligence Unit, 2012). The United States, tied with the United Arab Emirates for an overall rank of 24th among the 45 countries, was ranked 28th for social context, 31st for availability, 16th for affordability, and 22nd for quality. The countries with the top five overall rankings were Finland, Sweden, Norway, the United Kingdom, and Belgium, all countries that put high value on state-supported early childhood education.

Much evidence indicates that low-income and racial minority students in the United States have less access to quality early childhood education than their age peers (Ravitch, 2013). Wealthy families are competing for slots for their young children in expensive preschool programs, called the "baby ivies," that provide highly enriched early learning environments, further advancing opportunities for children in privileged families (Kozol, 2005). Middle-class families, as well as impoverished families, are increasingly unable to access quality early childhood education; 78% of families who earned more than $100,000 per year in 2004 sent their young children to early childhood educational programs compared with less than half of families earning less than $50,000 per year (Calman & Tarr-Whelan, 2005).

One longitudinal study followed a group of children who attended the High/Scope Perry Preschool Program in Ypsilanti, Michigan, until they reached the age of 40 (Schweinhart et al., 2005). From 1962 to 1967, the researchers identified a sample of 123 low-income African American children who had been assessed to be at high risk of school failure. They randomly assigned 58 of these children to attend a high-quality 2-year preschool program for 2- and 3-year-olds, while the other 65 attended no preschool program. The program met for 2½ hours per day, 5 days a week, and teachers made home visits every 2 weeks. The teachers in the preschool program had bachelor's degrees and education certification. No more than eight children were assigned to a teacher, and the curriculum emphasized giving children the opportunity to plan and carry out their own activities. By age 40, the preschool participants, on average, were doing better than the nonparticipants in several important ways:

- They were more likely to have graduated from high school (65% vs. 45%).
- They were more likely to be employed (76% vs. 62%).
- They had higher median annual earnings ($20,800 vs. $15,300).
- They were more likely to own their own home (37% vs. 28%).
- They were more likely to have a savings account (76% vs. 50%).
- They had fewer lifetime arrests (36% vs. 55% arrested five or more times).
- They were less likely to have spent time in prison or jail (28% vs. 52% never sentenced).

The researchers report that the preschool program cost $15,166 per child and the public gained $12.90 for every dollar spent on the program by the time the participants were 40 years old. The savings came from reduced special education costs, increased taxes derived from higher earnings, reduced public assistance costs, and reduced costs to the criminal justice system. Nobel Prize–winning economist James Heckman and colleagues (Heckman, Moon, Pinto, Savelyev, & Yavitz, 2010) have reanalyzed the data to rule out alternative assumptions and report estimated rates of social return of 7% to 10%.

Another longitudinal study began in North Carolina in 1972, when 112 low-income infants were randomly assigned to either a quality preschool program or no program (Masse & Barnett, 2002). The group assigned to the preschool program was enrolled in the program for 5 years instead of the 2 years in the High/Scope Perry study. The participants in this study were followed to the age of 21. The children who participated in the preschool program were less likely to repeat grades, less likely to be placed in special education classes, and more likely to complete high school. It is important to note that the researchers in this study also investigated the impact of the preschool program on the mothers. They found that the preschool program mothers earned $3,750 more per year than the mothers whose children did not attend the program, for a total of $78,750 more over 21 years.

The previous two longitudinal studies investigated the impact of quality preschool education on low-income children, but there is also preliminary evidence of the benefit of early childhood education on all children. A study conducted at Georgetown University has examined the effect of prekindergarten (PK) programs in Tulsa, Oklahoma (Gromley, Gayer, Phillips, & Dawson, 2005). These programs are considered high quality because teachers are required to have a bachelor's degree, there are no more than 10 children per teacher, and teachers are paid on the same scale as public school teachers. The researchers found that children who attended PK scored better on letter-word identification, spelling, and applied problems than children of the same age who had not attended PK. This was true regardless of race or socioeconomic status. Results from other research indicate that public funding of early childhood education can help close the gap in preschool education between low-income and higher-income children (Greenberg, 2010).

These studies suggest that early childhood education programs are good for children, for families, for communities, and for society. With such evidence in hand, social workers can join with other child advocates to build broad coalitions to educate the public about the multilevel benefits and to push for public policy that guarantees universal quality early childhood education.

TODDLERHOOD AND EARLY CHILDHOOD IN THE MULTIGENERATIONAL FAMILY

Curiosity and experimentation are the hallmarks of toddlerhood and early childhood. Young children are sponges, soaking up information about themselves, their worlds, and their relationships. They use their families as primary sources of information and as models for relationships. Where there are older siblings, they serve as important figures of identification and imitation. Aunts, uncles, cousins, and grandparents may also serve this role, but parents are, in most families, the most important sources of information, support, and modeling for young children.

Parents play two very important roles for their 2- to 6-year-old child: educator and advocate (Newman & Newman, 2012). As educators, they answer children's big and little questions, ask questions to stimulate thinking and growth in communication skills, provide explanations, and help children figure things out. They teach children about morality and human connectedness by modeling honest, kind, thoughtful behavior and by reading to their children about moral dilemmas and moral action. They help children develop emotional intelligence by modeling how to handle strong feelings and by talking with children about the children's strong feelings. They take young children on excursions in their real physical worlds as well as in the fantasy worlds found in books. They give children opportunities to perform tasks that develop a sense of mastery.

Not all parents have the same resources for the educator role or the same beliefs about how children learn. And some parents take their role as educators too seriously, pushing their young children into more and more structured time with higher and higher expectations of performance. The concern is that these children are deprived of time for exploration, experimentation, and fantasy.

In the contemporary era, infants, toddlers, and young children are moving into organized child care settings at earlier ages. As they do so, parents become more important as advocates who understand their children's needs. The advocate role is particularly important for parents of young children with disabilities. These parents may need to advocate to ensure that all aspects of early childhood education programs are accessible to their children.

For some children, like Ron and Rosiland Johnson, it is the grandparent and not the parent who serves as the central figure. Estimates are that in 2011, 7.7 million children were living with a grandparent or other relative, with 3 million of these children being cared for primarily by that grandparent. Both of these numbers rose rapidly after the recession of 2008. In 80% of the cases where children live with a grandparent, at least one of the child's parents is also living in the household. Many of the parents in these households are in need of assistance: 44% had a baby as a teen, 12% have a disability, 21% are unemployed, and 29% have less than a high school education (Livingston, 2013). Some custodial grandparents describe an increased purpose for living, but others describe increased isolation, worry, physical and emotional exhaustion, and financial concerns (Clarke, 2008). These are some of the same concerns expressed by Ms. Johnson in the third case study at the beginning of this chapter. In addition, grandparents caring for children with psychological and physical problems experience high levels of stress (Sands & Goldberg, 2000).

The literature indicates that young children often do better under the care of grandparents than in other types of homes. However, children like Ron and Rosiland, who are parented by their grandparents, must often overcome many difficult emotions (Smith, Dannison, & Vach-Hasse, 1998). These children struggle with issues of grief and loss related to loss of their parent(s) and feelings of guilt, fear, embarrassment, and anger. These feelings may be especially strong for young children who feel they are somehow responsible for the loss of their parent(s). Although children in this age group are capable of labeling their feelings, their ability to discuss these feelings with any amount of depth is very limited. In addition, grandparents may feel unsure about how to talk about the situation with their young grandchildren. Professional intervention for the children is often recommended. Some mental health practitioners have had success providing group sessions that help grandparents gain control over their grandchildren's behavior, resolve clashes in values between themselves and their grandchildren, and help grandparents avoid overindulgence and set firm limits.

Grandparents are often important figures in the lives of young children even when they do not serve as primary caregivers; they provide practical support, financial support, and emotional support. They may offer different types of practical support, coming to the aid of the family when needs arise. Or they may serve as the child care provider while parents work or provide babysitting services in the evening. They also provide financial support, depending on their financial circumstances. They may provide cash assistance or buy things such as clothes and toys for the children; it is distressing to some grandparents if they lack the financial resources to buy things for their grandchildren. Grandparents may also provide emotional support and advice to parents of young children; this is something that can be done at a distance by a variety of electronic technologies when grandparents live at some distance from the children (Clarke, 2008).

CRITICAL THINKING Questions 12.4

Based on the research noted earlier, what types of social policies would you like to see enacted in early childhood education? The United States has less vigorous state support for early childhood education than many other wealthy nations. What factors do you think influence the policy decisions about early childhood education in the United States and other wealthy nations? How could a social worker help Ron and Rosiland Johnson and their grandmother to thrive while Ron and Rosiland's mother is incarcerated?

RISKS TO HEALTHY DEVELOPMENT IN TODDLERHOOD AND EARLY CHILDHOOD

This section addresses a few risk factors that social workers are likely to encounter in work with toddlers and young children and their families: poverty, homelessness, ineffective discipline, divorce, and violence (including child abuse). The section that follows outlines protective factors that ameliorate the risks.

POVERTY

Examining the social science evidence about the effects of family life on physical and mental health, Repetti, Taylor, and Seeman (2002) made the following observation: "The adverse effects of low SES [socioeconomic status] on mental and physical health outcomes are as close to a universal truth as social science has offered" (p. 359). When a family is impoverished, the youngest are the most vulnerable, and, indeed, children birth to age 3 have the highest rates of impoverishment around the world (Addy & Wight, 2012; UNICEF, 2012a). Although there are many ways of measuring poverty, it is generally agreed that 1 billion children across the world live in poverty, representing 1 in 2 children (Global Issues, 2013). Although children living in the poorest countries are much more likely than children living in wealthy countries to be poor, the proportion of children living in poverty has been rising in many of the wealthiest nations (UNICEF, 2012b). Using a relative measure of poverty as income below 50% of the national median income, the UNICEF researchers found that the percentage of children living in poverty in 35 economically advanced countries ranged from 4.7% in Iceland to 25.5% in Romania. The United States had the second highest rate, 23.1%. Fourteen countries, including most European countries, had child poverty rates of less than 10%.

In the United States, the National Center for Children in Poverty (NCCP) estimates that families need an income about 2 times the U.S. federal poverty level to meet basic needs, and they refer to families below this level as low income (Addy & Wight, 2012). NCCP reports that, in 2010, of the more than 11 million infants and toddlers in the United States, 5.7 million (48%) lived in low-income families, and 3.0 million (25%) lived in families below the poverty level (Addy & Wight, 2012). Six million children (25%) younger than age 6 lived in poverty in 2011, and about 49% of children younger than age 6 lived in low-income families, with incomes below 200% of the poverty level. Seventy percent of American Indian and Black children younger than age 6 lived in low-income households, compared with 67% of Hispanic, 35% of White, and 30% of Asian children. Young children with immigrant parents are more likely than young children with native-born parents to live in low-income families, 63% compared with 46%.

Children living in poverty often suffer the consequences of poor nutrition, inadequate health care, and overcrowding. Undernutrition in infancy, toddlerhood, and early childhood is a major risk factor for serious health problems at later stages of life, especially if it is combined with prenatal undernutrition (Barker & Thornburg, 2013). In 2011, 22% of households with children younger than age 18 were food insecure for some part of the year. The research indicates that families with food insecurity usually attempt to provide adequate nutrition to the youngest children, with parents and older children making sacrifices to feed younger children (Child Trends, 2013a). A study of the Northern Cheyenne Indian reservation in southeastern Montana found that 70% of all households were food insecure (Whiting & Ward, 2008). Inadequate nutrition is a serious threat to all aspects of early childhood development. Inadequate health care means that many acute conditions become chronic. Overcrowding is problematic to young children in that it restricts opportunities for play, the means through which most development occurs.

Negative associations between family poverty and children's cognitive development begin to emerge by the end of the second year of life. By age 2, poor toddlers score 4.4 points lower on IQ tests than nonpoor toddlers. In addition, poor infants and toddlers are more likely to demonstrate emotional and behavioral problems than nonpoor infants and toddlers. Three-year-olds who live in deep poverty have been found to display more internalizing behavior symptoms, such as anxiety, withdrawal, and depression, than other children of the same age (Barajas, Philipsen, & Brooks-Gunn, 2008). Children who experience poverty during their early years are less likely to complete school than children whose initial exposure to poverty occurred in the middle childhood years or during adolescence. Researchers have also found that children who live in poverty are at high risk for low self-esteem, peer conflict, depression,

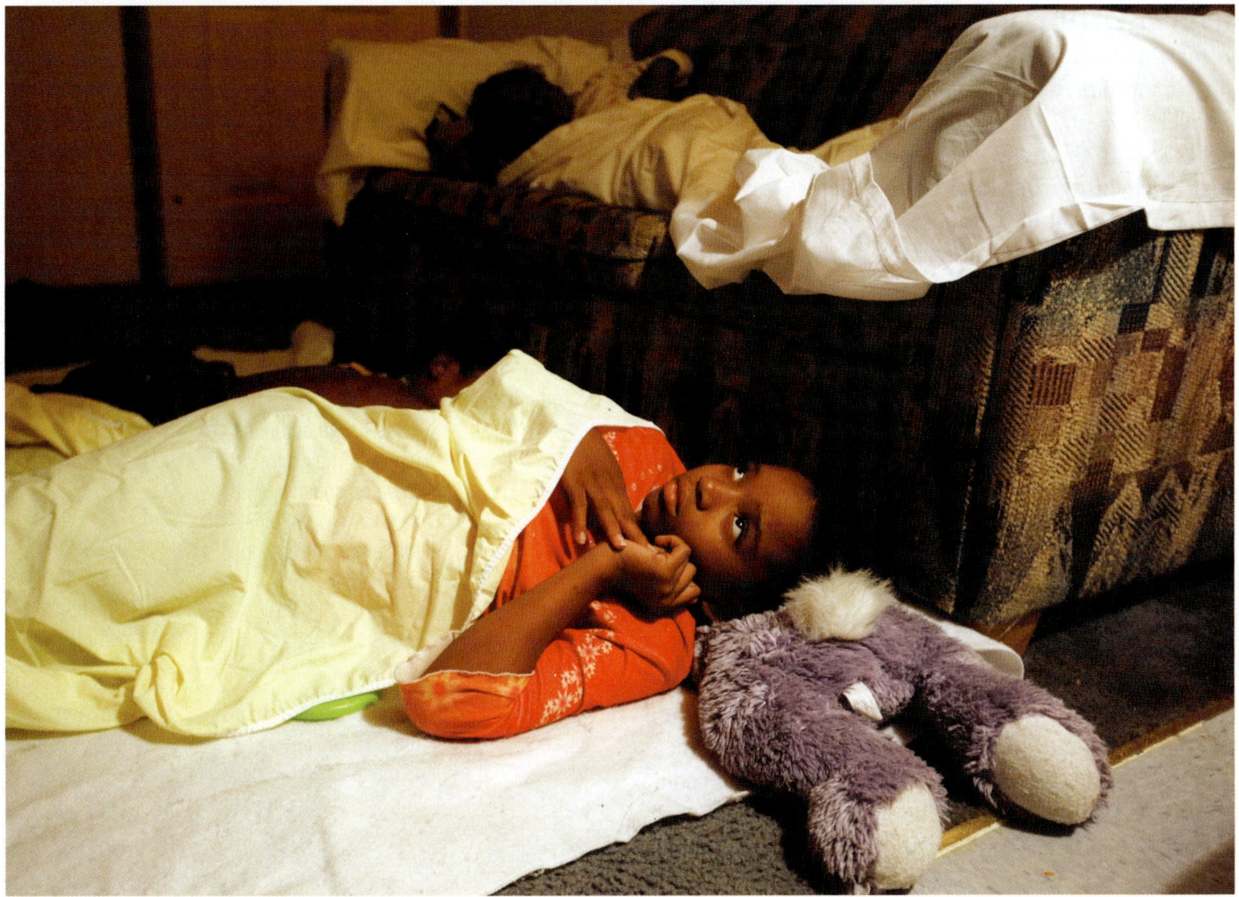

Children birth to age 3 have the highest rates of impoverishment around the world.

and childhood psychological disorders. Children are affected not only by the direct consequences of poverty but also by indirect factors such as family stress, parental depression, and inadequate or nonsupportive parenting (Davies, 2011). Irma Velasquez's depression and anxiety will affect her relationship with Henry. Poor children are also more likely to be exposed to environmental toxins (Hetherington & Boddy, 2013).

Not all young children who live in poverty fare poorly, however. In their longitudinal study of 180 children born into poverty, Sroufe et al. (2005) report that four groups emerged by early childhood: they grouped 70 children into a very competent cluster who were high in enthusiasm, persistence, compliance, and affection for the mother. They grouped another 25 children into a very incompetent cluster characterized by high negativity and low compliance and affection. The other almost half of the children were grouped into two clusters that fell between very competent and very incompetent.

HOMELESSNESS

Families with children make up one third of the homeless population. It is estimated that 42% of homeless families have children younger than age 6. Homeless children are sick more often, are exposed to more violence, and experience more emotional and behavioral problems and more delayed development than low-income housed children. Their school attendance is often disrupted because they need to change schools, but often because of transportation problems as well (Paquette & Bassuk, 2009).

Kristen Paquette and Ellen Bassuk (2009) note that parents' identities are often closely tied to relationships they maintain, especially with their children, and that homelessness undermines their ability to protect those they have a responsibility to protect. Like all parents, homeless parents want to provide their children with basic necessities. Being homeless presents dramatic barriers and challenges for parents, who too often lose the ability to provide essentials for their children, including shelter, food, and access to education. They must look for jobs and housing while also adhering to shelter rules. Their parenting is public, easily observed, and monitored by others. What they need is to be involved with a meaningful social support system that links them to organizations and professionals in the community who might offer resources and options that support them to engage in effective parenting.

INEFFECTIVE DISCIPLINE

A once-popular guidebook for parents declared, "Under no circumstances should you ever punish your child!!" (Moyer, 1974, p. 40). Punishment implies an attempt to get even with the child, whereas **discipline** involves helping the child overcome a problem. Parents often struggle with how forceful to be in response to undesired behavior. The Smiths are a good example of this struggle. And, indeed, the research on parental styles of discipline is finding that the question of the appropriate style of parenting young children is very complex.

A good place to begin this discussion is with the work of Diana Baumrind (1971), who, after extensive research, described three parenting styles—authoritarian, authoritative, and permissive—that use different combinations of two factors: warmth and control (see Exhibit 12.3). The **authoritarian parenting** style uses low warmth and high control. These parents favor punishment and negative reinforcement, and children are treated as submissive. Children reared under an authoritarian parenting style have been found to become hostile and moody and have difficulty managing stress (Carey, 1994). Baumrind considered the **authoritative parenting** style, in which parents consider the child's viewpoints but remain in control, to be the most desirable approach to discipline and behavior management. The authoritative parenting style has been found to be associated with academic achievement, self-esteem, and social competence (see Domenech Rodriguez, Donovick, & Crowley, 2009). The **permissive parenting** style accepts children's behavior without attempting to modify it. Baumrind suggested that children reared from the permissive parenting orientation are cheerful but demonstrate little if any impulse control. In addition, these children are overly dependent and have low levels of self-reliance. The Smiths' style of parenting probably fits here. Certainly, Terri Smith's behavior mirrors behavior exhibited by children reared with the permissive style. In later work, Baumrind (1991) presented a fourth parenting style, **disengaged parenting**, parents who are aloof, withdrawn, and unresponsive. Baumrind's typology of parenting styles has been the building block of much theorizing and research on parenting styles and child outcomes.

Stephen Greenspan (2006) questions Baumrind's suggestion that authoritative parenting is the best parenting. He suggests that Baumrind paid too little attention to the context in which parental discipline occurs, arguing that there are times to exercise control and times to tolerate a certain level of behavioral deviance and that a wise parent knows the difference between these types of situations. Greenspan proposes that another dimension of parenting should be added to Baumrind's two dimensions of warmth and control. He calls this dimension "tolerance" and recommends a style of parenting called "harmonious." He suggests that harmonious parents are warm and set limits when they feel they are called for, overlooking some child behaviors in the interests of facilitating child autonomy and family harmony. It seems that many parents, like Terri Smith's parents, struggle with knowing which situations call for firm control and which ones call for tolerating some defiance.

EXHIBIT 12.3 • Three Parenting Styles

PARENTING STYLE	DESCRIPTION	TYPE OF DISCIPLINE
Authoritarian	Parents who use this type of parenting are rigid and controlling. Rules are narrow and specific, with little room for negotiation, and children are expected to follow the rules without explanation.	Cold and harsh Physical force No explanation of rules provided
Authoritative	These parents are more flexible than authoritarian parents. Their rules are more reasonable, and they leave opportunities for compromises and negotiation.	Warm and nurturing Positive reinforcement Set firm limits and provide rationale behind rules and decisions
Permissive	The parents' rules are unclear, and children are left to make their own decisions.	Warm and friendly toward their children No direction given

SOURCE: Adapted from Baumrind, 1971.

Parenting styles are prescribed in part by the community and the culture; therefore, it is not surprising that there is growing sentiment that Baumrind's parenting typology may be a good model for understanding parenting in White, middle-class families but may not work as well for understanding parenting in other cultural groups. We examine two streams of research that have explored racial and ethnic variations in parenting styles: research on Latino families and research on African American families.

Strong support has not been found for Baumrind's parenting typology in research on Latino parenting styles. Some researchers have described Latino parenting as permissive and others have described it as authoritarian. One research team (Domenech Rodriguez et al., 2009), like Greenspan, suggests that another dimension of parenting should be added to Baumrind's two-dimension model of warmth and control. They call this dimension "autonomy granting," which they describe as allowing children autonomy of individual expression in the family. This seems to be very close to what Greenspan meant by "tolerance," because he writes of tolerance of emotional expression in the spirit of autonomy. Domenech Rodriguez and colleagues (2009) suggest that these three dimensions—warmth, control, and autonomy granting—can be configured in different ways to produce eight different parenting styles:

Authoritative: high warmth, high control, high autonomy granting

Authoritarian: low warmth, high control, low autonomy granting

Permissive: high warmth, low control, high autonomy granting

Neglectful: low warmth, low control, low autonomy granting

Protective: high warmth, high control, low autonomy granting

Cold: low warmth, high control, high autonomy granting

Affiliative: high warmth, low control, low autonomy granting

Neglectful II: low warmth, low control, high autonomy granting

In their preliminary research, which involved direct observation of 56 first-generation Latino American families, they found that the majority (61%) used a protective parenting style but had different expectations for male and female children. There seems to be merit in adding the dimension of autonomy granting, because it may help to capture the parenting styles of cultural groups that are less individualistic than European American culture.

There is a relatively long line of research that has questioned the appropriateness of applying Baumrind's model to understand African American parenting, and the issues are proving to be complex. Much of this research has looked at the use of physical discipline, with the finding that physical discipline causes disruptive behaviors in White families but not Black families (see Lau, Litrownik, Newton, Black, & Everson, 2006, for a review of this research). Researchers have suggested that Black children may regard physical discipline as a legitimate parenting behavior because there is a culture of using physical discipline out of "concern for the child": high levels of firm control are used along with high levels of warmth and affection. Conversely, it is argued that White children may regard physical discipline as an act of aggression because it is often used when parents are angry and out of control (Lansford, Deater-Deckard, Dodge, Bates, & Pettit, 2004). The idea is that the context of the physical discipline and the meaning made of it will influence its impact. However, research by Lau et al. (2006) did not replicate earlier research that found that the effects of physical discipline differed by race. They found that for both Black and White children, physical discipline exacerbated impulsive, aggressive, and noncompliant behaviors for children who had exhibited behavioral problems at an early age. However, they also found that parental warmth protected against later problems in White children but seemed to exacerbate early problems in Black children. The researchers concluded that professionals must recognize that parenting may need to take different forms in different communities. Clearly, this is an issue that needs further investigation.

Research has also indicated differences in parenting style based on the socioeconomic environment in which parenting occurs (Slatcher & Trentacosta, 2012). Low-income parents have been noted to be more authoritarian than more economically advantaged parents. Using observation methods, one research team found that the socioeconomic differences in parenting styles is not that straightforward, however. They found that middle-class parents routinely use subtle forms of control while, at the same time, trying to instill autonomy in their children. Their children spend a large portion of their time under adult supervision, in one activity or another. The researchers also found that low-income parents tend to value conformity but allow their school-aged children to spend considerable leisure time in settings where they do not have adult supervision, consequently affording them considerable autonomy (Weininger & Lareau, 2009).

Findings from studies about punishment and young children indicate that punishment is often used in response to early childhood behavior that is age appropriate. So rather than encouraging the independence that is otherwise expected for a child, such age-appropriate behavior is discouraged (Culp, McDonald Culp, Dengler, & Maisano, 1999). In addition, evidence indicates that brain development can be affected by the stress created by punishment or physical discipline (Glaser, 2000). Harsh punishment and physical discipline interfere with the neural connection process that begins in infancy and continues throughout early childhood. But for many low-income parents, harsh punishment may be less an issue of control or "bad parenting" than an effort to cope with a desperate situation.

As you can see, there are many controversies about effective parenting for young children, and this is an issue about which parents and professionals often have strong feelings. Research is beginning to recognize that different parenting styles may work well in different developmental niches.

DIVORCE

It is estimated that more than half of the children born in the 1990s spent some of their childhood in a single-parent household. Compared with parents in two-parent families, single parents work longer hours, experience greater stress, have more economic problems, and have less emotional support (Anderson & Anderson, 2011). Following divorce, about two thirds of children live with their mother, and most women and children experience a sharp and, unfortunately, long-term decline in economic well-being after divorce (Fine et al., 2010).

Researchers have come to very different conclusions about the effects of divorce on children. Some have found that children have severe and long-term problems following divorce (Wallerstein & Blakeslee, 1989). Others, using larger and more representative samples, have found less severe and more short-term effects of divorce on children (Barber & Demo, 2006). It has been suggested that the negative effects children experience may actually be the result of parents' responses to divorce rather than the divorce itself (Hetherington & Kelly, 2002). (See Chapter 7 in this book for further discussion of children's reactions to divorce.)

Several factors may protect children from long-term adjustment problems when their parents divorce. One significant parental issue is the relationship the parents maintain during and after the divorce. With minimal conflict between the parents about custody, visitation, and child-rearing issues, and with parents' positive attitude toward each other, children experience fewer negative consequences (Hetherington & Kelly, 2002). Unfortunately, many children end up as noncombatants in the middle of a war, trying to avoid or defuse raging anger and disagreement between the two parents. Other protective factors are higher levels of predivorce adjustment, adequate provision of economic resources, and nurturing relationships with both parents (Fine et al., 2010).

Children who live in families where divorce results in economic hardship are at special risk. Chronic financial stress takes its toll on the mental and physical health of the residential parent, who is usually the mother. The parent often becomes less supportive and engages in inconsistent and harsh discipline. In these situations, children become distressed, often developing difficulties in cognitive and social development (Fine et al., 2010).

In toddlerhood and early childhood, children are more vulnerable than older children to the emotional and psychological consequences of separation and divorce (Wallerstein & Corbin, 1991). One reason may be that young children have difficulty understanding divorce and often believe that the absent parent is no longer a member of the family and will never be seen again. In addition, because of young children's egocentrism, they often feel that the divorce is a result of their behavior and experience the absent parent's leaving as a rejection of them.

VIOLENCE

Many parents complain that keeping violence away from children requires tremendous work even in the best of circumstances. Irma Velasquez has lost all confidence that she can protect Henry from neighborhood violence. Children witness violence on television and through video and computer games and hear about it through many other sources. In the worst of circumstances, toddlers and young children not only are exposed to violence but become victims of it as well, as happened to Henry Velasquez's older sister. This section discusses three types of violence experienced by many young children: community violence, domestic violence, and child maltreatment.

Community Violence

In some neighborhoods, acts of violence are so common that the communities are labeled "war zones." However, most residents prefer not to be combatants. When surveyed, mothers in a Chicago housing project ranked neighborhood violence as their number one concern and as the condition that most negatively affects the quality of their life and the lives of their children (Dubrow & Garbarino, 1989). Unfortunately, neighborhood violence has become a major health issue for children around the world (Krug, Dahlberg, Mercy, Zwi, & Lozano, 2002).

The kinds of conditions that Henry Velasquez's family struggles with are not favorable for adequate child development (Krug et al., 2002). Investigations into the effects of living in violent neighborhoods support this claim. Children who grow up in a violent environment are reported to demonstrate symptoms of distress, deficient social skills, and poor peer relationships. For many children living in violent neighborhoods, the death of a close friend or family member is commonplace. When the second author (David) was employed at a community child guidance center, he found that appointments were often canceled so the parents could attend funerals. Living so intimately with death has grave effects on young children. In one study of young children whose older siblings had been victims of homicide, the surviving siblings showed symptoms of depression, anxiety, psychosocial impairment, and post-traumatic stress disorder (Freeman, Shaffer, & Smith, 1996). (Henry Velasquez was too young to understand what happened when his sister was shot, but he has spent most of his first 14 months in a household whose functioning was seriously impaired by the traumatic loss of his sister.) The symptoms noted earlier are similar to those observed in young children in situations of political and military violence—for example, in Palestinian children in the occupied West Bank (Qouta, Punamaki, & El-Sarraj, 2003) and in children in Cape Town, South Africa (Shields, Nadasen, & Pierce, 2008). Perhaps the label "war zone" is an appropriate one for violent

Karl Merton Ferron/TNS/Newscom

Neighborhood violence is a serious risk to the quality of life for young children in some neighborhoods.

communities. However, positive, affectionate, caregiving relationships—whether by parents or other family members or individuals in the community—can play an important mediating role in how violence is managed by young children (Shields et al., 2008).

Domestic Violence

As discussed in Chapter 7 in this book, family relationships are some of the most violent relationships in many societies. Domestic violence may take the form of verbal, psychological, or physical abuse, although physical abuse is the form most often implied. An estimated 275 million children worldwide are exposed each year to violence in their home (UNICEF, 2006).

Young children respond in a number of ways during violent episodes (Smith, O'Connor, & Berthelsen, 1996). Some children display fright—that is, they cry and scream. Others attempt to stop the violence by ordering the abuser to stop, by physically placing themselves between the victim and the abuser, or by hitting the abuser. Many children attempt to flee by retreating to a different room, turning up the volume on the TV or trying to ignore the violence.

The effects of domestic violence on children's development are well documented. Distress, problems with adjustment, characteristics of trauma, and increased behavior problems have all been observed in children exposed to domestic violence (Turner, Finkelhor, & Ormrod, 2006). In addition, these children develop either aggressive behaviors or passive responses, both of which make them potential targets for abuse as teens and adults (Baldry, 2003). Unfortunately, researchers are finding that children who witness intimate partner violence at home are also more likely to be victimized in other ways, including being victims of child maltreatment and community violence. The accumulation of victimization produces great risk for a variety of mental health problems in children (Turner et al., 2006).

Young children are more vulnerable than school-age children to the effects of living with domestic violence (O'Keefe, 1994). Younger children simply have fewer internal resources to help them cope with the experience. In addition, older children have friendships outside the family for support, whereas younger children rely primarily on the family. Many parents who are victims of domestic violence become emotionally unavailable to their young children. Battered mothers, for example, often become depressed and preoccupied with the abuse and their personal safety, leaving little time and energy for the attention and nurturing needed by young children. Another reason that young children are more vulnerable to the effects of domestic violence is that they lack the skills to verbalize their feelings and thoughts. As a result, thoughts and feelings about the violence get trapped inside and continually infringe on the child's thoughts and emotions. Finally, as in the case of divorce, because of their egocentrism, young children often blame themselves for the domestic abuse.

Domestic violence does not always affect children's long-term development, however. In one study, one third of the children seemed unaffected by the domestic violence they witnessed at home; these children were well adjusted and showed no signs of distress, anxiety, or behavior problems (Spilsbury et al., 2008). Two factors may buffer the effect domestic violence has on children (O'Keefe, 1994):

1. *Amount of domestic violence witnessed by the child.* The more violent episodes children witness, the more likely they are to develop problematic behavior.
2. *Relationship between the child and the mother*, assuming the mother is the victim. If the mother–child relationship remains stable and secure, the probability of the child developing behavioral difficulties decreases significantly—even when the amount of violence witnessed by the child is relatively high.

Child Maltreatment

It is difficult to estimate the rate of **child maltreatment**, because many incidences are never reported and much that is reported is not determined to be child maltreatment. Approximately 3.4 million referrals were made to Child Protective Services in 2012 involving 6.3 million children (U.S. Department of Health and Human Services, Administration on Children, Youth, and Families, 2012). An estimated 1,640 children died as a result of abuse and/or neglect, and 70% of these victims were younger than 3 years of age. The most prevalent forms of child maltreatment described by the U.S. Children's Bureau include neglect, physical abuse, sexual abuse, and emotional maltreatment. Slightly more girls were victims of child maltreatment in 2012, but boys had a higher incidence of fatal injuries. National incidence data indicate that the majority of child victims in 2012 were either White (44%), African American (21%), or Hispanic (22%). Poverty and the lack of economic resources are correlated with maltreatment, especially physical abuse and neglect (L. Berger, 2005). In addition, family isolation and lack of a support system, parental drug and alcohol abuse, lack of knowledge regarding child-rearing, and parental difficulty in expressing feelings are all related to child maltreatment (L. Berger, 2005).

Child maltreatment creates risks to all aspects of growth and development, as shown in Exhibit 12.4, but children ages birth to 6 are at highest risk of having long-lasting damage (Pecora & Harrison-Jackson, 2011). In their longitudinal research of 180 children born into poverty, Sroufe et al. (2005) found that young children who had been physically abused as toddlers had higher levels of negativity, noncompliance, and distractibility than other children. Those whose mothers were psychologically unavailable demonstrated more avoidance of and anger toward the mother. Children with a history of all types of maltreatment had lower self-esteem and agency and demonstrated more behavior problems than other children. Children with a history of neglect were more passive than other children.

PROTECTIVE FACTORS IN TODDLERHOOD AND EARLY CHILDHOOD

A number of factors have been found to promote resiliency during the toddler and early childhood years (Jenson & Fraser, 2016).

- *Social support.* Social support mediates many potential risks to the development of young children. The presence of social support increases the likelihood of a positive outcome for children whose parents divorce, moderates the effects for children who experience violence, facilitates better outcomes for children of mothers with mental illness, and is even thought to reduce the continuation of abuse for 2- and 3-year-olds who have experienced parental abuse during the first year of life. Social support aids young children in several ways. Having a consistent and supportive aunt or uncle or preschool teacher who can set firm but loving limits, for example, may buffer the effects of a parent with ineffective skills. At the community level, preschools, religious programs, and the like may help to enhance physical and cognitive skills, self-esteem, and social development.

- *Positive parent–child relationship.* A positive relationship with at least one parent helps children to feel secure and nurtured.

- *Effective parenting.* In early childhood, children need the opportunity to take initiative but also need firm limits, whether they are established by parents or grandparents or someone else who adopts the parent role. Terri Smith, for example, has not been able to establish self-control because her boundaries are not well defined. Effective parenting promotes self-efficacy and self-esteem and provides young children with a model of how they can take initiative within boundaries.

EXHIBIT 12.4 • Potential Effects of Child Abuse on Growth and Development

PHYSICAL IMPAIRMENTS	COGNITIVE IMPAIRMENTS	EMOTIONAL IMPAIRMENTS
PHYSICAL ABUSE AND NEGLECT		
Burns, scars, fractures, broken bones, damage to vital organs and limbs Malnourishment Physical exposure Poor skin hygiene Poor (if any) medical care Poor (if any) dental care Serious medical problems Serious dental problems Failure-to-thrive syndrome Death	Delayed cognitive skills Delayed language skills Mental retardation Delayed reality testing Overall disruption of thought processes	Negative self-concept Increased aggressiveness Poor peer relations Poor impulse control Anxiety Inattentiveness Avoidant behavior
SEXUAL ABUSE		
Trauma to mouth, anus, vaginal area Genital and rectal pain Genital and rectal bleeding Genital and rectal tearing Sexually transmitted disease	Hyperactivity Bizarre sexual behavior	Overly adaptive behavior Overly compliant behavior Habit disorders (nail biting) Anxiety Depression Sleep disturbances Night terrors Self-mutilation
PSYCHOLOGICAL/EMOTIONAL ABUSE		
	Pessimistic view of life Anxiety and fear Distorted perception of world Deficits in moral development	Alienation Intimacy problems Low self-esteem Depression

- *Self-esteem.* A high level of self-worth may allow young children to persist in mastery of skills despite adverse conditions. Perhaps a high level of self-esteem can enhance Ron's and Rosiland's development despite the disruptions in their lives. In addition, research indicates that self-esteem is a protective factor against the effects of child abuse.

- *Intelligence.* Even in young children, a high IQ serves as a protective factor. For example, young children with high IQs were less likely to be affected by maternal psychopathology. Others suggest that intelligence results in success, which leads to higher levels of self-esteem. For young children, then, intelligence may contribute to mastery of skills and independence, which may enhance self-esteem. Intelligence may also protect children through increased problem-solving skills, which allow for more effective responses to adverse situations.

CRITICAL THINKING Questions 12.5

What type of parenting style do you think your parent(s) used when you were a child? Did both parents, if involved, use the same parenting style? Do you think the parenting style(s) used by your parent(s) was effective? How do you think the parenting style of your parent(s) was affected by culture? Would you want to use the same parenting style that your parent(s) used if you were a parent? Why or why not?

IMPLICATIONS FOR SOCIAL WORK PRACTICE

Knowledge about toddlerhood and early childhood has several implications for social work practice with young children.

- Become well acquainted with theories and empirical research about growth and development among toddlers and young children.
- Continue to promote the elimination of poverty and the advancement of social justice.
- Collaborate with other professionals in the creation of laws, interventions, and programs that assist in the elimination of violence.
- Create and support easy access to services for toddlers, young children, and their parents.
- Assess toddlers and young children in the context of their environment.
- Become familiar with the physical and emotional signs of child abuse.
- Directly engage toddlers and young children in an age-appropriate intervention process.
- Provide support to parents and help facilitate positive parent–child relationships.
- Encourage and engage both mothers and fathers in the intervention process, where appropriate and possible.
- Provide opportunities for toddlers and young children to increase self-efficacy and self-esteem.
- Help parents understand the potential effects of negative environmental factors on their children.

KEY TERMS

authoritarian parenting, 396
authoritative parenting, 396
blooming, 374
child maltreatment, 400
developmental delays, 390
discipline, 396
disengaged parenting, 396
empathy, 381
fine motor skills, 375
gross motor skills, 375
hostile aggression, 384
instrumental aggression, 384
lateralization, 375
learning play, 389
permissive parenting, 396
perspective taking, 381
physical aggression, 384
preconventional level of moral reasoning, 381
preoperational stage, 378
prosocial, 380
pruning, 374
relational aggression, 384
self-esteem, 386
self-theory, 386
sociodramatic play, 389
symbolic play, 389
toddler, 373
transitional object, 384

ACTIVE LEARNING

1. Watch any child-oriented cartoon on television or the Internet. Describe the apparent and implied messages (both positive and negative) available in the cartoon about race and ethnicity and gender differences. Consider how these messages might affect gender and ethnic development in young children.
2. In groups of three or four, talk about what you have observed about the use of communication technology by toddlers and young children. What have you seen that seemed to suggest a positive benefit of this technology for healthy development? What have you seen that seemed to suggest the use of this technology by toddlers and young children can be detrimental to healthy development?
3. The case studies at the beginning of this chapter (Henry, Terri, and Ron and Rosiland) do not specify race or ethnicity of the families. How important an omission did that appear to you? What assumptions did you make about the racial and/or ethnic background of the families? On what basis did you make those assumptions?

WEB RESOURCES

American Academy of Child & Adolescent Psychiatry

www.aacap.org

Site presented by the American Academy of Child & Adolescent Psychiatry contains concise and up-to-date information on a variety of issues facing children and their families, including day care, discipline, children and divorce, child abuse, children and TV violence, and children and grief.

Children's Defense Fund

www.childrensdefense.org

Site presented by the Children's Defense Fund, a private nonprofit child advocacy organization, contains information on issues, the Black Community Crusade for Children, the Child Watch Visitation Program, and a parent resource network.

National Family Resiliency Center (NFRC)

http://nfrchelp.org

Site presented by the NFRC contains information about support groups, resources for professionals, and frequently asked questions.

Play Therapy International

www.playtherapy.org

Site presented by Play Therapy International contains reading lists, articles and research, news, and information about training and careers in play therapy.

U.S. Department of Health & Human Services

www.dhhs.gov

Site maintained by the U.S. Department of Health & Human Services contains news and information on health topics, prevention, and safety.

SAGE edge™ Sharpen your skills with SAGE edge at edge.sagepub.com/hutchisoness2e

SAGE edge for students provides a personalized approach to help you accomplish your coursework goals in an easy-to-use learning environment. watch listen read

LEARNING OBJECTIVES	FOR FURTHER EXPLORATION AND APPLICATION
LO 12.1: Compare and contrast one's emotional and cognitive reactions to three case studies.	(read) Emotions in Toddlerhood
LO 12.2: Summarize typical physical, cognitive and language, moral, personality and emotional, and social development during toddlerhood and early childhood.	(read) 12–24 Months: Socioemotional Development (watch) Body Proportions in Infancy and Early Childhood (watch) Fostering Gross Motor Skills in Early Childhood (watch) Checklist of Motor Skill Development (watch) Developing Body Awareness (watch) Strategies for Encouraging Your Child's Speech and Language Development
LO 12.3: Analyze the role of play in toddler and early childhood development.	(watch) Gender Schemas and Play Preferences
LO 12.4: Identify major social policies regarding developmental disruptions during toddlerhood and early childhood.	(read) How Trauma Affects Child Brain Development
LO 12.5: Evaluate the possible benefits of early childhood education.	(listen) Why Preschool Can Save the World (read) The Influence of Immigration Status on Early Childhood Education and Care Enrollment (watch) Inclusion (watch) Intergenerational Relationships (watch) School Gardens (watch) Child-Oriented Preschool
LO 12.6: Identify some special issues that face the multigenerational family with toddlers and young children.	(read) Multigenerational Households and the School Readiness of Children Born to Unmarried Mothers (watch) Resisting Temptation
LO 12.7: Give examples of risk factors and protective factors during toddlerhood and early childhood.	(read) Expanding Early Care and Education for Homeless Children (watch) Divorce: Parent's Perspective
LO 12.8: Apply knowledge of toddlerhood and early childhood to recommend guidelines for social work assessment and intervention.	(watch) Early Recognition of Child Development Problems (listen) Developmental and Mental Health Screening in Child Welfare: Implications for Young Children in Rural Settings

Road Roll

13

Middle Childhood

Leanne Wood Charlesworth

Learning Objectives

LO 13.1 Compare and contrast one's emotional and cognitive reactions to three case studies.

LO 13.2 Describe how the social context of middle childhood has changed over time and place.

LO 13.3 Identify some ways the multigenerational family influences middle childhood development.

LO 13.4 Summarize typical physical, cognitive, cultural identity, emotional, social, and spiritual development during middle childhood.

LO 13.5 Analyze the role of formal schooling in middle childhood development.

LO 13.6 Analyze special challenges to middle childhood development.

LO 13.7 Give examples of risk factors and protective factors in middle childhood.

LO 13.8 Apply knowledge of middle childhood to recommend guidelines for social work assessment and intervention.

Acknowledgments: The author would like to acknowledge the past contributions of Jim Wood and Pamela Viggiani and would like to thank Meena Lall for assistance in writing this chapter.

CASE STUDY 13.1

ANTHONY BRYANT'S IMPENDING ASSESSMENT

Anthony is a 6-year-old boy living in an impoverished section of a large city. Anthony's mother, Sephora, was 14 when Anthony was born. Anthony's father, James, 15 when Anthony was born, has always spent a great deal of time with Anthony. Although James now also has a 2-year-old daughter from another relationship, he has told Sephora that Anthony and Sephora are the most important people in his life. Once Anthony was out of diapers, James began spending even more time with him, taking Anthony along to visit friends and, occasionally, on overnight outings.

James's father was murdered when James was a toddler and he rarely sees his mother, who struggles with a serious substance addiction and is known in the neighborhood as a prostitute. James lived with his paternal grandparents until he was in his early teens, when he began to stay with a favorite uncle. Many members of James's large extended family have been incarcerated on charges related to their involvement in the local drug trade. James's favorite uncle is a well-known and widely respected dealer. James himself has been arrested a few times and is currently on probation.

Sephora and Anthony live with her mother. Sephora obtained her general equivalency diploma after Anthony's birth, and she has held a variety of jobs at local fast-food chains. Sephora's mother, Cynthia, receives Supplemental Social Security Income/Disability because she has been unable to work for several years because of her advanced rheumatoid arthritis, which was diagnosed when she was a teenager. Sephora remembers her father only as a loud man who often yelled at her when she made noise. He left Cynthia and Sephora when Sephora was 4 years old, and neither has seen him since. Cynthia seemed pleased when Anthony was born and she has been a second mother to him, caring for him while Sephora attends school, works, and socializes with James and her other friends.

Anthony has always been very active and energetic, frequently breaking things and creating "messes" throughout the apartment. To punish Anthony, Cynthia spanks him with a belt or other object—and she sometimes resorts to locking him in his room until he falls asleep. Sephora and James are proud of Anthony's wiry physique and rough and tough play; they have encouraged him to be fearless and not to cry when he is hurt. Both Sephora and James use physical punishment as their main discipline strategy with Anthony, but he usually obeys them before it is needed.

Anthony entered kindergarten at a local public school last fall. When he started school, his teacher told Sephora that he seemed to be a very smart boy, one of the only boys in the class who already knew how to write his name and how to count to 20. It is now spring, however, and Sephora is tired of dealing with Anthony's teacher and other school staff. She has been called at work a number of times, and recently the school social worker requested a meeting with her. Anthony's teacher reports that Anthony will not listen to her and frequently starts fights with the other children in the classroom. Anthony's teacher also states that Anthony constantly violates school rules, like waiting in line and being quiet in the hallways, and he doesn't seem bothered by threats of punishment. Most recently, Anthony's teacher has told Sephora that she would like Anthony assessed by the school psychologist.

CASE STUDY 13.2

BRIANNA SHAW'S NEW SELF-IMAGE

When Brianna was born, her mother, Deborah, was 31 years old with a 13-year-old daughter (Sienna) from a prior, short-lived marriage. Deborah and Michael's relationship was relatively new when Deborah became pregnant with Brianna. Shortly after Deborah announced the pregnancy, Michael moved into her mobile home. Michael and Deborah initially talked about setting a wedding date and pursuing Michael's legal adoption of Sienna, whose father had remarried and was no longer in close contact.

Michael made it clear throughout Deborah's pregnancy that he wanted a son. He seemed very content and supportive of Deborah until around the time the couple found out the baby was a girl. In Sienna's view, Michael became mean and bossy in the months that followed. He started telling Sienna what to do, criticizing Deborah's appearance, and complaining constantly that Deborah wasn't any fun anymore since she stopped drinking and smoking while she was pregnant.

During Brianna's infancy, the couple's relationship began to change even more rapidly. Michael was rarely home and instead spent most of his free time hanging out with old friends. When he did come by, he'd encourage Deborah to leave Brianna with Sienna so the two of them could go out like "old times." Even though her parents were Deborah's full-time day care providers and both Brianna and Sienna were thriving, Deborah was chronically exhausted from balancing parenting and her full-time job as a nursing assistant. Soon, whenever Michael came by, the couple frequently argued and their shouting matches gradually escalated to Michael threatening to take Brianna away. Michael was soon dating another woman, and his relationship with Deborah and Sienna became increasingly hostile during the following 4 years.

The summer that Brianna turned 5, the local hospital closed down and Deborah lost her job. After talking with her parents, Deborah made the decision to move her daughters to Fairfield, a city 4 hours away from home. An old high school friend had once told Deborah that if she ever needed a job, the large hospital her friend worked for had regular openings and even offered tuition assistance. Within 2 months, Deborah had sold her mobile home, obtained a full-time position with her friend's employer, and signed a lease for a small townhouse in a suburb known for its high-quality school system.

When Brianna started kindergarten in their new town, her teacher described her to Deborah as shy and withdrawn. Deborah remembered reading something in the school newsletter about a social skills group run by a school social worker, and she asked if Brianna could be enrolled. Gradually, the group seemed to make a difference and Brianna began to act more like her old self, forming several friendships during the following 2 years.

Today, Brianna is 8 years old and has just entered third grade. Brianna usually leaves for school on the bus at 8:00 a.m., and Deborah picks her up from an afterschool program at 5:45 p.m. When possible, Sienna picks Brianna up earlier, after her own classes at a local community college are over. Brianna still spends summers with her grandparents in the rural area where she was born. Academically, she has thus far excelled in school, but a new concern is Brianna's weight. Brianna is 49 inches tall and weighs 72 pounds. Until the last year or so, Brianna seemed unaware of the fact that many people viewed her as overweight. In the last several months, however, Brianna has told Sienna and Deborah various stories about other children calling her "fat" and making other comments about her size. Deborah feels that Brianna is increasingly moody and angry when she is home. Brianna recently asked Deborah why she is "fat" and told Sienna that she just wishes she were dead.

CASE STUDY 13.3

MANUEL VEGA'S DIFFICULT TRANSITION

Slightly built 11-year-old Manuel is in sixth grade in Greenville, Mississippi. He was born in Texas where his mother, Maria, and father, Estaban, met. For Estaban, it has been an interesting journey from his hometown in Mexico to Mississippi. For generations, Estaban's family lived and worked near Izucar de Matamoros, a small city in Mexico on the Inter-American Highway. By the time he was in his early 20s, Estaban began to look for better-paying work and was able to get his license to haul products from Izucar de Matamoros to larger cities, including Mexico City. Estaban and one of his four brothers eventually moved to a medium-sized city where his employer, the owner of a small trucking company, provided an apartment for several of his single truckers.

After 3 productive years in the trucking industry, the company went bankrupt. Estaban wanted to pursue his dream of owning his own trucking company but instead began working as a day laborer and eventually made his way to Laredo, Texas, where he met and married Maria. Although both Maria and Estaban's formal schooling ended relatively early, both acquired a basic command of English while living in Laredo. Aware of the family's financial challenges, Maria's uncle Arturo urged the family to move to the Mississippi Delta where he owns a Mexican restaurant and wholesale business. Uncle Arturo was hopeful that Maria would enrich his menu with her mastery of Mexican cuisine, and he promised employment for Estaban, hauling Mexican specialty food staples to the growing number of Mexican restaurants in the Delta, ranging from Memphis to Biloxi.

Almost 3 years ago, Estaban and Maria decided to take Arturo up on his offer, and together with their two sons, they moved to Greenville. Their older son, Carlos, never adjusted to school life in Mississippi. Now 16, Carlos did not return to school this fall. Instead, he began working full-time for his father loading and unloading the truck and providing his more advanced English language capacity to open up new business markets. At first Maria and Estaban resisted the idea

(Continued)

(Continued)

of Carlos dropping out of school, but he was insistent. Carlos knows the family finances are in peril and that he is needed. Manuel yearns to be like his older brother, but Carlos has always considered it his job to protect and care for his younger brother. He tells Manuel that he must stay in school to acquire the "book learning" that he could never grasp.

Leaving the warm embrace of their former neighborhood in Texas for the Mississippi Delta has been hard for Manuel. In Manuel's old school, most students and teachers spoke or knew how to speak Spanish, and Manuel always felt he fit in. Now, Manuel is one of a small percentage of Spanish-speaking students in his new school, where the vast majority of students and staff are African American and speak only English.

In the school setting, Manuel's new English as a second language (ESL) teacher, Ms. Jones, is concerned about him. His teacher reports that he often seems sullen. Ms. Jones has observed that Manuel frequently appears to be daydreaming, and when teachers try to talk with him, he seems to withdraw further. Ms. Jones knows that Manuel's records from Texas indicate that he was a successful, socially adjusted primary-school student. However, his records also show that his reading and writing performance was below grade level starting in first grade. Ms. Jones has found that if she speaks with Manuel in Spanish while taking a walk around the school, he will share stories about his family and his old neighborhood and friends.

HISTORICAL PERSPECTIVE ON MIDDLE CHILDHOOD

Historically, middle childhood represented a period during which children became increasingly able to play a role in maintaining or improving the economic status of the family and community (Fass & Mason, 2000). Beginning in the early 20th century, however, a radical shift occurred in the Western world's perceptions of children. Children passing through middle childhood became categorized as "school age," and their education became a societal priority. Child labor and compulsory education laws supported and reinforced this shift in societal values.

In parts of the United States and world, however, children continue to play important economic roles for families. Many children from the most impoverished families live and work on the streets, and in countries striving toward universal primary school education, children must balance their economic productivity with time spent in school (Karraker, 2013). Although this significant diversity exists among children, middle childhood is generally viewed in the United States as a time when education, play, and social activities should dominate daily life (Cole & Durham, 2008).

The age range classified as middle childhood is subject to debate. In the United States, it is most often defined as the period beginning at approximately ages 5 or 6 and ending at approximately ages 10 to 12 (Marotz & Allen, 2013). It is common to think of middle childhood as consisting of an early (ages 6 through 8) and later (ages 9 through 11) phase.

Images of middle childhood often include children who are physically active and intellectually curious, making new friends and learning new things. But as Anthony Bryant, Brianna Shaw, and Manuel Vega demonstrate, middle childhood is filled with both opportunities and challenges. For some children, it is a period of particular vulnerability.

MIDDLE CHILDHOOD IN THE MULTIGENERATIONAL FAMILY

During middle childhood, the child's social world expands dramatically. Although the family is not the only relevant force in a child's life, it remains an extremely significant influence on development. Families are often in a constant state of change, and so the school-age child's relationships with family members and the environment the family inhabits are likely to be different from the child's first experiences of family. For example, consider the changes in Anthony Bryant's, Brianna Shaw's, and Manuel Vega's families over time and the ways in which family relationships have been continually evolving.

Despite the geographical distances that often exist between family members today, nuclear families are still emotional subsystems of extended, multigenerational family systems. The child's nuclear family is significantly shaped by past, present, and anticipated future experiences, events, and relationships (McGoldrick, Carter, & Garcia-Preto, 2011b). Profoundly important factors such as historical events, culture, and social structure, as well as family members' experiences and characteristics, often influence children through their family systems. Relatives' experiences or characteristics may be biological and therefore fairly obvious, or they may include more nebulous qualities such as acquired emotional strengths or wounds. For example, consider Brianna's maternal grandfather, who is African American and grew up with the legacy of slavery under Jim Crow laws and legal segregation in the United States, or Anthony's maternal grandmother, who as a child was repeatedly victimized sexually. Children become connected to events or phenomena such as a familial history of child abuse or a group history of discrimination and oppression (restrictions and exploitation), even in the absence of direct experiences in the present generation (see Miller & Garran, 2008).

Thus, the developing school-age child is shaped not only by events and individuals explicitly evident in the present time and physical space but also by those events and individuals who have more directly influenced the lives of their parents, grandparents, great-grandparents, and beyond. These influences—familial, cultural, and historical—shape all aspects of every child's development in an abstract and complex fashion.

CRITICAL THINKING Questions 13.1

When you think of middle childhood for Anthony Bryant, Brianna Shaw, and Manuel Vega, do you think of it as a time of promise or a time of vulnerability? Explain. What do you see as the strengths in their multigenerational families? What do you see as the special challenges in their multigenerational families?

DEVELOPMENT IN MIDDLE CHILDHOOD

New developmental tasks are undertaken in middle childhood, and development occurs within multiple dimensions. Although each developmental domain is considered separately for our analytical purposes, changes in the developing child reflect the dynamic interaction continuously occurring across these dimensions.

PHYSICAL DEVELOPMENT

During middle childhood, physical development typically continues steadily, but children of the same chronological age may vary greatly in stature, weight, and sexual development. For most children, height and weight begin to advance less rapidly than during prior developmental phases, but steady growth continues. The nature and pace of physical growth during this period are shaped by both genetic and environmental influences in interaction (Jurimae, 2013).

As children progress from kindergarten to early adolescence, their fine and gross motor skills typically advance. In the United States today, children in this age range are often encouraged to gain a high level of mastery over physical skills associated with a particular interest such as dance, sports, or music. However, medical professionals caution that school-age children continue to possess unique physical vulnerabilities related to the growth process and thus are susceptible to injuries associated with excessive physical activity or training (Jurimae, 2013).

Middle childhood is a developmental phase of entrenchment or eradication of many potent risk or protective factors manifesting in this developmental domain (Mah & Ford-Jones, 2012). Focusing on risk, for children residing in chronically impoverished countries and communities, issues such as malnutrition and disease threaten physical health. Seemingly innocuous issues such as poor dental hygiene or mild visual impairment may become more serious as they begin to impact other areas of development such as cognitive, emotional, or social well-being. In the United States, health issues such as asthma and obesity are of contemporary concern and often either improve or become more severe during middle childhood. Susceptibility to risk varies across socioeconomic and ethnic groups. Unintentional death and physical injury (for example, motor vehicle injuries, drowning, playground accidents, and sports-related traumatic brain injury) represent a major threat to well-being among school-age children in general (Gilchrist, 2012). Moreover, as children move into middle childhood they gain other new risks: approximately one third of rapes occur before age 12, homicide risk increases, and among children ages 10 to 14, suicide is a leading cause of death (Black et al., 2011).

Some of the physical injuries unique to middle childhood may be indirectly facilitated by declines in adult supervision and adult overestimation of children's safety-related knowledge and ability to implement safety practices. In addition, children's continued physical and cognitive (specifically, judgment and decision-making processes) vulnerabilities combine, potentially, with an increasing propensity to engage in risk-taking activities and behaviors (Berk, 2012).

Many children experience puberty during middle childhood. Focusing on racial differences, several studies have found that in the United States, non-Hispanic African American girls begin puberty earlier than other children (National Institutes of Health, 2013; Reynolds & Juvonen, 2012). A trend toward earlier age of puberty onset, particularly among girls, has brought much attention to the potential causes. Most recently, research on this topic has examined in more depth the linkages between obesity and puberty onset among girls (Aleccia, 2013) and has also begun to reflect new interest in early puberty onset among boys (American Academy of Pediatrics, 2012). A wide variety of multidisciplinary researchers across the globe are examining available data regarding the causes of puberty onset. It is evident that a complex range of interacting factors, crossing the biopsychosocial spectrum, are relevant to understanding puberty onset. Wang, Needham, and Barr (2005) identify nutritional status; genetic predisposition, including race/ethnicity; and environmental chemical exposure as associated with age of puberty onset.

It should be noted that careful examination of puberty onset trends suggests that the "trend toward earlier onset of puberty in U.S. girls over the past 50 years is not as strong as some reports suggested" (Kaplowitz, 2006, p. 487). Specifically, the average age of menarche decreased from

New developmental tasks are undertaken in middle childhood, and development occurs within interacting developmental domains.

approximately 14.8 years in 1877 to about 12.8 years in the mid-1960s (Kaplowitz, 2006). Most researchers have concluded that the general trend observed during this broad historical time period is the result of health and nutrition improvement within the population as a whole. Recent examination of available data concludes that there is little evidence to support a significant continued decline in more recent years. Nevertheless, some have suggested that our public education and health systems should consider early health education for children because the onset of puberty may impact social and emotional development and has traditionally been associated with a variety of "risky and unhealthy behaviors" (Wang et al., 2005, p. 1101).

Indeed, a relationship, albeit complex, appears to exist between puberty and social development for both boys and girls (Santrock, 2009). During middle childhood, girls experiencing early onset puberty may be at particular risk (Mendle, Turkheimer, & Emery, 2007). Intervention focused on self-protection and individual rights and responsibilities may be beneficial, and schools committed to the safety of their students must diligently educate staff and students about sexual development and risk.

Middle childhood is the developmental phase when increased public attention and self-awareness is directed toward various aspects of physical growth, skill, or activity patterns and levels deemed outside the normal range. Because physical development is outwardly visible, it affects perceptions of self and the way a child is viewed and treated by peers and adults. School-age children constantly compare themselves with others, and physical differences are often the topic of discussion. Many children worry about being "normal." Reassurance by adults that physical development varies among people and that all development is "normal" is crucial.

COGNITIVE DEVELOPMENT

For most children, the acquisition of cognitive abilities that occurs early in middle childhood allows the communication of thoughts with increasing complexity. Formal education plays a major role in the cognitive development of children in the United States, if only because most children attend school throughout the formative years of such development. When Anthony Bryant, Brianna Shaw, and Manuel Vega first entered school, their readiness to confront the challenges and opportunities that school presents was shaped by prior experiences. Anthony, for example, entered school generally prepared for the academic emphases associated with kindergarten. He was perhaps less prepared for the social expectations present in the school environment.

Jean Piaget (1936/1952) played a significant role in our understanding of the cognitive development of children. In his terms, children start school during the second stage (preoperational thought) and finish school when they are completing the fourth and final stage of cognitive development (formal operations). In the third stage (**concrete operations stage**), children are able to solve concrete problems using logical problem-solving strategies. By the end of middle childhood, they enter the formal operations stage and become able to solve hypothetical problems using abstract concepts (refer back to Exhibit 4.1 in Chapter 4 for an overview of Piaget's stages of cognitive development). Examples of expanding cognitive capacity include pondering complex conceptual questions, advancing skill in categorizing and analyzing complicated systems of ideas or objects, and enhanced ability to solve problems. As you observe children moving into and through middle childhood, you will note these rapid gains in intellectual processes (Adler-Tapia, 2012). These brain-produced shifts in the child's understanding of himself or herself and the surrounding world are consistent with the transition into Piaget's concrete operational and formal operations stages of cognitive development.

Beyond Piaget's ideas, brain development and cognitive functioning during middle childhood traditionally received less attention than research devoted to brain development in prior developmental phases. By middle childhood, a child's brain development and functioning have been profoundly shaped by the nature of earlier experiences and development. And yet remarkable brain plasticity continues, with brain structure and functioning capable of growth and refinement throughout life (National Research Council, 2012). The conceptual framework perhaps most useful to understanding this potential and the processes at play is nonlinear dynamic systems theory, also known as complexity or chaos theory (see Chapter 2 in this book for a discussion of chaos theory) (Applegate & Shapiro, 2005). Applied to this context, this theoretical perspective proposes that changes in one area or aspect of the neurological system may stimulate or interact with other neurological or broader physiological system components in an unpredictable fashion, potentially leading to unanticipated outcomes. Brain development follows a coherent developmental process, but brain plasticity in particular demonstrates the role of complex nonlinear neurological system dynamics and processes.

At least two aspects of brain development are of particular interest when we focus on middle childhood. The first is the idea that different brain regions appear to develop according to different timelines. In other words, middle childhood may be a "sensitive period" for certain aspects of brain development not yet clearly understood. The second important idea is the notion that brain synapses (connections between cells in the nervous system) that are initially present as children enter this developmental phase may be gradually eliminated if they are not used. As reported in Chapter 12, there seems to be a pattern of *synaptogenesis*, or creation and fine-tuning of brain synapses, in the human cerebral cortex during early childhood, which appears to be followed by a gradual pruning process that eventually reduces the overall number of synapses to their adult levels (National Research Council, 2012).

The **cerebral cortex** is the outer layer of gray matter in the human brain thought to be responsible for complex, high-level intellectual functions such as memory, language, and reasoning. Ongoing positive and diverse learning opportunities during middle childhood may help facilitate continued brain growth and optimal refinement of existing structures. Variations in brain development and functioning play a critical role in learning, emotional responses, and patterns of behavior (Davidson & Begley, 2012; Kahneman, 2011). During middle childhood, identification and potential diagnosis of special needs, including issues such as ADHD, typically peaks. In recent years, an area of public interest is gender- or sex-based differences in brain functioning and, possibly, learning styles. This interest has been stimulated in part by evidence suggesting that in some countries, such as the United States, boys are currently at higher risk than girls for poor literacy performance, special education placement, and school dropout (Weaver-Hightower, 2008).

It has been suggested that brain-based behavior and learning style differences may be responsible for the somewhat stable trends observed in gender differences in educational achievement (Gurian, 2011). The importance of sex or gender in shaping the human experience cannot be overstated. Gender is a profoundly influential organizing factor shaping human development, and its biological correlates may impact behavior and learning processes in ways we do not clearly understand. However, gender is but one of several personal and group characteristics relevant to understanding educational privilege specifically as well as risk and protection generally. Unfortunately, developmental research historically lacked rigor and did not devote sufficient attention to females and children belonging to nondominant groups.

A number of contemporary developmental theorists have focused on assessing the relevance and applicability of traditional developmental tasks to all children. Most agree that the central ideas of the theorists summarized in Exhibit 13.1 continue to be meaningful. For example, Erikson's thoughts remain widely recognized as relevant to our understanding of school-age children. In some areas, however, these developmental theories have been critiqued and subsequently expanded. This is particularly true in the area of moral development.

The best-known theory of moral development is Lawrence Kohlberg's stage theory (for an overview of this theory, refer back to Exhibit 4.3 in Chapter 4). Kohlberg's

EXHIBIT 13.1 • Theories on Phases and Tasks of Middle Childhood

THEORIST	PHASE OR TASK	DESCRIPTION
Freud (1938/1973)	Latency	Sexual instincts become less dominant; superego develops further.
Erikson (1950)	Industry versus inferiority	Capacity to cooperate and create develops; result is sense of either mastery or incompetence.
Piaget (1936/1952)	Concrete operational	Reasoning becomes more logical but remains at concrete level; principle of conservation is learned.
Piaget (1932/1965)	Moral realism and autonomous morality	Conception of morality changes from absolute and external to relative and internal.
Kohlberg (1969)	Preconventional and conventional morality	Reasoning based on punishment and reward is replaced by reasoning based on formal law and external opinion.
Selman (1976)	Self-reflective perspective taking	Ability develops to view one's own actions, thoughts, and emotions from another's perspective.

research on moral reasoning found that children do not enter the second level of *conventional moral reasoning*, or morality based on approval of authorities or upon upholding societal standards, until about age 9 or 10, some time after they have the cognitive skills for such reasoning. Robert Coles (1987, 1997) expanded on Kohlberg's work and emphasized the distinction between moral imagination—the gradually developed capacity to reflect on what is right and wrong—and moral conduct, pointing out that a "well-developed conscience does not translate, necessarily, into a morally courageous life" (p. 3). Analyses of the interplay of imagination and conduct within more recent research supports Coles's initial ideas in this area (Gutzwiller-Helfenfinger, Gasser, & Malti, 2010). Moral *behavior* is shaped by daily experiences, typically reflecting the way the child is treated in his or her various environments such as home and school. The school-age child often pays close attention to the discrepancies between the "moral voices" and actions of the adults in his or her world, including parents, friends' parents, relatives, teachers, and coaches. Each new and significant adult sets an example for the child, sometimes complementing and sometimes contradicting the values emphasized in the child's home environment.

As noted in Chapter 4 in this book, Carol Gilligan (1982) extensively criticized Kohlberg's theory of moral development as paying inadequate attention to girls' "ethic of care" and the keen emphasis girls often place on relationships and the emotions of others. Consistent with Gilligan's ideas, a number of developmental theorists have argued that girls possess heightened **interrelational intelligence**, which is based on emotional and social intelligence and is similar to Howard Gardner's concept of interpersonal intelligence (Borysenko, 1996). Such developmentalists, drawing on feminist scholarship, point out that both girls and boys advance rapidly in the cognitive and moral developmental domains during middle childhood, but the sexes may be distinct in their approaches to social relationships and interactions, and such differences may shape the nature of development in all domains (Borysenko, 1996; Gilligan, 1982; Taylor, Gilligan, & Sullivan, 1995). It is also important to note that collectivist-oriented societies put a high value on connectedness, and research with groups from collectivist societies indicates that they do not score well on Kohlberg's model of moral development. Some scholars argue that moral development must be understood in cultural context (Gardiner & Kosmitzki, 2011; Haidt, 2013).

As children's cognitive abilities advance, understanding of group identities shifts. Children become much more aware of ethnic identities and other aspects of diversity (such as socioeconomic status and gender identities) during their middle childhood years. Cultural awareness and related beliefs are shaped by the nature of experiences such as exposure to diversity within the family and community, including school, contexts. Unlike the preschoolers' attraction to "black-and-white" classifications, children progressing through middle childhood are increasingly capable of understanding the complexities of group memberships; in other words, they are cognitively capable of rejecting oversimplistic stereotypes and recognizing the complexities present within all individuals and groups (Davies, 2011).

McAdoo (2001) asserts that, compared with children who identify with the majority group, children from nondominant groups are much more likely to possess awareness of their own group identity or identities as well as majority group characteristics. Thus, a now widely recognized developmental task associated with middle childhood is the acquisition of positive group identity or identities (Azzi, 2011). The terms *bicultural* or *multicultural competence* are used to refer to the skills children from nondominant groups must acquire in order to survive and thrive developmentally (Lum, 2011).

Middle childhood is a critical time for children to acquire a sense of self-confidence and develop conceptual thought.

Manuel speaks English as a second language and in some ways is representative of many school-age children. In the United States, approximately 20% of all children ages 5 through 17 enrolled in school speak a language other than English at home; this figure is expected to continue to increase steadily in the future (Kominski, Shin, & Marotz, 2008). Multilingual and bilingual children in the United States were traditionally thought to be at risk of developmental deficits. However, significant research demonstrates that bilingualism may have a positive impact on cognitive development. When controlling for socioeconomic status, bilingual children may perform better than monolingual children in certain areas of intellectual and academic performance (Korkman et al., 2012; Yow & Markman, 2011). With growing understanding of the way that environmental demands change brain structures, researchers have begun to explore the relationship between bilingualism and the brain. They have found that learning a second language increases the density of gray matter in the left inferior parietal cortex. The earlier a second language is learned and the more proficient the person becomes, the more benefit to brain development (Levine & Munsch, 2011).

CULTURAL IDENTITY DEVELOPMENT

For many European American children, ethnicity does not lead to comparison with others or exploration of identity (Tatum, 2003). But for most children who are members of nondominant groups, ethnicity or race may be a central part of the quest for identity that begins in middle childhood and continues well into adolescence and young adulthood. During middle childhood, cognitive advances allow children to view themselves and others as capable of belonging to more than one "category" at once, as capable of possessing two or more heritages simultaneously (Butler-Sweet, 2011; Nuttgens, 2010). As children mature, they may become more aware not only of dual or multiple aspects of identity but also of the discrimination and inequality to which they may be subjected. Such issues may in fact present overwhelming challenges for the school-age child belonging to a nondominant group. At a time when development of a sense of belonging is critical, these issues set some children apart from members of dominant groups and may increase the challenges they experience.

Segregation based on ethnicity/race and social class is common in friendships at all ages, including middle childhood. Like adults, children are more likely to hold negative attitudes toward groups to which they do not belong (Haidt, 2013). However, children, like adults, vary in the extent to which they hold ethnic and social class biases. Verbalized prejudice declines during middle childhood as children learn to obey social norms against overt prejudice. However, children belonging to nondominant groups continue to face institutional discrimination and other significant challenges throughout this period of the life course (Dulin-Keita, Hannon, Fernandez, & Cockerham, 2011; Harry & Klingner, 2006).

A particular challenge for children such as Anthony Bryant or Manuel Vega may be blending contradictory values, standards, or traditions. Some children respond to cultural contradictions by identifying with the mainstream American culture (*assimilation*) in which they are immersed or by developing negative attitudes about their subcultural group memberships either consciously or subconsciously (*stereotype vulnerability*). Individual reactions, such as those of Manuel, will be shaped by the child's unique experiences and social influences. It is a major developmental task to integrate dual or multiple identities into a consistent personal identity as well as a positive ethnic or racial identity (Vera et al., 2011). Many models of identity exist for children of mixed ethnicity, with new ideas and theories constantly emerging. It is clear that identity development for such children is diverse, extremely complex, and not well understood. As always, however, parents and professionals must start where the child is, with a focus on facilitating understanding and appreciation of heritage to promote development of an integrated identity and positive self-regard (Chung, Bemak, & Grabosky, 2011). Children should be provided with opportunities to explore their dual or multiple heritages and to select their own terms for identifying and describing themselves (Nuttgens, 2010; Rollins & Hunter, 2013). Although studies have produced diverse findings, the most positive outcomes seem to be associated with supportive family systems and involvement in social and recreational activities that expose children to their heritage and lead to self-affirmation (Hagelskamp, Suárez-Orozco, & Hughes, 2010; Lunkett, Behnke, Sands, & Choi, 2009). The family environment plays a critical role in shaping all aspects of development, and the family is the primary vehicle through which cultural identity is transmitted. Children typically learn, through their families, how to view their own ethnicity/race and that of others as well as coping strategies to respond to potential or direct exclusion, discrimination, or racism (Ponterotto, 2010).

Key tasks for all adults include educating children about family histories and supporting the creation of an integrated sense of self. Individuals and organizations within the child's social system can provide support by being sensitive to issues related to ethnic/racial origin and ethnic/racial distinctions; they can also help by celebrating cultural diversity and trying to increase the cultural sensitivity of all children. Such interventions appear to encourage fewer negative stereotypes of peers belonging to nondominant groups (Isenberg & Jolongo, 2003). In general, it is critical to the positive identity development of all children, but particularly those from nondominant groups, that schools value diversity and offer a variety of experiences that focus on positive identity development. Ensuring that schools respect nondominant cultures and diverse learning styles is an important step. For schools to do this, all school staff must develop self-awareness. A variety of materials have been designed to facilitate this process among educators (see Banks & Banks, 2010).

EMOTIONAL DEVELOPMENT

As most children move from early childhood into and through middle childhood, they experience significant gains in their ability to identify and articulate their own emotions as well as the emotions of others. Exhibit 13.2 summarizes several gains school-age children often make in the area of emotional functioning. It is important to recognize, however, that culture and other aspects of group identity may shape emotional development. For example, cultures vary in their acceptance of expressive displays of emotion.

EXHIBIT 13.2 • Common Emotional Gains During Middle Childhood

- Ability to mentally organize and articulate emotional experiences
- Cognitive control of emotional arousal
- Ability to remain focused on goal-directed actions
- Ability to delay gratification based on cognitive evaluation
- Ability to understand and use the concept of planning
- Ability to view tasks incrementally
- Use of social comparison
- Influence of internalized feelings (e.g., self-pride, shame) on behavior
- Capacity to tolerate conflicting feelings
- Increasingly effective defense mechanisms

SOURCE: Davies, 2011, pp. 360–363.

Many children in this age range develop more advanced coping skills that help them when encountering upsetting, stressful, or traumatic situations. As defined by Daniel Goleman (2006), *emotional intelligence* refers to the ability to "motivate oneself and persist in the face of frustrations, to control impulse and delay gratification, to regulate one's moods and keep distress from swamping the ability to think, to empathize and to hope" (p. 34) (see Chapter 4 in this book for a discussion of emotional intelligence). To Goleman (2006), emotional and social intelligence are inextricably linked, and many other developmentalists agree. As a result, interventions used with children experiencing social difficulties often focus on enhancing some aspect of emotional intelligence (see, for example, Birknerová, 2011).

Goleman also asserts that social and emotional intelligence are key aspects of both moral reasoning and moral conduct. In other words, although often it may seem that advancing capacities in the moral domain occur naturally for children, positive conditions and interactions must exist in a child's life in order for optimal emotional and social competencies to develop. Thus, a child like Anthony Bryant, with seemingly great academic promise, may not realize his potential without timely intervention targeting the development of critical emotional and social competencies. These competencies include, for example, self-awareness; impulse control; and the ability to identify, express, and manage feelings, including love, jealousy, anxiety, and anger. Healthy emotional development can be threatened by a number of issues, including challenges such as significant loss and trauma. We increasingly recognize the vulnerability of school-age children to serious emotional and mental health issues. Assessment approaches that incorporate awareness of and attention to the possible existence of such issues are critical.

Fortunately, a substantial knowledge base regarding the promotion of positive emotional development exists. Richard Davidson and Sharon Begley (2012) have written extensively about the concept of emotional style and effective approaches to changing one's emotional style. Many emotion-focused intervention strategies appear effective, particularly when they are preventive and provided during or before middle childhood (see Colle & Del Giudice, 2011).

For example, Brianna Shaw, like too many children—particularly girls her age—is at risk of developing depression and could benefit from intervention focusing on the development of appropriate coping strategies. A number of interacting, complex biopsychosocial-spiritual factors shape vulnerability to ailments such as depression. Davidson and Begley assert that an individual's unique brain-based emotional style reflects a combination of six components, or substyles. These six (outlook, attention, sensitivity to context, social intuition, resilience, and self-awareness) interact to produce our emotional style, and although it is not easy, we are capable of changing our style. (See Exhibit 4.7 in Chapter 4 in this book for definitions of these six components of emotional style.)

Goleman (2006) specifically argues that many cases of depression arise from deficits in two key areas of emotional competence: relationship skills and cognitive, or interpretive, style. In short, many children suffering from—or at risk of developing—depression likely possess a depression-promoting way of interpreting setbacks. Children with a potentially harmful outlook attribute setbacks in their lives to internal, personal flaws. Appropriate preventive intervention, based on a cognitive behavioral approach, teaches children that their emotions are linked to the way they think and facilitates productive, healthy ways of interpreting events and viewing themselves. For Brianna, such cognitive-behavioral-oriented intervention may be helpful. Brianna also may benefit from a gender-specific intervention, perhaps with a particular focus on relational resilience. Gender-specific interventions are often most appropriate when the social problem is experienced primarily by one gender (Perry-Parrish & Zeman, 2011; Potter, 2004). Eating disorders and depression are two examples of issues disproportionately impacting girls. Identifying the relevance of gender issues to Brianna's current emotional state and considering a gender-specific intervention strategy therefore may be appropriate. The concept of relational resilience is built on relational-cultural theory's belief that "all psychological growth occurs in relationships"; the building blocks of relational resilience are "mutual empathy, empowerment, and the development of courage" (see Chapter 2 in this book for a discussion of relational-cultural theory) (Jordan, 2005, p. 79).

Many school-age girls and boys also experience depression and other types of emotional distress because of a variety of factors, including **trauma** (severe physical or psychological injury) or significant loss. Children with close ties to extended family are particularly likely to experience loss of a close relative at a young age and therefore are more prone to this sort of depression. Loss, trauma, and violence may present serious obstacles to healthy emotional development. Research demonstrates the remarkable potential resilience of children (see Goldstein & Brooks, 2013; Luthar, 2003; Werner & Brendtro, 2012), but both personal and environmental attributes play a critical role in processes of resilience. To support the healthy emotional development of children at risk, appropriate multilevel prevention and intervention efforts are crucial.

Peter Dazeley/Photographer's Choice/Getty Images

Gender-specific interventions are often most appropriate when a socio-emotional problem is experienced primarily by one gender. Eating disorders and depression are two examples of issues disproportionately affecting girls.

CRITICAL THINKING Questions 13.2

How would you describe the physical, cognitive, cultural identity, and emotional development of Anthony Bryant, Brianna Shaw, and Manuel Vega? In what areas do they each show particular strengths? In what areas do they each show particular challenges? How could a social worker help each child to enhance development in areas where he or she is particularly challenged?

SOCIAL DEVELOPMENT

Perhaps the most widely recognized developmental task of this period is the acquisition of feelings of *self-competence.* Traditional developmentalists have pointed out that the school-age child searches for opportunities to demonstrate personal skills, abilities, and achievements. This is what Erik Erikson (1963) was referring to when he described the developmental struggle of middle childhood as *industry versus inferiority* (refer back to Exhibit 4.11 in Chapter 4 for a description of all eight of Erikson's psychosocial stages).

Industry refers to a drive to acquire new skills and do meaningful "work." The experiences of middle childhood may foster or thwart the child's attempts to acquire an enhanced sense of *mastery* and self-efficacy. Family, peer, and community support may enhance the child's growing sense of competence; lack of such support undermines this sense. The child's definitions of self and accomplishment vary greatly according to interpretations in the surrounding environment. But superficial, external bolstering of self-esteem is not all that children of this age group require. External appraisal must be supportive and encouraging but also genuine for children to value such feedback.

Some theorists argue that children of this age must learn the value of perseverance and develop an internal drive to succeed (Seligman, Reivich, Jaycox, & Gillham, 2007; Snyder et al., 2013). Opportunities to both fail and succeed must be provided, along with sincere feedback and support. Ideally, the developing school-age child acquires the sense of personal competence and tenacity that will serve as a protective factor during adolescence and young adulthood.

Families play a critical role in supporting development of this sense. For example, as the child learns to ride a bike or play a sport or musical instrument, adults can provide specific feedback and praise. They can counter the child's frustration by identifying and complimenting specific improvements and emphasizing the role of practice and perseverance in producing improvements. Failures and setbacks can be labeled as temporary and surmountable rather than attributed to personal flaws or deficits. The presence of such feedback loops is a key feature of high-quality adult–child relationships, in the family, at school, and beyond.

Children are not equally positioned to acquire feelings of self-competence as they enter this developmental phase, as Anthony Bryant's, Brianna Shaw's, and Manuel Vega's stories suggest. Developmental pathways preceding entry into middle childhood are extremely diverse. Children experience this phase of life differently based not only on differences in the surrounding environment—such as family structure and socioeconomic status—but also on their personality differences. A particular personality and learning style may be valued or devalued, problematic or nonproblematic, in each of the child's expanding social settings (Berk, 2012). Thus, although Anthony, Brianna, and Manuel are moving through the same developmental period and facing many common tasks, they experience these tasks differently and will emerge into adolescence as unique individuals.

Each individual child's identity development is highly dependent on social networks of privilege and exclusion. A direct relationship exists between the level of control and power a child experiences and the degree of balance achieved between feelings of power (privilege) and powerlessness (exclusion) (Johnson, 2006; Tatum, 2007). As children move toward adolescence and early adulthood, the amount of emotional, social, spiritual, and economic **capital**, or resources, acquired determines the likelihood of socioeconomic and other types of success as well as feelings of competence to succeed. Experiencing economically and socially just support systems is critical to optimum development.

Advancing language capability in middle childhood serves not only as a communication tool but also as a vehicle for more sophisticated introspection. Language is also a potential tool for positive assertion of self and more complex personal opinions as the child's social world expands (Coles, 1987, 1997; Gutzwiller-Helfenfinger et al., 2010). In recent years, many elementary schools have added **character education** to their curricula. Such education often consists of direct teaching and curriculum inclusion of mainstream moral and social values thought to be universal in a community (e.g., kindness, respect, honesty). Renewed focus on children's character education is in part related to waves of school violence, harassment, and bullying. Survey research with children suggests that, compared with children in middle and high school settings, children in elementary school settings are at highest risk of experiencing bullying, as either a perpetrator or a victim (Espelage & Swearer, 2011).

At a broader level, legislative initiatives have encouraged school personnel to confront bullying and harassment in the school setting (Piacenti, 2011). Schools have been particularly responsive to these initiatives in the wake of well-publicized incidents of school violence. Today, most schools have policies in place designed to facilitate efficient and effective responses to aberrant behavior, including bullying and violence. The content and implementation details of such policies, of course, vary widely.

During the late 20th century, changes occurred within our views and understanding of bullying (Espelage & Swearer, 2011). In general, the public has become less tolerant of bullying, perhaps because of a fairly widespread belief that school shootings (such as the Chardon, Ohio, school shootings and the Columbine High School massacre) can be linked to bullying. Bullying is today recognized as a complex phenomenon, with both **direct bullying** (physical) and indirect bullying viewed as cause for concern. **Indirect bullying** refers to verbal, psychological, and social or "relational" bullying tactics and includes cyberbullying (Englander, 2013).

In recent years, new interest has centered on the ways in which technology influences social relationships among children and youth as well as gender differences in relationships and bullying. Initially, attention was drawn to the previously underrecognized phenomenon of girls experiencing direct bullying, or physical aggression and violence, at the hands of other girls (Garbarino, 2007). Although both direct and indirect bullying crosses genders, more recent attention has centered on the

Bubbles Photolibrary/Alamy Stock Photo

Bullying today is recognized as a complex phenomenon, with both direct bullying and indirect bullying viewed as causes for concern.

widespread existence of indirect, or relational, bullying among all children, but particularly among girls, and its potentially devastating consequences (Chesney-Lind & Jones, 2010; Pepler, 2012; Simmons, 2011). One positive outcome of recent attention to bullying is interest in establishing "best practices" in bullying prevention and intervention. The current knowledge base suggests that the most effective approach to reducing bullying within a school is implementation of a comprehensive, schoolwide prevention and intervention plan that addresses the contributing factors within all levels of the school and community environment (Klein, 2012).

Communities possess great potential to provide important support and structure for children. Today, however, many communities provide as many challenges as opportunities for development. Communities in which challenges outweigh opportunities have been labeled as "socially toxic," meaning they threaten positive development (Garbarino, 1995). In contrast, within a socially supportive environment, children have access to peers and adults who can lead them toward more advanced moral and social thinking. This development occurs in part through the modeling of *prosocial behavior*, which injects moral reasoning and social sensitivity into the child's accustomed manner of reasoning and behaving. Thus, cognitive and moral development is a social issue. The failure of adults to take on moral and spiritual mentoring roles contributes significantly to the development of socially toxic environments.

Mentoring takes place in the **zone of proximal development**—the theoretical space between the child's current developmental level and the child's potential level if given access to appropriate models and experiences in the social environment (Vygotsky, Hanfmann, Vakar, & Kozulin, 2012). The child's competence is ideally impacted through such interactions in a dynamic and positive fashion, resulting in developmental progress.

The Peer Group

Nearly as influential as family members during middle childhood are *peer groups*: collections of children with unique values and goals. As children progress through middle childhood, peers have an increasingly important impact on such everyday matters as social behavior, activities, and dress. By this phase of development, a desire for group belongingness is especially strong. Within peer groups, children potentially learn three important lessons. First, they learn to appreciate different points of view. Second, they learn to recognize the norms and demands of their peer group. And third, they learn to have closeness to a same-sex peer (Newman & Newman, 2012). Whereas individual friendships facilitate the development of critical capacities such as trust and intimacy, peer groups foster learning about cooperation and leadership.

Throughout middle childhood, the importance of *group norms* is highly evident (von Salisch, Haenel, & Freund, 2013). Children are sensitive, sometimes exceedingly so, to their peers' standards for behavior, appearance, and attitudes. Brianna Shaw, for instance, is beginning to devalue herself because she recognizes the discrepancy between her appearance and group norms. Often it is not until adolescence that group norms may become more flexible, allowing for more individuality. This shift reflects the complex relationship among the developmental domains. In this case, the association between social and cognitive development is illustrated by simultaneous changes in social relationships and cognitive capacities.

Gains in cognitive abilities promote more complex communication skills and greater social awareness. These developments, in turn, facilitate more complex peer interaction, which is a vital resource for the development of **social competence**—the ability to engage in sustained, positive, and mutually satisfactory peer interactions. Positive peer relationships reflect and support social competence because they potentially discourage egocentrism, promote positive coping, and ultimately serve as a protective factor during the transition to adolescence (Spencer, Harpalani, Fegley, Dell'Angelo, & Seaton, 2003).

Gender and culture influence the quantity and nature of peer interactions observed among school-age children (Perry-Parrish & Zeman, 2011). Sociability, intimacy, social expectations and rules, and the value placed on various types of play and other social activities are all phenomena shaped by both gender and culture.

Spencer et al. (2003) point out that children from nondominant groups are more likely to experience dissonance across school, family, and peer settings; for example, such children may experience language differences, misunderstandings of cultural traditions or expressions, and distinct norms, or rules, regarding dating behavior, peer intimacy, or cross-gender friendships. These authors also assert that although many youth experiencing dissonance across school, family, and peer systems may suffer from negative outcomes such as peer rejection or school failure, some may learn important coping skills that will serve them well later in life. In fact, the authors argue that given the clear trend toward increasing cultural diversity around the globe, "experiences of cultural dissonance and the coping skills they allow youth to develop should not be viewed as aberrant; instead, privilege should be explored as having a 'downside' that potentially compromises the development of coping and character" (Spencer et al., 2003, p. 137).

However, a persistent finding is that, across gender and culture, peer acceptance is a powerful predictor of psychological adjustment. One well-known study asked children to fit other children into particular categories. From the results, the researchers developed five general categories of social acceptance: popular, rejected, controversial, neglected, and average (Coie, Dodge, & Coppotelli, 1982). Common predictors of popular status include physical appearance and prosocial behaviors in the social setting (Kupersmidt & Dodge, 2004; Rotenberg et al., 2004). Rejected children are those who are actively disliked by their peers. Rejected status is strongly associated with poor academic and social outcomes (Lev-Wiesel, Sarid, & Sternberg, 2013). For this reason, we should be concerned about Brianna Shaw's growing sense of peer rejection.

Support for rejected children may include interventions to improve peer relations and psychological adjustment. Most of these interventions are based on social learning theory and involve modeling and reinforcing positive social behavior—for example, initiating interaction and responding to others positively. Such programs are capable of helping children develop social competence and gain peer approval (Mikami et al., 2013; Mikami, Lerner, & Lun, 2010).

Friendship and Intimacy

Throughout middle childhood, children expand their ability to look at things from others' perspectives. In turn, their capacity to develop more complex friendships—based on awareness of others' thoughts, feelings, and needs—emerges (von Salisch et al., 2013; Zelazo, Chandler, & Crone, 2010). As a result, for many children, more complex and stable friendships begin to form for the first time in middle childhood. Although skills such as cooperation and problem solving are learned in the peer group, close friendships facilitate understanding and promote trust and reciprocity. Most socially competent children maintain and nurture both close friendships and effective peer-group interaction.

As children move through middle childhood, friendship begins to entail mutual trust and assistance and acquires a more intense emotional component (Jobe-Shields, Cohen, & Parra, 2011). As children move toward adolescence, they may gain close friendships based on the emotional support provided for one another as much as, if not more than, common interests and activities. The concept of friend is transformed from the playmate of early childhood to the confidant of middle childhood. The role of emotional support and intimacy in friendship becomes even more pronounced, and children increasingly value mutual understanding and loyalty in the face of conflict among peers (Woods, 2013).

Participating in team sports can contribute to improved capacity for interdependence, cooperation, comprehension of division of labor, and healthy competition.

Team Play

The overall incidence of aggression during peer activities decreases during middle childhood, and friendly rule-based play increases. This transition is due in part to the continuing development of a perspective-taking ability, the ability to see a situation from another person's point of view. In addition, most school-age children are exposed to peers who differ in a variety of ways, including ethnicity and personality.

Developmental changes result in shifts in group communication and interaction, reflecting an enhanced ability to understand the role of multiple participants in activities. These developments facilitate the transition to participation in more complex rule-based activities, such as team sports. Despite occasional conflict with peers, involvement with team sports may provide great enjoyment and may have long-term benefits. Research suggests linkages between physical activity in adulthood and participation in sports and other forms of regular exercise during childhood and adolescence (Mäkinen et al., 2010; Ortega et al., 2013). While participating in team sports and other similar group activities, other potential positive outcomes include the capacity for interdependence, cooperation, comprehension of division of labor, and healthy competition (American Alliance for Health, Physical Education, Recreation and Dance, 2013).

Gender Identity and Gender Roles

Although most children in middle childhood have a great deal in common based on their shared developmental phase, girls and boys differ significantly in areas ranging from their self-understanding and social relationships to school performance, interests, and life aspirations (Perry-Parrish & Zeman, 2011). Among most school-age children, gender identity, or an "internalized psychological experience of being male or female," is quite well-established (Diamond & Savin-Williams, 2003, p. 105). This is not, however, the case for all children. Many children experience a fluid sense of gender identity, particularly prior to the onset of puberty. Research indicates that the greater the **gender dysphoria** (the feeling that one's emotional and psychological identity as male or female is opposite one's assigned biological identity) experienced as a young child, the more likely it is that the child will continue to experience gender variance through adolescence (Wallien & Cohen-Kettenis, 2008). Transgender children and youth are particularly vulnerable to social isolation and other developmental challenges associated with negative experiences in family and school settings (Burgess, 2009).

Our understanding of the structure of gender roles is derived from various theoretical perspectives (Bromberg & O'Donohue, 2013). An anthropological or social constructionist orientation illuminates the ways in which gender shapes familial and societal systems and inevitably impacts individual development in an intangible yet profound fashion (Gardiner & Kosmitzki, 2011). Cognitive theory suggests that at the individual level, self-perceptions emerge. Gender, as one component of a psychological sense of self, joins related cognitions to guide children's gender-linked behaviors. A behavioral perspective suggests that gender-related behaviors precede self-perception in the development of gender role identity; in other words, at a very young age, girls start imitating feminine behavior and later begin thinking of themselves as distinctly female, and boys go through the same sequence in developing a masculine identity. Gender schema theory (see Bem, 1993, 1998), an information-processing approach to gender, combines behavioral and cognitive theories, suggesting that social influences and cognition work together to perpetuate gender-linked perceptions and behaviors.

Feminist psychodynamic theorists such as Nancy Chodorow (1991, 1999) have proposed that whereas boys typically begin to separate psychologically from their female caregivers in early childhood, most girls deepen their connection to and identification with their female caregivers throughout childhood. Such theorists propose, then, that as girls and boys transition into adolescence and face a new level of individuation, they confront this challenge from very different psychological places, and adolescent girls are more likely to find the task emotionally confusing if not deeply overwhelming. This feminist, psychoanalytic theoretical orientation represents one approach used to explain not only gender identity and role development but also differences between boys and girls in their approaches to relationships and emotional expressiveness.

Women's studies experts have pointed out that school-age girls often seem to possess a "confident understanding of self," which too often disintegrates as they increasingly "discredit their feelings and understandings, experiencing increased self-doubt" during early adolescence and subsequently becoming susceptible to a host of internalizing and externalizing disorders linked to poor self-esteem (Potter, 2004, p. 60). A number of studies and theories attempt to explain this shift in girls' self-image and mental health as they transition to adolescence (Perry-Parrish & Zeman, 2011; Simmons, 2011), but Potter (2004) cautions against overgeneralization of the phenomena and in particular suggests that the trend may not apply widely across girls from differing ethnic groups, socioeconomic statuses, and sexual orientations.

During middle childhood, often boys' identification with "masculine" role attributes increases whereas girls' identification with "feminine" role attributes decreases (Potter, 2004). For instance, boys are more likely than girls to label a chore as a "girl's job" or a "boy's job." As adults, females are the more androgynous of the two genders, and this movement toward androgyny appears to begin in middle childhood (Diamond & Savin-Williams, 2003).

These differences have multiple causes, from social to cognitive forces. In the United States, during middle childhood and beyond, cross-gender behavior in girls is more socially acceptable than such behavior among boys. Diamond and Savin-Williams (2003) use the term *gender typicality*, or the "degree to which one's appearance, behavior, interests, and subjective self-concept conform to conventional gender norms" (p. 105). Research suggests that for both genders, a traditionally "masculine" identity is associated with a higher sense of overall competence and better academic performance (Boldizar, 1991; Newcomb & Dubas, 1992). Diamond and Savin-Williams (2003) also emphasize the role of culture in this relationship, pointing out that this is likely because the traits associated with male status are those most valued in many communities. These traits include qualities such as athleticism, confidence, and assertiveness. Indeed, local communities with "more entrenched sexist ideologies" regarding male versus female traits are those in which boys exhibiting "feminine" behaviors are likely to suffer (Diamond & Savin-Williams, 2003, p. 107).

In general, because of expanding cognitive capacities, as children leave early childhood and progress through middle childhood, their gender stereotypes gradually become more flexible, and most school-age children begin to accept that males and females can engage in the same activities (Kahraman & Başal, 2012). The relationships between gender identity, gender stereotyping, and individual gender role adoption are not clear-cut. Even children well aware of community gender norms and role expectations may not conform to gender role stereotypes in their actual behavior

(Brinkman, Jedinak, Rosen, & Zimmerman, 2011; Gerouki, 2010). Our understanding of the complexities of gender and sexual identity development—and the relationships between the two during the life course—is in its infancy.

Technology and Social Development

In recent years, there has been intense interest in the ways in which technology impacts child development. In affluent nations, many children are technologically savvy by the time they enter middle childhood. Technological advances in social media, gaming, television, and the music industry are just a few examples of the ways in which digital media impact children (Turkle, 2011). An extensive body of research suggests both positive and negative implications for child development.

Technology presents children and the adults in their lives with opportunities for social connection that did not exist in the past (Singer & Singer, 2011). Children can maintain and develop relationships despite geographical or other separations. Social support positively influences children, and these relationships may promote the development of communication skills not supported through relationships initiated or maintained solely through in-person interaction.

Some argue that technology presents children with positive opportunities for social interaction that does not "fit" in the busy weekly schedule of today's often overscheduled school-age child (Singer & Singer, 2011). In addition, some children report that use of technology allows them to explore aspects of their identity in a safe way not possible through in-person interactions. Indeed, personal identity development in areas such as sexuality and ethnicity can be informed in both positive and negative ways via media exposure. Some children also report that technology enables them to relax or escape from stressors associated with family, peer relationships, or other challenges (Singer & Singer, 2011).

Turkle (2011) explains the ways in which a variety of new toys and virtual creatures, enhanced by technology, promote prosocial behavior in young children. However, like the violent video game controversy, some question whether young children should be exposed to the complex ethical issues inherent in such toys or entertainment. In particular, is it appropriate to allow "tech creatures" to die when neglected, potentially harming children's developing capacity for empathy and understanding of the nature of human life? A related but distinct question to ponder is whether the attachments to

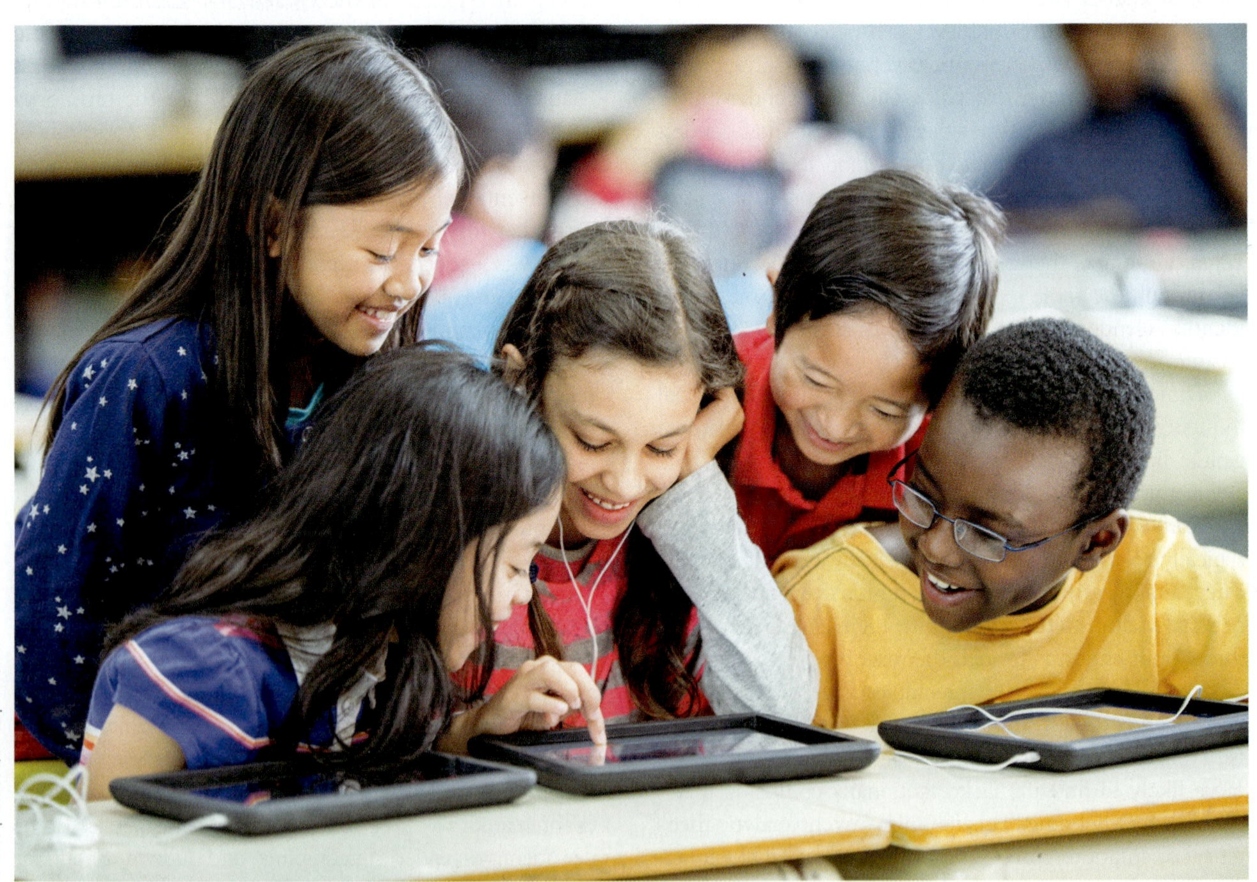

In affluent nations, many children are technologically savvy by the time they enter middle childhood.

"virtual" friends or creatures alter the nature of human attachment or attachment style among such children in some way.

Some children, like adults, report potentially unhealthy outcomes of technology use such as feeling more comfortable existing or interacting in a virtual rather than "real" environment and feeling more comfortable in a virtual identity (e.g., an avatar). Children are easily able to access an overwhelming quantity of media-based information, appropriate or inappropriate. Although there is evidence to support the harmful effects of such information access, evidence also supports the ways in which such media access can be positive, such as enhanced cognitive and moral development (Turkle, 2011). In addition, some research suggests that most children are more capable of strategizing through unwanted media-based information and messages than most adults think (Singer & Singer, 2011).

Children are impacted by technology in other less obvious ways as well. For example, parents are increasingly distracted by media, finding it difficult to "turn off" or "unplug" from work and social connections (Turkle, 2011). And yet information about effective parenting strategies and social support for isolated parents is facilitated by access to media and new technologies. Similarly, parents are capable of using technology to monitor or connect with their children more than ever before.

Focusing solely on the relationship between technology and social development, neuroscientists argue that children and adults struggle to unplug because of the dopamine release associated with human connection, and received texts and e-mails elicit this pleasure response to the point of addiction (Turkle, 2011). Our knowledge of neurobiology suggests that the human relationship with technology is shaping the development of school-age children in a complex and profound fashion.

SPIRITUAL DEVELOPMENT

Spiritual development, historically neglected or subsumed within other developmental domains, is now widely recognized as a critical aspect of child development. Robert Coles (1990) is identified as one of the first Western developmentalists to draw connections between moral and spiritual development. Benson, Scales, Syvertsen, and Roehlkepartain (2012) define spiritual development as comprising awareness or awakening, interconnecting and belonging, and a way of life; or more specifically a synergistic process of "becoming aware of one's potential and possibility; becoming aware of the intersection of one's life with others, nature, and the universe; connecting and linking the self and one's potentials to ideals and narratives; and developing a life orientation that generates hope, purpose, and compassion" (p. 457).

A significant body of research suggests that spirituality functions as a protective factor for children as well as adults. Spirituality has been established as supporting adaptive coping, and Clinton (2008) specifically found that among children suffering experiences of trauma in early childhood, higher levels of spiritual awareness are associated with more adaptive behavior, including more effective coping and resilience over time.

Holder, Coleman, and Wallace (2010) examined the differences between children's religiosity and spirituality as well as connections between spirituality and happiness in a sample of 8- to 12-year-old children. In their study, spirituality remained a significant happiness predictor even after controlling for individual temperament. Similar to scholars investigating adult spirituality and happiness, the researchers found that two particular aspects of spirituality—children's assessment of the value of life and the quality of interpersonal relationships (also labeled the "personal" and "communal" domains of spirituality)—were particularly good predictors of happiness.

Lipscomb and Gersch (2012) have engaged in qualitative research employing a spiritual listening approach, which they describe as an attempt to elicit children's views "about the meanings they attach to their lives, their essential drives, motivation and desires . . . a method of tapping into children's individual spiritual journey at a particular point in their lives" (p. 8). In a study with participants ages 10 and 11, Lipscomb and Gersch (2012) employed spiritual listening to inquire about identity, purpose, happiness, destiny, drive, and transition. Children shared views about identity, such as identity is "like an oyster" and "at first I was happy and I knew just what I was doing, but then people started bullying me just because of my skin color and then I started to think, who am I, what am I and why am I in this world" (Lipscomb & Gersch, 2012, p. 12). They also spoke about purpose, with such comments as "My purpose of life is having a mission. I don't really know what it is but I know it's a mission. I think my mission is to help other people, which is like my identity" (Lipscomb & Gersch, 2012, p. 13). The researchers noted that all children in the study were able to relate to questions about these abstract and complex concepts in an individual and relevant way. It is interesting to note that one of the strategies children used to connect philosophical ideas back to their concrete experiences was by referencing popular culture, including themes they had observed in television and films. Of particular relevance to social work is the authors' conclusion that the technique of spiritual listening may support children's development as it facilitates children's ability to link the concrete nature of their lives to the metaphysical.

CRITICAL THINKING Questions 13.3

Why do you think peer acceptance is a powerful predictor of psychological adjustment in middle childhood? Why do you think cross-gender behavior is more socially acceptable for girls than for boys in the United States? How do you think Anthony Bryant, Brianna Shaw, and Manuel Vega would respond to spiritual questioning?

MIDDLE CHILDHOOD AND FORMAL SCHOOLING

Before discussing the role of formal schooling in the life of the school-age child in the United States and other relatively affluent societies, it is important to note that there continue to be large global gaps in opportunities for education. Although educational participation is almost universal from ages 5 to 14 in affluent countries, many of the world's children do not receive even a primary education. In the current context of a knowledge-based global economy, the importance of formal schooling during middle childhood cannot be overstated, and yet a widening gap exists in average years of education between rich and poor countries (Gardiner & Kosmitzki, 2011; World Bank, 2013b).

Children entering school must learn to navigate a new environment quite different from the family. In school, they are evaluated on the basis of how well they perform tasks; people outside the family—teachers and other school staff as well as peers—begin shaping the child's personality, dreams, and aspirations. For children such as Manuel Vega, the environmental adjustment can be even more profound in part because the educational attainment of family members may be limited (Crouse, 2010). At the same time, the school environment has the potential to serve as an important resource for the achievement of the physical, cognitive, emotional, social, and spiritual developmental tasks of middle childhood for all children, regardless of the previous schooling available to their parents.

Success in the school environment is very important to the development of self-esteem. Anthony Bryant, Brianna Shaw, and Manuel Vega illustrate the potentially positive as well as painful aspects of schooling. Manuel and Brianna seem increasingly distressed by their interactions within the school environment. Often, difficulties with peers create or compound academic challenges. Brianna's school experience is becoming threatening enough that she may begin to withdraw from the environment, which would represent a serious risk to her continued cognitive, emotional, and social development. As children move through the middle years, they become increasingly aware that they are evaluated on the basis of what they are able to do. In turn, they begin to evaluate themselves based on treatment by teachers and peers and on self-assessments of what they can and cannot do well (Garralda & Raynaud, 2010).

In the past few decades, school-age children have benefited from new research and theory focusing on the concept of intelligence. Howard Gardner's work represented a paradigm shift in the field of education. He proposed that intelligence is neither unitary nor fixed and argued that intelligence is not adequately or fully measured by IQ tests. More broadly, in his theory of *multiple intelligences*, intelligence is "the ability to solve problems or fashion products that are of consequence in a particular cultural setting or community" (Gardner, 1993, p. 15). Challenging the idea that individuals can be described, or categorized, by a single, quantifiable measure of intelligence, Gardner proposed at least eight critical intelligences: linguistic, logical/mathematical, visual-spatial, bodily kinesthetic, musical, intrapersonal, interpersonal, and naturalist (Campbell, Campbell, & Dickinson, 2004; Zeidner, Matthews, & Roberts, 2012) (see Exhibit 4.2 in Chapter 4 for an overview of these eight intelligences). In its practical application, multiple intelligence theory calls for the use of a wide range of instructional strategies that engage the range of strengths and intelligences of each student (Ghazi, Shahzada, Gilani, Shabbir, & Rashid, 2011). In addition to calling for innovative and diverse instructional strategies, multiple intelligence theory suggests achievement evaluation should consist of comprehensive assessments examining diverse areas of performance.

Many schools are ill-equipped to respond to the issues confronting children such as Manuel. If Manuel is not supported and assisted by his school system, his educational experience may assault his healthy development. But if Manuel's personal and familial support systems can be tapped and mobilized, they may help him overcome his feelings of isolation in his new school environment. Carefully constructed and implemented interventions must be used to help Manuel.

Today in the United States, Manuel's situation is not rare. About 1 in 5 U.S. students speak a language other than English at home (Skinner, Wight, Aratani, Cooper, & Thampi, 2010). Overall, the percentage of children living in the United States with at least one foreign-born parent rose from 15% in 1994 to 24% in 2012 (Federal Interagency Forum on Child and Family Statistics, 2013). In general, students in the United States are more diverse than ever before (U.S. Department of Health and Human Services, 2011). Many challenges face children who have recently arrived in the United States, particularly those fleeing war-torn countries. Research suggests that immigrant and refugee children are at heightened risk of

Brian van der Brug/Contributor/Los Angeles Times/Getty Images

As children get older, schools are the primary context for development in middle childhood.

experiencing mental health challenges and school failure (Briggs, 2011; Henderson, 2008).

Language difficulties and their consequences among such children are also increasingly recognized. It has been established that children are best served when they are able to speak both their native language and the language of their host country (Auerbach & Collier, 2012). The need for specific strategies to acknowledge and honor the "informal language register," while teaching the formal, has been identified by several literacy researchers (see Gee, 2012; Maier, Vitiello, & Greenfield, 2012). These researchers emphasize the importance of teaching children to recognize their internal, or natural, "speech" and the "register" they use in the school environment. Identifying and mediating these processes is best accomplished in the context of a caring relationship (Noddings, 2013). By sensitively promoting an awareness of such differences in the home and school, social workers and other adults can help children experience less confusion and alienation.

Other aspects of the link between school and home are important as well because school and home are the two major spheres in which children exist during middle childhood. The more similar these two environments are, the more successful the child will be at school and at home. Students who experience vastly different cultures at home and at school are likely to have difficulty accommodating the two worlds (Gregory, 2000). A great deal of learning goes on before a child enters school. By the time Anthony Bryant, Brianna Shaw, and Manuel Vega began school, they had acquired routines; habits; and cognitive, social, emotional, and physical styles and skills (Hayes, 2011). The transition to school is relatively easy for many students because schools typically present a mainstream model for behavior and learning. As most parents interact with their children, they model and promote the behavior that will be acceptable in school. Children are well prepared for the school environment when, quite simply, they understand the rules because the school is then accepting of them (Howard, 2010; Payne, 2013).

In contrast, children not fluent in mainstream speech patterns or not extensively exposed to school rules or materials such as scissors and books typically possess skills and curiosity but are often viewed as inferior in some way by school personnel (Crouse, 2010; Murillo, 2010). Because the school environment does not support the home environment and the home environment does not support the school environment, these children face an increased risk of poor school outcomes. Schools that recognize the contribution of home to school success typically seek family involvement (Constable, 2006; Fan, Williams, & Wolters, 2012). Indeed, parental involvement in school is associated with better school performance (Duncan & Murnane, 2011). Schools serving diverse populations are becoming increasingly creative in their approaches to encouraging parent involvement, including the development of sophisticated interpretation and translation infrastructures (McNeal, 2012).

The U.S. educational system today struggles to correct its traditional structure, which both reflected and supported racial, ethnic, and class divisions within U.S. society (Darling-Hammond, 2010; Frankenberg & Debray, 2011; Kozol, 2005; Orfield, Kucsev, & Siegal-Harvey, 2012). For example, *full-service schools* attempt to provide school-based or school-linked health and social services for schoolchildren and their families (Dyson, 2011). This push for educational accountability and its impact on the lives of children is complex and highly controversial. The application of the No Child Left Behind Act's standards spurred a number of organizations and states to either sue the federal government or sharply criticize the act for raising state achievement requirements without adequate supporting funds or as a violation of states' rights.

No Child Left Behind reforms gained momentum with the U.S. Department of Education (2013) providing Race to the Top funds as an incentive to states to adopt particular programs designed to raise student achievement outcomes. Many states have won significant competitive grants for increasing charter school options and negotiating merit-based teacher contracts tied, in part, to students' achievement growth on standardized tests. Such tests are linked to the new national Common Core Curriculum that, as of 2015, had been adopted by 42 states and the District of Columbia.

The testing regimen to assess student knowledge of the Common Core has created the most controversy, continuing age-old states' rights concerns (Rich, 2013). Many believe such reforms will ultimately benefit diverse students like Anthony, Brianna, and Manuel, whereas others are convinced that most of the reforms will leave struggling students further behind.

In recent years, funding from government and corporate sources is increasingly directed at poor, low-resourced school districts. The idea is to use such funding to increase community partnerships designed to serve historically excluded students and their families as well as expanding preschool options and building more instructional technology infrastructure. In addition, many schools have responded to calls for educational reform by implementing innovative practices designed to raise achievement of basic skills while attempting to meet the educational needs of all students (Sherer, 2009; U.S. Department of Education, 2010). However, educational research has not had time to conclusively measure the long-range effects of such practices on a wide range of students. (See Chapter 9 in this book for further discussion of educational policy.)

CRITICAL THINKING Questions 13.4

Think about your own middle childhood years, ages 6 to 12. What are some examples of school experiences that helped you to feel competent and confident? What are some examples of school experiences that lead you to feel incompetent and inferior? What biological, family, cultural, and other environmental factors led to success and failure in school?

SPECIAL CHALLENGES IN MIDDLE CHILDHOOD

In the last several decades in the United States, family structures have become more diverse than ever. Although the percentage of children living with both parents has steadily declined during the last four to five decades, according to the U.S. Census Bureau, approximately two thirds of children live with married parents and one quarter live with one parent (Vespa, Lewis, & Kreider, 2013). Exhibit 13.3 shows trends in living arrangements of children from 1958 to 2008.

Social and economic trends require more parents of very young children to participate in the workforce in order to make ends meet. Legislation requires single parents who receive public assistance to remain engaged in or to reenter the workforce (Parham, Quadagno, & Brown, 2009). The school day often does not coincide with parents' work schedules, and recent research suggests that as a result of parental employment, more than half of school-age children regularly need additional forms of supervision when school is not in session. Most of these children either participate in a before-school or afterschool program (also known as wrap-around programs) or receive care from a relative; many low- and middle-income families struggle to find affordable child care and often are forced to sacrifice quality child care for economic reasons (Lippman, Vandivere, Keith, & Atienza, 2008; National Association of Child Care Resources and Referral Agencies, 2012). Unfortunately, available data suggest that the quality of child care experienced by the average child in the United States is less than ideal (Lippman et al., 2008).

This fact is particularly troubling because child care quality has been linked to children's physical health as well as cognitive, emotional, and social development. These findings apply not only to early childhood programs but also to before-school and afterschool programs for older children. Moreover, as children move from the early (ages 5 to 9) to later (10 to 12) middle childhood years, they are increasingly likely to take care of themselves during the before-school and afterschool hours. Regular participation in a high-quality

EXHIBIT 13.3 • Trends in Living Arrangements of Children Under 18

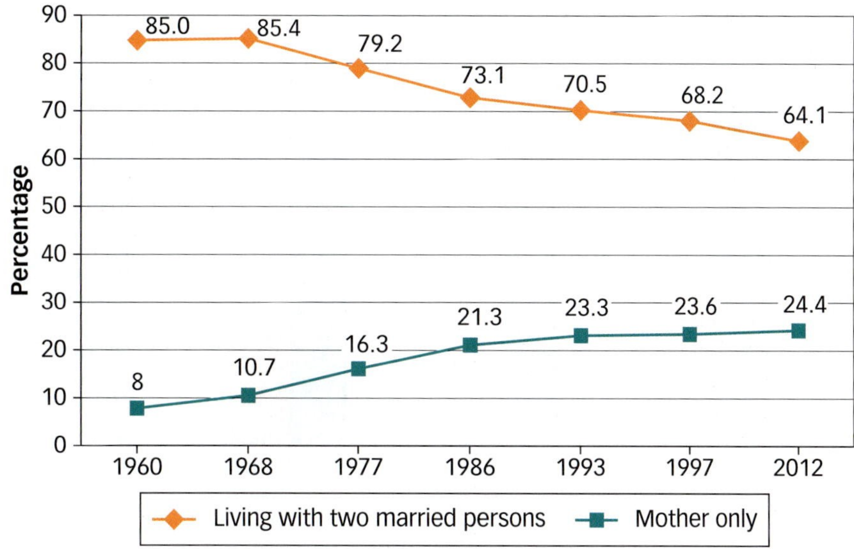

SOURCE: Based on Child Trends, 2013b.

before-school and afterschool program is positively associated with academic performance, and a significant body of research suggests that how school-age children spend their afterschool hours is strongly associated with the likelihood of engaging in risky behaviors (Lyn, 2009).

Inadequate and low-quality child care is just one of the challenges facing school-age children—along with their families and communities—in the 21st century. Other challenges include poverty, family and community violence, mental and physical challenges, and family disruption.

POVERTY

Poverty is the most significant human rights challenge facing the world community and potentially threatens positive development in all domains (see Ortiz, Daniels, & Engilbertsdóttir, 2012). It is estimated that half of the children of the world live in poverty, many in extreme poverty. That children should be protected from poverty is not disputed; in the United States, this societal value dates back to the colonial period (Trattner, 1998). The nature of policies and programs targeted at ensuring the minimal daily needs of children are met, however, has shifted over time, as has our success in meeting this goal (Bailey & Danziger, 2013).

In the United States, the late 20th century brought a dramatic rise in the child poverty rate, which peaked in the early 1990s, declined for approximately a decade, and has gradually increased during the 21st century (Wight, Chau, & Aratani, 2011). The percentage of children living in low-income families (both poor and near poor) increased from 40% in 2006 to 45% in 2011 (Addy, Engelhardt, & Skinner, 2013).

As illustrated in Exhibit 13.4, children in the middle childhood age range are less likely to live in low-income or poor families than their younger counterparts, and this trend continues as children grow toward adulthood. Caucasian children comprise the majority of poor children in the United States. Young children and children from minority groups, however, are statistically overrepresented among the population of poor children (Addy et al., 2013). (See Exhibit 13.5 for the percentage of children in low-income and poor families by race or ethnicity in 2011.) This is a persistent contemporary trend; in other words, although in absolute numbers Caucasian children consistently comprise the majority of poor children, children from Latino and African American families are consistently significantly overrepresented among all children in poverty.

Anthony Lake (2013), the executive director of the United Nations' Children's Fund, points out that although the causes of inequality are many, the outcomes are the same. Today, the richest approximately 20% of the global population enjoy about 70% of the world's total income. These disparities exist in the United States as well. Lake warns that the divisions resulting from such disparities "could continue to reverberate through future generations at great cost to us all" (para. 36).

In general, the risk factors associated with child poverty are numerous, especially when poverty is sustained. A number of perspectives attempt to explain the ways in which poverty impacts child development (see Duncan & Magnuson, 2011; Wagmiller & Adelman, 2009). Limited income constrains a family's ability to obtain or invest in resources that promote positive development. Poverty detrimentally impacts caregivers' emotional health and parenting practices. Poverty is correlated with inadequate family, school, and neighborhood resources, and thus children

EXHIBIT 13.4 • Percentage of Children in Low-Income and Poor Families by Age, 2011

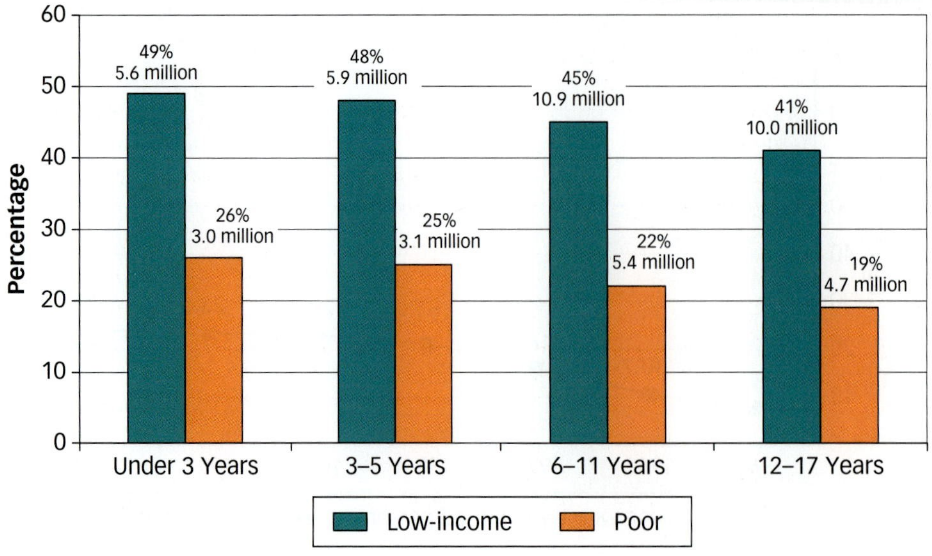

SOURCE: Addy et al., 2013.

experiencing family poverty are likely experiencing additional, cumulative risk factors. In sum, poverty threatens optimal child development in a complex, synergistic fashion. Research suggests that children affected by three or more risk factors are significantly more likely to experience school failure and to employ maladaptive coping strategies associated with a variety of negative outcomes (Robbins, Stagman, & Smith, 2012). Children who have spent any part of their prenatal period, infancy, or early childhood in poverty have often already encountered several developmental challenges by the time middle childhood begins. Children who enter, progress through, and leave middle

EXHIBIT 13.5 • Percentage of Children in Low-Income and Poor Families by Race or Ethnicity, 2011

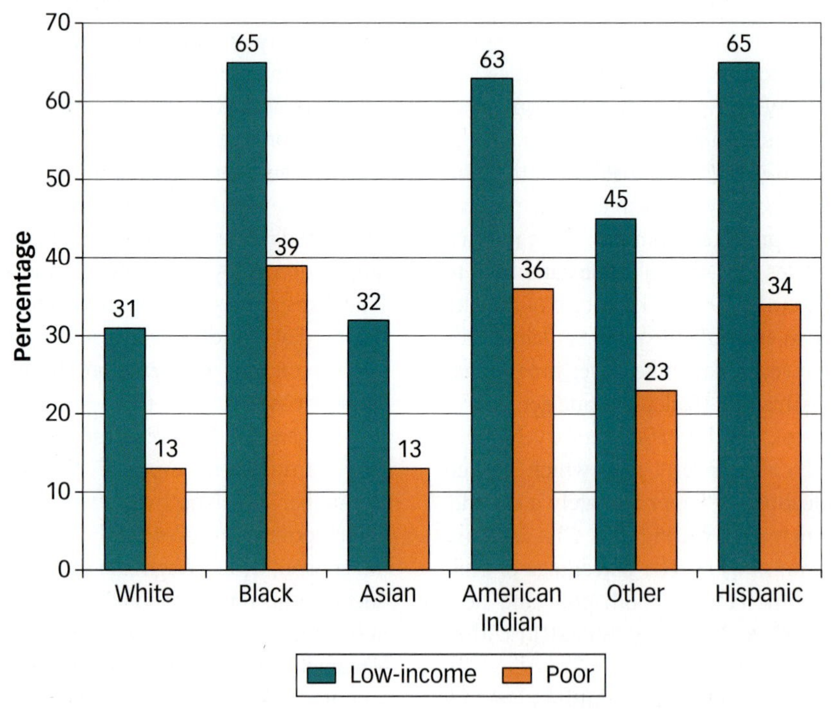

SOURCE: Addy et al., 2013.

childhood in poverty are at much greater risk of negative developmental outcomes than those who briefly enter and then exit poverty while still in middle childhood (Moore, Redd, Burkhauser, Mbwana, & Collins, 2009).

Persistent and "deep," or extreme, poverty poses the most significant threat to healthy child development. For example, extreme family poverty is correlated with homelessness, and poverty and homelessness combined increase a child's risk of abrupt family separation and experiencing or witnessing forms of trauma such as physical or sexual assault (Schneir, 2009).

But what does it actually mean, to a child, to be poor? Being poor is a relative concept, the meaning of which is defined by perceptions of and real exclusion (DiNitto, 2011; Kozol, 2005). In most communities, one must be *not* poor in order to be fully engaged and included. Lack of income and certain goods deprive poor people of what is expected among those who belong; thus, poverty results in perceived and real inabilities and inadequacies. For example, children often participate in extracurricular activities such as sports, music, or art. These programs often involve registration, program, and equipment fees that are prohibitive to impoverished families. This is the essence of **relative poverty**, or the tendency to define one's poverty status in relation to others within one's social environment. Fundamentally, then, poverty is as much a social as an economic phenomenon. Payne (2013) argues that economic poverty often includes emotional, spiritual, and support system impoverishment. Such deficits in a child's background accumulate and too often result in impediments to the development of critical capacities. James Garbarino (1995), a researcher who has studied causes of violent behavior among children, points to an innocent question once asked of him by a child: "When you were growing up, were you poor or regular?" (p. 137). As a child struggles with the developmental tasks of feeling included and socially competent, relative poverty sends a persistent message of social exclusion.

FAMILY AND COMMUNITY VIOLENCE

Witnessing violence deeply affects children, particularly when the perpetrator or victim of violence is a family member. Children are increasingly witness or subject to violence in their homes, schools, and neighborhoods (Finkelhor, Turner, Ormrod, Hamby, & Kracke, 2009). Although child maltreatment and domestic violence have always existed, they have been recognized as social problems only recently. Community violence is slowly becoming recognized as a social problem of equal magnitude, affecting a tremendous number of children and families. Exposure to violence is a particular problem in areas where a lack of economic and social resources already produces significant challenges for children. Children are most likely to experience "polyvictimization" beginning in the middle childhood years (Finkelhor, Turner, Hamby, & Ormrod, 2011). The atrocities witnessed or experienced by children from war-torn countries are often unimaginable to children and adults who have resided in the United States all of their lives (United Nations, 2011).

Many school-age children witness violence on a regular basis, an experience that threatens their healthy development (Children's Defense Fund, 2012; Tomoda, Polcari, Anderson, & Teicher, 2012). In the United States, children appear most susceptible to nonfatal physical abuse from ages 6 to 12. Some speculate that in the United States, at least, this association may be due to increased likelihood of public detection through school contact during these years. The number of children reported to Child Protective Services (CPS) agencies annually is staggering. Child neglect is consistently the most common form of documented maltreatment, but it is important to note that victims typically experience more than one type of abuse or neglect simultaneously and therefore are appropriately included in more than one category (Children's Defense Fund, 2013; U.S. Department of Health and Human Services, Administration on Children, Youth, & Families, 2012). Maltreatment subtype trends are relatively stable over time; victims of child neglect consistently account for more than half of all child maltreatment victims (see Exhibit 13.6).

African American and Native American children are consistently overrepresented among confirmed maltreatment victims. Careful examination of this issue, however, has concluded that although children of color are disproportionately represented within the child welfare population, studies that are cognizant of the relationship between culture and parenting practices, that control for the role of poverty, and that examine child maltreatment in the general population find no association between a child's race or ethnicity and likelihood of child maltreatment. Thus, it is likely that the disproportionate representation of children of color within the child welfare system is caused by the underlying relationship between poverty and race or ethnicity (Derezotes, Testa, & Poertner, 2005; Martinez, Gudiño, & Lau, 2013).

A variety of factors contribute to child maltreatment and family violence (Institute of Medicine and National Research Council, 2012). These factors include parental, child, family, community, and cultural characteristics. Typically, the dynamic interplay of such characteristics leads to maltreatment, with the most relevant factors varying significantly depending on the type of maltreatment examined. Thus, multiple theoretical perspectives, particularly the life course, ecological, systems, and stress and coping perspectives, are helpful for understanding situations of child maltreatment.

The impact of child maltreatment varies based on a number of factors, including but certainly not limited to the

EXHIBIT 13.6 • Selected Maltreatment Types of Victims by Age, 2011

AGE	MEDICAL NEGLECT		NEGLECT		PHYSICAL ABUSE		PSYCHOLOGICAL MALTREATMENT		SEXUAL ABUSE	
	NUMBER	%	NUMBER	%	NUMBER	%	NUMBER	%	NUMBER	%
<1–2	5,212	34.6	159,753	30.1	28,565	24.0	12,946	21.3	1,650	2.7
3–5	2,313	15.3	110,335	20.8	19,394	16.3	11,767	19.3	8,585	14.0
6–8	2,046	13.6	86,282	16.2	19,644	16.5	10,787	17.7	9,978	16.2
9–11	1,820	12.1	68,212	12.8	16,779	14.1	9,782	16.1	11,347	18.5
12–14	1,965	13.0	58,603	11.0	18,207	15.3	8,976	14.8	16,178	26.3
15–17	1,695	11.2	46,660	8.8	15,579	13.1	6,377	10.5	13,411	21.8
Unborn, Unknown, and 18–21	23	0.2	1,568	0.3	657	0.6	204	0.3	323	0.5
Total	15,074		531,413		118,825		60,839		61,472	
Percentage		100.0		100.0		100.0		100.0		100.0

SOURCE: U.S. Children's Bureau, 2012.

type of maltreatment; the age of the child; and many other child, family, and community characteristics (Cicchetti, 2013). The Centers for Disease Control and Prevention (2013i) provides a helpful overview of child maltreatment consequences, pointing out that experiencing maltreatment as a child is associated with an overwhelming number of negative health outcomes as an adult. These outcomes include an increased likelihood of using or abusing alcohol and other substances, disordered eating, depression, and susceptibility to certain chronic diseases.

Children who experience trauma, induced by either indirect or direct exposure to violence, may experience *post-traumatic stress disorder* (PTSD)—a set of symptoms that includes feelings of fear and helplessness, reliving of the traumatic experience, and attempts to avoid reminders of the traumatic experience (Foa, Keane, Friedman, & Cohen, 2010). Researchers have found changes in the brain chemistry of children exposed to chronic violence (Matto, Strolin-Goltzman, & Ballan, 2014). Witnessing or experiencing violence adversely affects children in a number of areas, including the ability to function in school and the ability to establish stable, healthy relationships (Lang et al., 2008; Tomoda et al., 2012). Children who directly experience violence are at high risk of negative outcomes, but secondary exposure to violence and trauma—such as when a child's parents are suffering from PTSD—also may lead to negative outcomes for children (Wasserman & McReynolds, 2011).

In general, the intergenerational nature of family violence has been established (Robboy & Anderson, 2011). Childhood exposure to violence significantly increases the likelihood of mental health difficulties and violence perpetration or revictimization. Currently, the focus is on understanding the specific pathways of intergenerational processes. It is clear that prolonged exposure to violence has multiple implications for child development. Children are forced to learn lessons about loss and death, perhaps before they have acquired the cognitive ability to understand. They may therefore come to believe that the world is unpredictable and violent, a belief that threatens children's natural curiosity and desire to explore the social environment. Multiple experiences in which adults are unable to protect them often lead children to conclude that they must take on such responsibility for themselves, a prospect that can easily overwhelm the resources of a school-age child. Experiencing such helplessness may also lead to feelings of incompetence and hopelessness, to which children who experience chronic violence react in diverse ways. Responses may be passive, including withdrawal symptoms and signs of depression; or they may be active, including the use of aggression as a means of coping with and transforming the overwhelming feelings of vulnerability (Charlesworth, 2007).

The emotional availability of a parent or other caretaker who can support the child's need to process traumatic events is critical. However, in situations of crisis stimulated by child maltreatment, domestic violence, and national or international violence, families are often unable to support their children psychologically. Even with the best of parental resources, moreover, children developing in violent and chronically dangerous communities continue to experience numerous challenges to development. The child's need for autonomy and independence is directly confronted by the parent's need to protect the child's physical safety. For example, hours spent indoors to avoid danger do not promote the much-needed peer relationships and sense of accomplishment, purpose, and self-efficacy so critical during this phase of development (Hutchison, 2007).

MENTAL AND PHYSICAL CHALLENGES

Although the term *disability* is still widely used in academic discourse and government policy, many are actively seeking to change popular discourse to reflect the need to see all children as possessing a range of physical and mental abilities. The use of the term *disability* establishes a norm within that range and labels those with abilities outside the norm as "disabled," which implies that group of individuals is "abnormal" and the group of individuals within the norm is "normal." These labels are not helpful for realizing a vision of a just and equal society, and yet information of relevance is shared within the confines of this terminology. In 2012, of the 62.2 million children younger than age 15, about 5.2 million or 8.4% had some kind of recognized disability. Half of children with a disability were classified with severe disabilities (Brault, 2012). During the last several years in the United States, the prevalence of developmental disabilities has increased (C. Boyle et al., 2011). Of particular note, ADHD and autism prevalence continues to increase.

Attention-Deficit/Hyperactivity Disorder (ADHD)

ADHD is a commonly diagnosed childhood behavioral disorder impacting learning in the school environment. ADHD includes predominately inattentive, predominately impulsive-hyperactive, and combined inattentive-hyperactivity (American Psychiatric Association, 2013). The Centers for Disease Control and Prevention (2013j) reports that approximately 11% of children 4 to 17 years of age (6.4 million) had been diagnosed with ADHD as of 2011. In 2011, boys (13.2%) were more likely than girls (5.6%) to have ever been diagnosed with ADHD. The average age of ADHD diagnosis was 7, but children reported by their parents as having more severe ADHD are typically diagnosed earlier. Prevalence of ADHD diagnosis varied substantially by state, from a low of 5.6% in Nevada to a high of 18.7% in Kentucky.

ADHD is associated with school failure or academic underachievement, but the relationship is complex in part because of the strong relationship between ADHD and a number of other factors also associated with school difficulties (Foley, 2011; Rietz, Hasselhorn, & Labuhn, 2012). Also, several studies suggest that the interpretation and evaluation of ADHD behaviors are significantly influenced by culturally linked beliefs (Rohde et al., 2005). In other words, the extent to which ADHD-linked behaviors are perceived as problematic varies according to individual and group values and norms.

Autism Spectrum Disorder (ASD)

In recent years, controversy has surrounded autism spectrum disorder, including definitions, causes, and diagnostic criteria (Grandin & Panek, 2013; Shannon, 2011). According to the Centers for Disease Control and Prevention (2013k), autism spectrum disorder is typically diagnosed by age 3 in about 1 in 88 children, and boys are approximately 5 times more likely to be diagnosed (1 in 54) than girls (1 in 252). Although autism spectrum disorder typically manifests and is diagnosed during or before early childhood, some children may not receive formal assessment or diagnosis until their early or middle childhood years. In general, autism spectrum disorder consists of impairment in social communication and social interaction across multiple contexts and restricted, repetitive patterns of behavior, interests, or activities (American Psychiatric Association, 2013). Like children with any special need or disability, children diagnosed with autism spectrum disorder are extremely diverse; in particular, such children vary widely in terms of their intellectual and communicative abilities, the nature and severity of behavioral challenges, and appropriate interventions (Herbert & Weintraub, 2012).

Emotional/Behavioral Disorder

In many schools, the children perhaps presenting the greatest challenge to educators and administrators are those who consistently exhibit disruptive or alarming behavior yet do not clearly fit the criteria for a disability diagnosis. Although the U.S. Individuals with Disabilities Education Act (IDEA) includes a definition for "seriously emotionally disturbed" children, not all school professionals and government education agencies consistently agree with or use this definition. The National Mental Health and Special Education Coalition has publicized a definition of "emotionally/behaviorally disordered" children, suggesting that this term and a set of diagnostic criteria could be used in place of the IDEA definition (Young, Marchant, & Wilder, 2004). This revised definition remains problematic, and because of definitional inconsistencies, it is extremely difficult to accurately estimate the number of school-age children falling within this population. Estimates range from 0.05% to 12% of preadolescent students (Bellenir, 2012; Walker & Melvin, 2010). It is estimated that approximately 15% of children 4 to 17 years old have parents or guardians who have talked with a health care provider or school staff about their child's emotional or behavioral difficulties (Simpson, Cohen, Pastor, & Reuben, 2008).

Early identification and intervention, or provision of appropriate supportive services, are key protective factors for a child with special needs. In addition, the social environment more generally may serve as either a risk or protective factor, depending on its response to the child with a special need. Although difference of any sort is often noticed by children and adults, students with special needs or chronic illness are at particular risk for being singled out by their peers, and middle childhood is a critical time for such children. For children to acquire a clear and positive sense of self, they need positive self-regard. The positive development of all children is facilitated by support at multiple levels to promote feelings of self-competence and independence. Educating all children and adults about special needs and encouraging the support of all students may help to minimize negative attitudes and incidents (Gargiulo & Kilgo, 2011; Painter, 2012).

Students who feel misunderstood by their peers are particularly likely to feel alone or isolated in the school setting. Students who are socially excluded by their peers often develop a dislike of school. Some students who are teased, isolated, or harassed on a regular basis may begin to withdraw or act out in order to cope with unpleasant experiences. Teachers, parents, and other school personnel who pay special attention to, and intervene with, students in this situation may prevent the escalation of such problems.

Children's adjustment to special needs is highly dependent on the adjustment of those around them. Families may respond in a number of ways to a diagnosis of a disability or serious illness. Often caregivers experience loss or grief stages; these stages may include the following: denial, withdrawal, rejection, fear, frustration, anger, sadness, adjustment, and acceptance (Ahmann, 2013; Richardson, Cobham, McDermott, & Murray, 2013). The loss and grief stages are not linear but can be experienced repeatedly as parents interface with educational, social, and medical institutions throughout their child's life. Awareness of and sensitivity to these reactions and the ongoing nature of grief and loss is critical for those assessing the need for intervention. Typically, parents are helped by advocacy and support groups and access to information and resources (McMillan, 2011).

Families of children with special needs also typically desire independence and self-determination for their children. Family empowerment was an explicit focus of the Education for All Handicapped Children Act (Pub. L. No. 94-142) of 1975, which stresses parental participation in the development of an **individual education plan (IEP)** for each child. The IEP charts a course for ensuring that each child achieves as much as possible in the academic realm. The need to include the family in decision making and planning is also embodied in the IDEA of 1990 (reauthorized in 1997 and 2004), which replaced the Education for All Handicapped Children Act (National School Board Association, 2013). The IDEA requires that the IEP include specific educational goals for each student classified as in need of special educational services. In addition, the IDEA assures all children the right to a free and appropriate public education and supports the placement of children with disabilities into integrated settings.

Prior to this act, the education of children with disabilities was left to individual states. As a result, the population labeled "disabled" and the services provided varied greatly. Today, however, through various pieces of legislation and several court decisions, society has stated its clear preference to educate children with special needs in integrated settings (*least restrictive environment*) to the maximum extent possible.

A recent examination of the nature of inclusion nationwide concluded that during the last few decades, students with special needs (including learning disabilities) were much more likely to be formally identified, but many states are not aggressively pursuing the ability to educate students with special needs in less restrictive settings (Aron & Loprest, 2012). Evaluations of the impact of inclusive settings on children's school success suggest positive academic gains for children with special needs and neutral impact on academic performance for children without identified special needs (Weigert, 2012). However, some caution is in order against a "one size fits all" model of inclusion for all students with special needs, arguing that assessment of the optimal educational setting must be thorough and individualized (Goodfellow, 2012).

FAMILY DISRUPTION

Throughout history, most nuclear and extended families have succeeded in their endeavor to adequately protect and socialize their young. For too many children, however, the family serves as both a protective and risk factor because of unhealthy family attributes and dynamics. In the specific realm of family disruption, divorce was traditionally viewed as a developmental risk factor for children. Today, among U.S. children with married parents, approximately one half experience the divorce of their parents (American Academy of Child & Adolescent Psychiatry, 2013). Many parents marry a second time, and thus approximately 10% of U.S. children live in blended family situations (U.S. Census Bureau, 2013f; Miller, 2010). Many children experience the dissolution of their parents' nonmarital romantic relationships, and related attachments, without being counted in official "children of divorce" statistics or research. Although no reliable data on similar nonmarital relationship patterns exist, we can assume that similar trends exist among children's nonmarried parents and other caregivers.

Divorce and other types of family disruption lead to new situations, including the introduction of new people, new housing and income arrangements, and new family roles and responsibilities (Ahrons, 2011).

Family disruption may also immerse the child in poverty (Ducanto, 2010). As the body of research on children and divorce has grown in depth and breadth, it has become apparent that divorce and other types of family disruption may detrimentally or positively impact children depending on the circumstances preceding and following the divorce (Stadelmann, Perren, Groeben, & von Klitzing, 2010). For example, if divorce brings an end to seriously dysfunctional spousal tension or violence and results in positive changes within the home environment, child outcomes may be positive. Alternatively, if the divorce disrupted a healthy, nurturing family system and led to declines in the emotional and financial health of the child's primary caregiver(s), child outcomes may be negative. (See Chapter 7 in this book for further discussion of divorce in family life.)

Historically, many children experienced family disruption because of the death of one or both parents (Amato, 2003). Although improvements in public health have significantly reduced the likelihood of parental death, a substantial number of children continue to experience the death of a primary caregiver. Compared with adults, children have fewer cognitive and other resources to cope with death and loss (Buchwald, Delmar, & Schantz-Laursen, 2012). For children coping with the death of a parent, the circumstances of the death and the adjustment of the remaining caregivers are critical variables impacting child outcomes. Also, in recent years, a number of studies have focused on "children of suicide." This literature notes the potential long-term impacts of parental suicide on surviving children and identifies the ways in which outcomes may be carried through generations (Bisagni, 2012).

Many school-age children experience disruption of attachment relationships through other means. Approximately 2 million children in the United States have one active-duty parent in the military. Children in military families are at heightened risk of frequent moves, parental absence, and parental emotional distress (Murphey, 2013). In any month in 2011, there were approximately 400,000 children in foster care (U.S. Children's Bureau, 2013). Some children spend lengthy periods of time in some type of foster care setting, whereas some children enter and leave foster care rapidly and only once during their childhoods, and still other children cycle in and out of their home and foster care settings repeatedly. Approximately one third of the children in foster care at any time have been in substitute care for 3 years or more; approximately one fifth of children in foster care are identified as unlikely to ever return home and are awaiting a permanent plan (Downs, Moore, & McFadden, 2010).

Family disruption is stressful for all children. Great variation exists, however, in the circumstances preceding and following the family disruption, the nature of the changes involved, and how children respond to this type of stress. Critical factors in outcomes for children include social supports within the family and surrounding community, the child's characteristics, the emotional well-being of caregivers, and in general the quality of care received following the family disruption. In addition, because middle childhood spans a wide age range, school-age children exhibit a wide range of cognitive, emotional, and behavioral responses to divorce and other types of family disruption. They may blame themselves and experience anxiety or other difficult emotions, or they may demonstrate a relatively mature understanding of the reasons behind the events.

Children experiencing family disruption without supports or those who have experienced difficulties preceding the disruption are most likely to experience long-term emotional and behavioral problems. Children placed in foster care or otherwise exposed to traumatic or multiple losses are more likely to fall into this group (Webb & Dumpson, 2006). These children are likely to face additional stress associated with the loss of familiar space, belongings, and social networks (Mallon & Hess, 2014). However, with appropriate support and intervention as well as the presence of other protective factors, many children experiencing family disruption adjust over time (see Guest, 2012).

RISK FACTORS AND PROTECTIVE FACTORS IN MIDDLE CHILDHOOD

School-age children face a variety of risks that undermine their struggles to develop a sense of purpose and self-worth. Risk factors are anything that increases the probability of a problem condition, its progression into a more severe state, or its maintenance (Luthar, 2003). Risk factors are moderated, however, by protective factors, either internal or external, that help children resist risk (Werner & Brendtro, 2012). Risk and protective factors can be biological, psychological, social, and spiritual, and like all influences on development, they span the micro to macro continuum (Bronfenbrenner, 1996). Dynamic, always-evolving interaction occurs among risk and protective factors present in each dimension of the individual child and his or her environment. During middle childhood, both risk factors and protective factors have been found at the child level, the family level, and the larger system level. As discussed earlier in this chapter, poverty, family and community violence, family disorganization and disruption, and mental and physical challenges serve as major risk factors. Good physical and mental health; good peer relationships; secure family and school attachment; family support and stability; and access to adequate educational, health, and social resources serve as protective factors.

Resilience—or "survival against the odds"—arises from an interplay of risk and protective factors and manifests as adaptive behavior producing positive outcomes (Jenson & Fraser, 2016). A variety of factors influence resilience during middle childhood. Whether a factor presents risk or protection often depends on its interaction with other factors influencing the individual child. For example, a highly structured classroom environment run by a "strict" teacher may function as a protective factor for one child while simultaneously functioning as a risk factor for another child.

The life course and systems perspectives provide tools for understanding positive development during middle childhood. These perspectives also facilitate assessment and intervention efforts. As social workers, we must recognize that resilience is rarely an innate characteristic. Rather, it is a process that may be facilitated by influences within the child's surrounding environment. Indeed, research suggests that high-risk behavior among children increases when they perceive declining family involvement and community support (Benson, Scales, & Roehlkepartain, 2011). A primary goal of the professions dedicated to child well-being must be facilitation of positive external supports for children and enhancement of the person–environment fit so as to maximize protective factors and minimize risk factors.

CRITICAL THINKING Questions 13.5

There is general agreement that poverty and child maltreatment are among the most serious threats to healthy child development. How does poverty threaten physical, cognitive, emotional, social, and spiritual development during middle childhood? How does child maltreatment threaten physical, cognitive, emotional, social, and spiritual development during middle childhood?

IMPLICATIONS FOR SOCIAL WORK PRACTICE

This discussion of middle childhood suggests several practice principles for social workers and other professionals working with children.

- Development is multidimensional and dynamic; recognize the complex ways in which developmental influences interact, and incorporate this understanding into your work with children.
- Support parents and other family members as critically important social, emotional, and spiritual resources for their children.
- Support family, school, and community attempts to stabilize environments for children.
- Incorporate identification of multilevel risk and protective factors into assessment and intervention efforts.
- Recognize and support resilience in children and families. Support the strengths of children and families and their efforts to cope with adversity.
- Recognize the critical influence of the school environment on growth and development, and encourage attempts by school personnel to be responsive to all children and families.
- Understand the important role of peer groups in social and emotional growth and development; facilitate the development and maintenance of positive peer and other social relationships.
- Understand the ways in which the organization of schools reflects and supports the social injustice present in society. Support schools in their efforts to end practices and policies that sustain or reinforce inequalities.
- Facilitate meaningful teacher–family–child communication and school responsiveness to children experiencing difficulties in the school environment.
- Understand the effects of family, community, and societal violence on children and establish prosocial, nurturing, nonviolent environments whenever possible; provide opportunities for positive nurturing and mentoring of children in the school and community environments.
- Become familiar with and implement best practices in areas such as trauma, loss and grief, social skill development, and character education.
- Promote cultural competency and help children and other adults recognize and respect all forms of diversity and difference.

KEY TERMS

capital, 416
cerebral cortex, 411
character education, 416
concrete operations stage, 411
direct bullying, 416
gender dysphoria, 419
indirect bullying, 416
individual education plan (IEP), 430
interrelational intelligence, 412
relative poverty, 427
social competence, 417
trauma, 415
zone of proximal development, 417

ACTIVE LEARNING

1. In small groups, compare and contrast the risk and protective factors present for Anthony Bryant, Brianna Shaw, and Manuel Vega. Brainstorm multilevel interventions you would consider if you were working with each child.
2. Working in pairs, consider the story of Anthony Bryant, Brianna Shaw, or Manuel Vega (as assigned by the instructor). Each pair should identify the relevance of the various developmental theorists discussed in the chapter to the assigned child, focusing on the theorist(s) whose idea(s) seem particularly relevant to the selected child. After approximately 20 minutes, form three small groups consisting of the pairs focusing on the same child. After comparing the similarities and differences in their assessments of the different theories, each group should report back to the full class.
3. As a class, create a list of debate topics raised directly or indirectly in the chapter (e.g., educational assessment/standardized testing, federal spending or programs to address child poverty, gun control to reduce violence against children, family structure and family disruption, inclusion for children with special needs). Debates can take place between teams or individuals. Each side will take 2 minutes to present their case, and each side will also have 1 minute for rebuttal.
4. Use task rotation for important chapter issues such as *family and community violence*: (1) How does child maltreatment or trauma impact childhood development? (2) How are child witnesses impacted by acts of violence? (3) What programs might schools employ to support students impacted by violence? (4) What interventions might a social worker pursue to help families impacted by violence? *Task rotation description*: Questions are posted on chart paper around the room. Each group starts at a question, discusses it, writes ideas in response on the chart paper, and then after a short time (less than 3 minutes) is stopped and rotated to the next chart. At the next chart, they are given a brief period of time to review the work of the previous group and add any ideas the first group missed. The groups are stopped and rotated until all groups have read and added to all issues listed on the charts. Whole-group review follows.

WEB RESOURCES

American Association of University Women

www.aauw.org

Site maintained by the American Association of University Women contains information on education and equity for women and girls, including a report card on Title IX, a law that banned sex discrimination in education.

Child Trauma Academy

www.childtraumaacademy.com

Site presented by the Child Trauma Academy contains information on the impact of child maltreatment on the brain and the physiological and psychological effects of trauma on children.

Child Welfare Information Gateway

www.childwelfare.gov

Site presented by the Administration for Children and Families contains information and resources to protect children and strengthen families, including statistics, prevention information, state statutes, family centered practice, and publications.

Forum on Child and Family Statistics

www.childstats.gov

Official website of the Federal Interagency Forum on Child and Family Statistics offers easy access to federal and state statistics and reports on children and families, including international comparisons.

Search Institute

www.search-institute.org

Site presented by the Search Institute, an independent, nonprofit, nonsectarian organization with the goal of advancing the well-being of adolescents and children, contains information on 40 developmental assets and methods for building assets for child and youth development.

SAGE edge™ Sharpen your skills with SAGE edge at edge.sagepub.com/hutchisoness2e

SAGE edge for students provides a personalized approach to help you accomplish your coursework goals in an easy-to-use learning environment. watch listen read

LEARNING OBJECTIVES	FOR FURTHER EXPLORATION AND APPLICATION
LO 13.1: Compare and contrast one's emotional and cognitive reactions to three case studies.	(read) Keeping It All Inside: Shyness, Internalizing Coping Strategies and Socioemotional Adjustment in Middle Childhood
LO 13.2: Describe how the social context of middle childhood has changed over time and place.	(listen) Roundtable Discussion—Childhood
LO 13.3: Identify some ways the multigenerational family influences middle childhood development.	(listen) When Grandma's House Is Home: The Rise of Grandfamilies
LO 13.4: Summarize typical physical, cognitive, cultural identity, emotional, social, and spiritual development during middle childhood.	(watch) Friendship (watch) Piaget's Conservation Tasks (read) Social Aggression and Social Position in Middle Childhood and Early Adolescence: Burning Bridges or Building Them?
LO 13.5: Analyze the role of formal schooling in middle childhood development.	(watch) Middle Years Pedagogy: Engaging Middle Years Learners (watch) Sociohistorical Influences on Development (watch) Transition to Middle School (watch) Bilingual Education
LO 13.6: Analyze special challenges to middle childhood development.	(read) The Multiple Contexts of Middle Childhood
LO 13.7: Give examples of risk factors and protective factors in middle childhood.	(read) Healthy People 2020—Early and Middle Childhood (watch) Temple Grandin: The World Needs All Kinds of Minds
LO 13.8: Apply knowledge of middle childhood to recommend guidelines for social work assessment and intervention.	(read) Spotlight on Middle Childhood

Visions of America/Contributor/Universal Images Group/Getty Images

WOMEN-POWER-STRONG
DAUGHTER-BEAUTY-JOY
LEE
COO
PER

Adolescence

Susan Ainsley McCarter

Learning Objectives

LO 14.1 Compare and contrast one's emotional and cognitive reactions to three case studies.

LO 14.2 Analyze how the status of adolescence has varied across time and place.

LO 14.3 Describe some of the transitions made in adolescence.

LO 14.4 Summarize biological, psychological, social, and spiritual development during adolescence.

LO 14.5 Analyze major themes in adolescent sexual development.

LO 14.6 Describe some major challenges to adolescent development.

LO 14.7 Give examples of risk factors and protective factors for adolescent development.

LO 14.8 Apply knowledge of adolescence to recommend guidelines for social work assessment and intervention.

CASE STUDY 14.1

DAVID'S COMING-OUT PROCESS

The social worker at Jefferson High School sees many facets of adolescent life. Nothing much surprises her—especially not the way some of the kids hem and haw when they're trying to share what's really on their mind. Take David Costa, for instance. When he shows up for his first appointment, he is simply asked to tell a bit about himself.

"Let's see, I'm 17," he begins. "I'm a center fielder on the varsity baseball team. What else do you want to know? My parents are from Bolivia and are as traditional as you can imagine. My dad, David Sr., teaches history and is the varsity soccer coach here at Jefferson. My mom is a geriatric nurse. I have a younger sister, Patti. Patti Perfect. She goes to the magnet school and is in the eighth grade."

"How are things at home?" his social worker asks.

"Whatever. Patti is perfect, and I'm a 'freak.' They think I'm 'different, arrogant, stubborn.' I don't know what they want me to be. But I don't think that's what I am. That may be because . . . because I'm gay. But I haven't come out to my parents. That's all I need!"

This is obviously a difficult confession for David to make to an adult, but with a little encouragement he continues: "There are a few other seniors at Jefferson who are out, but they aren't student athletes and so I don't really spend any time with them. Basically when the whole baseball team is together or when I'm with other kids from school, I just act straight. I talk about girls' bodies just like the other guys. I think that is the hardest, not being able to be yourself. It was really hard when I was about 13. I was so confused. I knew that men were supposed to be with women, not other men. What I was feeling was not 'normal,' and I thought I was the only one. I wanted to kill myself. That was a bad time."

David's tone changes. "Let's talk about something good. Let me tell you about Theo. I think Theo is hot! He's got a great body. I wonder if he'd like to hang out together—get to know me. He's a junior, and if we got together, I would hear about it. But I keep thinking about him and looking at him during school. I just need to say something to him. There's a club downtown that has an all ages night, maybe I could get him in."

CASE STUDY 14.2

CARL'S STRUGGLE FOR IDENTITY

Whereas David seeks out the social worker, Carl Fleischer, another 17-year-old, is sent to the social worker's office at the high school. He matter-of-factly shares that he is "an underachiever." He used to get an occasional B in his classes, but now it's mostly C's with an occasional D.

When Carl is asked what he likes to do in his spare time, he replies, "I get high and play Xbox." Further probing elicits one-word answers until the social worker asks Carl about relationships. His face contorts as he slaps his ample belly: "I'm not exactly a sex symbol. According to my doctor, I'm a fatso. He says normal boys my age and height weigh at least 50 pounds less than I do. He also tells me to quit smoking and get some exercise. Whatever. My mom says I'm big-boned. She says my dad was the same way. I wouldn't know. I never met the scumbag. He left when my mom was pregnant. But you probably don't want to hear about that."

Carl won't say more on that topic, but with more prodding, he finally talks about his job, delivering pizzas two nights a week and on the weekends. "So if you need pizzas, call me at Antonio's. I always bring pies home for my mom on Tuesday and Friday nights. She works late those nights and so we usually eat pizza and catch the Tuesday and Friday night lineups on TV. She lets me smoke in the house—cigarettes, not weed. Although I have gotten high in the house a couple times. Anyway, I am not what you would call popular. I am just a fat, slow geek and a pizza guy. But there are some heads who come into Antonio's. I exchange pies for dope. Works out pretty well: They get the munchies, and the pies keep me in with the heads!"

CASE STUDY 14.3

MONICA'S QUEST FOR MASTERY

Monica Golden, a peer counselor at Jefferson High, hangs around to chat after a meeting of the peer counselors. Monica is the eldest and tallest daughter in a family of five kids. Monica's mother is the assistant principal at Grover Middle School, and her father works for the Internal Revenue Service. This year, in addition to being a Jefferson peer counselor, Monica is the vice president of the senior class, the treasurer for the Young Republicans, a starter on the track team, and a teacher at Sunday school.

When the social worker comments on the scope of these activities, Monica replies, "I really do stay busy. I worked at the mall last year, but it was hard to keep my grades up. I'm trying to get into college, so my family and I decided I shouldn't work this year. So I just babysit sometimes. A lot of my aunts and uncles have me watch their kids, but they don't pay me. They consider it a family favor. Anyway, I am waiting to hear back from colleges. They should be sending out the letters this week. You know, the fatter the envelope the better. It doesn't take many words to say, 'No. We reject you.' And I need to either get into a state school or get a scholarship so that I can use my savings for tuition."

Next they talk a little about Monica's options, and she shares that her first choice is Howard University. "I want to surround myself with Black scholars and role models, and my dream is to be a pediatrician, you know. I love kids," Monica says. "I tried tons of jobs—that's where I got the savings. And, well, those with kids I enjoyed the most. Like I said, I've worked retail at the mall. I've worked at the supermarket as a cashier. I've worked at the snack bar at the pool. And I've been babysitting since I was 12. That's what I like the most.

"I'd love to have kids someday. But I don't even have a boyfriend. I wear glasses. My parents say I don't need contacts; they think I'm being vain. Not that I don't have a boyfriend because I wear glasses. Guys think I'm an overachiever. They think I'm driven and demanding and incapable of having fun. That's what I've been told. I think I'm just ambitious and extroverted. But really, I just haven't had much time to date in high school. I've been so busy. Well, gotta run."

THE SOCIAL CONSTRUCTION OF ADOLESCENCE ACROSS TIME AND SPACE

If we were asked to describe David Costa, Carl Fleischer, and Monica Golden, attention would probably be drawn to their status as adolescents. Worldwide, the current generation of adolescents is the largest in history, and youth ages 10 to 24 comprise one quarter of the world's population. Nearly 90% of these youth live in low-income and middle-income countries, where they comprise a much larger proportion of the population than they do in high-income countries (Sawyer et al., 2012).

The adolescent status has changed across time and cultures. Adolescence was invented as a psychosocial concept in the late 19th and early 20th centuries as the United States made the transition from an agrarian to an urban-industrial society (Choudhury, 2010). Prior to this time, adolescents worked beside adults, doing what adults did for the most part (Leeder, 2004). This is still the case for adolescents in many nonindustrial societies today, and in some cultures adolescence is not recognized as a stage at all (Gardiner & Kosmitzki, 2011). As the United States and other societies became urbanized and industrialized, child labor legislation and compulsory education policies were passed, and adolescents were moved from the workplace to the school and became economically dependent on parents. The juvenile justice system was created in the United States in 1899 because youthful offenders had come to be regarded as different from adult offenders, with less culpability for their crimes because of their immaturity.

In 1904, G. Stanley Hall, the first president of the American Psychological Association, published a book about adolescence in which he proposed that adolescence is a period of "storm and stress," a period when hormones cause many psychological and social difficulties. Hall was later involved in the eugenics movement, a movement that intended to improve the human population by controlled selective breeding, and there seems to be racist and classist bias in his work on adolescence, which was not unusual in his time. His discussion suggests that poor youth are at risk of trouble because of their heredity whereas middle-class youth are at risk of being corrupted by the world around them (Finn, 2009). Janet Finn (2009) argues that the public, professional, and scholarly conversations about adolescence in the 20th and beginning of the 21st century have focused on adolescents as "trouble."

© iStockphoto.com/4x6

Adolescence is a period filled with transitional themes in every dimension of life: biological, psychological, social, and spiritual.

Jane Kroger (2007) suggests that many societies are clear about what they want their adolescents to avoid (alcohol and other drugs, delinquency, and pregnancy) but not as clear about what positive things they would like their youth to achieve. There is growing agreement that the societal context in which adolescence is experienced in the United States and other wealthy nations is becoming increasingly less supportive for adolescent development (Choudhury, 2010). This concern has led, in recent years, to the construction of a positive youth development movement, which has focused on youth "as resources to be developed, and not as problems to be managed" (Silbereisen & Lerner, 2007a, p. 7).

Perhaps no life course phase has been the subject of more recent empirical research than adolescence. Most prominently, the National Longitudinal Study of Adolescent Health (Add Health) was initiated at the Carolina Population Center in 1994. It is a study of a representative sample of adolescents in Grades 7 through 12 during the 1994–1995 school year. This cohort was followed into young adulthood in 2008, when the sample was 24 to 32 years of age. The Add Health study includes measures of social, economic, psychological, and physical well-being as well as contextual information on the family, neighborhood, community, school, friendships, peer groups, and romantic relationships. Add Health data are now generating large numbers of research reports, a partial list of which can be retrieved at the website listed at the end of this chapter.

THE TRANSITION FROM CHILDHOOD TO ADULTHOOD

The word *adolescence* originates from the Latin verb *adolescere*, which means "to grow into maturity." It is a period of life filled with transitional themes in every dimension of the configuration of person and environment: biological, psychological, social, and spiritual. These themes do not occur independently or without affecting one another. For example, David Costa's experience may be complicated because he is gay and because his family relationships are strained, but it is also strengthened by his supportive friendships and his participation in sports. Carl Fleischer's transition is marked by several challenges—his weight, his substance use, his lack of a relationship with his father, his academic performance—but also by the promise of his developing computer expertise and entrepreneurial skills. Monica Golden's movement through adolescence may be eased by her academic, athletic, and social success, but it also could be taxed by her busy schedule and high expectations for herself.

Many cultures have specific **rites of passage**—ceremonies that demarcate the transition from childhood to adulthood. Often these rites include sexual themes, marriage themes, themes of becoming a man or a woman, themes of added responsibility, or themes of increased insight or understanding. Such rites of passage are found in most nonindustrialized societies (Gardiner & Kosmitzki, 2011). For example, among the Massai ethnic group in Kenya and Tanzania, males and females are both circumcised at about age 13, and males are considered junior warriors and sent to live with other junior warriors (Leeder, 2004). For the most part, the transition from adolescence to adulthood is not marked by such clearly defined rituals in North America and many other Western countries, but some groups in North America continue to practice rites of passage (Gardiner & Kosmitzki, 2011). Some scholars who study adolescence have suggested that where there are no clear-cut puberty rituals, adolescents will devise their own rituals, such as "hazing, tattooing, dieting, dress, and beautification rituals" (Kroger, 2007, p. 41).

Even without a cultural rite of passage, all adolescents experience profound biological, psychological, social, and spiritual changes. In economically advanced societies, these changes have been divided into three phases: early adolescence (ages 11 to 14), middle adolescence (ages 15 to 17), and late adolescence (ages 18 to 22). Exhibit 14.1 summarizes the typical biological, psychological, and social developments in these three phases. Of course, adolescent development varies from person to person and with time, culture, and other aspects of the environment. Yet deviations from the normative patterns of adolescent change may have psychological ramifications, because adolescents are so quick to compare their own development with that of their peers and because of the cultural messages they receive about acceptable appearance and behavior.

BIOLOGICAL ASPECTS OF ADOLESCENCE

Adolescence is a period of great physical change, marked by a rapid growth spurt in the early years, maturation of the reproductive system, redistribution of body weight, and continuing brain development. Adequate care of the body during this exciting time is of paramount importance.

EXHIBIT 14.1 • Typical Adolescent Development

STAGE OF ADOLESCENCE	BIOLOGICAL CHANGES	PSYCHOLOGICAL CHANGES	SOCIAL CHANGES
Early (11–14)	Hormonal changes Beginning of puberty Physical appearance changes Possible experimentation with sex and substances	Reactions to physical changes, including early maturation Concrete/present-oriented thought Body modesty Moodiness	Changes in relationships with parents and peers Less school structure Distancing from culture/tradition Seeking sameness
Middle (15–17)	Completion of puberty and physical appearance changes Possible experimentation with sex and substances	Reactions to physical changes, including late maturation Increased autonomy Increased abstract thought Beginning of identity development Preparation for college or career	Heightened social situation decision making Continue to renegotiate family relationships More focus on peer group Beginning of one-to-one romantic relationships Moving toward greater community participation
Late (18–22)	Slowing of physical changes Possible experimentation with sex and substances	Formal operational thought Continuation of identity development Moral reasoning	Very little school/life structure Beginning of intimate relationships Renewed interest in culture/tradition

PUBERTY

Puberty is the period of the life course in which the reproductive system matures. It is a process that begins before any biological changes are visible and occurs through interrelated neurological and endocrinological changes that affect brain development, sexual maturation, levels and cycles of hormones, and physical growth. The hypothalamus, pituitary gland, adrenal glands, and **gonads** (ovaries and testes) begin to interact and stimulate increased hormone production. It is the increase of these hormones that leads to the biological changes. Although androgens are typically referred to as male hormones and estrogens as female hormones, males and females in fact produce all three major **sex hormones**: androgens, progestins, and estrogens. Sex hormones affect the development and functioning of the gonads (including sperm production and ova maturation) and mating and child-caring behavior.

During puberty, increased levels of androgens in males stimulate the development and functioning of the male reproductive system; increased levels of progestins and estrogens in females stimulate the development and functioning of the female reproductive system. Specifically, the androgen testosterone, which is produced in males by the testes, affects the maturation and functioning of the penis, prostate gland, and other male genitals; the secondary sex characteristics; and the sex drive. The estrogen estradiol, which is produced in females by the ovaries, affects the maturation and functioning of the ovaries, uterus, and other female genitals; the secondary sex characteristics; and child-caring behaviors.

Primary sex characteristics are those directly related to the reproductive organs and external genitalia. For boys, these include growth of the penis and scrotum. During adolescence, the penis typically doubles or triples in length. Girls' primary sex characteristics are not so visible but include growth of the ovaries, uterus, vagina, clitoris, and labia.

Secondary sex characteristics are those not directly related to the reproductive organs and external genitalia. Secondary sex characteristics are enlarged breasts and hips for girls, facial hair and deeper voices for boys, and hair and sweat gland changes for both sexes. Female breast development is distinguished by growth of the mammary glands, nipples, and areolae. The tone of the male voice lowers as the larynx enlarges and the vocal cords lengthen. Both boys and girls begin to grow hair around their genitals and then under their arms. This hair begins with a fine texture and light color and then becomes curlier, coarser, and darker. During this period, the sweat glands also begin to produce noticeable odors.

Puberty is often described as beginning with the onset of menstruation in girls and production of sperm in boys, but these are not the first events in the puberty process. Menstruation is the periodic sloughing off of the lining of the uterus. This lining provides nutrients for the fertilized egg. If the egg is not fertilized, the lining sloughs off and is discharged through the vagina. However, for a girl to become capable of reproduction, she must not only menstruate but also ovulate. Ovulation, the release of an egg from an ovary, usually does not begin until several months after **menarche**, the onset of menstruation. For boys to reproduce, **spermarche**—the onset of the ability to ejaculate mobile sperm—must occur. Spermarche does not occur until after several ejaculations.

Girls typically first notice breast growth, then growth of pubic hair, and then body growth, especially hips. They then experience menarche; then growth of underarm hair; and finally, an increase in production of glandular oil and sweat, possibly with body odor and acne. Boys typically follow a similar pattern, first noticing growth of the testes; then growth of pubic hair; body growth; growth of penis; change in voice; growth of facial and underarm hair; and finally, an increase in the production of glandular oil and sweat, possibly with body odor and acne. Girls experience the growth spurt before they have the capacity for reproduction, but the opposite is the case for boys (Kroger, 2007).

Pubertal timing varies greatly. Generally, girls begin puberty about 2 years earlier than boys. Normal pubertal rates (meaning those experienced by 95% of the population) are for girls to begin menstruating between the ages of 9 and 17 and for boys to begin producing sperm between the ages of 11 and 16 (Rew, 2005). The age at which puberty begins has been declining in this century, but there is some controversy about the extent of this shift. There is evidence that puberty arrives earlier in economically advanced countries than in low-income countries and that nutrition and other living conditions play a role (Newman & Newman, 2012).

In addition to changes instigated by sex hormones, adolescents experience growth spurts. Bones are augmented by cartilage during adolescence, and the cartilage calcifies later, during the transition to adulthood. Typically, boys develop broader shoulders, straighter hips, and longer forearms and legs; girls typically develop narrower shoulders and broader hips. These skeletal differences are then enhanced by the development of additional upper body musculature for boys and the development of additional fat deposits on thighs, hips, and buttocks for girls. These changes account for differences in male and female weight and strength.

THE ADOLESCENT BRAIN

As recently as 30 years ago, it was thought that human brain development was finalized by early childhood (Choudhury, 2010). In the past 15 years, however, neuroimaging techniques have allowed researchers to study how the brain changes across the life course, and there is no doubt that the brain changes a great deal during adolescence (Colver & Longwell, 2013). Researchers are now able to study the adolescent brain using both magnetic resonance imaging (MRI), which provides an image of brain structure, and functional magnetic resonance imaging (fMRI), which provides a picture of metabolic function under specific circumstances (Blakemore, 2012). As discussed in earlier chapters, researchers have known for some time that the brain overproduces gray matter from development in the womb to about the age of 3 years, is highly plastic and thus shaped by experience, and goes through a pruning process. The neural connections or synapses that get exercised are retained during pruning, whereas the ones that are not exercised are eliminated. New brain research suggests that the adolescent brain undergoes another period of overproduction of gray matter just prior to puberty, peaking at about 11 years of age for girls and 12 years for boys, followed by another round of pruning. This process, like the infant's, is also affected by the individual's interactions with the outside world (Colver & Longwell, 2013).

Much interest surrounds recent findings about frontal lobe development during adolescence. The pruning process just described allows the brain to be more efficient to change in response to environmental demands and also facilitates improved integration of brain activities. Recent research indicates that pruning occurs in some parts of the brain earlier than in others, in general progressing from the back to the front part of the brain, with the frontal lobes among the latest to show the structural changes. The frontal lobes are key players in the "executive functions" of planning, working memory, and impulse control, and the latest research indicates that they may not be fully developed until about age 25 (Blakemore & Robbins, 2012). Because of the relatively late development of the frontal lobes, particularly the prefrontal cortex, different neuronal circuits are involved in the adolescent brain under different emotional conditions. Researchers make a distinction between "cold cognition" problem solving and "hot cognition" problem solving during adolescence. Cold-cognition problem solving occurs when the adolescent is alone and calm, as he or she typically would be in the laboratory. Conversely, hot-cognition problem solving occurs in situations where teens are with peers, emotions are running high, they are feeling sexual tension, and so on. The research indicates that in situations of cold cognition, adolescents or even preadolescents as young as 12 or 13 can reason and problem solve as well as or better than adults. However, in situations of hot cognition, adolescent problem solving is much more impulsive (Blakemore & Robbins, 2012).

Similar to all social mammals, human adolescents tend to demonstrate increased novelty seeking, increased risk taking, and greater affiliation with peers (Colver & Longwell, 2013). Yet, for most individuals, these activities peak in adolescence and then taper off as newly formed identities set and youth mature out of these tendencies (Spear, 2010; Steinberg, 2009). Brain research does not yet allow researchers to make definitive statements about the relationship between these adolescent behavior changes and changes in the brain, but these connections are being studied. Overall, as compared with adults, three themes have emerged: (1) adolescents do not yet have adult levels of maturity, responsibility, impulse control, and self-regulation; (2) adolescents are less autonomous and more susceptible to outside pressures (such as those from their peers) than adults; and (3) adolescents are less capable than adults of weighing potential consequences and considering future implications of their behavior (McCarter & Bridges, 2011; Spear, 2010). The emerging research on the adolescent brain is raising issues about social policy related to adolescents and is being used in ways that may be both helpful and hurtful to adolescent development (Steinberg, 2009). This is illustrated by two examples from the past 15 years. In 2005, the U.S. Supreme Court heard the case of *Roper v. Simmons* (543 U.S. 551), involving 17-year-old Christopher Simmons, who had been convicted of murdering a woman during a robbery. He had been sentenced to death for his crime. His defense team argued that his still developing adolescent brain made him less culpable for his crime than an adult, and therefore he should not be subject to the death penalty. The neuroscience evidence may have tipped the scales in the Supreme Court's decision to overturn the death penalty for Simmons and all other juveniles (Haider, 2006). In another example, in 2006, the state of Kansas used an interpretation of neuroscience research to stipulate that "sexual acts with individuals under 16 years of age are illegal regardless of the age of the defendant." This would include any consensual touching by youth and classify such as criminal statutory rape except in instances where the individuals are married (Kansas Statutes, § 21-3502 and § 21-3504; Johnson, Blum, & Giedd, 2009).

The question being raised is, what is the extent of human agency, the capacity for decision making, among adolescents? The answer to that question will vary from adolescent to adolescent. There is great risk that neuroscience research will be overgeneralized to the detriment of adolescents. Johnson et al. (2009) caution that it is important to put the adolescent brain in context, remembering that there are complex interactions of the brain with other biological systems as well as with "multiple interactive influences including experience, parenting, socioeconomic status, individual agency and self-efficacy, nutrition, culture, psychological well-being, the physical and built environments, and social relationships and interactions" (p. 219). Johnson and colleagues also recommend that we avoid focusing on pathology and deficits in adolescent development and use neuroscience to examine the unique strengths and potentials of the adolescent brain. Colver and Longwell (2013) argue that though the adolescent brain leads to greater risk taking, it supports the challenges specific to adolescence and allows adolescents to "push ideas and boundaries to the limit" (p. 905). That perspective is in keeping with the increasing focus on positive psychology and the related positive youth development movement.

NUTRITION, EXERCISE, AND SLEEP

At any stage along the life course, the right balance of nutrition, exercise, and sleep is important. As the transition from childhood to adulthood begins, early adolescent bodies undergo significant biological changes from their brains to the hair follicles on their legs and everywhere in between. Yet it appears that few adolescents maintain a healthy balance during their time in adolescent flux.

In many parts of the world, adolescents simply cannot get access to an adequate diet, resulting in high levels of anemia and youth who are underweight and overweight (Sawyer et al., 2012). In economically advanced nations, there is enough to eat, but adolescents often do not have a satisfactory diet to support the adolescent growth and development. In the United States, the Department of Health and Human Services (HHS) and the Department of Agriculture (USDA) worked together to develop the Dietary Guidelines for Americans (which is to be updated every 5 years; see http://health.gov/dietaryguidelines). For older children and adolescents (ages 4 to 18), they recommend that 45% to 65% of one's diet be from carbohydrates, 10% to 30% be from proteins, and 25% to 35% from fats. Additionally, adolescents should consume 2 cups of fruit (not from juice) and 2½ cups of vegetables a day (for a 2,000-calorie intake); choose a variety of fruits and vegetables each day; choose from all five vegetable subgroups—dark green, orange, legumes, starchy vegetables, and other vegetables—several times a week; consume 3 or more ounce equivalents of whole-grain products per day; consume 3 cups per day of fat-free or low-fat milk or equivalent milk products; consume most of their fat intake from sources of polyunsaturated and monounsaturated fatty acids, such as fish, nuts, and vegetable oils; and consume less than 2,300 mg (approximately 1 teaspoon of salt) of sodium per day (U.S. Department of Agriculture & U.S. Department of Health and Human Services [USDA/USDHHS], 2010).

The National Youth Risk Behavior Survey (YRBS) for 2011 (Eaton et al., 2012) suggests that in the United States only 22.4% of young people in Grades 9 to 12 had eaten at least five fruits and vegetables a day in the past 7 days, and 13.1% of students had not eaten breakfast at least once in the past 7 days. This is unfortunate, given the need for well-balanced diets and increased caloric intake during a period of rapid neurobiological and physical growth. Many U.S. youth say they don't have time to eat breakfast or that they aren't hungry in the morning. Yet the research is rather convincing, indicating that adolescent students who eat breakfast report higher energy and less fatigue and perform better on cognitive tests than students who do not eat breakfast (Cooper, Bandelow, & Nevill, 2011).

During adolescence, the right balance of nutrition, exercise, and sleep are important.

The recommendation is for most people of every age to engage in regular physical activity and reduce sedentary activities to promote health, psychological well-being, and a healthy body weight. Physical fitness should be achieved by including cardiovascular conditioning, stretching exercises for flexibility, and resistance exercises or calisthenics for muscle strength and endurance. The specific recommendation for adolescents (6 to 17 years old) is to engage in at least 60 minutes of physical activity on most, preferably all, days of the week (USDA/USDHHS, 2010).

Again, the data are not promising. Nationwide, 49.5% of high school students reported being physically active for a total of at least 60 minutes a day on at least 5 of the 7 days preceding the survey. Conversely, 31.1% of students played video or computer games, or used the computer for something other than schoolwork, for 3 hours or more on an average school day, and 32.4% watched television for 3 hours or more on an average school day (Eaton et al., 2012).

Along with other changes of puberty, there are marked changes in sleep patterns (National Sleep Foundation, 2013). Changes in circadian rhythms create a tendency to be more alert late at night and to wake later in the morning. Given the mismatch of these sleep patterns with the timing of the school day, adolescents often doze off during the school day. Sleep researchers suggest that adolescents require 8½ to 9¼ hours of sleep each night (National Sleep Foundation, 2013).

Researchers have found that typical adolescents in the United States are chronically sleep-deprived (Moreno, Furtner, & Rivara, 2010). Survey data show that only 15% of U.S. adolescents get at least 8½ hours of sleep on school nights (National Sleep Foundation, 2013).

Moreover, sleep deprivation has recently been linked to poor food choices. In their 2013 study of 13,284 teens, Krueger, Reither, Peppard, Krueger, and Hale found that 18% of youth slept less than 7 hours a night. Adolescents with sleep deprivation were less likely than well-slept adolescents to eat healthy food throughout the week and were more likely to eat fast food at least twice a week

(Krueger et al., 2013). School performance is affected by insufficient sleep (Wong et al., 2013). One research team found that cognitive performance was impaired in Spanish male adolescents who slept less than 8 hours a day, but this was not found to be the case for female adolescents (Ortega et al., 2010). Mood is also improved by sufficient sleep (Wong et al., 2013). As suggested, the risks of sleep deprivation are varied, and they can be serious (National Sleep Foundation, 2013). Drowsiness or falling asleep at the wheel is a principal cause of at least 100,000 U.S. police-reported traffic collisions annually. Sleep deficit contributes to acne, aggressive behavior, eating too much or unhealthy foods, illness, and unsafe use of equipment. It also heightens the effects of alcohol and can lead to increased use of caffeine and nicotine (National Sleep Foundation, 2013).

CRITICAL THINKING Questions 14.1

What are the implications of recent research findings about the adolescent brain for social policy? This research is leading to a number of policy discussions about several issues, including the timing of the school day; regulations for adolescent driving, including the legal age of driving, whether evening driving should be allowed, whether other adolescents can be present in the car of an adolescent driver, and so on; the drinking age; and the age when a juvenile can be tried as an adult in a court of law. What opinions do you hold about these issues? How are those opinions shaped by recent brain research?

PSYCHOLOGICAL ASPECTS OF ADOLESCENCE

Psychological development in adolescence is multifaceted. Adolescents have psychological reactions, sometimes dramatic, to the biological, social, and cultural dimensions of their lives. They become capable of and interested in discovering and forming their psychological selves. They may show heightened creativity as well as interest in humanitarian issues; ethics; religion; and reflection and record keeping, as in a diary (Rew, 2005). There is evidence that adolescence is a time of increased emotional complexity and a growing capacity to understand and express a wider range of emotions and to gain insight into one's own emotions (Silvers et al., 2012). Three areas of psychological development are particularly noteworthy: psychological reactions to biological changes, changes in cognition, and identity development.

PSYCHOLOGICAL REACTIONS TO BIOLOGICAL CHANGES

"Will my body ever start changing? Will my body ever stop changing? Is this normal? Am I normal? Why am I suddenly interested in girls? And why are the girls all taller (and stronger) than me? How can I ask Mom if I can shave my legs?" These are some of the questions mentioned when Jane Kroger (2007, pp. 33–34) asked a class of 12- and 13-year-old adolescents what type of questions they think most about. As you can see, themes of biological changes were pervasive. If you can remember your own puberty process, you probably are not surprised that researchers have found that pubertal adolescents are preoccupied with physical changes and appearances (Price, 2009). Young adolescents are able to reflect on and give meaning to their biological transformations. Of course, responses to puberty are influenced by the way other people, including parents, siblings, teachers, and peers, respond to the adolescent's changing body. In addition, reactions to puberty are influenced by other events in the adolescent's life, such as school transition, family conflict, and peer relationships. Media images also play an important role (Krayer, Ingledew, & Iphofen, 2008).

It appears that puberty in the United States is usually viewed more positively by boys than by girls, with boys focused on increased muscle mass and physical strength and girls focused on increased body weight and fat deposits (Price, 2009). For girls, body dissatisfaction and self-consciousness peaks from ages 13 to 15. There is evidence that African American adolescent girls are more satisfied with their body image and less inclined to eating disorders than Caucasian American girls, most likely due to a different cultural valuing of thinness in females (Franko & Striegel-Moore, 2002). Reactions to menstruation are often mixed (Uskul, 2004). One study of Chinese American adolescent girls found 85% reported that they were annoyed and embarrassed by their first menstruation, but 66% also reported positive feelings (Tang, Yeung, & Lee, 2003). In a focus group of 53 women from 34 different countries, most of the participants had vivid memories of their first menstruation. They reported both positive and negative emotions, but negative reactions (such as embarrassment, shame, fear, shock, and confusion) were more often noted. Reactions to menarche were greatly affected by the type of information and level of support that the young women received from their mothers (Uskul, 2004). Research shows that pubescent girls talk with parents and friends about their first menstruation, but pubescent boys do not discuss with anyone their first ejaculation, an event sometimes seen as the closest male equivalent to first menstruation (Kroger, 2007). Pubescent boys may receive less information from adults about nocturnal ejaculations than their sisters receive about menarche.

Because the onset and experience of puberty vary greatly, adolescents need reassurance regarding their own growth patterns. Some adolescents will be considered early maturers, and some will be considered late maturers. Timing and tempo of puberty are influenced by genetics, and there are ethnic differences, as well. On average, African American adolescents enter puberty earlier than Mexican American adolescents, who enter puberty earlier than Caucasian Americans (Chumlea et al., 2003). There are psychological and social consequences of early maturing for both male and female adolescents, but the research findings are not always consistent. A recent longitudinal study of Australian children found that those who experienced early puberty had more adjustment problems than their age peers; this was true for both boys and girls (Mensah et al., 2013). The researchers found, however, that the children who entered puberty early demonstrated more adjustment problems from early childhood through early adolescence. They concluded that the data support a "life course hypothesis that differences in pubertal timing and childhood adjustment may at least in part result from genetic and environmental factors early in life" (Mensah et al., 2013, p. 122). Further longitudinal research is needed to provide better understanding of the early risk factors for a difficult transition to puberty.

CHANGES IN COGNITION

Adolescence is considered to be a crucial phase in cognitive development, with development occurring in three main areas (Sanders, 2013):

1. *Improved reasoning skills*: the ability to consider a range of possibilities, to think hypothetically, and to engage in logical analysis
2. *Abstract thinking*: the ability to imagine things not seen or experienced
3. *Meta-cognition*: the ability to think about thinking

These abilities are components of Jean Piaget's fourth stage of cognitive development called formal operational thought (see Exhibit 4.1 in Chapter 4 in this book for an overview of Piaget's stages of cognitive development). *Formal operational thought* suggests the capacity to apply hypothetical reasoning to various situations and the ability to use symbols to solve problems.

Whereas younger children focus on the here-and-now world in front of them, the adolescent brain is capable of hypothesizing beyond the present objects. This ability also allows adolescents to engage in decision making based on a cost-benefit analysis. As noted, brain research indicates that adolescent problem solving is as good as adult problem solving in cold-cognition situations but is not equally sound in hot-cognition situations. Furthermore, brain development alone does not result in formal operational thinking. The developing brain needs social environments that encourage hypothetical, abstract reasoning and opportunities to investigate the world (Cohen & Sandy, 2007; Gehlbach, 2006). Formal operational thinking is more imperative in some cultures than in others but is most imperative in many fields in the changing economic base of postindustrialized societies. One research team found that Taiwanese adolescents, who are reared in a collectivist culture, exercise formal operational thinking but rely on parents and other important people to validate their thoughts (Lee & Beckert, 2012). More research is needed to explore cultural variations in cognitive autonomy. It is also important to remember that although contemporary education is organized to facilitate formal operational thinking, students in the United States and around the world do not have equal access to sound curriculum and instruction.

Recent research is suggesting that adolescence is a period of profound advancements in social cognition, which is the processing, storing, and using of information about other people. Brain researchers are identifying the brain regions that are involved in *mentalizing*, or the ability to think about the mental states and intentions of others, and finding that these regions of the brain continue to develop throughout adolescence (Blakemore & Robbins, 2012). They argue that this helps to explain why adolescents are more sociable, form more complex peer relationships, and are more sensitive to peer acceptance and rejection than younger children (Blakemore, 2012). One research team has investigated another way of thinking about changes in social cognition during adolescence. They found that group identity becomes a dominant theme in early adolescence, and automatic evaluations develop based on in-group and out-group memberships, with a tendency for positive evaluation of in-group members and negative evaluation of out-group members. They found that although younger children are aware of group identities, they do not develop automatic evaluations based on them (Degner & Wentura, 2010). This would suggest that early adolescence is a good time to help young people think about their automatic evaluations related to group identity.

IDENTITY DEVELOPMENT

There is growing agreement that identity is a complex concept. **Psychological identity** is a "person's self-definition as a separate and distinct individual" (Gardiner & Kosmitzki, 2011, p. 165). **Social identity** is the part of the self-concept that comes from knowledge of one's membership in a social group and the emotional significance of that membership (Gardiner & Kosmitzki, 2011). Lene Arnett Jensen (2003) suggests that adolescents increasingly develop multicultural identities as they are exposed to diverse cultural beliefs, either through firsthand experience or through the media. She argues that the process of developing an identity presents new challenges to adolescents in a global society. Jensen gives the example of arranged marriage in India, noting that on the one hand, Indian adolescents grow up with cultural values favoring arranged marriage, but on the other hand, they are increasingly exposed to values that emphasize freedom of choice. But identity is even more complex than that; it is increasingly examined from an *intersectional* perspective that recognizes the multiple social identities we must integrate, including gender identity, ethnic/racial identity, religious identity, social class identity, national identity, regional identity, and so on (see Shade, Kools, Weiss, & Pinderhughes, 2011).

Theories of Self and Identity

A number of prominent psychologists have put forward theories that address self or psychological identity development in adolescence. Exhibit 14.2 provides an overview of six theorists: Freud, Erikson, Kegan, Marcia, Piaget, and Kohlberg. All six help to explain how a concept of self or identity develops, and all six suggest that it cannot develop fully before adolescence. Piaget and Kohlberg suggest that some individuals may not reach higher levels of identity development at all.

Sigmund Freud (1905/1953) thought of human development as a series of five psychosexual stages in the expression of libido (sensual pleasure). The fifth stage, the genital stage, occurs in adolescence, when reproduction and sexual intimacy become possible.

Building on Freud's work, Erik Erikson (1950, 1959, 1963, 1968) proposed eight stages of psychosocial development (refer back to Exhibit 4.11 in Chapter 4 in this book for a summary of Erikson's eight stages). Erikson's fifth stage, identity versus identity diffusion, is relevant to adolescence. The developmental task is to establish a coherent sense of identity; failure to complete this task successfully leaves the adolescent without a solid sense of identity.

Robert Kegan (1982, 1994) asserts that there should be another stage between middle childhood and adolescence in Erikson's model. He suggests that before working on psychological identity, early adolescents face the psychosocial conflict of affiliation versus abandonment. The main concern is being accepted by a group, and the fear is being left behind or rejected. Successful accomplishment of group membership allows the young person to turn to the question of "Who am I?" in mid- and late adolescence.

James Marcia (1966, 1980) expanded on Erikson's notion that adolescents struggle with the issue of identity versus identity diffusion, and his theory is the most researched of adolescent identity. Marcia proposed that adolescents vary in how easily they go about developing a personal identity, and he described four identity statuses based on two aspects of identity development—the amount of exploration being done toward identity development and the amount of commitment to a particular identity:

1. *Identity diffusion*: no commitment made to roles and values, with or without exploration
2. *Foreclosure*: commitment made to roles and values without exploration
3. *Moratorium*: exploration of roles and values without commitment
4. *Identity achievement*: exploration of roles and values followed by commitment

Jean Piaget proposed four major stages leading to adult thought (refer back to Exhibit 4.1 in Chapter 4 in this book for an overview of Piaget's stages). He expected the last stage, the **formal operations stage**, to occur in adolescence, enabling the adolescent to engage in more

EXHIBIT 14.2 • Theories of Self or Identity in Adolescence

THEORIST	DEVELOPMENTAL STAGE	MAJOR TASK OR PROCESS
Freud	Genital stage	To develop libido capable of reproduction and sexual intimacy
Erikson	Identity versus identity diffusion	To find one's place in the world through self-certainty versus apathy, role experimentation versus negative identity, and anticipation of achievement versus work paralysis
Kegan	Affiliation versus abandonment (early adolescence)	To search for membership, acceptance, and group identity, versus a sense of being left behind, rejected, and abandoned
Marcia	Ego identity statuses	To develop one of these identity statuses: identity diffusion, foreclosure, moratorium, or identity achievement
Piaget	Formal operational thought	To develop the capacity for abstract problem formulation, hypothesis development, and solution testing
Kohlberg	Postconventional morality	To develop moral principles that transcend one's own society: individual ethics, societal rights, and universal principles of right and wrong

abstract thinking about "who I am." Piaget (1972) also thought that adolescents begin to use formal operational skills to think in terms of what is best for society.

Lawrence Kohlberg (1976, 1984) expanded on Piaget's ideas about moral thinking to describe three major levels of moral development (refer back to Exhibit 4.3 in Chapter 4 in this book for an overview of Kohlberg's stage theory). Kohlberg thought that adolescents become capable of **postconventional moral reasoning**, or morality based on moral principles that transcend social rules, but that many never go beyond conventional morality, or morality based on social rules.

Scholars generally agree that identity formation is structured by the sociocultural context (see Gardiner & Kosmitzki, 2011; Kroger, 2007). Thus, the options offered to adolescents vary across cultures. Societies such as North American and other Western societies that put a high value on autonomy offer more options for adolescents than more collectivist-oriented societies. Some writers suggest that having a large number of options increases stress for adolescents (Gardiner & Kosmitzki, 2011). Think about the case studies of David Costa, Carl Fleischer, and Monica Golden. What is the sociocultural context of their identity struggles? What choices do they have, given their sociocultural contexts?

For those aspects of identity that we shape ourselves, individuals have four ways of trying on and developing a preference for certain identities.

1. *Future orientation.* By adolescence, youth have developed two important cognitive skills: They are able to consider the future, and they are able to construct abstract thoughts. These skills allow them to choose from a list of hypothetical behaviors based on the potential outcomes resulting from those behaviors. David Costa demonstrates future orientation in his contemplation regarding Theo. Adolescents also contemplate potential future selves.

2. *Role experimentation.* According to Erikson (1963), adolescence provides a psychosocial moratorium—a period during which youth have the latitude to experiment with social roles. Thus, adolescents typically sample membership in different cliques, build relationships with various mentors, take various academic electives, and join assorted groups and organizations—all in an attempt to further define themselves. Monica Golden, for instance, sampled various potential career paths before deciding on becoming a pediatrician. She may reassess this goal during her college years.

3. *Exploration.* Whereas role experimentation is specific to trying new roles, exploration refers to the comfort an adolescent has with trying new things. The more comfortable the individual is with exploration, the easier identity formation will be.

4. *Self-evaluation.* During the quest for identity, adolescents are constantly sizing themselves up against their peers. Erikson (1968) suggested that the development of identity is a process of personal reflection and observation of oneself in relation to others. George Herbert Mead (1934) suggested that individuals create a **generalized other** to represent how others are likely to view and respond to them. The role of the generalized other in adolescents' identity formation is evident when adolescents act on the assumed reactions of their families or peers. For example, what Monica Golden wears to school may be based not on what she thinks would be most comfortable or look the best but rather on what she thinks her peers expect her to wear. Recent attention has been paid to identity as a life story that begins to be told in late adolescence, a story one tells oneself about one's past, present, and anticipated future (see McLean & Mansfield, 2012). This is called narrative identity.

Gender Identity

Adolescence, like early childhood, covered in Chapter 12, is a time of significant gender identification. **Gender identity**, the internalized understanding of one's gender, begins in early childhood but is elaborated on and revised during adolescence (Steensma, Kreukels, de Vries, & Cohen-Kettenis, 2013). Efforts are made to integrate the biological, psychological, and social dimensions of sex and gender. *Gender expression* refers to how individuals express their socially constructed gender and may include how they dress, their general appearance, the way they speak, or the way they carry themselves. *Gender roles* are societal expectations of how individuals should act, think, or feel based on their assigned gender or biological sex (and based on the predominant binary system: male/female). Culture plays a large role in gender identity, gender expression, and gender roles. Gender roles can be a source of painful culture clash for some immigrant groups who are migrating to North America and Europe, harder for some ethnic groups than for others. But there is evidence that many immigrant families and individuals learn to be bicultural in terms of gender expectations, holding on to some traditional expectations while also innovating some new ways of doing gender roles (see Denner & Dunbar, 2004).

In the majority of cases, gender identity develops in accordance with physical characteristics, but this does not always happen. Surprisingly little is known about the influences on adolescent gender identity development (Steensma et al., 2013). In recent years, the term *cisgender* has been used to describe situations in which people's gender identity matches their assigned gender or biological sex. *Trans* is an umbrella term used to include transgender, transsexual, and transvestite persons as well as other gender nonconformists. *Transgender* describes youth who have been assigned a gender (based on their genitalia at birth) and identify as the "opposite" gender.

These individuals may or may not alter their bodies through surgery or hormones. *Transsexuals* are folks who wish to alter their physical bodies through surgery and/or hormones to have their bodies match their internalized gender identities. *Transvestite* refers to people who wear the clothing of the "opposite" gender and may also identify as cross-dressers or drag kings/queens. One study followed the adjustment of 20 adolescent transsexuals who had sex-reassignment surgery. In the 1 to 4 years of follow-up, the adolescents were doing well, and none of them had regrets about the decision to undergo the sex change (Smith, van Goozen, & Cohen-Kettenis, 2001).

As noted in Chapter 3 in this book, gender identity is not the same as sexual orientation. Gender identity is how I consider myself—man, woman, somewhere in between, or neither—and sexual orientation refers to whether I am sexually attracted to members of the same sex, the opposite sex, or both. As we work with adolescents and strive to be responsive to their stories, we must allow youth to share their identities (if they are known) with us and not assume that they are cisgender or heterosexual. Some adolescents will still be questioning and, thus, are unsure about their sexual orientation or gender identity. Sexual orientation is discussed later in the Adolescent Sexuality section.

Cultural Identity

Research indicates that ethnic origin is not likely to be a key ingredient of identity for Caucasian North American adolescents, but it is often central to identity in adolescents of ethnic minority groups (Branch, Tayal, & Triplett, 2000). Considerable research indicates that adolescence is a time when young people evaluate their ethnic background and explore ethnic identity (see French, Seidman, Allen, & Aber, 2006; Phinney, 2006). The development of ethnic identity in adolescence has been the focus of research across Canada, the United States, and Europe in recent years as ethnic diversity increases in all of these countries (see, e.g., Street, Harris-Britt, & Walker-Barnes, 2009). Ethnic minority youth are challenged to develop a sense of themselves as members of an ethnic minority group while also coming to terms with their national identity (Lam & Smith, 2009). Adolescents tend to have wider experience with multicultural groups than when they were younger and may be exposed to ethnic discrimination, which can complicate the development of cultural pride and belonging (Costigan, Su, & Hua, 2009).

Consider Monica Golden, who is an upper-middle-class African American teenager in a predominantly White high school. What are some of the potential added challenges of Monica's adolescent identity formation? Is it any wonder she is hoping to attend Howard University, a historically Black school, where she could surround herself with African American role models and professional support networks?

Researchers have found that ethnic minority adolescents tend to develop strong ethnic identity, but there is also variability within ethnic groups in terms of extent of ethnic identity. Costigan and colleagues (2009) reviewed the literature on ethnic identity among Chinese Canadian youth and concluded that the evidence indicates a strong ethnic identity among these youth. Conversely, there was much variability in the extent to which these youth reported a Canadian national identity. Adolescents negotiated ethnic identity in diverse ways across different settings, with different approaches being used at home versus in public settings. Lam and Smith (2009) studied how African and Caribbean adolescents (ages 11 to 16) in Britain negotiate ethnic identity and national identity and had similar findings to those for Chinese Canadian youth. They found that both groups of adolescents, African and Caribbean, rated their ethnic identity higher than their national identity and reported more pride in their ethnic heritage than in being British. The researchers found, however, that girls reported stronger ethnic identity than boys. Using in-depth interviews rather than standardized instruments, Rivas-Drake (2008) found three different styles of ethnic identity among Latinos in one public university in the United States. One group reported high individualistic achievement motivation and alienation from other Latinos. A second group reported strong identification with Latinos and was motivated to remove perceived barriers for the group. A third group reported strong connection to Latinos but was not motivated to work to remove barriers for the group.

Cultural identity usually develops within the context of the family, and there has been a general belief that children of immigrants acculturate more quickly than their parents do, leaving parents with a stronger ethnic identity than their children. Some research in Canada questions that belief. Costigan and Dokis (2006) found that Chinese Canadian mothers and children indicated stronger ethnic identity than the fathers, and mothers and children did not differ from each other. Interestingly, they found that the adolescents tended to report stronger ethnic identity than their parents in families characterized by high levels of warmth. This finding may reflect the Canadian cultural context: Canada has an official policy of multiculturalism, which promotes the maintenance of one's cultural heritage. Conversely, researchers in the United States have found that African American parents are more likely than parents in other ethnic groups to feel the need to prepare their adolescents for racial bias as a part of their racial and ethnic socialization (Hughes, Hagelskamp, Way, & Foust, 2009). This most likely reflects a more hostile environment for African American youth in the United States than for the Chinese Canadian youth.

The available research on cultural identity among ethnic minority youth indicates that most of these youth cope by becoming bicultural, developing skills to operate within at least two cultures. Research indicates that family conflict can arise when there are discrepancies in cultural identity between adolescents and their parents. One research team found that parent–adolescent discrepancies in ethnic identity were associated with elevated depression and social stress in female adolescents but not in male adolescents (Ansary, Scorpio, & Catanzariti, 2013). This research should alert social workers to tune in to the process of ethnic identity development when they work with ethnic minority youth. It appears that ethnic identity is a theme for both David Costa and Monica Golden. They both appear to be developing some comfort with being bicultural, but they are negotiating their bicultural status in different ways. Discussion about their ethnic identity might reveal more struggle than we expected. Some youth may be more likely to withdraw from the challenges of accessing mainstream culture rather than confronting these challenges and seeking workable solutions. We must be alert to this possibility.

CRITICAL THINKING Questions 14.2

What do you recall about your own psychological reactions to your changing body during puberty? What factors do you think influenced your reactions? With which groups did you identify during adolescence? What were your multiple social identities? Which identities were most important to you during adolescence? Which identities are important to you now?

SOCIAL ASPECTS OF ADOLESCENCE

The social environment—family, peers, organizations, communities, institutions, and so on—is a significant element of adolescent life. For one thing, as already noted, identity develops through social transactions. For another, as adolescents become more independent and move into the world, they develop their own relationships with more elements of the social environment.

RELATIONSHIPS WITH FAMILY

Answering the question "Who am I?" includes a consideration of the question "How am I different from my brothers and sisters, my parents, and other family members?" For many adolescents, this question begins the process of **individuation**—the development of a self or identity that is unique and separate. David Costa seems to have started the process of individuation; he recognizes that he may not want to be what his parents want him to be. He does not yet seem comfortable with this idea, however. Carl Fleischer is not sure how he is similar to and different from his absent father. Monica Golden has begun to recognize some ways that she is different from her siblings, and she is involved in her own personal exploration of career options that fit her disposition. It would appear that she is the furthest along in the individuation process.

The concept of independence is largely influenced by culture, and mainstream culture in the United States places a high value on independence. However, as social workers, we need to recognize that the notion of pushing the adolescent to develop an identity separate from family is not acceptable to all cultural groups in the United States or other places around the world (Gardiner & Kosmitzki, 2011). One research team found that African American adolescents have less decision-making autonomy in middle adolescence than European American adolescents (Gutman & Eccles, 2007). Peter Nguyen (2008; Nguyen & Cheung, 2009) has studied the relationships between Vietnamese American adolescents and their parents and found that a majority of the adolescents perceived their fathers as using a traditional authoritarian parenting style and see this as posing problems for the adolescents' mental health in the context of the multicultural society in the United States. Latino families in the United States have been found to keep very close boundaries around the family during adolescence (Garcia-Preto, 2011). Filial piety, respect for parents and ancestors, is a strong value in East Asian cultures (Schneider, Lee, & Alvarez-Valdivia, 2012). Our assessments of adolescent individuation should be culturally sensitive. Likewise, we must be realistic in our assessments of the ability of adolescents with cognitive, emotional, and physical disabilities to function independently.

Overall, families tend to respond to the adolescent desire for greater independence by renegotiating family roles and opening family boundaries to allow for the adolescent's greater participation in relationships outside the family (Garcia-Preto, 2011). The research literature on the relationships between parents and their adolescents indicates that, in general, these relationships are "close, supportive, and warm" (Galambos & Kotylak, 2012). However, many families with adolescents have a high level of conflict. Conflict is particularly evident in families experiencing additional stressors, such as divorce and economic difficulties (Fine et al., 2010). Conflict also plays out differently at different points in adolescence. Research suggests that conflicts with parents increase around the time of puberty but begin to decrease after that (Galambos & Kotylak, 2012). Both parents and adolescents need some time to adjust to this new life stage.

Adolescent struggles for independence can be especially potent in multigenerational contexts (Garcia-Preto, 2011). These struggles typically come at a time when parents are in midlife and grandparents are entering late adulthood and both are facing stressors of their own. Adolescent demands for independence may reignite unresolved conflicts between the parents and the grandparents and stir the pot of family discord. Sibling relationships may also change in adolescence. Longitudinal research indicates that, compared with middle childhood, adolescents report lower levels of positive sibling relationships during early adolescence, followed by increased intimacy in midadolescence (Shanahan, Waite, & Boyd, 2012).

The Society for Research on Adolescence prepared an international perspective on adolescence in the 21st century and reached three conclusions regarding adolescents and their relationships with their families:

- Families are and will remain a central source of support to adolescents in most parts of the world. A great majority of teenagers around the world experience close and functional relationships with their parents.

- Adolescents are living in a wider array of diverse and fluid family situations than was true a generation ago. These include divorced, single-parent, remarried, gay and lesbian, and multilocal families. More adolescents live in households without men. As a result of AIDS, regional conflicts, and migratory labor, many adolescents do not live with their parents.

- Many families are becoming better positioned to support their adolescents' preparation for adulthood. Smaller family sizes result in adults devoting more resources and attention to each child. Parents in many parts of the world are adopting a more responsive and communicative parenting style, which facilitates development of interpersonal skills and enhances mental health (Larson, Wilson, & Mortimer, 2002).

RELATIONSHIPS WITH PEERS

In the quest for autonomy and identity, adolescents begin to differentiate themselves from their parents and associate with their peers. Peer influence is strongest in early adolescence (Hafen, Laursen, & DeLay, 2012). Early adolescents are likely to select friends that are similar to them in gender and interests, but by middle adolescence, the peer group often includes opposite-sex friends as well as same-sex friends (Seiffge-Krenge & Shulman, 2012). Most early adolescents have one close friend, but the stability of these friendships is not high. In early adolescence the peer

Peer relationships are a fertile testing ground for youth and their emerging identities.

group tends to be larger than in middle childhood; these larger peer groups are known as *cliques*. By midadolescence, the peer group is organized around common interests; these groups tend to be even larger than cliques and are generally known as *crowds* (Brown & Klute, 2003). David Costa hangs out with the athletic crowd but seeks support from gay peers. Carl Fleischer is making contact with the "heads" crowd. Monica Golden's crowds would include peer counselors and the Young Republicans. Peer relationships contribute to adolescents' identities, behaviors, and personal and social competence.

Peer relationships are a fertile testing ground for youth and their emerging identities. Many adolescents seek out a peer group with compatible members, and inclusion or exclusion from certain groups can affect their identity and overall development. For some adolescents, participation in certain peer groups influences their behavior negatively. Peer influence may not be strong enough to undo protective factors, but if the youth is already at risk, the influence of peers becomes that much stronger. Sexual behaviors and pregnancy status are often the same for same-sex best friends. Substance use is also a behavior that most often occurs in groups of adolescents. The same is true for violent and delinquent behaviors. Researchers debate whether selection (choosing friends based on shared delinquent behaviors) or socialization (peer influence) plays a more important role here (Hafen et al., 2012).

ROMANTIC RELATIONSHIPS

Until recently, adolescent romantic relationships received little or no attention from researchers. Since the beginning of the 21st century, theories of adolescent romantic relationships have been developed and a great number of studies have been conducted. Both the theories and the research have typically focused on heterosexual romantic relationships. The following discussion of heterosexual romantic relationships in adolescence is based on a review of the research on the topic by Seiffge-Krenge and Shulman (2012). Although same-sex romantic relationships are becoming more visible, there is very little research on same-sex romantic relationships in adolescence. What research there is has tended to focus on same-sex attractions in adolescence from a risk perspective. The following discussion of same-sex romantic relationships in adolescence is based on a review of research on the topic by Russell, Watson, and Muraco (2012).

With the hormonal changes of adolescence, youth begin to be interested in sexual gratification and emotional union with a partner. This typically begins with romantic fantasies in early adolescence, fantasies that are often shared in same-gender friendship groups. As they move into mixed-gender groups in midadolescence, heterosexual youth have an opportunity to meet potential romantic partners. Researchers in the United States have found that nearly all 13- and 14-year-old adolescents report romantic fantasies and a desire to date. By late adolescence, most youth in the United States have been involved in some kind of romantic relationship, and the rates are similar in other economically advanced countries. The duration of romantic relationships is about 3 months in early adolescence and from 1 to 2 years in middle and late adolescence. Research indicates that most people have at least one romantic breakup during adolescence and that a breakup is a highly stressful event. (See Seiffge-Krenge & Shulman, 2012, for a fuller discussion of the research on adolescent heterosexual romantic relationships.) It is important to remember that in the United States and many other societies, romantic relationships develop through a dance of flirtation and dating, but in some cultures, the romantic relationship develops in the context of an arranged marriage.

In contrast to the burgeoning research on adolescent heterosexual romantic relationships, there is very little research on adolescent same-sex romantic relationships. There are a number of reasons why that research is hard to do, but an important reason is that, because of stigma and internalized homophobia, many youth with same-sex attractions do not "come out." Most of the research on this topic is based on small samples. Research is indicating, however, that as society becomes more accepting, U.S. youth with same-sex attractions are becoming more likely to act on those attractions. One longitudinal study of a cohort born in the mid-1990s found that less than 10% of youth with same-sex attractions reported ever having a same-sex romantic relationship, and a majority of these youth reported ever having a heterosexual romantic relationship. Another study, conducted 10 years later, found that a majority of same-sex-attracted youth were currently or had recently been in a same-sex romantic relationship. Research finds that one issue for youth with same-sex attractions is the relatively small pool of potential romantic partners. One study found that gay male youth typically begin the romantic relationship with a sexual experience, and lesbian youth typically begin as close friends. Another study found that youth with same-sex attractions who reported heterosexual dating had higher levels of internalized homophobia than similar youth who did not engage in heterosexual dating. (See Russell et al., 2012, for a fuller discussion of the research on adolescent same-sex romantic relationships.)

RELATIONSHIPS WITH ORGANIZATIONS, COMMUNITIES, AND INSTITUTIONS

As adolescents loosen their ties to parents, they develop more direct relationships in other arenas such as school, the broader community, employment, and social media/technology.

School

In the United States, as well as in other wealthy nations, youth are required to stay in school through a large portion of adolescence. The situation is quite different in many poor nations, however, where children may not even receive a primary school education. In their time spent at school, adolescents are gaining skills and knowledge for their next step in life, either moving into the workforce or continuing their education. In school, they also have the opportunity to evolve socially and emotionally; school is a fertile ground for practicing future orientation, role experimentation, exploration, and self-evaluation.

Middle schools in the United States usually have a structured format and environment; high schools are less structured in both format and environment, allowing a gradual transition to greater autonomy. The school experience changes radically, however, at the college level. Many college students are away from home for the first time and are in very unstructured environments. David Costa, Carl Fleischer, and Monica Golden have had different experiences with structure in their environments to date. David's environment has required him to move flexibly between two cultures. That experience may help to prepare him for the unstructured college environment. Carl has had the least structured home life. It remains to be seen whether that has helped him to develop skills in structuring his own environment or left him with insufficient models for doing so. Monica is accustomed to juggling multiple commitments and expectations. Time management skills will help with the transition to college, but she may struggle with having freedom from pressing family and community expectations for the first time.

School is also an institutional context in the United States where cultures intersect, which may create difficulties for students whose appearance or behavior is different from the Eurocentric, female-centered education model. You may not realize how culturally specific the educational model in the United States is until you view it through a different cultural lens. We can use a Native American lens as an example. Michael Walkingstick Garrett (1995) uses the experiences of the boy Wind-Wolf as an example of the incongruence between Native American culture and the typical education model:

> Wind-Wolf is required by law to attend public school. . . . He speaks softly, does not maintain eye contact with the teacher as a sign of respect, and rarely responds immediately to questions, knowing that it is good to reflect on what has been said. He may be looking out the window during class, as if daydreaming, because he has been taught to always be aware of changes in the natural world. These behaviors are interpreted by his teacher as either lack of interest or dumbness. (p. 204)

Children in the United States spend less time in school-related activities than do German, Korean, and Japanese children and have been noted to put less emphasis on scholastic achievement. Some researchers attribute oft-noted cross-cultural differences in mathematics achievement to these national differences in emphasis on scholastics (D. Newman, 2012). For adolescents, scholastic interest, expectations, and achievements may also vary, based not only on nationality but also on gender, race, ethnicity, economic status, and expectations for the future.

Most youth who drop out of school in the United States do so in high school, but worldwide, the concern is for youth who leave school before completing primary school or who fail to enroll in school at all. The United Nations Educational, Scientific, and Cultural Organization (UNESCO) compiles global education statistics. They report that in 2010, there were 31.2 million "early school leavers" in the world, a drop-out rate of 42% in Sub-Saharan Africa, 33% in South and West Asia, 17% in Latin America and the Caribbean, and 13% in Arab states (UNESCO, 2012). Worldwide, girls are less likely than boys to enter primary school, but boys are more likely to repeat grades or leave school early once enrolled. Also, compared with youth who attend the appropriate grade for their age, overage pupils are more likely to leave school early. Finally, children from poor and rural households are also at an increased risk of leaving school before completing primary education (UNESCO, 2012).

The Broader Community

Recent studies have considered the ways adolescents attempt to make a contribution to society and found that they are increasingly using technology to engage in such activities as signing petitions and expressing opinions about societal issues (van Goethem et al., 2012). Adolescents and young adults were on the forefront of social unrest across North Africa and the Middle East in 2010 and 2011 and were able to use communication technologies to organize protest activities. Although they experienced success in their activism, they also faced serious threats to their lives (Sawyer et al., 2012).

In the United States, the participation of high school students in volunteer work in the community is becoming common, much more so than in Europe. Indeed, community service is required in many U.S. high schools. Flanagan (2004) argues that community volunteer service provides structured outlets for adolescents to meet a wider circle of community people and to experiment with new roles. The community youth development movement is based on the belief that such community service provides an opportunity to focus on the strengths and competencies of youth rather than on youth problems (see Villarruel, Perkins, Borden, & Keith, 2003). One research team found that participation in community service and volunteerism assisted in identity clarification and in the development of political and moral interests (McIntosh, Metz, & Youniss, 2005).

Another way adolescents can have contact with the broader community is through a mentoring relationship with a community adult. The mentoring relationship may be either formal or informal. The mentor becomes a role model and trusted adviser. Mentors can be found in many places: in part-time work settings, in youth-serving organizations, in religious organizations, at school, in the neighborhood, and so on. There is unusually strong evidence for the positive value of mentoring for youth. Here are some examples of research in this area. Longitudinal research found that natural mentoring relationships with nonparental adults were associated with greater psychological well-being (DuBois & Silverthorn, 2005). Another study found that perceived mentoring from an unrelated adult in the work setting was associated with psychosocial competencies and adjustment in both U.S. and European samples (Vazsonyi & Snider, 2008). Longitudinal research with foster care youth has found that youth who had been mentored had better overall health, less suicidal ideation, fewer sexually transmitted infections (STIs), and less aggression in young adulthood than foster care youth who had not been mentored (Ahrens, DuBois, Richardson, Fan, & Lozano, 2008). Another study investigated the mentor relationship between an adolescent survivor of acquired brain injury and an adult mentor who was also a survivor of this injury. The researchers found that both the mentors and the adolescents derived benefit from the relationship, with the adolescents reporting gains in social and emotional well-being and identity development (Fraas & Bellerose, 2010). One last study of adolescents identified as "at risk" and involved in an 8-month mentoring program designed to prevent substance abuse found that the mentors helped the youth to improve relationships with family and at school and to increase their overall life skills (Zand et al., 2009).

Work

Like many adolescents, Carl Fleischer and Monica Golden also play the role of worker in the labor market. Limited employment, no more than 20 hours per week, can provide an opportunity for social interaction and greater financial independence. It may also lead to personal growth by promoting notions of contribution, responsibility, egalitarianism, and self-efficacy and by helping the adolescent to develop values and preferences for future jobs—answers to questions like "What kind of job would I like to have in the future?" and "What am I good at?" (Mortimer, 2004). For example, Monica tried many jobs before deciding that she loves working with children and wants to become a pediatrician. In addition, employment may also offer the opportunity to develop job skills, time management skills, customer relation skills, money management skills, market knowledge, and other skills of value to future employers.

The U.S. Department of Labor has launched an initiative called YouthRules! that seeks to promote positive and safe work experiences for young workers (www.youthrules.gov). These guidelines are the social policy result of research that suggests that for youth, work, in spite of some positive benefits, may also detract from development by cutting into time needed for sleep, exercise, maintenance of overall health, school, family relations, and peer relations. Unfortunately, the types of work available to adolescents are usually low-skill jobs that offer little opportunity for skill development. Some researchers have found that working more than 10 hours per week puts adolescents at risk for a number of physical and mental health problems (see Entwisle, Alexander, & Olson, 2005; Marsh & Kleitman, 2005), but as noted, longitudinal research suggests that working less than 20 hours per week is not detrimental (Mortimer, 2004). Although we cannot draw causal conclusions, Carl Fleischer works more than 10 hours a week and also has declining grades and uses tobacco and marijuana.

Information and Communication Technologies (ICTs)

According to *Teens and Technology 2013*, research produced by the Pew Research Center and the Berkman Center for Internet and Society at Harvard University, over 95% of U.S. teens report using the Internet and being online (Madden, Lenhart, Duggan, Cortesi, & Gasser, 2013). The mechanisms teens use to go online have changed over time, however. In the early 2000s, Internet usage was mostly obtained through desktop computers, and it is now through ICTs (information and communication technologies), primarily smartphones. Thirty-four percent of girls ages 14 to 17 report that they mostly go online using their cell phone as compared with 24% of boys the same age, even though girls and boys are equally likely to own smartphones (Madden et al., 2013). Overall, in 2011, 78% of adolescents ages 12 to 17 had cell phones and used them to text a median number of 60 times a day (Lenhart, 2012). Here are other findings about how adolescents, ages 12 to 17, use ICTs to communicate every day (Lenhart, 2012):

- 63% exchange text messages every day
- 39% make cell phone calls
- 29% engage in social network site messaging
- 22% engage in instant messaging
- 19% make landline calls
- 6% use e-mail

The 2011 YRBS reports that 32.8% of students had texted or e-mailed while driving a car or other vehicle on at

Adolescents are prolific users of text messaging, bringing a high level of connectedness.

least 1 day during the last 30 days. This rate was higher for boys (35%) than girls (30%), higher for White youth (36%) than Hispanic (30%) or Black youth (24%), and highest for 12th graders (58%), followed by 11th graders (43%), 10th graders (23%), and 9th graders (12%) (Eaton et al., 2012).

These technologies are bringing both benefit and risk to adolescent development. They offer another level of connectedness, with potential benefits such as maintaining distant relationships, keeping parents updated on their child's whereabouts or needs, and providing broader social networks. They also introduce potential risks, such as driving while texting, mental and physical (primarily thumbs) fatigue, social disconnectedness, and instant gratification. Sherry Turkle (2011), professor of social studies of science and technology at the Massachusetts Institute of Technology, has been studying the impact of ICTs on human behavior since the 1990s. She acknowledges that the Internet fosters social connections, identity development, and access to information of almost any kind. She also suggests that, like adults, today's adolescents are tethered to their technologies, living in a constant state of waiting for connection and endangering themselves by texting while walking or driving. Some adolescents complain that their technologies mean they are always "on call" to parents and friends alike. They work on identity development in an era when photos or messages can be sent to audiences they did not select. They are often physically present in one setting while mentally present in one or more other settings, and they interact with both parents and friends who are physically present while being mentally present elsewhere.

Parents, school officials, and legislators have become increasingly concerned that adolescents will see sexually explicit material on the Internet and be sexually exploited or otherwise harassed via the Internet. The Crimes Against Children Research Center reports that Internet sex crimes are more often cases of statutory rape where adult offenders meet, develop relationships with, and openly seduce teenagers (Wolak, Finkelhor, Mitchell, & Ybarra, 2008).

CRITICAL THINKING Questions 14.3

Children and adolescents in the United States spend less time on school-related activities than students in most other industrialized countries. Do you think children and adolescents in the United States should spend more time in school? How would you support your argument on this issue? How could high schools in the United States do a better job of supporting the cognitive development of adolescents? Should the high school be concerned about supporting emotional and social development of adolescents? Why or why not?

ADOLESCENT SPIRITUALITY/RELIGIOSITY

As adolescents develop greater capacity for abstract thinking, they often search for meaning in life experiences, and some researchers consider adolescence to be the most sensitive life stage for spiritual exploration (Kim & Esquivel, 2011; Magaldi-Dopman & Park-Taylor, 2010). In recent years, behavioral scientists and mental health professionals have developed an interest in spirituality/religiosity (S/R) as a source of resilience for adolescents (Kim & Esquivel, 2011). *Spirituality* is a personal search for meaning and relationship with the sacred, whether that is found in a deity or some other life force. *Religiosity* comprises beliefs and actions associated with an organized religious institution (Good, Willoughby, & Busseri, 2011). S/R includes both personal and institutional ways of connecting with the sacred.

Research on adolescent S/R is still in its infancy, and very little is known. In an attempt to fill this gap, a Canadian research team undertook a longitudinal study to explore multiple dimensions of S/R (Good et al., 2011). They studied 756 students in Grade 11 and the same students again in Grade 12 and found that at both time periods, the youth fell into a five-cluster typology of S/R:

1. Neither spiritual nor religious (14.2% of 11th graders and 13.4% of 12th graders)
2. Disconnected wonderers (35.9% of 11th graders and 44.6% of 12th graders)
3. High spirituality/high religiosity (16.7% of 11th graders and 8.3% of 12th graders)
4. Primarily spiritual (24.3% of 11th graders and 25.8% of 12th graders)
5. Meditators (9.0% of 11th graders and 7.9% of 12th graders)

The largest cluster at both time periods was the disconnected wonderers, a group that was not involved in any form of spiritual or religious practices but reported often wondering about spiritual issues. The meditators may or may not have been meditating as a spiritual practice; meditating may have been related to a physical fitness or other type of physical and/or mental health regimen.

The National Study of Youth and Religion (NSYR) is the most comprehensive longitudinal study of spirituality and religion among U.S. adolescents. Supported by the Lilly Endowment, this study began in August 2001 and was funded through December 2013. The NSYR's study found that the vast majority of U.S. teenagers (aged 13 to 17) identify themselves as Christian (56.4% Protestant [various denominations], 19.2% Catholic). Fifteen percent are not religious. In addition, 2.3% are Mormon/Latter-Day Saints, 1.5% are Jewish, and other minority faiths (Jehovah's Witness, Muslim, Eastern Orthodox, Buddhist, Pagan or Wiccan, Hindu, Christian Science, Native American, Unitarian Universalist, or two affiliations) each comprised less than 1% of the representative sample. Four out of 10 U.S. adolescents say they attend religious services once a week or more, pray daily or more, and are currently involved in a religious youth group. Eighty-four percent of the surveyed youth believe in God, whereas 13% are unsure about belief in God, and 3% do not believe in God (Denton, Pearce, & Smith, 2008). The researchers found that the single most important social influence on the religious and spiritual lives of adolescents is their parents.

For many youth, spirituality may be closely connected to culture. Interventions with adolescents and their families should be consistent with their spirituality and religion, but knowing someone's cultural heritage will not always provide understanding of their religious or spiritual beliefs. For example, it is no longer safe to assume that all Latino Americans are Catholic. Today, there is much religious diversity among Latino Americans who increasingly have membership in Protestant denominations such as Methodist, Baptist, Presbyterian, and Lutheran, as well as in such religious groups as Mormons, Seventh-Day Adventists, and Jehovah's Witnesses. Moreover, the fastest growing religions among Latino Americans are the Pentecostal and evangelical denominations (Garcia, 2011). Many Latino Americans, particularly Puerto Ricans, combine traditional religious beliefs with a belief in spiritualism, which is a belief that the visible world is surrounded by an invisible world made up of good and evil spirits who influence human behavior. Some Latino Americans practice Indigenous healing rituals, such as Santeria (Cuban American) and *curanderismo* (Mexican American). In these latter situations, it is important to know whether adolescents and their families are working with an Indigenous folk healer (Ho, Rasheed, & Rasheed, 2004). Although adolescents may not seem to be guided by their spirituality or religiosity, they may have underlying spiritual factors at work. As with any biological, psychological, or social dimensions of the individual, the spiritual dimensions of youth must be considered to gain the best understanding of the whole person.

ADOLESCENT SEXUALITY

With the changes of puberty, adolescents begin to have sexual fantasies, sexual feelings, and sexual attractions. They will come to understand what it means to be a sexual being and, similar to other facets of their identity, will explore their sexual identity. They will consider the kinds of people they find sexually attractive. Some will make decisions about engaging in various sexual behaviors. In this experimentation, some adolescents will contract sexually transmitted infections (STIs) and some will become pregnant. Unfortunately, some will also experience unwanted sexual attention and become victims of sexual aggression.

SEXUAL DECISION MAKING

Transition into sexual behavior is partly a result of biological changes. The amount of the sex hormone DHEA in the blood peaks between the ages of 10 and 12, a time when both boys and girls become aware of sexual feelings. The way that sexual feelings get expressed, however, can depend largely on sociocultural factors. Youth are influenced by the attitudes toward sexual activity that they encounter in their environment, at school; among peers, siblings, and family; in their clubs or organizations; in the media; and so on. When and how they begin to engage in sexual activity are closely linked to what they perceive to be the activities of their peers (Hafen et al., 2012). Research also suggests that youth who are not performing well in school are more likely to engage in sexual activity than are those who are doing well (Rew, 2005). Finally, beliefs and behaviors regarding sexuality are also shaped by one's culture, religion/spirituality, and value system. Adolescents report a variety of social motivations for engaging in sexual intercourse, including developing new levels of intimacy, pleasing a partner, impressing peers, and gaining sexual experience (Impett & Tolman, 2006).

As the pubertal hormones cause changes throughout the body, most adolescents spend time becoming familiar with those changes. For many, exploration includes **masturbation**, the self-stimulation of the genitals for sexual pleasure. In the most comprehensive U.S. sex study in decades, the National Survey of Sexual Health and Behavior conducted in 2009 included a nationally representative sample of 14- to 17-year-olds and questions about masturbation (Herbenick et al., 2010). Seventy-four percent of boys and 48% of girls reported ever masturbating.

The gender difference has been found to be even greater in Bangkok, Thailand, where 79% of male secondary students report masturbating, compared with 9% of females (O-Prasetsawat & Petchum, 2004). Masturbation has negative associations for some adolescents. Thus, masturbation may have psychological implications for adolescents, depending on the way they feel about it and how they think significant others feel about it. Female college students who are high in religiosity report more guilt about masturbation than female college students who are low in religiosity (J. Davidson, Moore, & Ullstrup, 2004).

The 2011 U.S. YRBS suggests that nationwide 47.4% of high school students reported having had sexual intercourse during their life, 6.2% had sexual intercourse for the first time before age 13, 15.3% have had sexual intercourse with four or more persons during their life, and 33.7% were sexually active during the last 3 months (Eaton et al., 2012). Of the 33.7% of high school students who indicated that they are currently sexually active, 60.2% report that either they or their partner used a condom during last sexual intercourse, 22.1% had drunk alcohol or used drugs before their last sexual intercourse, and 12.9% reported not using any method to prevent pregnancy during their last sexual intercourse (Eaton et al., 2012).

International data suggest that, on average, adolescents in the United States experience first sexual intercourse at about the same age as youth in other economically advanced countries. Data from 26 countries in 2007 indicate that the average age for first sexual intercourse was 18 years in the United States, compared with 17.9 years in Australia, 17.3 years in Austria, 18.5 years in France, 17.6 years in Germany, and 18.3 years in the United Kingdom (Durex Network, 2007). (It should be noted that Durex is a condom manufacturer that does annual surveys of adolescent sexuality in a number of countries.) The same data set indicates that females are more likely than males to feel pressured into having sex, with 27.2% of females and 15% of males reporting that they felt pressured into their sexual debut. Females were also more likely than males to have negative feelings about their first sexual experience, 42% versus 32%. U.S. data indicate that adolescents are slightly less likely than in the past to report that first sex is involuntary (Guttmacher Institute, 2013c). A study of first sexual experiences of youth ages 14 to 18 in the Philippines, El Salvador, and Peru found that approximately one fifth of the sample of both male and female adolescents regretted the experience (Osorio et al., 2012).

Regardless of nation or milieu, there is most certainly a need for adolescents to develop skills for healthy management of sexual relationships. Early engagement in sexual intercourse has some negative consequences. One research team studied early adolescent sexual initiation in five countries, the United States, Finland, France, Poland, and Scotland, and found it to be a risk factor for substance abuse and poor school attachment (Madkour, Farhat, Halpern, Godeau, & Gabhainn, 2010). They also found that early sexual initiation was disruptive to the parent–adolescent relationship, particularly for female adolescents in the United States but not in the other countries.

Rates of sexual activity among teens in the United States are fairly comparable to those in western Europe, yet the incidence of adolescent pregnancy and childbearing in the United States exceeds that in other economically advanced countries (Martinez, Copen, & Abma, 2011). For instance, the teen birth rate in the United States in 2009 was almost 3 times the rate in Canada, 3 times the rate in Germany, and about 5.7 times the rate in Italy. This discrepancy is probably related to three factors: teenagers in the United States make less use of contraception than teens in European countries, reproductive health services are more available in European countries, and sexuality education is more comprehensively integrated into all levels of education in most of Europe than in the United States (Durex Network, 2010; Guttmacher Institute, 2013c).

SEXUAL ORIENTATION

As they develop as sexual beings, adolescents begin to consider sexual attraction. **Sexual orientation** refers to erotic, romantic, and affectionate attraction to people of the same sex (gay or lesbian), the opposite sex (heterosexual), or both sexes (bisexual). There are also questioning adolescents who are less certain of their sexual orientation than those who label themselves as heterosexual, bisexual, or gay/lesbian (Poteat, Aragon, Espelage, & Koenig, 2009). Research indicates that the current generation of lesbian, gay, bisexual, and questioning youth uses the Internet to get information about sexual orientation and to begin the coming-out process. This provides a safe and anonymous venue for exploration and questioning as well as for initiating the coming-out process; it can lead to greater self-acceptance before coming out to family and friends (Bond, Hefner, & Drogos, 2009). Researchers are currently focusing on three indicators of sexual orientation: same-sex attractions; same-sex sexual behaviors; and self-labels as gay, lesbian, or bisexual (see Russell et al., 2012; Saewyc, 2011). Glover, Galliher, and Lamere (2009) suggest that sexual orientation should be conceptualized as a "complex configuration of identity, attractions, behaviors, disclosure, and interpersonal explorations" (pp. 92–93).

Theory and research about adolescent sexual orientation are not new, but there has been a very large increase in research on the topic in the past 15 years. The following discussion presents the major themes of Elizabeth Saewyc's (2011) comprehensive review of the research on adolescent sexual orientation published in the decade from 1998 to 2008. Researchers are still trying to untangle the multiple influences on sexual orientation, but there is general agreement that both genetic and environmental influences are involved. Researchers have struggled with how to define and measure sexual orientation, for example, whether to use measures of attraction, self-identity, or sexual behavior. Even though different measures are used across different studies, researchers consistently find that adolescents with a sexual orientation other than heterosexual report less supportive environments and less nurturing relationships with their parents than heterosexual youth. The research also consistently indicates that sexual minority youth have increased risk for developmental stressors and compromised health.

Research also suggests that sexual minority youth are coming out at earlier ages than in previous eras, but there is still much heterogeneity in the coming-out process. Those who come out earlier appear to be more comfortable with their sexual orientation status but also face increased rejection and harassment from family and peers. African American and Latino youth have a similar trajectory of sexual orientation development as White youth in most ways, but they are more delayed in making public disclosure, and they are less likely to be involved in gay-related social networks that tend to have mostly White membership.

Some evidence contends that most people remain consistent in their sexual attractions across the adolescent and young-adult periods, but youth with a sexual orientation other than heterosexual are much more likely than heterosexual youth to change their self-identification and sexual behavior over a 10-year period. Bisexuality has received much less research attention than homosexuality.

Research from a number of countries indicates that sexual minority youth have a higher prevalence of emotional distress, depression, self-harm, suicidal thinking, and suicidal attempts than heterosexual youth. They also have a higher prevalence of smoking and alcohol and other drug use, are likely to report an earlier sexual debut and to have more sexual partners, and have a higher prevalence of sexually transmitted infections. They are also more likely to be the targets of violence (Saewyc, 2011).

It is important to note that although sexual minority youth face increased risks to physical and mental health, most are successful in navigating the challenges they face and achieve similar levels of well-being as heterosexual youth. Several protective factors have been found to promote resilience in sexual minority youth, including supportive family relationships, supportive friends, supportive relationships with adults outside the family, positive connections with school, and spirituality/religiosity. These are the same protective factors that have been found to promote resilience in all youth, and, unfortunately, the research indicates that sexual minority youth, on average, receive less support in all of these areas than heterosexual youth. Research indicates, however, that many sexual minority youth have protective factors specific to their sexual orientation, including involvement in gay-related organizations and attending schools with gay-straight alliances or schools where the staff is trained to make the school a safe zone for sexual minority youth. Consider David Costa's conflict over his sexual orientation. What do you see as the risk and protective factors he faces as he struggles with this aspect of identity?

There is hope that the changing legal status of same-sex relationships and the increased visibility of positive sexual minority role models will lead to decreased risk and increased protection for sexual minority youth. There is some evidence that growing numbers of the current generation of adolescents do not consider sexual orientation as central an identity concept as earlier generations and are less prone to make negative judgments about sexual orientations other than heterosexual.

Saewyc's (2011) research review indicates the important influence of school climate on the well-being of sexual minority youth. For more than a decade, GLSEN (the Gay, Lesbian, and Straight Education Network) has conducted a National School Climate Survey (NSCS) to document the unique challenges that 6th- to 12th-grade LGBT students face and to identify interventions that can improve school climate. In the 2011 NSCS (Kosciw, Greytak, Bartkiewicz, Boesen, & Palmer, 2012), 84.9% of LGBT students reported hearing homophobic or negative remarks regarding sexual orientation or gender expression at school, and 56.9% of students reported hearing these types of comments from their teachers or other school staff. Sexual orientation and gender expression can also compromise adolescents' safety at school. The 2011 NSCS found that 63.5% of the LGBT students surveyed felt unsafe because of their sexual orientation (43.9% because of their gender expression). Over 80% of these students were verbally harassed because of their sexual orientation, 38.3% were physically harassed (e.g., pushed, shoved), and 18.3% were physically assaulted (punched, kicked, injured with a weapon). Moreover, 60.4% of the students who were harassed or assaulted at school did not report the incident to school personnel because they believed little or no action would be taken or the situation would be exacerbated if reported. These data indicate the serious risk that the school climate imposes on sexual minority youth, but the 2011 survey also found some hopeful signs. This was the first school climate survey to show both a decrease in negative indicators of school climate and also a continued increase in school supports for sexual minority youth.

To forestall potential rejection from family and friends, and at school, Parents, Families, and Friends of Lesbians and Gays (PFLAG), a support, education, and advocacy organization with the goal of promoting a more supportive environment for lesbian, gay, bisexual, and transgender people, was founded in 1972. The organization's website, http://community.pflag.org, contains information on frequently asked questions, facts, resources, and advocacy issues.

Tammy Camp/Alamy Stock Photo

Attending schools with gay-straight alliances or schools where the staff is trained to make the school a safe zone for sexual minority youth serves as a protective factor for these youth.

PREGNANCY AND CHILDBEARING

In 2012, there were 305,420 babies born to adolescent girls aged 15 to 19 in the United States (Hamilton, Martin, & Ventura, 2013). This is a birth rate of 29.4 per 1,000 15- to 19-year-old girls. Of these births, approximately 89% occurred outside of marriage and 17% were to girls who already had a child. The teen pregnancy rate in the United States has declined relatively consistently since the early 1990s (the 1991 rate was 61.8/1,000), but it is still higher than the rate in many other economically advanced countries (Hamilton et al., 2013). Teenage pregnancy rates and birth rates vary considerably by race and ethnicity as well as by region of the country. In 2012, Hispanic/Latino girls had the highest birth rate (46.3 per 1,000) and Black girls had the second highest rate (43.9 per 1,000), followed by their White counterparts (20.5 per 1,000). The national Office of Adolescent Health (U.S. Department of Health and Human Services, Office of Adolescent Health [DHHS/OAH], 2013) reports that the lowest teen birth rates were reported in the Northeast, and the highest teen birth rates were from the southern region of the United States. (See how your state compares on pregnancy rates, birth rates, sexual activity, and contraceptive use at www.hhs.gov/ash/oah/resources-and-publications/facts.)

Adolescent pregnancies carry increased risks to the mother, including delayed prenatal care; higher rates of miscarriage, anemia, toxemia, and prolonged labor; and increased likelihood of being a victim of intimate partner violence (Pinzon & Jones, 2012). They also carry increased risks to the infant, including perinatal mortality, preterm birth, low birth weight, and developmental delays and disabilities (Pinzon & Jones, 2012). In many Asian, eastern Mediterranean, African, and Latin American countries, the physical risks of adolescent pregnancy are mitigated by social and economic support (Hao & Cherlin, 2004). In the United States, however, adolescent mothers are more likely than their counterparts elsewhere to drop out of school; be unemployed or underemployed; receive public assistance; have subsequent pregnancies; and have children with poorer educational, behavioral, and health outcomes (U.S. DHHS/OAH, 2013). Teenage fathers may also experience lower educational and financial attainment (Pinzon & Jones, 2012).

The developmental tasks of adolescence are typically accomplished in this culture by going to school, socializing with peers, and exploring various roles. For the teenage mother or father, these avenues to development may be radically curtailed. The result may be long-lasting disadvantage. Consider the story of Chris Johnson in Case Study 11.3 in Chapter 11. He attends school for half the day, works a part-time job the other half, and then cares for Sarah in the evenings. Although he is determined to do the best he can by Sarah, he still mourns the loss of his freedom and "carefree" lifestyle.

SEXUALLY TRANSMITTED INFECTIONS

Youth have always faced pregnancy as a possible consequence of their sexual activity, but other consequences include infertility and death as a result of **sexually transmitted infections (STIs)**, also known as sexually transmitted diseases (STDs). Adolescents aged 15 to 24 comprise almost half of the 20 million new cases of STIs each year in the United States, and 4 out of every 10 sexually active teenaged girls have had an STI that can cause infertility or even death (CDC, 2012e). Girls aged 15 to 19 have the highest rates of chlamydia and gonorrhea of any age or gender group (Martinez et al., 2011).

Research has found several contextual and personal factors to be associated with STIs, including housing insecurity, exposure to crime, childhood sexual abuse, gang participation, frequent alcohol use, and depression (Buffardi, Thomas, Holmes, & Manhart, 2008). The Centers for Disease Control and Prevention (2012e) adds that the "higher prevalence of STDs among adolescents also may reflect multiple barriers to accessing quality STD prevention services, including lack of health insurance or ability to pay, lack of transportation, discomfort with facilities and services designed for adults, and concerns about confidentiality" (para. 1).

Data collection on STIs is complicated for several reasons. State health departments have different requirements about which STIs must be reported. STIs are not always detected and reported. Some STIs, such as chlamydia and HPV (human papillomavirus), are often asymptomatic and go undetected. In addition, many surveys are not based on representative samples. The best estimates available indicate that adolescents and young adults ages 15 to 24 constitute 25% of the sexually active population but account for almost half of the STI diagnoses each year (CDC, 2012e).

Unfortunately, HIV/AIDS is also a risk to adolescent health around the world. In 2012, there were 32.2 to 38.8 million people living with HIV worldwide, according to the Joint United Nations Programme on HIV/AIDS (UNAIDS, 2013). The rate of HIV diagnoses increased in youth ages 15 to 19 and 20 to 24 from 2006 to 2009. Despite only comprising about 20% of the 13- to 19-year-old U.S. population, 70% of the 13- to 19-year-olds diagnosed with HIV are Black teens. Almost 80% of the HIV+ adolescents are boys, and 90% of male HIV infections result from male-to-male sexual contact. See Exhibit 14.3 for the racial and ethnic distribution of HIV in U.S. adolescents aged 13 to 19. The highest concentrations of HIV diagnoses among adolescents were located in the southeastern United States—notably Florida, South Carolina, and Louisiana. Of the more than 1.2 million people living with HIV in the United States, approximately 1 in 5 (~220,000) doesn't know she or he is infected. The CDC estimates that half of all undiagnosed HIV infections are youth aged 13 to 24 (Torian, Chen, & Hall, 2011). Many of these individuals contract the disease in their teen years and don't learn they have the virus until they become adults. Fortunately, 84% of students responding to the YRBS reported that they received HIV/AIDS education in school, and 12.9% state that they have been tested for HIV (Eaton et al., 2012).

CRITICAL THINKING Questions 14.4

What sources of information did you use to learn about human sexuality when you were an adolescent? Which sources were the most useful and accurate? If you were to teach a human sexuality class to adolescents, what types of sources would you draw from?

POTENTIAL CHALLENGES TO ADOLESCENT DEVELOPMENT

Many adjustments have to be made during adolescence in all areas of life. Adjustments to biological changes are a major developmental task of adolescence, family relationships are continuously renegotiated across the adolescent phase, and career planning begins in earnest for most youth in mid- to late adolescence. Most adolescents have the resources to meet these new challenges and adapt. But many adolescents engage in risky behaviors or experience other threats to physical and mental health. We have already looked at risky sexual behavior. Nine other threats to social, physical, and mental health are discussed briefly here: substance use and abuse, juvenile delinquency, bullying, school-to-prison pipeline, community violence, dating violence and statutory rape, poverty and low educational attainment, obesity and eating disorders, and depression and suicide.

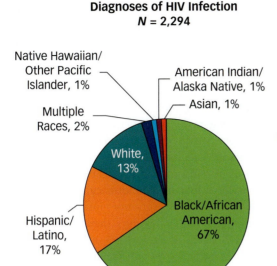

EXHIBIT 14.3 • Diagnoses of HIV Infection and Population Among Adolescents Aged 13 to 19, by Race or Ethnicity, in the United States, 2011

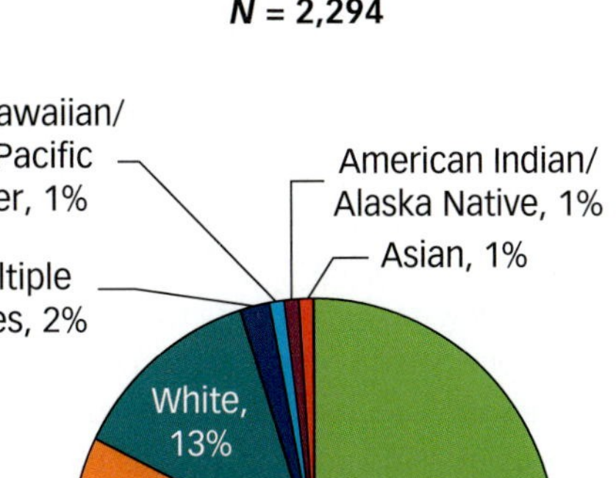

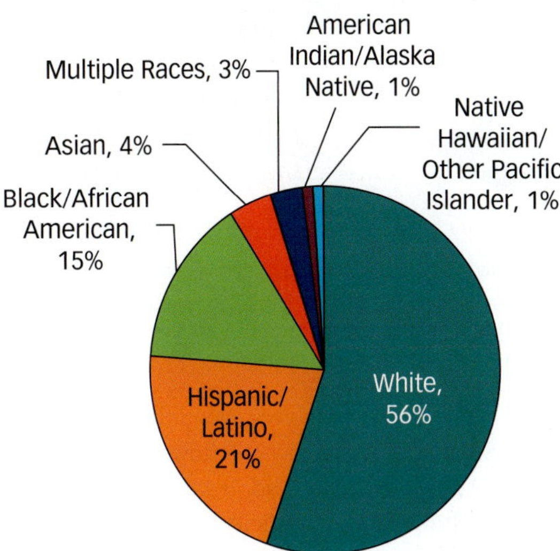

SOURCE: Centers for Disease Control and Prevention, 2012d.

SUBSTANCE USE AND ABUSE

In adolescence, many youth experiment with nicotine, alcohol, and other psychoactive substances with the motivation to be accepted by peers or to cope with life stresses (Weichold, 2007). For example, Carl Fleischer's use of tobacco and marijuana has several likely effects on his general behavior. Tobacco may make him feel tense, excitable, or anxious, and these feelings may amplify his concern about his weight, his grades, and his family relationships. Conversely, the marijuana may make Carl feel relaxed, and he may use it to counteract or escape from his concerns.

The rate of illicit drug use among U.S. adolescents aged 12 to 17 has remained at about 10% since 2002 according to the Substance Abuse and Mental Health Services Administration's *National Survey on Drug Abuse and Health* (Substance Abuse and Mental Health Services Administration [SAMHSA], 2013). Earlier research suggested that high school students in the United States maintain a higher rate of illicit drug use than youth in other economically developed countries (Johnston, O'Malley, Bachman, & Schulenberg, 2004, 2005). More recent research indicates that rates of adolescent use of illicit substances are lower in Latin America than in the United States (Torres, Peña, Westhoff, & Zayas, 2008). Overall, in 2012, SAMHSA reports that for those aged 12 to 17 in the United States, 7.2% used marijuana, 2.8% used prescription-type drugs for nonmedical purposes, 0.8% used inhalants, 0.6% used hallucinogens, and 0.1% used cocaine (SAMHSA, 2013). Alcohol continues to be the most widely used of all substances for adolescents. An estimated 9.3 million (underage) people aged 12 to 20 report drinking currently (24.3% of this age group reported drinking alcohol in the past month), according to 2012 statistics (SAMHSA, 2013). Furthermore, approximately 5.9 million (15.3%) considered themselves binge drinkers, and 1.7 million (4.3%) stated they were heavy drinkers. Meanwhile, tobacco use has steadily but only slightly declined over time. In 2011, 18.1% of 9th- to 12th-grade students had smoked cigarettes on at least one day in the previous month, and 7.7% of students had used smokeless tobacco on at least one day in the previous month.

When asked why youth choose to use alcohol, adolescents cite the following reasons: to have a good time with friends, to appear adultlike, to relieve tension and anxiety, to deal with the opposite sex, to get high, to cheer up, and to alleviate boredom. When asked why youth use cocaine, the additional responses were to get more energy and to get away from problems. Drug use at a party is also cited quite often as a reason (Engels & Knibbe, 2000). The following factors appear to be involved in adolescents' choice of drugs: the individual characteristics of the drug, the individual characteristics of the user, the availability of the drug, the current popularity of the drug, and the sociocultural traditions and sanctions regarding the drug (Segal & Stewart, 1996).

Some adolescents are clearly more at risk for substance abuse than others. National survey data indicate that Native American adolescents (47.5%) have

Burger/Phanie/Photo Researchers, Inc./Science Source

In adolescence, many youth experiment with nicotine, alcohol, and other psychoactive substances with the motivation to be accepted by peers or to cope with life stresses.

the highest prevalence of past year alcohol and other drug use of U.S. youth ages 12 to 17, followed by White adolescents (39.2%), Hispanic adolescents (36.7%), adolescents of multiple race or ethnicity (36.4%), African American adolescents (32.2%), and Asian or Pacific Islander adolescents (23.7%) (Wu, Woody, Yang, Pan, & Blazer, 2011). The same survey found racial and ethnic disparities in the prevalence of youth meeting the diagnostic criteria for substance-related disorders: Native American youth had the highest prevalence (15.0%), followed by adolescents of multiple race or ethnicity (9.2%), White adolescents (9.0%), Hispanic adolescents (7.7%), African American adolescents (5.0%), and Asian or Pacific Islander adolescents (3.5%).

Although these data indicate that many adolescents use alcohol and other substances, not all of them get into trouble with their usage, except for the potential legal trouble related to the illegality of their use of these substances. Problematic alcohol and drug use, however, can have a negative influence on adolescents, their families, and their communities. Because alcohol and illicit drugs alter neurotransmission, regular use can have harmful effects on the developing brain and nervous system (Wu et al., 2011). Early substance use increases the risk for later addiction and depression (Esposito-Smythers, Kahler, Spirito, Hunt, & Monti, 2011). Use of alcohol and other drugs can also affect the immune system and emotional and cognitive functioning, including sexual decision making (Weichold, 2007).

JUVENILE DELINQUENCY

Almost every adolescent breaks the rules at some time—disobeying parents or teachers, lying, cheating, and perhaps even stealing or vandalizing. Many adolescents smoke cigarettes and drink alcohol and use other drugs; some skip school or stay out past curfew. For some adolescents, this behavior is a phase, passing as quickly as it appeared. Yet for others, it becomes a pattern. Although most juvenile delinquency never meets up with law enforcement, the more times young people offend, the more likely they are to come into contact with the juvenile justice system.

In the United States, persons older than 5 but younger than 18 can be arrested for anything for which an adult can be arrested. (Children younger than 6 are said not to possess mens rea, which means "guilty mind," and thus are not considered capable of criminal intent.) In addition, they can be arrested for what are called **status offenses**, such as running away from home, skipping school, violating curfew, and possessing tobacco or alcohol—behaviors not considered crimes when engaged in by adults. When adolescents are found guilty of committing either a crime (by adult standards) or a status offense, we refer to their behavior as **juvenile delinquency**.

The Office of Juvenile Justice and Delinquency Prevention (OJJDP) reports that the number of delinquency cases, at about 1.5 million, increased from 1985 through 1997 and declined from 1997 to 2009 (Knoll & Sickmund, 2012). Juveniles (persons younger than 18) accounted for 13.7% of all violent crime arrests and 22.5% of all property crime arrests in 2010. And in that same year, 784 juveniles were arrested for murder, 2,198 were arrested for forcible rape, and 35,001 were arrested for aggravated assault (Federal Bureau of Investigation, 2011). Although the rate of delinquency among girls has increased (from 19% in 1985 to 28% in 2009), it is still a relatively small proportion of the overall delinquency caseload at 415,600 in 2009 (as compared with 1,088,600 for boys in that same year) (Knoll & Sickmund, 2012). And, of the total U.S. adolescent population in 2009, White youth comprised 78%, Black youth comprised 16%, Asian youth (including Native Hawaiian and other Pacific Islander) comprised 5%, and Native American (including Alaska Native) comprised 1%. However, 64% of the delinquency cases handled in 2009 were for White youth, 34% were for Black youth, 1% were for Asian American youth, and 1% were for Native American youth. Despite similar offending patterns and rates of self-reported crime, the rate at which Black youth were referred to juvenile court for a delinquency offense was more than 150% greater than the rate for White youth. The rate at which petitioned cases were waived to criminal court was 5% greater for Black youth than the rate for White youth, and the rate at which youth in adjudicated cases were ordered to residential placement was 23% greater for Black youth than for White youth in a phenomenon called disproportionate minority contact (Knoll & Sickmund, 2012; McCarter, 2011).

For years, the United States was the only country in the world to sentence juveniles to life imprisonment without parole, even some for nonhomicide offenses, and all of these youth were Black or Latino. This practice was ruled unconstitutional by the U.S. Supreme Court in 2010 and made retroactive in 2016 (Stevenson, 2015). Many

unique to adolescence include pervasive inability to experience pleasure, severe psychomotor retardation, delusions, and a sense of hopelessness (Sadock & Sadock, 2007). Depressed adolescents often present with irritable rather than depressed mood (Thapar et al., 2012).

The many challenges of adolescence sometimes prove overwhelming. We have already discussed the risk of suicide among gay male and lesbian adolescents. In the United States during the 12 months preceding the 2011 YRBS survey, 28.5% of high school students reported having felt so sad or hopeless almost every day for 2 weeks or more that they stopped doing some usual activities (Eaton et al., 2012). Furthermore, 15.8% had seriously considered attempting suicide; 12.8% had made a suicide plan; 7.8% had actually attempted suicide; and 2.4% had made a suicide attempt that resulted in an injury, poisoning, or overdose that had to be treated by a doctor or nurse (Eaton et al., 2012).

Overall, suicide is the third leading cause of death for adolescents in the United States. About 4,600 youth ages 15 to 24 take their own lives each year. The top three methods that youth use in suicide are firearm (45%), suffocation (40%), and poisoning (8%). Boys are about 4 times as likely as girls to die by suicide, but girls are more likely to attempt suicide. Native American/Alaskan Native youth have the highest rates of suicide-related deaths, and Hispanic youth are more likely to report attempting suicide than Black and White non-Hispanic youth (Centers for Disease Control and Prevention, 2014b). Cheryl King and Christopher Merchant (2008) have analyzed the research on factors associated with adolescent suicidal thinking and behavior and identified a number of risk factors: social isolation, low levels of perceived support, childhood abuse and neglect, and peer abuse.

RISK FACTORS AND PROTECTIVE FACTORS IN ADOLESCENCE

There are many pathways through adolescence; both individual and group-based differences result in much variability. Some of the variability is related to the types of risk factors and protective factors that have accumulated prior to adolescence. In addition, as we have seen throughout this chapter, the journey through adolescence is impacted by the risk and protective factors encountered during this phase of life. Social disadvantage and negative experiences in infancy and early childhood put a child at risk of poor peer relationships and poor school performance during middle childhood, which increases the likelihood of risky behaviors in adolescence (Sawyer et al., 2012). Emmy Werner and associates (see Werner & Smith, 2001) have found, in their longitudinal research on risk and protection, that girls have a better balance of risk and protection in childhood, but the advantage goes to boys during adolescence. Their research indicates that the earlier risk factors that most predict poor adolescent adjustment are a childhood spent in chronic poverty, alcoholic and psychotic parents, moderate to severe physical disability, developmentally disabled siblings, school problems in middle childhood, conflicted relationships with peers, and family disruptions. The most important earlier protective factors are easy temperament, positive social orientation in early childhood, positive peer relationships in middle childhood, non-sex-typed extracurricular interests and hobbies in middle childhood, and nurturing from nonparental figures.

Much attention has also been paid to the increase in risk behaviors during adolescence (Silbereisen & Lerner, 2007b). Attention has been called to a set of factors that are risky to adolescent well-being and serve as risk factors for adjustment in adulthood as well. These factors include use and abuse of alcohol and other drugs; unsafe sex, teen pregnancy, and teen parenting; school underachievement, failure, and dropout; delinquency, crime, and violence; youth poverty and undernutrition; and marketing of unhealthy products and lifestyles (Sawyer et al., 2012). The risk and resilience research indicates, however, that many youth with several of these risk factors overcome the odds. Protective factors that have been found to contribute to resilience in adolescence include family creativity in coping with adversity, good family relationships, spirituality and religiosity, social support in the school setting, and school-based health services. Giving adolescents a voice in society has also been identified as a potential protective factor. As social workers, we will want to promote these protective factors while at the same time work to prevent or diminish risk factors.

CRITICAL THINKING Questions 14.5

Adolescence is a time of rapid transition in all dimensions of life—physical, emotional, cognitive, social, and spiritual. What personal, family, cultural, and other social factors help adolescents cope with all of this change? What factors lead to dissatisfaction with body image and harmful or unhealthy behaviors? How well does contemporary society support adolescent development?

IMPLICATIONS FOR SOCIAL WORK PRACTICE

Adolescence is a vulnerable period. Adolescents' bodies and psyches are changing rapidly in transition from childhood to adulthood. Youth are making some very profound decisions during this life course period. Thus, the implications for social work practice are wide ranging.

- When working with adolescents, meet clients where they are physically, psychologically, and socially—don't assume that you can tell where they are, and be aware that that place may change frequently.
- Be familiar with typical adolescent development and with the possible consequences of deviations from developmental timelines.
- Be aware of, and respond to, the adolescent's level of cognition and comprehension. Assess the individual adolescent's ability to contemplate the future, to comprehend the nature of human relationships, to consolidate specific knowledge into a coherent system, and to envision possible consequences from a hypothetical list of actions.
- Recognize that the adolescent may see you as an authority figure who is not an ally. Develop skills in building rapport with adolescents. Avoid slang terms until you have immersed yourself in adolescent culture long enough to be certain of the meaning of the terms you use.
- Assess the positive and negative effects of the school climate on the adolescent in relation to such issues as early or late maturation, popularity/sociability, culture, and gender identity/sexual orientation.
- Consider how to advocate for change in maladaptive school settings, such as those with Eurocentric models or homophobic environments.
- Seek appropriate resources to provide information, support, or other interventions to assist adolescents in resolving questions of gender identity and sexual decision making.
- Link youth to existing suitable resources or programs, such as extracurricular activities, education on STIs, prenatal care, and LGBTQQ (lesbian/gay/bisexual/transgender/queer/questioning) support groups.
- Provide information, support, or other interventions to assist adolescents in making decisions regarding use of alcohol, tobacco, or other drugs.
- Develop skills to assist adolescents with physical and mental health issues, such as nutritional problems, obesity, eating disorders, depression, and suicide.
- Participate in research, policy development, and advocacy on behalf of adolescents.
- Work at the community level to develop and sustain recreational and social programs and safe places for young people.

KEY TERMS

acquaintance rape, 464
anorexia nervosa, 465
binge eating disorder, 465
bulimia nervosa, 465
formal operations stage, 447
gender identity, 448
generalized other, 448
gonads, 442
individuation, 450
juvenile delinquency, 462
masturbation, 456
menarche, 442
postconventional moral reasoning, 448
primary sex characteristics, 442
psychological identity, 446
puberty, 442
rites of passage, 441
secondary sex characteristics, 442
sex hormones, 442
sexual orientation, 457
sexually transmitted infections (STIs), 460
social identity, 446
spermarche, 442
status offenses, 462
statutory rape, 464

ACTIVE LEARNING

1. Working in groups of three or four, recall your own high school experiences and discuss which case study individual you most identify with—David, Carl, or Monica. For what reasons? How can you keep your personal experiences with adolescence from biasing your social work practice? How could a social worker have affected your experiences?
2. Janet Finn (2009) argues that the public, professional, and scholarly conversations about adolescence in recent times have focused on adolescents as "trouble." In groups of three or four discuss any recent news stories, movies, or other media with adolescent themes. Do these public depictions of adolescence present adolescents as "trouble" or as a resource for society? Explain.

3. Divide into groups of three or four and develop an outline of a 6-week course about adolescent substance abuse to be presented to a group of adolescent high school students. Now design an outline for a 6-week course on the same topic for a group of parents of high school students. How would the courses be similar and different? For what reasons?

WEB RESOURCES

ABA's Juvenile Justice Committee

apps.americanbar.org/dch/committee.cfm?com=CR200000

Site presented by the American Bar Association's Juvenile Justice Committee contains links to juvenile justice–related sites.

Add Health

www.cpc.unc.edu/projects/addhealth

Site presented by the Carolina Population Center contains a reference list of published reports of the National Longitudinal Study of Adolescent Health (Add Health), which includes measures of social, economic, psychological, and physical well-being.

Adolescent and School Health

www.cdc.gov/healthyyouth

Site maintained by the Centers for Disease Control and Prevention contains links to a variety of health topics related to adolescents, including alcohol and drug use, sexual behavior, nutrition, youth suicide, and youth violence.

Sexually Transmitted Infections Information

www.ashastd.org

Site maintained by the American Sexual Health Association, which is dedicated to improving sexual health, contains information about sexual health, STDs, and publications.

SAGE edge™ **Sharpen your skills with SAGE edge at edge.sagepub.com/hutchisoness2e**

SAGE edge for students provides a personalized approach to help you accomplish your coursework goals in an easy-to-use learning environment. watch listen read

LEARNING OBJECTIVES	FOR FURTHER EXPLORATION AND APPLICATION
LO 14.1: Compare and contrast one's emotional and cognitive reactions to three case studies.	(listen) Adolescence, the Age of Opportunity
LO 14.2: Analyze how the status of adolescence has varied across time and place.	(read) The Invention of the Teenager
LO 14.3: Describe some of the transitions made in adolescence.	(watch) Coming of Age: Bat Mitzvah (watch) Teen Girls' Transitions Into Adulthood "Untangled" (listen) Getting a Tattoo Is an Unlikely Rite of Passage
LO 14.4: Summarize biological, psychological, social, and spiritual development during adolescence.	(watch) Self-Concept in Adolescence (watch) School Lunches (watch) Formal Operations (watch) Recognizing a Crowd (read) Rites of Passage and the Story of Our Times
LO 14.5: Analyze major themes in adolescent sexual development.	(read) Sexual Development and Puberty (read) Mixed Drinks and Mixed Messages: Adolescent Girls' Perspectives on Alcohol and Sexuality
LO 14.6: Describe some major challenges to adolescent development.	(watch) Alarming Rise in Teens Reporting Dating Violence
LO 14.7: Give examples of risk factors and protective factors for adolescent development.	(read) Risk and Protective Factors
LO 14.8: Apply knowledge of adolescence to recommend guidelines for social work assessment and intervention.	(read) Effects of Adolescent Physical Abuse, Exposure to Neighborhood Violence, and Witnessing Parental Violence on Adult Socioeconomic Status

"YOU HAVE TO TRUST, MARTINE. EVERYTHING HAPPENS FOR A REASON."
LAUREN
JOHN
GIRAFFE

Young and Middle Adulthood

Elizabeth D. Hutchison and Holly C. Matto

Learning Objectives

LO 15.1 Compare and contrast one's emotional and cognitive reactions to three case studies.

LO 15.2 Define adulthood.

LO 15.3 Analyze the merits of four theoretical approaches to adulthood (Jung's, Erikson's, Levinson's, and Arnett's).

LO 15.4 Give examples of variations in the transition to adulthood.

LO 15.5 Summarize biological functioning, cognition, personality and identity, and spirituality in young and middle adulthood.

LO 15.6 Describe major themes of relationships in young and middle adulthood.

LO 15.7 Analyze major challenges related to work in young and middle adulthood.

LO 15.8 Give examples of risk factors and protective factors for young and middle adulthood.

LO 15.9 Apply knowledge of young and middle adulthood to recommend guidelines for social work assessment and intervention.

AP Photo/Jack Dempsey

GET MORE OUT OF YOUR STUDY TIME.

The **SAGE Interactive eBook** provides one-click access to integrated study tools that will enrich your understanding of course content.

- **Watch** video clips to learn actively
- **Think Critically** with SAGE Journals
- **Explore Further** with SAGE Reference
- **Connect** with relevant web resources
- **Listen** to podcasts for real-world context

CASE STUDY 15.1

SHEILA HENDERSON, COMING HOME AT 25

Sheila Henderson, 25 years old, her boyfriend, David, 27 years old, and her 4-year-old daughter, Johanna, from a previous relationship, all said goodbye at the Family Readiness Center at Fort Bragg, North Carolina, 18 months ago, as Sheila departed for her second tour to Afghanistan as a lieutenant in the infantry division of the United States Army. The family hasn't seen each other since, although they have participated in weekly family video calls. While Sheila was on tour, she sustained a minor closed-head injury when she was participating in a training exercise with her unit in Afghanistan. Her injury was deemed "minor" and not likely to cause significant or long-term impairment, but Sheila can't help but notice a change in her ability to handle emotions. She notices new limitations in her ability to concentrate and says she becomes easily agitated or "set off" over minor inconveniences, which is "not like her." And she cries more than she used to. She is opposed to calling her injury a disability and can't help but think that maybe it's just all in her mind anyway. She regularly experiences a variety of emotions, from frustration, anger, and resentment at her time spent away from family and friends, to loyalty and pride in serving her country. She occasionally feels guilty for taking so much time to "dwell" on her own challenges when she knows so many others have died or have been more seriously incapacitated while serving their country in Afghanistan and Iraq.

Now that she is returning from tour, Sheila knows she will struggle with transitioning back into life with her family but is giddy with excitement to be reunited with her daughter, who will be turning 5 shortly and entering kindergarten in the fall, and to rejoin her boyfriend whom she says has had the most difficulty with her absence. Her boyfriend, though officially a civilian working as an accountant, considers the military community where they live to be family. There is an informal ethos in their community that military families care for each other's children when one or more parents are deployed, and David has benefited from this support while Sheila's been away. What concerns him most is Sheila's transition back into their family life. He can't help but wonder how she will respond to the year and a half of developmental changes Johanna has gone through and how she will jump back into the role of disciplining her behavior and facilitating the family routines and schedule that David has worked so hard to establish. In fact, of Johanna's 4½ years, Sheila has really only been physically present for about a year and a half of that time. David wonders how the routine will play itself out now and how the family will reunite together. There is also the lingering anticipation and unpredictability of the next possible deployment, and that keeps him up at night. He wonders why Sheila seems so at ease with the uncertainty, and he hopes he will be able to gain her strength in negotiating the ambiguity of their family's shared life space in the future. But for now, he's overjoyed that she's coming home. They have a lot of catching up to do.

CASE STUDY 15.2

VIKTOR SPIRO, FINDING STABILITY AT 44

Viktor Spiro was born in a village outside of Tirana, Albania, and lived his early life, as did many Albanians in the Stalinist state, amid very impoverished conditions. He was the youngest of four children, with two sisters and a brother 12 years his senior. Viktor describes his childhood as "normal," until he sustained a serious head injury after falling from a tractor when he was 13.

He experienced an increasing depression following his hospitalization; his school performance declined and he withdrew from his friends. When Viktor was 20, his older brother died from a rare gastrointestinal illness, another traumatic event that exacerbated Viktor's depression and substance abuse. He subsequently went absent without leave (AWOL) from his military post and fled to Greece, where he continued to drink heavily and was reportedly hospitalized at a psychiatric facility.

Because his father was a U.S. citizen, Viktor was able to immigrate to the United States in his late 20s after the dissolution of Albania's repressive communist regime. He secured a job as a painter, but the language barrier and fast-paced life left him feeling vulnerable. Struggling to cope, Viktor made a series of suicide attempts and was arrested after lunging for the gun of a police officer who was trying to help him. Viktor claims that he did not intend to harm the officer but that he saw the gun as a quick means to end his own life. Viktor's suicide attempts and arrest led to the beginning of a long relationship with mental health services (MHS). He was diagnosed with bipolar I disorder with psychotic features, made more suicide attempts, was hospitalized, and lived in a group home.

After a few years, Viktor's father and mother, Petro and Adriana, moved to the United States to reunite with Viktor and his sister Maria. Viktor moved into an apartment with his parents and showed some signs of improved adjustment, including advances in his use of English and steady employment secured through the MHS job service program. However, his firsthand exposure to the worsening state of Petro's vascular dementia proved very traumatic, and he made another suicide attempt. Then, Petro broke his hip and was in a nursing home briefly. Viktor and his father were both referred to a residential program to obtain counseling and case management services. His social worker learned that Viktor had accrued more than $140,000 in hospital bills and was still on "medical leave" from his job. The family had no significant income other than Petro's monthly $400 social security check and Adriana's stipend from Social Services to "take care" of her husband. Viktor shared that he had deep regrets about his latest suicide attempt and could not put himself or his family through this again. He felt that he was at a turning point and needed to take on more responsibility as he approached 40, especially with caring for his ailing parents.

As Viktor and his social worker met regularly, Viktor became more aware of his mother's struggles to fulfill family needs and began to do more in the house. It became clear to the social worker that Adriana was the backbone of the family and that she found purpose and meaning in her role as keeper of the house. Adriana began to trust the social worker's commitment to her family, and with Viktor translating, she recounted the death of her firstborn, the chronic depression and strokes that had afflicted her husband over the past 40 years, and Viktor's ongoing struggles with his mental illness. The social worker saw that although the Spiro family clearly had experienced much suffering and trauma, their incredible strength, resolve, and affection were impressive.

Viktor began to reveal a more reflective, insightful side during his recovery. He confided to his treatment team that he was hearing voices for nearly 6 months prior to his last suicide attempt but didn't tell anyone. He hoped the voices would just "go away." His social worker and job coach assisted him with transition back into the workforce, and he eventually obtained the medical clearance to return to his dishwashing job, resuming the role as the primary breadwinner for the family. This was a real lift to Viktor's self-esteem. The Spiro family experienced another financial lift with the news of a total forgiveness of Viktor's outstanding hospital bills.

While the Spiro family was enjoying their improving situation, the treatment team worked with Viktor to expand his social network outside the family. Viktor had been spending all of his time with his parents in their apartment when he was not working. As his confidence grew with his psychiatric improvement, however, he became more receptive to suggestions about weekend social activities coordinated by the agency. He tried out a couple of the groups and enjoyed the activities and chance to form new relationships. He quickly immersed himself in a variety of weekend activities that involved shopping, movies, athletics, and cultural events. The social worker assisted Viktor with the long process of reapplying for naturalization, after learning that he did not provide INS with the required documents on his previous application. With his improved mental state, Viktor was able to concentrate on studying for the citizenship test, which he passed. His citizenship ceremony was a wonderful day for Viktor and his family, and he made a poignant speech about dreaming of this day as a teenager watching *CHiPS* reruns in Albania.

The Spiro family clearly enjoyed the series of positive events for Viktor, but soon they faced another change of events. Petro had a series of strokes, was in and out of hospice several times, and ultimately died of heart failure in his home with his wife and son by his side. Viktor grieves for his father, but his handling of Petro's health crises and death is a remarkable change from the impulsive and often dangerous behavior he had previously exhibited when responding to stressful situations. Today, Viktor has balance in his life, working part-time in a grocery store, spending time with his mother, doing household chores, and attending church. Although he sees mental health workers less than he once did, he continues to attend a day program for people with serious mental illness, where he enjoys the social opportunities, friends, and varied community outings. He plays the guitar and sings American pop as well as traditional Greek and Albanian songs. Currently, his biggest struggles are medication side effects and trying to care for his mother, who is having a hard time with the loss of her caregiving role. The agency social worker is trying to help her get more connected to the church and the Albanian community, where her inability to speak English would not be a barrier.

—Derek Morch

CASE STUDY 15.3

MICHAEL BOWLING, SWALLOWING HIS PRIDE AT 57

Michael Bowling always thought that if you are willing to work hard, you will never need public assistance. He realizes now that he made judgments about other people's lives without really knowing much about them. And he is convinced that his very life depends on getting some public assistance. Here is his story.

Michael grew up in a small town in Missouri, the oldest of five children. His parents were hardworking factory workers who had grown up in the midst of the Great Depression. His dad had to turn down a college scholarship to work odd jobs to help scrape together enough to feed the family. Michael's parents were determined to give their children an easier time, and though it was never easy, at least Michael and his siblings never went to bed hungry. They always felt loved, and their parents had high hopes for their children's futures.

Michael started working 20 hours a week when he was 16 to help his parents pay a hospital bill for one of his younger brothers. When he graduated from high school, he joined the U.S. Army, hoping that might provide some financial security for him and his family. He stayed in the U.S. Army for 4 years and then returned to his hometown. He soon found that there were no good jobs there for him, and he decided to move to a nearby college town to begin to study for a college degree. He found a low-paying job for 30 hours per week, so it took him 7 years to earn his engineering degree.

When he graduated from college, he married the woman he had been dating and found an engineering job in a larger city. The marriage lasted for 7 years, there were no children, and the divorce was friendly. The career went well and Michael moved up the ranks in small and moderate-size firms. He was able to buy a small house. He never married again, but he has been very close to a younger sister who lives in the same city, and he became a kind of substitute dad to her son and daughter after her husband left the family. His parents lived long enough to see him doing well and took pride in his success. Both parents died at a relatively young age, however, his dad of a stroke at age 55 and his mother of breast cancer at age 58, after moving in with Michael and using hospice care during her final 5 months.

In early 2007, at the age of 50, Michael got his dream job in a very large engineering firm. Life was good! And then, the deep recession of 2008 hit, and as one of the last hired, Michael was one of the first to be laid off. He had some savings, so he could make his mortgage payments and put food on the table. He cut where he could, things like his gym membership and cable television, but held on to the car and cell phone because he would need them for the job search. He put out 10 resumes a day and made two cold calls per day. He felt lucky when he found temporary jobs, but these projects never lasted long, and they never offered health insurance. For the first 2 years after he was laid off, he bought a very expensive individual health insurance policy, but as his savings diminished, he dropped the policy.

Then in October 2011, Michael awoke one morning with a severe headache, numbness in the right side of his face, and weakness in his right arm and leg. Because of his earlier experience with his father's stroke, Michael recognized these symptoms as warning signs of a stroke. He also knew that it was imperative that he get immediate medical care; he called 911 and was taken to the comprehensive hospital a few blocks from his home. Over the next 2 years, Michael used all of his savings and took a second mortgage on his house to pay his hospital and rehabilitation bills. He was lucky that his stroke was not as serious as the one that had killed his dad, and that he knew to get immediate help, and he has made a good recovery. The only remaining noticeable symptom is some right-sided weakness, particularly when he is tired. As he recovered from the stroke, he resumed the job search but, to date, has only found one very short-term project. His two brothers have helped him out a little, when they realized that he was choosing between buying food or his medication to prevent another stroke. But Michael knows that his brothers struggle financially, and he finally realized that he had to swallow his pride and apply for SNAP (food stamps) and energy assistance. At the same time, he signed up for health insurance through the Affordable Care Act's federal marketplace. He is sad that he is not able to help send his niece and nephew to college as he had expected to do, but he is still very involved in their lives. Michael is grateful to have survived his stroke, and he says that one bright spot is that he has begun a daily meditation practice, which he finds spiritually, emotionally, and physically beneficial. He credits this practice for helping him to stay calm in the midst of the stresses in his life, and he adds that it has helped him develop better understanding of himself and his life journey. It has also helped him to pay attention to what is happening in his body. He attends a stroke recovery support group at the rehabilitation center and has developed some close friendships in the group.

THE MEANING OF ADULTHOOD

You have just read about three lives in process, the lives of Sheila Henderson, Viktor Spiro, and Michael Bowling. With such different histories and current circumstances, they are likely to have very different futures. Despite the many differences in their life course trajectories, we think of each of them as an adult.

But what exactly does it mean to be an adult? Although much has been written about adult development in the past few decades, definitions of adulthood are rare. In an edited book (Erikson, 1978) written over 3 decades ago for the purpose of clarifying the meaning of adulthood, the following phrases were used, some repeatedly, by the various authors: "grown up," "a fully grown individual," "mature," "responsible," and "age of majority."

The limited attempts to define adulthood have been based on biological age, psychological age, or social age. In terms of *biological age*, Katchadourian (1978) proposes that any definition of adulthood must include "completion of growth and reproductive capacity" (p. 54). That definition raises the question of whether Sarah Johnson's parents, from Case Study 11.3 in Chapter 11, should have been considered adults when they became teen parents. Katchadourian (1978) acknowledges the difficulty with this biological definition of adulthood, commenting that a comprehensive definition will be based not only on biology but also on psychosocial characteristics and "mind and spirit that lend meaning to life" (p. 54).

And what of attempts to define *psychological* adulthood? Stegner (1978) suggests several traits that are identified with psychological adulthood: sanity, morality, rationality, sobriety, continuity, responsibility, and wisdom, a list that may have Western culture biases (Lapidus, 1978). Some have suggested that any listing of adult psychological qualities serves only as an ideal type; it does not accurately reflect the psychological state of many persons considered adult (for example, see Bouwsma, 1978). Indeed, governments often reserve the right to declare an age-qualified adult to be incompetent, but secular laws rely on vague, ambiguous, and unreliable psychiatric models for making evaluations of mental status. For example, do you think Viktor Spiro should have been considered a competent adult during his most suicidal period?

Social definitions of adulthood focus on family and work roles. Benchmarks such as financial independence, "a place of my own," and marriage and parenthood have been a part of the informal social definition of adulthood, but these benchmarks have been shifting in recent decades (Settersten, Furstenberg, & Rumbaut, 2005). Social definitions of adulthood are also formalized by secular law, which specifies who is recognized by government as adults. To be an adult in the eyes of secular law, one must have reached the *statutory age of majority*, which is based solely on chronological age. The statutory age of majority has changed over time, varies from place to place, and sometimes varies within a given locality for different purposes. For example, the U.S. federal voting age was reduced from 21 to 18 in 1971 by the Twenty-Sixth Amendment to the Constitution, but federal legislation in the 1980s resulted in states establishing 21 as the drinking age.

Simone Scherger (2009) examined the timing of young-adult transitions (moving out of parental home, marriage, becoming a parent) among 12 cohorts in West Germany. Cohorts of a 5-year range (e.g., born 1920–1924) were used for the analysis, beginning with the cohort born from 1920 to 1924 and ending with the cohort born from 1975 to 1979. This research found a greater variability in the timing of transitions among the younger cohorts than among the older cohorts. Scherger also found that the transitions were influenced by gender (men made the transitions later than women) and education level (higher education was associated with delay in the transitions). It is important to note, however, that another research team found that young-adult transitions have remained stable in the Nordic countries where strong welfare institutions provide generous supports for the young-adult transition (K. Newman, 2008). It is also important to note that within cultures, there is much diversity in the sequencing and timing of adult life course markers.

Obviously, definitions of adulthood are somewhat arbitrary. In this book, we use a chronological definition that begins at approximately age 18 and ends when life ends. This is a very long period that can span 80 years and more. In this chapter, we discuss the years between approximately age 18 and age 65, covering what is usually considered young and middle adulthood. Late adulthood is discussed in Chapter 16.

THEORETICAL APPROACHES TO ADULTHOOD

Religious, philosophical, and literary texts suggest that humans have long contemplated questions about their personal biographies and the adult life course. But early psychological theorizing, influenced by Freud, paid little attention to life after adolescence, and young and middle adulthood have received less scholarly attention than other periods of life, including late adulthood. It was not until the 1960s that adulthood became the subject of scholarly inquiry. Since that time, theorizing about the adult life course has grown steadily in the behavioral sciences. This chapter does not attempt a thorough discussion of recent theorizing about adulthood but summarizes the central ideas from the theories of Carl Jung, Erik Erikson, and Daniel Levinson. It also presents recent theorizing about the transition to adulthood, Arnett's theory of emerging adulthood.

JUNG'S ANALYTIC PSYCHOLOGY

The work of Swiss psychoanalyst Carl Jung is considered here because he played an important role in stimulating interest in adult development among behavioral scientists and has been referred to as "the father of the modern study of adult development" (cited in Austrian, 2008). Unlike his mentor, Sigmund Freud, who thought that no significant personality development happened after adolescence, Jung came to think that personality development had barely begun by the end of adolescence (Jung, 1933a, 1933b).

Although Jung may be best known for his typology of introvert and extrovert personality types and his use of the concept of collective unconscious, the concepts of differentiation and individuation are central to his theory and most pertinent to discussion of adulthood (Jung, 1939). He proposed that **differentiation** is the process by which humans develop unique patterns and traits. **Individuation** is the full development of all aspects of the self into a unique and harmonious whole that gives expression to repressed attributes and desires. Gender roles come into better balance as do introversion and extroversion. Jung believed that individuation does not happen before age 40. He thought that the adult years before age 40, by necessity, are focused on breaking away from parents and meeting responsibilities to family, work, and community. Once those tasks have been accomplished, the individual can work on greater understanding and acceptance of the self. He saw middle adulthood as a time when we discover and reclaim parts of the self that were repressed in the search for conformity in the first half of life.

ERIKSON'S PSYCHOSOCIAL LIFE SPAN THEORY

Erik Erikson's psychosocial theoretical framework is probably one of the most universally known approaches to understanding life course development (Erikson, 1950, 1959, 1982). As reported earlier, Erikson describes a sequence of eight psychosocial stages across the life span that result from the interaction between internal instincts and drives and external social and cultural demands. Elements of this theory have been discussed in earlier chapters and summarized in Exhibit 4.11 in Chapter 4.

A major focus of Erikson's theory is the development of **identity**, a concept that he never explicitly defines but that appears to include a sense of self that distinguishes "who I am" from other people and that is enduring over time. Identity develops as the person encounters physiological changes and the changing demands of society, demands that produce a **psychosocial crisis**—a struggle or turning point that defines the particular stage. A well-resolved psychosocial crisis leads to strength; a poorly resolved psychosocial crisis sets the stage for psychopathology. The last three stages of Erikson's theory are adult stages, generally referred to as the stages of young adulthood, middle adulthood, and later adulthood.

According to Erikson, the psychosocial struggle in young adulthood is *intimacy versus isolation*. It is the time when individuals move from the identity fragmentation, confusion, and exploration of adolescence into more intimate engagement with significant others (Erikson, 1968, 1978). **Intimacy** can be defined as a sense of warmth or closeness and involves three components: interdependence with another person, self-disclosure, and affection (Perlman & Fehr, 1987). Exhibit 15.1 lists some of the tasks involved in fostering an intimate relationship with someone.

Like many military families, Sheila Henderson and her boyfriend, Daniel, must work on developing and maintaining intimacy in the context of periodic lengthy separations. The weekly video calls during Sheila's recent deployment allowed them to remain connected and to express affection, but we can see that Daniel is concerned about how things will go as they reestablish a relationship based on shared daily activities.

Individuals who successfully resolve the crisis of intimacy versus isolation are able to achieve the virtue of love. An unsuccessful effort at this stage may lead the young adult to feel alienated, disconnected, and alone. A fear that exists at the core of this crisis is that giving of oneself through a significant, committed relationship will result in

EXHIBIT 15.1 • Tasks in Fostering Intimacy

Effectively negotiating expectations for the relationship
Negotiating roles and responsibilities
Making compromises
Prioritizing and upholding values
Deciding how much to share of oneself
Identifying and meeting individual needs
Identifying and meeting partnership needs
Renegotiating identity
Developing trust and security
Allowing for reciprocal communication
Making time commitments to partner
Effectively resolving conflict and solving problems
Demonstrating respect, support, and care

a loss of self and diminution of one's constructed identity. To successfully pass through this stage, young adults must try out new relationships and attempt to find a way to connect with others in new ways while preserving their individuality (Erikson, 1978; J. W. Fowler, 1981).

According to Erikson, the psychosocial struggle of middle adulthood is generativity versus stagnation. **Generativity** is the ability to transcend personal interests to provide care and concern for younger and older generations; it encompasses "procreation, productivity, and creativity, and thus the generation of new beings, as well as of new products and new ideas, including a kind of self-generation concerned with further identity development" (Erikson, 1982, p. 67). Generative adults provide "care, guidance, inspiration, instruction, and leadership" for future generations (McAdams, 2001, p. 395). Failure to find a way to contribute to future generations, or to make a contribution to the general well-being, results in self-absorption and a sense of stagnation. Erikson saw generativity as an instinct that works to perpetuate society. With some help, Viktor Spiro began to practice generativity in his relationship with his parents as he entered middle adulthood. Michael Bowling found meaning in acting as a substitute dad for his sister's children, and he continues to be a strong force in their lives even though he is not able to offer the financial help he once did. As a social worker, however, you will most likely encounter people who struggle with a sense of stagnation in middle adulthood.

Dan McAdams and Ed de St. Aubin (de St. Aubin, McAdams, & Kim, 2004; McAdams, 2006; McAdams & de St. Aubin, 1992, 1998) have presented a model of generativity that includes the seven components found in Exhibit 15.2. McAdams and de St. Aubin (1992, 1998) see generativity coming from both the person (personal desire) and the social and cultural environment (social roles and cultural demand).

EXHIBIT 15.2 • McAdams and de St. Aubin's Seven Components of Generativity

1. Inner desire for immortality and to be needed
2. Cultural demand for productivity
3. Concern for the next generation
4. Belief in the species
5. Commitment
6. Action: creating, maintaining, or offering
7. Development of a generative life story

SOURCE: Adapted from McAdams, Hart, & Maruna (1998).

Even though Erikson outlined middle-adult generativity in 1950, generativity was not a subject of empirical investigation until the 1980s (Peterson & Duncan, 2007). There is limited longitudinal research to answer the question of whether midlife adults are more generative than people in other life course phases. Most of the cross-sectional research on generativity reports greater generativity during middle adulthood than in young adulthood or late adulthood (An & Cooney, 2006; McAdams, 2001; Zucker, Ostrove, & Stewart, 2002), but other researchers have found that generativity continues to grow past middle adulthood (Sheldon & Kasser, 2001), and there is growing interest in generativity in older adults (Bates & Goodsell, 2013; Ehlman & Ligon, 2012). Researchers have also found some evidence of generative concern and motivation in late adolescence and young adulthood, while also finding that middle-aged adults have a greater sense of capacity for generativity than these younger groups (Lawford, Pratt, Hunsberg, & Pancer, 2005; Matsuba et al., 2012).

Research also finds that generativity is associated with gender, class, and race. Several researchers (Marks, Bumpass, & Jun, 2004; McAdams & de St. Aubin, 1992; McKeering & Pakenham, 2000) have found that men who had never been fathers scored particularly low on measures of generativity, but not being a mother did not have the same effect for women. However, An and Cooney (2006) did not find parenting to be more associated with generativity for men than women but did find that midlife women are more involved in both private and public caring than midlife men. Another recent research project found that as generativity increases for adults from ages 35 to 74, so does psychological well-being, and this association between generativity and well-being is equally strong for childless adults as for parents (Rothrauff & Cooney, 2008). Generativity has been found to increase with educational level (Keyes & Ryff, 1998) and income level (Jones & McAdams, 2013). Consistent with other research that found Black adults to score higher on some measures of generativity than White adults, Jones and McAdams (2013) found that African American late midlife adults reported higher levels of generativity, political and civic engagement, public service motivation, and religious engagement than White late midlife adults.

LEVINSON'S THEORY OF SEASONS OF ADULTHOOD

Although Erikson's psychosocial theory has had the most influence on stage theories of adulthood, Daniel Levinson's theory of seasons of adulthood is one of the best known and most often quoted stage theories (D. Levinson, 1978, 1980, 1986, 1990, 1996). Levinson (1996) conceptualizes the life course as a sequence of eras (see Exhibit 15.3), each with its own biopsychosocial character, with major changes from one era to the next and smaller changes within eras. The eras are partially overlapping, with cross-era transitions, in which characteristics of both the old era and the new are evident, lasting about 5 years. Adult life is, therefore, composed of alternating periods of relative stability and periods of transition. Every era begins and ends at a clearly defined average age, with a range of approximately 2 years above and below this average.

Levinson (1996) postulated that the eras and the cross-transition periods are universal, found in all human lives, but they accommodate innumerable "variations related to gender, class, race, culture, historical epoch, specific circumstances, and genetics" (p. 5). Just consider the variations at age 25 among the three people whose stories you read at the beginning of the chapter. Sheila Henderson is a mother coming home with a closed-head injury from deployment in a war zone; Viktor Spiro had recently lost a brother, gone AWOL from the military, and was struggling with depression and substance abuse; and Michael Bowling had completed four years in the military and was working almost full time while attending college, putting off marrying for a few years.

Levinson (1996) initially developed his theory based on interviews with men about their adult experiences; later, he included women in the research. From his

EXHIBIT 15.3 • Levinson's Seasons of Adulthood

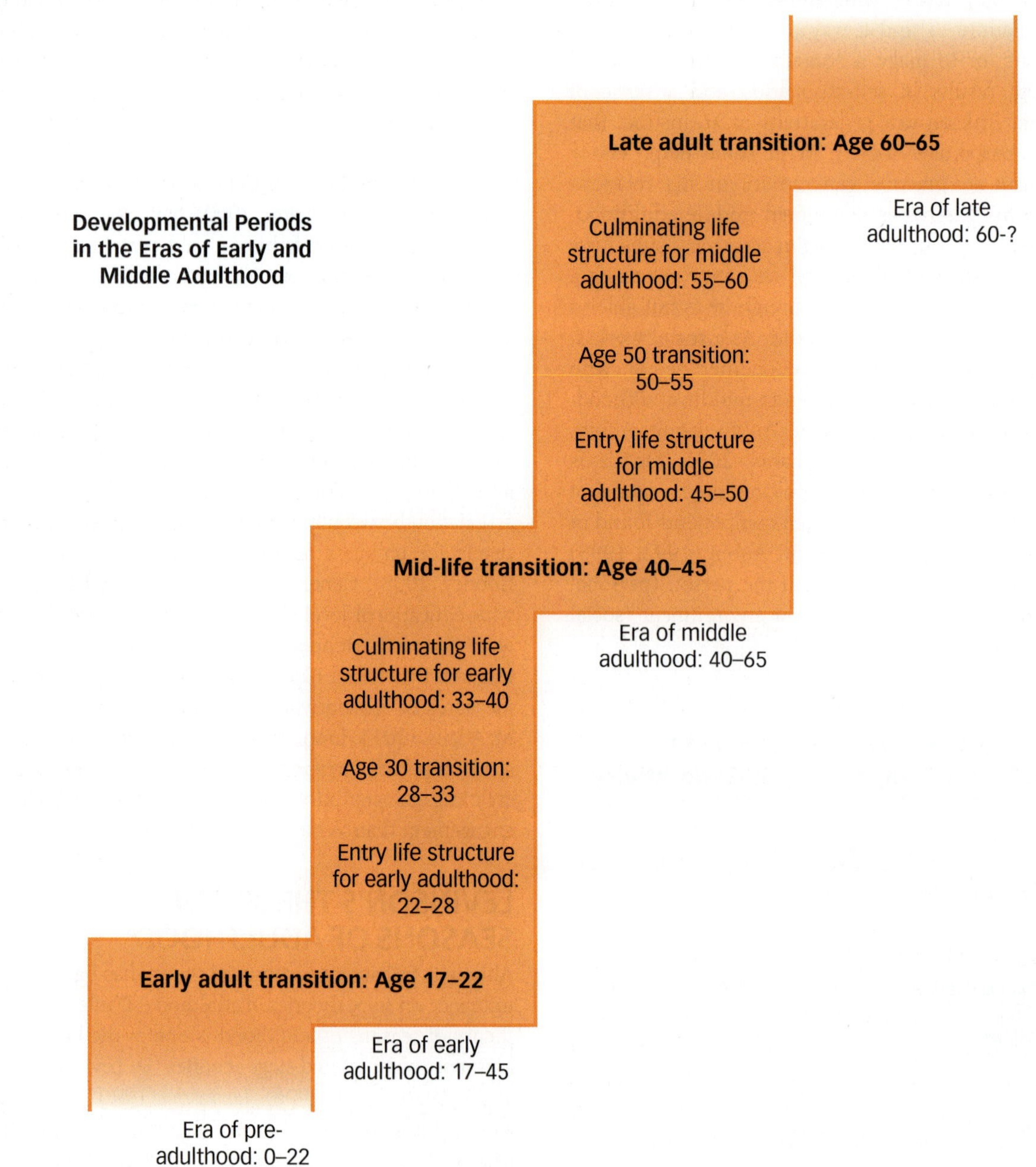

SOURCE: Levinson (1996).

research, he developed the concept of **life structure**, by which he means "the underlying pattern or design of a person's life at a given time" (p. 22). Levinson uses the concept of *central components* to designate the relationships that have the greatest significance to a life structure. He suggests that usually no more than two central components exist in a life structure, but the structure may also have peripheral components and unfulfilled components. In most cases, family and occupation are the central components in the life structure, but people vary widely in how much weight they assign to each. These variations are quite evident in the life course trajectories of Sheila Henderson, Viktor Spiro, and Michael Bowling. Work is a central part of Sheila's life, and her work has taken her to a place far from her daughter and boyfriend for a long period of time. Viktor's mental health problems have made it impossible for him to keep a sustained connection to work, but family is central to his life structure. Work was very important to Michael, and he would love to return to work, but for the moment, rehabilitation activities have become central to his life. Family seems to have been a continuous central component of his life structure.

Levinson considered the ages of 17 to 33 to be the *novice phase* of adulthood. The transition into young adulthood, which occurs during the ages of 17 to 22, includes the tasks of leaving adolescence and making preliminary decisions about relationships, career, and belief systems; the transition out of this phase, which occurs around the age of 30, marks significant changes in life structure and life course trajectory. During the novice phase, young persons' personalities continue to develop, and they prepare to differentiate (emotionally, geographically, financially) from their families of origin (Levinson, 1978). Levinson suggested that it may take up to 15 years for some individuals to resolve the transition to adulthood and to construct a stable adult life structure.

According to Levinson (1996), the early adulthood era, from about 17 to 45, is the adult era of greatest vigor but also of "greatest contradiction and stress" (p. 19). The 20s and 30s are peak years biologically. Psychosocially, early adulthood offers only limited life experience for making crucial decisions about domestic partnerships, family, work, and lifestyle. Heavy financial obligations are likely to be incurred, but earning power is still comparatively low. Both the rewards and costs of this era are enormous.

The era of middle adulthood, from about 40 to 65, is a time of reduced biological capacities but also a period when many people are energized by satisfying intimate relationships and gratifying contributions at work and in the community. This was true for Michael Bowling in the early years of this era. It appears that this may be an improved era for Viktor Spiro. For some, however, middle adulthood is a time of progressive decline, self-absorption, and emptiness. Michel Bowling seems determined to avoid this trajectory following a period of losses. In a similar way to Jung, Levinson suggests that during the transition to middle adulthood, individuals often try to give greater attention to previously neglected components. He sees this transition as balancing four opposing aspects of identity: young versus old, creation versus destruction, feminine versus masculine, and attachment versus separation (Levinson, 1977).

Building on Levinson's concepts, others have noted that cultural and societal factors affect life structure choices during adulthood by constraining or facilitating opportunities (Newman & Newman, 2012). For example, socioeconomic status, parental expectations, availability of and interactions with adult role models, neighborhood conditions, and community and peer group pressures may all contribute to a young person's decisions about whether to marry early, get a job or join the military before pursuing a college education or advanced training, or delay childbearing. Social and economic factors may directly or indirectly limit a young person's access to alternative choices, thereby rigidifying a young person's life structure. Along these lines, many researchers discuss the strong link between social capital and human capital, suggesting that a family's "wealth transfer" or extent of familial assets, such as the ability to pay for children's college education, is influential in opening up or limiting young adults' opportunities for advanced education and viable employment (Lui, Robles, Leondar-Wright, Brewer, & Adamson, 2006).

Sheila Henderson has spent her young-adult transition juggling a military career, parenthood, and a new romantic relationship. Viktor Spiro's young-adult transition was negatively impacted by poverty and political unrest, as well as by trauma, depression, and substance abuse. Michael Bowling joined the army after high school, hoping to provide some financial stability not only for himself but also for his family. Especially in young adulthood, life structures are in constant motion, changing with time and evolving as new life circumstances unfold. Decisions made during the young-adulthood transition, such as joining the military, foregoing postsecondary education, or delaying childbearing, may not accurately or completely represent a young person's desired life structure or goals.

ARNETT'S "EMERGING" ADULTHOOD

A number of prominent developmental scholars who have written about the stages of adolescence and young adulthood in advanced industrial countries have described phenomena called "prolonged adolescence," "youthhood," or "psychosocial moratorium," which represent an experimentation phase of young adulthood (Arnett, 2000; Erikson, 1968; Settersten et al., 2005; Sheehy, 1995). This is consistent with Levinson's conceptualization of a novice phase of adulthood. Jeffrey Jensen Arnett has gone one step further, defining a phase he terms **emerging adulthood** in some detail (Arnett, 2000, 2004; Arnett & Tanner, 2005). He describes emerging adulthood as a developmental phase distinct from both adolescence and young adulthood, occurring between the ages of 18 and 25 in industrialized societies (Arnett, 2000). Arnett (2000) notes that there is considerable variation in personal journeys from emerging adulthood into young adulthood, but most individuals make the transition by age 30. He conceptualized this new phase of life based on research showing that a majority of young persons ages 18 to 25 believe they have not yet reached adulthood and that a majority of people in their 30s do agree they have reached adulthood.

According to Arnett (2006, 2007), identity exploration has become the central focus of emerging adulthood, not of adolescence. Emerging adulthood is a period of prolonged exploration of social and economic roles where young people try out new experiences related to love, work, financial responsibilities, and educational interests without committing to any specific lasting plan. The social role experimentation of adolescence becomes further refined, more focused, and more intense, although commitment to adult roles is not yet solidified. Arnett explains this adulthood transition using an organizing framework that includes cognitive, emotional, behavioral, and role transition elements (Arnett & Taber, 1994).

Most young persons in emerging adulthood are in education, training, or apprenticeship programs working toward an occupation; most individuals in their 30s have established a more solid career path and are moving through occupational transitions (e.g., promotion to leadership positions and recognition for significant accomplishments). Studies do show more occupational instability during the ages of 18 to 25 as compared to age 30 (Rindfuss, Cooksey, & Sutterlin, 1999). Indeed, Arnett (2007) suggests that emerging adulthood can be an "unstructured time" characterized by a lack of attachment to social institutions, where young people are moving out from their families of origin; have not yet formed new families of their own; and are moving out of prior educational systems and into new vocational, educational, or employment sectors.

Although marriage has traditionally been cited as a salient marker in the adulthood transition, current research shows that marriage has not retained its high status as the critical benchmark of adulthood. Today, independent responsibility for decision making and finances seems to be more significant in marking this transition than marriage is (Arnett, 1998). Overall, the emphasis in emerging adulthood is on trying out new roles without the pressure of making any particular commitment (Schwartz, Cote, & Arnett, 2005). The transition, then, from *emerging* adulthood into *young* adulthood is marked by solidifying role commitments. Newer research shows that, across race and ethnicity, the difference between those who follow a **default individualization** pathway (adulthood transitions defined by circumstance and situation, rather than individual agency) versus a **developmental individualization** pathway (adulthood transitions defined by personal agency and deliberately charted growth opportunities in intellectual, occupational, and psychosocial domains) is a firmer commitment to goals, values, and beliefs for those in the developmental individuation pathway (Schwartz et al., 2005, p. 204). In addition, these researchers found that personal agency, across race and ethnicity, is associated with a more flexible and exploratory orientation to adulthood commitments and is less associated with premature closure and circumscribed commitment.

Residential stability and mobility is another theme of this transition. Emerging adults in their early 20s may find themselves at various times living with family, living on their own in independent housing arrangements yet relying on parents for instrumental support, and living with a significant partner or friends. Indeed, residential instability and mobility is typically at its height in the mid-20s (Rindfuss et al., 1999). Thus, a traditional definition of the separation-individuation process may not be appropriately applied to emerging adulthood. True "separation" from the family of origin may appear only toward the end of young adulthood or, perhaps for some, during the transition to middle adulthood.

Demographic changes over the past several decades, such as delayed marriage and childbearing, have made young adulthood a significant developmental period filled with complex changes and possibilities (Arnett, 2000; Sheehy, 1995). Current global demographic trends suggest a similar picture. Globally, family size has decreased; the timing of first marriage is being delayed, including a decrease in teenage marriages; and there are overall decreases in adolescent labor accompanied by increases in educational attainment. However, in some newly industrializing countries, the delay in first marriage has been attributed to a rise in the rate of adolescent girls in the labor market (see C. B. Lloyd, Behrman, Stromquist, & Cohen, 2006; N. R. White, 2003).

CRITICAL THINKING Questions 15.1

Which transitional markers do you see as the best indicators that one has become an adult? Explain why you chose these particular markers. How do the stories of Sheila Henderson, Viktor Spiro, and Michael Bowling when each was age 25 fit with developmental markers you have chosen? What societal and institutional barriers might contribute to stagnation in middle adulthood? Under what conditions, and for what groups, might these be particularly challenging barriers?

VARIATIONS IN THE TRANSITION TO ADULTHOOD

The theory of emerging adulthood recognizes that there is much diversity of experience with this transition. Individual routes of development (the timing and sequence of transitions) are contingent on socialization processes experienced within family, peer groups, school, and community. Environmental opportunities, expressed community attitudes, and family expectations may all influence the timing and sequencing of transitions during emerging adulthood. Socially constructed gauges of adulthood—such as stable and independent residence, completion of education, entry into a career path, and marriage or significant partnership—hold varying importance across families, cultures, and historical time.

For some young persons, decisions may be heavily weighted toward maintaining family equilibrium. For example, some may choose not to move out of the family home and establish their own residence in order to honor the family's expectation that children will continue to live with their parents, perhaps even into their 30s. For others, successful adult development may be defined through the lens of pragmatism; a young person may be expected to make decisions based on immediate, short-term, utilitarian outcomes. For example, the person may be expected to enter the labor force and establish a career in order to care for a new family and release the family of origin from burden. Michael Bowling's decision to enter the military after high school was based largely on a desire to bring financial security to his family of origin.

One study examined the home-leaving behavior of poor and nonpoor emerging adults in the United States. Using a longitudinal data set and a family economic status measure that included a federal poverty line indicator and childhood public assistance receipt, the authors found significant home-leaving and returning differences between poor and nonpoor emerging adults (De Marco & Cosner Berzin, 2008). Specifically, having a family history of public welfare assistance, dropping out of high school, and becoming a teen parent were the characteristics most likely to predict leaving the family home before age 18 years. Repeated home-leaving (leaving, returning, leaving again) was more frequent for nonpoor as compared to poor emerging adults. And when they left home, nonpoor emerging adults were more likely than poor emerging adults to transition to postsecondary educational opportunities (De Marco & Cosner Berzin, 2008).

International research that has focused specifically on foster youth aging out of care suggests that such youth face significant transitioning risks, such as homelessness, substance abuse, and involvement with the criminal justice system (Tweddle, 2007). More successful transitioning outcomes for former foster youth, such as finding stable housing and employment, are associated with having had a strong social support system and problem-solving skill development before leaving care (M. Stein, 2005; Tweddle, 2007).

Culture and gender also have significant influence on young-adult roles and expectations (Arnett & Taber, 1994). Social norms may sanction the postponement of traditional adult roles (such as marriage) or may promote marriage and childbearing in adolescence. There may be different family expectations about what it means to be a "good daughter" or "good son," and these expectations may be consistent or inconsistent with socially prescribed gender roles, potentially creating competing role demands.

Here are a couple of examples of cultural variations in the young-adult transition. One research team studied 450 college students in one southeastern U.S. state and found that African American, Latino, and Asian American students were more likely than White students to perceive themselves as adults, whereas the White students were more likely to perceive themselves as emerging adults. Likewise, low-income students were more likely than other students to perceive themselves as adults. The ethnic minority students were more likely than White students to put high value on family obligations. Students who perceived themselves as adults were less likely to binge drink, smoke cigarettes, and gamble than students who perceived themselves as emerging adults (Blinn-Pike, Worthy, Jonkman, & Smith, 2008). In another study examining the life course priorities of Appalachian emerging adults aged 19 to 24, Brown, Rehkopf, Copeland, Costello, and Worthman (2009) found that high family poverty, and particularly the combination of poverty and parental neglect, was associated with emerging adults' lower educational goals. In addition, the experience of traumatic stressors was associated with lowered economic attainment priorities among Appalachian emerging adults.

Some environments may offer limited education and occupational opportunities. Economic structures, environmental opportunities, family characteristics, and individual abilities all contribute to variations in transitioning during emerging adulthood. Young adults with developmental disabilities tend to remain in high school during the adulthood transitioning years of 18 to 21, as compared to their peers without such disabilities who are more likely to continue on to college or enter the workforce. Research suggests that more inclusive postsecondary environments, that offer higher education opportunities for young adults with developmental disabilities, and the necessary accommodations for such adults to succeed, can increase their social and academic skills, as well as facilitate productive interactions between young adults with and without disabilities (Casale-Giannola & Kamens, 2006). Some studies have shown that Latina mothers of young adults with developmental disabilities encourage family centered adulthood transitioning, with less emphasis on traditional markers of independence and more emphasis on the family's role in the young adults' ongoing decision making, with such mothers reporting that their young adults' social interactions were more important to them than traditional measures of productivity (Rueda, Monzo, Shapiro, Gomez, & Blacher, 2005).

Individuals who grow up in families with limited financial resources, or who are making important transitions during an economic downturn, have less time for lengthy exploration than others do and may be encouraged to make occupational commitments as soon as possible. Indeed, research shows that childhood socioeconomic status is an important mediating factor in young-adult transitions (Smyer, Gatz, Simi, & Pedersen, 1998). One research team (Astone, Schoen, Ensminger, and Rothert, 2000) found that an educational system that offers opportunities for school reentry across the life course may be beneficial to young people who do not immediately enter higher education due to family or economic reasons. They found that military service after high school increased the probability of returning to higher education for men but not for women. A family's economic background and resources are strongly associated with the adult status of the family's children; high correlations exist between parents' income and occupational status and that of their children (Rank, 2005). Individuals with greater financial stability often have more paths to choose from and may have more resources to negotiate the stressors associated with this developmental period.

BIOLOGICAL FUNCTIONING IN YOUNG AND MIDDLE ADULTHOOD

Physical functioning is typically at its height during early adulthood. Most biological systems reach their peak performance in the mid-20s. But as young adults enter their 30s, an increased awareness of physical changes—changes in vision, endurance, metabolism, and muscle strength—is common (e.g., Bjorklund, 2011).

There have been dramatic changes in the last few decades in the number of adults who enjoy healthy and active lives in the years between 45 and 65 and beyond. However, some physical and mental decline does begin to occur. Age-related changes are usually gradual, accumulating at different rates in different body systems. The changes are the result of interactions of biology with psychological, sociocultural, and spiritual factors, and individuals play a very active role in the aging process throughout adulthood. However, by the age of 50, the accumulation of biological change becomes physically noticeable in most people.

The biggest changes in biological functioning and physical and mental health in middle adulthood are in physical appearance; mobility; the reproductive system; and health, more specifically the beginnings of chronic disease. There are enormous individual differences in the timing and intensity of these changes, but some changes affect almost everyone, such as *presbyopia* (difficulty seeing close objects) for both men and women and menopause for women. Typical biological changes in middle adulthood are summarized in Exhibit 15.4.

HEALTH MAINTENANCE IN YOUNG AND MIDDLE ADULTHOOD

With new role responsibilities in family, parenting, and career, young adults may spend less time in exercise and sports activities than during adolescence and pay less attention to their physical health. At the same time, young adults ages 18 to 34 have historically been the least insured when it comes to health care coverage (Draut, 2005). With the Affordable Care Act enacted in 2010,

EXHIBIT 15.4 • Biological Changes in Middle Adulthood

CHANGES IN PHYSICAL APPEARANCE	CHANGES IN MOBILITY	CHANGES IN REPRODUCTIVE SYSTEM AND SEXUALITY
Skin begins to sag and wrinkle. Brown pigmentation appears in spots exposed to sunlight. Skin becomes drier. Hair on head becomes thinner and grayer. Hair may appear in unwanted places (ears, chin). Body build changes, with height loss and weight gain (increased body fat).	Progressive loss of muscles leads to loss of strength. Progressive loss of bone mineral leads to less strong, more brittle bones. Cartilage that protects joints begins to degenerate, interfering with ease of movement.	Women: Supply of egg cells is depleted, and ovarian production of hormones slows; women gradually lose capacity to conceive children, which ends with menopause (cessation of menstruation); vaginal dryness results. Men: Testes shrink gradually; volume of seminal fluid declines; testosterone level declines; frequency and intensity of orgasm decreases; erection becomes more difficult to achieve.

AP Photo/PHIL COALE

Young adults may choose to get more actively involved in community recreational leagues.

young adults are able to stay on their parents' health insurance until age 26. Official Obamacare enrollment numbers indicate that from 2010 to 2015, 5.7 million young adults (aged 19–25) stayed on their parents' plan, and the percentage of young adults between the ages of 18 and 25 who were uninsured dropped from 23.5% to 16.8% between 2013 and 2015. The most uninsured group in 2015 was the 26 to 34 age group, with 20.8% uninsured, down from 28.2% uninsured in 2013 (Obamacare Health Plans, 2016). Whether insured or uninsured, many young adults make an effort to maintain or improve their physical health, committing to exercise regimens and participating in wellness classes (such as yoga or meditation). They may choose to get more actively involved in community recreational leagues in such sports as hockey, soccer, racquetball, and ultimate Frisbee. Sometimes physical activities are combined with participation in social causes, such as Race for the Cure runs, AIDS walks, or organized bike rides to benefit a charity.

By middle adulthood, the need for good health maintenance activities becomes more imperative. To prevent unnecessary wear and tear on joints, it is important to wear the proper footwear when engaging in exercise activities and to avoid repetitive movements of the wrists. Flexibility exercises help to expand the range of motion for stiff joints. Exercises to strengthen the muscles that support joints also help to minimize the mobility problems associated with changes in joints. By engaging in strength training, midlife adults can minimize the loss of muscle mass. An effective strength training program involves two or three workouts per week.

The physical changes in middle adulthood require some adjustments in the sexual lives of midlife men and women. Many couples adjust well to these changes, however, and with children out of the home, may find that their sexual lives become less inhibited and more passionate. The sex lives of midlife adults may benefit from improved self-esteem that typifies middle adulthood and, in relationships of some longevity, from better understanding of the desires and responses of the sexual partner.

PHYSICAL AND MENTAL HEALTH IN YOUNG AND MIDDLE ADULTHOOD

Behavioral risks to health in emerging and young adulthood may include unprotected sex and substance abuse. The potential for sexually transmitted infections (STIs), including HIV, is related to frequent sexual experimentation, substance use (particularly binge drinking), and smoking or use of other tobacco products.

According to the Substance Abuse and Mental Health Administration's data from the National Survey on Drug Use and Health, one fifth (21.3%) of young adults ages 18 to 25 years used illicit drugs in 2012, which was higher than the rate for youth ages 12 to 17 (9.5%) and for adults older than 26 (7.0%). The nonmedical use of pain medications for this age group during 2012 was 5.3%, up from 4.1% in 2002. Illicit drug use for adults aged 18 years and older showed the highest rates for the unemployed (18.1%) and lower rates for part-time (12.5%) and full-time (8.9%) employment status (Substance Abuse and Mental Health Services Administration, 2013).

Research has shown physical and psychosocial interactions in producing health status. For example, obesity in adolescence is correlated with depression and lower social attainment (i.e., educational, economic, work satisfaction) in young adulthood for females but not males (Merten, Wickrama, & Williams, 2008). Important associations exist between being overweight and having depression in adolescence and young adulthood for African American and Caucasian females (Franko, Striegel-Moore, Thompson, Schreiber, & Daniels, 2005).

The changing economic environment, particularly the recent economic volatility experienced globally, has been found to affect physical health. According to the 2008 National Study of the Changing Workplace (Aumann & Galinsky, 2011), workers' overall health declined from 2002 levels, with an increase in frequency of minor health problems (such as headaches), rising obesity rates, and rising stress levels (41% reported significant stress). Of those workers who experience chronic health problems, most often reported conditions include high blood pressure (21%), high cholesterol (14%), diabetes (7%), heart condition (3%), or a mental health disorder (4%).

In working with young adults who have a physical or mental illness, social workers will want to assess the client's relationship to the illness and evaluate how the treatments are affecting the psychosocial developmental tasks of young adulthood. For example, an illness may increase a young person's dependence on others at a time when independence from parents is valued, and individuals may have concerns about finding a mate. Societal stigma associated with the illness may be intense at a time when the individual is seeking more meaningful community engagements, and adjustment to the possibilities of career or parenthood delays may be difficult. Increasingly, online social networking sites like PatientsLikeMe (www.patientslikeme.com) are being used by young adults with chronic health conditions to create online communities to promote social interaction and information exchange. Users can create a shared health profile and find other users who have the same health condition to share treatment experiences. Examples of current disease communities include HIV/AIDS, fibromyalgia, mood conditions, and multiple sclerosis. Currently, about one third (34%) of the PatientsLikeMe member base is under age 39, and the majority (72%) are women.

For several years now, many young adults in the United States have been returning from war zones with a variety of serious injuries, some of which will require long-term treatment and involve chronic impairment and disability. The two most pressing concerns are for returning soldiers with traumatic brain injury and post-traumatic stress disorder. Sheila Henderson has returned home having sustained a minor closed-head brain injury and is hopeful that her current symptoms will improve with time.

Young-adult partners who struggle with infertility problems may have to confront disappointment from family members and adjust to feelings of unfulfilled social and family expectations. Costs of treatment may be prohibitive, and couples may experience a sense of alienation from peers who are moving rapidly into parenthood and child-rearing. (See Chapter 11 in this book for further discussion of infertility.)

Health during middle adulthood is highly variable. There are some positive changes: The frequency of accidents declines, as does susceptibility to colds and allergies. On the other hand, although many people live through middle adulthood with little disease or disability, the frequency of chronic illness, persistent symptoms, and functional disability begins to rise during this time, and the death rate increases continuously over the adult years. There are significant gender and race/ethnicity differences in the death rates in middle adulthood, with men having higher death rates than women in Black, Asian and Pacific Islander, and White populations, and Blacks of both genders having alarmingly higher death rates than Whites.

In the past century, there has been a change in the types of diseases that are likely to affect health across the life course in affluent countries. In the early 1900s, when life expectancy was in the mid-40s, most deaths were caused by infectious diseases, such as pneumonia, tuberculosis, and influenza (Sapolsky, 2004). With the increase in life expectancy, chronic disease plays a more important role in the great stretch of middle adulthood and beyond. People are now living long enough to experience a chronic illness: "We are now living well enough and long enough to slowly fall apart. . . . The diseases that plague us now are ones of slow accumulation of damage—heart disease, cancer, cerebrovascular disorders" (Sapolsky, 2004, p. 3).

It is important to note that there are some global differences in causes of death. The World Health Organization (WHO, 2012b) reports on the leading causes of death in low-income, lower-middle-income, upper-middle-income, and high-income countries. In high-income and lower-middle-income countries, heart disease is the number one cause of death, and cerebrovascular disease (stroke) is the number two cause of death. In upper-middle-income countries, the situation is reversed, with stroke the number one cause and heart disease the number two cause. In low-income countries, however, lower respiratory infection (pneumonia) is the number one cause and HIV/AIDS is the number two cause. These data indicate that chronic illness is the major cause of death in high-income and middle-income countries, but infectious diseases continue to be a major challenge in less affluent nations.

Death is not the only outcome of chronic illness. As Sapolsky (2004) suggests, chronic disease often has a slow course and involves some level of disability over a number of years. The WHO uses the concept of disability-adjusted life year (DALY) to measure the sum of the years lost due to premature death *plus* the number of years spent in states of poor health or disability. There is much international evidence that socioeconomic position is a powerful predictor of both mortality and poor health (morbidity) (Marmot & Fuhrer, 2004). The WHO has calculated the worldwide causes of DALYs for low-income countries, lower-middle-income countries, upper-middle-income countries, and high-income countries. The leading worldwide causes are presented in Exhibit 15.5, which also shows how these causes are distributed across countries of different income levels. It is important to note that the WHO data include mental and behavioral health as well as physical health conditions, whereas health statistics in the United States typically do not. Therefore, the WHO data are useful because they give a better picture of the impact of mental and behavioral health conditions on global health. Unlike his father, Michael Bowling survived a stroke in his 50s, but he has devoted considerable time to rehabilitation and continues to have minor symptoms.

The story of Viktor Spiro demonstrates the important impact that mental health conditions can have on life trajectories. There is evidence that baby boomers in the United States and Europe have higher rates of depression and substance abuse than previous generations (Piazza & Charles, 2006). A longitudinal study in the Netherlands found that mental health tends to improve across the life course, but a minority of midlife adults show persistently high levels of depressive symptoms and loneliness across the middle-adult years (Deeg, 2005). These researchers, like many others who study middle adulthood, emphasize that reporting average results can mask the great variability in middle-adult trajectories. Researchers have also found that "midlife is a particularly high-risk period for either delayed onset or reactivated PTSD" (Solomon & Mikulincer, 2006, p. 664). A longitudinal investigation of PTSD symptoms among combat veterans found that the symptoms decreased by the 3rd year following combat trauma but had been reactivated in many veterans in the 20-year follow-up (Solomon & Mikulincer, 2006). It is important for social workers to recognize the possibility of delayed and reactivated PTSD in their midlife clients. This will be particularly important in the years ahead as veterans of the Iraq and Afghanistan wars become clients in every social service sector.

EXHIBIT 15.5 • Leading Causes of Disease Burden (DALYs) Worldwide and for Low-Income Countries, Lower-Middle-Income Countries, Upper-Middle-Income Countries, and High-Income Countries, 2011

CAUSE	WORLD (%)	LOW-INCOME COUNTRIES (% TOTAL)	LOWER-MIDDLE-INCOME COUNTRIES (% TOTAL)	UPPER-MIDDLE-INCOME COUNTRIES (% TOTAL)	HIGH-INCOME COUNTRIES (% TOTAL)
Infectious and parasitic diseases	16.5	30.9	19.3	7.5	2.3
Cardiovascular disease	13.8	5.7	11.6	21.2	18.4
Injuries	10.8	9.1	10.7	12.6	10.0
Cancers	8.1	3.3	4.7	12.8	18.3
Neonatal conditions	8.4	12.9	11.3	3.8	1.1
Mental and behavioral disorders	7.2	4.2	5.8	9.6	12.1
Respiratory infections	6.3	10.0	7.8	2.0	1.8
Respiratory disease (COPD)	4.9	3.1	5.4	5.1	5.7
Musculoskeletal disease	4.0	1.9	2.7	5.4	8.6

SOURCE: Based on World Health Organization, 2012c.

Viktor Spiro struggled with depression and substance abuse before he immigrated to the United States, and, as happens with many immigrants, the multiple losses and demands associated with the immigration experience exacerbated his mental health problems. As Karen Aroian and Anne E. Norris (2003) note, "Depression significantly impairs immigrants' ability to adapt to the new country and has serious emotional and economic consequences for immigrants and their families" (p. 420). Aroian and Norris found high levels of depression in a sample of immigrants from the former Soviet Union; they also found that the severity and longevity of depressive symptoms were correlated with the level of immigration-related stressors. They concluded that mental health interventions with depressed immigrants should focus on relieving these stressors by focusing on such practical issues as learning English and obtaining employment, as well as on emotional issues like loss, trauma, and feeling at home in the new country. Viktor was lucky to find mental health professionals who did just this, assisting him to get debt forgiveness and attain citizenship, while also working on issues of emotion regulation and expanding his social network.

COGNITION IN YOUNG AND MIDDLE ADULTHOOD

Young adulthood is a time when individuals expand, refine, and challenge existing belief systems, and the college environment is especially fertile ground for such broadening experiences. Late adolescents and young adults are also entering Piaget's formal operations stage, during which they begin to develop the cognitive ability to apply abstract principles to enhance problem solving and to reflect on thought processes (refer back to Exhibit 4.1 in Chapter 4 for an overview of Piaget's stages of cognitive development). These more complex cognitive capabilities, combined with a greater awareness of personal feelings, characterize cognitive development in young adulthood (Gardiner & Kosmitzki, 2011).

The abstract reasoning capabilities of adulthood and the awareness of subjective feelings can be applied to life experiences in ways that help individuals negotiate life transitions, new roles, stressors, and challenges (Labouvie-Vief, 2005). You might think of the development in cognitive processing from adolescence to young adulthood as a gradual switch from obtaining information to using that information in more applied ways (Arnett & Taber, 1994). Young adults are better able to see things from multiple viewpoints and from various perspectives than adolescents are.

With increasing cognitive flexibility, young adults begin to solidify their own values and beliefs. They may opt to retain certain traditions and values from their family of origin while letting go of others in order to make room for new ones. During this sorting out process, young adults are also defining what community means to them and what their place in the larger societal context might be like. Individuals begin establishing memberships in, and attachments to, selected social, service, recreational, and faith communities. Research indicates that religious beliefs, in particular, are reevaluated and critically examined in young adulthood, with individuals sorting out beliefs and values they desire to hold on to and those they choose to discard (Arnett & Jensen, 2002). However, there is a danger that discarded family beliefs may not be replaced with new meaningful beliefs (Arnett, 2000). Many emerging adults view the world as cold and disheartening and are somewhat cynical about the future. With this common pitfall in mind, we can take comfort from Arnett's finding that nearly all the 18- to 24-year-olds who participated in his study believed that they would ultimately achieve their goals at some point in the future (Arnett, 2000).

Perhaps no domain of human behavior in middle adulthood arouses more concern than intellectual functioning. And yet, middle-aged adults are often at the peak of their careers and filling leadership roles. Most of the recent presidents of the United States were men older than 50. Most multinational corporations are run by midlife adults.

Research on cognitive changes in middle adulthood is recent, but there is growing and clear evidence that cognitive performance remains stable for the majority of midlife adults (Martin & Zimprich, 2005; Willis & Schaie, 2005). However, a significant subset of midlife adults shows important gain in cognitive functioning, and another significant subset shows important decline (Willis & Schaie, 2005). The amount of gain and decline varies across different types of cognitive functioning. For example, one study found that, depending on the specific cognitive skill, the proportion of midlife adults who were stable in performance ranged from 53% to 69%, the proportion who gained ranged from 6% to 16%, and the proportion who declined ranged from 15% to 31% (Willis & Schaie, 2005).

Researchers are finding that individual differences in intellectual performance increase throughout middle adulthood (Martin & Zimprich, 2005). These increasing variations are related to both biological and environmental factors. Several biological risk factors have been identified for cognitive decline in midlife—including hypertension, diabetes, high cholesterol, and the APOE gene (a gene that has been associated with one type of Alzheimer's disease). Adverse circumstances early in life, including low socioeconomic position during childhood, have also been found to be a risk for midlife cognitive decline (Osler, Avlund, & Mortensen, 2012). Several protective factors have also been identified, including education; work or other environments that demand complex cognitive work; control beliefs; social support; cognitive exercise, including computer use; and physical exercise (Agrigoroaei & Lachman, 2011; Lachman, Agrigoroaei, Murphy, & Tun, 2010; Tun & Lachman, 2010; Willis & Schaie, 2005). These findings are consistent with the increasing evidence of brain plasticity throughout the life course and suggest that cognitive decline can be slowed by engaging in activities that train the brain. The news on this front keeps getting better. Lachman and colleagues (2010) have found that frequent cognitive activity, such as writing, reading, attending lectures, or playing word games, can compensate for lower education.

The Seattle Longitudinal Study (SLS) studied intellectual changes from the early 20s to very old age by following the same individuals over time as well as drawing new samples at each test cycle. Willis and Schaie (2006) summarized the findings about changes for selected mental abilities across the life course, paying attention to gender differences. By incorporating data on new participants as the survey progresses, they were also able to study generational (cohort) differences, addressing the question of whether the current baby boom midlife cohort is functioning at a higher intellectual level than their parents' generation.

Willis and Schaie (2005, 2006) summarize the findings for six mental abilities:

1. *Vocabulary:* ability to understand ideas expressed in words
2. *Verbal memory:* ability to encode and recall language units, such as word lists
3. *Number:* ability to perform simple mathematical computations quickly and accurately
4. *Spatial orientation:* ability to visualize stimuli in two- and three-dimensional space
5. *Inductive reasoning:* ability to recognize and understand patterns in and relationships among variables to analyze and solve logical problems
6. *Perceptual speed:* ability to quickly make discriminations in visual stimuli

The research shows that middle adulthood is the period of peak performance of four of the six mental abilities: inductive reasoning, spatial orientation, vocabulary, and verbal memory. Two of the six mental abilities, perceptual speed and numerical ability, showed decline in middle adulthood, but the decline in perceptual speed is much more dramatic than the decline in numerical ability. The question is how much the culture values speed. In the United States, speed is highly valued, and quick thinking is typically seen as an indication of high intelligence. In many non-Western countries, perceptual speed is not so highly valued (Gardiner & Kosmitzki, 2011). Willis and Schaie (2005) note that the mental abilities that improve in middle adulthood—inductive reasoning, spatial orientation, vocabulary, and verbal memory—are among the more complex, higher-order mental abilities. Some evidence indicates that cognitive decline in middle adulthood is predictive of cognitive impairment in late adulthood (Willis & Schaie, 2005).

Willis and Schaie (2005, 2006) found gender differences in the changes in mental abilities during middle adulthood. On average, men were found to reach peak performance somewhat earlier than women. Men reach peak performance on spatial orientation, vocabulary, and verbal memory in their 50s, and women reach peak performance on these same mental abilities in their early 60s. Conversely, on average, women begin to decline in perceptual speed somewhat earlier than men, in their 20s compared to the 30s for men. The improvement in mental abilities in middle adulthood is more dramatic for women than for men. Across the adult life course, women score higher than men on vocabulary, verbal memory, perceptual speed, and inductive reasoning. Men, conversely, score higher than women across the adult life course on spatial orientation.

Willis and Schaie (2006) also report on cohort differences in the selected mental abilities. They found that the baby boom cohort scored higher on two of the abilities, verbal memory and inductive reasoning, than their parents' generation did at the same chronological age. The baby boomers also scored higher than their parents on spatial orientation, but these differences were smaller than those for verbal memory and inductive reasoning. There were virtually no cohort differences on vocabulary and perceptual speed. The boomers did not score as well as their parents' generation on numerical ability, and the authors note that this is a continuation of a negative trend in numerical ability since the early 1900s found in other studies.

Recent longitudinal research in Germany explored cognitive change during middle adulthood but used a different classification of dimensions of cognition than used in the SLS. Zimprich and Mascherek (2010) studied four dimensions of cognition: fluid intelligence (the ability to think quickly and think abstractly), crystallized intelligence (the ability to use knowledge from accumulated learning), processing speed, and memory. They found that over a 12-year period in middle adulthood, research participants showed significant declines in fluid intelligence, processing speed, and memory. In contrast, they showed gains in crystallized intelligence.

Currently, intense research efforts are exploring what is happening in the middle-aged brain (see Strauch, 2010, for a summary of the research). It is clear that some brains age better than others, resulting in much variability in middle-aged brains. Researchers are finding evidence of both loss and gain, but on balance, the news is good. Part of memory wanes, most notably the part that remembers names. But the ability to make accurate judgments about people and situations gets stronger. In summarizing this situation, Barbara Strauch (2010) notes that "this middle-aged brain . . . just as it's forgetting what it had for breakfast can still go to work and run a multinational bank or school or city . . . then return home to deal with . . . teenagers, neighbors, parents" (pp. xvi–xvii). Neuroscientists are suggesting that as we reach midlife, our brains begin to reorganize and behave in a different way. Most notably, people in middle age begin to use both sides of their brains to solve problems for which only one side was used in the past, a process called bilateralization. The two hemispheres of the brain become better integrated. Research also indicates that starting in middle age, the brain's ability to tune out irrelevant material wanes, leading to more time in daydream mode but also greater capacity to capture "the big picture." Researchers are not certain about the most protective things that can be done for the aging brain, but the best evidence to date indicates that education buffers the brain, and physical exercise is a "potent producer of new neurons" (Strauch, 2010, p. 128).

CRITICAL THINKING Questions 15.2

How does culture influence the reactions of midlife adults to the biological changes that occur in this life phase? How are the reactions to these changes affected by socioeconomic status? What images of these changes are presented in the popular media in the United States? How have your ideas about middle adulthood been influenced by the popular media?

PERSONALITY AND IDENTITY IN YOUNG AND MIDDLE ADULTHOOD

Some theorists and researchers focus on how personality changes and stays the same across adulthood. Others focus specifically on identity in adulthood. Freud's psychoanalytic theory saw personality as determined sometime in middle childhood, and personality change in adulthood was seen as practically impossible. Some psychoanalysts broke with Freud and proposed that personality continues to change across adulthood. Regarding identity, Erikson's work resulted in identity development being associated with adolescence and seen as a discrete developmental marker, rather than as a process spanning all stages of the life course. However, recent theorists see ongoing identity development as necessary to make adult commitments possible, to allow individuals to abandon the insular self and embrace connection with important others (see Glover, 1996; Kroger, 2007). Identity is further shaped by the work adults do. Research shows that social networking media sites, such as Facebook, that allow the development of and participation in Internet communities, have significant impact on emerging adults' identity and social development (Pempek, Yermolayeva, & Calvert, 2009).

Dan McAdams and Bradley Olson (2010) suggest that the theoretical attempts to address the question of whether personality is stable or dynamic during adulthood can be divided into three main categories, which we call the trait approach, the human agency approach, and the life narrative approach.

TRAIT APPROACH

According to the trait approach, personality traits are enduring characteristics rooted in early temperament and influenced by genetic and organic factors. A large and growing international research literature focuses on the degree to which individuals exhibit five broad personality traits, often referred to as the Big Five personality traits (see, for example, Hampson & Goldberg, 2006; Lucas & Donnellan, 2011; Pulkkinen, Kokko, & Rantanen, 2012):

1. *Neuroticism:* tendency to be moody, anxious, hostile, self-conscious, and vulnerable
2. *Extroversion:* tendency to be energetic, outgoing, friendly, lively, talkative, and active
3. *Conscientiousness:* tendency to be organized, reliable, responsible, hardworking, persistent, and careful
4. *Agreeableness:* tendency to be cooperative, generous, cheerful, warm, caring, trusting, and gentle
5. *Openness to experience:* tendency to be curious, imaginative, creative, intelligent, adventurous, and nonconforming

Research on the Big Five personality traits suggests long-term stability in terms of the ranking of the traits for a given individual. For example, a person who is high in agreeableness at one point in adulthood will continue to be high in agreeableness across the life course (Lucas & Donnellan, 2011). However, research also suggests that there may be some gender differences in the stability of trait ranking, with men showing more consistency than women (Pulkkinen et al., 2012) and some traits (extroversion and conscientiousness) showing more consistency than others (Hampson & Goldberg, 2006). Studies of identical and fraternal twins suggest that adult personality traits have a large genetic base, with about a 50% heritability quotient (McAdams & Olson, 2010). That, of course, leaves a great deal of room for environmental influences, but scholars who favor the idea that personality is stable across adulthood argue that people with particular personality traits choose environments that reinforce those traits.

Another way to look at the question of stability or change in personality traits in adulthood is to look at mean levels of particular traits at different points in the adult life course. A number of both cross-sectional and longitudinal studies have done this and found that mean levels of extroversion and openness to experience decline with age starting in middle adulthood. Conversely, the mean level of agreeableness has been found to increase with age, and mean levels of conscientiousness and emotional stability have been found to peak in middle adulthood (see Lucas & Donnellan, 2011). What's more, these patterns of age-related changes in personality have been found in cross-cultural research that included samples from Croatia, Germany, Italy, Portugal, South Korea, and the United States (Gardiner & Kosmitzki, 2011). These findings suggest that some personality change does occur in young and middle adulthood, but McAdams and Olson (2010) note that studies of mean changes are unable to tell the more complex story of middle adult personality. Some people change more than others and sometimes in ways that are not consistent with overall trends. Social workers should be aware of overall trends but pay close attention to the specific story lines of unique individuals.

It is also important to note that some researchers have found gender differences in personality traits to be greater than age-related differences (Lachman & Bertrand, 2001). Women score higher than men in agreeableness, conscientiousness, extroversion, and neuroticism. Men, conversely, score higher than women in openness to experience. These gender differences in personality have been found in 26 cultures, but the magnitude of differences varied across cultures. The researchers were surprised to find that the biggest gender differences occurred in European and North American cultures, where traditional gender roles are less pronounced than in many other countries (Costa, Terracciano, & McCrae, 2001).

HUMAN AGENCY APPROACH

Other personality psychologists, consistent with life course scholars, have recently placed human agency at the center of adult personality development, focusing on how human agency facilitates change in midlife personality (McAdams & Pals, 2006). They are interested in motives, goals, plans, strategies, values, schemas, and choices and see these as important forces in adult personality. They recognize the ways that culture influences motives, goals, and the like (McAdams & Olson, 2010). Researchers in this vein of thought have found that middle-aged adults, on average, focus their goals on the future of their children and on prosocial societal engagement (Freund & Riediger, 2006). You probably recognize that this is the essence of generativity as presented by Erikson (1950). Researchers have also found that whereas young adults set goals to expand the self and change the environment to fit their goals, midlife adults are more likely to set goals that involve changing the self to adjust to the environment (Wrosch, Heckhausen, & Lachman, 2006).

The concept of human agency is consistent with humanistic models of personality that see middle adulthood as an opportunity for continued growth. It is also consistent with the work of neo-Freudians like Carl Jung, Erik Erikson, and George Vaillant who propose that middle adulthood is a time when the personality ripens and matures. Vaillant (1977, 2002, 2012) suggests that with age and experience, **coping mechanisms**, or the strategies we use to master the demands of life, mature. He divides coping mechanisms into *immature mechanisms* (denial, projection, passive aggression, dissociation, acting out, and fantasy) and *mature mechanisms* (sublimation, humor, altruism, and suppression). (See Exhibit 15.6 for a definition of these coping mechanisms.) He proposes that as we age across adulthood, we make more use of mature coping mechanisms such as altruism, sublimation, and humor and less use of immature coping mechanisms such as denial and projection. One research team found evidence of personality growth throughout middle adulthood, with slow and steady favorable resolution of earlier life tasks

EXHIBIT 15.6 • Coping Mechanisms

IMMATURE COPING MECHANISMS

Acting out. Ideas and feelings are acted on impulsively rather than reflectively.

Denial. Awareness of painful aspects of reality are avoided by negating sensory information about them.

Dissociation. Painful emotions are handled by compartmentalizing perceptions and memories and detaching from the full impact.

Fantasy. Real human relationships are replaced with imaginary friends.

Passive aggression. Anger toward others is turned inward against the self through passivity, failure, procrastination, or masochism.

Projection. Unacknowledged feelings are attributed to others.

MATURE COPING MECHANISMS

Altruism. Pleasure is attained by giving pleasure to others.

Mature humor. An emotion or thought is expressed through comedy, allowing a painful situation to be faced without individual pain or social discomfort.

Sublimation. An unacceptable impulse or unattainable aim is transformed into a more acceptable or attainable aim.

Suppression. Attention to a desire or impulse is postponed.

SOURCE: Vaillant, 1977, 2002, 2012.

(suggested by Erikson) of industry, identity, and intimacy, suggesting that work on these tasks continues into middle adulthood (Whitbourne, Sneed, & Sayer, 2009). They also found that midlife change in regard to these life tasks was influenced by life history, a finding consistent with the life narrative approach.

LIFE NARRATIVE APPROACH

Beginning in the 1980s, personality psychologists began to develop new theories of personality development that conceptualize the developing person as a storyteller who puts together characters, plots, and themes to develop an evolving story of the self, a life narrative (McAdams, 1985, 2006; McLean, Pasupathi, & Pals, 2007). These stories may include high points, low points, turning points, and intersecting plot lines. McAdams and Olson (2010) suggest that in modern societies, people begin to put together their life narratives, which can be thought of as narrative identities, in adolescence or young adulthood. They suggest that in the construction of the life narrative, adults draw on stories from childhood, stories rooted in culture, but identity changes as new experiences are added to the life story.

In contrast to the trait approach, which has received considerable longitudinal research attention, there has been little longitudinal research to explore the changes in life narratives across adulthood. Cross-sectional research has suggested that midlife adults construct more complex and coherent life narratives than adolescents and young adults (Baddeley & Singer, 2007), with increased tendency to draw summary conclusions about the self from the narrative (McLean et al., 2007). One research team found that the life narratives of midlife adults older than age 50 used more positive and fewer negative emotional words than the life narratives of young-adult college students (Singer, Rexhaj, & Baddeley, 2007). McAdams and Olson (2010) note that culture provides the menu of stories from which individuals choose to develop their own life narratives. They further note that identity choices are shaped by the confluence of social locations—gender, race, ethnicity, social class, geographical location, and so on—in which a particular person exists.

Research on life narratives shows much diversity in midlife narrative identities. For many midlife adults, life narratives are full of themes of agency, relationships, generativity, and personal growth, of forgiveness and overcoming obstacles. For others, depression, depletion, stagnation, and life gone bad are the content of the life narrative (McAdams & Olson, 2010). One research team examined the effect of major stressful life events on personality development in middle adulthood (Sustin, Costa, Wethington, & Eaton, 2010). They found that sometimes, major stressful events are viewed as lessons learned, and other times they are viewed as negative turning points. Michael Bowling seems to be thinking in terms of lessons learned from the crisis of a stroke.

Although there is evidence that midlife adults often engage in review and reappraisal, there is much disagreement about whether that review and reappraisal is serious enough to constitute the midlife crisis proposed by some theorists. Most researchers who have studied this issue take a middle ground, suggesting that some midlife adults do reach crisis level in midlife, but in general, the idea of a midlife crisis has been greatly overstated (see, e.g., Sterns & Huyck, 2001). One research team found that turning points are most likely to occur in young adulthood (Wethington, Kessler, & Pixley, 2004), but another research team found that when older adults were asked to identify turning points in their lives, there was some clustering of situations in their middle adulthood (Cappeliez, Beaupré, & Robitaille, 2008).

Sheila Henderson appears to be trying to incorporate the implications of her closed-head injury and its aftermath into her life narrative, and we can hope that she receives adequate medical assistance to monitor the situation. For Viktor Spiro, the tractor accident at age 13 and the death of his brother when he was 20 appear to have been interpreted as negative turning points. (Of course, it is important to remember that the adolescent accident involved a head injury that may have influenced Viktor's storytelling.) These events appear to have contributed to growing neuroticism and deterioration in conscientiousness. It could be argued that his relocation to the United States was a mixed turning point, offering possibilities as well as great stress. It seems clear, however, that Viktor's immediate response was growing neuroticism. With the help of mental health professionals and psychotropic medications, Viktor appears to be developing more positive themes for his life narrative, and he has shown great growth in conscientiousness in recent years. Michael Bowling faced a pileup of highly stressful events in his early 50s. We could understand if he interpreted this confluence of stressful events as a negative turning point, but the way he tells his story does not seem to indicate that it has resulted in any major personality change to date. He continues to demonstrate the high level of conscientiousness that has been evident in each stage of his life. It might be helpful to Michael to have an opportunity to talk with a professional mental health worker about what story he is telling himself about this unfortunate turn of events—and perhaps this has happened. A chance to engage in this kind of reflection can help him develop a survivor rather than victim narrative.

YOUNG- AND MIDDLE-ADULT SPIRITUALITY

Institutional religion is a source of social belonging for Viktor Spiro. For Michael Bowling, a personal meditation practice has been a source of spiritual growth and emotional regulation. There are two different models of spiritual development in adulthood (Wink & Dillon, 2002). James Fowler's (1981) theory of faith stages, presented in Chapter 5 in this book, can be called a growth model, an approach that sees spiritual growth as a positive outcome of a maturation process. The other model sees increased spirituality across the adult life course as an outcome of adversity (Wink and Dillon call it an adversity model) rather than as a natural maturation process; in this view spirituality becomes a way to cope with losses, disappointments, and difficulties. One rare longitudinal study of spiritual development across the adult life course found evidence for both of these models (Wink & Dillon, 2002). The researchers found a strong tendency for increased spirituality beginning in late middle adulthood, something that occurred among all research participants but was more pronounced among women than men. They also found that experiencing negative life events in early adulthood was associated with higher levels of spirituality in middle and late adulthood. Perhaps Michael Bowling's motivation for a daily meditation practice includes both a drive for spiritual growth and a resource for coping with loss and difficulty.

Although Fowler's conceptualization of faith included both religious faith as well as the more personal, nonreligiously based search for purpose and meaning, commonly referred to as spirituality, most of the research on faith development across the life course has focused on the concept of religiousness or religiosity. This research suggests that for most people, religiousness is quite stable across the life course, meaning that people who are highly religious relative to their peers at any given point in time are likely to be more highly religious than their peers at any other point in time (McCullough et al., 2005; Roberts & Yamane, 2012). Much of the existing longitudinal research indicates that, on average, adults in the United States become more religious over time, but for most people "religiosity does not proceed in a straight line" (Roberts & Yamane, 2012, p. 97) but is punctuated by temporary increases or reductions related to life events and life transitions (McCullough et al., 2005). Viktor Spiro was raised in a very religious family, lost contact with his religious faith and community during his most serious mental health crises, and has reconnected with this aspect of his life as his mental health improved.

Some research suggests that it may be even more complex than this. Using longitudinal data over a 60-year time span for two cohorts, one born in the early 1920s and the other born in the late 1920s, Dillon and Wink (2007) found a U-curve of religiousness over the life course. Religiousness was high in adolescence and late adulthood but, on average, lower in middle adulthood. Another research team used longitudinal data from the Terman study, begun in 1921, of highly intelligent children and adolescents (McCullough et al., 2005). These researchers found three distinct trajectories of religious development during adulthood. A first group, making up 40% of the sample, entered adulthood as slightly religious but became more religious throughout midlife and declined in religiousness after that. A second group, 41% of the sample, had low levels of religiousness in young adulthood and became less religious over time. A third group, 19% of the sample, entered adulthood with relatively high levels of religiousness that increased throughout adulthood. The researchers note that their sample was less religious than the U.S. general population, and representative samples look more like the third group.

The two longitudinal studies noted in the previous paragraph indicate both cohort and other group-based differences in religiousness in middle adulthood. In the report of their findings, McCullough and colleagues (2005) note that the trend toward increasing religiousness across the life course is more pronounced in Japan than in the United States but does not show up at all in research with adults in the Netherlands. The Dillon and Wink (2007) study found that although both cohorts in their study showed a U-curve pattern in religiousness, the decline in religiousness began in the younger cohort while they were in their 30s, but the decline in the older cohort did not begin until the late 40s. They suggest that the different ages of these two cohorts during the Great Depression and World War II may have been an influential factor in this difference.

CRITICAL THINKING Questions 15.3

Erik Erikson suggested that identity development occurred in adolescence, but recent theory and research suggests that identity is open and flexible and continues to develop across adulthood. What do you think about this recent suggestion that identity development is an ongoing process? What types of experiences in young and middle adulthood might affect identity development? Do you think that your identity has changed since late adolescence? If so, which aspects of your identity have changed? What impact do you think that new technologies, particularly cell phones and the Internet, have on adult identity development?

RELATIONSHIPS IN YOUNG AND MIDDLE ADULTHOOD

Social relationships play a major role in life satisfaction and physical well-being across the life course. The life course perspective reminds us that relationships in adulthood have been shaped by relationships in earlier life phases, in the attachment process in infancy, as well as in family and peer relationships in childhood and adolescence (Blieszner & Roberto, 2006). Although current relationships are shaped by our experiences with earlier relationships, longitudinal research indicates that it is never too late to develop new relationships that can become turning points in the life course (Vaillant, 2002; E. E. Werner & Smith, 2001).

Numerous studies have examined how social networks change over the life course. Researchers have been interested in different types of social networks and have used the term *global network* to indicate all existing social relationships that a person has with such people as family members, spouses and romantic partners, friends, coworkers, neighbors, religious congregations, and so forth. The *personal network* is a subnetwork of the closest relationships. Most of us are involved in a number of subnetworks, such as friendship networks, family networks, and work-related networks. Researchers have been interested in the changing size of social networks and the changing nature of specific subnetworks (Wrzus, Hänel, Wagner, & Neyer, 2013).

Two main theories have been used to think about how social networks change over the life course: socioemotional selectivity theory and social convoy theory. **Socioemotional selectivity theory** proposes that social goals change over the life course based on shifts in perspectives about how much time one has left to live, and changes in social goals result in changes in social networks (Carstensen, 1995). More specifically, this theory suggests that during adolescence and young adulthood, when life left to live seems unlimited, people focus on gathering information and resources from a large network of diverse relationships. Beginning with midlife, when life ahead begins to seem increasingly limited, people focus more on the emotional aspects of relationships and the social network decreases in size as peripheral relationships decrease but close relationships do not. **Social convoy theory** suggests that we each travel through life with a *convoy*, or a network of social relationships that protect, defend, aid, and socialize us (Antonucci & Akiyama, 1987, 1997; Antonucci, Akiyama, & Takahashi, 2004). Relationships in the convoy differ in level of closeness and are affected in different ways across the life course. The closest relationships are expected to be stable over time, but the more peripheral relationships are assumed to be less stable and prone to drop away over time with changing circumstances. Social convoy theory acknowledges that the convoy can have damaging effects on individuals, contributing more stress than support and creating problems rather than solving them.

Cornelia Wrzus and colleagues (2013) point out that, even though they propose different reasons for the changes, both socioemotional selectivity theory and social convoy theory indicate that the global network becomes

Research finds a lot of intergenerational solidarity in contemporary families.

smaller across adulthood, with a continuous decrease in peripheral relationships, but close relationships with family and close friends remain. They conducted a meta-analysis of 277 studies, which included both Western and non-Western samples, of age-related changes in social networks to test these ideas. Both cross-sectional and longitudinal studies found that the global network size increased during adolescence and emerging adulthood, plateaued in the mid-20s and early 30s, and continuously decreased after that. The size of personal and friendship networks decreased across adulthood. The size of family networks was highly consistent across adulthood, however. In middle adulthood, new relationships are often added to the family network, with adult children marrying and having children of their own, but there are also losses of parents and other older relatives. The meta-analysis also revealed that personal and friendship networks were significantly smaller in more recent studies. It also indicated that there were no significant differences in family network size between countries with collectivist values and those with more individualistic values. The global and personal networks were larger, however, in more individualistically oriented countries. It is important to note that studies from non-Western countries were scarce in the database used for the meta-analysis.

Some research has found racial and ethnic differences as well as social class differences in reported convoys in the United States. Whites have been found to have larger convoys than African Americans, and the convoys of African American adults as well as adults with low incomes have a higher proportion of kin in them than the convoys of higher-income White adults (Ajrouch, Antonucci, & Janevic, 2001; Antonucci, Akiyama, & Merline, 2001; Montague, Magai, Consedine, & Gillespie, 2003).

There is much popular speculation that family ties are weakening as geographic mobility increases. Research suggests, however, that there is more intergenerational solidarity than we may think (Kohli & Künemund, 2005; Wrzus et al., 2013). Certainly, we see much intergenerational solidarity in the families of Viktor Spiro and Michael Bowling. The available research indicates that the most important relationships in adulthood are romantic relationships, relationships with parents (mothers, specifically), relationships with children, relationships with grandchildren, relationships with siblings, and relationships with friends.

ROMANTIC RELATIONSHIPS

Romantic relationships are a key element in the development of intimacy during young adulthood. **Romantic love**, also called passionate love, has been defined as "a state of intense longing for union with another" (Hatfield, Bensman, & Rapson, 2012, p. 144). Social scientists have suggested two components of romantic love: infatuation ("overwhelming, amorous feeling") and attachment (emotional bonding) (Langeslag, Muris, & Franken, 2013, p. 739). Other social scientists emphasize that romantic love and sexual desire are separate relational processes that often, but not always, occur together (Gonzaga, Turner, Keltner, & Campos, 2006).

Anthropologist Helen Fisher (2004) suggests that the choice of romantic partners is based on three distinct emotional systems: lust, attraction, and attachment. *Lust* is sexual attraction and is associated with androgen hormones. *Attraction* involves feeling great pleasure in the presence of the romantic interest and thinking of the other person all the time. Fisher suggests that attraction is associated with increased levels of dopamine and norepinephrine and decreased levels of serotonin, which are neurotransmitters in the brain. Fisher's description of *attachment* is similar to Bowlby's concept described in Chapter 11 of this book. It involves a sense of security when in the presence of the attachment figure, which is the romantic partner in this discussion. Attachment has been associated with the hormone oxytocin. Brain changes related to romantic love and sexual attraction may be more complex than this and are still being studied (deBoer, van Buel, & Horst, 2012).

In the United States, heterosexual romantic love has traditionally been considered a precursor to marriage. However, a recent trend in romantic relationships is to have sex earlier but marry later, and same-sex marriage is now legal. It is important to remember, however, that in many parts of the world and among many recent immigrant groups to the United States, marriage is arranged and not based on romantic courtship. Many other variations in relationship development exist as well. Chapter 7 in this book discusses some of these variations, including couples with no children, lone-parent families, stepfamilies, and same-sex partner families.

Each person brings prior relationship experiences to partner relationships of all types. Möller and Stattin (2001) reviewed the empirical literature on these relationships and identified a number of characteristics of prior relationships that have been found to influence partner relationships in adulthood. For example, affection and warmth in the household during the preschool years have been associated with long and happy partnerships in adulthood. Interactions with peers during adolescence help to build the social skills necessary to sustain partner relationships. Based on these findings, Möller and Stattin engaged in longitudinal research with a Swedish sample to investigate the links between early relationships and later partner relationships. They found that warm relationships with parents during adolescence are associated with later satisfaction in the partner relationship. Relationships with fathers were more strongly related to partner satisfaction for males than for females. Contrary to previous research, Möller and Stattin found that the quality of parents' marital relationship was not associated with the quality of later partner relationships. The parent–child relationship was a better predictor of later partner relationships than the quality of the parents' marital relationships.

For heterosexual marriages, a long line of research indicates a U-shaped curve in marital happiness, with high marital satisfaction in the early years of marriage, followed by a decline that hits bottom in early midlife but begins to rise again in the postparental years. However, one longitudinal research project, one of the few studies to use a national representative sample, found no upturn in marital satisfaction in later life. As found in other studies, satisfaction took a steep decline over the first 5 years of marriage. This was followed by a gradual decline during the next 20 years, after which marital satisfaction leveled off for a few years but declined again beginning at 40 years of marriage (VanLaningham, Johnson, & Amato, 2001). There was some indication that more recent cohorts have lower marital satisfaction than earlier cohorts. Other research has found that lesbian partners report no change in relationship quality in the first 10 years of partnership (Kurdek, 2004).

Midlife adults are balancing a variety of roles: family roles, work roles, and community roles, and this requires partners to coordinate their role enactments. There is evidence that unmarried partners tend to be more egalitarian in the division of household activities than married couples (T. Simmons & O'Connell, 2003); there is also considerable evidence that African American married couples engage in more egalitarian role sharing than White married couples (Coltrane, 2000). Likewise, gay and lesbian partnerships have been found to be more egalitarian than married heterosexual couples (Kurdek, 2004).

The current generation of midlife adults has more complex marital biographies than earlier generations. The baby boomers were the first cohort to divorce and remarry in large numbers during young adulthood, and remarriages are 2.5 times as likely to end in divorce as first marriages. From 1980 to 2010, the percentage of midlife remarriages rose from 18% to 32%. One in four persons who divorced in 2010 was 50 years old or older, compared with 1 in 10 in 1990 (Brown & Lin, 2012). The overall divorce rate is higher for women than men, higher for Blacks than for

Whites or Hispanics, and higher for those with a high school education compared with those with a college education. Men report more marital satisfaction than women in the United States and Chinese Malaysia (Mickelson, Claffey, & Williams, 2006; Ny, Loy, Gudmunson, & Cheong, 2009), and most divorces are initiated by women (McGoldrick, Carter, & Garcia-Preto, 2011b).

Although there is a period of adjustment to divorce, midlife adults cope better with divorce than young adults (Greene, Anderson, Forgatch, DeGarmo, & Hetherington, 2012). Some individuals actually report improved well-being after divorce. Women have been found to be more adversely affected by a distressed marriage and men more adversely affected by being divorced (Hetherington & Kelly, 2002). However, the financial consequences of divorce for women are negative. After divorce, men are more likely to remarry than women, and Whites are more likely to remarry than African Americans.

RELATIONSHIPS WITH CHILDREN

Parenting is an interactive process, with reciprocal parent–child and child–parent influences (Maccoby, 2002b). The multiple role transitions that mark entry into parenthood during young adulthood can be both exciting and challenging, as new familial interdependencies evolve. New social obligations and responsibilities associated with caregiving affect the relationship between the young-adult partners and between the young adults and their parents. Often, the nature of the partners' relationship before parenthood will determine how partners will manage the demands of these changing roles (Durkin, 1995).

In a comprehensive review of the effects of minor children on parents, Anne-Marie Ambert (2001) suggests that parent–minor child relationships are influenced by characteristics of the child, characteristics of the parent, and the ways a society is organized to meet the needs of parents and children. Ambert proposes some societal traits that will produce more positive outcomes for both children and parents: adequate, affordable, and accessible housing, child care alternatives, schools, health and mental health resources, and recreational facilities; work opportunities that do not put parents at a disadvantage; safe neighborhoods; positive peer group cultures for children and adolescents; positive mass media; and societal regard for the contributions of parents. Currently, our social institutions are falling short in many of these areas, making them fruitful areas for social work planning and advocacy.

Research about the costs and benefits of parenting indicate that the benefits are primarily cognitive and emotional, such as more hopeful anticipation of the future, more complex thinking, greater self-awareness and maturity in identity, improved emotional regulation, more sense of responsibility, more playfulness, and more physical affection. Most of the costs appear to be in three primary areas: finances, personal freedom, and time. In agrarian societies, children are financial benefits, but they become financial costs in industrialized, urbanized societies. The research indicates that the costs in personal freedom and time are experienced more by mothers than by fathers, because mothers continue to be the primary caregivers in most families (Ambert, 2001).

There has been interest in recent years in the role of fathers in the lives of children, and father involvement has been shown to have a positive effect on children in such areas as academic success and reducing likelihood of delinquency and substance abuse (cited in Jones & Mosher, 2013). A National Survey of Family Growth examined U.S. fathers' (ages 15 to 44) involvement with their children from 2006 to 2010 (Jones & Mosher, 2013). This study included both biological and nonbiological fathers and coresidential fathers as well as nonresidential fathers. A larger percentage of non-Hispanic White fathers had coresidential children than either non-Hispanic Black or Hispanic fathers. As might be expected, a higher percentage of coresidential fathers (90%) were involved in bathing, diapering, or dressing their children than nonresidential fathers (31%). Among coresidential fathers, Black fathers (70%) were more likely than White (60%) or Hispanic (45%) fathers to bathe, dress, diaper, or help their children use the toilet. Likewise, Black nonresidential fathers (66%) were more likely than White nonresidential fathers (61%) and Hispanic nonresidential fathers (34%) to be involved in these activities with children in the past 4 weeks. On the other hand, coresidential Hispanic fathers (71%) were more likely than coresidential White fathers (64%) to eat daily meals with their children. Fathers who lived with their children were twice as likely as fathers who did not live with their children to perceive themselves as doing a very good job as a father. Other research has shown that very young fathers have significant mental health needs (Weinman, Buzi, & Smith, 2005).

Recently, Kathryn Edin and Timothy Nelson (2013) contributed an in-depth examination of fatherhood and the meaning it plays in low-income men's lives. Over 7 years, Edin and Nelson document the lived experiences of unmarried low-income fathers and their perceptions of parenting children in the urban environments of Philadelphia and Camden, New Jersey. When asked, "What would your life be like without your children?" fathers explained that they did not see their children "as millstones but as life preservers, saviors, redeemers" (Edin & Nelson, 2013, p. 58). Children, the interviews showed, facilitated a connection to life and love, helped men stay out of institutions (jails, drug rehabs), and motivated in men a commitment to doing well by and for their children.

As for mothers, the evidence suggests that maternal employment may have a positive influence on her sense of self, leading to better outcomes for her children. Given that the vast majority of women with children younger than age 6 are employed in the workforce, it is therefore

© Blend Images/Alamy Stock Photo

Research indicates that maternal employment may have a positive influence on a mother's sense of self, leading to better outcomes for her children, but there is also much evidence that mothers are more likely than fathers to experience time pressure and loss of personal freedom.

important to understand how workplace policies and conditions support or undermine parenting, particularly for low-income workers for whom employment is often characterized by unpredictable schedules and who often have little control or input into their day-to-day work routine (Gassman-Pines, 2013). Research has found that, indeed, mothers who were in emerging adulthood and working in low-wage jobs experienced significant distress in mother–child interactions related to both high and low workload stressors, as compared with mothers in other socioeconomic classes and as compared with older mothers.

Helping young adults to develop parenting efficacy may help them overcome environmental conditions and improve their children's well-being. Unfortunately, research shows that one of the biggest gaps in independent living services for young adults transitioning out of foster care is in parenting skills development (the other was housing preparation) (Georgiades, 2005). Another study compared the effects of increasing the mother's parenting efficacy in White and Black families characterized by a weak marriage and living in economically disadvantaged neighborhoods (Ardelt & Eccles, 2001). The Black families showed greater benefits in the form of increased academic success for their children. Parenting efficacy also contributed more to positive child outcomes in Black families with a compromised marriage than in Black families where the marriage was strong and secure. Parenting-related protective factors in Latino families include respect, familism, and biculturalism (Chapman & Perreira, 2005).

Although a growing number of midlife adults are parenting young or school-age children, most midlife parents are parents of adolescents or young adults. Delayed childbearing increases the likelihood that midlife adults will be stretched to provide care to their aging parents while also engaged in intense parenting to young children (Fingerman, Pillemer, Silverstein, & Suitor, 2012). Parenting adolescents can be a challenge if parent–child conflict escalates. Launching young-adult offspring from the nest is a happy experience for most families, but it is a family transition that has been undergoing changes in the past 20 years, coming at a later age for parents and becoming more fluid in its timing and progress (Newman, 2008). Data from 2012 indicate that 36% of U.S. young adults ages 18 to 31 lived in their parents' home, the highest percentage in at least 4 decades (Fry, 2012). A majority, 56%, of emerging adults ages 18 to 24 lived with their parents, a phenomenon more common among young men than young women. A similar trend exists in northern Europe, and young adults are even more likely to live with their parents in Spain and Italy (Kohli & Künemund, 2005). In general, parents are more positive than their young-adult children about living together (Blieszner & Roberto, 2006).

In a summary of findings of three studies, Fingerman and colleagues (2012) report that the current generation of midlife adults is much more involved in the lives of their adult children than their parents were with them, a trend that began when their offspring were young children. Providing support to children is associated with better psychological well-being in midlife adults, and receiving various kinds of support from their midlife parents is associated with better adjustment and well-being of young adults. In general, mothers have closer relationships with their young-adult children than fathers. Midlife parents help their young-adult children in different ways, depending on the resources they have to share.

Research also indicates that midlife adults can be negatively affected by their relationships with their adult children. For example, Greenfield and Marks (2006) found that midlife adults whose adult children have problems such as chronic disease or disability, emotional problems, problems with alcohol or other substances, financial problems, work-related problems, partner relationship problems, and so on report lower levels of well-being than midlife adults who do not report such problems in their adult children. Findings like this suggest a need for social service support for midlife parents whose adult children are facing ongoing challenges.

RELATIONSHIPS WITH PARENTS

More young adults in the United States are living in the parental home than in previous decades. However, in today's society, young persons are increasingly becoming primary caretakers for elderly family members. Such responsibilities can dramatically affect a young adult's developing life structure. Family life, relationships, and career may all be affected (Dellmann-Jenkins & Blankemeyer, 2009; Dellmann-Jenkins, Blankemeyer, & Pinkard, 2001). The demographic trend of delaying childbearing, with an increase of first births for women in their 30s and 40s, suggests that young adults are likely to face new and significant role challenges as primary caretakers for their own aging parents. This can result in young adults caring for the generation ahead of them as well as the generation behind them.

The concern is that young adults will face a substantial caregiving burden, trying to help their aging parents with later-in-life struggles while nurturing their own children. We might see a shorter period of "emerging" adulthood for many people, which would mean that they have less opportunity to explore, to gain a sense of independence, and to form new families themselves. There may be less support for the notion of giving young people time to get on their feet and establish a satisfactory independent adulthood.

Most research shows that middle-aged adults are deeply involved with their aging parents (Fingerman et al., 2012). As suggested in the stories of Viktor Spiro and Michael Bowling, the nature of the relationship with aging parents changes over time. A cross-national study of adults in Norway, England, Germany, Spain, and Israel found that across countries, support was bidirectional, with aging parents providing emotional and financial support to their midlife adult children and also receiving support from them (Lowenstein & Daatland, 2006). As the parents' health begins to deteriorate, they turn more to their midlife children for help, as is currently the case for Viktor Spiro and was earlier the case for Michael Bowling. A German study found that caring for elderly family members peaks between ages 50 and 54 (Kohli & Künemund, 2005).

Traditionally, and typically still, caregivers to aging parents are daughters or daughters-in-law (Fingerman, VanderDrift, Dotterer, Birditt, & Zarit, 2011). This continues to be the case, even though a great majority of midlife women are employed full-time. This does not tell the whole story, however. The baby boom cohort has more siblings than earlier and later cohorts, and there is some evidence that caregiving is often shared among siblings, with sisters serving as coordinators of the care (Hequembourg & Brallier, 2005). In spite of competing demands from spouses and children, providing limited care to aging parents seems to cause little psychological distress. Extended caregiving, conversely, has been found to have some negative effects as midlife adults try to balance a complex mix of roles (Savia, Almeida, Davey, & Zant, 2008), but there is also some evidence of rewards of caregiving (Robertson, Zarit, Duncan, Rovine, & Femia, 2007).

Most of the research on caregiving focuses on *caregiver burden*, or the negative effects on mental and physical health caused by caregiver stress. Compared with matched comparison groups who do not have caregiving responsibilities, caregivers of elderly parents report more depressive symptoms, taking more antidepressant and antianxiety medication; poorer physical health; and lower marital satisfaction (Sherwood, Given, Given, & Von Eye, 2005). Savia et al. (2008) found that psychological distress was greater on days that adult children provided assistance to aging parents, but they also found more distressed mood among caregivers with higher caregiving demands and lower resources. Another research team studying caregiver burden in caregivers of individuals with dementia found that the number of hours devoted to caregiving was a significant predictor of caregiver burden. They also found that having multiple helpers did not relieve caregiver burden and that caregivers who lived with the care recipient had higher levels of caregiver burden (Kim, Chang, Rose, & Kim, 2012).

Although this research is not as prevalent, some researchers have been interested in a phenomenon they call *caregiver gain* or *caregiver reward*. One early proponent of this line of inquiry found that the majority of caregivers have something positive to say about their caregiving experiences (Kramer, 1997). One group of researchers was interested in the balance of positive and negative emotions in family caregivers of older adults with dementia (Robertson et al., 2007). They found considerable variation in the responses of caregivers in terms of the balance of stressful and positive experiences of caregiving. The stressful experiences included behavior problems of the care receiver; need to provide personal assistance with activities such as eating, dressing, grooming, bathing, toileting, and transferring into bed; role overload; and role captivity (feeling trapped in caregiver role). The positive experiences of caregiving included caregiving rewards such as growing personally, repaying care receiver, fulfilling duty, and getting perspective on what is important in life; sense of competence; and positive behaviors in care receiver. The researchers identified different groups of caregivers in terms of their levels of distress. The most well-adjusted group had more resources in terms of health, education, and so on and reported fewer behavior problems and fewer needs for personal assistance of the care recipients.

Culture appears to play a role in whether providing care to aging parents is experienced as burden or gain. For example, Lowenstein and Daatland (2006) found a strong expectation of providing care for parents in Spain and Israel but a more negotiable obligation in northern Europe. In countries where caregiving is normalized, caregiving is often provided out of affection, not obligation;

may be shared among family members; and may be less likely to be experienced as burden. This seems to have been the case for Michael Bowling when he cared for his mother. Evans and colleagues (Evans, Crogan, Belyea, & Coon, 2009) report that Hispanic caregivers have been found to have slightly less caregiver burden than Anglos. Fingerman et al. (2011) found that middle-aged Blacks, on average, give more support of all kinds to aging parents and are also more likely to report an expectation that one support one's parents and that personal rewards are found in providing such support. Very individualistic families value individual independence and may find elder care particularly troublesome to both caregiver and care recipient. However, there is evidence that both individualistically oriented families and collectivist-oriented families experience negative effects of long-term, intensive caregiving, especially those families with few economic and social resources (Robertson et al., 2007).

OTHER FAMILY RELATIONSHIPS

Family relationships other than marital relationships and parent–child relationships have received little research attention. The grandparent–grandchild relationship has received the greatest amount of research attention, followed by a growing body of research on sibling relationships. Let's look first at the research on sibling relationships in adulthood.

Sibling relationships have been found to be the closest just before leaving the parental home. One study found that sibling relationships can help to compensate for poor relationships with parents in emerging adulthood (Milevsky, 2005). Siblings often drift apart in young adulthood, but contact between siblings increases in late midlife (McGoldrick & Watson, 2011). Sibling relationships have been found to be important for the well-being of both men and women in midlife. Midlife adults are often brought together around the care and death of aging parents, and research indicates that sibling contact decreases again after the death of the last parent (Khodyakov & Carr, 2009). Sibling collaboration in the care of aging parents may bring them closer together or may stir new as well as unresolved resentments. Pillemer and colleagues (Pillemer, Suitor, Pardo, & Henderson, 2010) found that midlife adults who recall their mothers playing favorites when they were children often have problematic relationships in midlife. Although stepsiblings and half siblings tend to stay connected to each other, their contact is less frequent than the contact between full siblings.

Research in the Netherlands found that brothers provide more practical support to siblings, and sisters provide more emotional support (Voorpostel & van der Lippe, 2007). In Taiwan, however, brother–brother dyads were found to provide the most companionship and emotional support of any dyad type (Lu, 2007). In the Netherlands, siblings seemed to overcome geographic distance to provide emotional support more easily than friends, but relationship quality was an important predictor of which sibling groups would offer emotional support (Voorpostel & van der Lippe, 2007).

Viktor Spiro's sister was an important lifeline for him when he immigrated to the United States, but tensions developed during the time when Viktor was suicidal. Their mutual concern about their father's health drew them closer again. Michael Bowling has close relationships with his siblings, and the closest relationship he has is with his younger sister.

In the United States, about three fourths of adults become grandparents by the time they are 65 (Bjorklund, 2011). For those adults who become grandparents, the onset of the grandparent role typically occurs in their 40s or 50s, or increasingly in their 60s. Grandparenthood has been reported to be among the top three most important roles among middle-aged men and women in the United States (Reitzes & Mutran, 2002). Baby boom grandparents are likely to have fewer grandchildren than their parents had, spend more years in the grandparent role, and share that role with more people, including stepgrandparents (Blieszner & Roberto, 2006). Vern Bengtson (2001) asserts that grandparents play an important socializing role in families and that this role is likely to grow in importance in the near future.

There are many styles of grandparenting and many cultures of grandparenting. In cultures with large extended families and reverence for elders—such as in China, Mexico, and many Asian and African countries—grandparents often live with the family. In the United States, Asian American, African American, Hispanic American, and Italian American grandparents are more likely to play an active role in the lives of grandchildren than other ethnic groups (Gardiner & Kosmitzki, 2011). Research has indicated gender differences in enactment of the grandparent role as well, with most research suggesting that grandmothers, particularly maternal grandmothers, play more intimate roles in their grandchildren's lives than grandfathers (Bjorklund, 2011). However, Bates and Goodsell (2013) argue that grandfathers have been underrepresented in research on grandparenting and recommend a more focused research effort to examine these relationships. In their own exploratory research, they found a wide variation in the nature of grandfather–grandson relationships, but grandsons saw grandfathers involved in seven domains of grandfathering work: lineage work, mentoring work, spiritual work, character work, recreation work, family identity work, and investment work. They concluded that "generative grandfathers provided grandsons with meaningful interactive experiences that built developmental competencies, including those that potentially might lead to strong generativity" (Bates & Goodsell, 2013, p. 46).

Researchers have noted two potential problems for contemporary grandparents. First, if adult children divorce, custody agreements may fail to attend to the rights of grandparents for visitation (Blieszner & Roberto, 2006). And baby boom adults are often serving as step-grandparents, a role that can be quite ambiguous. Second, if adult children become incapacitated by substance abuse, illness, disability, or incarceration, grandparents may be recruited to step in to raise the grandchildren. The number of children cared for by grandparents in the United States has risen dramatically in the past 30 years. About 2.4 million baby boom grandparents are serving as the primary caregiver to grandchildren. Racial and ethnic minority grandparents are 2 to 3 times more likely than European American grandparents to be serving in this role (Blieszner & Roberto, 2006). Unfortunately, grandparents with the fewest resources are often the ones called on to become primary caregivers to their grandchildren.

RELATIONSHIPS WITH FRIENDS

There is some evidence that the frequency of interaction with friends declines over the course of adulthood, but closeness does not decline, and friends continue to play an important role in adult well-being (Carstensen, 1995). Midlife adults have fewer friends in their social convoys than do adolescents and young adults, but they also continue to report at least a few important friendships (Wrzus et al., 2013). Baby boom midlife adults are good friends with about seven people on average; these friends are usually of the same age, sex, race or ethnicity, social class, education, and employment status (Blieszner & Roberto, 2006). Some boomers also maintain cross-sex friendships, and these are particularly valued by men who are more likely than women to see a sexual dimension to these relationships (Monsour, 2002). It has been suggested that midlife adults have less time than other adult age groups for friendships.

Friendships appear to have an impact on midlife well-being for both men and women, although they do not seem to be as important as close familial relationships. For instance, the adequacy of social support, particularly from friends, at age 50 predicts physical health for men at age 70 (Vaillant, 2002). Likewise, midlife women who have a confidant or a close group of female friends report greater well-being than midlife women without such interpersonal resources (McQuaide, 1998). Women who report positive feelings toward their women friends also have fewer depressive symptoms and higher morale than women who report less positive feelings toward female friends (Paul, 1997). Whether good feelings toward friends protect against depression or depression impairs the quality of friendships remains to be determined, however.

We might expect that Sheila Henderson has been able to develop friendships with colleagues in her military unit, as well as on the base back home as it appears her partner David has done. Viktor Spiro's recent participation in social events is providing him an opportunity to expand his social convoy and appears to be adding an important dimension to his life circumstances. Michael Bowling has developed some close friendships in the stroke recovery support group, and given what we know about Michael, we can suspect that he is giving as well as receiving support from this group.

It appears that the importance of friends in the social convoy varies by sexual orientation, race, and marital status. Friends are important sources of support in the social convoys of gay and lesbian midlife adults, often serving as an accepting "chosen family" for those who have traveled the life course in a homophobic society (Croghan, Moone, & Olson, 2014). These chosen families provide much care and support to each other, as evidenced by the primary caregiving they have provided in times of serious illness such as AIDS and breast cancer (Muraco & Fredriksen-Goldsen, 2011). Taking care of friends is often seen as a responsibility in some LGBT friend networks, and one research team found that midlife individuals reported that helping friends in their LGBT network raises their esteem. On average, they also reported tenuous ties to the family networks (Muraco & Fredriksen-Goldsen, 2011). Friends also become family in many African American families. The literature on African American families often calls attention to the "nonblood" family members as a strength for these families (Boyd-Franklin & Karger, 2012). Friendships also serve an important role in the social convoys of single midlife adults, serving as a chosen family rather than a "poor substitute" for family (Berliner, Jacob, & Schwartzberg, 2011). Friends often become chosen family on military bases as well.

CRITICAL THINKING Questions 15.4

The research indicates that family ties remain strong in societies around the world. What do you think about this? Do you think the family ties are strong in your multigenerational family? Are there family members who play a key role in maintaining multigenerational ties? If so, who are they, and what kinds of things do they do to keep relationships strong? What have you observed about your own friendship networks over time?

WORK IN YOUNG AND MIDDLE ADULTHOOD

It appears that Sheila Henderson's military career is important to her. Viktor Spiro's return to his dishwashing job

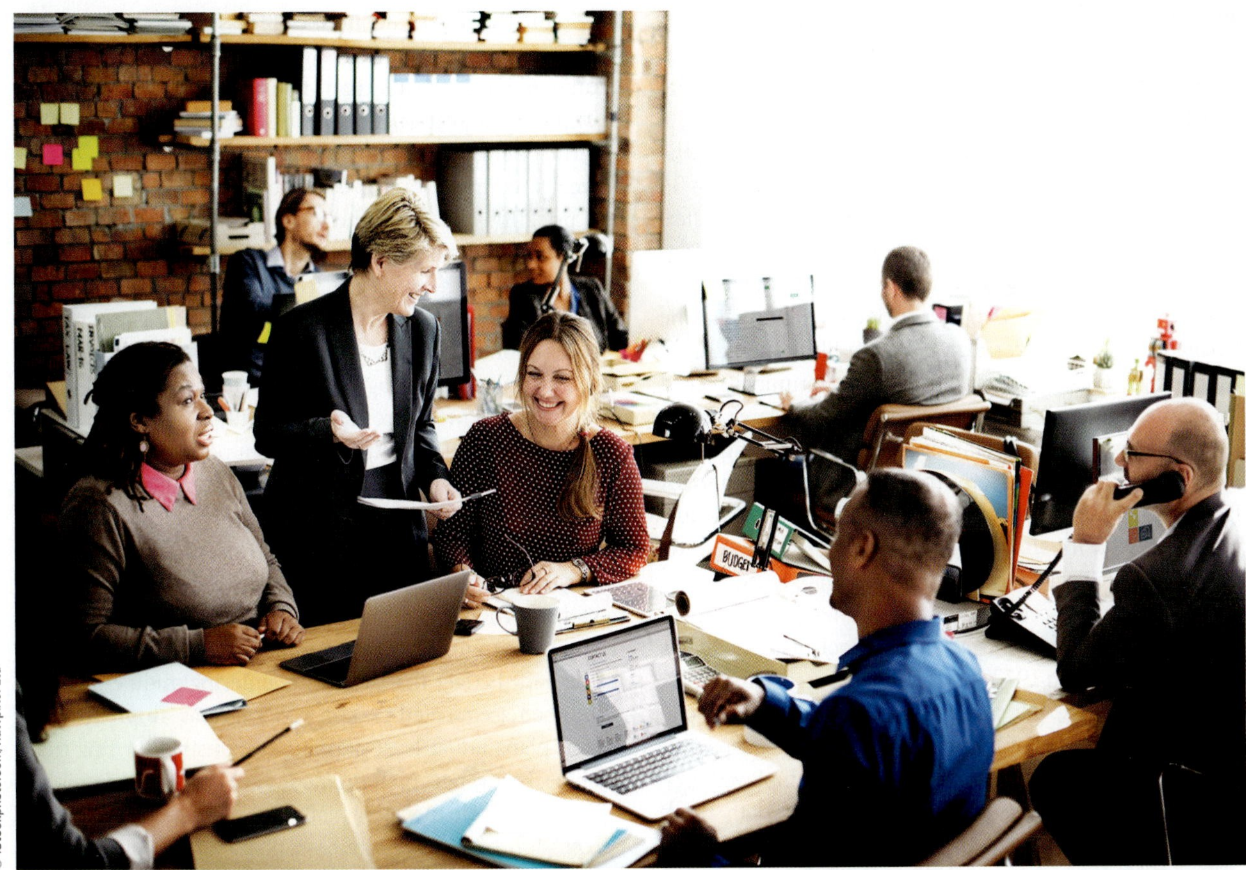
© iStockphoto.com/Rawpixel Ltd

One key marker of the transition to adulthood is achieving success in the labor market.

has been a real lift to his self-esteem. Michael Bowling had found his dream job just before the deep recession of 2008, but he has not been able to establish steady employment again since being laid off from that job. His ability to secure steady employment was further eroded by the stroke and the need for rehabilitation. Work has different meanings for different people. Here are some of the meanings that work can have: a source of income, a life routine and way of structuring time, a source of status and identity, a context for social interaction, or a meaningful experience that provides a sense of accomplishment (Friedmann & Havighurst, 1954). Given these meanings, employment is an important role for young and midlife adults, for men and women alike. What about for you? What meaning does work have for you? Involuntary unemployment can be a source of great stress.

A number of U.S. economists have referred to the decade of 2000–2010 as the "lost decade." After 2 decades of new job gains of about 20 million new jobs per decade, there was a loss in the total number of wage and salary jobs in the decade 2000–2010. During this decade, the employment rates of working-age Americans declined for all age groups under the age of 57, while the employment rates of the 57-and-older group increased. The greatest declines in employment rates occurred in the 16–19 age group, followed by young adults ages 20–24. There was a 10.7% decline in employment rates for the age group 20–24, with decline for males (12.8%) steeper than the decline for females (8.7%). There was a similar pattern of decline for all but 5 wealthy countries in the Organisation for Economic Co-operation and Development (OECD), but the United States saw more decline than some other countries, falling from 5th in overall employment rate in 2000 to 13th in 2012 (Sum, Khatiwada, & McHugh, 2014).

Danziger and Ratner (2010) note that "one key marker of the transition to adulthood is achieving success in the labor market" (p. 134). Failure to meet that marker interferes with the ability to meet other adult transition markers such as living independently, marriage, and parenthood. They call attention to the decline in labor market involvement of emerging and young adults noted in the previous paragraph and suggest several trends in the economic institution that are driving this decline: increased use of labor-saving technologies, increased globalization, declining unionization, failure of the minimum wage to keep up with inflation, increased use of casual (e.g., part-time, short-term) versus permanent employment, and an increasing portion of workers working in low-wage jobs as the bulk of economic gains go to the wealthiest families and highest earners. Over the past 3 decades, young males with a high school education are taking longer to reach economic self-sufficiency than they did in earlier eras, and young women are more likely to attain economic self-sufficiency than they did in earlier eras. During this period, median earnings increased for women but were largely unchanged for men.

Danziger and Ratner (2010) analyzed declines in the employment rate of high school graduates ages 25–34 between 1979 and 2007 and found racial/ethnic differences. Among men, the employment rate fell 23% for non-Hispanic Black males, 7.3% for non-Hispanic Whites, and 4.4% for Hispanics. Danziger and Ratner report that the dramatic rise in incarceration of young Black men during this period, and the negative effect of a criminal record on future employment opportunities, was a large factor in the greater decline in employment among young Black men. Employer racial discrimination is another important factor. Among women, employment rates increased during this period for all three groups, Non-Hispanic White, non-Hispanic Black, and Hispanic.

There were also declines in inflation-adjusted median annual earnings of employed high school male graduates ages 25–34 between 1973 and 2007. Earnings declined 26% for White non-Hispanic males, 25% for Black non-Hispanic males, and 29% for Hispanic males. During the same period, inflation-adjusted median annual earnings of employed high school female graduates increased by 7% for both Black and Hispanic women and by 37% for White women. For college-educated men ages 25–34, the inflation-adjusted median earnings remained about the same between 1973 and 2007, and the earnings for college-educated women improved at about the same rate as for high school–educated women (Danziger & Ratner, 2010).

The decline in employment opportunities has enormous ramifications for the trajectory of young adults in the labor market. The situation has been exacerbated by changes in secondary education, where tuitions have been increasing and financial aid has been declining. Many college graduates, particularly those who come from low-income families who are not able to subsidize their higher education, graduate with enormous student loan debt, only to struggle to find a foothold in the labor market. Besides young adults with criminal records, several other groups of young adults have been found to be particularly vulnerable in the tight labor market:

- Youth aging out of foster care (Hook & Courtney, 2011)
- Young adults with physical and mental disabilities (Verhoof, Maurice-Stam, Heymans, & Grootenhuis, 2012)
- Young adults who experienced a variety of types of childhood adversity (Lund, Andersen, Winding, Biering, & Labriola, 2013)
- Young adults who were early onset persistent problem drinkers (Paljärvi et al., 2015)

In the deep economic recession that began in December 2007, workers age 45 and older had a lower unemployment rate than younger workers, but they were disproportionately represented among the long-term unemployed, out of work for an average of 22.2 weeks, compared with 16.2 weeks for younger workers (Luo, 2009). In 2011, the median duration of unemployment for job seekers age 55 and older was 35 weeks, compared with 26 weeks for younger job seekers (U.S. Government Accountability Office, 2012). These midlife baby boomers are too young to draw a pension or social security (before the age of 62) or to have medical coverage through Medicare. Therefore, it is no surprise that in the first 3 months of the enrollment period for the Affordable Care Act's federal and state marketplaces, 55% of enrollees were ages 45 to 64 (Shear & Pear, 2014).

In affluent societies, the last decades of the 20th century saw a continuing decline in the average age of retirement, particularly for men (Moen, 2003). This trend exists alongside trends of longer midlife and late-adulthood periods and the fact that adults are entering midlife healthier and better educated than in previous eras. Improved pension plans are at least partially responsible for this trend of declining age of retirement. But with the demise of defined-benefit pension plans, and particularly since the recession of 2008, retirement plans have been changing again, with older adults remaining engaged in the workforce later in life (Carr & Kail, 2012).

Overall, the work patterns of middle-aged workers in the United States have changed considerably in the past 3 decades. Four trends stand out:

1. *Greater job mobility among middle-aged workers.* Changes in the global economy have produced job instability for middle-aged workers. In the late 20th century, corporate restructuring, mergers, and downsizing revolutionized the previous lockstep career trajectories and produced much instability in midcareer employment (Ritzer, 2013a). Midlife white-collar workers who, like Michael Bowling, had attained midlevel management positions in organizations have been vulnerable to downsizing and reorganization efforts aimed at flattening organizational hierarchies. Midlife blue-collar workers have been vulnerable to changes in job skill requirements as the global economy shifts from an industrial base to a service base. Within these broad trends, gender, class, and race have all made a difference in the work patterns of midlife adults (Newman, 2012). Women are more likely than men to have job disruption throughout the adult life course, although those with higher education and higher income are less vulnerable to job disruption. In the recent recession, however, men were more vulnerable to job loss than women. Race is a factor in the midlife employment disruption for men but not for women. Although Black men have more job disruptions

than White men, there are no race differences for women when other variables are controlled. Research indicates that loss of work in middle adulthood is a very critical life event that has negative consequences for emotional well-being (Dittmann-Kohli, 2005).

2. *Greater variability in the timing of retirement.* Some midlife workers retire in their late 50s. Today, many other midlife adults anticipate working into their late 60s or early 70s. The decision to retire is driven by both health and financial status (more particularly, the availability of pension benefits). At the beginning of the 21st century, the National Academy on an Aging Society (Sterns & Huyck, 2001) found that 55% of persons in the United States who retired at ages 51 to 59 reported a health condition as a major reason for retirement. Although availability of a pension serves as inducement for retirement, men and women who work in physically demanding jobs often seek early retirement whether or not they have access to a pension. Some leave the workforce as a result of disability and become eligible for social security disability benefits.

3. *Blurring of the lines between working and retirement.* Many people now phase into retirement (Carr & Kail, 2012). Some middle-aged retirees return to work in different occupational fields than those from which they retired. Others leave a career at some point in middle adulthood for a part-time or temporary job. Increasing numbers of middle-aged workers leave a career position because of downsizing and reorganization and find reemployment in a job with less financial reward, a "bridge job" that carries them into retirement.

4. *Increasing educational reentry of midlife workers.* This trend has received little research attention. However, workers with high levels of educational attainment prior to middle adulthood are more likely than their less-educated peers to retrain in middle adulthood (Luo, 2009). This difference is consistent with the theory of cumulative advantage; those who have accumulated resources over the life course are more likely to have the resources for retraining in middle adulthood. But in this era of high job obsolescence, relatively few middle-aged adults will have the luxury of choosing to do one thing at a time; to remain marketable, many middle-aged adults will have to combine work and school.

These trends aside, there is both good news and bad news for the middle-aged worker in the beginning of the 21st century. Research indicates that middle-aged workers have greater work satisfaction, organizational commitment, and self-esteem than younger workers (Dittmann-Kohli, 2005). However, with the current changes in the labor market, employers are ambivalent about middle-aged employees. Employers may see middle-aged workers as "hard-working, reliable, and motivated" (Sterns & Huyck, 2001, p. 476). But they also often cut higher-wage older workers from the payroll as a short-range solution for reducing operating costs and staying competitive.

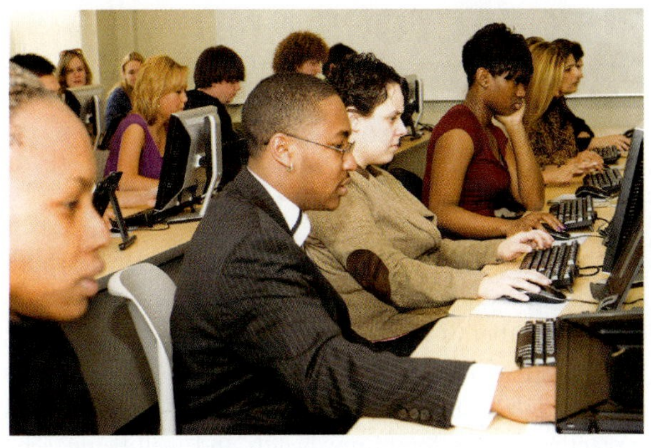

Changes in the global economy have produced job instability for middle-aged workers, and job retraining often becomes essential.

For some midlife adults, such as Viktor Spiro, the issue is not how they will cope with loss of a good job but rather how they can become established in the labor market. In the previous industrial phase, poverty was caused by unemployment. In the current era, the major issue is the growing proportion of low-wage, no-benefit jobs. Black men with a high school education or less have been particularly disadvantaged in the current phase of industrialization, largely because of the declining numbers of routine production jobs. Adults such as Viktor, with disabilities, have an even harder time finding work that can support them. In June 2013, the unemployment rate for persons with a disability was 13.4% compared with 7.9% for persons with no disability (U.S. Bureau of Labor Statistics, 2013b). Even with legislation of the past few decades, much remains to be done to open educational and work opportunities to persons with disabilities. In addition, Viktor has had to contend with language and cultural barriers.

Thus, middle-aged workers, like younger workers, are deeply affected by a changing labor market. Like younger workers, they must understand the patterns in those changes and be proactive in maintaining and updating their skills. However, that task is easier for middle-aged workers who arrive in middle adulthood with accumulated resources. Marginalization in the labor market in adulthood is the result of "cumulative disadvantage" over the life course. Unfortunately, adults such as Viktor Spiro who have employment disruptions early in the adult life course tend to have more job disruption in middle adulthood as well. But Michael Bowling's situation shows that even college-educated people with a strong work history can be vulnerable in times of economic downturn.

RISK FACTORS AND PROTECTIVE FACTORS IN YOUNG AND MIDDLE ADULTHOOD

From a life course perspective, adult behavior has both antecedents and consequences. Earlier life experiences can serve either as risk factors or as protective factors for health and well-being during adulthood. And behaviors at one adult phase can serve either as risk factors or as protective factors for future health and well-being. The rapidly growing body of literature on risk, protection, and resilience based on longitudinal research has recently begun to add to our understanding of the antecedents of young-adult and middle-adult behavior.

One of the best-known programs of research is a longitudinal study begun by Emmy Werner and associates with a cohort born in 1955 on the island of Kauai, Hawaii. The research participants turned 40 in 1995, and Emmy Werner and Ruth Smith (2001) capture their risk factors, protective factors, and resilience in *Journeys From Childhood to Midlife*. They summarize their findings by suggesting that the participants "taught us a great deal of respect for the self-righting tendencies in human nature and for the capacity of *most* individuals who grew up in adverse circumstances to make a successful adaptation in adulthood" (Werner & Smith, 2001, p. 166). The risk factors and protective factors that influence adjustment in young adulthood and middle adulthood are summarized in Exhibit 15.7.

One study (Ringeisen, Casanueva, Urato, & Stambaugh, 2009) found that although about half (48%) of young adults with a child maltreatment history had mental health problems, only 25% of these young adults received treatment services for their problems. In particular, there was a significant decline from those receiving services in adolescence (47.6%) to those continuing to receive such services in adulthood (14.3%). Data suggest that there is a significant risk of losing continuity of mental health services when making the move out of adolescence and into young adulthood, with data showing particularly high risk for non-Whites and those without Medicaid assistance (Ringeisen et al., 2009).

Other studies of youth aging out of the foster care system have found similar declining trends in mental health service utilization during the adolescent–adult transition. A study by McMillan and Raghavan (2009) found that 60% of 19-year-old foster youth dropped out

EXHIBIT 15.7 • Risk Factors and Protective Factors Affecting Adjustment in Young and Middle Adulthood

ANTECEDENTS TO YOUNG-ADULT ADJUSTMENT		ANTECEDENTS TO MIDDLE-ADULT ADJUSTMENT	
RISK FACTORS	**PROTECTIVE FACTORS**	**RISK FACTORS**	**PROTECTIVE FACTORS**
• Low family income during infancy • Poor reading achievement by age 10 • Problematic school behavior during adolescence • Adolescent health problems • For men: an excessive number of stressful events, living with an alcoholic or mentally ill father, and substance abuse • For women: a sibling death in early childhood, living with an alcoholic or mentally ill father, and a conflicted relationship with the mother	• Successful early social, language, and physical development • Stable maternal employment when the child was 2 to 10 years old • Access to nurturing, caring adults in the community • Good problem-solving skills in middle childhood • Access to a variety of social support sources and a sense of belonging with the family unit at age 18 • Educational and work expectations and plans by age 18 • Social maturity and a sense of mastery and control in late adolescence	• Severe perinatal trauma • Small-for-gestational-age birth weight • Early childhood poverty • Serious health problems in early childhood • Problems in early schooling • Parental alcoholism and/or serious mental illness • Health problems in adolescence • Health problems in the 30s	• Competent, nurturing caregiver in infancy • Emotional support of extended family, peers, and caring adults outside the family • Continuing education at community college • Military service • Marriage to a stable partner • Religious conversion • Survival despite a life-threatening illness or accident

SOURCE: Based on E. E. Werner & R. S. Smith (2001).

of services during the transition from pediatric system care to the adult service system. This is significant given that tens of thousands of youth age out of foster care each year and that former foster youth (ages 19–30) have twice the rate of post-traumatic stress disorder as U.S. war veterans (Pecora et al., 2005). In addition, they have more severe mental health and behavioral problems than the general population and than children who have a maltreatment history but not foster care placement (Lawrence, Carlson, & Egeland, 2006).

A study of the effects of war on adult mental health reveals other risk factors of which social workers should be aware. Although some researchers have found that military service often provides youth with a positive opportunity to transition into adulthood (Werner & Smith, 2001) and frequently leads to facilitating a young adult's return to higher education (Astone et al., 2000), the ravages of war experienced during military service can pose significant mental health risk. For example, Hoge, Auchterlonie, and Milliken (2006) examined the prevalence of mental health problems and service utilization among military personnel who recently returned from service in Iraq and found that one fifth (19.1%) had at least one mental health problem, with about one third (35%) of those adults accessing mental health services during their first year back home. In addition, those personnel who were assessed as having a mental health condition were more likely to subsequently leave the military as compared to those personnel who returned home without a mental health condition. Therefore, it appears that although military service can be a positive path for many transitioning youth, the nature and quality of a youth's military experience may influence later physical and mental health outcomes, as well as work trajectory decisions (e.g., to leave the military early). It appears that military service in a time of war may be a risk factor rather than protective factor, but without longitudinal data, we do not know how many military personnel entered service with an existing mental health problem. In addition, the availability of, access to, and quality of mental health care for military personnel upon their return home may also contribute to the severity of wartime service as a risk factor.

At age 40, compared to previous decades, the overwhelming majority of the participants in the Emmy Werner and Ruth Smith (2001) study reported "significant improvements" in work accomplishments, interpersonal relationships, contributions to community, and life satisfaction. Most adults who had a troubled adolescence had recovered by midlife. Many of these adults who had been troubled as youth reported that the "opening of opportunities" in their 20s and 30s had led to major *turning points* (Werner & Smith, 2001, p. 168). Such turning points included continuing education at community college, military service, marriage to a stable partner, religious conversion, and survival despite a life-threatening illness or accident. As noted in Exhibit 15.7, at midlife, participants were still benefiting from having had a competent, nurturing caregiver in infancy, as well as from the emotional support along the way of extended family, peers, and caring adults outside the family. Although this research is hopeful, Werner and Smith also found that 1 of 6 of the study cohort was doing poorly at work and in relationships at age 40.

Viktor Spiro's early life produced several of the risk factors noted in Exhibit 15.7: early childhood poverty, health problems in adolescence, and his father's chronic depression. It is interesting to note that Werner and Smith found that the long-term negative effects of serious health problems in early childhood and adolescence were just beginning to show up at age 40. We are also learning that some negative effects of childhood and adolescent trauma may not present until early midlife.

Studies have also examined the effects of midlife behavior, specifically the effects on subsequent health (see Dioussé, Driver, & Gaziano, 2009). They have found a number of health behaviors that are risk factors for more severe and prolonged health and disability problems in late adulthood. These include smoking, heavy alcohol use, diet high in fats, overeating, and sedentary lifestyle. Economic deprivation and high levels of stress have also been found to be risk factors throughout the life course. Health behaviors that are receiving much research attention as protective factors for health and well-being in late adulthood are a healthy diet; a physical fitness program that includes stretching exercises, weight training, and aerobic exercise; meditation; and giving and receiving social support (Cohen, 2012; Davidson & Begley, 2012).

CRITICAL THINKING Questions 15.5

What have you observed about the work life of the young and midlife adults in your family? How has the work life of the adults in your family been affected by growing insecurity in the labor market, if at all? How are the adults in your family working to balance family and work? How well are their efforts working?

What developmental risk factors do you see in the stories of Sheila Henderson, Viktor Spiro, and Michael Bowling? What developmental protective factors do you see in each of their stories? How would you evaluate the balance of risk factors and protective factors in each of their lives? What evidence do you see of current behaviors that might have consequences, either positive or negative, for their future life course?

IMPLICATIONS FOR SOCIAL WORK PRACTICE

This discussion has several implications for social work practice with young and midlife adults.

- Be familiar with the unique pathways your clients have traveled to reach adulthood.
- Recognize that social roles during emerging adulthood may be different from those later in young adulthood.
- Explore cultural values, family expectations, attitudes toward gender roles, and environmental constraints/resources that may influence life structure decisions and opportunities when working with adult clients.
- Where appropriate, help young adults to master the tasks involved in developing intimate relationships.
- Help midlife clients to think about their own involvement in generative activity and the meaning that this involvement has for their lives.
- Understand the ways that social systems promote or deter people from maintaining or achieving health and well-being.
- Be aware of both stability and the capacity for change in personality in middle adulthood.
- Engage midlife clients in a mutual assessment of their involvement in a variety of relationships, including romantic relationships, relationships with parents, relationships with children, relationships with other family relationships, relationships with friends, and community/organizational relationships.
- Collaborate with social workers and other disciplines to advocate for governmental and corporate solutions to work and family life conflicts.

KEY TERMS

coping mechanisms, 489
default individualization, 480
developmental individualization, 480
differentiation (Jung), 476
emerging adulthood, 480
generativity, 477
identity, 476
individuation (Jung), 476
intimacy, 476
life structure, 479
psychosocial crisis, 476
romantic love, 493
social convoy theory, 492
socioemotional selectivity theory, 492

ACTIVE LEARNING

1. Working in groups of three or four, choose one of the case studies at the beginning of the chapter (Sheila Henderson, Viktor Spiro, or Michael Bowling). Change the gender for that case without changing any other major demographic variable. Explore how your assumptions change about the individual's problems, challenges, and potential. Now choose a different case. Change the race or ethnicity for that case and again explore your assumptions. Finally, choose a third case, change the SES, and again explore how your assumptions change. Discuss why these changes make a difference in your assumptions about the cases.
2. Working in groups of three or four, identify one current social issue as portrayed in the media (e.g., housing, immigration policies, health care access or coverage or affordability, living wage) and explore how this social issue uniquely affects young adults.
3. Draw your social convoy as it currently exists with three concentric circles:
   - Inner circle of people who are so close and important to you that you could not do without them
   - Middle circle of people who are not quite that close but are still very close and important to you
   - Outer circle of people who are not as close and important as those in the two inner circles but still close enough to be considered part of your support system

   What did you learn from engaging in this exercise? Do you see any changes you would like to make in your social convoy?

WEB RESOURCES

Midlife in the United States

www.midus.wisc.edu

Site presented by Midlife Development in the U.S. (MIDUS) contains an overview of recent research on midlife development, multimedia presentations, featured publications, and links to other human development research projects.

National Fatherhood Initiative

www.fatherhood.org

Site of the National Fatherhood Initiative provides numerous resources and links to other fatherhood sites and discusses educational and outreach campaigns under way to promote involved fathering and family well-being.

National Survey of Family Growth

http://www.cdc.gov/nchs/nsfg.htm

Site of the National Center for Health Statistics offers reports, other publications, and data from their CDC-sponsored survey documenting family formation issues in adulthood, such as fertility and family planning, sexual behavior, and health.

Network on Transitions to Adulthood

http://www.transitions2adulthood.com

Site examines the policies, programs, and institutions influencing the adulthood transition and contains fast facts and information on research initiatives. The network is funded by the John D. and Catherine T. MacArthur Foundation and focuses on six areas: education, labor economics, social history, changing attitudes and norms, developmental changes, and ethnography.

Work and Family Researchers Network

workfamily.sas.upenn.edu

Site of the international membership organization of interdisciplinary work on the family and work (formerly the Sloan Work and Family Research Network) contains news, frequently asked questions, an online repository of research on work and the family, a literature database, a research newsletter, resources for teaching, research profiles, and work and family links. Part of the network's mission is to inform policymakers on key family-work issues.

SAGE edge™ **Sharpen your skills with SAGE edge at edge.sagepub.com/hutchisoness2e**

SAGE edge for students provides a personalized approach to help you accomplish your coursework goals in an easy-to-use learning environment. watch listen read

LEARNING OBJECTIVES	FOR FURTHER EXPLORATION AND APPLICATION
LO 15.1: Compare and contrast one's emotional and cognitive reactions to three case studies.	(listen) Eight Ways You Can Survive—and Thrive in—Midlife
LO 15.2: Define adulthood.	(read) When Are You Really an Adult?
LO 15.3: Analyze the merits of four theoretical approaches to adulthood (Jung's, Erikson's, Levinson's, and Arnett's).	(watch) Emerging Adulthood (read) Carl Jung's Stages of Life
LO 15.4: Give examples of variations in the transition to adulthood.	(watch) Emerging Adulthood: Choosing a Major (watch) Balancing College and Career in Emerging Adulthood (read) The Markers and Meanings of Growing Up: Contemporary Young Women's Transition From Adolescence to Adulthood
LO 15.5: Summarize biological functioning, cognition, personality and identity, and spirituality in young and middle adulthood.	(watch) Personality in Midlife (watch) Spirituality and Aging in Middle Adulthood
LO 15.6: Describe major themes of relationships in young and middle adulthood.	(watch) Romantic Relationships in Early Adulthood (watch) Relationships With Adult Children (read) The Dynamics of Young Adult Relationships
LO 15.7: Analyze major challenges related to work in young and middle adulthood.	(watch) Economic Challenges of Young Adults (listen) Balancing Work and Home Life (watch) Planning for Parenthood and Work-Life Balance (watch) Returning to School in Midlife
LO 15.8: Give examples of risk factors and protective factors for young and middle adulthood.	(watch) Resilience: Family Tragedy and Returning to School (read) Difficulties: Knights Without Armor in a Savage Land
LO 15.9: Apply knowledge of young and middle adulthood to recommend guidelines for social work assessment and intervention.	(read) Middle Adulthood

Late Adulthood

Matthias J. Naleppa, Pamela J. Kovacs, and Annemarie Conlon

Learning Objectives

LO 16.1 Compare and contrast one's emotional and cognitive reactions to three case studies.

LO 16.2 Summarize major themes in older adult demographic characteristics.

LO 16.3 Describe how old age is culturally constructed.

LO 16.4 Summarize the major biological changes, psychological changes, and role transitions and life events in late adulthood.

LO 16.5 Describe the search for personal meaning in late adulthood.

LO 16.6 Compare and contrast formal and informal resources for meeting the needs of elderly persons.

LO 16.7 Summarize what social workers need to know about the dying process.

LO 16.8 Summarize what social workers need to know about loss, grief, and bereavement.

LO 16.9 Give examples of risk factors and protective factors of late adulthood.

LO 16.10 Apply knowledge of late adulthood, dying, and bereavement to recommend guidelines for social work assessment and intervention.

Acknowledgments: The authors wish to thank Dr. Peter Maramaldi, Dr. Michael Melendez, and Rosa Schnitzenbaumer for contributions to this chapter.

GET MORE OUT OF YOUR STUDY TIME.

The **SAGE Interactive eBook** provides one-click access to integrated study tools that will enrich your understanding of course content.

- **Watch** video clips to learn actively
- **Think Critically** with SAGE Journals
- **Explore Further** with SAGE Reference
- **Connect** with relevant web resources
- **Listen** to podcasts for real-world context

CASE STUDY 16.1

MS. RUBY JOHNSON IS PROVIDING CARE FOR THREE GENERATIONS

Ms. Ruby Johnson is a handsome woman who describes herself as a "hard-boiled, 71-year-old African American" who spent the first 30 years of her life in Harlem, until she settled in the Bronx, New York. She married at 19 and lived with her husband until her 30th birthday. During her initial assessment for case management services, she explained her divorce with what appeared to be great pride. On her 29th birthday, Ruby told her husband that he had one more year to choose between "me and the bottle." She tolerated his daily drinking for another year, but when he came home drunk on her 30th birthday, she took their 6-year-old daughter and left him and, she explained, "never looked back."

Ruby immediately got a relatively high-paying—albeit tedious—job working for the postal service. At the same time, she found the Bronx apartment, in which she has resided for the past 41 years. Ruby lived there with her daughter, Darlene, for 18 years until she "put that girl out" on what she describes as the saddest day of her life.

Darlene was 21 when she made Ruby the grandmother of Tiffany, a vivacious little girl in good health. A year later, Darlene began using drugs when Tiffany's father abandoned them. By the time Darlene was 24, she had a series of warnings and arrests for drug possession and prostitution. Ruby explained that it "broke my heart that my little girl was out there sellin' herself for drug money." Continuing the story in an unusually angry tone, she explained that "I wasn't gonna have no 'hoe' live in my house."

During her initial interview, Ruby's anger was betrayed by a flicker of pride when she explained that Darlene, now 46, has been drug-free for more than 20 years. Tiffany is 25 and lives with her husband and two children. They have taken Darlene into their home to help Ruby. Ruby flashed a big smile when she shared that "Tiffany and Carl [her husband] made me a great-grandma twice, and they are taking care of Darlene for me now." Darlene also has a younger daughter—Rebecca—from what Ruby describes as another "bad" relationship with a "no-good man." Rebecca, age 16, has been living with Ruby for the past 2 years since she started having difficulty in school and needed more supervision than Darlene was able to provide.

In addition, about a year ago, Ruby became the care provider for her father, George. He is 89 and moved into Ruby's apartment because he was no longer able to live independently after his brother's death. On most weeknights, Ruby cooks for her father, her granddaughter, and everyone at Tiffany's house as well. Ruby says she loves having her family around, but she just doesn't have half the energy she used to have.

Ruby retired 5 years ago from the postal service, where she worked for 36 years. In addition to her pension and social security, she now earns a small amount for working part-time providing child care for a former coworker's daughter. Ruby explains that she has to take the extra work in order to cover her father's prescription expenses not covered by his Medicare benefits and to help pay medical and prescription bills for Tiffany's household. Tiffany and Carl receive no medical benefits from their employers and are considering lowering their income in order to qualify for Medicaid benefits, because they are not sure if they can afford insurance under the Affordable Care Act. Ruby wants them to keep working, so she has been trying to use her connections to get them jobs with the postal service. Ruby reports this to be her greatest frustration, because her best postal service contacts are "either retired or dead."

Although Ruby's health is currently stable, she is particularly concerned that it may worsen. She is diabetic and insulin dependent and worries about all the family members for whom she feels responsible. During the initial interview, Ruby confided that she thinks that her physical demise has begun. Her greatest fear is death—not for herself, she says, but for the effect it would have on her family. She then asked her social worker to help her find a way to ensure their well-being after her death.

—Peter Maramaldi

CASE STUDY 16.2

MARGARET DAVIS STAYS AT HOME

Margaret Davis has lived in her small, rural community in southern West Virginia for all of her 85 years. It is in this Appalachian mountain town that she married her grade school sweetheart, packed his pail for long shifts in the mine, and raised their four children. It has been over 30 years since she answered the door to receive the news that her husband had perished in an accident at the mine. She remains in that same house by herself, with her daughter living in a trailer on the same property and one of her sons living just down the road. Her other son recently moved to Cleveland to find work, and her other daughter lives in the same town but has been estranged from the family for several years.

Ms. Davis has hypertension and was recently diagnosed with type 2 diabetes. The nurse from the home health agency is assisting her and her daughter with learning to give insulin injections. It is the nurse who asks for a social work consult for Ms. Davis. The nurse and Ms. Davis's daughter are concerned that she is becoming increasingly forgetful with her medications and often neglects her insulin regime. They also suspect that she is experiencing some incontinence, as her living room couch and carpet smell of urine.

Ms. Davis and her daughter Judy greet the social worker at Ms. Davis's home. They have been baking this morning and offer a slice of peanut butter pie. Judy excuses herself to go to her trailer to make a phone call. The social worker asks Ms. Davis about how her insulin regime has been going and if she felt that she could keep up with the injections. She responds that she has learned to give herself the shots and "feels pretty fair." The social worker conveys the concern that she may be missing some of the injections and other medications as well. To this she replies, "Oh, don't worry about me. I'm fine." The social worker proceeds to ask the sensitive question as to whether she has been having trouble with her bladder or getting to the bathroom. This causes Ms. Davis to become very quiet. Looking up at the social worker, she shares that witches have been visiting her house late at night and have been urinating in her living room. The witches are very "devious," but because she is a very religious person, she does not feel that they will harm her.

Judy returns to the home and joins her mother and the social worker. Judy voices her concern about her mother's safety, noting the problems with medications and with general forgetfulness. Judy is able to prepare meals, dispense the medications, and give insulin injections in the morning because she works evenings at a factory. Judy's daughter Tiffany has been staying overnight in the home but complains of her grandmother's wandering and confusion late at night. As a result, she is often exhausted during her day shifts at a nursing home in the next county and in caring for her small children. When asked about Ms. Davis's son's involvement in her care, Judy responds, "He works and is in the Guard some weekends. He handles Mom's money mostly, and his wife, well, she has her own problems." Judy also reports that her mother has Medicare, but she was not sure if that would be sufficient to pay for all her mother's care long-term. Judy is also worried because her old car has been giving her problems lately, and the repairs are becoming expensive. She concludes by stating, "We promised Mom that she would never go to a home. . . . We take care of our own."

—Kristina Hash and Meenakshi Venkataraman

CASE STUDY 16.3

BINA PATEL OUTLIVES HER SON

Bina Patel is a 90-year-old immigrant who moved to the United States 25 years ago from India with her son and his family. Like many other South Asian older adults, Ms. Patel prefers to reside with her adult children and values the mutual interdependency among generations common in their culture. Upon arriving in this country at age 65, Ms. Patel, a widow, played a critical role in the family, providing child care, assisting with meals and various household tasks, and offering companionship and support for her adult children. True to her cultural tradition, Ms. Patel expects adult children—especially sons—to provide for parents in their old age and believes that the role of the elder is to provide crucial functions, such as passing on wisdom and guidance to children and grandchildren, and be constantly available to them.

(Continued)

(Continued)

Ms. Patel had been in remarkably good health until she had a mild stroke last year. She was managing well at home with weekly physical therapy and her family's assistance with bathing. She and her family have been unprepared for her longevity, and in fact it appears that she will outlive her son, who at age 69 was recently diagnosed with pancreatic cancer with a prognosis of 6 to 12 months to live. Her daughter-in-law is home full-time with Ms. Patel but does not drive and currently is emotionally distraught over her husband's rapid decline. Ms. Patel's two grandchildren, who are in their 30s, have relocated with their own families due to employment. They are in frequent telephone contact, but they live a 2 hour plane ride away and are busy with work and children's school and activities. Although this family has traditionally handled their family needs on their own or with the help of a small South Asian network, the son's decline in health has caused tremendous concern regarding Ms. Patel's future well-being.

The hospital social worker has been asked to meet with the son and daughter-in-law during his hospitalization to explore possible sources of assistance throughout the son's pending decline as well as to help strategize for Ms. Patel's anticipated increased need of physical care, given her recent decline in cognitive and physical capacity.

DEMOGRAPHICS OF THE OLDER-ADULT POPULATION

For Ruby Johnson, Margaret Davis, and Bina Patel, more years of life stretch behind them than lay ahead of them, but, like all other individuals, their day-to-day lives incorporate past, present, and future orientations (Mayer et al., 1999). Research from the longitudinal Berlin Aging Study has been able to dispel some commonly held beliefs about older adults. According to this research as well as findings from other studies, older adults

- are not preoccupied with death and dying;
- are able and willing to learn new things;
- still feel that they can and want to be in control of their life;
- still have life goals;
- do not live primarily in the past; and
- still live an active life, their health permitting.

The term *late adulthood* covers about one quarter to one third of a person's life and includes active and less active, healthy and less healthy, and working and non-working persons. Late adulthood encompasses a wide range of cohort-related life experiences. Someone reaching late adulthood today and having lived in the United States has experienced school segregation and busing for the purposes of integration, as well as Martin Luther King's "I have a dream" speech, but also the election of the first African American president and the appointment of the first Latina Supreme Court justice. He or she may have experienced the Dust Bowl and two world wars and would have grown up listening to radio shows before TV existed. The person may have been at Woodstock and could be in the age cohort of Mick Jagger and Bob Dylan. Every client in the case studies earlier could be considered old, and yet they are functioning in different ways and at different levels. In the context of U.S. society, the term *old* can have many meanings. These meanings reflect attitudes, assumptions, biases, and cultural interpretations of what it means to grow older. In discussing life course trajectories, we commonly use the term *older population* or *elderly persons* to refer to those over 65 years of age. But an Olympic gymnast is "old" at age 25, a president of the United States is "young" at age 50, and a 70-year-old may not consider herself "old" at all.

Late adulthood is perhaps a more precise term than *old*, but it can still be confusing because of the 50-year range of ages it may include. Late adulthood is considered to start at 65 and continue through to the end of life. Considering age 65 as the starting point for late adulthood is somewhat arbitrary, because there is no sudden change to our physiology, biology, or personality at this time. Rather, that age can be traced back to Bismarck's social insurance schemes in Germany more than 100 years ago and the introduction of the Social Security Act in the United States in 1935. In both cases, 65 years was selected for retirement based on population statistics and expected survival rates. Many people today reach the life stage of late adulthood. In 2013, there were approximately 579 million people 65 years or older in the world, and by 2050 this number is expected to increase to 1.6 billion (U.S. Census Bureau, 2014). In 2012, the World Health Organization (2012d) estimated that, worldwide, adults aged 65 and older will outnumber children younger than age 5 within 5 years, and by 2050, older adults will outnumber children younger than age 14. The United States has a fairly young population as wealthy nations go, with just over 13% of its population age 65 and older in 2011 (Administration on Aging, 2012). Most European countries average 15% of their population 65 or older. Japan's and Italy's older population stood at 20% of the total population in 2008 (Federal Interagency Forum on Aging-Related Statistics, 2008).

According to the U.S. Census Bureau, the 85-and-older population is the fastest-growing segment of the aging population, projected to increase from 4.2 million in 2000 to 14.1 million in 2040 (Administration on Aging, 2012). There are increasing numbers of people who are 100 years and older (called *centenarians*), a staggering 117% increase from 1990 figures (Administration on Aging, 2008). As of 2011, persons reaching age 65 have an average life expectancy of an additional 19.2 years (20.4 years for females and 17.8 for males). A child born in 2011 could expect to live 78.7 years, about 30 years longer than a child born in 1900 (Administration on Aging, 2012).

Increased life expectancy is a product of a number of factors: decreased mortality in children and young adults, decreased mortality among older adults, improved health technology, and other factors. The enormous increase in life expectancy is not unique to the United States. Indeed, recent research found that the United States has the lowest average life expectancy of 17 high-income countries. The researchers speculated that these cross-national differences in life expectancy were related to differences in access to health care, health behaviors, income inequality, and physical environments (dependence on automobiles) (Woolf & Aron, 2013). But increasing life expectancy is not just happening in high-income countries. Currently, 60% of the population older than 65 lives in low- and middle-income countries, and this may increase to 75% by 2020 (Hooyman & Kiyak, 2011). However, the average life expectancy at birth is 55 in the least economically advanced countries, compared with an average of 77 in the most economically advanced countries (Hooyman & Kiyak, 2011).

Life expectancy in the United States varies by race, gender, and socioeconomic status. In 2010, the overall life expectancy at birth in the United States was 78.7 years (Hoyert & Xu, 2012). It was 86.5 for Asian Americans, 82.8 for Latinos, 78.9 for Whites, 76.9 for Native Americans, and 74.6 for African Americans (Henry J. Kaiser Family Foundation, 2013). Females had an average life expectancy at birth of 81.0 years compared with an average of 76.2 years for males (Hoyert & Xu, 2012). Life expectancy increases with socioeconomic advantage, and recent research indicates that as income inequality grows, life expectancy is actually falling in some segments of the U.S. working class. In 2008, U.S. men and women with less than 12 years of education had life expectancies at the level experienced in the 1950s and 1960s (Olshansky et al., 2012). Researchers have noted the current health advantage of U.S. Latinos over other groups, except for Asian Americans, but predict that this advantage will disappear as second- and third-generation Latino immigrants reach late adulthood (Olshansky et al., 2012).

Age structure, the segmentation of society by age, will affect the economic and social condition of the nation, especially as it regards dependence. An interesting side effect of the growing elderly population is a shifting **dependency ratio**—a demographic indicator that expresses the degree of demand placed on society by the young and the aged combined, the ratio of dependent age groups to the working-age population. There are three dependency ratios: the old-age dependency ratio, the number of elders 65 and older per 100 people ages 20 to 64; the youth dependency ratio, the number of children under 20 per 100 persons ages 20 to 64; and the total dependency ratio, the combination of both of these categories (U.S. Census Bureau, 2010).

The nature of the U.S. dependency ratio has changed gradually over the past century as the percentage of children and adolescents in the population has decreased and the percentage of dependent older adults has increased. As Exhibit 16.1 demonstrates, the old-age dependency ratio is predicted to continue to increase at a fairly rapid pace in the near future. The overall dependency ratio is expected to stabilize to about 85 youth and older adults per 100 persons ages 20 to 64 between 2030 and 2050 (U.S. Census Bureau, 2010). The social and economic implications of this increase in the dependency ratio are the focus and concern of many scholars and policymakers.

The older population encompasses a broad age range and is often categorized into subgroups: the young-old (ages 65 to 74), the middle-old (ages 75 to 84), and the oldest-old (over 85). Ruby Johnson exemplifies the young-old, Margaret Davis is on the cusp of middle-old and oldest-old, and Bina Patel is among the oldest-old.

There have always been those who outlive their cohort group, but greater numbers of people are surpassing the average life expectancy and more are becoming centenarians. Although very few 100-year-old people were known to exist in the United States in 1900, there were 53,364 of them in 2010. The majority of these centenarians were women (82.8%) and were ages 100 to 104 (92%) (U.S. Census Bureau, 2012b). By 2050, it is estimated that more than 442,000 people in the United States will reach the century mark (U.S. Census Bureau, 2013g). Worldwide, more than 6 million are expected to reach age 100 by 2050 (U.S. Census Bureau, 2013h).

A small number of these centenarians, those aged 110 and older, are considered supercentenarians. As of January 2013, there were 63 validated supercentenarians throughout the United States, 58 women and 5 men (Coles, 2013). The Gerontology Research Group (2013) estimates that there are approximately 300 to 400 supercentenarians throughout the world.

The United States is one of the most racially and ethnically diverse societies in the world and becoming more so every day. The aging population reflects the shifting racial and ethnic trends in the general population, with racial and ethnic minority persons projected to become 42% of the old-age population by 2050 (U.S. Census Bureau, 2010). Exhibit 16.2 demonstrates the profound shift in the racial and ethnic makeup of the older-adult

EXHIBIT 16.1 • Youth and Old-Age Dependency Ratios in the United States, 1900, 1995, 2010, and 2030

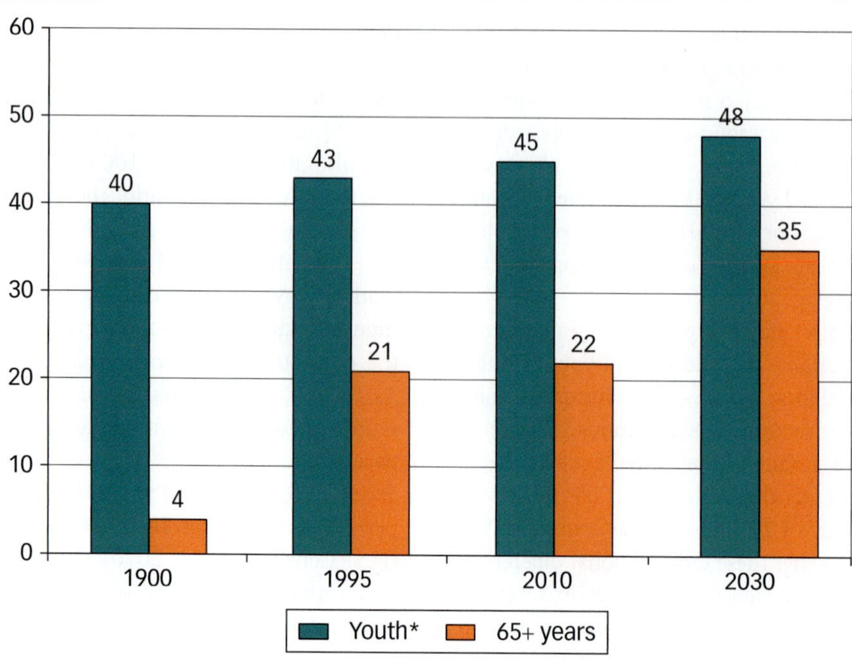

SOURCE: U.S. Census Bureau, 2010.

*1900 AND 1995 YOUTH DEPENDENCY BASED ON NEWBORNS TO 17-YEAR-OLDS, 2010 AND 2030 YOUTH DEPENDENCY BASED ON NEWBORNS TO 19-YEAR-OLDS.

population projected to occur from 2010 to 2050. The share of the population 65 and older that is White is projected to decrease by 10%, the share that is Hispanic is projected to increase from 7% to 20%, the share that is Black is expected to increase from 9% to 12%, and the share that is Asian is projected to increase from 3% to 9%. Although their numbers will remain small, large growth is projected in the older-adult population of American Indian and Alaska Natives, Native Hawaiian and other Pacific Islanders, and individuals of two or more races.

Among the older population in the United States, women—especially those in very late adulthood (85 and older)—continue to outnumber men across all racial and ethnic groups. Census data analyzed in 2012 indicate that older women (23.4 million) outnumber older men (17.9 million) (Administration on Aging, 2012). In 2007, the sex ratio among older adults stood at 137 females per 100 males. The female-to-male ratio increases with age, ranging from 114 females per 100 males for the 65-to-69 age group to a high of 210 females per 100 males for those 85 and older (Administration on Aging, 2008). Female centenarians outnumber males 9 to 1 (Harvard Health Letter, 2002).

One of the biggest gender differences in life circumstances of older adults relates to marital status. Older men are more likely to be married than older women. According to data from 2012, 72% of men 65 and older were married as compared to 45% of women in the same age group. The proportion of older adults living with a spouse decreased with age, more severely for women than for men; only 32% of women over age 75 lived with a spouse (Administration on Aging, 2012).

In 2012, 9.1% of the U.S. elderly population was living in poverty. Gender, race, and ethnicity have a significant effect on the economic status of elderly individuals. In 2010, the poverty rate for women age 65 and older was 60% higher than for older men, 10.7% compared with 6.7% (Women's Legal Defense and Education Fund, 2012). The rates of poverty were higher for older women and men living alone, 18.9% for women and 11.9% for men (Entmacher, Robbins, Vogtman, & Fohlich, 2013). There are also significant racial and ethnic differences in poverty rates among older adults. In 2012, 7.8% of White elderly lived in poverty, compared with 12.4% of Asian, 18.3% of African American, and 20.6% of Hispanic older adults (U.S. Census Bureau, 2013a).

CULTURAL CONSTRUCTION OF LATE ADULTHOOD

The ethnic/racial diversity of the older population in the United States underscores the complexity and importance of taking cultural differences in perceptions

© Stockbyte/ThinkStock

© Creatas Images/ThinkStock

The ethnic/racial diversity of the older population in the United States underscores the importance of taking cultural differences in perceptions of aging into account.

of aging into account. A salient example of cultural differences in approaches to aging is the contrast between traditional Chinese and mainstream U.S. beliefs and values. China has been described in anthropological literature as a "gerontocracy," wherein older people are venerated, given deference, and valued in nearly every task. Benefiting from the Confucian value of filial piety, older people hold a revered position in the family and society.

By contrast, consider the traditional cultural influences in the United States, where individualism, independence, and self-reliance are core values that inherently conflict with the aging process. In the United States, older people have traditionally been collectively regarded as dependent, and cultural values dictate that older people living independently are given higher regard than those requiring assistance. As people age, they strive to maintain independence and avoid—at all costs—becoming a burden to their family. Older people in the United States typically resort to intervention from private or social programs to maintain their independence rather than turning to family. By contrast, Chinese elders traditionally looked forward to the day when they would become part of their children's household, to live out their days being venerated by their families (Gardiner & Kosmitzki, 2011).

No discussion of comparisons between cultures would be complete without mention of differences that occur within groups. An individual Chinese person might value independence, whereas an individual in the United States might be closer to the Confucian value of filial piety than traditional U.S. values. Additionally, processes such as acculturation, assimilation, and bicultural socialization further influence the norms, values, expectations, and beliefs of all cultural groups, including that which is considered the dominant cultural norm. Globalization of economic and information exchange also impacts and changes the cultural norms of all countries (Gardiner & Kosmitzki, 2011). In fact, U.S. values of aging appear to be shifting, influenced in part by political and market forces. In the United States, we are now bombarded with contradictory information about aging—media presentations of long-lived, vibrant older adults are juxtaposed with media presentations of nursing home horror stories.

In his book *Aging Well*, George Vaillant (2002) raises the question, "Will the longevity granted to us by modern medicine be a curse or a blessing?" (p. 3). The answer, he suggests, is influenced by individual, societal, and cultural values, but his research makes him optimistic. Vaillant (2002, 2012) reports on the most long-term longitudinal research available, the Study of Adult Development. The study includes three separate cohorts of 824 persons, all of whom have been studied since adolescence. A significant limitation of the study is the lack of racial and ethnic diversity among the participants, who are almost exclusively White. The great strength of the study is its ability to

EXHIBIT 16.2 • Racial or Ethnic Makeup of Elderly U.S. Population 2010–2050

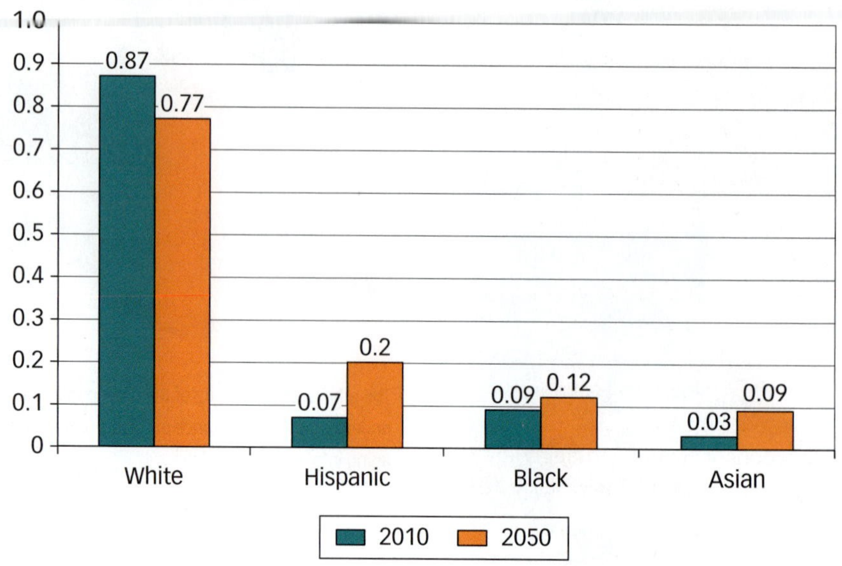

SOURCE: U. S. Census Bureau, 2010.

control cohort effects by following the same participants over such a long period of time.

Much of the news from the Study of Adult Development is good. Vaillant reminds us that Immanuel Kant wrote his first book of philosophy at 57, Titian created many artworks after 76, Ben Franklin invented bifocals at 78, Will Durant won a Pulitzer Prize for history at 83, Frank Lloyd Wright designed the Guggenheim Museum at age 90, the great surgeon Dr. Michael DeBakey obtained a patent for a surgical innovation when he was 90, Leopold Stokowski signed a 6-year recording contract at 94, and Grandma Moses was still painting at 100. Unless they develop a brain disease, the majority of older adults maintain a "modest sense of well-being" until a few months before they die (Vaillant, 2002, p. 5). Older adults are also less depressed than the general population and have a tendency to remember pleasant more than unpleasant events (Vaillant, 2012). Many older adults acknowledge hardships of aging but also see a reason to continue to live. Vaillant (2002) concludes that "positive aging means to love, to work, to learn something we did not know yesterday, and to enjoy the remaining precious moments with loved ones" (p. 16). Although he found many paths to successful aging, Vaillant identifies six traits for "growing old with grace," found in Exhibit 16.3.

Another recent study using longitudinal data from the Americans' Changing Lives study (ACL) continues to examine the question of the impact of life expectancy and quality of life as a person ages. This is a nationally representative sample of adults age 25 years and older, first interviewed in 1986 and reinterviewed in 1989, 1994, and 2001–2002 (House, Lantz, & Herd, 2005). The ACL was designed to address one central dilemma of research on aging and health: whether increased life expectancy in the United States and other economically advanced nations foreshadowed a scenario of longer life but worsening health with the result of increasing chronically ill and functionally limited and disabled people requiring expensive medical and long-term care—or whether, through increased understanding of psychosocial as well as biomedical risk factors, the onset of serious morbidity and attendant functional limitation and disability could be potentially postponed or "compressed."

These authors focused on socioeconomic disparities in health changes through the middle and later years. They represent a set of scholars who are examining a theoretical concept of cumulative advantage and disadvantage and its role in understanding differential aging among various populations (Schöllgen, Huxhold, & Tesch-Römer, 2010). (See Chapter 10 for a discussion of these concepts.) They

EXHIBIT 16.3 • Six Traits for Growing Old With Grace

Caring about others and remaining open to new ideas
Showing cheerful tolerance of the indignities of old age
Maintaining hope
Maintaining a sense of humor and capacity for play
Taking sustenance from past accomplishments while remaining curious and continuing to learn from the next generation
Maintaining contact and intimacy with old friends

SOURCE: Vaillant (2002, pp. 310–311).

argue that multiple interacting factors throughout the life course impact the quality of the health of older individuals. For example, early poverty, lifetime of poverty, poor environmental conditions, poor education, race, and gender have a direct impact on how a person will age. It is not a simple linear, causal track but instead reflects the complexity of interacting risk and protective factors.

Reviewing research findings from the ACL study, House et al. (2005) examined the impact of two factors related to socioeconomic status (SES), education and income, on poor health. They found that overall socioeconomic disparities do impact health outcomes rather than the reverse. Additionally, they found that education has a greater impact than income on the onset of functional limitations or disabilities. Finally, the impact of educational disparities on the onset of functional limitations increased strikingly in later middle and early old age, with more highly educated individuals postponing limitations and thus compressing the number of years spent with limitations (House et al., 2005). Other authors (see George, 2005) raise the question as to whether race and gender are more fundamentally associated with illness and poor quality of aging than the more general category of SES.

PSYCHOSOCIAL THEORETICAL PERSPECTIVES ON SOCIAL GERONTOLOGY

How social workers see and interpret aging will inspire our interventions with older adults. **Social gerontology**—the social science that studies human aging—offers several theoretical perspectives that can explain the process of growing old. Nine predominant theories of social gerontology are introduced here.

1. *Disengagement theory.* Disengagement theory suggests that as elderly individuals grow older, they gradually decrease their social interactions and ties and become increasingly self-preoccupied (Cumming & Henry, 1961). This is sometimes seen as a coping mechanism in the face of ongoing deterioration and loss (Tobin, 1988). In addition, society disengages itself from older adults. Although it was the first comprehensive theory trying to explain the aging process (Achenbaum & Bengtson, 1994), disengagement theory has received much criticism and little research support (see, for example, Cornwell, Laumann, & Schumm, 2008). Disengagement theory is now widely discounted by gerontologists (Hooyman & Kiyak, 2011).

2. *Activity theory.* Activity theory states that higher levels of activity and involvement are directly related to higher levels of life satisfaction in elderly people (Havighurst, 1968). If they can, individuals stay active and involved and carry on as many activities of middle adulthood as possible. There is growing evidence that physical activity is associated with postponing functional limitation and disability (Benjamin, Edwards, & Bharti, 2005). Activity theory has received some criticism, however, for not addressing relatively high levels of satisfaction for individuals like Ms. Johnson, whose level of activity is declining, arguing that the theory satisfies U.S. society's view of how people *should* age (Moody & Sasser, 2012). It also does not address the choice made by many older individuals to adopt a more relaxed lifestyle.

3. *Continuity theory.* Continuity theory was developed in response to critiques of the disengagement and activity theories. According to continuity theory, individuals adapt to changes by using the same coping styles they have used throughout the life course, and they adopt new roles that substitute for roles lost because of age (Neugarten, Havighurst, & Tobin, 1968). Individual personality differences are seen as a major influence in adaptation to old age.

4. *Social construction theory.* Social construction theory aims to understand and explain the influence of social definitions, social interactions, and social structures on the individual elderly person. This theoretical framework suggests that ways of understanding aging are shaped by the cultural, social, historical, political, and economic conditions in which knowledge is developed, and thus values are associated with various ways of understanding (Dean, 1993). The recent conceptualization of "gerotranscendence" is an example of the application of social constructionist theory to aging. The idea of gerotranscendence holds that human development extends into old age and does not simply end or diminish with aging (Hooyman & Kiyak 2011; Tornstam, 2005). According to this theory, aging persons evaluate their lives in terms of the time they have ahead and try to derive a sense of identity, self, and place in the world and universe (Degges-White, 2005; Tornstam, 2005).

5. *Feminist theory.* Proponents of feminist theories of aging suggest that gender is a key factor in understanding a person's aging experience. They contend that because gender is a critical social stratification factor with attendant power, privilege, and status that produces inequalities and disparities throughout the life course, we can only understand aging by taking gender into account (Arber & Ginn, 1995). Gender is viewed as influencing the life course trajectory by impacting access and opportunity, health disparities, and disparities in socioeconomic opportunities, and by creating a lifelong condition of "constrained choice" (Rieker & Bird, 2005). Gabriela Spector-Mersel (2006) argues that in Western societies, older persons have been portrayed as "ungendered." Older men are in a paradoxical position because the metaphors for old age are the opposite of the metaphors for masculinity in these societies.

6. *Social exchange theory.* Social exchange theory is built on the notion that an exchange of resources takes place in all interpersonal interactions (Blau, 1964; Homans, 1961). Individuals will only engage in an exchange if they perceive a favorable cost-benefit ratio or if they see no better alternatives (Hendricks, 1987). As individuals become older, the resources they are able to bring to the exchange begin to shift. Social exchange theory bases its explanation of the realignment of roles, values, and contributions of older adults on this assumption. As social workers, then, it is important to explore how older couples are dealing with the shift in resources within their relationships. Several studies indicate that maintaining reciprocity is important for older individuals (Fiori, Consedine, & Magai, 2008). For example, a recent study of reciprocity among residents of assisted living looked at the positive contributions of aging care recipients to their social relationships, including their interactions with caregivers (Beel-Bates, Ingersoll-Dayton, & Nelson, 2007).

7. *Life course perspective.* From the life course perspective, the conceptual framework used in this section of the book, aging is a dynamic, lifelong process (Greve & Staudinger, 2006). Individuals go through many transitions over their life course (Hendricks & Hatch, 2006). The era they live in, the cohort they belong to, and personal and environmental factors influence individuals during these transitions. "Life course capital" is a contemporary addition to the life course perspective. The theory states that people, over the course of their life, accumulate human capital, that is, resources that they can use to address their needs. This capital can take on various forms—for example, it may be social, biological, psychological, or developmental human capital (Hooyman & Kiyak, 2011). This accumulation of life course capital has an impact on a person's aging, for instance, on health (e.g., morbidity, mortality) or wealth (e.g., standard of living in retirement).

8. *Age stratification perspective.* The framework of age stratification falls into the tradition of the life course perspective (Foner, 1995; Riley, 1971). Stratification is a sociological concept that describes a given hierarchy that exists in a given society. Social stratification is both multidimensional and interactive, in that individuals occupy multiple social locations with varying amounts of power, privilege, and status. The age stratification perspective suggests that, similar to the way society is structured by socioeconomic class, it is also stratified by age. Roles and rights of individuals are assigned based on their membership in an age group or cohort. The experience of aging differs across cohorts because cohorts differ in size, composition, and experience with an ever-changing society.

9. *Productive aging.* Productive aging theory focuses on the positive changes that have occurred to the older adult population. A new generation of older adults is more independent and better off than previous cohorts in many areas, including health, economic status, mobility, and education (Kaye, 2005). This approach maintains that the focus of aging theories has been too much on the losses, crises, and problems of aging, while neglecting the positive side of becoming older.

CRITICAL THINKING Questions 16.1

At what age will you consider yourself old? What do you think your favorite activity will be when you are "old"? What do you think your biggest challenge will be? What do you think will be important to you when you reach old age? Where do you get your ideas about old age?

BIOLOGICAL CHANGES IN LATE ADULTHOOD

Every day, our bodies are changing. In a sense, then, our bodies are constantly aging. In general, all persons experience **primary aging**, or changes that are a normal part of the aging process. In addition, many experience **secondary aging** caused by health-compromising behaviors such as smoking or environmental factors such as pollution (Bjorklund, 2011). As social workers, however, we need not be concerned with the body's aging until it begins to affect the person's ability to function in her or his world, which typically begins to occur in late adulthood.

HEALTH AND LONGEVITY

The **mortality rate**—the ratio of deaths in an area to the population of that area—has declined significantly for all segments of the population in the United States during the last century. Between 1981 and 2009, the overall age-adjusted death rates for all causes of death for individuals 65 years and older declined by 25%. In this age bracket, death rates from heart disease and stroke declined by more than 50%. However, the death rates for some diseases increased; death rates from chronic lower respiratory diseases increased by 57% and death rates from diabetes mellitus were higher in 2009 than in 1981 but lower than in 2001. In 2009, the leading causes of death for people 65 and older were, in descending order, heart disease, cancer, chronic lower respiratory diseases, stroke, Alzheimer's disease, and influenza/pneumonia. Diabetes was the sixth leading cause of death among non-Hispanic Whites but the fourth leading cause of death among non-Hispanic Blacks and Hispanics. Overall death rates in 2009 were higher for older men than for older women (Federal Interagency Forum on Aging-Related Statistics, 2012).

As mortality has decreased, **morbidity**—the incidence of disease—has increased. In other words, the proportion of the population suffering from age-related chronic conditions has increased in tandem with the population of elderly persons. In 2009–2010, for people 65 years or older, the most prevalent and debilitating chronic conditions in descending order were hypertension (54% of men, 57% of women), arthritis (45% of men, 56% of women), heart disease (37% of men, 26% of women), cancer (28% of men, 21% of women), and diabetes (24% of men, 18% of women). Chronic illnesses are long-term, rarely cured, and costly (Federal Interagency Forum on Aging-Related Statistics, 2012).

The prevalence of chronic conditions varies significantly by gender, race, and ethnicity. For example, older women report higher levels of asthma, arthritis, and hypertension than do older men. Older men are more likely to identify heart disease, cancer, and diabetes. Racial and ethnic differences also exist. Non-Hispanic Blacks report higher levels of hypertension (69% compared with 54%) and diabetes (32% compared with 18%) than non-Hispanic Whites. Hispanics report higher levels of diabetes than Whites (33% compared with 18%). Physical decline is also associated with SES, but it is difficult to separate SES from race and ethnicity because minority groups tend to be overrepresented in lower SES groups (Wilmoth & Longino, 2006).

A chronic condition can have considerable impact on a family system. In Ms. Johnson's case, the seven people for whom she cares—including two toddlers, an adolescent, an adult daughter who is functionally impaired, a granddaughter and her husband who both are at risk of leaving the workforce, and an aging father—are all affected by her chronic diabetes. This case illustrates the untold impact of chronic conditions in aging populations that are rarely described by national trend reports.

For many people, illness and death can be postponed through lifestyle changes. In recent years, the importance of preventing illness by promoting good health has received considerable attention. The goals of health promotion for older adults include preventing or delaying the onset of chronic disease and disability; reducing the severity of chronic diseases; and maintaining mental health, physical health, and physical functioning as long as possible. Ways to promote health in old age include improving dietary habits, increasing activity levels and physical exercise, stopping smoking, and obtaining regular health screenings (blood sampling, blood pressure measurement, cancer screening, glaucoma screening) (CDC, 2013m; Erickson, Gildengers, & Butters, 2013). An important finding has been the roles of self-efficacy, sense of mastery, positive attitude, and social supports in improving the quality of life and delaying functional limitation and disability (Meisner, 2012).

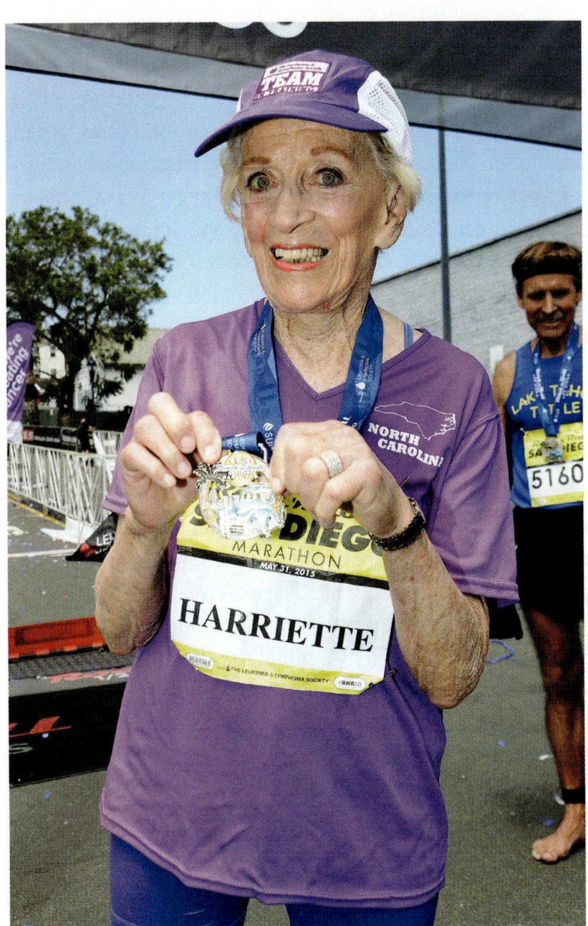

Jerod Harris/Stringer/Getty Images Entertainment/Getty Images

92-year-old Harriett Thompson becomes the oldest woman to finish a marathon at the Suja Rock 'n' Roll San Diego Marathon on May 31, 2015.

AGE-RELATED CHANGES IN PHYSIOLOGY

All systems of the body appear to be affected during the aging process. Consider the *nervous system*. In the brain, neurons and synapses are the transmitters of information throughout the nervous system. The number of neurons decreases throughout the life span; the result is a slow decrease of brain mass after age 30. Because we are born with many more neurons and synapses than we need to function, problems usually do not arise, but nerve cells may begin to pass messages more slowly than in the past (Dugdale, 2012a). If the older adult develops brain deficits in one area of the brain, he or she may make up for these deficits by increasing activity in other brain regions. However, a neurological injury or disease may result in more permanent and serious consequences for an older person. This is just one of the changes that may affect the brain, spinal cord, nerves, and mechanisms controlling other organs in the body. We look more closely at changes in the brain and neurodegenerative diseases in the next section.

Our *cardiovascular system* also changes in several ways as we become older. The cardiac output—the amount of blood pumped per minute—decreases throughout adult life, and the pulse slows with age. The arteries become less elastic and harden, which can result in arteriosclerosis. Fatty lipids accumulate in the walls of the blood vessels and make them narrower, which can cause atherosclerosis. As a result of these changes, less oxygen is available for muscular activities. With advancing age, it takes longer for the blood pressure and heart rate to return to normal resting levels after stressful events (Dugdale, 2012b).

The *respiratory system* too changes with age. Beginning at about 20 to 25 years of age, a person's lung capacity decreases throughout the life span. Breathing becomes a bit more labored. Respiratory muscle strength decreases with age and can interfere with effective coughing (Sharma & Goodwin, 2006). There is great variation in the effect of lung function, however; in healthy older adults who do not smoke, respiratory function is quite good enough for daily activities (Bjorklund, 2011; Sharma & Goodwin, 2006).

The most important age-related change in our *skeletal system* occurs after age 30, when the destruction of bones begins to outpace the reformation of bones. The gradual decrease in bone mass and bone density can cause osteoporosis, a condition in which the bones become brittle and fragile. Osteoporosis occurs in 20% of women older than 50 and half of women older than 80 (Bjorklund, 2011). It is estimated that bone mineral content decreases by 5% to 12% per decade from the 20s through the 90s. One result is that we get shorter as we age. As the cartilage between the joints wears thin, arthritis, a chronic inflammation of the joints, begins to develop. Although many individuals suffer from some form of arthritis in their 40s, the symptoms are often not painful until late adulthood. Some of these changes can be ameliorated by diet and exercise and by avoiding smoking and alcohol.

With increasing age, the *muscular system* declines in mass, strength, and endurance. As a consequence, an elderly person may become fatigued more easily. In addition, muscle contractions begin to slow down, which contributes to deteriorating reflexes and incontinence. However, the muscular system of older individuals can be successfully strengthened through weight training and changes in diet and lifestyle (Bjorklund, 2011).

Changes in the neurological, muscular, and skeletal systems have an impact on the *sensory system* and the sense of balance, which contributes to the increase in accidental falls and bone fractures in late adulthood. Vision decreases with age, and older persons need more light to reach the retina in order to see. The eye's adaptation to the dark slows with age, as does visual acuity, the ability to detect details. Age-related decreases in hearing are caused by degenerative changes in the spiral organ of the ear and the associated nerve cells. Many older adults have a reduced ability to hear high-pitched sounds. By age 65, about one third of adults have significant hearing loss, with men being more likely than women to suffer hearing loss (Federal Interagency Forum on Aging-Related Statistics, 2012). Age-related changes in taste appear to be minimal. The smell receptors in the nose can decrease with age, however, and become less sensitive (Hooyman & Kiyak, 2011).

The *integumentary system* includes the skin, hair, and nails. The skin comprises an outer layer (epidermis) and an inner layer (dermis). With age, the epidermis becomes thinner and pigment cells grow and cluster, creating age spots on the skin (Bjorklund, 2011). The sweat and oil-secreting glands decrease, leaving the skin drier and more vulnerable to injury. Much of the fat stored in the hypodermis, the tissue beneath the skin, is lost in age, causing wrinkles. The skin of an older person often feels cool because the blood flow to the skin is reduced (Bjorklund, 2011).

Sexual potency begins to decline at age 20, but without disease, sexual desire and capacity continue in late adulthood. Vaillant (2002) reports that *frequency* of sexual activity decreases, however. He found that partners in good health at 75 to 80 often continue to have sexual relations but that the average frequency is approximately once in every 10 weeks. Some illnesses and some medications can affect the ability of older adults to have and enjoy sex, as can problems in the relationship (National Institute on Aging, 2013a).

Contemporary views on the physiology of aging focus on longevity. For the past 2 decades, an anti-aging medicine movement has focused on developing biomedical interventions that will delay or reverse the biological changes of aging. Currently there are more than 26,000 members of the American Academy of Anti-Aging Medicine, and anti-aging medicine is a big business (Flatt, Settersten, Ponsaran, & Fishman, 2013). Science and technology are creating possibilities that show promise for the future, but there is no evidence that these gains have increased the maximum life span of humans.

FUNCTIONAL CAPACITY IN VERY LATE ADULTHOOD

Although persons who reach 85 years of age and older demonstrate resilience in the simple fact of their longevity, they continue to face an increased incidence of chronic illness and debilitation with age. The prevalence of older adults with a disability and those needing assistance with **instrumental activities of daily living (IADLs)**, activities that are not necessary for fundamental functioning but do allow an individual to live independently, increases steadily with age. Of those ages 65 to 69, 35% report a disability with 6.9% needing assistance; of those ages 70 to 74, 42.6% report a disability with 10.8% needing assistance; of those 75 to 79, 53.6% report a disability with 15.4% needing assistance; and of those age 80 and older, 70.5% report a disability with 30.2% needing assistance (Brault, 2012). Limitations in **activities of daily living (ADLs)**, basic care activities, also increase with age; 1.6%

of those ages 65 to 74, 3.5% of those ages 75 to 84, and 9.7% of those age 85 and older need assistance with three or more activities (National Center for Health Statistics, 2009). (Exhibit 16.4 lists common ADLs and IADLs.)

Although late adulthood is a time of loss of efficiency in body systems and functioning, the body is an organism that repairs and restores itself as damage occurs. Those persons who live to be 85 and older may be fortunate enough to have a favorable genetic makeup. But they may also have found ways to compensate, to prevent, to restore, and to maintain other health-promoting behaviors. Most very-late-life adults come to think of themselves in ways that fit their circumstances. They narrow the scope of their activities to those that are most cherished, and they carefully schedule their activities to make the best use of their energy and talents.

Sooner or later, however, most very-late-life adults come to need some assistance with ADLs and IADLs. As a society, we must grapple with the question of who will provide that assistance. Currently, most of the assistance is provided by family members. But as families grow smaller, fewer adult children exist to provide such care. A number of family theorists have begun to wonder how multigenerational families might adjust their relationships and better meet long-distance caregiving needs (Cagle, 2008; Harrigan & Koerin, 2007).

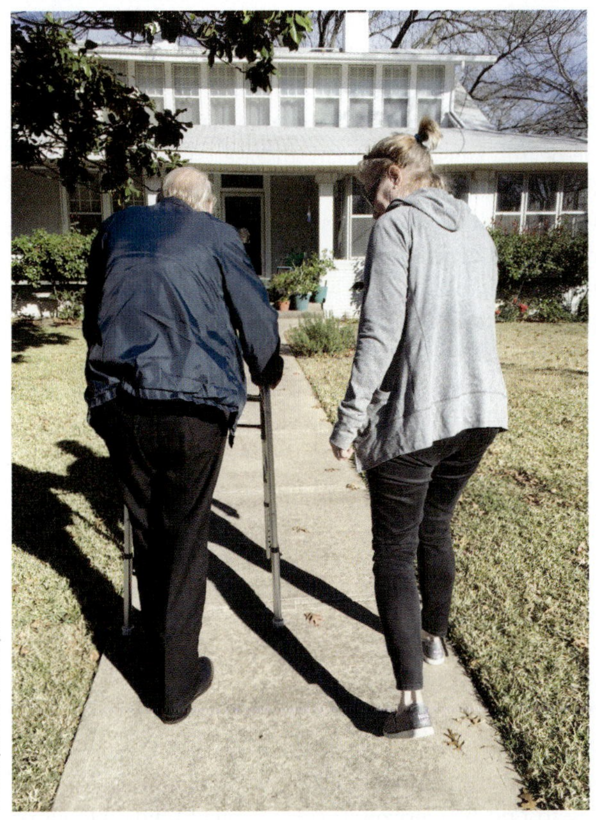

© iStockphoto.com/theresajam1

Social workers need to be concerned with aging if and when it affects a person's ability to function in his or her world.

EXHIBIT 16.4 • Common Activities of Daily Living (ADLs) and Instrumental Activities of Daily Living (IADLs)

ACTIVITIES OF DAILY LIVING
Bathing
Dressing
Walking a short distance
Shifting from a bed to a chair
Eating
INSTRUMENTAL ACTIVITIES OF DAILY LIVING
Doing light housework
Doing the laundry
Using transportation
Handling finances
Using the telephone
Taking medications

THE AGING BRAIN AND NEURODEGENERATIVE DISEASES

Before discussing the most common neurodegenerative diseases, dementia, Alzheimer's, and Parkinson's disease, we suggest you review the discussion of the nervous system in Chapter 3. Several changes occur to the brain as we age. Between ages 20 and 90, the brain loses 5% to 10% of its weight (Palmer & Francis, 2006). The areas most affected by this decrease are the frontal lobe and the hippocampus. A general loss of neurons also occurs. At the same time, the normal aging brain does not appear to lose synapses (Palmer & Francis, 2006). The transmission of information between neurons through the neurotransmitters can also decrease in some brain regions as we age. Furthermore, there is less growth of new capillaries and a reduced blood flow caused by narrowing arteries in the brain. Plaques and tangles develop in and around the neurons (see discussion of Alzheimer's disease in the next section), and inflammation and damage by free radicals increase (Alzheimer's Association, 2013). At the same time, the effects of these changes on performing tasks and memory are generally fairly small. Scores for task performance, for example, are similar for younger and older adults, when the older group is provided with additional time. Older adults can compensate and adapt well to many age-related brain changes. Part of this adaptation occurs through changes in the brain. Neuroimaging shows that some brain functions seem to get reorganized as the brain ages (Reuter-Lorenz, 2002). Imaging results point to a process in which the aging brain starts using areas of the two hemispheres that were previously not focusing on performing those tasks to compensate for age-related loss (Li, 2006). Negative changes can also be offset by age-related overall improvements in some cognitive areas such as verbal knowledge or vocabulary (Alzheimer's Association, 2013). Other brain changes, however, can become more challenging. We now turn to some of these neurodegenerative diseases.

Dementia

Dementia is the term for brain disease in which memory and cognitive abilities deteriorate over time. It may be significantly unrecognized and undiagnosed in many older adults. In 2005, it was estimated that 24.3 million people worldwide had dementia, and one new case is occurring every 7 seconds. A majority, 60%, of people with dementia live in low-income countries. It is forecasted that the number of people with dementia will increase by 100% between 2001 and 2040 in high-income countries and by more than 300% in India, China, and south Asia (Ferri et al., 2005). The first nationally representative population-based study of the prevalence of dementia in the United States, conducted in 2007, found the prevalence among persons aged 71 and older to be 13.9%. The prevalence increased with age; it was 5.0% for older adults aged 71 to 79 and 37.4% for those aged 90 or older (Plassman et al., 2007). Reversible dementia is caused by factors such as drug and alcohol use, a brain tumor, subdural hematomas, meningiomas, hypothyroid, syphilis or AIDS, or severe depression, and the cognitive decline is reversible if identified and treated early enough (Joshi & Morley, 2006; Yousuf et al., 2010). Irreversible dementia is not curable. In the advanced stages, the person may repeat the same words over and over again, may have problems using appropriate words, and may not recognize a spouse or other family members. At the same time, the person may still be able to recall and vividly describe events that happened many years ago.

The initial stage of cognitive dysfunction is called *age-associated memory impairment* (AAMI). It is followed by even greater memory loss and diagnosed as *mild cognitive impairment* (MCI), which may progress to dementia. The rate of decline in cognitive and functional skills is predictive of mortality among nondemented older adults (Schupf et al., 2005). AAMI and MCI involve primarily memory loss, whereas dementia results in disruption of daily living and difficulty or inability to function normally. MCIs have been thought not to constitute dementia but to be a transitional stage between normal cognitive functioning and Alzheimer's disease. Studies have identified one subtype of MCI, called nonamnestic, as evidence of early stage Alzheimer's disease (Petersen, 2011).

Risk factors for cognitive decline and dementia include age, family history, Down syndrome, alcohol use, atherosclerosis, high or low blood pressure, high levels of low-density lipoprotein (LDL) cholesterol, depression, diabetes, high estrogen levels, elevated blood levels of homocysteine, obesity, and smoking (Mayo Clinic, 2013). No positive answer has yet been found for how to prevent dementia. However, several studies suggest that social engagement as well as physical and intellectual activity may slow cognitive decline and the progression of dementia (Renaud, Bherer, & Maquestiaux, 2010; Savica & Petersen, 2011).

It is important to recognize the distinction between dementia and **delirium**, which is characterized by an impairment of consciousness. Unlike dementia, delirium has a sudden onset (a few hours or days), then follows a brief and fluctuating course that includes impairment of consciousness, and has the potential for improvement when the causes are treated. Prevalent causative factors of delirium include not only central nervous system disturbances but also outside factors such as toxicity from medications, low oxygen states, infection, retention of urine and feces, undernutrition and dehydration, and metabolic conditions (Joshi & Morley, 2006). The prevalence of delirium is high among hospitalized elderly persons, with approximately 50% of hospital patients over age 65 experiencing an episode following surgery during their hospital stay, compared to 15% to 25% of other patients (Berthold, 2009).

Alzheimer's disease (AD) is the most common type of dementia, accounting for about 70% of cases. In 2013, care for people with AD in the United States was estimated to cost $203 billion, and it is projected that the annual cost will rise to $142 trillion by 2050 (Alzheimer's Association, 2013; Plassman et al., 2007). The number of deaths caused by heart disease, stroke, and many forms of cancer has seen significant reductions during the first half decade of this century and has continued to decline. In contrast, deaths caused by AD increased 68% from 2000 to 2010 (Alzheimer's Association, 2013). As populations around the world age, this trend can be seen on a global level as well. AD is characterized by a progression of stages. A general distinction is made between mild, moderate, and severe stages of AD, although the description of the symptoms shows that the stages are not completely distinct. Exhibit 16.5 provides an overview of the three stages of Alzheimer's disease and the related symptoms.

Early detection and diagnosis of Alzheimer's disease is still difficult. The time period from the diagnosis of Alzheimer's disease to death ranges from 3 to 4 years up to 10 years, depending on the person's age. However, it is believed that the changes in the brain that cause Alzheimer's disease begin 10 or even 20 years before its onset. Consequently, there is a strong focus on trying to find biomarkers in cerebrospinal fluids, blood, or urine that may help to detect the presence of developing Alzheimer's disease. It is important that Margaret Davis

EXHIBIT 16.5 • Stages and Symptoms of Alzheimer's Disease

STAGE OF ALZHEIMER'S DISEASE	TYPICAL SYMPTOMS
Mild or early stage	• Memory loss • Confusion about location of familiar places • Taking longer for routine daily tasks • Trouble handling money and bills • Loss of spontaneity • Repeating questions • Losing things • Mood and personality changes • Increased anxiety and aggression
Moderate stage	• Increased memory loss and confusion • Problems recognizing friends and family members • Inability to learn new things • Inability to cope with new or unexpected situations • Hallucinations, delusions, suspiciousness, paranoia • Loss of impulse control • Inability to carry out complex tasks requiring multiple steps
Severe or late stage	• Weight loss • Seizures • Skin infections • Difficulty swallowing • Groaning, moaning, grunting • Increased sleeping • Lack of bladder and bowel control • Inability to communicate

SOURCE: Based on National Institute on Aging, 2013b.

receive good diagnostic services to determine whether her problems in functioning are related to AD or some other type of dementia.

In the mild or early stage, the first signs of the disease, such as forgetfulness, confusion, and mood and personality changes, appear. This stage may be the most stressful for many persons afflicted with Alzheimer's disease, because they often are very aware of the changes happening to their mind. Fluctuations in the severity of symptoms are common, both within a day and between days. Oftentimes the person will start to experience significant anxiety related to these changes.

Moderate-stage Alzheimer's disease is characterized by increased memory loss, problems organizing thoughts and language, difficulty recognizing friends and family members, and restlessness. As the disease progresses the person may exhibit reduced impulse control, repetitive behavior and speech, hallucinations, delusion, and suspiciousness.

In late-stage Alzheimer's disease, a person is often bedridden and has increasing health difficulties. The most common reason for death in the late stage is aspiration pneumonia, when the person can no longer swallow properly and fluids and food end up in the lungs (Alzheimer's Association, 2013).

Despite significant progress in researching the disease and trying to find possible cures, much is still unknown. Current thinking is that multiple factors, not one single cause, are involved in the development of AD. Research shows that brains of persons with Alzheimer's disease have an unusual accumulation of two substances: neurofibrillary tangles and amyloidal plaques. Amyloidal plaques are a substance building up *outside* the neuron cells. The plaques develop when amyloidal peptides, proteins associated with the cell membrane of neurons, divide improperly and turn into beta amyloid, which in turn is toxic to neurons. The neurons die and together with the proteins create these lumps (Alzheimer's Association, 2013). Neurofibrillary tangles form inside the neurons. These tangles are caused by a protein (tau) breaking down and sticking together with other tau proteins to create tangled clumps *inside* the neuron cells. When these tangles develop, they reduce the neurons' ability to communicate with other neurons. The neuron cells eventually die, which over time leads to brain atrophy (Alzheimer's Association, 2013). The role of the plaques and tangles is still not well understood, but scans show that the brains of people with advanced AD have dramatic shrinkage from cell loss and widespread debris from dead and dying neurons. Several medications are available for persons with AD, including Donepezil (Aricept), Galantamine (Razadyne), and Rivastigmine (Exelon). All of these medications can slow the progression of the disease, but none can reverse or cure it.

Parkinson's Disease

Parkinson's disease (PD) is a chronic and progressive movement disorder that primarily affects older adults over the age of 70. However, as in the case of movie star Michael J. Fox, it can afflict persons earlier in life as well. It is estimated that 7 to 10 million people worldwide have PD and that about 1 million people in the United States live with the disease. Approximately 60,000 people in the United States are diagnosed with PD each year (Parkinson's Disease Foundation, 2010).

Symptoms of PD include tremors (arms, legs, head), rigidity (stiffness of limbs), bradykinesia (trouble with and slowness of movement), and postural instability (insecure gait and balance). It can also cause language problems and

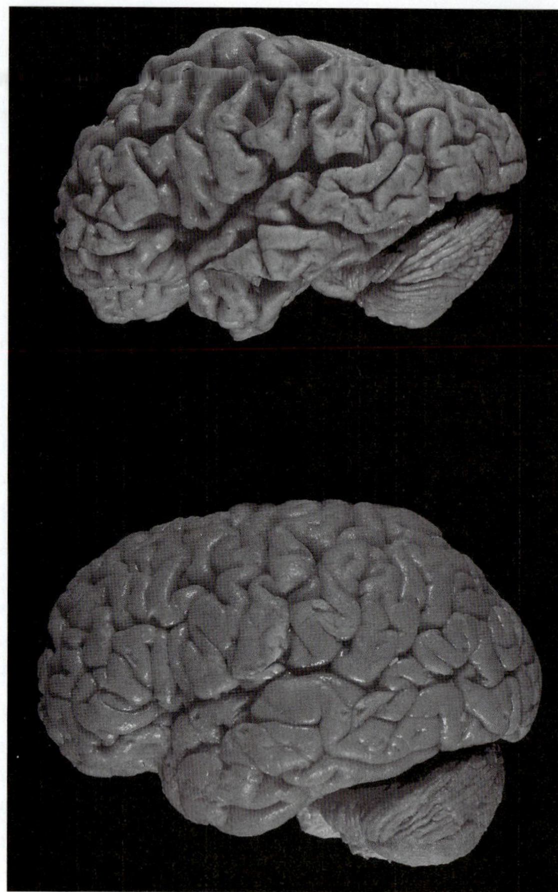

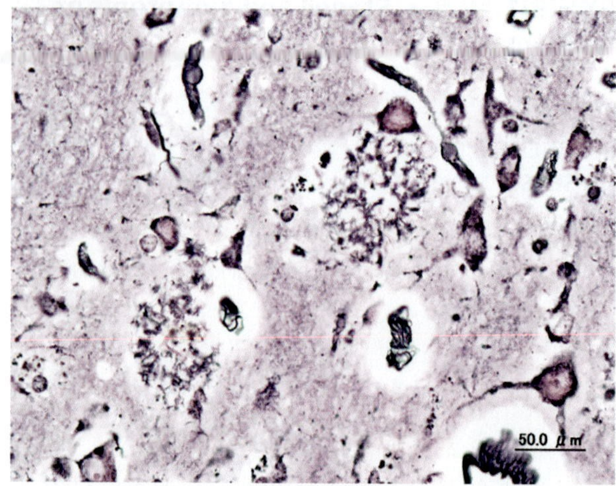

The photo on the left shows a healthy brain (*bottom*) versus the brain of a donor with Alzheimer's disease (*top*), demonstrating the shrinkage that occurred with Alzheimer's disease. The image on the right demonstrates plaques seen in the cerebral cortex in a patient with presenile onset of Alzheimer's disease.

cognitive difficulties and in extreme cases lead to a complete loss of movement. The disease is difficult to accurately diagnose, because some features of the normal aging process can be mistaken for PD (Parkinson's Disease Foundation, 2014). Tremors, slower movements, or insecure walking all may be part of normal aging, symptoms of depression, or medication-induced side effects. Even though PD is a neurodegenerative movement disorder, it often has mental health consequences. For example, cognitive impairment, dementia, depression, and sleep disorders may be associated with or co-occur with PD.

PD is caused by a gradual loss of cells that produce dopamine in a part of the brain called the basal ganglia, which is located at the base of the frontal brain area and is involved in coordinating a body's movements. The chemical dopamine is a neurotransmitter that transmits information about movement in the brain. A decrease in neurons that transmit information with the help of dopamine alters the processing of information related to physical movement (Playfer, 2006). Losing neurons in the substantia nigra, which is a part of the basal ganglia, is part of normal aging. We are born with 400,000 neurons in this part of the brain; at age 60 we have about 250,000 neurons left. However, research indicates that persons afflicted with Parkinson's disease may have as little as 60,000 to 120,000 neurons present in this part of the brain (Palmer & Francis, 2006). Research has also found a decrease in the nerve endings that produce norepinephrine, a neurotransmitter responsible for some of the body's automatic functions like blood pressure and pulse (National Institute of Neurological Disorders and Stroke [NINDS], 2013b). The brain cells of a person with PD also include abnormal clumps of a protein (synuclein) called Lewy bodies. It is not clear whether this contributes to the disease by preventing the cells from working correctly or whether it is an attempt of the body to bind these harmful proteins to keep other cells working (NINDS, 2013b).

Several drugs are available to address PD. A combination of these drugs with physical rehabilitation has shown great success in reducing the symptoms of the disease (Playfer, 2006). One group of medications works on increasing the dopamine levels in the brain. Levodopa is an example of such a drug. It is the most common medication for treating Parkinson's disease and has been used with success for more than 40 years (Playfer, 2006). A second type of drug mimics dopamine (dopamine antagonists) or inhibits dopamine breakdown (NINDS, 2013b). A more recent approach to treating the effects of PD is deep brain stimulation. Using this method, a tiny electrode is surgically implanted into the brain. Through a pulse generator this implant then stimulates the brain and stops many of the symptoms (NINDS, 2013b). Results of deep brain simulation show a positive effect on cognitive functions (Zangaglia et al., 2009). Anticolinergics and MAO-B and COMT inhibitors are also used to treat the symptoms and slow progression of the disease (Parkinson's Disease Foundation, 2013).

CRITICAL THINKING Questions 16.2

Would you like to know that your aging process could be reversed with anti-aging medicine? What are the reasons for your answer? How would society be affected if more of us could live to be well past 100 years of age? What social justice issues might arise regarding access to anti-aging medicine?

PSYCHOLOGICAL CHANGES IN LATE ADULTHOOD

Without good longitudinal research, it has been difficult to understand psychological changes in late adulthood. Because cross-sectional research cannot control for cohort effects, we need to exercise great caution in interpreting findings of age differences in human psychology. Three areas that have received a lot of attention are changes in personality, changes in intellectual functioning, and mental health and mental disorders in late adulthood. The Berlin Aging Study, one of the largest studies of older adults, included numerous measures of psychological aging. Findings suggest that one should not think about a uniform process of psychological aging (Baltes & Mayer, 1999). Rather, changes in areas such as cognition, social relationships, self, and personality occur to a large extent independent of each other.

PERSONALITY CHANGES

A couple of theorists have addressed the issue of how the personality changes as individuals age. Erik Erikson's (1950) life span theory proposes that the struggle of late adulthood is *ego integrity versus ego despair.* **Integrity** involves the ability to make peace with one's "one and only life cycle" and to find unity with the world (refer back to Exhibit 4.11 in Chapter 4 for an overview of Erikson's stages of psychosocial development). Erikson (1950) also noted that from middle adulthood on, adults participate in a "wider social radius," with an increasing sense of social responsibility and interconnectedness. Some support was found for this notion in a 50-year follow-up study of adult personality development (Haan, Millsap, & Hartka, 1986). The researchers found that in late adulthood, three aspects of personality increased significantly: outgoingness, self-confidence, and warmth. A more recent study examining the association of chronological aging with positive psychological change supported the idea that some forms of positive psychological change are normative across the life span, that older people know clearly what values are most important, and that they pursue these objectives with a more mature sense of purpose and ownership (Sheldon, 2006). As Erik and Joan Erikson (1997) moved into their 8th decade, they began writing about a ninth stage. Joan published this previously unfinished work in 1997 following Erik's death in 1994 at the age of 92. She revisits the meaning of wisdom and integrity in light of the losses that occur with time and, despite the challenges, declares that "to grow old is a great privilege" (p. 128).

George Vaillant (2002, 2012) has also considered the personality changes of late adulthood. He found that for all three of the cohorts in the Study of Adult Development, mastery of generativity tripled the likelihood that men and women would find their 70s to be a time of joy instead of despair. He also proposed that another life task, *guardian*, comes between generativity and integrity. Guardianship involves taking on the task of passing on the traditions of the past to the next generation, and guardians extend their concern to the culture as a whole. In addition, Vaillant (2002) suggests that humans have "elegant unconscious coping mechanisms that make lemonade out of lemons" (p. 91). As discussed in Chapter 15, Vaillant (2012) reports that with age and experience, individuals tend to use more adaptive coping mechanisms.

Vaillant (2002) found that over a 25-year period, his sample of Harvard men made significant increases in their use of altruism and humor and significant decreases in their use of projection and passive aggression. Overall, he found that 19 of 67 Harvard men made significant gains in use of mature coping mechanisms between the ages of 50 and 75, 28 men were already making strong use of mature mechanisms at age 50, use of mature mechanisms stayed the same for 17 men, and only 4 out of the 67 men used less mature coping mechanisms with advancing age. Vaillant (1993) in part attributed this maturation in coping to the presence of positive social support and the quality of the men's marriages. These findings are consistent with results from another longitudinal study of aging that found that in late adulthood, participants became more forgiving, more able to meet adversity cheerfully, less prone to take offense, and less prone to venting frustrations on others (McCrae et al., 1999). Langle and Probst (2004) suggest that this might be the result of older adults being required to face fundamental questions of existence, because coping with the vicissitudes of life loom ever larger during aging.

In Chapter 15, we read that there are controversies about whether personality changes or remains stable in middle adulthood. There are similar controversies in the literature on late adulthood. Findings from the large-scale Berlin Aging Study indicate that, on the whole, self and personality change only a little with age (Staudinger, Freund, Linden, & Maas, 1999). Vaillant (2002, 2012), conversely, found evidence for both change and continuity. He suggests that personality has two components: temperament and character. Temperament, he concludes, does not change, and adaptation in adolescence is one of the best predictors of adaptation in late adulthood. Studies on depression, anxiety, and suicidal ideation in late adulthood support this idea that coping and adaptation in adolescence are a good predictor of later-life temperament. Conversely, character, or adaptive style, does change, influenced by both experiences with the environment and the maturation process. Vaillant (2002) attributes this change in adaptive style over time to the fact that many genes are "programmed to promote plasticity," or the capacity to be shaped by experience. One personality change that was noted in Chapter 15 to occur in middle age is gender role expansion, with women becoming more dominant and men becoming more passive. This pattern has also been noted in late adulthood (Vaillant, 2012).

INTELLECTUAL CHANGES, LEARNING, AND MEMORY

Answering the question about how intellectual capabilities change in late adulthood is a complex and difficult task. One often-cited study on age-related intellectual changes found that fluid intelligence declines with age, but crystallized intelligence increases (Horn, 1982). **Fluid intelligence** is the capacity for abstract reasoning and involves such things as the ability to "respond quickly, to memorize quickly, to compute quickly with no error, and to draw rapid inferences from visual relationships" (Vaillant, 2002, p. 238). **Crystallized intelligence** is based on accumulated learning and includes the ability to reflect and recognize (e.g., similarities and differences, vocabulary) rather than to recall and remember. This theory has received much criticism, however, because it was based on a cross-sectional comparison of two different age groups who may have had very different educational experiences. Researchers who followed a single cohort over time found no general decline of intellectual abilities in late adulthood (Schaie, 1984). Rather, they found considerable individual variation. Other longitudinal research has found that fluid intelligence declines earlier than crystallized intelligence, which has been found to remain the same at 80 as at 30 in most healthy older adults (Vaillant, 2002). Aspects of crystallized intelligence, such as world knowledge, continue to grow into the 60s and show only gradual declines in the 70s (Ornstein & Light, 2010).

Learning and memory are closely related; we must first learn before we can retain and recall. Memory performance,

Memory performance demonstrates a wide degree of variability in late adulthood.

like the impact of aging on intelligence, demonstrates a wide degree of variability. When we process information, it moves through several stages of memory (Bjorklund, 2011; Hooyman & Kiyak, 2011).

- *Sensory memory.* New information is initially recorded in sensory memory. Unless the person deliberately pays attention to the information, it is lost within less than a second. There seems to be little age-related change in this type of memory.
- *Primary memory.* If the information is retained in sensory memory, it is passed on to the primary memory, also called recent or short-term memory. Primary memory has only limited capacity; it is used to organize and temporarily hold information.
- *Working memory.* This refers to the process of actively reorganizing and manipulating information that is still in primary memory. Although there are some age-related declines in working memory, there seems to be little age-related decline in primary memory.
- *Secondary memory.* Information is permanently stored in secondary memory. This is the memory we use daily when we remember an event or memorize facts for an exam. The ability to recall seems to decline with age, but recognition capabilities stay consistent.
- *Tertiary memory.* Information is stored for extended periods, several weeks or months, in tertiary memory, also called remote memory. This type of memory experiences little age-related changes.

Another way to distinguish memory is between intentional and incidental memory. **Intentional memory** relates to events that you plan to remember. **Incidental memory** relates to facts you have learned without the intention to retain and recall. Research suggests that incidental memory declines with old age, but intentional memory does not (Direnfeld & Roberts, 2006).

Another element of intellectual functioning studied in relation to aging is *brain plasticity*, the ability of the brain to change in response to stimuli. Research indicates that even older people's brains can rewire themselves to compensate for lost functioning in particular regions and in some instances may even be able to generate new cells. As a result, people are capable of lifelong learning, despite myths to the contrary. Adult education and intellectual stimulation in later life may actually help maintain cognitive health. Not only are humans capable of lifelong learning, but the stimulation associated with learning new things may also reduce the risk of impairments (Willis, Schaie, & Martin, 2009).

MENTAL HEALTH AND MENTAL DISORDERS

A number of longitudinal studies indicate that, without brain disease, mental health improves with age (Vaillant, 2012). Older adults have a lower prevalence of mental disorders than young and middle-age adults. This finding is supported by virtually all epidemiological studies ever conducted (Bengtson, Gans, Putney, & Silverstein, 2009). Although older adults are at greater risk for certain brain diseases such as dementia, these disorders are not a part of the normal aging process. It is estimated that 15% to 25% of older adults living in the community have some type of mental health disorder, but higher rates are found among older adults living in long-term care facilities, where an estimated 10% to 40% have mild to moderate impairment and 5% to 10% have serious impairment (Hooyman & Kiyak, 2011). About 20% of first admissions to psychiatric hospitals are adults aged 65 and older. It is estimated that only about 25% of older adults who need mental health services ever receive them. However, many of the more common mental disorders associated with older age can be diagnosed and treated in elderly persons much as they would be in earlier adulthood (Rodda, Walker, & Carter, 2011). Given the aging of the population, the need for geropsychiatric research and clinical practice is likely to increase.

CRITICAL THINKING Questions 16.3

George Vaillant suggests that his longitudinal research indicates that humans have "elegant unconscious coping mechanisms that make lemonade out of lemons." Think of a late-life adult whom you know who has or is making lemonade out of lemons. What challenges has this person faced in earlier life or in late adulthood? What is it about this late-life adult that makes you think of her or him as making lemonade out of lemons? What types of coping mechanisms do you think this person uses to deal with adversities?

SOCIAL ROLE TRANSITIONS AND LIFE EVENTS OF LATE ADULTHOOD

Transitions are at the center of the life course perspective, and people experience many of them, some very abrupt, in late adulthood. Retirement, death of a spouse or partner, institutionalization, and one's own death are among the most stressful events in human existence, and they are clustered in late adulthood. Despite the concern of the impact of the loss of social roles, studies have demonstrated that older adults generally adapt to late-life role transitions and maintain emotional well-being (Hinrichsen & Clougherty, 2006).

Social isolation is considered to be a powerful risk factor not only for the development of cognitive and intellectual decline in very late adulthood but also for physical illness (McInnis-Dittrich, 2009; Steptoe, Shankar, Demakakos, & Wardle, 2013). A sense of connectedness with family and friends can be achieved in person; on the phone; and more recently via e-mail, Facebook, chat rooms, blogs, Skype, and other social networking technology. The focus in this section is on relationships with people; however, remember that pets, plants, and other connections with nature bring comfort to any age group, including older adults.

FAMILIES IN LATER LIFE

As you saw with the case studies of Ruby Johnson, Margaret Davis, and Bina Patel, families continue to play an important role in the life of an older person. With increased longevity, however, the post–empty nest and postretirement period lengthens (Walsh, 2011). Thus, the significance of the marital or partner relationship increases in late adulthood. As older individuals are released from their responsibilities as parents and members of the workforce, they are able to spend more time together. Overall satisfaction with the quality of life seems to be higher for married elderly individuals than for the widowed or never married. For married couples, the spouse is the most important source of emotional, social, and personal support in times of illness and need of care.

About 28% of noninstitutionalized U.S. older adults live alone. The most common living arrangement for men over 65 is with their wife; in 2012, 72% of men over 65 lived with their spouse (Administration on Aging, 2012). The picture is different for older women; only 45% of women age 65 and older live with a spouse, and by age 75, almost half (46%) of women live alone.

Living arrangements for older adults vary by race and ethnicity in the United States. In 2008, the proportion of White (41%) and Black (42%) women living alone was

Social isolation is a powerful risk factor for physical illness as well as cognitive and intellectual decline in very late adulthood.

similar, about 41%. Fewer older Hispanic women lived alone (27%), and even fewer Asian and Pacific Islander women lived alone (22%) (Jacobsen, Mather, Lee, & Kent, 2011). Older Black women (25%) are less likely than Asian (45%), White (44%), and Hispanic (41%) women to live with a spouse (Jacobsen et al., 2011). White women (13%) are less likely than Black (32%), Asian (32%), or Hispanic (31%) women to live with relatives other than a spouse. Black men (30%) are more likely to live alone than White (18%), Hispanic (13%), or Asian (11%) men. Black men (54%) are also less likely than Asian (77%), White (74%), and Hispanic (67%) men to live with a spouse. Men of every race and ethnicity are less likely than women of the same race and ethnicity to live with a relative other than their spouse (Jacobsen et al., 2011). A complex relationship among culture, socioeconomic status, and individual personality has to be considered in accounting for the ethnic and racial differences in living arrangements. Drawing inferences based solely on cultural differences is overly simplistic given the use of ethnic and racial categories devised by the U.S. Census Bureau as proxies for cultural identity.

Family relationships have been found to be closer and more central for older women than for older men. Mother–daughter relationships have been found to be particularly strong (Silverstein & Bengtson, 2001). Additionally, friendship appears to be a more important protective factor for older women than for older men. Friendships have been associated with lower levels of cognitive impairment and increased quality-of-life satisfaction (Beland, Zunzunegui, Alvarado, Otero, & del Ser, 2005).

The never married constitute a very small group of the current elderly population. It will further decrease for some time as the cohort of baby boomers, with its unusually high rate of marriage, enters late adulthood (Bjorklund, 2011). However, the proportion of elderly singles and those never married will probably increase toward the middle of the next century, because the cohort that follows the baby boomers has had an increase in the number of individuals remaining single.

Singlehood caused by divorce in late adulthood is increasing, however, as divorce is becoming more socially accepted in all population groups. As in all stages of life, divorce in later life may entail financial problems, especially for older women, and it may be especially difficult to recuperate financially postretirement. Divorce also results in a change of kinship ties and social networks, which are important sources of support in later life. The incidence of remarriage after divorce or widowhood is significantly higher for older men than for older women. The fact that there are more elderly women than men contributes to this trend. Even if older adults are not themselves divorced, they may need to adjust to the enlarged and complicated family networks that come from the divorces and remarriages of their children and grandchildren (Walsh, 2011).

Until very recently, very little research focused on aging among LGBT individuals; currently this is a small but growing area of research. The current generation of LGBT older adults in the United States and some other countries is experiencing rapid social change in their visibility and acceptance in society. They have lived through the modern construction of "the homosexual," the medicalization of homosexuality as a mental disorder, the impact of HIV/AIDS, the rise of the gay liberation movement, and increasing visibility in the political conversation (Van Wagenen, Driskell, & Bradford, 2013). In recent years, many older gay and lesbian couples have been able to marry, some after several decades of partnership.

The small research literature on LGBT older adults indicates that they have faced serious adversities throughout their lives, and this has resulted in compromised mental and physical health. They have faced barriers to receiving informal caregiving from loved ones and prejudice and discrimination from health and social service providers (Institute of Medicine, 2011). They also have demonstrated strength and resilience, building robust social networks of chosen families and developing skills for coping with disease (van Wagenen et al., 2013). During later life, many LGBT adults and their families have been able to find and model new ways of disclosure and living authentically (Ashton, 2011). Even though sexual minorities are facing less prejudice and discrimination in recent years, recent research indicates that they still face limited access to LGBT-sensitive social services and long-term care (Hughes, Harold, & Boyer, 2011; Jihanian, 2013).

Sibling relationships play a special role in the life of older adults. Siblings share childhood experiences and are often the personal tie with the longest duration. Siblings are typically not the primary source of personal care, but they often play a role in providing emotional support. Sibling relationships often change over the life course, with closer ties in pre-adulthood and later life and less involvement in early and middle adulthood. Women's ties with siblings have been found to be more involved than those of men (Bjorklund, 2011).

Coresidence of multiple generations of the family has been gradually decreasing in Western societies since the 19th century, but the multigenerational family household has been making a comeback in Europe and the United States in recent years (Albuquerque, 2011). The percentage of persons living in multigenerational family households decreased in the United States from 24.7% in 1950 to 12.1% in 1980, but by 2010 it had increased again to 16.1%. This can be attributed to several factors, including demographic changes, the burst of the housing market and increase of foreclosures, higher unemployment rates since the onset of the last recession, and a high rate of immigration from Latin America and Asia (Pew Center for Social and Demographic Trends, 2013). The resurgence of multigenerational households has resulted in more interactions and exchanges across generations. Contrary to common belief, intergenerational exchanges between adult children and elderly parents are not one-directional. Children often take care of their elderly parents, but healthy elderly persons also provide significant assistance to their adult children, as is the case with Ms. Johnson. Research with multigenerational households in Portugal found that resources flowed both ways, particularly when the older generation was still young-old. Some contributions that the older generation provided to the household include income from employment, child care, and household chores (Albuquerque, 2011). As seen in Bina Patel's case, families with a collectivist heritage prefer to have elderly parents reside with their grown children.

GRANDPARENTHOOD

As people live longer, increasing numbers are becoming grandparents and great-grandparents. Ruby Johnson, Margaret Davis, and Bina Patel are all great-grandparents as well as grandparents. The current cohort of older adults is spending more years as grandparents than earlier cohorts did (Bjorklund, 2011). The transition to grandparenthood typically occurs in middle adulthood, and grandparents may be in their 30s or over 100 or anywhere in between (Hooyman & Kiyak, 2011). The grandchildren of older adults are more likely to be adolescents and young adults than to be young children. Great-grandchildren, however, are likely to be young.

In some cases, older people such as Ms. Johnson are assuming full responsibility for parenting their grandchildren, because their children have problems with drugs, HIV infection, or crime. Beginning in the early 1990s, the U.S. Census Bureau began to note an increasing number of children younger than 18 living with grandparents, rising from 3% in 1970 to 5.5% in 1997 (Bryson & Casper, 1999). Today, approximately 10% of children in the United States are living with a grandparent, and a grandparent is the primary caregiver for a large minority of these children. However, the majority of these grandparent coresiders are younger than age 60; 25% of grandparent caregivers are ages 60 to 69, and another 9% of grandparent caregivers are age 70 or older (Livingston, 2013). This has been viewed by some as a negative trend, but there is no inherent reason why grandchildren receiving care from grandparents is problematic, and, indeed, across time and place, grandparents have sometimes been seen as appropriate caregivers. Many cultural groups often have multigenerational households that are not predicated on dysfunction within the family. Recall that large percentages of Asian, Hispanic, and Black elders live with family members not their spouse. It does appear, however, that the current trend is influenced by the growth of drug use among parents, teen pregnancy, the rapid rise of single-parent families, and recent economic conditions (Hooyman & Kiyak, 2011; Livingston, 2013). As a result, new physical, emotional, and financial demands are placed on grandparents with already limited resources. Sometimes custodial grandparents are also caring for their own impaired adult child. Compared with their noncustodial counterparts, custodial grandparents have a higher rate of physical and mental health problems (Hayslip & Kaminski, 2005). However, many custodial grandparents and their grandchildren benefit or even thrive from the circumstance, and the parenting outcomes are often very positive. Parsons and Peluso (2013) compiled a list of famous custodial grandchildren that includes the likes of George Washington, Barack Obama, Bill Clinton, Clarence Thomas, Eric Clapton, Oprah Winfrey, Pierce Brosnan, Tammy Wynette, and Tipper Gore. They all have in common the fact that they were raised by their grandparents. Conversely, Margaret Davis's granddaughter, Tiffany, is an important part of Ms. Davis's caregiving system.

Grandparenthood is a normative part of the family life cycle, but the majority of grandparents do not coreside with their grandchildren. In general, being a grandparent is a welcome and gratifying role for most individuals, but it may increase in significance and meaning for an older person. Many grandparents today are maintaining relationships with grandchildren by means of various technologies, including texting, social networking sites, and webcam interactions.

Even when they do not coreside with their grandchildren, grandparents can play an important role in their grandchildren's lives. Here are some examples from research. Candace Kemp (2005) found that both adult grandchildren and their grandparents see their relationship as a safety net that can be tapped when needed. Another research team found that emerging adults who had lived with a single parent or in a stepparent home had fewer depressive symptoms if they had a strong relationship with a grandparent (Ruiz & Silverstein, 2007). Another study found that the quality of the relationship with the maternal grandmother predicted the psychological adjustment of emerging adults after parental divorce (Henderson, Hayslip, Sanders, & Louden, 2009). And another study found that adolescents in single-parent homes had fewer difficulties with school conduct and peer relations if they had high levels of involvement with grandparents (Attar-Schwartz, Tan, Buchanan, Flouri, & Griggs, 2009). One last study found that grandparents play a critical role when a grandchild has a disability, and the grandparent derives much joy and satisfaction from the grandparent–grandchild relationship (Woodbridge, Buys, & Miller, 2011).

Research demonstrates that the grandparent role may be played in many ways. A number of factors may influence the style of grandparenting, including culture, geographic proximity, ages of grandparents and grandchildren, number of grandchildren, and family rituals. For example, one research team investigated Chinese American grandmothering and found that these grandmothers spent significant amounts of time with their grandchildren and considered their grandparenting style to be based on a sense of responsibility to teach their grandchildren to have good character and to honor filial piety. Their high involvement with their grandchildren was formal and hierarchical, unlike the friendly companionate style characterized by many European American grandparents (Nagata, Cheng, & Tsai, 2010). The researchers caution not to assume that formal and detached relationships necessarily result in low involvement. They also note language and acculturation issues that can interfere with grandparent–grandchild relationships in immigrant families.

Grandparents can play an important role in their grandchildren's lives.

WORK AND RETIREMENT

Until the 20th century, the average worker retired about 3 years before death. Increased worker productivity, mass longevity, and social security legislation changed that situation, however. The labor force participation of men aged 65 or older declined steadily from 1900, when it was about 66%, to 1985, when it was 15.8%. From 1986 to 2002, it stabilized at 16% to 18% but began to increase after 2002. The labor force participation of women aged 65 and older rose slightly from 1900 to 1956, from about 8% to 10.8%. It fell to 7.3% in 1985, remained at 7% to 9% from 1986 to 2002, and then began to rise. In 2012, 18.5% of adults aged 65 and older were in the labor force, including 23.6% of men and 14.4% of women (Administration on Aging, 2012). It is thought that this recent upward shift in the labor force participation of older adults is related to both financial considerations and improved health. Changes to social security policy allowed older adults to continue working and still receive partial social security benefits, but two other changes have increased the financial necessity for older adults to stay in the labor force: a reduction in pension plans and the scheduled increase in age for receiving full social security benefits. In addition, many older adults faced losses in savings, investments, and home equity during the economic recession that started in 2007 (Bjorklund, 2011).

Retirement patterns vary with social class. Vaillant (2002) found that only 20% of his sample of surviving inner-city men were still in the workforce at age 65, but half of the sample of Harvard men were still working full-time at 65. The inner-city men retired, on average, 5 years earlier than the Harvard men. Poor health often leads to earlier retirement among less advantaged adults (Hooyman & Kiyak, 2011). In addition, higher levels of education make workers eligible for more sedentary jobs, which are a better fit with the declining energy levels in late adulthood (Vaillant, 2002).

The "appropriate" age for retirement in the United States is currently understood to be age 65. This cultural understanding has been shaped by social security legislation enacted in 1935. However, the 1983 Social Security Amendments included a provision for a gradual increase in the age at which a retired person could begin receiving social security retirement benefits. Exhibit 16.6 shows the schedule of the increased retirement age for receiving full benefits. In arguing for this legislative change, members of Congress noted increased longevity and improved health among older adults.

Older adults who continue to work fall into two groups: those who could afford to retire but choose to continue working and those who continue to work because of financial need. Because economic status in old age is influenced by past employment patterns and the

EXHIBIT 16.6 • Amended Age to Receive Full Social Security Benefits (1983)

YEAR OF BIRTH	FULL RETIREMENT AGE
1937 and earlier	65
1938	65 and 2 months
1939	65 and 4 months
1940	65 and 6 months
1941	65 and 8 months
1942	65 and 10 months
1943–1954	66
1955	66 and 2 months
1956	66 and 4 months
1957	66 and 6 months
1958	66 and 8 months
1959	66 and 10 months
1960 and later	67

SOURCE: Social Security Administration, 2013.

resultant retirement benefits, the second group consists of individuals who had lower-paying employment throughout their lives. This group also includes elderly divorced or widowed women who depended on their husband's retirement income and are now faced with poverty or near poverty. Lifelong gender inequality in wages contributes to inequality in pension and retirement funds (Hooyman & Kiyak, 2011). Ruby Johnson continues to be employed on a part-time basis out of financial necessity.

There are many ways of retiring from the workforce. Some individuals cease work completely, but others continue with part-time or part-year employment. Others may retire for a period and then reenter the labor market. Retirement is a socially accepted way to end an active role in the workforce. Most persons retire because of advancing age, mandatory retirement policies, health problems, a desire to pursue other interests, or simply a wish to relax and lead the life of a retiree.

Individuals vary in whether they view retirement as something to dread or something to look forward to. Most often, however, retirement is a positive experience. Vaillant (2002) found no evidence in his longitudinal research that retirement is bad for physical health. For every person who indicated that retirement was bad for her or his health, four retirees indicated that retirement had improved their health. Vaillant noted four conditions under which retirement is perceived as stressful: retirement was involuntary or unplanned, there are no means of financial support besides salary, work provided an escape from an unhappy home life, or retirement was precipitated by preexisting bad health.

CAREGIVING AND CARE RECEIVING

As retirement unfolds, declining health may usher in a period of intensive need for care. The majority of older adults with disabilities live in the community and receive predominantly informal care from spouses, children, and extended family. Among older adults who need care and live in the community, about 9% rely exclusively on formal care, and about 70% rely exclusively on informal care. It is estimated that if informal care was unavailable, long-term care costs would double (Hooyman & Kiyak, 2011). Women are the primary source of caregiving in old age. Daughters are more likely than sons to take care of elderly parents. Moreover, elderly men tend to be married and thus are more likely to have a wife available as caregiver (Walsh, 2011).

Caregiving can be an around-the-clock task and often leaves caregivers overwhelmed and exhausted (see Chan, Malhotra, Malhotra, Rush, & Ostbye, 2013). Margaret Davis's family is a good example of the burden that can be experienced by family caregivers. Programs that can assist caregivers in reducing their exceptional levels of stress have received much attention. Many programs combine educational components—for example, information about and training in adaptive coping skills—with ongoing support through the opportunity to share personal feelings and experiences. In recent years, social workers have been using telephone and computer-mediated support groups to assist family caregivers and have found many benefits of these virtual groups (Jones & Meier, 2011; Toseland & Larkin, 2010). Respite programs for caregivers are also available. In-home respite programs provide assistance through a home health aide or a visiting nurse (Petrovic, 2013). Community-based respite is often provided through adult day care and similar programs. It is important to remember that not all caregivers have the same reactions to their caregiving responsibilities, and there are gains as well as losses associated with the caregiver role.

Based on their research on the topic, Rhonda Montgomery and Karl Kosloski (2000, 2009) developed a caregiver identity theory. Their framework consists of seven "career markers," stages that individuals typically move through in their career as caregivers. The first marker signifies the time when the dependency situation begins. One person needs assistance with routine activities and another person starts performing caregiving tasks. The second marker is reached when the self-definition as a caregiver begins; that is, the person incorporates the role of caregiver into his or her personal and social identity.

The third marker is characterized by the performance of personal care tasks. At this time, caregiving family members begin to evaluate whether to continue as caregivers or seek alternatives. The next marker is reached when outside assistance is sought and formal service use is considered. Considering nursing home placement is the fifth marker. Although the institutional placement is considered at earlier phases, the decision now is more imminent. Nursing home placement is the sixth marker. When caregiving becomes too overwhelming, a nursing home placement may be pursued. Caregiving often continues after a family member enters a nursing home. Although many individuals will spend some time in a nursing home, others never enter such an institution and die at home. The final marker in Montgomery and Kosloski's (2000) caregiver identity theory is the termination of the caregiver role. This may occur due to recovery or death of the care recipient or through "quitting" as a caregiver.

Stress and burden are not experienced only by the caregiver. Although there has been very little research on the topic, it is suggested that the care recipient also experiences significant strain. Requiring care is a double loss: the person has lost the capability to perform the tasks for which he or she needs assistance and the person has also lost independence. Having to rely on others for activities that one has carried out independently throughout one's adult life can be the source of tremendous emotional and psychological stress. Some individuals respond by emotional withdrawal, whereas others become agitated and start blaming others for their situation. Still others make the best of the situation and even find benefits, such as being able to reside in the community, reducing the economic costs of care, and becoming closer to caregivers (Bjorklund, 2011).

INSTITUTIONALIZATION

One myth of aging is that older individuals are being abandoned and neglected by their families and being pushed into nursing homes to get them out of the way. Fewer elderly persons are institutionalized than we generally assume, but the risk for entering a nursing home increases significantly with age. The percentage of older people living in nursing homes in the United States actually declined from 5.1% in 1990 to 3.6% in 2011 (Administration on Aging, 2012). Only 1% of older adults ages 65 to 74, compared with 11% of those 85 and older, lived in nursing homes. U.S. Census (2012a) data show that 37.5% of female centenarians and 23.3% of male centenarians were living in a nursing or group residence compared with 20.8% of females and 11.9% of males ages 90 to 94. Additionally, 2.7% of older adults live in self-described senior housing with at least one supportive service (Administration on Aging, 2012). It is important to note that these data reflect the number of older adults living in institutional settings at a given point in time. The data do not reflect the movement in and out of such facilities, and it is estimated that 39% of people aged 65 and older will spend some time in a nursing home at some point; the percentage rises to 49% at age 85 (Hooyman & Kiyak, 2011). About three quarters of the residents of nursing homes are women, and about 86% are White (Hooyman & Kiyak, 2011).

Most children and spouses do not use nursing homes as a dumping ground for their elderly relatives. They turn to nursing homes only after they have exhausted all other alternatives. Nor is institutionalization a single, sudden event. It is a process that starts with the need to make a decision, continues through the placement itself, and ends in the adjustment to the placement (Naleppa, 1996).

Researchers have taken a close look at the factors that predict a person's entry into a nursing home. Among the most important are the condition and needs of the elderly individual. Functional and behavioral deficits, declining health, previous institutionalization, and advanced age all contribute to the decision to enter a nursing home. Family characteristics that are good predictors of institutionalization include the need for 24-hour caregiving, caregiver feelings of distress, caregiver health and mental status, and caregiving environment (Naleppa, 1996). The placement decision itself is emotionally stressful for all involved and can be viewed as a family crisis (Chang & Schneider, 2010). Yet it can be considered a normative part of the family life cycle. The process of making a placement decision itself unfolds in stages: initiating the placement decision, assessing and weighing the decision, finalizing the decision, and evaluating the decision (Chang & Schneider, 2010). Because many nursing home placements are arranged from the hospital for an elderly individual who entered the hospital expecting to return home, many older adults and their families may not have time to progress well through these stages. For those who unexpectedly enter a nursing home from the hospital, it may be advisable to arrange a brief visit home to say farewell to their familiar environment. Although society has developed rituals for many occasions, unfortunately no rituals exist for this difficult life transition.

Entering a nursing home means losing control and adjusting to a new environment, but the culture of nursing homes is changing. Increasingly, nursing homes focus on resident-centered care that offers more choices in such matters as waking and eating times. The new culture emphasizes a more homelike atmosphere, including companion animals, breaking large facilities into smaller communities, and humanizing staff–care recipient relationships. Evaluation of the impact of these changes on residents and staff indicate lower levels of boredom and helplessness among residents and less job turnover among staff (Hooyman & Kiyak, 2011). How well a person adjusts to moving to a nursing home depends on many factors. If the elderly individual sees entering the nursing home in a favorable light and feels in control, adjustment may proceed well. Frequent visits by relatives and friends also help in the adaptation to the new living arrangement.

THE SEARCH FOR PERSONAL MEANING

As adults become older, they spend more time reviewing their life achievements and searching for personal meaning. In gerontology, the concept of **life review** as a developmental task of late adulthood was introduced by Robert Butler (1963). He theorized that this self-reflective review of one's life is not a sign of losing short-term memory, as had been assumed. Rather, life review is a process of evaluating and making sense of one's life. It includes a reinterpretation of past experiences and unresolved conflicts. Newer forms of clinical interventions rooted in narrative theory underscore the importance of providing structure, coherence, and opportunity for making meaning of one's experience that "storying" provides (Madigan, 2011). Social workers can influence a more positive outcome of a life review through relationship, empathic listening and reflection, witnessing to the story, and providing alternative reframes and interpretations of past events. For example, promoting a story of resiliency as a lifelong process helps to reframe stories that support successful mastery of challenges and compensatory recovery in the face of adversity (O'Leary & Bhaju, 2006; Wadensten, 2005).

The life review can lead to diverse outcomes, including depression, acceptance, or satisfaction (Butler, 1987). If the life review is successful, it leads the individual to personal wisdom and inner peace. But the reassessment of one's life may also lead to despair and depression. This idea that the process of a life review may lead to either acceptance or depression is similar to the eighth stage of Erikson's theory of adult development; through the life review, the individual tries to work through the conflict between ego integrity (accepting oneself and seeing one's life as meaningful) and despair (rejecting oneself and one's life).

The ways in which individuals review their lives differ considerably. Some undertake a very conscious effort of assessing and reevaluating their achievements; for others, the effort may be subtle and not very conscious. Life review is believed to be a common activity for older adults, regardless of how they pursue it across cultures and time.

The concept of **reminiscence** is closely related to life review. Most older persons have a remarkable ability to recall past events. They reminisce about the past and tell their stories to anyone who is willing to listen, but they also reminisce when they are on their own. This reminiscing can serve several functions (Sherman, 1991):

Reminiscing can assist in the life review, as a way to achieve ego integrity.

- Reminiscing may be an enjoyable activity that can lift the spirits of the listener and of the person telling the story.
- Some forms of reminiscing are directed at enhancing a person's image of self, as when individuals focus on their accomplishments.
- Reminiscing may help the person cope with current or future problems, letting her or him retreat to the safe place of a comfortable memory or recall ways of coping with past stressors.
- Reminiscing can assist in the life review, as a way to achieve ego integrity.

Reminiscing combines past, present, and future orientations (Sherman, 1991). It includes the past, which is when the reviewed events occurred. However, the construction of personal meaning is an activity also oriented to the present and the future, providing purpose and meaning to life. One study examined the association between reminiscence frequency, reminiscence enjoyment or regret, and psychological health outcomes. The study found that high frequency of reminiscence and having regret were associated with poor psychological health. Reminiscence enjoyment, conversely, was positively associated with psychological health outcomes (Mckee et al., 2005).

Another factor in the search for personal meaning is religious or spiritual activity. Cross-sectional research has consistently found that humans become more religious or spiritual in late adulthood (Moody & Sasser, 2012). There seems to be consensus in the cross-sectional research from the United States that religiosity increases in late adulthood, with a short period of health-related drop-off in attendance at religious services at the end of life. Older adults are also more likely than other age groups to participate in private religious behaviors such as prayer, reading of sacred texts, or meditation (Bjorklund, 2011). One longitudinal study that followed a sample of men and women from ages 31 to 78 found that women and men tend to increase in spirituality between the mid-50s and mid-70s (Wink & Dillon, 2002). Vaillant's (2012) longitudinal research did not find support for this idea among his sample of Harvard men, and he suggests that the nature of the sample may be an important factor in this finding.

Often when faced with crises—particularly those of severe illness, disability, and/or loss—one tends to reexamine the meaning of life. And although illness, disability, and loss occur throughout life, these challenges tend to accumulate and come at a faster pace during very late adulthood. Spirituality late in life is often associated with loss (Armatowski, 2001). Over time, losses accumulate in relationships, status and roles, health, and independence.

RESOURCES FOR MEETING THE NEEDS OF ELDERLY PERSONS

The persons in the case studies at the beginning of this chapter need several kinds of assistance. Ruby Johnson requires a level of assistance most practically provided by effective and comprehensive case management; she is specifically asking for help in planning for the well-being of her multigenerational family after she dies. Margaret Davis's daughter and granddaughter are providing assistance with her daily care, and they could use a variety of services to assist them in their attempt to care for her at home. There is a strong need for assistance in managing her multiple chronic health problems. Finding accessible, affordable services in her rural community could be a real challenge for Ms. Davis's social worker. Until recently, Bina Patel provided as much assistance as she received, but her deteriorating health now poses a special challenge to her and her family in the face of her son's terminal illness. This family will need emotional support as well as practical assistance in planning for her future care.

The types of support and assistance that elderly persons receive can be categorized as either formal or informal resources. *Formal resources* are those provided by formal service providers. They typically have eligibility requirements that a person has to meet in order to qualify. Some formal resources are free, but others are provided on a fee-for-service basis, meaning that anyone who is able to pay can request the service. *Informal resources* are those provided through families, friends, neighbors, churches, and so forth. Elderly persons receive a considerable amount of support through these informal support networks. As the society ages, more attention will need to be paid to the interaction between the informal and formal support systems (Wacker & Roberto, 2014).

Many types of formal services are available, but the social worker's most daunting task is often assessing the elderly person's needs. It may also be a challenge, however, to find quality services that are affordable. Thus, advocacy on behalf of older adults remains a concern of the social work profession.

Some elderly persons have difficulty managing their legal and financial affairs. A **power of attorney (POA)** is a legal arrangement by which a person appoints another individual to manage his or her financial and legal affairs. The person given the POA should be someone the client knows and trusts. Standard POA forms can usually be found at office supply stores or on websites for state bar associations, but legal advice is highly recommended for specific situations. A POA can be limited (in scope or for a certain time period), general (no restrictions), or durable (begins after the client reaches a specified level of disability).

CRITICAL THINKING Questions 16.4

At what age do you expect to retire? If you were promised a full pension that would allow you to stop working now, would you want to continue to work? Why or why not? What does work mean to you? Do you work to live or live to work? What factors do you think a person should consider when making decisions about retirement?

THE DYING PROCESS

The topic of death and dying is almost always in the last chapter of a human behavior textbook, reflecting the hope that death will come as late as possible in life. Obviously, people die at all stages of life, but very late adulthood is the time when dying is considered "on time."

Despite our strong cultural predisposition toward denial of the topic, and perhaps in response to this, there have been a plethora of efforts to talk about death, starting most notably with Elisabeth Kübler-Ross's book *On Death and Dying* in 1969. Beginning in the late 1990s, initiatives such as the Project on Death in America (PDIA) funded by the Soros Foundation and end-of-life initiatives funded by the Robert Wood Johnson Foundation set out to change mainstream attitudes. The mission of PDIA was to understand and transform the culture and experience of dying and bereavement.

On a more individual level, many factors influence the ways in which a person adjusts to death and dying, including one's religion and philosophy of life, personality, culture, and other personal traits. Adjustment may also be affected by the conditions of dying. A person with a prolonged terminal illness has more time and opportunity to accept and prepare for his or her own death, or that of a loved one, than someone with an acute and fatal illness or sudden death.

The following adjectives used to describe death are found in both the professional and popular literature: *good*, *meaningful*, *appropriate*, *timely*, *peaceful*, *sudden*, and *natural*. One can be said to die well, on time, before one's time, and in a variety of ways and places. This terminology reflects an attempt to embrace, acknowledge, tame, and integrate death into one's life. Other language is more indirect, using euphemisms, metaphors, medical terms, and slang, reflecting a need to avoid directly talking about death—suggesting that the person is "lost," has "passed away," or has "expired" (DeSpelder & Strickland, 2005). It is important for a social worker to be attentive to words that individuals and families choose because they often reflect one's culture and/or religious background and comfort level (Bullock, 2011).

As with life, the richness and complexity of death are best understood from a multidimensional framework involving the biological, psychological, social, and spiritual dimensions (Bern-Klug, 2004). The following conceptualizations of the dying process help capture the notion that dying and other losses, and the accompanying bereavement, are processes that differ for each unique situation yet share some common aspects.

In *On Death and Dying*, Kübler-Ross (1969) described stages that people tend to go through in accepting their own inevitable death or that of others, summarized in Exhibit 16.7. Although these stages were written with death in mind, they have application to other loss-related experiences, including the aging process. Given time, most individuals experience these five reactions, although not necessarily in this order. People often shift back and forth between the reactions rather than experience them in a linear way, get stuck in a stage, and/or skip over others. Kübler-Ross suggests that, on some level, hope of survival persists through all stages.

Although these reactions may fit people in general, very-late-life adults appear to experience far less denial about the reality of death than other age groups (McInnis-Dittrich, 2009). As they confront their limitations of physical health and become socialized to death with each passing friend and

EXHIBIT 16.7 • Stages of Accepting Impending Death

STAGE	DESCRIPTION
Denial	The person denies that death will occur: "This is not true. It can't be me." This denial is succeeded by temporary isolation from social interactions.
Anger	The individual asks, "Why me?" The person projects his or her resentment and envy onto others and often directs the anger toward a supreme being, medical caregivers, family members, and friends.
Bargaining	The individual starts bargaining in an attempt to postpone death, proposing a series of deals with God, self, or others: "Yes, me, but I will do _______ in exchange for a few more months."
Depression	A sense of loss follows. Individuals grieve about their own end of life and about the ones that will be left behind. A frequent reaction is withdrawal from close and loved persons: "I just want to be left alone."
Acceptance	The person accepts that the end is near and the struggle is over: "It's okay. My life has been . . . "

SOURCE: Based on Kübler-Ross (1969).

family member, most very-late-life adults become less fearful of death. Unfortunately, some professionals and family members may not be as comfortable expressing their feelings related to death and dying, which may leave the elder feeling isolated.

In addition to expressing feelings about death, some very-late-life adults have other needs related to dying. A fear of prolonged physical pain or discomfort, as well as fear of losing a sense of control and mastery, trouble very-late-life adults most. Some have suggested that older adults who are dying need a safe and accepting relationship in which to express the fear, sadness, anger, resentment, or other feelings related to the pending loss of life and opportunity, especially separation from loved ones (Agronin, 2011; Bowlby, 1980).

ADVANCE DIRECTIVES

On a more concrete level, social workers can help patients and families discuss, prepare, and enact health care **advance directives**, or documents that give instructions about desired health care if, in the future, individuals cannot speak for themselves. Such discussions can provide an opportunity to clarify values and wishes regarding end-of-life treatment. Ideally, this conversation has been started prior to very late adulthood. If not, helping people to communicate their wishes regarding life-sustaining measures, who they want to act on their behalf when they are no longer competent to make these decisions, and other end-of-life concerns helps some people feel more empowered.

Since the passage of the Patient Self-Determination Act in 1990, hospitals and other health care institutions receiving Medicare or Medical Assistance funds are required to inform patients that should their condition become life-threatening, they have a right to make decisions about what medical care they would wish to receive (McInnis-Dittrich, 2009). The two primary forms of advance directives are the living will and the durable power of attorney for health care.

A **living will** describes the medical procedures, drugs, and types of treatment that one would choose for oneself if able to do so in certain situations. It also describes the situations for which the patient would want treatment withheld. For example, one may instruct medical personnel not to use any artificial means or heroic measures to keep one alive if the condition is such that there is no hope for recovery. Whereas a living will allows an individual to speak for oneself in advance, a durable power of attorney designates someone else to speak for the individual.

The promotion of patient rights as just described has helped many patients feel empowered and has comforted some family members, but this topic is not without controversy. Because the laws vary from state to state, laypersons and professionals must inquire about the process if one relocates. Also, rather than feeling comforted by knowing a dying person's wishes, some family members experience the burden of difficult decision making that once was handled by the physician. Advance directives are not accepted or considered moral by some ethnic, racial, and religious groups. Because of historical distrust of the White medical establishment, some African American and Hispanic families have preferred life-sustaining treatment to the refusal of treatment inherent in advance directives. Among some religious groups, the personal control represented in advance directives is seen to interfere with a divine plan and is considered a form of passive suicide. As discussed shortly, social workers must approach each patient and family with an openness to learn about their values and wishes. Volker (2005) cautions health care providers to consider the relevancy of Western values, such as personal control over one's future, in the lives of non-Western patient groups.

CARE OF PEOPLE WHO ARE DYING

Although some associate hospice and palliative care with "giving up" and there being "nothing left to do," in fact hospices provide **palliative care**—a form of care focusing on pain and symptom management as opposed to curing disease. The focus is on "caring, not curing" (National Hospice and Palliative Care Organization [NHPCO], 2012), when curative-focused treatment is no longer available or desired. Palliative care attends to the psychological, social, and spiritual issues in addition to the physical needs. The goal of palliative care is achievement of the best possible quality of life for patients and their families.

Hospice is one model of palliative care, borrowed from the British, that began in the United States in the mid-1970s to address the needs of dying persons and their loved ones. It is more a philosophy of care than a place, with the majority of persons receiving hospice services where they live, whether that is their private residence (41.6%), a nursing or residential facility (24.9%), or inpatient hospice facility (NHPCO, 2012). Hospice services are typically available to persons who have received a prognosis of 6 months or less to live and who are no longer receiving care directed toward a cure. For instance, the hospital social worker may want to give Bina Patel and her daughter-in-law information about hospice care, as an additional support during Ms. Patel's son's illness.

The National Hospice and Palliative Care Organization (2012) estimates that the United States had 5,300 hospice programs in 2011 serving most rural, suburban, and urban communities in all 50 states. In 2011, approximately 1.65 million patients, representing approximately 46.6% of all deaths in the United States, received hospice services. Four out of five hospice patients are 65 years of age or older, and about 39.3% are 85 and older. When hospice care was first established in the United States in the 1970s, cancer patients accounted for the majority of hospice admissions. Over time, hospices responded to the needs of others with end-stage disease (e.g., AIDS, dementia, heart disease, lung disease, and stroke as well as others), and in 2011, cancer accounted for less than half (37.7%) of all admissions (NHPCO, 2012).

Health disparities have been noted in hospice care, as in other health care settings, with persons of color historically being underserved. Initiatives through NHPCO,

Palliative care focuses on providing pain and symptom management when cure of disease is no longer an option. The patient and the family are the unit of care.

the Soros Foundation's Faculty Scholar program, and the Robert Wood Johnson Foundation's Promoting Excellence in End-of-Life Care have focused on program development specific to the needs of patients and families in African American, Hispanic, Native American, and other communities that have been underserved by more traditional hospice programs (Crawley et al., 2000; NHPCO, 2012).

Palliative care programs are emerging in hospital settings to address pain and symptom management in patients who might not fit the hospice criteria. Some hospitals have palliative care units specializing in management of short-term, acute symptoms; others have palliative care consultative services that bring their expertise to medical, oncology, pediatric, and other units throughout the hospital (Reith & Payne, 2009).

END-OF-LIFE SIGNS AND SYMPTOMS

Family members and others caring for a person who is dying often experience a great deal of anxiety when they do not have adequate information about the dying process. Most families appreciate knowing what to expect, and honest, factual information can help allay their fears of the unknown (Cagle & Kovacs, 2009; Proot et al., 2004). Many hospice services provide written information about symptoms of impending death for those families anticipating the death of a loved one at home. Exploring how much information people have and want is an important part of the social worker's assessment. Obviously, each individual situation will differ, but general information about symptoms of impending death, summarized in Exhibit 16.8, helps people prepare (Lamers, 2013; Reith & Payne, 2009).

EXHIBIT 16.8 • Signs and Symptoms of Impending Death

Lowered temperature and slowed circulation
Deeper and longer periods of sleep
Decreased acuity of vision and hearing
Increased secretions in the mouth and congestion
Incontinence
Restlessness and confusion
Reduced need for eating and drinking and difficulty swallowing
Irregular and interrupted breathing
Increased signs of pain

SOURCE: Lamers, 2013; Reith & Payne, 2009.

Dying may take hours or days; no one can predict the time of death, even when the person is exhibiting signs and symptoms of dying. The following are signs that death has occurred:

- Breathing stops.
- Heart stops beating.
- Bowel or bladder control is lost.
- There is no response to verbal commands or shaking.
- Eyelids may be slightly open with eyes fixed on a certain spot.
- Mouth may fall open slightly as the jaw relaxes.

Such explicit discussion of death with those attending a dying family member or close friend may seem upsetting, but this knowledge is also comforting and can help ease the anxiety related to the fear of the unknown. Dying persons are also comforted knowing that their family members have the informational, medical, and social support they need to help them in their caregiving role. It is also helpful to have funeral plans in place so that one phone call to the mortuary facilitates the process, rather than facing difficult and emotional decision making at the time of death.

LOSS, GRIEF, AND BEREAVEMENT

Loss is a common human experience. There is a great deal of evidence that people of all cultures have strong, painful reactions to the death of the people to whom they are emotionally attached (Doka & Tucci, 2009). Sadness, loneliness, disbelief, and anxiety are only a few of the feelings a person may experience in times of bereavement. The challenge is to refrain from making grief the problem, thereby pathologizing someone's experience, and to understand the complexities related to death in a society that has grown increasingly old-age and death avoidant (Jenkinson, 2012). So, we offer the following, cautioning against turning someone's grief into a problem and encouraging readers to help others understand grief as a normal part of life.

Grief, *bereavement*, and *mourning* are words often used interchangeably, perhaps because no one word "reflects the fullness of what a death introduces into the life of an individual, family or community" (Silverman, 2004, p. 226). The following definitions help distinguish the various aspects of this process.

- **Loss.** The severing of an attachment an individual has with a loved one; a loved object (such as a pet, home, or country); or an aspect of one's self or identity (such as a body part or function; physical or mental capacity; or role or position in family, society, or other context) (Stroebe, Stroebe, & Hansson, 1993). P. R. Silverman (2004) suggests that loss doesn't *happen* to us; rather, it is "something we must make sense out of, give meaning to, and respond to" (p. 226).
- **Bereavement.** The state of having suffered a loss.
- **Grief.** The normal internal reaction of an individual experiencing a loss. Grief is a complex coping process, is highly individualized (Stroebe et al., 1993), and is an expected period of transition (Silverman, 2004).
- **Mourning.** The external expression of grief (Stroebe et al., 1993); the "mental work following the loss of a loved one [a] . . . social process including the cultural traditions and rituals that guide behavior after a death" (Silverman, 2004, p. 226).

The rituals associated with death vary in historical and cross-cultural context (Bullock, 2011; Doka & Tucci, 2009). In some cultures, the dead are buried; in other cultures, the dead are burned and the ashes are spread. In some places and times, a surviving wife might have been burned together with her husband. In the United States, death rituals can be as different as a traditional New Orleans funeral, with street music and mourners dressed in white, or a somber and serene funeral with hushed mourners dressed in black. Some cultures prescribe more emotional expression than others. Some cultures build ritual for expression of anger, and some do not.

Throughout life, we are faced with many losses, some that occur by death, but many that occur in other ways as well. For example, Ruby Johnson has faced loss through divorce, disappointment and estrangement with her daughter, and retirement. Margaret Davis lost her husband to death, but she has also lost a daughter through estrangement and faced much loss of independence and privacy as she increasingly needed assistance from her children and grandchildren. Bina Patel lost her husband, lost a homeland when she immigrated to be near her children, and lost some physical functioning after her stroke. Recently, the burgeoning literature on loss, grief, and bereavement has recognized that there may be similar processes for grieving all losses, including those that occur for reasons other than death. Loss is one of the most important themes in our work as social workers. For example, we encounter loss due to foster care placement, divorce, disease and disability, migration and immigration, unemployment, and so on.

Many factors influence the way in which a person adjusts to death and dying, including one's religion and philosophy of life, personality, and other traits.

THEORIES AND MODELS OF LOSS AND GRIEF

A variety of theorists have sought to make sense of the complex experience of loss. Much of the literature on grief and bereavement for the past century has been influenced by Sigmund Freud's (1917/1957) classic article "Mourning and Melancholia." Freud described the "work of mourning" as a process of severing a relationship with a lost person, object, or ideal. He suggested that this happens over time as the bereaved person is repeatedly faced with situations that remind him or her that the loved person (or object or ideal) has, indeed, been lost. From this classic work came the idea of a necessary period of **grief work** to sever the attachment bond, an idea that has been the cornerstone of a number of stage models of the grief process.

In the United States, Erich Lindemann (1944) was a pioneer in grief research. Through his important study of families of people who died in a fire at the Cocoanut Grove Lounge in Boston, he conceptualized grief work as both a biological and psychological necessity. The common reactions to loss that he identified include the following:

- Somatic distress, occurring in waves lasting from 20 minutes to an hour, including tightness in throat, choking and shortness of breath, need for sighing, empty feeling in abdomen, lack of muscular power, and intense subjective distress
- Preoccupation with image of deceased, yearning for the lost one to return, wanting to see pictures of the deceased or touch items that are associated with the deceased
- Guilt
- Hostile reactions, toward the deceased as well as toward others
- Loss of patterns of conduct, where the ability to carry out routine behaviors is lost

Lindemann (1944) proposed that grief work occurs in stages, an idea that has been popular with other theorists and researchers since the 1960s. A number of stage models of grief have been proposed, and four are presented in Exhibit 16.9. As you can see, although the number and names of stages vary somewhat among theorists and researchers, in general the stage models all agree that grief work progresses from disbelief and feelings of unreality, to painful and disorganizing reactions, to a kind of "coming to terms" with the loss. Stages or phases run the risk of being misused when taken too literally; however, they have served to remind us that grief is a process with different parts that people experience in their own time (Winokuer & Harris, 2012).

J. William Worden (2009) took a somewhat different approach, writing about the "tasks of mourning" rather than stages of mourning. He considered *task* to be more consistent with Freud's concept of grief work, given that the mourner needs to take action and do something rather than passively move through grief. Worden suggests that the following four tasks of mourning are important when a person is adapting to a loss:

Task I: to accept the reality of the loss. Working through denial takes time, because this involves an intellectual and an emotional acceptance. Some people have traditional rituals that help with this process.

Task II: to work through the pain of grief. Because people are often uncomfortable with the outward displays of grief, our society often interferes with this task. People often seek a geographic cure or quickly replace the lost person in a new relationship but often still have this task to complete.

Task III: to adjust to an environment in which the deceased is missing. This includes filling roles previously filled by the deceased and making appropriate adjustments in daily activities. In terms of roles, many widows report being thrown the first time they have to cope with a major home repair. Regarding adjustments in daily activities, many bereaved persons report that they find themselves automatically putting the favorite foods of the deceased in their grocery carts.

Task IV: to emotionally relocate the deceased and move on with life. This task was best described by Sadie Delany after the loss of her beloved sister, Bessie: "I don't want to get over you. I just want to find a way to live without you" (Delany, 1997).

In the past couple of decades, there has been a critique of the idea of grief work. A highly influential article, "The Myths of Coping With Loss" (Wortman & Silver, 1989), disputed two major themes of the traditional view of grief work: Distress is an inevitable response to loss, and the failure to experience distress is a sign of improper grieving. In fact, a number of researchers have found that those who show the highest levels of distress immediately following a loss are more likely than those who show little distress to be depressed several years later. In another vein, Silverman (2004) challenges the notion of "tasks," which suggests something can be completed, recommending that we focus instead on "issues and processes" (p. 237).

EXHIBIT 16.9 • Four Stage Models of Grief

TYPICAL STAGES OF GRIEF	ERICH LINDEMANN (1944)	ELISABETH KÜBLER-ROSS (1969)	JOHN BOWLBY (1980)	THERESE RANDO (1993)
Disbelief and feelings of unreality	Shock and disbelief	Denial and isolation	Numbness	Avoidance
Painful and disorganizing reactions	Acute mourning	Anger Bargaining Depression	Yearning Disorganization Despair	Confrontation
A kind of "getting over" the loss	Resolution	Acceptance	Reorganization	Accommodation

Given the tremendous diversity among individuals based on gender, culture, personality, and life experience, as well as the various circumstances surrounding a loss, the grieving process is not easily defined, but theorists and practitioners continue to try to provide some framework for understanding the process. Camille Wortman and Roxanne Silver (1990) proposed that at least four patterns of grieving are possible: normal, chronic, delayed, and absent. Worden (2009) elaborated on these patterns:

1. *Normal or uncomplicated grief*. Relatively high level of distress soon after the loss encompassing a broad range of feelings and behaviors, followed by a relatively rapid recovery.
2. *Chronic or prolonged grief*. High level of distress continuing over a number of years without coming to a satisfactory conclusion.
3. *Delayed grief (or inhibited, suppressed, or postponed grief)*. Little distress in the first few months after the loss, but high levels of distress at some later point.
4. *Absent grief*. No notable level of distress either soon after the loss or at some later time. Some question this notion and wonder if it is not absent but masked or delayed; observation over time is important.

In their research, Wortman and Silver (1990) found absent grief in 26% of their bereaved participants, as well as a high rate (over 30%) of chronic grief.

Given these critiques of traditional models of grief, theorists and researchers have looked for other ways to understand the complex reactions to loss. The study of bereavement has been influenced by developments in the study of stress and trauma reactions. Research on loss and grief has produced the following findings (Bonanno & Kaltman, 1999):

- It is the evaluation of the nature of the loss by the bereaved survivor that determines how stressful the loss is.
- How well a coping strategy works for dealing with loss depends on the context and the nature of the person–environment encounter.
- Maintaining some type of continued bond with the deceased, a strong sense of the continued presence of the deceased, may be adaptive.
- The capacity to minimize negative emotions after a loss allows the bereaved to continue to function in areas of personal importance.
- Humor can aid in the grief process by allowing the bereaved to approach the enormity of the loss without maximizing psychic pain or alienating social support.
- In situations of traumatic loss, there is a need to talk about the loss, but not all interpersonal relationships can tolerate such talk.

Martin and Doka's (2000) model of adult bereavement explores the roles of gender, culture, and other characteristics that influence a person's grieving style. This model includes two adaptive grieving styles that they theorize to be at two ends of a continuum: the internal experience of loss and the outward expression relating to the loss. Martin and Doka (2000) suggest that adaptive grieving styles exist on a continuum with intuitive grievers at one end and instrumental grievers at the other end. Intuitive grievers experience and express their grief primarily through emotion, and instrumental grievers experience and express their grief primarily through a cognitive, behavioral, problem-solving approach. They suggest that few people tend to be at either extreme of the continuum, but rather most tend to have a blended style of grieving, using both intuitive and instrumental strategies (Doughty, 2009). They assert that the difficulty may arise when an individual for whatever reason uses a grieving style that is in conflict with his or her more natural adaptive style.

In summary, grief is a multidimensional process—a normal life experience—that theorists and practitioners continue to try to understand (Gordon, 2013). There seems to be general agreement that culture, past experience, gender, age, and other personal characteristics influence how one copes with loss.

CULTURE AND BEREAVEMENT

Some suggest that all people feel the same pain with grief but that cultural differences shape our mourning rituals, traditions, and behavioral expressions of grief (K. Walsh, 2012). Although there are good sources for exploring ethnic variations related to death and grief (see Irish, Lundquist, & Nelsen, 1993), we hesitate to provide overviews of various cultural groups, because of the diversity within groups, as well as increasing cultural diversity in most communities. So instead we suggest you come to each encounter with an openness and curiosity, acknowledging people as the experts about what has been helpful in the past and inquiring about what you need to know to best work with them now. Hooyman and Kramer (2006) provide detailed suggestions for conducting a good cross-cultural assessment and communication (see pp. 174–178), some of which include the following:

- Do your homework before talking to members of the group.
- Begin by listening to their story using open-ended questions.

- Approach them with humility and caution, recognizing them as "insiders" who have the more immediate and critical knowledge of their experience.
- Never judge or have predetermined ideas of what they should feel or do.
- Recognize potential cultural conflicts and respect their decisions and choices.
- Use and train qualified interpreters, understanding the benefits and limitations of doing so.

Important components of an assessment include reactions to loss; mourning style; level of acculturation; cultural history; the role and presence of religion and/or spirituality; grieving rituals; family dynamics, including intergenerational relationships; and other components of any good multidimensional assessment such as social support, financial resources, strengths, and personality. Inquire more specifically about the following:

- Their interpretation of the illness and/or death (asking what they call it, think caused it, think will help, fear most)
- Questions relevant to the care of the body after the death and related beliefs and rituals
- How people in their family and culture commonly express grief (i.e., who, when, how long)

Knowledge about beliefs, values, and customs puts certain behaviors in a context that will help guide you in your work.

A few examples of important components of some cultural norms that may be helpful to consider include the following:

- In the United States, the dominant culture tends to psychologize grief, understanding it in terms of sadness, depression, anger, and other emotions.
- In China and other Eastern societies, grief is often somatized, or expressed in terms of physical pain, weakness, and other physical discomfort (K. Walsh, 2012).
- Gender differences exist in many cultures, including the dominant U.S. culture, where men have learned to be less demonstrative with emotions of grief and sadness than women (K. Walsh, 2012).

Mourning and funeral customs also differ a great deal even within groups. For example, among African Americans, customs vary depending on whether the family is Southern Baptist, Catholic, Unitarian Universalist, Muslim, or Pentecostal; in fact, "religion may be a stronger determining factor than race alone" (Barrett, 2009, p. 85). Perhaps because of some vestiges of traditional African culture and slavery and a strong desire to celebrate the person's life and build up a sense of community, funerals are important external expressions of mourning in many Black communities.

Tremendous diversity exists within the Latino cultures in the United States, depending on country of origin and degree of acculturation; however, for the most part these subgroups share Latino values, language, religion, and traditional family structure. Some Latino cultural themes that can influence care at the end of life include *familismo* (emphasis of family over individual), *personalismo* (trust building over time based on mutual respect), *jerarquismo* (respect for authority and hierarchy), *presentismo* (focus on present more than past or future), *espiritismo* (belief that good and evil spirits can impact health), and *fatalism* (fate determines life outcomes) (Sandoval-Cros, 2009).

Given approximately 350 distinct Native American tribes in the United States and more than 596 bands among the First Nations in Canada, and because of the differing degrees of acculturation and religious practices from one group to another, it is difficult to provide useful generalizations about this cultural group (Brokenleg & Middleton, 1993). Most understand death as a natural end of life, not fearing it, and although it may be a painful separation for the living who are left behind, rituals exist to help with the transition (Cox, 2009).

A good source of more specific information about rituals and practices is websites on particular cultural/ethnic groups such as Hmong Americans: Dying and Death Rituals (http://sfsuyellowjournal.wordpress.com/2011/11/17/hmong-americans-dying-and-death-ritual). Sites such as these are often written by members of the respective community, and they too remind you of the great diversity among their members. The complex and at times impersonal health care system in the United States can be inadvertently insensitive to important cultural traditions. For example, in some cultures, proper handling of the body, time to sit with the deceased, and other traditions are valued. For one specific example, the Hmong believe that proper burial and worship of ancestors directly influence the safety and health of the surviving family members. They believe that the spiritual world coexists with the physical world and that each person has several souls that must be appropriately sent back to the spiritual world.

These are only a few examples of the rich diversity and complexity you will face in working in our increasingly multiethnic society. You cannot possibly know all the specific traditions, so start by knowing you do not know, and do your homework on their world, including being open to their story and teachings. It is exciting to think of how much there is to learn about how others make sense of these mysterious times of life.

RISK FACTORS AND PROTECTIVE FACTORS IN LATE ADULTHOOD

Chapter 15 suggests that young- and middle-adult behavior has both antecedents and consequences. The same can be said for late adulthood. Early life experiences can serve either as risk factors or as protective factors for health and well-being during late adulthood.

As the longest-term longitudinal research available on late-adult behavior, Vaillant's (2002, 2012) Study of Adult Development provides the clearest understanding of the antecedents of late-adult well-being. Like Emmy Werner, who has studied a cohort until midlife (see Chapter 15), Vaillant is impressed with the self-righting tendencies in human nature. He suggests that what goes right in childhood is more important for life in late adulthood than what goes wrong. A warm relationship with their mothers was a strong protective factor at age 80 for his sample of Harvard men (Vaillant, 2012). He also suggests that unhappy childhoods become less important over the stages of adulthood. Consequently, Vaillant suggests that it is more important to count up the protective factors than to count up the risk factors. Although he found childhood experiences to diminish in importance over time, Vaillant also found that much of the resilience, or lack thereof, in late adulthood is predicted by factors that were established by age 50. He suggests that risk factors and protective factors change over the life course. He emphasizes that longitudinal research demonstrates that "everything affects everything else" (2012, p. 258) and that the "etiology of successful aging is multifactorial" (2012, p. 259).

Exhibit 16.10 lists six variables that Vaillant (2002, 2012) was surprised to find did not predict healthy aging and seven factors that he did find to predict healthy aging. Some of the factors that did not predict healthy aging did predict good adjustment at earlier adult stages. In terms of stress, Vaillant found that if we wait a few decades, many people recover from psychosomatic illness. In terms of parental characteristics, he found that they are still important for predicting adaptation at age 40 but not by age 70. In terms of both childhood temperament and general ease in social relationships, he found that they are strong predictors of adjustment in young adulthood but no longer important at age 70.

Conversely, Vaillant found that the seven factors on the right side of Exhibit 16.10, collectively, are strong predictors of health 30 years in the future. He also found that each variable, individually, predicted healthy aging, even when the other six variables were statistically controlled. Vaillant has chosen to frame each of these predictive factors in terms of protection; he sees risk as the flip side of protection. He notes the danger of such a list of protective factors: that it is used to "blame the victim" rather than provide guidance

EXHIBIT 16.10 • Variables That Affect Healthy Aging

VARIABLES THAT DO NOT PREDICT HEALTHY AGING	VARIABLES THAT DO PREDICT HEALTHY AGING
Ancestral longevity	Not smoking, or stopping young
Cholesterol	Using mature coping mechanisms
Stress	Not abusing alcohol
Parental characteristics	Healthy weight
Childhood temperament	Stable marriage
General ease in social relationships	Some exercise
	Years of education

SOURCE: Vaillant, 2002.

for aging well. He sees the list of predictors as "good news," however, because they all represent something that can be controlled to some extent.

THE LIFE COURSE COMPLETED

In the last seven chapters of this book, we have explored the seasons of the life course. These seasons have been and will be altered by changing demographics. Recent demographic trends have led to the following predictions about the future of the life course (Hogstel, 2001):

- The size and inevitable aging of the baby boom generation will continue to drive public policy debate and improve services for very-late-life adults.
- Women will continue to live longer than men.
- Educational attainment levels of the very-late-life adult will increase, with more women having been in the labor force long enough to have their own retirement income.
- Six-generation families will be common, although the generations will live in geographically dispersed settings, making care for very-late-life adults difficult.
- Fewer family caregivers will be available for very-late-life adults because the baby boomers and their children tended to marry later and have fewer children. At the same time, the need for informal or family caregiving to supplement formal care will increase.
- Assessment and management of health care, as well as health care education, will increasingly

be available via telephone, computer/Internet, and television, providing greater access in remote areas but running the risk of rendering the service more impersonal.

As a society, we have a challenge ahead of us, to see that newborns begin the life course on a positive foot and that everyone reaches the end of life with the opportunity to see his or her life course as a meaningful whole. As social workers, we have a responsibility to take a look at our social institutions and evaluate how well they guarantee the opportunity for each individual to meet basic needs during each season of life, as well as whether they guarantee the opportunity for interdependence and connectedness appropriate to the season of life.

CRITICAL THINKING Questions 16.5

What does death mean to you? Is it the final process of life, the beginning of life after death, a joining of the spirit with a cosmic consciousness, rest and peace, a continuation of the spirit, or something else? How has culture influenced your understanding of the meaning of death? How has religion influenced your understanding of the meaning of death? How might your understanding of the meaning of death affect your work with someone who is dying? What does it mean to live a good life?

IMPLICATIONS FOR SOCIAL WORK PRACTICE

Several practice principles for social work with older adults can be recommended.

- When working with an older adult, take into account the person's life history.
- Develop self-awareness of your views on aging and how different theoretical perspectives may influence your practice.
- Be conscious that age-related social roles change over time and that they vary for different cohorts.
- Identify areas in which you can assist an elderly client in preventing future problems, such as health-related difficulties.
- Develop an understanding of and skills to assess the differences among the physical, biological, psychological, and socioemotional changes that are part of normal aging and those that are indicative of a problematic process.
- Develop an understanding of the retirement process and how individuals adjust differently to this transition.
- Carefully assess an elderly person's caregiving network. Be conscious of the difficulties that the caregiving situation poses for both the caregiver and the care recipient. Familiarize yourself with local caregiver support options.
- Develop an understanding of the process of institutionalizing an older adult. Develop an understanding of the process of adaptation to nursing home placement and skills to assist an older adult and his or her family with that adaptation.
- When assessing the need for service, be conscious of the availability of formal and informal support systems. Develop an understanding and knowledge of the formal service delivery system.
- Avoid treating older persons as if they were incapable of making decisions simply because they may not be able to carry out the decision. Rather, involve them to the maximum extent possible in any decisions relating to their personal life and care, even if they are not able to carry out the related actions.
- Assess the impact of loss in the lives of your very-late-life clients—loss of partners, friends, children, and other relationships, but also loss of role, status, and physical and mental capacities.
- Be aware of your own feelings about death and dying so that you may become more comfortable being physically and emotionally present with clients and their loved ones.

KEY TERMS

activities of daily living (ADLs), 518
advance directives, 533
Alzheimer's disease, 520
bereavement, 536
crystallized intelligence, 524
delirium, 520
dementia, 520
dependency ratio, 511
fluid intelligence, 524
grief, 536
grief work, 536
hospice, 534
incidental memory, 524
instrumental activities of daily living (IADLs), 518
integrity, 523
intentional memory, 524

life review, 531
living will, 534
loss, 536
morbidity, 517
mortality rate, 516
mourning, 536
palliative care, 534
power of attorney (POA), 532
primary aging, 516
reminiscence, 531
secondary aging, 516
social gerontology, 515

ACTIVE LEARNING

1. Think about the three case studies presented at the outset of this chapter (Ruby Johnson, Margaret Davis, and Bina Patel). Which theory or theories of social gerontology seem to be the best fit with each of these individuals?
2. Think about your own extended family. What roles do the members of the oldest generation play in the family? How do the different generations interact, exchange resources, and influence each other? How do the different generations deal with their role changes and life transitions as they age? In what ways do the different generations support and hinder each other in life transitions?
3. Think about possible relationships among poverty, gender, sexual orientation, and race as one ages in the United States today. Working in small groups, identify ways that social workers can influence policies that affect housing, health care, and other essential services directly related to quality of life in very-late-life adulthood.

WEB RESOURCES

Administration on Aging

www.aoa.gov

Site accesses information about the Older Americans Act, other federal legislation, and a range of programs and statistics.

AgingStats.gov

www.agingstats.gov

Site presented by the Federal Interagency Forum on Aging-Related Statistics covers 31 key indicators of the lives of older people in the United States and their families.

American Association of Retired Persons

www.aarp.org

Organizational site provides a wide range of resources on health technology, travel, law, and policy and advocacy.

American Society on Aging

www.asaging.org

Site provides general information about aging-related services, including a link to the LGBT Aging Issues Network (LAIN) and LGBT Aging Resources Clearinghouse (LARC) and information on older adults, alcohol, medication, and other drugs.

Center on an Aging Society—Older Hispanic Americans

https://hpi.georgetown.edu/agingsociety/pubhtml/hispanics/hispanics.html

Site presents research results on chronic conditions of older Latino Americans.

Hospice Foundation of America

www.hospicefoundation.org

Site contains information on locating hospice programs, a newsletter, and links to resources.

National Academy on an Aging Society

www.agingsociety.org

Organization provides clear, unbiased research and analysis focused on public policy issues arising from the aging of America's and the world's population.

National Caregivers Library

www.caregiverslibrary.org

Site maintained by FamilyCare America makes resources available to caregivers through alliances with professionals, businesses, and other organizations serving seniors and caregivers.

National Caucus and Center on Black Aging

www.ncba-aged.org

Site contains aging news for policymakers, legislators, advocacy groups, minority professionals, and consumers that addresses finances, caregiving, intergenerational issues, and governmental programs.

National Center for Gerontological Social Work Education

http://www.cswe.org/CentersInitiatives/GeroEdCenter.aspx

Site maintained by the Council on Social Work Education Gero-Ed Center (National Center for Gerontological Social Work Education) provides resources for aging and end-of-life care.

National Council on Aging

www.ncoa.org

Site contains information on advocacy, programs, and publications and a number of good links to other aging resources.

National Hospice and Palliative Care Organization

www.nhpco.org

Site contains information on the history and current development of hospice and palliative care programs, advance directives, grief and bereavement, caregiving, and other related topics.

National Institute on Aging

www.nia.nih.gov

Site contains information about the U.S. National Institutes of Health National Institute on Aging (NIA), news and events, health, research programs, research funding and training, and the National Advisory Council on Aging.

SAGE edge™ **Sharpen your skills with SAGE edge at edge.sagepub.com/hutchisoness2e**

SAGE edge for students provides a personalized approach to help you accomplish your coursework goals in an easy-to-use learning environment. watch listen read

LEARNING OBJECTIVES	FOR FURTHER EXPLORATION AND APPLICATION
LO 16.1: Compare and contrast one's emotional and cognitive reactions to three case studies.	(read) Older Adults Coping with Negative Life Events
LO 16.2: Summarize major themes in older adult demographic characteristics.	(read) An Aging Nation: The Older Population in the United States
LO 16.3: Describe how old age is culturally constructed.	(watch) How Societies Can Grow Old Better
LO 16.4: Summarize the major biological changes, psychological changes, and role transitions and life events in late adulthood.	(read) Alzheimer's Association (watch) Aging and Physical Development (watch) Grandparenthood (listen) Memory Maintenance
LO 16.5: Describe the search for personal meaning in late adulthood.	(listen) People Who Feel They Have a Purpose in Life Live Longer
LO 16.6: Compare and contrast formal and informal resources for meeting the needs of elderly persons.	(read) Housing America's Older Adults: Meeting the Needs of an Aging Population (listen) Health Literacy in Older Adults
LO 16.7: Summarize what social workers need to know about the dying process.	(watch) Supporting Clients and Families Through the Dying Process (watch) Caring for Ill Older Adults
LO 16.8: Summarize what social workers need to know about loss, grief, and bereavement.	(watch) Dealing With a Parent's Death (watch) The Adventure of Grief (read) Bereavement Among African American and White Older Adults
LO 16.9: Give examples of risk factors and protective factors of late adulthood.	(listen) Emergency Preparedness Concerns for Older Adults
LO 16.10: Apply knowledge of late adulthood, dying, and bereavement to recommend guidelines for social work assessment and intervention.	(read) Questioning the Evidence for Service Assumptions: Audit of Transfers From a Hospice to Nursing Home Care

GLOSSARY

ABC-X model of family stress and coping A way of viewing families that focuses on stressor events and crises, family resources, family definitions and beliefs, and outcomes of stress pileup.

Accommodation (cognitive) The process of altering a schema when a new situation cannot be incorporated within an existing schema.

Accommodation (cultural) Process of partial or selective cultural change in which members of nondominant groups follow the norms, rules, and standards of the dominant culture only in specific circumstances and contexts.

Acculturation A process of changing one's culture by incorporating elements of another culture; a mutual sharing of culture.

Acquaintance rape Forced, manipulated, or coerced sexual contact by someone who is known to the victim.

Acquired immunodeficiency syndrome (AIDS) Disease caused by the human immunodeficiency virus (HIV); involves breakdown of the immune system.

Activities of daily living (ADLs) Basic self-care activities, such as bathing, dressing, walking a short distance, shifting from a bed to a chair, using the toilet, and eating.

Adaptation A change in functioning or coping style that results in a better adjustment of a person to his or her environment.

Advance directives Documents that give instructions about desired health care if, in the future, an individual cannot speak for herself or himself.

Age norm The behaviors expected of people of a specific age in a given society at a particular point in time.

Age structuring The standardizing of the ages at which social role transitions occur, by developing policies and laws that regulate the timing of these transitions.

Agency The capacity to intentionally make things happen.

Alzheimer's disease The most common type of dementia; a progressive and incurable deterioration of key areas of the brain.

Anorexia nervosa An eating disorder characterized by a distorted body image and excessive dieting that results in severe weight loss. It involves a pathological fear of becoming fat.

Antibodies Protein molecules that attach to the surface of specific antigens in an effort to destroy them.

Antigens Foreign substances such as bacteria, fungi, protozoa, and viruses that cause the immune system to react.

Assimilation (cognitive) In cognitive theory, the incorporation of new experiences into an existing schema.

Assimilation (cultural) The process of change whereby individuals of one society or ethnic group are culturally incorporated or absorbed into another by adopting the patterns and norms of the host culture.

Assisted reproductive technologies (ART) A range of techniques in which the egg and sperm are handled to help a couple who is infertile to conceive and give birth.

Assistive devices Those products designated by the medical community to help an impaired person to communicate, see, hear, or maneuver.

Assumption Something taken to be true without testing or proof.

Atria (singular: atrium) The two upper, thin-walled chambers of the heart.

Attachment An enduring emotional bond between two people who are important to each other. Provides affection and a sense of security.

Authoritarian parenting A parenting style, identified by Baumrind, that involves unresponsive, inflexible, harsh, and controlling interactions with the child.

Authoritative parenting A parenting style, identified by Baumrind, that involves responsive and supportive interactions with the child while also setting firm limits. Thought to be the most effective parenting style.

Autoimmune diseases Diseases that occur when the immune system wrongly attacks systems that it should be protecting.

Axon A conduction fiber that conducts impulses away from the body of a nerve cell.

Behavior settings theories Theories that propose that consistent, uniform patterns of behavior occur in particular places, or behavior settings.

Bereavement The state of having suffered a loss.

Bicultural socialization Process whereby members of nonmajority groups master both the dominant culture and their own culture.

Binge eating disorder An eating disorder characterized by recurring episodes of eating significantly excessive amounts of food in a short period of time; the episodes are accompanied by feelings of lack of control.

Biological age A person's level of biological development and physical health, as measured by the functioning of the various organ systems.

Biophilia A genetically based need of humans to affiliate with nature.

Blood pressure Measure of the pressure of the blood against the walls of a blood vessel.

Blooming A period of overproduction of brain synapses during infancy, followed by a period of synapse pruning.

Bonding social capital Community relationships that are inward looking and tend to mobilize solidarity and in-group loyalty; they lead to exclusive identities and homogenous communities.

Boundary An imaginary line of demarcation that defines which human and nonhuman elements are included in a given system and which elements are outside the system.

Brain injury (BI) Damage to the brain arising from head trauma (falls, automobile accidents), infections (encephalitis), insufficient oxygen (stroke), or poisoning.

Bridging social capital Community relationships that are outward looking and diverse and that link community members to assets and information across community boundaries.

Built environment The portion of the physical environment attributable solely to human effort.

Bulimia nervosa An eating disorder characterized by episodes of binge eating followed by behaviors such as self-induced vomiting at least once a week to avoid weight gain.

Bureaucracy A form of organization, considered by Max Weber to be the most efficient form for goal accomplishment, based on formal rationality.

Capital A term used in different ways by different disciplines but generally refers to having the potential, capacity, and resources to function, produce, or succeed; in the social sciences, refers to possession of attributes associated with civic engagement and economic success.

Cardiovascular system Biological system made up of the heart and the blood circulatory system.

Cerebral cortex The outer layer of gray matter in the human brain thought to be responsible for complex, high-level intellectual functions such as memory, language, and reasoning.

Chaos theory A theory that emphasizes systems processes that produce change, even sudden, rapid change.

Character education The direct teaching and curriculum inclusions of mainstream values thought to be universal by a community (e.g., kindness, respect, tolerance, and honesty).

Child maltreatment Physical, emotional, and sexual abuse and neglect of children, most often by adult caregivers. Definitions vary by culture and professional discipline but typically entail harm, or threatened harm, to the child.

Classical conditioning theory A theory in the social behavioral perspective that sees behavior as the result of the association of a conditioned stimulus with an unconditioned stimulus.

Cognition Conscious thinking processes; mental activities of which the individual is fully aware. These processes include taking in information from the environment, synthesizing that information, and formulating plans of action based on that synthesis.

Cognitive social learning theory A theory in the social behavioral perspective that sees behavior as learned by imitation and through cognitive processes.

Cohabiting When a couple lives together in a romantic relationship without marriage.

Cohort Group of persons who are born in the same time period and who are of the same age group at the time of specific historical events and social changes.

Cohort effects The effects of social change on a specific cohort.

Collective efficacy The ability of community residents to engage in collective action to gain control of the neighborhood.

Colonialism The practice of dominant and powerful nations going beyond their boundaries; using military force to occupy and claim less dominant and powerful nations; imposing their culture, laws, and language upon the occupied nation.

Common sense Shared ways of perceiving reality and shared conclusions drawn from lived experience; an organized body of culture-bound beliefs that members of a community or society believe to be second nature, plain, obvious, and self-evident.

Community People bound either by geography or by webs of communication, sharing common ties, and interacting with one another.

Concept A word or phrase that serves as an abstract description, or mental image, of some phenomenon.

Concrete operations stage The third stage in Piaget's theory of cognitive development. School-age children (ages 7 to 11) begin to use logical reasoning at this stage, but their thinking is not yet abstract.

Conflict perspective An approach to human behavior that draws attention to conflict, dominance, and oppression in social life.

Conservative thesis A philosophy that inequality is the natural, divine order, and no efforts should be made to alter it.

Control theories Theories that focus on the issue of how much control one has over the physical environment and the attempts one makes to gain control.

Coping A person's efforts to master the demands of stress, including the thoughts, feelings, and actions that constitute those efforts.

Coping mechanisms Strategies used to master the demands of life.

Countermovement A social movement that arises to oppose a successful social movement.

Crisis A major upset in psychological equilibrium as a result of some hazardous event, experienced as a threat or loss, with which the person cannot cope.

Critical consciousness The ongoing process of reflection and knowledge seeking about mechanisms and outcomes of social, political, and economic oppression; requires taking personal and collective action toward fairness and social justice.

Critical perspective on organizations A perspective that sees formal organizations as instruments of domination.

Critical race theory A theory proposed by legal scholars who wanted to draw attention to racial oppression in law and society, calling attention to microaggressions, brief, everyday exchanges that send denigrating messages and insults to people of color or members of any other minority identity group.

Critical theorists Theorists who argue that as capitalism underwent change, people were more likely to be controlled by culture and their consumer role than by their work position.

Critical thinking Engaging in a thoughtful and reflective judgment about alternative views and contradictory information; involves thinking about your own thinking and the influences on that thinking, as well as a willingness to change your mind.

Crowding Unpleasant experience of feeling spatially cramped.

Crystallized intelligence The ability to use knowledge from accumulated learning.

Cultural framing (CF) perspective An approach to social movements that asserts that they can be successful only when participants develop shared understandings and definitions of some situation that impels the participants to feel aggrieved or outraged, motivating them to action.

Cultural hegemony The all-encompassing dominance of particular structures in society. Not limited to political control but includes a way of seeing the world that includes cultural and political dominance.

Cultural innovation A process of adapting, modifying, and changing culture through interaction over time.

Cultural relativism The position that behavior in a particular culture should not be judged by the standards of another culture.

Culture Shared cognitive and emotional frames and lenses that serve as the bases for an evolving map for living. It is constructed from the entire spectrum of human actions and the material circumstances of people in societies as they attempt to create order, meaning, and value.

Culture of poverty A term coined by Oscar Lewis to describe the unique culture and ways of those who are impoverished; it has been used over time to look at impoverished people as having cultural deficits.

Cumulative advantage The accumulation of increasing advantage as early advantage positions an individual for later advantage.

Cumulative disadvantage The accumulation of increasing disadvantage as early disadvantage positions an individual for later disadvantage.

Customs Beliefs, values, and behaviors, such as marriage practices, child-rearing practices, dietary preferences, and attire, that are handed down through generations and become a part of a people's traditions.

Deductive reasoning A method of reasoning that lays out general, abstract propositions that can be used to generate specific hypotheses to test in unique situations.

Default individualization One possible pathway in young adulthood, which involves making transitions defined by circumstance and situation.

Defense mechanisms Unconscious, automatic responses that enable a person to minimize perceived threats or keep them out of awareness entirely.

Delirium Syndrome characterized by an impairment of consciousness. It has a sudden onset (a few hours or days), follows a brief and fluctuating course that includes impairment of consciousness, and has the potential for improvement when causes are treated. Prevalence of delirium is high among hospitalized elderly persons; toxicity from prescribed medications is a common cause.

Dementia Impairment or loss of cognitive functioning caused by damage in the brain tissue. Dementia is not part of the brain's normal aging process, but its prevalence increases with age.

Density Ratio of persons per unit area of a space.

Dependency ratio A demographic indicator expressing the degree of demand placed on society by the dependent young and the dependent elderly combined.

Determinism A belief that persons are passive products of their circumstances, external forces, or internal urges.

Developmental delays Delays in developing skills and abilities in infants and preschoolers.

Developmental individualization One possible pathway in young adulthood, which involves making transitions defined by personal agency and deliberately charted growth opportunities in intellectual, occupational, and psychosocial domains.

Developmental niche The cultural context into which a particular child is born; guides every aspect of the developmental process.

Developmental perspective An approach that focuses on how human behavior changes and stays the same across stages of the life cycle.

Diabetes mellitus A disease of the endocrine system resulting from insulin deficiency or resistance to insulin's effects.

Differentiation (Jung) The process by which humans develop unique patterns and traits.

Differentiation of self In family systems theory, the process of learning to differentiate between thoughts and feelings and to follow one's own beliefs rather than making decisions based on reactivity to the cues of others or the need to win approval.

Dimension A feature that can be focused on separately but that cannot be understood without considering its embeddedness with other features.

Direct bullying Intentionally inflicting emotional or physical harm on another person through fairly explicit physical or verbal harassment, assault, or injury.

Discipline Action taken by a child's caretaker to help the child correct behavioral problems.

Disengaged parenting Aloof, withdrawn, and unresponsive parenting.

Diversity Patterns of group differences.

Ecocentric Perspective that the ecosphere and everything on earth has its own intrinsic worth and should be valued and cared for, including earth (Gaia) itself; recognition that humans are only one part of the interconnected web of life.

Ecocritical theories Theories that call attention to the ways human behavior degrades and destroys the natural world, the unequal burden of environmental degradation on different groups, and ethical obligations humans have to nonhuman elements of the natural environment.

Economic institution The social institution with primary responsibility for regulating the production, distribution, and consumption of goods and services.

Ecotherapy Exposure to nature and the outdoors as a component of psychotherapy.

Educational institution The social institution responsible for passing along formal knowledge from one generation to the next.

Efficacy expectation In cognitive social learning theory, the expectation that one can personally accomplish a goal.

Ego A mental structure of personality that is responsible for negotiating between internal needs of the individual and the outside world.

Ego psychology A theory of human behavior and clinical practice that views activities of the ego as the primary determinants of behavior.

Embryo The stage of prenatal development beginning in the 2nd week and lasting through the 8th week.

Emerging adulthood A developmental phase distinct from both adolescence and young adulthood, occurring between the ages of 18 and 25 in industrialized societies.

Emotion A feeling state characterized by one's appraisal of a stimulus, changes in bodily sensations, and expressive gestures.

Emotional intelligence A person's ability to process information about emotions accurately and effectively, and consequently to regulate emotions in an optimal manner.

Emotion-focused coping Coping efforts in which a person attempts to change either the way a stressful situation is attended to (by vigilance or avoidance) or the meaning of what is happening. Most effective when situations are not readily controllable by action.

Empathy Ability to understand another person's emotional condition.

Empirical research A careful, purposeful, and systematic observation of events with the intent to note and record them in terms of their attributes, to look for patterns in those events, and to make one's methods and observations public.

Empowerment theories Theories that focus on processes by which individuals and collectivities can recognize patterns of inequality and injustice and take action to increase their own power.

Endocrine system The biological system that is involved in growth, metabolism, development, learning, and memory. Made up of glands that secrete hormones into the blood system.

Ethnocentrism Considering one's own culture as superior and judging culturally different practices (beliefs, values, behavior) by the standards and norms of one's own culture.

Event history The sequence of significant events, experiences, and transitions in a person's life from birth to death.

Exchange and choice perspective A category of behavioral science theory that shares the common focus on the processes whereby individual and collective actors seek and exchange resources and the choices made in pursuit of those resources.

Exchange theory (small groups) Focuses on power issues in small groups, who gets valued resources and how fairly they are perceived as being distributed.

Faith As defined in Fowler's theory of faith development, a generic feature of the human search for meaning that provides a centering orientation from which to live one's life. May or may not be based in religious expression.

Faith stages Distinct levels of faith development, each with particular characteristics, emerging strengths, and potential dangers. Fowler identifies seven faith stages in his theory of faith development.

Family A social group of two or more persons, characterized by ongoing interdependence with long-term commitments that stem from blood, law, or affection.

Family ecomap Visual representation of how a family is connected to other individuals and social systems; uses circles, lines, and arrows to show family relationships and the strength and directional flow of energy and resources to and from the family.

Family economic stress model A model of family stress that suggests that economic hardship leads to economic pressure, which leads to parent distress, which leads to disrupted family relationships, which leads to child and adolescent adjustment problems.

Family investment model Theoretical model that proposes that families with greater economic resources can afford to make large investments in the development of their children.

Family life cycle perspective An approach that looks at how families change over time and proposes normative changes and tasks at different stages.

Family of origin The family into which one is born and in which one was raised, when the two are the same.

Family resilience perspective An approach to family that seeks to identify and strengthen family processes that allow families to bear up under and rebound from distressing life experiences.

Family systems perspective A way of understanding families that focuses on the family as a social system, with patterns of interaction and relationships, and on changes in these patterns over time.

Family timeline A visual representation of important dates and events in a family's life over time.

Feedback control mechanism The mechanism by which the body controls the secretion of hormones and therefore their actions on target tissues.

Feedback mechanism A process by which information about past behaviors in a system is fed back into the system in a circular manner.

Feminist perspective on families A perspective that proposes that families should not be studied as whole systems, with the lens on the family level, but rather as patterns of dominance, subjugation, and oppression, particularly as those patterns are tied to gender.

Feminist theories Theories that focus on male domination of the major social institutions and present a vision of a just world based on gender equity.

Fetal viability The capability of the fetus to survive outside the womb, typically requiring at least 25 weeks' gestation.

Fetus The developing organism from the 9th week of pregnancy to birth.

Fine motor skills Skills based on small muscle movements, particularly in the hands, as well as eye–hand coordination.

First force therapies Therapies based on dynamic theories of human behavior, with the prime concern being about repression and solving instinctual conflicts by developing insights.

Fluid intelligence Abstract reasoning skills.

Formal operations stage The fourth and final stage in Piaget's theory of cognitive development, generally experienced in adolescence. Involves the capacity to apply hypothetical reasoning and to use symbols to solve problems.

Formal organization A collectivity of people, with a high degree of formality of structure, working together to meet a goal or goals.

Four quadrants From Wilber's integral theory, the four most important dimensions of existence. The upper-left quadrant represents the interior of individuals, or the subjective aspects of consciousness or awareness; the upper-right quadrant represents the exterior of individuals, including the objective biological and behavioral aspects; the lower-left quadrant represents the interior of collectives, or the values, meanings, worldviews, and ethics that are shared by groups of individuals; the lower-right quadrant represents the exterior, material dimensions of collectives, including social systems and the environment.

Fourth force therapies Therapies that specifically target the spiritual dimension, focusing on helping the person let go of ego attachments and transcend the self through various spiritually based practices.

Fulcrum In Wilber's full-spectrum model of consciousness, a specific turning point in development, where the person must go through a three-step process of fusion/differentiation/integration in order to move from one level of consciousness to another.

Gender dysphoria Feeling one's emotional and psychological identity as male or female to be opposite of one's assigned biological identity.

Gender identity Understanding of oneself as a male or female.

Generalized other A construction that represents how others might view and respond to one's behavior.

Generativity The ability to transcend personal interests to provide care and have concern for generations to come.

Genogram A visual representation of the multigenerational family system, using squares, circles, and relationship lines.

Gestation The length of maturation time from conception to birth. In humans, it averages 280 days, with a range of 259 to 287 days.

Gini index An index that measures the extent to which the distribution of income within a country deviates from a perfectly equal distribution; scores range from 0 (perfect equality) to 100 (perfect inequality).

Globalization The process by which the world's people are becoming more interconnected economically, politically, environmentally, and culturally.

Gonads Sex glands—ovaries in females and testes in males.

Government and political institution The social institution responsible for how decisions are made and enforced for the society as a whole.

Grief The normal internal reaction of an individual experiencing a loss, a complex process that is highly individualized.

Grief work A necessary period of working to sever the attachment bond to a lost person or object.

Gross motor skills Skills based upon large muscle group movements and most easily observed during whole-body movements, such as hopping, skipping, and running.

Group cohesiveness A sense of solidarity or "we-ness" felt by group members toward the group.

Group work A recognized social work method that involves teaching and practicing social work with groups.

Health care institution The social institution with primary responsibility for promoting the general health of a society.

Heterogeneity Individual-level variations, differences among individuals.

Hierarchy of needs Abraham Maslow's humanistic theory that suggests that higher needs cannot emerge until lower needs have been satisfied; the hierarchy runs from physiological needs at the bottom, to safety needs, belongingness and love needs, and esteem needs, with self-actualization needs at the top.

High blood pressure (hypertension) Blood pressure greater than 140/90; the leading cause of strokes and a major risk factor for heart attacks and kidney failure.

Hospice Program that provides care to the terminally ill. Patients typically receive treatment by a team of doctors, nurses, social workers, and care staff through inpatient or outpatient care.

Hostile aggression Aggression that is an attack meant to hurt another individual.

Human agency The use of personal power to achieve one's goals.

Human immunodeficiency virus (HIV) The virus that causes acquired immunodeficiency syndrome (AIDS).

Humanistic perspective An approach that sees human behavior as based on freedom of action of the individual and focuses on the human search for meaning.

Hypotheses Tentative statements to be explored and tested.

Identity A sense of self that distinguishes "who I am" from other people and that is enduring over time.

Ideology A particular body of ideas or outlook; a person's specific worldview.

Immune system Organs and cells that interact and work together to defend the body against disease.

Incidental memory Memory that relates to facts a person has learned without the intention to retain and recall.

Indirect bullying Less explicit and less detectable than direct bullying, including subtler verbal, psychological, and social or "relational" bullying tactics.

Individual education plan (IEP) An individualized, collaboratively developed plan that focuses on facilitating achievement and is designed to respond to the unique needs of a child with a disability in the school setting. Such plans are mandated by the Individuals with Disabilities Education Act of 1990.

Individuation The development of a self and identity that are unique and separate.

Individuation (Jung) The full development of all aspects of the self into a unique and harmonious whole that gives expression to repressed attributes and desires; does not occur before age 40.

Infant A young child in the first year of life.

Infant mortality The death of a child before his or her first birthday.

Infertility The inability to create a viable embryo; can also include situations where women can get pregnant but are unable to stay pregnant.

Instrumental activities of daily living (IADLs) More complex everyday tasks such as doing light housework, doing the laundry, using transportation, handling finances, using the telephone, and taking medications.

Instrumental aggression Aggression that occurs while fighting over things like toys and space.

Integrity The ability to make peace with one's "one and only life cycle" and to find unity with the world; the task Erik Erikson associated with late adulthood (integrity versus despair).

Intentional memory Memory that relates to events that a person plans to remember.

Interactional/interpretive perspective on organizations A perspective that sees formal organizations as social constructions of reality, providing members with a sense of connection and reflecting the worldviews of the creators.

Interpretist perspective Ways of understanding human behavior that share the assumption that reality is based on people's definition of it.

Interrelational intelligence Based on emotional and social intelligence and similar to Howard Gardner's concept of interpersonal intelligence.

Intersectionality feminist theory A feminist theory that suggests that no single category is sufficient to understand social oppression and that categories such as gender, race, and class intersect to produce different experiences for women of various races and classes.

Intersectionality theory A pluralist theory of social conflict that recognizes numerous vectors of oppression and privilege, including but not limited to gender, class, race, global location, sexual orientation, and age; recognizes that individuals often hold cross-cutting and overlapping memberships in different status groups.

Intimacy Characteristic of close interpersonal relationships, includes interdependence, self-disclosure, and affection.

Juvenile delinquency Acts that, if committed by an adult, would be considered crimes, plus status offenses such as running away from home, skipping school, violating curfew, and possession of tobacco or alcohol.

Lateralization Process in which the two hemispheres of the brain begin to operate slightly differently during early childhood.

Learned helplessness In cognitive social learning theory, a situation in which a person's prior experience with environmental forces has led to low self-efficacy and efficacy expectation.

Learning play Play that is focused on language and thinking skills.

Levels of consciousness From Wilber's integral theory, overall stages of awareness and being; moving from the prepersonal to the personal and transpersonal phases, each with multiple levels of development.

Life course perspective An approach to human behavior that recognizes the influence of age but also acknowledges the influences of historical time and culture.

Life event Incident or event that is brief in scope but is influential on human behavior.

Life review A process of evaluating and making sense of one's life. It includes a reinterpretation of past experiences and unresolved conflicts. The process of life review relates to the eighth stage of Erikson's theory of adult development (ego integrity versus ego despair).

Life structure In Levinson's seasons of adulthood theory, the patterns and central components of a person's life at a particular point in time.

Linear time Time based on the past, present, and future.

Lines of consciousness From Wilber's integral theory, the approximately two dozen relatively independent developmental lines or streams that can evolve at different rates, with different dynamics, and on different time schedules; examples include cognitive, moral, interpersonal, self-identity, and socioemotional capacity.

Living will A document that describes the medical procedures, drugs, and types of treatment that an individual would choose for oneself if able to do so in certain situations. It also describes the situations for which this individual would want treatment withheld.

Lone-parent families Families composed of one parent and at least one child residing in the same household, headed by either a divorced or unmarried parent.

Loss The severing of an attachment an individual has with a loved one, a loved object, or an aspect of one's self or identity.

Lymphocytes White blood cells, which fight infection in the body.

Mass media institution In a democratic society, the social institution responsible for managing the flow of information, images, and ideas.

Masturbation Self-stimulation of the genitals for sexual pleasure.

Menarche The onset of menstruation.

Mobilizing structures (MS) perspective An approach to social movements that suggests that they develop out of existing networks and formal organizations.

Morbidity The incidence of disease and illness in a population group.

Mortality rate The ratio of deaths in an area to the population of that area.

Motor skills Control over movements of body parts.

Mourning The external expression of grief, also a process, influenced by the customs of one's culture.

Multidetermined behavior A view that human behavior is developed as a result of many causes.

Multidimensional Having several identifiable dimensions.

Multilevel family practice model A way of viewing a family that focuses on stress from and resources provided (or not provided) by patterns and institutions within larger social systems, including the neighborhood, local community, state, nation, and global socioeconomic system.

Multiple intelligences The eight distinct biopsychosocial potentials, as identified by Howard Gardner, with which people process information that can be activated in cultural settings to solve problems or create products that are of value in the culture.

Multiple psychological senses of community (MPSOC) The idea that individuals participate in multiple communities and consequently have multiple senses of community.

Musculoskeletal system Muscles that are attached to bone and cross a joint. Their contraction and relaxation are the basis for voluntary movements.

Natural environment The portion of the environment influenced primarily by geological and nonhuman biological forces.

Neocolonialism The practice of dominant and powerful nations going beyond their boundaries, utilizing international financial institutions such as the World Bank and the International Monetary Fund to exert influence over impoverished nations and to impose their culture, laws, and language upon the occupied nation through the use of financial incentives (loans) and disincentives.

Neoliberal philosophy A philosophy that governments should keep their hands off the economic institution.

Neonate Infant up to 1 month of age.

Nervous system The biological system responsible for processing and integrating incoming sensory information; it influences and directs reactions to that information.

Neuron Nerve cell that is the basic working unit of the nervous system. Composed of a cell body, dendrites (receptive extensions), and an axon.

Neuroplasticity The ability of the brain to change its structure and patterns of activity in significant ways throughout life.

Neurotransmitters Messenger molecules that transfer chemical and electrical messages from one neuron to another.

Nonnormative stressors Unexpected stressful events that can quickly drain a family's resources.

Nonspecific immunity Immunity that includes physical barriers to infection, inflammation, and phagocytosis. Does not include antibodies or cell-mediated immunity.

Normative stressors The stressors families face as a result of typical family life cycle transitions.

Norms Culturally defined standards or rules of conduct.

Object permanence The ability to understand that objects exist even when they cannot be seen.

Objective reality The belief that phenomena exist and have influence, whether or not one is aware of them.

Operant conditioning theory A theory in the social behavioral perspective that sees behavior as the result of reinforcement.

Oppression The intentional or unintentional act or process of placing restrictions on an individual, group, or institution; may include observable actions but more typically refers to complex, covert, interconnected processes and practices (such as discriminating, devaluing, and exploiting a group of individuals) reflected in and perpetuating exclusion and inequalities over time.

Palliative care Active care of patients who have received a diagnosis of a serious, life-threatening illness; a form of care focusing on pain and symptom management as opposed to curing disease.

Performance expectations The expectations group members have of other group members in terms of how they will act or behave in the group or how well they will perform a task.

Permissive parenting A parenting style, identified by Baumrind, that involves no limit setting on the part of the parent.

Personal space The physical distance one chooses to maintain in interpersonal relationships.

Perspective taking The ability to see a situation from another person's point of view.

Phenomenal self An individual's subjectively felt and interpreted experience of "who I am."

Physical aggression Aggression against another person using physical force.

Place attachment A process in which individuals and groups form bonds with places.

Place identity A process in which the meaning of a place merges with one's self-identity.

Political opportunities (PO) perspective An approach to social movements that suggests that they develop when windows of political opportunity are open.

Population pyramid A chart that depicts the proportion of the population in each age group.

Positive psychology An approach to psychology that focuses on people's strengths and virtues and promotes optimal functioning of individuals and communities.

Positivist perspective The perspective on which modern science is based. Assumes objective reality, that findings of one study should be applicable to other groups, that complex phenomena can be studied by reducing them to some component part, and that scientific methods are value-free.

Postconventional moral reasoning Third and final level of Lawrence Kohlberg's stage theory of moral development; morality based on moral principles that transcend societal rules.

Postmodernism A term used to describe contemporary culture as a postindustrial culture in which people are connected across time and place through global electronic communications; emphasis is on the existence of different worldviews and concepts of reality.

Power of attorney (POA) A person appointed by an individual to manage his or her financial and legal affairs. A POA can be limited (for a limited time period), general (no restrictions), or durable (begins after the individual reaches a specified level of disability).

Practice orientation A way of thinking about culture that recognizes the relationships and mutual influences among structures of society and culture, the impact of history, and the nature and impact of human action.

Preconscious Mental activity that is outside of awareness but can be brought into awareness with prompting.

Preconventional level of moral reasoning First level of moral reasoning in Lawrence Kohlberg's stage theory of moral reasoning; morality based on what gets rewarded or punished or what benefits either the child or someone the child cares about.

Preoperational stage The second stage in Piaget's theory of cognitive development. Young children (ages 2 to 7) use symbols to represent their earlier sensorimotor experiences. Thinking is not yet logical at this stage.

Primary aging Changes that are a normal part of the aging process.

Primary emotions Emotions that developed as specific reactions and signals with survival value for the human species. They serve to mobilize an individual, focus attention, and signal one's state of mind to others; examples include anger, fear, sadness, joy, and anticipation.

Primary sex characteristics Physical characteristics that are directly related to maturation of the reproductive organs and external genitalia.

Privilege Unearned advantage enjoyed by members of some social categories.

Problem-focused coping Coping efforts in which the person attempts to change a stress situation by acting on the environment. Most effective when situations are controllable by action.

Propositions Assertions about a concept or about the relationship between concepts.

Prosocial Behaving in a helpful or empathic manner.

Protective factors Personal and societal factors that reduce or protect against risk.

Pruning Reduction of brain synapses to improve the efficiency of brain functioning; follows a period of blooming of synapses.

Psychoanalytic theory A theory of human behavior and clinical intervention that assumes the primacy of internal drives and unconscious mental activity in determining human behavior.

Psychodynamic perspective An approach that focuses on how internal processes motivate human behavior.

Psychodynamic theory (small groups) Focuses on the relationship between emotional unconscious processes and the nature and quality of interpersonal communication in the group.

Psychological identity Self-definition as a separate and distinct person.

Psychological age The capacities that people have and the skills they use to adapt to changing biological and environmental demands, including skills in memory, learning, intelligence, motivation, and emotions; also the age people feel.

Psychology The study of the mind and mental processes.

Psychosocial crisis A struggle or turning point that defines a particular stage in Erik Erikson's developmental model.

Puberty Stage during which individuals become capable of reproduction.

Qualitative methods of research Research methods that use flexible modes of data collection, seek holistic understanding, present findings in words rather than numbers, and attempt to account for the influence of the research setting and process on the findings.

Quantitative methods of research Research methods, based on the tenets of modern science, that use quantifiable measures of concepts, standardize the collection of data, attend only to preselected variables, and use statistical methods to look for patterns and associations.

Race A system of social identity based on biological markers such as skin color that influence economic, social, and political relations.

Radical antithesis Philosophy that equality is the natural, divine order and that inequality is based on abuse of privilege and should be minimized.

Rational perspective on organizations A perspective that sees formal organizations as goal-directed, purposefully designed machines that maximize efficiency and effectiveness.

Reciprocity A norm that receiving resources in social exchange requires giving resources of relatively equal value, proposed by social exchange theory.

Reflex An involuntary response to a simple stimulus.

Relational aggression Aggression that involves behaviors that damage relationships without physical force, such as threatening to leave a relationship unless a friend complies with demands, or using social exclusion or the silent treatment to get one's way.

Relational community A community based on voluntary association rather than geography.

Relational coping Coping that takes into account actions that maximize the survival of others as well as oneself.

Relational theory A theory that proposes that the basic human tendency is relationships with others, and that personalities are formed through ongoing interactions with others.

Relative poverty A conceptualization of poverty that emphasizes the tendency to define one's poverty status in relation to others within one's social environment.

Religion A systematic set of beliefs, practices, and traditions experienced within a particular social institution over time.

Religious institution The social institution with primary responsibility for answering questions about the meaning and purpose of life.

Reminiscence Recalling and recounting past events. Reminiscing serves several functions: It may be an enjoyable activity, it may be directed at enhancing a person's self-image, it may serve as a way to cope with current or future problems, and it may assist in the life review as a way to achieve ego integrity.

Resilience Healthy development in the face of risk factors; thought to be the result of protective factors that shield the individual from the consequences of potential hazards.

Risk factors Personal or social factors at one stage of development that increase the likelihood of a problem occurring or being maintained at later stages.

Rites of passage Ceremonies that demarcate transition from one role or status to another.

Role A set of usual behaviors of persons occupying a particular social position.

Romantic love An intimate relationship that is sexually oriented.

Schema (plural: schemata) An internalized representation of the world, including systematic patterns of thought, action, and problem solving.

Science A set of logical, systematic, documented methods for answering questions about the world.

Second force therapies Therapies based on behavioral theories; they focus on learned habits and seek to remove symptoms through various processes of direct learning.

Secondary aging Changes caused by health-compromising behaviors such as smoking or environmental factors such as pollution.

Secondary emotions Emotions that are socially acquired. They evolved as humans developed more sophisticated means of learning, controlling, and managing emotions to promote flexible cohesion in social groups. Examples include envy, jealousy, anxiety, guilt, shame, relief, hope, depression, pride, love, gratitude, and compassion.

Secondary sex characteristics Physical characteristics associated with sexual maturation that are not directly related to the reproductive organs and external genitalia.

Self An essence of who one is that is more or less enduring.

Self-categorization theory A theory of small groups that proposes that in the process of social identity development, one comes to divide the world into in-groups (those to which one belongs) and out-groups (those to which one does not belong) and to be biased toward in-groups.

Self-efficacy A sense of personal competence.

Self-esteem The way one evaluates the self in relation to others.

Self-system In Wilber's full-spectrum model of consciousness, the active self or person who moves through the stages of consciousness and mediates between the basic and transitional structures of development.

Self-theory An organized understanding of the self in relation to others; begins to develop in early childhood.

Sense of community A feeling of belonging and mutual commitment.

Sensorimotor stage The first stage in Piaget's theory of cognitive development. Infants (ages 0 to 2 years) learn through sensory awareness and motor activities.

Sensory system The system of senses: hearing, sight, taste, smell, touch, responsiveness to the body's position, and sensitivity to pain.

Separation anxiety When an infant becomes anxious at the signs of an impending separation from parents, at about 9 months of age.

Sex hormones Hormones that affect the development of the gonads, functioning of the gonads, and mating and child-caring behavior; includes androgens, progestins, and estrogens.

Sex ratio The number of males per 100 females in a population.

Sexual orientation Erotic, romantic, and affectionate attraction to people of the same sex, the opposite sex, or both sexes.

Sexually transmitted infections (STIs) Infectious diseases that are most often contracted through oral, anal, or vaginal sexual contact. Also called venereal diseases.

Small group A small collection of individuals who interact with each other, perceive themselves as belonging to a group, are interdependent, join together to accomplish a goal, fulfill a need through joint association, or are influenced by a set of rules and norms.

Social age Age measured in terms of age-graded roles and behaviors expected by society—the socially constructed meanings of various ages.

Social behavioral perspective An approach that sees human behavior as learned when individuals interact with their environments.

Social capital Connections among individuals based on reciprocity and trustworthiness.

Social class A particular position in a societal structure of inequality.

Social competence The ability to engage in sustained, positive, and mutually satisfactory peer interactions.

Social constructionist perspective An approach that focuses on how people learn, through their interactions with each other, to classify the world and their place in it.

Social convoy theory A theory that suggests that one travels through life with a *convoy,* or a network of social relationships that protect, defend, aid, and socialize, with the closest relationships remaining stable over time and peripheral relationships being less stable.

Social exchange theory A theory in the rational choice perspective that sees human behavior as based on the desire to maximize benefits and minimize costs in social interactions.

Social gerontology The social science that studies human aging.

Social identity The part of the self-concept that comes from knowledge of one's membership in a social group and the emotional significance of that membership.

Social institutions Patterned ways of organizing social relations in a particular sector of social life.

Social movements Large-scale collective actions to make change, or resist change, in specific social institutions.

Social network The people with whom a person routinely interacts; the patterns of interaction that result from exchanging resources with others.

Social network theory A developing theory in the rational choice perspective that focuses on the pattern of ties that link persons and collectivities.

Social structure A set of interrelated social institutions developed by humans to impose constraints on human interaction for the purpose of the survival and well-being of the collectivity.

Social support The interpersonal interactions and relationships that provide people with assistance or feelings of attachment to others they perceive as caring.

Social welfare institution The social institution in modern industrial societies that promotes interdependence and provides assistance for issues of dependency.

Sociodramatic play Fantasy play in a group, with the group coordinating fantasies; important type of play in early childhood.

Socioemotional selectivity theory A theory that proposes that social goals change over the adult life course based on shifts in perspectives about how much time one has left to live, and changes in social goals result in changes in one's social network.

Specific immunity Immunity that involves cells (lymphocytes) that not only respond to an infection but also develop a memory of that infection and allow the body to defend against it rapidly during subsequent exposure.

Spermarche Onset of the ability to ejaculate mobile sperm.

Spiritual age The position of a person in the ongoing search for meaning and fulfilling relationships.

Spiritual bypassing Use of spiritual beliefs or practices to avoid dealing in any significant depth with unresolved issues and related emotional and behavioral problems; includes attempts to prematurely transcend the ego.

Spirituality A search for purpose, meaning, and connection between oneself and other people, the universe, and the ultimate reality, which can be experienced within either a religious or a nonreligious framework.

State A personality characteristic that changes over time, depending on the social or stress context.

States of consciousness From Wilber's integral theory, an understanding of experience that includes both ordinary (waking, sleeping, and dreaming) and nonordinary experiences (peak experiences, religious experiences, altered states, and meditative or contemplative states).

Status A specific social position.

Status characteristics In status characteristics and expectation states theory, any characteristics that are evaluated in the broader society to be associated with competence.

Status characteristics and expectation states theory (small groups) A theory of basic group process that assumes that the influence and participation of group members during initial interactions are related to their status and to expectations others hold about their ability to help the group accomplish tasks.

Status offenses Behaviors that would not be considered criminal if committed by an adult but are considered delinquent if committed by an adolescent—for example, running away from home, skipping school, violating curfew, and possessing tobacco or alcohol.

Statutory rape A criminal offense that involves an adult engaging in sexual activities with a minor or a mentally incapacitated person.

Stimulation theories Theories that focus on the physical environment as a source of sensory information that is necessary for human well-being.

Stranger anxiety When an infant reacts with fear and withdrawal to unfamiliar persons, at about 9 months of age.

Stress Any biological, psychological, or social event in which environmental demands or internal demands, or both, tax or exceed the adaptive resources of the individual.

Stress pileup When a series of crises over time depletes a family's resources and exposes the family to increasing risk of very negative outcomes.

Subjective reality The belief that reality is created by personal perception and does not exist outside that perception; the same as the interpretist perspective.

Symbol Something verbal (language, words) or nonverbal (such as a flag) that comes to stand for something else; a way of expressing meaning.

Symbolic interaction theory (small groups) Focuses on the small group as a place where symbols are created, exchanged, and interpreted.

Symbolic play Fantasy play; begins around the age of 2.

Synapse In the nervous system, the gap between an axon and a dendrite; the site at which chemical and electrical communication occurs.

Synaptogenesis The creation of synapses (neural connections).

Systems perspective An approach that sees human behavior as the outcome of reciprocal interactions of persons operating within organized and integrated social systems.

Systems perspective on organizations A perspective that focuses on formal organizations in constant interaction with multiple environments.

Technology The tools, machines, instruments, and devices developed and used by humans to enhance their lives.

Temperament A person's disposition and primary behavioral characteristics.

Teratogen Anything present during prenatal life that adversely affects normal cellular development in form or function in the embryo or fetus.

Territorial community A community based on geography.

Territoriality A pattern of behavior of a group or individual that involves marking or personalizing a territory to signify ownership and engaging in behaviors to protect it from invasion.

Testes Male gonads, primarily responsible for producing sperm (mature germ cells that fertilize the female egg) and secreting male hormones called androgens.

Theory A logically interrelated set of concepts and propositions, organized into a deductive system, that explains relationships among aspects of one's world.

Third force therapies Therapies rooted in experiential/humanistic/existential theories that focus on helping a person deal with existential despair, and that seek the actualization of the person's potential through techniques grounded in immediate experiencing.

Time orientation The extent to which individuals and collectivities are invested in three temporal zones: past, present, and future time.

Toddler A young child from about 12 to 36 months of age.

Tradition A process of handing down from one generation to another certain cultural beliefs and practices. In particular, a process of ratifying certain beliefs and practices by connecting them to selected social, economic, and political practices.

Trait A stable personality characteristic.

Trajectories Long-term patterns of stability and change based on unique person–environment configurations over time.

Transition points Times when families face a transition in family life stage or in family composition.

Transitional object Comfort object, such as a favorite blanket or stuffed animal, that toddlers often use to help them cope with separations from parents.

Transitions Changes in roles and statuses that represent a distinct departure from prior roles and statuses.

Transpersonal approach An approach to human behavior that includes levels of consciousness or spiritual development that move beyond rational-individuated-personal personhood to a sense of self that transcends the mind/body ego—a self-identity also referred to as transegoic.

Trauma A physical or mental injury generally associated with violence, shock, or an unanticipated situation.

Traumatic stress Stress associated with events that involve actual or threatened severe injury or death of oneself or significant others.

Triangulation A process that occurs when two family members (a family subsystem) inappropriately involve another family member to reduce the anxiety in the dyadic relationship.

Turning point A special event that produces a lasting shift in the life course trajectory.

Unconscious Mental activities of which one is not aware but that influence behavior.

Uterus Also called the womb, serves as the pear-shaped home for the fetus for the 9 months between implantation and birth.

Ventricles The two lower, thick-walled chambers of the heart.

Voluntarism The belief that persons are free and active agents in the creation of their behaviors.

Working model Model for relationships developed in the earliest attachment relationship.

Worldcentric Identification beyond the "me" (egocentric), or the "us" (ethnocentric), to identification and concern for "all of us" (worldcentric), or the entire global human family; a moral stance that is characteristic of higher levels of spiritual development.

Zone of proximal development According to Vygotsky, the theoretical space between the child's current developmental level (or performance) and the child's potential level (or performance) if given access to appropriate models and developmental experiences in the social environment.

Zygote A fertilized ovum cell.

REFERENCES

Abma, J., & Martinez, G. (2006). Childlessness among older women in the United States: Trends and profiles. *Journal of Marriage and Family, 68*, 1045–1056.

Abrams, D., Hogg, M., Hinkle, S., & Otten, S. (2005). The social identity perspective on small groups. In M. Poole & A. Hollingshead (Eds.), *Theories of small groups: Interdisciplinary perspectives* (pp. 99–137). Thousand Oaks, CA: Sage.

Achenbaum, W. A., & Bengtson, V. C. (1994). Re-engaging the disengagement theory of aging: Or the history and assessment of theory development in gerontology. *The Gerontologist, 34*, 756–763.

Acierno, R., Hernandez, M., Amstadter, A., Resnick, H., Steve, K., Muzzy, W., & Kilpatrick, D. G. (2010). Prevalence and correlates of emotional, physical, sexual, and financial abuse and potential neglect in the United States: The National Elder Mistreatment Study. *American Journal of Public Health, 100*(2), 292–297.

Adams, R., Boscarino, J., & Figley, C. (2006). Compassion fatigue and psychological distress among social workers: A validation study. *American Journal of Orthsopsychiatry, 78*(1), 103–108.

Addams, J. (1910). *Twenty years at Hull House*. New York, NY: MacMillan.

Addy, S., Engelhardt, W., & Skinner, C. (2013). *Basic facts about low income children: Children under 18 years, 2011*. National Center for Children in Poverty. Retrieved from www.nccp.org/publications/pdf/text_1074.pdf

Addy, S., & Wight, V. (2012). *Basic facts about low-income children, 2010: Children under age 3.* New York: National Center for Children in Poverty. Retrieved from http://www.nccp.org/publications/pdf/text_1056.pdf

Adler, N., & Stewart, J. (2010a). Preface to the biology of disadvantage: Socioeconomic status and health. *Annals of the New York Academy of Sciences, 1186*, 1–4.

Adler, N., & Stewart, J. (2010b). Health disparities across the lifespan: Meaning, methods, and mechanisms. *Annals of the New York Academy of Sciences, 1186*, 5–23.

Adler-Tapia, R. (2012). *Child psychotherapy: Integrating developmental theory into clinical practice.* New York, NY: Springer.

Administration on Aging. (2008). *A profile of older Americans: 2008*. Retrieved from http://www.nowaa.org/Document.Doc?id=69

Administration on Aging. (2012). *A profile of older Americans: 2012*. Retrieved from http://www.aoa.gov/Aging_statistics/Profile/2012/docs/2012profile.pdf

Agrigoroaei, S., & Lachman, M. (2011). Cognitive functioning in midlife and old age: Combined effects of psychosocial and behavioral factors. *The Journals of Gerontology, Series B: Psychological Sciences and Social Sciences, 66B*(S1), i130–i140.

Agronin, M. E. (2011). *How we age: A doctor's journey into the heart of growing old.* Philadelphia, PA: Da Capo Press.

Aguilar, M. A. (2001). Catholicism. In M. Van Hook, B. Hugen, & M. Aguilar (Eds.), *Spirituality within religious traditions in social work practice* (pp. 120–145). Pacific Grove, CA: Brooks/Cole.

Ahmann, E. (2013). Making meaning when a child has mental illness: Four mothers share their experiences. *Pediatric Nursing, 39*(4), 202–205.

Ahmed-Mohamed, K. (2011). Social work practice and contextual systemic intervention: Improbability of communication between social work and sociology. *Journal of Social Work Practice, 25*(1), 5–15.

Ahrens, K., DuBois, D., Richardson, L., Fan, M., & Lozano, P. (2008). Youth in foster care with adult mentors during adolescence have improved adult outcomes. *Pediatrics, 121*(2), 246–252.

Ahrons, C. R. (2011). Divorce: An unscheduled family transition. In M. McGoldrick, B. Carter, & N. Garcia-Preto (Eds.), *The expanded family life cycle: Individual, family, and social perspectives* (4th ed., pp. 292–316). Boston, MA: Allyn & Bacon.

Ainsworth, M., Blehar, M., Waters, E., & Wall, S. (1978). *Patterns of attachment: A psychological study of the strange situation*. Hillsdale, NJ: Erlbaum.

Ajrouch, K., Antonucci, T., & Janevic, M. (2001). Social networks among Blacks and Whites: The interaction between race and age. *Journal of Gerontology: Social Sciences, 56*, S112–S118.

Albuquerque, P. (2011). Grandparents in multigenerational households: The case of Portugal. *European Journal of Ageing, 8*(3), 189–198.

Aldwin, C. M. (2007). *Stress, coping, and development: An integrative perspective* (2nd ed.). New York, NY: Guilford Press.

Aldwin, C. M., & Yancura, L. A. (2004). Coping and health: A comparison of the stress and trauma literatures. In P. Schnurr & B. Green (Eds.), *Trauma and health: Physical health consequences of exposure to extreme stress* (pp. 99–125). Washington, DC: American Psychological Association.

Aleccia, J. (2013, November 4). *Obesity linked to early puberty in girls, study finds*. Retrieved from http://www.nbcnews.com/health/obesity-linked-early-puberty-us-girls-study-finds-8C11514727

Alink, L., Mesmon, J., & van Zeijl, J. (2006). The early childhood aggression curve: Development of physical aggression in 10- to 50-month-old children. *Child Development, 77*(4), 954–966.

Alio, A. P., Lewis, C. A., Scarborough, K., Harris, K., & Fiscella, K. (2013). A community perspective on the role of fathers during pregnancy: A qualitative study. *British Medical Journal: Pregnancy and Childbirth, 12*(1), 1–11.

Allen, K. R., Lloyd, S., & Few, A. (2009). Reclaiming feminist theory, method, and praxis for family studies. In S. Lloyd, A. Few, & K. R. Allen (Eds.), *Handbook of feminist family studies* (pp. 3–17). Thousand Oaks, CA: Sage.

Almaas, A. H. (1995). *Luminous night's journey*. Berkeley, CA: Diamond Books.

Almaas, A. H. (1996). *The point of existence*. Berkeley, CA: Diamond Books.

Alperovitz, G. (2005). *America beyond capitalism: Reclaiming our wealth, our liberty, and our democracy*. Hoboken, NJ: Wiley.

Altman, I. (1975). *The environment and social behavior: Privacy, personal space, territory, and crowding*. Monterey, CA: Brooks/Cole.

Alwin, D. (2012). Integrating varieties of life course concepts. *The Journals of Gerontology, Series B: Psychological Sciences and Social Sciences, 67*(2), 206–220.

Alwin, D., & McCammon, R. (2003). Generations, cohorts, and social change. In J. Mortimer & M. Shanahan (Eds.), *Handbook of the life course* (pp. 23–49). New York, NY: Kluwer Academic/Plenum Publishers.

Alwin, D., McCammon, R., & Hofer, S. (2006). Studying baby boom cohorts within a demographic and developmental context: Conceptual and methodological issues. In S. Whitbourne & S. Willis (Eds.), *The baby boomers grow up: Contemporary perspectives on midlife* (pp. 45–71). Mahwah, NJ: Erlbaum.

Alzheimer's Association. (2013). *2013 Alzheimer's Disease facts and figures*. Chicago, IL: Author.

Amato, P.R. (2003). Family functioning and child development: The case of divorce. In R. M. Lerner, F. Jacobs, & D. Wertlieb (Eds.), *Handbook of applied developmental science, Vol. 1* (pp. 319–338). Thousand Oaks, CA: Sage.

Amato, P., & Irving, S. (2006). Historical trends in divorce and dissolution in the United States. In M. Fine & J. Harvey (Eds.), *Handbook of divorce and relationship dissolution* (pp. 41–57). Mahwah, NJ: Erlbaum.

Ambert, A. (2001). *Effect of children on parents* (2nd ed.). New York, NY: Haworth Press.

Amenta, E., Caren, N., & Stobaugh, J. (2012). Political reform and the historical trajectories of U.S. social movements in the twentieth century. *Social Forces, 90*(4), 1073–1100.

American Academy of Child & Adolescent Psychiatry. (2013). *Facts for families: Children & divorce*. Retrieved from www.aacap.org/APP_Themes/AACAP/docs/facts_for_families/01_children_and_divorce.pdf

American Academy of Pediatrics. (2012). *American Academy of Pediatrics study documents early puberty onset in boys*. Retrieved from http://www.aap.org/en-us/about-the-aap/aap-press-room/pages/AAP-Study-Documents-Early-Puberty-Onset-In-Boys.aspx

American Alliance for Health, Physical Education, Recreation and Dance. (2013). *Maximizing the benefits of youth sport* (position statement). Retrieved from http://www.aahperd.org/naspe/publications/teachingTools/coaching/upload/Maximizing-the-Benefit-of-Youth-Sport-ADA-Approved.pdf

American Civil Liberties Union. (2013). *What is the school-to-prison pipeline?* Retrieved from http://www.aclu.org/racial-justice/what-school-prison-pipeline

American College of Medical Genetics. (2013). *ACMG releases policy statement on noninvasive prenatal screen (NIPS)*. Retrieved from www.acmg.net/docs/NIPS_Release.pdf

American College of Nurse-Midwives. (2013). Miscarriage. *Journal of Midwifery & Women's Health, 58*(4), 479–480.

American College of Obstetricians and Gynecologists. (2013). Benefits and risks of sterilization. *Obstetrics and Gynecology, 121*(2), 392–404.

American Diabetes Association. (2013). *The cost of diabetes*. Retrieved from http://www.diabetes.org/advocate/resources/cost-of-diabetes.html

American Heart Association. (2013a). *Heart disease and stroke statistics—2014 update: A report from the American Heart Association*. Retrieved from http://circ.ahajournals.org/content/early/2013/12/18/01.cir.0000441139.02012.80.citation

American Heart Association. (2013b). *High blood pressure and African Americans*. Retrieved from http://www.heart.org/HEARTORG/Conditions/HighBloodPressure/UnderstandYourRiskforHighBloodPressure/High-Blood-Pressure-and-African-Americans_UCM_301832_Article.jsp

American Heart Association. (2013c). *Statistical fact sheet 2013 update: High blood pressure*. Retrieved from https://www.heart.org/idc/groups/heart-public/@wcm/@sop/@smd/documents/downloadable/ucm_319587.pdf

American Pregnancy Association. (2012). *Preimplantation genetic diagnosis: PGD*. Retrieved from http://americanpregnancy.org/infertility/preimplantiongeneticdiagnosis.html

American Psychiatric Association. (2013). *Diagnostic and statistical manual of mental disorders* (5th ed.). Washington, DC: Author.

American Psychological Association. (2013). *Gun violence research: History of the federal funding freeze*. Retrieved from http://www.apa.org/science/about/psa/2013/02/gun-violence.aspx

American Psychological Association. (2015). Guidelines for psychological practice with transgender and gender nonconforming people. *American Psychologist, 70*(9), 832–864.

American Society for Reproductive Medicine. (2013). Consideration of the gestational carrier: A committee opinion. *Fertility and Sterility, 99*(7), 1838–1841.

Amole, D. (2005). Coping strategies for living in student residential facilities in Nigeria. *Environment & Behavior, 37*(2), 201–219.

An, J., & Cooney, T. (2006). Psychological well-being in mid to late life: The roles of generativity development and parent–child relationships across the lifespan. *International Journal of Behavioral Development, 30*(5), 410–421.

Anandarajah, G., & Hight, E. (2001). Spirituality and medical practice: Using the HOPE questions as a practical tool for spiritual assessment. *American Family Physician, 63*(1), 81–99.

Anderson, C. (2010). *The importance of nutrition in pregnancy for lifelong health*. United States Department of Agriculture: Agricultural Research Service. Retrieved from http://www.ars.usda.gov/News/docs.htm?docid=20977&pf=1&cg_id=0

Anderson, C. (2012). The diversity, strengths, and challenges of single-parent households. In F. Walsh (Ed.), *Normal family processes: Growing diversity and complexity* (4th ed., pp. 128–148). New York, NY: Guilford Press.

Anderson, C., & Anderson, M. (2011). Single-parent families: Strengths, vulnerabilities, and interventions. In M. McGoldrick, B. Carter, & N. Garcia-Preto (Eds.), *The expanded family life cycle: Individual, family, and social perspectives* (4th ed., pp. 307–316). Boston, MA: Allyn & Bacon.

Anderson, H. (2009). A spirituality for family living. In F. Walsh (Ed.), *Spiritual resources in family therapy* (2nd ed., pp. 194–211). New York, NY: Guilford Press.

Anderson, K. F. (2013). Diagnosing discrimination: Stress from perceived racism and the mental and physical health effects. *Sociological Inquiry, 83*(1), 55–81.

Anderson, P. (2008). *The powerful bond between people and pets: Our boundless connections to companion animals*. Westport, CT: Praeger.

Andrew, M., & Ruel, E. (2010). Intergenerational health selection in wealth: A first look at parents' health events and *inter vivos* financial transfers. *Social Science & Research, 39*, 1126–1136.

Angers, M. E. (2008). Psychoanalysis, politics, and "the repressed feminine": Toward a psychoanalytically informed sociology of knowledge. *Issues in Psychoanalytic Psychology, 30*(2), 137–155.

Anguita, M. (2014). The future of contraception: The male contraceptive pill. *Nurse Prescribing, 12*(1), 6–8.

Annie E. Casey Foundation. (2013). *The 2013 kids count data book*. Retrieved from http://datacenter.kidscount.org/publications/databook/2013

Ansary, N., Scorpio, E., & Catanzariti, D. (2013). Parent-adolescent ethnic identity discrepancies and adolescent psychosocial maladjustment: A study of gender differences. *Child and Adolescent Social Work Journal, 30*, 275–291.

Antonucci, T., & Akiyama, H. (1987). Social networks in adult life and a preliminary examination of the convoy model. *Journal of Gerontology: Social Sciences, 42*, S519–S527.

Antonucci, T., & Akiyama, H. (1997). Concern with others at midlife: Care, comfort, or compromise? In M. Lachman & J. James (Eds.), *Multiple paths of midlife development* (pp. 145–169). Chicago, IL: University of Chicago Press.

Antonucci, T., Akiyama, H., & Merline, A. (2001). Dynamics of social relationships in midlife. In M. Lachman (Ed.), *Handbook of midlife development* (pp. 571–598). New York, NY: Wiley.

Antonucci, T., Akiyama, H., & Takahashi, K. (2004). Attachment and close relationships across the life span. *Attachment & Human Development, 6*(4), 353–370.

Applegate, J. S., & Shapiro, J. R. (2005). *Neurobiology for clinical social work: Theory and practice.* New York, NY: Norton.

Arber, S., & Ginn, J. (1995). *Connecting gender and aging: A sociological approach.* Philadelphia, PA: Open University Press.

Ardelt, M., & Eccles, J. S. (2001). Effects of mothers' parental efficacy beliefs and promotive parenting strategies on inner-city youth. *Journal of Family Issues, 22*(8), 944.

Argyris, C. (1999). *On organizational learning.* Cambridge, MA: Blackwell.

Argyris, C., & Schön, D. (1978). *Organizational learning: A theory of action perspective.* Reading, MA: Addison-Wesley.

Argyris, C., & Schön, D. (1996). *Organizational learning II: Theory, method, and practice.* Reading, MA: Addison-Wesley.

Armatowski, J. (2001). Attitudes toward death and dying among persons in the fourth quarter of life. In D. O. Moberg (Ed.), *Aging and spirituality: Spiritual dimensions of aging theory, research, practice, and policy* (pp. 71–83). New York, NY: Haworth Pastoral Press.

Arnett, J. J. (1998). Learning to stand alone: The contemporary American transition to adulthood in cultural and historical context. *Human Development, 41*(5), 295–297.

Arnett, J. J. (2000). Emerging adulthood: A theory of development from the late teens through the twenties. *American Psychologist, 55*(5), 469–480.

Arnett, J. J. (2004). *Emerging adulthood: The winding road from the late teens through the twenties.* New York, NY: Oxford University Press.

Arnett, J. J. (2006). G. Stanley Hall's adolescence: Brilliance and nonsense. *History of Psychology, 9,* 186–197.

Arnett, J. J. (2007). Suffering, selfish, slackers? Myths and reality about emerging adults. *Journal of Youth and Adolescence, 36,* 23–29.

Arnett, J. J., & Jensen, L. (2002). A congregation of one. *Journal of Adolescent Research, 17*(5), 451–467.

Arnett, J. J., & Taber, S. (1994). Adolescence terminable and interminable: When does adolescence end? *Journal of Youth & Adolescence, 23*(5), 517–538.

Arnett, J. J., & Tanner, J. L. (2005). *Emerging adults in America: Coming of age in the 21st century.* Washington, DC: American Psychological Association.

Aroian, K., & Norris, A. E. (2003). Depression trajectories in relatively recent immigrants. *Comprehensive Psychiatry, 44*(5), 420–427.

Aron, L., & Loprest, P. (2012). Disability and the education system. *Future of Children, 22*(1), 97–122.

Arsenio, W., & Gold, J. (2006). The effects of social injustice and inequality on children's moral judgments and behavior: Towards a theoretical model. *Cognitive Development, 21,* 388–400.

Ashford, J., LeCroy, C., & Lortie, K. (2010). *Human behavior in the social environment* (4th ed.). Belmont, CA: Cengage.

Ashkanani, H. R. (2009). The relationship between religiosity and subjective well-being: A case of Kuwaiti car accident victims. *Traumatology, 15*(1), 23–28.

Ashton, D. (2011). Lesbian, gay, bisexual, and transgender individuals and the family life cycle. In M. McGoldrick, B. Carter, & N. Garcia-Preto (Eds.), *The expanded family life cycle: Individual, family, and social perspectives* (4th ed., pp. 115–132). Boston, MA: Allyn & Bacon.

Assagioli, R. (1965). *Psychosynthesis: A manual of principles and techniques.* New York, NY: Viking.

Assagioli, R. (1973). *The act of will.* New York, NY: Penguin.

Assagioli, R. (1989). Self-realization and psychological disturbances. In S. Grof & C. Grof (Eds.), *Spiritual emergency: When personal transformation becomes a crisis* (pp. 27–48). Los Angeles, CA: Jeremy P. Tarcher.

Astone, N. M., Schoen, R., Ensminger, M., & Rothert, K. (2000). School reentry in early adulthood: The case of inner-city African Americans. *Sociology of Education, 73,* 133–154.

Attar-Schwartz, S., Tan, J., Buchanan, A., Flouri, E., & Griggs, J. (2009). Grandparenting and adolescent adjustment in two-parent biological, lone parent, and step-families. *Journal of Family Psychology, 23,* 67–75.

Auerbach, S., & Collier, S. (2012). Bringing high stakes from the classroom to the parent center: Lessons from an intervention program for immigrant families. *Teachers College Record, 114*(3), 1–40.

Aumann, K., & Galinsky, E. (2011). *The state of health in the American workforce: Does having an effective workplace matter?* New York, NY: Families and Work Institute. Retrieved from http://www.familiesandwork.org/downloads/StateofHealthinAmericanWorkforce.pdf

Aussie Childcare Network. (2015). *Fine motor development for toddlers 2-3.* Retrieved from http://aussiechildcarenetwork.com/au/articles/child-development/fine-motor-development-for-toddlers-2-3-year-olds

Austrian, S. (2008). Adulthood. In S. Austrian (Ed.), *Developmental theories through the life cycle* (pp. 201–283). New York, NY: Columbia University Press.

Averill, J. R. (2012). The future of social constructionism: Introduction to a special section of *Emotion Review. Emotion Review, 4*(3), 215–220.

Azrin, N., & Foxx, R. (1989). *Toilet training in less than a day.* New York, NY: Simon & Schuster.

Azzi, A. E. (2011). *Identity and participation in culturally diverse societies: A multidisciplinary perspective.* Malden, MA: Wiley-Blackwell.

Bäckström, C., & Hertfelt Wahn, E. (2011). Support during labour: First-time fathers' descriptions of requested and received support during the birth of their child. *Midwifery, 27,* 67–73.

Baddeley, J., & Singer, J. (2007). Charting the life story's path: Narrative identity across the life span. In J. Clandinin (Ed.), *Handbook of narrative research methods* (pp. 177–202). Thousand Oaks, CA: Sage.

Bahrick, L., Lickliter, R., & Flom, R. (2006). Up versus down: The role of intersensory redundancy in the development of infants' sensitivity to the orientation of moving objects. *Infancy, 9,* 73–96.

Bailey, M., & Danziger, S. (Eds.). (2013). *Legacies of the war on poverty.* New York, NY: Russell Sage.

Baillargeon, R. (2004). Infants' physical world. *Current Directions in Psychological Science, 13,* 89–94.

Baker, E., Barton, P., Darling-Hammond, L., Haertel, E., Ladd, H., Linn, R., . . . Shepard, L. (2010). *Problems with the use of student test scores to evaluate teachers.* Washington, DC: Economic Policy Institute.

Baker, M., Das, D., Venugopal, K., & Howden-Chapman, P. (2008). Tuberculosis associated with household crowding in a developed country. *Journal of Epidemiology and Community Health, 62*(8), 715–721.

Baldry, A. (2003). Bullying in schools and exposure to domestic violence. *Journal of Child Abuse & Neglect, 27* (7), 713–732.

Baldur-Felskov, B., Kjaer, S., Albieri, V., Steding-Jessen, M., Kjaer, T., Johansen, C., . . . Jensen, A. (2013). Psychiatric disorder in women with fertility problems: Results from a large Danish register-based cohort study. *Human Reproduction, 28*(3), 683–690.

Ballantine, J., & Roberts, K. (2014). *Our social world: Introduction to sociology* (4th ed.). Thousand Oaks, CA: Pine Forge.

Balsam, K., Beauchaine, T., Rothblum, E., & Solomon, S. (2008). Three-year follow-up of same-sex couples who had civil unions in Vermont, same-sex couples not in civil unions, and heterosexual married couples. *Developmental Psychology, 44*(1), 102–116.

Baltes, P.B., & Mayer, K. U. (Eds.). (1999). *The Berlin Aging Study: Aging from 70 to 100.* Cambridge, UK: Cambridge University Press.

Bandura, A. (1977a). Self-efficacy: Toward a unifying theory of behavioral change. *Psychological Review, 84*, 191–215.

Bandura, A. (1977b). *Social learning theory.* Englewood Cliffs, NJ: Prentice Hall.

Bandura, A. (1986). *Social foundations of thought and action: A social cognitive theory.* Englewood Cliffs, NJ: Prentice Hall.

Bandura, A. (2001). Social cognitive theory: An agentic perspective. *Annual Review of Psychology, 52*, 1–26.

Bandura, A. (2002). Social cognitive theory in cultural context. *Applied Psychology: An International Review, 51*(2), 269–290.

Bandura, A. (2006). Toward a psychology of human agency. *Perspectives on Psychological Science, 1*(2), 164–180.

Banerjee, M. M., & Canda, E. R. (2009). Spirituality as a strength of African-American women affected by welfare reform. *Social Thought, 28*(3), 239–262.

Banerjee, M. M., & Canda, E. (2012). Comparing Rawlsian justice and the capabilities approach to justice from a spiritually sensitive social work perspective. *Journal of Religion & Spirituality in Social Work: Social Thought, 31*(1–2), 9–31.

Banik, S., Gupta, A., Habib, M., & Mousumi, R. (2013). Determination of active personal space based on emotion when interacting with a service robot. *International Journal of Advanced Robotic Systems, 10*, 1–7.

Banks, J. A., & Banks, C. A. M. G. (2010). *Multicultural education: Issues and perspectives.* Hoboken, NJ: Wiley.

Barajas, R., Philipsen, N., & Brooks-Gunn, J. (2008). Cognitive and emotional outcomes for children in poverty. In D. Crane & T. Heaton (Eds.), *Handbook of families and poverty* (pp. 311–333). Thousand Oaks, CA: Sage.

Barak, A., & Grohol, J. (2011). Current and future trends in Internet-supported mental health interventions. *Journal of Technology in Human Services, 29*(3), 155–196.

Barbaro, J., & Dissanayake, C. (2012). Early markers of autism spectrum disorders in infants and toddlers prospectively identified in the Social Attention and Communication Study. *Autism, 17*(1), 64–86.

Barber, B., & Demo, D. (2006). The kids are alright (at least, most of them): Links between divorce and dissolution and child well-being. In M. Fine & J. Harvey (Eds.), *Handbook of divorce and relationship dissolution* (pp. 289–311). Mahwah, NJ: Erlbaum.

Barbu, S., Le Maner-Idrissi, G., & Jouanjean, A. (2000). The emergence of gender segregation: Towards an integrative perspective. *Current Psychology of Letters: Behavior, Brain, and Cognition, 3*, 7–18.

Barclay, L. (2009). ACOG issues guidelines for stillbirth management. *Obstetrics & Gynecology, 113*, 748–761.

Barker, D., & Thornburg, K. (2013). The obstetric origins of health for a lifetime. *Clinical Obstetrics and Gynecology, 56*(3), 511–519.

Barker, R. G. (1968). *Ecological psychology: Concepts and methods for studying the environment of human behavior.* Palo Alto, CA: Stanford University Press.

Barnard, M., & McKeganey, N. (2004). The impact of parental drug use on children: What is the problem and what can be done to help? *Addiction, 99*, 552–559.

Barnekow, K., & Kraemer, G. (2005). The psychobiological theory of attachment. A viable frame of reference for early intervention providers. *Physical & Occupational Therapy in Pediatrics, 25*(1–2), 3–15.

Barnes, P.M., Bloom, B., & Nahin, R. (2008, December 10). Complementary and alternative medicine use among adults and children: United States, 2007. *CDC National Health Statistics Report #12.* Retrieved from https://nccih.nih.gov/sites/nccam.nih.gov/files/news/nhsr12.pdf

Barnoff, L., & Moffatt, K. (2007). Contradictory tensions in anti-oppression practice in feminist social services. *Affilia, 22*(1), 56–70.

Barret, R., & Barzan, R. (1996). Spiritual experiences of gay men and lesbians. *Counseling and Values, 41*, 4–15.

Barrett, R. (2009). Sociocultural considerations: African Americans, grief, and loss. In D. J. Doka & A. S. Tucci (Eds.), *Living with grief: Diversity and end-of-life care* (pp. 79–91). Washington, DC: Hospice Foundation of America.

Barsky, A. (2013, March 18). Episode 115. Online social work with individuals, families, and groups: Ethical issues and responses. *inSocialWork Podcast Series* [Audio Podcast]. Retrieved from http://www.socialwork.buffalo.edu/podcast/episode.asp?ep=115

Bartholomae, S., & Fox, J. (2010). Economic stress and families. In S. Price, C. Price, & P. McKenry (Eds.), *Families & change: Coping with stressful events and transitions* (4th ed., pp. 185–209). Thousand Oaks, CA: Sage.

Barton, B. (2010). "Abomination"—Life as a Bible belt gay. *Journal of Homosexuality, 57*, 465–484.

Barton, J., & Pretty, J. (2010). What is the best dose of nature and green exercise for improving mental health? A multi-study analysis. *Environmental Science and Technology, 44*, 3947–3955.

Barton, P., & Coley, R. (2010). *The Black-White achievement gap: When progress stopped.* Princeton, NJ: Educational Testing Service.

Bates, J., & Goodsell, T. (2013). Male kin relationships: Grandfathers, grandsons, and generativity. *Marriage & Family Review, 49*, 26–50.

Bauldry, S., Shanahan, M., Boardman, J., Miech, R., & Macmillan, R. (2012). A life course model of self-rated health through adolescence and young adulthood. *Social Science & Medicine, 75*, 1311–1320.

Baum, F. (1999). The role of social capital in health promotion. Australian perspectives. *Health Promotion Journal of Australia, 9*(3), 171–178.

Baumrind, D. (1971). Current patterns of parental authority. *Developmental Psychology Monographs, 41*(1, Pt. 2), 1–103.

Baumrind, D. (1991). The influence of parenting style on adolescent competence and substance use. *Journal of Early Adolescence, 11*(1), 56–95.

Baxter, L., & Braithwaite, D. (2006). Introduction: Metatheory and theory in family communication research. In D. Braithwaite & L. Baxter (Eds.), *Engaging theories in family communication: Multiple perspectives* (pp. 1–15). Thousand Oaks, CA: Sage.

BBC News. (2006, June 22). *The popularity of "time" unveiled.* Retrieved from news.bbc.co.uk/2/hi/5104778.stm

Beard, V., & Sarmiento, C. (2010). Ties that bind: Transnational community-based planning in Southern California and Oaxaca. *International Development Planning Review, 32*(3–4), 207–224.

Beauchemin, K., & Hays, P. (1998). Dying in the dark: Sunshine, gender, and outcomes in myocardial infarction. *Journal of the Royal Society of Medicine, 91*, 352–354.

Beck, A. T. (1976). *Cognitive therapy and the emotional disorders.* New York, NY: International Universities Press.

Beck, J. S. (2005). *Cognitive therapy for challenging problems.* New York, NY: Guilford Press.

Beck, S., Wojdyla, D., Say, L., Betran, A., Merialdi, M., Requejo, J., . . . Van Look, P. (2010). The worldwide incidence of preterm birth: A systematic review of maternal mortality and morbidity. *Bulletin of World Health Organization, 88*, 31–38.

Beck, U. (1992). *Risk society: Towards a new modernity.* Thousand Oaks, CA: Sage.

Becker, D. (2004). Post-traumatic stress disorder. In P. J. Caplan & L. Cosgrove (Eds.), *Bias in psychiatric diagnosis* (pp. 207–212). Lanham, MD: Jason Aronson.

Becker, D. (2005). *The myth of empowerment: Women and the therapeutic culture in America*. New York, NY: New York University Press.

Becker, H. (1957). Current sacred–secular theory and its development. In H. Becker & A. Boskoff (Eds.), *Modern sociological theory in continuity and change* (pp. 137–185). New York, NY: Dryden.

Beel-Bates, C. A., Ingersoll-Dayton, B., & Nelson, E. (2007). Deference as a form of reciprocity on aging. *Research on Aging, 29*, 626–643.

Behrens, K., Hesse, E., & Main, M. (2007). Mothers' attachment status as determined by the Adult Attachment Interview predicts their 6-year-olds' reunion responses: A study conducted in Japan. *Developmental Psychology, 43*(6), 1553–1567.

Beksinska, M., Smit, J., Greener, R., Piaggio, G., & Joanis, C. (2015). The female condom learning curve: Patterns of female condom failure over 20 years. *Contraception, 91*(1), 85–90.

Beland, F., Zunzunegui, M., Alvarado, B., Otero, A., & del Ser, T. (2005). Trajectories of cognitive decline and social relations. *Journals of Gerontology: Series B: Psychological Sciences and Social Sciences, 60*(6), 320–330.

Belanger, K., Copeland, S., & Cheung, M. (2009). The role of faith in adoption: Achieving positive adoption outcomes for African American children. *Child Welfare, 87*(2), 99–123.

Belcher, J. R., Fandetti, D., & Cole, D. (2004). Is Christian religious conservatism compatible with the liberal social welfare state? *Social Work, 49*(2), 269–276.

Belden, A., Thompson, N., & Luby, J. (2008). Temper tantrums in healthy versus DSM-IV depressed and disruptive preschoolers: Defining tantrum behaviors associated with clinical problems. *Journal of Pediatrics, 152*, 117–122.

Bell, K. (2012). Towards a post-conventional philosophical base for social work. *British Journal of Social Work, 42*, 408–423.

Bell, L. (2009). Mindful psychotherapy. *Journal of Spirituality in Mental Health, 11*(1–2), 126–144.

Bellenir, K. (2012). *Mental health disorders sourcebook: Basic consumer health information about healthy brain functioning and mental illnesses, including depression, bipolar disorder, anxiety disorders, posttraumatic stress disorder, obsessive-compulsive disorder, psychotic and personality disorders, eating disorders, impulse control disorders* (5th ed.). Detroit, MI: Omnigraphics.

Bell-Toliver, L., & Wilkerson, P. (2011). The use of spirituality and kinship as contributors to successful therapy outcomes with African American families. *Journal of Religion & Spirituality in Social Work, 30*(1), 48–70.

Bem, S. L. (1993). *The lenses of gender: Transforming the debate on sexual inequality*. New Haven, CT: Yale University Press.

Bem, S. L. (1998). Gender schema theory and its implications for child development: Raising gender-aschematic children in a gender-schematic society. In D. L. Anselmi & A. L. Law (Eds.), *Questions of gender: Perspectives and paradoxes*. Boston, MA: McGraw-Hill.

Benasich, A., & Leevers, H. (2003). Processing of rapidly presented auditory cues in infancy: Implications for later language development. In H. Hayne & J. Fagen (Eds.), *Progress in infancy research* (Vol. 3, pp. 245–288). Mahwah, NJ: Erlbaum.

Benavides, L. E. (2012). A phenomenological study of spirituality as a protective factor for adolescents exposed to domestic violence. *Journal of Social Service Research, 38*(2), 165–174.

Ben-David, V. (2011). Social constructions of reality and narratives of parental incapability in the process of adjudicating the adoption of minors in Israel. *Child and Family Social Work, 16*, 402–411.

Bender, C. (2010). *The new metaphysicals: Spirituality and the American religious imagination*. Chicago, IL: University of Chicago Press.

Benedict, R. (1946). *The chrysanthemum and the sword*. Boston, MA: Houghton Mifflin.

Benedict, R. (1989). *Patterns of culture*. Boston, MA: Houghton Mifflin. (Original work published 1934)

Bengtson, V. L. (2001). Beyond the nuclear family: The increasing importance of multigenerational bonds. *Journal of Marriage and Family, 63*, 1–16.

Bengtson, V. L., Gans, D., Putney, N. M., & Silverstein, M. (2009). *Handbook of theories of aging* (2nd ed.). New York, NY: Springer.

Benjamin, K., Edwards, N. C., & Bharti, V. K. (2005). Attitudinal, perceptual, and normative beliefs influencing the exercise decisions of community-dwelling physically frail seniors. *Journal of Aging and Physical Activity, 13*(3), 276–293

Benner, A. (2011). The transition to high school: Current knowledge, future directions. *Educational Psychology Review, 23*, 299–328.

Bennett, S., Sheridan, M. J., & Richardson, F. (2014). Caregiving as ministry: Perceptions of African Americans providing care for elders. *Families in Society: The Journal of Contemporary Social Services, 95*(1), 51–58.

Bennett, W. L. (2004). Communicating global activism: Strength and vulnerabilities of networked politics. In W. van de Donk, B. Loader, P. Nixon, & D. Rucht (Eds.), *Cyberprotest: New media, citizens and social movements* (pp. 109–126). London, UK: Routledge.

Benson, P. L., Scales, P. C., & Roehlkepartain, E. C. (2011). *A fragile foundation: The state of developmental assets among American youth* (2nd ed.). Minneapolis, MN: Search Institute.

Benson, P. L., Scales, P. C., Syvertsen, A. K., & Roehlkepartain, E. C. (2012). Is youth spiritual development a universal developmental process? An international exploration. *Journal of Positive Psychology, 7*(6), 453–470.

Bentley, K. J., & Walsh, J. (2014). *The social worker & psychotropic medication: Toward effective collaboration with mental health clients, families, and providers* (4th ed.). Pacific Grove, CA: Brooks/Cole.

Bergen, D., & Davis, D. (2011). Influences of technology-related playful activity and thought on moral development. *American Journal of Play, 4*(1), 80–99.

Berger, L. (2005). Income, family characteristics, and physical violence toward children. *Child Abuse & Neglect, 29*(2), 107–133.

Berger, P. L. (1969). *The sacred canopy: Elements of a sociological theory of religion*. Garden City, NY: Doubleday.

Berger, P. L., & Luckmann, T. (1966). *The social construction of reality*. Garden City, NY: Doubleday.

Bergman, K., Rubio, R., Green, R., & Padrón, E. (2010). Gay men who become fathers via surrogacy: The transition to parenthood. *Journal of GLBT Family Studies, 6*, 111–141.

Berk, L. E. (2005). *Infants, children, and adolescents* (5th ed.). Boston, MA: Pearson.

Berk, L. E. (2012). *Infants, children, and adolescents* (7th ed.). Boston, MA: Pearson/Allyn & Bacon.

Berliner, K., Jacob, D., & Schwartzberg, N. (2011). Single adults and the life cycle. In M. McGoldrick, B. Carter, & N. Garcia-Preto (Eds.), *The expanded family life cycle: Individual, family, and social perspectives* (4th ed., pp. 163–175). Boston, MA: Allyn & Bacon.

Berman, M., Kross, E., Krpan, K., Askren, M., Burson, A., Deldin, P., . . . Jonides, J. (2012). Interacting with nature improves cognition and affect for individuals with depression. *Journal of Affective Disorder, 140*, 300–305.

Bern-Klug, M. (2004). The ambiguous dying syndrome. *Health and Social Work, 29*(1), 55–65.

Berry, M. E. (2009). *The sacred universe: Earth, spirituality, and religion in the 21st century.* New York, NY: Columbia University Press.

Bertalanffy, L. V. (1969). *General systems theory.* New York, NY: George Braziller.

Berthold, J. (2009). Dealing with delirium in older hospitalized adults. *ACP Hospitalist.* Retrieved May 16, 2010, from http://www.acphospitalist.org/archives/2009/06/delirium.htm

Berzoff, J. (2011). Why we need a biopsychosocial perspective with vulnerable, oppressed, and at-risk clients. *Smith College Studies in Social Work, 81*, 132–166.

Besthorn, F. H. (2012). Deep ecology's contributions to social work: A ten-year retrospective. *International Journal of Social Welfare, 21*, 248–259.

Besthorn, F. H. (2013). Radical equalitarian ecological justice: A social work call to action. In M. Gray, J. Coates, & T. Hetherington (Eds.), *Environmental Social Work* (pp. 31–45). New York, NY: Routledge.

Biblarz, T., & Savci, E. (2010). Lesbian, gay, bisexual, and transgender families. *Journal of Marriage and Family, 72*, 480–497.

Bidart, C., & Lavenu, D. (2005). Evolutions of personal networks and life events. *Social Networks, 27*(4), 359–376.

Bierut, L. (2011). Genetic vulnerability and susceptibility to substance dependence. *Neuron, 69*, 618–627.

Billingsley, A. (1999). *Mighty like a river: The black church and social reform.* New York, NY: Oxford University Press.

Biorck, G. (1977). The essence of the clinician's art. *Acta Medica Scandinavica, 201*(3), 145–147.

Birknerová, Z. (2011). Social and emotional intelligence in school environment. *Asian Social Science, 7*(10), 241–248.

Bisagni, F. (2012). Shrapnel: Latency, mourning and the suicide of a parent. *Journal of Child Psychotherapy, 38*(1), 22–31.

Bjorklund, B. (2011). *The journey of adulthood* (7th ed.). Boston, MA: Prentice Hall.

Black, B., Holditch-Davis, D., & Miles, M. (2009). Life course theory as a framework to examine becoming a mother of a medically fragile preterm infant. *Research in Nursing & Health, 32*, 38–39.

Black, M. C., Basile, K. C., Breiding, M. J., Smith, S. G., Walters, M. L., Merrick, M. T., . . . Stevens, M. R. (2011). *The National Intimate Partner and Sexual Violence Survey (NISVS): 2010 Summary Report.* Atlanta, GA: National Center for Injury Prevention and Control, Centers for Disease Control and Prevention. Retrieved from http://www.cdc.gov/violenceprevention/pdf/nisvs_report2010-a.pdf

Blackmon, S., & Vera, E. (2008). Ethnic and racial identity development in children of color. In J. Asamen, M. Ellis, & G. Berry (Eds.), *The SAGE handbook of child development, multiculturalism, and the media* (pp. 47–61). Thousand Oaks, CA: Sage.

Blakemore, S. (2012). Imaging brain development: The adolescent brain. *Neuroimaging, 61*, 397–406.

Blakemore, S., & Robbins, T. (2012). Decision-making in the adolescent brain. *Nature Neuroscience, 15*(9), 1184–1191.

Blasco-Fontecilla, H., Delgado-Gomez, D., Legido-Gil, T., Leon, J., Perez-Rodriguez, M., & Baca-Garcia, E. (2012). Can the Holmes-Rahe Social Readjustment Rating Scale (SRRS) be used as a suicide risk scale? An exploratory study. *Archives of Suicide Research, 16*, 13–28.

Blasi, J., Freeman, R., & Kruse, D. (2013). *The citizen's share.* New Haven, CT: Yale University Press.

Blau, P. M. (1964). *Exchange and power in social life.* New York, NY: Wiley.

Blieszner, R., & Roberto, K. (2006). Perspectives on close relationships among the baby boomers. In S. Whitbourne & S. Willis (Eds.), *The baby boomers grow up: Contemporary perspectives on midlife* (pp. 261–281). Mahwah, NJ: Erlbaum.

Blinn-Pike, L., Worthy, S., Jonkman, J., & Smith, G. R. (2008). Emerging adult versus adult status among college students: Examination of explanatory variables. *Adolescence, 43*(171), 577–591.

Blumenthal, P. D., Voedisch, A., & Gemzell-Danielsson, K. (2011). Strategies to prevent unwanted pregnancy: Increasing use of long-acting reversible contraceptives. *Human Reproduction Update, 17*(1), 121–137.

Blumer, H. (1998). *Symbolic interactionism: Perspective and method.* Berkeley, CA: University of California Press.

Blunden, S., Thompson, K., & Dawson, D. (2011). Behavioural sleep treatments and night time crying in infants: Challenging the status quo. *Sleep Medicine Reviews, 15*, 327–334.

Boas, F. (1948). *Race, language and culture.* New York, NY: Free Press. (Original work published 1940)

Boase, J. (2008). Personal networks and the personal communication system: Using multiple media to connect. *Information, Communication & Society, 11*(4), 490–508.

Boase, J., Horrigan, J., Wellman, B., & Rainie, L. (2006). *The strength of Internet ties: The Internet and email aid users in maintaining their social networks and provide pathways to help when people face big decisions.* Washington, DC: Pew Internet & American Life Project. Retrieved from www.pewinternet.org/files/old-media/Files/Reporrts/20067/PIP-Internet_ties.pdf.pdf

Boat, A. C., Sadhasivam, S., Loepke, A. W., & Kurth, C. D. (2011). Outcome for the extremely premature neonate: How far do we push the edge? *Pediatric Anesthesia, 21*(7), 765–770.

Boddie, S. C., & Cnaan, R. A. (Eds.). (2006). *Faith-based social services: Measures, assessments, and effectiveness.* Binghamton, NY: Haworth Press.

Boddie, S. C., Hong, P. Y. P., Im, H., & Chung, S. (2011). Korean-American churches as partners in community development. *Social Work & Christianity, 38*(4), 395–416.

Bogovic, A., Mihanovic, M., Jokic-Begic, N., & Svagelj, A. (2013). Personal space of male war veterans with posttraumatic stress disorder. *Environment and Behavior.* Retrieved from eab.sagepub.com/content/46/8/929.full.pdf+html

Bohannan, P. (1995). *How culture works.* New York, NY: Free Press.

Boivin, A., Zhong-Cheng, L., Audibert, F., Masse, B., Lefebreve, F., Tessier, R., & Nuyt, A. M. (2012). Pregnancy complications among women born preterm. *Canadian Medical Association Journal, 184*(16), 1777–1784.

Boldizar, J. P. (1991). Assessing sex typing and androgyny in children: The children's sex role inventory. *Developmental Psychology, 27*, 505–515.

Bonanno, G., & Kaltman, S. (1999). Toward an integrative perspective on bereavement. *Psychological Bulletin, 125*(6), 760–776.

Bond, B., Hefner, V., & Drogos, K. (2009). Information-seeking practices during the sexual development of lesbian, gay, and bisexual individuals: The influence and effects of coming out in a mediated environment. *Sexuality & Culture, 13*, 32–50.

Bonduriansky, R. (2012). Rethinking heredity, again. *Trends in Ecology & Evolution, 27*(6), 330–336.

Boonstra, H. (2010). Sex education: Another big step forward—and a step back. *The Guttmacher Policy Review, 13*(2), 27–28.

Booth, R., & O'Brien, P. J. (2008). An holistic approach for counsellors: Embracing multiple intelligences. *International Journal of Advising and Counselling, 30*, 79–92.

Borden, W. (2009). *Contemporary psychodynamic theory and practice.* Chicago, IL: Lyceum Books.

Borgatti, S., & Halgin, D. (2011). On network theory. *Organization Science, 22*(5), 1168–1181.

Bornstein, A. (2009). N30 + 10: Global civil society, a decade after the Battle of Seattle. *Dialectical Anthropology, 33*, 97–108.

Bornstein, M., & Bradley, R. (Eds.). (2003). *Socioeconomic status, parenting, and child development*. Mahwah, NJ: Erlbaum.

Boroditsky, L., Fuhrman, O., & McCormick, K. (2011). Do English and Mandarin speakers think about time differently? *Cognition, 118*, 123–129.

Borysenko, J. (1996). *A woman's book of life: The biology, psychology, and spirituality of the feminine life cycle*. New York, NY: Riverhead Books.

Bos, H., van Balen, F., & van den Boom, D. (2007). Child adjustment and parenting in planned lesbian-parent families. *American Journal of Orthopsychiatry, 77*, 38–48.

Boss, P. (2006). *Loss, trauma, and resilience: Therapeutic work with ambiguous loss*. New York, NY: Norton.

Boswell, J. (1994). *Same-sex unions in premodern Europe*. New York, NY: Random House.

Bottoms, B. L., Nielsen, M., Murray, R., & Filipas, H. (2003). Religion-related child physical abuse: Characteristics and psychological outcomes. *Journal of Aggression, Maltreatment & Trauma, 8*(1–2), 87–114.

Bourdieu, P. (1977). *Outline of a theory of practice*. New York, NY: Cambridge University Press.

Bouwsma, W. (1978). Christian adulthood. In E. H. Erikson (Ed.), *Adulthood* (pp. 81–96). New York, NY: Norton & Norton.

Bowen, M. (1978). *Family therapy in clinical practice*. New York, NY: Aronson.

Bowland, S., Biswas, B., Kyriakakis, S., & Edmond, T. (2011). Transcending the negative: Spiritual struggles and resilience in older female trauma survivors. *Journal of Religion, Spirituality & Aging, 23*(4), 318–337.

Bowlby, J. (1969). *Attachment and loss*. New York, NY: Basic Books.

Bowlby, J. (1980). *Attachment and loss: Loss, sadness, and depression* (Vol. 3). New York: Basic Books.

Bowlby, J. (1982). *Attachment and loss* (Vol. 1). New York, NY: Basic Books.

Bowler, D., Buyung-Ali, L., Knight, T., & Pullin, S. (2010). A systematic review of evidence for the added benefits of health and exposure to natural environments. *BMC Public Health, 10*, 456.

Boyd, D., & Ellison, N. (2008). Social network sites: Definition, history, and scholarship. *Journal of Computer-Mediated Communication, 13*(1), 210–230.

Boyd-Franklin, B., & Karger, M. (2012). Intersections of race, class, and poverty: Challenges and resilience. In F. Walsh (Ed.), *Normal family processes* (4th ed., pp. 273–296). New York, NY: Guilford.

Boyle, C. A., Boulet, S., Schieve, L., Cohen, R. A., Blumberg, S. J., Yeargin-Allsopp, M., . . . Kogan, M. D. (2011). Trends in the prevalence of developmental disabilities in US children, 1997–2008. *Pediatrics, 127*(6), 1034–1042. doi:10.1542/peds.2010–2989

Boyle, M. H., Miskovic, V., Van Lieshout, R., Duncan, L., Schmidt, L. A., Hoult, L., . . . Saigal, S. (2011). Psychopathology in young adults born at extremely low birth weight. *Psychological Medicine, 41*(8), 1763–1774.

Bozard, R. L., & Sanders, C. J. (2011). Helping Christian lesbian, gay, and bisexual clients recover religion as a source of strength: Developing a model for assessment and integration of religious identity in counseling. *Journal of LGBT Issues in Counseling, 5*(1), 47–74.

Bradley, R., & Corwyn, R. (2002). Socioeconomic status and child development. *Annual Review of Psychology, 53*, 371–399.

Bradley, S. (2000). *Affect regulation and the development of psychopathology*. New York, NY: Guilford Press.

Bradshaw, Y., Healey, J., & Smith, R. (2001). *Sociology for a new century*. Thousand Oaks, CA: Pine Forge.

Brain Injury Association of America. (2013). *Brain injury facts*. Retrieved from http://www.biausa.org/glossary.htm

Branch, C., Tayal, P., & Triplett, C. (2000). The relationship of ethnic identity and ego identity status among adolescents and young adults. *International Journal of Intercultural Relations, 23*, 777–790.

Brandon, D. (1976). *Zen in the art of helping*. New York, NY: Delta/Seymour Lawrence.

Brantley, J., Doucette, D., & Lindell, A. (2008). Mindfulness, meditation, and health. In A. L. Strozier & J. E. Carpenter (Eds.), *Introduction to alternative and complementary therapies* (pp. 9–29). New York, NY: Haworth Press.

Branum, A. M., & Jones, J. (2015). *Trends in long-acting reversible contraception use among U.S. women aged 15–44*. NCHS Data Brief, No. 188. Hyattsville, MD: National Center for Health Statistics.

Braude, A. (1997). Women's history is American religious history. In T. A. Tweed (Ed.), *Retelling U.S. religious history* (pp. 87–107). Berkeley, CA: University of California Press.

Brault, M. W. (2012). *Americans with disabilities 2010: Household economic studies: Current population report*. Washington, DC: U.S. Census Bureau. Retrieved from http://www.census.gov/prod/2012pubs/p70–131.pdf

Brautigam, D. (2009). *The dragon's gift: The real story of China in Africa*. Oxford, UK: Oxford University Press.

Braver, S., Shapiro, J., & Goodman, M. (2006). Consequences of divorce for parents. In M. Fine & J. Harvey (Eds.), *Handbook of divorce and relationship dissolution* (pp. 313–337). Mahwah, NJ: Erlbaum.

Brawley, E. (2006). *Design innovations for aging and Alzheimer's*. Hoboken, NJ: Wiley.

Brawley, E. (2009). Enriching lighting design. *NeuroRehabilitation, 25*, 189–199.

Breitman, B. E. (1995). Social and spiritual reconstruction of self within a feminist Jewish community. *Woman and Therapy: A Feminist Quarterly, 16*(2/3), 73–82.

Brennan, D., & Spencer, A. (2009). Life events and oral-health-related quality of life among young adults. *Quality of Life Research, 18*(5), 557–565.

Brent, J. (1997). Community without unity. In P. Hoggett (Ed.), *Contested communities: Experiences, struggles, policies* (pp. 68–83). Bristol, UK: Policy Press.

Brewer, M. (1999). The psychology of prejudice: Ingroup love or outgroup hate? *Journal of Social Issues, 55*, 429–444.

Bridgett, D., Gartstein, M., Putnam, S., McKay, T., Iddins, E., Robertson, C., . . . Rittmueller, A. (2009). Maternal and contextual influences and the effect of temperament development during infancy on parenting in toddlerhood. *Infant Behavior & Development, 32*, 103–116.

Briggs, L. (2011). Demoralization and psychological distress in refugees: From research to practice. *Social Work in Mental Health, 9*(5), 336–345. doi:10.1080/15332985.2011.569444

Brinkman, B. G., Jedinak, A., Rosen, L. A., & Zimmerman, T. S. (2011). Teaching children fairness: Decreasing gender prejudice among children. *Analyses of Social Issues & Public Policy, 11*(1), 61–81.

Brockington, I. F., Aucamp, H. M., & Fraser, C. (2006). Severe disorders of the mother-infant relationship: Definitions and frequency. *Archives of Women's Mental Health, 9*(5), 243–251.

Brodsky, A. (2009). Multiple psychological sense of community in Afghan context: Exploring commitment and sacrifice in an underground resistance community. *American Journal of Community Psychology, 44*, 176–187.

Brokenleg, M., & Middleton, D. (1993). Native Americans: Adapting, yet retaining. In D. Irish, K. Lundquist, & V. Nelsen (Eds.), *Ethnic variations in dying, death, and grief: Diversity in universality* (pp. 101–112). Washington, DC: Taylor & Francis.

Bromberg, D. S., & O'Donohue, W. T. (2013). *Handbook of child and adolescent sexuality: Developmental and forensic psychology*. Boston, MA: Elsevier.

Bronfenbrenner, U. (1993). The ecology of cognitive development: Research models and fugitive findings. In R. Wozniak & K. Fischer (Eds.), *Development in context: Acting and thinking in specific environments* (pp. 3–44). Hillsdale, NJ: Erlbaum.

Bronfenbrenner, U. (1996). *The ecology of human development: Experiments by nature and design.* Cambridge, MA: Harvard University Press.

Bronfenbrenner, U. (2005). *Making human beings human: Bioecological perspective on human development.* Thousand Oaks, CA: Sage.

Bronfenbrenner, U., & Morris, P. (1998). The ecology of developmental processes. In W. Damon (Series Ed.) & R. M. Lerner (Vol. Ed.), *Handbook of child psychology: Vol 1. Theoretical models of human development* (5th ed., pp. 993–1028). New York, NY: Wiley.

Bronfenbrenner, U., & Morris, P. A. (2006). The bioecological model of human development. In W. Damon & R. M. Lerner (Eds.), *Handbook of child psychology, Vol. 1: Theoretical models of human development* (6th ed., pp. 793–828). New York: John Wiley.

Brown, B. B., & Klute, C. (2003). Friendships, cliques, and crowds. In G. Adams & M. Berzonsky (Eds.), *Blackwell handbook of adolescence* (pp. 330–345). Oxford, UK: Blackwell.

Brown, G. (2009). NICU noise and the preterm infant. *Neonatal Network, 28*(3), 165–173.

Brown, G., Lawrence, T., & Robinson, S. (2005). Territoriality in organizations. *Academy of Management Review, 30*(3), 577–594.

Brown, J. (2003). The self-enhancement motive in collectivistic cultures: The rumors of my death have been greatly exaggerated. *Journal of Cross-Cultural Psychology, 34*, 603–605.

Brown, J., Dutton, K., & Cook, K. (2001). From the top down: Self-esteem and self-evaluation. *Cognition and Emotion, 15*, 615–631.

Brown, R. A., Rehkopf, D. H., Copeland, W. E., Costello, E. J., & Worthman, C. M. (2009). Lifecourse priorities among Appalachian emerging adults: Revisiting Wallace's organization of diversity. *ETHOS, 37*(2), 225–242.

Brown, S., & Lin, I.-F. (2012). The gray divorce revolution: Rising divorce among middle-aged and older adults, 1990–2010. *The Journals of Gerontology, Series B: Psychological Sciences and Social Sciences, 67*(6), 731–741.

Bruce, S., & Muhammad, Z. (2009). The development of object permanence in children with intellectual disability, physical disability, autism, and blindness. *International Journal of Disability, Development & Education, 56*(3), 229–246.

Bruce, S., & Vargas, C. (2013). Teaching object permanence: An action research study. *Journal of Impairment & Blindness, 107*(1), 60–64.

Brückner, H., & Mayer, K. (2005). De-standardization of the life course: What it might mean? And if it means anything, whether it actually took place? In R. MacMillan (Ed.), *The structure of the life course: Standardized? Individualized? Differentiated?* (pp. 27–53). New York, NY: Elsevier.

Bryck, R. L., & Fisher, P. A. (2012). Training the brain: Practical applications of neural plasticity from the intersection of cognitive neuroscience, developmental psychology, and prevention science. *American Psychologist, 67*(2), 87–100.

Bryson, K., & Casper, L. (1999). *Coresident grandparents and grandchildren.* Washington, DC: U.S. Census Bureau.

Buchwald, D., Delmar, C., & Schantz-Laursen, B. (2012). How children handle life when their mother or father is seriously ill and dying. *Scandinavian Journal of Caring Sciences, 26*(2), 228–235. doi:10.1111/j.1471-6712.2011.00922.x

Buechler, S. (2011). *Understanding social movements: Theories from the classical era to the present.* Boulder, CO: Paradigm.

Buffardi, A., Thomas, K., Holmes, K., & Manhart, L. (2008). Moving upstream: Ecosocial and psychosocial correlates of sexually transmitted infections among young adults in the United States. *American Journal of Public Health, 98*(6), 1128–1136.

Bullis, R. K. (1996). *Spirituality in social work practice.* Washington, DC: Taylor & Francis.

Bullock, K. (2011). The influence of culture on end-of-life decision making. *Journal of Social Work in End-of-Life & Palliative Care, 7*, 83–98.

Burgess, W. C. (2009). Internal and external stress factors associated with the identity development of transgender and gender variant youth. In G. P. Mallon (Ed.), *Social work practice with transgender and gender variant youth* (pp. 53–62). London, UK: Routledge.

Burke, M. T., Chauvin, J. C., & Miranti, J. G. (2005). *Religious and spiritual issues in counseling: Applications across diverse populations.* New York, NY: Brunner/Routledge.

Burtless, G. (2012). *Life expectancy and rising income inequality: Why the connection matters for fixing entitlements.* Retrieved from http://www.brookings.edu/research/opinions/2012/10/23-inequality-life-expectancy-burtless

Bush, K., Bohon, S., & Kim, H. (2010). Adaptation among immigrant families: Resources and barriers. In S. Price, C. Price, & P. McKenry (Eds.), *Families & change: Coping with stressful events and transitions* (4th ed., pp. 285–310). Thousand Oaks, CA: Sage.

Bussolari, C., & Goodell, J. (2009). Chaos theory as a model of life transitions counseling: Nonlinear dynamics and life's changes. *Journal of Counseling & Development, 87*, 98–107.

Butler, R. N. (1963). The life review: An interpretation of reminiscence in the aged. *Psychiatry, 26*, 65–70.

Butler, R. N. (1987). Life review. In G. L. Maddox (Ed.), *The encyclopedia of aging: A comprehensive resource in gerontology and geriatrics* (2nd ed., pp. 397–398). New York, NY: Springer.

Butler-Sweet, C. (2011). "Race isn't what defines me": Exploring identity choices in transracial, biracial, and monoracial families. *Social Identities: Journal for the Study of Race, Nation and Culture, 17*(6), 747–769. doi:10.1080/13504630.2011.60667

Buzzell, L., & Chalquist, C. (Eds.). (2009). *Ecotherapy: Healing with nature in mind.* San Francisco, CA: Sierra Club Books.

Byoung-Suk, K., Ulrich, R., Walker, V., & Tassinary, L. (2008). Anger and stress: The role of landscape posters in an office setting. *Environment & Behavior, 40*(3), 355–381.

Cacioppo, J. T., Bernston, G. G., Sheridan, J. F., & McClintock, M. K. (2000). Multilevel integrative analysis of human behavior: Social neuroscience and the complementary nature of social and biological approaches. *Psychological Bulletin, 126*(6), 829–843.

Cagle, J. G. (2008). *Informal caregivers of advanced cancer patients: The impact of geographic proximity on social support and bereavement adjustment* (Unpublished doctoral dissertation). Virginia Commonwealth University, Richmond, VA. Retrieved January 8, 2010, from https://digarchive.library.vcu.edu/bitstream/10156/1974/1/caglejg_phd.pdf

Cagle, J. G., & Kovacs, P. J. (2009). Education: A complex and empowering social work intervention at the end of life. *Health & Social Work, 34*(1), 17–27.

Cairns, D. B. (2005). The journey to resiliency: An integrative framework for treatment for victims and survivors of family violence. *Social Work & Christianity, 32*(4), 305–320.

Calkins, S., & Hill, A. (2007). Caregiver influences on emerging emotion regulation: Biological and environmental transactions in early development. In J. Gross (Ed.), *Handbook of emotion regulation* (pp. 229–248). New York, NY: Guilford Press.

Calman, L., & Tarr-Whelan, L. (2005). *Early childhood education for all: A wise investment.* Retrieved from http://web.mit.edu/workplacecenter/docs/Full%20Report.pdf

Cameron, J. (1992). *The artist's way: A spiritual path to higher creativity.* New York, NY: Putnam.

Cameron, J., Alvarez, J., Ruble, D., & Fuligni, A. (2001). Children's lay theories about ingroups and outgroups: Reconceptualizing research on prejudice. *Personality and Social Psychology Review, 5*, 118–128.

Campbell, D. (1997). *The Mozart effect: Tapping the power of music to heal the body, strengthen the mind, and unlock the creative spirit.* New York, NY: Harper Trade.

Campbell, L., Campbell, B., & Dickinson, D. (2004). *Teaching & learning through multiple intelligences.* Boston, MA: Allyn & Bacon.

Campbell, S. (2002). *Behavioral problems in preschool children* (2nd ed.). New York, NY: Guilford Press.

Canda, E. R. (1983). General implications of shamanism for clinical social work. *International Social Work, 26*(4), 14–22.

Canda, E. R., & Furman, L. D. (1999). *Spiritual diversity in social work practice: The heart of helping.* New York, NY: Free Press.

Canda, E. R., & Furman, L.D. (2010). *Spiritual diversity in social work practice: The heart of helping* (2nd ed.). New York, NY: Oxford University Press.

Canda, E. R., & Phaobtong, T. (1992). Buddhism as a support system for Southeast Asian refugees. *Social Work, 37*, 61–67.

Canda, E. R., Shin, S., & Canda, H. (1993). Traditional philosophies of human services in Korea and contemporary social work implications. *Social Development Issues, 15*(3), 84–104.

Canda, E. R., & Yellow Bird, M. J. (1996). Cross-tradition borrowing of spiritual practices in social work settings. *Society for Spirituality and Social Work Newsletter, 3*(1), 1–7.

Cannon, W. B. (1924). *Bodily changes in pain, hunger, fear, and rage.* New York, NY: Appleton.

Cao, C., & O'Brien, K. O. (2013). Pregnancy and iron homeostasis: An update. *Nutrition Reviews, 71*(1), 35–51.

Caplan, G. (1990). Loss, stress, and mental health. *Community Mental Health Journal, 26*, 27–48.

Caplan, G., & Caplan, R. B. (2000). The future of primary prevention. *Journal of Primary Prevention, 21*(2), 131–136.

Cappeliez, P., Beaupré, M., & Robitaille, A. (2008). Characteristics and impact of life turning points for older adults. *Ageing International, 32*, 54–64.

Cappicci, A., Chadha, J., Bi Lin, M., & Snyder, F. (2012). Using critical race theory to analyze how Disney constructs diversity: A construction for Baccalaureate human behavior in the social environment curriculum. *Journal of Teaching in Social Work, 32*(1), 46–61.

Cardoso, C., Ellenbogen, M., Serravalle, L., & Linnen, A. M. (2013). Stress-induced negative mood moderates the relation between oxytocin administration and trust: Evidence for the tend-and-befriend response to stress? *Psychoneuroendocrinology, 38*(11), 2800–2804.

Carey, T. A. (1994). "Spare the rod and spoil the child." Is this a sensible justification for the use of punishment in child rearing? *Child Abuse and Neglect, 18*, 1005–1010.

Carnes, R., & Craig, S. (1998). *Sacred circles: A guide to creating your own women's spirituality group.* San Francisco, CA: HarperSanFrancisco.

Carnoy, M., & Rothstein, R. (2013). *What do international tests really show about U.S. student performance?* Washington, DC: Economic Policy Institute. Retrieved from www.epi.org/publications/us-student-performance-testing

Carolan, M. T., Bagherinia, G., Juhari, R., Himelright, J., & Mouton-Sanders, M. (2000). Contemporary Muslim families: Research and practice. *Contemporary Family Therapy, 22*(1), 67–79.

Caron, S. L. (2011). *Sex around the world: Cross-cultural perspectives on human sexuality* (4th ed.). Upper Saddle River, NJ: Pearson/Prentice Hall.

Carpentier, N., Bernard, P., Grenier, A., & Guberman, N. (2010). Using the life course perspective to study the entry into the illness trajectory: The perspective of caregivers of people with Alzheimer's disease. *Social Science & Medicine, 70*, 1501–1508.

Carr, D., & Kail, B. (2012). The influence of unpaid work on the transition out of full-time paid work. *The Gerontologist, 53*(1), 92–101.

Carstensen, L. (1995). Evidence for a life-span theory of socioemotional selectivity. *Current Directions in Psychological Science, 4*, 151–156.

Carter, B., McGoldrick, M., & Petkov, B. (2011). Becoming parents: The family with young children. In M. McGoldrick, B. Carter, & N. Garcia-Preto (Eds.), *The expanded family life cycle: Individual, family, and social perspectives* (4th ed., pp. 211–231). Boston, MA: Allyn & Bacon.

Carter, R. (2009). *The human brain book* London, UK: DK Adults.

Casale-Giannola, D., & Kamens, M. W. (2006). Inclusion at a university: Experiences of a young woman with Down syndrome. *Mental Retardation, 44*(5), 344–352.

Case, A., & Deaton, A. (2015). Rising morbidity and mortality in midlife among white non-Hispanic Americans in the 21st century. *Proceedings of the National Academy of Sciences.* Retrieved from www.pnas.org/cgi/doi/10.1073/pnas.1518393112

Casey, T., & Maldonado, L. (2012). *Worst off single-parent families in the United States: A cross-national comparison of single parenthood in the U.S. and sixteen other high-income countries.* Legal Momentum: The Women's Legal Defense and Education Fund. Retrieved from https://www.legalmomentum.org/sites/default/files/reports/worst-off-single-parent.pdf

Castells, M. (2012). *Networks of outrage and hope.* Boston, MA: Polity.

Catalano, S. (2012). *Intimate partner violence, 1993–2010.* U.S. Department of Justice. Retrieved from www.bjs.gov/content/pub/pdf/pv9310.pdf

Cattich, J., & Knudson-Martin, C. (2009). Spirituality and relationship: A holistic analysis of how couples cope with diabetes. *Journal of Marital & Family Therapy, 35*(1), 111–124.

Ceelen, M., van Weissenbruch, M. M., Vermeiden, J. P.W., van Leeuwen, F. E., & Delemarre-van de Waal, H. A. (2008). Growth and development of children born after in vitro fertilization. *Fertility and Sterility, 90*(5), 1662–1673.

Center for Economic and Policy Research. (2009). *Parental leave policies in 21 countries.* Washington, DC: Author.

Center for Human Reproduction. (2013a). *Male infertility.* Retrieved from http://www.centerforhumanreprod.com/male_infertility.html

Center for Human Reproduction. (2013b). *IVF success rates.* Retrieved from https://www.centerforhumanreprod.com/ivf-success-rates.html

Centers for Disease Control and Prevention. (2011). *Diagnosis during pregnancy: Prenatal testing.* Retrieved from http://www.cdc.gov/ncbddd/birthdefects/diagnosis.html

Centers for Disease Control and Prevention. (2012a). *Sexual risk behavior: HIV, STD, & teen pregnancy prevention.* Retrieved from http://www.cdc.gov/HealthyYouth/sexualbehaviors

Centers for Disease Control and Prevention. (2012b). *2011 YRBS results: Sexual behaviors that contribute to unintended pregnancy and sexually transmitted diseases, including HIV infection.* Retrieved from www.cdc.gov/healthyyouth/yrbs/slides/sexual_slides_yrbs.ppt

Centers for Disease Control and Prevention. (2012c). Abortion surveillance—United States, 2009. *Morbidity and Mortality Weekly Report (MMWR), 61*(SS-8), 1–44.

Centers for Disease Control and Prevention. (2012d). *Developmental monitoring and screening*. Retrieved from http://www.cdc.gov/ncbddd/childdevelopment/screening.html

Centers for Disease Control and Prevention. (2012e). *Sexually transmitted disease surveillance 2011*. Retrieved from http://www.cdc.gov/std/stats11/surv2011.pdf

Centers for Disease Control and Prevention. (2013a). *Injury prevention & control: Traumatic brain injury*. Retrieved from http://www.cdc.gov/traumaticbraininjury

Centers for Disease Control and Prevention. (2013b). *Diagnoses of HIV infection in the United States and dependent areas, 2011. HIV Surveillance Report: Vol. 23*. Retrieved from http://www.cdc.gov/hiv/library/reports/surveillance/2011/surveillance_Report_vol_23.html

Centers for Disease Control and Prevention. (2013c). *HIV in the United States: At a glance*. Retrieved from http://www.cdc.gov/hiv/statistics/basics/ataglance.html

Centers for Disease Control and Prevention. (2013d). CDC health disparities and inequalities report—United States, 2013. *Morbidity and Mortality Weekly Report, 62*(Suppl. 3), 1–187.

Centers for Disease Control and Prevention. (2013e). *FastStats: Infertility*. Retrieved from http://www.cdc.gov/nchs/fastats/fertile.htm

Centers for Disease Control and Prevention. (2013f). *What is ART?* Retrieved from http://www.cdc.gov/art

Centers for Disease Control and Prevention. (2013g). *Prematurity campaign*. Retrieved from http://www.marchofdimes.com/mission/the-economic-and-societal-costs.aspx

Centers for Disease Control and Prevention. (2013h). *QuickStats: Infant mortality rates, by race and Hispanic ethnicity of mother—United States, 2000, 2005, and 2009*. Retrieved from http://www.cdc.gov/mmwr/preview/mmwrhtml/mm6205a6.htm

Centers for Disease Control and Prevention. (2013i). *Child maltreatment: Consequences*. Retrieved from http://www.cdc.gov/violenceprevention/childmaltreatment/consequences.html

Centers for Disease Control and Prevention. (2013j). *Attention deficit hyperactivity disorder: Data and statistics*. Retrieved from http://www.cdc.gov/ncbddd/adhd/data.html

Centers for Disease Control and Prevention. (2013k). *Autism spectrum disorders: Data and statistics*. Retrieved from http://www.cdc.gov/ncbddd/autism/data.html

Centers for Disease Control and Prevention. (2013l). Homicide rates among persons aged 10–24 years—United States 1981–2010. *Morbidity and Mortality Weekly Report (MMWR), 62*(27), 545–548.

Centers for Disease Control and Prevention. (2013m). *The state of aging and health in America 2013*. Atlanta, GA: Centers for Disease Control and Prevention, U.S. Department of Health and Human Services.

Centers for Disease Control and Prevention. (2013n). *Childhood obesity facts*. Retrieved from http://www.cdc.gov/healthyyouth/obesity/facts.htm

Centers for Disease Control and Prevention. (2014a). *Breastfeeding report card: United States/2014*. Retrieved from http://www.cdc.gov/breastfeeding/pdf/2014breastfeedingreportcard.pdf

Centers for Disease Control and Prevention. (2014b). *Youth suicide*. Retrieved from http://www.cdc.gov/violenceprevention/pub/youth_suicide.html

Centers for Disease Control and Prevention. (2015a). *Key statistics for the National Survey of Family Growth (2011–2013)*. Retrieved from http://www.cdc.gov/nchs/nsfg/key_statistics/c.htm#currentuse

Centers for Disease Control and Prevention. (2015b). *Contraception: How effective are birth control methods?* Retrieved from http://www.cdc.gov/reproductivehealth/unintendedpregnancy/contraception.htm

Centers for Medicare and Medicaid Services. (2012). *Strong start for mothers and newborns*. Retrieved from http://innovations.cms.gov/initiatives/strong-start/index.html

Central Intelligence Agency. (2012). *The world factbook* (Chapter 11). Retrieved from http://www.cia.gov/library/publications/the-world-factbook

Central Intelligence Agency. (2013a). *The world factbook: Country comparison: Distribution of income: Gini index*. Retrieved from https://www.cia.gov/library/publications/the-world-factbook/rankorder/2172rank.html

Central Intelligence Agency. (2013b). *The world factbook: Country comparison: Life expectancy at birth*. Retrieved from https://www.cia.gov/library/publications/the-world-factbook/rankorder/2012rank.html

Central Intelligence Agency. (2013c). *The world factbook*. Retrieved from https://www.cia.gov/library/publications/the-world-factbook/fields/2177.html

Cervigni, F., Suzuki, Y., Ishii, T., & Hata, A. (2008). Spatial accessibility to pediatric services. *Journal of Community Health, 33*, 444–448.

Chamie, J., & Mirkin, B. (2011). Same-sex marriage: A new social phenomenon. *Population and Development Review, 37*(3), 529–551.

Chamiec-Chase, R. (2009). Developing a scale to measure social workers' integration of spirituality in the workplace. *Journal of Religion & Spirituality in Social Work, 28*(3), 284–305.

Chan, A., Malhotra, C., Malhotra, R., Rush, A., & Ostbye, T. (2013). Health impacts of caregiving for older adults with functional limitations: Results from Singapore survey on informal caregiving. *Journal of Aging and Health, 25*(6), 998–1012.

Chang, L. (2001). The development of racial attitudes and self-concepts of Taiwanese preschoolers (China). *Dissertation Abstracts International: Section A: Humanities & Social Sciences, 61*(8-A), 3045.

Chang, Y., & Schneider, J. (2010). Decision-making process of nursing home placement among Chinese family caregivers. *Perspectives in Psychiatric Care, 46*(2), 108–118.

Chapin, L., & Altenhofen, S. (2010). Neurocognitive perspectives in language outcomes of Early Head Start: Language and cognitive stimulation and maternal depression. *Infant Mental Health Journal, 31*(5), 486–498.

Chapman, M. V., & Perreira, K. M. (2005). The well-being of immigrant Latino youth: A framework to inform practice. *Families in Society, 86*, 104–111.

Charles, P., & Perreira, K. (2007). Intimate partner violence during pregnancy and 1-year post-partum. *Journal of Family Violence, 22*(7), 609–619.

Charlesworth, L. (2007). Child maltreatment. In E. Hutchison, H. Matto, M. Harrigan, L. Charlesworth, & P. Viggiani (Eds.), *Challenges of living: A multidimensional working model for social workers* (pp. 105–139). Thousand Oaks, CA: Sage.

Charon, J. (1998). *Symbolic interactionism: An introduction, an interpretation, and integration* (6th ed.). Englewood Cliffs, NJ: Prentice Hall.

Chen, X. (2009). The linkage between deviant lifestyles and victimization: An examination from a life course perspective. *Journal of Interpersonal Violence, 24*(7), 1083–1110.

Cheng, J., & Monroe, M. (2012). Connection to nature: Children's affective attitude toward nature. *Environment and Behavior, 44*(1), 31–49.

Cherlin, A. J. (2010). Demographic trends in the United States: A review of research in the 2000s. *Journal of Marriage and Family, 72*, 403–419.

Chesney-Lind, M., & Jones, N. (2010). *Fighting for girls: New perspectives on gender and violence*. Albany, NY: State University of New York Press.

Chibucos, T., & Leite, R. (2005). *Readings in family theory*. Thousand Oaks, CA: Sage.

Child Trends. (2013a). *Food insecurity*. Retrieved from http://www.childtrends.org?indicators=food-insecurity

Child Trends. (2013b). *Family structure: Indicators on children and youth*. Retrieved from www.childtrends.org/?indicators=family-structure

Child Trends Data Bank. (2013). *Low and very low birth weight infants: Indicators on children and youth*. Retrieved from http://www.childtrends.org/wp-content/uploads/2012/11/57_Low_Birth_Weight.pdf

Child Welfare Information Gateway. (2011). *How many children were adopted in 2007 and 2008?* Washington, DC: U.S. Department of Health and Human Services. Retrieved from https://www.childwelfare.gov/pubs/adopted0708.pdf

Child Welfare Information Gateway. (2016). *Foster care statistics 2014*. Retrieved from https://www.childwelfare.gov/pubs/factsheets/foster

Children's Defense Fund. (2012). *The state of America's children handbook of 2012*. Retrieved from http://www.childrensdefense.org/library/data/soac-2012-handbook.pdf

Children's Defense Fund. (2013). *Children in the United States*. Retrieved from www.childrensdefense.org/child-research-data-publications/data/state-data-repository/cits/2013/2013-united-states-children-in-the-states/pdf

Children's Therapy & Family Resource Centre. (2015a). *Toddler developmental milestones: Gross motor skills*. Retrieved from http://www.kamloppschildrenstherapy.org/gross-motor-skills-milestones-toddler

Children's Therapy & Family Resource Centre. (2015b). *Toddler developmental milestones: Fine motor skills*. Retrieved from http://www.kamloopschildrenstherapy.org/fine-motor-skills-toddler-milestones

Chodorow, N. (1991). *Feminism and psychoanalytic theory*. New Haven, CT: Yale University Press.

Chodorow, N. (1999). *The reproduction of mothering: Psychoanalysis and the sociology of gender*. Berkeley, CA: University of California Press.

Chomsky, N. (1968). *Language and mind*. New York, NY: Harcourt Brace Jovanovich.

Chong, J., Fortier, Y., & Morris, T. L. (2009). Cultural practices and spiritual development for women in a Native American alcohol and drug treatment program. *Journal of Ethnicity in Substance Abuse, 8*(3), 261–282.

Choudhury, S. (2010). Culturing the adolescent brain: What can neuroscience learn from anthropology? *SCAN, 5*, 159–167.

Christen, M., & Narvaez, D. (2012). Moral development in early childhood is key for moral enhancement. *AJOB Neuroscience, 3*(4), 25–26.

Chugani, H., Behen, M., Muzik, O., Juhasz, C., Nagy, F., & Chugani, D. (2001). Local brain functional activity following early deprivation: A study of post-institutional Romanian orphans. *Neuroimage, 14*, 1290–1301.

Chumlea, W. C., Schubert, C. M., Roche, A. F., Kulin, H. E., Lee, P.A., Himes, J. H., & Sun, S. S. (2003). Age at menarche and racial comparisons in U.S. girls. *Pediatrics, 111*(1), 110–113.

Chung, D. K. (2001). Confucianism. In M.V. Hook, B. Hugen, & M. Aguilar (Eds.), *Spirituality within religious traditions in social work practice* (pp. 73–97). Pacific Grove, CA: Brooks/Cole.

Chung, G., Tucker, M., & Takeuchi, D. (2008). Wives' relative income production and household male dominance: Examining violence among Asian American enduring couples. *Family Relations, 57*, 227–238.

Chung, I. W. (2006). A cultural perspective on emotions and behavior: An empathic pathway to examine intergenerational conflicts in Chinese immigrant families. *Families in Society, 87*(3), 367–376.

Chung, R., Bemak, F., & Grabosky, T. (2011). Multicultural-social justice leadership strategies: Counseling and advocacy with immigrants. *Journal for Social Action in Counseling & Psychology, 3*(1), 86–102.

Cicchetti, D. (2013). Annual research review: Resilient functioning in maltreated children—past, present, and future perspectives. *Journal of Child Psychology & Psychiatry, 54*(4), 402–422. doi:10.1111/j.1469-7610.2012.02608.x

Clammer, J. (2009). Sociology and beyond: Towards a deep sociology. *Asian Journal of Social Science, 37*(3), 332–346.

Clare, R., Mazzucchelli, T., Studman, L., & Sanders, M. (2006). Behavioral family intervention for children with developmental disabilities and behavioral problems. *Journal of Clinical Child and Adolescent Psychology, 35*(2), 180–193.

Clark, C. C. (2002). *Health promotion in communities: Holistic and wellness approaches*. New York, NY: Springer.

Clark, J. L. (2007). Listening for meaning: A research-based model for attending to spirituality, culture, and worldview in social work practice. *Critical Social Work, 7*(1). Retrieved February 26, 2010, from http://www.uwindsor.ca/criticalsocialwork/2006-volume-7-no-1

Clark, K., & Clark, M. (1939). The development of consciousness of self and the emergence of racial identification in Negro preschool children. *Journal of Social Psychology, 10*, 591–599.

Clark, R., Glick, J., & Bures, R. (2009). Immigrant families over the life course. *Journal of Family Issues, 30*(6), 852–872.

Clarke, L. (2008). Grandparents: A family resource? In D. R. Crane & T. Heaton (Eds.), *Handbook of families & poverty* (pp. 365–380). Thousand Oaks, CA: Sage.

Clean Clothes Campaign. (2009, October 5). *Asia wage demand put to Euro retailers*. Retrieved from http://archives.cleanclothes.org/media-inquiries/press-releases/asia-wage-demand-put-to-euro-retailers

Clearfield, M., & Nelson, N. (2006). Sex differences in mothers' speech and play behavior with 6-, 9-, and 14-month-old infants. *Sex Roles, 54*(1/2), 127–137.

Cleland, K., Raymond, E. G., Westley, E., & Trussell, J. (2014). Emergency contraception review: Evidence-based recommendations for clinicians. *Clinical Obstetrics & Gynecology, 57*(4), 741–750.

Cleveland Clinic. (2014). *Pulse and target heart rate*. Retrieved from http://my.clevelandclinic.org/services/heart/prevention/exercise/pulse-target-heart-rate

Clinton, J. (2008). Resilience and recovery. *International Journal of Children's Spirituality, 13*(3), 213–222. doi:10.1080/13644360802236474

Coates, J. (2007). From ecology to spirituality and social justice. In J. Coates, J. R. Graham, B. Swartzentruber, & B. Ouelette (Eds.), *Spirituality and social work: Selected Canadian readings* (pp. 213–227). Toronto, ON: Canadian Scholars' Press.

Cockerham, W. (2012). Current direction in medical sociology. In G. Ritzer (Ed.), *The Blackwell encyclopedia of sociology* (pp. 385–401). Malden, MA: Blackwell.

Cohen, J., & Manning, W. (2010). The relationship context of premarital serial cohabitation. *Social Science Research, 39*, 766–776.

Cohen, J., & Sandy, S. (2007). The social, emotional and academic education of children: Theories, goals, methods and assessments. In R. Bar-On, J. Maree, & M. Elias (Eds.), *Educating people to be emotionally intelligent* (pp. 63–77). Westport, CT: Praeger.

Cohen, P. (2012). *In our prime: The invention of middle age*. New York, NY: Scribner.

Coholic, D. (2011). Exploring how young people living in foster care discuss spiritually sensitive themes in a holistic arts-based group program. *Journal of Religion & Spirituality in Social Work, 30*(3), 193–211.

Coie, J. D., Dodge, K. A., & Coppotelli, H. (1982). Dimensions and types of social status: A cross-age perspective. *Developmental Psychology, 18*, 557–570.

Colby, I. C., Dulmus, C. N., & Sowers, K. M. (2012). *Social work and social policy: Advancing the principles of economic and social justice.* Somerset, NJ: Wiley.

Cole, J., & Durham, D. L. (2008). *Figuring the future: Globalization and the temporalities of children and youth.* Santa Fe, NM: School for Advanced Research Press.

Cole, P., Luby, J., & Sullivan, M. (2008). Emotions and the development of childhood depression: Bridging the gap. *Child Development Perspectives, 2*(3), 141–148.

Coleman, J. (1990). *Foundations of social theory.* Cambridge, MA: Belknap Press.

Coleman, M., Ganong, I., & Warzinik, K. (2007). *Family life in 20th- century America.* Westport, CT: Greenwood.

Coles, L. S. (2013). Validated worldwide supercentenarians, living and recently deceased. *Rejuvenation Research, 16*(1), 82–84.

Coles, R. (1987). *The moral life of children.* Boston, MA: Houghton Mifflin.

Coles, R. (1990). *The spiritual life of children.* Boston, MA: Houghton Mifflin.

Coles, R. (1997). *The moral intelligence of children.* New York, NY: Random House.

Colin, A. A., McEvoy, C., & Castile, R. C. (2010). Respiratory morbidity and lung function in preterm infants of 32 to 36 weeks' gestational age. *Pediatrics, 126*(1), 115–128.

Collado, S., Staats, H., & Corraliza, J. (2013). Experiencing nature in children's summer camps: Affective, cognitive and behavioral consequences. *Journal of Environmental Psychology, 33*, 37–44.

Colle, L., & Del Giudice, M. (2011). Patterns of attachment and emotional competence in middle childhood. *Social Development, 20*(1), 51–72.

Collins, G. (2009). *When everything changed: The amazing journey of American women from 1960 to the present.* New York, NY: Little, Brown.

Collins, P. H. (2000). It's all in the family: Intersections of gender, race, and nation. In U. Narayan & S. Harding (Eds.), *Decentering the center: Philosophy for a multicultural, postcolonial, and feminist world* (pp. 156–176). Bloomington, IN: Indiana University Press.

Collins, P. H. (2012). Looking back, moving ahead: Scholarship in service to social justice. *Gender & Society, 26*, 14–22.

Collins, R. (2004). *Interaction ritual chains.* Princeton, NJ: Princeton University Press.

Coltrane, S. (2000). Research on household labor: Modeling and measuring the social embeddedness of routine family work. *Journal of Marriage and the Family, 62*, 1208–1233.

Colver, A., & Longwell, S. (2013). New understanding of adolescent brain development: Relevance to transitional healthcare for young people with long term conditions. *Archives of Disease in Childhood, 98*, 902–907.

Condon, J. (2006). What about Dad? Psychosocial and mental health issues for new fathers. *Australian Family Physician, 35*(9), 690–692.

Conger, R., & Conger, K. (2008). Understanding the processes through which economic hardship influences families and children. In D. R. Crane & T. Heaton (Eds.), *Handbook of families & poverty* (pp. 64–81). Thousand Oaks, CA: Sage.

Conger, R., & Elder, G. (1994). *Linking economic hardship to marital quality and instability. Families in troubled times: Adapting to change in rural America.* New York, NY: Aldine De Gruyter.

Conger, R., Wallace, L., Sun, Y., Simons, R., McLoyed, V., & Brody, G. (2002). Economic pressure in African American families: A replication and extension of the family stress model. *Developmental Psychology, 38*, 179–193.

Congress.gov. (2013). *S.252. PREEMIE Reauthorization Act.* Retrieved from http://beta.congress.gov/bill/113th-congress/senate-bill/252

Conrad, P. (2007). *The medicalization of society: On the transformation of human conditions into treatable disorders.* Baltimore, MD: Johns Hopkins University Press.

Constable, R. T. (2006). *School social work: Practice, policy, and research.* Chicago, IL: Lyceum Books.

Cook, K. (Ed.). (1987). *Social exchange theory.* Newbury Park, CA: Sage.

Cook, K., Hardin, R., & Levin, M. (2005). *Cooperation without trust?* New York, NY: Russell Sage Foundation.

Cooley, C. (1964). *Human nature and the social order.* New York, NY: Scribner's. (Original work published 1902)

Cooper, P. G., & RelayHealth (2013). Natural family planning. *CRS-Adult Health Advisor.* Retrieved from http://eds.a.ebscohost.com.proxy.lib.odu.edu/ehost/detail/detail?vid=20&sid=ff7b13ed-7c67-41b1-8a1c-e5e4f8cec223%40sessionmgr4002&hid=4210&bdata=JnNpdGU9ZWhvc3QtbGl2ZSZzY29wZT1zaXRl#AN=36257585&db=hxh

Cooper, S., Bandelow, S., & Nevill, M. (2011). Breakfast consumption and cognitive function in adolescent school children. *Physiology and Behavior, 103*(5), 431–439.

Corbett, J. M. (1997). *Religion in America* (3rd ed.). Upper Saddle River, NJ: Prentice Hall.

Corcoran, J., & Walsh, J. (2010). *Clinical assessment and diagnosis in social work practice* (2nd ed.). New York, NY: Oxford.

Cornwell, B., Laumann, E. O., & Schumm, L. P. (2008). The social connectedness of older adults: A national profile. *American Sociological Review, 73*(2), 185–203.

Corsaro, W. (2011). *The sociology of childhood* (3rd ed.). Los Angeles, CA: Sage.

Cortright, B. (1997). *Psychotherapy and spirit: Theory and practice in transpersonal psychotherapy.* Albany, NY: SUNY Press.

Coser, L. (1956). *The functions of conflict.* New York, NY: Free Press.

Costa, P., Terracciano, A., & McCrae, R. (2001). Gender differences in personality traits across cultures: Robust and surprising findings. *Journal of Personality and Social Psychology, 81*(2), 322.

Costas, O. E. (1991). Hispanic theology in North America. In L. M. Getz & R. O. Costa (Eds.), *Strategies for solidarity: Liberation theologies in tension* (pp. 63–74). Minneapolis, MN: Fortress Press.

Costigan, C., & Dokis, D. (2006). Similarities and differences in acculturation among mothers, fathers, and children in immigrant Chinese families. *Journal of Cross-Cultural Psychology, 37*, 723–741.

Costigan, C., Su, T., & Hua, J. (2009). Ethnic identity among Chinese Canadian youth: A review of the Canadian literature. *Canadian Psychology, 50*(4), 261–272.

Coulton, C., Jennings, M. Z., & Chan, T. (2013). How big is my neighborhood? Individual and contextual effects on perceptions of neighborhood scale. *American Journal of Community Psychology, 51*, 140–150.

Council for a Parliament of the World's Religions. (2015). *About us.* Retrieved from http://www.parliamentofreligions.org/index.cfm?n=1

Council on Social Work Education. (2015). *Educational policy.* Alexandria, VA: Author.

Courage, M., & Howe, M. (2010). To watch or not to watch: Infants and toddlers in a brave new electronic world. *Developmental Review, 30*, 101–115.

Courage, M., & Setliff, A. (2009). Debating the impact of television and video material on very young children: Attention, learning, and the developing brain. *Child Development Perspectives, 3*(1), 72–78.

Cousins, L. (1994). *Community high: The complexity of race and class in a Black urban high school* (Unpublished doctoral dissertation). University of Michigan, Ann Arbor.

Cousins, L. (2013). Deservingness, children in poverty, and collective well being. *Children and Youth Services Review, 35*, 1252–1259.
Cowley, A. S. (1993). Transpersonal social work: A theory for the 1990s. *Social Work, 38*, 527–534.
Cowley, A. S. (1996). Transpersonal social work. In F. J. Turner (Ed.), *Social work treatment: Interlocking theoretical approaches* (4th ed., pp. 663–698). New York, NY: Free Press.
Cowley, A. S. (1999). Transpersonal theory and social work practice with couples and families. *Journal of Family Social Work, 3*(20), 5–21.
Cowley, A. S., & Derezotes, D. (1994). Transpersonal psychology and social work education. *Journal of Social Work Education, 30*, 32–39.
Cox, D., & Pawar, M. (2013). *International social work: Issues, strategies, and programs* (2nd ed.). Thousand Oaks, CA: Sage.
Cox, G. R. (2009). Death, dying, and end of life in American-Indian communities. In D. J. Doka & A. S. Tucci (Eds.), *Living with grief: Diversity and end-of-life care* (pp. 107–115). Washington, DC: Hospice Foundation of America.
Cox, K. (2000). Parenting the second time around for parents in recovery: Parenting class using the twelve-step recovery model. *Sources, 10*, 11–14.
Cox, T., Jr. (1993). *Cultural diversity in organizations: Theory, research, and practice*. San Francisco, CA: Berrett-Koehler.
Cox, T., Jr. (2001). *Creating a multicultural organization: A strategy for capturing the power of diversity*. San Francisco, CA: Jossey-Bass.
Coyle, J., Nochajski, T., Maguin, E., Safyer, A., DeWit, D., & Macdonald, S. (2009). An exploratory study of the nature of family resilience in families affected by parental alcohol abuse. *Journal of Family Issues, 30*(12), 1606–1623.
Coyne, R. (2014). *Group work leadership: An introduction for helpers*. Los Angeles, CA: Sage.
Cozolino, L. (2014). *The neuroscience of human relationships: Attachment and the developing social brain* (2nd ed.). New York, NY: W.W. Norton & Company.
Crabtree, S. A., Husain, F., & Spalek, B. (2008). *Islam and social work: Debating values, transforming practice*. Bristol, UK: Policy Press.
Crain, R. (1996). The influences of age, race, and gender on child and adolescent multidimensional self-concept. In B. Bracken (Ed.), *Handbook of self-concept* (pp. 395–420). New York, NY: Wiley.
Crawley, L., Payne, R., Bolden, J., Payne, T., Washington, P., & Williams, S. (2000). Palliative and end-of-life care in the African American community. *Journal of the American Medical Association, 284*(19), 2518–2521.
Cressey, T., & Lallemant, M. (2007). Pharmacogenetics of antiretroviral drugs for the treatment of HIV-infected patients: An update. *Infection, Genetics and Evolution, 7*(2), 333–342.
Crisp, B. (2010). *Spirituality and social work*. Burlington, VT: Ashgate.
Croghan, C., Moone, R., & Olson, A. (2014). Friends, family, and caregiving among midlife and older lesbian, gay, bisexual, and transgender adults. *Journal of Homosexuality, 61*, 79–102.
Cromley, T., Neumark-Sztainer, D., Story, M., & Boutelle, K. (2010). Parent and family associations with weight-related behaviors and cognitions among overweight adolescents. *Journal of Adolescent Health, 47*(3), 263–269.
Cronley, C. (2010). Unraveling the social construction of homelessness. *Journal of Human Behavior in the Social Environment, 20*(2), 319–333.
Crook, W. (2001). Trickle-down bureaucracy: Does the organization affect client responses to programs? *Administration in Social Work, 26*(1), 37–59.
Cross, W., Parham, T., & Black, E. (1991). The stages of Black identity development: Nigrescence models. In R. Jones (Ed.), *Black psychology* (3rd ed., pp. 319–338). Berkeley, CA: Cobb & Henry.
Croteau, D., Hoynes, W., & Milan, S. (2012). *Media/society* (4th ed.). Los Angeles, CA: Sage.
Crouse, J. S. (2010). *Children at risk: The precarious state of children's well-being in America*. New Brunswick, NJ: Transaction.
CTParenting.com. (2014). *Toddler cognitive development—Thinking and problem-solving*. Retrieved from http://www.ctparenting.com/toddlercognitivedevelopmentthinking.php
Cuba, L., & Hummon, D. (1993). A place to call home: Identification with dwelling, community, and region. *Sociological Quarterly, 34*(1), 111–131.
Culp, R., McDonald Culp, A., Dengler, B., & Maisano, P. (1999). First-time young mothers living in rural communities use of corporal punishment with their toddlers. *Journal of Community Psychology, 27*(4), 503–509.
Cumming, E., & Henry, W. (1961). *Growing old*. New York, NY: Basic Books.
Curra, J. (2011). *The relativity of deviance*. Thousand Oaks, CA: Pine Forge Press.
Czarniawska, B. (2007). Has organization theory a tomorrow? *Organization Studies, 28*, 27–29.
Dahlberg, G., Moss, P., & Pence, A. (2007). *Beyond quality in early childhood education and care: Postmodern perspectives* (2nd ed.). New York, NY: Routledge Falmer.
Daniels, K., Daugherty, J., & Jones, J. (2014). Current contraceptive status among women aged 15–44: United States, 2011–2013. *NCHS Data Brief, 173*. Retrieved from http://www.cdc.gov/nchs/data/databriefs/db173.pdf
Dannefer, D. (2003a). Toward a global geography of the life course: Challenges of late modernity for life course theory. In J. Mortimer & M. Shanahan (Eds.), *Handbook of the life course* (pp. 647–659). New York, NY: Kluwer Academic/Plenum.
Dannefer, D. (2003b). Whose life course is it, anyway? Diversity and "linked lives" in global perspective. In R. Settersten, Jr. (Ed.), *Invitation to the life course: Toward new understandings of later life* (pp. 259–268). Amityville, NY: Baywood.
Dannefer, D. (2003c). Cumulative advantage/disadvantage and the life course: Cross-fertilizing age and social science theory. *Journal of Gerontology: Social Sciences, 58B*, S327–S337.
Danziger, S., & Ratner, D. (2010). Labor market outcomes and the transition to adulthood. *The Future of Children, 20*(1), 133–158.
Darling-Hammond, L. (2010). *The flat world and education: How America's commitment to equity will determine our future*. New York, NY: Teachers College Press.
Datar, A., Liu, J., Linnemayr, S., & Stecher, C. (2013). The impact of natural disasters on child health and investments in rural India. *Social Science & Medicine, 76*, 83–91.
Davidson, J., Moore, N., & Ullstrup, L. (2004). Religiosity and sexual responsibilities: Relationships of choice. *Journal of Health Behavior, 28*(4), 335–346.
Davidson, R. J., & Begley, S. (2012). *The emotional life of your brain*. New York, NY: Plume.
Davidson, R. J., Kabat-Zinn, J., Schumacher, J., Rosenkranz, M., Muller, D., Santorelli, S. F., . . . Sheridan, J. F. (2003). Alterations in brain and immune function produced by mindfulness meditation. *Psychosomatic Medicine, 65*(4), 564–570.
Davies, D. (2011). *Child development: A practitioner's guide* (3rd ed.). New York, NY: Guilford.
Davies, S. (2006). *Challenging gender norms: Five genders among the Bugis in Indonesia*. Belmont, CA: Wadsworth.
Davis, G., McAdam, D., Scott, W. R., & Zald, M. (2005). *Social movements and organization theory*. Cambridge, UK: Cambridge University Press.
Davis, J., & Bauman, K. (2013). *School enrollment in the United States: 2011*. U.S. Census Bureau. Retrieved from

www.census.gov/prod/2013pubs/p20-571.pdf
Davis, M. (2006). *Planet of slums*. London, UK: Verso.
Day, P., & Schuler, D. (2004). *Community practice in the network society: Local action/global interaction*. New York, NY: Routledge.
Dean, R. G. (1993). Teaching a constructivist approach to clinical practice. In J. Laird (Ed.), *Revisioning social work education: A social constructionist approach* (pp. 55–75). New York, NY: Haworth Press.
Dean, R. G. (2001). The myth of cross-cultural competence. *Families in Society, 82*(6), 623–630.
Deater-Deckard, K. (2004). *Parenting stress*. New Haven, CT: Yale University Press.
deBoer, A., van Buel, E., & Horst, G. (2012). Love is more than just a kiss: A neurobiological perspective on love and affection. *Neuroscience, 201*, 114–124.
De Brucker, M., Haentjens, P., Evenepoel, J., Devroey, P., Collins, J., & Tournaye, H. (2009). Cumulative delivery rates in different age groups after artificial insemination with donor sperm. *Human Reproduction, 24*(8), 1891–1899.
Declercq, E. (2012). Trends in midwife attended births in the United States, 1989–2009. *Journal of Midwifery and Women's Health, 57*(4), 321–326.
Declercq, E., Sakala, C., Corry, M., Applebaum, S., & Herrlich, A. (2013). *Listening to mothers III: Pregnancy and birth*. New York, NY: Childbirth Connection.
Deeg, D. (2005). The development of physical and mental health from late midlife to early old age. In S. Willis & M. Martin (Eds.), *Middle adulthood: A lifespan perspective* (pp. 209–241). Thousand Oaks, CA: Sage.
Degges-White, S. (2005). Understanding gerotranscendence in older adults: A new perspective for counselors. *Adultspan Journal, 4*(1), 36–48.
Degner, J., & Wentura, D. (2010). Automatic prejudice in childhood and early adolescence. *Journal of Personality and Social Psychology, 98*(3), 356–374.
Delany, S., with Hearth, A. (1997). *On my own at 107: Reflections on life without Bessie*. New York, NY: HarperCollins.
Delaunay-El Allam, M., Marlier, L., & Schaal, B. (2006). Learning at the breast: Preference formation for the artificial scent and its attraction against the odor of maternal milk. *Infant Behavior and Development, 29*(3), 308–321.
Delgado, M. (1988). Groups in Puerto Rican spiritism: Implications for clinicians. In C. Jacobs & D. D. Bowles (Eds.), *Ethnicity and race: Critical concepts in social work* (pp. 34–37). Silver Spring, MD: NASW Press.
Delgado, M., & Staples, L. (2013). Youth-led organizing, community engagement, and opportunity creation. In M. Weil, M. Reisch, & M. Ohmer (Eds.), *The handbook of community practice* (2nd ed., pp. 547–565). Los Angeles, CA: Sage.
Dell'Amore, C. (2012, February 29). Women can make new eggs after all, stem-cell study hints finding may one day help delay menopause, improve fertility. *National Geographic News*. Retrieved from http://news.nationalgeographic.com/news/2012/02/120229-women-health-ovaries-eggs-reproduction-science
della Porta, D., & Diani, M. (2006). *Social movements: An introduction* (2nd ed.). Malden, MA: Blackwell.
della Porta, D., Kriesi, H., & Rucht, D. (2009). *Social movements in a globalising world*. New York, NY: Palgrave Macmillan.
Dellmann-Jenkins, M., & Blankemeyer, M. (2009). Emerging and young adulthood and caregiving. In K. Shifren (Ed.), *How caregiving affects development: Psychological implications for child, adolescent, and adult caregivers* (pp. 93–117). Washington, DC: American Psychological Association.
Dellmann-Jenkins, M., Blankemeyer, M., & Pinkard, O. (2001). Incorporating the elder caregiving role into the developmental tasks of young adulthood. *International Journal of Aging and Human Development, 52*(1), 1.
De Marco, A. C., & Cosner Berzin, S. (2008). The influence of family economic status on home-leaving patterns during emerging adulthood. *Families in Society, 89*(2), 208–218.
Demo, D., & Fine, M. (2010). *Beyond the average divorce*. Thousand Oaks, CA: Sage.
DeNavas-Walt, C., Proctor, B., & Hill Lee, C. (2006). *Income, poverty, and health insurance coverage in the United States: 2005*. Washington, DC: U.S. Census Bureau.
DeNavas-Walt, C., Proctor, B., & Smith, J. (2013). *Income, poverty, and health insurance coverage in the United States: 2012*. Washington, DC: U.S. Census Bureau.
Deng, J., Lian, Y., Shen, C., Zhang, M., Wang, Y., & Zhou, H. (2012). Adverse life event and risk of cognitive impairment: A 5-year prospective longitudinal study in Chongqing, China. *European Journal of Neurology, 19*(4), 631–637.
Denner, J., & Dunbar, N. (2004). Negotiating femininity: Power and strategies of Mexican American girls. *Sex Roles, 50*, 301–314.
Dennis, C., & Chung-Lee, L. (2006). Postpartum depression help-seeking barriers and maternal treatment preferences: A qualitative systematic review. *Birth, 33*(4), 323–331.
Dennison, B., Edmunds, L., & Stratton, H. (2006). Rapid infant weight gain predicts childhood overweight. *Obesity, 14*(3), 491–499.
Denton, M. L., Pearce, L. D., & Smith, C. (2008). *Religion and spirituality on the path through adolescence* (Research report No. 8). National Study of Youth and Religion, University of North Carolina at Chapel Hill. Retrieved from www.youothandreligion.org/sites/youthandreligion.org/files/imported/publication/docs/w2_pub_report_final.pdf
DePoy, E., & Gilson, S. F. (2004). *Rethinking disability: Principles for professional and social change*. Belmont, CA: Wadsworth.
DePoy, E., & Gilson, S. F. (2007). *The human experience: Description, explanation, and judgment*. New York, NY: Rowman & Littlefield.
DePoy, E., & Gilson, S. F. (2011). *Studying disability: Multiple theories and responses*. Thousand Oaks, CA: Sage.
DePoy, E., & Gilson, S. F. (2012). *Human behavior theory and applications: A critical thinking approach*. Thousand Oaks, CA: Sage.
Derezotes, D., Testa, M., & Poertner, J. (2005). *Race matters in child welfare: The overrepresentation of African American children in the system*. Washington, DC: CWLA Press.
Derezotes, D. S. (2001). Transpersonal social work with couples: A compatibility-intimacy model. In E. R. Canda & E. D. Smith (Eds.), *Transpersonal perspectives on spirituality in social work* (pp. 163–174). Binghamton, NY: Haworth Press.
Derezotes, D. S. (2006). *Spiritually oriented social work practice*. Boston, MA: Pearson.
DeSpelder, L. A., & Strickland, A. L. (2005). *The last dance: Encountering death and dying* (7th ed.). Boston, MA: McGraw-Hill.
de St. Aubin, E., McAdams, D., & Kim, T. (2004). *The generative society: Caring for future generations*. Washington, DC: American Psychological Association.
Destefanis, J., & Firchow, N. (2013). *Developmental milestones: Ages 3 through 5*. Retrieved from http://www.greatschools.org/special-education/health/724-devel opmental-milestones-ages-3-through-5.gs?page=all
Devereux, E. (2013). *Understanding the media* (3rd ed.). Thousand Oaks, CA: Sage.
DeVries, C., & De Vries, R. (2007). Childbirth education in the 21st century: An immodest proposal. *Journal of Perinatal Education, 16*(4), 38–48.

Dewey, D., Creighton, D., Heath, J. A., Wilson, B. N., Anseeuw-Deks, D., Crawford, S. G., Sauve, R. (2011). Assessment of developmental coordination in children born with extremely low birth weights. *Developmental Neuropsychology, 36*(1), 42–56.

Diamond, L. M., & Fagundes, C. P. (2010). Psychobiological research on attachment. *Journal of Social and Personal Relationships, 27*(2), 218–225.

Diamond, L. M., & Savin-Williams, R. C. (2003). Gender and sexual identity. In R. M. Lerner, F. Jacobs, & D. Wertlieb (Eds.), *Handbook of applied developmental science* (Vol. 1, pp. 101–121). Thousand Oaks, CA: Sage.

Dick-Read, G. (1944). *Childbirth without fear: Principles and practices of natural childbirth*. New York, NY: Harper & Row.

Dillon, M., & Wink, P. (2007). *In the course of a lifetime: Tracing religious belief, practice, and change*. Berkeley, CA: University of California Press.

DiNitto, D. M. (2011). *Social welfare: Politics and public policy*. Boston, MA: Allyn & Bacon.

Dioussé, L., Driver, J., & Gaziano, J. (2009). Relation between modifiable lifestyle factors and lifetime risk of heart failure. *Journal of American Medical Association, 302*(4), 394–400.

DiPrete, T., Gelman, A., McCormick, T., Teitler, J., & Zheng, T. (2011). Segregation in social networks based on acquaintanceship and trust. *American Journal of Sociology, 116*(4), 1234–1283.

Direnfeld, D., & Roberts, J. (2006). Mood congruent memory in dysphoria: The roles of state affect and cognitive style. *Behavior Research and Therapy, 44*(9), 1275–1285.

Disabled Peoples' International. (2013). *About us*. Retrieved from http://dpi.org/AboutUs

Dittmann-Kohli, F. (2005). Middle age and identity in a cultural and lifespan perspective. In S. Willis & M. Martin (Eds.), *Middle adulthood: A lifespan perspective* (pp. 319–353). Thousand Oaks, CA: Sage.

divorcesource.com. (n.d.). *U.S. divorce rates and statistics*. Retrieved from http://www.divorcesource.com/ds/main/u-s-divorce-rates-and-statiscs-1037.shtml

Dixon, J., Dogan, R., & Sanderson, A. (2005). Community and communitarianism: A philosophical investigation. *Community Development Journal, 40*(1), 4–16.

Doka, K. J., & Tucci, A. S. (2009). *Living with grief: Diversity and end-of-life care*. Washington, DC: Hospice Foundation of America.

Domenech Rodriguez, M., Donovick, M., & Crowley, S. (2009). Parenting styles in a cultural context: Observations of "protective parenting" in first-generation Latinos. *Family Process, 48*(2), 195–210.

Dominelli, L. (2012). *Green social work: From environmental crises to environmental justice*. Cambridge, UK: Polity Press.

Donleavy, G. (2008). No man's land: Exploring the space between Gilligan and Kohlberg. *Journal of Business Ethics, 80*, 807–822.

Doughty, E. A. (2009). Investigating adaptive grieving styles: A Delphi study. *Death Studies, 33*, 462–480.

Downs, S., Moore, E., & McFadden, E. J. (2010). *Child welfare and family services: Policies and practice*. Boston, MA: Pearson.

Drake, R. E., Mueser, K. T., Brunette, M. F., & McHugo, G. J. (2004). A review of treatments for people with severe mental illnesses and co-occurring substance use disorders. *Psychiatric Rehabilitation Journal, 27*(4), 360.

Draut, T. (2005). *Strapped: Why America's 20- and 30-somethings can't get ahead*. Garden City, NY: Doubleday.

Drehmer, M., Duncan, B. B., Kac, G., & Schmidt, A. I. (2013). Association of second and third trimester weight gain in pregnancy with maternal and fetal outcomes. *PLoS One, 8*(1), 1–8.

Drescher, K. D, Burgoyne, M., Casas, E., Lovato, L., Curran, E., Pivar, I., & Foy, D. W. (2009). Issues of grief, loss, honor, and remembrance: Spirituality and work with military personnel and their families. In S. M. Freeman, B. A. Moore, & A. Freeman (Eds.), *Living and surviving in harm's way: A psychological treatment handbook for pre- and post-deployment of military personnel* (pp. 437–466). New York, NY: Routledge.

Drosdzol, A., & Skrzypulec, V. (2008). Quality of life and sexual function of Polish infertile couples. *European Journal of Contraceptive and Reproductive Health Care, 13*, 271–281.

Drucker, P. (1954). *The practice of management*. New York, NY: Harper.

Duba, J. D., & Watts, R. E. (2009). Therapy with religious couples. *Journal of Clinical Psychology, 65*(2), 210–223.

DuBois, D., & Silverthorn, N. (2005). Characteristics of natural mentoring relationships and adolescent adjustment: Evidence from a national study. *Journal of Primary Prevention, 26*, 69–92.

Dubrow, N., & Garbarino, J. (1989). Living in the war zone: Mothers and young children in a public housing development. *Child Welfare, 68*, 3–20.

Ducanto, J. N. (2010). Divorce and poverty are often synonymous. *American Journal of Family Law, 24*(2), 87–94.

Dugdale, D. (2012a). Aging changes in the nervous system. *MedlinePlus*. U.S. National Library of Medicine/National Institutes of Health. Retrieved from www.nlm.nih.gov/medlineplus/ency/article/004023.htm

Dugdale, D. (2012b). Aging changes in the heart and blood vessels. *MedlinePlus*. U.S. National Library of Medicine/National Institutes of Health. Retrieved from http://www.nlm.nih.gov/medlineplus/ency/article/004006.htm

Dulin-Keita, A., Hannon, L., III, Fernandez, J. R., & Cockerham, W. C. (2011). The defining moment: Children's conceptualization of race and experiences with racial discrimination. *Ethnic & Racial Studies, 34*(4), 662–682.

Duncan, G. J., & Magnuson, K. (2011, Winter). The long reach of early childhood poverty. *The Stanford Center on Poverty and Inequality Pathways Magazine*, 22–27.

Duncan, G. J., & Murnane, R. J. (2011). *Whither opportunity? Rising inequality, schools, and children's life chances*. New York, NY: Russell Sage Foundation.

Dupre, M. (2008). Educational differences in health risks and illness over the life course: A test of cumulative disadvantage theory. *Social Science Research, 37*, 1253–1266.

Duran, E., & Duran, B. (1995). *Native American postcolonial psychology*. Albany, NY: State University of New York Press.

Durex Network. (2007). *The face of global sex 2007: First sex: An opportunity of a lifetime*. Retrieved from http://www.durexnetwork.org/SiteCollectionDocuments/Research%20-%Face%20of%20Global%20sex%202007.pdf

Durex Network. (2010). *The face of global sex 2010: They won't know unless we tell them*. Retrieved from http://www.durexnetwork.org/SiteCollectionDocuments/The%20Face%20of%20Global20%20sex%202010.pdf

Durkin, K. (1995). *Developmental social psychology*. Malden, MA: Blackwell.

Duvall-Early, K., & Benedict, J. (1992). The relationship between privacy and different components of job satisfaction. *Environment and Behavior, 24*, 670–679.

Dybicz, P. (2011). Anything goes? Science and social constructions in competing discourses. *Journal of Sociology & Social Welfare, 38*(3), 101–122.

Dylan, A., & Coates, J. (2012). The spirituality of justice: Bringing together the eco and the social. *Journal of Religion & Spirituality in Social Work, 31*(1–2), 128–149.

Dyson, A. (2011). Full service and extended schools, disadvantage, and social justice. *Cambridge Journal of Education, 41*(2), 177–193. doi:10.1080/0305764X.2011.572864

Eacott, M., & Easton, A. (2012). Remembering the past and thinking about the future: Is it really about time? *Learning and Motivation, 43*, 200–208.

Eagle, M., & Wolitzky, D. L. (2009). Adult psychotherapy from the perspectives of attachment theory and psychoanalysis. In J. H. Obegi & E. Berant (Eds.), *Attachment theory and research in clinical work with adults* (pp. 351–378). New York, NY: Guilford Press.

Early Intervention Support. (2013). *How children develop*. Retrieved from http://www.earlyinterventionsupport.com/how-children-develop

Eaton, D., Kann, L., Kinchen, S., Shanklin, S., Flint, K., Hawkins, J., . . . Centers for Disease Control and Prevention (CDC). (2012). Youth risk behavior surveillance—United States 2011. *Morbidity and Mortality Weekly Report (MMWR), 61*(4), 1–168.

Eberhard, J. (2008). *Brain landscape: The coexistence of neuroscience and architecture*. New York, NY: Oxford University Press.

Eckerd, A., & Keeler, A. (2012). Going green together? Brownfield remediation and environmental justice. *Policy Science, 45*, 293–314.

Economist Intelligence Unit. (2012). *Starting well: Benchmarking early education across the world*. Retrieved from www.lienfoundaton.org/pdf/publica tons/sw_report.pdf

Edin, K., Kefalas, M., & Reed, J. (2004). A peek inside the black box: What marriage means for poor unmarried parents. *Journal of Marriage and the Family, 66*, 1007–1014.

Edin, K., & Nelson, T. J. (2013). *Doing the best I can: Fatherhood in the inner city*. Berkeley, CA: University of California Press.

Edin, K., & Reed, J. (2005). Why don't they just get married? Barriers to marriage among the disadvantaged. *The Future of Children, 15*(5), 117–137.

Edmiston, B. (2010). Playing with children, answering with our lives: A Bakhtinian approach to coauthoring ethical identities in early childhood. *British Journal of Educational Studies, 58*(2), 197–211.

Edwards, G. (2014). *Social movements and protest*. New York, NY: Cambridge University Press.

Eggerston, L. (2012). Hospital noise: Increasingly, it hinders communication and puts patients at risk. *Canadian Nurse, 108*(4), 28–31.

Egley, A., Jr., & Howell, J. C. (2013, September). *Highlights of the 2011 National Youth Gang Survey*. Washington, DC: U.S. Department of Justice, Office of Justice Programs, Office of Juvenile Justice and Delinquency Prevention. Retrieved from http://www.ojjdp.gov/pubs/242884.pdf

Ehlman, K., & Ligon, M. (2012). The application of a generativity model for older adults. *International Journal of Aging and Human Development, 74*(4), 331–344.

Eidelman, A., & Schanler, R. (2012). Breastfeeding and the use of human milk. *Pediatrics, 129*(5), 827–841.

Eilperin, J. (2016, January 26). Obama bans solitary confinement for juveniles in federal prisons. *The Washington Post*. Retrieved from https://www.washingtonpost.com/politics/obama-bans-solitary-confinement-for-juveniles-in-federal-prisons/2016/01/25/056e14b2-c3a2-11e5-9693-933a4d31bcc8_story.html

Eisenberg, N. (2000). Emotion, regulation, and moral development. *Annual Review of Psychology, 51*, 665–697.

Eisenberg, N., Guthrie, I., Murphy, B., Shepard, S., Cumberland, A., & Carlo, G. (1999). Consistency and development of prosocial dispositions: A longitudinal study. *Child Development, 70*, 1360–1372.

Elder, G. H., Jr. (1974). *Children of the Great Depression: Social change in life experience*. Chicago, IL: University of Chicago Press.

Elder, G., Jr. (1994). Time, human agency, and social change: Perspectives on the life course. *Social Psychology Quarterly, 57*(1), 4–15.

Elder, G., Jr. (1998). The life course as developmental theory. *Child Development, 69*(1), 1–12.

Elder, G. H., Jr., & Giele, J. (Eds.). (2009a). *The craft of life course research*. New York, NY: Guilford Press.

Elder, G., & Giele, J. (2009b). Life course studies: An evolving field. In G. Edler & J. Giele (Eds.), *The craft of life course research* (pp. 1–24). New York, NY: Guilford.

Ellison, C. G., & Levin, J. S. (1998). The religion–health connection: Evidence, theory, and future directions. *Health, Education, and Behavior, 25*(6), 700–720.

Ellison, J. W., & Plaskow, J. (Eds.). (2007). *Heterosexism in contemporary world religion: Problem and prospect*. Cleveland, OH: Pilgrim Press.

Ellison, N., Steinfield, C., & Lampe, C. (2007). The benefits of Facebook "friends": Social capital and college students' use of online social network sites. *Journal of Computer-Mediated Communication, 12*, 1143–1168.

El-Messidi, A., Al-Fozan, H., Lin Tan, S., Farag, R., & Tulandi, T. (2004). Effects of repeated treatment failure on the quality of life of couples with infertility. *Journal of Obstetrics and Gynaecology Canada, 26*, 333–336.

Emery, R. (1999). *Marriage, divorce, and children's adjustment* (2nd ed.). Thousand Oaks, CA: Sage.

Engel, R., & Schutt, R. (2013). *The practice of research in social work* (3rd ed.). Thousand Oaks, CA: Sage.

Engel, S. (2005). *Real kids: Creating meaning in everyday life*. Cambridge, MA: Harvard University Press.

Engels, F. (1892). *The condition of the working class in England in 1844* (F. K. Wischnewtzky, Trans.). London, UK: Sonnenschein.

Engels, F. (1970). *The origins of the family, private property and the state*. New York, NY: International Publishers. (Original work published 1884)

Engels, R., & Knibbe, R. (2000). Alcohol use and intimate relationships in adolescence: When love comes to town. *Addictive Behavior, 25*, 435–439.

Englander, E. K. (2013). *Bullying and cyberbullying: What every educator needs to know*. Cambridge, MA: Harvard University Press.

Entmacher, J., Robbins, K., Vogtman, J., & Fohlich, L. (2013). *Insecure & unequal: Poverty and income among women and families 2000–2012*. Washington, DC: National Women's Law Center. Retrieved from http://www.nwlc.org/sites/default/files/pdfs/fina_2013_nwlc_poverty report.pdf

Entwisle, D., Alexander, K., & Olson, L. (2005). Urban teenagers: Work and dropout. *Youth and Society, 37*, 3–32.

Epstein, S. (1973). The self-concept revisited: Or, a theory of a theory. *American Psychologist, 28*, 404–416.

Epstein, S. (1991). Cognitive-experiential self-theory: An integrative theory of personality. In R. Cutis (Ed.), *The self with others: Convergences in psychoanalytic, social, and personality psychology* (pp. 111–137). New York, NY: Guilford Press.

Epstein, S. (1998). Cognitive-experiential self-theory. In D. Barone & M. Hersen (Eds.), *Advanced personality* (pp. 211–238). New York, NY: Plenum.

Erickson, K., Gildengers, A., & Butters, M. (2013). Physical activity and brain plasticity in late adulthood. *Dialogues in Clinical Neuroscience, 15*(1), 99–108.

Erikson, E. (1950). *Childhood and society*. New York, NY: Norton.

Erikson, E. (1959). The problem of ego identity. *Psychological Issues, 1*, 101–164.

Erikson, E. (1963). *Childhood and society* (2nd ed.). New York, NY: Norton.

Erikson, E. (1968). *Identity: Youth and crisis*. New York, NY: Norton.

Erikson, E. (Ed.). (1978). *Adulthood*. New York, NY: Norton.

Erikson, E. (1982). *The life cycle completed*. New York, NY: Norton.

Erikson, E. H., & Erikson, J. M. (1997). *The life cycle completed: Extended version with new chapters on the ninth stage of development*. New York, NY: W. W. Norton.

Ernst, J. (2000). Mapping child maltreatment: Looking at neighborhoods in a suburban county. *Child Welfare, 79*, 555–572.

Esbjörn-Hargens, S. (Ed.). (2010). *Integral theory in action: Applied, theoretical, and constructive perspectives on the AQAL model*. Albany, NY: SUNY Press.

Espelage, D. L., & Swearer, S. M. (2011). *Bullying in North American schools*. New York, NY: Routledge.

Esposito-Smythers, C., Kahler, C., Spirito, A., Hunt, J., & Monti, P. (2011). Treatment of co-occurring substance abuse and suicidality among adolescents: A randomized trial. *Journal of Consulting and Clinical Psychology, 79*(6), 728–739.

European Commission: Employment, Social Affairs & Inclusion. (2013). *Social protection & social inclusion*. Retrieved from http://ec.europa.eu/social/main.jsp?catId=750

Evans, B., Crogan, N., Belyea, M., & Coon, D. (2009). Utility of the life course perspective in research with Mexican American caregivers of older adults. *Journal of Transcultural Nursing, 20*(1), 5–14.

Evans, C. J., Boustead, R. S., & Owens, C. (2008). Expressions of spirituality in parents with at-risk children. *Families in Society: The Journal of Contemporary Social Services, 89*(2), 245–252.

Evans, G. W., Lepore, S., & Allen, K. (2000). Cross-cultural differences in tolerance for crowding: Fact or fiction? *Journal of Personality and Social Psychology, 79*(2), 204–210.

Evans, G. W., & Saegert, S. (2000). Residential crowding in the context of inner city poverty. In S. Wapner, J. Demick, T. Yamamoto, & H. Minami (Eds.), *Theoretical perspectives in environment-behavior research: Underlying assumptions research problems, and methodologies* (pp. 247–267). New York, NY: Kluwer Academic.

Exner-Cortens, D., Eckenrode, J., & Rothman, E. (2013). Longitudinal associations between teen dating violence victimization and adverse health outcomes. *Pediatrics, 131*(1), 71–78.

Fabelo, T., Thompson, M. D., Plotkin, M., Carmichael, D., Marchbanks, M. P., & Booth, E. A. (2011). *Breaking Schools' rules: A statewide study of how school discipline relates to students' success and juvenile justice involvement*. New York: Council of State Governments Justice Center. Retrieved from http://csgjusticecenter.org/wpcontent/uploads/2012/08/Breaking_Schools_Rules_Report_Final.pdf

Faber, A., Willerton, E., Clymer, S., MacDermid, S., & Weiss, H. (2008). Ambiguous absence, ambiguous presence: A qualitative study of military reserve families in wartime. *Journal of Family Psychology, 22*(2), 222–230.

Fadiman, A. (1998). *The spirit catches you and you fall down: A Hmong child, her American doctors, and the collision of two cultures*. New York, NY: Farrar, Straus and Giroux.

Fairbrother, M., & Martin, I. (2013). Does inequality erode social trust? Results from multilevel models of US states and counties. *Social Science Research, 42*, 347–360.

Falicov, C. (2005). The Latino family life cycle. In B. Carter & M. McGoldrick (Eds.), *The expanded family life cycle: Individual, family, and social perspectives* (3rd ed., pp. 141–152). Boston, MA: Allyn & Bacon.

Falicov, C. (2011). Migration and the life cycle. In M. McGoldrick, B. Carter, & N. Garcia-Preto (Eds.), *The expanded family life cycle: Individual, family, and social perspectives* (4th ed., pp. 336–347). Boston, MA: Allyn & Bacon.

Families USA. (2015). *A 50-state look at Medicaid expansion*. Retrieved from http://familiesusa.org/product/50-state-look-medicaid-expansion

Fan, F., Zou, Y., Ma, A., Yue, Y., Mao, W., & Ma, X. (2009). Hormonal changes and somatopsychologic manifestations in the first trimester of pregnancy and post partum. *International Journal of Gynecology and Obstetrics, 105*(1), 46–49.

Fan, W., Williams, C. M., & Wolters, C. A. (2012). Parental involvement in predicting school motivation: Similar and differential effects across ethnic groups. *Journal of Educational Research, 105*(1), 21–35.

Farmer, R. (2009). *Neuroscience and social work practice: The missing link*. Thousand Oaks, CA: Sage.

Farrelly-Hansen, M. (2009). *Spirituality and art therapy: Living the connection*. London, UK: Jessica Kingsley.

Farroni, T., Menon, E., Rigato, S., & Johnson, M. H. (2007). The perception of facial expressions in newborns. *European Journal of Developmental Psychology, 4*(1), 2–13.

Fass, P., & Mason, M. (Eds.). (2000). *Childhood in America*. New York, NY: New York University Press.

Faver, C. A., & Trachte, B. L. (2005). Religion and spirituality at the border: A survey of Mexican-American social work students. *Social Thought, 24*(4), 3–18.

Federal Bureau of Investigation. (2011). *Crime in the United States 2010*. Uniform Crime Reports. Washington, DC: U.S. Department of Justice. Retrieved from www.fbi.gov/about-us/cjis/ucr/crime-in-the-u.s/2010/crime-in-the-u.s.-2010/index-page

Federal Interagency Forum on Aging-Related Statistics. (2008). *Older Americans 2008: Key indicators of well-being*. Retrieved from http://www.agingstats.gov/agingstatsdotnet/Main_Site/Data/2008_Documents/OA_2008.pdf

Federal Interagency Forum on Aging-Related Statistics. (2012). *Older Americans 2012: Key indicators of well-being: Health status*. Retrieved from www.agingstats.gov/Main_Site/Data/2012_Documents/Health_Status.Aspx

Federal Interagency Forum on Child and Family Statistics. (2013). *America's children: Key national indicators of well-being*. Washington, DC: U.S. Government Printing Office. Retrieved from http://www.childstats.gov/pdf/ac2013/ac_13.pdf

Feldman, R. (1990). Settlement-identity: Psychological bonds with home places in a mobile society. *Environment and Behavior, 22*(2), 183–229.

Feldman, R. (2004). Mother–infant skin-to-skin contact and the development of emotion regulation. In S. Shohov (Ed.), *Advances in psychology research* (Vol. 27, pp. 113–131). Hauppauge, NY: Nova Science.

Felsten, G. (2009). Where to take a study break on college campus: An attention restoration theory perspective. *Journal of Environmental Psychology, 29*, 160–176.

Ferguson, K. M., Wu, Q., Dryrness, G., & Spruijt-Metz, D. (2007). Perceptions of faith and outcomes in faith-based programs for homeless youth: A grounded theory approach. *Journal of Social Service Research, 33*(4), 25–43.

Fergusson, D. M., Horwood, L. J., & Boden, J. (2009). Reactions to abortion and subsequent mental health. *The British Journal of Psychiatry, 195*, 420–426.

Ferraro, K., & Shippee, T. (2009). Aging and cumulative inequality: How does inequality get under the skin? *The Gerontologist, 49*(3), 333–343.

Ferree, M. M., & Martin, P. Y. (1995). *Feminist organizations: Harvest of the new women's movement*. Philadelphia, PA: Temple University Press.

Ferri, C., Prince, M., Brayne, C., Brodaty, H., Fratiglioni, L., Ganguli, M., . . . Alzheimer's Disease International. (2005). Global prevalence of dementia: A Delphi consensus study. *The Lancet, 366*, 2112–2117.

Figueiredo, B., & Conde, A. (2011). Anxiety and depression in women and men from early pregnancy to 3-months postpartum. *Archives of Women's Mental Health, 14*(3), 247–255.

Figueiredo, B., Pacheco, A., Costa, R., Conde, A., & Teixeira, C. (2010). Mother's anxiety and depression during the third pregnancy trimester and neonate's mother versus stranger's face/voice visual preference. *Early Human Development, 86*, 479–485.

Fine, M., Ganong, L., & Demo, D. (2010). Divorce: A risk and resilience perspective. In S. Price, C. Price, & P. McKenry (Eds.), *Families & change: Coping with stressful events and transitions* (4th ed., pp. 211–233). Thousand Oaks, CA: Sage.

Finger, W., & Arnold, E. M. (2002). Mind–body interventions: Applications for social work practice. *Social Work in Health Care, 35*(4), 57–78.

Fingerman, K., Cheng, Y. P., Wesselmann, E., Zarit, S., Furstenberg, F., & Birditt, K. (2013). Helicopter parents and landing pad kids: Intense parental support of grown children. *Journal of Marriage and Family, 74*, 880–896.

Fingerman, K., Pillemer, K., Silverstein, M., & Suitor, J. (2012). The baby boomers' intergenerational relationships. *The Gerontologist, 52*(2), 199–209.

Fingerman, K., VanderDrift, L., Dotterer, A., Birditt, D., & Zarit, S. (2011). Support to aging parents and grown children in Black and White families. *The Gerontologist, 51*(4), 441–452.

Finkelhor, D., Ormrod, R., Turner, H., & Hamby, S. (2005). The victimization of children and youth: A comprehensive national survey. *Child Maltreatment, 10*, 5–25.

Finkelhor, D., Turner, H., Hamby, S., & Ormrod, R. (2011, October). Polyvictimization: Children's exposure to multiple types of violence, crime and abuse. *Juvenile Justice Bulletin*. Retrieved from https://www.ncjrs.gov/pdffiles1/ojjdp/235504.pdf

Finkelhor, D., Turner, H., Ormrod, R., Hamby, S., & Kracke, K. (2009, October). Children's exposure to violence: A comprehensive national survey. *Juvenile Justice Bulletin*. Retrieved from https://www.ncjrs.gov/pdffiles1/ojjdp/227744.pdf

Finn, J. L. (2009). Making trouble. In L. Nybell, J. Shook, & J. Finn (Eds.), *Childhood, youth, and social work in transformation: Implications for policy and practice* (pp. 37–66). New York, NY: Columbia University Press.

Fiori, J. L., Consedine, N. S., & Magai, C. (2008). Ethnic differences in patterns of social exchange among older adults: The role of resource context. *Ageing & Society, 28*, 495–524.

Firestein, S. (2012). *Ignorance: How it drives science*. New York, NY: Oxford University Press.

First Ladies Community Initiative. (2013). *Birth shelter*. Retrieved from www.1stladies.org/programs/birthing-shelter

Fischer, D. (1989). *Albion's seed: Four British folkways in America*. New York, NY: Oxford University Press.

Fischer, J., Lyness, K., & Engler, R. (2010). Families coping with alcohol and substance abuse. In S. Price, C. Price, & P. McKenry (Eds.), *Families & change: Coping with stressful events and transitions* (4th ed., pp. 141–162). Thousand Oaks, CA: Sage.

Fisek, M. H., Berger, J., & Moore, J. (2002). Evaluations, enactment, and expectations. *Social Psychology Quarterly, 65*(4), 329–345.

Fisher, C., Hauck, Y., Bayes, S., & Byme, J. (2012). Participants experience of mindfulness-based childbirth education: A qualitative study. *British Medical Journal, 12*(1), 126–135.

Fisher, H. (2004). *Why we love: The nature and chemistry of romantic love*. New York, NY: Holt.

Fisher, R., & Karger, H. (1997). *Social work and community in a private world*. New York, NY: Longman.

Fisher, R., & Shragge, E. (2000). Challenging community organizing: Facing the 21st century. *Journal of Community Practice, 8*(3), 1–19.

Fitzgerald, J. (1997). Reclaiming the whole: Self, spirit, and society. *Disability and Rehabilitation, 19*(10), 407–413.

Flacks, R. (2004). Knowledge for what? Thoughts on the state of social movement studies. In J. Goodwin & J. Jasper (Eds.), *Rethinking social movements: Structure, meaning, and emotion* (pp. 135–153). Lanham, MD: Rowman & Littlefield.

Flake, E., Davis, B., Johnson, P., & Middleton, L. (2009). The psychosocial effects of deployment on military children. *Journal of Developmental & Behavioral Pediatrics, 30*(4), 271–278.

Flanagan, C. (2004). Institutional support for morality: Community-based and neighborhood organizations. In T. A. Thorkildsen & H. Walberg (Eds.), *Nurturing morality* (pp. 173–183). New York, NY: Kluwer Academic/Plenum.

Flatt, M., Settersten, R., Ponsaran, R., & Fishman, J. (2013). Are "anti-aging medicine" and "successful aging" two sides of the same coin? Views of anti-aging practitioners. *The Journals of Gerontology, Series B: Psychological Sciences and Social Sciences, 68*(6), 944–955.

Floyd, K., & Morman, M. (Eds.). (2006). *Widening the family circle: New research on family communication*. Thousand Oaks, CA: Sage.

Foa, E. B., Keane, T. M., Friedman, M. J., & Cohen, J. A. (2010). *Effective treatments for PTSD: Practice guidelines from the international society for traumatic stress studies*. New York, NY: Guilford.

Fogarty, R. (2009). *Brain compatible classrooms* (3rd ed.). Thousand Oaks, CA: Corwin.

Foley, M. (2011). A comparison of family adversity and family dysfunction in families of children with attention deficit hyperactivity disorder (ADHD) and families of children without ADHD. *Journal for Specialists in Pediatric Nursing, 16*(1), 39–49. doi:10.1111/j.1744-6155.2010.00269.x

Follett, M. P. (1918). *The new state: Group organization, the solution of popular government*. London, UK: Longman, Green.

Follett, M. P. (1924). *Creative experience*. New York, NY: Longman, Green.

Foner, A. (1995). Social stratification. In G. L. Maddox (Ed.), *The encyclopedia of aging: A comprehensive resource in gerontology and geriatrics* (2nd ed., pp. 887–890). New York, NY: Springer.

Fordham, S. (1996). *Blacked out: Dilemmas of race, identity, and success at Capital High*. Chicago, IL: University of Chicago Press.

Forsyth, D. (2011). The nature and significance of groups: In R. Coyne (Ed.), *The Oxford handbook of group counseling* (pp. 19–35). New York, NY: Oxford University Press.

Fowler, J. W. (1981). *Stages of faith: The psychology of human development and the quest for meaning*. San Francisco, CA: Harper.

Fowler, J. W. (1995). *Stages of faith: The psychology of human development and the quest for meaning*. New York, NY: HarperCollins.

Fowler, J. W. (1996). *Faithful change: The personal and public challenges of postmodern life*. Nashville, TN: Abingdon Press.

Fraas, M., & Bellerose, A. (2010). Mentoring programme for adolescent survivors of acquired brain injury. *Brain Injury, 24*(1), 50–61.

Frame, M. W. (2003). *Integrating religion and spirituality into counseling: A comprehensive approach*. Pacific Grove, CA: Brooks/Cole Thompson Learning.

Francescato, D., & Tomai, M. (2001). Community psychology: Should there be a European perspective? *Journal of Community & Applied Social Psychology, 11*, 371–380.

Francis, A. (2013). *Saving normal*. New York, NY: HarperCollins.

Frank, A. (1967). *Capitalism and development in Latin America*. New York, NY: Monthly Review Press.

Frankenberg, E., & Debray, E. H. (2011). *Integrating schools in a changing society: New policies and legal options for a multiracial generation*. Chapel Hill, NC: University of North Carolina Press.

Franklin, R. M. (1994). The safest place on earth: The culture of Black congregations. In J. P. Wind & J. W. Lewis (Eds.), *American congregations* (Vol. 2, pp. 257–260). Chicago, IL: University of Chicago Press.

Franko, D. L., & Striegel-Moore, R. (2002). The role of body dissatisfaction as a risk factor for depression in adolescent girls: Are the differences Black and White? *Journal of Psychosomatic Research, 53*, 975–983.

Franko, D. L., Striegel-Moore, R. H., Thompson, D., Schreiber, G. B., & Daniels, S. R. (2005). Does adolescent depression predict obesity in Black and White young adult women? *Psychological Medicine, 35*, 1505–1513.

Fraser, C., McIntyre, A., & Manby, M. (2009). Exploring the impact of parental drug/alcohol problems on children and parents in a Midlands county in 2005/06. *British Journal of Social Work, 39*, 846–866.

Freedberg, S. (2007). Re-examining empathy: A relational-feminist point of view. *Social Work, 52*(3), 251–259.

Freedom House. (2015a). *2015 Freedom of the Press Data*. Retrieved from http://www.freedomhouse.org/report-types/freedom-press

Freedom House. (2015b). *Freedom on the net 2015*. Retrieved from https://freedomhouse.org/report/freedom-net/freedom-net-2015

Freeman, D. R. (2006). Spirituality in violent and substance-abusing African American men: An untapped resource in healing. *Social Thought, 25*(1), 3–22.

Freeman, E., & Couchonnal, G. (2006). Narrative and culturally based approaches in practice with families. *Families in Society: The Journal of Contemporary Social Services, 87*(2), 198–208.

Freeman, L., Shaffer, D., & Smith, H. (1996). Neglected victims of homicide: The needs of young siblings of murder victims. *American Journal of Orthopsychiatry, 66*, 337–345.

Fremeaux, I. (2005). New Labour's appropriation of the concept of community: A critique. *Community Development Journal, 40*(3), 265–274.

French, S., Seidman, E., Allen, L., & Aber, J. (2006). The development of ethnic identity during adolescence. *Developmental Psychology, 42*, 1–10.

Freud, S. (1927). Some psychological consequences of the anatomical distinction between the sexes. *International Journal of Psycho-Analysis, 8*, 133–142.

Freud, S. (1928). *The future of an illusion*. London, UK: Hogarth Press and Institute of Psychoanalysis.

Freud, S. (1953). Three essays on the theory of sexuality. In J. Strachey (Ed. & Trans.), *The standard edition of the complete psychological works of Sigmund Freud* (Vol. 7, pp. 135–245). London, UK: Hogarth Press. (Original work published 1905)

Freud, S. (1957). Mourning and melancholia. In J. Strachey (Ed. & Trans.), *The standard edition of the complete psychological works of Sigmund Freud* (Vol. 14, pp. 237–258). London, UK: Hogarth. (Original work published 1917)

Freud, S. (1973). *An outline of psychoanalysis*. London, UK: Hogarth Press. (Original work published 1938)

Freud, S. (1978). *The interpretation of dreams* (A. A. Brill, Trans.). New York, NY: Modern Library. (Original work published 1899)

Freund, A. M., & Riediger, M. (2006). Goals as building blocks of personality and development in adulthood. In D. K. Mroczek & T. Little (Eds.), *Handbook of personality development* (pp. 353–372). Mahwah, NJ: Lawrence Erlbaum.

Frey, L., & Sunwolf. (2005). The symbolic-interpretive perspective of group life. In M. Poole & A. Hollingshead (Eds.), *Theories of small groups: Interdisciplinary perspectives* (pp. 185–239). Thousand Oaks, CA: Sage.

Friedman, S. H., & Boyle, D. E. (2008). Attachment in US children experiencing nonmaternal care in the early 1990s. *Attachment & Human Development, 10*(3), 225–261.

Friedman, S. H., Kessler, A. R., & Martin, R. (2009). Psychiatric help for caregivers of infants in neonatal intensive care. *Psychiatric Services, 60*(4), 554.

Friedmann, E., & Havighurst, R. (1954). *The meaning of work and retirement*. Chicago, IL: University of Chicago Press.

Fry, R. (2012). *A rising share of young adults live in their parents' home*. Pew Social Trends. Retrieved from http://www.pewsocialtrends.org/2013/08/01/a-rising-share-of-young-aduls-live-in-their-parents-home

Fuchs, A. (2013). *Nonlinear dynamics in complex systems theory and applications for the life-, neuro- and natural sciences*. New York, NY: Springer.

Fukuyama, M. A., & Sevig, T. D. (1999). *Integrating spirituality into multicultural counseling*. Thousand Oaks, CA: Sage.

Furman, L. E., & Chandy, J. M. (1994). Religion and spirituality: A long-neglected cultural component of rural social work practice. *Human Services in the Rural Environment, 17*(3/4), 21–26.

Gaard, G. (2011). Ecofeminism revisited: Rejecting essentialism and re-placing species in a material feminist environmentalism. *Feminist Formations, 23*(2), 26–53.

Galambos, N., & Kotylak, L. (2012). Transformations in parent-child relationships from adolescence to adulthood. In B. Laursen & W. A. Collins (Eds.), *Relationship pathways from adolescence to young adulthood* (pp. 23–42). Los Angeles, CA: Sage.

Gale, J. (2009). Meditation and relational connectedness: Practices for couples and families. In F. Walsh (Ed.), *Spiritual resources in family therapy* (2nd ed., pp. 247–266). New York, NY: Guilford Press.

Galinsky, E., Aumann, K., & Bond, J. (2011). *Times are changing: Gender and generation at work and at home*. Washington, DC: Families and Work Institute. Retrieved from familiesandwork.org/downloads/TimesAreChanging.pdf

Gallagher, L. (2013). *The end of the suburbs: Where the American dream is moving*. New York, NY: Penguin.

Gallup. (2013). *Abortion. Gallop historical trends*. Retrieved from http://www.gallup.com/poll/1576/abortion.aspx

Gallup. (2014). Religion. Retrieved from http://www.gallup.com/poll/1690/religion.aspx

Gallup, G. H. (2002). *Americans feel need to believe*. Retrieved from http://www.gallup.com/poll/5617/americans-feel-need-believe.aspx

Gallup, G. H., & Lindsay, D. M. (1999). *Surveying the religious landscape: Trends in U.S. beliefs*. Harrisburg, PA: Morehouse.

Galvin, K. (2006). Joined by hearts and words: Adoptive family relationships. In K. Floyd & M. Morman (Eds.), *Widening the family circle: New research on family communication* (pp. 137–152). Thousand Oaks, CA: Sage.

Galvin, K., Bylund, C., & Brommel, B. (2003). *Family communication: Cohesion and change* (6th ed.). New York, NY: Allyn & Bacon.

Galvin, K., Dickson, F., & Marrow, S. (2006). Systems theory: Patterns and wholes in family communication. In D. Braithwaite & L. Baxter (Eds.), *Engaging theories in family communication: Multiple perspectives* (pp. 309–324). Thousand Oaks, CA: Sage.

Gamson, W., & Meyer, D. (1996). Framing political opportunity. In D. McAdam, J. McCarthy, & M. Zald (Eds.), *Comparative perspectives on social movements* (pp. 273–290). New York, NY: Cambridge University Press.

Gannett, L. (2008). The Human Genome Project. *Stanford encyclopedia of philosophy*. Retrieved from http://plato.stanford.edu/entries/human-genome/#BriHisHumGenPro

Garad, R., McNamee, K., Bateson, D., & Harvey, C. (2012). Update on contraception. *Australian Nursing Journal, 20*(4), 34–37. Retrieved from http://eds.a.ebscohost.com.proxy.lib.odu.edu/ehost/pdfviewer/pdfviewer?vid=8&sd=d3435761-6486-48cc-bbd0-f0d56d1daa2e%40sessionmgr4004&hid=4210

Garbarino, J. (1995). *Raising children in a socially toxic environment.* San Francisco, CA: Jossey-Bass.

Garbarino, J. (2007). *See Jane hit: Why girls are growing more violent and what we can do about it.* New York, NY: Penguin Books.

Garcia, B. (2011). Cultural competence with Latino Americans. In D. Lum (Ed.), *Culturally competent practice* (4th ed., pp. 302–332). Belmont, CA: Brooks/Cole.

Garcia, D., & Siddiqui, A. (2009). Adolescents' psychological well-being and memory for life events: Influences on life satisfaction with respect of temperamental dispositions. *Journal of Happiness Studies, 10*(4), 407–419.

Garcia-Preto, N. (2011). Transformation of the family system during adolescence. In M. McGoldrick, B. Carter, & N. Garcia-Preto (Eds.), *The expanded family life cycle: Individual, family, and social perspectives* (4th ed., pp. 232–246). Boston, MA: Allyn & Bacon.

Garcia-Preto, N., & Blacker, L. (2011). Families at midlife: Launching children and moving on. In M. McGoldrick, B. Carter, & N. Garcia-Preto (Eds.), *The expanded family life cycle: Individual, family, and social perspectives* (4th ed., pp. 247–259). Boston, MA: Allyn & Bacon.

Gardiner, H. W., & Kosmitzki, C. (2011). *Lives across cultures: Cross-cultural human development* (5th ed.). Boston, MA: Pearson.

Gardner, H. E. (1993). *Multiple intelligences: The theory in practice.* New York, NY: Basic Books.

Gardner, H. E. (1999). *Intelligence reframed: Multiple intelligences for the 21st century.* New York, NY: Basic Books.

Gardner, H. E. (2006). *Multiple intelligences: New horizons.* New York, NY: Basic Books.

Gargiulo, R. M., & Kilgo, J. L. (2011). *An introduction to young children with special needs: Birth through age 8.* Belmont, CA: Wadsworth/Cengage Learning.

Gariepy, A. M., Creinin, M. D., Smith, K. J., & Xiao, X. (2014). Probability of pregnancy after sterilization: A comparison of hysteroscopic versus laparoscopic sterilization. *Contraception, 90*(2), 174–181.

Garland, D. R., Myers, D. M., & Wolfer, T. A. (2008). Social work with religious volunteers: Activating and sustaining community involvement. *Social Work, 53*(3), 255–265.

Garner, R., & Zald, M. (2012). Now we are almost fifty! Reflections on a theory of the transformation of social movement organizations. *Social Forces, 91*(1), 3–11.

Garner, S. (2014). Contraception update. *Practice Nurse, 44*(6), 24–27.

Garralda, M. E., & Raynaud, J.-P. (2010). *Increasing awareness of child and adolescent mental health.* Lanham, MD: Jason Aronson.

Garrett, B. (2009). *Brain and behavior: An introduction to biological psychology* (2nd ed.). Thousand Oaks, CA: Sage.

Garrett, K. (2004). Use of groups in school social work: Group work and group processes. *Social Work With Groups, 27*(2/3), 75–92.

Garrett, M. W. (1995). Between two worlds: Cultural discontinuity in the dropout of Native American youth. *The School Counselor, 10*, 199–208.

Garrow, E., & Hasenfeld, Y. (2010). Theoretical approaches to human service organizations. In Y. Hasenfeld (Ed.), *Human services as complex organizations* (2nd ed., pp. 33–57). Thousand Oaks, CA: Sage.

Gartstein, M., Gonzales, C., Carranza, J., Adaho, S., Rothbart, M., & Yang, S. (2006). Studying cross-cultural differences in the development of infant temperament: People's Republic of China, the United States of America, and Spain. *Child Psychiatry and Human Development, 37*, 145–161.

Gartstein, M., Knyazev, G., & Slobodskaya, H. (2005). Cross-cultural differences in the structure of temperament: United States of America (U.S.) and Russia. *Infant Behavior and Development, 28*, 54–61.

Gartstein, M., Peleg, Y., Young, B., & Slobodskaya, H. (2009). Infant temperament in Russia, United States of America, and Israel: Differences and similarities between Russian-speaking families. *Child Psychiatry and Human Development, 40*, 241–256.

Gassman-Pines, A. (2013). Daily spillover of low-income mothers' perceived workload to mood and mother-child interactions. *Journal of Marriage and Family, 75*, 1304–1318.

Gates, G. (2013). *LGBT parenting in the United States.* The Williams Institute. Retrieved from williamsinstitute.law.ucla.edu/wp-content/uploads/LGBT-Parenting.pdf

Geary, S., & Moon, Y. S. (2006). The human embryo in vitro: Recent progress. *Journal of Reproductive Medicine, 51*(4), 293–302.

Gee, J. P. (2012). *Social linguistics and literacies: Ideology in discourse* (4th ed.). New York, NY: Routledge.

Geertz, C. (1983). Common sense as a cultural system. In C. Geertz (Ed.), *Local knowledge: Further essays in interpretive anthropology* (pp. 73–93). New York, NY: Basic Books.

Gehlbach, H. (2006). How changes in students' goal orientations relate to outcomes in social studies. *Journal of Education Research, 99*, 358–370.

Geiger, B. (1996). *Fathers as primary caregivers.* Westport, CT: Greenwood.

Geller, M. (2005). The psychoanalytic perspective. In S. Wheelan (Ed.), *The handbook of group research and practice* (pp. 87–105). Thousand Oaks, CA: Sage.

Gelles, R. (2010). Violence, abuse, and neglect in families and intimate relationships. In S. Price, C. Price, & P. McKenry (Eds.), *Families & change: Coping with stressful events and transitions* (4th ed., pp. 119–139). Thousand Oaks, CA: Sage.

George, L. K. (1993). Sociological perspectives on life transitions. *Annual Review of Sociology, 19*, 353–373.

George, L. K. (2005). Socioeconomic status and health across the life course: Progress and prospects. *The Journal of Gerontology: Series B: Psychological Sciences and Social Sciences, 60B*, 135–139.

George, L. K. (2009). Conceptualizing and measuring trajectories. In G. Elder Jr. & J. Giele (Eds.), *The craft of life course resource* (pp. 163–186). New York, NY: Guilford.

Georgiades, S. D. (2005). Emancipated young adults' perspectives on independent living programs. *Families in Society, 86*(4), 503–510.

Gerdes, K., & Segal, E. (2011). Importance of empathy for social work practice: Integrating new science. *Social Work, 56*(2), 141–148.

Gergen, K. (1985). The social constructionist movement in modern psychology. *American Psychologist, 40*, 266–275.

Gerhardt, S. (2004). *Why love matters: How affection shapes a baby's brain.* New York, NY: Brunner-Routledge.

Germain, C., & Gitterman, A. (1996). *The life model of social work practice* (2nd ed.). New York, NY: Columbia University Press.

Gerontology Research Group. (2013). *Current validated living supercentenarians.* Retrieved from http://www.grg.org/Adams/E.HTM

Gerouki, M. (2010). The boy who was drawing princesses: Primary teachers' accounts of children's non- conforming behaviours. *Sex Education, 10*(4), 335–348. doi:10.1080/14681811.2010.51.5092

Ghazi, S., Shahzada, G., Gilani, U., Shabbir, M., & Rashid, M. (2011). Relationship between students' self-perceived multiple intelligences and their academic achievement. *International Journal of Academic Research, 3*(2), 619–623.

Giang, T., Karpyn, A., Laurison, H., Hillier, A., & Perry, D. (2008). Pennsylvania's Fresh Food Financing Initiative. *Journal of Public Health Management and Practice, 14*, 272–279.

Gibbs, J. C., Basinger, K. S., Grime, R. L., & Snarey, J. R. (2007). Moral judgement development across cultures: Revisiting Kohlberg's universality claims. *Developmental Review, 27*, 443–500.

Gibbs, N. (2009, October 14). What women want now. *Time*. Retrieved from content.time.com/time/specials/packages/article/0,28804,1930277_1930145_1930309,00.html

Gibson, M. (1988). *Accommodation without assimilation: Sikh immigrants in an American high school*. Ithaca, NY: Cornell University Press.

Gibson-Davis, C., Edin, K., & McLanahan, S. (2005). High hopes but even higher expectations: The retreat from marriage among low-income couples. *Journal of Marriage and Family, 65*(5), 1301–1312.

Giddens, A. (1979). *Central problems in social theory: Action, structure, and contradiction in social analysis*. Berkeley, CA: University of California Press.

Giddens, A. (2000). *Runaway world: How globalization is reshaping our lives*. New York, NY: Routledge.

Gielen, U., & Markoulis, D. (2001). Preference for principled moral reasoning: A developmental and cross-cultural perspective. In L. Adler & U. Gielen (Eds.), *Cross-cultural topics in psychology* (2nd ed., pp. 81–101). Westport, CT: Praeger/Greenwood.

Gifford, R. (2007). *Environmental psychology: Principles and practice* (4th ed.). Colville, WA: Optimal Books.

Gilchrist, J. (2012). Trends in child injury deaths United States, 2000–2009. *Morbidity and Mortality Weekly Report*. Retrieved from http://www.cdc.gov/stltpublichealth/townhall/presentations/2012/04_2012_Child_Injury.pdf

Gill, S. (2010). *Developing a learning culture in nonprofit organizations*. Thousand Oaks, CA: Sage.

Gilligan, C. (1982). *In a different voice: Psychological theory and women's development*. Cambridge, MA: Harvard University Press.

Gilligan, C. (1988). Remapping the moral domain: New images of self in relationship. In C. Gilligan, J. V. Ward, & J. M. Taylor (Eds.), *Mapping the moral domain* (pp. 3–20). Cambridge, MA: Harvard University Press.

Gilman, S. (2012). The successes and challenges of life course epidemiology: A commentary on Gibb, Fergusson and Horwood. *Social Science & Medicine, 75*, 2124–2128.

Gilson, S. F., & DePoy, E. (2000). Multiculturalism and disability: A critical perspective. *Disability & Society, 15*(2), 207–218.

Gilson, S. F., & DePoy, E. (2002). Theoretical approaches to disability content in social work education. *Journal of Social Work Education, 37*, 153–165.

Ginath, S., Lerman-Sagle, T., Haratz Krajden, K., Lev, D., Cohen-Sacher, B., Bar, J., & Malinger, G. (2013). The fetal vermis, pons and brainstem: Normal longitudinal development as shown by dedicated neurosonography. *Journal of Maternal-Fetal and Neonatal Medicine, 26*(8), 757–762.

Gitterman, A. (2009). The life model. In A. R. Roberts (Ed.), *Social workers' desk reference* (2nd ed., pp. 231–235). New York, NY: Oxford University Press.

Glaser, D. (2000). Child abuse and neglect and the brain—A review. *Journal of Child Psychology and Psychiatry, 41*(1), 97–116.

Gleason, P., Clark, M., Clark Tuttle, C., Dwoyer, E., & Silberberg, M. (2010). *The evaluation of charter school impacts*. Washington, DC: U.S. Department of Education. Retrieved from files.eric.ed.gov/fulltext/ED510573.pdf

Gleick, J. (2008). *Chaos: Making a new science*. New York, NY: Penguin.

Global Issues. (2013). *Poverty facts and stats* (Chapter 12). Retrieved from http://www.globalissues.org/article/26/poverty-facts-and-stats

Global Poverty Project. (2013). *1.4 billion reasons*. Retrieved from http://www.globalpovertyproject.com/pages/presentation

Glover, J., Galliher, R., & Lamere, T. (2009). Identity development and exploration among sexual minority adolescents: Examination of a multidimensional model. *Journal of Homosexuality, 56*, 77–101.

Glover, R. (1996). Religiosity in adolescence and young adulthood: Implications for identity formation. *Psychological Reports, 78*, 427–431.

Glynn, S. (2012). *Fact sheet: Child care*. Center for American Progress. Retrieved from https://www.americanprogress.org/issues/labor/news/2012/08/16/11978/fact-sheet-child-care/

Godsall, R., Jurkovic, G., Emshoff, J., Anderson, L., & Stanwyck, D. (2004). Why some kids do well in bad situations: Relation of parental alcohol misuse and parentification to children's self-concept. *Substance Use & Misuse, 39*(5), 789–809.

Godwyn, M., & Gittell, J. (2012). Introduction. In M. Godwyn & J. Gittell (Eds.), *Sociology of organizations: Structures and relationships* (pp. xi–xxiv). Thousand Oaks, CA: Sage.

Goffman, E. (1959). *Presentation of self in everyday life*. Garden City, NY: Archer.

Goldberg, A. (2010). Lesbian- and gay-parent families: Development and functioning. In S. Price, C. Price, & P. McKenry (Eds.), *Families & change: Coping with stressful events and transitions* (pp. 263–284). Thousand Oaks, CA: Sage.

Goldenring, J. (2011). *Infant reflexes*. MedlinePlus medical encyclopedia. Retrieved from http://www.nlm.nih.gov/medlineplus/ency/article/003292.htm

Goldman, J. (1996). *Healing sounds: The power of harmonics*. Rockport, MA: Element Books.

Goldstein, D. (1996). Ego psychology theory. In F. Turner (Ed.), *Social work treatment* (4th ed., pp. 191–217). New York, NY: Free Press.

Goldstein, E. (1995). *Ego psychology and social work practice* (2nd ed.). New York, NY: Free Press.

Goldstein, E. G. (2001). *Object relations theory and self psychology in social work practice*. New York, NY: Free Press.

Goldstein, E. G. (2009). The relationship between social work and psychoanalysis: The future impact of social workers. *Clinical Social Work Journal, 37*(1), 7–13.

Goldstein, S., & Brooks, R. B. (2013). *Handbook of resilience in children*. New York, NY: Springer.

Goleman, D. (2005). *Emotional intelligence* (10th anniv. ed.). New York, NY: Bantam.

Goleman, D. (2006). *Social intelligence: The new science of human relationships*. New York, NY: Bantam.

Gong, F., Xu, J., Fujishiro, K., & Takeuchi, D. (2011). A life course perspective on migration and mental health among Asian immigrants: The role of human agency. *Social Science & Medicine, 73*, 1618–1626.

Gonzaga, G., Turner, R., Keltner, D., & Campos, B. (2006). Romantic love and sexual desire in close relationships. *Emotion, 6*(2), 163–179.

Good, M., Willoughby, T., & Busseri, M. (2011). Stability and change in adolescent spirituality/religiosity: A person-centered approach. *Developmental Psychology, 47*(2), 538–550.

Goodenough, W. (1996). Culture. In D. Levinson & M. Ember (Eds.), *Encyclopedia of cultural anthropology* (Vol. 1, pp. 291–298). New York, NY: Holt.

Goodfellow, A. (2012). Looking through the learning disability lens: Inclusive education and the learning disability embodiment. *Children's Geographies, 10*(1), 67–81. doi:10.1080/14733285.2011.638179

Gopaul-McNicol, S. (1988). Racial identification and racial preference of Black preschool children in New York and Trinidad. *Journal of Black Psychology, 14*(2), 65–68.

Gordon, J. D., DiMattina, M., Reh, A., Botes, A., Celia, G., & Payson, M. (2013). Utilization and success rates of unstimulated in vitro fertilization in the United States: An analysis of the society for

reproductive technology database. *Fertility and Sterility, 100*(2), 392–395.
Gordon, J. R., Pruchno, R. A., Wilson-Genderson, M., Murphy, W. M., & Rose, M. (2010). Balancing caregiving and work: Role conflict and role strain dynamics. *Journal of Family Issues, 33*(5), 662–689.
Gordon, M. (1964). *Assimilation in American life: The role of race, religion, and national origins.* New York, NY: Oxford University Press.
Gordon, T. A. (2013). Good grief: Exploring the dimensionality of grief experiences and social work support. *Journal of Social Work in End-of-Life & Palliative Care, 9*, 27–42.
Gordon, W., Zafonte, R., Cicerone, K., Cantor, J., Brown, M., Lombard, L., ... Chanda, T. (2006). Traumatic brain injury rehabilitation: State of the science. *American Journal of Physical Medicine & Rehabilitation, 85*(4), 343–382.
Gotham, K. (2013). Contrasts of carnival: Mardi Gras between the modern and the postmodern. In P. Kivisto (Ed.), *Illuminating social life: Classical and contemporary theory revisited* (6th ed., pp. 319–344). Los Angeles, CA: Sage.
Gotta, G., Green, R., Rothblum, E., Solomon, S., Balsam, K., & Schwartz, P. (2011). Heterosexual, lesbian, and gay male relationships: A comparison of couples in 1975 and 2000. *Family Process, 50*(3), 353–376.
Gould, D. (2004). Passionate political processes: Bring emotions back into the study of social movements. In J. Goodwin & J. Jasper (Eds.), *Rethinking social movements: Structure, meaning, and emotion* (pp. 155–175). Lanham, MD: Rowman & Littlefield.
Grandin, T., & Panek, R. (2013). *The autistic brain: Thinking across the spectrum.* Boston, MA: Houghton Mifflin Harcourt.
Gray, M., Coates, J., & Hetherington, T. (2013). *Environmental social work.* New York, NY: Routledge.
Greeff, A. P., & Fillis, A. J. (2009). Resiliency in poor single-parent families. *Families in Society: The Journal of Contemporary Social Services, 90*(3), 279–285.
Green, D., & McDermott, F. (2010). Social work from inside and between complex systems: Perspective on person-in-environment for today's social work. *British Journal of Social Work, 40*, 2414–2430.
Green, R. (2012). Gay and lesbian family life: Risk, resilience, and rising expectations. In F. Walsh (Ed.), *Normal family processes: Growing diversity and complexity* (4th ed., pp. 172–193). New York, NY: Guilford Press.
Greenberg, J. (2010). Assessing policy effects on enrollment in early childhood education and care. *Social Service Review, 84*(3), 461–490.
Greenberg, L. S. (2011). *Emotion-focused therapy.* Washington, DC: American Psychological Association.
Greene, G., & Lee, M. Y. (2011). *Solution-oriented social work practice: An integrative approach to working with client strengths.* New York, NY: Oxford University Press.
Greene, R. R., & Cohen, H. L. (2005). Social work with older adults and their families: Changing practice paradigms. *Families in Society, 86*(3), 367–373.
Greene, S., Anderson, E., Forgatch, M., Degarmo, D., & Hetherington, E. M. (2012). Risk and resilience after divorce. In F. Walsh (Ed.), *Normal family processes: Growing diversity and complexity* (4th ed., pp. 102–127). New York, NY: Guilford Press.
Greenfield, E., & Marks, N. (2006). Linked lives: Adult children's problems and their parents' psychological and relational well-being. *Journal of Marriage and Family, 68*, 442–454.
Greenspan, S. (2006). Rethinking "harmonious parenting" using a three-factor discipline model. *Child Care in Practice, 12*(1), 5–12.
Greenwald, H. (2008). *Organizations: Management without control.* Thousand Oaks, CA: Sage.
Gregory, S. T. (2000). *The academic achievement of minority students: Perspectives, practices, and prescriptions.* Lanham, MD: University Press of America.
Greil, A. L., McQuillan, J., Lowry, M., & Shreffler, K. M. (2011). Infertility treatment and fertility-specific distress: A longitudinal analysis of a population-based sample of U.S. women. *Social Science and Medicine, 73*(1), 87–94.
Greve, W., & Staudinger, U. M. (2006). Resilience in later adulthood and old age: Resources and potentials for successful aging. In D. Cicchetti & D. J. Cohen (Eds.), *Developmental psychopathology, Vol. 3: Risk, disorder and adaptation* (pp. 796–840). Hoboken, NJ: Wiley.
Griswold, W. (2013). *Cultures and societies in a changing world* (4th ed.). Thousand Oaks, CA: Sage.
Grof, S. (2003). Physical manifestations of emotional disorders: Observations from the study of non-ordinary states of consciousness. In K. Taylor (Ed.), *Exploring holotropic breathwork: Selected articles from a decade of The Inner Door.* Santa Cruz, CA: Hanford Mead Publishers.
Grof, S., & Bennett, H. Z. (1992). *The holotropic mind: The three levels of human consciousness and how they shape our lives.* New York, NY: HarperCollins.
Gromley, W., Gayer, T., Phillips, D., & Dawson, B. (2005). The effects of universal pre-K on cognitive development. *Developmental Psychology, 41*(6), 872–884.
Grossman, P., Niemann, L., Schmidt, S., & Walach, H. (2004). Mindfulness-based stress reduction and health benefits: A meta-analysis. *Journal of Psychosomatic Research, 57*(1), 35–43.
Gudmunson, C., Beutler, I., Israelsen, C., McCoy, J., & Hill, E. (2007). Linking financial strain to marital instability: Examining the roles of emotional distress and marital interaction. *Journal of Family and Economic Issues, 28*(3), 357–376.
Guest, Y. (2012). Reflections on resilience: A psycho-social exploration of the life long impact of having been in care during childhood. *Journal of Social Work Practice, 26*(1), 109–124.
Gunnar, M. R., & Quevedo, K. (2007). The neurobiology of stress and development. *Annual Review of Psychology, 58*, 145–173.
Guralnick, M., Neville, B., Hammond, M., & Connor, R. (2008). Continuity and change from full-inclusion early childhood programs through the early elementary period. *Journal of Early Intervention, 30*(3), 237–250.
Gurian, M. (2011). *Boys and girls learn differently! A guide for teachers and parents.* San Francisco, CA: Jossey-Bass.
Gutiérrez, L. (1990). Working with women of color: An empowerment perspective. *Social Work, 35*(2), 149–153.
Gutiérrez, L. (1994). Beyond coping: An empowerment perspective on stressful life events. *Journal of Sociology and Social Welfare, 21*(3), 201–219.
Gutman, H. (1976). *The Black family in slavery and freedom, 1750–1925.* New York, NY: Pantheon.
Gutman, L., & Eccles, J. (2007). Stage-environment fit during adolescence: Trajectories of family relations and adolescent outcomes. *Developmental Psychology, 43*, 522–537.
Gutman, L., McLoyd, V., & Tokoyawa, T. (2005). Financial strain, neighborhood stress, parenting behaviors, and adolescent adjustment in urban African American families. *Journal of Research on Adolescence, 15*(4), 425–449.
Guttmacher Institute. (2012). *In brief: Facts on American teens' sources of information about sex.* Retrieved from http://www.guttmacher.org/pubs/FB-Teen-Sex-Ed.pdf
Guttmacher Institute. (2013a). *Facts on American teens' sexual and reproductive health.* Retrieved from http://www.guttmacher.org/pubs/FB-ATSRH.pdf

Guttmacher Institute. (2013b). *Facts on unintended pregnancy in the United States*. Retrieved from http://www.guttmacher.org/pubs/FB-Unintended-Pregnancy-US.html

Guttmacher Institute. (2013c). *Facts on American teens' sexual and reproductive health*. Retrieved from http://www.gutmmacher.org/pub/FB-ATSRh.html

Guttmacher Institute. (2015a). *Fact sheet: Contraception in the United States*. Retrieved from http://www.guttmacher.org/pubs/fb_contr_use.html

Guttmacher Institute (2015b). *Fact sheet: Induced abortion in the United States*. Retrieved from http://www.guttmacher.org/pubs/fb_induced_abortion.html

Gutzwiller-Helfenfinger, E., Gasser, L., & Malti, T. (2010). Moral emotions and moral judgments in children's narratives: Comparing real-life and hypothetical transgressions. *New Directions for Child & Adolescent Development, 129*, 11–31.

Haan, N. (1991). Moral development and action from a social constructivist perspective. In W. Kurtines & J. Gewirtz (Eds.), *Handbook of moral behavior and development: Theory* (Vol. 1, pp. 251–273). Hillsdale, NJ: Erlbaum.

Haan, N., Millsap, R., & Hartka, E. (1986). As time goes by: Change and stability in personality over fifty years. *Psychology and Aging, 1*, 220–232.

Habermas, J. (1984). *The theory of communicative action, Vol. 1: Reason and the rationalization of society*. Boston, MA: Beacon Press.

Habermas, J. (1987). *The theory of communicative action, Vol. 2: Lifeworld and system: A critique of functionalist reason* (T. McCarthy, Trans.). Boston, MA: Beacon Press. (Original work published 1981)

Haddad, Y. Y. (1997). Make room for the Muslims? In W. H. Conser Jr., & S. B. Twiss (Eds.), *Religious diversity and American religious history: Studies in traditions and cultures* (pp. 218–261). Athens, GA: University of Georgia Press.

Hafen, C., Laursen, B., & DeLay, B. (2012). Transformations in friends' relationships across the transition into adolescence. In B. Laursen & W. A. Collins (Eds.), *Relationship pathways from adolescence to young adulthood* (pp. 69–89). Los Angeles, CA: Sage.

Hagelskamp, C., Suárez-Orozco, C., & Hughes, D. (2010). Migrating to opportunities: How family migration motivations shape academic trajectories among newcomer immigrant youth. *Journal of Social Issues, 66*(4), 717–739. doi:10.1111/j.1540-4560.2010.01672.x

Haider, A. (2006). *Roper v. Simmons*: The role of the science brief. *Ohio State Journal of Criminal Law, 375*, 369–377.

Haidt, J. (2013). Moral psychology for the twenty-first century. *Journal of Moral Education, 42*(3), 281–297.

Haig-Brown, C. (1988). *Resistance and renewal: Surviving the Indian residential school*. Vancouver, BC, Canada: Tillacum Library.

Hall, E. (1966). *The hidden dimension*. Garden City, NY: Doubleday.

Hall, G. S. (1904). *Adolescence: Its psychology and its relations to physiology, anthropology, sociology, sex, crime, religion, and education*. New York, NY: Appleton.

Hall, J., Jaekel, J., & Wolke, D. (2012). Gender distinctive impacts on prematurity and small for gestational age (SGA) on age-6 attention problems. *Child and Adolescent Mental Health, 17*(4), 238–245.

Hall, K. S., Trussell, H., & Schwartz, E. B. (2012). Progestin-only contraceptive pill use among women in the United States. *Contraception, 86*(6), 653–658.

Halloran, L. (2013, December 24). "Living wage" effort eclipsed by minimum-pay battles. *NPR*. Retrieved from http://www.npr.org/2013/12/24/256879640/living-wage-effort-eclipsed-by-minimum-pay-battles

Hames, A. M., & Godwin, M. C. (2008). The "out of control" balloon: Using spirituality as a coping resource. In C. F. Sori, & L. L. Hecker (Eds.), *The therapist's notebook: More homework, handouts, and activities for use in psychotherapy* (pp. 171–176). New York, NY: Routledge/Taylor & Francis.

Hamilton, B. E., Martin, J. A., & Ventura, S. J. (2013). Births: Preliminary data for 2012. *National Vital Statistics Reports, 62*(3). Retrieved from http://www.cdc.gov/nchs/data/nvsr/nvsr62/nvsr62_03.pdf

Hampson, S., & Goldberg, L. (2006). A first large cohort study of personality trait stability over the 40 years between elementary school and midlife. *Journal of Personality and Social Psychology, 91*(4), 763–779.

Hampton, K., Sessions, L., Her, E. J., & Rainie, L. (2009, November 4). *Social isolation and new technology*. Washington, DC: Pew Internet & American Life Project.

Hampton, K., & Wellman, B. (2003). Neighboring in Netville: How the Internet supports community and social capital in a wired suburb. *City & Community, 2*(4), 277–311.

Hane, A., Cheah, C., Rubin, K., & Fox, N. (2008). The role of maternal behavior in the relation between shyness and social reticence in early childhood and social withdrawal in middle childhood. *Social Development, 17*(4), 795–811.

Hankivsky, O. (2012). Women's health, men's health, and gender and health: Implications of intersectionality. *Social Science & Medicine, 74*, 1712–1720.

Hansen, C., & Zambo, D. (2007). Loving and learning with Wemberly and David: Fostering emotional development in early childhood education. *Early Childhood Education Journal, 34*(4), 273–278.

Hansen, D., Larson, R., & Dworkin, J. (2003). What adolescents learn in organized youth activities: A survey of self-reported developmental experiences. *Journal of Research on Adolescence, 13*(1), 25–55.

Hansen, J. E., & Lambert, S. M. (2011). Grief and loss of religion: The experiences of four rural lesbians. *Journal of Lesbian Studies, 15*, 187–196.

Hao, L., & Cherlin, A. J. (2004). Welfare reform and teenage pregnancy, childbirth, and school dropout. *Journal of Marriage and Family, 66*, 179–184.

Hareven, T. (Ed.). (1978). *Transitions: The family and the life course in historical perspective*. New York, NY: Academic Press.

Hareven, T. (1982a). American families in transition: Historical perspectives on change. In F. Walsh (Ed.), *Normal family processes* (pp. 446–466). New York, NY: Guilford Press.

Hareven, T. (1982b). *Family time and industrial time: The relationship between the family and work in a New England industrial community*. New York, NY: Cambridge University Press.

Hareven, T. (Ed.). (1996). *Aging and generation relations over the life course: A historical and cross-cultural perspective*. New York, NY: Walter de Gruyter.

Hareven, T. K. (2000). *Families, history, and social change: Life-course and cross-cultural perspectives*. Boulder, CO: Westview Press.

Harkness, S., & Super, C. (2003). Culture and parenting. In M. Bornstein (Ed.), *Handbook of parenting* (2nd ed., Vol. 2, pp. 253–280). Mahwah, NJ: Erlbaum.

Harrigan, M. P., & Koerin, B. B. (2007). Long-distance caregiving: Personal realities and practice implications. *Reflections, 13*(2), 5–16.

Harrison, R., & Thomas, M. (2009). Identity in online communities: Social networking sites and language learning. *International Journal of Emerging Technologies & Society, 7*(2), 109–124.

Harry, B., & Klingner, J. K. (2006). *Why are so many minority students in special education? Understanding race & disability in schools*. New York, NY: Teachers College Press.

Hart, J. (1970). The development of client-centered therapy. In J. T. Hart &

T. M. Tomlinson (Eds.), *New directions in client-centered therapy* (pp. 3–22). Boston, MA: Houghton Mifflin.

Hartman, A., & Laird, J. (1983). *Family-centered social work practice*. New York, NY: Free Press.

Harvard Health Letter. (2002). Aging—Living to 100: What's the secret? *Harvard Health Letter, 27*(3), 1–3.

Harvard Pluralism Project. (2005). *Native American religious and cultural freedom: An introductory essay*. Retrieved from pluralism.org/reports/view/176

Harvard School of Public Health. (2012). *Child obesity*. Retrieved from http://www.hsph.harvard.edu/obesity-prevention-source/obesity-trends/global-obesity-trends-in-children

Harwood, R. (1992). The influence of culturally derived values on Anglo and Puerto Rican mothers' perceptions of attachment behavior. *Child Development, 63*, 822–839.

Hasenfeld, Y. (2010a). The attributes of human service organizations. In Y. Hasenfeld (Ed.), *Human services as complex organizations* (2nd ed., pp. 9–32). Thousand Oaks, CA: Sage.

Hastings, M. (1998). Theoretical perspectives on social movements. *New Zealand Sociology, 13*(2), 208–238.

Hatfield, E., Bensman, L., & Rapson, R. (2012). A brief history of social scientists' attempts to measure passionate love. *Journal of Social and Personal Relationships, 29*(2), 143–164.

Hattier, M., Matson, J., Sipes, M., & Turygin, N. (2011). Communication deficits in infants and toddlers with development disabilities. *Research in Developmental Disabilities, 32*, 2108–2113.

Hauser, M., Cushman, F., Young, L., Mikhail, J., & Jin, R. K. (2007). A dissociation between moral judgments and justifications. *Mind & Language, 22*(1), 1–21.

Havighurst, R. J. (1968). Personality and patterns of aging. *The Gerontologist, 8*, 20–23.

Havnen, K., Breivik, K., Stormark, K., & Jakobsen, R. (2011). Why do children placed out-of-home because of parental substance abuse have less mental health problems than children placed for other reasons? *Children and Youth Services Review, 33*, 2010–2017.

Hay, D., & Nye, R. (2006). *The spirit of the child* (Rev. ed.). London, UK: Jessica Kingsley.

Hay, D., Nye, R., & Murphy, R. (1996). Thinking about childhood spirituality: Review of research and current directions. In L. J. Francis, W. K. Kay, & W. S. Campbell (Eds.), *Research in religious education* (pp. 47–71). Macon, GA: Smyth & Helwys.

Hayes, D. (2011). Predicting parental home and school involvement in high school African American adolescents. *High School Journal, 94*(4), 154–166.

Hayslip, B., & Kaminski, P.L. (2005). Grandparents raising their grandchildren: A review of the literature and suggestions for practice. *The Gerontologist, 45*, 262–269.

Hayward, R., Miller, S., & Shaw, T. (2013). Social work education on the environment in contemporary curricula in the USA. In M. Gray, J. Coates, & T. Hetherington (Eds.), *Environmental social work* (pp. 246–259). New York, NY: Routledge.

Healey, J. (2012). *Race, ethnicity, gender, and class: The sociology of group conflict and change* (6th ed.). Los Angeles, CA: Sage.

Health Resources and Services Administration. (2010, September 20). Affordable Care Act Maternal, Infant, and Early Childhood Home Visiting Program. Retrieved from http://www.hrsa.gov/grants/apply/assistance/homevisiting/homevisitingsupplemental.pdf

Healthychildren.org. (2013). *Newborn reflexes*. Retrieved from http://www.healthychildren.org/English/ages-stages/baby/pages/Newborn-Reflexes.aspx

Healthy People. (2014). *Access to health services*. Retrieved from http://www.healthypeople.gov/2020/topicsobjectives2020/overview.aspx?topicid=1

Hearn, J., & Parkin, W. (1993). Organizations, multiple oppressions and postmodernism. In J. Hassard & M. Parker (Eds.), *Postmodernism and organizations* (pp. 148–162). Newbury Park, CA: Sage.

Heckman, J. (2006). Skill formation and the economics of investing in disadvantaged children. *Science, 312*(5782), 1900–1902.

Heckman, J. (2008). *Schools, skills, and synapses*. National Bureau of Economic Research. Retrieved from www.nber.org/papers/w14064.pdf?new_windows=1

Heckman, J., Moon, S., Pinto, R., Savelyev, P., & Yavitz, A. (2010). The rate of return to the HighScope Perry Preschool Program. *Journal of Public Economics, 94*, 114–128.

Hedberg, P., Brulin C., & Alex, L. (2009). Experiences of purpose in life when becoming and being a very old woman. *Journal of Women & Aging, 21*(2), 125–137.

Hederman, R., & Rector, R. (1999). *Income inequality: How census data misrepresent income distribution*. Retrieved from http://www.heritage.org/research/reports/1999/09/Income-Inequality

Hegtvedt, K. A. (1994). Justice. In M. Foshci & E. J. Lawler (Eds.), *Group processes: Sociological analyses* (pp. 177–204). Chicago, IL: Nelson-Hall.

Heisler, E. J. (2012). *The United States infant mortality rate: International comparisons, underlying factors, and federal programs*. Congressional Research Service. Retrieved from http://www.fas.org/sgp/crs/misc/R41378.pdf

Heimpel, S., Wood, J., Marshall, J., & Brown, J. (2002). Do people with low self-esteem really feel better? Self-esteem differences in motivation to repair negative moods. *Journal of Personality and Social Psychology, 82*, 128–147.

Helbig, A., Kaasen, A., Mait, U. F., & Haugen, G. (2013). Does antenatal maternal psychological distress affect placental circulation in the third trimester? *PLoS One, 8*(2), 1–7.

Henderson, C., Hayslip, B., Sanders, L., & Louden, L. (2009). Grandmother-grandchild relationship quality predicts psychological adjustment among youth from divorced families. *Journal of Family Issues, 30*(9), 1245–1264.

Henderson, L. (2000). The knowledge and use of alternative therapeutic techniques by social work practitioners: A descriptive study. *Social Work in Health Care, 30*(3), 55–71.

Henderson, S. W. (2008). *Refugee mental health*. Philadelphia, PA: Saunders.

Hendricks, J. (1987). Exchange theory in aging. In G. L. Maddox (Ed.), *The encyclopedia of aging* (pp. 238–239). New York, NY: Springer.

Hendricks, J., & Hatch, L. R. (2006). Lifestyle and aging. In R. H. Binstock & L. K. George (Eds.), *Handbook of aging and the social sciences* (pp. 301–319). Amsterdam: Elsevier.

Henrich, J., Heine, S., & Norenzayan, A. (2010). The weirdest people in the world? *Behavioral and Brain Sciences, 33*(2–3), 61–83.

Henry J. Kaiser Family Foundation. (2013). *Life expectancy at birth (in years) by race/ethnicity*. Retrieved from kff.org/other/state-indicator/life-expectancy-by-re

Hepworth, D., Rooney, R., Rooney, G. D., & Strom-Gottfried, K. (2013). *Direct social work practice: Theory and skills* (9th ed.). Independence, KY: Cengage Learning.

Hequembourg, A., & Brallier, S. (2005). Gendered stories of parental caregiving among siblings. *Journal of Aging Studies, 19*, 53–71.

Herbenick, D., Reece, M., Schick, V., Sanders, S., Dodge, B., & Fortenberry, J. D. (2010). Sexual behavior in the United States: Results from a national probability sample of men and women ages 14–94. *Journal of Sexual Medicine* (Suppl. 5), 255–265.

Herbert, M. R., & Weintraub, K. (2012). *The autism revolution: Whole-body strategies for making life all it can be*. New York, NY: Ballantine Books.

Herberth, G., Weber, A., Röder, S., Elvers, H. E., Krämer, U., Schins, R., LISAplus Study Group. (2008). Relation between stressful life events, neuropeptides and cytokines: Results from the LISA birth cohort study. *Pediatric Allergy & Immunology, 19*(8), 722–729.

Hetherington, E. M., & Kelly, J. (2002). *For better or for worse: Divorce reconsidered*. New York, NY: Norton.

Hetherington, T., & Boddy, J. (2013). Ecosocial work with marginalized populations: Time for action on climate change. In M. Gray, J. Coates, & T. Hetherington (Eds.), *Environmental social work* (pp. 46–61). New York, NY: Routledge.

Heuveline, P., & Timberlake, J. (2004). The role of cohabitation in family formation: The United States in comparative perspective. *Journal of Marriage and Family, 66*, 1214–1230.

Heymann, J., Earle, A., & Hayes, J. (2007). *The work, family, and equity index. How does the United States measure up?* Boston, MA: Project on Global Working Families, Harvard School of Public Health. Retrieved from www.mcgill.co/files/ihsp/WFEI2007.pdf

Hickson, J., & Phelps, A. (1998). Women's spirituality: A proposed practice model. In D. S. Becvar (Ed.), *The family, spirituality, and social work* (pp. 43–57). Binghamton, NY: Haworth Press.

Hill, A. J., & Donaldson, L. P. (2012). We shall overcome: Promoting an agenda for integrating spirituality and community practice. *Journal of Religion & Spirituality in Social Work: Social Thought, 31*(1–2), 67–84.

Hill, R. (1949). *Families under stress*. Westport, CT: Greenwood.

Hill, R. (1958). Generic features of families under stress. *Social Casework, 49*, 139–150.

Hillier, A. (2007). Why social work needs mapping. *Journal of Social Work Education, 43*(2), 205–221.

Hillier, A., Cole, B., Smith, T., Williams, J., Grier, S., Yancey, A., & McCarthy, W.J. (2009). Clustering of unhealthy advertisements around child-serving institutions: A three-city study. *Health and Place, 15*, 935–945.

Hillier, A., & Culhane, D. (2013). GIS applications and administrative data to support community change. In M. Weil, M. Reisch, & M. Ohmer (Eds.), *The handbook of community practice* (2nd ed., pp. 827–844). Los Angeles, CA: Sage.

Hing, B. (2004). *Defining America through immigration policy*. Philadelphia, PA: Temple University Press.

Hinrichsen, G. A., & Clougherty, K. F. (2006). Role transitions. In *Interpersonal psychotherapy for depressed older adults* (pp. 133–152). Washington, DC: American Psychological Association.

Hitchcock, J. (2006). *Net crimes and misdemeanors: Outmaneuvering web spammers, stalkers, and con artists*. Medford, NJ: CyberAge Books.

Hitlin, S., & Elder, G., Jr. (2007). Time, self, and the curiously abstract concept of agency. *Sociological Theory, 25*(2), 170–191.

Ho, M., Rasheed, J., & Rasheed, M. (2004). *Family therapy with ethnic minorities* (2nd ed.). Thousand Oaks, CA: Sage.

Hobfoll, S. E. (1996). Social support: Will you be there when I need you? In N. Vanzetti & S. Duck (Eds.), *A lifetime of relationships* (pp. 46–74). Belmont, CA: Thomson Brooks/Cole.

Hobsbawm, E. (1983). Introduction: Inventing tradition. In E. Hobsbawm & T. Ranger (Eds.), *The invention of tradition* (pp. 1–14). New York, NY: Cambridge University Press.

Hodge, D. R. (2005a). Developing a spiritual assessment toolbox: A discussion of the strengths and limitation of five different assessment methods. *Health & Social Work, 30*(4), 314–323.

Hodge, D. R. (2005b). Social work and the House of Islam: Orienting practitioners to the beliefs and values of Muslims in the United States. *Social Work, 50*(2), 162–173.

Hodnett, E., Downe, S., & Walsh, D. (2012). Alternative versus conventional institutional settings for birth. *Cochrane Database System Review*, 8, CD000012. doi:10.1002/14651858.CD000012.pub4

Hodnett, E., Gates, S., Hofmeyr, J., Sakala, C., & Weston, J. (2012). Continuous support for women during childbirth. *Cochrane Database System Review*. doi:10:CD003766. Retrieved from http://www.ncbi.nlm.nih.gov/pubmed/21328263

Hoff, E. (2003). The specificity of environmental influence: Socioeconomic status affects early vocabulary development via maternal speech. *Child Development, 74*, 1368–1378.

Hoff, E. (2005). *Language development*. Belmont, CA: Wadsworth/Thomson Learning.

Hoff, E. (2006). How social contexts support and shape language development. *Developmental Review, 26*, 55–88.

Hoff, E. (2009). *Language development* (4th ed.). Pacific Grove, CA: Cengage.

Hoffman, A., Rüttler, V., & Nieder, A. (2011). Ontogeny of object permanence and object tracking in the carrion crow. *Animal Behavior, 82*, 359–367.

Hofstede, G. (1996). An American in Paris: The influence of nationality on organization theories. *Organization Studies, 17*(13), 525–537.

Hofstede, G. (2001). *Culture's consequences: Comparing values, behaviors, institutions and organizations across nations* (2nd ed.). Thousand Oaks, CA: Sage.

Hofstede, G. (2010). *Cultures and organizations: Software of the mind* (3rd ed.). Boston, MA: McGraw-Hill.

Hoge, C. W., Auchterlonie, J. L., & Milliken, C. S. (2006). Mental health problems, use of mental health services, and attrition from military service after returning from deployment to Iraq or Afghanistan. *Journal of the American Medical Association, 295*(9), 1023–1032.

Hogg, M. (2005). The social identity perspective. In S. Wheelan (Ed.), *The handbook of group research and practice* (pp. 133–157). Thousand Oaks, CA: Sage.

Hogstel, M. (2001). *Gerontology: Nursing care of the older adult*. Albany, NY: Delma-Thompson Learning.

Holder, D. W., Durant, R. H., Harris, T. L., Daniel, J., Obeidallah, D., & Goodman, E. (2000). The association between adolescent spirituality and voluntary sexual activity. *Journal of Adolescent Health, 26*(4), 295–302.

Holder, M. D., Coleman, B., & Wallace, J. M. (2010). Spirituality, religiousness, and happiness in children aged 8–12 years. *Journal of Happiness Studies, 11*(2), 131–150.

Hollinghurst, S., Kessler, D., Peters, T., & Gunnell, D. (2005). Opportunity cost of antidepressant prescribing in England: Analysis of routine data. *British Medical Journal, 330*(7948), 999–1000.

Holm, J., & Bowker, J. (Eds.). (1994). *Women in religion*. New York, NY: Pinter.

Holmes, T. (1978). Life situations, emotions, and disease. *Psychosomatic Medicine, 19*, 747–754.

Holmes, T., & Rahe, R. (1967). The social readjustment rating scale. *Journal of Psychosomatic Research, 11*, 213–218.

Holtzworth-Munroe, A., & Stuart, G. (1994). Typologies of male batterers: Three subtypes and the differences among them. *Psychological Bulletin, 116*(3), 476–497.

Homans, G. (1958). Social behavior as exchange. *American Journal of Sociology, 63*, 597–606.

Homans, G. C. (1961). *Social behavior: Its elementary forms*. New York, NY: Harcourt Brace Jovanovich.

Hook, J., & Courtney, M. (2011). Employment outcomes of former foster youth as young adults: The importance human, personal, and social capital. *Children and Youth Services Review, 33*, 1855–1865.

Hooyman, N. R., & Kiyak, H. A. (2011). *Social gerontology: A multidisciplinary perspective* (9th ed.). Boston, MA: Allyn & Bacon.

Hooyman, N. R., & Kramer, B. J. (2006). *Living through loss: Interventions across the life span*. New York, NY: Columbia University Press.

Horn, A. W., & Alexander, C. I. (2005). Recurrent miscarriage. *Journal of Family Planning and Reproductive Health Care, 31*(2), 103–107.

Horn, J. L. (1982). The theory of fluid and crystallized intelligence in relation to concepts of cognitive psychology and aging in adulthood. In F. I. M. Craik & S. Trehub (Eds.), *Aging and cognitive processes* (pp. 237–278). New York, NY: Plenum.

Hornsey, M. J. (2008). Social identity theory and self-categorization theory: A historical review. *Social and Personality Psychology Compass, 2*(1), 204–222.

House, J. S., Lantz, P. M., & Herd, P. (2005). Continuity and change in the social stratification of aging and health over the life course: Evidence from a nationally representative longitudinal study from 1986 to 2001/2002 (Americans' Changing Lives Study). *The Journal of Gerontology: Series B: Psychological Sciences and Social Sciences, 60B*, 15–26.

Houston, J. B., Pfefferbaum, B., Sherman, M., Meison, A., Jeon-Slaughter, H., Brand, M., & Jarman, Y. (2009). Children of deployed National Guard troops: Perceptions of parental deployment to Operation Iraqi Freedom. *Psychiatric Annals, 39*(8), 805–811.

Hovens, J., Giltay, E., Wiersma, J., Spinhoven, P., Penninx, B., & Zitman, F. (2012). Impact of childhood life events and trauma on the course of depressive and anxiety disorders. *Acta Psychiatrica Scandinavica, 126*, 198–207.

Howard, T. C. (2010). *Why race and culture matter in schools: Closing the achievement gap in America's classrooms*. New York, NY: Teachers College Press.

Howell, D., Wysocki, K., & Steiner, M. (2010). Toilet training. *Pediatrics in Review, 31*(6), 262–263.

Hoyert, D., & Xu, J. (2012). Deaths: Preliminary data for 2011. *National Vital Statistics Reports, 61*(6), 1–51. Retrieved from http://www.cdc.gov/nchs/data/nvsr/nvsr61/nvsr61_06.pdf

Hser, Y., Longshore, D., & Anglin, M. (2007). The life course perspective on drug use. *Evaluation Review, 31*(6), 515–547.

Hsu, S. H., Grow, J., Marlatt, A., Galanter, M., & Kaskutas, L. A. (Eds). (2008). *Research on Alcoholics Anonymous and spirituality in addiction recovery*. New York, NY: Springer Science.

Huang, P., Smock, P., Manning, W., & Bergstrom-Lynch, C. (2011). He says, she says: Gender and cohabitation. *Journal of Family Issues, 32*(7), 876–905.

Huber, M. S., Egeren, L., Pierce, S., & Foster-Fishman, P. (2009). GIS applications for community based research and action: Mapping change in a community-building initiative. *Journal of Prevention & Intervention in the Community, 27*, 5–20.

Huebner, A., & Garrod, A. (1993). Moral reasoning among Tibetan monks. A study of Buddhist adolescents and young adults in Nepal. *Journal of Cross-Cultural Psychology, 24*, 167–185.

Hughes, A., Harold, R., & Boyer, J. (2011). Awareness of LGBT aging issues among aging services network providers. *Journal of Gerontological Social Work, 54*(7), 650–677.

Hughes, D., Hagelskamp, C., Way, N., & Foust, M. (2009). The role of mothers' and adolescents' perceptions of ethnic-racial socialization in shaping ethnic-racial identity among early adolescent boys and girls. *Journal of Youth and Adolescence, 38*, 605–626.

Hughes, F. (2010). *Children, play, and development* (4th ed.). Thousand Oaks, CA: Sage.

Hughes, S., Williams, B., Molina, L., Bayles, C., Bryant, L., Harris, J., . . . Watkins, K. (2005). Characteristics of physical activity programs for older adults: Results of a multisite survey. *The Gerontologist, 45*(5), 667–675.

Huinink, J., & Feldhaus, M. (2009). Family research from the life course perspective. *International Sociology, 24*(3), 299–324.

Human Rights Campaign. (2015). Love wins. Retrieved from http://www.hrc.org/campaigns/stand-for-marriage

Hunler, O. S., & Gencoz, T. (2005). The effect of religiousness on marital satisfaction: Testing the mediator role of marital problem solving between religiousness and marital satisfaction relationship. *Contemporary Family Therapy, 27*(1), 123–136.

Hunter, A., & Riger, S. (1986). The meaning of community in community mental health. *Journal of Community Psychology, 14*, 55–71.

Hunter, J. D. (1994). *Before the shooting begins: Searching for democracy in America's culture wars*. New York, NY: Free Press.

Hurdle, D. E. (2002). Hawaiian traditional healing: Culturally based interventions for social work practice. *Social Work, 47*(2), 183–192.

Hurst, J. (2007). Disability and spirituality in social work practice. *Journal of Social Work in Disability & Rehabilitation, 6*(1/2), 179–194.

Husain, S. A. (2012). Trauma, resiliency and recovery in children: Lessons from the field. *Psychiatria Danubina, 24*(Suppl. 3), 277–284.

Hutchison, E. (1987). Use of authority in direct social work practice with mandated clients. *Social Service Review, 61*(4), 581–598.

Hutchison, E. (2007). Community violence. In E. Hutchison, H. Matto, M. Harrigan, L. Charlesworth, & P. Viggiani (Eds.), *Challenges of living: A multidimensional working model for social workers* (pp. 71–104). Thousand Oaks, CA: Sage.

Hutchison, E. (2012). Spirituality, religion, and progressive social movements: Resources and motivation for social change. *Journal of Religion & Spirituality in Social Work: Social Thought, 31*, 105–127.

Hutchison, E. (2014). Adult criminal justice system. In H. Matto, J. Strolin-Goltzman, & M. Ballan (Eds.), *Neuro-science for social work* (pp. 355–378). New York, NY: Springer.

Hutchison, E., & Charlesworth, L. (2000). Securing the welfare of children: Policies past, present, and future. *Families in Society, 81*(6), 576–586.

Hutchison, E., Charlesworth, L., Matto, H., Harrigan, M., & Viggiani, P. (2007). Elements of knowing and doing in social work. In E. Hutchison, H. Matto, M. Harrigan, L. Charlesworth, & P. Viggiani, *Challenges of living: A multi-dimensional working model for social workers* (pp. 13–33). Thousand Oaks, CA: Sage.

Hutchison, E., Matto, H., Harrigan, M., Charlesworth, L., & Viggiani, P. (2007). *Challenges of living: A multidimensional working model for social workers*. Thousand Oaks, CA: Sage.

Huynh-Nhu, L., Ceballo, R., Chao, R., Hill, N., Murry, V., & Pinderhughes, E. E. (2008). Excavating culture: Disentangling ethnic differences from contextual influences in parenting. *Applied Developmental Science, 12*(4), 163–175.

Hyde, J. (2005). The gender similarities hypothesis. *American Psychologist, 60*, 581–592.

Iannello, K. (1992). *Decisions without hierarchy: Feminist interventions in organization theory and practice*. New York, NY: Routledge.

Imdad, A., & Bhutta, Z. A. (2012). Maternal nutrition and birth outcomes: Effect of balanced protein-energy supplementation. *Paediatric and Perinatal Epidemiology, 26*(Suppl.), 178–190.

Impett, E., & Tolman, D. (2006). Late adolescent girls' sexual experiences and sexual satisfaction. *Journal of Adolescent Research, 21, 628–646.*

Ingstad, B., & Whyte, S. (Eds.). (1995). *Disability and culture*. Berkeley, CA: University of California Press.

Institute of Medicine. (2006). *Preterm birth: Causes, consequences and prevention.*

Washington, DC: National Academies Press.

Institute of Medicine. (2011). *The health of lesbian, gay, bisexual, and transgender people: Building a foundation for better understanding*. Washington, DC: National Academies Press.

Institute of Medicine and National Research Council. (2012). *Child maltreatment research, policy, and practice for the next decade: Workshop summary*. Washington, DC: National Academies Press.

International Institute for Democracy and Electoral Assistance. (2011). *Voter turnout*. Retrieved from www.idea.int/vt/countryview.cfm?id

Irish, D., Lundquist, K., & Nelsen, V. (1993). *Ethnic variations in dying, death, and grief: Diversity in universality*. Washington, DC: Taylor & Francis.

Irvin, M. (2012). *Shocking divorce statistics*. Retrieved from http://www.mckinleyirvin.com/blog/divorce/32-shocking-divorce-statistics

Isenberg, J. P., & Jolongo, M. (2003). *Major trends and issues in early childhood education: Challenges, controversies, and insights* (2nd ed.). New York, NY: Teachers College Press.

Jackson, M. A. (2002). Christian womanist spirituality: Implications for social work practice. *Social Thought, 21*(1), 63–76.

Jacobsen, L., Mather, M., Lee, M., & Kent, M. (2011). America's aging population. *Population Bulletin, 66*(1), 1–18. Retrieved from www.prb.org

Jacobstein, R., & Polis, C. B. (2014). Progestin-only contraception: Injectables and implants. *Best Practice and Research: Clinical Obstetrics & Gynaecology, 28*(6), 795–806.

Jahromi, L., Putnam, S., & Stifter, C. (2004). Maternal regulation of infant reactivity from 2 to 6 months. *Developmental Psychology, 40*, 477–487.

Jain, R. B. (2013). Effect of pregnancy on the levels of blood cadmium, lead, and mercury for females 17–39 years old: Data from National Health and Nutrition Survey 2003–2010. *Journal of Toxicology and Environmental Health, Part A, 76*(1), 58–59.

James, K., & Bose, P. (2011). Self-generated actions during learning objects and sounds create sensori-motor systems in the developing brain. *Cognition, Brain, Behavior, 15*(4), 485–503.

James, R., & Gilliland, B. (2013). *Crisis intervention strategies* (7th ed.). Belmont, CA: Brooks/Cole.

James, W. (1890). *Principles of psychology*. New York, NY: Holt.

Jandt, F. (2010). *An introduction to intercultural communication: Identities in a global community* (6th ed.). Thousand Oaks, CA: Sage.

Janssen, R., Saxell, L., Page, L. A., Klein, M. C., Liston, R. M., & Lee, S. K. (2009). Outcomes of planned home birth with registered midwife versus planned hospital birth with midwife or physician. *Canadian Medical Association Journal, 191*, 377–383.

Jaskyte, K. (2012). Exploring potential for technology innovation in nonprofit organizations. *Journal of Technology in Human Services, 30*, 118–127.

Jean, A., & Stack, D. (2012). Full-term and very-low-birth-weight preterm infants' self-regulating behaviors during a still-face interaction: Influences of maternal touch. *Infant Behavior and Development, 35*, 779–791.

Jeffers, E. (2013). Banking deregulation and the financial crisis in the US and France. *Comparative Economic Studies, 55*, 479–500.

Jenkins, W. (2008). *Ecologies of grace: Environmental ethics and Christian theology*. Oxford, UK: Oxford University Press.

Jenkinson, S. (2012). *The skill of brokenheartedness: Euthanasia, palliative care and power*. Retrieved from http://www.youtube.com/watch?v=6dbmXWLCaRg

Jensen, L. A. (2003). Coming of age in a multicultural world: Globalization and adolescent cultural identity formation. *Applied Developmental Science, 7*, 188–195.

Jenson, J., & Fraser, M. (2016). *Social policy for children and families: A risk and resilience perspective* (3rd ed.). Thousand Oaks, CA: Sage.

Jihanian, L. (2013). Specifying long-term care provider responsiveness to LGBT older adults. *Journal of Gay & Lesbian Social Services, 25*(2), 210–231.

Jobe-Shields, L., Cohen, R., & Parra, G. R. (2011). Patterns of change in children's loneliness: Trajectories from third through fifth grades. *Merrill-Palmer Quarterly, 57*(1), 25–47.

Johnson, A. G. (2006). *Privilege, power, and difference*. Boston, MA: McGraw-Hill.

Johnson, A. N. (2008). Engaging fathers in the NICU: Taking down the barriers to the baby. *Journal of Perinatal and Neonatal Nursing, 22*(4), 302–306.

Johnson, G. R., Jang, S. J., Larsen, D. B., & De Li, S. (2001). Does adolescent religious commitment matter? A re-examination of the effects of religiosity on delinquency. *Journal on Research in Crime and Delinquency, 38*(1), 22–43.

Johnson, H. C. (2004). *Psyche and synapse expanding worlds: The role of neurobiology in emotions, behavior, thinking, and addiction for non-scientists* (2nd ed.). Greenfield, MA: Deerfield Valley.

Johnson, M. (Ed.). (1992). *People with disabilities explain it all for you*. Louisville, KY: Advocado Press.

Johnson, M. (1995). Patriarchal terrorism and common couple violence: Two forms of violence against women. *Journal of Marriage and the Family, 57*(2), 283–294.

Johnson, S. B., Blum, R., & Giedd, J. (2009). Adolescent maturity and the brain: The promise and pitfalls of neuroscience research in adolescent health policy. *Journal of Adolescent Health, 45*, 216–221.

Johnson, S. K. (1997). Does spirituality have a place in rural social work? *Social Work and Christianity, 24*(1), 58–66.

Johnston, L., O'Malley, P., Bachman, J., & Schulenberg, J. (2004). *Monitoring the future national results on adolescent drug use: Overview of key findings, 2003* (NIH Publication No. 04–5506). Bethesda, MD: National Institute on Drug Abuse.

Johnston, L., O'Malley, P., Bachman, J., & Schulenberg, J. (2005). *Monitoring the future national results on adolescent drug use: Overview of key findings, 2004* (NIH Publication No. 04–5506). Bethesda, MD: National Institute on Drug Abuse.

Johnstone, B., Yoon, D. P., Rupright, J., & Reid-Arndt, S. (2009). Relationships among spiritual beliefs, religious practices, congregational support and health for individuals with traumatic brain injury. *Brain Injury, 23*(5), 411–419.

Joint United Nations Programme on HIV/AIDS. (2013). *Global report: UNAIDS report on the global AIDS epidemic—2013*. Geneva, Switzerland: UNAIDS.

Jones, A., & Meier, A. (2011). Growing www.parentsofsuicide: A case study of an online support community. *Social Work With Groups, 34*, 101–120.

Jones, B., & McAdams, D. (2013). Becoming generative: Socializing influences recalled in late stories in late midlife. *Journal of Adult Development, 20*, 158–172.

Jones, J., & Mosher, W. (2013). Fathers' involvement with their children: United States, 2006–2010. *National Health Statistics Reports No. 71*. Hyattsville, MD: National Center for Health Statistics.

Jones, J., Mosher, W., & Daniels, K. (2012, May 18). Current contraceptive use in the United States, 2006–2010 and changes in patterns of use since 1995. *National Health Statistics Report, 60*. Retrieved from http://www.cdc.gov/nchs/data/nhsr/nhsr060.pdf

Jones, T. (2005). Mediating intragroup and intergroup conflict. In S. Wheelan (Ed.), *The handbook of group research and practice* (pp. 463–483). Thousand Oaks, CA: Sage.

Jordan, J. V. (2005). Relational resilience in girls. In S. Goldstein & R. B. Brooks

(Eds.), *Handbook of resilience in children* (pp. 79–90). New York, NY: Kluwer Academic/Plenum.

Joshi, S., & Morley, J. (2006). Cognitive impairment. *Medical Clinics of North America, 90*(5), 769–787.

Joss-Moore, L., & Lane, R. (2009). The developmental origins of adult diseases. *Current Opinions in Pediatrics, 21*(2), 230–234.

Joye, Y. (2007). Architectural lessons from environmental psychology: The case of biophilic architecture. *Review of General Psychology, 11*(4), 305–328.

Judd, R. G., & Johnston, L. B. (2012). Ethical consequences of using social network sites for students in professional social work programs. *Journal of Social Work Values & Ethics, 9*(1), 5–12.

Jung, C. (1933a). *Modern man in search of a soul*. New York, NY: Harcourt, Brace & World.

Jung, C. (1933b). *Psychological types*. New York, NY: Harcourt, Brace.

Jung, C. (1939). Conscious, unconscious and individuation. In *The collected works of C. G. Jung* (Vol. 9i). Princeton, NJ: Princeton University Press.

Jung, C. (1969). *The archetypes and the collective unconscious* (R. F. C. Hull, Trans.). Princeton, NJ: Princeton University Press. (Original work published 1959)

Jurimae, J. (2013). *Growth, physical activity, and motor development in prepubertal children*. Ipswich, MA: Ebsco.

Kagan, J. (2007). *What is emotion? History, measures, and meanings*. New Haven, CT: Yale University Press.

Kahn, J., & Pearlin, L. (2006). Financial strain over the life course and health among older adults. *Journal of Health & Social Behavior, 47*(1), 17–31.

Kahneman, D. (2011). *Thinking fast and slow*. New York, NY: Farrar, Straus and Giroux.

Kahneman, D., & Tversky, A. (1982). The psychology of preferences. *Scientific American, 246*, 160–173.

Kahneman, D., & Tversky, A. (1984). Choices, values, and frames. *American Psychologist, 39*, 341–350.

Kahraman, P., & Başal, H. (2012). Sex stereotypes of seven-eight year old girls and boys living in urban and rural areas. *International Journal of Human Sciences, 9*(1), 46–60.

Kaitz, M., Bar-Haim, Y., Lehrer, M., & Grossman, E. (2004). Adult attachment style and interpersonal distance. *Attachment & Human Development, 6*(3), 285–304.

Kalkhoff, W., & Barnum, C. (2000). The effects of status-organizing and social identity processes on patterns of social influence. *Social Psychology Quarterly, 63*, 95–115.

Kamerman, S. (1996). Child and family policies: An international overview. In E. Zigler, S. Kagan, & N. Hall (Eds.), *Children, families, and government: Preparing for the twenty first century* (pp. 31–48). New York, NY: Cambridge University Press.

Kamp Dush, C. (2011). Relationship-specific investments, family chaos, and cohabitation dissolution following a nonmarital birth. *Family Relations, 60*, 586–601.

Kamp Dush, C., & Amato, P. (2005). Consequences of relationship status and quality for subjective well-being. *Journal of Social and Personal Relationship, 22*(5), 607–627.

Kapit, W., Macey, R. I., & Meisami, E. (2000). *The physiology coloring book* (2nd ed.). Cambridge, MA: HarperCollins.

Kaplan, J., Aziz-Zadeh, L., Uddin, L., & Iacoboni, M. (2008). The self across the sense: An fMRI study of self-face and self-voice recognition. *Social Cognitive & Affective Neuroscience, 3*, 218–223.

Kaplan, S., & Berman, M. (2010). Directed attention as a common resource for executive functioning and self-regulation. *Perspectives on Psychological Science, 6*(1), 43.

Kaplowitz, P. (2006). Pubertal development in girls: Secular trends. *Current Opinions in Obstetrics and Gynecology, 18*, 487–491.

Karenga, M. (1995). Making the past meaningful: Kwanzaa and the concept of Sankofa. *Reflections: Narratives of Professional Helping, 1*(4), 36–46.

Karger, H., & Stoesz, D. (2014). *American social welfare policy: A pluralist approach* (7th ed.). Boston, MA: Pearson.

Karjane, N. W., Stovall, D. W., Berger, N. G., & Svikis, D. S. (2008). Alcohol abuse risk factors and psychiatric disorders in pregnant women with a history of infertility. *Journal of Women's Health, 17*(10), 1623–1627.

Karls, J. M., & O'Keefe, M. (2008). *Person-in-environment system manual* (2nd ed.). Washington, DC: NASW Press.

Karlsson, M., Nilsson, T., Lyttkens, C., & Leeson, G. (2010). Income inequality and health: Importance of a cross-country perspective. *Social Science & Medicine, 70*, 875–885.

Karmanov, D., & Hamel, R. (2008). Assessing the restorative potential of contemporary urban environment(s): Beyond the nature versus urban dichotomy. *Landscape and Urban Planning, 86*, 115–125.

Karpowitz, C., Mendelberg, T., & Shaker, L. (2012). Gender inequality in deliberative participation. *American Political Science Review, 106*(3), 533–547.

Karraker, M. (2013). *Global families* (2nd ed.). Los Angeles, CA: Sage.

Kasee, C. R. (1995). Identity, recovery, and religious imperialism: Native American women and the New Age. *Women and Therapy: A Feminist Quarterly, 16*(2–3), 83–93.

Katchadourian, H. (1978). Medical perspectives on adulthood. In E. H. Erikson (Ed.), *Adulthood* (pp. 33–60). New York, NY: Norton & Norton.

Kaur, P., Shorey, L., Ho, E., Dashwood, R., & Williams D. E. (2013). The epigenome as a potential of cancer and disease prevention in prenatal development. *Nutritional Reviews, 71*(7), 441–457.

Kay, A. (2006). Social capital, the social economy and community development. *Community Development Journal, 41*(2), 160–173.

Kaya, N., & Burgess, B. (2007). Territoriality: Seat preferences in different types of classroom arrangements. *Environment & Behavior, 39*(6), 859–876.

Kaya, N., & Weber, M. (2003). Territorial behavior in residence halls: A cross-cultural study. *Environment and Behavior, 35*(3), 400–414.

Kaye, L. W. (2005). The emergence of the new aged and the productive aging perspective. In L. W. Kaye (Ed.), *Perspectives on productive aging: Social work with the new aged* (pp. 3–18). Washington, DC: NASW.

Keane, C. (1991). Socioenvironmental determinants of community formation. *Environment and Behavior, 23*(1), 27–46.

Kearney, A. (2006). Residential development patterns and neighborhood satisfaction: Impacts of density and nearby nature. *Environment and Behavior, 38*(1), 112–139.

Keefe, T. (1996). Meditation and social work treatment. In F. J. Turner (Ed.), *Social work treatment: Interlocking theoretical approaches* (4th ed., pp. 434–460). New York, NY: Free Press.

Keenan, T., & Evans, S. (2016). *An introduction to child development* (3rd ed.). Thousand Oaks, CA: Sage.

Kegan, R. (1982). *The evolving self: Problem and process in human development*. Cambridge, MA: Harvard University Press.

Kegan, R. (1994). *In over our heads: The mental demands of modern life*. Cambridge, MA: Harvard University Press.

Kelly, G. (2014, February 22). SeaTac: The small US town that sparked a new movement against low wages. *The Observer*. Retrieved from http://www.theguardian.com/world/2014/feb/22/setac-minimum-wage-increase-washington

Kelly, Y., Sacker, A., Schoon, I., & Nazroo, J. (2006). Ethnic differences in achievement of developmental milestones by 9 months of age: The Millennium Cohort Study. *Developmental Medicine & Child Neurology, 48*, 825–830.

Kemp, C. (2005). Dimensions of grandparent-adult grandchild relationships: From family ties to intergenerational friends. *Canadian Journal on Aging, 24*(2), 161–177.

Kent, S. (1991). Partitioning space: Cross-cultural factors influencing domestic spatial segmentation. *Environment and Behavior, 23*, 438–473.

Keutzer, C. (1982). Physics and consciousness. *Journal of Humanistic Psychology, 22*, 74–90.

Keyes, C., & Ryff, C. (1998). Generativity in adult lives: Social structural contours and quality of life consequences. In D. McAdams & E. de St. Aubin (Eds.), *Generativity and adult development: How and why we care for the next generation* (pp. 227–263). Washington, DC: American Psychological Association.

Khaw, L., & Hardesty, J. (2007). Theorizing the process of leaving: Turning points and trajectories in the stages of change. *Family Relations, 56*, 413–425.

Khodyakov, D., & Carr, D. (2009). The impact of late-life parental death on adult sibling relationships. *Research on Aging, 31*(5), 495–519.

Khubchandani, J., Price, J., Thompson, A., Dake, J., Wiblishauser, M., & Telljohann, S. (2012). Adolescent dating violence: A national assessment of school counselors' perceptions and practices. *Pediatrics, 130*(2), 202–210.

Kihlström, A. (2012). Luhmann's system theory in social work: Criticism and reflections. *Journal of Social Work, 12*(3), 287–299.

Kim, H., Chang, M., Rose, K., & Kim, S. (2012). Predictors of caregiver burden in caregivers of individuals with dementia. *Journal of Advanced Nursing, 68*(4), 846–855.

Kim, S., & Esquivel, G. (2011). Adolescent spirituality and resilience: Theory, research, and educational practices. *Psychology in the Schools, 48*(7), 755–765.

King, C., & Merchant, C. (2008). Social and interpersonal factors relating to adolescent suicidality: A review of the literature. *Archives of Suicide Research, 12*, 181–196.

King, W. (2009). Toward a life-course perspective of police organizations. *Journal of Research in Crime and Delinquency, 46*(2), 213–244.

Kissman, K., & Maurer, L. (2002). East meets West: Therapeutic aspects of spirituality in health, mental health and addiction recovery. *International Social Work, 45*(1), 35–43.

Kitayama, S., Karasawa, M., & Mesquita, B. (2004). Collective and personal processes in regulating emotions: Emotion and self in Japan and the United States. In P. Philippot & R. Feldman (Eds.), *The regulation of emotion* (pp. 251–276). Mahwah, NJ: Erlbaum.

Kivel, P. (1991). Men, spirituality, and violence. *Creation Spirituality, 7*(4), 12–14, 50.

Kjellgren, A., & Buhrkall, H. (2010). A comparison of the restorative effect of a natural environment with that of a simulated natural environment. *Journal of Environmental Psychology, 30*, 464–472.

Klein, D., Mok, D., Chen, J., & Watkins, K. (2013). Age of language learning shapes brain structure: A cortical thickness study of bilingual and monolingual individuals. *Brain & Language*. Retrieved from http://dx.doi.org/10.1016/j.bandl.2013.05.014

Klein, J. (2012). *The bully society: School shootings and the crisis of bullying in America's schools*. New York, NY: New York University Press.

Kneas, D., & Perry, B. (2011). *Using technology in the early childhood classroom*. Retrieved from http://teacher.scholastic.com/professional/bruceperry/using_technology.htm

Knodel, J., Kespichayawattana, J., Saengtienchai, C., & Wiwatwanich, S. (2010). How left behind are rural parents of migrant children? Evidence from Thailand. *Ageing and Society, 30*(5), 811–841.

Knoll, C., & Sickmund, M. (2012). *Delinquency cases in juvenile court, 2009*. Washington, DC: U.S. Department of Justice, Office of Justice Programs, Office of Juvenile Justice and Delinquency Prevention. Retrieved from http://www.ojjdp.gov/pubs/239081.pdf

Kochanska, G. (1997). Multiple pathways to conscience for children with different temperaments: From toddlerhood to age 5. *Developmental Psychology, 33*, 228–240.

Kochanska, G., Forman, D., Aksan, N., & Dunbar, S. (2005). Pathways to conscience: Early mother–child mutually responsive orientation and children's moral emotion, conduct, and cognition. *Journal of Child Psychology and Psychiatry, 46*, 19–34.

Koehn, M. (2008). Contemporary women's perceptions of childbirth education. *Journal of Perinatal Education, 17*(1), 11–18.

Koenig, H. G. (2005). *Faith and mental health: Religious sources for healing*. Philadelphia, PA: Templeton Foundation Press.

Koenig, H. G., King, D. E., & Carson, V. B. (2012). *Handbook of religion and health* (2nd ed.). New York, NY: Oxford University Press.

Kogler Hill, S. (2013). Team leadership. In P. Northouse (Ed.), *Leadership: Theory and practice* (6th ed., pp. 287–318). Los Angeles, CA: Sage.

Kohlberg, L. (1969). *Stages in the development of moral thought and action*. New York, NY: Holt, Rinehart and Winston.

Kohlberg, L. (1976). Moral stages and moralization: The cognitive-developmental approach. In T. Lickona (Ed.), *Moral development and behavior: Theory, research, and social issues* (pp. 31–53). New York, NY: Holt.

Kohlberg, L. (1984). *Essays on moral development: Vol. 2. The psychology of moral development*. San Francisco, CA: Harper & Row.

Kohli, M., & Albertini, M. (2009). Childlessness and intergenerational transfers: What is at stake? *Ageing & Society, 29*, 1171–1183.

Kohli, M., & Künemund, H. (2005). The midlife generation in the family: Patterns of exchange and support. In S. Willis & M. Martin (Eds.), *Middle adulthood: A lifespan perspective* (pp. 35–61). Thousand Oaks, CA: Sage.

Kohut, H. (1971). *The analysis of the self*. New York, NY: International Universities Press.

Kolman, K. B., Hadley, S. K., & Jordahllafrato, M. A. (2015). Long-acting reversible contraception: Who, what, when, and how. *Journal of Family Medicine, 64*(8), 479–484.

Kominski, R., Shin, H., & Marotz, K. (2008, April 16–19). *Language needs of school-age children*. Paper presented at the Annual Meeting of the Population Association of America, New Orleans, LA. Retrieved January 19, 2010, from http://www.census.gov/population/www/socdemo/lang_use.html

Kondrat, M. E. (1999). Who is the "self" in self-aware: Professional self-awareness from a critical theory perspective. *Social Service Review, 73*(4), 451–477.

Kondrat, M. E. (2008). Person-in-environment. In T. Mizrahi & L. Davis (Eds.), *Encyclopedia of social work* (20th ed., Vol. 3, pp. 349–354). New York, NY: NASW Press/Oxford Press.

Koopmans, R. (2004). Political opportunity structure: Some splitting to balance the lumping. In J. Goodwin & J. Jasper (Eds.), *Rethinking social movements: Structure, meaning, and emotion* (pp. 61–73). Lanham, MD: Rowman & Littlefield.

Korkman, M., Stenroos, M., Mickos, A., Westman, M., Ekholm, P., & Byring, R. (2012). Does simultaneous bilingualism aggravate children's specific language problems? *Acta Paediatrica, 101*(9), 946–952. doi:10.1111/j.1651-2227.2012.02733.x

Korosi, A., & Baram, T. Z. (2010). Plasticity of the stress response early in life: Mechanisms and significance.

Developmental Psychobiology, 52(7), 661–670.

Kosciw, J., Greytak, E., Bartkiewicz, M., Boesen, M., & Palmer, N. M. (2012). *The 2011 National School Climate Survey: The experiences of lesbian, gay, bisexual and transgender youth in our nation's schools.* New York, NY: GLSEN. Retrieved from http://glsen .org/research

Kosmin, B., & Keysar, A. (2009). *American Religious Identification Survey (ARIS 2008).* Retrieved from http:// commons.trincoll.edu/aris/2011/08/ ARIS_Report_2008.pdf

Koss, M., & Figueredo, A. (2004). Change in cognitive mediators of rape's impact on psychosocial health across 2 years of recovery. *Journal of Counseling and Clinical Psychology, 72*(6), 1063–1072.

Kossek, E., Lobel, S., & Brown, J. (2006). Human resource strategies to manage workforce diversity: Examining "the business case." In A. Konrad & J. Pringle (Eds.), *Handbook of workplace diversity* (Vol. 1, pp. 53–74). Thousand Oaks, CA: Sage.

Kottak, C. P. (2008). *Anthropology: The exploration of human diversity* (12th ed.). Boston, MA: McGraw-Hill.

Kottak, C. P., & Kozaitis, K. (2008). *On being different: Diversity and multiculturalism in the North American mainstream.* Boston, MA: McGraw-Hill.

Kottler, J., & Englar-Carlson, M. (2010). *Learning group leadership: An experiential approach.* Thousand Oaks, CA: Sage.

Kovács, Á., & Mehler, J. (2009). Flexible learning of multiple speech structures in bilingual infants. *Science, 325*, 611–612.

Kowalski, K. (2003). The emergence of ethnic and racial attitudes in preschool-aged children. *Journal of Social Psychology, 143*, 677–690.

Kozhimannil, K. B., Law, M. R., & Virniq, B. A. (2013). Cesarean delivery rates vary tenfold among U.S. hospitals; reducing variation may reduce quality and cost issues. *Health Affiliates, 32*(3), 527–535.

Kozol, J. (2005). *The shame of the nation: The restoration of apartheid schooling in America.* New York, NY: Crown.

Kramer, B. (1997). Gain in the caregiving experience: Where are we? What next? *The Gerontologist, 37*, 218–232.

Kravetz, D. (2004). *Tales from the trenches: Politics and practice in feminist service organizations.* Lanham, MD: University Press of America.

Krayer, A., Ingledew, D., & Iphofen, R. (2008). Social comparison and body image in adolescence: A grounded theory approach. *Health Education Research, 23*(5), 892–903.

Kriesi, H. (1996). The organizational structure of new social movements in a political context. In D. McAdam, J. McCarthy, & M. Zald (Eds.), *Comparative perspectives on social movements* (pp. 152–184). New York, NY: Cambridge University Press.

Krill, D. (1996). Existential social work. In E. J. Turner (Ed.), *Social work treatment* (4th ed., pp. 250–281). New York, NY: Free Press.

Kristof, N., & WuDunn, S. (2009). *Half the sky: Turning oppression into opportunity for women worldwide.* New York, NY: Vintage.

Kroeber, A., & Kluckhohn, C. (1963). *Culture: A critical review of concepts and definitions.* New York, NY: Vintage.

Kroeber, A., & Kluckhohn, C. (1978). *Culture: A critical review of concepts and definitions.* Cambridge, MA: Peabody Museum. (Original work published 1952)

Kroger, J. (2007). *Identity development: Adolescence through adulthood* (2nd ed.). Thousand Oaks, CA: Sage.

Kroll, B. (2004). Living with an elephant: Growing up with parental substance misuse. *Child and Family Social Work, 9*, 129–140.

Krueger, A. K., Reither, E., Peppard, P. E., Krueger, P. M., & Hale, L. (2013). Do sleep-deprived adolescents make less healthy food choices? *Proceedings of the annual SLEEP Conference*, Baltimore.

Krug, E., Dahlberg, L., Mercy, J., Zwi, A., & Lozano, R. (2002). *World report on violence and health.* Geneva, Switzerland: World Health Organization.

Kübler-Ross, E. (1969). *On death and dying.* New York, NY: Macmillan.

Kupersmidt, J. B., & Dodge, K. A. (2004). *Children's peer relations: From development to intervention.* Washington, DC: American Psychological Association.

Kupritz, V. (2003). Accommodating privacy to facilitate new ways of working. *Journal of Architectural and Planning Research, 20*(2), 122–135.

Kurcinka, M. S. (2006). *Sleepless in America: Practical strategies to help your family get the sleep it deserves.* New York, NY: HarperCollins.

Kurdek, L. (2004). Are gay and lesbian cohabiting couples *really* different from heterosexual married couples? *Journal of Marriage and the Family, 66*, 880–900.

Kurdek, L. (2006). Differences between partners from heterosexual, gay, and lesbian cohabiting couples. *Journal of Marriage and Family, 68*, 509–528.

Kurlanski, S., & Ibay, A. (2012). Seasonal affective disorder. *American Family Physician, 86*(1), 1037–1041.

Kurtz, L. (2012). *Gods in the global village: The world's religions in sociological perspective* (3rd ed.). Los Angeles, CA: Sage.

Kurtz, S. (2002). *Workplace justice: Organizing multi-identity movements.* Minneapolis, MN: University of Minnesota Press.

Kurzweil, R. (2012). *How to create a mind: The secret of human thought revealed.* New York, NY: Viking.

Kvarfordt, C. L. (2010). Spiritual abuse and neglect of youth: Reconceptualizing what is known through an investigation of practitioners' experiences. *Journal of Religion & Spirituality in Social Work: Social Thought, 29*(2), 143–164.

Kvarfordt, C., & Sheridan, M. J. (2007). The role of religion and spirituality in working with children and adolescents: Results of a national survey. *Social Thought, 26*(3), 1–23.

Labouvie-Vief, G. (2005). Self-with-other representations and the organization of the self. *Journal of Research in Personality, 39*, 185–205.

Lachman, M., Agrigoroaei, S., Murphy, C., & Tun, P. (2010). Frequent cognitive activity compensates for education differences in episodic memory. *American Journal of Geriatric Psychiatry, 18*(1), 4–10.

Lachman, M., & Bertrand, R. (2001). Personality and the self in midlife. In M. Lachman (Ed.), *Handbook of midlife development* (pp. 279–309). New York, NY: Wiley.

LaDue, R. A. (1994). Coyote returns: Twenty sweats does not an Indian expert make. *Women & Therapy, 15*(1), 93–111.

Lagan, B., Sinclair, M., & Kernohan, W. (2010). Internet use in pregnancy informs women's decision-making: A web-based survey. *Birth, 37*(2), 106–115.

Lajoie, D. H., & Shapiro, S. I. (1992). Definitions of transpersonal psychology: The first twenty-three years. *Journal of Transpersonal Psychology, 4*, 79–98.

Lake, A. (2013). *Growing gulf between rich and poor reproach to the promise of the United Nations.* United Nations General Assembly GA11391. Retrieved from http://www.un.org/News/Press/ docs/2013/ga11391.doc.htm

Lakoff, G. (2006). *Whose freedom? The battle over America's most important ideas.* New York, NY: Farrar, Straus & Giroux.

Lakoff, G. (2011). How Occupy Wall Street's moral vision can beat the disastrous conservative world view. *AlterNet.* Retrieved from www.alternet.org/story/152800/ lakoff%3A_how_occupy_wall_ street's_moral_vision_can_beat_the_ disastrous_conservative_worldview

Lally, J. R. (2011). The link between consistent caring interactions with babies, early brain development, and school readiness. In E. Zigler, W. S. Gilliam, & W. S. Barnett (Eds.), *The pre-K debates: Current controversies and issues* (pp. 159–162). Baltimore, MD: Paul H. Brooks.

Lam, C., & McHale, S. (2012). Developmental patterns and family predictors of adolescent weight concerns: A replication and extension. *International Journal of Eating Disorders, 45*(4), 524–530.

Lam, V., & Smith, G. (2009). African and Caribbean adolescents in Britain: Ethnic identity and Britishness. *Ethnic and Racial Studies, 32*(7), 1248–1270.

Lamaze, F. (1958). *Painless childbirth: Psychoprophylactic method* (L. R. Celestin, Trans.). London, UK: Burke.

Lamers, W. (2013). *Signs of approaching death.* Washington, DC: Hospice Foundation of America. Retrieved from http://www.hospicefoundation.org/dyingsigns

Lane, C. (2007). *Shyness: How normal behavior became a sickness.* New Haven, CT: Yale University Press.

Lane, J., Wellman, H., Olson, S., LaBounty, J., & Kerr, D. (2010). Theory of mind and emotion understanding predict moral development in early childhood. *British Journal of Development Psychology, 28,* 871–889.

Lane, K. L., Wehby, J., Menzies, H. M., Doukas, G. L., Munton, S. M., & Gregg, R. M. (2003). Social skills instruction for students at risk for antisocial behavior. The effects of small-group instruction. *Behavioral Disorders, 28*(3), 229–248.

Lang, A. J., Aarons, G. A., Gearity, J., Laffaye, C., Satz, L., Dresselhaus, T. R., & Stein, M. B. (2008). Direct and indirect links between childhood maltreatment, posttraumatic stress disorder, and women's health. *Behavioral Medicine, 33*(4), 125–135.

Langeslag, S., Muris, P., & Franken, I. (2013). Measuring romantic love: Psychometric properties of the infatuation and attachment scales. *Journal of Sex Research, 50*(8), 739–747.

Langle, A., & Probst, C. (2004). Existential questions of the elderly. *Archives of Psychiatry and Psychotherapy, 6*(2), 15–20.

Lansford, J., Deater-Deckard, K., Dodge, K., Bates, J., & Pettit, G. (2004). Ethnic differences in the link between physical discipline and later adolescent externalizing behaviors. *Journal of Child Psychology and Psychiatry, 45,* 801–812.

Lantz, J., & Walsh, J. (2007). *Short-term existential intervention in clinical practice.* Chicago, IL: Lyceum Books.

Lapidus, I. (1978). Adulthood in Islam: Religious maturing in the Islamic tradition. In E. H. Erikson (Ed.), *Adulthood* (pp. 97–112). New York, NY: Norton & Norton.

Larson, R. W., Wilson, S., & Mortimer, J. T. (2002). Adolescence in the 21st century: An international perspective—Adolescents' preparation for the future. *Journal of Research on Adolescence, 12*(1), 159–166.

Latva, R., Lehtonen, L., Salmelin, R. K., & Tamminen, T. (2007). Visits by the family to the neonatal intensive care. *Acta Paediatrica, 96*(2), 215–220.

Lau, A., Litrownik, A., Newton, R., Black, M., & Everson, M. (2006). Factors affecting the link between physical discipline and child externalizing problems in Black and White families. *Journal of Community Psychology, 34*(1), 89–103.

Lau, C., Ambalavanan, N., Chakraborty, H., Wingate, M. S., & Carlo, W. A. (2013). Extremely low birth weight and infant mortality rates in the United States. *Pediatrics, 131*(5), 855–860.

Lau, J. T., Wang, Q., Cheng, Y., Kim, J., Yang, X., & Tsui, H. (2008). Infertility-related perceptions and responses and their associations with quality of life among rural Chinese infertile couples. *Journal of Sexual and Marital Therapy, 34,* 248–267.

Lau, J. Y. F., Eley, T. C., & Stevenson, J. (2006). Examining the state–trait anxiety relationship: A behavioural genetic approach. *Journal of Abnormal Child Psychology, 34*(1), 19–27.

Lau, W., Chan, C., Li, J., & Au, T. (2010). Effectiveness of group cognitive-behavioral treatment for childhood anxiety in community clinics. *Behavior Research and Therapy, 28,* 1067–1077.

Lauritsen, J., & Rezey, M. (2013). *Measuring the prevalence of crime with the National Crime Victimization Survey.* Washington, DC: U.S. Department of Justice, Office of Justice Programs, Bureau of Justice Statistics. Retrieved from http://www.bjs.gov/content/pub/pdf/mpcncvs.pdf

Lawford, H., Pratt, M., Hunsberg, B., & Pancer, S. M. (2005). Adolescent generativity: A longitudinal study of two possible contexts for learning concern for future generations. *Journal of Research on Adolescence, 15*(3), 261–273.

Lawrence, C., & Andrews, K. (2004). The influence of perceived prison crowding on male inmates' perception of aggressive events. *Aggressive Behavior, 30*(4), 273–283.

Lawrence, C. R., Carlson, E. A., & Egeland, B. (2006). The impact of foster care on development. *Development and Psychopathology, 18*(1), 57–76.

Lazarus, R. S. (2001). Relational meaning and discrete emotions. In K. R. Scherer, A. Schorr, & T. Johnstone (Eds.), *Appraisal processes in emotion: Theory, methods, research* (pp. 37–67). New York, NY: Oxford University Press.

Lazarus, R. S. (2007). Stress and emotion: A new synthesis. In A. Monat, R. S. Lazarus, & G. Reevy (Eds.), *The Praeger handbook on stress and coping* (Vol. 1, pp. 33–51). Westport, CT: Praeger/Greenwood.

Le Brocque, R. M., Hendrikz, J., & Kenardy, J. A. (2010). The course of posttraumatic stress in children: Examination of recovery trajectories following traumatic injury. *Journal of Pediatric Psychology, 35*(6), 637–645.

Lederberg, A., Schick, B., & Spencer, P. (2013). Language and literacy development of deaf and hard-of-hearing children: Successes and challenges. *Developmental Psychology, 49*(1), 15–30.

Lee, C., Tsenkova, V., & Carr, D. (2014). Childhood trauma and metabolic syndrome in men and women. *Social Science & Medicine, 105,* 122–130.

Lee, B., & Campbell, K. (1999). Neighbor networks of Black and White Americans. In B. Wellman (Ed.), *Networks in the global village* (pp. 119–146). Boulder, CO: Westview Press.

Lee, C., & Beckert, T. (2012). Taiwanese adolescent cognitive autonomy and identity development: The relationship of situational and agential factors. *International Journal of Psychology, 47*(1), 39–50.

Lee, J. (2001). *The empowerment approach to social work practice: Building the beloved community.* New York, NY: Columbia University Press.

Lee, K. H. (2011). The role of spiritual experience, forgiveness, and religious support on the general well-being of older adults. *Journal of Religion, Spirituality & Aging, 23*(3), 206–223.

Lee, M. (2008). A small act of creativity: Fostering creativity in clinical social work practice. *Families in Society, 89*(1), 19–31.

Lee, M. Y., Ng, S., Leung, P. P. Y., & Chan, C. L. W. (2009). *Integrative body-mind-spirit social work: An empirically based approach to assessment and treatment.* New York, NY: Oxford University Press.

Lee, Y. (2010). Office layout affecting privacy, interaction, and acoustic quality in LEED-certified buildings. *Building and Environment, 45,* 1594–1600.

Leeder, E. (2004). *The family in global perspective: A gendered journey.* Thousand Oaks, CA: Sage.

Leisering, L. (2003). Government and the life course. In J. Mortimer & M. Shanahan (Eds.), *Handbook of the life course* (pp. 205–225). New York, NY: Kluwer Academic/Plenum.

Lengermann, P., & Niebrugge-Brantley, G. (2007). Contemporary feminist theories. In G. Ritzer (Ed.), *Contemporary sociological theory and its classical roots* (2nd ed., pp. 185–214). Boston, MA: McGraw-Hill.

Lenhart, A. (2012, March). *Teens, smartphones & texting*. PewResearch Internet Project. Retrieved from www.pewinternet.org/2012/03/19/teens-smartphones-texting

Lenski, G. (1966). *Power and privilege*. New York, NY: McGraw-Hill.

Leonard, K. (2015, June 25). Supreme court upholds Obamacare subsidies. *U.S. News*. Retrieved from http://www.usnews.com/news/articles/2015/06/25/supreme-court-upholds-obamacare-subsidies-in-king-v-burwell

Leonard, K., & Eiden, R. (2007). Marital and family processes in the context of alcohol use and alcohol disorders. *Annual Review of Clinical Psychology, 3*, 285–310.

LePoire, B. (2006). *Family communication: Nurturing and control in a changing world*. Thousand Oaks, CA: Sage.

Leung, P.P.Y., & Chan, C. L.W. (2010). Utilizing Eastern spirituality in clinical practice: A qualitative study of Chinese women with breast cancer. *Smith College Studies in Social Work, 80*(2–3), 159–183.

Leung, P.P.Y., Chan, C. L.W., Ng, S. M., & Lee, M.Y. (2009). Towards body-mind-spirit integration: East meets West in clinical social work practice. *Clinical Social Work Journal, 37*(4), 303–311.

Levi, D. (2014). *Group dynamics for teams* (4th ed.). Los Angeles, CA: Sage.

Levine, L. E., & Munsch, J. (2011). *Child development: An active learning approach*. Thousand Oaks, CA: Sage.

Levine, S. (1999). Children's cognition as the foundation of spirituality. *International Journal of Children's Spirituality, 4*(2), 121–140.

Levinson, D. (1977). The mid-life transition. *Psychiatry, 40*, 99–112.

Levinson, D. (1978). *The seasons of a man's life*. New York, NY: Knopf.

Levinson, D. (1980). Toward a conception of the adult life course. In N. J. Smelser & E. H. Erikson (Eds.), *Themes of work and love in adulthood* (pp. 265–290). Cambridge, MA: Harvard University Press.

Levinson, D. (1986). A conception of adult development. *American Psychologist, 41*(1), 3–13.

Levinson, D. (1990). A theory of life structure development in adulthood. In C. N. Alexander & E. J. Langer (Eds.), *Higher stages of human development* (pp. 35–54). New York, NY: Oxford University Press.

Levinson, D., with Levinson, J. (1996). *The seasons of a woman's life*. New York, NY: Ballantine Books.

Levitt, H., & Ippolito, M. (2014a). Being transgender: Navigating minority stressors and developing authentic self-presentation. *Psychology of Women Quarterly, 38*(1), 46–64.

Levitt, H., & Ippolito, M. (2014b). Being transgender: The experience of transgender identity development. *Journal of Homosexuality, 61*(12), 1727–1758.

Lev-Wiesel, R., Sarid, M., & Sternberg, R. (2013). Measuring social peer rejection during childhood: Development and validation. *Journal of Aggression, Maltreatment & Trauma, 22*(5), 482–492.

Lewandowski, C. A., & Canda, E. R. (1995). A typological model for the assessment of religious groups. *Social Thought, 18*(1), 17–38.

Lewicka, M. (2011). Place attachment: How far have we come in the last 40 years? *Journal of Environmental Psychology, 31*, 207–230.

Lewis, M. (2005). The child and its family: The social network model. *Human Development, 48*, 8–27.

Lewis, T. (1994). A comparative analysis of the effects of social skills training and teacher-directed contingencies on social behavior of preschool children with disabilities. *Journal of Behavioral Education, 4*, 267–281.

Li, S.-C. (2006). Biocultural co-construction of life span development. In P.B. Baltes, P.A. Reuter-Lorenz, & F. Rössler (Eds.), *Life span development and the brain: The perspective of biocultural co-constructivism* (pp. 40–60). Cambridge, UK: Cambridge University Press.

Liang, K. (2014). The cross-domain correlates of subjective age in Chinese oldest-old. *Aging & Mental Health, 18*(2), 217–224.

Lichter, D., & Qian, Z. (2008). Serial cohabitation and the marital life course. *Journal of Marriage and Family, 70*, 861–878.

Lichter, D., Turner, R., & Sassler, S. (2010). National estimates of the rise of serial cohabitation. *Social Science Research, 39*, 754–765.

Lieberman, M. (2013). *Social: Why our brains are wired to connect*. New York, NY: Crown.

Lie, K. K., Groholt, E. K., & Eskild, A. (2010). Association of cerebral palsy with Apgar score in low and normal birthweight infants: Population based cohort study. *British Medical Journal, 341*. Retrieved from http://www.bmj.com/content/341/bmj.c4990

Lightfoot, C., Lalonde, C., & Chandler, M. (Eds.). (2004). *Changing conceptions of psychological life*. Mahwah, NJ: Erlbaum.

Lima-Pereira, P., Bermudez-Tamayo, C., & Jasienska, G. (2012). Use of the internet as a source of health information amongst participants of antenatal classes. *Journal of Clinical Nursing, 21*(3–4), 322–330.

Limb, G. E., & Hodge, D. R. (2008). Developing spiritual competency with Native Americans: Promoting wellness through balance and harmony. *Families in Society: The Journal of Contemporary Social Services, 89*(4), 615–622.

Lindell, G., Marsal, K., & Kallen, K. (2012). Impact of maternal characteristics on fetal growth in the third trimester: A population-based study. *Ultrasound in Obstetrics and Gynecology, 40*(6), 680–687.

Lindemann, E. (1944). Symptomatology and management of acute grief. *American Journal of Psychiatry, 101*, 141–148.

Linver, M. R., Brooks-Gunn, J., & Kohen, D. (2002). Family processes as pathways from income to young children's development. *Developmental Psychology, 38*, 719–734.

Lipka, M. (2013). What surveys say about worship attendance – and why some stay home. Pew Research Center. Retrieved from http://www.pewresearch.org/fact-tank/2013/09/13/what-surveys-say-about-worship-attendance-and-why-some-stay-home/

Lippa, R. A. (2005). *Gender, nature, and nurture* (2nd ed.). Mahwah, NJ: Erlbaum.

Lippman, L., Vandivere, S., Keith, J., & Atienza, A. (2008). Child care use by low income families: Variations across states. *Child Trends Research Brief #2008-23*. Retrieved from www.childtrends.org/wp-content/uploads/2013/07/2008-23ChildcareLow-Income.pdf

Lipscomb, A., & Gersch, I. (2012). Using "spiritual listening tools" to investigate how children describe spiritual and philosophical meaning in their lives. *International Journal of Children's Spirituality, 17*(1), 5–23.

Litty, C., & Hatch, J. A. (2006). Hurry up and wait: Rethinking special education identification in kindergarten. *Early Childhood Education Journal, 33*(4), 203–208.

Livingston, G. (2013). *At grandmother's house we stay*. PewResearchCenter. Retrieved from www.pewsocial trends.org/files/2013/09/grandparents_report_final_ 2013.pdf

Living Wage Action Coalition. (n.d.). *Student worker solidarity resource center*. Retrieved from http://www.livingwageaction.org

Living Wage Aotearoa New Zealand. (2014). *About*. Retrieved from http://www.livingwagenx.org.nz/about.php

Living Wage Foundation. (2014). *History*. Retrieved from http://www.livingwage.org.uk/history

Lloyd, C. B., Behrman, J. R., Stromquist, N. P., & Cohen, B. (2006). *The changing transitions to adulthood in developing countries: Selected studies*. Washington, DC: National Research Council.

Lloyd, S., Few, A., & Allen, K. (2009). Preface. In S. Lloyd, A. Few, & K. Allen (Eds.),

Handbook of feminist family studies. Thousand Oaks, CA: Sage.

Loftin, R. W., Habli, M., & DeFranco, E. A. (2010). Late preterm births. *Review in Obstetrics and Gynecology, 3*(1), 10–19.

Logan, G. (2000). Information-processing theories. In A. E. Kazdi (Ed.), *Encyclopedia of psychology* (Vol. 4, pp. 294–297). Washington, DC: American Psychological Association.

Logan, S. L. (1997). Meditation as a tool that links the personal and the professional. *Reflections: Narratives of Professional Helping, 3*(1), 38–44.

Logan, S. L. (Ed.). (2001). *The Black family: Strengths, self-help, and positive change* (2nd ed.). Boulder, CO: Westview Press.

Lombardi, J. (2012). The federal policy environment. In Institute of Medicine and National Research Council, *From neurons to neighborhoods: An update: Workshop summary* (pp. 26–30). Paper presented at Committee on From Neurons to Neighborhoods: Anniversary Workshop, Washington, DC. Washington, DC: The National Academies Press.

Loomis, E. (2013). The global water crisis: Privatization and neocolonialism in film. *Radical History Review, 116*, 189–195.

Lothian, J. A. (2008). Choice, autonomy, and childbirth education. *Journal of Perinatal Education, 17*(1), 35–38.

Loureiro, T., Ferreira, A. F. A., Ushokov, F., Montenegro, N., & Nicolaides, K. H. (2012). Dilated fourth ventricle in fetuses with trisomy 18, trisomy 13 and triploidy at 11–13 weeks' gestation. *Fetal Diagnosis and Therapy, 32*(3), 186–189.

Lovaglia, M. (1995). Power and status: Exchange, attribution, and expectation states. *Small Group Research, 26*, 400–426.

Lovaglia, M., Mannix, E., Samuelson, C., Sell, J., & Wilson, R. (2005). Conflict, power, and status in groups. In M. Poole & A. Hollingshead (Eds.), *Theories of small groups: Interdisciplinary perspectives* (pp. 63–97). Thousand Oaks, CA: Sage.

Low, S., & Altman, I. (1992). Place attachment: A conceptual inquiry. In I. Altman & S. Low (Eds.), *Place attachment* (pp. 1–12). New York, NY: Plenum.

Lowe, J., Erickson, S., MacLean, P., & Duvall, S. (2009). Early working memory and maternal communication in toddlers born very low birth weight. *Acta Paediatrica, 98*, 660–663.

Lowe, J., MacLean, P., Duncan, A., Aragón, C., Schrader, R., Caprihan, A., & Phillips, J. (2012). Association of maternal interaction with emotional regulation in 4- and 9-month infants during the Still Face Paradigm. *Infant Behavior and Development, 35*, 295–302.

Lowenstein, A., & Daatland, S. (2006). Filial norms and family support in a comparative cross-national context: Evidence from the OASIS study. *Ageing and Society, 26*, 203–223.

Lownsdale, S. (1997). Faith development across the lifespan: Fowler's integrative work. *Journal of Psychology and Theology, 25*, 49–63.

Lowry, B., Cao, J., & Everard, A. (2011). Privacy concerns versus desire for interpersonal awareness in driving the use of self-disclosure technologies: The case of instant messaging in two cultures. *Journal of Management Information Systems, 27*(4), 163–200.

Lu, P. (2007). Sibling relationships in adulthood and old age: A case study in Taiwan. *Current Sociology, 55*(4), 621–637.

Lubin, H., & Johnson, D. R. (1998). Healing ceremonies. *Family Networker, 22*(5), 38–39, 64–67.

Lucas, R., & Donnellan, M. B. (2011). Personality development across the life span: Longitudinal analyses with a national sample from Germany. *Journal of Personality and Social Psychology, 101*(4), 847–861.

Luchowski, A. T., Anderson, B. L., Power, M. L., Raglan, G. B., Espey, E., & Schulkin, J. (2014). Obstetrician-gynecologists and contraception: Long-acting reversible contraception practices and education. *Contraception, 89*(6), 578–583.

Luhmann, N. (2011). *Introduction to systems theory.* New York, NY: Polity Press.

Lui, M., Robles, B., Leondar-Wright, B., Brewer, R., & Adamson, R. (2006). *The color of wealth.* New York, NY: The New Press.

Lum, D. (2011). *Culturally competent practice: A framework for understanding diverse groups and justice issues* (4th ed.). Belmont, CA: Thomson.

Lund, L. K., Vik, T., Skranes, J., Brubakk, A. M., & Indredavik, M. S. (2011). Psychiatric morbidity in two low birth weight groups assessed by diagnostic interview in young adulthood. *Acta Paediatricia, 100*(4), 598–604.

Lund, T., Andersen, J., Winding, T., Biering, K., & Labriola, M. (2013). Negative life events in childhood as risk indicators of labour market participation in young adulthood: A prospective birth cohort study. *PLoS One, 8*(9), 1–7.

Lunkett, S., Behnke, A., Sands, T., & Choi, B. (2009). Adolescents' reports of parental engagement and academic achievement in immigrant families. *Journal of Youth & Adolescence, 38*(2), 257–268. doi:10.1007/s10964-008-9325-4

Luo, M. (2009, April 12). Longer unemployment for those 45 and older. *New York Times.* Retrieved from http://www.nytimes.com/2009/04/13/us/13age.html?pagewanted=all&_r=0

Luthar, S. (Ed.). (2003). *Resilience and vulnerability: Adaptation in the context of childhood adversities.* New York, NY: Cambridge University Press.

Lutz, A., Dunne, J. D., & Davidson, R. J. (2007). Meditation and the neuroscience of consciousness. In P. Zelazo, M. Moscovitch, & E. Thompson (Eds.), *The Cambridge handbook of consciousness* (pp. 499–552). Cambridge, UK: Cambridge University Press.

Lyn, A. (2009). *Middle childhood matters: An inventory of full-week after school programs for children 6–12 years old in Toronto.* Toronto, ON: Community Social Planning Council of Toronto.

Lyon, L. (1987). *The community in urban society.* Philadelphia, PA: Temple University Press.

Lyotard, J. (1984). *The postmodern condition.* Minneapolis, MN: University of Minnesota Press.

Maccoby, E. (2002a). Gender and group processes: A developmental perspective. *Current Directions in Psychological Science, 11*, 55–58.

Maccoby, E. (2002b). Parenting effects: Issues and controversies. In J. G. Borkowski, S. Landesman Ramey, & M. Bristol-Power (Eds.), *Parenting and the child's world* (pp. 35–45). Mahwah, NJ: Erlbaum.

MacDorman, M., Mathews, M., & Declercq, E. (2012). Home births in the United States, 1990–2009. *NCHS Data Brief*, No. 84. Hyattsville, MD: National Center for Health Statistics. Retrieved from www.cdc.gov/nchs/data/databriefs/db84.htm

Mackay, G., & Neill, J. (2010). The effect of "green exercise" on state anxiety and the roles of exercise duration, intensity, and greenness: A quasi-experimental study. *Psychology of Sport and Exercise, 22*, 238–245.

MacKinlay, E. (Ed.). (2006). *Aging, spirituality and palliative care.* Binghamton, MA: Haworth Press.

Madden, M., Lenhart, A., Duggan, M., Cortesi, S., & Gasser, U. (2013, March). *Teens and technology 2013.* Pew Research Center and Berkman Center for Internet & Society at Harvard University. Retrieved from http://www.pewinternet.org/Reports/2013/Teens-and-Tech.aspx

Mader, S., & Windelspecht, M. (2012). *Human biology* (12th ed.). New York, NY: McGraw-Hill.

Madigan, S. (2011). *Narrative therapy.* Washington, DC: American Psychological Association.

Madigan, S., Moran, G., & Pederson, D. R. (2006). Unresolved states of mind, disorganized attachment relationships, and disrupted interactions of adolescent mothers and their infants. *Developmental Psychology, 42*(2), 293–304.

Madkour, A., Farhat, T., Halpern, C., Godeau, E., & Gabhainn, S. (2010). Early adolescent sexual initiation as a problem behavior: A comparative study of five nations. *Journal of Adolescent Health, 47*, 389–398.

Magai, C. (2001). Emotions over the life span. In J. E. Birren & K. W. Schale (Eds.), *Handbook of the psychology of aging* (5th ed., pp. 399–426). San Diego, CA: Academic Press.

Magaldi-Dopman, D., & Park-Taylor, J. (2010). Sacred adolescence: Practical suggestions for psychologists working with adolescents' religious and spiritual identity. *Professional Psychology: Research and Practice, 41*(5), 382–390.

Maggiolo, F., & Leone, S. (2010). Is HAART modifying the HIV epidemic? *The Lancet, 376*(9740), 14–20.

Mah, V., & Ford-Jones, E. (2012). Spotlight on middle childhood: Rejuvenating the "forgotten years." *Paediatrics & Child Health, 17*(2), 81–83.

Maier, M. F., Vitiello, V. E., & Greenfield, D. B. (2012). A multilevel model of child- and classroom-level psychosocial factors that support language and literacy resilience of children in Head Start. *Early Childhood Research Quarterly, 27*(1), 104–114.

Mak, W., Cheung, R., & Law, L. (2009). Sense of community in Hong Kong: Relations with community-level characteristics and residents' well-being. *American Journal of Community Psychology, 44*, 80–92.

Mäkinen, T. E., Borodulin, K., Tammelin, T., Rahkonen, O., Laatikainen, T., & Prättälä, R. (2010). The effects of adolescence sports and exercise on adulthood leisure-time physical activity in educational groups. *International Journal of Behavioral Nutrition & Physical Activity*. Retrieved from link.springer.com/article/10.1186%2F1479-5868-7-27#page-1

Malanga, S. (2003, Winter). How the "living wage" sneaks socialism into cities. *City Journal*, 1–8. Retrieved May 17, 2010, from http://www.city-journal.org/html/13_1_how_the_living_wage.html

Maller, C., Townsend, M., Pryor, A., Brown, P., & St. Leger, L. (2005). Healthy nature healthy people: "Contact with nature" as an upstream health promotion intervention for populations. *Health Promotion International, 21*(1), 45–54.

Mallon, G. P., & Hess, P. M. C. (2014). *Child welfare for the twenty-first century: A handbook of practices, policies, and programs*. New York, NY: Columbia University Press.

Malti, T., Gasser, L., & Buchmann, M. (2009). Aggressive and prosocial children's emotion attributions and moral reasoning. *Aggressive Behavior, 35*(1), 90–102.

Mandy, G. T. (2013). Small for gestational age infant. *UpToDate*. Retrieved from http://www.uptodate.com/contents/small-for-gestational-age-infant

Mann, C. (2011). *1493: Discovering the new world Columbus created*. New York, NY: Knopf.

Mann, S. (2011). Pioneers of U.S. ecofeminism and environmental justice. *Feminist Formations, 23*(2), 1–25.

Mann, W. C., Belchior, P., Tomita, M. R., & Kemp, B. J. (2005). Computer use by middle-aged and older adults with disabilities. *Technology and Disability, 17*(1), 1–9.

Manning, L. K. (2010). An exploration of paganism: Aging women embracing the divine feminine. *Journal of Religion, Spirituality & Aging, 22*(3), 196–210.

Manning, M., Cornelius, L., & Okundaye, J. (2004). Empowering African Americans through social work practice: Integrating an Afrocentric perspective, ego psychology, and spirituality. *Families in Society: The Journal of Contemporary Social Services, 85*(2), 229–235.

Mano, R. (2009). Information technology, adaptation and innovation in nonprofit human service organizations. *Journal of Technology in Human Services, 27*, 227–234.

Mapp, S. (2008). *Human rights and social justice in a global perspective: An introduction to international social work*. New York, NY: Oxford University Press.

March, J., & Simon, H. (1958). *Organizations*. New York, NY: Wiley.

March of Dimes. (2010). *Pregnancy loss: Stillbirth*. Retrieved from www.marchofdimes.com/loss/stillbirth.aspx

March of Dimes. (2012a). *Born too soon: The global action report of preterm birth*. Retrieved from http://www.marchofdimes.com/glue/files/BornToSoonGARonPretermBirth_05212012.pdf

March of Dimes. (2012b). *March of Dimes 2012 Premature birth report card*. Retrieved from http://www.marchofdimes.com/peristats/pdflib/998/US.pdf

March of Dimes. (2012c). *Prematurity campaign*. Retrieved from http://www.marchofdimes.com/mission/march-of-dimes-prematurity-campaign.aspx

Marcia, J. E. (1966). Development and validation of ego-identity status. *Journal of Personality and Social Psychology, 3*, 551–558.

Marcia, J. E. (1980). Identity in adolescence. In J. Adelson (Ed.), *Handbook of adolescent psychology* (pp. 159–187). New York, NY: Wiley.

Marecek, J., Kimmel, E. B., Crawford, M., & Hare-Mustin, R. T. (2003). Psychology of women and gender. In D. K. Freedheim (Ed.), *Handbook of psychology: History of psychology* (Vol. 1, pp. 249–268). Hoboken, NJ: Wiley.

Markovitzky, G., & Mosek, A. (2005). The role of symbolic resources in coping with immigration. *Journal of Ethnic & Cultural Diversity in Social Work, 14*(1–2), 145–158.

Marks, G., & McAdam, D. (2009). On the relationship of political opportunities to the form of collective action: The case of the European Union. In D. della Porta, H. Kriesi, & D. Rucht (Eds.), *Social movements in a globalising world* (pp. 97–111). New York, NY: Palgrave Macmillan.

Marks, N., Bumpass, L., & Jun, H. (2004). Family roles and well-being during the middle life course. In O. Brim, C. Ryff, & R. Kessler (Eds.), *How healthy are we? A national study of well-being at midlife* (pp. 514–549). Chicago, IL: University of Chicago Press.

Markus, H., & Kitayama, S. (2003). Models of agency: Sociocultural diversity in the construction of action. In G. Berman & J. Berman (Eds.), *Cross-cultural differences in perspectives on the self* (pp. 2–57). Lincoln, NE: University of Nebraska Press.

Markus, H., & Kitayama, S. (2009). Culture and the self: Implications for cognition, emotion, and motivation. In P. Smith & D. Best (Eds.), *Cross-cultural psychology* (Vol. 1, pp. 265–320). Thousand Oaks, CA: Sage.

Marmot, M., & Fuhrer, R. (2004). Socioeconomic position and health across midlife. In O. Brim, C. Ryff, & R. Kessler (Eds.), *How healthy are we? A national study of well-being at midlife* (pp. 64–89). Chicago, IL: University of Chicago Press.

Marotz, L. R., & Allen, K. E. (2013). *Developmental profiles: Pre-birth through adolescence*. Belmont, CA: Wadsworth/Cengage Learning.

Marsh, H., & Kleitman, S. (2005). Consequences of employment during high school: Character building, subversion of academic goals, or a threshold? *American Educational Research Journal, 42*, 331–370.

Marsh, V. R. (2005). Story sharing, voice fatigue, and moving forward after divorce: When women resist being defined by their tragedies. *Reflections: Narratives of Professional Helping, 11*(1), 86–91.

Marshall, V., & Mueller, M. (2003). Theoretical roots of the life-course perspective. In W. Heinz & V. Marshall (Eds.), *Social dynamics of the life course: Transitions, institutions, and interrelations* (pp. 3–32). New York, NY: Aldine de Gruyter.

Marti, I., Etzion, D., & Leca, B. (2008). Theoretical approaches for studying corporations, democracy, and the public good. *Journal of Management Inquiry, 17*, 148–151.

Martin, J. A., Hamilton, B. E., Ventura, S. J., Osterman, M. J. K., Wilson, E., & Mathews, T. J. (2012). Births: Final data for 2010. *National Vital Statistics Reports, 61*(1). Retrieved from http://www.midwife.org/CNM/CM-attended-Birth-Statistics

Martin, J. A., & Sherman, M. (2010). The impact of military duty and military life on individuals and families. In S. Price, C. Price, & P. McKenry (Eds.), *Families & Change: Coping with stressful events and transitions* (4th ed., pp. 381–397). Thousand Oaks, CA: Sage.

Martin, J. J. (2013). Benefits and barriers to physical activity for individuals with disabilities: A social-relational model of disability perspective. *Disability and Rehabilitation: An International, Multidisciplinary Journal, 35*(24), 2030–2037.

Martin, M., & Zimprich, D. (2005). Cognitive development in midlife. In S. Willis & M. Martin (Eds.), *Middle adulthood: A lifespan perspective* (pp. 179–206). Thousand Oaks, CA: Sage.

Martin, T. L., & Doka, K. J. (2000). *Men don't cry . . . women do: Transcending gender stereotypes of grief.* Philadelphia, PA: Brunner/Mazel.

Martinez, G., Copen, C., & Abma, J. (2011). Teenagers in the United States: Sexual activity, contraceptive use, and childbearing, 2006–2010 National Survey of Family Growth. National Center for Health Statistics. *Vital Health Statistics, 23*(31). Retrieved from www.cdc.gov/nchs/data/series/sr_23_031.pdf

Martinez, J. I., Gudiño, O. G., & Lau, A. S. (2013). Problem-specific racial/ethnic disparities in pathways from maltreatment exposure to specialty mental health service use for youth in child welfare. *Child Maltreatment, 18*(2), 98–107.

Martinez-Brawley, E. (2000). *Close to home: Human services and the small community.* Washington, DC: NASW Press.

Martz, E. (2004). Do reactions of adaptation to disability influence the fluctuation of future time orientation among individuals with spinal cord injuries? *Rehabilitation Counseling Bulletin, 47*(2), 86–95.

Marx, G., & McAdam, D. (1994). *Collective behavior and social movements: Process and structure.* Englewood Cliffs, NJ: Prentice Hall.

Marx, J. (2012). *American social policy in the 60's and 70's*: The Social Welfare History Project. Retrieved from http://www.socialwelfarehistory.com/eras/american-social-policy-in-the-60s-and-70s

Marx, K. (1967). *Capital: A critique of political economy* (S. Moore & E. Aveling, Trans; Vol. 1). New York, NY: International. (Original work published 1887)

Mascarenhas, M. N., Flaxman, S. R., Boerma, T., Vanderpoel, S., & Stevens, G. A. (2012). National, regional, and global trends in infertility prevalence since 1990: A systematic analysis of 277 health surveys. *PLoS One.* Retrieved from http://www.plosmedicine.org/article/info%3Adoi%2F10.1371%2Fjournal.pmed.1001356

Maslow, A. (1962). *Toward a psychology of being.* New York, NY: Van Nostrand.

Maslow, A. (1971). *Farther reaches of human nature.* New York, NY: Viking.

Masse, L., & Barnett, W. S. (2002). *A benefit cost analysis of the Abecedarian Early Childhood Intervention.* Retrieved September 13, 2011, from http://nieer.org/docs/?DocID=57

Maternal and child nutrition. (2013). *The Lancet.* Retrieved from http://www.thelancet.com/series/maternal-and-child-nutrition

Matheson, L. (1996). Valuing spirituality among Native American populations. *Counseling and Values, 41*, 51–58.

Mathews, T. J., & MacDorman, M. F. (2013). Infant mortality statistics from the 2009 period linked birth/infant death data set. *National Vital Statistics Reports, 61*(8). Retrieved from http://www.cdc.gov/nchs/data/nvsr/nvsr61/nvsr61_08.pdf

Matson, J., Fodstad, J., & Dempsey, T. (2009). What symptoms predict the diagnosis of autism or PDD-NOS in infants and toddlers with developmental delays using the baby and infant screen for autism traits. *Developmental Neurorehabilitation, 12*(6), 381–388.

Matsuba, M. K., Pratt, M., Norris, J., Mohle, E., Alisat, S., & McAdams, D. (2012). Environmentalism as a context for expressing identity and generativity: Patterns among activists and uninvolved youth and midlife adults. *Journal of Personality, 80*(4), 1091–1115.

Matthews, D. A., McCullough, M. E., Larson, D. B., Koenig, H. G., Swyers, J. P., & Milano, M. G. (1998). Religious commitment and health status: A review of the research and implications for family medicine. *Archives of Family Medicine, 7*(2), 118–124.

Matto, H., Berry-Edwards, J., Hutchison, E. D., Bryant, S. A., & Waldbillig, A. (2006). An exploratory study on multiple intelligences and social work education. *Journal of Social Work Education, 42*(2), 405–416.

Matto, H., Strolin-Goltzman, J., & Ballan, M. (Eds.). (2014). *Neuroscience for social work: Current research and practice.* New York, NY: Springer.

Maxwell, L. (2003). Home and school density effects on elementary school children: The role of spatial density. *Environment and Behavior, 35*(4), 566–578.

May, A., Duivenvoorden, H., Korstjens, I., van Weert, E., Hoekstra-Weebers, J., van den Borne, B., . . . Ros, W. (2008). The effects of group cohesion on rehabilitation outcome in cancer survivors. *Psycho-Oncology, 17*, 917–925.

Mayer, K. U., Baltes, P. B., Baltes, M., Borchelt, M., Delius, J., Helmchen, H., . . . Wagner, M. (1999). What do we know about old age and aging? Conclusions from the Berlin Aging Study. In P. B. Baltes & K. U. Mayer (Eds.), *The Berlin Aging Study: Aging from 70 to 100* (pp. 475–519). Cambridge, UK: Cambridge University Press.

Maynard, M., & Taylor, C. (1996). A comparative analysis of Japanese and U.S. attitudes toward direct marketing. *Journal of Direct Marketing, 10*(1), 34–44.

Mayo, E. (1933). *The human problems of an industrial civilization.* New York, NY: Macmillan.

Mayo, K. R. (2009). *Creativity, spirituality, and mental health: Exploring connections.* Surrey, UK: Ashgate.

Mayo Clinic. (2013). *Dementia: Risk factors.* Retrieved from www.mayoclinc.com/health/dementia/DS01131/DSECTION=risk-factors

Mayo Clinic. (2015). *Withdrawal method.* Retrieved from www.mayoclinic.org/tests-procedures/withdrawal-method/basics/what-you-can-expect/prc.-20020661

Mayo Foundation for Medical Education and Research. (2012). *Multiple sclerosis: Symptoms.* Retrieved from http://www.mayoclinic.com/health/multiple-sclerosis/DS00188/DSECTION=symptoms

McAdam, D. (1996a). Conceptual origins, current problems, future directions. In D. McAdam, J. McCarthy, & M. Zald (Eds.), *Comparative perspectives on social movements* (pp. 23–40). New York, NY: Cambridge University Press.

McAdam, D. (1996b). The framing function of movement tactics: Strategic dramaturgy in the American civil rights movement. In D. McAdam, J. McCarthy, & M. Zald (Eds.), *Comparative perspectives on social movements* (pp. 338–355). New York, NY: Cambridge University Press.

McAdam, D., McCarthy, J., & Zald, M. (1996). Introduction: Opportunities, mobilizing structures, and framing processes: Toward a synthetic, comparative perspective on social movements. In D. McAdam, J. McCarthy, & M. Zald (Eds.), *Comparative perspectives on social movements* (pp. 1–20). New York, NY: Cambridge University Press.

McAdams, D. (1985). *Power, intimacy, and the life story: Personological inquires into identity*. New York, NY: Guilford.

McAdams, D. (2001). Generativity in midlife. In M. Lachman (Ed.), *Handbook of midlife development* (pp. 395–443). New York, NY: Wiley.

McAdams, D. (2006). *The redemptive self: Stories Americans live by*. New York, NY: Oxford University Press.

McAdams, D., & de St. Aubin, E. (1992). A theory of generativity and its assessment through self-report, behavioral acts, and narrative themes in autobiography. *Journal of Personality and Social Psychology, 62*, 1003–1015.

McAdams, D., & de St. Aubin, E. (Eds.). (1998). *Generativity and adult development: How and why we care for the next generation*. Washington, DC: American Psychological Association.

McAdams, D., Hart, H., & Maruna, S. (1998). The anatomy of generativity. In D. McAdams & E. de St. Aubin (Eds.), *Generativity and adult development: How and why we care for the next generation* (pp. 7–43). Washington, DC: American Psychological Association.

McAdams, D., & Olson, B. (2010). Personality development: Continuity and change over the life course. *Annual Review of Psychology, 61*, 517–542.

McAdams, D., & Pals, J. (2006). A new big five: Fundamental principles for an integrative science of personality. *American Psychologist, 61*, 204–217.

McAdoo, H. P. (2001). Parent and child relationships in African American families. In N. B. Webb (Ed.), *Culturally diverse parent–child and family relationships: A guide for social workers and other practitioners* (pp. 89–106). New York, NY: Columbia University Press.

McAvoy, M. (1999). *The profession of ignorance: With constant reference to Socrates*. Lanham, MD: University Press of America.

McBee, L., Westreich, L., & Likourezos, A. (2004). A psychoeducational relaxation group for pain and stress management in the nursing home. *Journal of Social Work in Long-Term Care, 3*(1), 15–28.

McCarroll, J., Ursano, R., Fan, Z., & Newby, J. (2004). Patterns of mutual and nonmutual spouse abuse in the U.S. Army (1998–2002). *Violence and Victims, 19*(4), 453–468.

McCarter, S. A. (2011). Disproportionate minority contact in the American juvenile justice system: Where are we after 20 years, a philosophy shift, and three amendments? *Journal of Forensic Social Work, 1*(1), 96–107.

McCarter, S. A., & Bridges, J. B. (2011). Determining the age of jurisdiction for adolescents: The policy debate. *Journal of Policy Practice, 10*(3), 168–184.

McClure, E. B. (2000). A meta-analytic review of sex differences in facial expression processing and their development in infants, children and adolescents. *Psychological Bulletin, 126*, 424–453.

McCormick, M. S., Litt, J. S., Smith, V. C., & Zupancic, A. F. (2011). Prematurity: An overview and public health implications. *Annual Review of Public Health, 32*, 367–379.

McCrae, R. R., Costa, P.T., de Lima, M. P., Simões, A., Ostendorf, F., Angleitner, A., Piedmont, R. L. (1999). Age differences in personality across the adult life span: Parallels in five cultures. *Developmental Psychology, 35*(2), 466.

McCreary, L., & Dancy, B. (2004). Dimensions of family functioning: Perspectives on low-income African American single-parent families. *Journal of Marriage and Family, 66*, 690–701.

McCubbin, H. I., & Figley, C. R. (1983). *Stress and the family, Vol. 1: Coping with normative transitions*. New York, NY: Brunner/Mazel.

McCubbin, H. I., & Patterson, J. M. (1983). The family stress process: The double ABCX model of adjustment and adaptation. In H. I. McCubbin, M. B. Sussman, & J. M. Patterson (Eds.), *Social stress and the family: Advances and developments in family stress theory and research* (pp. 7–37). New York, NY: Haworth.

McCullough, M., Enders, C., Brion, S., & Jain, A. (2005). The varieties of religious development in adulthood: A longitudinal investigation of religion and rational choice. *Journal of Personality and Social Psychology, 89*(1), 78–89.

McDermott, M. L. (1997). Voting cues in low-information elections: Candidate gender as a social information variable in contemporary United States elections. *American Journal of Political Science, 41*(1), 270–283.

McFarland, M., Pudrovska, T., Schieman, S., Ellison, C., & Bierman, A. (2013). Does a cancer diagnosis influence religiosity? Integrating a life course perspective. *Social Science Research, 42*, 311–320.

McFarlin, B. L. (2009). Solving the puzzle of prematurity. *American Journal of Nursing, 109*(1), 60–63.

McGoldrick, M., & Ashton, D. (2012). Culture: A challenge to concepts of normality. In F. Walsh (Ed.), *Normal family processes: Growing diversity and complexity* (4th ed., pp. 249–272). New York, NY: Guilford.

McGoldrick, M., Carter, B., & Garcia-Preto, N. (2011a). *The expanded family life cycle: Individual, family, and social perspectives* (4th ed.). Boston, MA: Allyn & Bacon.

McGoldrick, M., Carter, B., & Garcia-Preto, N. (2011b). Overview: The family life cycle in its changing context: Individual, family, and social perspectives. In M. McGoldrick, B. Carter, & N. Garcia-Preto (Eds.), *The expanded family life cycle: Individual, family, and social perspectives* (4th ed., pp. 1–19). Boston, MA: Allyn & Bacon.

McGoldrick, M., & Watson, M. (2011). Siblings and the life cycle. In M. McGoldrick, B. Carter, & N. Garcia-Preto (Eds.), *The expanded family life cycle: Individual, family, and social perspectives* (4th ed., pp. 149–162). Boston, MA: Allyn & Bacon.

McGregor, D. (1960). *The human side of enterprise*. New York, NY: McGraw-Hill.

McHale, S., Crouter, A., & Whiteman, S. (2003). The family contexts of gender development in childhood and adolescence. *Social Development, 12*, 125–148.

McHale, S., Updegraff, K., Ji-Yeon, K., & Cansler, E. (2009). Cultural orientations, daily activities, and adjustment in Mexican American youth. *Journal of Youth and Adolescence, 38*(5), 627–641.

McInnis-Dittrich, K. (2009). *Social work with elders: A biopsychosocial approach to assessment and intervention* (2nd ed.). Boston, MA: Allyn & Bacon.

McIntosh, D., Poulin, M., Silver, R., & Holman, E. A. (2011). The distinct roles of spirituality and religiosity in physical and mental health after collective trauma: A national longitudinal study of responses to the 9/11 attacks. *Journal of Behavioral Medicine, 34*, 497–507.

McIntosh, H., Metz, E., & Youniss, J. (2005). Community service and identity formation in adolescence. In J. Mahoney, R. Larson, & J. Eccles (Eds.), *Organized activities as contexts of development: Extracurricular activities, after-school and community programs* (pp. 331–351). Mahwah, NJ: Erlbaum.

McIntosh, P. (1988). *White privilege: Unpacking the invisible knapsack*. (Available from Peggy McIntosh, Wellesley College Center for Research on Women, Wellesley, MA 02181.)

McIntosh, P. (2007). White privilege: Unpacking the invisible knapsack. In P. Rothenberg (Ed.), *Race, class, and gender in the United States* (6th ed., pp. 177–182). New York, NY: Worth.

Mckee, K. J., Wilson, F., Chung, C. M., Hinchliff, S., Goudie, F., Elford, H., & Mitchell, C. (2005). Reminiscence, regrets and activity in older people in residential care: Associations with psychological health. *British Journal of Clinical Psychology, 44*(4), 543–561.

McKeering, H., & Pakenham, K. (2000). Gender and generativity issues in parenting: Do fathers benefit more than mothers from involvement in child care activities? *Sex Roles, 43*(7–8), 459–480.

McKee-Ryan, F., Song, Z., Wanberg, C., & Kinicki, A. (2005). Psychological and physical well-being during unemployment: A meta-analytic study. *Journal of Applied Psychology, 90*(1), 53–76.

McKenna, J. (2002). Breastfeeding and bedsharing: Still useful (and important) after all these years. *Mothering, 114*, 28–37.

McKnight, P., Snyder, C., & Lopez, S. (2007). Western perspectives on positive psychology. In C. Snyder & S. Lopez (Eds.), *Positive psychology: The scientific and practical explorations of human strengths* (pp. 23–35). Thousand Oaks, CA: Sage.

McLean, K., & Mansfield, C. (2012). The co-construction of adolescent narrative identity: Narrative processing as a function of adolescent age, gender, and maternal scaffolding. *Developmental Psychology, 48*(2), 436–447.

McLean, K., Pasupathi, M., & Pals, J. (2007). Selves creating stories creating selves: A process model of self- development. *Personality and Social Psychology Review, 11*, 262–278.

McLeod, P., & Kettner-Polley, R. (2005). Psychodynamic perspectives on small groups. In M. S. Poole & A. B. Hollingshead (Eds.), *Theories of small groups* (pp. 63–99). Thousand Oaks, CA: Sage.

McMahon, S. (2013). Enhancing motor development in infants and toddlers: A multidisciplinary process for creating parent education materials. *Newborn & Infant Nursing Reviews, 13*, 35–41.

McMichael, P. (2012). *Development and social change: A global perspective* (5th ed.). Los Angeles, CA: Sage.

McMillan, D. (1996). Sense of community. *Journal of Community Psychology, 24*, 315–325.

McMillan, D. (2011). *Challenge and resiliency: The stories of primary caregivers of people with Asperger's syndrome*. Auckland, New Zealand: University of Auckland.

McMillan, D., & Chavis, D. (1986). Sense of community: A definition and theory. *Journal of Community Psychology, 14*, 6–23.

McMillan, J. C., & Raghavan, R. (2009). Pediatric to adult mental health service use of young people leaving the foster care system. *Journal of Adolescent Health, 44*, 7–13.

McNeal, R. B. (2012). Checking in or checking out? Investigating the parent involvement reactive hypothesis. *Journal of Educational Research, 105*(2), 79–89.

McPherson, M., Smith-Lovin, L., & Brashears, M. (2006). Social isolation in America: Changes in core discussion networks over two decades. *American Sociological Review, 71*(3), 353–375.

McQuaide, S. (1998). Women at midlife. *Social Work, 43*(1), 21–31.

Mead, G. H. (1934). *Mind, self and society*. Chicago, IL: University of Chicago Press.

Mead, G. H. (1959). *The philosophy of the present*. LaSalle, IL: Open Court.

Medical News Today. (2013). *What is a miscarriage? What causes a miscarriage?* Retrieved from http://www.medicalnewstoday.com/articles/262941.php

MedLinePlus. (2011). *Small for gestational age*. U.S. National Library of Medicine. Retrieved from http://www.nlm.nih.gov/medlineplus/ency/article/002302.htm

Meek, M. (2000). Foreword. In K. Roskos & J. Christie (Ed.), *Play and literacy in early childhood: Research from multiple perspectives* (pp. vii–xiii). Mahwah, NJ: Erlbaum.

Mehall, K., Spinrad, T., Eisenberg, N., & Gaertner, B. (2009). Examining the relations of infant temperament and couples' marital satisfaction to mother and father involvement: A longitudinal study. *Fathering, 7*(1), 23–48.

Meisenhelder, J. B., & Marcum, J. P. (2009). Terrorism, post-traumatic stress, coping strategies, and spiritual outcomes. *Journal of Religion and Health, 48*(1), 46–57.

Meisner, B. (2012). A meta-analysis of positive and negative age stereotype priming effects on behavior among older adults. *The Journals of Gerontology, Series B: Psychological Sciences and Social Sciences, 67*(1), 13–17.

Melchert, T. (2013). Beyond theoretical orientations: The emergence of a unified scientific framework in professional psychology. *Professional Psychology: Research and Practice, 44*(1), 11–19.

Melton, J. G. (1993). *Encyclopedia of American religion*. Detroit, MI: Gale Research.

Meltzoff, A. (2002). Imitation as a mechanism of social cognition: Origins of empathy theory of mind, and the representation of action. In U. Goswami (Ed.), *Blackwell handbook of childhood cognitive development* (pp. 6–25). Malden, MA: Blackwell.

Memmi, D. (2006). The nature of virtual communities. *AI & Society: Journal of Knowledge, Culture and Communication, 20*, 288–300.

Mendle, J., Turkheimer, E., & Emery, R. E. (2007). Detrimental psychological outcomes associated with early pubertal timing in adolescent girls. *Developmental Review, 27*(2), 151–171.

Menezes, P., Scazufca, M., Rodrigues, L., & Mann, A. (2000). Household crowding and compliance with outpatient treatment in patients with non-affective functional psychoses. *Social Psychiatry and Psychiatric Epidemiology, 35*(3), 116–120.

Mensah, F., Bayer, J., Wake, M., Carlin, J., Allen, N., & Patton, G. (2013). Early puberty and childhood social and behavioral adjustment. *Journal of Adolescent Health, 53*, 118–124.

Mercadante, L. (2014). *Belief without borders: Inside the minds of the spiritual but not religious*. New York, NY: Oxford University Press.

Merce, L. T., Barco, M. J., Alcazar, J. L., Sabatel, R., & Trojano, J. (2009). Intervillous and uteroplacental circulation in normal early pregnancy and early pregnancy loss assessed by 3-dimensional power Doppler angiography. *Journal of Obstetrics and Gynecology, 200*(3), 315.e1–8.

Mercer, J. (2013). *Child development: Myths and misunderstandings* (2nd ed.). Los Angeles, CA: Sage.

Merten, J., Wickrama, K. A. S., & Williams, A. L. (2008). Adolescent obesity and young adult psychosocial outcomes: Gender and racial differences. *Journal of Youth & Adolescence, 37*, 1111–1122.

Merton, R. (1968). The Matthew Effect in science: The reward and communications systems of science. *Science, 199*, 55–63.

Messinger, L. (2004). Comprehensive community initiatives: A rural perspective. *Social Work, 49*(4), 529–624.

Meyer, C. (1993). *Assessment in social work practice*. New York, NY: Columbia University Press.

Meyer, D. (2004). Tending the vineyard: Cultivating political process research. In J. Goodwin & J. Jasper (Eds.), *Rethinking social movements: Structure, meaning, and emotion* (pp. 47–59). Lanham, MD: Rowman & Littlefield.

Mezzich, A., Tarter, R., Kirisci, L., Feske, U., Day, B., & Gao, Z. (2007). Reciprocal influence of parent discipline and child's behavior on risk for substance disorder: A nine-year prospective study. *American Journal of Drug and Alcohol Abuse, 33*(6), 851–867.

Michinov, N., Michinov, E., & Toczek-Capell, M. (2004). Social identity, group processes and performance in synchronous computer-mediated communication. *Group Dynamics: Theory, Research, and Practice, 8*(11), 27–39.

Mickelson, K., Claffey, S., & Williams, S. (2006). The moderating role of gender and gender role attitudes on the link between spousal support and marital quality. *Sex Roles, 55*, 73–82.

Middleton, K., & Craig, C. D. (2012). A systematic literature review of PTSD among female veterans from 1990 to 2010. *Social Work in Mental Health, 10*(3), 233–252.

Migration Policy Centre. European University Institute. (2013). *Syrian refugees: A snapshot of the crisis in the Middle East and Europe*. Retrieved from syrianrefugees.eu

Migration Policy Institute. (2013). *Immigration data hub: Migration facts, stats, and maps*. Retrieved from http://www.migrationinformation.org/datahub

Mijares, S. G., & Khalsa, G. S. (2005). *The psychospiritual clinician's handbook: Alternative methods for understanding and treating mental disorders*. New York, NY: Haworth Reference Press.

Mikami, A., Griggs, M., Lerner, M. D., Emeh, C. C., Reuland, M. M., Jack, A., & Anthony, M. R. (2013). A randomized trial of a classroom intervention to increase peers' social inclusion of children with attention-deficit/hyperactivity disorder. *Journal of Consulting & Clinical Psychology, 81*(1), 100–112.

Mikami, A., Lerner, M. D., & Lun, J. (2010). Social context influences on children's rejection by their peers. *Child Development Perspectives, 4*(2) 123–130.

Miklowitz, D., & Johnson, B. (2009). Social and familial factors in the course of bipolar disorder: Basic processes and relevant interventions. *Clinical Psychology: Science & Practice, 16*(2), 281–296.

Mikulas, W. L. (2002). *The integrative helper: Convergence of Eastern and Western traditions*. Pacific Grove, CA: Brooks/Cole Thompson Learning.

Miles, M. (1995). Disability in an Eastern religious context: Historical perspectives. *Disability and Society, 10*, 49–69.

Milevsky, A. (2005). Compensatory patterns of sibling support in emerging adulthood: Variations in loneliness, self-esteem, depression, and life satisfaction. *Journal of Social and Personal Relationships, 22*, 743–755.

Miller, A. K. (2010). Young adult daughters' accounts of relationships with nonresidential fathers: Relational damage, repair, and maintenance. *Journal of Divorce & Remarriage, 51*(5), 293–309.

Miller, D., Warren, L., & Owen, E. (2011). *Comparative indicators of education in the United States and other G-8 countries: 2011*. National Center for Education Statistics, U.S. Department of Education. Retrieved from nces.ed.gov/pubs2012/2012007.pdf

Miller, J., & Garran, A. M. (2008). *Racism in the United States: Implications for the helping professions*. Belmont, CA: Thomson Brooks/Cole.

Miller, L., Davies, M., & Greenwald, S. (2000). Religiosity and substance use and abuse among adolescents in the National Comorbidity Survey. *Journal of the American Academy of Child and Adolescent Psychiatry, 19*(9), 1190–1197.

Miller, W. D., Pollack, C. E., & Williams, D. R. (2011). Healthy homes and communities. *American Journal of Preventive Medicine, 40*, S48–S57.

Min, J., Silverstein, M., & Lendon, J. (2012). Intergenerational transmission of values over the family life course. *Advances in Life Course Research, 17*(3), 112–120.

Mishel, L. (2013). *The CEO-to-worker compensation ratio in 2012 of 273 was far above that of the late 1990s and 13 times the ratio of 20.1 in 1965*. Economic Policy Institute. Retrieved from www.epi.org/publications/the-ceo-to-worker-compensation-ratio-in-2012-of-2731

Mishra, G., Cooper, R., & Kuh, D. (2010). A life course approach to reproductive health: Theory and methods. *Maturita, 65*, 92–97.

Mistry, R., Lowe, D., Renner, A., & Chien, N. (2008). Expanding the Family Economic Stress Model: Insights from a mixed-methods approach. *Journal of Marriage and Family, 70*(1), 196–209.

Moen, P. (2003). Midcourse: Navigating retirement and a new life stage. In J. Mortimer & M. Shanahan (Eds.), *Handbook of the life course* (pp. 269–291). New York, NY: Kluwer Academic/Plenum.

Mohai, P., & Saha, R. (2007). Racial inequality in the distribution of hazardous waste: A national-level reassessment. *Social Problems, 54*(3), 343–370.

Mohamed, N., & Ahmad, I. (2012). Information privacy concerns, antecedents and privacy measure use in social networking sites: Evidence from Malaysia. *Computers in Human Behavior, 28*, 2366–2375.

Mokrova, I., O'Brien, M., Calkins, S., Leerkes, E., & Marcovitch, S. (2012). Maternal expressive style and children's emotional development. *Infant and Child Development, 21*, 617–633.

Möller, K., & Stattin, H. (2001). Are close relationships in adolescence linked with partner relationships in midlife? A longitudinal prospective study. *International Journal of Behavioral Development, 25*(1), 69–77.

Mongillo, E., Briggs-Gowan, M., Ford, J., & Carter, A. (2009). Impact of traumatic life events in a community sample of toddlers. *Journal of Abnormal Child Psychology, 37*(4), 455–468.

Monsour, M. (2002). *Women and men as friends: Relationships across the life span in the 21st century*. Mahwah, NJ: Erlbaum.

Montague, D., Magai, C., Consedine, N., & Gillespie, M. (2003). Attachment in African American and European American older adults: The roles of early life socialization and religiosity. *Attachment and Human Development, 5*, 188–214.

Montgomery, R. J. V., & Kosloski, K. (2000). Family caregiving: Change, continuity and diversity. In P. Lawton & R. Bubenstein (Eds.), *Alzheimer's disease and related dementias: Strategies in care and research*. New York, NY: Springer.

Montgomery, R. J. V., & Kosloski, K. (2009). Caregiving as a process of changing identity: Implications for caregiver support. *Generations, 33*, 47–52.

Moody, H. R., & Sasser, J. (2012). *Aging: Concepts and controversies* (7th ed.). Los Angeles, CA: Sage.

Moore, K. L., Redd, Z., Burkhauser, M., Mbwana, K., & Collins, A. (2009). *Children in poverty: Trends, consequences, and policy options*. Washington, DC: Child Trends. Retrieved from www.childtrends.org/wp-contnet/uploads/2013/11/2009-11ChildreninPoverty.pdf

Moraru, L., Sameni, R., Schneider, U., Haueisen, J., Schleußner, E., & Hoyer, D. (2011). Validation of fetal auditory evoked cortical responses to enhance the assessment of early brain development using fetal MEG measurements. *Physiological Measurement, 32*(11), 1847–1868.

Mor Barak, M. (2014). *Managing diversity: Toward a globally inclusive workplace* (3rd ed.). Thousand Oaks, CA: Sage.

Mor Barak, M., & Travis, D. (2010). Diversity and organizational performance. In Y. Hasenfeld (Ed.), *Human services as complex organizations* (2nd ed., pp. 341–378). Thousand Oaks, CA: Sage.

Moren-Cross, J. L., & Lin, N. (2006). Social networks and health. In R. H. Binstock & L. K. George (Eds.), *Handbook of aging and the social sciences* (6th ed., pp. 111–126). Amsterdam: Elsevier.

Moreno, M., Furtner, F., & Rivara, F. (2010). Information about adolescent sleep. *Archives of Pediatric and Adolescent Medicine, 164*(7), 684–687.

Morgan, G. (2006). *Images of organizations* (Updated ed.). Thousand Oaks, CA: Sage.

Morgan, J. P. (2002). Dying and grieving are journeys of the spirit. In R. B. Gilbert (Ed.), *Health care and spirituality: Listening, assessing, caring* (pp. 53–64). Amityville, NY: Baywood.

Morreale, D. (Ed.). (1998). *The complete guide to Buddhist America*. Boston, MA: Shambhala.

Morris, A. (2004). Reflections on social movement theory: Criticisms and proposals. In J. Goodwin & J. Jasper (Eds.), *Rethinking social movements*

(pp. 233–246). Lanham, MD: Rowman & Littlefield.
Morris, P.M. (2002). The capabilities perspective: A framework for social justice. *Families in Society, 83*(4), 365–373.
Morris, T., & McInerney, K. (2010). Media representations of pregnancy and childbirth: An analysis of reality television programs in the United States. *Birth, 37*(2), 134–140.
Mortimer, J. (2004). *Working and growing up in America.* Boston, MA: Harvard University Press.
Morton, C., & Hsu, C. (2007). Contemporary dilemmas in American childbirth education: Findings from a comparative ethnographic study. *Journal of Perinatal Education, 16*(4), 25–37.
Mosbacher, D., Reid, F., & Rhue, S. (1996). *All god's children.* [Video recording]. Available from Woman Vision, http://www.womanvision.org
Mosher, W. D., Jones, J., & Abma, J. C. (2012). *Intended and unintended births in the United States: 1982–2010.* Retrieved from http://www.cdc.gov/nchs/data/nhsr/nhsr055.pdf
Moyer, K. (1974). Discipline. In K. Moyer (Ed.), *You and your child: A primer for parents* (pp. 40–61). Chicago, IL: Nelson-Hall.
Mueller, P.C., Plevak, D. J., & Rummans, T. A. (2001). Religious involvement, spirituality, and medicine: Implications for clinical practice. *Mayo Clinical Proceedings, 76*(12), 1225–1235.
Muir, D., & Lee, K. (2003). The still face effect: Methodological issues and new applications. *Infancy, 4,* 483–491.
Mukhopadhyay, C. C., Henze, R., & Moses, Y.T. (2007). *How real is race: A sourcebook on race, culture and biology.* Lanham, MD: Rowman & Littlefield Education.
Mulligan, K., & Scherer, K. R. (2012). Toward a working definition of emotion. *Emotion Review, 4*(4), 345–357.
Mullings, L. (2005). Interrogating racism: Toward an antiracist anthropology. *Annual Review of Anthropology, 34,* 667–693.
Munakata, Y., McClelland, J., Johnson, M., & Siegler, R. (1997). Rethinking infant knowledge: Toward an adaptive process account of successes and failures in object permanence tasks. *Psychological Review, 104*(4), 618–713.
Muraco, A., & Fredriksen-Goldsen, K. (2011). "That's what friends do": Informal caregiving for chronically ill midlife and older lesbian, gay, and bisexual adults. *Journal of Social and Personal Relationships, 28*(8), 1073–1092.
Murillo, E. G. (2010). *Handbook of Latinos and education: Theory, research and practice.* New York, NY: Routledge.
Murphey, D. (2013). Home front alert: The risks facing young children in military families. *Child Trends Research Brief.* Retrieved from http://www.childtrends.org/wp-content/uploads/2013/07/2013-31MilitaryFamilies.pdf
Murray, B. (2001). Living wage comes of age: An increasingly sophisticated movement has put opponents on the defense. *The Nation, 273*(4), 24.
Myers, B. K. (1997). *Young children and spirituality.* New York, NY: Routledge.
Nagai, C. (2007). Culturally based spiritual phenomena: Eastern and Western theories and practices. *Psychoanalytic Social Work, 14*(1), 1–22.
Nagata, D., Cheng, W., & Tsai, A. (2010). Chinese-American grandmothering: A qualitative exploration. *Asian American Journal of Psychology, 1*(2), 151–161.
Naidoo, R., & Adamowicz, W. (2006). Modeling opportunity costs of conservation in transitional landscapes. *Conservation Biology, 20*(2), 490–500.
Nakagawa, F., Miners, A., Smith, C., Simmons, R., Lodwick, R., Cambiano, V., ... Phillips, A. (2015). Projected lifetime healthcare costs associated with HIV infection. *PLoS One, 10*(4), e0125018. doi: 10.1371/journal.pone.0125018
Naleppa, M. J. (1996). Families and the institutionalized elderly: A review. *Journal of Gerontological Social Work, 27,* 87–111.
Nappi, R.E. (2013). Counseling on vaginal delivery of contraceptive hormones: Implications for women's body knowledge and sexual health. *Gynecological Endocrinology, 29*(13), 1015–1021.
National Alliance to End Homelessness (NAEH). (2013a). *Frequently asked questions.* Washington, DC: Author. Retrieved from http://www.endhomelessness.org/pages/faqs
National Alliance to End Homelessness (NAEH). (2013b). *Snapshot of homelessness.* Washington, DC: Author. Retrieved from http://www.endhomelessness.org/pages/snapshot_of_homelessness
National Alliance to End Homelessness (NAEH). (2013c). *Cost of homelessness.* Washington, DC: Author. Retrieved from http://www.endhomelessness.org/pages/cost_of_homelessness
National Association of Child Care Resources and Referral Agencies. (2012). *Child care in America: 2012 state fact sheets.* Retrieved from www.naccrra.org/sites/default/files/default_site_pages/2012/full2012cca_state_factsheetbook.pdf
National Association of Social Workers. (2002). *NASW priorities on faith-based human services initiatives.* Retrieved February 26, 2010, from http://www.socialworkers.org/advocacy/positions/faith.asp
National Association of Social Workers. (2006). *Tell the president and Congress to oppose government-funded religious discrimination!* Retrieved from http://www.socialworkers.org/advocacy/alerts-012606.asp
National Association of Social Workers. (2008). *Code of ethics* (Rev.). Washington, DC: Author.
National Business Group on Health. (2009). *Preventing prematurity and adverse birth outcomes: What employers should know.* Center for Prevention and Health Services. Retrieved from http://www.businessgrouphealth.org/pub/f314b76e-2354-d714-5142-0b6fe2192d60
National Center for Complementary and Alternative Medicine. (n.d.). *Complementary, alternative, or integrative health: What's in a name?* Retrieved from http://nccam.nih.gov/health/whatiscam
National Center for Health Statistics. (2009). *Limitations in activities of daily living and instrumental activities of daily living, 2003–2007.* Retrieved from http://www.cdc.gov/nchs/health_policy/ADL_tables.htm
National Conference of State Legislatures. (2014). *State laws regarding marriages between first cousins.* Retrieved from http://www.ncsl.org/research/human-services/state-laws-regarding-marriages-between-first-cousi.aspx
National Healthy Marriage Resource Center. (2009). *Stepfamilies in the United States: A fact sheet.* Retrieved from www.healthymar riageinfo.org/resources-detail/index.aspx?id=3002
National Hospice and Palliative Care Organization. (2012). *NHPCO facts and figures: Hospice care in America 2011.* Alexandria, VA: National Hospice and Palliative Care Organization.
National Human Genome Research Institute. (2013). *All about the Human Genome Project (HGP).* Retrieved from http://www.Genome.gov/10001772
National Institute of Diabetes & Digestive & Kidney Diseases. (2011). *National Diabetes Information Clearinghouse: Fast facts on diabetes.* Retrieved from diabetes.niddk.nih.gov/dm/pubs/statistics/#fast
National Institute of Neurological Disorders and Stroke. (2013a). *Multiple sclerosis: Hope through research.* Retrieved from http://www.ninds.nih.gov/disorders/multiple_sclerosis/detail_multiple_sclerosis.htm#240043215
National Institute of Neurological Disorders and Stroke. (2013b). *Parkinson's disease: Hope through research.* Retrieved from www.ninds.nih.gov/disorders/parkinson_disease/detail_parkinsons_disease_htm
National Institute on Aging. (2013a). *Health & aging: Menopause.* Retrieved

from http://www.nia.nih.gov/health/publication/menopause
National Institute on Aging. (2013b). *About Alzheimer's disease: Symptoms*. Retrieved from http://www.nia.nih.gov/alzheimers/topics/symptoms?utm_source= ad_fact_sheet&utm_medium=web&utm_content=symptoms&utm_campaign=top_promo_box#very
National Institutes of Health. (2010). *Fact sheet: Human Genome Project*. Retrieved from http://report.nih.gov/nihfactsheets/Pdfs/HumanGenomeProject%28NHGRI%29.pdf
National Institutes of Health. (2013). *Puberty and precocious puberty: Overview*. Retrieved from http://nichd.nih.gov/health/topics/puberty/Pages/default.aspx
National Multiple Sclerosis Society. (n.d.). *Epidemiology of MS*. Retrieved from http://www.nationalmssociety.org/about-multiple-sclerosis/what-we-know-about-ms/who-gets-ms/epidemiology-of-ms/index.aspx
National Network of Libraries of Medicine. (2013). *Health literacy*. Retrieved from http://nnlm.gov/outreach/consumer/hlthlit.html
National Newborn Screening and Global Resource Center (NNSGRC). (2013). *Newborn screening*. Retrieved from http://genes-r-us.uthscsa.edu/sites/genes-r-us/files/nbsdisorders.pdf
National Priorities Project. (2015). *U.S. and world military spending*. Retrieved from https://www.nationalpriorities.org/campaigns/us-military-spending-vs-world/
National Religious Partnership for the Environment. (2014). *About*. Retrieved from http://www.nrpe.org/about.html
National Research Council. (2012). *From neurons to neighborhoods: An update: Workshop summary*. Washington, DC: National Academies Press.
National School Board Association. (2013). *Issue brief. Individuals with Disabilities Education Act (IDEA): Early preparation for reauthorization*. Retrieved from http://www.nsba.org/Advocacy/Key-Issues/SpecialEducation/NSBA-Issue-Brief-Individuals-with-Disabilities-Education-Act-IDEA.pdf
National Sleep Foundation. (2013). *Teens and sleep*. Retrieved from http://www.sleepfoundation.org/article/sleep-topics/teens-and-sleep
Navarro, V., Muntaner, C., Borrell, C., Benach, J., Quiroga, A., Rodriguez-Manz, M., . . . Pasarín, M. I. (2006). Politics and health outcomes. *The Lancet, 368*(9540), 1033–1037.
Neal, J. (2000). Work as service to the divine: Giving our gifts selflessly and with joy. *American Behavioral Scientist, 43*(8), 1316–1333.
Nechamkin, Y., Salganik, I., Moadai, I., & Ponizovsky, A. (2003). Interpersonal distance in schizophrenic patients: Relationship to negative syndrome. *International Journal of Social Psychiatry, 49*, 116–174.
Needham, A. (2001). Object recognition and object segregation in 4.5-month-old infants. *Journal of Experimental Child Psychology, 78*, 3–24.
Neff, K. D., & Helwig, C. C (2002). A constructionist approach to understanding the development of reasoning about rights and authority in cultural contexts. *Cognitive Development, 17*, 1429–1450.
Negy, C., Shreve, T. L., Jensen, B. J., & Uddin, N. (2003). Ethnic identity, self-esteem, and ethnocentrism: A study of social identity versus multicultural theory of development. *Cultural Diversity and Ethnic Minority Psychology, 9*(4), 333–344.
Nelson, C. (2001). The development and neural bases of face recognition. *Infant and Child Development, 10*, 3–18.
Nelson-Becker, H. B. (2006). Voices of resilience: Older adults in hospice care. *Journal of Social Work in End-of-Life & Palliative Care, 2*(3), 87–106.
Nesdale, D. (2004). Social identity processes and children's ethnic prejudice. In M. Bennett & M. Sani (Eds.), *The development of the social self* (pp. 219–245). New York, NY: Psychology Press.
Netting, F. E., O'Connor, M. K., & Singletary, J. (2007). Finding homes for their dreams: Strategies founders and program initiators use to position and sustain faith-based programs. *Families in Society: The Journal of Contemporary Social Services, 88*(1), 19–29.
Neugarten, B. L., Havighurst, R. J., & Tobin, S. S. (1968). Personality and patterns of aging. In B. L. Neugarten (Ed.), *Middle age and aging*. Chicago, IL: University of Chicago Press.
Newcomb, N., & Dubas, J. S. (1992). A longitudinal study of predictors of spatial ability in adolescent females. *Child Development, 63*, 37–46.
Newman, B., & Newman, P. (2012). *Development through life: A psychosocial approach* (11th ed.). Belmont, CA: Wadsworth/Cengage Learning.
Newman, D. (2012). *Sociology: Exploring the architecture of everyday life* (9th ed.). Los Angeles, CA: Sage.
Newman, K. (2008). Ties that bind: Cultural interpretations of delayed adulthood in Western Europe and Japan. *Sociological Forum, 23*(4), 645–669.
Newport, F. (2014). *The new era of communication among Americans*. Retrieved from http://www.gallup.com/poll/179288/new-era-communication-americans.aspx?version=print
Nguyen, P. (2008). Perceptions of Vietnamese fathers' acculturation levels, parenting styles, and mental health outcome in Vietnamese American adolescent immigrants. *Social Work, 53*(4), 337–346.
Nguyen, P., & Cheung, M. (2009). Parenting styles as perceived by Vietnamese American adolescents. *Child and Adolescent Social Work Journal, 26*, 505–581.
Nichols, M., & Schwartz, R. (2006). *Family therapy: Concepts and methods* (7th ed.). Boston, MA: Allyn & Bacon.
Nicotera, N. (2005). The child's view of neighborhood: Assessing a neglected element in direct social work practice. *Journal of Human Behavior in the Social Environment, 11*(3/4), 105–133.
Niemann, S. (2005). Persons with disabilities. In M. T. Burke, J. C. Chauvin, & J. G. Miranti (Eds.), *Religious and spiritual issues in counseling: Applications across diverse populations* (pp. 105–133). New York, NY: Brunner-Routledge.
Nishitani, S., Miyamura, T., Tagawa, M., Sumi, M., Takase, R., Doi, H., . . . Shinohara, K. (2009). The calming effect of a maternal breast milk odor on the human newborn infant. *Neuroscience Research, 63*(1), 66–71.
Nobles, W. W. (1980). African philosophy: Foundations for Black psychology. In R. L. Jones (Ed.), *Black psychology* (2nd ed., pp. 23–36). New York, NY: Harper & Row.
Noddings, N. (2002). *Starting at home: Caring and social policy*. Berkeley, CA: University of California Press.
Noddings, N. (2005). *Educating citizens for global awareness*. New York, NY: Teacher's College Press.
Noddings, N. (2013). *Caring: A relational approach to ethics and moral education*. Berkeley, CA: University of California Press.
Norcross, J. C., & Wampold, B. E. (2011). Evidence-based therapy relationships: Research conclusions and clinical practices. *Psychotherapy, 48*(1), 98–102.
Norton, C. (2009). Ecopsychology and social work: Creating an interdisciplinary framework for redefining person-in-environment. *Ecopsychology, 1*(3), 138–145.
Novelli, D., Drury, J., & Reicher, S. (2010). Come together: Two studies concerning the impact of group relations on "personal space." *British Journal of Social Psychology, 49*, 223–236.
Nowell, B., Berkowitz, S., Deacon, Z., & Foster-Fishman, P. (2006). Revealing the cues within community places: Stories of identity, history, and possibility. *American Journal of Community Psychology, 37*(1–2), 29–46.

Nussbaum, M. (2001). *Women and human development: The capabilities approach*. New York, NY: Cambridge University Press.

Nussbaum, M. (2011). *Creating capabilities: The human development approach*. Cambridge, MA: The Belknap Press of the Harvard University Press.

Nuttgens, S. (2010). Biracial identity theory and research juxtaposed with narrative accounts of a biracial individual. *Child & Adolescent Social Work Journal, 27*(5), 355–364.

Ny, K., Loy, J., Gudmunson, C., & Cheong, W. (2009). Gender differences in marital and life satisfaction among Chinese Malaysians. *Sex Roles, 60*, 33–43.

Nybell, L., Shook, J., & Finn, J. (Eds.). (2009). *Childhood, youth, and social work in transformation: Implications for policy and practice*. New York, NY: Columbia University Press.

Obamacare Health Plans. (2016). *Obamacare enrollment numbers*. Retrieved from http://obamacarefacts.com/sign-ups/obamacare-enrollment-numbers/

O'Brien, P. (1992). Social work and spirituality: Clarifying the concept for practice. *Spirituality and Social Work Journal, 3*(1), 2–5.

O'Brien, P. (2001). Claiming our soul: An empowerment group for African-American women in prison. *Journal of Progressive Human Services, 12*(1), 35–51.

Obst, P., & Tham, N. (2009). Helping the soul: The relationship between connectivity and well-being within a church community. *Journal of Community Psychology, 37*(3), 342–361.

Obst, P., & White, K. (2004). Revisiting the Sense of Community Index: A confirmatory factor analysis. *Journal of Community Psychology, 32*(6), 691–705.

Obst, P., Zinkiewicz, L., & Smith, S. (2002a). Sense of community in science fiction fandom, Part 1. Understanding sense of community in an international community of interest. *Journal of Community Psychology, 30*(1), 87–103.

Obst, P., Zinkiewicz, L., & Smith, S. (2002b). Sense of community in science fiction fandom, Part 2. Comparing neighborhood and interest group sense of community. *Journal of Community Psychology, 30*(1), 105–117.

Ochshorn, J., & Cole, E. (Eds.). (1995). *Women's spirituality, women's lives*. Binghamton, NY: Haworth Press.

O'Connor, M. K., & Netting, F. E. (2009). *Organization practice: A guide to understanding human service organizations* (2nd ed.). Hoboken, NJ: Wiley.

Odgers, C. Moffitt, T., Tach, L., Sampson, R., Taylor, A., Matthews, C., Caspi, A. (2009). The protective effects of neighborhood collective efficacy on British children growing up in deprivation: A developmental analysis. *Developmental Psychology, 45*(4), 942–957.

OECD Family Database. (2013). *Cohabitation rate and prevalence of other forms of partnership*. Retrieved from www.oecd.org/els/soc/SF3_3_Cohabitation_rate_and_prevalence_other_forms_of_partnerships_Jan2013.pdf

Office of Faith-Based and Neighborhood Partnerships. (2009). *Preserving our constitutional commitments and values*. Retrieved from http://www.whitehouse.gov/administration/eop/ofbnp/values

Ogbu, J. U. (2003). *Black American students in an affluent suburb: A study of academic disengagement*. Mahwah, NJ: Erlbaum.

Ogden, J., Stavrinaki, M., & Stubbs, J. (2009). Understanding the role of life events in weight loss and weight gain. *Psychology, Health, & Medicine, 14*(2), 239–249.

O'Keefe, M. (1994). Adjustment of children from maritally violent homes. *Families in Society, 75*, 403–415.

Oldmeadow, J., Platow, M., Foddy, M., & Anderson, D. (2003). Self-categorization, status, and social influence. *Social Psychology Quarterly, 66*(2), 138–152.

O'Leary, V. E., & Bhaju, J. (2006). Resilience and empowerment. In J. Worell & C. D. Goodheart (Eds.), *Handbook of girls' and women's psychological health: Gender and well-being across the life span* (pp. 157–165). New York, NY: Oxford Press.

Olshansky, S. J., Antonucci, T., Berkman, L., Binstock, R., Boersch-Supan, A., Cacioppo, J., . . . Rowe, J. (2012). Differences in life expectancy due to race and educational differences are widening, and many may not catch up. *Health Affairs, 31*(8), 1803–1810.

Olusanya, B. (2010). Is undernutrition a risk factor for sensorineural hearing loss in early infancy? *British Journal of Nutrition, 103*, 1296–1301.

Ombelet, W. (2014). Is global access to infertility care realistic? The Walking Egg Project. *Reproductive BioMedicine Online, 28*, 267–272.

O-Prasetsawat, P., & Petchum, S. (2004). Sexual behavior of secondary school students in Bangkok metropolis. *Journal of the Medical Association of Thailand, 87*(7), 755–759.

O'Rand, A. (2009). Cumulative processes in the life course. In G. Elder & J. Giele (Eds.), *The craft of life course research* (pp. 121–140). New York, NY: Guilford.

Orbuch, T., & Brown, E. (2006). Divorce in the context of being African American. In M. Fine & J. Harvey (Eds.), *Handbook of divorce and relationship dissolution* (pp. 481–498). Mahwah, NJ: Erlbaum.

O'Reilly, B. (2007). *Culture warrior*. New York, NY: Broadway Books.

Orfield, G., Kucsev, J., & Siegal-Harvey, G. (2012). E Pluribus . . . separation: Deepening double segregation for more students. The Civil Rights Project. Retrieved from http://civilrightsproject.ucla.edu/research/k-12-education/integration-and-diversity/mlk-national/e-pluribus...separation-deepening-double-segregation-for-more-students

Organisation for Economic Co-operation and Development. (2011). Growing income inequality in OECD countries: What drives it and how can policy tackle it? Retrieved from http://www.oecd.org/els/47723414.pdf

Organisation for Economic Co-operation and Development. (2012). *Key characteristics of parental leave systems*. Retrieved from www.oecd.org/social/soc/PF2.1_Parental_leave_systems%20–20%update%20%2018_July_2012.pdf

Organisation for Economic Co-operation and Development. (2013a). *Education at a glance 2013: OECD indicators*. OECD Publishing. Retrieved from http://dx.doi.org/10.17871/eag-2013-en

Organisation for Economic Co-operation and Development. (2013b). *OECD: StatExtracts: Trade union density*. Retrieved from https://stats.oecd.org/Index.aspx?DataSetCode=UN_DEN

Organisation for Economic Co-operation and Development. (2013c). *Health at a glance 2012: OECD indicators*. OECD Publishing. Retrieved from http://dx.doi.org/a0.1787/health_glance-2013-en

Organisation for Economic Co-operation and Development. (2013d). *Dataset: Social expenditure—Aggregated data*. Retrieved from stats.oecd.org/Index.aspx?datasetcode=SOCX.AGG

Ornstein, P., & Light, L. (2010). Memory development across the life span. In R. Lerner (Series Ed.) & W. Overton (Vol. Ed.), *Handbook of life-span development: Vol. 1. Biology, cognition, and methods across the life span*. Hoboken, NJ: Wiley.

Orr, S. T., James, S. A., & Reiter, J. P. (2008). Unintended pregnancy and prenatal behaviors among urban, black women in Baltimore, Maryland: The Baltimore preterm birth study. *Annals of Epidemiology, 18*(7), 545–551.

Ortega, F. B., Konstabel, K., Pasquali, E., Ruiz, J. R., Hurtig-Wennlöf, A., Mäestu, J., . . . Sjöström, M. (2013). Objectively measured physical activity and sedentary time during childhood, adolescence and young adulthood: A cohort study. *PLoS One, 8*(4), 1–8.

Ortega, F. B., Ruiz, J., Castillo, R., Chillón, P., Labayen, I., Martínez-Gómez, D., . . . AVENA Study Group. (2010). Sleep duration and cognitive performance in adolescents: The AVENA study. *ACTA Paediatrica, 99*, 454–456.

Ortiz, I., Daniels, L. M., & Engilbertsdóttir, S. (Eds.). (2012). *Child poverty and inequality: New perspectives.* New York, NY: United Nations Children's Fund.

Ortner, S. B. (1984). Theory in anthropology since the sixties. *Comparative Studies in History and Society, 26*(1), 126–166.

Ortner, S. B. (1989). *High religion: A cultural and political history of Sherpa Buddhism.* Princeton, NJ: Princeton University Press.

Ortner, S. B. (1996). *Making gender: The politics and erotics of culture.* Boston, MA: Beacon Press.

Ortner, S. B. (2006). *Anthropology and social theory: Culture, power, and the acting subject.* Durham, NC: Duke University Press.

Osler, M., Avlund, K., & Mortensen, E. (2012). Socio-economic position early in life, cognitive development and cognitive change from young adulthood to middle age. *European Journal of Public Health, 23*(6), 974–980.

Osorio, A., Burgo, C., Carlos, S., Ruiz-Canela, M., Delgado, M., & Irala, J. (2012). First sexual intercourse and subsequent regret in three developing countries. *Journal of Adolescent Health, 50*, 271–278.

Osterweil, N. (2013, November 6). Genetic anomalies account for majority of miscarriages. *Ob.Gyn News.* Retrieved from http://www.obgynnews.com/single-view/genetic-anomalies-account-for-majority-of-miscarriages/64d9325e6b83614b2d1aca488b2fd98.html

Ostrov, J., Crick, N., & Stauffacher, K. (2006). Relational aggression in sibling and peer relationships during early childhood. *Journal of Developmental Psychology, 27*(3), 241–253.

Oudekerk, B., Farr, R., & Reppucci, N. D. (2013). Is it love or sexual abuse? Young adults' perceptions of statutory rape. *Journal of Child Sexual Abuse, 22*(7), 858–877.

Ozdemir, A. (2008). Shopping malls: Measuring interpersonal distance under changing conditions and cultures. *Field Methods, 20*(3), 226–248.

Ozorak, E. W. (1996). The power, but not the glory: How women empower themselves through religion. *Journal for the Scientific Study of Religion, 35*(1), 17–29.

Padden, D., & Agazio, J. (2013). Caring for military families across the deployment cycle. *Journal of Emergency Nursing, 39*(6), 562–569.

Page, A., Milner, A., Morrell, S., & Taylor, R. (2013). The role of under-employment and unemployment in recent birth cohort effects in Australian suicide. *Social Science & Medicine, 93*, 155–162.

Painter, K. (2012). Outcomes for youth with severe emotional disturbance: A repeated measures longitudinal study of a wraparound approach of service delivery in systems of care. *Child & Youth Care Forum, 41*(4), 407–425.

Paljärvi, T., Martikainen, P., Pensola, T., Leinonen, T., & Herttua, K. (2015). Life course trajectories of labour market participation among young adults who experienced severe alcohol-related health outcomes: A retrospective cohort study. *PLoS One, 10*(5), 1–14.

Palmer, A. M., & Francis, P. T. (2006). Neurochemistry of aging. In J. Pathy, A. J. Sinclair, & E. J. Morley (Eds.), *Principles and practice of geriatric medicine* (4th ed., pp. 59–67). Chichester, UK: Wiley.

Panksepp, J. (2008). The affective brain and core consciousness: How does neural activity generate emotional feelings? In M. Lewis, J. M. Havilland-Jones, & L. F. Barrett (Eds.), *Handbook of emotions* (3rd ed., pp. 47–67). New York, NY: Guilford Press.

Papell, D., & Prodan, R. (2011). *The statistical behavior of GDP after financial crises and severe recessions.* Paper prepared for the Federal Reserve Bank of Boston conference Long-Term Effects of the Great Recession, October 18–19, 2011. Retrieved from www.bostonfed.org/economics/conf/LTE2011/papers/Papell_Prodan.pdf

Paquette, K., & Bassuk, E. (2009). Parenting and homelessness: Overview and introduction to the special edition. *American Journal of Orthopsychiatry, 79*(3), 292–298.

Paradies, Y. (2006). A systematic review of empirical research on self-reported racism and health. *International Journal of Epidemiology, 35*(4), 888–901.

Parappully, J., Rosenbaum, R., van den Daele, L., & Nzewi, E. (2002). Thriving after trauma: The experience of parents of murdered children. *Journal of Humanistic Psychology, 42*(1), 33–70.

Pargament, K. I. (1997). *The psychology of religious coping: Theory, research, practice.* New York, NY: Guilford Press.

Pargament, K. I. (2007). *Spiritually integrated psychotherapy: Understanding and addressing the sacred.* New York, NY: Guilford Press.

Pargament, K. I. (2008). The sacred character of community life. *American Journal of Community Psychology, 41*(1–2), 22–34.

Pargament, K. I., Koenig, H. G., & Perez, L. M. (2000). The many methods of religious coping: Development and initial validation of the RCOPE. *Journal of Clinical Psychology, 56*, 519–543.

Parham, L., Quadagno, J., & Brown, J. (2009). Race, politics, and social policy. In J. Midgley & M. Livermore (Eds.), *The handbook of social policy* (2nd ed., pp. 263–278). Thousand Oaks, CA: Sage.

Parham, P. (2009). *The immune system* (3rd ed.). New York, NY: Garland Science, Taylor & Francis.

Paris, P. J. (1995). *The spirituality of African peoples: The search for a common moral discourse.* Minneapolis, MN: Fortress Press.

Parish, S., Saville, A., & Swaine, J. (2011). Policies and programs for children and youth with disabilities. In J. Jenson & M. Fraser (Eds.), *Social policy for children and families: A risk and resilience perspective* (2nd ed., pp. 236–269). Los Angeles, CA: Sage.

Parish, S., Saville, A., Swaine, J., Igdalsky, L. (2016). Policies and programs for children and youth with disabilities. In J. Jenson & M. Fraser (Eds.), *Social policy for children and families: A risk and resilience perspective* (3rd ed., pp. 236–269). Los Angeles, CA: Sage.

Parish, S. L., Magana S., & Cassiman, S. A. (2008). It's just that much harder: Multi-layered hardship experiences of low-income mothers with disabilities. *AFFILIA: Journal of Women and Social Work, 23*(1) 51–65.

Park, R. (1936). Human ecology. *American Journal of Sociology, 17*, 1–15.

Parkinson, B., Fischer, A. H., & Manstead, A. S. R. (2005). *Emotion in social relations: Cultural, group, and interpersonal processes.* New York, NY: Psychology Press.

Parkinson's Disease Foundation. (2010). *Understanding Parkinson's: Parkinson's FAQ.* Retrieved from http://www.pdf.org/pdf/fs_frequently_asked_questions_10.pdf

Parkinson's Disease Foundation. (2013). *Prescription medications.* Retrieved from http://www.pdf.org/parkinson_prescription_meds

Parkinson's Disease Foundation. (2014). *Diagnosis.* Retrieved from http://www.pdf.org/en/diagnosis

Parra-Cordeno, M., Rodrigo, R., Barja, P., Bosco, C., Rencoret, G., & Sepulveda Martinez, A. (2013). Prediction of early and late pre-eclampsia from maternal characteristics, uterine artery Doppler and markers of vasculogenesis during first trimester of pregnancy. *Ultrasound in Obstetrics and Gynecology, 41*(5), 538–544.

Parreñas, R. (2001). *Servants of globalization: Women, migration, and domestic work.* Palo Alto, CA: Stanford University Press.

Parreñas, R. (2008). *The force of domesticity: Filipina migrants and globalization.* New York, NY: New York University Press.

Parrillo, V. (2009). *Diversity in America* (3rd ed.). Thousand Oaks, CA: Pine Forge.

Parsons, M., & Peluso, P. R. (2013). Grandfamilies and their grand challenges. In P. R. Peluso, R. E. Watts,

& M. Parsons (Eds.), *Changing aging, changing family therapy* (pp. 45–61). New York, NY: Routledge.
Pasley, K., & Lee, M. (2010). Stress and coping within the context of stepfamily life. In S. Price, C. Price, & P. McKenry (Eds.), *Families & change: Coping with stressful events and transitions* (4th ed., pp. 235–261). Thousand Oaks, CA: Sage.
Passel, J., & Cohn, D. (2008). *Immigration to play lead role in future U.S. growth*. Retrieved from www.pewhispanic.org/2008/02/11/us-population-projections-2005-2050
Paul, E. (1997). A longitudinal analysis of midlife interpersonal relationships and well-being. In M. Lachman & J. James (Eds.), *Multiple paths of midlife development* (pp. 171–206). Chicago, IL: University of Chicago Press.
Paulino, A. (1995). Spiritism, santeria, brujeria, and voodooism: A comparative view of indigenous healing systems. *Journal of Teaching in Social Work, 12*(1–2), 105–124.
Payne, K., & Gibbs, L. (2013). *Economic well-being and the great recession: Dual earner married couples in the U.S., 2006 and 2011.* (FP-13-05). National Center for Family & Marriage Research. Retrieved from http://ncfmr.gbsu.edu/pdf/family_profiles/file126564.pdf
Payne, R. A. (2000). *Relaxation techniques: A practical handbook for the health care professional* (2nd ed.). Edinburgh, NY: Churchill Livingstone.
Payne, R. K. (2013). *A framework for understanding poverty: A cognitive approach* (5th ed.). Highlands, TX: Aha! Process.
Pearlin, L., & Skaff, M. (1996). Stress and the life course: A paradigmatic alliance. *The Gerontologist, 36*(2), 239–247.
Pearlstein, T., Howard, M., Salisbury, A., & Zlotnick, C. (2009). Pospartum depression. *American Journal of Obstetrics & Gynecology, 200*(4), 357–364.
Pearson, J. (1996). *Discovering the self through drama and movement: The Sesame Approach*. London, UK: Jessica Kingsley.
Pecora, P. J., & Harrison-Jackson, M. (2011). Child welfare policies and programs. In J. Jenson & M. Fraser (Eds.), *Social policy for children and families: A risk and resilience perspective* (2nd ed., pp. 57–112). Thousand Oaks, CA: Sage.
Pecora, P. J., Kessler, R. C., Williams, J., O'Brien, K., Downs, A. C., English, D., … Holmes, K. (2005). *Improving family foster care: Findings from the Northwest Foster Care Alumni Study*. Seattle, WA: Casey Family Programs.
Pedrotti, J., Snyder, C., & Lopez, S. (2007). Eastern perspectives on positive psychology. In C. Snyder & S. Lopez (Eds.), *Positive psychology: The scientific and practice explorations of human strengths* (pp. 37–50). Thousand Oaks, CA: Sage.
Pempek, T. A., Yermolayeva, Y. A., & Calvert, S. L. (2009). College students' social networking experiences on Facebook. *Journal of Applied Developmental Psychology, 30*, 227–238.
Peng, G., & Wang, W. (2011). Hemisphere lateralization is influenced by bilingual status and composition of words. *Neuropsychologia, 49*, 1981–1986.
Pepino, M. Y., & Mennella, J. A. (2006). Children's liking of sweet tastes: A reflection of our basic biology. In W. Spillane (Ed.), *Optimising sweet taste in foods* (pp. 54–65). Cambridge, UK: Woodhead.
Peplau, L., & Fingerhut, A. (2007). The close relationships of lesbians and gay men. *Annual Review of Psychology, 58*, 373–408.
Pepler, D. J. (2012). *The development and treatment of girlhood aggression*. New York, NY: Psychology Press.
Perkins, T. (2012). Women's pathways into activism: Rethinking the women's environmental justice narrative in California's San Joaquin Valley. *Organization & Environment, 25*(1), 76–94.
Perlman, D., & Fehr, B. (1987). The development of intimate relationships. In D. Perlman & S. Duck (Eds.), *Intimate relationships: Development, dynamics, and deterioration* (pp. 13–42). Newbury Park, CA: Sage.
Perrig-Chiello, P., & Perren, S. (2005). Impact of past transitions on well-being in middle age. In S. Willis & M. Martin (Eds.), *Middle adulthood: A lifespan perspective* (pp. 143–178). Thousand Oaks, CA: Sage.
Perry, A. V., & Rolland, J. S. (2009). The therapeutic benefits of a justice-seeking spirituality: Empowerment, healing, and hope. In F. Walsh (Ed.), *Spiritual resources in family therapy* (2nd ed., pp. 379–396). New York, NY: Guilford Press.
Perry, B. (2002). Childhood experience and the expression of genetic potential: What childhood neglect tells us about nature and nurture. *Brain & Mind, 3*(1), 79–100.
Perry, M. (2015). Contraception: Choices and contraindications. *Nurse Prescribing, 13*(5), 236–240.
Perry-Parrish, C., & Zeman, J. (2011). Relations among sadness regulation, peer acceptance, and social functioning in early adolescence: The role of gender. *Social Development, 20*(1), 135–153. doi:10.1111/j.1467-9507.2009.00568.x
Peteet, J., Lu, F., & Narrow, W. (2011). *Religious and spiritual issues in psychiatric diagnosis: A research agenda for DSM-V*. Washington, DC: American Psychiatric Publishing.
Petersen, R. (2011). Mild cognitive impairment. *The New England Journal of Medicine, 364*(23), 2227–2234.
Peterson, B., & Duncan, L. (2007). Midlife women's generativity and authoritarianism: Marriage, motherhood, and 10 years of aging. *Psychology and Aging, 22*(3), 411–419.
Peterson, B., Newton, C., & Rosen, K. (2003). Examining congruence between partners' perceived infertility-related stress and its relationship to marital adjustment and depression in infertile couples. *Family Process, 42*, 59–70.
Petrovic, K. (2013). Respite and the internet: Accessing care for older adults in the 21st century. *Computers in Human Behavior, 29*, 2448–2452.
Petty, T. C. (n.d.). *The second breath of life*. Retrieved from http://www.nlhep.org/Documents/SecondBreath.pdf
Pew Center for Social and Demographic Trends. (2013). *The return of the multi-generational family household*. Retrieved from http://www.pewsocialtrends.org/2010/03/18/the-return-of-the-multi-generational-family-household
Pew Forum on Religion & Public Life. (2008). *U.S. religious landscape survey: Religious affiliation—diverse and dynamic*. Washington, DC: Author.
Pew Research Center. (2009). *Views of religious similarities and differences: Muslims widely seen as facing discrimination*. Retrieved from http://www.pewforum.org/files/2009/09/survey0909.pdf
Pew Research Center. (2010). *Millennials: A portrait of generation next. Confident. Connected. Open to change*. Retrieved from http://pewresearch.org/millennials
Pew Research Center. (2015a). *America's changing religious landscape*. Retrieved from http://www.pewforum.org/files/2015/05/RLS-08-26-full-report.pdf
Pew Research Center. (2015b). *The future of world religions: Population growth projections, 2010–2050*. Retrieved from http://www.pewforum.org/2015/04/02/religious-projections-2010-2050/
Pew Research Center's Religion & Public Life Project. (2010). *World religion makeup*. Retrieved from http://www.globalreligiousfutures.org/explorer#/?subtopic=15&chartType=pie&year=2010&data_type=percentage&religious_affiliation=all&destination=to&countries=Worldwide
Pew Research Center's Religion & Public Life Project. (2012). *"Nones" on the rise*.

Retrieved from http://www.pewforum.org/2012/10/09/nones-on-the-rise

Pew Research Center's Religion & Public Life Project. (2014, February 5). *Gay marriage around the world.* Retrieved from http://www.pewforum.org/2013/12/19/gay-marriage-around-the-world-2013

Pew Research Hispanic Center. (2013). *Statistical portrait of the foreign-born population in the United States, 2011.* Retrieved from http://www.pewhispanic.org/files/2013/02/statistical-portrait-of-the-foreign-born-population-in-the-United-States-2011_Final.pdf

Pew Research Hispanic Trends Project. (2013). *A nation of immigrants: A portrait of the 40 million, including 11 million unauthorized.* Retrieved from http://www.pewhispanic.org/2013/01/29/a-nation-of-immigrants

Pew-Templeton Global Religious Futures Project. (2014). Retrieved from http://www.globalreligiousfutures.org/explorer#/?subtopic=15&chartType=pie&year=2010&data_type=percentage&religious_affiliation=all&destination=to&countries=Worldwide.

Pfeffer, J. (1982). *Organizations and organization theory.* Boston, MA: Pitman.

Pharr, S. (1988). *Homophobia: A weapon of sexism.* Inverness, CA: Chardon Press.

Pharris-Ciurej, N., Hirschman, C., & Willhoft, J. (2012). The 9th grade shock and the high school dropout crisis. *Social Science Research, 41*, 709–730.

Phinney, J. (2006). Ethnic identity exploration in emerging adulthood. In J. Arnett & J. Tanner (Eds.), *Emerging adults in America: Coming of age in the 21st century* (pp. 117–134). Washington, DC: American Psychological Association.

Piacenti, R. (2011). Toward meaningful response to the problem of anti-gay bullying in American public schools. *Virginia Journal of Social Policy & the Law, 19*(1), 58–108.

Piaget, J. (1952). *The origins of intelligence in children.* New York, NY: International Universities Press. (Original work published 1936)

Piaget, J. (1965). *The moral judgment of the child.* New York, NY: Free Press. (Original work published 1932)

Piaget, J. (1972). Intellectual evolution from adolescence to adulthood. *Human Development, 15*, 1–12.

Piazza, J., & Charles, S. (2006). Mental health among baby boomers. In S. Whitbourne & S. Willis (Eds.), *The baby boomers grow up: Contemporary perspectives on midlife* (pp. 111–146). Mahwah, NJ: Erlbaum.

Pickering, J., Kintrea, K., & Bannister, J. (2012). Invisible walls and visible youth: Territoriality among young people in British cities. *Urban Studies, 49*(5), 945–960.

Pierce, B. (2012). *Genetics: A conceptual approach.* New York, NY: W. H. Freeman.

Pierce, K. (2011). Early functional brain development in autism and the promise of sleep fMRI. *Brain Research, 1380*, 162–174.

Pillemer, K., Suitor, J., Pardo, S., & Henderson, C. (2010). Mothers' differentiation and depressive symptoms among adult children. *Journal of Marriage and the Family, 72*, 333–345.

Pinker, S. (2011). *The better angels of our nature: Why violence has declined.* New York, NY: Viking.

Pinzon, J., & Jones, V. (2012). Care of adolescent parents and their children. *Pediatrics, 130*(6), 1743–1756.

Pirog, M., & Ziol-Guest, M. (2006). Child support enforcement: Programs and policies, impacts and questions. *Journal of Policy Analysis and Management, 25*, 943–990.

Plassman, B., Langa, K., Fisher, G., Heeringa, S., Weir, D., Ofstedal, M., . . . Wallace, R. (2007). Prevalence of dementia in the United States: The aging, demographics, and memory study. *Neuroepidemiology, 29*, 125–132.

Playfer, J. R. (2006). Parkinson's disease and Parkinsonism in the elderly. In J. Pathy, A. J. Sinclair, & E. J. Morley (Eds.), *Principles and practice of geriatric medicine* (4th ed., pp. 765–776). Chichester, UK: Wiley.

Plutchik, R. (2005). The nature of emotions. In P. W. Sherman & J. Alcock (Eds.), *Exploring animal behavior: Readings from American Scientist* (4th ed., pp. 85–91). Sunderland, MA: Sinauer Associates.

Pokorná, J., Machala, L., Řezáčová, P., & Konvalinka, J. (2009). Current and novel inhibitors of HIV protease. *Viruses, 1*(3), 1209–1239.

Pons, F., Laroche, M., & Mourali, M. (2006). Consumer reactions to crowded retail settings: Cross-cultural differences between North America and Middle East. *Psychology & Marketing, 23*(7), 555–572.

Ponterotto, J. G. (2010). *Handbook of multicultural counseling.* Thousand Oaks, CA: Sage.

Posmontier, B., & Horowitz, J. (2004). Postpartum practices and depression prevalences: Technocentric and ethnokinship cultural perspectives. *Journal of Transcultural Nursing, 15*, 34–43.

Poteat, V. P., Aragon, S., Espelage, D., & Koenig, B. (2009). Psychosocial concerns of sexual minority youth: Complexity and caution in group differences. *Journal of Consulting and Clinical Psychology, 77*(1), 196–201.

Potter, C. C. (2004). Gender differences in childhood and adolescence. In P. Allen-Meares & M. W. Fraser (Eds.), *Intervention with children and adolescents: An interdisciplinary perspective* (pp. 54–79). Boston, MA: Allyn & Bacon.

Potter, T. (2005, Fall). Bringing foster care management into the 21st century with GIS. *ArcNews Online.* Retrieved from http://www.esri.com/news/arcnews/fall05articles/bringing-foster.html

Premberg, A. (2006). Fathers' experience of childbirth education. *Journal of Perinatal Education, 15*(2), 21–28.

Premberg, A., Carlsson, G., Hellström, A., & Berg, M. (2011). First-time fathers' experiences of childbirth: A phenomenological study. *Midwifery, 27*, 848–853.

Premberg, A., Hellström, A.-L., & Berg, M. (2008). Experiences of the first year as father. *Scandinavian Journal of Caring Sciences, 22*(1), 56–63.

Prezza, M., & Costantini, S. (1998). Sense of community and life satisfaction: Investigation in three different territorial contexts. *Journal of Community and Applied Social Psychology, 8*(3), 181–194.

Price, B. (2009). Body image in adolescents: Insights and implications. *Paediatric Nursing, 21* (5), 38–43.

Price, S. J., Price, C., & McKenry, P. (2010). *Families & change: Coping with stressful events and transitions* (4th ed.). Thousand Oaks, CA: Sage.

Price, S. K. (2008a). Stepping back to gain perspective: Pregnancy loss history, depression, and parenting capacity in the Early Childhood Longitudinal Study, Birth Cohort (ECLS-B). *Death Studies*, 32(2), 97–122.

Price, S. K. (2008b). Women and reproductive loss: Client-worker dialogues designed to break the silence. *Social Work*, 53(4), 367–376.

Procidano, M. E., & Smith, W. W. (1997). Assessing perceived social support: The importance of context. In G. R. Pierce, B. Lakey, & B. R. Sarason (Eds.), *Sourcebook of social support and personality* (pp. 93–106). New York, NY: Plenum.

Proescholdbell, R., Roosa, M., & Nemeroff, C. (2006). Component measures of psychological sense of community among gay men. *Journal of Community Psychology, 34*(1), 9–24.

Proot, I. M., Abu-Saad, H. H., ter Meulen, R. H. J., Goldsteen, M., Spreeuwenberg, C., & Widdershoven, G. A. M. (2004). The needs of terminally ill patients at home: Directing one's life, health and things related to beloved others. *Palliative Medicine, 18*, 53–61.

Puchalski, C., & Romer, A. L. (2000). Taking a spiritual history allows clinicians to understand patients more fully. *Journal of Palliative Medicine, 3*(1), 129–137.

Pulkkinen, L., Kokko, K., & Rantanen, J. (2012). Paths from socioemotional behavior in middle childhood to personality in middle adulthood. *Developmental Psychology, 48*(5), 1283–1291.

Putnam, R. (1993). *Making democracy work.* Princeton, NJ: Princeton University Press.

Putnam, R. (2000). *Bowling alone: The collapse and revival of American community.* New York, NY: Simon & Schuster.

Qouta, S., Punamaki, R., & El-Sarraj, E. (2003). Prevalence and determinants of PTSD among Palestinian children exposed to military violence. *European Psychiatry and Adolescent Psychiatry, 12*(6), 265–272.

Quigley, B. (2001). The living wage movement. *Blueprint for Social Justice, LIV*(9), 1–7.

Raanaas, R., Evensen, K., Rich, D., Sjostrom, G., & Patil, G. (2011). Benefits of indoor plants on attention capacity in an office setting. *Journal of Environmental Psychology, 31*, 99–105.

Rabkin, J., Balassone, M., & Bell, M. (1995). The role of social workers in providing comprehensive health care to pregnant women. *Social Work in Health Care, 20*(3), 83–97.

Raines, J. (1997). Co-constructing the spiritual tree. *Society for Social Work and Social Work Newsletter, 4*(1), 3, 8.

Rakison, D., & Poulin-Dubois, D. (2001). Developmental origin of the animate-inanimate distinction. *Psychological Bulletin, 127*, 209–228.

Ramirez, R. (1985). Hispanic spirituality. *Social Thought, 11*(3), 6–13.

Rampage, C., Eovaldi, M., Ma, C., Foy, C., Samuels, G., & Bloom, L. (2012). Adoptive families. In F. Walsh (Ed.), *Normal family processes: Growing diversity and complexity* (4th ed., pp. 222–246). New York, NY: Guilford.

Ramsey, J., Langlois, J., Hoss, R., Rubenstein, A., & Griffin, A. (2004). Origins of a stereotype: Categorization of facial attractiveness by 6-month-old infants. *Developmental Science, 7*, 201–211.

Rando, T. (1993). *Treatment of complicated mourning.* Champaign, IL: Research Press.

Rank, M. R. (2005). *One nation, underprivileged: Why American poverty affects us all.* New York, NY: Oxford University Press.

Rapoport, A. (1990). *Meaning of the built environment.* Tucson: University of Arizona Press.

Rapoport, J., Jacobs, P., & Jonsson, E. (2009). *Cost containment and efficiency in national health systems.* Hoboken, NJ: Wiley-Blackwell.

Raustiala, K. (2005). The evolution of territoriality. *International Studies Review, 7*, 515–519.

Ravitch, D. (2010). *The death and life of the great American school system: How testing and choice are undermining education* (Revised and expanded). New York, NY: Basic Books.

Ravitch, D. (2013). *Reign of error: The hoax of the privatization movement and the danger to America's public schools.* New York, NY: Knopf.

Rawls, J. (1971). *A theory of justice.* Cambridge, MA: Harvard University Press.

Rawls, J. (2001). *Justice as fairness: A restatement.* Cambridge, MA: The Belknap Press of Harvard University.

Ray, O. (2004). How the mind hurts and heals the body. *American Psychologist, 59*(1), 29–40.

Ray, R., Gornick, J., & Schmitt, J. (2009). *Parental leave policies in 21 countries: Assessing generosity and gender equality.* Washington, DC: Center for Economic and Policy Research. Retrieved from http://cepr.net/documents/publications/parental_2008_09.pdf

Raza, M., & Velez, P. (Directors). (2002). *Occupation: The Harvard University living wage sit-in* [Motion Picture]. Waterville, ME: EnMasse Films.

Reardon, S. (2011). The widening academic achievement gap between the rich and the poor: New evidence and possible explanations. In G. Duncan & R. Murname (Eds.), *Whither opportunity? Rising inequality, schools, and children's life chances* (pp. 91–116). New York, NY: Russell Sage Foundation.

Rector, R., Johnson, K., & Fagan, P. (2008). Increasing marriage would dramatically reduce child poverty. In D. R. Crane & T. Heaton (Eds.), *Handbook of families and poverty* (pp. 457–470). Thousand Oaks, CA: Sage.

Redman, D. (2008). Stressful life experiences and the roles of spirituality among people with a history of substance abuse and incarceration. *Social Thought, 27*(1–2), 47–67.

Reese, D. J., & Kaplan, M. S. (2000). Spirituality, social support, and worry about health: Relationships in a sample of HIV+ women. *Social Thought, 19*(4), 37–52.

Regoeczi, W. (2008). Crowding in context: An examination of the differential responses of men and women to high-density living environments. *Journal of Health and Social Behavior, 49*(3), 254–268.

Reichert, E. (2006). *Understanding human rights: An exercise book.* Thousand Oaks, CA: Sage.

Reilly, P. (1995). The religious wounding of women. *Creation Spirituality, 11*(1), 41–45.

Reinhardt, U., Hussey, P., & Anderson, G. (2002). Cross-national comparisons of health systems using OECD data, 1999. *Health Affairs, 21*(3), 169–181.

Reinhardt, U., Hussey, P., & Anderson, G. (2004). U.S. health care spending in an international context. *Health Affairs, 23*(3), 10–25.

Reisch, M., & Jani, J. (2012). The new politics of social work practice: Understanding the context to promote change. *British Journal of Social Work, 42*, 1132–1150.

Reith, M., & Payne, M. (2009). *Social work in end-of-life and palliative care.* Chicago, IL: Lyceum Books.

Reitzes, D., & Mutran, E. (2002). Grandparenthood: Factors influencing frequency of grandparent–grandchildren contact and grandparent role satisfaction. *Journals of Gerontology: Social Sciences, 59B*, S9–S16.

Renaud, M., Bherer, L., & Maquestiaux, F. (2010). A high level of physical fitness is associated with more efficient response preparation in older adults. *The Journals of Gerontology: Psychological Sciences, 65B*, 756–766.

Repetti, R., Taylor, S., & Seeman, T. (2002). Risky families: Family social environments and the mental and physical health of offspring. *Psychological Bulletin, 18*, 330–366.

Reporters Without Borders. (2015). *World Press Freedom Index 2015.* Retrieved from http://en.rsf.org

Reproductive Health Access Project. (2014). *Your birth control choices.* Retrieved from http://www.reproductiveaccess.org/resource/birth-control-choices-fact-sheet/?gclid=COHmuuTWhsgCFQwYHwodonABaA

Reuter-Lorenz, P. A. (2002). New visions of the aging mind and brain. *Trends in Cognitive Sciences, 6*, 394–400.

Reuther, R. (1983). *Sexism and God-talk: Toward a feminist theology.* Boston, MA: Beacon Press.

Rew, L. (2005). *Adolescent health: A multidisciplinary approach to theory, research, and intervention.* Thousand Oaks, CA: Sage.

Reynolds, B., & Juvonen, J. (2012). Pubertal timing fluctuations across middle school: Implications for girls' psychological health. *Journal of Youth & Adolescence, 41*(6), 677–690.

Rich, M. (2013, August 15). School standards' debut is rocky, and critics pounce. *New York Times.* Retrieved from http://www.nytimes.com/2013/08/16/education/new-education-standards-face-growing-opposition.html?_r=0

Richardson, M., Cobham, V., McDermott, B., & Murray, J. (2013). Youth mental illness and the family: Parents' loss and grief. *Journal of Child & Family Studies, 22*(5), 719–736.

Richman, J. M., Rosenfeld, L. B., & Hardy, C. J. (1993). The Social Support Survey: A validation study of a clinical measure of the social support process. *Research on Social Work Practice, 3*, 288–311.

Richmond, M. (1901). Charitable cooperation. In *Proceedings of the National Conference of Charities and Corrections* (pp. 298–313). Boston, MA: George H. Elles.

Rieker, P.R., & Bird, C.E. (2005). Rethinking gender differences in health: Why we need to integrate social and biological perspectives. *The Journal of Gerontology: Series B, Psychological Sciences and Social Sciences, 60B*, 40–47.

Riera, C. (2005). Social policy and community development in multicultural contexts. *Community Development Journal, 40*(4), 433–438.

Rieser-Danner, L. (2003). Individual differences in infant fearfulness and cognitive performance: A testing, performance, or competence effect? *Genetic, Social, and General Psychology Monographs, 129*(1), 41–71.

Rietz, C., Hasselhorn, M., & Labuhn, A. (2012). Are externalizing and internalizing difficulties of young children with spelling impairment related to their ADHD symptoms? *Dyslexia (10769242), 18*(3), 174–185.

Riley, M.W. (1971). Social gerontology and the age stratification of society. *The Gerontologist, 11*, 79–87.

Rindfuss, R. R., Cooksey, E. C., & Sutterlin, R. L. (1999). Young adult occupational achievement: Early expectations versus behavioral reality. *Work & Occupations, 26*(2), 220–263.

Ringeisen, H., Casanueva, C. E., Urato, M., & Stambaugh, L. F. (2009). Mental health service use during the transition to adulthood for adolescents reported to the child welfare system. *Psychiatric Services, 60*(8), 1084–1091.

Ripley, A. (2013). *The smartest kids in the world: And how they got that way.* New York, NY: Simon & Schuster.

Ritzer, G. (2013a). *Introduction to sociology.* Thousand Oaks, CA: Sage.

Ritzer, G. (2013b). *The McDonaldization of society* (20th anniv. ed.). Los Angeles, CA: Sage.

Rivas-Drake, D. (2008). Perceived opportunity, ethnic identity, and achievement motivation among Latinos at a selective public university. *Journal of Latinos and Education, 7*(2), 113–128.

Robbins, S., Chatterjee, P., & Canda, E. (2012). *Contemporary human behavior theory: A critical perspective for social work* (3rd ed.). Boston, MA: Allyn & Bacon.

Robbins, T., Stagman, S., & Smith, S. (2012). *Young children at risk: National and state prevalence of risk factors.* New York, NY: Columbia University National Center on Children in Poverty.

Robboy, J., & Anderson, K. G. (2011). Intergenerational child abuse and coping. *Journal of Interpersonal Violence, 26*(17), 3526–3541.

Roberson, W.W. (2004). *Life and livelihood: A handbook for spirituality at work.* Harrison, PA: Morehouse Publishing.

Roberts, E., Burchinal, M., & Bailey, D. (1994). Communication among preschoolers with and without disabilities in same-age and mixed-age classes. *American Journal on Mental Retardation, 99*, 231–249.

Roberts, K., & Yamane, D. (2012). *Religion in sociological perspective* (5th ed.). Los Angeles, CA: Sage.

Robertson, S., Zarit, S., Duncan, L., Rovine, M., & Femia, E. (2007). Family caregivers' patterns of positive and negative affect. *Family Relations, 56*, 12–23.

Robinson, T.L. (2000). Making the hurt go away: Psychological and spiritual healing for African American women survivors of childhood incest. *Journal of Multicultural Counseling and Development, 28*(3), 160–176.

Robinson, T.R. (2010). *Genetics for dummies* (Kindle Locations 2036–2039). Hoboken, NJ: Wiley. Kindle Edition.

Rodda, J., Walker, Z., & Carter, J. (2011). Depression in older adults. *British Medical Journal, 343*, 683–687.

Roehlkepartain, E. C., King, P.E., Wagener, L., & Benson, P.L. (2006). *Spiritual development in childhood and adolescence.* Thousand Oaks, CA: Sage.

Rogers, C. (1951). *Client-centered therapy.* Boston, MA: Houghton Mifflin.

Rogers-Sirin, L., & Gupta, T. (2012). Cultural identity and mental health: Different trajectories among Asian and Latino youth. *Journal of Counseling Psychology, 59*(4), 555–566.

Roggman, L., Boyce, L., Cook, G., Christiansen, K., & Jones, D. (2004). Playing with daddy: Social toy play, early head start, and developmental outcomes. *Fathering, 2*, 83–108.

Rogoff, B., & Chavajay, P. (1995). What's become of research on the cultural basis of cognitive development? *American Psychologist, 50*, 859–873.

Rohde, L., Szobot, C., Polanczyk, G., Schmitz, M., Martins, S., & Tramontina, S. (2005). Attention-deficit/hyperactivity disorder in a diverse culture: Do research and clinical findings support the notion of a cultural construct for the disorder? *Biological Psychiatry, 57*, 1436–1441.

Roksa, J., & Velez, M. (2012). A late start: Delayed entry, life course transitions and bachelor's degree completion. *Social Forces, 90*(3), 769–794.

Rollero, C., & Piccoli, N. (2010). Place attachment, identification and environment perception: An empirical study. *Journal of Environmental Psychology, 30*, 198–205.

Rollins, A., & Hunter, A. G. (2013). Racial socialization of biracial youth: Maternal messages and approaches to address discrimination. *Family Relations, 62*(1), 140–153.

Ronen, T., & Freeman, A. (Eds.). (2007). *Cognitive behavior therapy in clinical social work practice.* New York, NY: Springer.

Rönkä, A., Oravala, S., & Pulkkinen, L. (2003). Turning points in adults' lives: The effects of gender and amount of choice. *Journal of Adult Development, 10*(3), 203–215.

Roof, W. C. (1999). *Spiritual marketplace: Baby boomers and the remaking of American religion.* Princeton, NJ: Princeton University Press.

Rooij, S., Wouters, H., Yonker, J., Painter, R., & Roseboom, T. (2010). Prenatal undernutrition and cognitive function in late adulthood. *Proceedings of the National Academy of Sciences, 107*(9), 16681–16886.

Roopnarine, J., Shin, M., Donovan, B., & Suppal, P. (2000). Sociocultural contexts of dramatic play: Implications for early education. In K. Roskos & J. Christie (Eds.), *Play and literacy in early childhood: Research from multiple perspectives* (pp. 205–220). Mahwah, NJ: Erlbaum.

Roosevelt, M. (2013, January 1). "Living-wage" movement growing in region. *Orange County Register.* Retrieved from http://www.ocregister.com/articles/wage-523783-living-long.htm

Roper v. Simmons, 543 U.S. 551 (2005).

Rose, S. (1992). *Case management and social work practice.* White Plains, NY: Longman.

Rose, S. (1994). Defining empowerment: A value-based approach. In S. P. Robbins (Ed.), *Melding the personal and the political: Advocacy and empowerment in clinical and community practice. Proceedings of the Eighth Annual Social Work Futures Conference*, May 13–14, 1993 (pp. 17–24), Houston, TX: University of Houston Graduate School of Social Work.

Rosenberg, S., Ellison, M., Fast, B., Robinson, C., & Lazar, R. (2013). Computing theoretical rates of Part C eligibility based on developmental delays. *Maternal and Child Health Journal, 17*, 384–390.

Rosenwald, M., Smith, M., Bagnoli, M., Ricceli, D., Ryan, S., Salcedo, L., ... Seeland, D. (2013). Relighting the campfire: Rediscovering activity-based group work. *Social Work with Groups, 36*(4), 321–331.

Rosenzweig, S. M., Breedlove, N.V., & Watson, M. R. (2010). *Biological psychology: An introduction to behavioral, cognitive, and clinical neuroscience* (6th ed.). Sunderland, MA: Sinauer Associates.

Rostow, W. (1990). *The stages of economic growth: A non-communist manifesto.* Cambridge, UK: Cambridge University Press.

Rotenberg, K., McDougall, P., Boulton, M., Vaillancourt, T., Fox, C., & Hymel, S. (2004). Cross-sectional and longitudinal relations among peer-reported trustworthiness, social relationships, and psychological adjustment in children and early adolescents from the United Kingdom and Canada. *Journal of Experimental Child Psychology, 88*, 46–67.

Rothenberg, P. (2010). *Race, class, and gender in the United States* (8th ed.). New York, NY: Worth.

Rothman, J. (2008). *Cultural competence in process and practice: Building bridges*. Boston, MA: Pearson.

Rothrauff, T., & Cooney, T. (2008). The role of generativity in psychological well-being. Does it differ for childless adults and parents? *Journal of Adult Development, 15*, 148–159.

Rothschild-Whitt, J., & Whitt, J. (1986). *The cooperative workplace*. Cambridge, UK: Cambridge University Press.

Rothstein, R. (2011). *Fact-challenged policy*. Economic Policy Institute. Retrieved from www.epi.org/publication/fact-challenged-policy

Roulstone, A. (2004). Employment barriers and inclusive futures? In *Disabling barriers—Enabling environments* (2nd ed., pp. 195–200). Thousand Oaks, CA: Sage.

Roy, J., & Chakraborty, S. (2012). Changing trends in emergency contraception. *Nepal Journal of Obstetrics and Gynaecology, 7*(1), 59–63.

Rudacille, D. (2005). *The riddle of gender: Science, activism, and transgender rights*. New York, NY: Pantheon.

Rueda, R., Monzo, L., Shapiro, J., Gomez, J., & Blacher, J. (2005). Cultural models of transition: Latina mothers of young adults with developmental disabilities. *Exceptional Children, 71*(4), 401–414.

Ruffman, T., Slade, L. & Redman, J. (2005). Young infants' expectations about hidden objects. *Cognitive, 97*, B35–B43.

Ruiz, S., & Silverstein, M. (2007). Relationships with grandparents and the emotional well-being of late adolescent and young adult grandchildren. *Journal of Social Issues, 63*, 793–808.

Russell, S., Watson, R., & Muraco, J. (2012). The development of same-sex intimate relationships during adolescence. In B. Laursen & W. A. Collins (Eds.), *Relationship pathways from adolescence to young adulthood* (pp. 215–233). Los Angeles, CA: Sage.

Rychtarik, R., McGillicuddy, N., & Barrick, C. (2013). Reaching women under stress from a partner's drinking problem: Assessing interest in online help. *Journal of Technology in Human Services, 31*(3), 185–196.

Sadock, B., & Sadock, V. (2007). *Kaplan & Sadock's synopsis of psychiatry: Behavioral sciences/clinical psychiatry* (10th ed.). Baltimore, MD: Wolters Kluwer.

Saewyc, E. (2011). Research on adolescent sexual orientation: Development, health disparities, stigma, and resilience. *Journal of Research on Adolescence, 21*(1), 256–272.

Saez, E. (2012). *Striking it richer: The evolution of top incomes in the United States* (Updated with 2009 and 2010 estimates). Retrieved from elsa.berkeley.edu/~saez/saez-UStopincomes-2010.pdf

Sagi, A., Koren-Karie, N., Gini, M., Ziv, Y., & Joels, T. (2002). Shedding further light on the effects of various types and quality of early child care on infant–mother attachment relationships: The Haifa study of early child care. *Child Development, 73*, 1166–1186.

Sahgal, N., & Smith, G. (2009). A religious portrait of African-Americans. Pew Research Center's Forum on Religion & Public Life. Retrieved from http://www.pewforum.org/A-Religious-Portrait-of-African-Americans.aspx

Sahlins, M. (1981). *Historical metaphors and mythical realities: Structure in the early history of the Sandwich Islands kingdom*. Ann Arbor: University of Michigan Press.

Saleebey, D. (2012). *The strengths perspective in social work practice* (6th ed.). Upper Saddle River, NJ: Pearson.

Sampson, R. (2003). The neighborhood context of well-being. *Perspectives in Biology and Medicine, 46*(3), S53–S65.

Sampson, R., Morenoff, J., & Earls, F. (1999). Beyond social capital: Spatial dynamics of collective efficacy for children. *Science, 277*, 918–924.

Sanders, R. (2013). Adolescent psychosocial, social, and cognitive development. *Pediatrics in Review, 34*, 354–359.

Sandoval-Cros, C. (2009). Hispanic cultural issues in end-of-life care. In D. J. Doka & A. S. Tucci, *Living with grief: Diversity and end-of-life care* (pp. 117–126). Washington, DC: Hospice Foundation of America.

Sands, R., & Goldberg, G. (2000). Factors associated with stress among grandparents raising their grandchildren. *Family Relations, 49*(1), 97–105.

Sang-Ho, Y. (2010). Hair nicotine levels in non-smoking pregnant women whose spouses smoke outside of the home. *Tobacco Control, 19*(4), 318–324.

Santrock, J. W. (2009). *Child development*. Boston, MA: McGraw Hill.

Sapolsky, R. (2004). *Why zebras don't get ulcers* (3rd ed.). New York, NY: Henry Holt.

Sarafino, E. P., & Smith, T. W. (2010). *Health psychology: Biopsychosocial interactions* (7th ed.). New York, NY: John Wiley & Sons.

Sarason, S. (1974). *The psychological sense of community: Prospects for a community psychology*. San Francisco, CA: Jossey-Bass.

Satir, V. (1983). *Conjoint family therapy* (3rd ed.). Palo Alto, CA: Science and Behavior Books.

Savia, J., Almeida, D., Davey, A., & Zant, S. (2008). Routine assistance to parents: Effects on daily mood and other stressors. *Journals of Gerontology Series B, Psychological Sciences & Social Sciences, 36B*(3), S154–S161.

Savica, R., & Petersen, L. C. (2011). Prevention of dementia. *Psychiatric Clinics of North America, 34*, 127–145.

Sawyer, S., Afifi, R., Bearinger, L., Blakermore, S., Dick, B., Ezeh, A., . . . Patton, G. (2012). Adolescence: A foundation for future health. *The Lancet, 379*, 1630–1641.

Sayer, L. (2006). Economic aspects of divorce and relationship dissolution. In M. Fine & J. Harvey (Eds.), *Handbook of divorce and relationship dissolution* (pp. 385–406). Mahwah, NJ: Erlbaum.

Scales, T. L., Wolfer, T. A., Sherwood, D. A., Garland, D. R., Hugen, B., & Pittman, S. W. (2002). *Spirituality and religion in social work practice: Decision cases with teaching notes*. Alexandria, VA: Council on Social Work Education.

Scannell, L., & Gifford, R. (2010a). Defining place attachment: A tripartite organizing framework. *Journal of Environmental Psychology, 30*, 1–10.

Scannell, L., & Gifford, R. (2010b). The relations between natural and civic place attachment and pro-environmental behavior. *Journal of Environmental Psychology, 30*, 289–297.

Scannell, L., & Gifford, R. (2013). Personality relevant climate change: The role of place attachment and local versus global message framing in engagement. *Environment and Behavior, 45*(1), 60–85.

Scarlett, A. G., Naudeau, S., Salonius-Pasternak, D., & Ponte, I. (2005). *Children's play*. Thousand Oaks, CA: Sage.

Schacter, S., & Singer, J. E. (1962). Cognitive, social, and physiological determinants of emotional states. *Psychological Review, 69*, 379–399.

Schaie, K. W. (1984). The Seattle Longitudinal Study: A 21-year exploration of psychometric intelligence in adulthood. In K. W. Schaie (Ed.), *Longitudinal studies of adult psychological development* (pp. 64–135). New York, NY: Guilford.

Schamess, G., & Shilkret, R. (2011). Ego psychology. In J. Berzoff, L. M. Flanagan, & P. Hertz (Eds.), *Inside out and outside in: Psychodynamic clinical theory and psychopathology in contemporary multicultural contexts* (3d ed., pp. 62–96). Lanham, MD: Rowman & Littlefield.

Schein, E. (1992). *Organizational culture and leadership* (2nd ed.). San Francisco, CA: Jossey-Bass.

Scherger, S. (2009). Social change and the timing of family transitions in West Germany: Evidence from cohort comparisons. *Time & Society, 18*(1), 106–129.

Schiller, J., Lucas, J., & Peregoy, J. (2012). Summary health statistics for U.S. adults: National Health Interview Survey, 2011. *Vital and Health Statistics, 10*(256). Hyattsville, MD: U.S. Department of Health and Human Services. Centers for Disease Control and Prevention.

Schmitz, C., & Hilton, A. (1996). Combining mental health treatment with education for preschool children with severe emotional and behavioral problems. *Social Work in Education, 18*, 237–249.

Schneider, B., Lee, M., & Alvarez-Valdivia, I. (2012). Adolescent friendship bonds in cultures of connectedness. In B. Laursen & W. A. Collins (Eds.), *Relationship pathways from adolescence to young adulthood* (pp. 113–134). Los Angeles, CA: Sage.

Schneider, J., & Cook, K. (1995). Status inconsistency and gender: Combining revisited. *Small Group Research, 26*, 372–399.

Schneir, A. (2009). *Psychological first aid for youth experiencing homelessness*. The National Child Traumatic Stress Network. Retrieved from www.hhyp.org/downloads/HHYP_PFA_youth.pdf

Schoech, D. (2013). Community practice in the digital age. In M. Weil, M. Reisch, & M. Ohmer (Eds.), *The handbook of community practice* (2nd ed., pp. 809–826). Los Angeles, CA: Sage.

Schöllgen, I., Huxhold, O., & Tesch-Römer, C. (2010). Socioeconomic status and health in the second half of life: Findings from the German Ageing Survey. *European Journal of Ageing, 7*, 17–28.

Scholz, R. W., Blumer, Y. B., & Brand, F. S. (2012). Risk, vulnerability, robustness, and resilience from a decision-theoretic perspective. *Journal of Risk Research, 15*(3), 313–330.

Schore, A. N. (2002). Dysregulation of the right brain: A fundamental mechanism of traumatic attachment and the psychopathogenesis of post-traumatic stress disorder. *Australian and New Zealand Journal of Psychiatry, 36*, 9–30.

Schroeder, R., Giordano, P., & Cernkovitch, S. (2010). Adult child-parent bonds and life course criminality. *Journal of Criminal Justice, 38*, 562–571.

Shuey, K., & Willson, A. (2008). Cumulative disadvantage and Black-White disparities in life-course health trajectories. *Research on Aging, 30*(2), 200–225.

Schupf, N., Tang, M., Albert, S., Costa, A. R., Andrews, H., Lee, J., . . . Mayeux, R. (2005). Decline in cognitive and functional skills increases mortality risk in nondemented elderly. *Neurology, 65*(8), 1218–1226.

Schutz, A. (1967). *The phenomenology of the social world* (G. Walsh & F. Lehnert, Trans.). Evanston, IL: Northwestern University Press. (Original work published 1932)

Schwalbe, M. (2006). Afterword: The costs of American privilege. In P. Rothenberg (Ed.), *Beyond borders: Thinking critically about global issues* (pp. 603–605). New York, NY: Worth.

Schwartz, S., Cote, J., & Arnett, J. (2005). Identity and agency in emerging adulthood: Two developmental routes in the individualization process. *Youth and Society, 37*(2), 201–229.

Schweinhart, L., Montie, J., Xiang, Z., Barnett, W., Belfield, C., & Nores, M. (2005). *Lifetime effects: The High/Scope Perry preschool study through age 40*. Ypsilanti, MI: High/Scope Educational Research Foundation.

Scott, M. (2005). A powerful theory and a paradox: Ecological psychologists after Barker. *Environment and Behavior, 37*(3), 295–329.

Scott, W. R. (2014). *Institutions and organizations: Ideas, interests, and identities* (4th ed.). Los Angeles, CA: Sage.

Seabrook, J., & Avison, W. (2012). Socioeconomic status and cumulate disadvantage processes across the life course: Implications for health outcomes. *Canadian Review of Sociology, 49*(1), 50–68.

Seccombe, K., & Warner, R. (2004). *Marriages and families: Relationships in social context*. New York, NY: Thomson Learning.

Sedgh, G., Singh, S., Shah, I. H., Ahman, E., Henshaw, S. K., & Bankote, A. (2012). Induced abortion: Incidence and trends worldwide from 1995 to 2008. *The Lancet, 379*(9816), 625–632.

Segal, B. M., & Stewart, J. C. (1996). Substance use and abuse in adolescence: An overview. *Child Psychiatry and Human Development, 26*(4), 193–210.

Segall, M., Dasen, P., Berry, J., & Poortinga, Y. (1999). *Human behavior in global perspective* (2nd ed.). Boston, MA: Allyn & Bacon.

Segerstrom, S. S., & Miller, G. E. (2004). Psychological stress and the human immune system: A meta-analytic study of 30 years of inquiry. *Psychological Bulletin, 130*(4), 601–630.

Seidman, E. (2012). An emerging action science of social settings. *American Journal of Community Psychology, 50*, 1–16.

Seiffge-Krenge, I., & Shulman, S. (2012). Transformations in heterosexual romantic relationships across the transition into adolescence. In B. Laursen & W. A. Collins (Eds.), *Relationship pathways from adolescence to young adulthood* (pp. 157–189). Los Angeles, CA: Sage.

Seligman, M. (1998). *Learned optimism: How to change your mind and your life* (2nd ed.). New York, NY: Pocket Books.

Seligman, M. (2002). *Authentic happiness: Using the new positive psychology to realize your potential for lasting fulfillment*. New York, NY: Free Press.

Seligman, M., Reivich, K., Jaycox, L., & Gillham, J. (2007). *The optimistic child: A proven program to safeguard children against depression and build lifelong resilience*. Boston, MA: Houghton Mifflin.

Selman, R. L. (1976). Social-cognitive understanding: A guide to educational and clinical practice. In T. Lickona (Ed.), *Moral development and behavior: Theory, research, and social issues* (pp. 219–316). New York, NY: Holt, Rinehart & Winston.

Selye, H. (1991). History and present status of the stress concept. In A. Monat & R. S. Lazarus (Eds.), *Stress and coping: An anthology* (3rd ed., pp. 21–35). New York, NY: Columbia University Press.

Sen, A. (1992). *Inequality reexamined*. Cambridge, MA: Harvard University Press.

Sen, A. (1999). *Development as freedom*. New York, NY: Anchor Books.

Sen, A. (2009). *The idea of justice*. Cambridge, MA: The Belknap Press of Harvard University.

Seng, J., Lopez, W., Sperlich, M., Hamam, L., & Meldrum, C. (2012). Marginalized identities, discrimination, burden, and mental health: Empirical exploration of an interpersonal-level approach to modeling intersectionality. *Social Science & Medicine, 75*, 2437–2445.

Sengane, M. (2009). The experience of Black fathers concerning support for their wives/partners during labour. *Curationis, 32*, 67–73.

Senge, P. (1990). *The fifth discipline*. New York, NY: Doubleday.

Sernau, S. (2014). *Social inequality in a global age* (4th ed.). Los Angeles, CA: Sage.

Settersten, R. A., Jr. (2003). Age structuring and the rhythm of the life course. In J. Mortimer & M. Shanhan (Eds.), *Handbook of the life course* (pp. 81–98). New York, NY: Kluwer Academic/Plenum.

Settersten, R. A., Jr., Furstenberg, F. F., & Rumbaut, R. G. (2005). *On the frontier of adulthood: Theory, research, and public policy*. Chicago, IL: University of Chicago Press.

Settersten, R. A., & Mayer, L. U. (1997). The measurement of age, age structuring, and the life course. *Annual Review of Sociology, 23*, 233–261.

Severson, K. (2011, July 5). Systematic cheating is found in Atlanta's school system. *New York Times*. Retrieved from www.nytimes.com/2011/07/06/education/06atlanta.html

Shade, K., Kools, S., Weiss, S., & Pinderhughes, H. (2011). A conceptual model of incarcerated adolescent fatherhood: Adolescent identity development and the concept of intersectionality. *Journal of Child and Adolescent Psychiatric Nursing, 24*, 98–104.

Shanahan, L., Waite, E., & Boyd, T. (2012). Transformations in sibling relationships from adolescence to adulthood. In B. Laursen & W. A. Collins (Eds.), *Relationship pathways from adolescence to young adulthood* (pp. 43–66). Los Angeles, CA: Sage.

Shanahan, M. (2000). Pathways to adulthood in changing societies: Variability and mechanisms in life course perspective. *Annual Review of Sociology, 27*, 667–692.

Shannon, J. B. (2011). *Autism and pervasive developmental disorders sourcebook*. Detroit, MI: Omnigraphics.

Sharma, G., & Goodwin, J. (2006). Effect of aging on respiratory system physiology and immunology. *Clinical Interventions in Aging, 1*(3), 253–260.

Shaw, B., Sivakumar, G., Balinas, T., Chipman, R., & Krahn, D. (2013). Testing the feasibility of mobile audio-based recovery material as an adjunct to intensive outpatients treatment for veterans with substance abuse disorders. *Journal of Technology in Human Services, 31*(4), 321–336.

Shear, M., & Pear, R. (2014, January 13). Older pool of health care enrollees stirs fears on costs. *New York Times*. Retrieved from http://www.nytimes.com/2014/01/14/us/health-care-plans-attracting-more-older-less-healthy-people.html?_r=0

Sheehy, G. (1995). *New passages*. New York, NY: Random House.

Shek, D. (2003). Economic stress, psychological well-being and problem behavior in Chinese adolescents with economic disadvantage. *Journal of Youth and Adolescence, 32*(4), 259–266.

Sheldon, K. (2006). Getting older, getting better? Recent psychological evidence. In M. Csikszentmihalyi & I. Csiksezentmihali (Eds.), *A life worth living: Contributions to positive psychology* (pp. 215–229). New York, NY: Oxford University Press.

Sheldon, K., & Kasser, T. (2001). Getting older, getting better? Personal striving and psychological maturity across the life span. *Developmental Psychology, 37*, 491–501.

Shepard, B. (2013). Community gardens, community organizing, and environmental activism. In M. Gray, J. Coates, & T. Hetherington (Eds.), *Environmental social work* (pp. 121–134). New York, NY: Routledge.

Sherblom, S. (2008). The legacy of the "care challenge": Re-envisioning the outcome of the justice-care debate. *Journal of Moral Education, 37*(1), 81–98.

Sherer, M. (2009). *Challenging the whole child: Reflections on best practices in learning, teaching and leadership*. Alexandria, VA: Association for Supervision & Curriculum Development.

Sheridan, M. J. (2002). Spiritual and religious issues in practice. In A. R. Roberts & G. J. Greene (Eds.), *Social workers' desk reference* (pp. 567–571). New York, NY: Oxford University Press.

Sheridan, M. J. (Ed.). (2014). *Connecting spirituality and social justice: Conceptualizations and applications for macro social work practice*. London, UK: Routledge.

Sherman, E. (1991). *Reminiscence and the self in old age*. New York, NY: Springer.

Sherry, A., Adelman, A., Whilde, M. R., & Quick, D. (2010). Competing selves: Negotiating the intersection of spiritual and sexual identities. *Professional Psychology: Research and Practice, 41*(2), 112–119.

Sherwood, P., Given, C., Given, B., & Von Eye, A. (2005). Caregiver burden and depressive symptoms: Analysis of common outcomes in caregivers of elderly patients. *Journal of Aging Health, 17*, 125–147.

Shields, N., Nadasen, K., & Pierce, L. (2008). The effects of community violence on children in Cape Town South Africa. *Child Abuse & Neglect, 32*(5), 589–601.

Shonkoff, J., & Phillips, D. (Eds.). (2000). *From neurons to neighborhoods: The science of early childhood development*. Washington, DC: National Academies Press.

Shore, R., & Shore, B. (2009). *Increasing the percentage of children living in two-parent families*. Baltimore: The Annie E. Casey Foundation. Retrieved December 9, 2009, from http://www.kidscount.org

Shorey, H. S., & Snyder, C. R. (2006). The role of adult attachment styles in psychopathology and psychotherapy outcomes. *Review of General Psychology, 10*(1), 1–20.

Shreffler, K. M., Greil, A. L., & McQuillan, J. (2011). Pregnancy loss and distress among U.S. women. *Family Relations, 60*(3), 343–355.

Shu, L., & Li, Y. (2007). How far is enough? A measure of information privacy in terms of interpersonal distance. *Environment & Behavior, 39*(3), 317–331.

Shweder, R. (1995). Anthropology's Romantic rebellion against the Enlightenment, or there's more to thinking than reason and evidence. In R. Shweder & R. LeVine (Eds.), *Culture theory: Essays on mind, self, and emotion* (pp. 27–66). New York, NY: Cambridge University Press. (Original work published 1984)

Sideridis, G. D. (2006). Coping is not an "either" "or": The interaction of coping strategies in regulating affect, arousal and performance. *Stress and Health: Journal of the International Society for the Investigation of Stress, 22*(5), 315–327.

Silbereisen, R., & Lerner, R. (2007a). *Approaches to positive youth development*. Thousand Oaks, CA: Sage.

Silbereisen, R., & Lerner, R. (2007b). Approaches to positive youth development: A view of the issues. In R. Silbereisen & R. Lerner (Eds.), *Approaches to positive youth development* (pp. 3–30). Thousand Oaks, CA: Sage.

Silverman, D. (1971). *The theory of organizations: A sociological framework*. New York, NY: Basic Books.

Silverman, D. (1994). On throwing away ladders: Re-writing the theory of organizations. In J. Hassard & M. Parker (Eds.), *Towards a new theory of organizations* (pp. 1–23). New York, NY: Routledge.

Silverman, P. R. (2004). Bereavement: A time of transition and changing relationships. In J. Berzoff & P. R. Silverman (Eds.), *Living with dying: A handbook for end-of-life healthcare practitioners* (pp. 226–241). New York, NY: Columbia University Press.

Silvers, J., Gabrieli, J., McRae, K., Gross, J., Remy, K., & Ochsner, D. (2012). Age-related differences in emotional reactivity, regulation, and rejection sensitivity in adolescence. *Emotion, 12*(6), 1235–1247.

Silverstein, M., & Bengtson, V. (2001). Intergenerational solidarity and the structure of adult child–parent relationships in American families. In A. Walker, M. Manoogian-O'Dell, L. McGraw, & D. L. White (Eds.), *Families in later life: Connections and transitions* (pp. 53–61). Thousand Oaks, CA: Pine Forge.

Simaika, J., & Samways, M. (2010). Biophilia as a universal ethic for conserving biodiversity. *Conservation Biology, 24*(3), 903–906.

Simeoni, U., Ligi, I., Buffat, C., & Boubred, F. (2011). Adverse consequences of accelerated neonatal growth: Cardiovascular and renal issues. *Pediatric Nephrology, 26*(4), 493–508.

Simmons, R. (2011). *Odd girl out: The hidden culture of aggression in girls*. Boston, MA: Mariner Books/Houghton Mifflin Harcourt.

Simmons, T., & O'Connell, M. (2003). *Married-couple and unmarried-partner households: 2000.* Washington, DC: U.S. Census Bureau.

Simon, H. (1957). *Administrative behavior* (2nd ed.). New York, NY: Macmillan.

Simpson, G. A., Cohen, R. A., Pastor, P.N., & Reuben, C. A. (2008). Use of mental health services in the past 12 months by children aged 4–17 years: United States, 2005–2006. NCHS Data Brief, 8, 1–8.

Sinetar, M. (2011). *Do what you love, the money will follow: Discovering your right livelihood.* New York, NY: Random House.

Singer, D., & Singer, J. (2011). *Handbook of children and the media* (2nd ed.). Thousand Oaks, CA: Sage.

Singer, J., Rexhaj, B., & Baddeley, J. (2007). Older, wiser, and happier? Comparing older adults' and college students' self-defining memories. *Memory, 15*, 886–898.

Singh, R. (2001). Hinduism. In M.V. Hook, B. Hugen, & M. Aguilar (Eds.), *Spirituality within religious traditions in social work practice* (pp. 34–52). Pacific Grove, CA: Brooks/Cole.

Sinha, S., & Mukherjee, N. (1996). The effect of perceived cooperation on personal space requirements. *Journal of Social Psychology, 136*, 655–657.

Sinha, S., & Nayyar, P. (2000). Crowding effects of density and personal space requirements among older people: The impact of self-control and social support. *Journal of Social Psychology, 140*(6), 721–726.

Sisson, G. (2012). Finding a way to offer something more: Reframing teen pregnancy prevention. *Sexuality Research and Social Policy, 9*, 57–69.

Skinner, C., Wight, V. R., Aratani, Y., Cooper, J. L., & Thampi, K. (2010). *English language proficiency, family economic security, and child development.* National Center for Children in Poverty. Retrieved from http://www.nccp.org/publications/pub_948.html

Skocpol, T. (2003). *Diminished democracy: From membership to management in American civil life.* New York, NY: Cambridge University Press.

Skocpol, T., & Williamson, V. (2012). *The Tea Party and the remaking of Republican conservatism.* New York, NY: Oxford University Press.

Slatcher, R., & Trentacosta, C. (2012). Influences of parent and child negative emotionality on young children's everyday behaviors. *Emotion, 12*(5), 932–942.

Slee, N. M. (1996). Further on from Fowler: Post-Fowler faith development research. In L. J. Francis, W. K. Kay, & W. S. Campbell (Eds.), *Research in religious education* (pp. 73–96). Leominster, UK: Gracewing.

Smink, E., van Hoeken, D., & Hoek, H. (2012). Epidemiology of eating disorders: Incidence, prevalence and mortality. *Current Psychiatry Reports, 14*(4), 406–414.

Smith, A., Dannison, L., & Vach-Hasse, T. (1998). When Grandma is Mom. *Childhood Education, 75*(1), 12–16.

Smith, C., & Denton, M. L. (2005). *Soul searching: The religious and spiritual lives of American teenagers.* New York, NY: Oxford University Press.

Smith, C. O., Smith, E. P., Levine, D. W., Dumas, J., & Prinz, R. J. (2009). A developmental perspective of the relationship of racial-ethnic identity to self-construct, achievement, and behavior in African American children. *Cultural Diversity and Ethnic Minority Psychology, 15*(2), 145–157.

Smith, E. D. (1995). Addressing the psychospiritual distress of death as reality: A transpersonal approach. *Social Work, 40*, 402–413.

Smith, G. (1996). Ties, nets and an elastic bund: Community in the postmodern city. *Community Development Journal, 31*(3), 250–259.

Smith, J., & Medalia, C. (2015, September). *Health insurance coverage in the United States: 2014.* Washington, DC: U.S. Census Bureau.

Smith, J., O'Connor, I., & Berthelsen, D. (1996). The effects of witnessing domestic violence on young children's psycho-social adjustment. *Australian Social Work, 49*(4), 3–10.

Smith, N. R. (2006). *Workplace spirituality: A complete guide for business leaders.* Lynn, MA: Axial Age.

Smith, R., Fortin, A., Dwamena, F., & Frankel, R. (2013). An evidence-based patient-centered method makes the biopsychosocial model scientific. *Patient Education and Counseling, 91*, 265–270.

Smith, Y., van Goozen, S., & Cohen-Kettenis, P. (2001). Adolescents with gender identity disorder who were accepted or rejected for sex assignment surgery: A prospective follow-up study. *Journal of the American Academy of Child and Adolescent Psychiatry, 40*, 472–481.

Smyer, M. A., Gatz, M., Simi, N. L., & Pedersen, N. L. (1998). Childhood adoption: Long-term effects in adulthood. *Psychiatry: Interpersonal and Biological Processes, 61*(3), 191.

Snarr, C. M. (2007). "Oh Mary, don't you weep": Progressive religion in the living wage movement. *Political Theology, 8*(3), 269–279.

Snipp, C. M. (1998). The first Americans: American Indians. In M. L. Andersen & P.H. Collins (Eds.), *Race, class, and gender: An anthology* (pp. 357–364). Belmont, CA: Wadsworth.

Snyder, C., & Lopez, S. (2007). *Positive psychology: The scientific and practical explorations of human strengths.* Thousand Oaks, CA: Sage.

Snyder, F.J., Acock, A. C., Vuchinich, S., Beets, M. W., Washburn, I. I., & Flay, B. R. (2013). Preventing negative behaviors among elementary-school students through enhancing students' social-emotional and character development. *American Journal of Health Promotion, 28*(1), 50–58.

Snyder, M. (2014). Self-fulfilling stereotypes. In P.S. Rothenberg (Ed.), *Race, class, and gender in the United States* (9th ed.). New York, NY: Worth.

Snyder, S., & Mitchell, D. (2001). Re-engaging the body: Disability studies and the resistance to embodiment. *Public Culture, 13*(3), 367–389.

Social Security Administration. (2013). *Retirement planner: Full retirement age.* Retrieved from www.ssa.gov/retire2/retirechart.htm

Social Trends Institute. (2012). *What do marriage & fertility have to do with the economy?* Retrieved from http://sustaindemographicdividend.org/wp-content-uploads/2012/07/SDD-2011-Final.pdf

Society for Neuroscience. (2012). *Brain facts: A primer on the brain and nervous system.* Washington, DC: Author. Retrieved from www.sfn.org

Solantaus, T., Leinonen, J., & Punamaki, R. (2004). Children's mental health in times of economic recession: Replication and extension of the Family Economic Stress Model in Finland. *Developmental Psychology, 40*(3), 412–429.

Sollod, R., Wilson, J., & Monte, C. (2009). *Beneath the mask: An introduction to theories of personality* (8th ed.). Hoboken, NJ: Wiley.

Solomon, B. (1976). *Black empowerment: Social work in oppressed communities.* New York, NY: Columbia University Press.

Solomon, B. (1987). Empowerment: Social work in oppressed communities. *Journal of Social Work Practice, 2*(4), 79–91.

Solomon, Z., Helvitz, H., & Zerach, G. (2009). Subjective age, PTSD and physical health among war veterans. *Aging & Mental Health, 13*(3), 405–413.

Solomon, Z., & Mikulincer, M. (2006). Trajectories of PTSD: A 20-year longitudinal study. *American Journal of Psychiatry, 163*(4), 659–666.

Sommer, R. (1969). *Personal space: The behavioral basis of design.* Englewood Cliffs, NJ: Prentice Hall.

Sommer, R. (2002). Personal space in a digital age. In R. Bechtel & A. Churchman (Eds.), *Handbook of environmental psychology* (pp. 647–660). New York, NY: Wiley.

Sompayrac, L. M. (2012). *How the immune system works.* Hoboken, NJ: Wiley & Sons.

Sonfield, A. (2010). The potential of health care reform to improve pregnancy-related services and outcomes. *Guttmacher Policy Review, 13*(3), 13–17.

Soulsby, A., & Clark, E. (2007). Organization theory and the post-socialist transformation: Contributions to organizational knowledge. *Human Relations, 60*(10), 1419–1442.

Spear, L. P. (2010). *The behavioral neuroscience of adolescence*. New York, NY: W. W. Norton.

Spector-Mersel, G. (2006). Never-aging stories: Western hegemonic masculinity scripts. *Journal of Gender Studies, 15*(1), 67–82.

Spence, K., Henderson-Smart, D., New, K., Evans, C., Whitelaw, J., Woolnough, R., & Australian and New Zealand Neonatal Network. (2010). Evidence-based clinical practice guideline for management of newborn pain. *Journal of Paediatrics and Child Health, 46*, 184–192.

Spencer, M. B. (1984). Black children's race awareness, racial attitudes and self concept: A reinterpretation. *Journal of Child Psychology and Psychiatry, 25*(3), 433–441.

Spencer, M. B., Harpalani, V., Fegley, S., Dell'Angelo, T., & Seaton, G. (2003). Identity, self, and peers in context: A culturally sensitive, developmental framework for analysis. In R. M. Lerner, F. Jacobs, & D. Wertlieb (Eds.), *Handbook of applied developmental science* (Vol. 1, pp. 123–142). Thousand Oaks, CA: Sage.

Speybroeck, N., Konings, P., Lynch, J., Harper, S., Berkvens, D., Lorant, V., . . . Hosseinpoor, A. (2010). Decomposing socioeconomic health inequalities. *International Journal of Public Health, 55*(4), 347–351.

Spiegel, D., & Classen, C. (2000). *Group therapy for cancer patients: A research-based handbook of psychosocial care*. New York, NY: Basic Books.

Spilsbury, J., Kahana, S., Drotar, D., Creeden, R., Flannery, D., & Friedman, S. (2008). Profiles of behavioral problems in children who witness domestic violence. *Violence and Victims, 23*(1), 3–17.

Spinrad, T., Eisenberg, N., Gaertner, B., Popp, T., Smith, C., Kupfer, A., . . . Hofer, C. (2007). Relations of maternal socialization and toddlers' effortful control to children's adjustment and social competence. *Developmental Psychology, 43*(5), 1170–1186.

Sroufe, L. A., Egeland, B., Carlson, E., & Collins, W. A. (2005). *The development of the person: The Minnesota study of risk and adaptation from birth to adulthood*. New York, NY: Guilford Press.

Stadelmann, S., Perren, S., Groeben, M., & von Klitzing, K. (2010). Parental separation and children's behavioral/emotional problems: The impact of parental representations and family conflict. *Family Process, 49*(1), 92–108.

Stanley, S., Markman, H., & Whitton, S. (2002). Communication, conflict, and commitment: Insights on the foundations for relationship success from a national survey. *Family Process, 41*, 659–675.

Stapleton, S. R., Osborne, C., & Illuzzi, J. (2013). Outcomes of care in birth centers: Demonstration of a durable model. *Journal of Midwifery and Women's Health, 58*(1), 3–14.

Starhawk. (1979). *The spiral dance: A rebirth of the ancient religion of the great Goddess*. San Francisco, CA: Harper & Row.

Statistic Brain. (2013). *Adoption statistics*. Retrieved from http://www.statisticbrain.com/adoption-statistics

Statistic Brain. (2014). *Facebook statistics*. Retrieved from http://www.statisticbrain.com/facebook-statistics

Staudinger, U. M., Freund, A. M., Linden, M., & Maas, I. (1999). Self, personality, and life regulation: Facets of psychological resilience in old age. In P. B. Baltes & K. U. Mayer (Eds.), *The Berlin Aging Study: Aging from 70 to 100* (pp. 302–328). Cambridge, UK: Cambridge University Press.

Steen, M., Downe, S., Bamford, N., & Edozien, L. (2012). Not-patient and not-visitor: A metasynthesis fathers' encounters with pregnancy, birth and maternity care. *Midwifery, 28*, 422–431.

Steensma, T., Kreukels, B., de Vries, A., & Cohen-Kettenis, P. (2013). Gender identity development in adolescence. *Hormones and Behavior, 64*, 288–297.

Stegner, W. (1978). The writer and the concept of adulthood. In E. H. Erikson (Ed.), *Adulthood* (pp. 227–336). New York, NY: Norton & Norton.

Stein, L. (2009). Social movement web use in theory and practice: A content analysis of U.S. movement websites. *New Media & Society, 11*(5), 749–771.

Stein, M. (2005). Resilience and young people leaving care: Implications for child welfare policy and practice in the UK. In R. J. Flynn, P. M. Dudding, & J. G. Barber (Eds.), *Promoting resilience in child welfare* (pp. 264–278). Ottawa, ON: University of Ottawa Press.

Steinberg, J., & Finer, L. (2011). Examining the association of abortion history and current mental health: A reanalysis of the National Comorbidity Survey using a common-risk-factors model. *Social Science & Medicine, 72*, 72–82.

Steinberg, L. (2009). Should the science of adolescent brain development inform public policy? *American Psychologist, 64*(8), 739–750.

Stephan, Y., Chalabaev, A., Kotter-Grühn, D., & Jaconelli, A. (2013). "Feeling younger, being stronger": An experimental study of subjective age and physical functioning among older adults. *The Journals of Gerontology, Series B: Psychological Sciences and Social Sciences, 68*(1), 1–7.

Stephan, Y., Demulier, V., & Terracciano, A. (2012). Personality, self-rated health, and subjective age in a life-span sample: The moderating role of chronological age. *Psychology and Aging, 27*(4), 875–880.

Stephens, N., Hamedani, M., Markus, H., Bergsieker, H., & Eloul, L. (2009). Why did they "choose" to stay? Perspectives of Hurricane Katrina observers and survivors. *Psychological Science, 20*(7), 878–886.

Steptoe, A., Shankar, A., Demakakos, P., & Wardle, J. (2013). Social isolation, loneliness, and all-cause mortality in older men and women. *Proceedings of the National Academy of Sciences, 110*(15), 5797–5801.

Sternberg, E. (2009). *Healing spaces: The science of place and well-being*. Cambridge, MA: Belknap Press.

Sterns, H., & Huyck, M. (2001). The role of work in midlife. In M. Lachman (Ed.), *Handbook of midlife development* (pp. 447–486). New York, NY: Wiley.

Stevenson, B. (2015). *Just mercy: A story of justice and redemption*. New York, NY: Spiegel & Grau.

Stewart, C., Koeske, G., & Pringle, J. L. (2007). Religiosity as a predictor of successful post-treatment abstinence for African-American clients. *Journal of Social Work Practice in the Addictions, 7*(4), 75–92.

Stewart, J. (2001). Radical constructivism in biology and cognitive science. *Foundations of Science, 6*(1–3), 99–124.

Stiglitz, J. (2012). *The price of inequality: How today's divided society endangers our future*. New York, NY: W. W. Norton.

Stillbirth Collaborative Research Network Writing Group. (2011). Causes of death among stillbirths. *Journal of the American Medical Association, 306*(22), 2459–2468.

Stirling, K., & Aldrich, T. (2008). Child support: Who bears the burden? *Family Relations, 57*, 376–389.

Stockard, J., & O'Brien, R. (2002). Cohort effects on suicide rates: International variation. *American Sociological Review, 67*, 854–872.

Stokols, D., & Montero, M. (2002). Toward an environmental psychology of the Internet. In R. Bechtel & A. Churchman (Eds.), *Handbook of environmental psychology* (pp. 661–675). New York, NY: Wiley.

Stone, D. (2012). *Policy paradox: The art of political decision making* (3rd ed.). New York, NY: Norton.

Strauch, B. (2010). *The secret life of the grown-up brain: The surprising talents of the middle-aged mind*. London, UK: Viking.

Street, J., Harris-Britt, A., & Walker-Barnes, C. (2009). Examining relationships between ethnic identity, family environment, and psychological outcomes for African American adolescents. *Journal of Child and Family Studies, 18*, 412–420.

Street, K., Harrington, J., Chiang, W., Cairns, P., & Ellis, M. (2004). How great is the risk of abuse in infants born to drug-using mothers? *Child Care, Health and Development, 30*(4), 325–330.

Streib, H. (2005). Faith development research revisited: Accounting for diversity in structure, content, and narrativity of faith. *International Journal for the Psychology of Religion, 15*, 99–121.

Streifel, C., & Servaty-Seib, H. L. (2009). Recovering from alcohol and other drug dependency: Loss and spirituality in a 12-step context. *Alcoholism Treatment Quarterly, 27*(2), 184–198.

Streri, A. (2005). Touching for knowing in infancy: The development of manual abilities in very young infants. *European Journal of Developmental Psychology, 2*, 325–343.

Strier, R. (2013). Responding to the global economic crisis: Inclusive social work practice. *Social Work, 58*(4), 344–353.

Stroebe, M., Stroebe, W., & Hansson, R. (1993). *Handbook on bereavement: Theory, research and intervention*. New York, NY: Cambridge University Press.

Substance Abuse and Mental Health Services Administration. (2013). *Results from the 2012 National Survey on Drug Use and Health: Summary of national findings*. NSDUH Series H-46, HHS Publication No. (SMA) 13-4795. Rockville, MD: Substance Abuse and Mental Health Services.

Sullivan, M. C., Msall, M. E., & Miller, R. J. (2012). 17-year outcome of preterm infants with diverse neonatal morbidities: Part I. Impact on physical, neurological, and psychological health. *Journal for Specialists in Pediatric Nursing, 17*(3), 226–241.

Sum, A., Khatiwada, I., & McHugh, W. (2014). Deteriorating labor market fortunes for young adults. *Challenge, 57*(3), 60–83.

Super, J. T., & Jacobson, L. (2011). Religious abuse: Implications for counseling lesbian, gay, bisexual, and transgender individuals. *Journal of LGBT Issues in Counseling, 5*, 180–196.

Sustin, A., Costa, P., Wethington, E., & Eaton, W. (2010). Turning points and lessons learned: Stressful life events and personality trait development across middle adulthood. *Psychology and Aging, 25*(3), 524–533.

Sutphin, S. (2010). Social exchange theory and the division of household labor in same-sex couples. *Marriage & Family Review, 46*(3), 191–206.

Sweet, S., & Meiksins, P. (2013). *Changing contours of work: Jobs and opportunities in the new economy* (2nd ed.). Los Angeles, CA: Sage.

Świątczak, B. (2012). Immune system, immune self: Introduction. *Avant: Journal of Philosophical-Interdisciplinary Vanguard, 3*(1), 12–18.

Swidler, A. (1986). Culture in action: Symbols and strategies. *American Sociological Review, 51*, 273–286.

Swift, D. C. (1998). *Religion and the American experience*. Armonk, NY: M.E. Sharpe.

Swinton, J. (2012). From inclusion to belonging: A practical theology of community, disability, and humanness. *Journal of Religion, Disability & Health, 16*(2), 172–190.

Sword, W., Watt, S., & Krueger, P. (2006). Postpartum health, service needs, and access to care experiences of immigrant and Canadian-born women. *Journal of Obstetric Gynecological and Neonatal Nurses, 35*(6), 717–727.

Szydlik, M. (2012). Generations: Connections across the life course. *Advances in Life Course Research, 17*, 100–111.

Taddio, A., Shah, V., Gilbert-Macleod, C., & Katz, J. (2002). Conditioning and hyperalgesia in newborns exposed to repeated heel lances. *Journal of the American Medical Association, 288*(7), 857–861.

Takahashi, K. (1990). Are the key assumptions of the "strange situation" procedure universal? A view from Japanese research. *Human Development, 33*, 23–30.

Tam, E., Rosenbluth, G., Rogers, E., Ferriero, D., Glidden, D., Goldstein, R., . . . Barkovich, A. (2011). Cerebellar hemorrhage on magnetic resonance imaging in preterm newborns associated with abnormal neurologic outcome. *The Journal of Pediatrics, 158*(2), 245–250.

Tamaru, S., Kikuchi, A., Takagi, K., Wakamatsu, M., Ono, K., Horikoshi, T., . . . Nakamura, T. (2011). Neurodevelopmental outcomes of very low birth weight and extremely low birth weight infants at 18 months corrected age associated with prenatal factors. *Early Human Development, 87*(1), 55–59.

Tan, P.P. (2006). Spirituality and religious beliefs among South-East Asians. *Reflections: Narratives of Professional Helping, 12*(3), 44–47.

Tang, C., Yeung, D., & Lee, A. (2003). Psychosocial correlates of emotional responses to menarche among Chinese adolescent girls. *Journal of Adolescent Health, 33*, 193–201.

Tangenberg, K. M. (2008). Saddleback Church and the P.E.A.C.E. plan: Implications for social work. *Social Work & Christianity, 35*(4), 391–412.

Tangenberg, K. M., & Kemp, S. (2002). Embodied practice: Claiming the body's experience, agency, and knowledge for social work. *Social Work, 47*(1), 9–18.

Tanielian, T., & Jaycox, L. (Eds.). (2008). *Invisible wounds of war: Psychological and cognitive injuries, their consequences, and services to assist recovery*. Santa Monica, CA: RAND Corporation.

Tanner, J. (2002). Do laws requiring higher wages cause unemployment? *CQ Researcher, 12*(33), 769–786.

Tarrow, S. (1994). *Power in movement: Social movements, collective action, and politics*. New York, NY: Cambridge University Press.

Tarrow, S. (1998). *Power in movement: Social movements and contentious politics* (2nd ed.). New York, NY: Cambridge University Press.

Tarrow, S. (2006). *The new transnational activism*. New York, NY: Cambridge University Press.

Tate, A., Dezateux, C., Cole, T., & The Millennium Cohort Study Child Health Group. (2006). Is infant growth changing? *International Journal of Obesity, 30*, 1094–1096.

Tatum, B. D. (2003). *"Why are all the black kids sitting together in the cafeteria?" And other conversations about race*. New York, NY: Basic Books.

Tatum, B. D. (2007). *Can we talk about race? And other conversations in an era of school resegregation*. Boston, MA: Beacon Press.

Tausch, C., Marks, L. D., Brown, J. S., Cherry, K. E., Frias, T., McWilliams, Z., . . . Sasser, D. D. (2011). Religion and coping with trauma: Qualitative examples from Hurricanes Katrina and Rita. *Journal of Religion, Spirituality & Aging, 23*(3), 236–253.

Taylor, A., & Kuo, F. (2009). Children with attention deficits concentrate better after walk in the park. *Journal of Epidemiology and Community, 56*, 913–918.

Taylor, F.W. (1911). *Principles of scientific management*. New York, NY: Harper & Row.

Taylor, J. M., Gilligan, C., & Sullivan, A. M. (1995). *Between voice and silence: Women and girls, race and relationship*. Cambridge, MA: Harvard University Press.

Taylor, P., & Cohn, D. (2012). *A milestone en route to a majority minority nation*. Pew Research Center. Retrieved from http://www.pewsocialtrends.org/2012/11/07/a-milestone-en-route-to-a-majority-minority-nation

Taylor, P., Fry, R., Cohn, D., Wang, W., Velasco, G., & Docterman, D. (2011). *Living together: The economics of cohabitation*. Pew Social & Demographic Trends. Retrieved from www.pewsocialtrends.org/files/2-11/06/pew-social-trends-cohabi tation-06-2011.pdf

Taylor, R. B. (1988). *Human territorial functioning: An empirical, evolutionary perspective on individual and small group territorial cognitions, behaviors, and consequences*. Cambridge, UK: Cambridge University Press.

Taylor, R. J., Chatters, L. M., & Levin, J. (2004). *Religion in the lives of African-Americans: Social, psychological, and health perspectives*. Thousand Oaks, CA: Sage.

Taylor, S. E., & Stanton, A. L. (2007). Coping resources, coping processes, and mental health. *Annual Review of Clinical Psychology, 3*, 377–401.

Teeple, G. (2000). *Globalization and the decline of social reform: Into the twenty-first century*. Aurora, ON, Canada: Garamond Press.

Terkel, S. (2003). *Hope dies last: Keeping the faith in difficult times*. New York, NY: The New Press.

Thapar, A., Collishaw, S., Pine, D., & Thapar, A. (2012). Depression in adolescence. *The Lancet, 379*, 1056–1067.

Thomas, A., Chess, S., & Birch, H. G. (1968). *Temperament and behavior disorders in children*. New York, NY: New York University Press.

Thomas, A., Chess, S., & Birch, H. G. (1970). The origin of personality. *Scientific American, 223*, 102–109.

Thomas, M. L. (2009). Faith collaboration: A qualitative analysis of faith-based social service programs in organizational relationships. *Administration in Social Work, 33*(1), 40–60.

Thomas, W. I., & Thomas, D. S. (1928). *The child in America: Behavior problems and programs*. New York, NY: Knopf.

Thompson Coon, J., Boddy, K., Stein, K., Whear, R., Barton, J., & Depledge, M. (2011). Does participating in physical activity in outdoor natural environments have a greater effect on physical and mental wellbeing than physical activity indoors? A systematic review. *Environmental Science & Technology, 45*, 1761–1772.

Thomson, R. G. (Ed.). (1996). *Freakery: Cultural spectacles of the extraordinary body*. New York, NY: New York University Press.

Thyer, B. A. (2005). The misfortunes of behavioral social work: Misprized, misread, and misconstrued. In S. A. Kirk (Ed.), *Mental disorders in the social environment: Critical perspectives* (pp. 330–343). New York, NY: Columbia University Press.

Tilly, C., & Wood, L. (2013). *Social movements 1768–2012*. Boulder, CO: Paradigm.

Tilton, J. (2009). Youth uprising: Gritty youth leadership development and communal transformation. In L. Nybell, J. Shook, & J. Finn (Eds.), *Childhood, youth, & social work in transformation: Implications for policy & practice* (pp. 385–400). New York, NY: Columbia University Press.

Tindall, D. (2004). Social movement participation over time: An ego-network approach to micro-mobilization. *Sociological Focus, 37*, 163–184.

Titone, A. M. (1991). Spirituality and psychotherapy in social work practice. *Spirituality and Social Work Communicator, 2*(1), 7–9.

Tobin, S. (1988). Preservation of the self in old age. *Social Casework: The Journal of Contemporary Social Work, 66* (9), 550–555.

Tomai, M., Veronica, R., Mebane, M., D'Acunti, A., Benedetti, M., & Francescato, D. (2010). Virtual communities in schools as tools to promote social capital with high school students. *Computers & Education, 54*, 265–274.

Tomoda, A., Polcari, A., Anderson, C. M., & Teicher, M. H. (2012). Reduced visual cortex gray matter volume and thickness in young adults who witnessed domestic violence during childhood. *PLoS One, 7*(12), 1–11. doi:10.1371/journal.pone.0052528

Tonnies, F. (1963). *Community and society* (C. P. Loomis, Ed.). New York, NY: Harper & Row. (Original work published 1887)

Toosi, N., Sommers, S., & Ambady, N. (2012). Getting a word in group-wise: Effects of racial diversity on gender dynamics. *Journal of Experimental Social Psychology, 48*, 1150–1155.

Torian, L., Chen, M., & Hall, H. (2011). HIV Surveillance—United States—1981–2008. *Morbidity and Mortality Weekly Report, 60*(21), 689–693. Retrieved from www.cdc.gov/mmwr/preview/mmwrhtml/mm6021a2.htm

Tornstam, L. (2005). *Gerotranscendence: A developmental theory of positive aging*. New York, NY: Springer.

Torres, L., Peña, J., Westhoff, W., & Zayas, L. (2008). A cross-national comparison of adolescent alcohol and drug use behaviors: U.S. Hispanics and youth in the Dominican Republic. *Journal of Drug Issues, 38*(1), 149–170.

Torrez, E. (1984). *The folk-healer: The Mexican-American tradition of curanderismo*. Kingsville, TX: Nieves Press.

Toseland, R. W., & Larkin, H. (2010). Developing and leading telephone groups. *Social Work with Groups, 34*(1), 21–34.

Toseland, R. W., & Rivas, R. F. (2012). *An introduction to group work practice* (7th ed.). Boston, MA: Allyn & Bacon.

Townley, G., & Kloos, B. (2011). Examining the psychological sense of community for individuals with serious mental illness residing in supported housing environments. *Community Mental Health Journal, 47*, 436–446.

Townley, G., Kloos, B., Green, E., & Franco, M. (2011). Reconcilable differences? Human diversity, cultural relativity, and sense of community. *American Journal of Community Psychology, 47*, 69–85.

Tracy, E., & Martin, T. (2007). Children's roles in the social networks of women in substance abuse treatment. *Journal of Substance Abuse Treatment, 32*, 81–88.

Trattner, W. (1998). *From poor law to welfare state: A history of social welfare in America* (6th ed.). New York, NY: Free Press.

Treyvaud, K., Doyle, L. W., Lee, K. J., Roberts, G., Cheong, J. L. Y., Inder, T. E., & Anderson, P. J. (2011). Family functioning, burden, and parenting stress 2 years after very preterm birth. *Early Human Development, 87*(60), 427–431.

Tripses, J., & Scroggs, L. (2009). Spirituality and respect: Study of a model school–church–community collaboration. *School Community Journal, 19*(1), 77–97.

Troiden, R. (1989). The formation of homosexual identities. *Journal of Homosexuality, 17*, 43–73.

Tucker, M. (2011). *Standing on the shoulders of giants: An American agenda for education reform*. Washington, DC: National Center on Education and the Economy.

Tun, P., & Lachman, M. (2010). The association between computer use and cognition across adulthood: Use it so you won't lose it? *Psychology and Aging, 25*(3), 560–568.

Turiel, E. (2004). Commentary: Beyond individualism and collectivism: A problem or progress? *New Directions in Child and Adolescent Development, 104*, 91–100.

Turkle, S. (2011). *Alone together: Why we expect more from technology and less from each other*. New York, NY: Basic Books.

Turner, H., Finkelhor, D., & Ormrod, R. (2006). The effect of lifetime victimization on the mental health of children and adolescents. *Social Science & Medicine, 62*(1), 13–27.

Turner, R. P., Lukoff, D., Barnhouse, R. T., & Lu, F. G. (1995). Religious or spiritual problem: A culturally sensitive diagnostic category in the DSM–IV. *Journal of Nervous and Mental Disease, 183*, 435–444.

Tweddle, A. (2007). Youth leaving care: How do they fare? *New Directions for Youth Development, 113*, 15–31.

Tweed, T. T. (1997). Asian religions in the United States. In W. H. Conser, Jr., & S. B. Twiss (Eds.), *Religious diversity and American religious history: Studies in traditions and cultures* (pp. 189–217). Athens, GA: University of Georgia Press.

Uchino, B. N. (2009). Understanding the links between social support and physical health: A life-span perspective with emphasis on the separability of perceived and received support. *Perspectives on Psychological Science, 4*(3), 236–255.

Uddin, L., Iacoboni, M., Lange, C., & Keenan, J. (2007). The self and social cognition: The role of cortical midline structures and mirror neurons. *Trends in Cognitive Sciences, 11*(4), 153–157.

Uhlenberg, P. (1996). Mutual attraction: Demography and life-course analysis. *The Gerontologist, 36*(2), 226–229.

Ulrich, R. (1984). View through a window may influence recovery from surgery. *Science, 224*, 420–421.

Ulrich, R. (2006). Evidence-based health-care architecture. *The Lancet, 368*, 538–539.

Ulrich, R., Simons, R., Losito, B., Fiorito, E., Miles, M., & Zelson, M. (1991). Stress recovery during exposure to natural and urban environments. *Journal of Environmental Psychology, 11*, 201–230.

UNAIDS. (2013). *Global report: UNAIDS reports on the global AIDS epidemic 2013*. Retrieved from www.unaids.org/en/resources/campaigns/globalreport2013/global report

UNESCO. (2012). *EFA global monitoring report 2012: Youth and skills: Putting education to work*. Paris: Author.

UNICEF. (2006). *Behind closed doors: The impact of domestic violence on children*. New York, NY: Author.

UNICEF. (2012a). *Measuring child poverty*. Florence, Italy: UNICEF Innocenti Research Center. Retrieved from www.unicef-irc.org/publications/pdf/rc10_eng.pdf

UNICEF. (2012b). *Report Card 10. Measuring child poverty: New league tables of child poverty in the world's rich countries*. Florence, Italy: UNICEF Innocenti Research Centre.

UNICEF. (2013a). *End child trafficking*. Retrieved from http://www.unicefusa.org/work/protection/child-trafficking/?gclid=CK2yt_-CorsQlafgodqlARw

UNICEF. (2013b). *Levels & trends in child mortality*. New York, NY: Author.

UNICEF. (2013c). *MDG related facts and figures*. Retrieved from http://www.unicef.org/media/media_45485.html

UNICEF. (2013d). *Child info: Monitoring the situation of children and women. Malnutrition*. Retrieved from http://www.childinfo.org/malnutriton_status.html

United Nations. (1948). *The universal declaration of human rights*. Retrieved from http://www.un.org/en/documents/udhr

United Nations. (2011). *Children and armed conflict*. Retrieved from http://childrenandarmedconflict.un.org/publications/StrategicFramework2011–2013.pdf

United Nations Development Programme. (2013). *Human development report 2013*. New York, NY: Author.

United Nations Educational, Scientific, and Cultural Organization, Institute for Statistics. (2012). *Opportunities lost: The impact of grade repetition and early school leaving*. Retrieved from http://www.uis.unesco.org/Education/GED%20Documents%20C/GED-2012-Complete-Web3.pdf

United Nations Enable. (2013). *Convention on the Rights of Persons with Disabilities*. Retrieved from http://www.un.org/disabilities/default.asp?id=150

United States v. Windsor. No. 12-307. June 26, 2013.

Urban Child Institute. (2013). *Baby's brain begins now: Conception to age 3*. Retrieved from http://www.urbanchildinstitute.org/why-0-3/baby-and-brain

Ursache, A., Blair, C., Stifter, C., & Voegtline, K. (2013). Emotional reactivity and regulation in infancy interact to predict executive functioning in early childhood. *Developmental Psychology, 49*(1), 127–137.

U.S. Bureau of Labor Statistics. (2013a). *Persons with a disability: Labor force characteristics summary*. Retrieved from http://www.bls.gov/news.release/disabl.nr0.htm

U.S. Bureau of Labor Statistics. (2013b). *Women in the labor force: A databook*. Retrieved from www.bls.gov/cps/wlf-databook-2012.pdf

U.S. Bureau of Labor Statistics. (2013c). *News release: Union members 2012*. Retrieved from www.bls.gov/news.release/pdf/union2.pdf

U.S. Bureau of Labor Statistics. (2013d). *Employment characteristics of families summary*. Retrieved from http://www.bls.gov/news.release/famee.nr0.htm

U.S. Census Bureau. (2010). *The next four decades: The older population in the United States: 2010 to 2050: Population estimates and projections*. Washington, DC: U.S. Department of Commerce, Economics and Statistics Administration, U.S. Census Bureau.

U.S. Census Bureau. (2012a). *Statistical abstract of the United States, 2012*. Retrieved from https:www.census.gov/compendia/stattab/2012edition.html

U.S. Census Bureau. (2012b). *2010 Census Special Reports, Centenarians: 2010*, C2010SR-03. Washington, DC: U.S. Government Printing Office. Retrieved from http://www.census.gov/prod/cen2010/reports/c2010sr- 03.pdf

U.S. Census Bureau. (2013a). *Asians fastest-growing race or ethnic group in 2012*. Retrieved from www.census.gov/newsroom/releases/archieves/population/cb13-112.html

U.S. Census Bureau. (2013b). *American Community Survey*. Retrieved from http://www.census.gov

U.S. Census Bureau. (2013c). *America's foreign born in the last 50 years*. Retrieved from http://www.census.gov/how/infographics/foreign_born.html

U.S. Census Bureau. (2013d). *American Community Survey Reports: The foreign-born population in the United States: 2010*. Washington, DC: Government Printing Office.

U.S. Census Bureau. (2013e). *Current population survey (CPS)—Definitions*. Retrieved from www.census.gov/cps/about/cpsdef.html

U.S. Census Bureau. (2013f). *Current population survey, annual social and economic supplements*. Retrieved from http://www.census.gov/prod/techdoc/cps/cpsmart13.pdf

U.S. Census Bureau. (2013g). *Annual estimates of the resident population by single year of age and sex for the United States: April 1, 2010 to July 1, 2012*. Retrieved from http://factfinder2.census.gov/faces/tableservices/jsf/pages/productview.xhtml?src=bkmk

U.S. Census Bureau. (2013h). *International data base*. Retrieved from http://www.census.gov/population/international/data/idb/informationGateway.php

U.S. Census Bureau. (2014). *International data base: World population by age and sex for 2013*. Retrieved from https://www.census.gov/population/international/data/idb/worldpopu.php

U.S. Children's Bureau. (2012). *Child maltreatment 2011*. Retrieved from https://www.acf.hhs.gov/sites/defaults/files/cb/cm11.pdf

U.S. Children's Bureau. (2013). How many children are in foster care in in the U.S.? In my state? In *Frequently asked questions*. Retrieved from http://www.acf.hhs.gov/programs/cb/faq/foster-care4

U.S. Commission on Human Rights. (1998). Indian tribes: A continuing quest for survival. In P.S. Rothenberg (Ed.), *Race, class and gender in the United States: An integrated study* (4th ed., pp. 378–382). New York, NY: St. Martin's Press.

U.S. Department of Agriculture and U.S. Department of Human Services. (2010). *Dietary guidelines for Americans 2010* (7th ed.). Washington, DC: U.S. Government Printing Office. Retrieved from http://www.health.gov/dietaryguidelines/dga/2010/DietaryGuidelines.2010/pdf

U.S. Department of Education. (2010). *Blueprint for reform of the Elementary and Secondary Education Act.* Retrieved from http://www2.ed.gov/policy/elsec/leg/blueprint/index.html

U.S. Department of Education. (2013). *Race to the top fund: Executive summary.* Retrieved from http://www2.ed.gov/programs/racetothetop/executive-summary.pdf

U.S. Department of Education Office for Civil Rights. (2013). *2006 civil rights data collection: Projects values for the nation.* Retrieved from http://ocrdata.ed.gov/downloads/projections/2006/2006-nation-projection.xls

U.S. Department of Health and Human Services. (2013). *Key features of the Affordable Care Act by year.* Retrieved from http://www.hhs.gov/healthcare/facts/timeline/timeline-text.html

U.S. Department of Health and Human Services. Administration on Children, Youth, and Families. (2012). *Child maltreatment 2011.* Retrieved from http://www.acf.hhs.gov/programs/cb/resource/child-maltreatment-2011

U.S. Department of Health and Human Services. Maternal and Child Health Bureau. (2011). *Child Health USA, 2011.* Rockville, MD: U.S. Department of Health and Human Services.

U.S. Department of Health and Human Services. Office of Adolescent Health. (2013). *State facts.* Retrieved from http://www.hhs.gov/ash/oah/resources-and-publications/facts

U.S. Department of Housing and Urban Development. (2011, December 5). Homeless Emergency Assistance and Rapid Transition to Housing Program; Defining "homeless." *Federal Register: The Daily Journal of the United States Government,* p. 75994. FR DOC # 2011-30942.

U.S. Department of Labor. (2014). *Federal minimum wage.* Retrieved from http://www.dol.gov/elaws/esa/flsa/minwage.htm

U.S. Department of Labor, Wage and Hour Division. (2015). *Minimum wage laws in the states – January 1, 2015.* Retrieved from http://www.dol.gov/whd/minwage/america.htm

U.S. Government Accountability Office. (2012). *Unemployed older workers: Many experience challenges regaining employment and face reduced retirement security.* Washington, DC: Author. Retrieved from www.gao.gov/assets/600/590408.pdf

Uskul, A. (2004). Women's menarche stories from a multicultural sample. *Social Science & Medicine, 59,* 667–679.

Vaillant, G. (1977). *Adaptation to life.* Boston, MA: Little, Brown.

Vaillant, G. (1993). *The wisdom of the ego.* Cambridge, MA: Harvard University Press.

Vaillant, G. (2002). *Aging well: Surprising guideposts to a happier life from the Landmark Harvard Study of Adult Development.* Boston, MA: Little, Brown.

Vaillant, G. (2012). *Triumphs of experience: The men of the Harvard Grant Study.* Cambridge, MA: Belknap Press.

Valsiner, J. (2000). *Culture and human development.* Thousand Oaks, CA: Sage.

van de Beek, C., Thijssen, J. H., Cohen-Kettenis, P.T., van Goozen, S. H., & Buitelaar, J. K. (2004). Relationships between sex hormones assessed in amniotic fluid, and maternal and umbilical cord serum: What is the best source of information to investigate the effects of fetal hormonal exposure? *Hormones and Behavior, 46*(5), 663–669.

VanDeMark, N., Russelol, L., O'Keefe, M., Finkelstein, N., Noether, C., & Gambell, J. (2005). Children of mothers with histories of substance abuse, mental illness, and trauma. *Journal of Community Psychology, 33,* 445–459.

van de Werfhorst, H., & Salverda, W. (2012). Consequences of economic inequality: Introduction to a special issue. *Research in Social Stratification and Mobility, 30,* 377–387.

Van Goethem, A., van Hoof, A., van Aken, M., Raajmakers, Q., Boom, J., & de Castro, B. (2012). The role of adolescents' morality and identity in volunteering: Age and gender differences in a process model. *Journal of Adolescence, 35,* 509–520.

VanLaningham, J., Johnson, D., & Amato, P. (2001). Marital happiness, marital duration, and the U-shaped curve: Evidence from a five-wave panel study. *Social Forces, 78*(4), 1313–1341.

Van Wagenen, A., Driskell, J., & Bradford, J. (2013). "I'm still raring to go": Successful aging among lesbian, gay, bisexual, and transgender older adults. *Journal of Aging Studies, 27,* 1–14.

Vazsonyi, S., & Snider, J. B. (2008). Mentoring, competencies, and adjustment in adolescents: American part-time employment and European apprenticeships. *International Journal of Behavioral Development, 32*(1), 46–55.

Vennemann, M., Hense, H., Bajanowski, T., Blair, P., Complojer, C., Moone, R., & kiechl-Kohlendorfer, U. (2012). Bed sharing and the risk of sudden infant death syndrome: Can we resolve the debate? *The Journal of Pediatrics, 160*(1), 44–50.

Vera, E. M., Vacek, K., Coyle, L. D., Stinson, J., Mull, M., Doud, K., . . . Langrehr, K. J. (2011). An examination of culturally relevant stressors, coping, ethnic identity, and subjective well-being in urban, ethnic minority adolescents. *Professional School Counseling, 15*(2), 55–66.

Verhoof, E., Maurice-Stam, H., Heymans, H., & Grootenhuis, M. (2012). Growing into disability benefits? Psychosocial course of life of young adults with a chronic somatic disease or disability. *ACTA Paediatrica, 101,* 19–26.

Verity, F., & King, S. (2007). Responding to intercommunal conflict—What can restorative justice offer? *Community Development Journal, 43*(4), 470–482.

Vespa, J. (2012). Union formation in later life: Economic determinants of cohabitation and remarriage among older adults. *Demography, 49,* 1103–1125.

Vespa, J., Lewis, J., & Kreider, R. (2013). *America's families and living arrangements: 2012.* U.S. Census Bureau. Retrieved from https://www.census.gov/prod/2013pubs/p20-570.pdf

Vetere, A. (2005). Structural family therapy. In T. Chibucos & R. Leite (Eds.), *Readings in family theory* (pp. 293–302). Thousand Oaks, CA: Sage.

Vickrey, B. G., Strickland, T. L., Fitten, L. J., Admas, G. R., Ortiz, F., & Hays, R. D. (2007). Ethnic variations in dementia caregiving experiences: Insights from focus groups. *Journal of Human Behavior in the Social Environment, 15*(2–3), 233–249.

Vikat, A., Speder, Z., Beets, G., Billari, F., & Buhler, C. (2007). Generations and Gender Survey (GGS): Towards a better understanding of relationships and processes in the life course. *Demographic Research Online, 17,* 389–440.

Villarruel, F., Perkins, D., Borden, L., & Keith, J. (2003). *Community youth development: Programs, policies, and practice.* Thousand Oaks, CA: Sage.

Vohra-Gupta, S., Russell, A., & Lo, E. (2007). Meditation: The adoption of Eastern thought to Western social practices. *Social Thought, 26*(2), 49–61.

Volker, D. L. (2005). Control and end-of-life care: Does ethnicity matter? *American Journal of Hospice & Palliative Care, 22*(6), 442–446.

Volling, B., Blandon, A., & Kolak, A. (2006). Marriage, parenting, and the emergence of early self-regulation in the family system. *Journal of Child and Family Studies, 15*(4), 493–506.

von Salisch, M., Haenel, M., & Freund, P. (2013). Emotion understanding and cognitive abilities in young children. *Learning & Individual Differences, 26*, 15–19.

Voorpostel, M., & van der Lippe, T. (2007). Support between siblings and between friends: Two worlds apart? *Journal of Marriage and Family, 69*, 1271–1282.

Voronin, Y., & Phogat, S. (2010). HIV/AIDS: Vaccines and alternate strategies for treatment and prevention. *Annals of the New York Academy of Sciences, 1205*(Suppl. 1), E1–E9.

Vosler, N. R. (1996). *New approaches to family practice: Confronting economic stress.* Thousand Oaks, CA: Sage.

Voss, K. (1996). The collapse of a social movement: The interplay of mobilizing structures, framing, and political opportunities in the Knights of Labor. In D. McAdams, J. McCarthy, & M. Zald (Eds.), *Comparative perspectives on social movements* (pp. 227–258). New York, NY: Cambridge University Press.

Voss, R. W., Douville, V., Little Soldier, A., & Twiss, G. (1999). Tribal and shamanic-based social work practice: A Lakota perspective. *Social Work, 44*(3), 228–241.

Vranic, A. (2003). Personal space in physically abused children. *Environment and Behavior, 35*(4), 550–565.

Vygotsky, L. S., Hanfmann, E., Vakar, G., & Kozulin, A. (2012). *Thought and language*. Cambridge, MA: MIT Press.

Waanders, C., Mendez, J., & Downer, J. (2007). Parent characteristics, economic stress and neighborhood context as predictors of parent involvement in preschool children's education. *Journal of School Psychology, 45*(6), 619–636.

Wacker, R., & Roberto, K. (2014). *Community resources for older adults: Programs and services in an era of change* (4th ed.). Thousand Oaks, CA: Sage.

Wadensten, B. (2005). Introducing older people to the theory of gerotranscendence. *Journal of Advanced Nursing, 52*(4), 381–388.

Wadsworth, M., & Santiago, C. (2008). Risk and resiliency processes in ethnically diverse families in poverty. *Journal of Family Psychology, 22*(3), 399–410.

Wadsworth, S., & Southwell, K. (2011). Military families: Extreme work and extreme "work-family." *The Annals of the American Academy of Political and Social Science, 638*, 163–183.

Wagmiller, R. L., & Adelman, R. M. (2009). *Childhood and intergenerational poverty: The long-term consequences of growing up poor.* New York, NY: Columbia University National Center on Children in Poverty.

Walch, J., Day, R., & Kang, J. (2005). The effect of sunlight on postoperative analgesic medication use: A prospective study of patients undergoing spinal surgery. *Psychosomatic Medicine, 67*, 156–163.

Walker, D., & Worrell, R. (2008). Promoting healthy pregnancies through perinatal groups: A comparison of Centering Pregnancy group prenatal care and childbirth education classes. *Journal of Perinatal Education, 17*(1), 27–34.

Walker, D. F., Reid, H. W., O'Neill, T., & Brown, L. (2009). Changes in personal religion/spirituality during and after childhood abuse: A review and synthesis. *Psychological Trauma: Theory, Research, Practice, and Policy, 1*(2), 130–145.

Walker, J., & Melvin, J. (2010). Emotional disorders in children and adolescents. In J. H. Stone & M. Blouin (Eds.), *International Encyclopedia of Rehabilitation.* Retrieved from http://cirrie.buffalo.edu/encyclopedia/en/article/7

Walker, L. (1989). A longitudinal study of moral reasoning. *Child Development, 5*, 33–78.

Waller, T. (2009). Modern childhood: Contemporary theories and children's lives. In T. Waller (Ed.), *An introduction to early childhood* (2nd ed., pp. 2–15). Thousand Oaks, CA: Sage.

Wallerstein, I. (1974). *The modern world system: Capitalist agriculture and the origins of the European world economy in the 16th century.* New York, NY: Academic Press.

Wallerstein, I. (1979). *The capitalist world economy.* London, UK: Cambridge University Press.

Wallerstein, I. (1980). *The modern world-system: Mercantilism and the consolidation of the European world economy, 1600–1750.* New York, NY: Academic Press.

Wallerstein, I. (1989). *The modern world-system: The second great expansion of the capitalist world-economy, 1730–1840's.* San Diego, CA: Academic Press.

Wallerstein, I. (2004). *World systems analysis: An introduction.* Durham, NC: Duke University Press.

Wallerstein, J. S., & Blakeslee, S. (1989). *Second chances: Men, women and children a decade after divorce.* New York, NY: Ticknor & Fields.

Wallerstein, J., & Blakeslee, S. (1990). *Second chances.* New York, NY: Ticknor & Fields.

Wallerstein, J. S., & Corbin, S. (1991). The child and the vicissitudes of divorce. In M. Lewis (Ed.), *Child and adolescent psychiatry: A comprehensive textbook* (pp. 1108–1118). Baltimore, MD: Williams & Wilkins.

Wallien, M. S., & Cohen-Kettenis, P. T. (2008). Psychosocial outcome of gender dysphoric children. *Journal of the American Academy of Child and Adolescent Psychiatry, 47*(12), 1413–1423.

Walsh, F. (2009a). Integrating spirituality in family therapy: Wellsprings for health, healing, and resilience. In F. Walsh (Ed.), *Spiritual resources in family therapy* (2nd ed., pp. 31–61). New York, NY: Guilford Press.

Walsh, F. (2009b). Spiritual resources in family adaptation to death and loss. In F. Walsh (Ed.), *Spiritual resources in family therapy* (2nd ed., pp. 81–102). New York, NY: Guilford Press.

Walsh, F. (2011). Families in later life: Challenges, opportunities, and resilience. In M. McGoldrick, B. Carter, & N. Garcia-Preto (Eds.), *The expanded family life cycle: Individual, family, and social perspectives* (4th ed., pp. 261–277). Boston, MA: Allyn & Bacon.

Walsh, F. (2012a). *Normal family processes* (4th ed.). New York, NY: Guilford.

Walsh, F. (2012b). The new normal: Diversity and complexity in 21st-century families. In F. Walsh (Ed.), *Normal family processes: Growing diversity and complexity* (4th ed., pp. 3–27). New York, NY: Guilford.

Walsh, F. (2012c). Family resilience: Strengths forged through adversity. In F. Walsh (Ed.), *Normal family processes: Growing diversity and complexity* (4th ed., pp. 399–427). New York, NY: Guilford Press.

Walsh, F. (2016). *Strengthening family resilience* (3rd ed.). New York, NY: Guilford Press.

Walsh, J. (2000). *Clinical case management with persons having mental illness: A relationship-based perspective.* Pacific Gove, CA: Brooks/Cole.

Walsh, J. (2014). *Theories for direct social work practice* (3rd ed.). Belmont, CA: Wadsworth.

Walsh, J., Meyer, A., & Schoonhoven, C. (2006). A future for organization theory: Living in and living with changing organizations. *Organization Science, 17*(5), 657–671.

Walsh, K. (2012). *Grief and loss: Theories and skills for the helping professions* (2nd ed.). New York, NY: Pearson.

Wamsley, G., & Zald, M. (1973). *The political economy of public organizations.* Lexington, MA: Heath.

Wang, R., Needham, L., & Barr, D. (2005). Effects of environmental agents on attainment of puberty: Considerations when assessing exposure to environmental chemicals in the National Children's Study. *Environmental Health Perspectives, 113*(8), 1100–1107.

Wang, Y., & Zhang, Q. (2006). Are American children and adolescents of low socioeconomic status at increased risk of obesity? Changes in the association between overweight and family income between 1971 and 2002. *American Journal of Clinical Nutrition, 84*(4), 707–716.

Wanyeki, I., Olson, S., Brassard, P., Menzies, D., Ross, N., Behr, M., & Schwartzman, K. (2006). Dwellings, crowding, and tuberculosis in Montreal. *Social Science & Medicine, 63*(2), 501–511.

Warboys, R. (2015). Breastfeeding as birth control. *Midwives, 18*, 72–73.

Warner, D., & Brown, T. (2011). Understanding how race/ethnicity and gender define age-trajectories of disability: An intersectionality approach. *Social Science & Medicine, 72*, 1236–1248.

Warner, S. R. (1993). Work in progress: Toward a new paradigm for the sociological study of religion in the United States. *American Journal of Sociology, 98*, 1044–1093.

Warren, R. (1963). *The community in America*. Chicago, IL: Rand McNally.

Warren, R. (1978). *The community in America* (2nd ed.) Chicago, IL: Rand McNally.

Warren, R. (1987). *The community in America* (3rd ed.). Chicago, IL: Rand McNally.

Warwick, L. L. (1995). Feminist Wicca: Paths to empowerment. *Women and Therapy: A Feminist Quarterly, 16*(2–3), 121–133.

Wasserman, G. A., & McReynolds, L. S. (2011). Contributors to traumatic exposure and posttraumatic stress disorder in juvenile justice youths. *Journal of Traumatic Stress, 24*(4), 422–429. doi:10.1002/jts.20664

Waterhouse, L. (2010). Multiple intelligences, the Mozart effect, and emotional intelligence: A critical review. *Educational Psychologist, 41*(4), 207–225.

Watson, M., Mann, M., Lloyd-Puryear, M., Rinaldo, P., & Howell, R. (2006). Newborn screening: Toward a uniform screening panel and system. *Genetics in Medicine, 8*(Suppl. 5), 1s–11s.

Watters, E. (2010). *Crazy like us: The globalization of the American psyche*. New York, NY: Free Press.

Weaver, H. (2011). Cultural competence with First Nations peoples. In D. Lum (Ed.), *Culturally competent practice: A framework for understanding diverse groups and justice issues* (4th ed., pp. 223–247). Belmont, CA: Thomson.

Weaver-Hightower, M. B. (2008). *The politics of policy in boys' education: Getting boys "right."* New York, NY: Palgrave Macmillan.

Webb, N., & Dumpson, J. (2006). *Working with traumatized youth in child welfare*. New York, NY: Guilford Press.

Weber, M. (1947). *The theory of economic and social organization*. New York, NY: Free Press.

Weber, M. (1958). *The Protestant ethic and the spirit of capitalism* (T. Parsons, Trans.). New York, NY: Scribner's. (Original work published 1904–1905)

Weichold, K. (2007). Prevention against substance misuse: Life skills and positive youth development. In R. Silbereisen & R. Lerner (Ed.), *Approaches to positive youth development* (pp. 293–310). Thousand Oaks, CA: Sage.

Weigert, S. C. (2012). Aligning and inventing practices to achieve inclusive assessment policies: A decade of work toward optimal access for US students with disabilities 2001–2011. *International Journal of Disability, Development & Education, 59*(1), 21–36. doi:10.1080/1034912X.2012.654935

Weininger, E., & Lareau, A. (2009). Paradoxical pathways: An ethnographic extension of Kohn's findings on class and childrearing. *Journal of Marriage and Family, 71*, 680–695.

Weinman, M. L., Buzi, R. S., & Smith, P. B. (2005). Addressing risk behaviors, service needs, and mental health issues in programs for young fathers. *Families in Society, 86*(2), 261–266.

Weisner, T. (2005). Attachment as cultural and ecological problem with pluralistic solutions. *Human Development, 48*, 89–94.

Weiss, D., & Lang, F. (2012). The two faces of age identity. *GeroPsych, 25*(1), 5–14.

Weitz, R. (2013). *The sociology of health, illness, and health care: A critical approach* (6th ed.). Boston, MA: Wadsworth.

Wellman, B. (1979). The community question. *American Journal of Sociology, 84*, 1201–1231.

Wellman, B. (1982). Studying personal communities. In P. Marsden & N. Lin (Eds.), *Social structure and network analysis* (pp. 61–80). Beverly Hills, CA: Sage.

Wellman, B. (1996). Are personal communities local? A Dumptarian reconsideration. *Social Networks, 18*, 347–354.

Wellman, B. (1999). The network community: An introduction. In B. Wellman (Ed.), *Networks in the global village* (pp. 1–47). Boulder, CO: Westview Press.

Wellman, B. (2005). Community: From neighborhood to network. *Communications of the ACM, 48*(10), 53–55.

Wellman, B., & Potter, S. (1999). The elements of personal communities. In B. Wellman (Ed.), *Networks in the global village* (pp. 49–81). Boulder, CO: Westview Press.

Wellman, B., & Wortley, S. (1990). Different strokes from different folks: Community ties and social support. *American Journal of Sociology, 96*, 558–588.

Welwood, J. (2000). *Toward a psychology of awakening: Buddhism, psychotherapy, and the path of personal and spiritual transformation*. Boston, MA: Shambhala.

Wenger, G. C. (2009). Childlessness at the end of life: Evidence from rural Wales. *Ageing and Society, 29*(8), 1243–1259.

Werbart, A., Levin, L., Andersson, H., & Sandell, R. (2013). Everyday evidence: Outcomes of psychotherapies in Swedish public health services. *Psychotherapy, 50*(1), 119–130.

Werner, E., & Brendtro, L. (2012). Risk, resilience, and recovery. *Reclaiming Children and Youth, 21*(1), 18–23.

Werner, E. E., & Smith, R. S. (2001). *Journeys from childhood to midlife*. Ithaca, NY: Cornell University Press.

Wethington, E., Kessler, R., & Pixley, J. (2004). Turning points in adulthood. In O. Brim, C. Ryff, & R. Kessler (Eds.), *How healthy are we? A national study of well-being at midlife* (pp. 586–613). Chicago, IL: University of Chicago Press.

Wethington, E., Moen, P., Glasgow, N., & Pillemer, K. (2000). Multiple roles, social integration, and health. In K. Pillemer, P. Moen, & N. Glasgow (Eds.), *Social integration in the second half of life* (pp. 48–71). Baltimore, MD: Johns Hopkins University Press.

Whitbourne, S., Sneed, J., & Sayer, A. (2009). Psychosocial development from college through midlife: A 34-year sequential study. *Developmental Psychology, 45*(5), 1328–1340.

White, J., Klein, D., & Martin, T. (2015a). The systems framework. In J. White, D. Klein, & T. Martin (Eds.), *Family theories* (4th ed., pp. 141–174). Thousand Oaks, CA: Sage.

White, J., Klein, D., & Martin, T. (2015b). The conflict framework. In J. White, D. Klein, & T. Martin (Eds.), *Family theories* (4th ed., pp. 175–206). Thousand Oaks, CA: Sage.

White, J., Klein, D., & Martin, T. (2015c). The rational choice and social exchange framework. In *Family theories* (4th ed., pp. 39–69). Thousand Oaks, CA: Sage.

White, J., Klein, D., & Martin, T. (2015d). *Family theories: An introduction* (4th ed.). Thousand Oaks, CA: Sage.

White, J., Klein, D., & Martin, T. (2015e). The feminist framework. In *Family theories* (4th ed., pp. 207–238). Thousand Oaks, CA: Sage.

White, M., Pahl, S., Ashbullby, K., Herbert, S., & Depledge, M. (2013). Feelings of restoration from recent nature visits. *Journal of Environmental Psychology, 25*, 40–51.

White, N. R. (2003). Changing conceptions: Young people's views of partnering & parenting. *Journal of Sociology, 39*(2), 149–164.

Whiting, E., & Ward, C. (2008). Food insecurity and provisioning. In D. R. Crane & T. Heaton (Eds.),

Handbook of families & poverty (pp. 198–219). Thousand Oaks, CA: Sage.

Wicker, A. (2012). Perspectives on behavior settings: With illustrations from Allison's ethnography of a Japanese Hostess Club. *Environment and Behavior, 44*(4), 474–492.

Wigert, H., Johannson, R., Berg, M., & Hellstrom, A. L. (2006). Mothers' experiences of having their children in a neonatal intensive care unit. *Scandinavian Journal of Caring Sciences, 20*(10), 35–41.

Wight, V. (2011). Adolescents and poverty. *The Prevention Researcher, 18*(4), 3–6.

Wight, V., Chau, M., & Aratani, Y. (2011). *Who are America's poor children? The official story*. National Center for Children in Poverty. Retrieved from http://www.nccp.org/publications/pub_1001.html

Wilber, K. (1977). *The spectrum of consciousness*. Chennai, India: Quest Books.

Wilber, K. (1995). *Sex, ecology, spirituality: The spirit of evolution*. Boston, MA: Shambhala.

Wilber, K. (1996). *A brief history of everything*. Boston, MA: Shambhala.

Wilber, K. (1997a). *The eye of spirit: An integral vision for a world gone slightly mad*. Boston, MA: Shambhala.

Wilber, K. (1997b). An integral theory of consciousness. *Journal of Consciousness Studies, 4*(1), 71–93.

Wilber, K. (2000a). *Integral psychology: Consciousness, spirit, psychology, therapy*. Boston, MA: Shambhala.

Wilber, K. (2000b). *Sex, ecology, spirituality: The spirit of evolution* (2nd ed.). Boston, MA: Shambhala.

Wilber, K. (2001). *A theory of everything: An integral vision for business, politics, science, and spirituality*. Boston, MA: Shambhala.

Wilber, K. (2006). *Integral spirituality*. Boston, MA: Integral Books.

Wilkin, A. C. (2009). Masculinity dilemmas: Sexuality and intimacy talk among Christians and Goths. *Signs, 34*(2), 343–368.

Williams, C. (2006). The epistemology of cultural competence. *Families in Society: The Journal of Contemporary Social Services, 87*(2), 209–220.

Williams, D., Mohammed, S., Leavell, J., & Collins, C. (2010). Race, economic status, and health: Complexities, ongoing challenges, and research opportunities. *Annals of New York Academy of Sciences, 1186*, 69–101.

Williams, M., Teasdale, J. D., Segal, Z., & Kabat-Zinn, J. (2007). *The mindful way through depression: Freeing yourself from unhappiness*. New York, NY: Guilford Press.

Williams, R. (1977). *Marxism and literature*. Oxford, UK: Oxford University Press.

Williams, R. (1983). *Key words: A vocabulary of culture and society* (Rev. ed.). New York, NY: Oxford University Press.

Williamson, J. S., & Wyandt, C. M. (2001). New perspectives on alternative medicines. *Drug Topics, 145*(1), 57–66.

Willis, S., & Schaie, K. W. (2005). Cognitive trajectories in midlife and cognitive functioning in old age. In S. Willis & M. Martin (Eds.), *Middle adulthood: A lifespan perspective* (pp. 243–275). Thousand Oaks, CA: Sage.

Willis, S., & Schaie, K. W. (2006). Cognitive functioning in the baby boomers: Longitudinal and cohort effects. In S. Whitbourne & S. Willis (Eds.), *The baby boomers grow up: Contemporary perspectives on midlife* (pp. 205–234). Mahwah, NJ: Erlbaum.

Willis, S., Schaie, K. W., & Martin, M. (2009). Cognitive plasticity. In V. Bengtson, D. Gans, N. Putney, & M. Silverstein (Eds.), *Handbook of theories of aging* (2nd ed., pp. 295–321). New York, NY: Springer.

Wills, T. A., Yaeger, A. M., & Sandy, J. M. (2003). Buffering effect of religiosity for adolescent substance abuse. *Psychology of Addictive Behaviors, 17*(1), 24–31.

Wilmoth, J. M., & Longino, C. F. (2006). Demographic trends that will shape U.S. policy in the twenty-first century. *Research on Aging, 28*(3), 269–288.

Wilson, C., Gutiérrez, F., & Chao, L. (2013). *Racism, sexism, and the media: Multicultural issues into the new communications age* (4th ed.). Los Angeles, CA: Sage.

Wilson, E. (2007). Biophilia and the conservation ethic. In D. Penn & I. Mysterud (Eds.), *Evolutionary perspectives on environmental problems* (pp. 249–257). New Brunswick, NJ: Transaction Publishers.

Wilson, G., & Baldassare, M. (1996). Overall "sense of community" in a suburban region: The effects of localism, privacy, and urbanization. *Environment and Behavior, 28*(1), 27–43.

Wink, P., & Dillon, M. (2002). Spiritual development across the adult life course: Findings from a longitudinal study. *Journal of Adult Development, 9*(1), 79–94.

Winokuer, H. R., & Harris, D. L. (2012). *Principles and practice of grief counseling*. New York, NY: Springer.

Winston, C. A. (2006). African American grandmothers parenting AIDS orphans: Grieving and coping. *Qualitative Social Work, 5*(1), 33–43.

Wisner, K., Chambers, C., & Sit, D. (2006). Postpartum depression: A major public health problem. *Journal of American Medical Association, 296*(21), 2616–2618.

Wisniewski, C. (2008). Applying complementary and alternative medicine practices in a social work context: A focus on mindfulness meditation. *Praxis, 8*, 13–22.

Wittine, B. (1987, September/October). Beyond ego. *Yoga Journal*, pp. 51–57.

Wolak, J., Finkelhor, D., Mitchell, K., & Ybarra, M. (2008). Online "predators" and their victims: Myths, realities and implications for prevention and treatment. *American Psychologist, 63*(2), 111–128.

Wolsko, C., & Hoyt, K. (2012). Employing the restorative capacity of nature: Pathways to practicing ecotherapy among mental health professionals. *Ecopsychology, 4*(1), 10–24.

Women's Legal Defense and Education Fund. (2012). *Reading between the lines: Women's poverty in the United States, 2010*. Retrieved from http://www.legalmomentum.org/sites/default/files/reports/reading-between-the-lines.pdf

Wong, M., Lau, E., Wan, J., Cheung, S., Hui, C. H., & Mok, D. (2013). The interplay between sleep and mood in predicting academic functioning, physical health and psychological health: A longitudinal study. *Journal of Psychosomatic Research, 74*, 271–277.

Wood, J. (2006). Critical feminist theories: A provocative perspective on families. In D. Braithwaite & L. Baxter (Eds.), *Engaging theories in family communication: Multiple perspectives* (pp. 197–212). Thousand Oaks, CA: Sage.

Woodbridge, S., Buys, L., & Miller, E. (2011). "My grandchild has a disability": Impact on grandparenting identity, roles and relationships. *Journal of Aging Studies, 25*, 355–363.

Woods, R. (2013). *Children's moral lives: An ethnographic and psychological approach*. Hoboken, NJ: Wiley.

Woolever, C. (1992). A contextual approach to neighbourhood attachment. *Urban Studies, 29*(1), 99–116.

Woolf, S., & Aron, L. (Eds.). (2013). *U.S. health in international perspective: Shorter lives, poorer health*. Washington, DC: Institute of Medicine.

Worden, J. W. (2009). *Grief counseling and grief therapy: A handbook for the mental health practitioner* (4th ed.). New York, NY: Springer.

World Bank. (2013a). *GDP per capita*. Retrieved from http://data.worldbank.org/indcator/NY.GDO.PCAP.CD

World Bank. (2013b). *Developing countries to receive over $410 billion in remittances in 2013, says World Bank*. Retrieved from http://www.world

bank.org/en/news/press-release/2013/10/02/developing-countries-remittances-2013-world-bank

World Bank. (2013c). *Mortality rate, under 5 (per 1,000 live births)*. Retrieved from http://data.worldbank.org/indicator/SH.DYN.MORT

World Bank. (2013d). *World Bank launches initiative on migration, releases new projections on remittance flows*. Retrieved from http://www.worldbank.org/en/news/press-release/2013/04/19/world-bank-launches-initiative-on-migration-releases-new-projections-on-remittance-flows

World Bank. (2013e). *Mortality rate, infant (per 1,000 live births)*. Retrieved from http://data.worldbank.org/indicator/SP.DYN.IMRT.IN

World Health Organization. (2012a). *Human trafficking*. Retrieved from www.who.int/iris/bitstream/10665/77394/1/WHO_RHR_12.42_eng.pdf

World Health Organization. (2012b). *The 10 leading causes of death by income group (2011)*. Retrieved from http://www.who.int/mediacentre/factsheets/fs310/index1.html

World Health Organization. (2012c). *Summary: DALYs (thousands) by cause and by World Bank income group*. Retrieved from www.who.int/healthinfo/global_burden/disease/estimates_regional/en/index.html

World Health Organization. (2012d). *Are you ready? What you need to know about ageing*. Retrieved from www.who.int/world-health-day/2012/toolkit/background/en

World Health Organization. (2013a). *World health statistics 2013*. Geneva: Author.

World Health Organization. (2013b). *Family planning*. Retrieved from http://www.who.int/mediacentre/factsheets/fs351/en/index.htm

World Health Organization. (2013c). *Stillbirths*. Retrieved from http://www.who.int/maternal_child_adolescent/epidemiology/stillbirth/en

World Health Organization. (2013d). *Preterm birth*. Retrieved from http://www.who.int/mediacentre/factsheets/fs363/en

World Health Organization Multicentre Growth Reference Study Group. (2006a). Assessment of differences in linear growth among populations in the WHO Multicentre Growth Reference Study. *Acta Paediatrica*(Suppl.), 450, 56–65.

World Health Organization Multicentre Growth Reference Study Group. (2006b). WHO motor development study: Windows of achievement for six gross motor developmental milestones. *Acta Paediatrica*(Suppl.), 450, 86–95.

World Health Organization Multicentre Growth Reference Study Group. (2006c). Assessment of sex differences and heterogeneity in motor milestone attainment among populations in the WHO Multicentre Growth Reference Study. *Acta Paediatrica*(Suppl.), 450, 66–75.

Wortman, C., & Silver, R. (1989). The myths of coping with loss. *Journal of Consulting and Clinical Psychology, 57*, 349–357.

Wortman, C., & Silver, R. (1990). Successful mastery of bereavement and widowhood. A life course perspective. In P. Baltes & M. Baltes (Eds.), *Successful aging: Perspectives from the behavioral sciences* (pp. 225–264). Cambridge, UK: Cambridge University Press.

Wright, P. M. (2011). Barriers to a comprehensive understanding of pregnancy loss. *Journal of Loss and Trauma, 16*(1), 1–12.

Wright, V. H. (2005). *The soul tells a story: Engaging spirituality with creativity in the writing life*. Downers Grove, IL: InterVarsity Press.

Wrigley, E. (1966). Family limitation in pre-industrial England. *Economic History Review, 19*, 82–109.

Wronka, J. (2008). *Human rights and social justice: Social action and service for the helping and health professions*. Thousand Oaks, CA: Sage.

Wrosch, C., Heckhausen, J., & Lachman, M. (2006). Goal management across adulthood and old age: The adaptive value of primary and secondary control. In D. K. Mroczek & T. Little (Eds.), *Handbook of personality development* (pp. 399–421). Mahwah, NJ: Lawrence Erlbaum.

Wrzus, C., Hänel, M., Wagner, J., & Neyer, F. (2013). Social network changes and life events across the life span: A meta-analysis. *Psychological Bulletin, 139*(1), 53–80.

Wu, L., Woody, G., Yang, C., Pan, J., & Blazer, D. (2011). Racial/ethnic variations in substance-related disorders among adolescents in the United States. *Archives of General Psychiatry, 68*(11), 1176–1185.

Wuthnow, R. (2001). *Creative spirituality: The way of the artist*. Berkeley, CA: University of California Press.

Wyckoff, A. (2013). AAP: Babies born at home must receive same standard of care as in medical facility. *American Academy of Pediatrics News, 34*(5), 29.

Xu, Q., Perkins, D., & Chow, J. (2010). Sense of community, neighboring, and social capital as predictors of local political participation in China. *American Journal of Community Psychology, 45*, 259–271.

Yarhouse, M. A., & Carr, T. L. (2012). MTF transgender Christians' experiences: A qualitative study. *Journal of LGBT Issues in Counseling, 6*, 18–33.

Yellow Bird, M. J. (1995). Spirituality in First Nations story telling: A Sahnish-Hidatsa approach to narrative. *Reflections: Narratives of Professional Helping, 1*(4), 65–72.

Yeung, D., Fung, H., & Kam, C. (2012). Age difference in problem solving strategies: The mediating role of future time perspective. *Personality and Individual Differences, 53*, 38–43.

Yost, C. (2012, May 23). 3 reasons why card-carrying capitalists should support paid family leave. *Forbes*. Retrieved from http://www.forbes.com/sites/work-in-progress/2012/05/23/3-reasons-why-card-carrying-capitalists-should-support-paid-family-leave

Young, J., Bruno, D., & Pomara, N. (2014). A review of the relationship between proinflammatory cytokines and major depressive disorder. *Journal of Affective Disorders, 169*, 15–20.

Young, K. R., Marchant, M., & Wilder, L. K. (2004). School-based interventions for students with emotional and behavioral disorders. In P. Allen-Meares & M. W. Fraser (Eds.), *Intervention with children and adolescents: An interdisciplinary perspective* (pp. 175–204). Boston, MA: Allyn & Bacon.

Yousuf, R., Fauzi, A., Wai, K., Amran, M., Akter, S., & Ramli, M. (2010). Potentially reversible causes of dementia. *International Journal of Collaborative Research on Internal Medicine & Public Health, 2*(8), 258–265.

Yow, W., & Markman, E. M. (2011). Young bilingual children's heightened sensitivity to referential cues. *Journal of Cognition & Development, 12*(1), 12–31. doi:10.1080/15248372.2011.539524

Yu, J., & Hu, X. H. (2013). Inappropriate use of combined hormonal contraceptives for birth control among women of reproductive age in the United States. *Journal of Women's Health, 22*(7), 595–603.

Zand, D., Thomson, N., Cervantes, R., Espiritu, R., Klagholz, D., Lablanc, L., & Taylor, A. (2009). The mentor-youth alliance: The role of mentoring relationships in promoting youth competence. *Journal of Adolescence, 32*, 1–17.

Zangaglia, R., Pacchetti, C., Pasotti, C., Mancini, F., Servello, D., Sinforiani, E., . . . Nappi, G. (2009). Deep brain stimulation and cognitive functions in Parkinson's disease: A three-year controlled study. *Movement Disorder, 11*, 1621–1628.

Zastrow, C. H. (2009). *Social work with groups: A comprehensive workbook* (7th ed.). Belmont, CA: Brooks/Cole.

Zeidner, M., Matthews, G., & Roberts, R. D. (2012). *What we know about emotional intelligence: How it affects learning, work, relationships, and our mental health*. Cambridge, MA: MIT Press.

Zeilmaker, M. J., Hoekstra, J., von Eijkeren, J. C. H., de Jong, N., Hart, A., Kennedy, M., . . . Gunnlaugsdottir, H. (2013). Fish consumption during child bearing age: A quantitative risk-benefit analysis on neurodevelopment. *Food and Chemical Toxicology, 54*, 30–34.

Zeisel, J. (2006). *Inquiry by design: Environment/behavior/neuroscience in architecture, interiors, landscape, and planning* (Rev. ed.). New York, NY: Norton.

Zeisel, J. (2009). *I'm still here: A breakthrough approach to understanding someone living with Alzheimer's.* New York, NY: Penguin Group.

Zelazo, P. D., Chandler, M. J., & Crone, E. (2010). *Developmental social cognitive neuroscience.* New York, NY: Psychology Press.

Zhang, B., Wang, Y., Vasilakos, A., & Ma, J. (2013). Mobile social networking: Reconnect virtual community with physical space. *Telecommunication Systems, 54*, 91–110.

Zhang, Y., Jin, X., Shen, X., Zhang, J., & Hoff, E. (2008). Correlates of early language development in Chinese children. *International Journal of Behavioral Development, 32*(2), 145–151.

Zigler, E., Finn-Stevenson, M., & Hall, N. (2002). *The first three years and beyond: Brain development and social policy.* Chicago, IL: R. R. Donnelly.

Zimbardo, P. (2007). *The Lucifer effect.* New York, NY: Random House.

Zimbardo, P., & Boyd, J. (2008). *The time paradox.* New York, NY: Free Press.

Zimprich, D., & Mascherek, A. (2010). Five views of a secret: Does cognition change during middle adulthood? *European Journal of Ageing, 7*, 135–146.

Ziv, M., & Frye, D. (2003). The relation between desire and false belief in children's theory of mind: No satisfaction? *Developmental Psychology, 39*, 859–876.

Zucker, A., Ostrove, J., & Stewart, A. (2002). College-educated women's personality development in adulthood: Perceptions and age differences. *Psychology and Aging, 17*(2), 236–244.

Zunkel, G. (2002). Relational coping processes: Couples' response to a diagnosis of early stage breast cancer. *Journal of Psychosocial Oncology, 20*(4), 39–55.

Zyskinsa, J., & Heszen, I. (2009). Resources, coping with stress, positive emotions, and health. Introduction. *Polish Psychological Bulletin, 40*(1), 1–5.

INDEX

ABOUT THE CONTRIBUTORS

Suzanne Baldwin, PhD, LCSW, MSW, BSN, RN, received her PhD in social work from the School of Social Work at Virginia Commonwealth University. She owns her own clinical social work practice, primarily focusing on working with families involved in the court systems and military family issues. She spent almost 2 decades working as a clinical nurse specialist in newborn intensive care units. She has taught human behavior, practice, communications, and research courses and supervised internships at Old Dominion University and at the School of Social Work at Virginia Commonwealth University. She is the mother of three adult children. Her oldest daughter was a patient in the neonatal intensive care unit (NICU), and her daughter's son spent a month in the NICU after his birth in 2009.

Leanne Wood Charlesworth, LMSW, PhD, is associate professor and director of the undergraduate program in the Department of Social Work at Nazareth College of Rochester, New York. Her areas of service and research interest include poverty and homelessness, and she primarily teaches human behavior and research courses.

Annemarie Conlon, PhD, MBA, LCSW, is assistant professor in the School of Social Work at Virginia Commonwealth University. Her clinical experience includes individual, family, and group practice at MD Anderson Cancer Center. Her major areas of interest include ageism in health care, end-of-life needs of older adults, and hospice and palliative care. She teaches social work practice, health care policy, and qualitative research and serves as preceptor for a geriatric interprofessional education assignment with faculty from medicine, nursing, and pharmacy.

Linwood Cousins, MSW, MA, PhD, is professor in the School of Social Work at Western Michigan University. He is a social worker and an anthropologist who has practiced in child welfare and family services. His research, teaching, and practice interests include the sociocultural manifestations of race, ethnicity, and social class as well as other aspects of human diversity in the community life and schooling of African Americans and other ethnic and economic minorities.

Elizabeth P. Cramer, MSW, PhD, LCSW, ACSW, is professor in the School of Social Work at Virginia Commonwealth University. Her primary scholarship and service areas are domestic violence, lesbian and gay male issues, and group work. She teaches in the areas of foundation practice, social justice, oppressed groups, interpersonal violence, and lesbian and bisexual women.

Cory Cummings, LCSW, is a doctoral candidate in the School of Social Work at Virginia Commonwealth University. He has worked in community mental health, providing individual and group interventions, case management, and administrative services for a number of years. His research interests include health disparities, health equity, and community-engaged interventions for people affected by serious and persistent mental health problems. Cory has adjunct teaching experience with social work methods and social justice and has participated in the design, development, and delivery of numerous in-service clinical trainings.

Stephen French Gilson, MSW, PhD, is professor and coordinator of interdisciplinary disability studies at the Center for Community Inclusion and Disability Studies; professor at the School of Social Work at the University of Maine; and senior research fellow at Ono Academic College Research Institute for Health and Medical Professions, Kiryat Ono, Israel. After he completed his undergraduate degree in art, he shifted his career to social justice, pursuing a masters in social work. Realizing that knowledge of human biology and physiology was foundational to his work, he completed a PhD in medical sciences. Synthesizing the diversity and richness of this scholarly background, Dr. Gilson engages in research in disability theory, disability as diversity, design and access, social justice, health and disability policy, and the atypical body. He teaches courses in disability as diversity, policy, and human behavior from a legitimacy perspective. In collaboration and partnership with his wife, Liz DePoy, Stephen is involved in the development and production of aesthetically designed mobility equipment and solutions to foster full participation for all people in all aspects of work, recreation, and social life. Also with Liz, Stephen is the owner of an adapted rescue farm in Maine. Two other major influences on Dr. Gilson's writing, research, and work include his passion for and involvement in adaptive alpine skiing and dressage.

Marcia Harrigan, MSW, PhD, is associate professor emeritus and former associate dean of student and academic affairs in the School of Social Work at Virginia Commonwealth University. She has practiced in child welfare, juvenile justice, and mental health. Her major areas of interest are nontraditional family structures, family assessment, multigenerational households, and long-distance family caregiving. She has taught human behavior and practice courses.

Pamela J. Kovacs, MSW, PhD, is former associate professor in the School of Social Work at Virginia Commonwealth University. Her practice experience includes work with individuals, families, and groups in oncology, hospice, and mental health settings. Her major areas of interest are HIV/AIDS, hospice and palliative care, volunteerism, caregiving, and preparing social workers for health care and other settings serving older adults. She has taught clinical practice, social work practice and health care, and qualitative research, and she additionally serves as a field liaison.

Holly C. Matto (MSW, University of Michigan; PhD, University of Maryland) is associate professor in the College of Health and Human Services Department of Social Work at George Mason University in Fairfax, Virginia. She has more than 15 years of research and practice experience in the field of addiction science and has conducted treatment intervention studies with diverse clinical populations. Recently she conducted a clinical trial with Inova Fairfax Hospital and Georgetown University's Center for Functional and Molecular Imaging that used neuroimaging technology to examine functional brain change associated with behavioral health interventions for substance-dependent adults. She is currently working on the development of a mobile device to manage stimulus cues and reduce drug relapse by detecting neurophysiological reactivity and delivering a device-activated personalized music and imagery intervention (a STEAM-H: Science, Technology, Engineering, Arts & Math–Health initiative).

Susan Ainsley McCarter, MS, MSW, PhD, is associate professor in the School of Social Work at the University of North Carolina at Charlotte. She has worked as a juvenile probation officer; mental health counselor for children, adolescents, and families; social policy analyst/advocate; and mother. Her major area of interest is risk and protective factors for adolescents, specifically disproportionate minority contact in the juvenile justice system. She currently teaches research methods and the MSW capstone course and has taught human behavior, social policy, and forensic social work courses at both the undergraduate and graduate levels.

Matthias J. Naleppa, MSW, PhD, is professor of social work at Baden-Württemberg State University Stuttgart, Germany, and a Hartford Geriatric Social Work scholar. For many years, he held a position in the School of Social Work at the Virginia Commonwealth University. His research focuses on geriatric social work, short-term treatment, and international social work. He regularly conducts workshops on task-centered practice and geriatric social work in the United States, Europe, and Asia. He has an MSW from the Catholic School of Social Work in Munich and a PhD from the University at Albany.

Michael J. Sheridan, MSW, PhD, is special advisor for diversity and wellness programs with the Office of Intramural Training & Education at the National Institutes of Health. In this capacity, she provides a variety of diversity and inclusion trainings, as well as offerings on stress management and self-care. She also facilitates a weekly mindfulness meditation group for NIH fellows. Her previous practice experience includes work in mental health, health, corrections, and youth and family services. As a former social work educator she taught courses on diversity and social justice, spirituality and social work, transpersonal theory, human behavior, international social development, research methods and statistics, and conflict resolution and peacebuilding. Her major research and scholarship focus has been on the ethical and effective integration of spirituality within social work practice and education.

Cara Wallace, PhD, LMSW, is an assistant professor in the School of Social Work at Saint Louis University. She graduated with her PhD from the University of Texas at Arlington. Her research agenda is related to overcoming barriers to end-of-life care, transitions to care, and the role of family in health care decision making. Recent research includes looking at factors that impact the timing of the decision for hospice care and gaining a deeper understanding of what hospice means to patients and families. She has practice experience in hospice, in hospital social work, and with at-risk youth. She teaches values and ethics as well as courses related to direct practice in health, end of life, and older adults.

Joseph Walsh, MSW, PhD, LCSW, is professor in the School of Social Work at Virginia Commonwealth University. He was educated at Ohio State University and has worked for 40 years in community mental health settings. His major areas of interest are clinical social work, serious mental illness, and psychopharmacology. He teaches courses in social work practice, human behavior and the social environment, and the dynamics of the social worker–client relationship, while maintaining a small clinical practice. Joe also performs 60s and 70s rock and roll music with his band Social Phobia.

David Woody III, PhD, LCSW, is chief services officer at The Bridge—Homeless Recovery Center, in Dallas, Texas. Several years in academia include social work education at Texas Christian University, the University of Texas at Arlington, and Baylor University. In addition to issues related to poverty, Dr. Woody's major areas of interest include research exploring affordable housing policy, transition from social work supervision to nonprofit leadership, and implementation of evidence-based practices in nonprofit settings.

Debra J. Woody, PhD, LCSW, is the associate dean for academic affairs in the School of Social Work at the University of Texas at Arlington. She is the director of the Center for Addictions and Recovery Studies that provides recovery and parenting services to mothers and their children, and school-based substance abuse prevention services to students and their families.

ABOUT THE CASE STUDY CONTRIBUTORS

Megan Beaman is a community-based civil rights attorney representing primarily low-income and immigrant clients and communities around Southern California, particularly in the Coachella Valley, and also leading and participating in community advocacy toward policy and systems change outside of the traditional legal context. Ms. Beaman is a longtime advocate for the rights of workers, immigrants, women, and low-income communities—and the combination of any or all of those groups. Her career and passion are rooted in her own rural, working-class upbringing, as well as the experiences she has shared with diverse communities and leaders around the country, all united in their commitments to justice and better lives.

Nicole Footen Bromfield, MSW, PhD, is associate professor and associate dean of academic affairs in the Graduate College of Social Work at the University of Houston. Nicole earned her PhD in public policy from Virginia Commonwealth University with a focus in health policy, and an MSW and BA in anthropology from West Virginia University. Nicole's research interests include issues relating to women's and children's health and social well-being. Her recent publications focus on human trafficking, global surrogacy, the lived experience of divorce for Arabian Gulf women, and child welfare issues such as intercountry adoption and infant and child car restraints, all from a policy perspective.

Kristina Hash, LICSW, PhD, is a professor and director of the Gerontology Certificate Program in the School of Social Work at West Virginia University. Her research interests include caregiving, LGBT issues, the use of technology in teaching and research, and geriatric education. Her practice background includes positions in home health care, social work continuing education, and research and program evaluation. Additionally, she has been involved in several volunteer activities with community-based agencies serving older adults. She primarily teaches courses in aging and human behavior in the social environment.

Beverly B. Koerin, MSW, PhD, is associate professor emerita in the School of Social Work at Virginia Commonwealth University (VCU). She practiced in public social services at the local and state levels. At VCU she taught policy, macro practice, and diversity courses and served as BSW program director, MSW program director, and associate dean. For more than 10 years, she was involved in research and service related to family caregiving and cofacilitated a caregiver support group for the Richmond Alzheimer's Association. She is an active community volunteer, working with Jewish Family Services, the Fan Free Clinic, St. Mary's Hospital, and the American Red Cross.

Peter Maramaldi, PhD, MPH, LCSW, is a professor at the Simmons School of Social Work in Boston, where he serves as the director of the PhD program. He also serves on the faculty at the Harvard School of Public Health in the Department of Social and Behavioral Sciences, where he teaches social welfare and has developed an opportunity for social work PhD students to earn the MPH degree during their training. Dr. Maramaldi also holds a faculty appointment at the Harvard School of Dental Medicine in oral health policy and epidemiology, where he mentors postdoctoral trainees and works with interdisciplinary teams on NIH-funded investigations. He is a Hartford faculty scholar and national mentor with expertise in behavioral oncology in older populations. As a social work behavioral scientist, he has had consistent NIH and foundation funding since 2003 for his work across disciplines on research initiatives focused on health promotion. He is currently working on an NIH-funded multiyear study to promote patient safety using medical informatics. Another current NIDCR-funded study is developing implementation strategies for improved diagnostic coding in electronic health records. Dr. Maramaldi is also working on a foundation-funded national demonstration project using behavioral interventions to reduce childhood caries in high-risk populations of children. Prior to returning to Columbia University to earn his PhD degree and launch an academic career, Dr. Maramaldi was a community organizer and clinical social worker in New York City for more than 25 years.

Derek Morch, LCSW, is a graduate of the School of Social Work at Virginia Commonwealth University. He has worked in a variety of settings providing mental health services, including outpatient psychotherapy, residential counseling, homeless outreach, and supporting families with children at risk for out-of-home placement. His areas of interest include ongoing practice with multicultural populations, co-occurring treatment, and housing issues for those with serious mental illness.

Meenakshi Venkataraman, PhD, is a lecturer in the Department of Social Work at Metropolitan State University of Denver. She has taught human behavior at the graduate and undergraduate levels. Her research interests include psychological, social, and spiritual aspects of adults with severe mental illness.

Maria E. Zuniga, MSW, PhD, is professor emeritus from the School of Social Work at San Diego State University, where she taught for 16 years, with an additional 11 years at Sacramento State University. Along with human behavior courses, Dr. Zuniga's areas of focus were direct practice, gerontological practice, and practice with multicultural populations, in particular practice with Latinos. She was also a member of the board of directors of the Council on Social Work Education (CSWE) and helped to develop a CSWE-sponsored conference on cultural competence held at the University of Michigan in 1999. She is a consultant on cultural competence for local, state, and national agencies and publishing houses.